House of Commons

Irish jury system : first and second reports of the Select Committee on magistrates and juries with minutes of evidence, etc

House of Commons

Irish jury system : first and second reports of the Select Committee on magistrates and juries with minutes of evidence, etc

ISBN/EAN: 9783741105289

Manufactured in Europe, USA, Canada, Australia, Japa

Cover: Foto ©ninafisch / pixelio.de

Manufactured and distributed by brebook publishing software
(www.brebook.com)

House of Commons

Irish jury system : first and second reports of the Select Committee on magistrates and juries with minutes of evidence, etc

FIRST, SECOND, AND SPECIAL

REPORTS

FROM THE

SELECT COMMITTEE

ON

JURIES (IRELAND);

TOGETHER WITH THE

PROCEEDINGS OF THE COMMITTEE,

MINUTES OF EVIDENCE,

AND APPENDIX.

Ordered, by The House of Commons, *to be Printed*,
7 *July* 1873.

Monday, 31st March 1873.

Ordered, That a Select Committee be appointed to inquire and report on the working of the Irish Jury System before and since the passing of the Act 34 & 35 Vict. c. 65, and whether any and what amendments in the Law are necessary to secure the due Administration of Justice.

Wednesday, 2nd April 1873.

Ordered, That the Committee do consist of Seventeen Members.

Committee nominated of –

The Marquis of Hartington.
Mr. Attorney General.
Dr. Ball.
Mr. Heron.
Mr. Bourke.
Viscount Crichton.
The O'Conor Don.
Sir Rowland Blennerhassett.
Lord Claud Hamilton.
Major O'Reilly.
Colonel Wilson Patten.
Mr. Downing.
Mr. Charles Lewis.
The O'Donoghue.
Colonel Vandeleur.
Mr. M'Mahon.
Mr. Bruen.

Ordered, That the Committee have power to send for Persons, Papers, and Records

Ordered, That Five be the Quorum of the Committee.

Tuesday, 29th April 1873.

Ordered, That Lord *Claud Hamilton* be discharged from further attendance on the Committee, and that Colonel *Forde* be added thereto.

Monday, 5th May 1873.

Ordered, That Mr. *M'Mahon* be discharged from further attendance on the Committee, and that Mr. *Henry Herbert* be added thereto.

Thursday, 15th May 1873.

Ordered, That the Committee have power to report their Observations from time to time to The House.

Monday, 16th June 1873.

Ordered, That the Committee have leave to make a Special Report.

Tuesday, 17th June 1873.

Ordered, That the Petition of the Ballinasloe Union Guardians, for alteration of the Juries (Ireland) Act (1871), and for relief, be referred to the Select Committee.

Monday, 7th July 1873.

Ordered, That the Committee have power to Report the Minutes of Evidence taken before them to The House.

FIRST REPORT.

THE SELECT COMMITTEE appointed to inquire and report on the working of the IRISH JURY SYSTEM before and since the passing of the Act 34 & 35 Vict. c. 65, and whether any and what amendments in the Law are necessary to secure the due Administration of Justice;——HAVE made progress in the matters to them referred, and have agreed to the following FIRST REPORT:—

1. YOUR Committee have examined several witnesses upon the practical working and effect of the Juries Act (Ireland), 1871, and propose to examine many others, amongst whom will be some of the Judges of the Superior Courts in Ireland. Under these circumstances your Committee do not feel prepared at present to give any opinion upon the measure which ultimately it may be expedient to recommend to Parliament in order to remedy the defects of the existing system; but without expressing any opinion on the main principles on which the Act was founded, are satisfied that the rating qualification for jurors fixed by that Act has placed on the jurors' books the names of persons who are not qualified in point of intelligence to serve as jurors.

2. Your Committee recommend that the amount of property qualification for common jurors in counties at large, in respect of premises which do not appear on the rate-book to be situate in any city, town, or village, should be raised.

3. Your Committee recommend that the amount of property qualification for special jurors in counties at large, in respect of premises not situate in towns, should be raised.

4. Your Committee are of opinion that persons unable to read or write the English language should be exempted from serving on juries, and that a judge should have the power of excusing a juror from serving in his court.

5 It has been stated in evidence that if a Bill be immediately passed for amending the Juries Act (Ireland), 1871, in the above particulars the jurors' books might be amended and corrected by expunging the names of persons not qualified under the provisions of the intended Act, and that the jurors' books so amended would be available at the approaching Quarter Sessions and Assizes.

6. Under these circumstances your Committee recommend that a Bill containing provisions of the character before suggested, but temporary and limited in its duration, should be at once introduced.

15 *May* 1873.

SECOND REPORT.

THE SELECT COMMITTEE appointed to inquire and report on the working of the IRISH JURY SYSTEM before and since the passing of the 34 & 35 Vict. c. 65, and whether any and what amendments in the Law are necessary to secure the due Administration of Justice;——HAVE made further progress in the matters to them referred, and have agreed to the following SECOND REPORT:—

1. YOUR Committee having by their First Report recommended that a Bill modifying, to a certain extent, the provisions of the Act 34 & 35 Vict. c. 65, but temporary, and limited in its duration, should be introduced, such a Bill has become law under the title of The Juries (Ireland) Act, 1873.

2. Your Committee are of opinion that before concluding their inquiry it may become necessary to examine Witnesses as to the practical operation of this Act, and that it may also be expedient that they should have an opportunity of considering some of the provisions of a Bill now before the House of Commons for amending and consolidating the Law relating to Juries in England, in case the same shall become law.

3. Your Committee have therefore agreed to report the Evidence taken before them to the House, and to recommend to the House the re-appointment of the Committee next Session.

7 July 1873.

SPECIAL REPORT.

THE SELECT COMMITTEE appointed to inquire and report on the working of the IRISH JURY SYSTEM before and since the passing of the Act 34 & 35 Vict. c. 65, and whether any and what amendments in the Law are necessary to secure the due Administration of Justice;——HAVE agreed to the following SPECIAL REPORT:—

THE Chairman having called the attention of the Committee to two documents purporting to be summonses issued by his direction as Chairman of the Committee, the one to John Fay, Esq., High Sheriff of the County of Cavan, the other to Theophilus Thompson, Esq., J.P., County of Cavan, directing them to attend as Witnesses before the Committee, which documents were issued without his authority or knowledge,—

Resolved, That the same be reported to The House, together with the documents referred to.

16 *June* 1873.

DOCUMENTS REFERRED TO.

Inns of Court Hotel, London,
13 June 1873.

My Lord,

I enclose a communication, in obedience to which I have come to London.

Mr. M'Kenna, the clerk at the Irish Office here, informs me that it is not an official document.

I pray your Lordship will direct my expenses to be paid, same as if I had been summoned.

I could not possibly have known that you did not direct me to be summoned.

Your obedient,
John Fay, Sheriff,
County Cavan.

The Right Hon.
The Marquis of Hartington.

Dublin Castle, Chief Secretary's Office,
10 June 1873.

Sir,

The Committee on Juries (Ireland) Act, have decided to receive your evidence as an experienced magestrate (*sic*) of Cavan, on certain subjects at present under their consideration, and that you are forthwith to repair to the House of Commons by desire of the Marquis of Hartington, and that the usual scale of expences (*sic*) shall be accorded to you.

I am, Sir,
Your obedient Servent (*sic*),
B. C. Cruse

To John Fay, Esq., J.P., High Sheriff,
Moyne Hall, Cavan

Ford Lodge, Cavan, Ireland,
13 June 1873.

Sir,

I have the honour to forward the enclosed letter as directed by your telegram just received.

I have the honour to be, Sir,
Your obedient Servant,
Theophilus Thompson,
5 o'clock P.M.

The Private Secretary,
Irish Office, London.

Dublin Castle, Chief Secretary's Office,
10 June 1873.

Sir,

The Committtee on Juries (Ireland) Act have decided to receive your evidence as an experianced (*sic*) magistrate of Cavan on certain subjects at present under their consideration, and that you are forthwith to repair to the House of Commons by desire of the Marquis of Hartington, and that the usual scale of expences (*sic*) shall be accorded to you.

I am, Sir,
Your obedient Servant,
B. C. Cruse.

To Theophelis (*sic*) Thompson, Esq., J.P., Cavan.

Ford Lodge, Cavan, 11 June 1873.

Sir,

I have the honour to acknowledge the receipt of the Chief Secretary's letter, dated yesterday, requiring my immediate attendance to give evidence before the Committee now sitting in the House of Commons on the Juries (Ireland) Act; and, in reply, I regret to have to inform you that I am at present confined to bed, and so ill that it would be utterly impossible for me to proceed to London.

I attach

I attach a certificate from my medical attendant, and have only to add that I should have much pleasure in attending were it possible for me to do so.

I have the honour to remain, Sir,
Your obedient Servant,
Theophilus Thompson, J.P.

Thomas H. Burke, Esq.,
Under Secretary, &c. &c. &c., Dublin Castle.

I hereby certify that Theophilus Thompson, Esq., J.P., County Cavan, Ireland, is now under my medical care, and that he is physically unable to leave his home, being confined to his room by a severe seizure of acute rheumatic gout.

I further certify that a journey from Cavan to London might be attended with danger to his life.

(signed) *Andrew Mease*, F.R.C.S.I., Surgeon,
County Cavan Infirmary, Ireland.

11 June 1873.

PROCEEDINGS OF THE COMMITTEE.

Friday, 4th April 1873.

MEMBERS PRESENT:

Mr. Bruen.	Mr. Heron.
Lord Crichton.	Colonel Wilson Patten.
Colonel Vandeleur.	Dr. Ball.
Mr. M'Mahon.	Mr. Bourke.
The O'Donoghue.	The Marquis of Hartington.

Marquis of HARTINGTON was called to the Chair.

[Adjourned till Thursday, 24th April, at Twelve o'clock.

Thursday, 24th April 1873.

MEMBERS PRESENT:

The Marquis of HARTINGTON in the Chair.

Colonel Wilson Patten.	Mr. Charles Lewis.
The O'Conor Don.	Mr. M'Mahon.
Mr. Heron.	The O'Donoghue.
Lord Crichton.	Dr. Ball.
Major O'Reilly.	Mr. Attorney General.
Mr. Bruen.	

The Committee deliberated.

Mr. *Charles Hemphill*, examined.

[Adjourned till Monday next, at Twelve o'clock.

Monday, 28th April 1873.

MEMBERS PRESENT:

The Marquis of HARTINGTON in the Chair.

Lord Crichton.	Mr. Bruen.
Major O'Reilly.	Mr. Bourke.
Dr. Ball.	Colonel Wilson Patten.
Mr. Heron.	The O'Conor Don.
Mr. Downing.	Lord Claud Hamilton.
The O'Donoghue.	

Mr. *Thomas De Molyns* and Mr. *James Charles Coffey* were severally examined.

The Committee deliberated.

[Adjourned till Thursday next, at Twelve o'clock.

Thursday, 1st *May* 1873.

MEMBERS PRESENT:

The Marquis of HARTINGTON in the Chair.

The O'Donoghue.
Major O'Reilly.
The O'Conor Don.
Mr. Bourke.
Dr. Ball.
Colonel Wilson Patten.
Mr. Bruen.
Colonel Vandeleur.
Sir Rowland Blennerhassett.
Colonel Forde.
Mr. Heron.
Mr. Downing.
Lord Crichton.
Mr. Charles Lewis.

Mr. Serjeant *Armstrong* and Mr. *J. P. Hamilton* were severally examined.

[Adjourned till Monday next, at Twelve o'clock.

Monday, 5th *May* 1873.

MEMBERS PRESENT:

The Marquis of HARTINGTON in the Chair.

Mr. Heron.
Lord Crichton.
Colonel Forde.
The O'Conor Don.
Mr. Bruen.
Major O'Reilly.
Colonel Vandeleur.
Mr. Bourke.
Mr. Downing.
The O'Donoghue.
Colonel Wilson Patten.
Sir Rowland Blennerhassett.
Dr. Ball.

Mr. *J. P. Hamilton* further examined.

[Adjourned till Thursday next, at Twelve o'clock.

Thursday, 8th *May* 1873.

MEMBERS PRESENT:

The Marquis of HARTINGTON in the Chair.

Colonel Wilson Patten.
Mr. Herbert.
The O'Conor Don.
Mr. Bruen.
Lord Crichton.
Colonel Forde.
Dr. Ball.
Colonel Vandeleur.
The O'Donoghue.
Mr. Attorney General.
Mr. Charles Lewis.
Sir Rowland Blennerhassett.
Mr. Bourke.

Dr. *George Battersby* and Mr. *Constantine Molloy* was severally examined.

[Adjourned till Monday next, at Twelve o'clock.

Monday, 12th May 1873.

MEMBERS PRESENT:

Colonel WILSON PATTEN, afterwards the Marquis of HARTINGTON, in the Chair.

Sir Rowland Blennerhassett.
Mr. Herbert.
Colonel Vandeleur.
Dr. Ball.
Lord Crichton.
Mr. Bruen.
The O'Donoghue.
Mr. Bourke.

Mr. *Lewis M. Buchanan* examined.

The Committee deliberated.

Mr. *William Henry McGrath* examined.

[Adjourned till Thursday next, at Twelve o'clock.

Thursday, 15th May 1873.

MEMBERS PRESENT:

The Marquis of HARTINGTON in the Chair.

Mr. Herbert.
Colonel Forde.
The O'Conor Don.
Mr. Heron.
Colonel Wilson Patten.
Mr. Bourke.
Mr. Bruen.
Lord Crichton.
Mr. Attorney General.
Dr. Ball.
Sir Rowland Blennerhassett.
Colonel Vandeleur.
The O'Donoghue.
Mr. Charles Lewis.

The Committee deliberated.

DRAFT REPORT proposed by the Chairman, read the first time, as follows:—

"1. Your Committee, without expressing any opinion on the main principles on which the Juries Act (Ireland), 1871, was founded, are satisfied that the rating qualification for jurors fixed by that Act has placed on the jurors' books the names of persons who are not qualified in point of intelligence to serve as jurors.

"2. Your Committee recommend that the amount of property qualification for common jurors in counties at large, in respect of premises which do not appear on the rate-book to be situate in any city, town, or village, should be raised.

"3. Your Committee recommend that the amount of property qualification for special jurors in counties at large, in respect of premises not situate in towns, should be raised.

"4. Your Committee are of opinion that persons unable to read or write the English language should be exempted from serving on juries, and that a judge should have the power of excusing a juror from serving in his court.

"5. It has been stated in evidence that if a Bill be immediately passed for amending the Juries Act (Ireland), 1871, in the above particulars the jurors' books might be amended and corrected by the chairmen of counties at the next Midsummer Quarter Sessions expunging the names of persons not qualified under the provisions of the intended Act, and that

that the jurors' books so amended would be available at the approaching assizes; and your Committee recommend that such a Bill should be immediately introduced in Parliament."

Question, "That the Draft Report be read a second time, paragraph by paragraph"—put, and *agreed to*.

Paragraph 1, amended, and *agreed to*.

Paragraphs 2—4, *agreed to*.

Paragraph 5, amended, and *agreed to*.

New Paragraph *added*.

Question, "That this Report, as amended, be the First Report of the Committee to The House"—put, and *agreed to*.

Ordered, To Report.

Mr. *James Morland* and Mr. *William Roche* were severally examined.

[Adjourned till Monday next, at Twelve o'clock

Monday, 19*th May* 1873.

MEMBERS PRESENT:

The Marquis of HARTINGTON in the Chair.

Mr. Heron.	Colonel Forde.
Mr. Downing.	The O'Donoghue.
Sir Rowland Blennerhassett.	Mr. Herbert.
Lord Crichton.	Colonel Vandeleur.
Mr. Bruen.	The O'Conor Don.
Colonel Wilson Patten.	Mr. Bourke.
Mr. Attorney General.	

Chief Justice *Monaghan*, Mr. Justice *Lawson*, and Mr. Justice *Morris* were severally examined.

[Adjourned till Thursday next, at Two o'clock.

Thursday, 22*nd May* 1873.

MEMBERS PRESENT:

The Marquis of HARTINGTON in the Chair.

Mr. Heron.	The O'Conor Don.
Mr. Downing.	Mr. Attorney General.
Mr. Bruen.	Sir Rowland Blennerhassett.
Lord Crichton.	Mr. Herbert.
Colonel Wilson Patten.	Colonel Forde.
Colonel Vandeleur.	The O'Donoghue.
Mr. Bourke.	Mr. Charles Lewis.

Mr. Justice *Morris* further examined.

Mr. Justice *Fitzgerald* examined.

[Adjourned till Monday next, at Twelve o'clock.

Monday, 26th *May* 1873.

MEMBERS PRESENT:

The Marquis of HARTINGTON in the Chair.

Mr. Heron.	The O'Donoghue.
Mr. Downing.	Colonel Forde.
Lord Crichton.	Sir Rowland Blennerhassett.
Mr. Bruen.	Mr. Attorney General.
Mr. Herbert.	Colonel Wilson Patten.

Mr. *H. H. Bottomley*, Mr. *J. B. Johnson*, and Mr. *A. Murphy*, were severally examined.

[Adjourned till Monday, 9th June, at Twelve o'clock.

Monday, 9th *June* 1873.

MEMBERS PRESENT:

The Marquis of HARTINGTON in the Chair.

Mr. Bruen.	Colonel Wilson Patten.
Major O'Reilly.	Mr. Downing.
Lord Crichton.	The O'Conor Don.
Sir Rowland Blennerhassett.	Mr. Charles Lewis.

Mr. *James Robinson*, Q.C., and Mr. *Thomas Wilkinson* were severally examined.

[Adjourned till Thursday next, at Twelve o'clock.

Thursday, 12th *June* 1873.

MEMBERS PRESENT:

The Marquis of HARTINGTON in the Chair.

Mr. Bruen.	Mr. Heron.
Mr. Herbert.	Mr. Downing.
Colonel Wilson Patten.	Lord Crichton.
Major O'Reilly.	Dr. Ball.
Colonel Vandeleur.	Sir Rowland Blennerhassett.

Mr. *William Flynn*, Chief Justice *Whiteside*, and Mr. *Frederick Hamilton*, were severally examined.

[Adjourned till Monday next, at Twelve o'clock.

Monday, 16th *June* 1873.

MEMBERS PRESENT:

The Marquis of HARTINGTON in the Chair.

Mr. Downing.	Colonel Wilson Patten.
Colonel Vandeleur.	Mr. Herbert.
Mr. Bruen.	Dr. Ball.
The O'Conor Don.	Mr. Attorney General.

The Committee deliberated.—The Chairman called the attention of the Committee to two documents purporting to have been issued from the Chief Secretary's Office, Dublin Castle, by direction of the Chairman, directing Mr. John Fay and Mr. Theophilus Thompson to attend and give evidence before the Select Committee, which documents were spurious, and had not emanated from the Irish Office in Dublin.—Motion made, and Question, That the Chairman be directed to move the House for leave to make a Special REPORT,—put, and *agreed to*. Special Report brought up and read as follows:—"The Chairman having called

called the attention of the Committee to two documents purporting to be summonses issued by his direction, as Chairman of the Committee, the one to John Fay, Esq., High Sheriff of the county of Cavan, the other to Theophilus Thompson, Esq., J.P., county of Cavan, directing them to attend as witnesses before the Committee, which documents were issued without his authority or knowledge.—*Resolved*, That the same be reported to the House, together with the documents referred to"—(Colonel *Wilson Patten*).—Question, That this be the Special Report of the Committee to the House, put, and *agreed to*.

Ordered, To Report.

Mr. *John Reilly* examined.

[Adjourned till Tuesday, the 24th, at Twelve o'clock.

Tuesday, 24*th June* 1873.

MEMBERS PRESENT:

The Marquis of HARTINGTON in the Chair.

Mr. Bruen.
The O'Conor Don.
Lord Crichton.
Colonel Vandeleur.
Dr. Ball.
Mr. Downing.
Colonel Wilson Patten.

Mr. *William Ormsby*, Mr. *William Mitchell*, and Mr. *J. D. Cope*, were severally examined.

[Adjourned till Friday, 4th July, at half-past Two o'clock.

Friday, 4*th July* 1873.

MEMBERS PRESENT:

The Marquis of HARTINGTON in the Chair.

Mr. Heron.
Colonel Vandeleur.
Major O'Reilly.
The O'Conor Don.
Sir Rowland Blennerhassett.
Mr. Bruen.
Mr. Downing.
Colonel Wilson Patten.
Mr. Bourke.

The Committee deliberated.

[Adjourned till Monday next, at half-past Two o'clock.

Monday, 7*th July* 1873.

MEMBERS PRESENT:

The Marquis of HARTINGTON in the Chair.

Mr. Downing.
Lord Crichton.
Mr. Bruen.
Mr. Herbert.
The O'Conor Don.
Major O'Reilly.
Sir Rowland Blennerhassett.

DRAFT REPORT proposed by the Chairman, read a first and second time, amended, and *agreed to*.

Question, That this Report, as amended, be the Second Report of the Committee to the House, put, and *agreed to*.

Ordered, To Report, together with the Minutes of Evidence and Appendix.

EXPENSES OF WITNESSES.

NAME of WITNESS.	Profession or Condition.	From whence Summoned.	Number of Days Absent from Home, under Orders of Committee.	Allowance during Absence from Home.	Expenses of Journey to London and back.	TOTAL Expenses allowed to Witness.
				£. s. d.	£. s. d.	£. s. d.
Mr. Charles Hemphill -	Queen's Counsel - -	Dublin -	3	9 9 -	5 9 -	14 18 -
Mr. Thomas de Moleyns	- ditto - - -	ditto -	7	22 1 -	5 9 -	27 10 -
Mr. James Charles Coffey.	- ditto - - -	ditto -	3	9 9 -	5 9 -	14 18 -
Mr. George Battersby, D.C.L.	- ditto - - -	ditto -	7	22 1 -	5 9 -	27 10
Mr. William Henry McGrath.	Solicitor - - -	ditto -	4	8 8 -	5 9 -	13 17 -
Mr. Louis M. Buchanan.	Deputy Clerk of Peace, and Deputy Clerk of Crown, for County Tyrone.	Tyrone -	6	6 6 -	6 10 -	*15 16 -
Mr. James Hamilton -	Barrister - - -	Dublin -	7	22 1 -	5 9 -	27 10 -
Mr. William Roche -	Crown Solicitor - -	ditto -	5	6 6 -	5 9 -	11 15 -
Right Hon. Mr. Justice Lawson.	- - -	ditto -	3	3 3 -	5 9 -	8 12 -
Right Hon. Mr. Justice Keogh.	- - -	ditto -	6	6 6 -	5 9 -	11 15 -
Right Hon. Lord Chief Justice Monahan.	- - -	ditto -	3	3 3 -	5 9 -	8 12 -
Right Hon. Mr. Justice Fitzgerald.	- - -	ditto -	6	6 6 -	5 9 -	11 15 -
Mr. H. H. Battersby -	Sub-Sheriff for County Antrim (Solicitor).	Belfast -	16	33 12 -	6 10 -	†44 6 -
Mr. J. B. Johnson -	Sub-Sheriff for County Cork.	Cork -	5	5 5 -	6 2 -	11 7 -
Mr. A. Murphy - -	Crown Solicitor - -	Dublin -	- -	- -	5 9 -	5 9 -
Mr. James Morland -	- ditto - - -	Downpatrick	5	5 5 -	6 5 6	11 10 6
Mr. William Flynn -	Gentleman - - -	Strokestown, County Roscommon.	4	4 4 -	7 16 -	12 - -
Mr. Thomas Wilkinson	Gentleman - - -	Enniscorthy	5	5 5 -	7 - -	12 5 -
Mr. James Robinson -	Queen's Counsel - -	Dublin -	4	12 12 -	5 9 -	18 1 -
Mr. Serjeant Armstrong	- - -	ditto -	3	9 9 -	5 9 -	14 18 -
Mr. John Reilly - -	Attorney - - -	Monaghan -	7	14 14 -	4 16 -	19 10 -
Mr. Frederick Hamilton	Solicitor - - -	Dublin -	3	6 6 -	5 - -	11 15 -
Mr. J. D. Cope - -	Clerk of Union - -	Kingstown -	3	3 3 -	5 9 -	8 12 -
Mr. William Ormsby -	Sub-Sheriff - - -	Dublin -	3	3 3 -	5 9 -	8 12 -
					£.	372 13 -

* Allowance for providing substitute for six days, for duties in connection with the Polling Districts Act - £. 3 - -
† Ditto - - ditto - two weeks - - - - ditto - - - - 4 4 -

MINUTES OF EVIDENCE.

LIST OF WITNESSES.

MINUTES OF EVIDENCE.

Thursday, 24th April 1873.

MEMBERS PRESENT:

Mr. Attorney General.
Dr. Ball.
Mr. Bruen.
Viscount Crichton.
The Marquis of Hartington.
Mr. Heron.
Mr. Charles Lewis.
Mr. M'Mahon.
The O'Conor Don.
The O'Donoghue.
Major O'Reilly.
Colonel Wilson Patten.

THE RIGHT HONOURABLE THE MARQUIS OF HARTINGTON, IN THE CHAIR.

Mr. CHARLES HARE HEMPHILL, called in; and Examined.

Mr. *C. H. Hemphill.*

24 April 1873.

1. *Chairman.*] I BELIEVE you are a Queen's Counsel?—Yes.

2. And Chairman of the county of Kerry?—Yes.

3. Will you have the goodness to state to the Committee what opportunity you have had of becoming acquainted with the practical working of the Juries Act, Ireland?—As chairman of quarter sessions in Kerry, of course I have had to preside at the quarter sessions, and as a member of the Leinster Circuit, and practising there, and also at nisi prius at the after sittings in Dublin, I have had an opportunity of judging of the Act on the civil side of the court.

4. Will you state to the Committee the result of your experience upon the subject as far as it has gone?—I will first state my experience as chairman of quarter sessions. I have been for some years now chairman of quarter sessions, indeed since 1864, and so far as one sessions enables me to form an opinion, I think that the Act has worked well in the county of Kerry. I have found that in Tralee, for instance, the grand jury, who are altogether new men, found the bills in a very intelligent manner. They threw out two bills, which I myself on reading the informations, had come to the conclusion beforehand ought to have been thrown out; and they found the other bills. And then with regard to the petty juries, there were five different indictments tried, and the juries appeared to me to act with fairness and discrimination; they convicted in three of the cases quite in conformity with the evidence, and they acquitted in two of the cases, where there should have been acquittals in my opinion. I found both the grand jury and the petty juries a little awkward in the mere mechanical part of the work, and of course it was necessary for me to explain to the grand jury, more fully than otherwise I should have done, the precise nature of their duties; and so also I had to explain, perhaps more at large than otherwise might have been necessary, to the common jury what their function was.

5. The grand jury that you speak of is the grand jury of the quarter sessions, I presume?—Yes. The grand jury at the quarter sessions are selected from the special jurors' list.

6. What change was made with regard to the grand jury of the quarter sessions by these late Acts?—The change was this: The grand jury of the quarter sessions were always selected from what was called the special jurors' list under the old statutes, and of course the change consisted in the change which has been created in the special jurors' list.

7. Were they selected by the sheriff from that list?—Yes, they were selected by the sheriff from that list, and were summoned by the sheriff. Of course the qualification was different. With regard to the civil side of the court, as chairman of quarter sessions, I may observe that our cases are not tried by juries as a general rule. There may be a jury, but a jury is very seldom resorted to. But on the Leinster Circuit, where I believe I was in almost every record that was tried, I found that the juries under the new system acted reasonably well; there were no disagreements that I can recollect, and the juries found verdicts which were quite reasonable and fair. And also, in Dublin, I would say at nisi prius that the juries under the new system have acted in a very reasonable manner.

8. Has it come under your observation that the class of jurors who attended were a very different class from those whom you have been accustomed to?—At quarter sessions the class of jurors that I have observed have always been of rather inferior character. Under the old system I have frequently known publicans to

serve

Mr. *C. H. Hemphill.*

24 April 1873.

serve upon juries at quarter sessions. I am speaking now of petty juries who try criminals at quarter sessions. The class that I observed under the new system were more of the agricultural and farming class, and not perhaps quite so smart, but I should say that they were equally fair and equally reasonable.

9. Do you suggest any alteration as to the disqualification or exemption of jurors?—I think that there should be a disqualification of a man who was not able to read and write. The present Act does not provide for that, but it would be what I would call an educational disqualification.

10. Did any cases come before you in which it appeared that the jurors could not read or write?—Yes; there was one remarkable case, a civil case, which I may mention. It was a fishery case in Clonmel, and was a very important case, in which I was for the defendant. A conditional order has been obtained by Mr. Butt to set aside the verdict which was found for the defendant, and one of the grounds stated by him (I am now speaking from hearsay, for I did not happen to be in court) was, that there was a juror who could not read or write upon the jury. But I would certainly suggest that if a case of that sort occurred, the judge should have the power to strike off a juror without the consent of either or both parties, which might be easily done.

11. Either party might strike him off, might they not?—Not as the law stands. It is not a ground of challenge at present, and I think there should be that change made.

12. But in a criminal prosecution the Crown Solicitor could set a juror aside, might he not, without the cause?—Yes, without assigning any cause in the case of a felony, but in a misdemeanour he could not, so that there should be some power given I think to strike off a juror who could not read and write. I would further suggest that at the revision by the chairman of quarter sessions, on its being established before him that a particular juror could not read and write, the chairman should be vested with the power to strike off that juror; but as the Act stands at present he cannot do so. I would further suggest, from my experience in Kerry, that if it were proved that a juror could not understand English, there should be a power both in the chairman on the revision, or if it escaped his observation, which it may possibly do, in the judge who tried the case to strike off that juror. I am sorry to say that there are many instances of apparently very respectable men in Kerry, who, when they come to be examined as witnesses, cannot either speak or understand English even now, strange as it may appear. At my quarter sessions I am obliged to have an interpreter in the outlying districts to take the evidence.

13. Mr. *Bruce.*] I suppose that would be more so in your district than in almost any district in Ireland?—I should say that in Kerry, or perhaps Mayo, it would be worse than in any other district, but I cannot speak from my experience of other counties.

14. Mr. *Heron.*] And also in the whole west of Galway that would be the case, would it not?—I believe so. In Dingle, in the county of Kerry, which is one of my quarter sessions' towns, and at Cahirciveen, almost every second case requires the intervention of an interpreter; I am of course not speaking of jurors now, but of witnesses.

15. *Chairman.*] You are now speaking, are you not, of the power which you think might be beneficially given to the judge, to set aside, on the spot, a juror who presented himself who was found to be unable to read or write?—Yes, I think that would be a most useful power, and would obviate a great many of the objections which I have seen stated about this new Act; the great advantage would be this, that at the trial, whether criminal or civil, it could be ascertained on the spot whether a man could read and write when he came to the book.

16. Mr. *Lewis.*] You would not propose to institute an examination in every case as to whether a juror, before he was sworn, could read or write?—Not in every case; but in the country especially there are always people in the court, or some of the officials, who would be likely to know whether a particular man was illiterate, or would suggest that it was so, and you might then institute an inquiry.

17. *Chairman.*] Would you place the inability to speak English in the same category as the inability to read or write?—Certainly; I think that that would occur very rarely, but I think it ought to be provided against.

18. Do you suggest any alteration as to the basis of the qualification, distinguishing urban from rural districts?—I would suggest that in addition to the present qualification of rated occupiers at a certain value there should be added, what I would call a household qualification; that is to say, that persons renting houses of from 12 *l.* to 15 *l.* a year, or whatever sum might be agreed upon, should be placed upon the common jury, in addition to the rated occupiers; and also that there should be a higher test for special juries. I think that the advantage of that would be that you would get a great number of intelligent townspeople who would be mixed with the rural and agricultural juries, and by their, perhaps, superior intelligence, there might be a great improvement in the juries. That would be very easily provided for without at all interfering with the principle or with the machinery of the present Act.

19. Will you state to the Committee what were the former qualifications under the old Act?—Under the Act, which was passed in 1833, the qualifications for a common juror were a 10 *l.* freeholder above what is called in the Act all reprizes, which means, clear of all incumbrances and charges, and a 15 *l.* leaseholder, and a householder, not holding by lease, of the clear annual value of 20 *l.*; there was no test of the Poor Law in those days. I think those were the qualifications for the common jury in the counties, and for the special jury the qualifications were very much the same, that is to say, what I call the honorary qualifications, were nearly, the same as in the present Act, such as the sons of peers, magistrates, baronets; they were, as they are in the present Act, put upon the special jury list, and also bankers and wholesale merchants and retailers, whose personal property was 5,000 *l.* at least. Those were the qualifications for special jurors in the counties.

20-21. Mr. *Bruce.*] Did I rightly understand you to say, that those honorary qualifications are continued as qualifications for special jurors?—Yes, I think so; that is my recollection of the present Act.

22. Mr. *Heron.*] And also the having been summoned as a grand juror?—Yes, an ex-grand juror

Mr. C. H. Hemphill.

24 April 1873.

juror and an ex-sheriff; but I say what are called the honorary qualifications were very much the same, with the addition, as the honourable Member for Tipperary says, that the former Act provided that any one who had served the office of sheriff or grand juror, should also be on the special jury list.

23. *The O'Donoghue.*] You spoke of certain changes being made in the machinery and principle of the Bill; what would you describe as the principle of the Bill?—The principle of the Bill is, I think, that the Poor Law valuation is made under this Bill the basis of the qualification.

24. *Chairman.*] Will you just state to the Committee by what machinery those old qualifications which you have mentioned, were ascertained?—Of course the machinery contemplated by the Act was what were called the Jury Sessions, that is sessions presided over by the magistrates, which took place on a certain day, appointed at the October quarter sessions of the peace; but I believe that, in fact and in practice, it was impossible to ascertain the existence of those qualifications which was one of the great objections, because it is very difficult to prove that a man has a freehold of 10 *l.* a year above all charges and incumbrances, and it was most difficult also to ascertain the leasehold qualification; and again, in the case of special jurors, I know myself by experience that some men acted upon the special jury in Dublin who were not worth 5,000 pence, not to say 5,000 *l.*, and I have no doubt that men were frequently put upon the jurors' book at the old Jury Sessions who had no property qualification at all, for there were no means of sifting it; that is what I think makes the present qualification superior, because it is uniform, and it is certain, and it is capable of being ascertained; there can be no doubt whether a man is a rated occupier to the extent of 20 *l.* a year.

25. Under the old system, might not the practical inconvenience have resulted that unqualified jurors' names got upon the list?—Yes; when once a man got upon the jurors' list, it was almost impracticable to object to him on the ground of want of qualification; if he got on the list there he would remain; the consequence was, especially in the City of Dublin, that there was a class of special jurors who unquestionably served for the mere sake of the guinea, who were devoid of the property qualification. That was a matter of notoriety to everyone practising in Dublin before this Act was passed; and that was one of the things that really led to the agitation for some change in the jury system.

26. Then I understand you to approve of the basis fixed by these Acts for the property qualification of jurors?—Yes; I think the basis should be the poor law valuation.

27. Dr. *Ball.*] In using the words "the poor law valuation," I presume that you do not mean the amount?—With regard to the amount, I can only speak from my own experience.

28. *Chairman.*] Have you any suggestions to make as to the amount?—I will take Kerry as an illustration, the amount there for a common juror, as it is in every other county, I believe, is a 20 *l.* valuation, and for a special juror 50 *l.* in Kerry. When I heard that I was to be examined before this Committee, I telegraphed to my clerk of the peace to ascertain the precise numbers under the new Act on the jurors' book, and his telegram, I think was, that there were 2,240 on the common jurors' book in Kerry, which is a large county, and 511 on the special jurors' book; that is to say, on the 50 *l.* and 20 *l.* valuation. In Tipperary the valuation is 100 *l.* for special jurors, and certainly one would expect that a man who occupied a farm rated at 100 *l.* a year ought to be as fit to serve on a jury as any person. If I were asked the question, I do not myself see that there is any necessity for raising the valuation, but I would certainly, as I have already stated, add a household qualification.

29. Mr. *Lewis.*] Do you mean to substitute that for the ingredient of rating?—No, quite independent of rating; there are very many respectable men in a country town who pay 15 *l.* a year for a house, of which the valuation might be only 10 *l.*, and under the present Act such a person could not serve; therefore, I think I would import the household qualification in addition, and I think that would be practicable for this reason, that in Ireland the houses are of inappreciable value in the rural districts; there is hardly any value put upon them at all. I am sorry to say that even on large substantial farms, the houses are comparatively very valueless.

30. Dr. *Ball.*] Have you not observed that a man who lives in one of those inferior houses is generally an uneducated man, even if he has land; but if he becomes educated and gains the feeling suitable to his position, he immediately improves his house, so that by giving a certain qualification for a house, you are likely to obtain a higher class of jurors in point of intelligence than by the mere valuation derived from land?—I do not think that, practically speaking, the house at all improves in proportion to the extent of the valuation of a farm; that is the result of my observation in the south of Ireland.

31. *Chairman.*] I do not quite understand what your suggestion is; I understand you to say that you do not propose to make the value of the house a part of the rated qualification?—I do not; what I propose is this: I would take, for argument sake, 15 *l.*; if it is proved before me in settling the list that a person pays for a house and premises attached to it 15 *l.* a year, I would add him to the list, even although the poor rate valuation might be considerably under 20 *l.* a year.

32. That would have the effect, in your opinion, of adding a certain number of intelligent persons to the panel?—Yes, of townspeople generally, in the county towns.

33. Have you any suggestion to make as to preventing the persons who are now said to be unfit to serve as jurors from getting on to the jurors' list; do you propose to raise the rating qualification?—I myself think that the way to do that is not by raising the valuation or the qualification, but by enabling the chairmen who now have the revision of the lists, to sift more closely the fitness of the jurors.

34. That I think is the second great change which has been made by these Acts?—Yes, substituting the chairman's court for the jury sessions.

35. Will you state to the Committee exactly what change was made in that respect by the Acts?—Formerly, the course of proceeding was this: at the general quarter sessions of the peace, the magistrates used to fix a day, generally six weeks or two months off, for the revision of the jurors' list, and then the county cess collectors had to make out lists of the various persons qualified

Mr. C. H. Hemphill.

24 April 1873.

qualified under the pre-existing Act, and those lists were revised by the magistrates at the jurors sessions. Independently of the jurors' book, there was what was called a special jurors' list, composed of those who had a special juror's qualification. Now, that jurisdiction is taken away altogether from the jury sessions, and the course of proceeding now is, for the clerk of the peace before the October sessions, to issue his precept to the clerks of unions who return lists of the various rated occupiers of 20 *l.* and upwards, and of 50 *l.* and upwards, to the clerk of the peace; he makes out the general jurors' list from those lists, and he selects out of the general jurors' list those who are rated at 50 *l.* and upwards, and those constitute the special jurors' list. Those lists are printed, and are submitted to the chairman of the county at the quarter sessions in October. The poor law collectors and the clerks of the unions attend, and those names are then called over, and if it is proved before the chairman that a juror is dead, for instance, he is struck off, but if no evidence is afforded to the chairman one way or the other, the list remains as it is printed.

36. Do you know whether the old revision sessions were an efficient process or not?—I think not, for this reason; that very often, as I have already stated, there were no means of ascertaining whether a juror possessed the qualification required by law. If the law said that a juror should have a particular qualification, I take it that it was essential that the existence of his qualification ought to be established, but in point of fact, there were no means of ascertaining it, and frequently persons got on what I call the special jurors' list who had not the qualification required by the Act.

37. Did anybody attend at those sessions to give information?—The county cess collectors did attend, and the magistrates depended very much on their local knowledge.

38. Are you not aware that, in many cases, this revision sessions had become very little more than a form?—In some cases, certainly, men got on who had no qualification at all.

39. Mr. *Lewis.*] Do you mean by that that they had no pecuniary qualification?—No legal qualification; legal is the correct phrase; I am assuming that it was desirable that they should have the qualification required by the Act of Parliament: I am not at all saying that a very intelligent juror might not get on the list, who had not the qualification; of course that might very often happen, and very frequently did happen, but I am assuming, that it was desirable, the Legislature having said so under the old Act, that a legal qualification should exist, otherwise, I am afraid, that you would have no rule at all to go by.

40. *Chairman.*] With regard to the revision provided by the late Act, have you any suggestions to make as to its improvement?—I think, as I stated, that if some machinery could be devised which would enable the chairman to ascertain the fitness of the jurors, better than exists under the Act at present, it would be desirable. The difficulty is, that the Act, of course, is framed in analogy to the register of voters, and the analogy is maintained between the register of voters and the register of jurors; but it is the object of every man to get on the voters' list, and it is the object of every man to get off the jurors' list, and therefore there is more difficulty in having that searching inquiry before the chairman in the latter; but I think that a great deal might be done in this way: if the clerks of unions were required to print before the name of every juror whom they conceived to be either incapable of reading or writing, or incapable of speaking English, or otherwise unfit to be put upon the jury, the word "objected." The word "objected" on the list would call the chairman's attention to the fact of the name being objected to, and then the poor law collector might be able to furnish the chairman with what would enable him to strike off the name. I think that that discretion might very fairly be vested in the chairman.

41. As it is at present the juror list, which is placed in your hands as chairman, gives you no information whatever?—No, it gives me no information, it is a mere printed list of names; these names are called out, and if anyone comes forward and says that such and such a man is dead, or that such and such a man is past 60, and if that is proved, I strike him off; but in the absence of any such evidence, or any such materials before me, my duty is to leave his name on, for instance, in the case of the register of voters, when a man has gone out of possession, it is the duty of the clerk of the union to put before such voter's name "objected," and then he is called upon at the revision to substantiate the objection; then he or the poor law collector states that the man has gone out of possession, or that he is underrated, or that his rating has been reduced; that enables me at once, in case of the register of the voters, to strike off his name. So with regard to the register of jurors, the poor law collector, who knows all about those country people better than anyone else, knows perfectly well whether a man can read and write, and whether a man can speak Irish only; if the clerk were to be required to put the word "objected" before the juror's name, that would call the chairman's attention to the fact, and he would ask the collector, on his oath, whether he could substantiate the objection.

42. Major *O'Reilly.*] Is not this a list from which it is his duty to exclude every person, or rather not to insert the name of any one person, who is exempt?—But he must have evidence of that.

43. Is it a list which contains a single name of a person over 60 years of age, or blind, or deaf, or anything of that sort?—The poor law collector's duty is not to return those names; but if he does return them, and they possibly may be returned, *per incuriam* or otherwise, the chairman cannot expunge them without evidence.

44. *Chairman.*] The chairman having no local knowledge?—No.

45. Will you state to the Committee exactly what you do on your revising the list?—The list is placed before me, and then anyone is invited to come forward who can state whether any of the jurors on that list are disqualified, or the jurors themselves can come forward and state that they are disqualified, and then if evidence is given which satisfies my mind, I strike the names off; for instance, I may mention what occurred in practice when I was revising the list last October for the present year. One gentleman on the special jury list was proved to be very deaf, and I struck him off as a matter of course; others were proved to be dead, and they were struck off as a matter of course, and so on; but unless such evidence was afforded to the chairman he could not expunge a man's name.

46. In

Mr. C. H. Hemphill.

24 April 1873.

46. In fact, unless the juror came forward himself, it was nobody's interest to object?—It was no one's interest to object.

47. Did you examine the poor law collectors generally, as to whether they had satisfied themselves that the lists were correct?—No; the lists were returned by them, and they were assumed to be correct in the absence of any evidence to the contrary.

48. But you did not go through, and could not have gone though, the list name by name, and have asked the poor law collectors to satisfy you that so and so were qualified?—No, that is not the course pursued.

49 Mr. *Brown*.] That would be impossible, would it not, with the number of names on the list?—Yes, it would be impossible with the number of names, and it would lead to nothing, because the clerk of the union, whose duty is pointed out by an earlier section, is to return, not merely everyone who is rated at 20 *l.* a year, or 50 *l.* a year, but to leave out from the list those who have passed 60 years of age, or those who labour under any physical disqualification.

50. *Chairman*.] Would you recommend that the chairman should have power to strike off the name of any person from any cause?—On sufficient proof I would; I think that that power might be safely vested in the chairman.

51. For instance, if it was alleged and proved to the satisfaction of the chairman, that a person on the list was imbecile, should he have power to strike him off?—That is provided for by the Act; but as to the education test, that is not provided for, and I would have no power as the law stands, to strike out a man, although I knew, or it was proved to demonstration, that he was incapable of reading and writing; nor would I have the power to strike off a purely Irish speaking juror. This might be remedied by putting in general words, enabling the chairman to strike off for any good and sufficient reason; I think that that discretion might be fairly vested in the chairman.

52. Viscount *Crichton*.] Would not that practically transfer to the chairman the power exercised by the sheriff under the old system?—No; the sheriff had no power to strike out a name. The power of the sheriff was in summoning; he had no control over the jurors' book. You might vest a large discretion in the chairman, but like every other discretion vested in him it should be a judicial discretion, and he could not strike out a name unless upon some evidence of unfitness.

53. *Chairman*.] Referring to the first great change made by the Act, that of depriving the sheriff of discretion in summoning jurors, do you approve of that change in principle?—I do decidedly; under the former Act, the sheriff had an absolute discretion in summoning whom he liked, and omitting to summon whom he pleased on the jurors' book. He had no control over the jurors' book, but he had absolute discretion in selecting the jurors for any particular assizes, and that I think was very often calculated to lead to injurious consequences.

54. Mr. *Brown*.] Do you know of any cases in which it did lead to injurious consequences? —I cannot mention instances, but, of course, there were many cases where one has heard of disagreements and trial after trial, under the old system; but I would not attribute that altogether to the discretion of the sheriff. But there was this tendency, that the sheriff used to summon generally those who were nearest home; and circuit after circuit, and sittings after sittings, one saw the same jury; there was no circulation of jurors at all. They were, generally speaking, the same men serving on the jury; the men whom the sheriff found it easiest to summon.

55. *Chairman*.] And so the whole duty fell upon a very limited number?—A very limited number; and besides which, in the case of political trials, undoubtedly it gave people, justly or not, an idea that the sheriff, if he happened to be of any particular political persuasion, might possibly pack the jury. I do not say that he did do so, but it had the tendency to inspire that feeling.

56. In your opinion did the system cast some doubt upon the impartiality of the juries who were summoned?—I think it did, particularly in political cases in Ireland where the people are prone to be very suspicious of persons in authority. It was an absolute discretion in the sheriff to select from the jurors' books any names that he pleased, and there was no controlling that discretion.

57. Do you know whether in practice that selection was generally left by the sheriff to the sub-sheriff?—In practice I may say always.

58. What sort of position did the sub-sheriffs hold?—The sub-sheriffs generally were solicitors who originally had been practicising solicitors in the county; and, of course, like most people in Ireland, they had their political biases, both on one side and on the other.

59. So that whether it happened or not, it was possible that the panel might be dependent upon the political views of the sub-sheriff?—Quite possible.

60. You have no doubt, I presume, that the change in that respect was a beneficial one?—I have no doubt that it was.

61. Whatever alteration may be found to be necessary in the Act, you would not advise a return in any shape to the principle of selection? —Certainly not.

62. What has been the operation of the present Act upon the duties of the sheriff; has it imposed upon him any additional labour?—It has imposed upon them additional labour and additional expense which has led to a good deal of discontent with the Act, I think, amongst the sheriffs. In this way that they are obliged to send to great distances to serve the summonses, for which they get no additional remuneration. In a county like Kerry, they are obliged to send sometimes 25 miles to serve a summons personally or at the dwelling-house of a juror, and that really is rather a hardship upon them.

63. How is personal service effected?—Either by serving the jurors personally in any place, or by serving a member of his family, or a servant at his dwelling-house.

64. By whom is that done?—By the sheriff's officer, by one of the sheriff's staff. There was another objection to the former system. Frequently there was great difficulty even in proving the service, and the consequence was that, practically, jurors were called on fines, but in 99 cases out of 100 the fines were never enforced in Ireland from the difficulty of proving the service.

65. Major *O'Reilly*.] Do you mean that to apply to the new Act?—No, to the old Act. I was speaking of the old Act in that respect.

66. *Chairman*.] Was personal service imposed by the new Act?—No, it was the same species of service under the old Act as under the new.

67. What is it that has so much increased the trouble?

Mr. *C. H. Hemphill.*

24 April 1873.

trouble?—The sheriff is obliged now to go in alphabetical series. If, we will say, the first juror on the list lives 25 miles off he must serve him, whereas under the old Act if he found that a juror lived 25 miles off, he would not serve him at all, but he would serve some person living within two or three miles, or perhaps living within a few yards of the court-house; but now if a juror lives 25 miles away, he is bound to follow in alphabetical, and I believe in dictionary order, no matter how remote, and no matter how expensive or inconvenient the service may be, if he discharges his duty he must serve him.

68. Is it not the case that for the quarter sessions jury, a juror can only be taken from the district?—From what is called the division; counties are divided generally into two or three divisions; for instance, in Kerry there are three divisions; there is the Killarney division, the Tralee division and the Listowel division; and the grand and petty jurors for the quarter sessions for those respective divisions must be summoned from the jurors living in those divisions, and not from the whole body of the county.

69. Then the inconvenience to the chairman, and the hardship to a juror being summoned from a great distance, does not arise in the case of quarter sessions juries?—Not at all to the same extent, it does to a certain extent, but not to the same extent.

70. Mr. *Lewis.*] Are the jurors alphabetically arranged in each of the divisions?—No, not in each of the divisions; they are alphabetically arranged from the body of the county, but then there is a provision in the Act that in summoning them for the quarter sessions, the sheriff has only to summon those from the book who live in the division, and he has the means of ascertaining that; he has that power of selection as far as the quarter sessions are concerned.

71. *Chairman.*] Have you any suggestion to make for the purpose of reducing this inconvenience?—Under Section 22 of the Act, I think it is, in the county of the City of Dublin, the sheriffs are enabled to serve by registered letter, and I would extend that privilege to every part of Ireland; I see no reason why the service of the summonses should not be by registered letter in every county in Ireland; the registrations under the Post Office are very perfect in even the remotest districts of Ireland; possibly some of those letters might not come to hand, but even so the sheriff could guard against that by summoning, perhaps, a greater number of jurors than otherwise might be absolutely necessary, and that would be no great inconvenience; but I am sure that if this principle which is recognised in the county and the City of Dublin were extended, it would be a great boon to the sheriffs, and I do not see why it should not be extended to the whole of Ireland.

72. Dr. *Ball.*] It was originally proposed in the House of Commons to extend it to all Ireland, but it was stated that the Post Office arrangements in Ireland were not in such a state of perfection as to make it quite certain as a universal rule that the letter would arrive at its destination, and that as there are not post offices near every place of residence, there might be a delay in the transmission of the letter; it was not any objection to the Post Office as a medium of communication, but solely on the ground that it was not safe to extend it to every part of the country that it was not done?—Of course; and therefore I say possibly some of the letters might miscarry, but I do not think that many would, and that could easily be obviated by the sheriff who has the power of summoning any number that he thinks fit; all that he is required to do is to summon a sufficient number, there is no number limited by this Act at all, and by issuing a few more summonses, he would guard against any public inconvenience.

73. *Chairman.*] I presume that it could be ascertained through the machinery of the Post Office, whether a summons had been received or not?—Yes; it could be ascertained, of course, when sent by a registered letter.

74. If the summonses were sent by registered letter, a receipt would be obtained, would it not, by the Post Office when the letter was delivered?—Yes.

75. So that for the purpose of finding, it would be effectually?—Yes, quite effectual; I am quite sure that it would be a great advantage and answer all practical purposes.

76. Dr. *Ball.*] Do you think that a farmer, who happened not to have a post office nearer than six or seven or eight miles from his house, which I know to be the case often, would send every day for his letters; do not you think, that unless the post-office system had post offices as numerous in other counties as they are in the county of Dublin, there would be great danger that the summonses would not be received in time, and it would be a question how to guarantee that, on the day of trial, a sufficient number of persons had personally received intimation that they would be obliged to attend? I think that it might be taken, that in the case of a juror, who would not be in the habit of sending to the post office every second day, at all events, his absence might be very well dispensed with.

77. Major *O'Reilly.*] If he only sent once a week, would the summons be sent out in time enough to ensure his attendance?—At present, I think four days is the time, but that might be extended.

78. Dr. *Ball.*] Take the county of Cork, and a summons sent from the town of Cork for a juror to attend in court, the farmer may reside in a most remote part of that county, and the post office may be many miles from his residence; from what you know of the habits of the people, do you believe that Irish farmers send to the post office often enough to lead to a certainty that that summons would reach him?—I think that now there is a post office certainly within four or five miles of every man who would be likely to be on the jurors' book, because a 20 *l.* valuation represents a certain amount of substance.

79. Are you sure that there is a post office within four or five miles of every farmer?—I think in most parts of Ireland there is, but there may be places where there is not.

80. The post-office arrangements in the counties round Dublin might render this clause operative, but that could not apply to distant counties, because it is not a fact that there would be a post office every four or five miles, especially in the case of the county of Donegal?—I only make this suggestion, because I think it would relieve the sheriffs of a great burden, a burden which they may reasonably complain of; and as I stated, very possibly some of those letters might miscarry, but I think that the great mass of them would be delivered in due time.

81. With respect to errors in the qualification, the

Mr. *C. H. Hemphill.*

24 April 1873.

the only machinery which you have suggested to aid the chairman in revising, is the poor law collector writing opposite the name the word "objected," wherever he is opinion that the party has not either sufficient education or intelligence to act as a juror?—Yes, as far as the chairman's revision goes; but of course I would also extend the same power to the judge at the trial.

82. Do you believe that the Irish poor law collectors would ever mark opposite any man's name, their own neighbour, or their own acquaintance probably, the word "objected"?—I believe that they would. I do not think that they would have the slightest scruple in doing it. It is done every day in the case of the register of voters.

83. But that is not an objection to a man's capacity, or an objection to a man's education; that is an objection to his property, which is a very fair and legitimate thing if he is not rated; but if the poor law collector did put opposite the farmer rated, say, at 40 *l.* or 50 *l.* a year, the word "objected," do you think that that would be done where the objection was an objection as to education or intelligence?—I do not think that they would have the slightest delicacy in stating it if they knew that a man could not read or write, because the word "intelligence" is somewhat larger than that. A man may be very intelligent, although he may not be able to read or write; but if you were to make reading and writing a test, which I think ought to be a necessary qualification, I do not think, speaking from my observation, that the poor law collectors would have the slightest delicacy in objecting.

84. Besides that mode of revision, you would give power to the judge at the trial to strike off a person whom they thought unfit?—Yes, I would.

85. How would the judge exercise that power?—I have mentioned a case which occurred in Clonmel, where on the application for a conditional order for a new trial, one of the jurors was alleged to be incapable of either reading or writing; and it was also alleged that the counsel for the defendant objected to having him put off on that ground, and Baron Fitzgerald, who tried the case, had no power to deal with it. He could not put the juror off on that ground as the law now stands; and I would alter the law, so that when such a case (if it occurred) arises again, the judge presiding should at once swear the juror, and say, "Can you read and write?" and if he he says not, should have power to strike him off forthwith.

86. Then you would impose the inability to read and write as a legal subjection?—Yes.

87. And you would give the judge arbitrary discretion to remove or retain a name whenever it is objected to?—No; there should be some ground for the exercise of discretion.

88. Then you would specify the ground of objection?—Yes; I would have it on certain specified grounds.

89. Mr. *Bruen.*] I think before you get a jury into the box there are three operations that have to be gone through; first, the formation of the general jurors' list; next, the summoning of the panel by the sheriff; and thirdly, the selection of the jurors by ballot from that panel?—Quite so. The names are put on slips of paper and put into the box, and called by ballot; that is before you empanel them for the trial of a civil cause, before you swear them.

90. *Chairman.*] Any name which comes out of the box may be objected to in certain cases, at any rate, by the counsel on either side?—Yes; if there is ground of challenge, what is called the challenge to the poll is to the individual juror. In the case I have mentioned, there would be no ground as the law stands, and therefore the whole jury might consist of persons who were incapable of reading and writing.

91. In certain cases which you have specified, the Crown counsel may order a juror to stand aside without alleging any cause?—Yes, in felonies the Crown counsel may.

92. Mr. *Bruen.*] The application of the principle of selection in the first process, that is, the formation of the general jurors' book, you would place in the hands of the chairman of quarter sessions?—Yes, I would, as the Act stands.

93. And you would specify the grounds upon which he should make his selection?—Yes.

94. That would, I suppose, be in the form of putting in the schedule of disqualification in the Act some additional grounds of disqualification?—Precisely so; what I would call the educational test.

95. So that you get upon the general jurors' book a list of men who would be fit, educationally speaking, and also who would be fit, so far as the property qualification would go?—Yes.

96. Is that a sufficient test of fitness in your opinion; are there not some other grounds of disqualification before you put a man upon the general jurors' book; for instance, do you think that a man who has committed offences against the law, we will say moral offences, is a fit person to be put upon a jury for the administration of the law?—I think as regards several offences, the 7th section provides for a person who has been convicted of offences against the law being disqualified.

97. Conviction of treason-felony, or any crime that is not moral?—Yes; that meets part of your question. As to moral offences, I think it would be too large a term, because it would be very difficult to test what a moral offence might be, so as to disqualify a man. The clause provides for treason or felony, and what is called an infamous crime; it does not provide for assault, which is a misdemeanour; and perhaps it would be no ground of disqualification to put off a man who had been convicted of assault. That could easily be cured by extending that section to anyone who was convicted of any misdemeanour. As far as I see, perhaps it might be safely extended to that.

98. You think that the disqualification might be somewhat extended?—I think so; I think that the advantage of the present Act is, that it gives a larger number of jurors, and that you may never be put to the risk of not having a sufficiency owing to disqualifications and exemptions. I wish to mention what I intended to mention before, that I think that publicans ought to be relieved by law from serving upon juries at all. They are not amongst the exempted class at present, but I think that they ought to have the privilege of being exempt.

99. *Chairman.*] Would you give it them as a privilege, or make it a disqualification?—I would call it a privilege, but it would have the same effect. If you will look at the schedule of exemptions, you will find that various professions are exempted, and I would make the trade of publican exempt, because unfortunately (especially if we have this household qualification which I recommend)

Mr. C. H. Hemphill.

24 April 1873.

I recommend) the number of public-houses is increasing in the south of Ireland in every town. We have in Tralee 107 or 109 public-houses, and in other small towns in proportion, and there is no possible means that I can see of checking their increase. While the Act suspending the licenses was in operation it was most useful.

100. *Mr. Bruen.*] With regard to the point of exemption, I received a letter from a member of the Royal College of Veterinary Surgeons, containing a reason for exemption from serving on juries, would you be inclined to express an opinion upon that point as to whether the veterinary surgeons should be exempted?—I think myself that they might be. They are not very numerous in the country parts of Ireland, and I think it might be extended to them. There might be cases in which it would not be fair to them to have their time taken up by a case which may last several days. That is the principle on which professional men, whose time is very precious to them, are exempted, and I think that the exemption might be safely and fairly extended to veterinary surgeons.

101. We have got so far as the formation of the general jurors' list in choosing the panels from the general jurors' list; would you give to any person whatsoever a discretion in the choice, or would you make the selection in strict dictionary order according to the present law?—I would leave the selection as it stands, in strict order, according as the book is made out.

102. Would it not be possible to conceive a case in which a whole district of country was very much interested in some trial that was to come off, we will say a trial of the right of way, in which the whole district of country had a strong personal interest, and would not there be a danger in selecting the jury to try that case, that by adopting the strict dictionary order you would get a number of men from that district to try the case?—I think, on the doctrine of chances, it would be very unlikely, because taking the A's, B's, C's and D's it would be very unlikely that each letter would be represented in that district; it would be barely possible, but very unlikely. On the contrary, in most parts of Ireland, we know that districts run in particular letters altogether; there are a great many clans; for instance, in parts of Cork they are all Sullivans or O'Sullivans, and in parts of the north the names all begin with M or Mac, and so on, and therefore I do not think that at all likely to happen. Of course the sheriff is bound to make out his summonses with A, B, C, D, all through the 26 letters; then he goes back to the second on the list, and so on, and, according to the ordinary doctrine of chances, it would be most unlikely that the 26 letters would have representatives in the same district; it is possible, but very unlikely, I think.

103. But it is almost a certainty, according to the doctrine of chances, that, we will say in the county of Cork, there would be some of the jurors of the same names as the suitors?—Yes.

104. If that district happened to be the district, you would have one or perhaps two men interested in the case on the jury?—Of course that might be possible, but I think that it would happen so rarely as not to affect the principle, and, on the other hand, if you give the sub-sheriff the arbitrary power of selection, and I am putting a possible case, he may be a friend of either of the suitors, and he may select jurors altogether favourable to one side of the question. I am speaking now of a civil case, just as you put a civil case with respect to a right of way. I do not say that it would happen, but it might happen, and I think that the sheriff having that power of selection would be a very great evil, because it would be trusting to an individual a very large discretion.

105. Discretion implies power, and you must place power in the hands of somebody?—The less power you place in anyone's hands the better.

106. I think that, in the beginning of your evidence, you stated that the grand jury of Tralee, under the new system, were all new men who had not served on juries before?—That is my impression; I was speaking of the quarter sessions grand jury.

107. The distinction between the quarter sessions grand jury and the grand jury at the assizes, is that the grand jury at the assizes is drawn from all parts of the country?—Yes; the grand jury at the assizes is not affected by this Act; it is the grand jury of the quarter sessions that is affected, and for this reason, that the grand jury were always selected from the special jurors' list, and of course anything that alters the constitution of the special jurors' list or book, alters the constitution of the grand jury at the quarter sessions.

108. But the jurors for general causes are drawn from the whole county, and I daresay you are aware that in the formation of the panel, the sheriff very often for the winter assizes, that is to say, the spring assizes, chose men on his panel who were near to the assize town?—Yes.

109. And in summer he chose men who lived at a distance, and in that way he afforded great convenience to the jurors?—I believe that that was the case.

110. Do not you think that that is a considerable advantage?—I think myself that the advantage is counterbalanced by the greater advantage of distributing over the whole body of the county the obligation of serving on juries, and that it would be much better for a man to have to serve once in three years, even though it might be in the winter coming from a distance, than to have to serve every recurring summer; so that even from the point of view of the convenience of the jurors, I think that the present system is better, because the probability is that if the Act is properly worked, according to its letter, the same juror would not be summoned more than once in every three years in a large county, and therefore he would only have, even in the spring, the inconvenience of attending once in three years.

111. Still it would be an advantage if it could be secured?—But I am afraid that it could not be secured consistently with taking away the discretion from the sheriff.

112. You spoke of honorary qualifications as being still continued under the new Act, as they were under the old; I am inclined to think that they have been abolished, because of what is said in the first schedule?—If you look at the section, you will observe that it points out what the clerk of the peace has to do in making the special jurors' books; you will find that he has to select the magistrates, and so forth; the ex-sheriffs and and the ex-grand jurors are not mentioned, and I certainly see no objection at all to enlarging this

by

Mr. C. H. Hemphill.

24 April 1873.

by including those persons, and that anyone who has served those high offices ought to be on the special jury, quite irrespective of any other qualification.

113. There is also the property qualification of 5,000 *l.*?—Yes; a retailer, as I read the old Act, was qualified who had personal property to the extent of 5,000 *l.*, and I think one of the greatest objections to the old system was, that it was impossible to ascertain whether a man was worth 5,000 *l.*, and consequently men got on the special jury who were not worth 5,000 pence; I am not speaking of country special jurors at all.

114. Referring to the possibility of certain interested persons getting upon juries through the want of the power of selection, would you as a counterbalance to that, give any right of challenge to parties in civil causes?—In the ordinary case of an action against a railway company, you always ask, are any of the jurors shareholders in the company, and, as a matter of course, they are put off; and so, if you could show anything like an interest, even a remote pecuniary interest in a juror, as a matter of course, the judge always says, "You need not serve;" and in civil cases even this constantly occurs in practice; if a juror states, "I have formed an opinion upon this case from having read about it in the newspapers," it is a matter of course that he would not be required to serve in civil cases; of course, if he be a relative, or agent, or anything of that sort, in practice it presents no difficulty; and there is no difficulty even in the way of that by the new Act any more than by the old; by a sort of comity between the judge and the counsel, that is always done.

115. Under the old system we got upon the jury list people not qualified; do you know any instances in which there was a failure of justice, or that improper persons got on by that means?—I can only say that there were many instances, and I suppose there would be many instances under the new Act, where juries disagreed both in civil and in criminal cases, and a disagreement is in many cases of evidence of a miscarriage; but anyone who knows anything about the special jurors in the city of Dublin, knows that some of them went by a particular name which was not very complimentary. It was a matter of notoriety, that in the Four Courts a few necessitous persons served upon special juries, and that unquestionably shook the confidence, not only of the counsel in the case, but of the suitors, and the public at large on their verdicts.

116. There is a disinclination to serve on petty juries, is there not?—Yes, there is on every jury, because it takes a man away from his business, and takes up his time, and sometimes a trial occupies a long time. I have known civil cases to occupy 19 days, and sometimes longer.

117. The only means of getting over that at present under the existing law, is the imposition of fines in the case of non-attendance?—*Yes*, that is the only way.

118. The imposition of that fine depends upon the certainty that the juror has been served with the summons?—Yes.

119. You suggest, do you not, that registered letters should be the means of service?—Yes.

120. In a country place you know that farmers very often do not call for their letters for some days together, perhaps three or four days, where the post offices are distant; and a farmer, who did not wish to serve upon a jury, if he thought it was at all likely that there was a summons lying for him in a registered letter at the nearest office, would not call for his letters till after the assizes, and then he would get off his fine?—That might happen. I would make the proof of sending a registered letter *primâ facie* evidence against a juror. Of course that is evidence which he might be able to rebut; but, practically, the inconvenience of that would not be very considerable, because even with the present service, which is a very large expense upon the sheriffs in Ireland, the fine never is levied. I have been a long time practising at the bar, and I do not know of an instance where the fine on a juror has actually been levied. They have been frequently called upon fines, and they have been frequently fined in court; but the very fact of proving personal service has generally been so difficult, or some of the judges have been so lenient, that in practice the fine is never levied.

121. *Chairman.*] To whom does the fine go?—It goes to the Queen through some process which is called Green Wax.

122. Dr. *Ball.*] It is laid out in paying the petty sessions' clerks, is it not?—Yes, under the Fines Act, but they are never in practice levied; I do not say that they ought not to be levied, because I think that if they were levied perhaps jurors would be more punctual in their attendance.

123. Mr. *Bruen.*] Attendance upon the assizes is, perhaps, more onerous upon the poorer class of jurors than upon the richer class of jurymen?—Still it is a public duty which they ought to be taught to discharge. I should say, with regard to your last question, that if jurors know that they are on the jury list, which they must be presumed to know, and if they know when the assizes are likely to take place, I would be very slow to listen to their saying, "I did not go to the post office to inquire for letters."

124. You would make it compulsory upon them to call upon the post office?—A sort of compulsion in that way; I would be very particular in receiving an excuse from them at the approach of the assizes, when they were aware that they were on the jury list, and when they were aware that by law a summons might be sent through the post.

125. *Chairman.*] Do you say that jurors are necessarily aware whether their names are on the list?—Yes.

126. How do they gain that knowledge?—They do not get personal knowledge, but the lists are printed and posted all through the district on the chapels, and so forth. They know perfectly well, because the people are generally very sharp and intelligent; although they may not read or write, in many cases they are very knowledgable about the law as a general rule.

127. You say that there is a natural disinclination to serve on juries?—Yes, there is generally so.

128. If the jurors are aware that they are on the list, and that by proving that they are disqualified they would be struck off the list, why do not they come forward to get their names struck off?—They may not have a ground of disqualification. I would suggest, as an illustration, that some persons appeared before me at the last revision of the jury list, to prove that they were over 60 years of age; that is a ground of disqualification, and as a matter of course, I struck them off when I was satisfied of the truth of their statements.

129. If

Mr. C. H. Hemphill.

24 April 1873.

129. If the suggested alteration were made, you might to a certain extent, might you not, trust to the jurors themselves to come forward and claim their exemption on the ground of ignorance?—But I would examine them on oath, and I would ascertain whether they were really as ignorant as they alleged themselves to be.

130. Mr. *Bruen.*] As to the effect of taking away, in criminal cases, from the sheriff the power of selecting panels, a gentleman, who was examined before a Committee, and whose evidence has been published about a couple of years ago, Mr. Seeds, stated that his horror at finding the panel of the county of Meath in a very bad state, that it was said that it was the duty of the sheriff to have such a panel framed as would enable the Crown to have a fair jury for the trial of political cases; but if that power is taken away from the sheriff, if a panel happens to be by this alphabetical process returned, which is manifestly one that would be partial to the prisoners, would it not throw upon the Crown officers, that is to say, upon the Crown solicitor, who has now the right of challenge, a very onerous duty, and one that would subject him to very great unpopularity as a Crown officer?—That duty was frequently exercised under the old law. I am afraid that it was one of those duties that a man cannot avoid sometimes. Although I am not Crown prosecutor, I have been for many years on the Leinster Circuit, one of the counties on which is Tipperary, where there used to be always very heavy calendars; and in the time of the late Mr. Kemmis, who was a most experienced Crown solicitor, he was constantly obliged to exercise the prerogative of the Crown of directing jurors to stand aside in Crown cases, in felonies; I do not think that ought to be considered an objection; people do not mind it; they are reasonable enough to know that a Crown official only discharges his duty as well as he can, and I do not think that it would subject him to unpopularity any more than the old system It was inevitable under the old system, and I think it would be inevitable in certain cases under the new; Crown solicitors are always obliged to do it. One of the good effects of this present system, and I think it is a very desirable effect, is, that you may on common juries have a combination of men of a very high class, with men of a very common place or ordinary class. I recollect at the last Waterford assizes, seeing a gentleman who is always on the grand jury for Tipperary, summoned on the petty jury in the county of Waterford; the two counties march with each other, and as I say, it is a great advantage to have an admixture of classes in the ordinary juries. In practice, we know that one or two leading minds really decide a case; although the law requires 12, and the law requires the unanimous opinion of the 12. Any one who has been much in the habit of dealing with juries, knows that there are one or two leading men upon every jury to whom the whole conduct of the case is ultimately surrendered; and it seems to me a great advantage under this new Act, that from the way in which the names must be summoned, you may have the very highest class of men with of course, men of a very opposite class; that is one of the things which is suggested in the English Jury Bill, so far as I could understand from the statement of the Attorney General for England.

131. You spoke of the very heavy expenses which are incurred by the sheriff under some of the provisions of the new Act, and which probably are incurred by one class of officers; would it in your opinion be possible for the chairmen of quarter sessions to revise those lists, and have them published together with the register of Parliamentary voters?—They are revised practically at the same time and on the same day. For instance, we generally fix our jury revision and our Parliamentary voters revision to take place on the same day, or the day after one another, but you never can obviate the necessity of having the two lists printed separately; you never could make a common list of both qualifications; the qualification is different; the voter's qualification is 12*l.* as an occupier, and the juror's qualification is 20*l.*

132. Could you not put the jurors in one column and the Parliamentary voters in another column?—That would create confusion. I do not think myself that much advantage would be ultimately gained in economy by it, and I am sure that it would lead to a great deal of confusion from one authority dealing with the jurors' lists and the election judges dealing with the Parliamentary lists.

133. *Chairman.*] The expense to the sheriff falls upon him personally, does it not?—Yes; it falls upon him personally.

134. And in the case of the other list it falls upon the county?—Yes.

135. The *O'Conor Don.*] Is not the sheriff paid out of the county rate, is he, for any extra labour?—No.

136. Are you aware that that has been done in some cases?—I am not aware that it has been done, and I do not believe that there is any power to do it.

137. I may state as a fact that it has been done?—Then I was not aware of it. I never happened to have heard of it.

138. Mr. *Lewis.*] I understand you to say that you are satisfied with the working of the present Juries Act?—I am, with such modifications as I have suggested.

139. In your opinion there has not been any change for the worse between the juries summoned under the old system and those under the new system?—I cannot say that I think there has been any change for the worse. I think that the new jurors require a little training, and that they are a little more awkward at first, and incidents have occurred in court which have led to a little laughter, and that sort of thing, but that will be very soon got over.

140. But as regards the intelligence and capacity of the jurors, has there been any difference?—The Act has not had a very long trial, and therefore every one's experience of the working of the system must be rather limited. My experience is derived from my own sessions in the county of Kerry, which is a large county, a first class county, and from being a counsel on the Leinster circuit in going round the six towns, and I can say that as far as the records go (I am not a Crown prosecutor), the verdicts were quite as satisfactory at those assizes as they were on any other occasion.

141. With regard to the criminal business of the sessions, I think you stated that you are quite satisfied?—I am quite satisfied.

142. In fact, you think that there is no real grievance under the new Juries Act as regards the failure of justice?—That is my impression.

143. You stated that one of the greatest objections

Mr. C. H. Hemphill.

24 April 1873.

jections to the old system was that men who ought to have had a pecuniary qualification, might get on the jury, although they did not possess that qualification?—Yes.

144. But you look upon that merely with regard to the proper observance of the law?—Yes, I think so; I think that it has enabled persons to get on the special jury list, merely for the sake of getting the guinea.

145. Do you know any class of men to whom that charge could apply?—I might mention two or three instances, but I should not wish to do so.

146. As regards the working of the administration of justice, has it led to unintelligent verdicts?—I do not know that the verdicts could be called unintelligent; but unquestionably one could not have the same confidence in a tribunal, if you knew that some of the men were really in a very necessitous state, especially on a special jury.

147. Does the present system prevent jurors being called in, who are in a deeply necessitous state?—I think it has a tendency to prevent it.

148. Are you able to say, from your experience in the county of Kerry, that the rating at 50 *l.* a year to the poor rate as a qualification prevents or is anything like a barrier to necessitous persons getting on the special jury list?—I do not think it is a necessary barrier, but I think it is some check

149. Is it any barrier at all?—I think so, because a man cannot be in the occupation of a farm rated at 50 *l.* a year without having some ostensible means of living. I have known jurors in Dublin (and it is a matter of notoriety to Irish counsel), who went about and actually insulted counsel by asking loans of money from them. I think the experience of some members of the Committee may bear me out in this.

150. In one of your answers which you gave to the noble Lord in the chair, you let drop this, that the chairman might have power to strike off jurors' names for any good and sufficient reason, in order that there may be no misconception; am I right in supposing that the latter part of your evidence narrowed down those words to these facts: inability to read or write, and I think also, no knowledge of the English language?—Yes.

151. You did not intend by those words to give any general discretion as to general incapacity, or want of honesty or fitness?—No; I do not think that we could be vested with that discretion

152. With regard to your suggestion that the collectors might write the word "objected" against such persons as he thought were liable to the remark that they could not read or write, or speak English; do you really believe that the body of poor rate collectors might be trusted to carry out such a duty without fear or favour?—I think they might from my experience of them in the register of voters, which is very considerable. My experience of the clerks of unions and poor law collectors in the county of Louth, of which I was chairman, and in the county of Leitrim, of which I was chairman, and in the county of Dublin, where I acted as deputy chairman before I was appointed regular chairman, and in the county of Kerry, is, that they are a very fair and intelligent body as a rule; and I find that they do not scruple to state the grounds of disqualification against voters upon the list; and I think that they would do the same with regard to jurors.

153. There is no sort of analogous disqualification on the list of voters as the inability to read or write?—No.

154. The disqualification of a voter purely relates to ownership or occupation?—Yes; all that the poor rate collector has to say is, that they had gone out of possession before a particular date, and objections of that nature.

155. But there is no slur upon a man's capacity by writing the word "objected" against a man's name on the list of voters?—No; I am sorry to say that they are not sufficiently advanced in the rural districts in Ireland to have what you would call a strong public opinion against a man's being unable to read or write.

156. The overseer writing "objected" against a man's name on the list of Parliamentary voters does not thereby cast a slur upon his capacity or his intelligence?—No.

157. But it does do so if he writes the word "objected," on the ground of inability to read or write, or to speak English, against a juror's name?—I do not think it would be regarded as a slur; that is my experience.

158. Do you think that it would be regarded as an advantage to a possible juror, and that he would thereby get off the list?—It might be so.

159. It might even be welcomed as a means of escape?—Yes, that might be so.

160. In the same way every poor rate collector would give a publican the privilege of being exempt whom he would desire to disqualify?—Yes.

161. You think that the privilege ought to be disqualification?—Yes, I do.

162. Has it ever occurred to you that the real way to improve the jurors' list is to destroy all exemptions?—I have heard that mooted, but I cannot say that I agree with it.

163. Have you ever considered what might be the effect upon the population of a country like Ireland, the exemption of all persons named in the second schedule to this Act, and how much that narrows down the qualified classes?—I do not think that you could conveniently remove any of those exemptions.

164. Have you ever really considered and looked through those exemptions, and seen how greatly the schedule sifts all the *primâ facie* intelligent classes of society?—It does unquestionably eliminate out of the list a great number of the most intelligent classes; it has that effect certainly.

165. But you would not be disposed individually to narrow those exemptions?—I would not.

166. *The O'Donoghue.*] I think I understood you to say that the system of registered letters might be advantageously used in summoning jurors?—That is what I meant to convey.

167. And also that the other difficulty which you experienced in the working of the Jury Act was, that an illiterate juror, or a person speaking only Irish, might be summoned?—Precisely so.

168. Do not you think that it would meet the difficulty, if, when a person came to the book, he was asked whether he could read or write, or whether he could speak English?—I think that would be in most cases sufficient. The advantage of having it previously sifted out is, that possibly it might escape notice until after the juror

Mr. C. H. Hemphill.

24 April 1873.

juror was sworn, if it were left to the trial. The advantage of sifting it beforehand is, that you have a double chance of avoiding such a juror.

169. Could not it be so arranged that the question should certainly be asked?—That might be arranged. There would be no practical difficulty in the registrar, or the officer who was swearing the juror, asking whether he could read or write.

170. *Chairman.*] But he would have had the trouble of summoning him uselessly?—Yes; so that I think it would be better to get him out of the list if possible beforehand.

171. *The O'Donoghue.*] On the whole you think that the Bill is an improvement?—I do.

172. You are of opinion, are you not, that the principle of the Bill, which prevents what is called selection, but what is popularly known as jury packing, should be preserved?—Yes, I think that that ought to be preserved.

173. Mr. *Heron.*] With regard to your own experience under the 12th section, at how many places in the County Kerry do you hold quarter sessions for revision purposes?—At five.

174. Do you consider that that is a sufficient number of places in the county for the purpose of revision?—I do.

175. I do not mean as regards yourself personally, but as regards the county generally?—Yes. The revision is held in the same places where the Parliamentary voters lists are revised, and it would be highly inconvenient to bring together the county staff of the Poor Law clerks and collectors, and so forth, of the different districts in the same union at any different time or place.

176. Did it ever occur to you that a limited power of revision might be given to the magistrates at petty sessions, and that men who themselves objected to be jurors for any reasons might come before the magistrates and state their disqualification, with an appeal to the chairman?—That would be going back to a certain extent, except so far as the appeal is concerned, to the old jury sessions. I think myself that the juror would be just as likely to come into the revision court, because the revision court is generally held at the same time with the general quarter sessions, which are in October; and in almost every part of Ireland, indeed I may say in every part of Ireland, the people flock in to the quarter sessions court, which is notoriously a court of long sitting; and I have no doubt that more publicity is given to the revision by the chairman than could be possibly given to a revision by the magistrates.

177. Do you see any objection to a juror being permitted to make a declaration of disqualification, and to that being sent to you, and you acting upon it?—I see no objection to that. He could be indicted for perjury upon it, if it was proved to be incorrect.

178. That would save the trouble of a personal appearance, and generally speaking it would be an accurate declaration?—Yes; and I think it would be sufficient for the chairman to act upon a statutory declaration.

179. With regard to sending registered letters as notices to jurors, from your experience of country people, do not you consider that the more remote the districts, and the fewer the letters received, it is generally better known whether a letter for such a person has arrived or not?—That is my experience, certainly; one neighbour tells it to another.

180. Invariably, in Roman Catholic districts, they come in on Sunday to mass, and the post office is generally very near the Roman Catholic chapel, is it not?—Yes, generally in Kerry.

181. Mr. Bruen referred to the possible unpopularity that might arise to the Crown Solicitor from exercising his right of challenge at trials; in your experience of the Leinster Circuit, before the passing of this Act, have you not known the right to challenge to be very largely exercised by Mr. Kemmis and others?—Yes, I have in almost all capital cases.

182. As far as you are aware, is it not the fact that in cases of charges for murder, or in any other serious cases, no unpopularity whatever has accrued from the exercise of the right of challenge?—No personal unpopularity whatever. The late Mr. Kemmis stood very well with the county people; he was a man of very large experience; he was Crown Solicitor for the whole circuit at that time.

183. During the great number of agrarian cases which occurred in different counties, he largely exercised the right of challenge, did he not?—Yes, and at the special commissions.

184. So that the selection by the sheriff did not in any way dispense with the necessity for exercising the right of challenge?—By no means, that is the result of my experience.

185. Did I understand you rightly to say that in ordinary cases you would disqualify publicans?—I think so. I think it is placing them in an invidious position to summon them as jurors, because the very class of prisoners at quarter sessions who are being tried are the customers of the publicans, and their friends are the best customers of the publicans. I used to find, before this new system, that nearly one half of those juries consisted of publicans, and the consequence was that it was very often very difficult to get a verdict. I am speaking now particularly of the quarter sessions. As I said, the experience of the working of the Act at the assizes has not been very great yet, the time has been so recent, but I anticipate, especially in the quarter sessions, a decided improvement from the new Act in the class of jurors.

186. You mean, I presume, because it will prevent the sheriff, for his own convenience, soliciting doubtful people?—Yes.

187. You found, did you not, when you sat at Clonmel, that most of the jurors were towns people?—Occasionally.

188. In fact, during the quarter sessions the publicans' houses are used as hotels, where the witnesses and friends of the parties who are being tried stay?—Yes.

189. And it is a very unfair thing then, is it not, to have them upon the juries?—Yes; but they could not well be let off under the old system, because there might not be a sufficient number of jurors without them. The great advantage of the new system is, that it gives a large body of jurors on the jurors' book. I understand that the contrast, in point of numbers, is very considerable between the new jurors' books and the old jurors' books.

190. When the honourable Member for Londonderry referred to the persons who are exempted by the second schedule to the Act from serving on juries, do you remember that at the last sittings at Nisi Prius, in Dublin, a number of

Mr. C. H. Hemphill.

24 April 1873.

of persons objected to serve, on the ground that they were attorneys' clerks, and bankers' clerks, and that they were exempted by the judges?—Yes, I recollect that having happened.

191. Do you consider that a person engaged as an attorney's clerk should still be liable to be summoned as a juror?—No; I would certainly not have attorneys' clerks summoned.

192. At the last sittings in Dublin they objected themselves, and their masters objected, and they were struck off the list, were they not?—Yes; I certainly would exclude them as far as I could; and the same with regard to bankers' clerks.

193. It is a tremendous public inconvenience, is it not, if they are prevented from attending their ordinary business?—Yes; with regard to attorneys' clerks, I think they should be exempted for the same reason as publicans; it would place them in an invidious position. I think that the great object in constituting a jury is to be sure that the verdict that they will find is based upon fair grounds, and not in any way influenced by personal interest or expectation of any advantage.

194. With regard to the service of the summons by post, have you had any communication with any sheriff or sub-sheriff of Ireland upon that subject?—The sub-sheriff of Kerry has complained to me very much that the privilege has been conceded to the county of the City of Dublin, and withheld from him and sheriffs like him.

195. Do you see any objection to putting upon the sub-sheriff himself the duty of registering and posting the registered letters, and then, before either the assizes or quarter sessions, making an affidavit of such registering and posting?—No; I think that that ought to be a complete service, and I am sure that it would answer all practical purposes.

196. With reference to the jurors in the county of Kerry, you say that the number of common jurors amounts to 2,240, and of special jurors to 511; in your opinion, is that in excess of the number required by the public service of the county?—I think not, so as to produce a proper circulation. The common jurors are mostly summoned in Kerry for the quarter sessions twice a year in four towns, and twice a year in five towns. I hold quarter sessions in four towns twice a year, and in five towns twice a year.

197. And therefore that number is required?—I think it is required in order to prevent the burthen being always cast upon the same individuals.

198. Have you made any calculation, or has any calculation been made for you, of the numbers that would be added to your list by putting on the 10 *l.* householders?—I confess that I have not; but if you exclude publicans, I apprehend that the addition would not be very considerable.

199. As regards the houses of farmers, except on some estates like Mr. Herbert's or Lord Lansdowne's, where great attention has been paid to building houses for the farmers, the houses are generally very poor, are they not?—Yes; their value is almost infinitesimally small as abstracted from their farms, and that arises not only from the farmhouses themselves not being of a very improved class, but also from the way in which the valuation was made originally. We know that Kerry particularly is valued very low in proportion to the actual value of the properties there. It was one of the first counties that was valued, and it was valued exceptionally low, so much so that the poor law valuation is a very uncertain criterion of the letting value of the properties in Kerry particularly, as compared with Tipperary or other counties.

200. Have you made any calculation, from your own experience at Nisi Prius, in Dublin, of the actual number of persons who, before the passing of the Act, used practically to discharge the entire duty of jurors for the city of Dublin?—I cannot say that I have made a calculation, but from my own experience, and recalling it now to mind, I think that the whole duty would be spread over some 40 or 50 men; that is my recollection of sittings after sittings.

201. And those used to go about from court to court, did they not?—Yes.

202. During the term they would sit in the consolidated Nisi Prius, and they would act as special jurors in the three Supreme Courts, and in the Probate Court, and as grand jurors in Green-street?—Yes, precisely so; that is my experience, especially in the Probate Court. The Probate Court jurors were always better, as a general rule, than the Nisi Prius Court jurors; but even under this new system I saw what I thought a very decided improvement in the Probate Court common juries; nothing could have been better that the special juries were in the Probate Court at all times, but during the last sittings of the Probate Court I saw a very marked improvement, as it appeared to me, in the common juries there.

203. As regards both the county and the city of Dublin, in the case of the common jurors at all events; has there not been a most decided improvement under the new Act?—My opinion is that there has been, and more especially in the consolidated Nisi Prius Court, which is a very important court now.

204. Under the old system, either at the Nisi Prius sittings in Dublin, or at the assizes, it was known what causes were to be tried, and the sheriff had the power of selecting from the general jurors' book the panel for the trial?—Yes, certainly.

205. You disapprove entirely of the old system?—Entirely.

206. You have no doubt that it led to grave suspicions of the purity of the administration of justice?—I have not the slightest doubt of it, and it was a matter of notoriety amongst the Bar, at all events, and the *habitués* of the Four Courts.

207. Speaking of other counties, are you aware of the sub-sheriff in other counties having been for years electioneering agents for the counties on the one side or the other?—I would rather not answer that question, for at present I cannot call to mind any particular instance of a sub-sheriff having been so employed.

208. *The O'Conor Don.*] I understand that your suggestion with regard to the house valuation entering into the qualification for a juror is in addition to the land valuation qualification?—Yes, as an addition to it.

209. But you would still preserve the qualification derivable from land?—Yes, I would; that is what I meant to convey.

210. Do you think that a man who lives in a house which is valued, we will say, under 15 *s.* a year, is likely to be a competent juror?—If he has a substantial farm, and if he has the test which I would add, of being able to read and write,

Mr. *C. H. Hemphill.*

24 April 1873.

write, I see no reason why he should not be a perfectly competent juror.

211. You do not think that the fact that a man lived in a miserable cabin ought to be considered as sufficient proof that he did not belong to the class from which jurors should be taken?—I should say not necessarily so, because my experience of the people in the south of Ireland is that, under a very rough exterior, and living in a very rude manner, they are extremely acute and intelligent.

212. Do not you think that a man's intelligence, such as would probably qualify him to serve on a jury, might be more safely gauged by the sort of house that he lives in, than by the amount of land he rents?—I would not be prepared to say that; unfortunately, the habits of the people admit of a very great deal of improvement in the direction of their homes, but I am afraid that we could not conclude that a person was unfit to serve upon a jury merely because he was not very particular or tidy about his house.

213. You do not think that the test of the house in which he lives is a good test irrespective of the land which he holds?—I do not.

214. Do you consider that if he holds a certain amount of land, no matter what sort of cabin or house he lives in, he ought to be placed upon the jurors' list?—If he does not come within any of the existing or suggested disqualifications.

215. You stated that the valuation of Kerry took place a very long time ago, and is very low, and you were asked that question, were you not, in connection with the valuation of the houses in Kerry?—Yes.

216. Are you, or are you not, aware that there is a revision of the valuation every year, and that when a house is improved, the improved value is added each year?—I believe so.

217. Consequently that objection with respect to the old date of the valuation of Kerry cannot apply to the valuation of buildings?—No; but in my suggestion about adding the householder class I did not go into the poor law valuation of the house at all; what I meant by adding the householder class was this, that by adding the class of persons who paid a certain rent for their houses; for instance, the inhabitants of the smaller country towns; they would, I think, be a very useful class to mix with the agricultural and rural class.

218. You stated, in answer to a question asked you by the honourable Member for the University of Dublin, that in your opinion the house did not increase in value in proportion to the size of the farm?—That is my experience; I may be wrong, but that is the result of my observation.

219. Is it the result of your observation that the character of the house does not improve in proportion to the intelligence of its occupier?—I am quite sure that it ought to do so; but I am afraid that my experience does not enable me to say that it does.

220. You desire that the poor rate collector should furnish information as to the intelligence and learning of the jurors to the barrister at the revising sessions?—Of their capacity to read and write. I would not go beyond that.

221. I understand you to argue that those poor rate collectors would discharge this duty well, because you have found them act satisfactorily as regards the voters' list?—That is my experience.

222. The voter's qualification depends upon his holding or occupying certain lands or houses?—Yes.

223. A voter having ceased to have that qualification, if the rate collector does not strike him off the list, he would have to collect the rate from him, would he not?—He may, or he may not, because we have no control over the poor rate collector, so far as the general discharge of his duty goes; that is, between him and the poor law guardians.

224. But if the poor rate collector keeps a man on the list, and returns him to the poor law guardians, would he not be bound to account to the poor law guardians for that rate, and to collect it from that man?—He would, of course.

225. Is not that the reason why the poor rate collectors always strike off a man who ceases to hold land, because they could not get the rate from him?—That would be a motive, certainly.

226. And that motive would not exist with regard to a juror who is unable to read or write?—Of course that same motive would not exist; but those poor law collectors are intelligent men, and they are fair, and anxious to assist the court, and I have no doubt that if the law cast upon them that obligation, they would fairly come forward and say to the revising chairman, Such-and-such a person I know to be incapable of reading and writing, or I believe him to be so.

227. Would you cast it upon him as an obligation?—I would, as a duty.

228. Under a penalty?—I would not put a pecuniary penalty, but I would say that they should do it, and then it would lie upon the poor law guardians to see that their officers carried out the dictates of the Legislature.

229. *Chairman.*] You do not think that it would be an unpopular thing for them?—I do not. I know, from the experience of hundreds of witnesses that have been examined before me, that so far from being ashamed at not being able to speak or understand English, their great struggle is to show that they cannot speak English or understand English.

230. Then the poor rate collector would be conferring a benefit upon the person whose name he struck off?—Yes; I am sorry to say that I think that in some parts of Ireland there are a great many people who hold comfortable farms, especially the middle-aged generation, who are not able to read or write; more than one would imagine.

231. *The O'Conor Don.*] If you throw the duty upon the poor rate collectors, do not you think that they would expect to be largely remunerated for the additional trouble that it would throw upon them?—I do not think they would, for this reason, that it would not really cast upon them any trouble; it would be merely calling upon them to give expression to their knowledge and information about a person.

232. But they would be obliged, would they not, to obtain that information?—But, practically, the poor rate collector knows every person in his parish.

233. Then would you give him no additional remuneration?—Not for that, certainly.

234. Are you aware that, owing to the duties thrown upon them under this Act, they have throughout Ireland sent in very large bills?—Because they have certain duties thrown upon them by the Act necessarily, which, of course, they ought to be paid for, but this mere addition which

Mr. C. H. Hemphill.

24 April 1873.

which I suggest now, I certainly think they would neither expect nor be entitled to be remunerated for, because they would be merely giving to the court the information which they have.

235. Would you not oblige them to seek that information if they did not happen to know it?—I think it would be desirable to point out that it would be their duty to ascertain if possible whether so and so could read or write.

236. If you were to require them to make those inquiries, that would be an additional duty, would it not, for which they would seek remuneration?—I think myself that they would know it very well without much inquiries, having regard to the habits of the people. Poor rate collectors are men that know almost every man and woman in the parish.

237. Did I rightly understand you to say that you do not consider that there is any power of remunerating the sub-sheriffs for their duties under this Act?—I am not aware of any in the Act. I may be mistaken in that; perhaps I may have overlooked it; but my answer was with reference to the service of jurors.

238. Is there any other duty thrown upon them by this Act which they had not before?—No, I do not think so; there is a change of duties, but no new duties.

239. I will read you the section, and then ask you your opinion upon it. Section 16 says:—"The expenses of this Act, so far as the same shall be incurred in connection with the duties hereby imposed on the clerks of the peace, shall be defrayed out of the grand jury cess, and it shall be lawful for the grand jury of every county, and for every town council empowered to make presentments, as the case may be, from time to time, at the next ensuing assizes or presenting term, and they are hereby required, without previous application at presentment sessions or otherwise, to present all such sums of money as they shall deem reasonable and necessary for defraying the expenses of any printing done in pursuance of this Act, and any other expenses attending the execution of this Act"?—I do not think that that would at all include the case of the service of the summonses by the sheriffs, because that was a duty which they previously had to exercise, and for which they got no remuneration.

240. Are you aware of any other duty that has been thrown upon the sheriff by this Act?—I am not aware that there is any.

241. You think that under these words no additional remuneration can be given to the sheriffs?—That is my impression.

242. You are probably not aware that in the county of Sligo the question was submitted to one of the judges at the late assizes, and he decided that the grand jury had the power under these words of remunerating the sheriffs for the additional expenses under the Act?—I was not aware of that. Of course I bow to any decision of the judges with the greatest possible deference.

243. But you are not aware of that as a matter of fact in the county of Sligo?—I was not aware of that as a matter of fact.

244. I think you stated that you calculated that a juror under the new Act would serve only once in three years?—I think it would be about that in Kerry. You should have at least 36 at each quarter sessions town; but that would be a very small number; in fact the old Act required that there should be not less than 36 and not more than 60. I think that the sheriff would not be doing his duty if he did not summon at least from 36 to 48 at the quarter sessions, because they may have to try felonies. At the quarter sessions every prisoner charged with a felony has the power of challenging 20 jurors, and therefore you must leave a balance for the trial of the case or the jury may be locked up considering a case, and another prisoner may be put upon his trial. Very frequently, in practice, the moment that one jury retires to consider their verdict I call a second jury to proceed with the next case so as not to lose time, so that there ought to be at least from 36 to 48 jurors at each town. I am putting that as the very minimum.

245. But you could not give a rough number of how many actual jurors served in the county in one year?—I have not made that calculation.

246. Do you think it an advantage to have different jurors on every occasion, and that a man should serve only once in three years?—That is my impression; there may be a difference of opinion upon that point, but you would want a jury who had reasonable intelligence, and who listened to the evidence (and there is no difficulty in attending to the evidence, and weighing the evidence), and also who paid a certain attention to the direction of the judge, in point of law. I would not have what you would call regular hack jurors, men who were always serving on juries.

247. There is a distinction between having regular hack jurors and men who serve only once in three years; do you consider that that is sufficiently often to give a man practical experience as a juror?—Quite sufficient in my opinion.

248. Major *O'Reilly*.] With regard to the suggestion of Dr. Ball, and some questions of the O'Conor Don, that a certain valuation should be made a necessary qualification, do you know particularly what sort of valuation is put upon houses in purely agricultural districts?—I believe that the value is very low indeed, and I am fortified in that by a conversation which I had with a very intelligent gentleman, one of the local Government inspectors, who stated that it would be desirable to have a household qualification for jurors, but that it would be impossible in the rural districts to get anything like a household test, the valuation was so very low; he knows a great deal more upon that subject than I can be possibly expected to know.

249. I do not know whether you have examined the valuation as I have done in certain counties, but it struck me that the value must be taken apparently as though a house would let for nothing without the land. In the county of Galway I was surprised on going over some large properties at finding that there was not a single house that was valued at more than 5 *l.* a year, although some of them were good two-storied houses which in any village would let at 25 *l.*; and in the same way I found that a gentleman's house, which would certainly cost from 4,000 *l.* to 6,000 *l.* to build, was valued at 20 *l.* a year. I ask you, therefore, whether you have looked over the valuation sufficiently to know that you could not classify the houses by valuation in country districts?—I have not looked over it with sufficient care to be able to answer the question satisfactorily.

250. Then you propose that there should be a special house qualification for jurors besides the land

Mr. *C. H. Hemphill.*

22 April 1873.

land qualification, in order to bring in another class of jurors?—Yes.

251. That you think would apply practically to towns?—Yes.

252. Have you at all considered what class of house you would think should qualify a man to be on the jury?—I think for a common jury a man paying, we will say, from 12 *l.* to 15 *l.* a year rent, and for a special juror, from 25 *l.* to 30 *l.* That would, I have no doubt, give a very fair class, in addition to the rural class.

253. As to the revision, I have not quite got it clearly what your suggestion of the power to the chairman to strike off a name should be. You said first, for any reasonable cause. Do you intend that in the Act the reasonable causes should be defined, or would you suggest such general words as you think would leave a discretion in the chairman?—Section 12 says that the chairman "shall upon sworn testimony, or any other evidence satisfactory to such chairman or barrister, amend the said lists by expunging therefrom the name of every man whose name shall appear therein respectively who shall be exempted, or who shall not be qualified under this Act, or who from lunacy, imbecility of mind, deafness, blindness, or other permanent infirmity, shall be unfit to serve as a juror." Those are the limits, and we cannot transcend those limits. My idea would be, that "or any other good and sufficient reason" should be added. I think that you might safely give a general discretion to the chairman; but at all events, if that was not desirable, you should extend that category by adding the educational test.

254 But yourself would suggest that there should be a general discretion given to the chairmen?—Yes, I think that it might be safely given to the chairmen considering their general position in relation to the county; they have no local connection with the counties; they are strangers there, and their only object would be to get as good a list as possible for the ordinary trial of cases.

255. Great distinction has been drawn between such discretionary power of the chairman and the present discretionary power of the sheriff, would there not be this broad distinction between them, that one would be discretion by the chairman exercised by a judicial functionary in open court on cause assigned, whereas the discretion exercised by the sheriff is exercised by a non-responsible person in private, without any obligation to state the grounds upon which he exercised it, or any check unless positive corruption shall be proved against him?—There would be that discretion clearly, and also there would be this further distinction, that practically, as I stated, a sheriff is a county man residing in the county.

256. You also suggested that a judge should have power to set aside a juror who could not read or write, or who could not speak English; would it be necessary or desirable, do you think, to give a judge the general power of setting aside a juror on those grounds, which is one which is practically exercised now?—I think that it would be desirable, for this reason, that as the law stands if the counsel on either side objected to the judge setting aside a juror (I am speaking of a civil case) on the ground that he could not read or write, the judge would not have power to do so.

257. Is it not practically the case that counsel never do make such an objection?—I do not know. They might, and I think myself that it would be better to give that power to the judge, because it could lead to no disadvantageous result. Cases may escape the chairman at the revision, no matter how vigilant he may be, from want of information. He may leave on a person of that nature, and then it would be very desirable when such a person came to take the book to be sworn, on a suggestion being made that he could neither read nor write, for the judge to put the question to him when he was there present, and, on ascertaining that he could not either read nor write, to strike him out. I think that that would be very useful.

258. But the law, as I take it, now is that the lists, as made out by the poor law collector, are not to contain the names of any persons who are exempt or who are disqualified by "lunacy, imbecility of mind, deafness, blindness, or other permanent infirmity." It has been stated in the public papers frequently that it is found in practice that those lists or jurors' books do contain the names of not only persons who are disqualified but even of persons who are dead; do you know at all, practically, how that has come to pass?—It has come to pass I know. In two or three instances persons beyond the age of 60 have been on the list before me, and it has been proved at the hearing before me that they were beyond the age of 60 and they were expunged, and I could only account for it in this way, that the collector had not the information.

259. Or that he did not take the trouble to inquire?—Or that he did not take the trouble.

260. There appears to me to be a deficiency in the Act with regard to which I should like to ask whether it has struck you in your experience, and that is that whilst the duty is cast upon the poor rate collector to revise those lists, and it is one which of course gives him trouble, there is in reality no penalty upon him for neglecting that duty, the penalties are otherwise contained in Clause 46, inasmuch as the words are put in "who shall wilfully omit any name," it would follow necessarily that, practically, the poor rate collector is not interested, or but rarely, in revising the list, in the way in which the act directs, and does it not arise from that fact that the poor rate collectors have not made out the lists properly?—It may possibly arise from their not having information, and perhaps it would be too strong to impose a penalty for that which might be the result of something beyond their control. That is the reason why, I apprehend, the word "wilfully" is inserted there.

261. Have you any suggestion to make with a view of insuring that those lists shall for the future be more accurately made out?—My only suggestion is what I have already stated, that there should be an instruction given to the clerks of union and poor rate collectors to bring before the chairman any objection to the fitness or qualification of the juror by printing the word "objected" before his name, and in that way it would impose upon the chairman at once the duty of asking the collector "Why do you do so and so?" And it would elicit from him the grounds on which he had so objected.

262. Do not you think it probable that there would be a greater amount of error of this sort by the inclusion of improper names in the first preparation of the list than are likely to continue, because while the poor rate collector may have returned a number of people over 60 years of age, they are otherwise disqualified

in

Mr. *C. H. Hemphill.*

24 April 1873.

in the first instance, those will naturally be all struck off upon the revision, and every subsequent list has a chance of being more perfect than the first one under the new Act?—Yes, I have no doubt that that would be so, the poor rate collectors would understand their business better after each revision; for instance, there were at the first revision one or two mistakes committed by some of the union clerks, in my county, from reading in the schedule of exemptions, "persons holding any paid judicial or other office belonging to any court of justice in Ireland," as excluding the ordinary unpaid magistrates, and I had myself to point out that error to them, and to add in manuscript to the printed list the names of magistrates who were some of the most valuable special jurors in the county; I only mention that just to illustrate what you say; now when we have got the register into better order, very few mistakes of that sort will be made, and I have no doubt that after three or four years we shall have those jury revision lists also much more perfect than could have been expected with altogether a new Act, and a new duty.

263. It is the duty, is it not, of the poor rate collectors to attend at the revisions?—Yes.

264. And if their lists have been found very inaccurate, they will make them more accurate next year?—Yes, I have no doubt that the chairman would point out any deficiency, and a great many of those difficulties I anticipate will be removed by time alone.

265. Who had the duty of making out the list of qualified jurors under the old system?—The magistrates at the jury sessions revised them.

266. Who made out the lists first?—The county cess collectors; they gave the information as to the occupiers, leaseholders, and freeholders.

267. Were the county cess collectors in a better position than the poor rate collectors are now for obtaining information?—I do not think that they were in so good a position. They could only have acted upon mere hearsay, whereas the present qualification cannot err, being uniform and certain, which I think is one great advantage in the new system.

268. What means had the magistrates at the juror sessions of practically and really revising the list?—Sometimes one got up and said, such and such a person has a freehold of 10 *l.* a *year*, on mere hearsay gossip, it might be. They had no means of really testing the fact.

269. Supposing that he found names on the list that were not qualified, what means had the magistrate of ascertaining whether that was the case or not?—Practically there were no means.

270. Have you any knowledge of what was the practical working of the justices jury sessions?—The practical working was this; that several persons got on the list who had no property qualification at all.

271. Do you know how far the magistrates attended and went over those lists?—I believe that in some counties they took that trouble, but in other counties it was looked upon as a mere matter of routine; one of the Acts repealed in the schedule to this Act was an Act enabling the Lord Lieutenant to appoint special revision sessions in cases where the magistrates had altogether omitted to revise the jury lists.

272. You would not be surprised to find that was my experience for very many years in the county attending the jury revising sessions, that there were hardly ever justices enough to revise, and there was practically no revision whatever?—I am quite sure that that is not only your experience, but the experience of a great number of other magistrates. When the 3rd and 4th of William the 4th was passed, the basis of qualification was not the poor law valuation, but I am quite certain that it would have been if the poor law had then existed in Ireland.

273. Then there was no such thing as the poor law in Ireland, and of course this ready mode of qualification was not attainable?—No.

274. Mr. Bruen suggested that an additional ground of disqualification should be the conviction of any offence against the law; do I take you as agreeing to that suggestion, that any one who had been convicted of any misdemeanour, should be disqualified to serve upon a jury?—I think myself that that would perhaps be going a little too far; because there are cases in the country very often of drunken riots, for instance, without very much moral turpitude in them; they are tried constantly at quarter sessions, where a very honest intelligent farmer may get three months with hard labour, and not be a bit the worse for it after he comes out; those are constantly cases tried at sessions; although perhaps I rather fell into the suggestion of the honourable Member, I would not like to extend that seventh section to a conviction for misdemeanour. I think myself that where you get treason or felony or an infamous crime provided against, it is sufficient. A person may commit a misdemeanour without being so immoral as to be unfit to serve upon a jury.

275. Mr. *Bruen*.] You will observe that I did not make use of the word "misdemeanour"?—No, I am aware that I used it; that was my impression at the time. The question came upon me rather by surprise, but I confess, when I reflect upon it, and knowing how many of those people live, I must admit that many things are punished as misdemeanours in the present state of society in Ireland without involving any real dishonesty or immorality.

276. Major *O'Reilly*.] Is it not a notorious fact that some members of the upper classes, perfectly honourable men, have been convicted of misdemeanour, such as quarrelling, and that many who are now in the commission of the peace in both countries have been convicted of misdemeanours?—Yes; one might bring up many instances of that.

277. Is not the essence of the difference between the system of this Jury Act, and the former system, that the power of the sheriff of selecting the panel is absolutely taken away?—That is the essence of it. There are three distinct and essential differences between the present and the former system; first, in the basis of qualification; next, in the tribunal for revising the jury lists; and thirdly, in what you have mentioned, namely, taking from the sheriff the absolute discretion as to who shall be summoned.

278. Some suggestions have been made as to the advantages accruing from leaving the sheriff the power of summoning whatever jurors he thought best out of the whole panel, and it was suggested that all the jurors from a particular district might be interested in a right of way, and that consequently, whilst the sheriff in the exercise

Mr. *C. H. Hemphill.*

24 April 1873.

exercise of a sound discretion would leave out all the jurors in that district, at least a certain number of them might now get on the panel; should you not consider it a problematical evil arising from that?—Yes.

279. Mr. *Attorney General.*] Might not that be met in Ireland by changing the venue as in this country?—Yes; we do constantly change the venue.

280. Major *O'Reilly.*] Would not all such cases be met at once by applying for a change of venue?—Yes; of course the court have abundant power to change the venue, on the slightest suggestion of any partiality.

281. And the advantage that the sheriff would summon the jurors who live nearer the town, in the winter, where the trial is held, is, you apprehend, to be considered a very slight advantage indeed?—Yes, and countervailed by the greater advantage of the jurors not having to serve so often.

282. You were asked whether you could state any bad result arising from the framing of the panel being in the discretion of the sheriff; whilst it would be impossible and wrong to say, that bad verdicts have been consequent on that discretion, is there any doubt that great discredit has been thrown upon the administration of justice, by the well-known fact that the sheriff could select a jury for a certain purpose?—It was the general idea in Ireland, that in any case of a political nature the sheriff might do so, and that created a feeling of distrust.

283. Is it not possible that he might do it in a civil case too?—Yes.

284. Have you heard of any instances in which such a suggestion was made in the newspaper, or otherwise, that such a thing might have occurred; whether truly or untruly, is immaterial?—I should be sorry to mention or refer in any way to any particular cases.

285. The honourable Member for Carlow referred to the evidence of Mr. Seed, a gentleman who was called before what was commonly called the Westmeath Committee in 1871; I think as illustrative of the advantage of discretion being vested in the sheriff, you were asked whether the sheriff selecting the panel did not obviate the necessity of the law officer of the Crown incurring unpopularity by desiring jurors to stand aside; what was your answer to that question?—My answer was that it was constantly exercised without incurring any personal unpopularity that I ever knew of.

286. Mr. Seed is Crown Solicitor, and not sub-sheriff, as I understand?—He is Crown Solicitor, he never was sub-sheriff.

287. Let me read you a little of his evidence as to the working of that system, and ask your opinion upon it; he said, in answer to Question 2356, "A class of jurors will be found on all the panels of petty jurors in Ireland as now constituted, who are wholly unfit to be trusted with the trial of any prisoner for an agrarian crime;" would not that imply that, in Mr. Seed's opinion, the selection of the panel by the sheriff had not obviated the necessity for some improvement in the system?—Certainly.

288. Then he goes on to say: "The formation of the petty jury panel is now entirely at the discretion of the sub-sheriff, who is often the friend of, and influenced by, the attorney for the prisoners;" he was asked at a subsequent question, number 2393, "Did I understand you to say that the sub-sheriff was frequently influenced by the solicitor employed for the accused," and he answered, "Most frequently; I know cases of it myself;" then the next question was, "Do you confine that observation to your own county, or do you say that it is a matter which has occurred elsewhere?" to which he replied, "I answer the question this way, I have seen by the acts of the sub-sheriff that he was influenced by the prisoner's attorney. I cannot prove that he receives money or that he is bribed by him, but for a person who attends the criminal courts so constantly as I do, it is very easy to observe the influence the prisoner has with the sub-sheriff;" I think you said that, practically, the discretion under the old law in selecting the panel was exercised by the sub-sheriff?—Yes; practically it is so altogether, and without any control.

289. Would not this evidence of Mr. Seed's go to show that in the opinion of a gentleman of such large experience as Mr Seed, that discretion was exercised to the disadvantage of, and not to the advantage of, justice?—Undoubtedly, that is the effect of the evidence.

290. Mr. *Attorney General.*] I think you said that one advantage of the present system was, that you might have upon the trial of common offences, or upon the trial of criminal offences, at all events, men of the highest capacity and intelligence by the formation of one list, upon which all jurors, whether belonging to the common jury class or to the special jury class, are alike to be found?—That is not exactly so. The clerk of the peace is to take out from the general book that is given in by the clerks of unions those who come under the denomination of special jurors.

291. Is the working of that system in Ireland the same as it is in most counties in England, that those who are so taken out of the general list no longer remain in it?—No, they are taken out of the general list for civil purposes; but as I read this Act, they still remain on it for criminal purposes.

292. Then this Act differs from the English law in that respect, that it makes by law a certain class of persons not liable to serve on common juries?—Yes, for civil causes.

293. Do you think that for all purposes it would be an advantage that there should be men of intelligence upon every jury?—I think so.

294. Has it ever occurred to you to consider whether that might be brought about by insisting upon a certain specified proportion of the two classes in each jury?—That, of course, would involve an organic change in the system hitherto existing in Ireland.

295. Not necessarily at all; supposing that there was but one list, and that in the list those who stood as common jurors, but with also a qualification to rank as special jurors, had a distinctive mark put against them, and supposing that, in selecting for a panel, an officer was bound, without giving any notice, to select a specified proportion of those marked with a special mark, would not that secure the object?—I think, myself, that that would be an improvement; I have always thought that there ought to be no such thing as a distinction between special and common jurors.

296. There is none in England by law, and I was not aware that there was any in Ireland until now?—Yes, there was always a "special jurors'" list put at the foot of the book.

297. As far as you can judge, you think that it

Mr. *C. H. Hemphill.*

24 April 1873.

it would be an improvement?—I think so, certainly.

298. Should you be afraid at all of the higher intelligence of a certain portion of the jury, having a bad and antagonistic effect upon the others?—No, I think not. I think that they would amalgamate very well.

299 Have you ever considered the question of unanimity?—I am in favour myself of unanimity, and I have considered it to some extent.

300. It would not do to have a specified proportion; and I do not say a bare majority, but simply that, after a certain time, and with the consent of the judge we will say, two men should not be permitted to nullify the verdict of 10?—My opinion is, that the suitor who was defeated would never be so well satisfied with a verdict of that nature, as under the present system; that is my objection to it. I think that it would prevent that which all judges are anxious to promote, namely, the finality of causes. Especially in Ireland, where people are not easily satisfied with a defeat, it would lead to the suitor saying, "Two men were for me;" and how could it be proved that those men were not right. I think, especially in Ireland, that that would be a dangerous experiment.

301. How would it be in criminal cases?—I think the same result would follow even in criminal cases, or rather it would be worse, because I think that in the case of a political offence, or an agrarian offence, if 12 men are found who convict, my experience and observation has been, that the public have always acquiesced in the justice of that conviction; but if there were two or three men on a jury who are known to be in the minority, I think that such a verdict would not be accepted by the portion of the public who may have sympathised with the accused. I think that that would be the result in Ireland especially.

302. Do you think it capable of defence in reason, that one man should practically prevent the result at which 11 have arrived?—That involves the whole question of trial by jury; it is difficult to say why, logically, it should be so.

303. Not necessarily, because you are aware that the system works so in Scotland?—I am aware that it does in Scotland, but they have a greater number of jurors in Scotland.

304. Of course, you are aware that the 12 was arrived at as the majority of a larger number?—Yes, of course.

305. So that in the institution of juries, the majority governed?—Twelve was arrived at by a sort of analogy to the grand juries finding bills. I have turned it over frequently in my mind, although not with reference to this present inquiry; and I think that in Ireland, at all events, it would lead to great dissatisfaction with the result of cases.

306. I suppose it would, in fact, produce the kind of difference of result which even now is arrived at?—Of course, there are cases where there have been disagreements, but on the other hand I have known in the most trying times in Tipperary, especially when agrarian outrage was at its height (happily now altogether, or nearly disappearing), juries in Nenagh and Clonmel unhesitatingly to convict prisoners, and there were very few cases of disagreement. That has been the result of my observation with a few exceptions.

307. I understood you rather to have given a clear opinion, that reading and writing should be a condition precedent for a juror?—Yes; I think so.

308. Do you really think, that in the majority of cases which have to be decided by common juries, reading and writing is necessary to the formation of a just opinion?—I think that a man that does not read or write, may possibly form an opinion, but a knowledge of reading and writing is a certain test.

309. I am supposing the case of a man who is sufficiently competent to be conducting a farm, and to be otherwise qualified for the purposes of life, and to be a juror; is it your experience really, that such men are incapable of forming a competent opinion upon the broad questions which are generally matters of fact?—They may be perfectly competent to form an opinion, but a juror may happen to be the foreman, the first who answers, and it certainly is very awkward for the foreman not to be able to read an issue paper which is handed up to him.

310. In England, we do it *viva voce*; is the practice different in Ireland?—In Ireland, the issues are on paper, and are handed up to the foreman.

311. Viscount *Crichton*.] Has it happened that the foreman has been unable to read?—Yes; I certainly think that a juror ought to be able to read and write.

312. Mr. *Attorney General*.] Do you seriously think from your experience of Irishmen, that a man who cannot read and write, is in the present day necessarily, or even probably, incompetent to form a reasonable judgment upon the simple matters of fact which are ordinarily presented to a common jury?—There are cases in which he may be competent.

313. Are there not a great many?—There are cases certainly of a simple character in which he may be competent; I will even admit a great many.

314. Would you go a little further, and say the majority of cases?—I would not say the majority.

315. Would it meet your views, do you think, that there should be one law, whatever it be for the two countries?—Decidedly, in every respect, if you could attain it.

316. You think that that would be an advantage?—I do; I have no hesitation in saying that.

317. I do not mean, of course, in detail, because the machinery in many respects, and the systems of the two countries, are different, but I mean substantially that the law should be the same?—I think that that would be very desirable.

318. Supposing it should be determined that a majority of a definite proportion should prevail in England, would you approve of that for Ireland?—I think it very desirable, for every reason, that the law should, when possible, be assimilated.

319. *Chairman*.] If what was suggested to you by the Attorney General were carried into effect, namely, that there should always be a certain number of special jurors on every jury, do you think that in Ireland they would be exposed at all to become marked men in agrarian or political cases?—No; I do not think so. I think myself that the Irish people accept patiently a verdict when given. My experience is that, as far as the juries are concerned, and as far as the judges are

Mr. C. H. Hemphill.

24 April 1873.

are concerned and any one connected with the necessary administration of justice, I have rarely known any particular odium cast upon them, even in the most troubled times. I have never known Crown prosecutors on circuit, or judges or jurors in the most troubled times, at all subject to any vexation.

320. You have known of juries threatened, have you not?—I have heard of some deterrent influences being used, but I think they have been very rare when they have occurred. I am not sure that they ever did take place, but as a general rule I think that there is a respect for the administrators of the law in Ireland, whatever feeling there may be with regard to the law itself, paradoxical as it may appear. There is no instance of an official being molested in Ireland, no matter what the result of the case has been.

321. I suppose that the suggestion could be carried into effect without much difficulty, but it would be necessary to alter the machinery of the Act?—As I understand for Crown purposes it does exist, because there is a general book consisting both of the common and special jurors' book. For Crown purposes that is the book that is used, although for a certain class of civil cases, as I read the Act, special jurors are eliminated from the general book, and formed into the special jurors' book.

322. I think that the Attorney General's suggestion goes a little further than that, if I did not misunderstand it; I think it was that on every jury there should be a certain number of special jurors?—So I understood the Attorney General.

323. And the special jurors may be on the jury trying a criminal case?—Yes, that is as I understand the Act.

324. But in order to secure the attendance of a certain number of special jurors on every jury, a considerable alteration of the machinery of the Act would be required, would it not?—It necessarily would, because you would require your panel to be made out of a certain proportion; I mean adopting the present machinery.

325. Major *O'Reilly*.] Is there anything in the Act which directs that a special juror's name shall not be on the general list?—As I collect from the Act it is this, the general jurors' book contains both the special and common jurors. Then the clerk of the peace under the 13th section, is to make out a special list of jurors; that special list of jurors is the only list for the trial of special civil cases. The general jurors' book containing both special and common jurors is the book that is used for Crown cases.

326. Mr. *Attorney General*.] Or for common jury civil cases?—Or for common jury civil cases; at the assizes the jury is taken from the common jurors' book.

327. Major *O'Reilly*.] Would not the common jurors' book contain the names of special jurors?—It does, certainly. My attention was confined to special jurors' lists and the special jury records. The common jurors' book contains the names of special jurors.

328. Mr. *Heron*.] In Section 13, it is put in this way, that the clerk of the peace "shall insert in a column for that purpose, in the 'general jurors' book,' the word 'special' opposite the name of every person whose name shall appear in both books, and the said clerk of the peace shall, on or before the 1st day of January in every year, deliver the said general jurors' book and special jurors' book to the sheriff," and so on?—Yes, that is so, but the mode of selection is regulated by the 19th section.

Monday, 28th April 1873.

MEMBERS PRESENT:

Dr. Ball.	Marquis of Hartington.
Mr. Bourke.	Mr. Heron.
Mr. Breen.	The O'Conor Don.
Viscount Crichton.	The O'Donoghue.
Mr. Downing.	Major O'Reilly.
Lord Claud Hamilton.	Colonel Wilson Patten.

THE RIGHT HONOURABLE THE MARQUIS OF HARTINGTON, IN THE CHAIR.

Mr. THOMAS DE MOLEYNS, called in; and Examined.

Mr. *De Moleyns.* 28 April 1873.

329. *Chairman.*] I BELIEVE you are a Queen's Counsel?—I am.

330. And Chairman of the County of Kilkenny?—Yes.

331. And a Crown Prosecutor?—Yes, for the City and County of Limerick.

332. You heard Mr. Hemphill's evidence on Thursday, did you not?—Yes, I was here on Thursday.

333. And you heard his statement as to the change which had been effected in the law by the recent Jury Acts?—Yes.

334. I think we need not go over that ground again, unless there was anything in his statement which you wish to add to with regard to the changes that have been effected in the law?—I think that he stated them quite correctly.

335. Have you had any experience of the working of the present Acts?—As Crown Prosecutor for the County and City of Limerick, I attended to prosecute on behalf of the Crown at the last Limerick assizes; the Munster circuit was the first circuit that went out, and consequently there was some interest excited as to the first working of the new Act in the country parts of Ireland. At Ennis, which was the first town in the circuit, there was no conviction at all; at Limerick there was a heavy calendar; there was one case of murder; three cases of manslaughter; several cases of very aggravated assaults, which are usually the most trying cases for jurors; and there were the ordinary class of common cases. The result I cannot say was a particularly happy one, at least in my opinion; there were several cases of acquittals, some disagreements, and only two convictions, and those certainly not in a very exciting class of cases; the one being for stealing a donkey, the other for stealing a cow; in all the other cases there were either acquittals or disagreements, with the exception of the two or three cases in which the prisoners pleaded guilty; but so far as regarded the operation of the Act by Juries, there were only those two convictions at Limerick, following the assizes at Ennis, in which there was no conviction.

336. Viscount *Crichton.*] How many cases were there altogether?—There were 21 cases in the county of Limerick; four or five of those were postponed, one or two persons pleaded guilty, and the results that I now state must be taken from about 14 cases, which either were actually tried, or in which the prisoners pleaded guilty.

337. *Chairman.*] What class of cases were they?—Generally speaking, of a serious character. But having stated thus much as to the result of this first trial at the assizes at Limerick, I should state that I think the Act hardly received a fair trial upon that occasion.

338. Will you be good enough to tell the Committee what opinion you formed of the intelligence and fitness of the juries; could you judge of the class of men from whom they were brought?—They certainly were of a very inferior class, those that actually attended. I was going to state that I think it was hardly a fair trial of the Act. In the first place, I think there was a great deal of preconceived prejudice against it; in the next place, there was a great deal of hostility, I think, which came out in strong relief at the first failures; but, above all, I should say that whilst, very much to their credit, the whole of the new class of jurors attended with great regularity in answer to their names, there was a marked absence of all the more experienced and older jurors; so marked, as to call for very strong observations from the presiding judge; and I certainly think that had this class attended they might probably have leavened the mass of jurors, and by their superior intelligence and experience have, in some cases, at least led to sounder conclusions than, I think, were arrived at in several of the cases which I have specified or generally mentioned. Perhaps I should add, that in all cases of great alterations in the law, there generally is a very strong prejudice at first as to their working.

339. Have you had any experience of the Act, as chairman?—As chairman, I have had experience to some extent at one sessions held in Kilkenny, but I should state that those particular quarter sessions following very closely upon the assizes, there were not many criminal cases for trial at the sessions; however, the experience

Mr. *De Moleyns.*

18 April 1873.

perience which I have had as to the working of the Act there is not at all so unfavourable as it was in the case of the assizes at Limerick. I believe I may add generally, that the experience of other chairmen has also been less unfavourable as to the class of jurors attending at sessions, as distinguished from assizes.

340. You had mentioned the absence of a particular class of jurors at the assizes, were any steps taken to correct that for the future?—As to the future, I do not know that any steps could be taken beyond that of fining them for non-attendance; the judge in several cases commented very strongly upon their absence, and directed them to be called upon fines, and they were fined. At a subsequent stage of the assizes they attended, and many of them pleaded that they were not at all aware that under the new Act they were to be called, for the first time, upon what is called the long jury panel for criminal trials. I may add, that I think it is one of the advantages of the new Act that by the 19th section, I think it is, all special jurors are included in the general panel; and the jurors are directed to be taken in the first instance for the trial of criminal business at the assizes.

341. Some jurors were actually fined, were they not?—Yes, many of the jurors were fined, but I believe the fines were remitted subsequently upon the statement which I have mentioned as to their not being aware that they were bound to attend, it being the first time the new Act came into operation.

342. You have also stated that you thought that there was a good deal of prejudice against the new Act; in what way did that operate unfavourably?—To this extent: I think that any shortcomings were rather ostentatiously paraded, and, I should say, made the most of. In fact, there was a general feeling to discredit the Act through the country. It is in that way that I alluded to what may be called a prejudice against it.

343. Was the power of ordering jurors to stand aside extensively used?—It was extensively used in a very serious case, the case of a son charged with poisoning his father, in which the jury eventually disagreed, and in which both challenges by the prisoner, and the power of setting aside jurors by the Crown, were extensively acted upon.

344. By whom is the power of ordering jurors to stand aside actually used, by the Crown Solicitor, or by the Crown Prosecutor?—By the Crown Solicitor upon his own responsibility.

345 As far as you were able to observe, was that power sufficiently and judiciously exercised?—Certainly.

346. Did you observe many cases in which the jurors appeared to be actually ignorant and unable to read or write?—I cannot specifically say that I am aware that any juror was unable to read or write.

347. But they appeared to be decidedly of a lower class than those whom you had been accustomed to see as jurors?—Certainly: and that was accounted for to some extent, by the fact, which I think is greatly to their credit, that they almost all attended, whilst the better class, the older and more experienced jurors, did not attend.

348. Have you formed any opinion as to the principle of the Act?—I must say that I think that the Act is quite correct in principle and in its conception. The principle appears to me to be to endeavour to secure fair, and what the law calls, though perhaps upon this occasion it is not a very happy term, "indifferent jurors," by extending the class, and by extending the area from which they are to be taken; and a second principle which is strongly kept in view throughout the Act, that the jurors that have once served should not be called upon again within a very long period to repeat their services. I think, however, that there is another and an equally important consideration to be kept in view, that the jurors should be capable, should be intelligent, should be, to some extent at all events, removed beyond the probable rank of the usual classes of offenders, and also above all, should be free from the chance of intimidation, and perhaps what is more to be feared, solicitations on the part of the friends of the prisoners; I speak more of the criminal business now than of the civil. I think that whilst the principle was correct, that some alterations certainly are required to ensure the Act working well.

349. Do you think that there was any great objection to the old system, on the score of want of qualification of many of the jurors?—I am not aware that there was any objection of that sort; I think that applied more, perhaps, to the City of Dublin jurors. I am not aware that there was any actual want of qualification complained of as regards the country parts of Ireland, at least in those parts with which I am familiar.

350. Was it not the fact, that it was very difficult to ascertain whether any particular person did possess the statutory qualification?—Yes, it was difficult to ascertain certainly, because there was no well-defined basis of qualification. A 10 *l.* freehold, a 15 *l.* leasehold, and a house worth 20 *l.* a year, were difficult matters to investigate by the magistrates at the sessions.

351. But you have no doubt about the propriety of the alteration which deprives the sheriff of the power of selection?—I think it was a very invidious power to give to any person, and that person generally one who has filled the office for several successive years; therefore it was a power which might be complained of very properly, as it would vest in him the full discretion year after year, not only as to the jurors to be summoned, but as to the jurors to be exempted from being summoned, which was equally a subject of complaint; I think some change was necessary, and the Act has made a change in the right direction by having a substantial basis of qualification, and extending the area from which they are to be taken.

352. There was, under the old system, a possibility, at all events, of the panel not being impartially framed?—There was that possibility; but at the same time, whilst I object to the system, I must add, with regard to the counties with which I am familiar, Limerick and Kilkenny, that I am not aware that any practical objection of that sort was ever made to the exercise of his discretion by the sheriff or under-sheriff.

353. Are you aware that in some counties that charge has been made?—I am aware that it has, whether rightly or wrongly.

354. Under the law as it stood, it was possible, was it not, that partiality might be exercised?—Yes, possible.

355. Will you state what modifications, in your opinion, are required?—The Act as at present framed appears to recognise an absolute

Mr. *De Moleyns.*

28 April 1873.

lute right upon the part of every man who is rated at a particular sum to serve as a juror, with certain very defined restrictions. Every person who is rated at 20 *l.* is returned as a juror, unless he is convicted of treason or felony, or unless he is an idiot, or a lunatic, or deaf, or blind, or afflicted with any other permanent infirmity. I think that the restrictions have been rather too jealously framed in that respect. I think that the office of a juror differs in many respects, we will say, from that of a Parliamentary elector; that it is not necessary to recognise an absolute right in every person who has a rateable qualification of 20 *l.* to fill so delicate and so difficult an office as to sit as a juror upon questions involving, sometimes, the life, and often the property and the liberty of his fellow subjects. I think that there should be, besides this rated qualification, some consideration, at all events, of ordinary personal fitness recognised.

356. Have you considered how that could be ascertained?—That is a most difficult question to answer; the only plan that occurs to me is this, that instead of the power of selection of individuals, as hitherto exercised by the sheriff, some power of selection must be given at an anterior period to the present revising tribunal; in fact, to the chairman.

357. In the first place, do you approve of the revising authority established under the Act?—At present, let me say in answer, that from the strict limitations, and I may almost say from the jealous way in which the Act has been framed, the office of chairman is almost nominal in revising the lists; the poor rate collectors naturally know all who have been convicted of those offences, or who are afflicted with any permanent infirmity, and consequently the list, as at present submitted to the chairman, imposes upon him merely a nominal duty. At my sessions in Kilkenny there were only two cases in which I was called upon to strike any person off the list, and those were brought forward by the under agent of Lord Bessborough, the one being a stonemason, I think, who was over 60 years of age, and the other being a person in his employ in a similar capacity, and also over the age; those were the only two instances in which I had to strike off any person

358. Dr. *Ball.*] They would have been on the panel otherwise?—Yes; if they had not personally appeared, and been brought forward to claim the exemption on account of age. I think there are difficulties in entrusting any person with what may be called an absolute discretion; but the only way that I see out of the difficulty is by entrusting to the chairman, who, at all events, would exercise his discretion judicially, the power of going beyond the strict disqualifications, and, by a few words introduced into the 12th section, meeting to some extent this difficulty. As the Act stands now, he is to expunge the name of every man who shall be exempted, or not qualified, or who is incapacitated from lunacy, imbecility of mind, deafness, blindness, or any other permanent infirmity; and there it stops short. I would merely add these words: "or from any other cause shall, in the judgment of such chairman, be unfit to serve as a juror." I think that I have said already that it is unpleasant for any person to exercise a discretion of this sort; but still I know of no other tribunal that can do it. The chairman, at all events, has considerable local knowledge and no local prejudices, and he sits in a court where he can be assisted by the poor rate collectors, and, I would also suggest, assisted by the local Crown solicitor, and by others who may give to him the necessary information, which, if he is given that discretion, would enable him to put aside many who I think, in the judgment of impartial men, might be unfit to serve as jurors, although they were neither deaf, nor blind, nor convicted of any infamous crime, or of treason, or of felony.

359. Is not it almost necessary that his attention should be called in some way on the list itself to the alleged disqualification of a juror?—I would rather object to that; I think that the machinery which has been recommended to the Committee, that is to say, throwing upon the poor rate collectors the duty of entering upon the list a column with the word "objected," would be to throw too great a responsibility upon them, considering the nature of the objections that might be gone into before the chairman. I think it would be very much better that, in a case of this sort, the poor rate collectors should be instructed to collect beforehand every information possible as to the condition in life, and so forth, of the juror; and that the chairman, sitting in his own court, with their assistance, should exercise that discretion which I have ventured to suggest would be the only remedy for the evil.

360. Mr. *Downing.*] The poor rate collector has nothing to say under this Act to the List of jurors?—No.

361. *Chairman.*] You would make the chairman dependent upon the assistance which he could get at the revision court itself?—I think he can get a great deal of information, and that he possesses a great deal of information. I would merely suggest, with the permission of the Committee, one or two instances: A man has not been convicted either of treason or felony, but he has been convicted, we will say, of a very aggravated assault, such as too often occurs in Ireland, for which he may be sentenced to five years' penal servitude; or he may be convicted of an assault of a less aggravated character, and sent for a year to prison; I do not myself think that five years' penal servitude, or confinement in prison for a year, exactly fits a man to take afterwards the office of a county juror; and, if the case came before me, I should certainly exercise the discretion which I ventured to suggest ought to be given by the Act, and I would expunge the name of such person from the list.

362. But do you think that, in the way which you propose, you could rely upon the facts being brought before you, because the chairman would not know of those things as facts within his own knowledge?—The chairman has very difficult questions to decide upon all sorts of conflicting facts and conflicting evidence.

363. The list of names conveys no idea to the chairman, I presume?—The list of names by itself would not, except as to some particular case that he may be familiar with, or perhaps as to a great many persons from his long knowledge of the county; but as to the difficulty of ascertaining truth by evidence, of course there is always some difficulty.

364. That is not my point; my point is, that the chairman would, of himself, very rarely know that John Murphy, say, was a person against whom there was any ground of objection?—Usually not.

Mr. *De Moleyns.*

28 April 1873.

365. And therefore he must depend, must he not, upon the information which he may be able to elicit upon the spot?—Upon information from various sources; from the poor rate collector, from the clerk of the peace, from the local Crown solicitor, and from what he has himself seen in the district upon previous criminal trials, as to previous jurors serving before him, and also upon his very great knowledge of the county, by means of the innumerable civil bills which he is called upon to decide; and, of course, he must depend to a very great extent upon the evidence that is presented before him.

366. Have you ever acted as the revising authority?—Yes; it is part of the duty of the chairman to revise the jury lists.

367. At your own sessions?—Yes.

368. Do you recollect how many names were on the list which you had to revise?—I have had a return from the sheriff of Kilkenny, and at present the total number of rated jurors over 20*l.* would be 3,283.

369. At how many places did you revise that list?—At seven different places.

370. So that you had, on the average, between 400 and 500 names to revise at each sessions?—Yes.

371. And you think that sufficient local information might be forthcoming at each of those sessions to enable you to revise thoroughly and completely those lists?—I would hardly say completely. It is a remedy which I would merely suggest, not a security that we shall be infallible, or that we shall be able to make what I may call a thoroughly pure and proper list. I think that if the chairman has that discretion he would be much more likely to err in the direction of not exercising it sufficiently, by allowing persons to remain on that are not exactly fit, rather than by expunging too many names.

372. Would you make inability to read and write a ground of disqualification?—I think so. With regard to the examination of Mr. Hemphill by the Attorney General, it occurs to me, that although in some cases possibly a person who cannot read or write may, from general intelligence, be a very good juror, yet it might as well be argued that he would therefore be, under all general circumstances, fit to serve as a juror, as that a person with one arm would be able to perform all the functions of life, although he might be very fit for certain things. I would merely add, recollecting that each juror is liable to serve on all classes of cases, how could a person who is not able to read or write try cases of forgery, or cases where comparisons of handwriting are required, and in all cases, both civil and criminal, comparisons of handwriting are now admitted. I think myself that that is a fair and proper ground of disqualification; that a person has no vested right to sit as a juror upon other persons, and that a test of his fitness ought to be applied for performing a delicate and difficult office, involving the interests of others.

373. Although there might be a few shrewd and intelligent men who might be excluded by such a test as that, you do not think that, on the whole, the county would lose a great deal?—I think not.

374. Is it not the fact that of the persons under 60 years of age, there are very few who are qualified by position or intelligence to serve as jurors, who cannot read or write?—I think that in the two counties that I am particularly acquainted with, Limerick and Kilkenny, they can read and write, and that educated intelligence is very generally diffused throughout Ireland.

375. The system of national education has been now very generally spread throughout Ireland?—Yes, I think there is a very extensive diffusion throughout Ireland both of natural intelligence and of educated intelligence; I may add that with regard to this discretion, what I should call rather "relieving" persons from the duty of serving on juries than any other term, I should say that probably there would be very little offence felt at the fact of their being removed; I would also suggest that an appeal should be given, and any person who might conceive himself aggrieved might come personally afterwards at any time before the chairman and submit himself for examination without any attorney, and claim his right to be retained on the list.

376. Would you exclude publicans from the list?—Certainly; I would make that a positive ground of disqualification, for the reasons given by Mr. Hemphill.

377. I understand you to object to a suggestion that was made, that the poor rate collector should place the word "objected" against the name of any person on the list?—I think that it would be better not; that suggestion has been taken, I think, from the Parliamentary Registration Act, where there are certain stringent clauses, that if a person claiming is out of possession, or is not rated, and so on, he is objected to, and there properly the word "objected" is put before his name to call the attention both of the claiming elector and of the chairman to the fact, but I think that that differs from what is now suggested as to jurors.

378. Would you see any objection to another column being added to the list which the poor rate collector has to prepare, in which he should state opposite to the juror's name any circumstance which in his opinion ought to be brought to the notice of the chairman, for instance, that he cannot read and write?—I think that it would be almost better if he received instruction as to this matter, to make every inquiry as to the circumstances, the intelligence, and so forth, of the juror, and then, as the poor rate collectors also attend the court, the chairman would, of course, have them before him, and the collector would state those same matters without writing formally the word "objected" upon the list; that, however, is a mere matter of opinion.

379. Do you think that there would be anything invidious about such a duty?—Of course, any objection to anybody is to some extent invidious, but I hardly think that it would be very invidious.

380. Would it be more invidious for the poor rate collector to have to state it formally upon the face of his list, than verbally before the chairman?—It occurs to me that however invidious or disagreeable to the individual it might be, all those considerations are quite subservient to the public duty of collecting intelligent and independent jurors.

381. Would it not be in many cases considered to be conferring a service upon the juror in removing him from the list?—Frequently, I think, it would; I do not think it is a duty which any person is particularly ambitious to perform.

382. Do you not think it probable that when the operation of the Act is more widely known, jurors

jurors will themselves come forward and ask to be excused?—At present they could not ask to be excused upon any grounds but the narrow ones which I have enumerated.

383. But if those grounds were extended, do you think that they would themselves come forward and claim exemption?—I am not certain that they would; they take very little interest in the business of the court of revision now; they seldom attend to it. I would suggest, in addition, that the basis of qualification should be raised. I think, if I might so phrase it, that too low a stratum has been arrived at, that is to say, that it has been brought down too low; I say this, of course, not in any offensive or invidious sense, but I mean too low in point of property qualification. The only two remedies that I can suggest, whilst freely approving of the principle of the Act, and its conception, are to raise the basis of qualification to some extent, and to give a power of selection in some shape or other beyond the narrow limits now given by the Act, so as to excuse persons who, although possessed of the property qualification, might be, in the judgment of other people, unfit to take the office.

384. Have you considered whether the household qualification might not be added to the basis?—I do not see my way to the household qualification; but I may remark, that on this head there is an omission which ought to be remedied. In the 4th Schedule of the Act, as to particular counties, there is a qualification which acts very well, I think. In the 4th Schedule, Class 1, there are 11 counties in which the qualification is 20 *l.*, "or a net annual value of 12 *l.* or upwards in respect of lands, tenements, or hereditaments appearing on the rate-book of any union to be situate in any city, town, or village within any of the said counties." That 12 *l.* qualification is a very valuable one, as it appears to me; it diversifies the class of jurors, and in general they are a very intelligent description of persons occupying those premises within the limits of towns or villages; but in Class 2, comprising a more numerous class of counties, the qualification is merely "a net annual value of 20 *l.* or upwards in respect of lands, tenements, or hereditaments within any of the said counties," stopping short of the 12 *l.* qualification, and I do not see villages within this class.

385. In Class 2 you get no townspeople, unless they are rated over 20 *l.*?—No, unless they are rated over 20 *l.*, or unless they are rated within what are called counties of cities or boroughs having separate sessions. What I venture to suggest is, in this class, that a rate of 12 *l.* in respect of tenements or hereditaments in any towns, &c., within any of the said counties also might be included; for instance, take the case of the county of Louth and the town of Dundalk; I do not see why you should not have this qualification in that case. Take the county of Tyrone, why not in Omagh also? and so going through them, assimilating, in fact, the second class of counties in this respect to the first class.

386. Have you considered how high you would raise the qualification?—I do not think that it could be safely raised higher than 30 *l.*, so as to secure a sufficient number of jurors; but I may add also, that I think in that respect the Act has gone rather too far in its anxiety to exempt jurors from serving more than once in three years. It occurs to me that they may very well be made to serve once in a year and a half, or two years, and probably raising the limit to 30 *l.* would not impose that obligation upon them oftener than once in two years. It appears that in Kilkenny, for instance, looking at a return from the sheriff, if the qualification were raised to 30 *l.* and upwards, there would be 2,198 jurors on the general list instead of 3,283, and upon making a computation, it appears that if they were all served as now directed, they would not be called upon to act more than once in two years. I think, with a view to ensure what I may call aptitude on the part of a juror, that limit of serving once only in three years is too extended, so that it does not occur to me that this objection to being called upon to serve more frequently than once in three years should be any argument against raising the qualification to a certain extent; I would say 30 *l.* in ordinary counties, and 70 *l.* for special jurors in the other class of counties; 100 *l.* applies to some counties, but with the other second class counties I would say 30 *l.* and 70 *l.*

387. Major *O'Reilly.*] What would you do with the other class of counties, where the present qualification is only 15 *l.*?—That only applies to one county Leitrim; and let me add also, that my experience is, that in the case of cities and towns, such as Kilkenny and Limerick, the Act works very well with the present qualifications; I am not aware that there has been any reason to complain of the working of the Act in cities or towns.

388. *Chairman.*] Then the qualification that you recommend would be 30 *l.* for jurors resident in the country, with an additional qualification of 12 *l.* in towns?—That is as to towns within Class 2 of the counties. Might I be allowed to suggest that I think it would be desirable that the principle of balloting from the list should be extended to criminal cases, under Section 41; at present it is held that it does not apply; they are called in alphabetical order now upon the trials; for instance, take the surname "Abraham," which was the first in the county of Limerick; he was always called upon every trial, as number one. Section 41 is held to apply only to the civil class of cases to be balloted for, and I think that the ballot should apply to all criminal cases, with the view of the attendance of what I call a higher class of jurors, and thereby a more experienced class.

389. Is there any other suggestion which you would wish to make to the Committee?—Not at present.

390. Dr. *Ball.*] Before the present Act jurors were taken by ballot in both criminal and civil case, were they not?—Yes, my recollection is so.

391. There has been, as I understand you, only one quarter sessions since the Act came into operation?—Only one.

392. And that quarter sessions followed the assizes?—Yes.

393. It is the duty of the judge, is it not, to clear the gaol of criminal cases?—Yes.

394. Therefore, at the last sessions in the Civil Bill Courts, there must have been a very slight trial of this Act in criminal cases?—So I have stated as regards Kilkenny, at all events.

395. Because there could be only those criminal cases which occurred between the judge clearing the gaol at the assizes and that sessions?—Certainly. Perhaps I may also add that the reverse state of things occurs at the summer assizes.

Mr. De Moleyns. 23 April 1873.

396. There are no jurors, I think, in ejectment cases in the Civil Bill Courts?—No; we are forbidden to employ them.

397. Had you any case of a civil character tried by a jury at all before you at your last sessions?—I sometimes wish, particularly in what are called warranty cases, to have the assistance of persons of a very intelligent character upon questions of fact that arise in those cases.

398. But you do not empanel 12, do you?—No.

399. Speaking now of the last sessions, had you any civil case with a jury at all?—Yes.

400-1. How many?—Three or four, that is all.

402. The rest were decided by yourself alone?—Yes; we have the power of calling in the assistance of a jury in all cases, except ejectment cases and land cases.

403. You are not obliged to have 12?—No; six where the parties apply themselves for a jury, and three or any other number where the chairman of his own accord wishes for the assistance of other persons upon matters of fact.

404. Before this recent Act was passed, were juries of the quarter sessions composed of the same class of jurors as constituted the panel at the assizes?—No.

405. Were they inferior in position?—Yes, they were inferior.

406. Then there could not have been as much difference between the juries that were formerly in the Civil Bill Courts and the new juries under this Act, as between juries that were formerly at assizes and juries under this Act at assizes?—That is so.

407. I think you stated that in criminal cases under this Act the panel ought to contain more jurors than for civil purposes; that is to say, it ought to contain some special jurors?—It does contain them under the section of the Act at assizes. The sheriff is directed not to eliminate any special jurors from the general Jurors' List for the criminal panel, and, in addition to that, he is directed to return this panel before he selects the special juries, properly so called, for the trial of special issues. Everything is done by that section that I think could be done for the purpose of securing, as far as the principle of the Act allows, a good class of jurors for the trial of criminal cases.

408. Then the criminal panel at the assizes, according to that Act, is superior to the panel for civil purposes at the same assizes?—Yes; the general panel for the trial of criminal cases is superior to the ordinary common panel for the trial of common issues, as containing some special jurors.

409. And if the panel in the criminal cases has turned out a failure, it must be so, *à multo fortiori*, in the civil cases?—With the exception, of course, that either party may apply for special jurors.

410. It being the actual fact that there is a higher panel for criminal cases, if that fails, you may infer that if it is an inferior panel for civil cases, *à fortiori*, that fails also?—I say, certainly, that with the addition of the special jurors the criminal panel is, as I have said, superior to the ordinary common panel.

411. In a county that has a great number of towns, have you not a much better chance of having a good panel at the assizes, under the present law, than in a county which is purely agricultural?—I should conceive so.

412. You get those men of intelligence, who are engaged in business in towns?—Yes, I think so; and a mixed class, which is always an advantage.

413. You said that you would raise the qualification, but you seem to doubt if the qualification ought to be based upon residence in a particular class of house; do not you think that the character of the house which a man occupies is much more a sign of his civilisation and refinement than the fact that he cultivates a certain amount of land?—I think so, unquestionably.

414. Do not you observe, that if a man gets a little civilisation, being a farmer, the very first thing he does is to improve his house?—I would not go to that extent in Ireland.

415. But still they do in some degree improve their houses?—It is a very remarkable fact how little you can judge of the wealth, or the circumstances of any person in Ireland, that is to say, in the south and west of Ireland, by the fact of his residence. It is to be lamented, but it is so.

416. Where they have good houses, do not you think that they are generally of a better class?—Yes, certainly.

417. What do you say as to the suggestion which has been made of compelling certain special jurors to serve upon every case, say three out of 12, or four out of 12?—These are matters of detail; but I doubt whether the respective classes would not become antagonistic to each other. Whilst I think that there is no such feeling in existence if they are selected indiscriminately from the general panel; the moment you get three persons who are said to be of a superior class, and are appointed as such, that moment there is an antagonism set up, as it appears to me.

418. *Mr. Bruen.*] I think you said that you had occasion to summon a grand jury at the quarter sessions at Kilkenny; did I understand you to say that that was a criminal case?—There were criminal cases.

419. Did you find that upon that grand jury there were some persons who were illiterate?—No; the grand jury at the sessions are directed to be taken from the special jurors, and I think it could hardly be anticipated that persons having rated qualifications of over 50 *l.*, and 100 *l.* in some counties, would be absolutely illiterate.

420. That absolutely contradicts what I have heard, that there was a grand juror at the last quarter sessions at Kilkenny who could not read or write?—I was not aware of it.

421. *Mr. Downing.*] The sheriff would scarcely empanel a person who could neither read nor write on the grand jury?—No; for the sessions he must take them from the special jurors. The sheriff has not the same discretion in selecting grand jurors for the sessions as he has for the assizes; at the assizes he may select any person, whereas at the sessions he must select from the special jurors.

422. *Mr. Bruen.*] What is the rule under which the sheriff must act in calling together the grand jury for quarter sessions?—He must select from the special jurors' list; and if a sufficient number cannot be obtained, then he may take them from the common jury list.

423. But first he has the power of selecting them at discretion, has he not?—I think not; I think that he follows by rotation, as it is called. The great principle of the act is what is called the rotatory clause, that of selection by rotation.

424. Supposing the fact to be true, which I have heard, that there was one illiterate man upon the grand jury, it would be owing to the sheriff

Mr. *De Moleyns.*

28 April 1873.

sheriff being obliged to select his grand jurors by rotation in accordance with the new Act of Parliament?—So I should assume, supposing the fact to be so.

425. As regards the qualification for jurors, I think you said that you approve very much of the qualification which was introduced into Class 1, in the first schedule of the Act, giving the qualification to persons having a nett annual valuation of 10 *l.* or upwards, in respect of hereditaments situate in cities, towns, and villages?—Yes.

426. Can you tell me how a village is to be defined: what is a village?—I think that the Ordnance Survey gives the limits; that is my impression.

427. But does the Ordnance Survey actually say what is a village, and what is not a village, in the case of a small collection of houses?—I am really not exactly aware how that may be, but I should imagine that there would be no practical difficulty in ascertaining it. Unless there is some such pratical difficulty as would render it impossible so to segregate them, I think it would be an advantage to the panel that there should be this class added in those counties that I have named in Class 2.

428. What difference would there be between a collection, we will say of 10 houses, which would come under the denomination of a village, and a collection of eight houses, which would not come under that denomination; there would be no particular difference in the class of men living there, would there?—Those are things which I think in practice do not create any difficulty, although, perhaps, defining them beforehand may be difficult; I think that we all know, popularly speaking, what is called a town, city, or village; it must at all events contain a sufficient number of tenements to give this qualification to a person inhabiting a house and premises.

429. I think you said that you considered that the Act was deficient in that it gave no power of selection to anybody?—To anybody as it stands now; I think that it has too jealously defined the different disqualifications.

430. Do you recommend that that power of selection should be lodged in the hands of the chairman?—I rather demur to the word "recommend." I merely suggest it as the only course which really occurs to my mind; I need hardly say that it is one that we are not anxious to assume, and one that would impose a great deal of trouble (if I may call any public duty a trouble), or a great deal of additional public duty upon us; the Act itself uses the word "selection," but it is a selection within very defined limits, that is to say, by alphabetical series.

431. It seems very much the same thing whether they select a certain number of persons by eliminating those that are not fit to serve, or whether they select those that are fit to serve out of a general list?—I should not, of course, venture to suggest that the chairman should return the panel of jurors, whilst I do not object under the circumstances to give him the power of expunging those whom he may think unfit, or whom it is not expedient to return.

432. In theory, the result of the process would be the same, that you retain upon the jurors' list those who would be fit to serve?—Yes, exercising a judicial discretion, and under the responsibility which that discretion always imposes.

433. Who are to make the objections before the chairman to the persons that are unfit to serve? I have already suggested, I think, the poor law collectors, the clerk of the union, and if necessary the clerk of the peace, and I would also add the local Crown solicitor; and you will remember also that the Act, as it at present stands in the section giving the power of revision, says that the chairman shall by evidence on oath, or from any other source (those are not the exact words) have the power to amend the list.

434. The Act does not make it compulsory on anybody, or the duty of anybody, to come forward and make objections?—No; the Act first of all enjoins the rate collectors and clerks of the union to return all persons except those exempt or disqualified. The lists are so returned to the chairman, and, practically speaking, as those disqualified are well known, he has nothing to do but to sign his name to the lists.

435. You suggest that besides that, there should be objections made before the chairman against those men on the list who are unfit to serve, and that those objections should be made by certain persons?—I say that the chairman should have the power of receiving objections from any of those persons who attend before him, who have local knowledge, and the chairman then to act upon his own discretion as to whether he does or does not think the objections so well founded as to render it inexpedient to retain the particular names on the jurors' list.

436. But you would not make it the duty of any of those officials to make the objections?—I would give certain instructions to them. Their duty now is defined by the Act to make those inquiries, and I would give instructions to them to be prepared, when they are attending before the chairman to be examined, as to the circumstances and other conditions of any jurors whom they may think not fit, from special causes, to serve.

437. Ought not those instructions to be given in any amendment of the Act of Parliament that might be advisable?—I think not; they could hardly be defined beforehand.

438. Who would give the instructions?—I think that the chairman might do that. If he is to be intrusted with the power at all, he might give to the clerk of the peace the instructions which he thinks ought to be given to the poor-rate collectors. A great deal might be done through the machinery of the county courts at present, which would be inexpedient to have specified upon the face of the Act.

439. Among those persons whose duty it was to make the objection, or rather who would be instructed, as I understood you to say, to make those objections, would you include the constabulary?—The constabulary are authorised in several cases now to object as to publicans' licenses and other things, and certainly the constabulary might give information as to convictions for assaults or convictions for misdemeanors; but I can hardly give a positive opinion as to whether it would be wise to be employing the constabulary in these cases generally.

440. Still the object is to get the greatest amount of information that you can?—In fact, I think, without specifying who should make the objections, the chairman might be at liberty to hear any evidence that was produced before him at the court; and I am quite certain that the constabulary would attend whenever there had been

Mr. *De Moleyns.*

28 April 1873.

been a conviction for any offence, and give evidence before him of the fact.

441. Do you think that those persons, living amongst the farmers against whom they would be required to make the objections, would do it unless they were actually instructed to do so by some binding authority?—I think they would; I find no difficulty of that sort; I think that they are all ready to give any evidence, and to further the views of the court, and the business of the court, in every way.

442. At the same time, in many cases it would be rather an invidious thing to do, would it not?—To a certain extent any objection is invidious, but I do not think there is much delicacy amongst those persons in doing what they consider their duty.

443. Do you think that they would be ready to come forward and make those objections without any actual authority to compel them?—I think that if the duty which I have suggested were thrown upon the chairman, he would feel it his duty to inform the poor-rate collectors that they should be prepared to state to him any objections they might think tenable to the fitness or the expediency of a particular person serving as a juror, and that they would state so to him, and he would have then to make his way as he best could according to the evidence, and discharge this duty, as he does many other difficult duties, as he best may; that is the only solution that I can offer to effect the object I have suggested.

444. Still there would be this general power of eliminating from the list those persons who were unfit to be jurors?—Or whom it is inexpedient, in the judgment of the chairman, to retain.

445. "From any other cause" are the words that you used?—Yes; I think that you never can define in an Act of Parliament every cause which might render it inexpedient to retain a person in such an office as that of a juror, which I think is quite different from that of a Parliamentary elector.

446. This revision carried on in the form that you say you admit, would be a very delicate thing, and to a certain extent invidious?—I do not say that on the part of the chairman; he must exercise the duty that is given him by the Act of Parliament, and I am sure that he would do it without any regard to considerations of that sort; he is a person greatly interested in the matter himself, and he would feel it his duty, by every means possible, to secure what is the greatest object, that is, a capable, intelligent, and independent class of jurors.

447. Viscount *Crichton.*] I suppose you find no jurors in your county that do not understand English?—I think none. We have no interpreter which is, perhaps, the best proof of that.

448. That would make a ground of disqualification, would it not?—Yes, that ought certainly to be a ground of disqualification.

449. With regard to the last assizes at Limerick, you stated that there were five cases postponed; were they postponed, or any of them, in consequence of the nature of the panel?—No, there were specific reasons for each of them, which, in the judgment of the Crown, rendered it expedient that they should be postponed; I think it better not to state those reasons, as the cases remain for trial.

450. Mr. *Downing.*] I think you fell into a mistake, which I think it right to give you an opportunity of correcting, in your answer to the honourable Member for the University of Dublin, in which you stated that the jurors in criminal cases were selected by ballot?—That is on actual trials: that is my impression, and Dr. Ball himself suggested that that was his experience also.

451. Have you ever seen it in your experience?—I think so; that is to say, the names are put into a box.

452. I think I can state from my own knowledge that it is not so?—I can only say that the right honourable Member for the University of Dublin, who was Crown prosecutor for a long time, had the same impression.

453. Mr. *Heron.*] They are always called in order upon the panel, are they not?—Very probably. I am obliged to the honourable Member for giving me an opportunity of correcting myself if I am wrong. At the time that I gave the evidence, I expressed some doubt and hesitation upon the point; but it is not a thing that really arrests the attention of the Crown prosecutor very much in what manner the jury is called, whether it is by name or whether it is by ballot.

454. Mr. *Downing.*] I think I understand from the evidence that you have given, that you approve of this Act on principle?—On principle certainly, and in its conception.

455. You think it is quite a right thing that the jurors should be selected as laid down in this Act, alphabetically?—I think so.

456. You are under the impression that a power to correct the jurors' list at quarter sessions by the chairman would really make the Act a very excellent and good working Act?—I should say that it would make it work very fairly; and I think also that the Act, in its working, is likely to improve with time.

457. You stated, did you not, that with every new Act, generally speaking, there was some difficulty in carrying it into operation?—There have been no great changes in the law that have not been attended with a great deal of animadversion; for instance, the original Jury Act of 1832, the Common Law Procedure Act, all those changes in the law I think led to a great deal of cavil and a good deal of opposition for some time.

458. Are you aware that the Act of the 3rd and 4th of William the Fourth, which was the Act in operation up to the passing of this Act, also was met by that same spirit of hostility which you have described that this Act has received in Ireland?—My recollection is so.

459. Are you aware that there was a Select Committee of the House of Lords in consequence to inquire into the operation of that Act?—I was not aware of that.

460. The honourable Member for the University of Dublin put a question to you as if you considered the Act a failure; I did not understand you to say that?—I did not say that; I thought that it had worked unsatisfactorily in the county of Limerick, but not in the city. Let me add, that I gave certain reasons why I thought that it had perhaps not had a fair trial upon its first working.

461. And you would recommend that the chairman at quarter sessions should have larger powers in forming the jury panel?—I have recommended that, and I have stated it unwillingly, because no person is willing to undertake a new jurisdiction.

462. The

Mr. De Moleyns.

28 April 1873.

462. The collector of the poor rate at present is under the Act bound, is he not, to make a return according to his knowledge, and to state those to whom he has an objection?—I am not aware of that, except as to the disqualifications mentioned in the Act.

463. He has to put opposite the name of the person to whom he objects, that he is not a proper person?—All that we have to deal with is the return of the clerk of the union.

464. Are you aware that the return is made to him by the poor rate collector?—I do not think that he is to make any entry of objections under the Act.

465. You will find that the poor rate collector makes a return to the clerk of the union?—But I am not aware that he strikes out those that he objects to.

466. He is not to return any of those parties specified in the Act?—That is what I say, that there is no column of "objected;" that it is his duty in the first instance not to return the particular classes of persons specified in the Act.

467. Have you been a member of any board of guardians in your lifetime?—A very great number of years back, during the famine years, I was a guardian in Kerry as a magistrate, but it is a very long time ago.

468. You are aware that every electoral division is represented upon the board of guardians?—Yes.

469. And the elected guardian of each division is supposed to have a very intimate knowledge of all the parties in his division?—Yes.

470. Would you approve of those lists after they are returned by the poor rate collector being brought before the board of guardians upon a given day, while the elected guardian of the division would be present, and would then and there state his own knowledge of whether such a man was not fit according to the terms of the Act of Parliament, or where there was any very great objection to him, that should be put on the list before it goes to you?—No, I would not, for this reason, that I think a person employed in any situation with a duty for which he is paid, would do his duty; but I do not think that any elected guardian would perform that duty; I think that his doing it would make him open to many of the objections that have been brought forward about the invidiousness of the task.

471. Do you think really that it is an invidious act on the part of any one to object to a juror; do not you think that he would be very much obliged to the party who would get him off?—I am not so certain of that; although a person, if he is returned, may be very glad not to attend, yet if once an objection is made, human nature is such, that he naturally thinks some affront is intended.

472. Supposing that the electoral guardian had not that objection, do not you think that it would give a very great object to the chairman to have that noted upon the list?—I think that if the elected guardian would exercise such a duty, and performed it fairly, it would be a form of information which would go a long way to assist the chairman.

473. If a person is called before the judge at the assizes, and he satisfies the judge that there was some defect, or that he was so wretchedly poor that he had not the means of remaining at the assize town, would you not give the judge power then to let him off, or strike him off the jurors' list?—Yes, certainly, and I would give it also to the chairman; I think that one of the reasons which ought to operate against a juror remaining on the list is inadequacy of means to enable him to attend.

474. But you would not do that, would you, without having an examination on oath?—Certainly not; I would let the man himself attend either before the chairman or before the judge.

475. With regard to the raising of the qualification, do you think that you would get a more intelligent man because he is rated at 30 *l.* than at 20 *l.*?—If the honourable Member by that question means to ask whether the difference between 20 *l.* and 30 *l.*, or whatever the specific amount may be, is to be a measure of intelligence, or whether a man who is rated at 1,000 *l.* a year is not likely to be more intelligent than a man rated at 20 *l.*, I think he is; I think the larger the rating and the larger the holding of a man, the more likely he is to be, at all events, independent of the influences which I have stated do operate, and naturally operate.

476. My question had reference to intelligence? I would say, yes, to some extent, even as to those particular limits.

477. Do not you think that the intelligence often depends much more upon a man's age than upon his valuation?—I do; I may say that it occurred to me, though I did not like to mention it, that to insert a lower age than 60 as the limit might also be a valuable suggestion; I think with regard to the farming classes, that their intelligence and activity of mind does not survive so long as in the case of those who are in the higher ranks of life, and who are not equally hard worked, perhaps; however, that may be a fanciful suggestion, and I do not bring it forward myself.

478. Have you not found in your experience as a judge, that men at the age of 40 or 45, or say from 30 to 50, are much more intelligent, and are, generally speaking, able to read and write, whereas men approaching the age of 60 and over are not?—Unquestionably so.

479. That arises, does it not, from the spread of education in the national schools?—Yes, from the continual spread of education; and, of course, that is a matter which has occurred to my own mind, though I do not suggest it, that lowering the limit of age might be a valuable amendment.

480. Are you aware that under this Act a number of men, who are considerably over 60 years of age, were returned and summoned?—I am not aware of that. I have stated already that there were only two cases of persons who claimed to be exempted upon that ground, and it would be contrary to the duty of the poor-rate collector and the clerk of the union to return any such persons.

481. You spoke, I think, of the judge making some observations with regard to persons of the higher classes not attending upon him at the assizes in obedience to their summonses?—Yes; they did not, in fact, attend.

482. Was that Judge Fitzgerald?—Yes.

483. Are you aware that he made similar observations at the Cork Assizes?—I think I have seen it in the public newspapers.

484. Are you aware that that judge, in discharging the jury at the assizes, complimented them very much upon their conduct and their verdicts?—So I also heard, and therefore I made those observations as to what occurred in the county

Mr. *De Moleyns.*

28 April 1873.

county of Limerick, and which were made by a judge whom I should not venture to differ from.

485. With regard to the qualification, are you aware that there was a Jury Bill brought in in the year 1854 by the present Chief Justice of the Court of Queen's Bench?—I have heard so, but I am not aware of the contents of the Bill.

486. Are you aware that the qualification in that Bill was 30 *l.*?—I am not aware of that; it is not upon that ground that I suggested it.

487. Are you aware that that Bill was amended in Committee, and that the qualification was reduced to 20 *l.*?—I am not aware of anything connected with it. I never saw it, or heard of it.

488. Are you aware of the Bill that was brought in by Mr. Whiteside and Mr. Napier in 1854?—No.

489. With regard to the fourth schedule of the Act, you made an observation which was perfectly correct; the first class was made on an amendment of mine in Committee, and it was a mere omission that the nett annual value of 12 *l.* was not extended to the second class; of course, Cork, Limerick, and Kilkenny are large towns, and those are in Class No. 2?—Yes.

490. Therefore, it would appear quite evident that it was a mere mistake not to extend the same rating to towns in the counties in Class No. 2?—The counties of Cork, Limerick, and Kilkenny are in the first class.

491. You approve of that, do you not?—Yes, I approve of that certainly. My evidence has been to the effect that I think it ought to be extended to the other counties.

492. You do not think that the qualification arising from house property in the agricultural districts could be at all enforced?—There is a separate rating, I understand, as to houses, but I do not think that there would be any extensive addition made by mere houses.

493. Are you aware that there are parties whose lands are valued at something like 60 *l.* or 70 *l.* a year whose house has not been valued at more than 30 *s.* a year?—I am sure that, in many cases, in the parts of Ireland that I am familiar with, such is the case.

494. Are you aware that in passing the Westmeath Peace Preservation Act that the imposition of a rate under that Act by the Committee was originally of a house rate, and that it was abandoned afterwards in the House, because it could not be enforced?—I was not aware of that.

495. You spoke of having the local Crown prosecutor to assist the chairman in revising the list; how could you have the local prosecutor for Cork attend your sessions?—He attends the quarter sessions, as it is.

496. But that is for criminal purposes only, is it not?—Yes.

497. You do not, then, revise your list?—He also practises in civil cases. Whenever they attend at those particular places the revision of the list occurs at the same time, either the day before or the day after, or in the middle of the sessions; and his attendance would not be inconvenient, I think.

498. Do you think that he has such a knowledge of the people living in distant parts of the county as to be of any service whatever to you?—He might be of some service, and I suggested that, as representing the Crown, he should attend.

499. To whom would you give the appeal?—My idea would be this, that any person who found his name omitted from the list as finally published should be at liberty to appear before the chairman personally without any formal appeal, and state that his name was omitted, and that he claimed to be retained upon the list.

500. That would be only after the lapse of a year?—No, at any quarter sessions.

501. The party whose name was struck off is not present at the time of striking off?—No, but he would see the list published, and the moment he sees that he is omitted, if he wishes to be retained he could appear before the chairman at the next quarter sessions, which would not be more than two months afterwards, and claim to be retained upon the list; the chairman would examine him, and see what his appearance and demeanour were when before him, and either retain him on the list, or continue the omission; I may add, that by the Act as it now stands a power is given both to the chairman and to the Court of Queen's Bench, or any judge of that court, if any person complains that he is either omitted or inserted by mistake, to order the list to be corrected or amended at any time, after examining the complainant.

502. Are you aware, from your experience, that the parties who are employed by the sheriff to summon jurors have been often tampered with, and induced not to summon certain parties?—I have heard of that, and I have no doubt that those things will occur whenever persons of a given class of life are intrusted with a duty of that description; as long as human nature is such as it is, there will always be abuses.

503. Would you substitute another mode of summoning jurors; would you suggest a summons being sent through the post office, and registered?—I have considered that matter, and I think that there would be very great difficulties and objections; I do not think the machinery of the post office is suited to it in the distant parts of Ireland. I think that there would be great difficulty in the way of a judge fining afterwards, and that it would, in effect, be to make the post office officials sheriffs' bailiffs for the purpose of serving the jurors. Let me also add, that at present a very expensive duty is thrown upon the sheriffs and sub-sheriffs in paying their bailiffs for the service of those persons. What I would suggest is this, although no doubt it would be received with great disfavour by the heads of the force, that the constabulary might very well be employed in serving those summonses. Let it be made a part of their patrol duties if necessary. I think that they object generally to the performance of any service that may be considered not within the sphere of their duties as connected with the preservation of the peace and repression of crime; but this being a duty concerning the administration of the criminal justice of the country, I think they might very fairly be employed in their own immediate district to serve those jurors, and to make a statutory declaration before a magistrate of their having done it. It appears to me that this would get rid of the post office difficulty, and of the expense and the difficulty which the sheriffs feel now to be so onerous.

504. You think that that would be much more satisfactory than the present system?—Yes; and it does not occur to me to be a difficult one, because in every village there is a constabulary station, and I think that it is a very important duty

Mr. *De Moleyns.*

28 April 1873.

duty concerning the administration of criminal justice in which they might peculiarly be employed, but I believe that there are objections made to employing them for anything out of the proper or primary business of the force.

505. *The O'Donoghue.*] I think you gave the Committee your opinion that no one should be allowed to serve upon a jury who could not read or write?—That is my impression, that it is a fair ground of disqualification, because of course there are many cases that they might be inadequate to decide upon.

506. You asked, I think, how a person not capable of reading and writing could form an opinion in a case of forgery or of disputed handwriting; do you mean that a juror should have ocular demonstration of the point that he had to decide?—He always has now ocular demonstration, at least by the Act of Parliament, wherever there is a case of forgery, or any case of that description, and in comparisons of disputed handwriting with handwriting proved to be unquestionably the handwriting of the individual. Comparison of handwriting is always admitted, and of course a person who could not write, could not bring the same degree of intelligence to the consideration of such a question as a person who could both read and write.

507. Could not he form an opinion in those cases upon the testimony of reliable witnesses, as well as in other cases?—He might, but he would not have the same amount of evidence before him that is now permitted to him by the Act; he might be capable, but he would not have the same amount of intelligence, and therefore upon all such cases I think it would be a very proper discretion not to admit him.

508. Is it not the fact, that under the old Jury Act the qualification for a juror was lower than that under the present law, but that the power of selection exercised by the sheriff made a man's legal qualification merely nominal?—I do not know whether the qualification could be called a lower one; it was a different kind of qualification; it was a 10 *l.* freehold, or a 15 *l.* leasehold, or a house of the value of 20 *l.*; the present system has the great advantage of being a permanent basis, and a basis that cannot be simulated; I may state that many men found their way on the jury lists formerly who had not in fact the qualification which the Act required, but there can be no mistake upon that point with the present basis of qualification, whatever may be the difficulty in other respects.

509. You approve of that portion of the present Act which has deprived the sheriff of the power of selection?—Yes, I think it was an objectionable principle: I have added that I have never known it to be improperly exercised, but I think it is one of those things which are objectionable in principle, and, therefore, ought to be removed.

510. Mr. *Heron.*] With reference to your last observation, the great objection to the sheriff absolutely returning the panel was, was it not, that he made out the panel after it was known what cases were to be tried at the assizes and at the sittings in Dublin?—He might, very possibly.

511. And therefore he always returned the panel knowing what cases were to be tried?—In many cases he did; he made out the panel, I think, 15 days before the assizes; of course he might not know all the cases that were to be tried.

512. But any remarkable cases were certainly known before to the sheriff?—Yes.

513. And it was impossible for him to return his panel without knowing what important cases were to be tried?—I think he must have known of them.

514. With reference to the districts from which your jurors come to the quarter sessions in the county of Kilkenny, is there any grave objection as to the distance which the jurors have to come?—The county of Kilkenny is not so extensive a county as some of the more remote counties, and our juries are taken from the divisions of the county; they must reside within the division, that is to say, the jurors for quarter sessions. Of course for the assizes they come from the body of the county.

515. As regards the quarter sessions jurors in large counties such as Donegal, Galway, and Cork especially, serious objections are made as to distances that the jurors have to come; would you give the chairman the absolute power of revision, or distribution, so as to take them alternately from any of the baronies?—I am aware that objections have been made, and the fact I believe exists, but I do not see my way to giving any power of direction in the matter, without disturbing the principle of the Act.

516. Supposing an alternative were suggested that they should come from certain arranged baronies, how would that answer?—Then the principle of what is called alphabetical selection must be departed from, which is now imposed upon the sheriff. The "strict alphabetical dictionary order," which is the ruling principle of the Act, must be departed from.

517. Even now if the sheriff's returns are correct or not, he only returns under Section 19, which says, "Provided further, that the persons to be selected to serve as grand jurors or petit jurors at any general sessions of the peace, or in any civil bill court, shall be resident within the division in and for which such sessions or civil bill court are or is holden"?—Let me say that if that principle could be extended in the way that you say, I see no objection to doing it; any thing that may meet the convenience of the jurors I think might reasonably be allowed if it could be done.

518. So far the sheriff has to deviate from the alphabetical order?—Yes.

519. It would be very convenient, would it not, if an extended power of sub-division were given to the chairman at quarter sessions, either associated with the justices or not, so as to subdivide by baronies the divisions of his county?—Yes, in large counties probably it might be convenient and desirable if it could be done.

520. Supposing that such a power were to be given, would you propose to give it to the chairman absolutely, or to the chairman associated with the justices at sessions?—I think that the chairman alone is a less cumbrous court.

521. With regard to introducing further exemptions or disqualifications, you mentioned publicans; would you disqualify them from serving on both civil and criminal juries?—Yes, I think that in the public interest, and in their own interest, it is desirable.

522. Under the old system, before the passing of the Act, did you know of any instances where, in consequence of publicans being on juries, there were acquittals which, in your opinion, ought not to have taken place?—I would not say that; I never

Mr. De Moleyns. 28 April 1873.

I never like to examine into the grounds of acquittals in criminal cases; I rather prefer to believe that it is a fair result at which the jury have arrived, and it is a safe rule I think.

523. Are you aware that in quarter session towns the witnesses and the men out on bail that came in to be tried used to lodge at the publican's houses and to use those houses as their inns?—Naturally in counties where the criminal business extended over more than one day.

524. With reference to the other persons that are exempted under the second schedule, namely, barristers, attorneys, and solicitors; at the last sittings in Dublin, we had constant requests from attorneys' clerks to be exempted and struck off the list, and that was always yielded to by consent; do you think that attorneys' clerks also should be in the same position as either barristers or attorneys and solicitors?—I think they are not proper jurors, but the case does not often arise in counties.

525. With regard to the service of the summonses upon jurors in remote districts, you are aware that an immense expense has been thrown upon the sheriffs in Ireland by the personal service being required?—So it appears.

526. Why do you think that service through the post office would not be an effectual service even in remote districts? I adopt the language of the section of the Act of Parliament, which says that in the county of Dublin they are to be delivered by "letter-carriers." I do not believe that in the remote parts of Ireland there is this delivery of letters by letter-carriers. Persons must be supposed to come in to inquire for their letters, a practice which we all know does not exist more than once a week, and which they would even abstain from doing before the assizes and sessions. Then the mere machinery of registration, I think, at those small county post offices would be very difficult to carry out, for in the section of the Act of Parliament which applies to the county of Dublin it mentions post offices where "savings banks" exist. I think that altogether in the country parts of Ireland it is too delicate and difficult a mode of service to be depended on in the present state of things.

527. Do you see any objection to carry out that mode of service in cities and towns, and districts where there are no letter-carriers?—No; but there the same reason would not exist, because there would be no difficulty in serving them without. I may be allowed to add this, which may probably interest some of the members of the Committee, that in the provision for serving by "registered letters," the section provides that the expense shall be paid in the same manner as the duties devolving upon the clerk of the peace under the Act of Parliament are to be provided for; that is to say, it would be thrown upon the county.

528. Do you think that that expense ought to be thrown upon the sheriff?—I mean that the expense of serving by registered letter is to be defrayed by the county, as the clerk of the peace's expenses are at present defrayed.

529. That is a great privilege for the city of Dublin, is it not?—Yes; but probably the country parts of Ireland would not consider it an equal privilege.

530. Do not you know that the Inspector General would be very much opposed to throwing this important duty of summoning the jurors upon the constabulary?—I believe that would be so, but I have added (whether right or wrong, that is my opinion) that it would be a fair duty to cast upon the constabulary. I think that they are resident in the districts, and they know a large class of jurors, and being a duty connected with the administration of the criminal justice of the county, it is one which might fairly be placed upon them.

531. Surely, in the cities of Cork and Limerick, and Galway and Belfast, and other considerable towns of Ireland, the constabulary ought not to be serving summonses, whilst we have a perfect mode of serving them by post?—I do not say in the towns. I mentioned those places where considerable expense and difficulty were cast upon the sheriff in effecting a service.

532. Do you see any objection to the chairman being allowed to make exemptions upon declarations made by the jurors themselves, and transmitted to you through the post?—I think not, as to the limits of age, and similar causes of exemption.

533. Would you allow any exemption to be made by the chairman, supposing that in agricultural counties men objected to be summoned as jurors from the great distance of their residence, and from their poverty?—Yes. At present I need not tell the honourable Member that under the Act that would not be a ground of exemption, nor could the chairman exercise a discretion to allow them to be put off the list, but perhaps that might be one of those causes which might influence the chairman if he had a discretion given him by the Act.

534. You think that that would be a fair reason for exemption, especially in the spring of the year, from being brought 50 or 60 miles from his home?—He would have power to do that under the discretion which I would vest in him.

535. You mentioned, with reference to the questions by the honourable Member for the University of Dublin and the honourable Member for Carlow, that persons ought to be disqualified for having committed some offence, if the proof is before you; do you see any objection to the clerk of the quarter sessions returning to you at the quarter sessions a list of all jurors against whom any conviction appears in their books?—I think that that might fairly be done.

536. But you would not require the constabulary to give you the information?—Yes; that is a definite duty which I think that they might fairly undertake.

537. It would not be a very onerous duty, would it?—No.

538. The clerk of the petty sessions in your county might send to you by post the convictions against the petty jurors?—Yes, the clerk of the petty sessions might transmit it to the clerk of the peace, not to the chairman. I think that would be a very fair thing.

539. The clerk of the petty sessions ought to know by looking at the roll whether a man has been convicted or not?—Yes.

540. Are there not other persons besides publicans and attorneys' clerks, who you suggest ought to be either exempted or disqualified?—Not positively in the Act.

541. We have in Dublin now objections from the Bank of Ireland, the Provincial Bank, and the National Bank, as to their clerks being summoned?—That applies to the city, and I daresay that in Dublin there would be no objection to their being exempted, where you have so very numerous a class of jurors.

542. They

Mr. *De Moleyns.*

28 April 1873.

542. They objected most strongly to their clerks being summoned, and, as a matter of courtesy, they were all let off, I think?—Yes.

543. Another class referred to by the Honourable Member for Carlow the other day, was veterinary surgeons; do you think that they ought to be either exempted or disqualified?—I think that perhaps they might fairly be exempted; they are not a very numerous class. I do not think it is of much importance one way or the other.

544. With regard to the 12 *l.* valuation, you are aware that in the valuation of Ireland there is a distinct class of valuation for house and land, and house and offices?—I believe so.

545. Would you give a qualification as juror, and to be put upon the general jurors' book, to every person throughout Ireland who had a net annual value of 12 *l.* for a house and offices?—I think that that would be a very proper addition to the qualification.

546. It would simplify the matter very much indeed, would it not, without putting down whether it was in a city, or a town, or a village, wherever there was a net annual value of 12 *l.* for a house and offices?—Yes, that comes to what is called the household qualification, and I think that it would be a valuable addition. The class of 12 *l.* householders would be at least as intelligent as the 20 *l.* rated land occupiers.

547. Do not you think that they would be a much superior class in point of intelligence?—I do not like to throw discredit upon any class by comparisons.

548. Under the present law, in the city of Armagh, the town of Carlow, the town of Ennis, the county of the town of Galway, the city of Londonderry, and in fact all the principal towns and boroughs in Ireland, they do not get the 12 *l.* house and office qualification?—No; 15 *l.*, I think it is.

549. It is 15 *l.* now in Carrickfergus and in Galway, I believe?—Class 3 stands at present at 15 *l.* for those particular towns.

550. Do not you think that in those towns this might be reduced to 12 *l.*?—Yes.

551. With regard to your raising the qualification in the county of Kilkenny, which you know so well, I think you stated that you adopt it as a rule that a juror ought to serve every two years?—I rather stated this, that if the raising of the qualification was supposed to involve their serving more frequently than once in three years, I did not think that that would be any objection by itself to raising the qualification, for that they might fairly be called upon without any great hardship to serve once in two years instead of once in three.

552. And that would be accomplished by raising the qualification to 30 *l.* per annum?—So it appears to me upon looking at the return furnished to me.

553. Do you see any objection to a juror being permitted to object to himself at petty sessions, in the first instance, before the justices?—At present the justices have no jurisdiction of the sort at petty sessions, and I think that it would be piecemeal legislation allowing anything to be gone into at petty sessions, unless the petty sessions had the power of revision; and it could be easily effected in another way by the man transmitting his objection to the chairman.

554. Supposing that the chairman strikes off the juror as exempt or disqualified, do you think that the juror should be permitted at the next sessions to come before the chairman and appeal?—Yes; of course no person likes to assume a jurisdiction without an appeal from him. My idea is that when the list is finally published, if a man sees that he is no longer on it, and he wishes to be retained, he should have nothing to do but to come then to the session, and state his wish to the chairman, and he should submit to be examined, and the chairman could order the list to be revised by retaining him on it.

555. Is it not your opinion that, generally speaking, the officials throughout Ireland, as far as you know personally, or have seen it in the public newspapers, were not very well disposed to give the Act a fair trial?—I will not go that length; I have already stated that I thought there was a preconceived prejudice against it, and that species of dislike to any extensive alteration of the law which prejudices a man's mind at first against its working; but I will not go the length of saying that there was any desire or any feeling that could be supposed to be against working it fairly.

556. Was there not rather an attempt to get up good stories about the working of the Act?—I think there was rather an ostentatious parading of any shortcomings, or any failures that may have arisen in connection with the Act; I also stated why I think that the Act hardly had a fair trial upon the first occasion of its being introduced.

557. With special reference to the county of Limerick, which you know so well, the special jurors of the county were, before the passing of this Act, the very highest class of country gentlemen, were they not?—Yes, the magistrates, and so on.

558. As you may remember, they took an interest, and one might almost say a pride, in attending at the assizes?—Yes; that is to say, the special jurors, or grand jurors; but they seldom served on criminal juries. I must add this, that even then there appeared to be always a strong feeling on their part against being on what is called the common or long panel, and in favour of being returned only on the special panel; whereas it would appear to me that the first duty of men of position in a county is to assist in the administration of criminal justice, which so closely concerns themselves and their properties; and that I have pointed to be one of the advantages of the present Act, that, as regards the criminal panel at the assizes, all persons are equally included.

559. Unless the doing away with the old power of selection by the sheriff is met by a willingness to attend, it would be impossible to get the high class of special jurors that used to be in the county of Limerick; I mean by the ordinary alphabetical order for special jurors?—Yes, certainly.

560. But if country gentlemen will attend on the general panel, especially on the criminal side of the court, on the whole, the constitution of the jury on the criminal side ought to be improved?—It is, perhaps, difficult to say that; but if some of those persons, in point of fact, were on the jury, I think that the constitution of the jury would be improved, because their intelligence and experience would naturally be guides to the class who I am sure would willingly defer in all proper cases to their opinion; without entirely submitting their own judgment to them, they would be guided

Mr. *De Moleyns.*

28 April 1873.

guided by them where they ought fairly to be influenced by their superior intelligence.

561. Do not you think it of great importance in a county like Limerick that the first gentlemen of the county, or a few of them, should occasionally serve with ordinary farmers, merchants, and shopkeepers, and should be returned in the jurors' list?—It would be not only of great importance, but of the greatest importance; I never could understand why there should be any objection to it; I have said already it so closely concerns both themselves and their properties, that I think it ought to be a privilege to them to serve, and as educated men, to assist others, perhaps, of an inferior class, in performing the duties which are now imposed upon them.

562. Mr. *Bourke.*] Did you go to the last Limerick assizes?—Yes.

563. There was one case which was reported in the newspapers which is not likely to be tried again, so that I may ask you about it; I think, as well as I recollect, that it was the case of a man who was indicted and tried, and the jury disagreed, and afterwards he pleaded guilty, and there were some strong observations made by the judge on the subject; do you recollect that case?—I do recollect that case, and it certainly is one of those cases upon which I have founded my strong opinion as to the way in which the assizes resulted at Limerick; it was a case of manslaughter; there had been a fight between the prisoner and the deceased man, an ordinary pugilistic fight, and the prisoner, who was tried for manslaughter, got the worst of the encounter; after being two or three times separated, they were finally parted, and the deceased man went on his way home; he was followed shortly afterwards by the prisoner, who was tried, and although no person saw the actual deed, yet within a very few minutes the man was found dead, lying by the roadside, weltering, I may say, in his blood, and with a stab in his neck two or three inches, at least, deep. I think the prisoner was proved to be either a gardener or a shoemaker, I forget which, and to have had in his possession a knife of a description similar to that which might have inflicted the wound. In addition to that, the man, who appears to have regretted what occurred, and which probably was the result of heated blood in the previous fight, came back and admitted what he had done, and asked the advice of some persons as to what he should do under the circumstances. The case was tried before a most eminent and experienced judge, who charged the jury, and left the matter to them; after some considerable time they returned, and stated that they disagreed, and that they could not agree; the judge then asked them, Did they believe the evidence of the man who was examined for the Crown, and who stated the admission made to him by the prisoner of the fact of his having killed the man; they stated that they did believe the witness. The judge then said, What difficulty can you have? They retired again, and again they stated that they could not agree, and at length they had to be discharged. The Crown, as was their duty, ordered the man to be put upon his trial by another jury the next morning, and some observations which you have alluded to were made by the presiding judge as to the result of the trial. I may state that the prisoner was defended by a very able and very experienced Queen's Counsel, who the next morning, in the exercise of his discretion, for which he was complimented by the judge, stated that upon consideration he thought it better that the man should withdraw his plea of not guilty, and admit his guilt, throwing himself upon the mercy of the court. Under all the circumstances of the case, and considering the previous fight that had occurred, the man was sentenced to 18 months' imprisonment. That was one of the cases upon which I founded my judgment as being the unfortunate result of the working of the Jury Act upon this its first operation.

564. Mr. *Downing.*] Was there any question raised in that case as to the admission of that evidence by the counsel?—I think not; there could not have been, because the man came back and acknowledged what he had done. One reason why I did not allude to that case was because the honourable Member for Tipperary was present, who was the able and experienced counsel to whom I have alluded.

565. Mr. *Bourke.*] Was there anything peculiar or strange apparently to you, as an experienced Crown Prosecutor, as to the constitution of that jury, because it was almost the first jury that you saw empaneled under the new Act; did they appear to be men of less intelligence and station in society, and less capable of forming a correct judgment upon the evidence than former juries?—In fact it was not one of the first juries, but followed upon four or five previous acquittals, and therefore, perhaps, attracted more attention; at all events, we considered on the part of the Crown, which was shown by the result, that there had been a miscarriage of justice; but, of course, miscarriages of justice have always prevailed, and will always prevail.

566. With regard to the other exemptions that you would suggest, would you propose that those persons whom you suggest should be exempt should be left out in the first instance, or should they be exempted by the barrister?—I think I have only suggested one additional exemption.

567. Those who cannot read and write, for instance?—That is a matter which I would rather leave to the discretion of the chairman; I would not go further than possible in defining with a jealous scrutiny any and every possible ground of disqualification. I think that, in addition to those that now exist, publicans might be exempted. I would not add to the actual disqualifications; I would leave the remainder to the discretion of the chairman.

568. In the way in which it is done at present, does the revising barrister take each name in the list?—That has only been done now once as to the jurors' list; all the persons who attend are sworn to answer all such questions as shall be administered to them, and they are then examined generally as to the correctness of the lists, and if no objection is made, the chairman then signs the lists according to the Act, and they are returned as being correct.

569. They are taken in bulk, in fact?—Yes, they are taken in bulk, unless any objection is made to the list, and they are asked whether there are any objections.

570. *The O'Conor Don.*] How long at your last sessions did it take you to make this revision?—I should say not long; but it was at seven different places.

571. In each place did it take you more than 10 minutes?—I should think it would not be more than 20 minutes. Of course, if there are

Mr. *De Moleyns.*

28 April 1873.

no objections made, our duty is merely nominal in consequence of the very narrow limits within which the Act is confined, so that you cannot go into anything beyond. There are not many men who are, in general, idiots or lunatics, or deaf or blind, or convicted of treason or felony; and, therefore, there are not many objections to be made.

572. Mr. *Heron.*] With reference to the case of Bourke, whom I defended at the last Limerick Assizes, do you remember that that man and his family had borne a very excellent character; that they had been shepherds on the Galtese, and that Captain Massey and Mr. John Massey, of Kingswell, gave them a most excellent character?—I remember that, or that one of those gentlemen was to have attended for that purpose.

573. And you allowed letters to be read?—Yes, I have no doubt that they were people of excellent character, and I believe you also stated to the jury that they and their ancestors had possessed property there for centuries.

574. And also, with regard to the quarrel out of which the unfortunate homicide arose, there was nothing of a party nature in it?—No, nothing.

575. The unfortunate man who lost his life and the prisoner had been on good terms, and they had been drinking together that day?—Yes.

576. That unfortunate homicide arose out of drunkenness, no doubt?—Yes.

577. There was nothing of an agrarian, or party, or sectarian character in the quarrel?—No; the man appeared to have deeply regretted what he had done, and he came back and consulted others as to what he should do.

578. Unfortunately, he was badly advised to plead guilty?—I will not say badly advised.

579. I mean to say that in that case there was nothing whatever of those ordinary matters which have caused disagreements of juries in Ireland?—There was nothing agrarian, but I would say that whenever a man is charged with manslaughter, or with an aggravated assault, that is the very thing which produces disagreement, because I think there exists what I may call a general prejudice of caste among that class of jurors, which indisposes them to convictions in cases of that nature, and which too often results in disagreements.

580. *The O'Conor Don.*] How many jury cases, criminal and civil, have you had at your sessions since the assizes?—The civil cases were merely those in which I had to call upon the jurors myself. I think, as well as I can recollect, there were three or four criminal cases; not more, because the sessions followed within two or three weeks of the assizes.

581. So that altogether you have had experience as chairman only in some seven or eight cases?—Not more than that, as the Act only came into operation on the 11th of January.

582. I understood you in answer to a question from the honourable Member for Cork, to say, that you considered that it would be an invidious thing on the part of the elected guardian of a union to raise an objection to a juror, on the ground of his not being able to read and write, or any other of those proposed disqualifications?—Yes, and I think also, that it is not a duty which is properly cast upon him, and not a duty for which he is elected. I think that no man likes to object to his neighbour when he conceives it to be a gratuitous act upon his part. I distinguish in that case, a guardian from a poor rate collector, who represents the public. A gentleman employed in a particular office would not have the same objection that a mere elected guardian would feel.

583. Would you impose it as a duty upon the poor law collector?—Yes.

584. And would you have him paid for it?—No, under the section as it at present stands, he is to be paid such compensation for the additional duties thrown upon him, as may be considered reasonable.

585. Would not this be an additional duty?—To some extent it would, but as he is bound already to attend at the sessions, I do not think that there would be any serious duty thrown upon him such as need alarm any county as to the additional expense.

586. When you say that he is bound already to attend, if you were to throw additional duty upon him, would you oblige him to initiate the objection, or would he only have to attend to answer questions that were asked him as regards individual jurors?—My idea is this, that if the duty is cast upon the chairman eventually, he should have instructions given to the poor law collector to make inquiries of a general description as to the fitness or unfitness of jurors, and that when he attends at the revising court, without making any preliminary formal objection on the record, if I may so say, or upon the return made by him, he should be examined by the chairman, and should state to him then orally what objections he entertains, if any, to any particular juror.

587. Then the initiation of the objections would come from the chairman, or should he ask whether the collector had any objection to so and so?—Yes; he might ask, Do you know anything about these particular persons, without defining particularly from whom that initiation should come. There are ways in which things are done that you cannot actually define or describe beforehand.

588. I want to know whether this poor rate collector is himself to state, I object to A. B., or C. D., because he is unable to read or write; or whether his duty would be simply confined to answering the questions that might be asked him?—I think that the latter would be a better way, because each chairman may entertain his views of what may in his opinion render it inexpedient that any particular juror should be upon the panel.

589. Do you consider that the collector himself should be required to state the objections to individuals from whom he collects the rates?—That is the way in which I should manage it myself, I think.

590. If this duty be thrown upon the poor rate collector of initiating the objections, do not you think that he would claim higher remuneration for having to make inquiries throughout the whole of the rate-paying people in the locality, as to their reading and writing for instance, and other disqualifications?—I think that he may claim, but I do not say to be highly remunerated; I very much question it. I do not like again to say that he is not entitled to it; he is already entitled to be paid. The grand jury have power under the new Act to pay for additional trouble.

591. You are going to throw additional burden upon the poor rate collector, and I want to have it clear whether that additional duty will require

Mr. *De Moleyns.*

28 April 1873.

require additional remuneration?—I think that a man who knows the circumstances and the conditions of every one, and who is bound to attend the court, cannot claim any additional remuneration for merely stating whether such and such a person has been convicted of an offence, and so on, or is illiterate.

592. Colonel *Wilson Patten.*] In your evidence you have suggested 30 *l.* as the qualification for a juror, and you stated that that would involve the necessity of service upon the jury once in 18 months, or, at the outside, once in two years?—I have said, that as regards the county of Kilkenny, from the return that has been made to me, and from the calculation that I have made as to the number of jurors to be returned for the assizes and sessions, that it might involve the attendance of each person about once in two years.

593. What is about the average attendance required from a juryman at present?—One of the complaints of the old system was that the same class of jurors were made almost constantly to attend.

594. What is the duration of attendance now, upon the average, that he is obliged to remain at the assizes or sessions?—That of course must depend very much upon the business; in the Belfast assizes, or in the northern counties, or in Cork, where they are very long and very protracted assizes, they may be detained many days; in the quarter sessions districts they are seldom kept much beyond a day or two; I endeavour so to manage it as to dismiss them always by night in order to avoid all the evils of public-houses, and a protracted stay in small country towns. Generally speaking, the mere criminal business can be got over in a day's long work in Kilkenny; I am speaking now only of Kilkenny.

595. At the Limerick assizes, with which you are most connected, what should you say is about the average service of a juryman? What time is he obliged to give up to that duty?—I should say from six to seven days at the ordinary assizes.

596. And that upon the average he would be required to give up that time once in two years?—Yes; I do not say positively that that would be so in Limerick, for I do not know the number of jurors on the panel at Limerick; perhaps I ought to state how many days he would be required in Kilkenny at the assizes; I should say that it would be from three to four days; three days probably.

597. If it was six days, would it not be considered rather a grievance for a juryman to be called up once in two years?—Some of those persons formerly attended more often than that, others did not attend at all; but still even if it was something of a grievance, I think that that ought to be subservient to raising the qualification so as to secure a somewhat more independent and intelligent class of jurors; of course if you reduce the number of jurors it must involve a more frequent attendance; it is, if I may so call it, the choice of an alternative.

598. Major *O'Reilly.*] The case which you mentioned, which occurred at the Limerick assizes under a new jury system, has been cited as a remarkable instance (which we must take it to be) of the failure of justice; from your extensive experience, do you think that it stands almost alone as such an instance of failure of justice in Ireland?—I think I have stated that there had been frequently failures of justice.

599. Under the old system of juries do you mean?—Yes, under the old system as well as under the present one; but this happens to be a remarkable one, and it did occur under the new system; and I also added that it followed upon a very large number of acquittals.

600. You have been asked whether you think there would be any difficulty in striking jurors off the jurors' book, and it has been suggested almost invariably that jurors would rather wish to get off than to be left on; is that your opinion?—I have not had sufficient experience since the passing of this Act, but I think that up to this, jurors were very anxious to get off; they do not consider it a privilege to serve at all, and I think naturally so.

601. Are you acquainted with the north of Ireland and the jury system there?—No.

602. Do I take it that your suggestion is, that the discretion should be left in the chairman of leaving out names from the jurors' book, for whatever might appear to him a good and sufficient ground; but that the ground should be stated publicly in court, and that his decision should be given publicly in court, and that he should say, for instance, that he left a man out because he could not read and write?—He naturally would say that.

603. Therefore, would not there be this broad distinction between any power of revision so exercised by the chairman and the power of selection now exercised by the sheriff or sub-sheriff, that the latter is exercised not in public and without any cause assigned, and without any means of knowing for what reason it is so exercised?—I think that there would be the broadest possible difference in every way, because there is in the first instance a public and judicial selection upon what the chairman considers sufficient grounds.

604. Is there any good reason why special jurors should be omitted from the panel, and should not take their turn of serving with common jurors for the ordinary discharge of justice in all those cases in which by section 15 they are exempt?—I think that, as regards the quarter sessions, it would be most important for the administration of justice that special jurors, with the exception of magistrates, who are prohibited from serving at all because they sit with the chairman, should take part in the administration of justice, and the more so as the proportion of cases tried at quarter sessions is about three or four times greater than those tried at the assizes; all cases, with the exception of homicides and one or two other classes of offences, being triable, and in fact tried, at quarter sessions, and the result was, I must say, that under the old system at quarter sessions in many divisions we had a very inferior class of jurors.

605. Would you extend your suggestion that it would be an advantage that the special jurors should serve on common juries beyond the quarter sessions, or is there any good reason why they should be exempt from serving on the trial of any issues to be tried by common jurors at Her Majesty's courts in Dublin?—I think it would, perhaps, be well if they were not exempt. I do not see why those rated above 50 *l.*, as well as those above 20 *l.*, should not take their share in the ordinary administration of justice.

606. Do you think it desirable that a special juror should take his share of the ordinary common administration of justice?—I think that it would be desirable in the interests of justice; perhaps not desirable to the juror himself.

607. *The*

Mr. De Moleyns.

28 April 1873.

607. *The O'Donoghue.*] Does your objection to summoning a juror by a registered letter arise from an apprehension that the juror might not receive the notice?—I think it would be very unsafe to calculate upon his receiving the notice, and I think that a duty would be thrown upon the post offices, which in the present state of Ireland they are not competent to fulfil.

608. Does not the Act require that the lists of those entitled to serve as jurors should be posted up in some public place, such as outside a chapel?—Yes; in the schedule of forms he is required to post up beforehand a list of all those persons who are returned by him.

609. I understood you not to agree with the honourable Member for Cork, when he suggested that persons would, as a general rule, regard it as a favour to be exempt from serving as jurors?—I think that up to this time they are very anxious not to serve as jurors; but, if they were subject to removal from the list, I think I said it was human nature that they should probably feel, then for the first time, rather a desire to be retained.

610. My impression was that you stated that they would not regard it as a favour to be exempt from serving; but, on the contrary, they would like to serve?—No; that was coupled with this fact, that if they were removed from the list, they might object to such removal.

611. Do not you think it almost certain that, if it was known that notices to them to serve as jurors were to be sent through the post, a man, on seeing his name on the list at the chapel door, would go and inquire at the post office whether there was a letter for him?—I can hardly state that; they are not a very particular class of people in that way; but that is a matter on which those familiar with the country are better judges than I can be as to how it would work.

612. *Chairman.*] Any amendment of the Act would require some time, would it not, before it could come into operation?—Yes, I think so. Supposing that there is to be a revision of the nature which I have indicated, there must be either a special sessions, or you must wait till the ordinary sessions in October.

613. And it could not come into operation before, say a year at the least?—It could not come into operation, then, in the ordinary course of things, till the next spring assizes. The list would be revised, and then whatever alteration was made would depend upon the passing of an Act of Parliament during this session, and a subsequent revision at the October sessions.

614. Supposing that no Act should be passed this Session, no alteration could take place for two years?—Certainly not, if it is not done till next session.

615. Have you considered whether, without going into a complete revision of the Act, such as you have suggested, any amendment might be suggested which would come into effect immediately, say, before the next assizes?—I think that it would be a difficult thing to do, except you specified some few more causes of disqualification, and unless you raised the rate qualification.

616. Might you not direct the sheriff, still selecting alphabetically from the jurors' list, to exclude the names of jurors rated under a certain sum?—That you might do, of course, because the present list specifies the amount at which they are rated. It begins only with the 20*l.* rate, and there is a column specifying the amount of rated qualification. Of course there is no difficulty in omitting any one.

617. But do you attribute any very great importance to the mere raising of the qualification?—I think myself that it would be important.

618. You perhaps have not very much considered whether any temporary measure should be passed?—I have not considered that.

619. *Mr. Downing.*] Did I understand you to say, in answer to the honourable Member for Tipperary, that you would take the return from the petty sessions of persons convicted of ordinary offences, common assaults, so as to exclude them from the panel?—No, the honourable Member for Tipperary merely asked whether I saw any objection to allowing the clerks of petty sessions to forward to the clerk of the peace a return of the convictions recorded against any individual. Then, of course, it would be in the discretion of the chairman to say whether such conviction would be sufficient to unfit a juror. It is merely one means of testing fitness that he proposed.

Mr. James Charles Coffey, Q.C., called in; and Examined.

Mr. J. C. Coffey, Q.C.

620. *Chairman.*] I believe you are Chairman of the County and the City of Londonderry?—I am.

621. For what period?—I think about seven years.

622. Previously you had been chairman of other counties, had you not?—Yes; I had been chairman of two counties, and acted previously as *locum tenens* in others.

623. Are you a Crown prosecutor?—I am Crown prosecutor for the county of Clare.

624. In those capacities have you had any experience of the operation of the Jury Act?—I have observed it, and as a matter of duty rather closely.

625. Have you also had any experience in Dublin?—Yes, considerable in the city of Dublin, in Nisi Prius practice there.

626. Of course you have had very extensive experience of the working of the old Act?—Yes, for a great number of years.

627. Will you be so good as to state shortly to the Committee your opinion of the operation of the change which has been brought about by the new Act?—I may say that I have upon the Munster Circuit gone through all the circuit towns from Clare to Cork; I practice in each of them, and I fill the rather exceptional position of special Crown prosecutor in heavy cases in addition. In Clare I am bound to say that it was impossible to see a worse description of jurors, as to appearance, clothing and matters of that description; it would strike you at once that they were of a very low average of intelligence and position, and the verdicts were on the whole unsatisfactory there. My friend, Mr. De Moleyns, is wrong in saying that we did not get any convictions, but they bore no proportion to what we thought we ought to have got; the class of jurors were better in Limerick. In Kerry they were very bad, and in Cork they improved wonderfully; that is my experience. I am bound to say that I think that the Act got no fair play whatever. I came to the conclusion, and I have taken the liberty to express it, that the grand juries in the county of Clare, the gentlemen of the

Mr. *J. C. Coffey*, Q.C.

18 April 1873.

the country, made a great mistake in abstaining from answering to their names on the panel, although they were called, and in fact allowed a class of jurors to have the entire transaction of the business of the assizes, to whom, in my humble judgment, if they regarded their own position, they ought not have remitted it; in consequence, no one of the usual jury class appeared at all in Clare, and that so much attracted the attention of the judges that one of them, who, as some members of the Committee are aware, is very cautious and very reticent in his language, that is Mr. Justice Fitzgerald, openly remarked upon this, and spoke of what he thought the duties of the country gentlemen were, and that in his judgment they were abandoning them.

628. Was it the common jury panel?—Yes; what we call the long panel in the Crown Court.

629. Viscount *Crichton*.] Was it the custom for the sheriff to summon the country gentlemen upon the jury panels under the old system?—It was; there was a great mixture: there were shopkeepers and country gentlemen, and magistrates, and every class represented under the old system; I do not think that in Her Majesty's dominions there could have been better jurors found than there were in Clare and in Limerick.

630. *Chairman*.] Did the country gentlemen, as a rule, attend under the old system, when they were summoned?—Yes, they did; I have seen magistrates sitting over and over again five or six upon each jury.

631. Do you know the reason why the country gentlemen did not attend at the late assizes?—I really would be very slow to assign any cause that is not absolutely within my knowledge; I can only mention the fact, a fact within the cognizance of every man in the county, and, as I said before, which caused a judge to speak in rather strong terms about what he thought a resignation of the duties that devolved upon the country gentlemen; that is the reason I have said that I do not think that the Act got a fair trial at all; and I may mention it now, in view of the question that was put by the noble lord in the Chair, to the former witness, with respect to amending the Jury Act in sufficient time for the next assizes; I anticipate that no such failure of justice will occur at the next assizes, because I think that the attention of the country gentlemen has been aroused by the observation of the judges; that they will conceive it their duty to be in attendance, so that you will have a sprinkling at all events of that superior class.

632. It could not have been from ignorance of the duty which the law cast upon them that they did not attend?—If you ask me my individual opinion I should say decidedly not; I think that it was some different cause.

633. Those gentlemen had been, up to the recent assizes, in the habit of acting as jurors?—Yes, certainly. Allow me to distinguish: what we call the long panel is different from that of the other jury panel. The long panel includes both special and common jurors, and you always have a sprinkling of each class on the long panel. The special jury is formed from a special class taken from the long panel itself.

634. Do you think that the disfavour with which the Act was regarded had any prejudicial effect upon its operation in any other way?—Except the natural feeling to make the best of a good story. There are very curious and ludicrous stories afloat, and two or three of them were most undoubtedly founded upon facts, and the working of the Act was made a joke and a piece of fun. I myself, in Clare, saw a judge direct an amputated hand to be sent back to the owner, who was the prisoner; he was acquitted; there was an order made to restore the property to the owner.

635. Did he not ask for it?—No, he did not; it was suggested to the judge that he ought to make that order. But I must say, in the presence of Mr. Heron and Dr. Ball, that although it was, in my humble judgment, a complete failure of justice, there was certainly this point in the case, which the Crown immediately recognised, and which was taken advantage of with great ability by Mr. FitzGibbon, who defended the prisoner. He was indicted for firing at Mr. Crea, a gentleman of the county, a deadly weapon loaded with ball or other destructive material. The police were hunting for three days to get the ball or slug, or anything else, but they failed to find it; and, accordingly, Mr. FitzGibbon argued that the weapon might not have been loaded with any deadly or destructive material at all, and that it might have been merely blank powder.

636. Did any circumstances come to your knowledge which made you suppose that the officers engaged in the preparation of the list had in any way failed in their duty?—No, I had not the slightest idea that there was any failure of duty upon the part of the officials.

637. Did there appear to be any jurors who were over 60 years of age?—I cannot say that that struck me; I could not say approximately, Yes, or No, to that question.

638. What is your opinion of the chief principles of the new Act?—I consider it a most valuable step in the right direction; and I know a great many, too, of officials connected with various parts of the country, and I know a great many sub-sheriffs of different politics, and I have not met one of them who wishes to revert to the old system; I think there is no man who has considered the subject with a view to the efficient administration of the law in Ireland who does not conceive it a valuable improvement to take the selection of the panel from an individual.

639 Did they consider the exercise of it to be a very invidious duty?—Yes; and they were very anxious to be relieved of it, for no matter how pure the motive is, in any sensational or political trial they are always subject to suspicion, and the verdict is never acquiesced in.

640. That is a feature of the Act which they consider most important?—Yes; I think that the others are matters of detail which can be readily amended, if there is a desire really to do that which it is to be hoped every right minded person is anxious for, namely, to secure the efficient administration of justice in the country.

641. The sub-sheriff is usually permanent, is he not?—Yes, although under the Act of Parliament he ought not to be so, but in Dublin we have the same sheriff, and I believe it is the same in every county of Ireland, for years and years, and that of course intensifies the suspicion which is excited, because there is no change; it is always in the same groove, and always the same individual.

642. Did the sheriff, as a rule, interfere with the selection of the panel?—No; the public had no security in that way from the character of the high sheriff. Of course he is a man of great social position and importance, but he never interfered, except in very rare exceptional cases; perhaps not once in 10 years does the high sheriff interfere in the formation of the panel, or has anything to do with it. Therefore the public have no security from his position or character.

643. I presume

Mr. *J. C. Coffey*, Q.C.

28 April 1873.

643. I presume that you have had a great deal to do with political and party trials?—Indeed I have had, unfortunately, in Ireland, a great deal of that, both in the north and in the south.

644. In the north, you have had more party cases, have you not?—Yes, they are chronic; they crop up constantly; in fact they are indigenous.

645. Are you aware that in political or party cases, the panel thus framed is looked upon with suspicion by the one side or the other?—I have no hesitation in saying so, that is my deliberate conviction, and I am bound further to say, that, from the necessities of the case, it was sometimes absolutely essential in criminal trials to exercise what of course every man who is clothed with responsibility considers to be a very invidious thing to do, that is to say, calling upon jurors to stand by, so that really the people who are charged with the defence or with the prosecution, feel in a very awkward and anxious position. There is no man who prosecutes or defends, that does not feel it to be most unpleasant, and that it is often calculated to imperil the efficient administration of justice.

646. Do you think that that is a state of things which gives confidence in the faithfulness and the impartiality of juries?—Certainly not; it is just like as if you were to empanel 12 blacks to try a white man, or 12 white men to try a black man; that is putting, in coarse but truthful language, the nature of the feeling that is produced by what is considered packing a jury.

647. There are two other principal changes that were made, besides the minor ones, and first of all the adoption of the rating qualification instead of the old qualification; in principle do you approve of that?—In principle I approve of the rating qualification; I think that it is sound, but in my judgment it is too low, and it must be raised; the class of jurors that we have in Clare, for example, would not I think appear in the jury box if that qualification were raised; and I cannot wonder at gentlemen objecting to sit and serve with people of that description and appearance; for some of the men were in habiliments that were scarcely decent.

648. Would you merely raise the standard of qualification, or would you make any distinction between the qualification as to lands and houses?—I have considered that matter, and I, this morning, discussed it with my friend, Mr. De Moleyns, and I also spoke to the gentleman who is supposed to have assisted in drafting the Bill; it has occurred to me that I could not see any reason for the exclusion of that household franchise; I think it is one of the most valuable parts of the first class in the fourth schedule to the Act; you get there the very best description of juror; you get intelligent shopkeepers, traders, merchants, and all that sort of persons; in the second class there is Londonderry, and I can speak personally as to that; and in that county what do you do? Take now Coleraine, a very thriving town, where there are plenty of merchants and people of that description; you exclude those men who absolutely are the most valuable element that you could have; take the county, with which the honourable Member for Cork is acquainted, viz., Kerry. This remarkable thing has occurred. I inquired from the sub-sheriff, who says, "We have a bad description of jury upon the panel, but then," he said, "you know what they were upon the former occasions, before this Act came into operation." In Tralee, a town with 9,000 inhabitants, with an extremely wealthy and extremely prosperous, and most intelligent and educated class of people, he tells me that all the jurors he can get out of that town are 12, the general rating being 10*s*. under 20*l*. In Coleraine and Magherafelt, and in Tralee, you are excluded from the advantage of having those jurors.

649. You have mentioned already that some of the jury panels of which you had experience were much superior to others; do you think that you would have superior jury panels if there was an admixture of the town element?—Certainly. In a case in which I was called to the assistance of the Crown, in Cork, we had a very important case tried, involving a very serious matter which occurred upon the high seas. There we had a mixed jury, and some of them were of the old panel; when I say that they were of the old panel, I say that they were jurors who were accustomed to attend before, and the others were new men, and the result of it was that we got on most satisfactorily, and the judge expressed his approval of the conduct of the jury, and was perfectly well satisfied with them.

650. In fact, in the county of Cork the 20*l*. valuation did include a considerable number of town jurors?—Yes, it did. Cork is in the first class; there are eleven counties in that class, and about 20 in the second, by which means the household qualification is excluded in the latter instance.

651. In the county of Clare you probably had very few town jurors?—We had none; they did not attend. Houses rated at 12*l*. in towns are generally two storied houses, and they represent about 20*l*. a year rental.

652. You would suggest that the 12*l*. qualification for lands, tenements, &c., appearing on the rate book, situate in any city, town, or village, should be extended throughout Ireland?—I would; I do not see why this class should be excluded from it. And allow me to say, as it is fresh in my recollection, there was some discussion about how a correct definition could be arrived at with respect to villages. There is no difficulty about that, because the rating book gives the description of villages, towns, and so on; it is so expressed in the rating book, in the heading of the columns.

653. At all events there is no difficulty, if it be necessary, to distinguish between country districts and towns?—No; the means exist for it in the public document, the rating valuation.

654. There seems to be some confusion as to the practice of balloting from the panels for jurors in criminal cases; can you throw any light upon that?—The long panel, as I tried to explain before, consists of the common jurors, and the special jurors. The sheriff will be obliged to take that panel under the new law, which will include in it the common jurors of low qualification, and the special jurors of high qualification (and, of course, they are an intermixed class) by the letters of the alphabet; but when you come to try a prisoner, you do not ballot, but you take and read the long panel, beginning at the first name and going down until you get a jury. Then there are a number of challenges. The Crown calls upon parties to stand by if they do not consider it advisable to have them. Then the prisoner challenges 20, in order to get at a particular friend who is probably low on the list, and in order to get him on the list; practically that is the way in which it works. You read the panel

Mr. *J. C. Coffey*, Q.C.

28 April 1873.

panel down from the first letter, and then the prisoner's attorney is instructed by the prisoner and his friends in this way: such and such a person is very favourable to us; he knows all our people and friends, or he is a first cousin to so-and-so, or is a third cousin of mine, and so on; and he struggles to get that man on the panel; then the Crown Solicitor, on the other hand, in order to do his duty, must, at the same time, exercise what I have already said I think highly obnoxious and disagreeable privilege, which produces a very bad effect, the duty of calling out one after another, "stand by, stand by," giving no reason and assigning no cause, but at his arbitrary will compelling people to stand by, and ultimately, when they have exhausted the whole panel, the Crown is obliged to come to challenge and challenges; there has occurred to me one way of remedying that evil (and anything that is done in that direction I take leave to say will be a very great benefit, and will be appreciated), and that is, doing in a criminal case what is done as a matter of course in a civil case, namely, balloting for the panel, and then no man knows when his friend is to turn up, and there would be no Crown solicitor saying, "stand by, stand by," and you would have no prisoner with his eye directed to the names striving to get down to a particular individual; as far as my experience goes, I can see no objection; I have tried to find out if there is any objection, but, at present, I see no objection to that plan, and I think that it is a step in the right direction.

655. If the jury were balloted for in criminal cases, it would take away altogether, would it not, the right of the Crown to order jurors to stand by?—No, it would not do that, but I say that it would take away the frequent necessity for resorting to what I consider a very bad and very vicious practice. The same inducements, and the same reasons, would not exist for it, because when you come to ballot, perhaps you get a special juror; you may get a man of intelligence, a person that you have every reason to believe to be a proper man to serve upon the jury, and he goes on, and there is no reason why the Crown should exercise the power of calling upon persons to stand by until you get to that person.

656. Would you leave the right of challenging and ordering a juror to stand by to remain as it is?—At present I would; I am not prepared to recommend, on my own responsibility, that the Crown should relinquish that power; that is more for the consideration of the executive officers than for me. I do not interfere with or touch the rights of the Crown at all in my recommendation or suggestion.

657. There was a suggestion made on Thursday by the Attorney General to Mr. Hemphill, that it should be necessary that a certain number of the special jurors should serve upon every jury; what do you think of that suggestion?—I do not know whether that would meet the approval of those who are charged with the consideration of the matter from a Government point of view, but I think it would be a most valuable improvement. You must understand that in litigation in civil cases for 20 *l.*, 10 *l.*, or 100 *l.*, it does not matter what the amount may be, the plaintiff or defendant may require the case to be tried by a special jury, and there is no power of withholding it, although afterwards it is in the discretion of the judge whether he will give the party the cost of increased expenses incurred thereby; but in a trumpery civil case, if you were trying the value of a portmanteau lost upon a railway, or anything else, you have the power of getting a special jury; but where a man's life or liberty is at stake, no such power exists. I would give, both to the Crown and to the prisoner, in cases of capital felonies, and treason and treason-felonies, and serious misdemeanors, the power of having the case tried by a special jury. The result of that would be, that the sheriff being obliged to return a large number of special jurors, you have at once at your command a high order of intelligence and no packing. You have men of property in the country; no question of religion enters into the case at all. You take them from the special jury lists, and I would humbly submit that it would be found a very vast improvement on the administration of the criminal law as it now exists.

658. Would not the Crown always ask for a special jury in important cases?—In important cases I take it for granted that they would; I know that if I were charged with the executive part of the duty, I certainly would in every serious case; and I would have it *ex termo* without going through any circumlocution, or any affidavits or applications upon motion, I would give it as a right, when the case was going to be tried, to the prisoner, to be tried by a special jury, and the Crown should have the same right.

659. Do you think that that would have the public confidence?—That is my impression; and I cannot see an answer to it.

660. Do you think that it would be an advantage to secure that a certain number, say three special jurors, should be on every jury?—That would be an advantage, because, of course, the higher the amount of intelligence you can command, the better security you have for coming to a correct conclusion, but the *modus operandi* is where I see difficulties arising; there is one thing that is worth observation, and I merely throw it out as a suggestion, that at present upon the grand jury, where property to large amount is involved, and considerable sums of money are disposed of, persons of social position without a rating qualification at all can be empaneled; the sons of peers, knights, baronets, magistrates; the eldest sons of baronets; the eldest sons of knights, or the eldest sons of magistrates, all those are qualified without any rating qualification to act as grand jurors.

661. In fact, there is no required qualification, is there, for a grand juror?—No, there is no qualification required; and as special jurors they are recognised throughout the present Act of Parliament as being special jurors, no matter what amount of rating qualification they may have, so that there, to that extent, the principle is adopted. Under this Act the sheriff is compelled to take all of those parties, and put them on the special jurors' list, independently of their rating qualification. They must be rated, but the amount does not signify. If you were to utilise them, being qualified grand jurors, make them special jurors as well, you would, in part, increase the number of special jurors in every county in Ireland.

662. Have you considered how high you would raise the qualification?—From any information or consideration that I have been able to give to the matter at present, I would raise the qualification for common jurors to 20 *l.*, adding the household qualification. I think that that would be, at all events, an experiment well worthy of trial in legislation.

663. You

Mr. J. C. Coffey, Q.C.

18 April 1873.

663. You think that 12*l* would be the rate of the household qualification?—Yes; it in reality means a habitation for which 20*l.* a year rent is paid; the rating qualification is always lower than the actual value.

664. The household qualification is not quite a correct expression, is it, because the valuation book, I believe, only gives the buildings?—There is a very happy expression, I think, in the poor rate valuation, where there is a heading for the class "of house, offices, and yard," that is connected with land, and that would have hit it off at once.

665. But there are only two headings in the valuation return, namely, land and buildings (*handing the Return to the Witness*)?—I find it is buildings here only. I thought it was houses also.

666. But at any rate, in towns a building valued at 12*l.* would be almost invariably a house?—That would be the case certainly; it is so defined in the rate book.

667. The third change which was made by that Act was the entrusting of the revision of the list to the chairman; do you approve of that?—Of course, this being our first revision, we have only had the opportunity of one sessions to do it in, and it was a mere matter of form. There was no person there to give information, and no inquiry was made, except of the parties coming before you.

668. There were parties there to give information, were there not?—Yes, the poor rate collector and the clerk of the union, but there was no person to volunteer information, or to suggest objections, or to tell you what a man's case was.

669. But under the Act there would have been no use in their telling you anything about a man, would there?—Supposing that the duty was efficiently performed, there would not have been put upon the list any of the persons exempted by the Act; that is to say, a blind man, or a deaf man, or a man who was over 60 years of age; and I would, therefore, expect that in the lists submitted to me for revision I should find the omission of the names of men who were permanently infirm, or blind, or over 60 years of age.

670. I think you have already stated that you have no knowledge that legally disqualified men have been placed upon the list?—No.

671. But supposing the necessary information to be given to the chairman, do you think that he is the proper authority to revise the list?—I think that he is the most proper person that I could possibly suggest; his is the immediate tribunal, the local court.

672. Would you propose to extend the power which the chairman possesses of exempting jurors?—I would very widely extend that power, and I would directly legislate that an illiterate person was not qualified to act as a juror, and I would make that a ground of disqualification; when I make that remark I am perfectly sensible that there is no such disqualification in England; I have read in the public journals of very extraordinary verdicts given by English juries, and I do not think that we have a monopoly of perverse verdicts or illiterate jurors in our country; I have read very curious observations made by jurors in England, but I would make the experiment in Ireland; I am strongly of opinion that a man who has no education, and who cannot read or write, is not a person to judge in matters of fact between parties, or understand points of evidence, and he should be disqualified; I am happy to think that that disqualification would not be very extensive, for the progress of education is something marvellous in our country.

673. Would you give any additional discretionary power to the chairman to disqualify or to exempt?—To excuse; I would prefer to use that word excuse; supposing that a man was in a very delicate state of health, or I was satisfied upon evidence that he was an habitual drunkard, I would not consider either a fit man to serve; I would give power to excuse on any reasonable ground that appeared sufficient to the chairman, and I would not tie him down too strictly; I entirely concur with Mr. De Moleyns that that power if it was given would be certainly exercised with discrimination and discretion.

674. You would give power to the chairman upon the allegations of incompetency being proved either by the juror himself or by any other person?—Upon due inquiry, I would say, because sometimes you cannot get sworn evidence of a fact that is notorious to everybody; I do not think that it would be dangerous to give that discretion to the chairman in that respect; of course he would only exercise it in plain cases.

675. Have you considered in what way the necessary information should be brought to the notice of the chairman?—I have; I conceive that the poor-rate collectors, who are familiar with every man upon the roll within their districts, and who with their own hands take money from them and give receipts to them, and who see them three or four times a year it may be, are just the very persons who, from their personal knowledge, could supply that information; the barony cess collectors are another class of men that come in immediate contact with those occupying-tenants, and they could give information; the clerk of the peace also has an extensive knowledge, generally speaking; and from those three sources I think you could get complete information, so as to enable a real revision of the jurors' list to be made.

676. Would you require the poor rate collectors to place the term "objected" against a juror's name, or would you rely upon his oral information at the revision sessions?—No, I think that I ought not to act without the man's knowledge, or in his absence, and I would compel the poor rate collector who objects to a man remaining upon the jurors' list, or being placed upon it, to put his objection in the margin opposite; say that the man is illiterate, if the Committee recommend Parliament to legislate in that direction, or that a man is infirm, or blind, or over 60 years of age, all this I would compel to be placed in the margin of the list, and placed before the chairman who has to revise the list.

677. How would it be brought to the juror's notice?—I think that it might be done by a printed notice being served by the constabulary upon the person objected to, and then if he does not come forward to rebut the objection that is made against him, he cannot say in a sense that you are acting capriciously; he has a knowledge of what is going on, and he submits to the objection if he does not think it right or proper to come forward and rebut it.

678. Those Poor Rate Collectors' Lists are not published, are they, until they have been revised by the chairman?—Yes, they are; a list is printed first of the persons who are intended to be placed upon the roll, in order to enable parties to apply to have themselves placed upon it if they

Mr. *J. G. Coffey*, Q.C.

28 April 1873.

they are omitted from it, and for all the public who are interested in it to object to any name upon it.

679. Are the lists put in some public place?—Yes, they are posted all over the county, and generally upon the police barracks.

680. Would you recommend that they should be publicly posted with those observations of the poor rate collector upon them?—I do not see how to avoid it consistently with doing what I think is the first principle of justice, which is to deal with no man's privileges without his complete and entire knowledge.

681. But it would be rather an invidious thing, would it not?—It would, but I cannot help that.

682. Would you expect that the poor rate collector would post upon the chapel door a list with the observation opposite the juror's name that he was an habitual drunkard?—That is the very strongest objection that could be raised, and I fully and fairly feel the force of it, but with that exception I do not see that there is anything very objectionable in writing opposite a man's name "illiterate" if he be illiterate, or the other disqualifications contained in the Act of Parliament.

683. Would not it be sufficient if you were to place opposite the name "objected"?—That might be so, I quite admit, but habitual intemperance is not a disqualification under the Act at present, it is a mere suggestion of my own that a man who is in that condition is not a person who is fit to be upon a jury.

684. Might not notice be served upon the juror to whom objection was taken without publishing it to all the world?—No doubt that may be and would be, I dare say, a very considerable improvement on what I have taken the liberty to suggest. If what was really an objection let the cause of objection be stated in a printed notice to the man himself.

685. Have the sub-sheriffs such local knowledge as would enable them to revise the lists with advantage?—I think that they have such local knowledge as would enable them to assist the chairman very materially.

686. The Act is not very popular with the sub-sheriffs, I believe?—In large counties they complain very much of the expense of serving of these notices. I may say that what operates as a peculiar hardship, and to which attention really ought to be called, is the necessity of calling these jurors on the quarter sessions from long distances, and keeping them for a day and night in the small towns, where there is very slight accommodation for them, and more particularly at this season of the year. That has been represented to me in a way that I certainly did feel a very great grievance, but there is a remedy already in existence under the Civil Bill Act, if it were put in operation. The Lord Lieutenant has the power, with the assent of the Privy Council, to sub-divide districts and to make additional districts. Under this Act the jurors at quarter sessions are drawn from distant districts, which is the cause of very serious complaint. I may exemplify what I mean from my own county of Londonderry. There are two towns, Coleraine and Magherafelt, in one division which contains half-a-dozen or more of baronies. The jurors, in order to comply with this Act of Parliament, are obliged to be drawn from Coleraine to Magherafelt, and *vice versâ* from Magherafelt to Coleraine, whereas, if those were made into separate divisions, they would be then taken from their own immediate vicinity. That is a matter which operates in every county in Ireland as a grievance and hardship.

687. Do you think that the post office might be made use of for serving notices upon the jurors?—I think that that would be wholly unworkable; anybody who understands the country must be aware of that. The peasants and those little country farmers have very little correspondence. Excepting that a man expects a letter from America, or something of that sort, he never thinks of going to the post at all; and if he does go to the post from curiosity to know if his neighbour's letter is received, it is on a Sunday when he goes to mass, that he goes into the post office to make inquiry, but as a rule they have no correspondence.

688. Do you think that the post office could be made use of, neither to serve jury summonses nor to serve notice of objection?—In the large towns there is no difficulty at all in making use of the post office, because the letter carrier goes about to each house; the objection only arises in villages and remote districts.

689. I think, from what you stated, that you would exempt publicans?—Certainly, in criminal cases. I do not see any objection to their serving on civil cases, but I see considerable objection to their serving in criminal cases.

690. Are there any other classes that you would exempt?—There is a class that I think are not exempted at present but who ought to be, that is, the clerks of attorneys. I do not know if they think that they ought to be disqualified, but I think that they ought not to be on juries for many reasons.

691. Is there any other class?—I am not aware of any.

692. From what you have said I think you do not consider that there is any very pressing or immediate necessity for a temporary amendment of the Act?—I think that, if things were to remain as experience has shown in the south of Ireland in the places that I have mentioned, it would be a very serious matter indeed to allow another assizes to pass without improving the jurors; but, as I said before, I am tolerably confident that, from the notoriety which the matter has acquired, and from the observations that have been made by the judges, we shall see a mixture of persons of higher education and higher social position attending and taking their part on juries, and then I think the whole danger would be removed, because from their intellectual superiority they would influence ignorant or inexperienced men on the jury.

693. Have you considered any mode in which some amendment might be effected before the next assizes?—The only way that occurs to me is by a short Act raising the standard of qualification in the schedules from 20 *l.* to 30 *l.*, and adding the town or house valuation, as I call it.

694. You could not have the new qualification added before another assizes, could you?—I am afraid not. The summer assizes would be about the end of July, or the beginning of August, and you would have to prepare the lists, which would take a considerable time, and I am afraid that it would be impracticable.

695. But you might use the existing jury book, only selecting from it jurors of a given qualification?—Yes, you might do that certainly, making mandatory upon the sheriff to return the jurors qualified at 30 *l.*, or above 30 *l.* a-year, and not under.

696. Would

Mr. *J. C. Coffey*, Q.C.

28 April 1873.

696. Would you recommend that?—I think it would be advisable to do it, and it would give time for the consideration of various questions that, of course, will impress themselves upon the Committee, more or less.

697. Have you ever considered the question which is now being considered in this country of adopting the principle of a majority in a jury?—I do not like a majority, I confess; I think that the abuses have not been so great as to render it advisable to alter the constitutional practice which has existed hitherto.

698. Then you are in favour of unanimity?—I am. I believe that now and then valuable and innocent lives have been saved by it.

699. Is there any other suggestion which you wish to make to the Committee?—No, I think not.

700. Dr. *Ball*.] With regard to the suggestion of yours about the power to name a special jury in particular criminal cases, if an application of that nature were made by the Crown, would you have it made on behalf of the Attorney General directly by counsel in open court, and not by mere serving a notice, or by his volition?—I would give it *ore tenus* at the assizes, the Attorney General, or his representative, to stand up and say, "I require this case to be tried by a special jury," which would render it necessary that the sheriff should have a special jury panel of a sufficient number, say 100, to meet every emergency, the prisoner to have a like right.

701. Mr. *Brown*.] In that case, would not it be likely to throw the trial of all criminal cases upon the special jury panel?—I think not; I think that for small misdemeanors, and certain things of that description, nobody would dream of having a special jury.

702. But in all serious and heavy cases, you think that it would be desirable?—Yes, I think it would, and I think it ought to be so.

703. With regard to the suggested temporary amendment of the Act by raising the property qualification for the next assizes; do you think that that would be at all a sufficient amendment of the Act?—Not at all; I would not stop there.

704. It is only just a temporary thing to stop the gap?—Just to stop the gap.

705. You mentioned, did you not, that the high sheriff never interferred with the formation of the panels?—As a rule he does not.

706. The original Act, the 3 & 4 Will. 4, though not actually in terms, yet in principle appears to suggest that the high sheriff should form the panel?—Yes; but in that Act you read "high sheriff" all through as "sub-sheriff."

707. In some parts of the Act, but not in all?—I have not referred to the Act for a long time; but be that as it may, the fact remains indisputable that the high sheriff as a rule never does interfere; that is the experience of every country gentleman.

708. Do not you think that that is rather a misfortune?—I think it is unavoidable; the high sheriff comes to the office with the greatest disadvantage; he practically knows nothing about the business that he has to perform; he is not trained to it; he has had no previous knowledge of it at all; and he must be very much dependent upon the permanent official; he goes to him for advice and assistance; and usually when we have confidence in a man we give him the whole conduct of the business we consult him upon.

709. Still you would have the assistant barrister to apply to the sub-sheriff to assist him in the revision of the jury list?—Yes; because the persons referred to are responsible officials in the public employment; they have responsible duties cast upon them, and they are under the sanction and obligation of an oath; you have that security in the information that they give you, and you act judicially upon that information.

710. But you do not think that the assistant barrister by himself, without any such assistance, could very well revise the lists?—Unless compelled I should altogether decline it; I would not initiate questions or seek out information; it is not my business to do that; it would be putting a very invidious task upon me.

711. Do you suggest any higher qualification for special jurors than those named in the Act?—No; I think it is just fairly; I would have them gradually ascending in that way; I do not think that the line ought to be drawn too fine, so as to exclude persons who are not very rich; but who may nevertheless be very intelligent and very honest.

712. You of course know the rates of qualification mentioned in the fifth Schedule?—Yes, I do.

713. And you think that those are good?—Yes, certainly.

714. Mr. *Downing*.] What do you mean by saying that you answered from a Government point of view?—I do not know what I did say about a Government point of view; I did not say, I think, I answered from a Government point of view; I think the noble Chairman was putting a question to me about recommending or advising the Crown about relinquishing some power.

715. It was with regard to the exercise by the Attorney General, or a person representing him with regard to special juries, and you added "taking the Government point of view," what did you mean by that?—I meant to say that if I were a Government official I consider that I do ample justice generally, and I consider that I do equal justice to the prisoners, and by adopting that suggestion I would put them in the same position as the Crown, and I would give the additional security of the Ballot between both parties.

716. I understood you to say that you approve of this Act on principle?—I do.

717. If you give power to the Crown to try a prisoner by special jury, would not that strike at the very root of the Act itself?—I think not; I think I do this, I prevent what I consider, I do not say a discreditable scene, but certainly an invidious proceeding; you often have a struggle between the prisoner and the Crown, the prisoner attempting to get on the jury persons who are not properly qualified to be on it as either being friends or relations of the prisoner, or from other causes that are perfectly well known to those who are entrusted with the duty of making inquiries. I think it would prevent that, and it also would prevent the Crown from calling out wholesale "Stand by, stand by;" by my plan I get a high order of intelligence, and by balloting them I prevent anything like the previous manipulation or the arrangement of the jurors, who are to try any particular case.

718. I understood you to say, in answer to the noble Chairman, that you would not interfere with the right of the Crown to put by, nor with the right of the prisoner's counsel to challenge?—So

Mr. *J. C. Coffey*, Q.C.

25 April 1873.

—So I stated, certainly; it is not my duty, sitting here as a witness upon the question, to suggest what authority I would take from the Crown, or whether I would circumscribe the right of the Crown.

719. Has not the prisoner the same right to challenge whilst you are drawing by ballot?—Yes, certainly.

720. What distinction do you draw between that system and the present?—As at present constituted, when the Clerk of the Crown takes the panel in his hands, he calls the first name upon it, and he goes in consecutive order through the whole of it. By what I suggest, namely, having this panel balloted for, it will prevent upon the one hand the Crown from calling out "Stand by, stand by, stand by," and it will prevent the prisoner from calling out "Challenge, challenge, challenge," until he comes to a name that particularly strikes his fancy. I think that by so doing you do equal justice between the Crown and the prisoner, not giving a tittle of advantage to one more than the other. You do not deprive any party of any right that they have at the present moment.

721. How is that possible; surely if a man's name on the list is John Murphy, if the prisoner, as you say, considers him his friend, what is to prevent him arriving at that man's name, and having him on the jury, as well by the ballot as by the present system, for this reason, that he challenges every man that is called by ballot till Murphy is drawn?—But before Murphy is drawn his challenges may be exhausted, unless, to use a familiar phrase, the dice are loaded.

722. Do you put the whole number on the panel into the box, or do you select from each letter: so many of letter A, so many of letter B, and so many of letter C?—Either way, because the question is not to destroy altogether the alphabetical arrangement, because the alphabetical arrangement compels the sheriff, instead of selecting originally the names, to bring in the names *par hasard*. It secures perfect impartiality, prevents selection, and prevents the sheriff doing what was most objectionable, naming his own panel.

723. Do not you get rid altogether of the alphabetical order when you throw the whole of the names into the box, for this reason, that you do not know but that that very name in the letter M may be first called?—That is the great advantage, that nobody knows who will come up.

724. You would allow the Crown to say "Stand by," and you would allow the prisoner to challenge?—Certainly.

725. How does that enable you to get a better jury?—Simply because the prisoner's attorney does not know in what order a particular man whom he wants to have upon the panel will come up, or whether he will come up at all till all his challenges are exhausted, and therefore he is acting upon mere chance if he goes on challenging against men, as to whom he has no real cause of objection.

726. Mr. *Heron*.] It would prevent capricious challenging, would it not?—Yes.

727. Mr. *Downing*.] Do you think that a man who can read, but cannot write, is not an intelligent juror?—I should be very sorry to say that; I certainly would modify my answer to this extent, that if I found that a man was capable of reading with reasonable facility, although he could not write, I would say that he was quite sufficiently intelligent to be on a jury. Of course a man with clumsy hands, and that sort of thing, may not be able to write, although he may use his hands very well in other respects.

728. Then you qualify your answer to this extent, that you think a man that could read with facility is a proper juror?—Yes

729. Do you expect that you will find more intelligence in jurors rated at 30 *l.* than at 20 *l.*?—I do.

730. Is that your experience?—It is, and what is more, a reason that occurs to me as an obvious one is that a man rated at 30 *l.* can afford to give his children a better education than a man rated at 20 *l.* He sends them to an excellent school and keeps them there, instead of having them at home labouring upon his farm. The observation which I have heard here is most perfectly accurate, that of the peasantry of Ireland up to 30 or 35 years of age, the exception are those who cannot read, and who are not intelligent; but I say that the higher the qualification goes, the better standard of education you are likely to get, and the higher the order of intelligence.

731. Have you made any calculation as to the number of special jurors that you can have upon the panel?—I can tell you in my own county that under the present system (I asked the sub-sheriff to let me know) there are 600 special jurors in the county of Londonderry.

732. Which is a very large county, is it not?—A very large county.

733. You would have those criminal cases, would you not, both at assizes and at sessions?—Yes, I would.

734. That would render it necessary that those men should be summoned repeatedly?—It would; but with what necessarily must follow, namely, dividing the quarter sessions into districts, that inconvenience would not exist; but they would be taken from the immediate neighbourhood, instead of coming from the county at large.

735. That would not apply, would it, to the assizes?—No, it would not; whatever be the inconvenience and hardship, it must arise at the assizes.

736. From your experience as a Crown prosecutor, if the Crown were to exercise the right which you would give them, to try a prisoner by a special jury, for you said you would give power to the Attorney General at the assizes to say, "I will try this man by a special jury," would not the prisoner be taken by surprise?—I think not, because if the law is that it is the right of the Attorney General in a certain defined class of cases to apply for a special jury, the prisoner and his attorney will know just as well as any man in the world the probability of the Crown applying to have him so tried.

737. Would he also know what is passing in the mind of the Attorney General?—Yes, if he be a man of sense and forethought, as far as those cases are concerned.

738. Do you think it would be satisfactory to public opinion that the Attorney General should have the right to call for the trial of a prisoner by a special jury?—Yes, if there is a corresponding right upon the part of the prisoner; I cannot see any objection to that, provided always that the jury is not packed; and I say that the valuable principle in this Act is that it takes away the opportunity and the power of selection.

739. Why

Mr. J. C. Coffey, Q.C.

28 April 1873.

739. Why not go at once according to your opinion, and let no man be summoned except under the fifth schedule, and make them all special jurors?—No; because in civil cases, and in ordinary small trumpery cases, nobody would think of resorting to a special jury.

740. But in criminal cases might not that be done?—In criminal cases, stealing a cow, or clothes off a bush, or petty larcenies, or picking pockets, nobody would dream of having a special jury.

741. Then you would only give it in political cases, would you?—Excuse me, I have not said that; I would give it in capital felonies, in serious misdemeanors and very high class misdemeanors, such as homicide, or treason, or treason-felony.

742. Is there not power already, in a case of treason-felony, to apply to have a special jury, or to change the venue?—Yes; but I would make it the ordinary operation of the law instead of having it in special cases.

743. Although you would do that, your opinion is that it would not affect the principle of the Act?—I think not.

744. Do you think that, as far as you have seen, a greater number of illiterate persons, and persons unfit to serve upon a jury, have been called under the recent Act than under the old Act, the 3rd and 4th of William the Fourth?—I cannot answer that question as fully as I would like, because exclusively those of the humbler classes attended in answer to the call, and there was no sprinkling, no admixture whatever of any other class, and therefore the same number would not have appeared, and there would have been an admixture if, as I think was their duty, the jurors of a higher class had attended.

745. I think your evidence is that in the county of Cork the Act works beneficially?—Yes.

746. Are you not aware yourself that in the County of Cork, at the last assizes the magistrates of the county served upon the juries?—I am not aware of that; if you mention a name to me I shall be able to say whether he was on it or not, because most of the names are familiar to me; the only person individually whom I could cite as having been on the jury (and that was in consequence of a conversation which I had with him) was Mr. Adams; I do not know whether he is a magistrate or not; he was foreman of the jury that tried the sea captain.

747. Did you see Mr. Carberry Egan?—No, I did not; but if you say he was there that is sufficient for me.

748. If other counties have found the Act to operate in the same way, I presume that you do not really see any very extensive amendment to be necessary?—I will tell you frankly, as a matter of fact, that if I were an inhabitant of the county of Clare, and if I were a gentleman there, waiting to be called upon a jury, if I saw the same individuals that were in the box, I would not like to sit in the box with them, nor would you.

749. Major Warburton, in his evidence before the Select Committee on the State of Ireland, stated, "The year after the 3rd and 4th of William the Fourth was passed, seven or eight men came to me with a petition to hand to the judge. They said, 'We are brought here as jurors; we literally are starving; we have no means of providing ourselves; we have come 40 miles.' I found out of the seven there were four who could not speak English, and the other three were illiterate." Have you seen anything of that kind under this Act?—If you ask me, I should say that I do not suppose that of the men that I saw in the box in the county of Clare on some of the trials, scarcely one of them could read or write, judging from their appearance; of course I had no other means of knowledge, and I venture to think that you would come to the same conclusion if you saw them.

750. Did you know Mr. Kemmis, the late Crown solicitor?—Yes, I did know him.

751. He said, in answer to a question which was put to him, "I have known persons returned to serve who were absolutely illiterate;" do you agree with that?—I am sure of it.

752. Do you know Mr. Seed?—Yes.

753. He said, "I have seen cases where the jurors could not read and write;" "some of them were very ignorant men;" do you believe that?—Yes, I believe it.

754. Then the same things existed under the 3 & 4 Will. 4 as exist now?—Unquestionably.

755. *The O'Donoghue.*] Is not the change that you propose, in fact, to return to the principle of selection?—No, I think not. I think that it is diametrically opposed to it; that is the conclusion that I have formed. I may be wrong, of course.

756. You will admit that there was selection under the old system?—Yes, and a very bad system it was.

757. It was selection in a particular sense, was it not?—It was. It left to the uncontrolled discretion of an individual the power and opportunity to pack his panel and to select his names without being responsible to anybody.

758. If that was selection in a particular sense, is not the change which you propose, selection in a general sense?—I think not.

759. Did I rightly understand you to say, with regard to what occurred in the county of Clare, that the character of the juries might have been different if many of those jurors who ought to have attended had attended?—Certainly, and the same evil consequences would not have followed; if you had had six and six, or four intelligent men, or four of a higher class, mixed with eight persons of the description alluded to, I have no doubt that their intelligence would have had its just influence.

760. Then the Act as it now exists was not altogether responsible for what occurred in Clare?—Undoubtedly not.

761. *The O'Conor Don.*] You stated that you would propose a 12 *l.* household qualification; do not you think that 12 *l.* is rather high, and that it might be reduced with regard to houses in Ireland which are generally valued too low?—You will observe that this is for towns and villages.

762. But even in towns and villages in the country parts of Ireland, are you not aware that the valuation of houses is very low?—Yes.

763. Would not the valuation of 12 *l.* shut out a great number of very intelligent jurors in small villages and in towns in the country?—It may be so, but that is a question of degree which I would not be prepared to give a dogmatic opinion upon at all; I have no means of testing or inquiring into that, so as to give a satisfactory answer.

Thursday, 1st May 1873.

MEMBERS PRESENT:

Dr. Ball.	The Marquis of Hartington.
Sir Rowland Blennerhassett.	Mr. Heron.
Mr. Bourke.	Mr. Charles Lewis.
Mr. Bruen.	The O'Conor Don.
Viscount Crichton.	The O'Donoghue.
Mr. Downing.	Major O'Reilly.
Colonel Forde.	Colonel Wilson Patten.
	Colonel Vandeleur.

THE RIGHT HONOURABLE THE MARQUIS OF HARTINGTON, IN THE CHAIR.

Mr. SERJEANT ARMSTRONG, called in; and Examined.

Mr. Serjeant *Armstrong.*

1 May 1873.

764. *Chairman.*] I BELIEVE you are a Queen's Counsel?—Yes, and first Serjeant of Law in Ireland.

765. Have you had considerable opportunities of observing the practical working of the Juries Act in Ireland?—I have had opportunities of observing it on three of the Irish circuits, and in the city of Dublin, and the county of Dublin.

766. Will you have the goodness to give the Committee the result of your experience of its operation?—In the first place, the novelty of the change attracted great and general attention, and the minds of the public were directed peculiarly to observe its working, so that some matters which occurred, and which were to the inexperienced people the aspect of novelties, were to my mind but a recurrence of difficulties that I had observed under the old system. I may state that with regard to the main principle of the Bill, I had opportunities of hearing, in many quarters, professional and unprofessional, the general feeling on the subject, and strange to say, there appears to be, as far as my own knowledge goes, a unanimity of feeling upon this one subject in Ireland, for I have not heard one dissentient voice as to the wisdom and propriety of distributing the business of jurymen over the whole county, and the principle sought to be carried out by this alphabetical selection appears to be universally approved of. But with reference to the qualification, I think that a very decided amendment, and a very marked amendment is absolutely necessary; and I think that that qualification should be made to be dependent, not altogether upon mere property, because, unfortunately at present in Ireland, at all events, the possession of large farms and of property realised upon them, in counties particularly, is not a test of that educational qualification which I think a man should possess to enable him to understand complicated matters of evidence, and particularly a line of reasoning leading to inductive conclusions which often arise.

767. In what circuits have you had experience?—I was special on the Home Circuit, special on the North-west Circuit, and I was on my own circuit, which I have never left, the Leinster Circuit.

768. Have you observed any practical failure in the working of the Act?—I would have a difficulty in answering that question, for this reason: I have met with disappointments, but as those were cases in which I happened to be professionally engaged, my mind might labour under a bias which, perhaps, it would not be fair to communicate; but this I will state in general terms, that in several instances the class of men who answered to the summonses were quite inadequate to the investigation of the cases which they were about to try, and in some instances which they were empanelled to try.

769. As a matter of opinion, you feel convinced that the average of the intelligence of the juries whom you have seen under the new Act, was not equal to that of the old juries?—I certainly think not; I think that the qualification ought to be raised, and very sensibly raised. My impression is, that you will not find a satisfactory common jury with a qualification of less than 50*l.* I would desire to say, with reference to this system, of what is called the distribution of the business by the alphabetical plan, that it has commanded, I think, the confidence of the country; it is a step in the right direction. It tends to put an end to what never was right, and never was desirable, and is no longer practicable, and that is anything like the packing of juries. I think that people are entitled, not only to have the administration of justice pure, but to have it conducted in such a way as to impress them with its fairness. And I think it is politic, for this reason also, that it tends to enlarge the area of persons taking a share in the administration of justice; and however some of them may complain of inconvenience, I am satisfied from observation that many a small shopkeeper, and so on, is very proud to act upon juries; they consider it a credit and an advantage to them in more ways than one; and it tends to identify them with the institutions of the country, and to make them more loyal and more contented men by taking some little share in the administration of justice. I think that in every respect therefore it is politic, but the qualification should be raised to secure intelligence.

770. Did you observe that there was a marked absence

Mr. Serjeant *Armstrong.*

1 May 1873.

absence of the better class of jurors at the last assizes, and that those who attended were almost exclusively composed of the lowest class upon the list?—I observed that particularly in one instance, and I think I can give a reason for it; it was particularly the case at Omagh, in a Crown case. I never saw anything like the absence of the better sort, and the swarming prevalence of men of the very obscurest positions.

771. Did you hear any observations made by the judges on the absence of the better class of jurors?—It did not happen to strike me; I never heard that; I heard observations of the converse character upon the nature and the style of the men who did appear; for instance, where men appealed to the judge to allow them to stand by as they could not read or write. I have noticed that myself at Nenagh particularly, where a man was complimented very highly by the Chief Justice upon his candour in informing the court of his practical incapacity to attend to his business, which it was very right of the man to do. But I may say that in Dublin particularly my experience amounts to this, that those who used in my early days to attend the special juries, had for a long time deliberately abandoned their duty, and neglected it *in toto*; and the consequence of that was, that the special juries in Dublin became, I may say, a regular set of men, quite well known, whom we would always expect to meet and to see. That was highly inconvenient, and I think that that very matter was one of the staring inconveniences which led to the present enactment.

772. A great number of persons made a kind of profession of it, did they not?—The better classes, the leading merchants of Dublin, the wealthy shopkeepers, who have large establishments in the town, and reside outside in villas round about, chose to absent themselves, and there was no pressure put upon them. The power of the judge to fine them never was exercised with anything like vigour, and the thing crept into a slipshod style, very much owing to the neglect of imposing fines, and insisting upon respectable people attending. A reason suggests itself to my mind for the absence of the better sort of people in Dublin, and I dare say it has been creeping into the country, and that is, the want of an adequate machinery of summoning; and I think it has been a great defect in this Act in not altering the machinery of summoning, and for this reason, after all the pains that are taken in selection, classification and qualification, and so on, you have a list made out of the summonses, but I have no doubt that in Dublin the practice has prevailed of intercepting the process server, who is a humble man, a common bailiff, who comes to serve the summons, and a very small consideration will induce him to pass by the door. He is told that the master is not at home, or he is not in his office, and the servant receipts the book, or the porter at the gate receipts the book, and the man goes away. For that I would substitute postal services all over the country. I think that a man who is so obscure as to be beyond the reach of postal communication is not fit to serve upon a jury at all. And I believe, having regard to the postal arrangements over the face of Ireland, that there would be no difficulty whatever in a registered letter, if that was thought desirable, reaching every man whose pretensions were at all adequate to serve upon any jury in the county.

773. In Dublin the service is through the post, is it not?—Yes, it is; and I wish to generalise it, because it is highly important, not only to have a number of the model sort of people, with the proper qualification, attending, but to ensure the attendance of the better class, who can now easily evade it by an arrangement with his servant, or a little understanding with the bailiff, and you do not find them attending at all, but they shirk the trouble.

774. Mr. *Bruen.*] Do you state that that is the case in practice?—It would be a delicate thing to say that I know it of my own knowledge; but I have had a great deal of observation, and, looking at the results, I have no doubt that it has been done, and done in such a way as not to infringe the law. A servant intercepts the man at the door with the summons, and says the master is not at home. Very well. "Here is a crown piece for you." I am not aware that that is against the law. And if the green wax process goes against a man who is supposed to be served, he conscientiously files an affidavit that he never heard of the summons.

775. *Chairman.*] Did I not understand you to say that you had observed the absence of the better class of jurors in Dublin also?—Yes; markedly; and in Dublin particularly so. Latterly it has become the habit to see a settled number of men, some of them undoubtedly highly respectable, and others of whom I will not say anything offensive, but whose time was not otherwise so engaged as to prevent their continuous attendance.

776. But in Dublin you have the postal service?—Yes; but you see the Act has had very little working in Dublin; there has been but one term of its operation as yet, and therefore very little experience of it. But in the county of Dublin cases particularly, the idea of a qualification of 20*l.* is perfectly absurd. There are many men in Dublin who, if the qualification was fixed at 100*l.*, would not be fit to serve. But recollect those are not anomalies arising from this new system merely. I recollect under the old system, in the remarkable Mount Garrett case, which settled the title of the estates of the Mount Garrett family, and gave the estates to the present Viscount Mount Garrett, on one of the trials there was a gentleman on the special jury who attended upon that jury, and acted upon it, who was twirling a straw hat without a band or ribbon upon it, and the collar of his shirt was lying open, and he had a beautiful red, well-tanned breast to expose, and although he could neither read nor write, yet he was one of the most wealthy farmers in Kilkenny, farming 800 acres of land in his own hand. Those things occasionally occur, and, therefore, there should be an educational qualification, because no amount of money or of property will occasionally prevent a man very inadequate indeed to perform such duties, being upon a jury.

777. Do you think that that juror whom you have just mentioned was not fit to act as a juror?—I do not think that he was fit to act as a juror. I am convinced that when that man got into the jury room he followed the leading grand juror or the leading man of position in the county, and just followed him as a sheep follows the bell wether. I am convinced that he was a capital judge of stock, live or dead, and knew right well how to cultivate land, but as to reasoning upon facts, he was quite incompetent.

Mr. Serjeant Armstrong.

1 May 1873.

778. *Dr. Ball.*] In the Mount Garrett case was it not a question of the Scotch law of marriage?—It was a very involved case. There were questions of law, and questions involving a great general knowledge of life, and of the intercourse of people of fashion in Edinburgh and in London, with fashionable women, and all that style of thing, and the man was utterly incompetent to judge upon such matters.

779. *Chairman.*] You would lay down as a general principle that a man who was not able to read and write should be disqualified?—I think he should be *ipso facto* disqualified, but I would do it in a way not to hurt his feelings; and therefore I would not propose to confer on the local guardian or on the board of guardians the least power of selection or of rejection. I would propose to fix a *bonâ fide* high and respectable qualification, and then I would have a return made, as now, to the chairman at sessions, and I think that there might be safely vested in the chairman, assisted by a staff of officers whom I would suggest, a discretion to reject any person without assigning any precise reason. If there be any judge of a secondary class who possesses the confidence of the county, it is the chairman of the county. I believe him to be beyond all exception in point of purity and integrity, and in the enjoyment of general public respect and confidence, and I am convinced that there is not a man in any county in Ireland who would not rather rejoice to hear that it was the chairman of the county, with proper assistance and proper information brought to aid him, who had the power of rejection. That could be done in a very simple way by a very few words in the 12th section, which says, "The clerks of unions, poor-rate collectors, and all persons who shall have assisted or taken part in preparing any of the said lists," "shall attend upon the chairman and shall answer upon oath all such questions as shall be put to them by the chairman or barrister presiding in such court, touching anything done by them in execution of the provisions of this Act; and such chairman or barrister shall at the said court, or at some lawful adjournment thereof, revise the said general list of jurors and list of special jurors respectively;" then I pass on, "and shall amend the said lists by expunging therefrom the name of every man whose name shall appear therein respectively who shall be exempted" (that is by the special words of the Act), "or who shall not be qualified under this Act, or who from lunacy, imbecility of mind, deafness, blindness, or other permanent infirmity, shall be unfit to serve as a juror;" I would introduce the words, "Or for any other reason appearing sufficient to the barrister or chairman in that behalf." I believe, further, that the chairmen would command the general confidence of the whole country, and no one would be shocked with an investigation which was made by him before he could exercise his discretion; but certainly the chairmen should be well informed and well assisted. They are, generally speaking, strangers in the county until they are appointed, but they rapidly become acquainted both with the country people and with the county, and I would propose to assist them in this way: I would have the chairman attended not only by the clerk of the peace and by the poor-rate collector, but by the sessional Crown solicitor, by the county inspector of constabulary, and by the county surveyor. I think that the county surveyor is a man who could well afford a day for such business, and who is about the best acquainted with the county of any man in it, because he comes in contact with every class of people in the county; he has constantly to ride over it. There is no one public officer whose duty it is to perambulate the county periodically in the manner that the county surveyor does, and he is peculiarly acquainted with it; therefore I would arm the chairmen with that discretion which, I think, nobody would be jealous of or shocked at; for, as I said before, the chairmen are emphatically gentlemen who enjoy the confidence of the whole county, and are entirely free from anything like imputations with regard to their integrity or purity of character. That being so, I say give them a proper staff of information to inform their minds. Give them the clerk of the peace, the deputy clerk of the peace, the sessional Crown prosecutor, the county constabulary inspector, and the sub-inspectors of constabulary, or the head constables, if you choose, who are men of sagacity themselves, and who know the men, and I would like them especially to have the assistance of the county surveyor. With that staff they would know almost everything about each man who was qualified in the county. Then, without anything offensive, instead of saying, "This man cannot read or write," they might draw their pen quietly through his name, and there is no offence given.

780. Would it not be necessary that the attention of the chairman should be directed to any one who was specially disqualified, by some mark upon the list itself?—That might be done, but I would not propose it. It is an invidious thing to ostracise a man by any reference to any peculiar disqualification. It is quite sufficient to put a tick opposite to his name, or you might put the word "exempt," or "query," or anything at all except "objected." I would not say "objected," because it is not an objection in the sense of any objection as to character.

781. Unless the Act directed the poor-rate collector to put even a tick or a query against the name of a juror, he would not be justified in doing so, would he?—No, he would not be justified in doing so; but by the plan that I am suggesting to the Committee I would impose upon the chairman the duty of investigating these matters. I do not think that it would be adequate to have him slurring over the thing and making a race over the list, assuming that it was all right if it was not objected to. I think that he should take the trouble of going through the list, name by name, and say, "Is there any objection to this man?" in the hearing of all those officers in attendance upon him, who should be sworn to give him information.

782. Would not it be an enormous task in some counties to go over the list name by name?—I do not think it would be any very great task, because, after all, the objections would be rare, and even if there were a little additional labour cast on the chairman, I think it is his duty, which he would cheerfully undertake in the interests of the public. I know of no better place to have it done, and they ought to do it. I have no sympathy with men in a public position not doing their duty, and I do not think that one of them would grumble at it. I would allow no consideration of labour or difficulty in the way of chairman or court to interfere with the ultimate object of having a respectable and competent and independent jury, and I think the machinery ought to be

Mr. Serjeant *Armstrong.*

1 May 1873.

be properly worked to create that result, but I would stand upon no difficulty as to giving trouble to anybody

783. I understand the chief suggestions that you make, to be the raising of the qualification and the extension of the power of revision?—Those are the two main ones, together with the postal summons instead of the present system, which is a mere evasion; but there are one or two little matters which are trifling, comparatively speaking, but I take leave, as I am here, to suggest them. In the first place, I have some doubts as to the prudence of an absolute declaration that no man shall serve but once in three years. Recollect this is a new system that has been introduced; you are widening the area of the system very much by bringing in many men who have never served before, and I think that that is very wholesome, for the reasons already given, but, after all, the business of a jury requires some little education. It is a very embarrassing thing to any counsel to have to address 12 men who were never before on a jury, and I think it would be a very convenient thing to have one or two who understand the routine business sufficiently, and, above all, who understand the use of ordinary terms. I remember one juror asking the judge what was the meaning of an information, and the judge had to explain it to him, and it was very embarrassing and very awkward. I think that we should have a better class than that. I doubt greatly whether it is expedient to continue this exclusion of men who have served within three years, because the result is that you would continually have new jurors, and it is very hard indeed to manage men who are not the least acquainted with the business. The man is expecting assistance from his neighbour which he finds he cannot obtain. Take the case of grand juries in Ireland; though they are all men of intelligence and men of position, we know that practically all the business and all the real working of the thing is done by a few leading experienced heads, whom the younger men are glad to be guided by and to follow, and they follow them very rightly and properly.

784. Would you approve of a suggestion which has been made, that it should be necessary that a certain number of jurors qualified as special jurors should serve upon every jury?—That would be one way of meeting the general difficulty, but I do not like to do anything that would necessitate an invidious comparison. It would be a sort of imputation upon the other jurors that they could not, in the absence of special jurors, get on with their duty; and I think that the necessity for such a plan would be obviated by an enlarged qualification. I would not like to do anything to set one section of the jury, even momentarily, above the other in point of position, or in point of prestige, because there would be a risk of those men assuming a superiority in the jury-room over the others, which I would avoid by a higher qualification generally.

785. Are you aware that that is the principle which the Attorney General proposes to introduce in England?—I have noticed it in the public papers. However, I will take the liberty, with great respect, of stating my own candid views on the matter, leaving every other gentleman to think for himself.

786. Do you think that there would be any special objection to it in Ireland, if the principle were adopted for England; do you think that the special jurors in any class of cases would become to any extent marked men?—I rather think so. I think that it would create an unpleasant distinction. I would not like to have a set of men, a section of the jury, recognised by the law as in some way superior to their fellows. I think that they should be associates in their duty. We call the grand jurors "you and your fellows," and the foreman talks of himself and fellows as finding a bill. I think that, as a point of principle, you should do nothing to elevate one section of the jury above the rest. It might lead to various irregularities; for instance, to a peculiar style of address to the section of the special jurors upon the jury. Experienced men might not fall into that difficulty, but inexperienced men might; and there is no necessity for it if you raise the qualification.

787. Major *O'Reilly*.] Have you any suggestion to make as to the practical way in which the object which you consider desirable, that some of the special jurors should serve more frequently, should be brought about?—I am not prepared to state the mechanism, so to say, but I am sure that it could be done.

788. *Chairman*.] What have you to say with regard to the suggestion that in criminal cases special juries might be required by the counsel on either side?—With regard to a special jury, I think that the idea that the defendant, or the traverser, or the prisoner, as the case may be, in a criminal case, applying for a special jury, is scarcely to be contemplated, and I do not think that it is ever likely to arise. I am afraid that applying for a special jury would sound very much like a foregone conclusion on the part of the authority, and a desire, as it were, to ensure a conviction, which would be an unwholesome feeling; and recollecting this, that the Crown can, in momentous cases, or cases of great public interest and involving serious questions, always resort to a special commission, I would rather leave it to that extraordinary prerogative of the Crown than introduce this new and marked distinction of trying a defendant by a special jury. I think it would be regarded by the people of Ireland as the worst system of packing that ever was heard of, and I should not like it.

789. You have mentioned the power of the Crown to have a special commission if necessary, but that does not affect the character of juries in any way, does it?—Under this Act it would not; but I think myself that the ancient prerogative of the Crown as to having a special commission should be left untouched and should be carefully guarded. The practice under a special commission was this: I do not say that there was any law in the Statute Book recognising it, but the practice was known, and it was this: men who were upon the grand jury panel of a county were summoned, and constituted a jury at a special commission; and we all know that in very bad times special commissions were unhappily necessary, and that they were sometimes attended by consequences very wholesome to society. We must all regret the necessity for them; but I think that the prerogative of the Crown in that respect ought never to have been touched, and that the ancient practice should be adhered to. At present, with a special commission, you have nothing but an ordinary jury in a case of treason or felony.

790. Then an alteration of the Act would be required

Mr. Serjeant Armstrong.

1 May 1873.

required for what you think proper?—I think that the qualification is the main point, with this power of selection vested in the responsible chairmen of the counties, who would be sure to do their duty, always supposing that they were well advised and well assisted by the sworn evidence of officials above all imputation or suspicion.

791. But you would not recommend that where a special commission is necessary the jury should be selected in any different way from the jury at ordinary assizes?—I am not prepared to say that I would, upon consideration. I think if you raised the qualification you would get a good and fair jury.

792. As to the postal summons, would there not be considerable difficulty in proving the receipt of the summons?—No; I have already stated that, if a man is so obscure and is so isolated as not to be accessible by the ordinary post, in my opinion he should not be on a jury at all; he must be some very low and coarse sort of personage. I would make the receipt of a registered letter *primâ facie* evidence of service. I would not require the man to answer it, but I would make the posting of the letter, upon the affidavit of the sheriff's bailiff, *primâ facie* evidence that it reached the man, and I would impose a fine if he did not answer it; but so long as the great point of insuring attendance is left in the hands of obscure bailiffs, you never can be certain of the summonses being served.

793. It is suggested that the summons should be served by the constabulary; what do you think of that?—I would prefer, myself, the postal service, in analogy to the Dublin regulation, and in analogy to the notice officer of the Court of Chancery, both of which work remarkably well; we never hear a complaint, and I never heard of any difficulty about the notices being served. I would have the summons stamped with a formal stamp, to give it the aspect of something very solemn and important, which would recommend it to the country people.

794. A receipt is required, is it not, for a registered letter?—It is.

795. Therefore, if the letter were delivered, it would be possible to prove that it had been received?—Quite so; what I meant to say was this, that I would make the posting of the registered letter *primâ facie* evidence that it reached the person to whom it was addressed, and, if it did not reach him, let him get out of it by an affidavit.

796. I understand from what you have said, that under no circumstances would you be in favour of reverting to the old system of selection of the jury panel by the sheriff?—I certainly would not. I think, in the first place, that that power led to a suspicion of unfairness, and I think that, next to the purity of the administration of justice, the next thing in point of importance is a popular feeling that there is nothing like corruption, or unfair play, on the jury panel. I think myself, from the observation of 25 years, that many alienations from adherence to lawful authority, or appeal to lawful authority, arose from the impression that the jury were unfairly empanelled, and that people would not get fair play.

797. Have you known cases in which there have been challenges to array?—Yes, repeatedly.

798. Have they been successful?—Yes, certainly; on the ground of the partiality or the unindifferency of the sheriff, that is the general ground; that is the common law rite, and it remains to the present day, and there is nothing to interfere with it.

799. You are not surprised that there should have been an impression that the panels were not impartially framed?—I am not in the least surprised; that is the great merit of the Act as it stands, that it strikes a decided blow at such a system. I have not the slightest hesitation in saying that under the old system cases occurred in which you could have a jury to order, and if you prescribed your jury, you might get it. I have not the slightest hesitation in saying so from my observation. I have been obliged in Dublin, myself, in a civil case, in consequence of a man that I saw about to be sworn upon the jury, to withdraw notice of trial, and never to proceed with it, knowing perfectly well that the man would find against my client, no matter what the consequence was. That arose from the persistent abstinence of respectable merchants and people of the town to come forward, and from their shirking their duty, and the reason, if you probed it to the bottom, was this, that they did not get the summonses owing to the manipulation which I have explained.

800. The selection was practically in the hands of the sub-sheriff, was it not?—Yes; the high sheriff is an honorary officer, and he knows nothing whatever of what is going on.

801. Do you think that that system worked against the impartiality of jury panels on both sides; might not that system tell in favour of the prisoner as well as in favour of the Crown?—I am not making a sweeping general accusation; I hope the Committee do not understand anything of that sort. I say that it was resorted to occasionally, and, I think, never in favour of the prisoner. I never heard of such a thing as that.

802. What class of men are the sub-sheriffs?—They are a highly respectable body of men, but they have their political prejudices and their local feelings, and they are greatly mixed up with the politics of the country, and they take strong views. Socially, they are always highly respectable persons, and very worthy men.

803. Were they generally country solicitors?—They did not practice as solicitors, at least until a very recent period; they could not whilst they were sub-sheriffs, but many of them were solicitors.

804. Has your attention been called to the evidence which was given before a Committee by Mr. Seed, the Crown Solicitor of Meath and Westmeath?—Nothing more than from newspaper report.

805. Are you aware that he said that he had known cases in which a jury panel was framed by a sub-sheriff, friendly to the solicitor for the prisoner, or for solicitors interested in cases to be tried?—I never have come in contact with the manipulation so as to be privy to anything of that sort, and I could not throw any light upon it. I only look at the result, and I see the plain result. There was another matter which I should like to mention to the Committee, it is a trifling matter; but if the Legislature are amending the Act at all, it might be as well to cure it, as it is a little blemish in that section with regard to view juries. At present the rule is to send six men to view the premises where it is desirable to

Mr. Serjeant Armstrong.

1 May 1873.

to have usual observation of the place. Supposing it is an action of trespass, or about a right of way, or the diverting of a water course, and either party desires to have a view, the present practice is to send six men to view, but the result is that the view is quite an abortion, for the other six men who are sworn upon the jury never saw the premises; they take the partial information of the six. I would have the whole jury sent. I never knew any reason for sending six. That is a minute matter; but, however, it might as well be done.

806. Have you any suggestion to make as to the special jury panel?—I would be greatly inclined to give the power of having a special jury, as under the old system, at the option of the party, without applying to the court at all. I would either abolish it altogether, or leave it optional with the party as it used to be. At present, there are occasional circumstances that render it desirable to have a jury under the old old system, which the Committee are well aware was arrived at in this way: 48 names were selected by the master of the court by ballot; the parties then attended before him, and by striking off 12 on each side reduced the number to 24, and the first 12 of those 24 who answered constituted the jury. Cases arise in which, owing to connections and relationships, and various matters, it is very desirable to have the power of striking off, for reasons satisfactory to one's own mind, but which would not be adequate as a ground of challenge if it came to a challenge of the unindifferency of the sheriff; and I would be disposed either to abolish it or to revert to the old law, and let anybody who wished it have a special jury, and have it without applying to the judge, because, really, it is nearly impossible to get it. Of late the practice has been to refuse it, unless in cases where strong political feeling, or religious feeling, intervenes. I would either abolish it altogether, or give it at the option of either party. Bearing this in mind, that it would not be frequently resorted to, because there is a great deal of expense attending it.

807. What have you to say with regard to the preparation of the special jurors' book?—I would raise the qualification of special jurors in proportion to that of common jurors. I think that any qualification under a rating of 100 *l.* a year would be perfectly idle in the case of special jurors.

808. In towns as well as in counties?—I am now speaking of counties. I have not considered such places as Drogheda, and many such small places as the town and county of the town of Galway, and those exceptional jurisdictions.

809. Dr. *Ball.*] That qualification would apply to Dublin, would it not?—In the county of the city of Dublin there is an excellent jury under the present system. I never saw a better. In a town it might be much lower; and if possible, I would introduce into the qualification the domicillary consideration, so to speak, and for this reason: You may find a man who is rated very high indeed to the relief of the poor, and who is a wealthy man; but he is a very ignorant man, and lives in a most filthy state, as I know many instances, and who have no cleanliness and no comfort in their houses, but are wallowing in dirt. You never find intelligence associated with that state of things. You will find that such a man has a neighbour, who has not one-tenth of his means, who has a neat respectable house, and is a man of superior intelligence. I always like, in estimating any man's moral calibre, if I may use the expression, and intellectual position, to look at how he lives; whether he is cleanly and comfortable in his house, and I would greatly prefer to make a portion of the qualification depend upon house property.

810. *Chairman.*] Two suggestions have been made to the Committee, one that the rating qualification should be a compound one; that a certain minimum qualification of rating for a house should be insisted upon, which I understand to be your suggestion?—I would highly approve of that for the reason I have given.

811. But another suggestion has been made, that in addition to the rating qualification of, say 30 *l.* or 40 *l.*, or 50 *l.*, whatever it may be, persons rated at 12 *l.*, for instance, for a house, only should form a supplementary class upon the jurors' book; would you approve of that suggestion?—I think that a 12 *l.* rating for a house in itself would not be likely to ensure any considerable amount of comfort and respectability.

812. Have you considered what minimum house qualification you would admit?—I would not go under 12 *l.*, if you make that a sole qualification, or under 10 *l.*, at all events.

813. I mean for your compound qualification?—If it were 50 *l.*, I would make the house at least 10 *l.* or 12 *l.* of that

814. Do you think that in many counties in Ireland you would get a sufficient number of jurors with such a qualification?—Yes, I think so.

815. Are you not aware that in the country the houses are generally rated at a very low figure indeed?—Yes, very low; it is a merely formal rating at present; but it would be very easy to direct the attention of the public valuator to those conditions of things, and indeed, perhaps, inquiry ought to precede legislation with a view of ascertaining whether, at a given figure, there would be a sufficient supply of jurors; because a good deal would depend upon that, and that inquiry could be very easily made.

816. Do you consider it very desirable that there should be on the book a sufficient number of jurors to secure a rotation of at least two years?—I think there ought to be.

817. Mr. *Bourke.*] A return has been furnished to the Committee showing the number of houses in each county at 10 *l.* and up to 15 *l.*; that would show, would it not, the number of jurors under this system (*handing a Return to the Witness*)?—Yes, that would supply me with the data. Anything that I have said must be taken subject to the qualification of there being an adequate supply. I could not undertake to investigate the figures at all. I have only suggested the principle; of course it must depend upon circumstances as to the practical working of it. If you have not the materials you must do without them. There is another matter with reference to the jury under the old system should continue. As the law stands at present there is very often a default when you come to trial, for this reason, that unless the jury answer, you cannot pray a *tales*. In an ordinary case, if the 12 jurors do not answer who are upon the panel, any other man who is upon the jurors' book, and happens to be attending in court, may be immediately called upon and sworn upon the jury, and that is called praying a *tales*. That does not obtain in a case of a jury struck under the old system. I have known a case to occur of only eight or nine answering,

Mr. Serjeant *Armstrong.*

1 May 1873.

answering, although there were 150 good jurors in court, and the case has been rendered abortive. I think that there should be the power of praying a *tales* in that case as well. It is a slight matter, but I have known it to be a practical inconvenience, and I see no objection to that power being given. I have know a jury to go off, and an important case has been obliged to stand over for want of jurors when there were 20 equally respectable and intelligent men there, owing to the peculiar wording of Perrin's Act. I apply that to every case.

818. Mr. *Heron.*] Would you give that power to both plaintiff and defendant in civil cases?—Yes, I would indeed. I think it is a great pity to have the thing rendered abortive after all the expense is incurred.

819. *Chairman.*] Have you considered the question of requiring unanimity in jurors?—Yes; I think that that is a very large question, and I see no sufficient reason to my mind for departing from the present rule of unanimity. I have heard a suggestion of some proposition and the judge giving a casting voice, but I think that that would put the judge in a most painful and invidious, if not to say dangerous, position. I would not ask a judge to take such a duty upon him at all.

820. If the change were made, as proposed in England, should you be in favour of adopting it in Ireland, so as to have uniformity of procedure?—I declare that my mind is so constituted that I am averse to any change unless I see good reason for it. I like to hold to old things unless there is some positive evil to be avoided, or some positive advantage that I can understand to be gained. I think that under this Act the great merit of it is that there was a great evil to be avoided, and a great advantage to be gained, by this alphabetical system and the distribution of the business. I think that is a great merit which outweighs any slight blemishes which no man could foresee, and which it required the practical working of the thing to develop.

821. Are there any other suggestions which you would wish to make and which I have not asked you about?—I think that I have quite thrown out to the Committee anything that has occurred to my mind, but if any question occurs to any honourable gentleman, I shall be very happy to answer it.

822. Colonel *Wilson Patten.*] The general purport of your evidence is to this effect, is it not, that you consider the new law an admirable law if properly administered?—Yes, administered through the medium of a higher qualified class of jurors with an effective service of summonses.

823. That is to say, it is merely the defective administration of the present law that you find fault with?—The defective qualification of jurors and the machinery by which their attendance is compelled. I think that the principle of the Act, namely, distributing the business amongst the respectable middle classes of the country is admirable. It tends to elevate them in their own idea, and to remove the notion that they are not fit to take a share in the administration of justice, and to make them satisfied with the institutions of the country, and to make them in some degree more loyal; and besides that, it ensures confidence in the minds of the people that justice is rightly administered, and that there is no packing under any pretence or any tendency to it. I think that that is the great glory of the Act.

824. Dr. *Ball.*] When you say a 50 *l.* qualification, you are aware that the rating bears quite a different proportion to the real value in different parts of Ireland?—Yes.

825. In the north of Ireland the rating is quite close to the letting value; but in the south of Ireland it is 25 per cent., and often one-third, below, and therefore, when you say a 50 *l.* rating qualification, I apprehend you mean a qualification in every county that would correspond, say, to the 50 *l.* rating in the north?—I do, indeed. If, owing to the system of valuation in other counties, intelligence would not be so represented by the 50 *l.* rating as it would in the north, I would increase the amount of the qualification in those places. I quite adopt what you say.

826. In challenging a jury under the old system, have you not sometimes observed that very respectable men were put out by both sides?—That is one of my reasons for suggesting, for the consideration of the Committee, the retention of any such jury at all, because, under the pretence of getting rid of persons who might be unindifferent and one-sided, or biased, the sheriff is made to weed out the respectability from the 48, and I have known it actually occur that both sides, for their own objects, and particularly the defendant it may be, will weed out all the respectable names, and they are struck out just because they are respectable, and then you have nothing but the residuum at the end to work with. Therefore I do not like the system at all, because I think that it is a remnant of the packing system.

827. With respect to the question of a majority of the jury, do not you think that there would be a great difference between considerations applicable to civil cases and those applicable to criminal cases, and that in criminal cases, whilst it would be objectionable to have a difference of opinion upon the jury as tending to create uncertainty and doubt, yet many civil cases might be decided by a majority?—I take the distinction, and I think it would be much more objectionable indeed in criminal cases. Possibly, in the progress of public opinion, it might be thought well that a majority in civil cases might decide; but, nevertheless, it is one of those ancient landmarks of the law which is as old as the jury system itself, and I do not like the notion of interfering with it. However, that is rather a question for a political lawyer than for a mere working man, as I am.

828. Supposing that that limited extent of alteration in the law was carried in England, is it not a very serious question whether we should not agree to it in Ireland, if it went no further than that it did not touch any criminal trials?—I would have no objection to having it tried in England; and, if it worked well there, having it extended to Ireland; but I would like to observe the experiment first. I would have no objection to letting the English try it. There is a great deal of precedent for it. Many statutes have been tried, and many legislative improvements have been introduced in England, and extended to Ireland when their good working was experienced.

829. Mr. *Bruen.*] Do you think that if it did work well it should be extended to Ireland?—I would be inclined to say so. I think that if it is found from experience that it worked well, and had the sanction of public opinion, there could

could be no reason why it might not be extended to Ireland in both classes of business, both civil and criminal; but I would be very slow to introduce it in criminal business. I never yet heard of any jury being assailed, or attacked, or annoyed for unanimity in conviction; but I am afraid that if the thing was decided by a majority, it would ooze out who were the majority; and they would be put in a very difficult position. It might tend to deter men from doing their duty as formerly. I think that the wisdom of having a jury is the distribution of responsibility over so many. They never attack 12 men, but they might attack one man individually. If they could tax a man and say, "Why did not you take such a view as such and such a man did?" he might suffer for it. These are political considerations far beyond my ken, or anything that I can offer an opinion about.

830. Did I understand you to say that you considered it would be desirable that a special jury might be obtained, as under the old system, without application to the judges?—Yes, if it is to be retained at all; but I entertain great doubts, because it is a constant habit to weed out of the 48 all the best of the jury; and the consequence is, that we have had a special jury with men who could not read or write, whose language it was perfectly alarming to hear spoken from the jury box; but the attorneys have attended and struck out all the respectable men out of the 48, and this was the jury residuum. Therefore I look with great suspicion upon that system altogether. I do not see the necessity for it, if you have a proper qualification pervading the whole country.

831. The Right Honourable Chairman examined you as to some evidence which Mr. Seed gave before a Committee that sat two or three years ago, with regard to an accusation made against the impartiality of the sub-sheriffs; are you aware that since that time every sub-sheriff in Ireland has signed a declaration that that accusation is utterly untrue?—I have heard of that just as a popular matter current through the country; but I have my own eyes and my own observation, and I draw my own inferences, no matter what anybody declares. I have had as much experience as most people on every circuit in Ireland, and I do not attend to declarations of that general description, unattended by the possibility of inquiring into particular cases. I believe that there are a good many engaged in such matters that are hardly aware that they are doing it, they are so much in the habit of it.

832. Do you think that the sub-sheriffs have been guilty of this partiality?—I think that in very Catholic counties I have seen a jury trying a Catholic, and in the whole jury there was not one Catholic, although there were plenty on the panel, but they were all Protestants.

833. But the sub-sheriff returns the panel, does he not?—Yes.

834. If there were plenty of Catholics on the panel, that was not the sub-sheriff's fault, was it?—But there might not have been an adequate proportion, or there might have been a large number who would be necessarily set aside, as publicans, who ought to be always excluded from every jury.

835. Under the old system of qualification, was it very often the case that there really was a majority of Protestants qualified, although there might have been a majority of Catholics in population, and that in that case the sub-sheriff would not have been guilty of partiality in returning a larger number of Protestants?—I would not be understood, as I have said already in a former part of my evidence, as making any sweeping accusation against all the sub-sheriffs in Ireland; but there were curious reasons which would lead the public mind to think that there was something wrong at the bottom, and I would put an end to that if possible.

836. Were these effects upon the public mind at all caused by the verdicts that were returned?—That is so often, but not so much from the verdicts as from the conduct and character of the jury. And with regard to what is very likely passing in your mind, if I may be pardoned for saying so, as to the right of the Crown to set aside jurors, I think that that right must be reserved, but it is a painful thing to be obliged to resort to it, and an unpleasant duty to be obliged to resort to it. I see no better way of avoiding the necessity, but I would preserve the right. There is no better way of rendering it unnecessary to resort to it than to have a good general class of jurors of whom you are not afraid. If you have a low qualification you must set aside extensively, or the whole thing would end in an abortion. Improve your qualification and set aside as little as you can.

837. I think you mentioned that the principal cases of the breach of indifference, if I may so say, and of sinning against that principle, occurred in Dublin, and I think you mentioned that you had been engaged in a remarkable case in Dublin in which you withdrew your case in consequence of the state of the panel?—Yes.

838. Did it ever happen to you in any other place than Dublin?—Never. Dublin was conspicuous in that respect; but still I would not say they were hack jurors, but gentlemen whose time was so completely at their own disposal that it was convenient to them to attend in the absence of the Guinnesses and the Pims, and perhaps of men of that class who would not take the trouble of coming down, and who I am sure the summonses never reached. They were only gentlemen who had plenty of time on their hands.

839. Was not that an infringement of the old law, which directed the sheriff to return his panel indifferently?—Yes, and so he did; but the summons when sent out never reached the respectable classes in many instances; and if it did reach them, they disregarded the small fine, and the fine, although small, was hardly ever levied. I have often told the judge personally that much of the dereliction of attendance on the part of the leading merchants and higher class of jurors of Dublin arose from the hesitation of the judges to impose the fines. They would speak very strongly upon that subject, and say what a scandalous thing it was that men of position would not answer to their names, and they would impose the fines; but the next thing I would hear was, that they were all remitted. There has been no enforcement of the fines.

840. I want to ascertain your opinion whether it was owing to the state of the panel, or because the summonses were not served that this breakdown of the system occurred?—That I could not tell; there were two cases that I might mention. In one instance I saw a gentleman about to answer to his name on a jury, and I knew perfectly well that if he were put upon the jury the verdict would be very unsatisfactory, if ever there was

Mr. Serjeant Armstrong.

1 May 1873.

was a verdict, and there was very great difficulty in knowing what to do. I have that case particularly in my mind. Another case was one in which I knew that if a gentleman who was ready to answer, and whom I saw hanging about the court, was put upon the jury, the result might be also very disastrous; and I withdrew the record, and it never went to trial. There were private reasons for that, which I would not like to state.

841. But supposing that a sheriff really did frame his panel partially, was not there always the remedy of challenge to the array?—Yes, certainly, and that right remains.

842. And that challenge has succeeded occasionally, has it not?—It has succeeded occasionally; but I must say that beyond any doubt those were exceptional cases.

843. Still it was a remedy?—Yes, certainly, by challenge to the array.

844. And one which was calculated to remove the bad effects of the partiality?—In the particular instance, it did; but it left an impression upon the general, and particularly upon the vulgar, mind, the mind of the body of the people, that things were not done fairly; and if possible that feeling ought to be got rid of. Make the people satisfied with the administration of the law in all its branches, and that will tend to make them loyal people, and content with the administration of the law.

845. But the packing of the jury is what was complained of by the people?—Just so.

846. Would not there be a danger under the new law of very much the same accusation being made; because, supposing the Crown exercised its right of challenge and setting aside of jurors, the accusation would be against the Crown, still, of packing the jury?—It is impossible, I think, to avoid that. I do not think that anyone acquainted with anything of the country would suggest the total abolition of the right to direct a man to stand aside. A man may be a very respectable-looking man, and a very well-to-do man, and he may be an opulent man, and yet it may be notorious that he is associated with some movement or another, and if he gets upon the jury there would be no result, no conclusion. You know that, for the sake of public justice, that man ought to be directed to stand aside. You cannot avoid that. I am convinced that there never was any strength of feeling arising upon the exercise of that prerogative on the part of the Crown at all, nor a suspicion that in the array of the panel there is any favouritism shown to one section of the community more than another. There never was any suspicion, or any difficulty, arising from the action of the Crown in setting aside jurors at all; but there clearly have been suspicions that the sheriff being a certain sort of man, had not done fairly in selecting a jury.

847. Then the objection was against the sheriff personally?—No, it was against the system. People had not confidence in the hands who had the administration of the selection of the jury.

848. But will not the right of challenge, and the right of selecting, if I may so say, the persons who are fit to serve as a jury, throw a greater burthen now upon the Crown officers than was the case before?—No, not upon the Crown officers. If I had my wish, I would have legislation to this effect: that the chairman of the county should have responsible officers who were sworn to give information, associated with him in revising the list.

849. My question was with reference to the jury panel, not to the jury list?—The sheriff would have no discretion; the alphabetical arrangement is conclusive as to his power. He has no general power. I would take away all power of selection from the sheriff.

850. So I understand; but still there might be improper persons returned upon the panel by the alphabetical process, and if that were so, it would be the duty of the Crown officers, would it not, to see that those men were set aside?—Yes, and for that very reason I would reserve the right, because, do all you can, there will always be some little imperfection. You cannot have perfection in any human process.

851. Would not that throw upon the Crown officers any odium that might be likely to arise from the exercise of that power?—I do not think that it would be regarded as an odious right. I never knew any bad feeling to arise from it.

852. And you do not think that it is likely to arise?—I do not. I would have the person pure and above suspicion who selected the jury, and the result would work out itself, and the people would be satisfied.

853. You, of course, remember very well the Fenian troubles and the Fenian trials in Ireland some time ago?—Yes.

854. In many of the districts of the country where those trials took place a very large body of the farmers in the country were Fenians?—So it was alleged; I do not know that.

855. In that case, if it had been the duty of the Crown officers to weed the panel by causing jurors to stand aside, would not that have thrown upon them a considerable amount of odium and unpopularity?—Perhaps it might have been so, but, however, I cannot speak of it, not having any practical knowledge, because it so happened that I never was engaged in any Fenian's case, either for the prosecution or the defence, to which I attribute a considerable portion of the popularity which I have the happiness to enjoy. I never was either for Fenians or against them, therefore I act for all parties.

856. You are not at all in favour of the right of trying certain cases by special juries?—Not at all. In criminal cases I would not approve of it; I think that it would look very much like a determination to have something very special done indeed.

857. With regard to the persons who are to assist the chairman in making the selection for the jury lists, you would require the attendance of the constabulary, the county surveyor, and other officers?—Yes, I would; the sessional Crown Solicitor, and other officers.

858. Would you require that by summons from the chairman himself, or would you make it compulsory upon them by a provision in the Act?—Compulsory, by a provision in the Act that they should have notice of the holding of the court, and attend upon it as part of it. I would define their duty to answer all such questions, and to give all information to enable the chairman fairly and faithfully to revise the list.

859. You think that the chairman is the best officer to exercise that power of revising the lists?—Yes; I think that there is universal confidence reposed in the chairmen of Ireland.

860. Should you say, for instance, that Ribbonmen and Fenians have absolute confidence in the chairman?

Mr. Serjeant Armstrong.

1 May 1873.

chairman?—I think they have, generally speaking. That class of question never arises in which Fenianism or Ribbonism, or serious felonies, are involved, they are are always relegated to the assizes; they do not come before the chairman, and the consequence is that the chairmen are very little mixed up judicially with those investigations. They dispense a vast amount of public business; in fact they are doing in the aggregate the general common run of business in the country, but they are away from those contentious which exite animosity, and the result, I think, is that there is great confidence reposed in them.

861. Would the fact of a man being a well-known Fenian or Ribbonman, be one of those circumstances which you think would cause the chairman to reject him from the jury list?—If the county inspector, on his oath, informed the chairman that a man was a suspicious character upon party grounds, I would not have the slightest hesitation in giving the chairman the power of putting him aside.

862. You would not get the perfect confidence of Ribbonmen or Fenians in any chairman at present?—When I speak of perfect confidence, I do not suppose that Ribbonmen and Fenians would have perfect confidence in anybody at all, but I am speaking, generally, of the prevailing sense of the people of Ireland with regard to the chairmen of counties. You find some disaffected people who would not have confidence in Divine Providence, or anything else.

863. You do not think that persons who had not any great confidence in, or are disaffected to, the present judicial system, would have any confidence in the chairman?—I think if you give the chairmen of counties such power as I have stated, you would find no considerable, respectable, recognisable class of society in Ireland to find any fault with them; that is my opinion.

864. In fact, all the unpopularity which has hitherto attended the execution of the law, would completely vanish?—I would rather hope for than expect those halcyon days. I have no such expectation that we are going to have perfection, by any means. You may do your best, but there will be malcontents at all times. But with reference to the chairmen, consider what a vast amount of business they dispatch, and the paucity of appeals; there is scarcely ever an appeal. They are so rare in some circuits, that there would not be perhaps half-a-dozen appeals from some hundreds and thousands of decisions, which is a convincing proof, I think, of the general satisfaction which is felt with the fairness and the sense of justice, as well as with the law and acquirements of the chairmen.

865. Your general impression of the working of the Act so far, I understand to be, that the class of jurors who appeared in the cases at the different assizes, and perhaps quarter sessions too, was a class inadequate to discharge the duties that were imposed upon them?—Yes; I except from that the special jurors except in the county of Dublin; that applies to the special juries in the county of Dublin in criminal cases only: but it does not apply to the special juries or to the common juries in the city of Dublin. I exempt the city of Dublin altogether, for it is done very well there. In the very first case under the new bankruptcy jurisdiction which enabled the bankruptcy judge to summon a jury and investigate questions of suggested fraud, we had as admirable a jury under the new system as I would ever wish to address.

866. It was in fact a very great improvement upon the rather corrupt system which existed there before?—It was an improvement upon the hackneyed system. I had the pleasure of seeing men of decided mercantile position and solvency and individual intelligence, for although they had never served upon juries before they were quite able to grapple with the subject at once, and one had the satisfaction of speaking to fresh minds who you knew could not be influenced in any way out of court.

867. Is two years the minimum period at which you think a juror should be summoned to perform his duties a second time? I think two years would be reasonable; I would not like to onerate those men by doing too much, and it may be necessary in order to effect the distribution to have a two years' limit.

868. You certainly think that experience is a useful thing in a juryman?—I do indeed; I think it is a very trying position for any counsel to be addressing 12 men who never sat upon a jury before, and to be explaining elementary principles to them. I think it would be well to have one or two who understand something of affairs.

869. Still, in that point of view, the old system did not act so badly in many cases, because it supplied experienced jurymen?—The old system acted very well in many cases, particularly in civil cases.

870. Viscount *Crichton*.] You mentioned three permanent county officers, who you suggest should give the chairman information about the qualification of jurors; would you exempt the poor-rate collector?—No; I said in addition to those who were mentioned in the Act. I would have the persons who are connected with furnishing the list, so that if any question arose as to their *bona fides*, they might come and explain matters. There should be the county inspector or any sub-inspector that the chairman might think fit to require, and the sessional Crown prosecutor and the county surveyor, who knows as much about the county as any one in it, being obliged to preambulate it all periodically, and the deputy clerk of the peace at least. With that assistance he should know every man with great ease.

871. Colonel *Forde*.] Did not you suggest the high constables of baronies?—I do not think I did, but I see no objection to them. They would be very proper persons, and if I omitted them I am obliged to the honourable Member for supplying the omission.

872. Sir *R. Blennerhassett*.] You mentioned, did you not, that the qualification should not be dependent upon property?—Not altogether; it should be an educational qualification.

873. And that that educational qualification should be that a man should be able to read and write?—Yes, I would have ignorance of reading and writing a disqualification by itself, but I would not cross-examine a man with regard to his literary attainments beyond that.

874. Do not you think that a man who is unable to read and write is incompetent to judge of evidence?—I do, and therefore I would disqualify him *ipso facto*.

875. Have not you known very intelligent people who could not read or write?—I think they are intelligent in their own concerns, and that gentleman in the Mount Garrett case that I mentioned,

Mr. Serjeant Armstrong.

1 May 1873.

mentioned, was, I daresay, one of the most successful farmers in Kilkenny. He occupied at least 800 acres of arable land with a fine stock, and there was something in the aspect of the man that showed that he was rich and happy, but he has not been able to follow a consecutive argument.

876. Do you think that a mere knowledge of reading and writing is a test of the cultivation of a man's mind?—I think it is a certain amount of test. It would never occur to me to put every one upon the panel who could read and write, because that would be making it a qualification, but I would insist that he should be disqualified unless he could read and write. You see there is a marked distinction in that; it is a disqualification that I would impose, and not a qualification.

877. Mr. *Downing*.] I understand you to convey to the Committee that a man's rating or valuation does not insure that he is possessed of intelligence?—Not always.

878. The man that you refer to upon the jury in the Mount Garrett case was a man holding 800 acres of land?—Yes, and one of the most successful farmers in the county, and one of the most respected men in fact.

879. I will direct your attention to a printed paper, which will perhaps induce you to qualify your opinion with regard to the valuation which should qualify a juror. Taking the county of Tyrone, which you have just mentioned, you will see in the very last column that the total number of jurors in the general jurors' book for the year for the county was 3,092?—Yes; I see that.

880. If you look at the column of the number rated at 30*l.*, and if you carry your eye down that column, you will find that it is 312?—Yes.

881. Then you find, do you not, in the third column, 1,531 rated at 20*l.* and under 30*l.*?—Yes.

882. Those must be deducted from the general number, must they not?—No doubt of it.

883. And so must the 312, must they not?—Yes.

884. You also see in another column that the number under 40*l.* is 740?—Yes.

885. If you add these three together, and then deduct 2,583 from the 3,092, you will leave upon the jurors' book 509, would that be a sufficient number for the county Tyrone?—I think it would; it is a great deal more than the sheriff ever returns, or ever did return. At the last assizes, when it was necessary to return a very large number, under special circumstances, he returned only 211.

886. But, according to your own view, you would not have the jurors called for two years?—Just so.

887. Taking your own figures; taking 211 for one assize from 509, that leaves only 298?—Quite so.

888. Take 211 for the next assizes, and you exhaust the panel?—Very true.

889. Then you exhaust it in the very first year?—That is a practical test arising upon figures, with reference to which I stated what I would wish and what I would recommend; but, of course, it must be subject to there being a supply adequate to the demand. I see that there might be a practical difficulty in working it out.

890. You stated that you would have special jurors rated at not less than 100*l.* a year?—Yes; that would be my inclination.

891. If you look again to that very county of Tyrone, I could give you a case which is much stronger; if you look at the number rated at 100*l.* a year in Tyrone you will find that they only amount to 69.

892. Would 69 special jurors be sufficient?—They never return more than 48.

893. In this Act, in what are called the special jurors marked upon the general panel, the sheriff is not confined to 48?—At the last assizes they returned more than 48 over the county, I think.

894. Taking the Act that we are discussing, that would be so?—Here is another crucial test as to whether they could be found in the county.

895. I could call your attention to a great many more, because you will see that it is a very extraordinary thing, speaking of the house qualification, that if you refer to page 5 of the Return, and will look under the head of Munster, at colum 5, you will find that in the whole of Munster there are only rated at 10*l.*, and under 12*l.* a year, 697?—Yes, so it appears; it was a 12*l.*, and above 12*l.* house qualification that I suggested.

896. I have now in my hand a Jury Bill, brought in in the year 1854 by the present Chief Justice of the Queen's Bench, and if you will be good enough to look at it, I will just call your attention to it so as to make it evidence; you will see that the qualification in that Bill, which was brought in by him, was a rating of 30*l.* a year?—Yes.

897. Are you aware that that was amended in Committee and reduced to 20*l.*?—So I always understood, and we think it was an unfortunate mistake.

898. Here is another Bill, which was brought in by Mr. Napier and Lord Naas, and you will find that the qualification in that was 30*l.*?—Yes, so I see.

899. Here is another, which was brought in by Mr. Attorney General Keogh, and you will see that the qualification in that was 20*l.*?—I observe it is; all of which are very good precedents for the present Act as it stands, and very strong reasons for suggesting why the qualification was fixed as it was, but then we have the practical working of the thing in answer to speculation.

900. The qualification in the Bill of Mr. Justice Fitzgerald, who was then Attorney General, was also 20*l.*, was it not?—Yes.

901. Therefore the gentlemen who filled the office of Attorney General never went beyond 30*l.* a year?—That is so.

902. With regard to the service of summonses, I presume there is no doubt that any one connected with the law in Ireland knows very well what exists with regard to paying the bailiff?—Yes, I always heard that that was done.

903. There are always policemen from every town attending the assizes, are there not?—Yes.

904. Do not you think that it would be an admirable plan if the police, who are obliged to attend the assizes on business, were employed for the purpose of of serving summonses in the immediate neighbourhood, they being so well acquainted with the people?—I cannot say that any insuperable objection occurs to me to the employment of the police in that way, but I do not think it would be very acceptable to the farmers to find the police coming up to their houses;

Mr. Serjeant Armstrong.

1 May 1873.

houses; the appearance of a policeman coming there, as he would, in his costume, very likely with his rifle with him, is never an acceptable sight. It might beget suspicion of the most innocent man in the county, and he might be under some cloud about it for a week. The neighbours would say, "The police are up at such and such a house; what are they doing there?" I think it would not be a pleasant thing to convert the police into process servers. I would rather have the post.

905. Would you have the letter sent as a registered letter?—Yes; the expense would be so inconsiderable, and it would be a greater security; and it would give a sanction to the thing, and it would call the attention of the jurors to it so as to impress it upon his mind, and his wife would not throw it in the fire.

906. Would there not be this disadvantage, that the postmaster would take a receipt for it?—Yes; but I would make the dispatch of it by post *primâ facie* evidence of service.

907. Mr. *Bruen*.] Then you would throw the onus of proving the negative upon the juror?—Yes; for instance, the general law of the land is this, that if I post a letter here addressed to a friend in Dublin, that would be *primâ facie* evidence that it reached him, because the regularity of the system is such that nobody doubts it, and if the juror has not received it let him come forward and say that he did not get it.

908. Mr. *Downing*.] With regard to the challenge to the array which the honourable Member for Carlow examined you upon, has that been generally successful?—Indeed the instances are very rare, but it has been successful.

909. You are aware, are you not, that in the year 1869 the challenge to the array was successful in the county of Monaghan?—Yes, very recently. I do not pin myself to the precise year.

910. Are you aware that the sheriff was, in consequence, removed from his office by the Lord Lieutenant of Ireland?—Yes, he was.

911. The honourable Member also asked you whether there would not be some danger now of packing the jury if the Crown exercised its undoubted right of saying, "Stand by," and you said, "No"?—No, I do not think there would be.

912. The panel is prepared by the sub-sheriff, and he might so arrange the names as that he may have, say 20 Roman Catholics upon the panel, and he may so place them as that it would be impossible that one could be on the panel after the challenges?—No doubt the cards might be so shuffled that that result might arrive.

913. But that could not happen now when they are taken in alphabetical order?—It could not.

914. Are you aware that in Scotland the Crown has only the same right to say "stand," as the prisoner has to challenge?—Just so.

915. Do not you think that that would be a fair alteration in the law with regard to Ireland, and that it would altogether remove the objection made by the honourable Member for Carlow?—You mean that as there are now 20 peremptory challenges, there should be 20 peremptory settings aside, with power to set aside for cause shown. I cannot say that I ever knew of any evil result from the present system of standing aside; and I think that it would be a very invidious thing indeed to put the Crown to assign a cause and have a contest in open court.

916. With regard to the evidence of Mr. Seed before the Westmeath Committee, do you remember the words which were used with reference to a particular trial to the Attorney General, now Judge Barry, "Leave it to me"?—Yes, it attracted attention at the time.

917. What would you understand by those words, "Leave it to me"?—That he would exercise his right to direct people to stand aside according to his discretion.

918. Until he got a proper jury?—According to his discretion.

919. Until he got the jury that he liked?—It is open to that construction.

920. Do not you think that it would be desirable to take away from the Crown solicitor such a power as that, by adopting what I have suggested; namely, to give the Crown the right to put by 20 peremptorily, and the prisoner the same, and afterwards to set aside for cause shown?—I think there are elements unhappily existing still in Ireland, and that the political atmosphere is not sufficiently cleared up to render it advisable to take away the ancient prerogative of the Crown, and I would preserve it. If you reduce it as you suggest, there would be 20 peremptory challenges and 20 peremptory standings aside, and cause shown afterwards. You may imagine the case of a man very respectable in his social position, upon whose character there was no blemish, and yet who was notoriously connected in private with some association or confederacy. I do not care whether it is Orange or Fenian, or what it is, and it might be very uncomfortable indeed to have a discussion upon that in open court; and I think that the evil of setting them aside quietly is more than counterbalanced by the absence, if it is an evil, of any such discussion; and on such occasions I would preserve that right to the Crown. I am afraid that you could not work criminal cases at all without it. Speaking from my own knowledge, and I am largely concerned in prosecutions myself, I am aware that there is a growing feeling on the part of the public prosecutors in Ireland to consider public feeling upon the subject, and only in case of necessity to resort to the system of setting aside. It is a thing that I never encourage myself; but I believe it is necessary to retain it.

921. Does the Crown solicitor exercise that right without consulting the senior Crown counsel?—Undoubtedly. It is very unusual for him to consult the senior Crown counsel or any Crown counsel. It has been done, and ought to be done. There ought to be the most entire confidence between the counsel and the solicitor in Crown cases, as well as in any other, but in the matter of setting aside jurors, the Crown counsel are not acquainted with the people; they do not know them; they come very much strangers to them, and I would manage it under the new system so as to make it optional with the Crown solicitor.

922. It was suggested by a witness on a former day that it would be very desirable that the jurors should be taken from a ballot box as in civil cases; what is your opinion of that; do you see that there would be any great advantage derived from it, where they are at present called alphabetically, if that is strictly pursued?—I see no reason for adopting the analogy of civil cases; I would

Mr. Serjeant *Armstrong.*

1 May 1873.

I would leave the matter as it is. As I have said already, I do not like change unless there is something worth changing for.

923. Are you aware that any of the judges of Ireland have expressed an opinion that, after the first name is called beginning with A. then the sheriff may go to any other person (say that there are four of letter A) after No. 1 is called?—I have heard in professional circles that some judges take that view, but that others do not.

924. You do not give it that construction, do you?—With the greatest deference to them, I take the other view.

925. If it was a really fair construction of the law it would altogether strike at the principle of the Act, would it not?—I think that if the Act is open to such a construction, it ought to be immediately reformed in that respect, because it would be shuffling the cards over again. I do not think that that ever was the intention, and if there is anything in the wording of the Act that would seem to justify it, the Act ought to be amended.

926. Mr. *Heron.*] With regard to what the honourable Member for Carlow referred to, namely, that the right of challenge may tend to cast an odium upon the Crown solicitor, do you remember that on the Leinster circuit, by a gentleman of the name of Mr. Hemmis, in agrarian cases a very large exercise of that power had repeatedly to be resorted to?—Yes.

927. Did you ever know the slightest odium of that kind to be cast upon him?—Never; he was a most deservedly popular man, a man in whom the highest confidence was always reposed by the public generally; he was a pre-eminently fair man, with a great spirit of justice, and a desire to have fair play.

928. When you have been special prosecutor, as you have been on every circuit in Ireland, have you ever known an instance of any odium attaching to the Crown solicitor in consequence of his largely exercising this right?—I never have.

929. And which power you think ought to be retained?—I do, indeed, if it is necessary. A time may come when it will not be necessary, but at present it is.

930. It was suggested the other day by Mr. Coffey that in criminal cases the names ought to be balloted for, as in civil cases, in place of calling them from the long panel; are you not aware that the system of calling from the long panel in the regular course is for convenience, as regards the right of challenge by the prisoner, and the right of standing by the Crown?—I have always understood that it is so.

931. The moment the names would be called from the ballot there would be a deal of confusion, and no real object gained?—No; I do not see anything to be gained by it.

932. With regard to the alleged partiality of the sub-sheriffs in Ireland, have you known instances, or understood that many of those gentlemen have been electioneering agents in their counties?—Yes; they have been in every way mixed up with strong political feeling, so that their names were never mentioned without a great body of people saying something antagonistic to them. There was a good deal of sentiment in it as well as reality; but I think it was a sentiment that deserves consideration.

933. Mr. *Bruen.*] Have you not known that the gentlemen who now fill the offices of county chairman and assistant barrister have also taken part in politics?—Not that I recollect as taking any very active part in politics. My memory at the present moment does not supply me with the name of any county chairman who has taken any very active part in politics. I think, on the contrary, there is a sort of feeling on their part rather to abstain from politics.

934. After they are chairmen, that may be so, but I mean before?—That would apply to others besides chairmen.

935. Had none of those gentlemen who now fill the office of county chairman ever taken an active part in politics before they were appointed?—I think that they might take a strong view for their own party, but never in any way I think so as to detract from their perfect impartiality at the present moment. I do not think that there is a man on what I may call the secondary judicial branch in Ireland, who owes his promotion to party services alone. I think that they are promoted by their friends in power, and that will be done I hope hereafter.

936. Mr. *Heron.*] Have you known that the sub-sheriffs of counties in many cases hold their office for 20 or 25 years?—Yes, perpetually, I may say.

937. And during that time they have been on one side or the other repeatedly, and they have been the great electioneering agents for their counties?—There is no doubt about it; it is not an unusual thing by any means. They are very influential men generally speaking; they are always in a good social position, and what are called right good fellows.

938. Major *O'Reilly.*] Have you ever known an instance in which a gentleman who has generally filled the office of sub-sheriff, has been a conducting agent for an election?—I think so; such cases have occurred.

939. Mr. *Heron.*] The honourable Member for Carlow referred to the challenge to the array for the unindifferency of the sheriff being a safeguard against the partiality of the sheriff, and a safeguard as regards the impartial array of the panel; in practice, do you not know that it is almost impossible to get the triers to find against the sheriff?—Yes, it is almost impossible to get the triers to find anything right; I have known most ridiculous conclusions found by the triers. I was special in a case in the Home Circuit; it was an ejectment case, in which there was a strong feeling about ejecting a tenant. The friends of the tenant, who was resisting the ejectment, got up a large subscription to defend the action, and to employ counsel. On the jury was called a gentleman, a large trader and proprietor and grazier, who had attended a meeting held for the purpose of getting funds, to which he himself largely subscribed. I thought that that was a fair ground of objection. He insisted upon sitting upon the jury, although he had subscribed 50*l.* towards the fund of the defendant. I, being counsel for the plaintiff, challenged him on the ground of unindifferency, and of his being a subscriber to the fund for the defence. There were two triers appointed; that gentleman was examined himself. I examined him, and he admitted upon oath that he had subscribed 50*l.*, and that he took the strongest interest in the defence; but the triers found that he was perfectly indifferent, and so he remained upon the jury. I relied upon his oath in addressing the jury, and strange to say, we got a verdict for the plaintiff; but

Mr. Serjeant *Armstrong*.

1 May 1873.

but it was a most ridiculous conclusion to arrive at, although I was successful. Anomalies occurred under the old system, and will occur under the present one; you need not expect to have perfection.

940. I want you to show exactly the power that the sheriff had under the old system; he always knew, did he not, what cases were to be tried before he arranged the panel?—Yes.

941. And then he had to select from the general juror's book any persons that he pleased?—Yes.

942. Therefore, in point of fact, as a matter of practice, he returned the panel with a view to the cases to be tried?—I believe that often occurred, and I have heard it said myself. The attorney would say to me, "We will have a right good jury; such and such a man is a particular friend of mine, and we will have a right good jury." "All right," I would say, of course. Counsel would say that we were quite glad at that, and we could not resist such an overture. We would have nothing to do with it, but we would have the satisfaction of knowing that we should have a right good jury. There was a significant nod of the head, and the thing was done.

943. That is now gone, is it not?—Yes; and I think that that is the great glory of this Act.

944. With reference to the service by registered letter, there are a great many districts in Ireland, are there not, where there is no regular service by letter carriers?—Yes.

945. Do you suggest that the mere posting of a registered letter should be good service, whether the man called for it at the post office or not?—I think it should be sent. Provision should be made that where a man was not in the habit of sending to the post office (assuming him to be in all other respects a qualified man), as the instances would be rare, never more, perhaps, than twice a year, it should be the duty of the postmaster to send the letter on; but I think that that would be a very exceptional case, because if a man is rated, as I suggest he ought to be, he would be in communication with the post office.

946. In the more remote districts, the fewer the letters there are the more it is known who has got a letter, is it not?—Yes, there would be very little difficulty about that.

947. The *O'Donoghue*.] I understand one of your suggestions to be that the jurors for each county should be selected by the chairman?—That he should have the power of objecting to them.

948. Of course, I understand that he should have the power of objecting to them, and that he should be assisted by a number of persons, who are supposed to be qualified to give him reliable information as to the fitness of the jurors?—That is my idea.

949. Would the evidence to be taken by the chairman be taken in open court, and on oath?—I think that they should all act under the sanction of an oath, and I think myself that it ought to be in open court; but it would attract very little attention, and I would not be afraid of that. I would give the chairmen the power, as I think that there is a power incident to every court to proceed in camera under certain circumstances, to retire from public observation, and I would leave that discretion with the chairmen to that extent, but it would be very rarely exercised. Every court may do it.

950. You assume that the very high character enjoyed by the chairmen generally would induce the community to acquiesce in such a power being placed in their hands?—I think that there would be the greatest confidence in them, for they are universally respected. I think that many of the chairmen are amongst the most popular men in the whole country.

951. You would not say, would you, that all chairmen enjoyed equal reputation?—Nor all the higher judges; there is a disparity, of course; but I think that, as to their integrity, there is not any exception.

952. Do not you think that the character of the duties is so serious that it would be dangerous to leave the great decisions involved in the working of the jury system solely dependent upon him, as it would be in such a case as this?—I do not think it would be; you cannot expect perfection. There must be a power of election vested somewhere, and I can suggest nothing better than men of undoubted respectability and position, and who stand well with the community in their respective counties. They are a particularly popular body of men, are the chairmen of Ireland, in their own counties.

953. You disapprove of the power of selection which existed under the old system, do you not?—I do disapprove of the sheriff's selection.

954. Would not what you propose simply transfer that power to the chairmen and a staff of officials?—Recollect the chairmen would be acting upon an alphabetical prepared list, and that you would be transferring to a chairman of respectable character who has no connection with the parties and no object to serve. No one would dare to make a suggestion to the chairman of a county as to striking off this man's name or that man's name. They are as much superior to such influences as the judges of the superior courts, and their perfect impartiality, I believe, would command the public confidence.

955. In case the chairman decided to take evidence in private, the public would have no means afterwards, would they, of getting at that evidence?—I would not allow them to have any means of getting at it. I think that what I am suggesting would be open of course to the observation which the honourable Member has made, but you must have power vested somewhere, and it is much better than the old hole-and-corner sheriff's room, where nobody was present.

956. Do you think that a man's not being able to read and write should be made a ground of exclusion from the jury list?—I would positively exclude him, but I am happy to think that, with the promise of education and with the rapid spread of it all over Ireland under the national system, it is a state of things which will not long continue; but at present I would make it a disqualification; it is a ridiculous thing to think that a man of education should be addressing them as gentlemen of the jury, and complimenting them, and endeavouring to persuade them, and yet the foreman, if he is called upon even to write his own name for self and fellows, cannot do it. It is a burlesque, I think.

957. Is it a ground of disqualification in England?—I do not know; I have not heard it; public attention has never been drawn to it.

958. I believe it is well known that it is not a ground of disqualification in England?—It could not be without my knowing it; I never heard of such

Mr. Serjeant *Armstrong.*

1 May 1873.

such a thing, and speaking as a lawyer, I am sure that it is not.

959. Do not you think that it might be left to either the plaintiff or the defendant, or to the prosecutor or the traverser, to object when a juror was called, and that he should be sworn as to whether he is able to read or write, and that the question of fact might be left to the judge?—That is to reserve the matter for investigation in open court.

960. I mean, that when a juror was called to be sworn it should be open to anyone, plaintiff or defendant, to object?—I would reserve the power to the judges, because, however active a chairman might be, he might not be fully informed. Some people might, from inadvertency, be upon the list who ought not to be on the list, and therefore I would give the judge the power, and impose the duty upon him of setting aside every such person upon an objection being made before him; but I would have the thing winnowed, so to speak, by the chairman. I would not reserve that to the judge. I would not have the time of the judge wasted in those minute investigations.

961. Would you be in favour of requiring a man to live in a house of a certain value to enable him to serve on a jury?—I would like very much that a portion of the qualification should be a compound qualification, compounded of a house rating and land, because I think that the domicile test is important. I have known many instances of men who have a good deal of land, and a good many pigs, and a good many horses and cows, but who live, as to animal comforts, very little better than those animals themselves; ill-clothed, ill-bedded, and in dirt and squalor; you will find them with their hands in their pockets, sneaking about with their two ideas, as they are called; but if you find a man with a neat, trim appearance, and a decent house, he is generally a smart and intelligent man, who knows something of the world, and is just the sort of person that one would wish to have upon a jury.

962. Do not you think that insisting upon a house qualification would, from the general character of houses in Ireland, exclude from the jurors' list men who are well qualified otherwise to serve as jurors?—It might have that tendency, but it must be a balance of inconvenience.

963. Do not you think that it would exclude a vast number of persons?—I do not know; that would depend upon the statistics, which I have had no opportunity of looking at, and that is a matter of detail. I suggest a certain supply, and the question is whether there is the material for that supply.

964. I understood the first answer you made to the noble Chairman to be, that one of the reasons why you approve so highly of this Bill was, that it distributed almost over the country generally the duty of serving occasionally upon juries?—Yes, that is the tendency of it; but still you must have the qualification.

965. If you put a house qualification, would not that greatly limit it?—Yes; but if I find two evils, I must choose the less, and it is the less evil of the two; and if the alternative is that you are to have a grossly ignorant person on the jury, I need not suggest which alternative you would adopt.

966. What figures would you put as the qualification?—I suggested 50*l.*, and I should be glad of a 10*l.* or 12*l.* a year house rating, but if upon the statistics of the county, and upon the revision of the valuation, the material is not existent, of course you would be obliged to lower your standard. If the higher standard is non-existent, and you are driven to what you can get, if you cannot get the best thing you get the next best; that is a matter of detail.

967. Colonel *Forde.*] Is there not an arrangement for the revision of the valuation now under the law?—That is constantly going on in Ireland. I see no difficulty at all in that.

968. Mr. *Bourke.*] Supposing that the Legislature adopts the suggestion which you have made, as well as other gentlemen who have been examined, as to raising the qualification of jurors, the jury panel will of course be by so much abridged, and I want to ask you whether you would suggest that, if a class of persons or classes of persons could be found without a rating qualification, but in other respects people who might serve as jurors, you would be disposed to add them to the common jury panel. I mean such persons as magistrates' sons, or grand jurors' sons, or many persons who we might find would be capable of acting upon the grand jury?—Yes; that is already provided for largely in the existing Act.

969. Might they not come upon the common jury panel?—I see no objection to that. I think that men might be very well qualified indeed, and highly intelligent, who are not possessed of actual property in their own immediate right, and I think that the same reason for having them upon special juries would apply to their being on common juries: intelligence and independence are the points to be arrived at.

970 With regard to the duties of the poor rate collectors, you would be disposed to leave their duties as they are at the present moment, without giving them any discretion to put any mark against any person's name for any cause whatever?—I would not confer any such discretion upon them; I would not allow men of that rank to trifle with the feelings of their neighbours I would leave it to a man of dignity, whose position would be a sufficient protection against anything hurtful, and whose opinion would be accepted in the county, and who does not live there; and to their honour be it said, as a general rule, they make it a point not to associate even with the gentry of their counties; it is a great privation to them, but still it is the fact.

971. The chairmen are allowed, are they not, to practice at the bar?—Yes, they certainly are, and unquestionably they should be, otherwise you would not find many men to accept the office of chairman. They never could, with merely the chairman's salary, think of retiring from their profession.

972. Do not you think that in view of those duties that they will have to perform, if your suggestion is adopted by the Legislature, it would be desirable to debar them from private practice?—I do not think that the duties would so onerate them as to make any material difference; it would not be a very onerous duty. I would not, with a view of allocating their time, so to speak, to this duty, think of preventing their practising; there is no necessity for that.

973. I mean with regard to any additional confidence that the public might gain in their being

being impartial?—I think that there is not the slightest apprehension of any such feeling arising from their continuing to practice.

974. Sir *R. Blennerhassett.*] Do they often practice in their own district?—They do not; but they can. As a general rule the chairman of each county declines, from a feeling of honour and delicacy, to take briefs from the solicitors of his own county. I believe that is the usual rule, and their own high feeling suggested it.

975. Mr. *Bourke.*] Considering the power that you suggested that the chairman of a county should have, do not you think it would be desirable that, in case the name of any person escaped the winnowing, as you term it, of the chairman, a similar power should be given to the judge?—I have distinctly suggested that in answer to The O'Donoghue, because, although, they may do their best at the earlier court, the court of primary instance, there may be lapses and oversights, and I would reserve to the judge the power to set aside any man upon just cause. I would have no triers. You might safely repose that confidence, or any other, in the judges.

976. Colonel *Vandeleur.*] When a jury is sworn, the first man sworn is generally the foreman, is he not?—Yes, unless he asks to have himself excused.

977. Are you aware that during the last assizes in my county the foreman on several occasions said that he was not able to read or write?—I know that to have occurred.

978. Would you consider it better to allow the foreman to be selected by the jury?—They do it by courtesy amongst themselves at the present moment; there is no magic in the circumstance of being a foreman at all; that gives them no additional weight or authority.

979 It happened in my own county on one occasion that the foreman handed the issue to the judge, and said that he had no learning, and he asked leave to hand it to somebody else; have you heard of that case?—Yes, I have heard of that.

980. If, by legislation, you get rid of such an occurrence, there would be no necessity, would there, for the alteration that you suggest?—I would get rid of such an accident happening as an illiterate person being on the jury at all; and then it would not be necessary to hold that sort of election of the foreman.

981. The jury are frequently led, are they not, by the foreman in forming their verdict?—I am not aware of that. I think it is not usual to find that the others are led by the foreman; but if the foreman is a man of superior intelligence, of course he would naturally have weight.

982. You stated, did you not, that there would be a good deal of objection to the summonses being served by the police?—I think that it would be rather an invidious thing to send the police round. They would not go through the country without their rifles, and it might be confounded with some summons upon litigious business, or something before the petty sessions.

983. You are aware that the police are at present employed upon various civil duties, such as serving voting papers at the poor law elections?—Yes.

984. And as they serve notices with regard to cleanliness, and statistical notices with regard to the crops, and so on, might not they equally well serve other notices?—I think if you could devise any plan whatever that would ensure the service of the summons in the best way, I would be satisfied to adopt it.

985. Would you not consider that the police were so very well acquainted with the country districts generally that they would know where to find the jurors, who are in many cases long distances from post offices, and would never call at the post office, and might never hear of the letters, and besides that there are in many districts many persons of the same name?—Yes; those are very fair reasons for introducing the assistance of the police. My object would be to ensure the arrival of the summons at its destination, and I think the less manipulation there is the better; but even the police might miscarry. The police are not all immaculate; a summons might go astray even in their hands; but I do not understand how it could go astray between the post master and the man to whom it is addressed. If a man is so obscure, and has so little acquaintance with life as not to have a communication with the post office, I do think that that in itself renders it not very desirable that he should be on a jury at the assizes, and I would sooner that he should stay at home; or if a man has so little correspondence that his letters must be stuck up in the window of the post office.

986. The sub-sheriff is nominated, is he not, by the high sheriff?—Yes, no doubt that is so.

987. And he is his servant for his period of office?—He is his agent.

988. Would you consider that it would be more eligible to make the sub-sheriff a permanent officer?—No, I see no reason in the world for that; at the present moment it is the high sheriff who is responsible for the due execution of all writs, and he is answerable to persons for the levying of their debts, and that sort of thing, and that is one of the reasons which renders it important to have a man of position and property at the head of the county as the sheriff to answer for the due execution of writs, and to make the sub-sheriff responsible would be anything but desirable.

989. It would be an additional expense upon the sheriff, would it not?—For that very reason gentlemen are particularly active in some places in observing the slightest blemish, and dragging them into public light, and running the Act down. It has been a very common thing to inveigh against this Act because it has given them a little more trouble, and they have been very active in finding fault where fault ought not to be found, perhaps.

990. You are aware, I dare say, that there was an Act of Parliament passed last year which considerably reduced the fees of the sub-sheriff?—Yes, no doubt that was so.

991. And has thrown a considerable amount of expense on the high sheriff?—No doubt. Many of the honourable Members who have served the office of sheriff know better than I do all about that; and you are quite aware of the arrangements between yourselves and your sub-sheriffs. I never heard that it costs the high sheriff much, and I should be very sorry that it should.

992. For your information, I may say that in my own county, of which I have been high sheriff, the sub-sheriff was very glad to do the business for nothing three years ago, and it cost the high sheriff nothing?—As I understand the question of the honourable Member, he would suggest that the sub-sheriff should be remunerated;

Mr. Serjeant *Armstrong.*

1 May 1873.

rated; but I say let him settle that with the sheriff.

993. *The O'Conor Don.*] Do you think that there is any provision in the Act of Parliament which empowers payment to be made now to the sub-sheriff for the additional duties which are thrown upon him under this Act?—I do not recollect that there is; perhaps there is, but it never struck me. If his duties were sensibly increased, it might be a very fair thing to make him some allowance for that.

994. I understood you to propose, that the qualification of a common juror should be raised to 50?—Yes, if the material exists to supply it.

995. Would you propose any difference in different counties?—Looking to the schedule of the Act that is a matter so dependent upon the position and the population, that I am not able to grapple with it; it depends so much upon local circumstances. You might find a class of men in one county rated at 30 *l.*, who would be quite equal to and above many who would be rated at 50 *l.* in another county; it depends, as I say, upon local considerations.

996. I presume that you have not given much attention yourself to the question of the valuation in different parts of Ireland?—I have not.

997. Therefore when you were asked a question with respect to the valuation of houses being much higher in the north of Ireland than in the south, your answer was not given from any practical information on the subject?—No; I was assuming the position of the honourable Member to be correct, and I do not know how that is, but I have no doubt that it is so from his suggesting it, for I am sure that he is well informed.

998. You propose, do you not, that the revising barrister should be assisted by certain county officers, and amongst others by the county surveyor?—Yes, I think he would be an excellent man, because he knows more about the country people generally than any man in the county, because he has to go over it by day and by night, and he perambulates the county periodically and knows everybody.

999. Do you think that the county surveyor would be willing to accept this duty without remuneration?—I would never ask him. I would impose the duty upon him, because what would it involve; it would involve perhaps, one day's attendance in the year, so that is really not worth talking about. Even supposing it took him two days, he might be allowed a guinea a day for his expenses, or something of that sort, for the special duty, but it would be quite a bagatelle. I would not propose to make any sensible increase to his salary for so trifling a duty. Remember this, I would not require him to make any preliminary investigations in the county *pro hâc* at all, but confine him to his general knowledge.

1000. *Major O'Reilly.*] An objection has been made to vesting the discretionary power which you propose, in the hands of the chairmen; and it has been suggested that it would be open to the same objection as to the power now vested in the hands of the sheriff; would not there be this difference, that whilst the sheriff now has the power of selecting the names for the panel out of the whole body of jurors, any discretion that was vested in the chairman would only apply to striking a certain number of names off the jurors' book; and that even if by mistake he strikes off some names he must leave a substantial body of jurors sufficient for all purposes?—It is an obvious distinction, and very well put, I think, and it makes it very clear.

1001. Your attention was called to the fact that it might take a very large part of the chairman's time going over the list of the jurors, name by name, and examining it; and you stated that you thought it necessary that they should do that; but would there not also be this to be observed, that whilst it might take a very long time at first when he would be going over the new jurors' book, with perhaps some thousands of names in it, the labour would be very much diminished after the first time, because the only names then to be investigated would be the new names on it?—Yes, you are quite right; I quite concur in that; it would become a simple, and in some degree a routine duty, after a little experience.

1002. Would you consider that in any question of remuneration for this duty, if any such should arise, it should be very carefully preserved in mind that the amount of labour should not be estimated merely from what it would be in the first instance?—I think that that should of course be borne in mind.

1003. *Chairman.*] Any alteration in the preparation of the jurors' book would necessarily be a considerable time before it came into operation, would it not?—Yes, unless you made special legislation; you might make it very prompt by immediate legislation.

1004. The alterations which you have suggested could not possibly come into operation, for instance, before the next assizes?—They could not; the only thing that you could do with reference to the next assizes, if you think the evil so great as to demand it, would be to direct all the jury panels that have been struck to be quashed, and to revert to the old system for the present assizes; but I am afraid that the idea of legislating in the meantime satisfactorily would be out of the question.

1005. From what you have yourself observed, should you suggest that some alteration which should come into operation at the next assizes, should be made?—It would be merely temporary. I have seen such exhibitions, that I really think it amounts to a burlesque to go to some places in Ireland under this Act, owing altogether to that one point, the lowness of the qualification, which was not a matter foreseen, and, indeed, I do not know how it could have been foreseen. It was an experiment well worth trying, but it is a result which makes people pause a little.

1006. As a temporary measure, might not the sheriff be directed, in framing the panel, to leave out the names of all jurors whose qualifications were below a certain figure?—That might answer the purpose, and in all other respects let the present Act stand, subject to future legislation.

1007. Do you think that the Act is likely to work better on a second trial than at the first?—I have no doubt that it may be made a most admirable Act.

1008. I mean, were some of the failures and difficulties which you observed owing to its being an entirely new Act, and that everybody concerned in its administration was rather unused to it?—I think that the low standard of qualification is an essential objection that ought to be removed, and I do not think that anything could

cure

Mr. Serjeant Armstrong.

1 May 1873.

cure it; time would not cure it. As it is at present, respectable people may not be served very often, for by a little scheming and a little arrangement with their gatekeepers or servants, and all that, the summonses do not reach them. There are twenty peremptory challenges in a criminal case, and then the Crown is obliged to set aside jurors, and you have what are humorously called "challenges to the array," that is, challenges to the appearance of a man, to his raiment, and looking to a man's ordinary costume. The very look of a man who had got no necktie, with rough corduroy breeches, very bad stockings, and a battered old hat, is enough; you are obliged to set him aside, and then you take a better-looking sort of man; but, after all, the qualification is too low. The respectable men do not come at all, and you have nothing but the residuum, and that is very bad.

1009. Would not an improvement be at once effected if the better class of jurors did attend?—It would be a step in the right direction, but it is necessary to enforce two things: first of all, the attendance of well-qualified people, and to take care that they are better served, and that they will be sure to come. That is to be insured by the delivery of the summons to them. There is a feeling that they do not care to be mixed up with men of inferior rank. It is very desirable that you should have such people, but you will never get it done unless you can make sure of the service of the summons upon them, and the judge ought to fine them when they do not attend.

1010. Dr. *Ball*.] It might be a good thing, might it not, for the next assizes to make the experiment of trying a higher qualification?—Yes.

1011. Because it would then be seen by experience whether it had ensured the result that you desire?—Yes; that is the suggestion of the noble Lord, as I understand it. In fact, I should not be at all astonished to find that it would require the test of further experience to lead to a modification of the Act, so as to make the thing permanently effective; it may require the test of experience and observation. It is not to be expected to have a perfect thing either in England or in Ireland. Recollect the general principle of it is a sound and solemn one, and all that you want to do is to get good jurors rightly summoned.

1012. Mr. *Bruen*.] You said you thought that the right of the Crown to issue a special commission should be preserved, and that in that case the old system of the trial by jury of civil cases should be preserved?—I wish to add to that, that if the qualification be raised to the figure that I have suggested, I think there would be no necessity for resorting to the grand panel of the county or to the old practice, and I would rather not see it resorted to.

1013. And then you qualify your former answer to that extent?—I will qualify it, if you will allow me. I think that if the qualification is made satisfactory there will be no necessity for resorting to the old grand jury panel in special commissions; but I would reserve the power of specials commissions on special occasions.

1014. Mr. *Heron*.] I think you said that the Crown should still retain the right of bringing cases to the Queen's Bench, and dealing with them by a special jury?—Yes. If a Crown case be brought to the Queen's Bench by *certiorari*, which the Crown can do, you cannot try it otherwise than by a special jury under the old system, and then the vice crops up of striking out every respectable man that is upon it.

1015. Mr. *Downing*.] Cannot you remove the trial from one county to another?—Yes, that remains, of course, in the power of the court.

Mr. James Hamilton, called in; and Examined.

Mr. J. Hamilton.

1016. *Chairman*.] You are a Queen's Counsel, are you not?—Yes.

1017. And you are Chairman of the county of Sligo?—Yes.

1018. And a practising barrister?—Yes.

1019. Have you had much experience in the operation of the Jury Act?—Yes, on my own circuit I have had very considerable experience of it; I may say that I was leading counsel on one side or the other in almost every civil case that was tried, and I also was in the Crown Court at the last assizes.

1020. Before asking you as to your experience of its operation, I may ask you generally whether you are favourable to the principles adopted in the Act?—So far as the preparation of the jury lists is concerned, I think that it is an admirable Act. I quite agree with Lord O'Hagan that, from the changes in the circumstances of the country, Perrin's Act has ceased to be applicable. We have lost that class of jurors, the freeholders and the leaseholders, who formed the jury list under it, and therefore I agree that, as far as the preparation of the lists is concerned, the present is an excellent Act.

1021. Do you approve of the substitution of the rating qualification for the old qualification?—Yes.

1022. Do you also approve of the adoption of the chairman's court as a court of revision?—Yes, I think so; it is a mere mechanical operation, the revision in the chairman's court.

1023. But have you any doubt as to the third principle of depriving the sheriff of the power of the selection of the panel?—I decidedly disapprove of depriving the sheriff of what I call the power of excluding the names of men, who he knows will not do justice between the parties, from his panel. I should retain the power in the hands of the sub-sheriff, which he formerly exercised.

1024. Will you tell the Committee what has been your experience as to the operation of the present Act?—My experience of the operation of the present Act is, to use the language of Serjeant Armstrong, that it has simply created a burlesque of justice. That is my experience on my own circuit. The jury box was crowded by men who were utterly unfit to discharge the duties of jurymen, on account of the low qualification.

1025. Has the Act very much altered the character of the juries which you have had in your own court?—In my own court, as chairman, I have had very little experience indeed of the working of the Act, because the first sessions in which we have had the Act in operation followed immediately after the assizes for each county, and I think, for my own part, that I have tried only one Crown case, and that one of very trifling

Mr. J. Hamilton. 1 May 1873.

trifling importance; and, in fact, I almost directed an acquittal, so that I have had no experience whatever in my own court of the operation of the Act.

1026. You had only one jury, as I understand you?—Only one jury.

1027. Then your experience of the juries under the present Act is almost entirely confined to your experience as a practising barrister?—Yes.

1028. Would you say that the character of the juries has very much deteriorated?—Very much deteriorated indeed, but not to the same degree in each county. For instance, on my own circuit I found that in counties like Londonderry, where there are a considerable number of thriving towns, the character of the juries had not by any means deteriorated so much as in the large agricultural counties without those elements.

1029. What are the counties in that circuit?—Longford is the first; but I omit Longford, because I do not believe that there was a single record tried at Longford at the last assizes; and I practised on the civil side of the court principally: the next county is Cavan.

1030. What sort of juries were they in Cavan?—They were very inferior to what they were; Cavan used to supply a very excellent jury on the civil side. The next county, Fermanagh, I think, has always supplied rather an inferior jury, inferior to Cavan, certainly; I did not observe very much difference, but it was certainly inferior to what it was before. The next county is Tyrone; I observed an immense change in the character of the juries there; there were no better juries in Ireland than in Tyrone formerly, in my opinion, but now they are very much inferior indeed. The next county is Donegal; I had, practically, very little experience in Donegal, because in consequence of the very protracted trial at Omagh, and of the fact that one judge was detained there until after the time for holding the Donegal assizes passed by, and we were obliged to adjourn, I may say, the whole assizes, and only a few trifling cases were tried. but from the appearance of the jurors that I saw at Lifford, the county town, and from the fact that I am a native of Donegal, and know the county very well, I think I am justified in saying that they were of a very inferior class indeed; they were a very wretchedly poor class, and they complained bitterly of the distances that they were obliged to walk to attend the assizes; those people really could not afford it, they had not the means of getting the common necessaries of life. The next county would be Londonderry; there was a very considerable amount of business there, and for the reason I have stated, that we had jurors from such towns as Londonderry itself, with a population of about 30,000 people, and from Coleraine, and from Newtownlimavady, and various other good towns in the county, and from their being a very prosperous class of farmers, the jurors had not deteriorated so much, but they had deteriorated; I am now giving, not only my own opinion, but the opinion of the majority of the circuit.

1031. Major *O'Reilly*.] You said that they were not quite as good a class as before in Londonderry; were they adequate to the discharge of their duties on those assizes?—I should prefer having them better; I should prefer the old jurors that we had, but Londonderry is a county that will not suffer much from the Act, I think.

1032. *Chairman*.] Could you describe to the Committee generally in what respect the juries had deteriorated; did they appear unintelligent?—They were grossly ignorant, and very badly dressed, and I may tell the Committee that, in following the example of the learned serjeant, we really turned the juries, in most instances, into complete ridicule. That was the tone adopted by my circuit towards the juries; we scarcely talked to them at all; we talked to the judge, and we simply chaffed the jury, because they could not understand us as a general rule, and in cases where there was no disturbing element they simply did what the judge told them, and they might as well not have been there at all; but in cases where there was a disturbing element (there were not many of that kind on my circuit), there was no agreement; they did not mind the judge at all, at least some of them did not.

1033. You think that in many cases they were not men competent to form an opinion upon the evidence brought before them?—I am perfectly certain about it.

1034. I understand you that they acted either in obedience to the directions of the judge, or in accordance with their own feelings or prejudices?—Yes, in accordance with their own prejudices or fears.

1035. And that to a certain extent, you think, was because they were not competent to form an opinion upon the evidence?—Yes, I do think that they were not competent to form an opinion upon the evidence, but I should add that I think that the Committee would be greatly led astray if they thought that ignorance was the principal evil that we have to deal with in Irish juries; on the contrary, I think that there is a large number of persons necessarily on those jury lists who either sympathise with lawlessness, or are under the influence of terror of secret societies, and, therefore, who either will not do their duty, or are afraid to do their duty; that, in my opinion, is the principal evil that you have to deal with in Ireland.

1036. What are the principal recommendations which you would make for the improvement of juries?—I am happy to say, for my own sake, that I agree almost entirely with the principles which Mr. Serjeant Armstrong announced; and Colonel Wilson Patten will excuse me if I say that I draw altogether a different conclusion from what he stated, from what Colonel Patten seemed to say, and that is, that the principle of this Act was very good, but that the administration was bad. I do not agree in that at all; I merely wish to guard myself against conveying a wrong impression. What I understood Mr. Serjeant Armstrong to say was that he would raise the qualification more than double, with a very stringent power of selection besides.

1037. Do you understand Mr. Serjeant Armstrong to recommend investing in anyone the power of selection?—You may call it selection; I think exclusion and selection come to the same thing; at least it strikes me so. Nobody imagines, I suppose, that any public officer would select an improper body of men to form the jury panel; that is entirely contrary to the experience of anybody; but if you allow a person to exclude a number of persons, it does amount to a selection of those that it leaves on. I would adopt the word exclusion, if your Lordship pleases.

1038. Mr. *Bourke*.] Have you any objection to

Mr. J. Hamilton.

1 May 1873.

to the word Revision?—I should prefer adopting the word that I believe Mr. Serjeant Armstrong used; he used either selection or exclusion; let us adopt exclusion; I say that I agree with him, and I think that you should raise the qualification, and that you should vest in somebody the power of excluding improper persons from the panel.

1039. *Chairman.*] That is to say, the raising of the qualification and the exclusion of unqualified persons, would affect the preparation of the jurors' book?—I think the great point is the panel.

1040. But those things would affect the preparation of the jurors' book, would they not?—My opinion is that you should raise the qualification, and then, of course, it would affect the jurors' book, but with regard to the power of excluding improper persons from the jury box, that should be done, in my opinion, in the preparation of the panel.

1041. I understand you to agree with Mr. Serjeant Armstrong, that the qualification should be raised?—Yes.

1042. And that the chairman or some person should also have the power of removing from the jurors' book the names of jurors who are not properly qualified?—Yes, I think that that would be also a useful thing.

1043. Do I understand that you go further, and are of opinion that in some person there must be vested a discretion in selecting the panel from the book?—I do not say in selecting the panel, but I will use this phrase: the sub-sheriff ought to have the power in forming his panel, to omit from his panel the names of persons who, as he knows, will not do justice.

1044. Although the names of those persons may be upon the jurors' book?—Yes.

1045. Then, in fact, you do not approve of the alphabetical process of selection contained in the Act?—I think no witness that I have heard yet can possibly approve of that when Mr. Coffey suggests such a power as that the Crown should have in every instance the right to try the prisoners by special juries, and when Mr. Serjeant Armstrong would give such a stringent power to the chairman of the county.

1046. What stringent power do you mean?—The stringent power of striking every name off the general list as to whom he could get evidence to show that the persons name ought not to be there for any cause.

1047. What connection has that proposal, to give to the chairman a stringent power in the preparation of the jurors' book, with the proposal to give somebody else the power of selecting a limited number of names from that purged jurors' book?—If you could so purge the jurors' book, which I believe you could not by any process, but if you could so purge the jurors' book as to leave no improper person on the panel, you would want no further safeguard; but, in my opinion, you could not so purge the jurors' book by any practicable means.

1048. Will you give your reasons for that opinion?—In the first place, with regard to the propositions of Serjeant Armstrong, that the county inspector, for instance, should come up and point out to me, as I sit revising those lists, that A. B. is a Ribbonman, and that C. D. is a Fenian, and that E. F. is a Master of an Orange Lodge, or something of that sort, and would be highly objectionable persons to have on the list. I do not believe that any county inspector, in the first place, would do such a thing; he would subject himself to an action of slander a hundred times at every revision of the books. I do not think that any public officer ought to be called upon to do that, and I do not think that any public officer would do it. Then how could you prove it to my satisfaction? Am I to take his *ipse dixit* that this person is a Fenian or a Ribbonman? It appears to me to be an utterly impracticable process. I think that the power of eliminating those objectionable persons from the jury panel must be exercised by some responsible official in private, as it is done by the sub-sheriff at present.

1049. As I understand, you think that the exclusion of ignorant or unintelligent persons would not be sufficient?—Clearly not. Ignorant and unintelligent jurors very often do what the judge tells them, and that is a very good thing, particularly in civil cases.

1050. But you think that some means ought to be adopted for excluding Ribbonmen and Fenians?—Yes, I do.

1051. And Orangemen?—I do, and Orangemen in cases where any question exciting their prejudices arose.

1052. In fact, the panel must be prepared with reference to the special cases which have to be tried?—No, I think not. The panel is not so prepared as a matter of fact, I believe. The special jury panel is prepared at the beginning of the year, without reference to any particular case, and without the knowledge of any case. I think that Mr. Serjeant Armstrong fell into an error with respect to that. The common jury panel is a general panel, not prepared for any particular case at the assizes, as I believe, but prepared for all cases.

1053. In your opinion, if the unintelligent and the uneducated were first eliminated from the jurors' book, and if the panel were then selected by lot or alphabetically, would there be no security in the power which still remains to the Crown solicitor to direct any juror to whom he objects to stand by?—Certainly there would; but as I have heard it stated, and as I agree myself, I think that that power, largely exercised by the Crown solicitor, throws a much greater suspicion on the administration of justice than the power exercised by the sub-sheriff in preparing the panel in the old way. I say, as a matter of experience, that where that power is largely exercised, for instance, in Fenian or agrarian cases, we have the whole national press coming out with the outcry that men were excluded from the jury box on account of their religion. That is the experience of everybody; and I think that if you take away the power from the sub-sheriff, you impose on the Crown solicitor the necessity of exercising that power of the Crown to order jurors to stand aside to a much greater extent than he is obliged to do it now; and you will bring greater odium on the administration of justice by that result than existed formerly. I think I may say this, that in all my experience it has never been the case, and I think, if the judges should happen to be examined before this Committee, you may ask their experience whether this preparation of the panel by the sub-sheriff ever produced an improper conviction of a prisoner. I should like to know a single instance where any judge would say so; and therefore I rather judge of the thing, as Mr. Serjeant

Mr. J. Hamilton.

May 1873.

Serjeant Armstrong says, by its practical results than by any mere speculation.

1054. Does the Crown solicitor, in directing jurors to stand by, act entirely upon his own responsibility?—He does it on his own knowledge, and on the information which he can obtain from persons best informed as to the character of the juror; he cannot receive that assistance from the Crown counsel, because the Crown counsel is a perfect stranger to the county; the Crown solicitor ought to be a person fully acquainted with the county, but I am sorry to say very often he is not.

1055. Although acting on his own knowledge and on the knowledge that he could obtain, does not he act to a certain extent under the direction of the Crown solicitor?—They act in accord. The Crown counsel and the Crown solicitor, in my opinion, never have a desire for an improper conviction, but they have a desire that men shall not be placed in the jury box who come there with preconceived opinions, and who will not do their duty fairly between the Crown and the prisoner.

1056. Then, in fact, I understand you to think that the mode of the selection of the panel from the jurors' book by the sub-sheriff ought to be reverted to? I do. I think that you will either be obliged to do that, or else to adopt such suggestions as Mr. Coffey made, to give the Crown right to try every prisoner for felony by a special jury, or to adopt the suggestion of Mr. Serjeant Armstrong, to raise the qualification to such an extent as to diminish the number of jurors, so that, according to what Mr. Downing demonstrated, you cannot get on with the present Act.

1057. Was your experience of the operation of the old system altogether favourable?—I am rather inclined to agree with Mr. Seed, that it operated rather much in favour of the prisoner; I think that the sub-sheriff scarcely eliminated his panel enough, because most unquestionably there were acquittals of the most absurd character, even under the old system, whilst there was no wrong conviction under the old system, I maintain, within the last 20 years in my experience.

1058. When you say you agree with Mr. Seed that it operated too much in favour of the prisoner, do you mean that cases came under your knowledge where the panel was prepared with the object of assisting the prisoner by a friend of the prisoner?—No, not at all; but I believe that such was the amount of popular jealousy, and perhaps alarm, about the press, and that sort of thing, that the sub-sheriff left on men very often that he ought rather to have struck out, and sometimes he did so from ignorance. In one of the worst cases of murder that I ever listened to, there was an absolute acquittal, because the first cousin of the prisoner was on the jury, and several of his neighbours. It was altogether from ignorance on the part of the Crown solicitor that he was kept on. We did not order him to stand by, through ignorance on the part of the sub-sheriff, who certainly ought to have kept those persons off his panel. I prosecuted in the case myself.

1059 As to that case, you say that it took place through ignorance on the part of the sub-sheriff?—Yes. The crime was committed in a very remote part of a very wild county. I am not ascribing blame to either the solicitor or the sub-sheriff, from not knowing this, and I unfortunately did not know it.

1060. I want to know whether what you say in that case was occasioned through ignorance, might not conceivably have taken place through partiality?—I really do not think that the sub-sheriffs of Ireland are liable to that imputation, if you will consider that they have no interest in the result of a trial, and if you consider that they are, generally speaking, men of a very respectable position, and solicitors of high standing, and who are made responsible by large security to the high sheriff for the proper discharge of their duty; in short, they are as trustworthy men, as a body, as I think exist in Ireland. I do not believe that they would be guilty of excluding a name from a panel or putting a name on a panel for the sake of doing any injustice; but I think that the motive which actuates the sub-sheriffs, especially with regard to criminal trials, is this: they are men who know the county thoroughly; the very nature of their duties, the execution of civil-bill processes, and the various duties that they have to discharge, make them thoroughly acquainted with almost every character in the county; and therefore, if there is an agrarian case to be tried, or a Ribbon case to be tried, or an Orange case to be tried, they will omit from their panel, and I think that they ought to omit from their panel, the names of men whom they know right well to be Orangemen, Ribbonmen, Fenians, or persons who have a sympathy with agrarian crime. That, in my opinion, is what they do.

1061. I understand you to say that you do not think that there is any ground for the imputation, such as has been made, upon the character of the sub-sheriffs of Ireland; putting aside for a moment the consideration of criminal cases, might it not happen that the sub-sheriff or his friends might be interested in the civil cases that were coming on for trial?—Quite so.

1062. Would not it be in his power to prepare the panel in such a way as to be likely to assist in obtaining a verdict favourable to the side in which he was interested?—Then you must remember the safeguards that exist in the challenge to the array. If the sheriff is a party to the suit, if he is related to the party to the suit, if he has any interest in the suit, and if any improper conduct with regard to framing the panel can be proved, the panel is quashed; that is, in my opinion, a sufficient safeguard. In almost any improper or partial conduct of the sheriff, you can get rid of the panel by a challenge to the array. The way that that challenge is tried is by appointing triers. I think at present, as Serjeant Armstrong says, the triers are sometimes a very absurd tribunal. I should give power to the judge to name the triers, and he should select the triers from persons of known respectability.

1063. Mr. *Heron*.] He does now, does he not?—Not always; they are generally taken from the jury, and my experience is that they are the two first names called upon the jury, as a general rule. There was a case I know in which a famous challenge which I can refer to was tried by two petty jurors; but I should not at all confine the judge to selecting two petty jurors; he should have the power of selecting two persons of acknowledged respectability to act as triers; and then if you secure a fair mode of trying the challenge, you at once counteract any improper conduct of the sheriff.

1064. *Chairman*.] I understand you think that the

Mr. *J. Hamilton.* 1 May 1873.

the old system worked well in practice; do you think that it did not throw any slur upon the impartiality of justice in public opinion?—If you speak of Irish public opinion, it is of a very composite character. I know that one portion of the press declares that there is no such thing as justice to be had in Ireland; if you always legislate entirely to get rid of popular cries, and I am afraid that that is rather a misfortune to us in Ireland, I am afraid that legislation would be very unsatisfactory.

1065. I suppose you only advocate that system as a necessary remedy for a great evil, but would you, on principle, for the purpose of getting a good jury, intrust the selection from the book, or the old panel, to any individual, however great your confidence might be in him?—I should, certainly. In the first place, from my experience, no injustice has ever been done to the prisoner by the selection of the panel in that way; and next, from the powerful control of public opinion now. You have three safeguards, further: first, in the challenge to the array; secondly, in the challenge to the poll; and thirdly, in the fact that you must have a unanimous jury before a man can be convicted. Thus I think that you have ample security against any chance of unfair conduct on the part of the individual to whom you may give the selection, or rather the arrangement of the jury panel.

1066. Do you think that under the old system persons were not habitually excluded in many cases who were perfectly competent to act as jurors, and who would have made good jurors?—I do not think so, as a rule. My belief is that the principal cause of the necessity for a change in the Jury Act was the fact that Perrin's Act was no longer applicable. That was an Act brought in by a very great lawyer, and who even as a judge would do nothing against the popular side of the question; but that Act became inapplicable in consequence of the diminution, to a very great extent, of the freeholders and leaseholders, and you had not materials under it for forming the panel. Next to that the cause has been the gross abuse of the jury system in the city of Dublin; and I agree with every word that Mr. Serjeant Armstrong said about the abuse in the city of Dublin, and that that caused very great discontent with the jury system; but I think that the old jury system operated very fairly and reasonably well in the counties in Ireland at the assizes.

1067. We are told that in many counties very nearly the same panels were returned one assizes after another, is that the fact?—Yes; I think to a considerable extent the sheriff, according to my experience (I am speaking now of my own circuit), was operated upon by two motives; first, to get intelligent, and proper, and respectable men, who would do their duty; and next, to get those men with as much convenience to themselves as possible; that is, men who resided as near the county town as he could. He did not bring men 40 or 50 miles, if he could help it.

1068. In your opinion ought the whole duty of serving on juries to be confined to persons who happened to live near the assize town?—No, I think that all men should serve in their turn on juries.

1069. I suppose you admit that there are probably properly qualified persons outside the limited panels returned at our assizes after another by the sub-sheriff?—I do not say that the old system was perfect, but I think it was as good a working system as you are likely to get by increasing the number of jurors as you do under this Act; and I do not think that any suspicion attached to it amongst right-minded people, except where it was abused, as in the city of Dublin, where it was grossly abused. In fact, there were professional juries in the city of Dublin, and all respectable men shirked attending; but that was the abuse of the system, and not the use of it.

1070. Was it not rather a plausible imputation for the disaffected to cast upon the administration of justice that the jury panels were selected by certain irresponsible individuals?—I do not think that it was a plausible imputation, to judge by the fact of the very small number of challenges to the array, and the fact that they were hardly ever successful. I think that if they were in reality suspected, you would have had a greater number of challenges, and if there was any ground for the suspicion, those challenges would have succeeded, but that was not the rule but the exception.

1071. Then challenges to the array did take place sometimes?—Yes, but very rarely.

1072. I believe that one took place in which you were concerned?—Yes; the Attorney General was good enough to remind me of that. Some years ago I remember drawing a challenge to the array myself in Omagh, and I will tell you what the result of that was, now that I remember it.

1073. This challenge is signed by yourself and Mr. Yates Johnstone, and it appears to allege "that the said sheriff, in the arraying and returning of the said panel, did array and return in the said panel certain persons whose names were not contained in the said jurors' book, or in any other jurors' book?"—That is so.

1074. And further, it appears to have alleged that "the said sheriff did act with partiality in arraying the said panel, for that he did omit therefrom the names of certain persons lawfully qualified to serve as jurors, because he, the said sheriff, deemed them more likely to acquit than to convict the said prisoner, and did insert and return thereon names of 'a large number of persons,' because he deemed them more likely to convict than to acquit the said prisoner, and because the said panel was so arrayed and returned by and through the agency of So-and-So, Esq., solicitor, sub-sheriff of the said county, and brother to the said So-and-So, being the attorney for the next of kin of the deceased, and actively assisting in the prosecution;" do you recollect what was the result of that challenge?—I do recollect it perfectly well. Of course, I merely drew that challenge upon the information supplied to me by my attorney.

1075. What was the result of it?—The Crown very foolishly, in my opinion, instead of taking issue as to whether it was true or not, demurred to it, and that demurrer was held bad in point of law; the challenge was good in form, and by their demurrer they admitted the truth of the statement, but whether it was true or not was never tried. They said that it was bad in point of law, but it proved good in point of law, and, therefore, the merits were never tried; and I remember that the sub-sheriff was outrageous about it, because he said he could have proved that there was not a word of truth in the challenge.

Mr. *J. Hamilton.*

1 May 1873.

1076. But the panel was quashed upon those allegations?—Yes, the panel was quashed; the allegations were never tried or proved.

1077. What do you think was the effect upon the minds of the people as regards the administration of justice in that county?—The effect is, that Tyrone is one of the most prosperous, peaceable and best conditioned counties in Ireland.

1078. Although you say that the truth of the accusations was never tried, you do not know to this day that they were not true?—I know nothing about it; the attorney supplied me with the statements, and I put them into legal form; that is the whole effect of it.

1079. Do not you think that the possibility of having such charges of partiality in the selection of the panel made, and in some instances as they were sustained, had any prejudicial effect upon the administration of justice?—We never had a perfect system, and you never will, at least for years to come. You will not convince the majority of the people in Ireland, under any system, that you are dealing fairly with them; because, if you read the weekly press, the burthen of their song from one year's end to the other is, that justice is unfairly administered in Ireland, and will be always unfairly administered under British rule. The great majority of the peasantry read nothing else, I believe, than those papers, and therefore you never will drive it out of their heads by any change in the law.

1080. Do not you think it possible that justice might be unfairly administered under such a system?—I do not believe that it is.

1081. You do not believe that in practice it is, but it is possible that it might be?—Scarcely possible; with the pressure of public opinion on public officers, with the utter absence of all interest in public officers to do anything that is wrong, and with the safeguards which the prisoner has, which I have already pointed out, of challenge to the array, and challenge for cause, and the unanimity of juries, I think it is scarcely possible that injustice can arise.

1082. Might not those facts, or facts similar to those to which I have referred, if that challenge had been true, have not come to the knowledge of the counsel for the prisoner?—Very unlikely. The attorney for the prisoner is, generally speaking, an exceedingly intelligent and active person, and he is certain to know quite well if anything wrong has been done with the jury panel.

1083. Is the prisoner always defended by an attorney?—Invariably, in serious cases, and if he is too poor to employ an attorney himself, in a capital case the court assigns an attorney and counsel to him, and pays them.

1084. You suggest that the qualification should be raised under the new Act?—Yes.

1085. Do you also suggest that it should consist in any part of a household qualification?—I should think that a compound qualification would be very desirable, because I entirely agree with Mr. Serjeant Armstrong, that if a man chooses to live in a hut with his own pigs, no matter what the extent of land that he possesses may be, he must be an unintelligent person, and behind the times, and, therefore, not fit to serve on a jury.

1086. Would you make the household qualification an additional qualification, as has been suggested by Mr. Coffey, I think?—No. I am now speaking of counties with few towns, where I think that the jurors are the worst; large agricultural wild counties like Donegal. I should prefer in that case a sort of compound qualification, composed of a rating of about 40*s.* for a house; that would be quite as high as you could practically go, and then you would have an additional land qualification of 30*l.*, say.

1087. Do you attach much importance to having a large jurors' book?—That would depend upon its materials. I prefer quality to quantity.

1088. Do you attach much importance to obtaining the power of relieving jurors from constant attendance?—I think so. I should like to relieve them as much as possible, provided you could do so consistently with preserving the proportion of the qualified class; but I should rather give them additional trouble than deteriorate the character of the jury very much, because, after all, they are most deeply interested in it.

1089. You do not think that the suggestion which was made that the Crown should have, as a matter of right, a special jury in every criminal case, would be advisable?—I think that that would be infinitely more unpopular than leaving the power in the sub-sheriff to arrange the panel; besides, it is one of those things that they would only resort to in the last instance.

1090. The special jurors' book in every county would contain the names of a large number of persons of all religions, would it not?—I should hope so. I am not sufficiently acquainted with Ireland to be able to give any answer that would be at all accurate upon that subject; but I should hope it would. I should be very sorry indeed that there should be a separation on account of religion.

1091. In every county in the north, and in the most Protestant counties in the north, the present special jurors' book would contain the names of a large number of Roman Catholics, would it not?—I am not capable of giving accurate information upon that subject.

1092. Supposing that to be the fact, would not it be more desirable that the prisoner should be tried by a jury selected from the special jurors' book than as may be now, by a jury selected from a panel which may be all of one political or religious complexion?—I am perfectly satisfied that the prisoner would prefer the old way of doing it, if you consulted the prisoner.

1093. He would prefer the old panel to a special jury from the special jurors' book?—I am satisfied of that, and if I was his counsel I should recommend it to him.

1094. Mr. *Bruen.*] Have you ever been counsel in cases for the prisoner?—I was counsel for the Ribbonmen of Donegal for years, and I knew them very well. I defended a great many Ribbonmen in the early part of my professional career.

1095. *Chairman.*] Have you any other suggestion to make before you are examined by any other member of the Committee?—I think I concur so entirely in everything that Mr. Serjeant Armstrong said, except with regard to substituting the chairman for the sub-sheriff, in which I differ from him altogether, that I think it would be only wasting the time of the Committee if I were to go into detail.

1096. Colonel *Wilson Patten.*] I understand you to say, that you agree with Mr. Serjeant Armstrong, that on the whole the present Act is a great improvement upon the old Act?—I did not understand him to say so; I do not think it is the case.

Mr. J. Hamilton.

1 May 1873.

case. I think that it is a decided disimprovement.

1097. That was not what Mr. Serjeant Armstrong said?—He certainly conveys that to my mind, when Mr. Serjeant Armstrong was obliged to lay down double the qualification in the present Act, and to suggest such powers as he suggested in order to counteract the mischief of the Act as it now stands. I understood him to describe it as much worse than the old Act.

1098. What are the points besides those which you have alluded to, in which you think that the present Act is inferior to the old Act?—I think that in its practical result, as Mr. Serjeant Armstrong said, it is a burlesque of justice as it stands.

1099. I think that you differ from Mr. Serjeant Armstrong in this, that the new Act is not so popular in Ireland as the old Act was, because he said that the principle of the Act had given satisfaction in Ireland?—That depends upon what he means by the principle.

1100. The chief principle is the absence of selection by the sub-sheriff?—The absence of selection by the sub-sheriff, in my opinion, is very popular with the criminal part of the population, but it is not popular with the orderly part of the population, according to my experience.

1101. I want to ascertain from you what are the other points in which you think that it is inferior to the old Act, because there are a great many other points in the Act?—It puts on a great amount of ignorance, prejudice, and sympathy with crime on the jury lists, in consequence of the extended area. As you go down in the social scale in Ireland, you reach a substratum of sympathy with lawlessness, and the vice of this Act is that it reaches that substratum. Of course if you raise the qualification, you, to a certain extent, get out of that.

1102. If you raise the qualification and give up the selection by the sub-sheriff, do you think that that would be sufficient?—The word selection is rather invidious, because what the sub-sheriff really did was to omit from his panel the names of men that he believed would not do justice.

1103. *Chairman.*] I understood you to say that what the sub-sheriff did was to omit from the panel the names of those whom he thought for any reasons disqualified?—Who he thought would not do justice between either of the parties, or the Crown and the prisoner.

1104. What were the number that were generally required on the panel at an average town in your assizes; would it be 200?—I really do not know with anything like accuracy.

1105. Take the county of Tyrone; what would be the number required on the panel?—I never had my attention called to the exact figures.

1106. Have you some idea?—Perhaps 150; I cannot give it with any great degree of accuracy. We have jurors enough to try all the cases, always.

1107. It appears from a return, taking the average of the three last years, that the number of jurors on the jurors' book in county Tyrone, was 1,153, and the sheriff had to frame a panel of about 150; in doing that he surely had names selected from the book, not merely omitting names not properly qualified as jurors?—The sheriff, as I mentioned to you, is a man who knows every man in the county; he knows the respectable men, and he would take them indifferently; but when he came to a man who he knew ought not to be on the jury, he omitted him, and then he came to the next, and so on.

1108. If he had to form a body of 150 men out of a body of 1,150, is not "selection" the proper name of that operation?—Indeed, it is a mere disputing about names.

1109. Is not that the proper name?—If you prefer it, I adopt it with pleasure, but the operation appears to me to be simply this. The sheriff has his list formed alphabetically, and he has the residences of the people; and he begins and finds A. B. a very proper man, and he puts him on his panel; he finds C. D., perhaps, a very improper man, and he drops him off his panel; in that way he selects them. The lists were always prepared alphabetically.

1110. Colonel *Wilson Patten.*] Was the panel prepared alphabetically?—No, the panel never was prepared alphabetically, but the lists were prepared alphabetically. The alphabetical preparation, so far as it does not make the thing a mere self-acting machine, and compel you to take a bad juror as well as a good one, is a convenient arrangement; but then its evils are greater than its benefits. On that account, in my opinion, the lists were prepared alphabetically under Perrin's Act.

1111. Dr. *Ball.*] There is some discussion about what is the principle of the existing Act; would not you say, putting aside the amount of qualification, that it was the absence or deprivation of any power of selection?—Yes; which I think is a very great defect.

1112. You condemn it, but others approve of it?—Yes.

1113. Would not it operate as the result of its being the great principle of this Act, that the choice of jurors is coercive and not in the discretion of any person or any body of men?—Yes, quite so.

1114. How long have you been chairman of Sligo?—Five years.

1115. From your experience as chairman of Sligo, do not you think that if an arbitrary power were given to you of leaving out persons from the list, who in your judgment ought not be on the jurors' list, you could very well exercise that discretion for the benefit of the community from the knowledge that you have now acquired of the persons in that county?—I should be perfectly incapable of exercising any such power from the knowledge that I have acquired of persons there.

1116. Would you say that if you had the assistance which was offered in the suggestion of Mr. Serjeant Armstrong, namely, calling in the constabulary inspector, the county surveyor, and other persons of that kind acquainted with the county?—I believe that those officers would naturally be exceedingly chary in coming forward in open court and pointing out to me men as guilty of what I may call crimes, which would enable me to exclude them from the jury list. I think that you could never expect the necessary information.

1117. Supposing that it was not to be in open court, but that discretion was given to you, and you had the power of consulting those people, do not you think that you could use that discretion so as to guard against persons being improperly placed upon the panel?—If you put me into a private chamber with those men, and let me have the whole police of the county, I could make you very good lists; but I should totally object to being

Mr. J. Hamilton.

1 May 1873.

being employed in any such office. I think that it would be a very degrading office to a chairman of a county to be what the public would call manipulating the jury lists or panels, and I would not do it. I would not execute such an office, and then try the prisoners with the lists so prepared.

1118. Do not you think that he would give a great deal more satisfaction than the sub-sheriff?—The sub-sheriff is grossly abused for what he does, and we should come in for it in a minor degree.

1119. It would come to this, would it not, that it must either be the sub-sheriff, or it must be a coercive representation by selection?—I think so; it comes to that.

1120. Do you think that it is necessary to have a large number brought into the assizes for the panel?—I think that you may fairly leave that to the experience of the sub-sheriff.

1121. Is it not a great hardship on men to be brought in if their presence turned out afterwards not to be required, and to be put to expense by being brought in?—Yes, it is of course, and they grumble very much about it. I must tell you that my experience of jurors is that, instead of being insulted or feeling aggrieved by being left off the panel, they are very much aggrieved by being put on it. If I were placed there to eliminate or expurgate those jury lists, my difficulty would be in keeping properly qualified men on, who would be very anxious to get off, or at least that would be one of my difficulties.

1122. Did you observe in the persons that you saw at the last assizes, that any of them were of such a class, that the necessity of residing in the assize-room for two or three days at their own expense, would be a very severe pressure upon them?—I not only observed it, but in Donegal several of them told me so, and it was notorious.

1123. In what county are you Crown prosecutor?—I am not Crown prosecutor in any county; but I am very often taken in to assist the Crown in important cases.

1124. Did you observe whether the last time there was rather more than the usual proportion of directions to the jurors to stand by?—At the last assizes I had not very much experience on the Crown side. I was more profitably engaged on the civil side, and therefore I avoided the Crown side to some extent.

Monday, 5th May 1873.

MEMBERS PRESENT:

Dr. Ball.
Sir Rowland Blennerhassett.
Mr. Bourke.
Mr. Bruen.
Viscount Crichton.
Mr. Downing.
Colonel Forde.
The Marquis of Hartington.
Mr. Heron.
The O'Conor Don.
The O'Donoghue.
Major O'Reilly.
Colonel Wilson Patten.
Colonel Vandeleur.

THE RIGHT HONOURABLE THE MARQUIS OF HARTINGTON, IN THE CHAIR.

Mr. JAMES HAMILTON, called in; and further Examined.

Mr. *J. Hamilton.*

5 May 1873.

1125. *Chairman.*] Is there anything which you wish to add to your evidence on the former day?—I forgot to add one other safeguard which I find against the malconstruction of the jury panel, which did exist in Perrin's Act, the 3rd and 4th of William the Fourth, chapter 91, section 15: "Provided always, and be it further declared and enacted that nothing herein contained shall be construed to prevent the Court of Queen's Bench, or any court of oyer and terminer, gaol delivery, or court of sessions of the peace, from respectively having and exercising the same power and authority as they may now have and exercise in issuing any writ or precept, or in making any award or order orally or otherwise for the return of a jury for the trial of any issue before any of such courts respectively, or for the amending or enlarging the panel of jurors returned for the trial of any such issue." The court had very extensive power under the late Act of amending and forming the jury panel.

1126. What were the proceedings in those cases?—On an application to the court or judge, it appears that he had the power mentioned in that section.

1127. Was that proceeding to be taken at the assizes?—So it appears by the wording of that section; it was to be either upon an application orally or otherwise.

1128. Have you, practically, seen that power to be put into operation?—No, I never have. I think it was generally considered that the power of challenge was quite a sufficient power to prevent injustice being done.

1129. Do I understand that it would have been possible for the purpose of trying cases which were to be tried at certain assizes, that the panel should be there and then amended?—I am sure it could. There is that power given in terms, and certainly by as able a lawyer as we ever had upon the Irish bench, afterwards Mr. Justice Perrin.

1130. Would not considerable delay have been caused by the use of that power?—The application might have been made before the assizes; the panel was known before the assizes took place, and if an improper panel was formed, an application under that section might have been made to the Court of Queen's Bench.

1131. Do I understand that the judge at the trial directed how the panel was to be amended?—According to the order of the court in the direction which the court thought right; the court's discretion appears to have been unfettered under that section.

1132. Major *O'Reilly.*] Does it not say any power which now exists?—Yes.

1133. What power had it?—It contemplates that power, and I have no doubt that the power existed. I cannot state what power existed, because I have not had an opportunity of seeing the old Acts, but I suppose Mr. Justice Perrin would not have introduced such a section, unless such a power existed; he was not such a fool as that.

1134. Mr. *Bruen.*] I think your general impression of the results of the change in the law have not been favourable to that change?—Extremely unfavourable; in fact, my impression is the same as Mr. Serjeant Armstrong's.

1135. Perhaps you would make one exception to that, namely, the case of the Dublin juries?—I do most decidedly; I think nothing could be worse than the Dublin common juries were.

1136. With regard to the juries in Dublin, there was no similarity between them and the circumstances under which they were brought together, and the circumstances under which the juries came into court in other parts of the country?—There was the greatest possible difference. I agree with Mr. Serjeant Armstrong in saying, that what was complained of in Dublin, was altogether an abuse of the old jury system; it was not fairly attributable to the principle of the Act, but it was altogether an abuse of the Act, and it consisted in this, as he told the Committee, that there are in Dublin a number of men who have not much to do, who are very anxious to serve upon juries, and to whom even the trifling sum that the jurors receive is an object. Those men were constantly in attendance, and the respectable merchants and traders of the city as constantly

Mr. J. Hamilton.

5 May 1873.

stantly absented themselves. Either as Serjeant Armstrong said, they managed the matter with the sheriff's bailiff not to be summoned, or being summoned, they did not attend; their names however were on the panel; it was no fault of the sub-sheriff in the arrangement of the panel; their names were there, but they did not attend; and the bar generally attributed considerable blame, I must say, to the chiefs of the three courts, who were content with the kind of juries that did attend, and who did not compel the attendance of respectable juries. It is perfectly obvious that the same result will follow under this Act, unless there is great vigilance exercised by those judges.

1137. In fact, unless the attendance of jurors is secured by the imposition of fines, it would be possible and probable that the respectable class of business men will not be likely to attend, and consequently the duty of serving on juries will be left to the residuum of the panel?—There will be precisely the same motive actuating both classes, and unless the presiding judges insist upon the attendance of respectable jurors, respectable jurors will not attend. I should add that, under the immediate operation of this Act, respectable people had attended so far; but if they find the same remissness as existed before as to the compulsion of attendance, of course they will drop off. I believe that the juries in the city of Dublin have been better under this Act than they were under the former; but, for the reason that I have mentioned, that respectable men had considered it necessary to attend.

1138. I want to draw your attention to a case that was mentioned by Mr. Serjeant Armstrong in his evidence, at Question 840; I asked him, "I want to ascertain your opinion whether it was owing to the state of the panel, or because the summonses were not served, that this breakdown of the system occurred," and the Serjeant answered, "That I could not tell; there were two cases that I might mention. In one instance I saw a gentleman about to answer to his name on a jury, and I knew perfectly well that if he were put upon the jury the verdict would be very unsatisfactory, if ever there was a verdict, and there was very great difficulty in knowing what to do. I have that case particularly in my mind. Another case was one in which I knew that if a gentleman who was ready to answer, and whom I saw hanging about the court, was put upon the jury, the result might also be very disastrous, and I withdrew the record, and it never went to trial." Is it not quite possible, and not only possible but very probable, that similar cases might occur under the provisions of the new law?—Of course, you will have the man who will have an interest in attending; that is the man to whom 1 *s.* 9 *d.* a case is important, and who have nothing else to do, and you will not have the respectable traders of the city attending, if they can help it.

1139. In the country parts, you found, did you not, that the mass of the jurors who attended were ignorant?—Yes.

1140. And that they were dependent, except in certain cases, on the directions of the judge?—Yes; quite so. We had the good fortune to have two extremely able and vigorous judges, and the verdicts were their verdicts, and not the verdicts of the jury. I do not mean to say that they interposed wrongly; on the contrary, they interposed in the most proper and beneficial manner, the verdicts were generally right, and there was scarcely a new trial motion from our circuit; but we neither treated the jury as intelligent persons in addressing them, nor did the judges. The verdicts were, in fact, I may say, directed by the judges, and very fortunately for the interests of justice.

1141. So that really it was, in fact, a misnomer to call it a jury system; it was not a jury system at all?—It was not a jury at all.

1142. Have you reason to believe that the system, as exhibited, had a mischievous effect, in that it excited great hopes, and fresh new life to certain secret societies?—I think it must have had that effect. I think that it has alarmed the orderly part of the population in Ireland immensely, and it has encouraged the disorderly part of the population.

1143. In fact, it being perfectly well known before hand who are to be upon the panel, the secret societies, or those who wish to exercise intimidation, could intimidate those jurors whose justice and whose independence they feared; they could exercise some sort of intimidation upon them, and dissuade them from attending?—I think, to use a phrase from the turf, they could "get at them" either by intimidation or solicitation.

1144. *Chairman.*] That is your opinion of what might have happened?—Yes; of what I have no doubt would happen.

1145. You have no knowledge that it has happened?—Jurors, especially poor jurors, have told me that they would be very much alarmed if they were asked to try a party or an agrarian case.

1146. Was that since the new Act, or before?—Since the new Act, and before too.

1147. Mr. *Bruce.*] In fact the class of jurors who are now brought in are more liable to intimidation, are they not, than those who were generally summoned before?—Yes, because the sheriffs, I repeat again, whose main object, as I believe, was to get independent men, and men who would do their duty fearlessly, cannot do that now. A lower class of jurors, and a more timid class of jurors, will appear, and a number of men will appear who have a sympathy with agrarian crime instead of a desire to repress it.

1148. The general consequence will be that if there is any political case, or any case in which a very strong sympathy is felt, those societies will visit those who are likely to be on the panel, and who they expect will be likely to give a verdict against them, and they will tell them that they had better stay at home, and they will not so dissuade those upon the panel who they believe will be their friends, and the consequence will be that only those would appear who are their friends?—I have no doubt of that, because when I find the public press endeavouring to intimidate the judges, I have no doubt of the operations which would be brought to bear upon the jurors.

1149. Did you remember in any of the counties in your circuit a disinclination on the part of the county gentlemen to attend?—There was one very remarkable case at Omagh, which had been tried before, and which had lasted a very long time, and which was a very disagreeable case, I have no doubt, for the jurors to try. It was a case of murder depending altogether upon circumstantial evidence, and I think that a great number of the old jurors did try to avoid that case; but

but I saw the gentry of the county, and saw respectable farmers of the county, whom I knew very well, and whom I knew on former juries. I saw them in Omagh in considerable numbers, and I think they did shirk that case.

1150. Supposing that they had attended, and had answered to their names, do you suppose that in political cases they would have been allowed to serve?—In political cases, what occurs is this; the Crown solicitor in the first place strikes off, or causes to stand by, to use the technical phrase, all those men who he thinks will not give a fair verdict, and of course the attorney for the prisoner challenges every man whom he thinks, from any cause, likely to find a verdict against his client; that is the process; and my experience is, that the men who are generally challenged by the prisoner are men in a high position, or a respectable position. And it is natural enough, because the prisoner generally comes from a low class, and probably thinks that the prejudices of the better classes are against him.

1151. So that as regards the verdict they would be powerless, that is to say, one or two possibly of the class which the prisoner challenges might escape the challenge, and might be left upon the jury, but from the greater attendance of the better classes, in obedience to the sheriff's summons, it does not in any way follow that they will be upon the jury; and if there are one or two on that jury, it will not affect the verdict?—It would not prevent disagreement.

1152. Mr. *Heron.*] If 30 or 40 gentlemen answered to their names, the prisoner could not challenge them all?—I do not think that the Crown Solicitor would put 30 or 40 gentlemen on a jury to try a peasant; I think that it would be a very objectionable process if he did it. The effect of this Act must necessarily be this; probably I may elucidate what the honourable Member for Carlow means, better by this observation. If you take away from all persons the power of leaving objectionable jurors off the panel, the necessity imposed upon the Crown Solicitor to challenge will be doubled, or trebled, and that as I have heard all the witnesses that I have heard examined say, casts very considerable suspicion upon the Crown. The national papers immediately cry out that men are ordered to stand by the Crown on account of their religion: and in order to get the enemies of the prisoner upon the jury. That is the universal outcry where the Crown solicitor exercises that power of challenge to a large extent; and it will throw, in my opinion, much greater suspicion on the Crown than the exercise of the office by the sub-sheriff, in what I will call clearing the panel quietly of objectionable men.

1153. Mr. *Bruen.*] As to the right of the Crown to try certain cases by a special jury, do you think that it would be more likely to be popular in Ireland than the old system of the sheriff returning the panel?—It would excite much greater outcry I am perfectly satisfied. I agree with Mr. Serjeant Armstrong in that.

1154. But that has been suggested as a remedy by some of the witnesses that have gone before you, I think?—It must have been from the consciousness of the badness of the Act. I would not suggest such an expedient.

1155. It seems to be a very extreme expedient, and one not at all consistent with the principle of trial by jury, which appears to be that a man shall be tried by his peers?—It is perfectly inconsistent with it, and it would bring great popular odium on the jury system in Ireland.

1156. But there seems to be a general concurrence in the necessity of some power by which the lists of jurymen shall be expurgated, if I may use such an expression, from those who are unfit to serve?—I have heard three witnesses examined, and I have remarked that everyone of them uses the term "selection," and insist upon it, that in addition to raising the qualification very considerably, there should be a power of selection somewhere.

1157. Do you think that the power of selection exercised upon the jury lists will be at all equal to the case, or will it be necessary to exercise that power of selection in the summons of the panel?—I do not think that the power of selection, as you call it, can be practically exercised upon the preparation of the jury lists.

1158. In order to exercise that power of selection, several witnesses who went before you suggest that certain officers should attend the court, and give their advice to the chairman, because the chairman himself cannot possibly have the knowledge which is necessary for him to select and revise the lists?—It is out of the question that the chairman could have any such knowledge.

1159. I suppose that, acting as chairman, and vested with the power of striking out of the jury list any person who, from any other "reasonable cause," which were the words, if you recollect, which were used by the witnesses, if you were to exercise that power, and you were to consider that a man was disaffected to the law, that would be a reasonable cause for striking him out of the jury list?—If it was proved to me that he belonged to some of these secret societies that were banded against the law I would; but I am for giving a man great latitude of opinion in all other matters.

1160. You will remember that a man being on the jury list gives him the right and the duty of trying cases in which the maintenance of the law is concerned, and that if you knew a man to be disaffected to the law, you would hardly consider him a fair juror, would you?—A man may think some laws very bad, and others tolerably good; I would require very strong grounds to be proved to me before I would deprive a man of any civil right. I would require some tangible proof to be given me of some very strong and tangible objection. I look upon that idea of the chairman clearing the list as absurd. I cannot use a milder phrase than that, and I should like to give my reasons for it. In the first place, the chairman of a county, as far as my experience goes, has very little personal knowledge of the men who serve on common juries, because he is not resident in the county; he merely runs down to the county from Dublin, and gets through his sessions, and immediately leaves the county; therefore he has not an opportunity of becoming acquainted with the characters of the men who serve on common juries. Then it is proposed that he should be aided by a whole staff of public officers, the constabulary and all the other public officers, including the county surveyor. It is proposed that he should read out each name from the list, and say, "Is there any objection to this man?" And then it is supposed that the county inspector of constabulary, or the county surveyor,

Mr. *J. Hamilton.*

5 May 1873.

veyor, or some other official, will come forward, and say, "There is a great objection to this man." Then the chairman says, "What is the objection?" "Oh, he is a Fenian." Then the chairman immediately says, "What evidence can you give of that?" It is impossible to prove it. In the first place he would not try to do it. I do not believe that any public officer would place himself in such an odious and intolerable position as that would place a public officer in. If he could not prove it, I should tell him at once that he was a very great fool for making these vague charges, which he could not substantiate, and then on would go the man. I think that the process would be perfectly ridiculous. Then Serjeant Armstrong proposed that perhaps it might be conducted in secret; that we might go into a chamber, and that the chairman, with the aid of the constabulary of the county, and those other public officers, should manage those lists in private; and then that, with his own lists so prepared in private, he should come out and try the prisoners. That, in my opinion, is one of the most unconstitutional propositions that I ever heard made, I think, and it would cover the administration of the law with odium; and I do believe that a great number of chairmen would not consent to do it. I think that it is impossible that any person can properly clear the panel of objectionable persons, except the public officer to whom you entrust the formation of the panel, he is the only person who can practically do it.

1161. It has been suggested by some of the witnesses that the sub-sheriff has an interest in these matters; in your experience, have you found the sub-sheriffs act in an interested manner in the execution of their duty?—Never. The sub-sheriff is placed in a peculiar position. As has been stated, he serves, generally speaking, for a great number of years, and he serves under high sheriffs of the most different views, political and religious; if, therefore, he acts as a violent partisan under one sheriff he would be certain to be dismissed under the next, who was a person of opposite views. It is therefore the interest of the sub-sheriff to preserve that amount of moderation which will recommend him to high sheriffs of all parties; and he does do so. I do not at all agree with the imputation thrown by Mr. Seed upon the sub-sheriffs. I know, and have known the sheriffs of five northern counties for the last 20 years, and I am confident of this, that there is no one of them who would be capable of manufacturing the panel with an unfair object.

1162. Of course the fact of the length of his service, and he has in many counties, as we know, served over 20 years, proves a great guarantee to the people that he is a person who exercises the duties of his office in a disinterested manner?—Yes; and I may add this as a reason which weighs very much on my mind in confirmation of my own experience, there never was a more strenuous asserter of popular rights than Mr. Perrin, who framed the Jury Act to which I have alluded. He was a man of a most powerful and vigorous order of mind, and vigorous enough not to give way to popular clamour unless there was some good foundation for it; and I find in this Jury Act which he passed, that he never thought of taking that power from the sub-sheriff. He introduces it into his own Act, and I believe that if any imputation could be made upon the sub-sheriffs now, they would have been more liable to it then, because the force of public opinion is much stronger now in keeping public men right than it was then.

1163. There has been a suggestion made of unpopularity as regards the execution of those rather onerous duties of challenge by the Crown Solicitor, or forming the panels by the sub-sheriff. It is your opinion, is it not, that that unpopularity is never a personal unpopularity; it is never directed to the person who exercises the duty?—Not at all, unless he introduces something personal into his own conduct. I think that the Irish people are very fair in this, that they give a public man credit for discharging the duties of his office, generally, fairly, and no personal unpopularity attaches to the discharge of a public duty, provided it is done in a fair manner.

1164. But that does not at all prevent unpopularity attaching to the system which the person executes?—No; they are a very quick and clever people, and they are very discriminating.

1165. So that if there is any unpopularity attaching to the system of the selection of jury panels by the sub-sheriff, that unpopularity as regards the law, is not at all likely to be diminished by shifting the duties which he now exercises to the Crown Solicitor, having to exercise an increased power of calling to stand aside?—I do not think that there is any very great outcry at all against the preparation of the panel by the sub-sheriff. I think that there is a much greater outcry against the exercise of challenge to a large extent by the Crown Solicitor. As I have said, if you leave this Act as it stands, you will impose double or treble the necessity for challenging, on the Crown Solicitor. He would be obliged, if he does his duty, to challenge to a very much greater extent than he formerly did, because there are a number of names presented to him by a self-acting process, and of course amongst them will be the very worst names of the county.

1166. The sub-sheriff has been charged with partiality, has he not, from the fact that in some counties he has held political opinions?—I did not hear any of the witnesses charge him with partiality. On the contrary, I noted that Mr. Serjeant Armstrong and the other gentlemen, whom I heard examined, used the word "suspicion" of it; but they never said that it was well founded.

1167. But it was said that the sub-sheriffs were sometimes election agents?—I have no doubt they have been.

1168. Have you ever known a Crown Solicitor or even a chairman taking a very strong part in politics?—I think it is rather the duty of a man to take a strong part in politics. But if you will allow me to say this, if there is one office in Ireland to which you appoint a man as the reward of political services more than another, it is the office of Crown Solicitor and Crown prosecutor at assizes and sessions. Everyone of them almost has obtained that appointment from both sides equally for strong political services; but at the same time no suspicion attaches itself to them, on that account on either side.

1169. You think it unfair to charge that undue partiality to the sub-sheriff, when the same partiality is not charged to other officers who have also strong political leanings?—There would be just the same reason for charging it to the one as to

Mr. *J. Hamilton.*

5 May 1873.

to the other; both charges would be without foundation in my opinion.

1170. If possibilities are contemplated, and it is asked whether juries appointed under the old system did not sometimes give unjust verdicts, may it not also be asked whether juries appointed under the new law may be capable of returning unjust verdicts? —Unless you reform this Act to a very large extent, there would scarcely be an intelligent or right verdict if it rested with the juries alone. But with the able and impartial judges that we have, probably by their assistance in ordinary cases, juries might be guided to what was right; but then it would be the verdicts of the judges, and not of the juries.

1171. As a matter of fact, is it not the case that since this new law has come into operation, very unjust verdicts have been returned, even in the opinion of the judges, and has it not been distinctly stated so by the judges? —I do not wish to answer a general question in general terms, because it would be conveying impressions of my own which might not be well founded. But I can mention one or two instances, and one very remarkable instance, in which the case is over. It was a case of ejectment, tried in the county of Roscommon, where the jury found a verdict directly in the teeth of the evidence. The only question, I believe, that the jury had to try was, whether a notice to quit was served or not. Motion for a new trial, I believe, was granted, and the Chief Justice stated that the verdict was a most disgraceful one; that it was against law, against evidence, and against the obligations of the jury in their oaths; and a new trial has been granted. In fact, there was nothing to try. And another was a case of ejectment. Ejectments are cases in which this new Jury Act will never work, nor any cases in which the rights of property are concerned. A juror stated that while the jury were in deliberation, they had agreed to write a letter to the defendant, who was a middle man. It was an action to set aside a lease made on very favourable terms to a person as being beyond a power in a settlement, and the jury had agreed to write a letter to the defendant, to say that if he would let his lands on reasonable terms to his under tenants, they would find for him; and they wanted the policeman to bring this letter out to the defendant, but he refused. I would rather not say where it was; but there are other persons who can testify to it as well as myself, it was a statement by one of the jurors.

1172. With regard to the system of summons of the jury panels by strict alphabetical rotation, if that is rigidly carried out, does not it throw a more heavy burden of service on the distant jurors, than on the jurors that live near to the town in which they have to serve?—In proportion to the distance, of course, it does.

1173. A distant man has a greater charge for travelling expenses, and he cannot return to his own home, and the consequence is that it is far more expensive and inconvenient to him than to a man that lives near the town, and can return to his home every night?—Of course, that is so.

1174. Then, as regards men in business, and men without constant occupation, a man in business who is obliged to serve once, say, in two years, has a far heavier burden thrown upon him, has he not, than a man who has not a regular occupation?—It is a matter of profit to one, and it is a matter of loss to the other. Still, I should do nothing to exempt men in business from serving on juries, for they are the best jurors.

1175. But still the burden is not equally distributed by that system of alphabetical rotation? —Of course not.

1176. I wish to read to you a letter on that point, and to ask you whether you think that it is a fair statement of the case; it is from a firm carrying on business in Dublin, Carson Brothers, Booksellers, of 7, Grafton-street, and they say, "Our grievance is as follows: We have received this day jury summonses for both members of our firm to attend at the Courts of Exchequer and Queen's Bench on the same day, and every day after, till discharged by the court. Now, the result of this would be, that our business would be left, perhaps for weeks, almost entirely to the care of apprentices, incompetent of course to undertake the management of its affairs, while the inconvenience to our customers, permanent injury to our business, and pecuniary loss to ourselves, which must inevitably result, is really to us a most serious consideration. The annoyance is augmented by the conviction that our being placed in this unpleasant predicament is not in any way necessary in the interests of justice, while it is obvious that should these proceedings become general, the effect upon commercial interests would be disastrous in the extreme. It is conceivable as a contingency, which in the present state of affairs may at any moment arise, that the entire staff of an establishment might be summoned to serve on juries at the same time. That no business could be carried on under such disadvantages, it is unnecessary for us to point out; as it would merely require that such oppressive measures should be repeated in order to paralyse the energy of the most vigorous and flourishing concern in the country." Is that a fair statement of the extreme pressure which the rigid system of rotation entails upon business men?—That is an obvious instance of one of the disadvantages of the Act, in the fact that both members of the same firm, brothers, both men whose names begin with the same letter, should be summoned That never would have occurred when the sheriff had the power; he never would have done so inconvenient a thing as summon the members of the same firm. Of course it may happen, and must happen, under the new system.

1177. Under the new system, where the names of both members of the firm are the same, it is an inevitable necessity that they should both be summoned at the same time, because, if you remember, the sheriff is directed to summon the man whose name begins with A., and then he goes down the list, and begins the list again, and he takes the man next below the man he first summoned; and of course, where the two names are the same, he must take the second member of the firm?—Yes; I can see that that will produce very considerable inconvenience to mercantile men; but at the same time, unless we get mercantile men to attend upon the juries, the jury system will be very bad.

1178. That does not affect, does it, the principle of selection being placed in the hands of some person in summoning the panel?—I am in favour of what I call a power to clear the jury panel of bad men, and avoiding inconveniences of that kind; no sheriff would summon two or three members of the same firm.

1179. *Chairman.*] Has anyone any power to excuse

Mr. J. Hamilton.

5 May 1873.

excuse a juror who has been summoned from attendance?—Unless for some very good cause, a judge will not excuse him.

1180. But the judge could do so, could he not?—I think he could.

1181. Under the circumstances stated in that letter, could a judge, if he thought fit, have excused the attendance of one?—I think that he might. I do not know that he would do it; the one is in the Queen's Bench and the other is in the Exchequer, and each judge would be likely to say, "I will keep you, Mr. So-and-So, and let my brother judge excuse your brother if he likes." But the judge could excuse him, of course.

1182. If a juror did not attend who had been summoned he could be fined, could he not?—Yes.

1183. Have you ever known a fine inflicted under such circumstances as non-attendance; would not the circumstances stated in that letter be considered a sufficient excuse?—That would depend very much upon whether a proper jury could be got without his attendance. I am sure that if a proper jury could be got without the attendance of one of those gentlemen, the judge would never think of inflicting a fine upon him. But it is not at all impossible that, if his absence caused the trial to be abortive, the judge might fine him.

1184. Mr. *Bruen.*] You have attended very frequently the courts in Dublin, have you not?—Yes.

1185. And you have heard juries summoned?—Yes.

1186. Have you not heard these pleas advanced by jurymen, that it is a very great inconvenience to them to attend; did you ever hear a juryman let off on that account?—I think it would be great weakness to let off a juryman on the ground of inconvenience.

1187. Mr. *O'Reilly.*] Have you ever known jurymen let off on those grounds?—I cannot recollect that sort of thing.

1188. Mr. *Bruen.*] At all events, if the judge exercised his power of letting off a juryman from reasons of this kind, it would be a departure, would it not, from the rigid system of alphabetical rotation?—Of course it would be.

1189. Are you aware that in the English Bill, which is now before Parliament, the system of alphabetical rotation is not proposed, and that selection is allowed to the sheriff?—It appears to give the sheriff the same power that he had under our former system.

1190. It is slightly modified; he is required, before summoning a man a second time, to summon every man on his panel who has not served?—Yes; that is an improvement. He is not to summon a man twice till he has gone through the list; that appears to be the effect of it.

1191. Viscount *Crichton.*] What, in your opinion, were the defects of Perrin's Act?—The defects of the late Act were these, that the qualification for a juror under it was, that he should be a freeholder or a leaseholder; and then those classes had so very much diminished in number that the Act ceased to be applicable, and the sheriffs often summoned men who were neither freeholders nor leaseholders; very respectable men, no doubt, but there would have been a cause for challenge to the array; it has been alleged as a ground of challenge to the array, and therefore it became necessary to enlarge the area; and, as I said before, I approve of the principle of this Act, so far as it enlarges the area of jurors beyond that in Perrin's Act. Then the other objection to Perrin's Act was the great abuse of it which existed principally in the city of Dublin, and which I have before described, that all the most proper men, virtually, never attended, and all the worst men did, in the city of Dublin.

1192. The evil effects were conspicuous in the city of Dublin?—Yes, in the county of Dublin that was not so; but now it is very curious that the effect of this Act in the county of Dublin is as prejudicial as it is beneficial in the city: the other day in the Court of Probate, Judge Warren, the judge of the Probate Court, a very calm and temperate judge, refused to allow a case to be tried by a county jury, as he said that the county juries that had been returned were perfectly incapable, as a rule, of trying the cases before him, and he refused on that account to allow the case to be tried before a jury of the county of Dublin.

1193. Was it not the abuse of the administration of that Act in the city of Dublin that principally raised the outcry against it?—It was unquestionably. I will tell you what it caused in the city of Dublin; a very low class of jurors created a very low class of business. It gave encouragement to speculative actions, and those speculative actions, I need not say, were not brought by respectable members of the attorney's profession. In my opinion it degraded the whole profession, or both professions, to a certain extent, and caused a great number of vexatious actions to be brought which otherwise would not have been brought.

1194. Is there any security in the present Act against a recurrence of the same abuse?—Not the smallest, and if the judges do not exercise an increased vigilance over this Act, the same result must follow in a short time.

1195. Mr. Serjeant Armstrong described the operation of the present Act as amounting to a burlesque almost. Do you attribute this result to any defect in the administration of the Act?—The administration has nothing to do with this Act. It is a self-acting affair; you cannot administer it; that is the vice of it.

1196. You do not expect that any better results will arise in course of time if the Act remains unaltered?—I think not.

1197. Did you observe a marked absence of respectable jurors at the last assizes?—I observed a marked absence of respectable jurors from the jury box; but in the towns, in Omagh, for instance, where Mr. Serjeant Armstrong says there was a great absence, I saw, and was conversing with a great number of respectable jurors who had served on juries in the olden times, and who were laughing at the present juries when they saw them. They were there, but they were not called under this rotatory system.

1198. Has the effect of the Act been to secure fairness or intelligence in juries, do you think?—Neither the one nor the other.

1199. With regard to the former method of preparation of the panel, do you think that any actual injustice followed from it in any cases?—I do not believe on the Crown side of the court that any injustice ever followed from it. I am perfectly satisfied of this, that if a judge indicated to any jury (at least, within my experience) in the slightest possible way, that he thought the evidence was weak against the prisoner, that prisoner

Mr. J. Hamilton.

5 May 1873.

prisoner would not be convicted by any jury that ever was in the box. There is always somebody on a jury, or more than one, who are timid, and are anxious to acquit rather than to convict.

1200. Have you known many challenges to the array?—Very few indeed; and I think that if it could be proved that the panel was unfairly managed, there would have been a greater number of challenges to the array. It is easy to allege a thing, but if it could have been proved there would have been a greater number of challenges to the array. Young barristers are very anxious to distinguish themselves by a thing of that sort. A successful challenge to the array would make a make a man's fortune almost at the bar as a junior.

1201. I do not know whether you heard Mr. Serjeant Armstrong say, in answer to Mr. Heron, at Question 919, "It is almost impossible to get the triers to find anything right; I have known most ridiculous conclusions found by the triers; do you agree in that?—Yes; I think that the system of the appointment of triers is very bad. You object to the array of a panel, and what do you do? You take the two first jurors upon that panel who answer to try this question. That appears to me a ridiculous mode of doing it. The judge ought to select two men beyond suspicion in the court, to try the challenge.

1202. Suggestions have been made before this Committee that the constabulary should be obliged to serve summonses to attend on juries. What is your opinion upon that point; do you think that they would be proper persons to serve summonses?—No; I agree with Mr. Serjeant Armstrong, that I think the service of the summons would be admirably managed through the post office; but I think that the service by the constabulary would be very objectionable. In the first place it would add very much to the expense, and this is a very expensive Act to administer. You would be obliged to bring in from the most remote districts, in a large county like Cork or Galway, nearly all the constabulary men, in order to prove the service of those summonses, and then I can imagine very ludicrous things occurring in the service. I can imagine a serjeant of the police going up to Rory of the Hills with a summons, inviting him to come and try one of his own gang before a judge at the assizes, and grins would be on the face of each of them as soon as this was done. That sort of thing would be a burlesque on justice in many instances.

1203. By a summons through the post office, I presume you mean a summons by registered letter?—The system which Mr. Serjeant Armstrong mentioned I think: that if there is any man so utterly obscure and remote as never to go to the post office, or that a letter could not reach him, he is just as well off a jury as on it. It is not that kind of person that we want.

1204. In your evidence the last day, I think you said that in Donegal, with which county you are connected, and know very well, many jurors "complained bitterly of the distances that they were obliged to walk to attend the assizes; those people really could not afford it; they had not the means of getting the common necessaries of life;" that was at assizes; would not that hardship be needlessly increased in the case of jurors summoned to attend on juries at quarter sessions?—I should recommend that no juror should be summoned to attend at quarter sessions out of his own division.

1205. I have received a communication from the Associated Law Clerks of Ireland. I do not know what that body may be, but I dare say you do. The secretary writes to me, and he states that numbers of the members of that association have been summoned to serve as jurors in cases in which they have had the conduct and management of the suit at the trial, and that he is prepared to depose to those facts if necessary. Do you agree in the suggestion that has been made that law clerks should be exempted from serving on juries?—I think so, and publicans also.

1206. And bank clerks; do you think that they ought to be exempt?—I do not know; banks are very rich bodies.

1207. Do not you think it would be a great inconvenience to the business of the country, if bank clerks were taken away from their duties?—Bank clerks are very intelligent men, and banks are very rich, and can very well afford to pay for the inconvenience by an increase of their staff. I should not agree in that suggestion.

1208. Do you think that the exemptions at present, numerous as they are, of a very large and intelligent body of men from serving on juries might be very usefully diminished?—I have not considered that part of the question sufficiently to give an answer that would be worth having.

1209. Mr. *Downing*.] As far as I understand your evidence, it would be rather favourable to the Act which is known as Perrin's Act?—Yes.

1210. And that that judge discharged his duties properly?—Yes, I think so; except for this: that I think the area had become contracted from which jurors were taken, and I approve of this Act as far as it increases the area.

1211. But, in truth, the state of things which we have just heard from yourself and from Mr. Serjeant Armstrong, arose from the judges in Dublin neglecting their duty?—I do not like to use such a phrase towards men of their eminence; but I think that finding a sufficient quantity of jurors, they were not energetic enough in compelling the attendance of better men, and that in so far they neglected their duty.

1212. We all know that in the city of Dublin there are a very large number of highly respectable commercial men, and men who are living upon their own means, who are bound to attend on the jury, and if they had been compelled to attend upon those juries the state of things which you have described could never have arisen?—I think not.

1213. I think I understood you to say that it was only in Dublin that that state of things was so very prominently observed? That is my own experience. We have not the same class of what I may call professional jurors on circuit.

1214. You have spoken of the very high character of the late Judge Perrin, and very rightly, as every one who knows him will say: are you aware that there was a committee of the House of Lords to inquire into that very Act of his?—I am not.

1215. Are you aware that it was condemned in terms much more severely than even you condemn this Act?—I am not aware of that; but I think that Judge Perrin was a man of that strong vigorous

Mr. *J. Hamilton.*

May 1873.

vigorous mind, that would not mind condemnation or popular clamour unless it had foundation.

1216. Allow me to ask your attention to some of the questions and answers given before the Committee upon that very Act; I think you said that you were the chairman for Sligo?—Yes.

1217. Mr. Fausset, one of the magistrates of that county was examined; I have a report here of the evidence, which I will hand in, if necessary, to make it evidence; he is asked, "For the last few years" (that was during the period in which the Act was in operation) "the petty jurors were of a lower class; not the same description of persons as formerly; many of them very illiterate, could not either read or write;" he is further asked, and he says, "There were 83 indictments found at last Sligo Assizes, and the number of convictions were, I believe, not more than six or seven;" that was a very lamentable state of things, was it not?—Yes.

1218. He says, "I recollect Mr. Dudgeon, the Crown solicitor, stating to me he thought it was useless to go to the expense of having assizes in Sligo;" that is worse than any state of things that you have seen?—I have seen nothing like that in Sligo; on the contrary, there is a very good state of things indeed there.

1219. He also says, "In Sligo in 1838 the number of persons committed was 224, indicted 155, and convicted 20 only;" that is still worse?—Yes.

1220. And he says, "The small number of convictions was attributable, probably, to the formation of the juries." Mr. Rowan, the resident magistrate, was examined, and he says, "I am very sorry to say the recent Jury Act has put a class of persons on the panel, many of whom are likely to be Ribbonmen;" that is exactly your point?—I am sure that there were frequently men of that class on the panel under the old Act. You could not possibly keep them off in every instance.

1221. Mr. Taheteau, the stipendiary magistrate said, "Juries since the new Act has come into force are of an inferior class; it is more difficult to obtain a verdict of guilty, though the evidence would lead you to consider it sufficient;" that is rather an unfortunate state of things, is it not?—Yes; but all I can say is that under the operation of that Act that state of things does not exist now; it has enormously improved. I suppose that Perrin's Act lowered the qualification from the prior one, and this Act, in order to make things better, lowers it still more.

1222. Are you aware that there was a Committee of the House of Commons in the year 1852, the Select Committee on Outrages (Ireland)?—I am not aware.

1223. There were upon that Committee the then Attorney General for Ireland, Mr. Napier, Mr. Caulfield, Mr. Scully, Mr. O'Flagherty, Mr. Leslie, Mr. Gould, Mr. Bright, Mr. Fortescue, Lord Naas, Sir James Graham, Sir William Somerville, Mr. Hatchell, and Judge Keogh, a vigorous judge, you admit?—Yes, a man I entirely respect.

1224. It was a strong Committee?—Yes; they were very great names.

1225. Will you allow me to read to you the conclusions that they came to. "That the juror's book be made up from a list of the names of all persons rated under the poor law valuation, to the amount of not less than *l.*, to be furnished to the clerk of the peace or other responsible officer, by the clerk of the union in which the rated property is situate," that is exactly what was done under this Act which we are now discussing?—Yes.

1226. "That there shall be but one panel of jurors to try issues, criminal and civil, at each assizes, in addition to any special jury which may be lawfully summoned, and that measures shall be adopted to secure strict impartiality in the selection of the jury panel," do you agree in that?—Certainly; that is most desirable, and I think that one of the means by which you should try to secure strict impartiality would be to keep off the panel men who would not honestly do their duty.

1227. That power you would give solely to the sub-sheriff, as the only fitting person that you think is capable of selecting the panel properly?—I do not say that you might not substitute somebody else for the sub-sheriff, if you thought you could find a more trustworthy public officer to prepare the panel; but what I say is, that it must be a person that shall do it properly, and nobody else can do it so well, practically; and, in so far as my experience goes, no actual injustice has followed from the way in which it has hitherto been done.

1228. Is it your present view, with regard to selection, that the one person who is fitted to discharge that duty is the sub-sheriff?—What I have said is, that I see no reason for changing the sub-sheriff; but I say that if this Committee, in its wisdom, shall find out any more trustworthy public officer to prepare the panel, of course that would be desirable.

1229. Would you assist the Committee in that, from your own knowledge, and name any person that you think is more fitted to discharge that duty than the sub-sheriff?—I cannot.

1230. You stated to-day that you knew five sub-sheriffs, and not one of them could be guilty of arranging the panel?—I said arranging the panel unfairly.

1231. You are acquainted, are you not, with the north of Ireland in particular?—Yes, it was those five counties that I am in the habit of going the circuit, and therefore I confine my observation to those five counties.

1232. What are these counties?—I omit Longford, because I am not in the habit of going there, but I believe that there is a very respectable sub-sheriff there. The counties that I go on my own circuit are Cavan, Fermanagh, Tyrone, Donegal, and Londonderry, and the only reason why I mention them is because I go that circuit, and have been going it for a great many years.

1233. Are you acquainted at all with the county of Monaghan?—No, I am quite unacquainted with Monaghan.

1234. I understand you, with regard to your experience of this Act, to say that, as chairman of Sligo, you have had none?—None, I may say: but my experience, as chairman, under the late Act, is very favourable to that county. I think that the jurors do their duty very fairly, and I have had party cases as well as others.

1235. As regards Longford, I understand you to say that you do not practice in the criminal court?—I have been in the criminal court in Longford, but I go very little to Longford, for the reason I mentioned, that there is scarcely ever any civil business in Longford.

1236. At the last assizes, there was not one record

Mr. *J. Hamilton.* 5 May 1873.

record tried there, I believe? — No, I was not there, and I very seldom go to Longford.

1237. As regards Fermanagh, I think you told the Committee that Fermanagh before gave a very indifferent jury? — I think so, and that is the opinion of the circuit, certainly inferior to Cavan and Tyrone.

1238. Were you at Fermanagh this last assizes? —I was.

1239. Were they about the same class of jurors as formerly? — I think they were rather worse, but the jurors in Fermanagh have had very little experience; there is scarcely ever a Crown case in Fermanagh, except about the 12th of July.

1240. As regards Londonderry, if you look at the returns you will find that there is a very small increase of jurors at all in that county?— I said, as well as I remember, that the difference in Londonderry was not very sensibly felt.

1241. You have no complaints about Londonderry? — No, and one reason why is, that the town itself is a very thriving town, and supplies most excellent jurors, and there are a great number of other thriving towns which supply excellent jurors.

1242. You stated that you were in the town of Lifford; were you engaged in any case there?— I was retained in several cases, but we were obliged to postpone the greater part of the Lifford assizes in consequence of the judge being detained in Tyrone, and unable to come on to Lifford, so that only very trifling cases were tried, and we had not much experience of the Act there; but I know that the county of Donegal jurors were worse. I saw that they were a very inferior class.

1243. It was there that you chaffed the jury, was it not?— No, that was at Omagh principally, but everywhere we did, we followed the example of Serjeant Armstrong.

1244. You were not quite prepossessed in favour of the Act, even before you had knowledge of its working? — I expected that bad results would follow from it in consequence of the lowering of the qualification of the jurors.

1245. You were in the committee-room on Thursday, when I referred to no less than eight Bills that were brought in by Mr. Whiteside, Mr. Napier, Mr. Fitzgerald, Mr. Keogh, and several other attorney generals and solicitor generals, and none of them raised the qualification beyond 30 *l.*? — Yes, I think that their Acts would have disappointed their expectations. I am sure that every one of the gentlemen that you have mentioned, including the framers of this Act, expected different results, but as Serjeant Armstrong said, the practical results are to be considered.

1246. As I understand, you approve of having an ignorant jury?—I do not. I think it would be very bad for the bar to have an ignorant jury, and for the country too.

1247. But I understood you to say that the jurors found verdicts that were directed by the judges?—I said that ignorance was not the worst fault; that an ignorant jury, where their passions or prejudices were not excited, generally did as the judges bid them do; and if they did that generally, you will observe that that would be ignoring trial by jury altogether.

1248. Do you mean the Committee to understand that you are an advocate for getting rid of trial by jury?—No, certainly not; on the contrary. What I should like would be as intelligent and fair a class of jurors as I could have; that would be much better for the bar, and much better for the public.

1249. As I understand you, you would wish, however it is to be arrived at, that all the panel should be prepared with the most perfect impartiality?— Surely; but then I attach to the word impartiality the meaning that every man on the panel will do his duty.

1250. Do you know Mr. Mitchell, the sub-sheriff of the county of Monaghan?—I do not.

1251. You are aware, are you not, that he was removed from office?—I was not aware that the sub-sheriff was removed. I am aware that the high sheriff was removed.

1252. Was that because he would not remove the sub-sheriff?—Yes.

1253. Do you know why he was removed?— The high sheriff was removed, because, as you say, he refused to remove the sub-sheriff, and the reason, I believe, that he was required to remove the sub-sheriff was, because a challenge to the array had succeeded at Monaghan.

1254. Was that because the sub-sheriff had returned a jury in the words of Serjeant Armstrong, "to order"?—I will not say that. I remember something about that challenge to the array. It was alleged that the panel was prepared so as to exclude men who ought to have been on it, and to put on men who ought not to have been on it, with the object of an unfair trial. It was a case of homicide, in which a Catholic, I think, had been killed by Orangemen, or Protestants.

1255. There was also a case, was there not, in which a Roman Catholic of the name of McKenna, was to be tried for the murder of a man named Clark?—I do not know about the last, but the former I know; and I know that this challenge came on to be tried in the usual way, the two first persons who answered to their names were the triers. They happened, I think, unfortunately, to be both Roman Catholics, one was a person who had taken an interest in the prosecution of the case, and they found, as I heard, and as was generally alleged, directly against the charge of the judge. The executive then communicated with the sheriff, desiring him to remove his sub-sheriff, but he refused to do it, and then they remove himself, and he complained that they did that without ever consulting the judge who had tried the case, as to whether he was satisfied with the finding of the triers. Those are the circumstances of the case that were most prominently before the public at the time.

1256. I think you said that you were not at Monaghan?—No.

1257. Then you are only giving us what you heard?—I say that those were the circumstances that were most prominently before the public, and what I heard from members of the bar who were there. The public complaint made by the high sheriff was, that he was dismissed without the judge being consulted as to the case that was tried before him.

1258. Are you aware that there were on the panel 250 names?—I could not tell you that, but I am sure that whatever you state is certain to be accurate.

1259. I will put it into your hands (*handing the panel to the Witness*); will you tell me how many there are there?—It appears to be 250 names.

1260. Keeping

Mr. *J. Hamilton.*

5 May 1873.

1260. Keeping in your recollection that Baird and his son were to be tried for the murder of a man of the name of Hughes, who was shot in the street, as was alleged; an innocent man, who had nothing to say to the riot, and that M'Kenna, a Roman Catholic, was to be tried for the murder of Clark, and that that panel contained 250 names, and, taking the whole population of Monaghan at 90,000, of whom 60,000 are Roman Catholics and 30,000 comprising all other denominations, do you think that it was a fair complaint that the sheriff had put only 40 Roman Catholics out of 250?—Without knowing the whole circumstances of the case, I will not say that it was fair or unfair. *Primâ facie*, it appears strange, that is all I can say; but I do not know any of the circumstances.

1261. As a lawyer, you would know that the jury is generally selected from about the first 48 or from that to 60 men?—Yes, I should say that they are most likely to be the persons to turn up, because, as you say, the panel is taken right from beginning to end; therefore I would approve of that suggestion of Mr. Coffey's, that they should be ballotted for.

1262. Where there were those very important trials, involving politics and religion, would you think it proper for the sub-sheriff to put on the first 48 names, two Roman Catholics, and those two men publicans who could not serve?—As I have said already, I think that it is most desirable to have mixed juries.

1263. I put a case to you; will you have the goodness to answer my question?—I cannot answer your question, because if I thought that the Roman Catholics were violent partizans, I would leave them off, whether they were Catholics or not; and if I thought that the Protestants were violent partizans, I would leave them off, whether they were Protestants or not.

1264. With great respect, you do not quite see my question; it is not leaving off or leaving on, because they were on the panel; do you think that the sheriff acted fairly and impartially in putting only two Roman Catholics on the first 48 names, of which the jury, you say, is selected? —It is perfectly impossible to answer that question, unless I knew the particular circumstances which may have been in the knowledge of the sheriff; for instance, if I was trying an Orangeman in a party case in the county of Down, I should take care not to put Orangemen first on the panel; I say most decidedly not; and if I was trying in another part of the county where I thought violent prejudices were the other way, I would keep the other side off.

1265. Will you answer me in this way: *prima facie*, does it appear to be a most unfair return? —*Prima facie*, it does not look well, but it is perfectly impossible to say whether it was right or not, unless you knew the circumstances of the case. I can quite imagine that it might have been perfectly right and perfectly fair.

1266. Let us see what the result was; do you think that it was satisfactory to the ends of justice, and that the people of Monaghan could have faith in the administration of the law, when they found, upon the trial of Baird and his son, 12 men who at all events were Protestants, and a great many of whom, as was believed, were Orangemen?—They would have been naturally dissatisfied.

1267. They were both acquitted, were they not?—I do not know that.

1268. Was it not after the two Bairds were acquitted by an exclusively Protestant or Orange jury that the challenge to the array was put in by Mr. Butt and my friend Mr. Heron?—I do not know anything about it.

1269. You read the papers?—Yes; but I am not sure that I ever read the newspapers about it, for I take very little interest in those kind of things.

1270. Were you acquainted with a gentleman who was very notorious (I do not say it in an offensive way), Mr. Samuel Grey, of Ballybay? —I am not acquainted with him; but I have heard of him over and over again.

1271. You are aware, are you not, that he was tried for the murder of a man of the name of Shevlin in the year 1856?—I cannot say that I am.

1272. Do not you remember that he was defended by Mr. Whiteside, and that it was a very remarkable trial?—I know nothing about it.

1273. Would you think that it would be calculated to impress people generally, with confidence in the administration of the criminal law, if there had been upon his trial 12 Protestants, or Orangemen?—If he was an Orangeman, and the other was not, and the jury were 12 Orangemen, I think that would be very wrong.

1274. He avowed himself one, and he never denied it?—I daresay he was; but I do not know whether the jury were or not.

1275. You are aware, are you not, that he was acquitted?—I am not sure about that; was not there some some question of law reserved and argued?

1276. That was another case, but he was allowed to challenge; he was tried three times? —I know nothing about that.

1277. Are you aware, for it is rather important that one of the grounds of challenge at the Monaghan Assizes, in the case of M'Kenna, was that the sub-sheriff was actually an Orangeman, and a member of an Orange lodge?—That is a ground which I was not aware of.

1278. And that the Crown did not traverse, but admitted the fact that he was a member of an Orange lodge?—I am not aware; I am not so intimately acquainted with it as that.

1279. Do not you know that he was examined, and he admitted that he was?—I do not remember that.

1280. Were you ever in an Orange lodge?—Never in my life.

1281. Have you heard that in all those cases in which an Orangeman is tried for any offence, his brethren collect a fund to defend him?—I do not believe that it is true in all cases, but I am sure that it is very general when he is tried for an Orange offence, that is, for a party procession, or anything of that sort, but I also know that there is the same thing done on the opposite side.

1282. When you talk of the very strong objections which you have to seeing a Fenian, or a Ribbonman, on a jury, I take it for granted that you have the same horror of seeing an Orangeman upon a jury?—Most unquestionably, in the trial of an Orangeman, or a man for an offence in which the sympathies of the Orangemen would be likely to be involved, precisely the same, and I should set him aside with exactly the same rigour.

1283. How are you to know him?—I should not

Mr. J. Hamilton. 5 May 1873.

not know him at all unless I was informed. You do not mean to insinuate that I am an Orangeman.

1284. How then do you know whether a man is a Ribbonman or an Orangeman?—I should rely upon the men who know every Orangeman and Ribbonman in the country. The constabulary know them well. Besides that, there is no concealment of the fact of a man being an Orangeman; but every man conceals that he is a Ribbonman; there is no difficulty about the one, and there is little practical difficulty about the other.

1285. You stated, did you not, in one of the first answers that you gave, that you were very glad to find that you agreed with Mr. Serjeant Armstrong in the evidence which he had given?—That is, as to the working of the Act; but I differ from him *in toto* about the mode of forming the panel; and I differ from him *in toto* about the possibility of the chairman being the person to select.

1286. Here is your answer to Question 1036, which the noble Chairman put to you: "What are the principal recommendations which you would make for the improvement of the juries?" and you say, "I am happy to say, for my own sake, that I agree almost entirely with the principles which Mr. Serjeant Armstrong announced"?—Those were the principles of increasing the qualification largely, and of selection.

1287. Only those?—That is all.

1288. Then you differ, do you not, from Serjeant Armstrong with regard to the arrangement of the alphabetical order?—I do, as far as the panel is concerned.

1289. You would not have the returns made in alphabetical order?—I would have the lists prepared in alphabetical order, as they were under Perrin's Act, and as they are under this, and then for the sheriff to form his panel as before.

1290. That is to say, the sheriff should return the panel as before?—Yes.

1291. Without reference to order or taking them alphabetically?—Yes.

1292. That strikes, does it not, at the principle of the whole Act?—No doubt; I think that the effects which Mr. Serjeant Armstrong and Mr. Coffey described, arose necessarily from the adoption of the principle of the Act that I object to.

1293. Mr. Serjeant Armstrong is perhaps a man of all the bar in Ireland that has the largest experience, as a *nisi prius* and criminal lawyer?—He certainly is.

1294. He said in Question 766, "I had opportunities of hearing in many quarters, professional and unprofessional, the general feeling on the subject, and strange to say there appears to be, as far as my own knowledge goes, a unanimity of feeling upon this one subject in Ireland, for I have not heard one dissenting voice as to the wisdom and propriety of distributing the business of jurymen over the whole county, and the principle sought to be carried out by this alphabetical selection, appears to be universally approved of?"—That is as I understand it as far as the preparation of the lists is concerned, and I agree with it.

1295. The alphabetical order of the selection?—I did not hear him use the word selection.

1296. He says, "The principles sought to be carried out by this alphabetical selection appears to be universally approved of"?—Then my experience is directly opposite. I hear the Act universally condemned on account of the results which have followed from this alphabetical selection; and when I find him raising the qualifications of common jurors to the qualification of special jurors, and insisting on the principle of selection himself, it appears to me that it is impossible that he can approve of the Act.

1297. He says he does; and you yourself, in the answer that you gave, admitted that it would be impossible to raise the qualification as Mr. Serjeant Armstrong recommended, because there would not be a sufficient number of persons to be found to sit on the jury?—Indeed, I think so. I think his qualification is impracticable, and that is the reason why I think it is so necessary to retain the old system, because you cannot get a qualification which, according to the opinion of Mr. Serjeant Armstrong, would give fair juries.

1298. You heard Mr. Serjeant Armstrong express a very strong opinion against giving the power of selection to the sheriff, and say that under no circumstances would he go back to that system?—I do; but I think he has gone to a worse one.

1299. In answer to a question put by the noble Chairman, Question 779, "You are not surprised that there should have been an impression that the panels were not impartially framed?" he said, "I am not in the least surprised; that is the great merit of the Act as it stands, that it strikes a decided blow at such a system. I have not the slightest hesitation in saying that, under the old system, cases occurred in which you could have a jury to order, and if you prescribed your jury you might get it. I have not the slightest hesitation in saying so, from my own observation, I have been obliged in Dublin;" and then he gives the Dublin case; do you agree, that even in Dublin that is the case, that you can get a jury to order?—The question is what he means by to order; I should like a more definite expression.

1300. If you prescribed your jury, you might get it?—Whom does he mean by "you"?

1301. Any person interested; the attorney?—Then I do not agree with him that you could get a jury to order. I do not believe that any subsheriff would so grossly violate his duty and his interest; and I may say that the force of public opinion is now so strong, that in my opinion no public officer could dare to violate his duty to that extent. We know that in former times the sheriff of London could hang anybody the Government liked, and we know that in former times the Prime Minister could corrupt half the House of Commons, and we know that in former times the judges were corrupt; but the force of public opinion is so strong now-a-days as to render those things perfectly impossible of recurrence. Therefore to argue that because abuses existed a great many years ago the same must crop up now is, I think, omitting to observe the progress of the times.

1302. In answer to Question 1045, "Then, in fact, you do not approve of the alphabetical process of selection contained in the Act?" you said, "I think no witness that I have heard as yet can possibly approve of that when Mr. Coffey suggested such a power as that the Crown should have, in every instance, the right to try the prisoners by special juries, and when Mr. Serjeant

Mr. *J. Hamilton.*

5 May 1873.

Serjeant Armstrong would give such a stringent power to the chairman of the county," you said that no witness had spoken in favour of the alphabetical process of selection?—Not as it stands in the Act when such tremendous remedies are proposed.

1303. The power given to the chairman does not in the slightest degree affect the selection, does it?—But if you do these two things: if you strike off the whole of the present common juries by raising the present qualification to 50 *l.*, which is the qualification proposed for special jurors, or if you adopt the principle of allowing the Crown to try every prisoner for a serious case by a special jury, you do not want selection, because you get a class of men who are not common jurors at all.

1304. You spoke of two cases; one of them in the county of Roscommon; that was an ejectment case, was it not?—Yes.

1305. Was not it a question of whether the notice had reached the hand of the tenant?—Yes.

1306. And that question was put by the judge to the jury?—Yes; but I believe that the tenant admitted that it had. The jury were called out by the judge to know what they were hesitating about, and he asked them whether they believed that the notice to quit had reached the hands of the defendant, and they said that they did. Then the judge told them that that was the only question to be tried; but still they went in and refused to find for the plaintiff.

1307. In your experience have you very often seen juries whom it was rather difficult to get to find a verdict in a particular way?—Of course. I do not mean to say that the former Act was perfect at all. Of course you cannot expect to find perfection in any Act.

1308. Mr. *Heron.*] I just wish to refer to this Monaghan assizes case in 1869, as I happened to be there, and as Mr. McCarthy Downing has called your attention to it; in the case of the two Bairds, they were to be tried, were they not, on an indictment for the murder of a Roman Catholic?—Yes.

1309. And McKenna was to be tried on an indictment for the murder of a Protestant and an Orangeman?—Yes; at least I suppose that was so.

1310. And the grand jury had found both bills?—Yes

1311. Then the first 48 names on the panel were all Protestants except two, who were publicans; have you a doubt in your own mind but that Mr. Mitchell, the sub-sheriff, did that by design?—If you mean to say that he knew he was doing that, of course he did, no doubt.

1312. He did that, did he not, to exclude Roman Catholics from the first 48 names on the panel?—Of course he must have done it for that purpose. I was engaged in the Fenian trials in Dublin, and it was alleged that when the Crown Solicitor came forward and ordered men to stand aside whom he knew, probably, to be sympathisers with the movement, not a religious movement at all, but if those men happened to be Roman Catholics, it was universally alleged that they were set aside by the Crown Solicitor because they were Roman Catholics. I do not believe that myself at all.

1313. On the panel at Monaghan it was proved that out of 250 there were at least 84 members of the Orange lodges at Monaghan or the neighbourhood of Monaghan?—Then that was entirely wrong, in my opinion.

1314. Mr. Mitchell also stated that he was himself, and had been for many years, an Orangeman, and had subscribed every year to the party procession?—Then it would have been much better that he should not have been the person to prepare that panel.

1315. On the whole, you have not a doubt but that that panel was properly quashed?—All those facts would certainly lead me to believe that the panel ought to be quashed, because I think that justice should be as far as possible beyond suspicion.

1316. Are you aware that Mr. Mitchell was the sub-sheriff when Sam Grey, of Ballybay was tried?—No, I do not know anything about Sam Grey or Mr. Mitchell. I never saw them in my life.

1317. You mentioned, I think, that the Fermanagh jurors under the old system were worse than the Cavan jurors?—I think that they were inferior in intelligence.

1318. And you were satisfied with the Cavan jurors?—Yes, fairly satisfied; although there have been gross failures of justice in Cavan.

1319. In the Queen and Fay, a case which was tried three times, the case against Fay was the alleged murder of a sweetheart; and I would refer you to the judgment of Chief Justice Whiteside and Mr. Justice Fitzgerald on the application to change the name, which is reported in the Irish Reports, Common Law Series, 6th volume, page 446. Mr. Justice Fitzgerald says: "I am amazed to hear that the practice in Cavan has been that the panel summoned to try criminal cases has always been selected from the lowest class of jurors. Now, I do not wish to say one word that would interfere with the proper discretion of sheriffs as to the manner in which they should summon juries, but I would express my opinion that if the panel has been selected from the lowest grade of jurors, the sheriffs' discretion has been most erroneously exercised. I do not say that it ought to be taken from the highest, but from both high and low impartially. The fault is probably due, not altogether to the sheriff, but in some degree to the gentry of the county, who shrink from the performance of a disagreeable duty, and in doing so commit a grave error." I also refer you to what Chief Justice Whiteside says: "The sub-sheriff, in his affidavit has described the condition of the jury panel of the county Cavan. He says that it is principally composed of small shopkeepers and tenant farmers, and that several of the jurors have stated to him that they would not find the prisoner guilty under any circumstances, as they were apprehensive that if they did so they might suffer injury in their persons or property. Now, the sheriff seems to think that he is bound to return such persons as he has thus described to serve as jurors in criminal cases, while by his own description they are most unfit persons;" do not you see that under the old system as regards the County of Cavan, nearly every evil that you have stated as applicable to the present system existed?—I do not see so. My experience of the jurors of the county of Cavan was that as a rule they did their duty very well. And I think that the judges might have added that there was another motive which influenced the sub-sheriffs, that is the tremendous abuse that would have been heaped upon them by a section of the press if they

Mr. *J. Hamilton.*

5 May 1873.

they summoned jurors of a high class alone to try peasants, and that that operated injuriously upon them.

1320. In the Monaghan case, there was only one magistrate summoned on the whole of the panel of nine, and the rest were very small shopkeepers and very small farmers?—I know nothing about Monaghan.

1321. In Cavan there was not a single magistrate upon the panel; do not you see that that made them as bad in Cavan as regards that case as could be?—I do not see that my experience is the opposite. The jurors in Cavan, generally speaking, did their duty very well. As to the fact, as to whether there was a failure of justice, I believe that the prisoner escaped each time by one juror, and one alone; and in most of those cases in which notorious criminals escape, it is through the medium of one or two jurors, and not of the whole panel at all. It is very difficult to make the panel good enough even where the sheriff has the power, but here you have no power over it at all, and therefore you have got evidently from bad to worse, if the former was bad.

1322. From your experience in the North-west circuit, do you mean to say that for the last 15 or 20 years you consider that the jurors have acted fairly in party cases, say in the July and August riots?—No, I do not go that length; I think there were many cases in which there ought to have been convictions of the rioters on both sides, in which they were not convicted. I will mention an expedient that was adopted at the last assizes at Omagh, in order to produce a better result. I was taken in to aid the Crown, the great body of Crown counsel being employed in that important case which I mentioned. We had a number of Protestants and a number of Catholics, who had had a fight; pistols had been fired, and blows struck; and on consultation we came to the conclusion that although we had prepared a number of indictments against the parties singly, and in batches, there was no use before the kind of jury that we had, in trying them in that way, and the only thing we tried them for was riot, and we put them altogether in the dock, Protestants and Catholics, altogether. And the result of that was, that through the ability of the judge, we managed to make, I believe, the Protestants on the jury convict the Catholics, and the Catholics convict the Protestants; so that we got a number of convictions by herding them altogether in the dock, but then we had to withdraw the more serious charges.

1323. That is since the new Act of Parliament, is it not?—Yes.

1324. Therefore, since the new Act, you have got a perfectly satisfactory verdict, finding them all guilty of riot, both Protestants and Catholics, from having a mixed jury?—It was by very dexterous management, and great vigour and skill, on the part of judge who tried the case.

1325. Viscount *Crichton*.] Could not you have done the same thing under the old Act?—Yes, of course, if we had done the same thing under the old Act, we should have had the same result; but we did do that which was a very serious thing; we had to withdraw the charges of firing pistols at each other, and that sort of thing, and the simple conviction was for riot.

1326. Mr. *Heron*.] What sentence did they get?—A very trifling sentence; it was considered a great piece of luck to get them convicted at all.

1327. Under the old Act, supposing the sheriff had the selection, would not that panel, as regards the first 50 names, in all probability have been a Protestant panel?—It would not; at least, I do not believe it would. I believe that the panel would have been fairly enough chosen, but there would have been names on it which would have had a tendency to acquit on either side. Perhaps you will allow me to mention as to that challenge of mine which was adverted to; it was not stated on the last occasion, and I forgot it at the time, that one great reason for the challenge there was, that it was a case in which an Orangeman was tried for the homicide of a Catholic. The sub-sheriff and his brother were both Catholics, and the prosecution was conducted, I may say, by the sub-sheriff's brother. I think that was the main ground of suspicion. In short, it was the sub-sheriff himself who was conducting the prosecution. He was a gentleman named John M'Crossan, whom I daresay you know, and his brother Charles M'Crossan was the sub-sheriff. John M'Crossan was a man of very great ability and a strong politician, and we were prepared to allege that he was the real prosecutor.

1328. Was not that most objectionable?—It was.

1329. Was not the panel in that case a departure from the previous panel?—If you will allow me to refer you to the challenge, you will find that all the causes were specifically mentioned in the challenge, but it is so long ago that I could not tell you from memory.

1330. Was not the attention of those who were advising you directed to the construction of the panel, because it varied from the usual and preceding panel?—I daresay that was so, but when we have the document it would be better to refer to it.

1331. At all events in that case the accusation was that the Roman Catholic sub-sheriff made the panel?—No doubt.

1332. And it was decided that he did so?—No, it was not; the merits of the case were never tried.

1333. The Crown admitted that it was so?—The Crown thought that the challenge was bad in point of form, and therefore they demurred to it, and the demurrer was held to be bad.

1334. Do you remember that the leading Crown prosecutor was Mr. Brooke?—No, it was Mr. Major and Mr. Smilley, both of them as fair men as ever lived. I do not mean to say that Mr. Brooke would have prosecuted unfairly, for there could not be a more impartial man than he is.

1335. Under the old system, had not the sub-sheriff the absolute power of packing the panel as he pleased?—Theoretically he had, but practically he had not.

1336. How do you mean that practically he had not?—Practically he would not dare to do so. Practically there were so many safeguards against it that he could not do it; and practically he did not do it, because he was continued in his office by Protestant high sheriffs, Catholic high sheriffs, Tory high sheriffs, Radical high sheriffs, and Whig high sheriffs, if there is a Whig in Ireland.

1337. To go back to the question that I asked you about juries under the former system; is it your

Mr. *J. Hamilton.*

5 May 1873.

your opinion that under the former system jurors acted in the party riots, or did they not usually convict Roman Catholics, and sometimes acquit Protestants?—The tendency of the Orangemen was to convict Roman Catholics, and the tendency of the Roman Catholics was to convict Orangemen.

1338. Do you ever remember a jury composed exclusively of Roman Catholics under the old system?—I never inquired into the religion of men on juries in all my life, and therefore I cannot tell you. But then these party riots, after all, are not of very much importance in the north; they make a great deal of noise, but after the month of July is over, they are as good friends as ever for the next year.

1339. But do they not lead to a lamentable loss of life every year?—No doubt, the Belfast riots were a dreadful thing.

1340. At Question 1047 you say, "If you could so purge the jurors' book, which I believe you could not by any process, but if you could so purge the jurors' book as to leave no improper person on the panel, you would want no further safeguard"?—I do not think you could; that is my decided opinion.

1341. I will put to you the first county alphabetically in the list, namely, Antrim, which has 7,836 jurors; do you mean to say that you could not get 3,000 who were fit to be on the book?—I think the honourable Member must misunderstand the effect of my answer altogether. The meaning of my answer was that you could not separate the good jurors from the bad.

1342. I want you to give an opinion as to the county of Antrim, in which there are on the jurors' book at this moment 7,836; do you not believe that you could get 3,000 fair and impartial jurors out of that number?—If your question means this, that there are 3,000 fair and impartial jurors on the jurors' book in the county of Antrim, I am satisfied that there are; but if your question means, could I pick out those 3,000 persons by any process as chairman of the county, I say it is impracticable.

1343. Never mind "as Chairman," but supposing 3,000 jurors were sufficient for the county of Antrim, and that by raising the qualification, and giving a limited power of exclusion or selection, whichever you like to call it, to the chairman, you got that 3,000, do not you think that 3,000 impartial jurors could be easily got out of 7,836?—That is, in other words, if you struck off all the jurors that the present Act contemplates as common jurors, they can be only special then. You are right if you adopt Serjeant Armstrong's view; no doubt, if you raised the qualification very much, the necessity for selection diminishes in proportion as you raise the qualification; but they are much fewer in number than you suppose, even as regards Antrim.

1344. What I mean, is this, that supposing now there are 7,800 in Antrim, and the county does not require so many, do not you think that in all probability you will get a very fair jurors' book by selecting 3,000?—Tell me the qualification of those 3,000, and then I shall be able to form something like an opinion.

1345. In Antrim probably you would get the 35*l.* qualification, in the case of the 3,000?—I think that the 40*l.* qualification in Antrim would do, because Antrim is a peculiarly situated county. You have near the great town of Belfast, which would give a very great supply.

1346. Belfast has its own jurors, amounting to 1,968?—Belfast supplies jurors for the county of Antrim. Then you have many very excellent towns in Antrim: you have Ballymena, and you have Larne, and you have a great many good towns in Antrim; but where you will find that this Act will not work at all, will be in the wild agricultural counties, like Donegal and Mayo and Galway.

1347. Donegal has 1,663 jurors now under the present Act?—Then I should say that one-half of them are not fit to serve. We have always bad juries in Donegal.

1348. You mentioned to-day, did you not, that you thought it would be most unconstitutional to allow the chairman to exclude persons from the jurors' book?—No, I did not say that. I said that it would be a very unconstitutional process for the chairman in a private chamber, as proposed by Mr. Serjeant Armstrong, with the aid of the constabulary and the public officers of the county, to prepare the lists, and then come out and try prisoners by the lists which he had so prepared in private. That, I say, is an unconstitutional proceeding.

1349. Do not you think that it is more unconstitutional for the sub-sheriff to have power to select 200 on the panel out of 500 on the jurors' book?—No, because the sub-sheriff does not try the prisoner. There is the unconstitutional part of it, the trying of a prisoner by a jury list made up by yourself, I am sure that it would create a tremendous outcry. What Mr. Serjeant Armstrong proposes to do is, to sweep off the jury lists all persons objectionable on account of their being members of secret societies or things of that sort. He proposed that if that could not be done in public, of which he appeared to have a misgiving, it should be done in private, and he proposed that the person who should do that in private, with the aid of the police, should be the chairman of the county; and then the chairman of the county having done that, should come out, and try with those lists the prisoners of the county. I am sure that that would create a very great outcry in Ireland, and properly so, because it would be really preparing the lists by the police, and not by the chairman; and I do not think that that would give public satisfaction in Ireland. The chairman would have to act solely on the information supplied to him by the police and those persons, so that virtually the preparation of all the lists would be by the police. I heard a celebrated judge say, that the government of Ireland was the government of Larcom and the police, and I must say that this would redouble that state of things.

1350. Are you really of opinion that in your time in Ireland, there never has been a sub-sheriff capable of packing a panel?—I would not say that; it is impossible to find perfection, but I say that as a general rule they are highly respectable men, and that they are as a body incapable of doing that.

1351. Have you any doubt that the jury that tried Mr. O'Connell was packed by the sheriff?—My impression is, that in a case which caused such an enormous amount of political excitement as that, what the sheriff did, was to leave off all partisans of Mr. O'Connell.

1352. You remember what Lord Denman said; but have you any doubt that there were partisans on the jury against Mr. O'Connell?—I do not know that jury at all.

1353. You

Mr. *J. Hamilton.*

3 May 1873.

1353. You do not consider that it was what we call in Ireland a packed jury? — I really cannot tell, because I do not know the men who were on it. I daresay that if you had selected the principal merchants of Dublin, Guinness, Pymm, Talbeau, and all those men, it would have been said that it had been a packed jury too.

1354. You give no opinion whether you consider that it was or was not?—No.

1355. Colonel *Forde.*] As to choosing the juries alphabetically, there are some letters in the alphabet naturally with more names than others? —Yes.

1356 So that virtually, when the jury list would be called over to the end, you would have the whole jury composed of the letter or letters which had the largest number; that would be the case, would it not?—I think that must follow.

1357. And the whole panel might be composed virtually of such letters?—Yes.

1358. Do not you think that something might be done to obviate that, if it is found to be necessary? — Yes, certainly. It would be very objectionable to have a jury panel composed of a single letter, because the chances are that in some counties those men would be all of the same clan.

1359. If, as in my county, there are somewhere about 700 and 800 M's, the jurors' book might be composed of that letter, should not something be done to modify that? — If that is the result, it is a very serious thing.

1360. Major *O'Reilly.*] On the last day of your examination, you said that the last assizes, as far as your experience went, the system was a burlesque of justice?—I adopted those words.

1361. Then you added another point; you said that where no disturbing elements arose, the juries followed the direction of the judge, but where disturbing elements arose there was no agreement; was that latter description applied to civil or to criminal cases?—It applied to both.

1362. You mentioned, I think, that you had not experience as to the criminal cases on the last assizes?—I had some, but not much; for instance, in Omagh I prosecuted for the Crown.

1363. What I want to know is this, whether that evidence that where disturbing elements existed no agreement arose at the last assizes, is founded on your own experience in criminal cases?—Not in cases that I was actually in, but of course I was aware of them.

1364. But you were present at the assizes?—Yes, I was present at the assizes.

1365. With regard to the question of the impartiality of the sub-sheriff, you have given several reasons for believing that, to use your own words, the sub-sheriffs of Ireland are not liable to even the imputation of partiality?—Not liable justly.

1366. I take some of those reasons, and there are one or two that I wish to ask you for some explanation of; one is that they are, generally speaking, men of very respectable position and solicitors of high standing; that, I think, requires no explanation; the second in the order in which I will take them is this, that, as a general rule, they have no interest in the results of the trial? —Yes.

1367. I wish to call your attention to a subsequent answer of yours, in which you say that the sub-sheriff or his friends might be interested in cases coming on for trial?—That is on the civil side; the other answer is confined more to the Crown side.

1368. Then do you mean your answer to be this: that as a general rule the sub-sheriff has no interest in the results of trials, to apply to the Crown and not to the civil side?—To apply to the Crown side, of course, most strongly; and then I think I may add that, with regard to the civil side, if an objectionable person is on the jury, and there is fair and reasonable ground for objecting to him, the counsel would have no difficulty in making the objection, and I think the judge would either recommend him or order him to stand aside.

1369. In a civil case, do you say that the judge would make him stand aside?—Yes. I have often seen an objection made to a juror in a civil case, as being connected with one of the parties, and the judge has told him, "You had better not serve."

1370. Do I understand you as stating that a judge has the power to set aside a juror in a civil case?—I was rather under the impression that he had, because I have seen a judge very often say to a juror, "Do not serve; there is no objection to you," and I have seen the juror immediately retire.

1371. You understand my question; has he the power to set aside a juror?—I do not know whether he has the power legally or not. Then I might add there would be the power of challenging the array, and in that case, if the sheriff was interested in a suit, or was related to one of the parties to the suit, and he had done anything unfair or improper you could challenge the array.

1372. Another reason that you gave why the impartiality of the sub-sheriffs might be relied upon was this: that in all cases of framing panels they were made responsible by large security to the high sheriffs for the proper discharge of their duties; does this security extend to framing them impartially?—I should think that if the high sheriff was involved in any pecuniary loss, a fine or anything of that sort, by his sub-sheriffs, they would have to pay it.

1373. For instance, in your challenge to the array which was successful, was the high sheriff involved in any pecuniary loss which was recouped by the sub-sheriff?—No, he was not; because, in that case, the merits of the thing were not tried at all; it was a mere dry question of law that was decided there.

1374. I want to know what penalty recoverable on this security the sub-sheriff would incur for partiality in framing his panel?—If the judge fined the sheriff for any impropriety of which the sub-sheriff was guilty, the sub-sheriff would have to pay it.

1375. Have you ever known an instance of that proposed even?—No, I never have; probably you might add, in terms to this Act, that if the sheriff knowingly and corruptly omitted from his panel any person that ought to be on it, or put on any person that ought not to be on it, the judge should have the power of fining him.

1376. Then comes the remedy in this case which you have stated for any impartiality on the part of the sheriff, nominally the sub-sheriff really, in framing the panel, which is the challenge to the array, and you said, "In my opinion, the challenge to the array is a sufficient safeguard"?—Coupled with all the others.

1377. That answer, of course, applied to the challenge to the array as it exists?—Yes.

1378. Allow me to call your attention to a further

Mr. *J. Hamilton.*

5 May 1873.

further statement of yours, that the way that a challenge to the array is tried is by appointing triers; and I think you mentioned that the triers sometimes are a very absurd tribunal; is it not rather anomalous, in your opinion, to state that a sufficient safeguard is contained in an appeal to a very absurd tribunal?—But the absurd tribunal is an abuse of the system. I never argue against a system from its abuse. I take its use, or its capability of being useful, and not its abuse, and that is an abuse.

1379. You mentioned, as a proof that no charge of partiality could fairly be brought against any sub-sheriff in Ireland, that challenges to the array were unfrequent, and very rarely successful?—Yes.

1380. Must not that proof be measured by the fact, that the safeguard which you have mentioned as rarely claimed, and still more rarely successful, was, as you have mentioned, an appeal to an absurd tribunal? It was not always an appeal to an absurd tribunal; it was not necessarily an absurd tribunal; sometimes it was badly administered. It was a ridiculous thing, in my opinion, for a judge to select as triers two of the first men that happened to be on the panel; that was objectionable.

1381. Would not that be the natural way of accounting for the rarity of challenges to the array, according to your own statement, that such challenge would at least sometimes have to be tried by a very absurd tribunal?—I think not; I think, on the contrary, that the true reason was that the challenge would not have succeeded whether the tribunal was absurd or not.

1382. I remark, that in the challenges which you drew, and which has been referred to, you alleged partiality on the part of the sub-sheriff; am I right in thinking that that is a necessary allegation?—No, not a necessary one.

1383. Then, in the Monaghan case, the mere allegation that the panel consisted of an undue proportion of Protestants and Roman Catholics, and an unfairly small proportion of Roman Catholics, or any similar facts connected with the panel, would not be a good ground for challenge, unless it was alleged that it arose from partiality on the part of the sheriff?—Partiality, of course, is a good ground for challenge, but it is not the only ground of challenge; there are other grounds of challenge; for instance, a panel was quashed the other day in the county of Down, because the sheriff had not followed exactly the alphabetical system; and it was not alleged that he had done that from partiality, or from any reason but a mistake. Another ground of challenge would be, if the sheriff unwittingly or ignorantly put persons on the panel who were not on the lists; and another ground of challenge would be want of qualification, and so on. Partiality is itself a ground, but the fact of merely putting Roman Catholics on to try a Protestant, or Protestants to try a Roman Catholic, would not of itself be a ground of challenge, unless it was done from a corrupt and improper motive.

1384. Is it not, naturally, immensely difficult to prove, in such a challenge to the array, the corrupt motive which in such a case would be a necessary element to be proved?—Yes, it is always difficult to prove a motive If the facts were glaring facts of constant occurrence, I have no doubt that they would be not only alleged, but that they would be proved, and panels quashed over and over again.

1385. The challenge must be to one panel, must it not, and how can facts of constant occurrence be alleged against one panel?—Facts of constant occurrence are alleged against different panels, panel after panel.

1386. Do you think that the fact of a series of panels having been challenged would influence the trial of the challenge to the rest of that series of panels?—No; but I mean to say that if this was not a cry without solid foundation, if it was a well-founded charge which was capable of proof, it would very frequently be made. As, in my opinion, it is not a well-founded charge, and incapable of proof, it is very seldom made.

1387. Are not the two things which you have coupled together perfectly distinguishable; may not a charge be perfectly well founded, and yet incapable of proof, and may not it be the latter cause which causes the rarity of challenges, and not the former?—I do not think that that observation would apply at all to the fact.

1388. Are they not distinguishable; a charge may be perfectly well founded, and incapable of proof?—That is quite true, but I do not think that that is the cause why challenges are so infrequent. For instance, in criminal law some crimes consist in the intent, and the intent is, as you know, very hard to prove, very often. Charges, however, are over and over again made, and men are over and over again convicted of crimes, of which the gist is the intent.

1389. Still, the rarity of challenges to the array, and their still more rare success, may be attributable to the difficulty of proof, and not to the absence of ground for the charge; but that they are due to the absence of good ground, and not to the rarity of proof, is your opinion, and not a matter of which you can adduce proof?—No, I cannot adduce proof, but I think it is obvious.

1390. I suppose you would consider that Mr. Serjeant Armstrong has had pretty considerable experience as to facts connected with the jury system in Ireland?—Very great indeed.

1391. Allow me to call your attention to an answer of his to Question 808, referring, I rather think, to cases of juries in civil cases, in which he says, "Cases arose in which, owing to connections and relationships, and various matters, it is very desirable to have the power of striking off for reasons satisfactory to one's mind, but which would not be adequate as a ground of challenge, if it came to a challenge, of the unindifferency of the sheriff"?—Yes, he is quite right in that.

1392. Is not that a proof that there might be good grounds for an objection to a panel which yet would be incapable of proof?—Clearly there might, no doubt; but in the majority of instances, if there were good grounds, they would be capable of proof.

1393. You have given as a ground for believing that there is no ground for the imputation of unfairness in framing panels in Ireland, and that is your own experience?—Yes.

1394. And you said in connection with that, "I judge of the thing, as Mr. Serjeant Armstrong says, by its practical results"; will you allow me to call your attention to Mr. Serjeant Armstrong's judgment upon the same point, in answer to a question which called his attention to the declaration made by the sub-sheriffs of Ireland as to their impartiality. In answer to

Mr. *J. Hamilton.*

5 May 1873.

Question 831, the learned Serjeant said, "I have heard of that just as a popular matter current through the country; but I have my own eyes and my own observation, and I draw my own inferences, no matter what anybody declares. I have had as much experience as most people on every circuit in Ireland, and I do not attend to declarations of that general description unattended by the possibility of inquiring into particular cases. I believe that there are a good many engaged in such matters that are hardly aware that they are doing it, they are so much in the habit of it." Then he is asked the question, "Do you think that the sub-sheriffs have been guilty of this partiality?" and he answers, "I think that in very Catholic counties I have seen a jury trying a Catholic, and in the whole jury there was not one Catholic, although there were plenty on the panel; but they were all Protestants"?—I see that he does not give a direct answer to the question.

1395. He says in answer to Question 799, "I have not the slightest hesitation in saying that under the old system cases occurred in which you could have a jury to order, and that if you prescribed your jury you might get it." That latter part of the answer appears to apply merely to the case of Dublin; do not those answers imply that Mr. Serjeant Armstrong's judgment, formed to use his own words, from those practicable results, differs from yours?—I think that if that was Mr. Serjeant Armstrong's opinion he would have given a direct answer to the question, which was a plain and clear one; and I attach very little importance to answers couched in vague and mysterious language, hinting a charge rather than making it.

1396. You said, "I do not think that any suspicion attaches to the exercise of the power of selection by the sub-sheriff amongst right-minded persons." Am I right in taking it that that is equivalent to saying that any persons who do entertain such suspicion, are not right-minded persons?—No, my answer was a more general one.

1397. Will you point out the difference between the two phrases?—Not speaking of individuals, but of classes. I think that the classes who are interested in the preservation of law and order in Ireland do not suspect the sub-sheriff; and I think that the classes who are interested the other way do.

1398 Then am I right in understanding that you would wish to qualify that answer, and to admit that amongst right-minded persons as a body there may be, as we know there are some, who entertain a very different opinion?—I should hope that I would have not been understood as meaning to say that there were not a great number of rightminded persons who not only entertain, but express the opinion, that it is a bad way of doing the thing.

1399. Does not the same explanation apply to this statement of yours, that "Nobody imagines, I suppose, that any public officer would select an improper body of men to form a jury panel"?—It is too general an expression, perhaps; but I meant to convey that the general impression of what I call the orderly classes is, that they do not do that. I judge very much from the results of my experience, and I have never known an instance of a man being unfairly convicted in all my life; I have known instances of men being improperly acquitted.

1400. I suppose you would consider that putting on improper persons on the panel, is equally a dereliction of duty on the part of the sub-sheriff as striking off proper persons?—They are both bad.

1401. I wish, in connection with that, to call your attention to an answer of your own, "I believe that such was the amount of popular jealousy, and perhaps alarm about the press, and that sort of thing, that the sub-sheriff left on a man very often, that he ought rather to have struck out"?—I think so; I am sure of that.

1402. Then it would not be a jealousy of any defect in the process as carried out by the sub-sheriff?—It was a disadvantage, but it was really the unreasoning suspicion which existed which I think led to the jealousy.

1403. You adduced, as a proof that it was not desirable to take away the power of selection from the sheriff, that Mr. Justice Perrin, a man well known for his support of popular liberties, did not propose in his Act to take that away; might not that be attributable to the fact that there was very little chance at that time of carrying such an Act; can it be taken as conclusive of Mr. Justice Perrin's own opinion upon the desirability of doing it?—I believe that he was the Attorney General of the Liberal Government at that time, and I think that his opinion would have had very great weight with his Government; if he had proposed it, I should say that it would have been carried.

1404. Would it have any weight with you if Mr. Justice Perrin had expressed an opinion adverse to the impartiality of the sub-sheriff in Ireland at any time?—Yes, of course it would; any statement, in fact, of Mr. Justice Perrin's would, because he was a very able man.

1405. With regard to the exercise of the power of setting aside jurors by the Crown, you said that under the present system the Crown would have to set aside far more men; I would like to know from you, practically, in the counties with which you are acquainted, what proportion of the jurors on the jurors' book, in round numbers, you would consider improper to be on a jury panel?—I could not possibly give you any accurate opinion upon that point, because it would involve an acquaintance with the characters of the jurors beyond anything that I have.

1406. Do not you conceive that that is essentially the same in considering the necessity of leaving the selection of the panel to any officer, because that argument must be grounded on the fact that the panels when formed under the present system from the jurors' books, would include so large a number of improper jurors, that the exercise of the power of setting aside by the Crown would have to be used to a very large extent?—Yes.

1407. Then, practically, the case depends entirely upon the probable proportion of improper jurors who would get on the panel from the jurors' book under the present system?—No question of it, if I may judge of it by the kind of jurors that I saw at the last assizes.

1408. Allow me to take the point in two different ways; and, first, as to the quality of the low class of jurors, that might be obviated, might it not, by raising the qualification?—Yes.

1409. But you mentioned another very weighty objection, which is, that a man, though coming up to any standard of qualification, might from other reasons, being a Ribbonman or an Orangeman, or other

Mr. *J. Hamilton.*

5 May 1873.

other reasons, be unfit to serve on a jury; what you saw of the panels at the last assizes would be evidence as regards the first class of disqualification, but what we want to get at is, what is the proportion of improper persons, although with a raised qualification, that might be counted as likely to get on the panel, with regard to whom in criminal cases the right of setting aside by the Crown must be exercised; can you give the Committee any information upon that point?—Not the smallest information that would lead you to anything like a right conclusion. You see that one of the reasons is, that as chairman of a court by myself, I could be of no use in settling this right.

1410. Is not that essential in order to be able to come to the conclusion which you have asked us to come to, that the Crown would have to set aside far more men in framing a jury than they have at present?—I think not; if even with the preparation of the lists by the sub-sheriff, even after the care that he takes to put off improper men, and by which even as it is he should incur suspicion; if even after all that is done, the Crown had to exercise its power very largely, is it not obvious that when that is not done, and when the jurors are huddled up together on this alphabetical system, it must exercise it still more largely.

1411. There is a decided presumption I admit, that they must exercise it more largely; but the extent to which they would have to exercise it manifestly depends upon the question upon which I have asked for information, and which you are not in a position to give?—No, I cannot.

1412. You mentioned that ejectments are a class of cases in which this Act would never work, for the reasons that you gave?—I think so.

1413. Is there not one thing peculiar about ejectment cases under the present law, and that is, that the venue cannot be changed?—There is a power of changing the venue, but it is only in extreme cases; but that would be getting out of the frying-pan into the fire. Under this Act there is no use in changing the venue at all.

1414. Will you be kind enough to explain to me what in your view the sheriff or the sub-sheriff really does; to use your own words in answer to Question 1109, you said, "The operation appears to me to be simply this: the sheriff has this list formed alphabetically," and he goes through that, and he leaves out the improper men?—Yes, from the panel.

1415. Do you take it that the sheriff in doing so simply goes through the book, leaving out the men whom he considers objectionable, and taking all the other men as they stand?—I think I said that other motives did influence him; for instance, I think he preferred summoning jurors who would find it more convenient to attend to summoning jurors from a very great distance in large counties; and that the jurors nearer the assize town, as a rule were more frequently summoned than jurors from a distance; but that was not from any improper motive.

1416. Then your statement that what he does is simply this, to go through the alphabetical list and leave out the improper men, would require qualification?—It would require modifying to the extent that I have mentioned. You see the sub-sheriff knows every man in the county thoroughly; he knows his circumstances; he knows his intelligence; he knows his politics, and he knows his character. There is no officer in the county who knows it so well as the sub sheriff. He has peculiar qualifications if he will only exercise them honestly for giving you a good panel.

1417. What I want to understand clearly is this, is it not apparent, from the facts that have come to your knowledge, that in framing the panel, which has never been framed alphabetically, what the sub-sheriff does (I will say in the very best way) is to select names out of the book, and not to go through the book, leaving out objectionable names?—I really think that the two processes are the same. He has the whole book before him, and he, as you say, selects the best names out of the book, leaving out the bad ones.

1418. Is it not manifest that, in the county of Antrim, it is a totally different thing to go through the book leaving out the objectionable names, and to take 250 out of it, whom he considers the best?—He does go through the book, and he does take out of the book the names that he considers, as I believe, will form the best jurors, and that is omitting the bad ones.

1419. With regard to the panel being framed with reference to cases to be tried, at Question 1052 you said that the panel is not so prepared with reference to the special cases which have to be tried as a matter of fact; and at a subsequent answer to Question 1060, you said, "If there is an agrarian case to be tried, or a Ribbon case to be tried, or an Orange case to be tried, they" (the sub-sheriffs) "will omit from their panel, and I think that they ought to omit from their panel, the names of men whom they know right well to be Orangemen, Ribbonmen, Fenians, or persons who have a sympathy with agrarian crime." And you expressed an opinion that they do do so?—Yes.

1420. I would ask you to explain the apparent discrepancy between those two statements?—I am obliged to you for putting the question; Mr. Serjeant Armstrong in an answer, seemed to convey that the sheriff prepared his panel for each particular case; and I meant to correct that by stating that the sheriff prepared it generally for the assizes, but that he prepared the common jury panel only a short time before the assizes, and if he had notice that there were cases of such a character as you have read to be tried, then he exercised and ought to exercise that discretion.

1421. What you mean is, that the panel is not prepared with regard to the particular case, but that it is prepared with a view to cases to be tried at the assizes?—Mr. Serjeant Armstrong said that the sheriff prepared his panel for each particular case; and first, he said that the special jury panel could be managed in the same way; the special jury panel I said was prepared at the beginning of the year, and therefore it was not at all liable to that objection. All that I meant to correct was his answer, which seemed to convey that the panel was prepared for each particular case, by telling you that the common jury panel was prepared for the assizes generally, and not for any particular case. Now I say, that if those exciting cases arise, before the sheriff prepares his general panel for the assizes, he does prepare it, and ought in my opinion to prepare it with the view to having those cases tried by fair jurors.

1422. If the sub-sheriff is, as was the case in Monaghan, an Orangeman, he knows the case in which the sympathies of the Orangemen and the Roman Catholics are enlisted, which are going to to be tried at the assizes, and he prepares his panel with a view to those cases; whether he prepares it rightly or not; that is so, is it not?—If an offence has taken place.

1423. He prepares it with a view to those cases?—Yes, exactly; if an offence has taken place before he prepares his panel, and he has a knowledge of it, he prepares his list with that knowledge.

1424. You said that the office of striking off names, so as to guard against a person being improperly placed upon the panel, you think is a degrading office for the chairman of a county, and that you would not do it; that you would not execute such an office; then the office which you describe, and as would be called by the public as manipulating the jury lists or panels, is an office that you propose to entrust to the sub-sheriffs of Ireland, is it not?—You omit a very important feature in the case, not intentionally, I am sure; but the context will show you what I was speaking about. Mr. Serjeant Armstrong had made a proposition that the chairman should retire if necessary into a private room, attended by the constabulary and the public officers of the county, and that he should there revise those lists, striking out of them every objectionable person. Then I say that that would, in point of fact, be the preparation of the lists by the constabulary, and that I should consider it a degrading office for a county judge to be engaged in that sort of thing, and then coming out and immediately trying prisoners with those lists. I think that that would be a degrading office to the judge; the sub-sheriff does not try prisoners. Once he has made his panel, he has no more to do with it.

1425. Is it quite correct to say that the chairman would go into a room in the case suggested, and prepare the jury lists, and then come out of that room and try the cases with those jury lists; would anything of the sort occur; would it not be the fact that he would prepare the jurors' book of the county for the following year, and that he would the following year try the cases by juries taken from a panel taken in alphabetical order out of that book, and is not that slightly different from the way in which you have put it?—Perhaps I put it a little too strongly, but it comes to the same thing; he would try prisoners of the county with lists prepared by himself, from a source which the people of Ireland would consider highly objectionable, and which, in my opinion, would bring greater odium on the administration of justice than any that attaches to it at present.

1426. Sir *R. Blennerhassett.*] Have you considered the question of requiring unanimity in juries?—Of course I have discussed it, and to some extent formed an opinion upon it. I should still require it in criminal cases; in civil cases it would be a question whether or not it would not be an improvement that the verdict of a certain proportion of the jury, if it met with the concurrence of the judge, should be given, say 9 out of 12; but I should rather, in criminal cases, adhere to the principle of requiring unanimity, because I do not want to frighten the people too much with the law.

1427. What would you think of the suggestion that there should be a certain number of qualified special jurors serving upon all juries?—I think that the same objection which Mr. Serjeant Armstrong mentioned would really apply to that, that very often it would have a tendency to prevent unanimity.

1428. Do you suggest that property should be the only qualification of jurors?—No; I entirely agree with the witnesses who would strike off illiterate persons. I would not allow any man to serve on a jury who could not read and write.

1429. I think you said, also, that one of the reasons of the failure of justice at the late assizes was not so much ignorance as sympathy with lawlessness on the part of the juries?—I think that that is one of the greatest causes of the failure of justice; either sympathy or terrorism.

1430. So far as sympathy with lawlessness is concerned, do not you think that the greater the number of people are that you interest in the administration of the law, the greater the number of people you get to support it and sympathise with it?—I quite agree with you. I should like to interest the whole population in the administration of the law; but I think you would do it at too great a sacrifice under present circumstances. I think that the circumstances of the country do not admit of what I agree is a correct and proper theory.

1431. I understand that you would wish to interest as great a number of people in the administration of the law as is possible, considering the circumstances of the case?—Yes, certainly.

1432. Viscount *Crichton.*] Do you recollect the effect of Judge Morris's charge to the triers in the Monaghan case?—All that I can remember of the matter is this, that I heard from members of the circuit, and from other persons, that the verdict of the triers was against the charge of the judge; it is, as a matter of law, no objection that the sheriff should have put on a man on account of his religion, or left him off on account of his religion; that has been decided.

1433. Would his opinion modify the opinion that you expressed, that the panel was properly quashed?—I merely assumed Mr. Heron's data when I spoke of propriety. I said that, *primâ facie*, it had a bad appearance, taking Mr. Heron's data; but I do not know anything of the merits of the case myself, and therefore I give no opinion upon the actual case. I might add that, *primâ facie*, the case of my own challenge had a bad appearance, but I do not mean to say that we should have sustained it in point of fact.

1434. Mr. *Bruen.*] You were asked whether the fact of the first 50 names on the panel being 48 Protestants, and the other two Roman Catholics, was a proof of partiality on the part of the sub-sheriff; the question I wish to put is, whether you are aware that, in forming panels, the sub-sheriff generally places first upon the panels those who are the highest rated of the whole number of those that are upon the panel?—I have understood so; but in answer to the other question, I should say that that fact of itself would not prove partiality.

1435. But that fact of itself, of the formation of panels in that way, would disprove the allegation of partiality on the part of the sub-sheriff, even supposing the first 48 names were Protestants?—It would give a good reason for his having properly done the thing.

Thursday, 8th May 1873.

MEMBERS PRESENT:

Mr. Attorney General.	Marquis of Hartington.
Dr. Ball.	Mr. Henry Arthur Herbert.
Sir Rowland Blennerhassett.	Mr. Lewis.
Mr. Bourke.	The O'Conor Don.
Mr. Bruen.	The O'Donoghue.
Viscount Crichton.	Colonel Wilson Patten.
Colonel Forde.	Colonel Vandeleur.

THE RIGHT HONOURABLE THE MARQUIS OF HARTINGTON, IN THE CHAIR.

Mr. GEORGE BATTERSBY, LL.D., called in; and Examined.

Mr. G. Battersby, LL.D.

8 May 1873.

1436. Mr. *Bruen*.] You are a Queen's Counsel, and are now Senior of the Home Bar, are you not?—I am.

1437. Have you not been for some years a Judge in the Consistorial Court?—Yes.

1438. And you are Crown Counsel for King's County, for Kildare, and for Westmeath?—Yes.

1439. You have had some experience, have you not, in your professional capacity, of the working of the new jury law?—Yes.

1440. Is your experience favourable or unfavourable to that law?—Unfavourable. In my opinion, it will be impossible to administer justice under that law as it stands.

1441. Have you come to the conclusion that life and property are not safe in the hands of those whom you have seen brought into the jury box through the operation of the law?—Yes, that is my opinion, and the reason why I have formed that opinion is this, that the great majority of the jurors under that Act will not have sufficient independence or intelligence to enable them to act so as to discharge their duties properly.

1442. I suppose you concur with one or two of the witnesses that have already been before the Committee, that the conduct of the juries at the last assizes was actually ludicrous. I may say that, in fact, it was a burlesque?—Ludicrous I think is the proper word to express it.

1443. In the cases which came under your observation, were there any serious cases?—On that circuit there were no cases that I would call serious. There were cases, of course, of some importance, but none of a very serious character, or involving any very excitable feelings.

1444. But supposing that there had been serious cases, are you of opinion that the result would have been disastrous?—In my opinion it would have been so.

1445. Have any particular instances come under your notice of the working of the Act?—Yes. In the first special jury case we tried at Trim the foreman of the jury who was unable to write down the word "plaintiff." After some little effort, the judge sent the crier into the jury box to assist him. The letters "the," preceding it be made some attempt at, with the assistance of the crier, but he broke down with the letter "P." He could not make a letter "P" at all. The judge had to get the crier to write it for him. I may add with regard to that county, that under the old administration of the law, the foreman of that jury would probably have been a gentleman of information and education, and of 1,000 *l.* or 2,000 *l.* a year income.

1446. In those special jury cases, then, under the old law, you found, did you not, that men of a very superior class of society were brought together to administer the law?—In that county especially, both in the civil and criminal courts, they were always men of intelligence and independent property. I do not remember to have seen a petty jury in that county, every man of whom had not at least 100 *l.* a year income, to my own knowledge, and I am personally acquainted with most of them.

1447. In this particular case which you have just mentioned to the Committee, this special juryman, who was the foreman of the jury under the new Act, must have been in possession of property, must he not, of the net annual value of 100 *l.* or upwards?—Yes, of the net annual value according to the valuation as it is entered in the ordnance valuation; but although entered there as having land of that net annual value, he may not have had a penny at all of his own out of it, because lands are usually let at rack-rent, and the tenant holding at rack rent may not have any profit at all.

1448. Do you think that the rating qualification is not a sufficient test of the fitness of the juror, even if you raise the qualification?—The rating at any lower amount is certainly not; the rating at a higher amount, of course, would be a better test than at the lower amount, but at a very low amount it is no test at all.

1449. Do you think that the rating qualification now made by this law would be a sufficient test?—I think that it ought not to be the only test, but that other tests ought to be adopted, as far as possible.

1450. Have any of the jurors who attended at the last assizes told you personally of the great difficulty that they had in being present to perform their duties?—Many of them from the neighbourhood of my country residence came to me, and applied to me in very earnest terms to try and get the judges to exonerate them from attendance. They said that they were not able

to

Mr. G. Battersby, LL.D.

8 May 1873.

to live in the town; they were not able to support themselves in it; that they came from a distance, which some of them did, from 11 to 20 miles; that they were unable to walk there and back again; that they had no horses, and that they had no railway. I did not interfere with them, because the judge would not have attended to me. I did in one particular case, in the county of Kildare. I did not know the man; but he applied to some of the barristers at the table, for God's sake, to help him to get home. He said that he had five children and a wife at home, and he had nobody to look after them, and he was not able to pay for his keep in the town. One of the barristers gave a shilling to pay the crier to make an affidavit, which was absolutely necessary, in order to make an application to the judge. He made an affidavit, and I applied to the judge, and he did excuse him. Some bystanders said that it was a mistake bringing him there, for he was not rated sufficiently within the meaning of the Act, and should not have been there; but it was the fault of the collector. However, on inquiry, it was found that he was rated, I think, at 17 *l.* Being resident in a town his qualification would be 12 *l.*; but the man was an object of charity to the people about him, and he received a shilling in charity to get him exonerated.

1451. Dr. *Ball.*] You have a country residence in Westmeath, have you not?—Yes; on the borders of Westmeath.

1452. Mr. *Bruen.*] You speak of those cases as coming actually within your own personal knowledge as regards the jurors themselves; you know them to be men of that class?—I know them to be persons of that class; I had conversations with a great number of them, that is to say, many of them applied to me, and I tried to induce them to believe that it was an honour and a privilege to be a juror, sitting there upon the property and lives of their neighbours and friends, and sitting so near the judge, but none of them would take that view of it; they all wanted to get home.

1453. Did it appear to you that they were entirely dependent upon the direction of the judge for the verdicts which they returned?—No, the way it stands is this: in indifferent matters, about which they had no feeling, they would follow the judge; but if any case of religion or politics, or between landlord and tenant arose, all the judges in the land could not lead them to find a verdict according to law, in most cases.

1454. Do those observations apply especially to the very lowest class of the jurors who came together at the last assizes, or would they also apply even to a higher rated class of men?—Men of a higher rate are many of them subject to strong prejudices; but generally speaking, if you find men of a higher rate, they are independent men of character, and you may rely upon them. I have seen juries from every section of the people, and where they were of a higher class, they act with perfect honesty and independence against their own prejudices.

1455. Have you thought of any remedies that you would apply, so as to bring the present law into a better shape?—Yes; since I have been here, I have been thinking about it, and there are some matters which I think would improve the present law, and might make it more workable, and if the Committee desire it, I will state what they are. First, I would raise the rating qualification, if practicable, to 100 *l.* for common jurors, or to some other more considerable amount than at present. I may say that, as regards specially Meath and Westmeath, I never saw a jury whose qualifications would be under that amount if they were inquired into under the old law. I am not speaking of what they would be under the new law; but they were persons who actually had that amount if they were asked. Secondly, I would compel all persons upon the panel who are summoned to attend. At all times there are a vast number of the better class of jurors that do not attend; some of them never attend, and if they really do attend they do not answer; they do not appear, and the judges are very unwilling to fine if they get a sufficient number of jurors in attendance. It does not concern the judge whether he has qualified men or not; if they answer they are put on the jury, and he is satisfied; and I think, perhaps, that might be corrected by imposing upon every juror who is summoned, and called, and did not answer or attend, a small fine, without consulting the judge at all, but making the juror liable to it. I would give power to the judge, if he thought fit, for any sufficient reason assigned, to remit it afterwards, or to impose a higher fine if he thought proper; but I would have it in the first instance as a matter to which he would be subject by not attending. Thirdly, I think the recommendation that I have heard made of having the summonses served by a post, ought to be adopted; I think that that would have a good result, and I have no doubt that in the most remote and secluded part of the country those summonses would reach the parties, for there are constantly communications by post from America, and they always get them, and if a summons such as that were sent out, marked on the back as being a summons, every man in the neighbourhood would know it; and if he knew that it had been sent through the post, he would call for it. That, I think, would be an effectual service. The only thing to be apprehended is that they would never take the summons, and would not ask for it; but then, if the mere sending by post were taken to be a service, they would then be sufficiently served. There is another recommendation, which I think would be a good one, and that is that either party, both in criminal and in civil cases, should be entitled to have a special jury struck under the old Act. It probably would not be resorted to very often, but it is the fairest way of striking a jury that can be imagined; because 48 names taken fairly from the panel, and each party striking off 12 without assigning any reason, and then balloting for the remaining 24, appears to be, and I have always observed it to be, as far as I could judge, the fairest way of striking a jury that can be thought of.

1456. Viscount *Crichton.*] Would that apply only to civil cases?—I would do it in both.

1457. *Chairman.*] Will you explain how the 48 names were first selected?—The panel of 48 is taken by the sheriff from amongst all the long panel of the county by ballot, and out of those 48 each party strikes off 12.

1458. Dr. *Ball.*] That is the mode at present in the Court of Chancery; when an issue is directed to a jury, the jury is struck in no other way; cards representing every name on the whole panel of the county are all put in the box, and the jury is taken from the 48 that first come out?—Yes, that has always been the practice in the

Mr. G. Battersby, LL.D.

8 May 1873.

the Court of Chancery, and it is the fairest course in the world; and unless the sheriff should, by some means or another, put together 48, I do not know how he could do it; but unless he could manage to do it, he could not return an unfair jury. The fifth recommendation is this: I would place upon the jurors' book, without any property qualification at all, the sons of peers, baronets, knights, magistrates (except stipendiary magistrates), and their respective eldest sons. I may observe that in the present Act their position is recognised, because they are directed to be placed before the others in the Act as it stands; but I would give them the privilege, if it be a privilege; I would make them jurors without requiring any qualification, because they would all have intelligence; then I would also place upon the book retired officers of the army and navy, graduates of the universities, merchants having 1,000 *l.* property, freeholders of 20 *l.* per annum, and leaseholders of the same amount, whose terms were originally created for not less than 21 years. There are many of those classes resident in the counties, who, by reason of their living on annuities or having let their lands, are not rated at all, or rated at something very low, and would not come under the present arrangement. There is no possible ground upon which any prejudice could be apprehended on the part of any of them in my view of the case. Sixthly, I would say, let the poor-rate collectors mark on their lists all persons who, from bodily or mental infirmity, poverty, inability to write or read, or absence from home, cannot well serve as jurors. Seventhly, let the constable in charge of every police district be furnished with a list of the proposed jurors within such district, and let them attend before the chairman and give such information as may be required, because he ought to know every man in his district. The inspectors and sub-inspectors of constabulary have been mentioned, but they do not know the people at all; whereas the man who is in charge of the police barrack of a district must of necessity, if he is any time there, know every man at once. It would not interfere with his duties or with his popularity, or interfere with him at all attending and giving this information to the chairman when he is settling the list.

1459. Colonel *Forde*.] Then you would suggest that the chairman should be the revising officer?—I assume that that is to continue. As I understood the examination upon the former day, the only question was in what way he should do so, and what means he should have for doing it; but as I understand it, nobody objected to his being the person to revise, provided he did it in open court and properly. Eighthly, the sheriff ought to be allowed, at the time of summoning, to omit names on his own responsibility. It appears to me that there must be a discretion somewhere; and it appears to me that there is no person in whom that discretion may be so safely vested as the sheriff; there is no other officer that I can recollect who could discharge the duty at all. It has been said that the county surveyor might know; but the county surveyor knows nothing on earth about the people; he knows nobody except the contractors under him. He drives through the country to see whether the roads are in order; and he sees the contractor who has agreed with the grand jury; but he knows no more of the people of the county, and he would be entirely incompetent to do it.

1460. *Chairman*.] I do not remember that it has been suggested that the county surveyor should exercise a discretion in summoning the jurors, but that the suggestion was that the county surveyor should attend and give information, with others, to the chairman?—The county surveyor could give no information, except as to the state in which the roads were. He knows nothing about the people in the county; but the constable in charge of the police district does know, and the collectors do know, and they would be the proper attendants upon the chairman.

1461. Are you not now making a recommendation that the sheriff, or some person, should have the discretion of omitting names which appear on the jurors' book?—Yes, that is my suggestion, and the ground upon which I suggest that is this. Heretofore the panel was framed, the men highest in position and highest in fortune being at the top of the list, and so descending till you came to the end. When they are called upon any trial for felony, the invariable practice is for the prisoners' advisers to strike off every independent man as far as their power of challenge exists, and if they can manage by that means to get one partisan of their own upon the jury there is no decision, and then they are safe in that way. If there are many challenges, that is to say, if there are three or four prisoners upon trial, they have a great chance of having the whole of the jury composed of their partisans, and under the present statute that is now before the Committee, that difficulty will be greatly increased, for this reason, that the great majority of the jurors will be of the lowest class, because of their being the lowest rated, and that will increase the chance of having a greater number of their partisans upon the jury, and therefore I think that it is quite impossible that calling them in the order of their names can work well. I think it would be quite impossible to convict felons wherever there was any question of an exciting character concerned in the matter; therefore I think, certainly, that we must choose in some other way a jury that will do impartial justice between the parties.

1462. Mr. *Bruen*.] You mean the panel?—Yes, I mean the panel; none of the remedies which I have heard suggested would in fact prevent the evil that I have mentioned. The Crown Solicitor does not know the whole county; probably he would know very little about it, but at all events he does not know them all, and therefore he cannot know the persons who ought not to be upon the jury at all. He may know some, or he may chance to be informed, but he does not in fact know them, and therefore that remedy of the Crown Solicitor challenging would be quite ineffectual, for persons will come in that nobody knows. I may mention an instance that occurred at the Mullingar assizes when the first Fenian was convicted; a man called himself Pagan O'Leary, and when he was put upon trial the first time, the jury differed in this way. One of the jurors came out immediately after they were discharged and told me how it occurred, and he said that I ought to know it, in order that there might be some remedy found if possible. One of the jurors was living in Mullingar in good business, and a rich man, and as soon as they retired into the jury room, somebody addressed this gentleman, and said, "We shall have no trouble in this case; it is clearly proved, and we

Mr. G. Battersby, LL.D.

8 May 1873.

we shall not be delayed by it." "Oh," said that gentleman, "the case is clearly proved; there is no doubt that the man has done all that they attribute to him, but I shall never find him guilty; he is a Fenian, and I will not convict a Fenian." So they sat down, and remained there until they were kept long enough, and then they were discharged. That man was a man of good position, but the Crown Solicitor did not know him. It is possible that the sheriff might have known him. That may happen for any number of times, because persons who are genuine partisans, as he was, have no regard for an oath, and will find a verdict, or refuse to find a verdict, as happens to suit their views.

1463. And that case may happen even if you raise the qualification to the extent that you suggest?—It might happen, no matter what the qualification was.

1464. It might happen without discretionary power upon the part of some officer in forming the panels?—Yes; certainly. It is impossible to guard against everything, but the present state of the law, in my view, increases greatly the difficulty in securing a fair trial.

1465. So that it is your opinion that raising the qualification, without some discretionary power, will not be sufficient to prevent a failure of justice?—Without some discretionary power somewhere.

1466. You mean, do you not, discretionary power in forming the jury panels?—Just so.

1467. Your first suggested remedy of raising the qualification to the extent, as you say, of 100 *l.* for common jurors and to 200 *l.* for special jurors, would very much diminish, would it not, the number of those who are qualified to serve?—Yes, of course it would.

1468. I presume that in some counties it would diminish the number almost too much?—That might be; but I think that the other qualifications which I have mentioned, not requiring property, would be a considerable set off against that, and would supplement it to some extent, and probably to a great extent.

1469. In the more backward parts of Ireland do you think that you could find persons possessing those honorary qualifications in sufficient number to supplement the deficiency?—I am not able to say with regard to the more remote parts of Ireland, as I do not know them; but I do not think there is any part of Ireland in which there are not persons of the classes that I have named residing, more or less.

1470. If you found, for instance, in the county of Cavan, that the 100 *l.* qualification would only put 91 upon the common jurors' book, do you suppose that the supplementary qualifications which you have mentioned would raise the number to a sufficient extent?—I cannot say; but I am surprised to hear that there are so few in the county of Cavan.

1471. I see by the return that in the county of Donegal those rated at 100 *l.* and upwards are only 108; would not there be the same difficulty there?—Of course, where that happens, you must have a lower qualification.

1472. My object in asking you these questions is to know whether, if you give this discretionary power to the sheriff in forming his panels, it would be necessary to raise the qualification so very much; but if the sheriff had the power of summoning his jury panels according to his judgment, you could afford to admit in the jury lists men of a much lower qualification than the rate which you have mentioned?—Yes, that would be so.

1473. You very often find, do you not, a man rated even as low as 30 *l.*, who is very well qualified to act as a juryman, although that would not be the rule?—A man may be rated at 30 *l.*, and yet have an income of 3,000 *l.* a year, as often happens to be the case, because he lets all his lands, and he is only rated for what he has in his own hand.

1474. Therefore, if you give the sheriff this discretionary power, you would be enabled by the lower rating qualification to include those men who would be quite fit to serve upon a jury, and it would lighten the burden upon other persons upon whom that burden has lain?—That would be so.

1475. With regard to the fine, you propose that a fine of 3 *l.* should be payable by any man who did not answer to his name?—Yes; it should be absolutely incurred by default.

1476. But, I suppose, you would allow it to be remitted if a man came forward and alleged a just reason why he was not present?—Yes, certainly.

1477. Would the failure of the service of the summons, in your opinion, be a sufficient cause for remitting the fine?—Yes, if it did not arise from his own default. I view it in this way. I have had a good deal of experience in the Ecclesiastical Court, in which I presided for some years, and there the summonses and everything were served in that way, and there never was an instance of a failure of service; and if these jury summonses were served in that way, I do not think that there would be a failure, except by a default of the party himself in avoiding the summons.

1478. But in the service of the summons by post in the more remote districts, you would make the sending of a registered letter to the post office, the summons?—Yes, that would be the summons.

1479. And you would throw the onus of proving the negotiation upon the juror?—Yes, I would.

1480. Is not that very often a very difficult thing to prove?—If the letter went, as it would go, being a registered letter, into the hands of the postmaster, and the postmaster could prove that he had it there for him, it would not be very difficult for him to prove that it was not his own default, and it would be for him to prove that he had not received it.

1481. In many of the backward parts of Ireland, we have had it in evidence that people do not go to the post for a week, very often?—That may be, but some of his neighbours do; and if there is anything for his benefit in the way of a letter that he ought to get, he always hears of it. If he does not go to the market, somebody else goes, or if he does not go to the town to buy things, somebody else does, and so they always know if there is a letter for them.

1482. Supposing he proved distinctly that he had not heard of that letter being at the post office, would that be a sufficient excuse?—If it was a *bonâ fide* excuse, that would be for the judge to determine.

1483. It is rather a difficult thing, is it not, to prove the *bonâ fides* of the matter, and to prove that he did not hear of it?—If he proved it by satisfactory evidence he might be excused; but

Mr. G. *Battersby*, LL.D.

8 May 1873.

if all his neighbours got summonses at the same time, and he knew that the assizes were approaching, if he did not go to the post office because he did not wish to get the letter, I think that that ought to be a satisfactory proof against him.

1484. That would seem to impose the necessity of his going to the post office as well?—He might very well go at the approach of the assizes. Certainly every man in the neighbourhood would know that the letters were coming, and every man in the neighbourhood ought to send to the post and inquire whether there was one for him There is a great objection now in the matter of the services. The expense is very great, because sometimes the sheriffs have to send 30 miles or more, in some cases with a special messenger, to have these services effected. Then the special messenger may not know the individual personality, and the special messenger very often, as somebody mentioned here in evidence, think, fails to give it to the juror, because he gets half-a-crown, or a crown, from somebody not to give it to him. I think, myself, that it would be a much more certain mode of service through the post.

1485. You propose that in criminal cases, as well as in civil cases, there should be a special jury at the option of either party?—Yes, I do.

1486. You are probably aware that Mr. Hamilton's objections to that, when he was examined the other day, were that it was an infringement of the principle of the law, which was that every man should be tried by his peers, and that in a special jury the class of men who would try a prisoner, probably one of the lowest class, would hadly come within that definition?—Commoners are all peers.

1487. Then you do not think that that would be an infringement of that principle?—I think not. I think that if I were to be tried I should like to be tried by a special jury.

1488. Do you think that in Ireland a feeling prevails that a poor man who was accused of a crime would be equally satisfied to be tried by a jury composed, we will say, of the gentlemen that special jurors generally are?—No; but this feeling prevails, and that is, that every man who is a very bad man, and a very dangerous man, thinks that he has a much better chance of getting off by having the lowest class of jurors that can be found, because they either sympathise with him in that case, or they are afraid, or are actuated by some other motive that deters them from doing justice; but I think that any fair class of men, wishing to have a fair jury, would rather be tried by gentlemen than others, if they really wished a fair trial.

1489. There were one or two questions asked about a case of which I think you have some personal knowledge, and that is a case which Mr. Seed referred to in his examination before the Westmeath Committee two years ago, a case in which he made some imputations upon the conduct of the sub-sheriff in forming the jury panels; you have personal knowledge of that case, I think?—Yes, I have personal knowledge of that case, and of all the parties concerned in it.

1490. Dr. *Ball.*] Were you the Crown prosecutor?—I was the counsel for the Crown in that case. I am the regular Crown prosecutor there, and I know all the parties. I know the high sheriff and the sub-sheriff, and most of the jurors, and I know Mr. Seed perfectly. There has been a great deal of misconception and misrepresentation about that case; and I know that very well, because I was at the consultation upon it that Mr. Seed speaks of. The sub-sheriff, after Mr. Seed gave his evidence, consulted me as to whether he should bring an action for libel against Mr. Seed. He gave me the whole of his version of the case, and I am perfectly acquainted with everything belonging to it; and really I am perfectly convinced beyond doubt that no party concerned in those transactions was in the least to blame, or did anything wrong. The way it occurred was this: at previous special commissions, the panel returned always included every man who was not actually sworn upon the grand jury, and the panel to try cases then consisted of the highest men in the county, and we went on until a sufficient number were had upon the jury; and not merely upon that occasion, but for many years before, when I first knew it, that had been the practice in Meath. Latterly, of the higher classes a good many have dropped off somehow or other, but upon this occasion a panel was furnished, which certainly was not such a panel as Mr. Seed had a right to expect. They were pretty decent people, but they were of an inferior class, most of them. Mr. Seed, when the matter was discussed at the consultation, made his observations, and said what occurred to him, and I think somebody said, of course I cannot pledge myself to the very words used, but somebody did say, "What is to be done?" Mr. Seed said, "Leave it to me, I will see to the jury." What Mr. Seed meant by that was that he would set aside the jurors who were not fit to try the case; and afterwards, at the trial, he set aside a good many, and he set them aside rightly. After all this, he gave his evidence, and there was a great outcry about it; and as I said, the sub-sheriff came to me, and consulted me as to whether he should not bring an action. What he did was perfectly fair, and fairly intended, and it was this: when he had made out his panel, he and the high sheriff, who is as honourable a man as any in the world, Mr. Preston, Lord Gormanstown's eldest son, went over the panel; and in order that they might be acting perfectly fair, and prevent any local prejudice, they took the jurors from every part of the county at random, and neither the one nor the other knew the men that they were choosing. Mr. Preston never associated with the petty jurors, nor did he know them, and the sub-sheriff had been recently appointed (his predecessor having been promoted to be clerk of the peace), and he never knew anything of the county; he was a practising attorney in a very limited practice in Trim, and he did not know the jurors; but it was in order to avoid all local prejudice that they took the jurors in that way at random. But the consequence was, that the jury was not such a jury as Mr. Seed had a right to expect, or that he had ever seen in the box before, and that led him to make those observations, I suppose, which do appear to be rather rash; but his intentions were right, he did nothing wrong, and he intended nothing wrong.

1491. Colonel *Wilson Patten.*] I do not quite understand why the sheriff threatened to bring an action upon the subject?—Because Mr. Seed said here that the attorney for the prisoner and the sub-sheriff he thought were to blame, or were too intimate, or something of that sort; I cannot pledge

Mr. *G. Battersby*, LL.D.

8 May 1873.

pledge myself to the very words of course; but really there was not any person concerned in that transaction that did anything in the least wrong, or had the slightest intention of doing wrong. Mr. Seed could no more have gone to the sub sheriff to get him to make the panel, or to alter the panel, than he could come to one of the Committee here. It could not be altered, for it was struck, and if it could, the sub sheriff would not have listened to him for an instant.

1492. Mr. *Bruen*.] So that the bad nature of the panel was owing to the sub-sheriff having chosen it on the principles of the new Act, instead of the old Act?—It was somewhat on the principles of the new Act; it was with a view to attain the same object.

1493. In your opinion the sub-sheriff was not guilty of any partiality whatever? — Not the slightest.

1494. Consequently, to rely upon that as one instance of the bad working of the late Act is not justifiable?—No. I may say that I never knew a sub sheriff pack a jury.

1495. Have you never known the sub-sheriffs being exposed to unpopularity in the exercise of their duty in forming the panels?—I never have, personally.

1496. But I suppose that there has been an outcry against the system when prisoners have been convicted?—There is nothing in Ireland against which there has not been some outcry sometimes by some party; but there being an outcry is no evidence that there is any foundation for the accusation.

1497. The slang term of "jury packing" is one that would be just as applicable to a jury formed by an extensive exercise of the right of calling jurors to stand aside, as by the exercise of the right of the sub-sheriff in forming his panel?—The exercise of the right to stand by is palpable, and seen by everybody; and if many are set aside there is always a complaint; but as regards the sheriff in the exercise of his discretion in forming the panel, I have never known any outcry about it.

1498. Have you thought about the effect of the system of calling jurors by strict alphabetical rotation, as regards men of business?—Every man of business, of course, may be inconvenienced by being called; but I do not know how that would be objectionable, because every man is bound to serve in his turn.

1499. Is not it a greater burden upon a man of business than upon middle men?—Of course.

1500. And it is a greater weight of burden upon a man who lives at a distance than upon a person who lives near the assize town?—Certainly.

1501. Do you think that that burden could in any way be equalised justly, so long as the efficiency of the administration of the law is not interfered with?—It might be remedied in this way, by not calling a second time the same man, except at some interval, so as not to oppress the same man by a constant attendance.

1502. Supposing the case of a man who had not very much to do, who was perfectly suitable as a juryman, and against whom no imputation of partiality could be alleged, and supposing the case of another man, who had a business which depended upon his personal superintendence, do you think it would be a fair thing to summon the man who had not much to do, and who did not object to it, rather oftener than the man who had a great deal to do, and who did object to it, and to whom it would be an injury to serve?—Yes; and that was the practice adopted to a considerable extent by the sheriffs heretofore. They usually summoned the men who could without any very great inconvenience attend, and who did not live too far away; and therefore, to some extent, they relieved the persons who ought to be relieved from attendance.

1503. You think that was not at all an unfair exercise of their discretion?—No; it appears to me to be quite harmless.

1504. Viscount *Crichton*.] It has been suggested to the Committee that no man, however highly rated he might be, should be on the panel, unless he possessed a house and offices rated at a certain amount; and I think that has been called the compound qualification; do you think that that would be a good plan?—I do not understand it all. Farm houses are taken into account in the valuation of a farm.

1505. Supposing a man had a farm of 800 acres, but lived in a mud hovel, as is sometimes the case, would not it be very desirable that that man should not be on the jury list; is not it generally the first effect of education upon a man to make him improve his dwelling-house?—I have not much considered that subject; but it strikes me that that distinction need not be taken, and that it would not be useful. I have known men live in very poor houses, because they liked to save money, and keep it; and a man having that disposition, I think, would not unfit him for a juryman.

1506. You suggested that the sons of knights, peers, and baronets, &c., should be placed on the jurors' book without any qualification; would there not be some difficulty about enforcing their attendance?—Not the least if they lived in the county. It would be as easily enforced as any other attendance.

1507. They might be living in their father's house, and have no property upon which any fine could be levied?—I do not know. It would be no great loss if that should happen; but it would very rarely happen, I believe.

1508. I asked Mr. Hamilton a question with reference to a communication which I received from the secretary of the Associated Law Clerks, who says that members of the association have been summoned to serve as jurors in cases where they have had the conduct and management of the suit at the trial; do you think it right that law clerks should be exempt from serving on juries?—I think so, and I think that domestic servants ought to be exempted, and also publicans ought to be exempted. No publican in the country parts of Ireland ought to be upon a jury, for unless they either are, or pretend to be, partisans and members of the secret societies, they would dispose of none of their whisky.

1509. Colonel *Forde*.] With regard to the qualification, which you put at 100 *l*. for a common juror, I see from the return that in the county of Limerick you would only have by that qualification 37; are you aware of that?—It appears to me very extraordinary; but if that be so, you must have a lower qualification in that county.

1510. When you say that 100 *l*. should be the qualification, you would classify the counties, would you not, very much as they are at present?—They must be classified so as to afford a sufficient number of jurors, whatever they might be.

1511. You

Mr. G. Battersby, LL.D.

8 May 1873.

1511. You would like to correct that answer as to the 100 *l.*; you would classify them to a certain extent?—So much as in each county would afford a sufficient number of jurors.

1512. Mr. *H. A. Herbert.*] You stated, did you not, that when a letter was sent to a juror through the post office, a neighbour might bring the man his letter, and he would be responsible for receiving that letter?—I did not say that the neighbour would bring it to him.

1513. If he did not go to the post office at all, how would he get it?—He would go if he wished to get a letter.

1514. He might not know it?—He would surely hear of it.

1515. In the remote parts of the country, such as the county of Kerry, where the post offices are a long way off, supposing a man did not go to the post office or any of his neighbours, would you then hold him responsible?—No. If it happened from circumstances such as that, that he was so remote from the post office as that neither he nor anybody else in the neighbourhood went, he ought not to be punished; because he would only have to satisfy the judge of the difficulty or impossibility, and the judge would remit the fine, but he would be a very singular subject, I think.

1516. I suppose you have not seen this Return of the jurors in the general jurors' book classified, have you?—I saw it, but I did not read it.

1517. When you suggested just now the increase of jurors, and you put certain qualifications to them, have you tried to form any idea of the number that have generally been put on the jury list?—I am not aware of the number; but in the county that I am acquainted with, there would be a sufficient number.

1518. You would be very much surprised to hear that in Kerry there would be only 91 jurors?—I am not surprised at anything, but I should have supposed that there would have been more, and if my supposition was wrong, of course it is my ignorance; I know nothing about it.

1519. In Kilkenny city I see there would be only three jurors altogether, under the qualification that you propose?—From all I have heard of the Kilkenny jurors, the fewer of them there were, the better; but I do not know what the number is.

1520. Colonel *Vandeleur.*] Would you include what we term the "immediate lessors," that is to say, persons who do not hold lands in their own hands, but let it to others?—They would come under the two classes that I have named, freeholders and termors for more than 21 years, or for 21 years.

1521. Would they come under the class of what we call in Ireland the 50 *l.* freeholders?—Yes, they would be included in my class of freeholders.

1522. That would considerably enlarge the number of jurors, would it not?—Yes, of course it would. There are a great number in every county of gentlemen who let their lands altogether, or nearly altogether, and yet have very fine estates, and good property, who are exempt now under this rating, and that would bring them all in.

1523. And there are a great many persons, are there not, who have houses in towns in the same way?—Yes.

1524. With regard to the police serving the notices, are you aware that the police serve the voting papers for the unions?—Yes.

1525. Are you aware that the police serve a great many other notices?—Yes.

1526. And that the police serve summonses upon their own account in police cases?—Yes, if they find pigs and dogs and things upon the roads.

1527. Do you consider that it would make the police unpopular?—I do not think it would.

1528. Would you consider, or not, that each policeman would, in his own respective district, serve the notices forwarded to him by the clerk of the peace?—Of course, if that practice were adopted, that would be the way to do it.

1529. Are you aware, also, that from every district, at assize times, some of the police generally attend the assizes?—Yes, always.

1530. I think you said before that every policeman in his own district is supposed to know the individuals?—The constable in charge of the district, as superior officer in the barrack or whatever it may be, is generally retained for a good while in the same situation, and of course he knows the men in the district.

1531. At present the summonses are sent out, are they not, and served by a messenger or bailiff from the county town?—Yes, that is so.

1532. On his return on having served, do you know the form that he signs?—I am not sure that there is any form; but where there is a bad attendance of jurors, and the judge wishes to inquire into it, he has that bailiff put upon the table and sworn as to the service of each individual.

1533. Are you aware that there has been a change lately made, that the bailiff comes before the judge and swears generally to all parties that he served, and not individually; that he has a list given to him and he swears to the list, that he served every person in that list?—I am not aware of that; but if it be so, it is not a satisfactory way of doing it.

1534. The constable of police would attend the assizes, and could do exactly the same, could he not, with much less trouble and much less expense?—No doubt.

1535. And more satisfactorily, because he would not receive the half-crowns which you said were very frequently given?—No; I am sure if the service were to be made in that way, it would be done in a more satisfactory manner, and without any great difficulty or trouble.

1536. With regard to the division of the jurors, have you ever sat in the Assistant Barrister's Court as chairman?—No, not as assistant barrister. I never was assistant barrister.

1537. Are you aware that the assistant barrister corrects the voters' list every October?—Yes.

1538. Would you conceive that the assistant barrister, at the same time, could correct the jurors' lists, they being all taken out of the same book?—That might be done at one time as well as another.

1539. The clerks of the union, the rate collectors, and the other officials being obliged to attend at the October sessions to instruct and give information to the barrister; the two revisions could be conducted, could they not, at one and the same time?—I see nothing to prevent it.

1540. *The O'Conor Don.*] I understood you, in answer to some of the honourable Members of the Committee, to say that with regard to those counties that you were asked about, you have not

Mr. G. Battersby, LL.D.

8 May 1873.

not made any inquiry as to the number of jurors that would be placed upon the book under your proposal?—No, I have not.

1541. Do I understand that you have considered that with respect to the counties with which you are more intimately connected?—I have not considered it with regard to the number who may be put on the jurors' book at any particular rate, but from my knowledge of those counties with which I am acquainted, I am sure that they would give a sufficient number of jurors for the purpose.

1542. You are most intimately acquainted with the county of Westmeath, I understand?—Yes.

1543. Have you considered how many jurors would be put on the book under those qualifications in the county of Westmeath?—No, I have not.

1544. Would you be surprised to learn that there would be only 273 common jurors, and only 96 special jurors under those qualifications in the county of Westmeath?—I am not aware of the fact; but I would have supposed that there would have been many more, because I have seen the jurors under the old law for many years, and I never saw anybody upon a jury there who had not a higher qualification in point of actual income than I have stated; but with regard to the number that would appear upon the rating, I cannot tell.

1545. How many jurors do you think there ought to be on the book for the county of Westmeath?—I do not know.

1546. Have you never turned your mind to the subject?—I have never calculated it, but I have seen the panels sometimes, and I think the number returned is generally about 140 at each assizes.

1547. Do you mean to say that you believe that there were no persons on the jurors' book in the county of Westmeath, under the old system, who did not possess the qualifications which you have mentioned?—I am sure that there were many on the jurors' book, but those who were returned to serve, and did serve, I am sure had that qualification, and more.

1548. I understand your proposal would be that this qualification should be for the making out of the jurors' book?—No doubt the qualification I proposed was so, and it would be a higher qualification as to freeholders and leaseholders than under the old law.

1549. It would be a high qualification for occupation, would it not, 100 *l.* for the common jurors, and 200 *l.* for special jurors?—I do not think that that upon house rating would be a very high qualification, upon this principle, that the persons rated are nearly all tenants, and tenants at rack rent, and although the farms may be of intrinsic value to that amount, their share of it may be very small.

1550. Are we to understand this 100 *l.* and 200 *l.* to be the rent, and not the valuation?—Rated upon the valuation.

1551. I did not understand your last answer, in which you said that those tenants were generally at rack rent, and their interest in them might be very small, because it is not by the rent that you calculate the 100 *l.* or the 200 *l.* qualification, but by the rating valuation?—By the rating in the ordnance valuation.

1552. Do you consider that the valuation of 100 *l.* for common jurors, and 200 *l.* for special jurors would be sufficiently low?—If the state of things would admit of it, I think that would be low enough.

1553. Is the Committee to understand that, in making those suggestions, you have never considered at all the number of jurors that would be placed upon the book by those qualifications?—No; I have no means of knowing, and I do not know.

1554. And have you never considered it?—I have never considered it.

1555. As I understand your proposal, under it the qualification for placing men upon the jurors' book would be raised considerably from what it has been up to the present time?—It would.

1556. And at the same time you would retain the power of the sheriff to omit from this restricted jurors' book any names that he thought proper in making out his panels?—Yes.

1557. So that you would restrict the number of jurors on the panel, and you would retain the present power of the sheriff over that restricted list?—I do not want to restrict the number; the full number should be still retained one way or another.

1558. Have you not admitted that practically your proposal would exclude many men from the jurors' book who are now on it?—No, my suggestion was attended with this, that where a sufficient number could not be had to satisfy the rate that I would put on then, the rate must be lowered so as to get a sufficient number. That is a matter of necessity.

1559. You have not given any consideration to what a sufficient number would be, or how much the rate should be lowered in different counties to meet the probable deficiency?—I have not considered how much it should be lowered in different counties.

1560. Nor the number of jurors that would be required in different counties?—No.

1561. Have you considered in any single county, even in your own, what the effect of your proposal would be with respect to the number of jurors?—No, I have not; I have only considered what class of man would probably be independent and discharge his duties fairly and independently.

1562. I do not exactly understand your proposal with respect to the leasehold qualification, which you mentioned; what is the exact character of it?—Every person holding upon a term originally created for not less than 21 years.

1563. No matter what his valuation was?—Yes, I put the same valuation as a freeholder.

1564. Do you mean every man who held land under a lease of 21 years or over, and valued at 20 *l.*?—Which is worth 20 *l.* to him, the holding being part of it; it is one of the old qualifications under the old Acts.

1565. How would you ascertain that?—The assistant barrister could ascertain it very well; the collectors could return a man as having that value, and any party might object, or he himself might change it before the assistant barrister, and he could easily determine it in the same way as he determines voters' qualifications for the counties and the like.

1566. Dr. *Ball.*] It is the voters' qualification in Ireland, is it not?—Yes, in the same way in rent charges it is.

1567. *The O'Conor Don.*] Leases and rent charges

Mr. G. Battersby, LL.D.

3 May 1873.

charges are different things, are they not?—They are generally freeholds.

1568. Is there such a qualification for voters at present in Ireland as a 20*l.* leasehold qualification?—For leaseholders I think not. I do not recollect that there is.

1569. I do not understand how the collector is to know whether a man has a 20*l.* interest in a lease or not?—The collectors generally know the situation and the circumstances of everybody.

1570. The collectors would know what is the valuation of a man's holding, but how would they know what interest he has in it?—They generally know very well what rent he pays; they generally hear of it; and the worst that could happen in a case of that kind would be, either that a man's name might be put upon the roll who had not the qualification for it, and that would not be any very great harm, or he might be omitted, and then he could claim to be put on.

1571. Would you allow any man who held upon lease in the district, and who paid a rent of 20*l.* a year, to be put upon the jurors' list?—Not unless he had 20*l.* for himself, after paying the rent.

1572. Do you think that a man who would have 20*l.* for himself after paying the rent would be a fit person, as a rule, to be made a juror?—I think they would be better on the average than those who were put on merely because they were rated at 20*l.*

1573. You think that a man who paid a rent of 20*l.* under a lease, and who had 20*l.* interest in it, would be more likely to be a good juror than a man who was rated, we will say, at 70*l.* or 80*l.*?—No, I do not say that.

1574. But you exclude a man who is rated at 70*l.* or 80*l.*, and you allow a man who has a leasehold of 20*l.* a year?—Yes, I would.

1575. What is your reason for that, if you do not think that the one is a better class than the other?—I think that a man who is merely rated has no certainty of profit; but a man who has a certainty of profit would be a qualified man.

1576. Then you attach the qualification to the certainty of profit?—Yes, I think that is the result.

1577. As soon as the landlord gives the tenant a lease, you think that the tenant, who before was disqualified, immediately, from the certainty of profit, becomes a qualified juror?—It might be so.

1578. But you are of opinion that it is so when you recommend it, I presume?—I only want to answer after forming a correct opinion, if I can.

1579. You consider that the qualification of jurors, as it appears to me from your answer, depends upon what you term a certainty of profit, and that a holder from year to year being rated, we will say, at 70*l.*, 80*l.*, or 90*l.*, is less likely to be a qualified juror, because he has no certainty of profit, than a farmer who farms land valued at 20*l.* under a lease of 21 years, on account, in his case, of his certainty of profit?—It is very difficult to say what the exact position would be; but I think a man who has a certainty of tenure, and a certain profit, is better qualified than a man who has neither, and who may not have any profit at all.

1580. *Chairman.*] You mean that his interest in the lease is to be 20 *l.*?—Yes.

1581. Although his actual holding would be valued at much more?—The actual holding would probably be rated at 30 *l.* or 40 *l.*, or more. I am trying to distinguish between the class of persons who should be taken according to their rated valuation, which rated valuation might give them no profit at all, and another class who have a certain profit, and who would be a different class in actual *bonâ fide* possession of land, and with an income of 20 *l.*

1582. *The O'Conor Don.*] I suppose you are aware of the very large sums that are given now in Ireland for the interest in farms merely held from year to year?—I am.

1583. Sometimes amounting almost to what the fee would sell for in the Landed Estates Court?—Sometimes actually more in some small farms.

1584. Would not that prove that if you are to allow jurors to be put upon the book on account of the interests that they have in their lands, tenants holding very small portions of land could be proved to have an interest with 20 *l.* a year in it?—I did not, I think, say anything as to the quantity of land to be held.

1585. Do you think that any man, no matter how small his holding, who could prove, first of all, that he has a lease for 31 years, and, secondly, that the lease is of the value of 20 *l.* more than his rent, should be placed upon the jury book?—If he has an actual value so as to make him an independent man, I think he ought to be put on the jurors' book.

1586. Would not that practically include almost every man in Ireland who has a 31 years' lease?—No, certainly not.

1587. Have you ever considered how many it would include?—I have not; I have no means of judging, but I know this as a matter of actual certainty, that a great majority of the tenants in Ireland holding land to that extent have hardly any profit at all.

1588. If they have hardly any profit at all how do you account for the enormous sums given for their interests?—It is only given in particular cases. People are always to be found in particular neighbourhoods to pay a good deal of money if they want to get possession of a piece of land that is near them, but if you were to bring into the market a large estate and divide it in that way, you could not get the same prices at all.

1589. In your opinion, with regard to the large sums of money given for what is called the tenant's interest in Ireland, those are only given in peculiar cases?—Only in peculiar cases.

1590. Are they not the exceptions?—Yes, they are. I have actually seen gentlemen trying to sell estates, to take advantage of that principle to which the honourable Member has been referring; and they could not sell them at all where there were many lots; they could not get purchasers for them.

1591. What were they generally selling?—Selling the fee simple.

1592. Another qualification that you proposed is with regard to merchants having 1,000 *l.* property of any kind; how is that to be ascertained?—Very easily. The collector would know a man that was likely to have it, and he could put him down, and if anybody objected, the chairman could put him off; and if anybody thought he had a right to claim it, he could go before the chairman, and could satisfy him. I do not see any difficulty about it; besides, that is one of the qualifications under the old Acts. Under the old Acts, 5,000 *l.* was the qualification

Mr. *G. Battersby*, LL.D.

8 May 1873.

tion for a special juror. I put it as 1,000 *l.* as being a fair sum for a common juror.

1593. You consider that there would be no objection to having persons tried by special jurors in all cases, if the Crown thought proper to do so?—I think that it would be a good thing to have the power. It probably would not be often acted upon; but if a gentleman were going to be tried, I think that he ought to be very glad to get a special jury to try him.

1594. Upon the same principle, do not you think that if a poor man were going to be tried, he would be very glad to have a jury composed of poor men to try him?—So he would; but the object would not be the same in both parties. The one would try to get an impartial jury, whereas the other would try to get a jury that would sympathise with himself as to the offence.

1595. Do not you think that the proposed trying persons by special juries would be unpopular in the country?—I do not think it would.

1596. Are you aware that there is any feeling against the old Act?—I am aware that there has been a feeling with a very large proportion of the people of the country against any trial at all or any law at all. There is no doubt about that.

1597. Do not you think that it would be a little beyond that?—It would be a little beyond that too; but I am sure that they all have it.

1598. You do not think that the feeling would be intensified by the idea that the Crown could try them always by a special jury?—I think not.

1599. You said, did you not, as far as your own knowledge goes, you never knew a sheriff attempt to pack a jury?—I never did.

1600. Did you ever hear of such a thing in Ireland?—I have often heard of such a thing; but I do not believe all I hear in Ireland.

1601. Mr. *Attorney General.*] You have been asked about the number of jurors that would remain in the various counties in Ireland under the general state of things that you have suggested; out of that number, I presume, are to be taken all the persons who are exempted?—Yes, of course.

1602. That would still further reduce the number, would it not?—It would.

1603. Has it ever occurred to you, as a wiser and better mode, that there should absolutely be no exemptions, but that everybody should take his turn?—No; I think the persons exempted by the Act ought to be exempt still.

1604. You know those exemptions, I take for granted?—I have read them.

1605. I do not presume to know how Irish society is, but does not it occur to you that this takes the very cream of society: for instance, all Members of Parliament, all clergymen, all persons holding any paid judicial or other office belonging to any court of justice in Ireland, barristers at law, attorneys, and solicitors, licensed medical practitioners, apothecaries, civil engineers, public notaries and actuaries, professors, schoolmasters, or teachers in any college, academy, or school, persons holding any public office under Her Majesty's Government, or any public department, or under any local authority, and paid from taxes general or local, stamp distributors, and other public officers paid by authorised fees or per-centage, masters of vessels, and duly licensed pilots, and persons heretofore exempted by virtue of any prescription, charter, grant, writ, or local Act of Parliament, are all exempt: in England that would sweep the jury list of almost all the people that we wish to have in it, how is it in Ireland?—Probably it would be better to have them all upon the juries, but they have been generally exempted in Ireland from service. There is no doubt that those persons come within the classes of persons who would be the most intelligent, and capable of serving as jurors.

1606. It never has occurred to you to consider the principle of the exemptions?—Possibly the thing may have occurred to me, but I never gave it much attention.

1607. At all events, it is plain that whatever plan you suggest, the number that would remain now would have to be further reduced by sweeping out of them the whole of those exempted classes?—Certainly; they never were included.

1608. Dr. *Ball.*] You cannot have any doubt that clergymen in Ireland ought not only to be exempt, but excluded from the jury box?—As regards clergymen in Ireland, I think the people are unanimous that no clergymen ought to be introduced into any position of the kind.

1609. With respect to other exemptions, in looking through them, I should think that they would not have much operation in a county, but a great deal of operation in a town?—It would be so; probably in a county there would not be more than 8 or 10 per cent. altogether coming within the exemptions.

1610. Of course, in towns like Dublin, or Belfast, or Cork there would be a great many?—Yes.

1611. As I understand you, you do not propose that the sheriff should select, but only that the sheriff should omit?—Yes.

1612. Do you think there would be more, or that there would be any use in providing that any act of that kind should be done by the high sheriff personally, and not by the sub-sheriff?—I think it might tend to a satisfactory result if the high sheriff were with his own hand to sign the panel, for the high sheriff is a person of high position, and generally the people have great confidence in him, and I think that the signing of the panel with his own hand would be a useful provision.

1613. Besides your knowledge of matters of this kind, from practising as a barrister, do you not reside a great part of the year in the country?—During the long vacation, I always do.

1614. You are a magistrate, are you not?—I am.

1615. And I think you attend the petty sessions?—Yes; I do, occasionally.

1616. Are you intimately acquainted with the farming class in Ireland?—Very intimately. I know nearly all the jurors in Meath and Westmeath.

1617. In giving your evidence as to the state of affairs, I take it that you were speaking principally of the home circuit counties, such as Dublin, which you know so well?—Yes, of course.

1618. You would not undertake to lay down a rule as to the remote districts in the west and south?—No, I have never been in Kerry or in Cork.

1619. I mean so as to amend the statutory provisions?—No.

1620. What you mean is from your experience in your own counties to suggest a kind of approximation of what ought to be enacted for all?—Just so, provided the materials are to be found there.

Mr. G. Battersby, LL.D.

8 May 1873.

1621. It has been said that 273, as I understand, would be the number in Westmeath; supposing that there were about 300 jurors, would not that be a very fair panel in a county like Westmeath?—It would be a sufficient panel; the number returned by the sheriff under the old system when I have seen it was about 140. I speak of the panel returned to try the cases, and not the number upon the books. I never saw the number upon the books.

1622. *The O'Conor Don.*] Your evidence with regard to the qualification was as to the qualification of those who were to be put upon the book?—Certainly. The general practice has been that nearly the same persons attended at every assizes, and there were many jurors who never attended at all.

1623. Dr. *Ball.*] The assizes at Mullingar, I think, only last about two days?—Seldom more.

1624. *The O'Conor Don.*] How long do the sessions last?—One day, or half a day in each quarter.

1625. Dr. *Ball.*] In the counties on the home circuit, except the last town, the assizes are generally not more than two days?—Yes; that is the only one that is longer.

1626. Colonel *Wilson Patten.*] Do you think that it would be impolitic to allow the present law to exist and for another assizes to pass under it?—I think that the sooner the present law is altered the better; in the present state of the country, so far as I know, there is not likely to be any very great pressure of heavy business of a criminal nature before the next assizes unless some change should take place. The business now at the assizes is very light; the offences are hardly any, and unless something extraordinary were to happen, there would not be any great pressure of business before the next assizes.

1627. *Chairman.*] I think you propose to add several qualifications to those which are now prescribed in the Act?—Yes, I would propose to add several without any property qualification at all.

1628. To whom would you entrust the duty of making those additions to the jurors' book?—To the chairman.

1629. But he cannot do that, can he, out of his own knowledge?—I would give him some information; he is to do it with the assistance of the knowledge of all the others. The collector of poor rates, the clerk of the poor law union, and the police could help him very much in it.

1630. Have you considered that much?—I have never considered very much about the Act at all, but I have been thinking of it since I was brought here, and I think it would be an improvement.

1631. As the basis is the existing jurors' book, the clerk of the union and the poor rate collector would have nothing to do but to take the rate-book; is not that so?—That is all the mechanical part of it.

1632. That is the basis?—Yes.

1633. But many of those names which you propose should be added might not appear on the rate-book at all?—No, they might not appear.

1634. What foundation is the clerk of the union and the poor rate collector to have to make out this new list?—If the collectors were desired to return such persons for the purpose of forming the jurors' list, they could easily do it, and if they did not do it, the police could do it very well.

1635. Would not it require a considerable knowledge of the private circumstances of a great many individuals?—Yes, everybody knows them. They could not settle them with perfect accuracy, of course, but as a matter of general knowledge, they have a general knowledge of everybody's affairs in the county.

1636. You could not secure that every one so qualified, as you propose, should appear on the jurors' list; that is to say, you could not make it incumbent upon the clerk of the union, could you, to return a complete list of those various qualifications?—If he were directed to do it; it is no part of his duty at present; but if every collector of poor rate were directed to do it, there is nothing to prevent him doing it that I can see.

1637. Would you impose a penalty on the clerk of the union if he omitted anyone?—If he corruptly and knowingly omitted, I would.

1638. Do not you think that that would be a very heavy addition to the duties of the clerk?—No, I should say not.

1639. Are there any qualifications in addition to the rating qualifications for Parliamentary voters now?—Yes, freeholders and rent-charges.

1640. Whose duty is it to make a list of the Parliamentary voters?—As to rated persons, the clerk of the union returns them, and they are made by the chairman, like what is being discussed in this Act; but a freeholder of 50 *l.* or a 20 *l.* annuitant applies at the quarter sessions to the chairman to be registered, and he gives notice to the clerk of the peace. He is the moving party himself.

1641. But do you think that he would have many applications from qualified persons to be placed on the jurors' book?—Not one; everybody that ever I saw in Ireland want to get off the jurors' book, and not on it.

1642. Do not you think that there might be some difficulty in having those additions made?—There would be some trouble: but, I think, not much difficulty.

1643. You think that, whatever alterations you may make in the jurors' book, you ought still to leave in some person the power of selecting the panel?—I think it is unavoidable; and I know no person to be entrusted with it except the sheriff. I have been turning it over in my mind, and I cannot call to mind any person who could possibly be entrusted with it. I should much rather dispense with sheriff's discretion altogether, and all discretion, if that could be; but I do not think it can be.

1644. You think that, however much you may raise the qualification, there are in Ireland only a limited number of persons who are qualified to act as impartial jurors?—I think so.

1645. And you think that the selection by the sheriff is the best way of securing that impartiality?—I think it is the only way.

1646. Is it a selection by the sheriff; is it not rather a selection by the sub-sheriff in practice?—The sub-sheriff is the sheriff for all purposes. The high sheriff never interferes; he does nothing but attend the judges. The sub-sheriff is the person who does everything, and he signs the high sheriff's name to the different documents and things.

1647. Dr. *Ball.*] But you approve of the suggestion that I made, that the high sheriff should be made to do it personally?—Yes, as regards the panels.

1648. *Chairman.*] But the high sheriff has so very

Mr. G. Battersby, LL.D.

8 May 1873.

very minute local knowledge except in his own immediate neighbourhood?—Commonly not; in fact in that case of Mr. Seed's that was spoken of, the high sheriff, although he examined the list, was not acquainted with the jurors.

1649. Then I understand you to think, as a rule, the sub-sheriff may be trusted to select the most impartial persons?—I think he may.

1650. It is placing very great power in the hands of the sub-sheriff, is it not?—It is; but it is a power that he always had, and which, I think, he seldom abused. It is the law of the land, and has been always; we got it from England.

1651. If he had any bias in favour of one section of the community rather than the other it would be possible, would it not, for him to frame his panel in accordance with his bias?—Certainly it would.

1652. And you think that in the north, for instance, the power of selecting panels to try party cases can, in all cases, be safely left to the sub-sheriff?—As far as my experience goes, it may. I went the North Eastern Circuit, which is the most troublesome part of the north, and I thought that the juries were very fair, and decided the cases very fairly.

1653. Dr. *Ball.*] You went as judge, did you not?—Yes; and there were some questions between Orangemen and Roman Catholics, and all sorts of things of that kind, but I saw no unfairness in the juries.

1654. *Chairman.*] Is it not a system that is rather calculated to throw doubt upon the impartiality of Irish juries, if the nomination and selection of the panel is left to a person who may be a partisan?—Everybody in Ireland may be a partisan, and most of them are; I do not know whom you could put in his place.

1655. You would not entrust the selection of the juries to everybody?—I would rather not leave the discretion to anybody, but I think it is impossible to avoid it.

1656. You think that the old system was an evil, but a necessary evil?—I do not think that the old system was an evil, but I think that the defect, or the possibility of defect, which has been pointed out, cannot be helped; it is human nature, and there will be defects in every human system.

1657. Without assuming that in many cases, or if you like you may assume that the sheriff never did act improperly, is it not calculated to throw doubt upon the impartiality of justice that such a thing should be possible; does not it weaken the confidence of the people in the administration of justice?—People will make imputations, and make them without foundation; you cannot prevent that.

1658. Even if you greatly raised the standard of qualification, and adopted several precautions to remove the names of improper persons from the list, you still would not trust to a panel selected by lot from that list; you do not think that the jury book can by any process be sufficiently purged?—Certainly not; it is quite impossible.

1659. Do you think that persons, even in a good position in Ireland, are not to be trusted to act with impartiality?—There are many in good positions who could not be trusted to act with impartiality.

1660. And who must be kept off?—Who ought to be kept off.

1661. Mr. *Bruen.*] In the case which you mentioned just now, the Fenian was in a good position, was he not?—A very good position.

1662. *Chairman.*] You think, do you not, that the power of the Crown Solicitor to order jurors to stand by is a very invidious power?—The exercise of it to any great extent is an invidious exercise.

1663. But in this case to which reference has just been made, it ought to have been exercised, ought it not?—Yes, if the Crown Solicitor had known the man, but he did not know him.

1664. The Crown Solicitor can easily make himself acquainted with the characters of all the jurors upon the panel, can he not?—No, not at all.

1665. Not through the constabulary?—The constabulary may give him information, but they do not do it always.

1666. If he asked for it, could he not obtain it?—It is very often difficult to get information, even though he asks for it, and he could not effectually do it, unless he has got the whole 140 names, and got all the police from the different parts of the county from which they came, and each to point out the man that he knew; and that would be quite impracticable, unless he had the whole body of police to instruct him in the room, and of course he could not have that.

1667. There are a considerable number of constabulary, are there not, from the different parts of the county at the assizes?—Yes, there are.

1668. How long is the panel struck before the assizes?—Seven days before.

1669. So that he has seven days to get information?—Yes.

1670. Do not you think that the Crown Solicitor might find out in the course of those seven days the names of any persons who ought not, under any circumstance, to be allowed to serve on a jury in a criminal case?—I do not think that he could, because he would have to see the constable in charge of every division in the county, and that would be a very onerous business.

1671. He might communicate with the head constable, might he not?—The head generally knows nothing about it; the inspectors, who are the principal officers in the county, sometimes know those who are residing in their own immediate neighbourhood, but they do not know the others at all.

1672. Do you think that the county inspector does not know anything about the Fenians in the county?—He knows that there are Fenians, but he does not know who they are.

1673. But do not you think that he ought to do?—He ought, if he could, find them out, but it is not so easy to get information of late years.

1674. Mr. *Bruen.*] With regard to the exemptions in the second schedule, about which the Attorney General asked you, are not those exemptions made on account of the interference with other public duties, and necessary duties, which those persons named in the schedule are obliged to perform?—Some of them are.

1675. Nearly all of them are, are they not; for instance, persons holding judicial and other offices in any court of justice in Ireland, and there are certain necessary public duties which probably would be interfered with if those persons were summoned on a jury, such as barristers-at-law, attorneys and solicitors, and licensed medical

Mr. G. *Battersby*, LL.D.

3 May 1873.

medical practitioners. There are public duties attaching to all those persons, and they might be seriously interfered with by the exercise of this other public duty?—Yes, they appear to be all public duties.

1676. The honourable and learned Member for the University of Dublin put a question to you as to the formation of the actual jury panel by omission, and not by selection; does not it come to the same thing: supposing that a panel is composed of 150 names, and the sheriff omitted 100 of them and allowed 50 to remain upon that panel, would not that be the same thing as if he selected the 50 out of the jury lists?—It would not be exactly the same thing, but it would come to pretty nearly the same.

1677. It would be the same thing in its practical results, would it not?—Possibly it might be said to be so.

1678. *The O'Donoghue.*] Do you think that under the present system the jurors would always lean to their own class?—Not all the jurors.

1679. The jurors, I mean, to whom you object?—They would not always do it, but there would be many of them, probably, who would.

1680. What would be the cases in which they would not do that?—In every class there are individuals above the prejudices and weaknesses of their particular class, who would act always rightly, but the feelings of the majority of that class would be in favour of the offender.

1681. Mr. *Attorney General.*] The cases, I presume, into which these feelings enter, which render impartiality difficult, are the exceptions, are they not?—They are.

1682. Might it not be put thus, that it is better to have a system which will be, at all events, certainly impartial in the great majority of cases, and run the chance of an occasional mistake in cases which you admit to be exceptional?—That is my view of it. I would want to have a higher class in every instance to try the cases if practicable.

1683. Assuming for the sake of argument, that the chance of the ballot or what not, might now and then produce a bad result, still what I want you to consider is, whether, allowing for the sake of argument that it might, in an exceptional case, now and then produce a deplorable result, it would not be better to have a system undeniably impartial, to which in the great majority of cases there could be no objection, and of which the exceptional cases might be very rare?—Undeniable impartiality is what ought to be sought for and effected, if possible.

1684. What I want to put to you is this, let it be governed by chance, and if those cases are exceptional cases, there is a chance, at all events, of securing an impartial selection in the great majority of cases, and although we may now and then fail to secure a right jury for a particular case, granting that difficulty, which I admit for the sake of argument, is it not better to adopt that which is undoubtedly a just rule in the majority of cases, even though here and there the application of that rule may turn out to bring forth an unfortunate result in a particular case, rather than have for every case a rule which is open to the objection that you are leaving the power of selection in possibly partial hands?—I think that as little ought to be left to chance as possible in any case, and I think that impartiality and fairness ought to be secured as far as practicable; as far as means will admit.

1685. Impartiality of selection is secured by chance, is it not; if nobody selects the names the selection must be made impartially, they may be fit or unfit when you have got them, but they must be at least impartially chosen if nobody chooses them?—Partiality of choice, which, according to my view of it, almost always insures partiality in action, ought not to be allowed.

1686. The great majority of cases are cases, are they not, in which there is no scope for what you call partiality of action, and the cases to which partiality of action applies are the exception, are they not?—They are few.

1687. In a case between A. and B. for goods sold and delivered, you do not suggest that there is partiality of action in Ireland any more than in this country?—No, in such cases I should say certainly not.

1688. Those are the majority of cases, are they not?—They are the most numerous, but they are the least important.

1689. May it not be better to have a rule which, at all events, selects impartiality in the majority of cases, even if, now and then, in the chances, it may perhaps, either in this or that case, fail, rather than have a rule which in every case is open to the suspicion that you have given to a particular person, who may be a partial man, the power of selecting the tribunal to try the case, when you really do not want it in the great majority of cases at all?—I do not think that the great majority of cases to be tried, being unimportant, ought to regulate the rule as to the administration of justice with respect to serious cases, although they may be fewer.

1690. Do not you feel that you may infect the very fountain of justice if you put into the hands of a possibly partial man the power of selecting the tribunal in every case; whereas, I understand you to admit that, in the great majority of cases, chance will select the tribunal perfectly well?—I cannot accept that view at all; but it is difficult to answer the position as put.

1691. Dr. *Ball.*] Besides impartiality, I understand you to aim at obtaining a considerable degree of intelligence?—Certainly, that is what I want.

1692. *Chairman.*] May you not secure sufficient intelligence for the purpose required by a careful revision of the jurors' book?—I think not. I think that the chairman will have no means to make a perfectly correct jury list.

1693. If you raise the standard of qualification, and if you adopt many of the propositions which have been made for striking off men who were unfit, and if you give an absolute discretion to the chairman to strike off anybody whom he considers unfit for the jury book, you may then secure sufficient intelligence, might you not?—If the chairman had the absolute control of absolute information, there might be such a list made, but he has not, and cannot have.

1694. If there were a possibility of making such a list, then you would not object to the panel being selected by lot from that list?—If you could have a correct and pure list, I should not object to ballot for it.

1695. But you do not think the list can be sufficiently purified?—I think not.

1696. Mr. *Bruen.*] Is not this your idea, that you want to get impartial juries, even if you get them by a system which is said to be theoretically imperfect, rather than to fail to get them by a system which is said to be theoretically imperfect?—Yes.

Mr. CONSTANTINE MOLLOY, called in; and Examined.

Mr. C. Molloy.

8 May 1873.

1697. *Chairman.*] You are a Practising Barrister, I believe?—Yes; of 14 years' standing, and a Member of the Home Circuit. I have also practised at Quarter Sessions on the Home Circuit.

1698. Did you assist in the preparation of the Juries Act?—I did. I prepared the draft Bill under Lord O'Hagan's instructions, with the assistance of Dr. Hancock and Mr. Piers White.

1699. Mr. Piers White is a barrister, is he not?—Yes; he is a barrister and a Queen's Counsel.

1700. Had you any occasion to observe the operation of the old system, and the necessity for a change in the law?—Yes; in my opinion a change in the law was absolutely necessary. From experience I saw that at quarter sessions criminal justice could not be administered, owing to the small number of persons who were qualified, so that a prisoner, if he wished to postpone his trial, had the means of doing it simply by exhausting the panel by his challenges for want of qualification, or by his peremptory challenges.

1701. Was it that the panels were too small?—In the quarter sessions district the sheriff only summoned those who were resident in that quarter sessions division, and the panel that he was so able to summon was very small, and after the 20 peremptory challenges, and those who were disqualified for want of qualification, he would not have remaining 12 jurors. I have known that to be the case.

1702. Even supposing the Crown set no one aside?—Yes, without the Crown setting any person aside. I have known it to occur in King's county; in each of the three quarter sessions division comprised in the county I have seen that, and probably it has occurred elsewhere.

1703. So that a prisoner had the power of getting his trial postponed?—Yes; I know one case where, at the October sessions, a man did not wish to be tried, and he applied for a postponement. The sessional Crown Solicitor opposed the postponement, and the jury were then called, and the prisoner exhausted the panel, and the Crown were obliged then to postpone the trial to the January sessions. At the January sessions the sheriff summoned every available person, and the very same thing occurred then, and the Crown had to bring the case to the adjoining quarter sessions division, and to have it tried there, where the prisoner made no objection to being tried.

1704. Were there very many objections to the old system on the ground of partiality, and so on?—Yes; I think the way in which the sheriff's function was exercised in forming the panel was a subject of well-founded complaint.

1705. Have you seen anything of the operation of the new Act?—Yes; I have on the last Home Circuit, and in Dublin. As regards the county of the city of Dublin, my own observation was that there was a great improvement in the class of jurors, common and special, that appeared in the box; but as regards the county juries, I think they were men of an inferior class. Then as regards two of the counties on the Home Circuit, Queen's County and Kildare, I did not notice any change in the class of jurors that appeared in court. They appeared to me to consist of the class that I saw usually attending.

1706. In the other counties how was it?—In the other four counties they were of an inferior class.

1707. Which were those counties?—Meath, Westmeath, King's County, and Carlow. I think it right also to state that the better class of jurors who were summoned in those counties at the last assizes, I think, from what I heard and saw, did not answer to their names when they were called; so that the jurors answering to their names were not a fair specimen of those returned on the panel, because the better class of jurors did not answer to their names.

1708. Do you attribute the defects which have appeared in the new system to any other causes besides the non-attendance of the better class of jurors?—I think that they resulted from three things: first, from the careless manner in which the jurors' lists were made out by the clerks of the unions and the poor rate collectors, which is the cause, as I think, of the very sad condition of the jurors' book at present. If there had been any care at all exercised in making out the lists, the books at present would not be in the condition that they are.

1709. You are of opinion that there was a want of care shown in the preparation of the lists?—In the county of Meath, I know from the sheriff that several persons who were not resident, persons who were dead, persons over the age of 60 years, and even so old as 80 years, were returned on the books, and some residences are not stated. In the county of Westmeath the sheriff showed me the jurors' book, and I saw myself, in court, that a large number of persons answering to their names were over age. Whilst one trial was going on, I recollect five or six persons, who were men of over age, interrupting the trial by applying to the judge to be excused from serving, and one of those men was certainly up to 80 years of age. On the jurors' book for the county of Westmeath, I saw that several persons were returned on it, and in the column for their place of abode it was stated to be unknown, and in other cases the place of abode was stated to be in the county of Meath. All these things showed that there must have been a very great want of care in the preparation of the lists. In the Queen's County the sheriff told me that when he came to make out his panel for the assizes, he found that a large number of persons resident in the adjoining county, King's County, were returned on the jurors' book, and he asked me what was he to do in the cases of those persons if he came to them in the alphabetical selection. I afterwards saw on the panel for the Queen's County, at the last assizes, two persons were returned on it with their residences stated to be in King's County. I saw in other counties in the circuit that men within the exempted classes, holding public offices, such as postmasters and others, were summoned. I see from the papers also, that persons on the staff of the militia, and holders of offices in the courts in Dublin, have been returned. All these things lead me to believe that there was very little care taken by the clerks of the unions, and the poor-rate collectors in making out the lists.

1710. Would those instances of carelessness affect the character of the jurors who appeared?—I think they would as regards those illiterate and non-English speaking persons who have turned up;

Mr. G. Molloy.

8 May 1873.

up; if no persons were returned on the list over 60 years of age, the great bulk of those illiterate and non-English speaking people would be got rid of. I saw several persons last circuit who said that they could not read or write, and in every one of those instances I saw that they were old men over 60 years of age, who ought not to have been on the list at all. If the jurors' book were corrected, and that might have been done at the January sessions, by removing those persons who ought not to be on it, according to the provisions of the Act, the great bulk of those illiterate persons would have been removed, and any of them who might have remained on the list could have been got rid of by the exercise of the Crown's right to order the jurors to stand by.

1711. Under the Act the chairman had the duty, had he not, of revising the list?—Yes; the power was given to him, by the 15th section, of correcting the list at any time that he held his court in the county.

1712. And clerks of the unions and the poor rate collectors were ordered to attend before him?—Yes, it might have been done at the January sessions. I know, from information that I have received from a reliable source, that at the last Dunshaughlin sessions, in the county of Meath, over 20 persons beyond the age applied to the chairman to have their names struck off the book.

1713. Unless the jurors came forward themselves and claimed exemption, or unless the officers came forward and gave the chairman the information, he had no means of correcting the list?—No, the chairman himself could not correct the list; but it would not be necessary for the person whose name was on the book to come forward. A complaint of his being inserted on the book might be made by any person.

1714. But no one, I presume, could be expected to make it except the clerks of the unions and the poor rate collectors, whose duty it was?—Or the sessional Crown Solicitor.

1715. Would you say, moreover, that the qualification which was adopted in the Act was too low?—Yes, I would. I think that the qualification for common jurors ought to be raised, I would say, to 30 *l.*, in all the counties except Leitrim, which is a county that is very peculiarly situated. Then it would be desirable to bring in town jurors at a rating of 12 *l.* and upwards; they would be a very desirable class to have mingled with the agricultural class.

1716. Those jurors rated at 12 *l.* in towns are only on the lists of certain counties, are they?—In the 11 counties mentioned in the first class.

1717. You have heard, have you not, a great part of the evidence which has been given before this Committee?—I have.

1718. Have you considered how the Act could be corrected partially, at all events so corrected so as to come into operation before the next assizes?—I have.

1719. Any general amendment of the Act which has been suggested could not possibly come into operation for some considerable period, even if the Act could be passed this Season?—It could not.

1720. Even the amendments, for instance, of the way in which the jury book is prepared?—It could not. The only amendment that could come into operation before the next assizes would be to correct the existing jurors' books, by expunging improper names from them.

1721. Will you explain how you think that they might be corrected before the next assizes?—If the clerks of the unions and the rate collectors were to go over the copy of the general list of jurors which the clerk of the union had made out last July, to examine it with a view to ascertain what persons were on it who were illiterate, who were over the age, who were not resident in the county and (if the qualification was to be raised) who did not possess the qualification such as would be required by the proposed Act, and were to make out a return of all the persons belonging to those classes, the rate collector and the clerk of the union could verify such a return by declaration before a magistrate in lieu of oath, and it could then be transmitted to the clerk of the peace, who could have it laid before the chairman on the first day of the ensuing Midsummer Sessions, and the chairman then could expunge from the book the name of every person returned on the list so transmitted to the clerk of the peace.

1722. And the next panels might then be selected, as directed by the Act, from the revised jurors' book?—Yes, from the revised jurors' book. If it so happened that a chairman had not expunged the list till the sheriff had made out his panel for the assizes, it could be provided for by enabling the court at which the panel was returned to amend it by striking out the names of any persons on the panel that had been in the meantime expunged from the book by the chairman.

1723. As to the time, have you considered whether what you suggest could be done so as to come into operation before the next assizes; when will the summer assizes begin?—Generally one circuit goes out in the latter end of the last week in June.

1724. When will the next sessions be held?—If we take them according to the circuits, county of Louth is the first county on the north-east circuit, and the sessions will be held there on the 17th June; that is the commencement of the quarter sessions in Louth.

1725. So that, according to your proposal, the clerks of the unions should have to revise the lists before the 17th of June in that county, at any rate?—They would. That is the first day of the sessions, and the sessions in that county would be over in a week, or about the 23rd or 24th June; so that, at all events, they should have it done before the 24th June.

1726. Is there anything in what you propose which would necessarily take the clerks of the unions and the poor rate collectors any considerable time?—The whole thing could be done by the clerks of the union and the poor rates collectors within less than a week.

1727. They would have nothing to deal with except the existing lists?—Nothing but the existing lists, copies of which they have preserved in the board-room.

1728. And they would have to expunge from those lists?—They would have to ascertain what persons on their lists belonged to the classes that I have mentioned, and to make a return of the persons that belonged to those classes.

1729. Do the jurors' lists show whether the rating qualification is in respect of a town or of a country holding?—The jurors' lists do not show that; but the clerk of a union who had prepared any jurors' lists would not have the slightest difficulty in a few minutes in ascertaining

ing whether the rating of an individual juror consisted partly of a town rating and partly of an agricultural rating, or solely of only one or other of those ratings.

1730. So that if what you propose were done, it would not necessarily expunge the names of those 12 *l.* town occupiers who have been generally said to be a very good class of jurors?—It would not. The jurors' list shows the place in which the rated property is situated, and the clerks of the unions are so familiar with every town land on the rate-books, that they would form a very good guess from simply seeing the name of the place where the property was situated, whether it was in a town or a village, and they would at once refer to the rate-book.

1731. *The O'Conor Don.*] Do you mean the jurors' or the voters' list?—The jurors' list.

1732. If you refer to the jurors' list at present, the persons who are rated at 12 *l.* do not appear in it at all, in some counties?—In the counties in Class I. they do.

1733. But in all the other counties they do not?—No.

1734. *Chairman.*] As I understand, your proposal would not place any new names upon the list?—No, not on the existing jurors' book.

1735. And it is impossible that the jurors' lists can be revised in such a way as to place new names upon them for a very considerable time, is it not?—Not until the book for next year is prepared.

1736. Is there any other suggestion which you would make for the amendment of the Act? I would recommend the raising of the qualification of both classes of jurors.

1737. There is no necessity, is there, for doing that immediately?—No, there is not.

1738. Would you give to the judge the power of excusing from further attendance any juror who might appear to be incompetent at the next assizes?—I would.

1739. Colonel *Vandeleur.*] What qualification do you recommend for special jurors?—£. 30 for agricultural ratings, and 12 *l.* for town ratings, for all counties at large, except Leitrim, and in Leitrim 20 *l.* for an agricultural rating and 12 *l.* for the town rating. Then, as to special jurors in counties at large, I would divide them into six classes, placing the counties of Antrim and Dublin in the first class, where the qualification would be highest, and there, I think, the qualification might be 150 *l.* for agricultural ratings and 50 *l.* for town ratings. In the second class, which would comprise the counties of Cork, Down, Kildare, Limerick, Londonderry, Meath, Tipperary, and Wicklow, I would have the agricultural rating 150 *l.* and the town rating 30 *l.* In the third class are Armagh, Carlow, Clare, Galway, Kilkenny, King's County, Louth, Queen's County, Roscommon, Tyrone, Waterford, Westmeath, and Wexford; there I would have 100 *l.* agricultural rating and 30 *l.* town rating. In the fourth class, including Cavan, Donegal, Fermanagh, Kerry, Longford, Monaghan, Mayo, and Sligo, I would have the agricultural rating 80 *l.* and the town rating 30 *l.* Then in the county of Leitrim, which would be a fifth class, the agricultural rating would be 50 *l.* and the town rating 20 *l.*

1740. *Chairman.*] On what principle do you propose different qualifications in the different counties?—Having regard to the number that they will produce. If they were all put in the first class, you would have no special jurors in some counties; or the number would be so small that you could not have a special jury.

1741. Do you find that that is necessary, both as regards the special and the common jurors?—Yes; and I think that the raising of the qualification in that way would have the very best effect upon the improvement of the class of jurors that I would have put upon the books.

1742. Do you think that a good many of the defects which have been alleged against the Act might be overcome by the use of the power of the Crown to order jurors to stand by?—I think that, no matter in what way the qualification of the juror is settled, it may so happen, as it did happen under the previous jury system, that unfit persons will be returned upon the panels, and I think that those cases could be met by the exercise of the Crown's right to stand by, and I think it is the only way in which those cases could be dealt with.

1743. Do you consider that the exercise of that power is very invidious?—I do not. During the 14 years that I have been practising as a barrister, I have watched very carefully its operation, and I have seen it frequently exercised, and largely exercised, and there was only one instance in which I think it was abused.

1744. How do you mean that it was abused?—In setting aside men who ought not to have been set aside.

1745. But although it may not be abused, the power may be very unpopular, may it not?—I think not; for I have seen it frequently exercised when I was defending a prisoner, and the persons about me could very well understand, or give a very good guess, at the reasons that operated in the Crown Solicitor's mind for setting aside a particular juror.

1746. Do you think that the Crown Solicitors would have much difficulty in informing themselves tolerably accurately before the assizes as to the character of the panel which had been struck?—I think not; the Crown Solicitor's rules, which have been prepared by Mr. Attorney General Warren, provide that four days before the commencement of the assizes the Clerk of the Crown is to give to the Crown Solicitor a copy of the panel, "and for the purpose of duly exercising the right of the Crown, to direct jurors to stand by, and, if need be, to challenge for cause, the Crown Solicitor shall make due inquiries in reference to the persons summoned; and when in any case he shall have sufficient reason to believe that any person coming to be sworn as a juror is open to challenge for affinity to the person on trial, partiality, bodily or mental infirmity rendering him unfit to serve as a juror, or other sufficient ground on which a challenge, if made, could be sustained, he shall direct such juror to stand by; and he shall also, in the exercise of a due discretion, direct to stand by all such persons as he shall have reason to believe are likely to be hindered from giving an impartial verdict by favour towards the accused, fear of the consequences to their persons, property, or trade, or other improper motive, although same may not amount to a legal ground of challenge, or may not admit of legal proof; and in the discharge of this duty the Crown Solicitors will not interfere, unless the circumstances of the case required it, and will then act with due care and caution, but also with promptness and decision; and, if time permit, should consult the leading

Mr. *C. Molloy.*

8 May 1873.

leading Crown Counsel in the case. In all cases of peculiar local excitement in any particular town or district of the county, it will be prudent, if the panel permit, to set aside all persons returned from such locality; and in all cases, every vintner, publican, and retailer of spiritual or malt liquors shall, as a matter of course, be ordered to stand by." I think that if the Crown Solicitor gets the panel within the time mentioned in that rule, he has only to consult the constabulary officers, who are in attendance at the assizes, and he gets full information as to the persons as to whom he ought to exercise his right.

1747. By whom were those rules issued?—By Mr. Attorney General Warren in 1868, and they are in force at present.

1748. You have mentioned to the Committee the way in which you would raise the qualifications under the Act; have you consulted any statistics, to show the number of jurors who would remain on the lists under the raised qualification?—With the assistance of Dr. Hancock, I have gone over the returns furnished to the Committee and the return of agricultural holdings made in 1870; we have estimated the number which would be produced under the proposed raising of the qualification which I have mentioned.

1749. You could probably put in a statement showing that?—Yes; I have a statement showing the estimated number of jurors that there would be under the proposed raising of the qualification.

1750. I believe you heard Mr. Serjeant Armstrong's evidence?—I did.

1751. Do you wish to make any explanation as to those defects which he pointed out as regards a view jury?—Mr. Serjeant Armstrong said that there was a blemish or defect in the Act, because in the case of a view jury he could only have one-half of the jury or six to view the place; but the section of the Act which deals with the question of a view jury is the 38th section, and that provides for having six or more of the jurors named as the viewers, viewing the place, so that there is no defect in the Act in that respect, because the parties can have six or the full jury, if they think proper, to view the place.

1752. Mr. *Bourke.*] Do you know what was the object of putting in six?—One-half of the jury was the number that used to be brought to view the *locus in quo*, and the general practise is to bring only six of them; the parties do not like the expense of bringing out the whole jury.

1753. *Chairman.*] Is there any other suggestion of Mr. Serjeant Armstrong's which you wish to make a remark upon?—Mr. Serjeant Armstrong made a suggestion that the Act should have provided for having a *tails* in the case of a jury struck according to the old system, but the law in that respect is not altered by the Act of 1871; it is the same as it had been previously from the first institution of the system.

1754. Is there anything else that you would like to add to your evidence?—With regard to the right of the Crown to order jurors to stand by, I took occasion when preparing the draft Bill to trace out the history of how that right grew up or was acquired by the Crown. If the Committee have no objection I would wish to give in a Paper, upon which I have traced the history of how the Crown acquired that right; and the conclusion at which I arrive is this, that I believe it was a privilege which was necessary to be entrusted to the public prosecutor, in order to secure the due administration of justice. (*The same was delivered in,* vide *Appendix.*)

1755. Dr. *Ball.*] I think that you either draughted, or assisted in draughting, this Act of Parliament?—I draughted the Act.

1756. You have no official position as draughtsman, have you?—No.

1757. There is a certain draughtsman belonging to the Irish Office, is there not?—Yes, Mr. O'Hara.

1758. You were brought in specially for the purpose of this particular Bill?—Yes.

1759. You have had a great deal of practice, have you not, in defending prisoners?—I have had.

1760. As you draughted the Bill, perhaps you can explain to me this matter in the Bill. I find that in 11 counties jurors occupying houses rated at 12 *l.* are entitled to act; but I find that in 24 counties any rating for houses is absolutely excluded. On what ground was the inclusion of the 11, and on what ground was the exclusion of the other 24 counties?—As I draughted the Bill, and as it passed the House of Lords, the figures in Class I. were 30 *l* and 20 *l.*, and they were changed in the House of Commons from 30 *l.* to 20 *l.*; and the 20 *l.*, as regards towns, into 12 *l.*

1761. I want to know why the 24 counties in the second class have no qualification from houses? They had the 20 *l.* qualification for houses, the same as it was in Class I. when it came from the House of Lords.

1762. Why is there not a similar qualification in Class II for houses?—I think if I had been aware of the change that was made in the House of Commons, by reducing the 20 *l.* to 12 *l.* in Class I., I would have suggested that a similar change should have been made for Class II. I think that it is rather inconsistent, saying that a man rated in respect of a 12 *l.* house in the counties class, in Class I., should be qualified as a juror, and not in Class II.

1763. *Chairman.*] Did Classes II. and III. stand as they were in the original Bill?—They did. The only alteration made was in the first class, by changing the figure 30 *l* into 20 *l.*, and the 20 *l* in the towns into 12 *l.*

1764 Dr. *Ball.*] Why should the county of Antrim have a franchise peculiar to a house, and the county of Armagh have no franchise peculiar to a house, although Armagh contains two towns, Portadown and Lurgan, in which you will find as great a number of qualified jurors as in any place in Ireland?—As the Bill was draughted by me, the town rating for the two classes on the Bill was the same; 20 *l.* for each of them. The Committee of the House of Commons made a change in Class I., and they made the jurors rated at 12 *l.* in towns qualified, and they did not introduce a corresponding amendment as regards Class II.

1765. You say that it was entirely done in the House of Commons?—Yes.

1766. And it was not in the original plan of the Bill?—Certainly not.

1767. Why, in the special jury qualification, is there no distinction between houses and land, although you have adopted that qualification according to your own statement in Class I. of the common jurors?—In Perrin's Act, the House qualification existed, 20 *l.* in towns, and we had no precedent in any former Bills for a town qualification as regards special jurors.

1768. But

Mr. *C. Molloy.*

8 May 1873.

1768. But in point of fact, do not you know that in the county of Dublin this 50 *l.* qualification brings in farmers and agriculturalists of a very uneducated class, and excludes merchants and traders, whose houses are rated at 50 *l.*, who live in the country?—It does.

1769. In short, do not you think that there ought to be house qualification? Yes; and I have suggested in Dublin and Antrim the 50 *l.* house qualification for special jurors.

1770. Have you seen how many that would be?—No return has been made to the Committee of the number of jurors on the special jurors' book for the county of Dublin, so that we can only make an estimate of the number that would be the result of that 150 *l.* agricultural and 50 *l.* town holding. We think they would come to between 500 and 600 in the county of Dublin.

1771. You admit the principle, do you not?—Yes, I do.

1772. Mr. *Bourke.*] Would not the proposal to put the household qualification at 50 *l.* exclude all those jurors that the honourable and learned Member for the University of Dublin has alluded to possessing a 30 *l.* household qualification?—Yes, for Antrim and Dublin it would.

1773. Dr. *Ball.*] Is that for the city or the county?—The county.

1774. Mr. *Bruen.*] That would assume that those who are rated under 50 *l.* were not fit men to serve?—It would that they were not qualified.

1775. You mentioned Dublin and Antrim, that they are to have for the special jurors a house qualification; are there any other counties than Dublin and Antrim to which you would give this household qualification for special jurors?—Yes, I think in all cases I would; the 50 *l.* is only in those two.

1776. Dr. *Ball.*] It suggested whether, for a house 50 *l.* is not too high?—I think that there are a very great number of houses rated in Antrim and in the county of Dublin at 50 *l.* For instance, houses in Rathmines, Rathgar, Kingstown, Monkstown, and towards Bray.

1777. Mr. *Bruen.*] As regards the house qualification, you propose a different qualification for the other counties?—There are five classes of counties for special jurors. In the first class the town qualification is 50 *l.*, and in the next three it is 30 *l.* Then, in the case of Leitrim, which is a peculiar county, it is 20 *l.*

1778. You think that the qualification for common jurors which is named in the Act, as it becomes law, is too low?—I think it is; but in justification of myself, I would like to mention that the Act has followed the precedents of the former Bills. There were nine Bills introduced by different Attorneys General and Secretaries for Ireland.

1779. Why do you think the 20 *l.* qualification for common jurors in Class I. of the Act too low?—For the 20 *l.* qualification in Class I., I am not responsible; for what I suggested in the draft of the Bill was 30 *l.* and 20 *l.*

1780. *Chairman.*] With 30 *l.* and 20 *l.* in Class I., do you think that you would be able to provide a sufficient number of jurors?—Yes, I have no desire to raise the qualification; and in reference to the 20 *l.* qualification for common jurors in Class II., I was there following the precedent of the previous Bills.

1781. Mr. *Bruen.*] Why do you think that the 20 *l.* qualification in Class I., is too low?—I have seen myself from experience in my own circuit a number of men who I believe come in under that 20 *l.* qualification, and whom I think it would be better to have removed from the book, which would be done by raising the qualification to 30 *l.*, which would get rid of a large number of those jurors.

1782. Do you mean that the large number that you wish to get rid of are not fit to serve as jurors?—I think you would be better without that class of jurors.

1783. Do you think that the administration of justice is not fit to be placed in their hands?—I would not go so far as saying that.

1784. For what reason is it that you think that they ought to be excluded?—I think that by going up to 30 *l.* you would get a much better class of jurors. I have watched the conduct of the juries on my own circuit of six counties, and at the last circuit I do not think there was anything in their conduct or their verdicts in one single instance that was open to objection.

1785. Then why do you wish to remove them if there was nothing in their conduct which was open to objection?—For the purpose of getting a better class of jurors.

1786. You must admit then that they are a worse class of jurors?—Yes, I do.

1787. Do you think that in the county of Leitrim, the men rated at 20 *l.* are a better class of men than the class rated at that amount elsewhere?—I do not; but Leitrim is a very peculiar county owing to the number of small holdings in it.

1788. *Chairman.*] Or rather the absence of large holdings?—Yes.

1789. Mr. *Bruen.*] You say as regards the other counties, that you think the 20 *l.* men are a worse class of men, and you wish to see them removed; but in Leitrim, do you mean to say, that the 20 *l.* men are not a worse class of men, or are they better than the 20 *l.* men elsewhere?—It would be a mere speculation for me to offer any opinion as to the people of Leitrim. I have never been in the county, and I do not know what sort of people they are there.

1790. Then it is merely for the look of the thing that you wish to do this?—It is for the number; I would like to improve the class of jurors as much as I could, having regard to the number that would be produced under the qualification that I suggest.

1791. Then you think that it would be better to have a large number of a worse class in Leitrim than to have a limited number of a better class?—No, I do not. Leitrim appears to me, from the ratings, to be a very peculiar county. If you adopted the 100 *l.* qualification for a special juror in Leitrim, I do not think you would have a special jury. The numbers are 37; and then you must take 40 per cent. off the gross number of ratings for persons who are exempt or disqualified.

1792. As regards the trial of causes in Leitrim, do you think that it would be quite safe to leave the trial of causes to juries composed partly of men rated at 20 *l.*, whereas in other counties you think that men rated at 20 *l.* are not quite safe to have the trial of causes entrusted to them?—I did not say that it was not quite safe; my experience of them is that it was quite safe.

1793. Then you can hardly see any reason for removing them?—My desire is to improve the class of jurors as much as possible, and that was the reason, as regards special jurors in Antrim and

Mr. C. Molloy.

8 May 1873.

and Dublin, of putting the house qualification up to 50*l*. instead of 30*l*., as it is in other counties. You cannot adopt the same uniform rule for all counties.

1794. Dr. *Ball*.] The plan of rating is different in different counties, is it not?—Yes, the counties vary very much.

1795. Mr. *Bruen*.] Are you prepared to say that the system of rating in Leitrim is sufficient to account for that?—No; it is rather the condition of the county; the absence of large holdings. The land in the county of Leitrim, I believe, is very poor, and it is only held by small farmers; whereas in Meath the land is first class, and there you have a large number of large holdings.

1796. Do you think that, no matter what system is pursued, there will still be some unfit persons who will find their way into the jury panels?—Yes, just as they existed under every previous system, and I think it was their presence on the jury panels that caused the exercise of the right of the Crown to make jurors to stand by. I cannot account for that right in any other way.

1797. Do you think it is more likely that those persons will find their way to the jury panels by alphabetical selection, which is more a matter of chance than anything else, or by a system under which some officer is entrusted with the power of selecting proper and fit persons?—I think that it may occur under the alphabetical system, and I have no doubt will occur just as it occurred in the case of the sheriffs.

1798. My question is, which do you think is the more likely?—I think it is as likely in the one case as in the other, from my own experience.

1799. You think that if the power of the sheriff if properly exercised, is as likely to place upon the panel unfit persons as the chance method of selection?—I think so, judging from experience. I have heard Dr. Battersby to-day mention O'Leary's case. I recollect that case perfectly well. The juror that he mentioned lived in the town, and the sub-sheriff put him on the panel. Living in the town, he must have been well acquainted with him, and I think that the exercise of the sheriff's discretion afforded no protection for keeping off unfit persons from the panel. I think that the real protection against such persons getting on the jury book is that provided for by the Crown Solicitor's rules, which I have read, and which were adopted by Mr. Seed in the case of his special commission.

1800. But if the sub-sheriff did not know that this man was a Fenian, or sympathised with the Fenians, how would the Crown Solicitor have a better opportunity of knowing it?—He would know it from the police.

1801. You think that the sub-sheriff in the formation of his panel would be better qualified to exercise the powers of selection if he consulted the police?—He would; but I do not think that the police would give him the information which they would give to the Crown Solicitor.

1802. Why not?—Because it would be to a certain extent confidential.

1803. Confidential to whom?—To the Crown Solicitor.

1804. Why not to the sub-sheriff?—I do not think it would do. It might result in this practical difficulty, that if the sheriff, instead of exercising his own discretion, exercised it at the advice, or under the discretion, of the police, some of whom might be engaged in the prosecution of the case to be tried; that might afford ground for challenge to the array. I have seen a case where two prisoners upon their trial were between them entitled to 40 challenges, and the Crown Solicitor and the prisoners each set aside man for man; the Crown Solicitor then set aside 36, and the panel was exhausted, and he had to return to those who were told to stand by, by the Crown Solicitor.

1805. Sir *R. Blennerhassett*.] What you have just mentioned with regard to the different qualifications in different classes of counties are suggestions for a temporary Act to be passed before the next assizes?—Yes, before the next assizes, to raise the qualification.

1806. I thought you said that there should be a general raising of the qualification to 30*l*.?—Yes; to 30*l*. in all counties, except Leitrim.

1807. And you stated, I think, that in Meath, Westmeath, and King's County the better class of jurors did not attend at the last assizes; what was the reason for that?—I can only account for it from a desire on their part to bring discredit upon the operations of the Act.

1808. *The O'Donoghue*.] Do not you think that the rating qualification must always be an uncertain and shifting test of the persons who are entitled to serve as jurors?—It may to a certain extent; but I do not think that you can select any better principle upon which to fix the jurors' qualification.

1809. For instance, might not a new valuation at once qualify those who are now disqualified, by raising the valuation from 15*l*. to 20*l*., and from 20*l*. to 30*l*., and so on?—Yes, it might.

1810. New valuations are likely to take place constantly, are they not?—No; the present valuation in the counties with which I have been acquainted has been in existence since 1851.

1811. It has been frequently proposed, has it not, to have the counties re-valued?—Yes, it has been, I know.

1812. And it has been delayed from year to year?—Yes.

1813. Do you think that any harm could arise from leaving the qualification as it is fixed by this new Act, and trust to the rapid progress of intelligence, and the spread of education, to secure a good class of jurors?—No, I think that, as regards the first class, it was a mistake to reduce the qualification from 30*l*. to 20*l*.

1814. But the new valuation will most likely place all those 20*l*. men into the 30*l*. class at once?—I do not know that it will.

1815. You are aware that there has been a great increase in the value of property, and that the valuation would be much higher than it was?—I would anticipate, if there was any re-valuation, that there would be an increase.

1816. Colonel *Forde*.] You stated that you would suggest that the clerks of the unions should at once have the duty to re-arrange the jurors' books according to the higher valuation?—Yes.

1817. And that they should be all brought before the assistant barrister at the next sessions?—At the next Midsummer Sessions.

1818. The criminal cases and civil cases to be tried by the assistant barrister are the same as at the assizes, are they not?—Yes, they are to a great extent.

1819. By the same juries, and from the same panel?—Yes.

1820. As

Mr. *C. Molloy.*

8 May 1873.

1820. As is usually the case, most of the Crown cases will be tried, will they not, by the assistant barristers at the quarter sessions this time?—A good number of them.

1821. Nearly all of them, in fact.

1822. So that you would allow most of the business to be transacted by the present juries, so far as the quarter sessions are concerned, but by a new and a higher panel, so far as the assizes are concerned?—No.

1823. You cannot bring in your higher scale of jurors before the quarter sessions, because they could not be summoned, as the assistant barrister is the man to select for the next quarter sessions?—The improvement in the panels that would result at the assizes by getting rid of those who are rated under 30*l.* for their different buildings, would also be effected at the quarter sessions, and then this could be done. Let the chairman exercise the power of expunging those persons from the list when he sits first; and no doubt before he did that the sheriffs would have selected their panels of jurors for the quarter sessions, but the Committee will recollect that I suggested, that where anything of that kind had occurred and the panel had been returned to any courts before the chairman had exercised the power of expunging those names from the list, the power should be given to the judge in the court to which the panel was returned to amend it by striking out the name of any person returned on it who had been expunged from the book, so that all that would be required, so far as the trials at the next quarter sessions were concerned, would be that the chairman before he went into his criminal business should deal with the expunging of those names from the books, and then having done that the sheriff and the clerk of the peace could at once call his attention to it, and say, on the panel that you are going to try this prisoner upon, there are four or five, or whatever the number may be, names of men who are expunged, and then the chairman would order them to amend the panel by striking out the names of those persons.

1824. But those persons would have been summoned, and been at the inconvenience of attending there and then?—No doubt that inconvenience would result to them, but that inconvenience will be put an end to, or rather the trouble to which they will be put from being jurors, will be put an end to at once by striking their names out of the panel, and they could get notice from the sheriff that they were discharged from further attendance.

1825. Then you would not agree with Mr. Serjeant Armstrong, where he suggests, at Questions 1004 and 1006, to alter the qualification of a juror as at present, and to revert to the old system for this one sessions and assizes, and for the sheriff to summon the jury, as he did before this Act was passed?—I do not recollect if Mr. Serjeant Armstrong proposed that.

1826. If you read Questions 1004 and 1006, I think you will see that what he says implies that?—Mr. Serjeant Armstrong certainly there spoke of reverting to the old system.

1827. Do not you think that it would save a great deal of trouble, supposing the suggestion of Mr. Serjeant Armstrong were adopted, inasmuch as you would not have to summon a great number of jurors at great inconvenience to attend. I do not want to insinuate that the sheriff hereafter should be the summoning officer, as I may call it; but that for this once it would save a great deal of trouble if we were to revert to the old system?—I think that, in order to do that, there should be a special Act of Parliament passed, and certain clauses in the present Act should be repealed, because, if the sheriff were then to summon a man out of his rotation, it would not be according to the Act.

1828. But you suggest that there must be a new Act of Parliament to meet the case?—There must.

1829. Do not you think it a choice of two evils, as you would have to put all the jurors to a very great deal of inconvenience, do not you think that it would be just as simple to hand over the thing for the one time, and let the sheriff summon as formerly?—I think not; the only additional trouble would be purging the jurors' books of the errors that at present prevail on them; and I think it is a reproach to the administration of justice in Ireland when the Legislature passes an Act of Parliament providing for the correction of the jurors' books, which are admittedly beyond all question in an improper state, that means are not taken to exercise this power, and to have the reproach of the condition that the juries' books are in put an end to as speedily as possible.

1830. Mr. *H. A. Herbert.*] You stated just now that a great many jurors did not answer to their names, in order to throw discredit upon the Act; do you mean to say that in every county in Ireland a party of respectable men got up and proposed, if possible, to make this Act fall to the ground?—I am only speaking of what I saw myself at the last assizes. Going down to the first town of the assizes, I went down the morning of the assizes, and there was a gentleman in the train with me, and I heard his observations about the Act, and about the class of jurors that it would produce. I saw that gentleman afterwards, and I heard his name called; and although I know him to be in the habit of serving, I saw him decline to answer to his name; and I cannot account for his conduct in another way than by supposing that it arose from a desire to bring discredit upon the operation of the Act; and I am confirmed in that opinion by the observations that I heard him make in the train. In the next county I saw gentlemen who were in the habit of serving upon juries, four or five of them, going round to the opposite side of the court and sitting opposite the jury box, and decline to answer to their names when they were called.

1831. You think that they did that entirely to bring discredit upon the Act?—I cannot account for it on any other grounds.

1832. Do not you think that the absence of that better class of jurors might arise from a dislike to being associated with the inferior class of men whom they expected to be on the jury?—It might, but I do not think it did.

1833. You admit that it might be also a very fair reason for their not answering to their names?—Yes. I should add that, until Judge Perrin's Act was passed, the jurors that were qualified to serve in the Record Court were of a superior class, higher rated, having a higher property qualification than those who were qualified to serve in the Crown Court, and I do not think that the superior class of men in the habit of serving in the Record Court were influenced by any feelings of that kind to abstain from answering to their names, because they would be associated with men of such humble means as 40 *s.* freeholders.

Mr. *C. Molloy.*

8 May 1873.

1834. *The O'Conor Don.*] Did you hear Mr. Coffey give his evidence upon this point?—I did.

1835. You do not agree with him in the evidence that he gave with respect to the particular reason for the upper classes not serving on the late occasions on the juries?—So far as my own observation upon circuit extended I would be very sorry to come to the conclusion that any gentleman refused to discharge his duty as a juror because he might happen to be associated or sit in the jury box with a small farmer.

1836. Mr. *H. A. Herbert.*] Do not you think that that might be just as good a reason as saying that they clubbed together in order to make this thing come to the ground, and that they agreed not to act properly?—I do not.

1837. When you devised this list, and you divided the counties into different classes, did you take into consideration that should the Valuation Bill, which is now before the House of Lords, be passed, there would be a great number more jurors on the list?—No, I did not.

1838. Therefore you had no idea in the county of Kerry, for instance, what number that new valuation would add on to the list?—No, I do not think that any person could form an opinion. I would take counties which I know myself, and the class of people that are in them, and the size of their holdings.

1839. Do not you think that for the coming assizes the most simple way to correct this would be to direct the sheriffs to strike off all under a valuation of 30*l.*?—The sheriffs have not the means of doing it.

1840. He might be directed by Parliament, might he not?—The question is how you are to provide the sheriff with the means of carrying out that direction. Take now the case of Antrim. If you directed him to strike off all persons rated under 30*l.*, he would strike off the 12*l.* town tenements; but he has not the means, unless he refers to the rate book, of ascertaining whether a man rated at 20*l.* is rated in respect of a town holding or not. I do not think that the sheriffs could do that, and if the duty was cast upon them it would be one which it would be impossible for them to discharge, because to be able to do it, they should have the rate books of every union in the county before them; and they are not men who are acquainted with the rate books, whereas it could be done in a very short time, say in a day or two, by the clerk of the union, but I do not think that the sheriff could do it himself without the assistance of the clerk of the union in a month, or two months.

1841. But with his aid he might do it, might he not?—With the aid of the clerk of the union he might do it.

1842. Colonel *Vandeleur.*] Could not the clerk of the union be directed to do it as you state in a week's time?—He could do it, I think, in two or three days, striking out, so far as the rating is concerned, but in making inquiries as to illiterates and persons over age, and non-residents, I think the whole of that thing could be done in a week by the clerk of the union.

1843. On this special occasion, would not that which the honourable Member suggests be sufficient, because that could scarcely be done as the next sessions, which will be all over in one week, and the assizes will begin on the 4th of July?—At the last assizes the Munster Circuit went out first, and they commenced in Clare; that will not be the first to go out this time, but I think that if the Act were passed, there would be ample time between this and the first day of any quarter sessions being held next June, if all the clerks of the unions were to make out the return that I suggested, and then it would not take the Chairman more than a day in any place to expunge the list.

1844. In Clare there would be about 2,000 on the book, and those divided between the three quarter sessions that are held in the county, there would be 300, or 320, at each sessions?—The chairman would do it all at one sessions, in the town of Kilrush, or whatever town the Chairman commenced to hold the June sessions in, he would there do the whole thing, not as he revises the lists now, by doing it in each town or place where he holds his sessions, he would do the whole thing in the first town wherever he commenced his sessions, whether it is Kilrush or Ennis, upon the first day of his holding the sessions in that town.

1845. *The O'Conor Don.*] I understand you to state that the clerks of the unions, according to your opinion, did not carry out the directions of the existing Act, with regard to expunging certain disqualified jurors from the list?—I think so; but it should be borne in mind that it was a duty which was cast upon them for the first time; the Act of last session only passed on the 27th of June, and it was not until some week or 10 days afterwards that the precepts were prepared and sent out by the clerks of the peace; and I know of my own knowledge that the first precepts sent out, in the vast majority of cases, were wrong, and had to be countermanded by the clerks of the peace; and a second precept in the proper form sent down to the clerks of the unions, and that diminished very much the time that they had for performing the duty, because the clerks of the union's duty was to be completed before the 1st of August; therefore the time was very much limited, and as it was the first time that they were called upon to discharge that duty, it must necessarily have been done in a hasty manner, and I think that that would account for the imperfections that undoubtedly exist in the lists as returned by them.

1846. Do you think that if a short Act were passed now, imposing additional duties upon them, they would be able to do them properly before the 17th of June?—I think they would.

1847. Do you think that they would do it?—I have no doubt at all that they would. As regards the mode in which the clerk of the unions discharge their duty with regard to making out the lists of Parliamentary voters, my experience is that they do it in an admirable manner, and give the greatest satisfaction in the several counties with which I am acquainted. I never heard a complaint made that they put into the voters' list any man who was not qualified, or kept a man off who was qualified.

1848. The qualification for voters is simply a rating qualification, is it not?—Yes.

1849. You propose to impose upon them the duty of finding out whether men are illiterate or disqualified in other ways besides rating?—I do; and for that purpose the Act proposed that they should have the assistance of the rate collector. The rate collector is a man who, in the discharge of his duty, must know the residence of each ratepayer within his district of collection. He must know it for the purpose of being able to serve the

Mr. *C. Molloy.*

8 May 1873.

the notice as regards the payment of rates at his residence. He comes in the collection of the rate into personal communication with each of the ratepayers in his district. He knows, or is able to form, a very good opinion of the age of a man from seeing him, and he knows perfectly well, I think, in almost every case (and in any case that he was not personally acquainted with he could ascertain it by inquiry), whether the party was illiterate or not.

1850. You propose, then, to raise the qualification to 30*l.* for the rural qualification, and to 12*l* for towns; do not you think that 12*l.* is rather high in most of the counties of Ireland for the town qualification?—I do not. I think it is the limit fixed for a qualification for a town commissioner.

1851. The 12*l.* includes house and lands in town, does it not?—Yes; a house and garden.

1852. Colonel *Vandeleur.*] In many small towns, like the town of Ennis or Kilrush, a house, the leasehold value of which was perhaps a couple of pounds, often may be worth 10*l.*?—I think not, speaking from my own native town, there are three or four very good gardens in it; but I do not think they are rated at more than three or four pounds per year.

1853. If it was a house with the land attached, that would make a difference?—It is rating lands, tenements, and hereditaments.

1854. *The O'Conor Don.*] Do you propose any alteration in the qualification as regards the towns in the county of Leitrim, different from the rest of Ireland?—No.

1855. Do not you think that it would be more likely to conduce to having good jurors in the county of Leitrim if you were to lower that qualification for the town holding, instead of lowering the qualification for the county holding 20*l.*?—The agricultural holding is proposed to be raised from 15*l.* to 20*l.*

1856. I understand you admitted that a man rated at 20*l.* in the country in Leitrim was not likely to be more eligible for a juror than a man rated at 20*l.* say, in Roscommon, the adjoining county, and yet you have proposed to allow this man in Leitrim to be a juror because there would not be enough of jurors without him. Is it not so?—It is so.

1857. I want to ask you whether a sufficient number of jurors, and a better class jurors, might not be got in Leitrim by lowering the town qualification from 12*l.* say, to 8*l.* or 10*l.*, than by making the county qualification in Leitrim 20*l.*?—I have no objection to lower the qualification for jurors in the towns in Leitrim.

1858. Mr. *Attorney General.*] I understood you to propose some temporary alteration of this Act for the coming assizes?—Yes, it is so.

1859. But that view of yours is founded upon the assumption that, at all events in some respects, the existing law has not worked well, and wants alteration?—I think first it is with reference to the preparation of the jurors' list, that is to say, to correct it in order to get rid of persons who have been improperly placed on the list. That is one immediate step that I suggested. The other is with reference to raising the qualification from 20*l.* to 30*l.*

1860. The old system which the new law, now under consideration superseded, whatever other defects it had, at least produced an intelligent set of jurymen, did it not?—Yes, it did.

1861. A great failing of the new law, whatever merits it may have, is that it has not produced an intelligent set of jurymen?—But under the old system, I have seen in many cases non-intelligent jurors.

1862. The merit of the old law amidst whatever defects there were, which I do not go into, was that the juries were fairly intelligent, and a defect of the present law, whatever other merits it may have, is that the juries are not fairly intelligent?—I have not seen, in my experience in my circuit, any want of intelligence on the part of the jury.

1863. Is not that what is alleged to be a defect, at any rate?—Yes.

1864. And, at any rate to some extent, you say that it is true that the juries were unintelligent?—I would prefer to have a somewhat better class of jurors, which I think would be accomplished by getting rid of those.

1865. Do you accept generally my proposition that whereas under the old law you had, with whatever defects it may have, intelligent juries, the defect of the present law is that in some instances to some extent the juries have a want of intelligence?—Yes.

1866. These premises being ascertained, and if it was also admitted that a temporary change is wanted for the next two or three assizes, I should like to hear from you, if you can tell me without trouble, what is the advantage that would result from the adoption of your suggestion, over the simple suggestion made by the honourable and gallant Member for Downshire, that you should go back for a time to the old law?—It involves the correction of the jurors' book by getting rid of those persons who ought not to be left upon it, and also the raising of the qualification; and then I do not see, once that this is done, any necessity for going back to the old system; because I think if that was done the great bulk of those matters that have given rise to complaint would then be obviated.

1867. What I meant was, what objection would there be to suspending the operation of the present law and reviving the old law for a time, and then take time to consider what would be the best system to enact for the future?—I think that if there was a proposal to return to the sheriff's discretion it would give rise to a great deal of dissatisfaction in Ireland.

1868. *Chairman.*] Even as a temporary measure?—Yes, even as a temporary measure.

1869. It would be a simple plan that would afford more time for the consideration of the amendments that are necessary in the original Act, would it not?—I think not, because it is not proposed to leave the jurors' books in the condition that they are at present, and the qualification unaltered; but it is proposed to correct them and to alter the qualification; and once that is done, I do not see then the necessity for restoring the sheriff's discretion now for a short period.

1870. Dr. *Ball.*] Do not you see that if there was a power of selection there would be no occasion to alter the book at all, because out of the existing book the sheriff could choose a most excellent panel inasmuch as the book includes, does it not, both high, low, educated and uneducated?—That is so.

1871. That is to say, when you were speaking before you were only speaking of a temporary measure. I want to point out to you that the figures which you have proposed, could only

Mr. C. Molloy.

8 May 1873.

answer for a temporary measure, because there is before Parliament a Bill for altering altogether the character of the rating in Ireland, and which even provides that it shall approximate to the rental; and the valuation approximating to the rental of 30*l.*, would have a tendency, would it not, to bring up the class that are now excluded altogether, and admit the persons that you want at the present moment to exclude?—No doubt it would have that effect; but when that result arises, it could be provided for by taking care that by the increase of the valuation, those parties that are now excluded should not be brought in.

1872. *Chairman.*] Then you would want another Act?—Yes.

1873. *The O'Donoghue.*] Do not you think that there has been very little opportunity of testing the working of the new system?—Only one assizes and one quarter sessions.

1874. That is a very slight experience to act upon, is it not?—It is.

1875. Do you think that any evil results would arise if this Committee were to suspend any decision until after another assizes, and the working of the Act has been tried again?—I should like to see that the juror books were corrected, and those improper persons removed off them. Their presence on the jury book, or their appearance upon the panels, will be just one of those grounds for discrediting the Act, whereas the Act is not responsible for those parties appearing, or rather their presence is not due to the Act.

1876. Dr. *Ball.*] Were you in that case in Dublin of attempted assassination, which was tried twice?—No.

1877. Did you know of college porters being on one of the juries?—No.

1878. Did you know whether there were any menial servants on the other jury?—Yes. Under the old system I have seen waiters and domestic servants serving on juries in the Four Courts.

1879. *Chairman.*] When would the next revision of the list take place under the present Act?—At the October sessions. In the first place, in next July, the clerk of the peace will send out his precept to the clerks of the union to have the lists made out from which the Jurors' books for 1874 will be made up, and those lists will be revised at the October sessions.

1880. And the panel for the next spring assizes would be taken out of that book, would it not?—Yes; that book would be made up before the 1st of December, and given to the sheriff before the 1st of January, and the jurors taken from that book will commence to serve on the 11th of January 1874.

1881. Colonel *Forde.*] With regard to the new book, it states in the act that the sheriff is to go from the next letter to where he left off; if it is a new jurors' book altogether how would he know where he left off?—He has the former book; he retains it in his office, and he should initial in the new book the men whom he had summoned this year.

1882. Supposing that a man whose name is "Adair" is the first on the list, and that then there is "Archer," and supposing that the sheriff goes down to Archer, and that through a change of tenancy another man named Adair comes in that has not been summoned before, the sheriff is obliged to go through the whole of the A's before he comes back to that man, and therefore that man who was first on the list would virtually be exempt, would be not, until his turn came round?—No, I do not understand the Act in that way. Take the case of our present book, and that the first name is Adair, and that the sheriff has gone down to Archer, and say that the last panel that he took this year ended with the letter M. in taking his first panel for the next year he should begin with the letter N; he would go down the letter N till he got to the last letter in the alphabet. Then he would find, probably, in the new book, that before Adair and Archer there was the name "Abbott," which was not there before. He would take him as the first in the A's, because he was the first name that he would come to, and he had not been previously summoned; and then he would go to the names in letter B.

1883. *Chairman.*] With regard to one point which was referred to in the examination of another witness, in some counties in Ireland there is an immense preponderance of names beginning with some particular letter, is there not, such as "M" or "O"?—Yes.

1884. Would not the effect of this alphabetical selection be, that after you had had a few panels all the other letters would be exhausted, and you would have the jury entirely of M's or O's?—I think not, because those are in large counties, and before you would come down to the residuum names on the book comprising one letter, the period of rotation would be exhausted, and you would begin again.

1885. What do you call the period of rotation?—The period of rotation was during the current and two preceding years.

1886. Mr. *Attorney General.*] Supposing that in a large county there were 140 names beginning with O to make the panel for the assize, you would have them all?—I think not. There are not so many names of any letter upon the book that they would all come upon the same panel.

1887. Mr. *Bruen.*] What do you mean by the period of rotation?—In Section 19, it says, "not already summoned during the current or next two preceding years."

1888. So that a great number of jurors who had not been summoned at the expiration of three years would not be summoned at all?—They would not be summoned at all.

Monday, 12*th May* 1873.

MEMBERS PRESENT:

Mr. Attorney General.	Mr. Henry Arthur Herbert.
Dr. Ball.	The O'Conor Don.
Sir Rowland Blennerhassett.	The O'Donoghue.
Mr. Bourke.	Major O'Reilly.
Mr. Bruen.	Colonel Wilson Patten.
Viscount Crichton.	Colonel Vandeleur.
Colonel Forde.	

THE RIGHT HONOURABLE THE MARQUIS OF HARTINGTON, IN THE CHAIR.

Mr. LEWIS M. BUCHANAN, called in; and Examined.

Mr. L. M. Buchanan.

12 May 1873.

1889. Colonel *Wilson Patten*.] WILL you state to the Committee the office that you hold in Ireland?—I am Deputy Clerk of the Peace, and Deputy Clerk of the Crown for the County of Tyrone; I am also Baronial Constable for two Baronies of the County.

1890. As baronial constable what is the nature of your duties?—As baronial constable under the old Act, prior to the passing of the late Act, I had the initiatory preparation of the jurors' lists for the baronies of which I am constable.

1891. In the first place, what is your opinion upon the operation of the old Act?—I believe that the qualifications under the old Act had become, (certainly as far as Tyrone was concerned,) so obsolete that enough jurors were not obtainable under it.

1892. For what reason?—The leaseholders and freeholders taken together have become progressively fewer in Tyrone, within my experience, and I do not think that there are more than, perhaps, 600 or 700, qualified to serve on juries.

1893. Under the present Act what is the state of affairs?—Under the present Act, with a qualification of 20 *l.*, the list of jurors is 3,092. In order to make the old lists sufficient, I travelled out of the precept, and, after returning the leaseholders and freeholders, I made up the deficiency by putting in the highest cess payers, and the most respectable men in the barony that I knew, but they were not legally qualified under the old Act

1894. Under the new Act do you think that the change has been a beneficial one?—As far as regards substituting a rating qualification for the former qualification, it was absolutely necessary.

1895. Taking the general result of the change, do you believe that it has been a beneficial one?—I do, but I believe that the qualification has been fixed at too low a figure, and that on that account the new jury list of the county is inferior to the old.

1896. What is the present number of men on the jury list?—Three thousand and ninety-two, but if the qualification were raised, so as only to have about as many jurors as were formerly upon the list, namely, from 1,000 to 1,200, you would have practically the same men as you had before, and as good men.

1897. How would you propose to amend the Act?—1. By raising the qualification. 2. By a searching revision before the chairman.

1898. Would you make any change in the qualification?—I think that as between the towns and the county ratings, there ought to be discrimination; for instance, the qualification in the county of Tyrone is now 20 *l.*, without making any distinction between town ratings and country ratings. In the towns in Tyrone a man rated at 20 *l.* is perfectly good material for a common juror, but a man rated at 20 *l.* for land is not by any means fit to be a common juror, therefore I should discriminate between house ratings in towns and country ratings, and I would have the one fixed at very much lower than the other, because the class of men who are so rated are very different indeed.

1899. Do you believe that 12 *l.* would be a good qualification for house property?—I should fix it at 15 *l.*

1900. Would you alter the rating in the county generally?—Yes, certainly.

1901. What rating would you adopt in the county for house property?—I should go as high for the qualification as would leave behind a jury sufficiently numerous for the duties of each county (having settled the number which was a sufficient jury on the rating qualification) and I would provide that number of men, and no more.

1902. Could you give the Committee any opinion of what number, for instance, a 12 *l.* rating would furnish?—It is impossible for me to give anything but an approximate idea of how many a 12 *l.* or 15 *l.* house rating would produce, because that has not up to the present time been dealt with in any of the Acts, but I should say that it would add considerably to the lists; although the towns in Tyrone are small, yet still I think it would add materially to the lists. I should recommend a 15 *l.* rating in towns, and not a 12 *l.* rating; I think 12 *l.* is too low.

1903. What rating do you propose for the county?—Certainly not under 30 *l.*

1904. Would you go above 30 *l.*?—If a higher qualification

Mr. *L. M. Buchanan.*

12 May 1873.

qualification would give a sufficient number I should go above 30*l.*

1905. Do you believe that with a qualification of 15*l.* in towns and 30*l.* in counties, it would furnish jurors of average intelligence?—I think it would give a very fair jury, I would say, a good jury in Tyrone; but if it were possible to raise the standard further I should be inclined to do so. That qualification in Tyrone would give 1,500 jurors, and I think that is too many.

1906. Would you have the rating in the counties a joint rating of household and land, or of household separate from land?—I should keep house ratings and land ratings distinct in towns, and if possible in counties, because a man might inhabit a very indifferent house in a town and be very indifferent material for a juror, and yet be returnable as a juror, by reason of his want of qualification as a householder being supplemented by perhaps so much more from a couple of fields in the neighbourhood.

1907. You say that you are not able to inform the Committee what would be about the number of jurors left on the list under a qualification of 15*l.* for a house and 30*l.* for the county?—I know exactly the number that would be left upon the list with a 30*l.* county rating.

1908. What would be left upon the list under a 30*l* county rating?—1,540.

1909. But you cannot say what addition would be made by a 15*l.* house rating?—No.

1910. Do you consider that 1,200 on the jury list would be sufficient for all the assize business and quarter sessions business of the county?—That depends upon what is considered the proper rotation of the jurors as to how often they shall serve; it all depends upon that. Of course, if jurors are required to serve once a year, a smaller list would do; but if you require them only to serve once in two years, you must have twice as large a list in order to keep up the rotation. Having regard to the fact that jurors under the old Act had to serve four times a year, I think it would not be considered a hardship by jurors under the new Act if they were asked to serve say once a year, and if they were asked to serve only once a year, 1,000 names upon the list would certainly be sufficient for the county of Tyrone.

1911. From the position which you hold in the county of Tyrone, I suppose you are aware of the general feeling with regard to the present jury law?—Quite so.

1912. What do you believe to be the general feeling throughout the county with regard to the operation of the present Act?—I believe that the principle of the Act is approved of universally almost.

1913. But it has been very much criticised, has it not, both by the press and by the bar?—It has been generally criticised by reason of the qualification having been made too low; principally that men were brought into the last assizes and sessions, particularly the assizes, who were not fit to be jurors. Their unfitness was much more apparent at the assizes than at any quarter sessions.

1914. In what way specially did it strike you as to their being unfit?—The position was quite novel to them; they did not know what they were doing; in fact, they had never heard that they were jurors until they were summoned. The first intimation that they got of being jurors was the summons from the sheriffs' bailiff, and they came in totally unacquainted with their duty as jurors; very anxious indeed to do their duty to the best of their ability, but quite unacquainted with their duty.

1915. In point of intelligence and education, did they appear to you generally to be up to the proper performance of their duty?—I think not.

1916. Did you see any instances which particularly attracted your notice, in which jurors showed a want of intelligence or a want of education that unfitted them to act as jurors?—I think generally that at the assizes their want of intelligence was apparent in most of the cases. They did not understand how to go about returning the issue for instance; they did not understand what was their duty. There is no provision in the late Act for selecting a foreman by any person in the court, and they were rather puzzled to know who should take the lead, or what they should do, that is to say, in small cases; I do not allude to the Montgomery trial which was quite different as far as regards the position of the jurors.

1917. In the present Act, is there any rule laid down for the selection of the foreman of a jury?—No, there is not.

1918. You recommend that there should be some rule laid down, by which a selection should be made?—Most decidedly.

1919. By whom would you have that selection made?—By the officer of the court.

1920. By what officer?—Either by the sub-sheriff, or by the clerk of the Crown, or the clerk of the peace at quarter sessions. I consider that it is a matter of importance.

1921. Have you any suggestion to make with regard to the examination of the lists, prior to their coming before the court?—I am of opinion that the first time the clerk of the union returns a man's name upon the jury list which he has to forward to the clerk of the peace, he should serve upon the man so returned, a printed notice, acquainting him with the fact that he is returned upon the list, and stating upon that notice the disqualifications which will entitle him to claim exemption from the list, and also stating upon the notice that if by reason of a qualification in any other union in the county he can claim to be put upon the special list, he can do so at the revision sessions, and stating any other things that may be useful to him as a juror.

1922. Do you believe that amongst the class that would have to serve on the jury it is rather an object of ambition to serve, or do you think that it is looked upon as an onerous duty?—I think that they would object to being excluded if they thought that they had a right to be on; I may state as a fact that I have been found fault with for having been supposed to have excluded persons from the jurors' list; not that I did so, but I have been found fault with in one or two instances for having been supposed to have done it.

1923. Have you any suggestions to make with regard to an alteration in the right of challenge which at present exists?—I think that the right of challenge ought to be limited to 12, and given to every prisoner; at present it is only extended to prisoners who are accused of felony. A man who is accused of what is technically called a misdemeanour, but what may be of tremendous consequence to him has no right of challenge, whilst a person accused of the smallest theft has; one great advantage also, in limiting the right of challenge, would be that it would do away with the necessity

for

Mr. I. M. Buchanan.

12 May 1873.

for so large a jury. At present the sheriff, by reason of a prisoner accused of felony having the right of challenge, has to provide a very large panel. The sheriff cannot tell till the assizes or the quarter sessions come on that there may not be such prisoners, and he is obliged to make provision for the possibility, because if he has not made provision for it, the counsel or attorney for the prisoner might, by making use of his challenge, postpone the trial indefinitely; therefore, he is obliged to summons not only as many as will exhaust the challenges, but enough to have a sufficient jury behind, and that repeated in four divisions of a county exhausts the lists to a very large extent unnecessarily.

1924. Under the modification of the present law which you suggest, that would not be so great a detriment as it was under the old Act, I presume, because you would have sufficient jurors under the present law, or under the modification which you suggest?—Quite sufficient.

1925. And that objection, which you have just stated, would, therefore, not apply in the same degree?—I make it apply in this way, that the fewer jurors that are required the higher the qualification may be. A smaller number will be sufficient for the purposes of the county, and then you may have a higher qualification.

1926. Have you observed any great difficulty of conviction to exist at the assizes and quarter sessions in the county of Tyrone on account of the want of intelligence or other defects of the juries?—At quarter sessions the jurors discharged their duties very well, better than either the chairman or I expected; but, I think, that from their inexperience they were over anxious to be guided by the opinion of the bench.

1927. Do you think that under the altered system the juries will be more independent and less anxious to be guided by the opinion of the judges or the chairman?—I do not mean that they were altogether guided, but they were apt from their own inexperience to take the opinion of the bench at once without any hesitation whatever; but, I think, with the alteration in the qualification which I propose, you will have men of more experience and intelligence; you would have a smaller jury list, and there will be some chance of the jurors becoming experienced by the rotation occurring more frequently, which, I think, a matter of great importance.

1928. How long have you had experience of the jury system in Ireland?—Twelve years.

1929. You have been a constant attendant at the quarter sessions and the assizes, have you not?—I believe I have sworn every jury myself during that time, certainly for the quarter sessions, and for the last seven years at the assizes.

1930. Has your observation led you to believe that any change in the general system of juries is required, for instance, in the unanimity which is required from a jury?—I have been for a long time of opinion that some modification would be desirable, but I am slow to give an opinion against that of men of so great eminence who have expressed themselves of the other opinion.

1931. What is your own private opinion?—My own private opinion is, that some modification as to the unanimity of jurors would conduce to the ends of justice in Ireland; for instance, a very largely preponderating majority, making room for men who, from some reason or other, find their way upon juries, and succeed in defeating the ends of justice.

1932. Sir *R. Blennerhassett*.] Are you speaking of criminal cases as well as civil cases?—Yes, but my experience of civil cases tried by jurors is very small indeed.

1933. Colonel *W. Patten*.] A good deal of evidence has been given to the Committee with regard to the person who should have the charge of the jury list; do you entertain any strong objections to the old system of the lists being in the charge of the sub-sheriff; do you think that the duties that were performed by the sub-sheriff under the old Act were satisfactorily performed with regard to selecting the lists?—I never knew an instance in which the sub-sheriff acted improperly, but still I believe that the power of selection should not remain with the sub-sheriff.

1934. In whose hands would you place it?—I should not give any power of selection to any officer.

1935. Would you, under no circumstances, allow a juror to be struck off the list?—I would give to the sheriff the power of omitting from the lists the names of those who he knew were dead, blind, or deaf, or otherwise physically disqualified, who in the process of revision had escaped the notice of the revision court, but I would not give the sheriff the power of selection; although I have never known that power abused, still it is open to animadversion, and more particularly where cases of a political or party character occur; the sheriff may act, and I believe certainly to my knowledge, not only in Tyrone, but in every other county in the north of Ireland that I am acquainted with, has acted with the most perfect purity and honour; but yet it is open to this, that he may do otherwise if he chooses.

1936. Do you believe that the absence of all power of striking a man off the jury would be compensated for by the challenge of 12, that you suggest?—That amongst other things.

1937. By what process would you eliminate from the jury lists the objectionable parties?—The first process would be to raise the qualification to as high a point as possible, and secondly, to have a very stringent revision of the lists; formerly the revision of the jury lists has been the merest matter of form; there was no real revision in my time, and there never was so bad a revision as the last time.

1938. In what way was it more defective than the former ones?—Because the lists were so enormous; I believe that the people did not know at the time of the revision that they were on the lists, and never heard that they were jurors; hundreds of men, I might say, who were over age and physically disqualified were on the lists, the chairman of the court, nor any one in the court, not knowing anything about them, and they remained upon the lists and attended at quarter sessions and the assizes; the sheriff, although he may have known something of it, was bound to summon those men, and I have known him of my own knowledge to summon men from his own neighbourhood who were over 80 years of age, because he could not help it.

1939. The present Act has been in operation only during one assizes, has it?—During a portion of the Hilary quarter sessions, during the last assizes, and during the Easter quarter sessions.

1940. At this assizes and at those quarter sessions, did you observe such a want of power to obtain

Mr. *L. M. Buchanan.*

12 May 1873.

obtain a just verdict from the jury, that you think some immediate alteration is required?—*Yes.*

1941. Will you state to the Committee what were the instances which have led you to that conclusion?—At the quarter sessions I cannot say that there was any failure of justice. At the assizes it so happened that almost all the prisoners who were tried by Baron Dowse pleaded guilty. The great case of Montgomery was a case where all the jurors came into court, and, on view, most of them were quite unfit material for jurors; at least, I think so.

1942. Was that a very important case?—Yes, it was a very important case. People were so impressed with its importance, that all the respectable jurors remained away, or tried to be excused so far as they could. The men who would have formed a very good jury to try the case, made various excuses in the court, with the object of getting off. But, speaking of the majority of the jurors, I believe that they were quite unfit to try a case of any magnitude.

1943. Supposing that there had been a compulsory service, the defect would not have existed?—Of course; but there would still be a large proportion of the men who were unfit to try that case.

1944. But the unwillingness to serve would not have operated?—If the unwillingness to serve had not operated, we should have had a much better jury.

1945. Can you mention any other instance at the assizes?—At the assizes there was another case, in which I was present in court, where the jury retired to their room and stayed there for three hours. The sheriff was sent for, and he went into the room, and returned into the court, stating that the jury had agreed, but that they did not know how to put their agreement upon paper, none of them having ever been on a jury before, they did not understand how to send back the issue paper. There was a good deal of confusion about it; it was understood throughout the case that there were several prisoners who were to be found guilty and others acquitted, so that there was some excuse for their not knowing what to do. It was rather complicated as far as regards the finding. There were 22 prisoners arraigned; some of them by the direction of Baron Dowse were to be acquitted, and the others were to be dealt with by the jury, and they did not know how to frame the issue paper, because of their inexperience, none of them ever having been on a jury before.

1946. Dr. *Ball.*] As I understand, the county of Tyrone is the county that you are connected with?—Yes.

1947. You are the deputy clerk of the Crown, are you not?—Yes, I am deputy clerk of the Crown, but I do the entire duty.

1948. Do you reside in the county?—Yes, I reside in the county.

1949. Have you land there?—Yes, I have.

1950. Are you acquainted with the value of land in the county?—I am.

1951. Where do you live in the county?—Within one mile of Omagh.

1952. You know the barony of Dungannon, do you not?—Yes.

1953. About what number of acres would there be in a farm in the county of Tyrone to correspond to a 30 *l.* rating?—The barony of Dungannon varies very considerably.

1954. Take fair land, how many acres, could you say?—I cannot speak positively, but I should say about 25 acres.

1955. Do you mean the Cunningham, the statute, or the imperial acre?—Statute, or English acre.

1956. In the case of a man who lives on a 25 acre farm, is not that man very little above a labourer in his appearance, in his dress, and his whole bearing?—I think he is very much above a labourer in Tyrone.

1957. Have they other business in Tyrone besides land and connected with it; are they in connection with the linen business?—Very little.

1958. What capital would a man require for a farm of 25 acres?—Very much more than he has; it depends upon what he supposed was proper farming.

1959. What would you say that a man with 25 acres of land ought to have in that county?—£. 10 an acre to begin with.

1960. What have they generally?—I cannot answer that question; there are so few cases come within my knowledge when they absolutely commence. You asked me what they would require at the commencement of the operation.

1961. I mean what capital have they invested in stock, implements, and the outgoing of wages through the year, before there is any return?—I should think, perhaps, one half of that, counting stock, implements, and wages; but in a farm of that sort the members of the family, the women and boys, to a very large extent provide the labour.

1962. Is there much flax-growing in Tyrone?—A great deal; it is either the second or the third county in Ireland, I think, as regards the growth of flax.

1963. There are three good towns in Tyrone, Omagh, Dungannon, and Cookstown?—Yes, and Strabane.

1964. The 20 *l.* rating applied to those towns ought to have given you a good many jurors from those four towns?—So it did.

1965. And that would go in some degree to improve the panel over a mere 20 *l.* rating in a farm, would it not?—So it did; the 20 *l.* town jurors were very fair jurors. If it were possible, I should leave it at 20 *l.* in towns, but if that were not sufficient, I would certainly not go below 15 *l.*

1966. Does not that case of the 22 prisoners that you mentioned, show that at the ordinary business of assizes cases of complication arise, and that the jurors ought to be persons of intelligence and education?—I quite think so.

1967. Do you know any part of Ireland except Tyrone?—I have a general knowledge of Ulster.

1968. Do you think that Tyrone ranks high in the scale of education?—I think it is equal to the average of Ulster.

1969. You would not put it over the average; take the barony of Dungannon?—I cannot say positively; but from my observation I should say that it is quite equal to the average. Of course, it is very much superior to Donegal.

1970. There have only been one assizes and one quarter sessions, have there, since the new Act?—One assizes and one quarter sessions entire, and a portion of another quarter sessions. The Act came into operation on the first day of Hilary Term, and that was in time for the Dungannon sessions.

1971. The assizes having cleared the gaol, that did not give you any great experience at quarter sessions?

Mr. L. M. Buchanan.

12 May 1873.

sessions?—Not very great experience, but there was a great deal to do at the January sessions upon that occasion; Dungannon is a very large division indeed.

1972. In that trial of Montgomery were there a very great number set aside by the Crown?—A great number.

1973. Could you at all tell the number; as you were clerk to the Crown, perhaps you may have observed it?—At this moment the number has escaped me, but I think it was between 30 and 40, say about 35 or 36; I am not quite sure. Mr. Magrath, the Crown solicitor, can state that better than I can.

1974. Had not the prisoner challenges besides?—Yes, the prisoner used the right of challenge to his utmost, and he challenged.

1975. Mr. *Bruen*.] I think you said that you have had 12 years' official experience?—Yes, I have had 12 years' experience.

1976. In both offices, as deputy clerk of the peace and deputy clerk of the Crown?—Seven years as deputy clerk of the Crown, and 12 years as deputy clerk of the peace.

1977. And you have also been barony constable?—Yes.

1978. In the formation of the list of jurors, do you think it at all advisable or possible that the lists of the jurors and the lists of the electors could be combined?—Quite possible, in their initiatory preparation.

1979. Do you think it would be possible that, the lists being so combined, the chairman of the quarter sessions could revise them both with greater facility than he is under the present Act obliged to do; he has to separately revise them under the present Act, has he not?—Naturally two separate lists must be made, and he would have the two lists to revise. At present he does revise them at the same time, in fact, and I do not suppose that it would make any difference.

1980. Do you mean to say that he does not take one list first, and go through it before he takes the other?—He revises them upon the same day, but at separate moments, for the convenience of the parties attending, and for the convenience of the court he fixes the same day.

1981. Do you happen to know the number of names on the electors' list for the county of Tyrone?—Eight thousand seven hundred and sixty-five.

1982. For the county of Tyrone, I see that the number of jurors is 3,092?—Yes.

1983. Do you mean to say that he can go over both those lists in one day?—The electors' lists are published and the objections are published along with them; the word "objected" is written opposite the name of every person to whom the clerk of the union makes any objection, or to whom any voter makes an objection, or to whom the clerk of the peace makes an objection. Those names are read out, and evidence is taken with regard to those names, and there being no objections to any other names, they are not read out; they remain on, as a matter of course, if there is no objection to them.

1984. Are there also claims to be inserted on the list?—Also the lists of claims are read out, but they are not very numerous. The revision of the voting lists in the county of Tyrone takes on an average half an hour for each of the four divisions. The three baronies of Dungannon, which comprise very nearly half the county, take an hour, and the three remaining divisions of the county average half an hour each.

1985. I presume that, at this revision of the list of voters, at all events, there is no very great contest between the parties?—None whatever.

1986. But supposing there were such a contest, would it not take a very much longer time?—Yes, very much. The borough of Dungannon has been watched very closely by both parties; and, at first, when there was a probability of a contest, the revision of that list for the borough alone occupied a day, and there are only 236 voters upon it. In all probability, any future revision for the county will occupy a very long time too.

1987. You think that it would be impossible, do you, to combine the two lists, so as to save the time of the officers who attend upon the chairman, and the chairman himself in revising the two lists?—I think that there would be no advantage whatever to combine them any more closely than they are at present; I would rather be inclined to make it much more separate if it would contribute to a more thorough revision.

1988. Can you suggest any means by which the expenses of this process can be reduced?—The expenses are matters with the grand juries and with the boards of guardians, as to how much they will allow for the work done.

1989. That is to say, it is a matter simple and easy to them; they have to pay?—Yes; they have to pay.

1990. You are aware, I suppose, that a very considerable amount of dissatisfaction was expressed on the part of the tax-payers at these expenses; what I want to know from you is, if you can suggest any means whereby those expenses could be in any way diminished?—By reducing the number upon the lists, they would be at once lightened; by raising the qualification the lists would be made much smaller, and the work would be rendered less, and the expense paid to the clerks of the unions and to the clerks of the peace would naturally be lowered in proportion.

1991. In your suggestion about going over and revising the lists of jurors by the chairman, I think you said that you recommended a very strict revision?—Yes, a very strict revision.

1992. And that would involve, would it not, going over almost every name?—Almost every name.

1993. That would take a very long time in many counties, would it not; for instance, in the county of Antrim, the first on the list, I see there are 7,800 names?—But by raising the qualification, you would probably get rid of one half of the jurors at once. I do not know anything about Antrim; but the mere act of raising the qualification in the book from 20 *l.* to 30 *l.*, disposes of just one-half of the list exactly in Tyrone.

1994. Your suggestion was a high qualification, and a stringent revision, was it not?—Yes.

1995. Have you any other suggestions to make as to the improvement of the Act?—It does not occur to me, except to modify the extent to which the qualification shall go, and the method in which the revision shall take place, and those to whom it should be intrusted, who are best capable of informing the court on the matter.

1996. I think you mentioned something about a diminution of the right of challenge which at present exists?—Yes; there would be less necessity for a large jury list; a smaller jury list would do.

1997. Do you think that that would in any way

Mr. *L. M. Buchanan.*

12 May 1873.

way diminish the rights and the safety of prisoners?—It would increase the rights of a vast number of prisoners, the majority of prisoners having now no right of challenge whatever.

1998. But you would give the right of challenge, would you not?—Yes; I would give the right of challenge in all cases, and limit it to 12.

1999. If that was given, and if it was exercised, in what way would the number of jurors be diminished?—At present the sheriff is obliged to make provision for challenges of 20.

2000. That is only in certain cases, is it not?—He does not know whether the cases to be tried will be felonies or not, and, therefore, he has to assume that there will be a necessity, and he has to summon sufficient jurors.

2001. But it is only in a certain class of cases?—Only in cases of felony; but he summonses a jury for all the cases.

2002. Then I understand you to say that you would give the right of challenge to a different class of cases?—Yes; but the fact of a man being challenged in one case would not exclude him from trying any other case that might happen to come; he would not be challenged for the remainder of the assizes or quarter sessions; he would be available for the next case that came on; 12 would try any particular case, and the remainder of the jury would be in court waiting to try the next case, in case the jury had retired to their room, and there was a new trial in the court.

2003. But at present that same possibility exists; supposing the prisoner exercises that right of challenging 20, those men who had been challenged would still remain to serve on other juries?—Yes, but a smaller panel would be sufficient to do the duty of the assizes or quarter sessions, as the case may be; by diminishing the right of challenge to 12, and the power of selection being taken away from the sheriff, there is not so great a necessity for a larger right of challenge. That was one of the reasons for conceding a right of challenge to prisoners; but when the power of selection is taken away from the sheriff, the necessity for challenge in all cases would, I imagine, be diminished.

2004. Then, if the necessity for challenge is diminished, why do you leave it at all?—I would leave, certainly, the right of challenge.

2005. You think that possibly there might get upon the panel persons who are not impartial?—I think so.

2006. Do you think that the alphabetical method of selection is not one which would entirely take away the partiality of the jurors who serve upon the panels?—It tends to make the list an impartial list; but, notwithstanding the list being taken in alphabetical order, it is quite possible that, in the alphabetical arrangement, men may get on, that ought to be excluded by some means or other.

2007. How would you exclude them?—By the right of challenge, after they came into court.

2008. Are there not cases in which several prisoners are all put upon their trial together, and all charged under one count or indictment, and have they not each of them the right of challenge separately?—I really cannot answer that question from memory.

2009. You are not conversant with the law upon that point?—I am conversant with the practice, but that is a point that never was raised in my time; I am not quite sure about it; I should imagine that they had separately the right of challenge.

2010. If they all exercised separately the right of challenge, they could set aside nearly the whole panel, could they not?—No doubt they could; they are asked by the officer of the court if they join in their challenges, if they refuse, they can challenge separately I believe.

2011. But you are of opinion, are you not, that the qualification should be raised as high as it is possible, so long as it provided a sufficient number of jurors?—That is a rule that I think should be laid down, and let every county stand upon its own requirements.

2012. Do you think that that is the proper consideration to apply, namely, that the qualification should be fixed with regard to the number of jurors, and not with regard to the fitness of those who possess it?—My object in raising the qualification is, that it is the best principle upon which you can go, that the higher the qualification *primâ facie* the better the jurors; I am of opinion that the qualification should be raised as high as possible, leaving behind a sufficient jury.

2013. Dr. *Ball.*] As high as would give a sufficient number?—Yes, as high as would give a sufficient number; I think I stated before that I would economise the summoning of juries, at least in one way, first, by limiting the right of challenge, and secondly, by doing away with the trial of prisoners in certain quarter sessions towns; speaking for Tyrone, the usual practice is to bring a prisoner returned for trial at Clogher, from Omagh to Clogher, and to try him in Clogher, and send him back to Omagh, although the following day we may come to Omagh and try the prisoners that are for trial at Omagh, at quarter sessions. This exhausts the panel to a very great extent, unnecessarily; and it very frequently happens that the sheriff, after summoning 36 men, which are usually sufficient for the grand jury, and the same number for the petty jury at quarter sessions, exhausting the panel to the extent of 72, there are no prisoners to be tried, the panel is exhausted to the extent of 72, the men are brought from their homes, and there is nothing for them to do.

2014. Colonel *Wilson Patten.*] Is that the only instance?—No, I am only instancing that as an example; that must be multiplied by four for the county of Tyrone; because there are four quarter sessions divisions at which prisoners are triable. By reducing that number to two, which would be quite ample (Strabane being a place where there is no Bridewell), by reducing the places at which the prisoners are tried to Omagh and Dungannon, you economise the panel to the extent of 144 at every quarter sessions.

2015. Mr. *Bruen.*] Then your recommendations also extend to the diminution of the number of places at which quarter sessions are held?—Certainly; because I think that it is intimately connected with the question. In order that a smaller panel may suffice, and a higher qualification consequently be adopted.

2016. Can you give the Committee any idea of the distances which the present courts of quarter sessions impose upon jurors and parties who attend and go there for the transaction of their business?—I should think, on the average, seven miles. It so happens that the towns are situated very near the centre of the divisions. Dungannon being a very large division, the distance is more than that; but in the three divisions of Omagh, Strabane, and Clogher, I should

should say that the average would be eight miles, and for Dungannon the average would be 10 miles.

2017. Therefore, in order to have a proper class of jurymen, you first of all wish to reduce the number of those who serve, and in order to reduce the number of those whom it is necessary to summon to serve, you would reduce the number of quarter sessions courts?—At which criminal business is tried only. I do not mean that to apply to civil cases; in fact, they would require, perhaps, to be increased.

2018. I suppose you are aware that many of the counties in Ireland are not so favourably circumstanced as regards distance as the county of Tyrone seems to be?—Of course, that is so.

2019. Therefore the diminution of the number of quarter sessions courts, which you recommend, might not be possible in other counties without very great inconvenience to the public?—It is merely for the trial of criminal business, not at all for the trial of civil cases.

2020. But still very great distances would impose considerable inconvenience upon the jurors, and also, I suppose, upon the police authorities and the Crown authorities, if the number of courts was seriously diminished?—It would not make it at all more inconvenient to the jurors, because the jurors are only summoned from their own divisions. For instance, if Strabane and Clogher were done away with as places at which criminal business at the quarter sessions took place, and all the business was transacted at Dungannon and Omagh, the jurors from the baronies of Dungannon and Omagh would do all that business. It would not make any difference.

2021. As regards the county of Tyrone, that is your evidence, but as regards other counties, where the distances are greater, I suppose you will not deny that it is a very great inconvenience to jurors to attend at the quarter sessions courts which are held at a great distance from their homes?—They would not have to attend any greater distance; they would have a few more cases to try by reason of some divisions being done away with. But at quarter sessions cases are tried by the jurors of particular divisions; they are not drawn from adjoining divisions.

2022. Then you would keep up the divisions for the purposes of summoning the jurors, and you would only have the jurors summoned from this one immediate division, and you would leave out the other divisions?—As at present, because the jurors of the other divisions would be summoned to the assizes as a matter of course; they would have their rotation; they would have to do it once, and when they had done it once their turn would be over; it would make no difference.

2023. In the case of Tyrone, you would diminish the number of those quarter sessions courts for the Crown business as well?—For Crown business only.

2024. Would the jurors, to serve at those two courts, be drawn from the districts of the other courts?—No; the present Act provides that the jurors shall be summoned from the quarter sessions divisions.

2025. Then as regards some divisions, there would be the liability to serve on those criminal cases on the jury, but there would be other divisions where they would not have any such liability at all?—But their turn would come, they would be summoned for the assizes; if they were omitted from the quarter sessions, they would be summoned for the assizes, because their names would be taken in turn. It would not impose any greater duty upon the jurors of one division over another.

Mr. *L. M. Buchanan.*

12 May 1873.

2026. Viscount *Crichton.*] You suggested, did you not, I think, a 15 *l.* rating for jurors living in towns?—Not lower than 15 *l.*

2027. Has it ever occurred to you that what has been called the compound qualification might be adopted with advantage in the country, that is to say, that no man however highly rated he might be, should be on the panel unless he had a house and offices rated at a certain amount?—Yes, I have considered that.

2028. Do you think that it would be an advantage?—I think it would be an advantage, but I am afraid that it would be very difficult to carry out, for this reason, the valuation books in the hands of the clerk of the union do not discriminate between the rating of houses upon the farm, and land upon the farm; there is the valuation in bulk, "houses, offices, and land," opposite the name of any particular person in the rate book; I believe that it would be a better criterion of a man's respectability and fitness for a juror if the rating of his homestead and farm buildings should be taken into account, but the rate books as at present drawn up do not discriminate between the one and the other, and it could not be adopted at present.

2029. The first effect of education upon a man is to make him improve his dwelling house, is it not?—Practically, I do not know that it is; in the county of Tyrone the farmers are of very considerable wealth, and yet their homesteads and farm buildings are not by any means in proportion to their wealth.

2030. You said that at the trial at Omagh the respectable jurors remained away in great numbers or made excuses; do you attribute that to any unwillingness on their part to serve?—I attribute it to a great unwillingness to serve in that particular case.

2031. Do you attribute it in any measure to their unwillingness to be associated with an inferior class of jurors?—Not at all: perhaps there was an instance or two, but I do not think that there was more.

2032. Sir *R. Blennerhassett.*] In your answer to the honourable Member for Carlow, I understood you do not seem to attach any importance whatever to having as many people as convenient in Ireland engaged in the administration of the law by serving as jurors, provided that they were competent of course for their duties?—Provided that they were competent; and the object is to obtain a competent and sufficient list.

2033. Your notion of competence appears to me to be by raising the qualification so high that as few as possible should be employed?—That is not my notion of competence, but as a matter of experience, the higher the qualification the more competent they will be, and there will be a better class of jurors, better educated, and more intelligent; a very stupid man indeed might be a man with a very high rating qualification.

2034. Was it at quarter sessions that you said that you observed that the jurors were unduly guided by the opinion of the bench?—I do not say that they were unduly guided, but that they appeared to place very great reliance upon the opinion of the bench.

2035. What objection have you to that?—Not the slightest objection, except that they were the persons who were sworn to give a verdict.

2036. I understood you to say, as one charge against those jurymen, that they were unduly guided by the opinion of the bench; what did you mean by making that remark?—I think they were so inexperienced that they were apt, because of their inexperience, to be entirely guided by the bench, and not to use their own intelligence to so great an extent as if those same men had been experienced jurors.

2037. Is not that a fault to be cured as the jurors acquire greater experience?—Certainly, but at present the rate of rotation is so slow that there is very little chance of any jurors becoming experienced.

2038. You would wish the foreman to be appointed by the officer of the court?—Yes.

2039. Would you suggest also that there should be a certain number of special jurors serving on a jury?—At present they are taken indiscriminately.

2040. I mean special jurors serving on all juries?—Yes, that is the present law.

2041. I mean that there should be on every jury a certain number of persons who are qualified to serve as special jurors?—If you mean that upon every jury there should be a proportion of men who were special jurors, naturally the more the better.

2042. *The O'Donoghue.*] I understand you to say that you approve of the principle of the Act?—Entirely.

2043. Might I ask what you describe as the principle of the Act?—The principle first of all is a rating qualification being substituted for a freehold and leasehold qualification, and the taking the names from the list by alphabetical arrangement, making all qualified persons serve in turn.

2044. In other words, taking away from the sheriff the power of selection?—Limiting the power of selection that he had before.

2045. Is that approved of by all classes in the county of Tyrone?—I believe that it has general approval of the people of the county of Tyrone; I believe they all approve of the principle of the Act; I have heard very many object to the Act on account of the men, who by the lowness of the qualification have been put upon the list, but at the same time they approve highly of the principle of the Act; but there is no doubt a feeling amongst a very large number of people, that some limited power of selection, or a general power of selection, in some cases should be left with the sheriff.

2046. But you likewise think that they would not wish to go back to the old system?—Quite so.

2047. Mr. *H. A. Herbert.*] Will you tell the Committee what your opinion is with regard to the qualification of special jurors; do you approve of the present qualification, or would you have it raised?—As to the special jurors, their insufficiency, if they be inefficient, is not so apparent; I should raise the qualification for special jurors, because I think that there are many men on the special jury panel who are not fit to be in the position of special jurors, and I would raise the qualification proportionately, leaving behind as many as would be sufficient for the duties of special jurors.

2048. Would you say that the qualification of a rating 100 *l.* in the county, and 30 *l.* in the towns, would be a fair estimate for a special juror?—I think that 30 *l.* would be too low in the towns, and that 100 *l.* would be too high in counties.

2049. What would you put it at in town and county?—Somewhere about 40 *l.* and 70 *l.*

2050. What number in the county of Tyrone would you generally have on the panel or on the list of special jurors?—By raising the qualification from what it is at present to 70 *l.*, it would take off, as nearly as possible, one half the panel of special jurors.

2051. How many would it leave?—It would leave about 260, which would be too few; but it would be greatly increased by the town qualification of 40 *l.*

2052. How many would that give?—I have no means of knowing that positively, but I should say that the special jury lists in Tyrone would amount, perhaps, to 350 upon both those qualifications, 70 *l.* and 40 *l.*

2053. Do you think that that would be a sufficient number for the county?—Yes, I think it would be quite sufficient. If anything, I think you might possibly go somewhat lower for the special jury panel in Tyrone; and that if 70 *l.* were found too high a figure at which to obtain a sufficient number, it would be safe to go as far as 60 *l.*

2054. When was the last general valuation of Tyrone, which was Griffits' valuation?—In 1859, I think it was.

2055. When you said that 30 *l.* was a sufficient rating for the counties, did you take into consideration that there was a Valuation Bill before this House, and that if it passes, most likely all the valuations will be raised; and did you take into consideration the extra number that that will put on the list?—I based it entirely upon the existing valuation; if the valuation be raised, making the existing 20 *l.*, 25 *l.* under the new valuation, the qualifications would have to be proportionately raised.

2056. If a new valuation was passed, and it became law, you think that the valuation ought to be raised considerably?—Certainly.

2057. Do you think that there would be any difficulty in printing the name of the townland opposite a man's name on the list of jurors, in order that the Crown solicitor might be able to obtain any information from the police with regard to him?—At present it is so placed; everything about him is placed upon the jurors' book.

2058. Colonel *Vandeleur.*] The ratepayers in towns and villages rated at 12 *l.* are liable to be called as jurors under the Act, are they not?—I think that that is only in some counties.

2059. Would you consider it advisable to include the word "villages," which at present is very indefinite, seeing that a village may be three houses at the corner of cross roads?—I think that it might possibly increase the panel, and I think that a man rated at 20 *l.* in a village would probably be as good material for a juror as a man rated at 20 *l.* in a town.

2060. Would not say 12 *l.* in a village if there were only two or three houses, which would leave it a very indefinite thing both for clerks of unions and poor-rate collectors to say what is a village, or what is not?—There is, no doubt, that it would be somewhat indefinite; but I have got what is practically a portion of the rate-book here, and the villages and towns are there mentioned.

2061. If you refer to the rate-book, I do not think

Mr. *L. M. Buchanan.*

12 May 1873.

think that "village" is mentioned?—Mine is the barony constable's book; I am not sure whether there are any villages in it, but as far as my recollection serves, I believe that where there is a village it is mentioned as a village; I think that a person rated at 15 *l.* in a village ought certainly to be put upon the list if you fix 15 *l.* as the rating for a man in a town.

2062. There are many farmers living in little villages, and one man living where three or four houses happen to be together is rated at 12 *l.* for house and premises, whereas the next man within a quarter of a mile of him, who has, perhaps, a better holding than he has a great deal, would not be rated at 12 *l.*, and would not come in except at 30 *l.*; is not that rather an invidious thing?—He is more likely to have land attached to his house by which the qualification would be raised sufficiently; if he be a farmer he would naturally have house and premises.

2063. Then you exclude the land, and take merely the house and premises?—Merely the house, if he be not a farmer.

2064. Would it be possible for the chairman, at the next sessions at Midsummer, to revise the jurors' book for the approaching sessions and assizes?—There would not be the least difficulty. Nothing could be more simple than revising the jurors' book at the next June sessions. Supposing that a valuation be fixed, excluding the lower valuations that are now upon the book, nothing could be simpler than to expunge their names, the chairman initialling the same up to the given qualification, and leaving behind him the rest; which would remain in as good an alphabetical arrangement as the present list.

2065. Would you recommend that that should be done at each sessions, or at the county sessions only?—It is merely a formal matter, and should be done at the first sessions.

2066. It was suggested that that should be done when the barrister went the county, and that it should be done at the first sessions that he attended; do you think that feasible?—It would be too late if it were not done at the first sessions. Judging from the Tyrone quarter sessions, that for the division of Dungannon, being almost half the county, would not take place in sufficient time, assuming that the assizes were at the usual time; this revision, therefore, could not take place in sufficient time so that the book should be revised and delivered to the sheriff, for him to send out his summonses for the assizes.

2067. Could you refer to a county as large as Cork, which has 8,000 names on the jurors' book?—I assume that it would be a mere formal striking out and initialling the names; there would be no putting on or taking off any names that were qualified above that, whatever valuation was fixed.

2068. You stated that you thought it very desirable that power should be given under the new Act to select the foreman?—Yes.

2069. Do you think that the foreman should be either named by the officer of the court, or that the jurors themselves should select their own foreman at once?—The jury, as far as my knowledge of juries goes, would much prefer that it was done for them.

2070. Do you consider that that would be a very essential point?—Yes, a very essential point.

2071. *Chairman.*] I understand that you stated that in Tyrone the special list will be exhausted this year?—It will.

2072. Will you state how that will occur?—The special list consists of only 500 names, and under the present Act as many special as common jurors (who number 3,092) are required for the business of the county, hence the disproportionate exhaustion of the list.

2073. That is as large a panel as is sufficient?—It is more than sufficient if the law were altered.

2074. Is it necessary that so large a list should be provided?—It is necessary to provide for the grand juries at four divisions of quarter sessions, and for the special juries at the assizes, and for the exhaustion of the special jurors upon the common jurors' book. When a man is summoned on a special jury for any cause whatever, a mark is put opposite his name in the general jurors' book, as well as in the special jurors' book, and the result is that the special jurors are exhausted far in advance of the common jurors upon the general jurors' book. At the next Tyrone assizes, if the law is not altered before then, there may be one or two, but I do not think there will be more, special jurors upon the crown panel.

2075. The principal cause then is the number of quarter sessions grand jurors?—That exhausts the list.

2076. What are the duties of the grand jury at the quarter sessions?—To find any bills of indictment that may be returned for trial at the particular division to which they have been summoned.

2077. The work is generally extremely light, I suppose?—Extremely; very frequently there is nothing whatever to be done, but yet they are summoned and must attend and exhaust the panel.

2078. How many districts are there in Tyrone?—Four quarter sessions.

2079. The jurors are only summoned from the district itself?—From the district.

2080. In most cases the duty of serving on quarter sessions grand juries does not occupy more than a day, I believe?—I have never known it to occupy a day.

2081. Should you say that it generally took a juror more than a day of his time coming and returning?—He loses his day by it; if there is much work to be done; if there are a good many bills to be found, it generally occupies till two or three in the afternoon. They have to come a considerable distance, seven, eight, or ten miles; an average of eight or nine miles, I should say, and the day is practically lost.

2082. Would you say it would be a hardship upon the special jurors that serving upon a quarter sessions grand jury should not count as serving on a jury?—I think it would be a hardship.

2083. You do not see any way to remedy this rapid exhaustion of the special jurors' list?—Except by doing away with the divisions which are not necessary; there is frequently nothing to be done, and almost always little or nothing.

2084. Have you given any evidence as to the cost of the working of a new Act?—The chief expense is the expense of the clerks of the union, which is borne by the poor rates. The expenses in future will not be so great as heretofore, because the difficulty in the preparation of the lists will not be so great, and the raising of the qualification

Mr *L. M. Buchanan.*

12 May 1873.

fication will so diminish the numbers on the list that there will not be so much to be done.

2085. Do you know what was the cost of the preparation of a juror's book?—I could make the calculation.

2086 Were the expenses paid through you?—No, not through me. The clerks of the union were paid by the various unions in Tyrone 145 *l.* The grand jury allowed me 100 *l.* The poor rate collectors were allowed among them (and there are a vast number of them), I should say, 100 *l.* more; say 350 *l.* altogether.

2087. But that cost was in many particulars exceptional, you think?—If the present Act remains in force the same amount of work will have to be done, and we who do it will expect to be paid for it at the same rate

2088. I understood you to say, that a good deal of the work had had to be done on the first occasion which would not have to be done again?—For that the grand jury of Tyrone allowed me 20 guineas extra, and they fixed my remuneration for all future years at 100 *l.* Of course it was on the assumption that the work would remain the same. If the work be diminished they might possibly think that they ought to diminish the remuneration.

2089. By whom was the remuneration allowed to the clerks of the unions?—By the boards of guardians.

2090. The grand jury had nothing to say to it?—They had nothing to say to the clerks of the unions; they had to allow the remuneration to the clerks of the peace and the poor rate collectors.

2091. Do you know at what rate the guardians remunerated the clerks?—The remuneration spread over the seven unions of the county amounted to 145 *l.*

2092. About 20 *l.* each?—Yes, the average is about 20 *l.* It is from 15 *l.* to, in some places, 30 *l.* It was a very large district where they got 30 *l.* The average is 20 *l.* to 22 *l.*

2093. What work had the clerks of the union to do except to put together the lists, which he gets from the poor rate collector?—The clerk of the union prepared the lists. He associated with himself in the preparation of those lists the poor rate collectors. The poor rate collectors were supposed to have assisted him. He himself had the preparation of the lists, and the poor rate collectors were associated with him in order that they, from their intimate knowledge of the people whose names were upon the list, might be able to tell the clerk of the union whom to exclude from their being over age or incapacitated.

2094. On a future occasion, he will have nothing to do but to go over his last list and make any additions or alterations which are necessary; he will not have to make a new list; the list for next year will be substantially what it was for this?—He would only have to make alterations; he would not have to write down the names on the old list, but he would have to examine every name with the aid of the poor-rate collectors, and the clerk of the peace will also have to do that.

2095. Should you say that 20 *l.* was an excessive payment for that work?—It certainly was not excessive for last year.

2096. For the preparation of the list in the first instance?—Certainly not; and I believe that had they been fixing the remuneration for one particular year, they would have fixed it much higher. It was by reason of its being likely to be permanent that they fixed it at that rate.

2097. Your own duty is to make the county list from all the lists received from the clerks of the unions?—Yes.

2098. Do you know whether other grand jurors have allowed about the same as has been allowed to yourself?—Some more, and some less. I think Tyrone is an average or better than the average; it is in proportion to the numbers upon the lists. The grand jurors had as much information as they could gain in the time

2099. You have to make out the long panel, the general list which contains common jurors and special jurors?—Yes.

2100. And then a special jurors' list?—Yes.

2101. And then a separate list for each division?—No.

2102. In summoning the jurors for the quarter sessions, the general list is used?—Every particular about every juror is stated on the face of the jurors' book.

2103. The general list is used?—The names of the jurors are extracted from their own particular division to serve in their own quarter sessions towns.

2104. The work would be reduced by raising the qualification?—By raising the rating, the list will be diminished in size, and the work will be reduced.

2105. Do you see any other way in which under the new system the work would be reduced?—I think there is no other way that the work could be reduced, and if a greater amount of attention is paid to the revision the work will be increased by the greatly increased care that it will be necessary to devote to the revision of the list, which I consider of very great importance indeed.

2106. Under any circumstances, you think that the new system must remain more expensive to the counties and to the ratepayers than the old one?—It naturally must.

2107. Do you think the clerks of the unions would have any difficulty, or would it be an invidious duty if they had to state any ground of objection which occurred to them against a particular juror in sending in their lists?—I think it would be an invidious duty.

2108. I understand you would leave the task of revision very much to the Crown solicitors?—I thought that the Crown solicitor, perhaps, was the best officer, but he being a Crown prosecutor at quarter sessions, possibly there might be an objection to him on that account, being an official of the Crown; but some official should be intrusted with a very careful examination of the lists, and should be empowered to require the aid of the parties who are most conversant with the people of the district before the list came on for revision.

2109. Is there any objection to the chairman actually revising the list, supposing he is provided with sufficient information?—No, I think not.

2110. Would you make it the duty of the Crown solicitor to obtain that information?—The three officials who I think would be perfectly qualified to do it would be the Crown solicitor, the sub-sheriff, or the clerk of the peace; either of the three would be fully qualified from their local knowledge to be entrusted with the preliminary revision, or the information which would enable the proper revision to be made.

2111. Do

Mr. *L. M. Buchanan.*

12 May 1873.

2111. Do I understand that you have sufficient individual knowledge of the jurors on the list to be able to tell the chairman of quarter sessions who would be in any way disqualified?—Personally, I believe none of those three officials would have that knowledge; but if there was associated with them either the constabulary, or the poor-rate collectors, or the baronial constables, there is no doubt they could gain sufficient knowledge.

2112. You could obtain the knowledge?—The knowledge could be obtained.

2113. You, in your own case, could obtain the necessary knowledge?—Yes; if it were entrusted to the clerks of the peace I could.

2114. Colonel *Vandeleur*.] You stated that you had 100 *l.* on your own account, for your own duties as clerk of the peace?—Yes.

2115. How much were you out of pocket?—I did a very large amount of the work myself; I had to pay for all the books, the printing and publishing, out of the money allowed me by the grand jury. I paid for all the printing and stationery, and other work connected with the formation of the lists, all the forms supplied to the clerks of the union; all the forms necessary to make up the returns afterwards were to be defrayed out of the expenses allowed to me.

2116. How much did the printing and copying come to, the clerks' work paid out of pocket?—I cannot tell exactly.

2117. Did not the grand jury require the printer's bill, or a statement of it?—They were furnished with an account detailing all the items, but I cannot recollect at this moment what the different items were. The bulk sum came to 130 *l.* odd; they fixed the remuneration at 100 *l.* and gave 20 *l.* this year for the extra trouble.

2118. How many names were there?—Three thousand and seventy-five names on the general jurors' book, and 505 upon the special jurors' book.

2119. How much did the poor-rate collectors claim?—They claimed sums averaging from 4 *l.* to 6 *l.* I think they got from 2 *l.* to 4 *l.*

2120. They were cut down to that?—I think so.

2121. *Chairman*.] You do not consider that you were overpaid for your share of the work?—No, I do not; it was a work of enormous trouble at first, and the strict alphabetical arrangement, as in a dictionary, was what made it such enormous trouble. The names had to be culled out in the strictest alphabetical order, not only of the surname, but of the christian name, and sometimes the alphabetical arrangement extended to the fifth or sixth letter. It was not the mere act of copying, but the act of arranging, which created the immense difficulty.

2122. Colonel *Vandeleur*.] The clerks of the unions had little or no trouble?—The clerks of the unions are not compelled to make out their lists in a dictionary order; they are compelled to make them out in alphabetical order only.

2123. The clerks of the unions have already a dictionary order, because they make out the voters' list?—Yes.

2124. They have it already; they have nothing to do but to copy that out, taking out the names of 20 *l.*, or 30 *l.*, and upwards?—They are not supposed to have the custody of any of the voters' lists; if they had, there is no doubt it would have saved them a great deal of trouble if they had culled them from the voters' lists.

2125. They make out the voters' list?—They correct the voters' list by a sufficient number of lists sent to them by the clerk of the peace at the time specified in the Act of Parliament.

2126. The clerks of the unions claimed a considerable sum of money for doing work which was very simple?—I do not think the clerks of the unions were overpaid for the work they did last year; if they had had the voters' lists they might have availed themselves of them, and it would have saved them a great deal of trouble, but they had not.

2127. *Chairman*.] I understand that they were paid for their own trouble and nothing else; they had no printing to do?—They had to print the lists, but they had not to pay for the printing of the lists. They had nothing but copying to do upon forms supplied by me.

2128. The 20 *l.* which they got upon the average was entirely for their own labour?—Entirely.

2129. In that 100 *l.* which you received there was a good deal of printing and other expenses? Printing, and other expenses; stationery.

2130. Is it left entirely to the grand jury?—Entirely; it does not go before the presentment sessions.

2131. Have you in your county a great preponderance of names beginning with any one letter?—"M," of course, an enormous preponderance.

2132. Will the effect of the rotation provided by the Act be to leave the last panel almost entirely composed of "M's"?—I should think the last two or three panels will be almost entirely composed of "M's." There are several letters already exhausted. There cannot be an alphabetical panel at present, further than the next unexhausted letter can be taken.

2133. The last two or three panels will be composed entirely of "M's"?—If the list remains at its present strength.

2134. *The O'Donoghue*.] Would not that be assuming that all the "M's" were qualified to serve as jurors?—The "M's" at present on the list. I am speaking of the present jurors' book.

Mr. William Henry M'Grath, called in; and Examined.

Mr. *W. H. M'Grath.*

2135. *Chairman*.] You are a Crown Solicitor?—Yes.

2136. For what counties? For the counties Fermanagh and Tyrone.

2137. During what time?—Since the year 1856.

2138. You have had a large experience of the old, and some experience of the new, system?—Yes.

2139. What is your opinion as to the principle of selection of the jury panel by the sheriff?—I think the uncontrolled selection of the jury panel by the sheriff was open to very great objection.

2140. Will you give your reasons?—Particularly in political or religious matters. It was always a cause of suspicion, whether there was any ground or not. There was no public confidence in trials under the circumstances.

2141. Was that a matter of notoriety?—Quite so, I think.

Mr. *W. H. M'Grath.*

12 May 1873.

2142. I do not understand you to say that there was any ground for such suspicion?—No; I do not mean to say that. It was always open to observation.

2143. Do you consider that verdicts obtained under that system in political or religious cases did not command the confidence of the public?—I do not think they did, generally speaking.

2144. In the counties with which you were acquainted, were the same jurors generally selected?—The same jurors were generally selected from year to year. At the assizes I have met the same persons constantly in criminal cases, in the county Tyrone particularly.

2145. You have nothing to do with the selection of the panel?—Nothing at all.

2146. Do you know the cause of the same jurors having always been selected in a large county like Tyrone?—The sub-sheriff selected men who were, as he knew, acquainted with the duties, and were on the spot.

2147. Was it considered a hardship by them?—Very often; I have heard them complain very often.

2148. Of what class was that panel?—In the county of Fermanagh generally, shopkeepers of Enniskillen, and some farmers in the county. In Tyrone they were generally the class of shopkeepers.

2149. Were farmers ever placed upon the panel?—Yes. In my own county, the county Clare, I have frequently seen upon both criminal and civil juries, magistrates, and gentlemen of the county, serving upon ordinary juries. I never saw the same class in either Fermanagh or Tyrone.

2150. They were not placed upon the panel?—They were not.

2151. That, I suppose, was a matter of custom in different counties?—Quite so. I think the practice was different in almost every county. It rested altogether with the sub-sheriff. Generally speaking, I do not think the high sheriff interfered with the panels.

2152. The high sheriff possibly did not usually possess sufficient local knowledge to interfere much?—I do not think he did.

2153. So that, practically, a good deal depended upon the sub-sheriff, and his idea of the way in which his duties should be discharged?—Yes.

2154. Have you formed any opinion of the present Jury Act?—Yes; I think it has been very unsatisfactory indeed in its working.

2155. As to its general principle?—I quite approve of the general principle. I do not think the Jury Act was done justice to previous to the last assizes. I do not think the proper revision contemplated by the Act took place. In Enniskillen, and also in Omagh, several were called from the jury list, and when they appeared in court they were at once put aside, for they appeared incompetent to try any case. Some of them excused themselves from age.

2156. They ought not to have been on the list?—They ought not to have been on the panel at all, or on the jurors' book, under the Act.

2157. That would be the fault of the poor-rate collectors, or of the clerks of unions?—Or of the revision; no proper revision took place.

2158. The revising officer, the chairman, had no knowledge of them?—He had not.

2159. He could not strike off the name of an unqualified person, unless he were informed of the disqualification?—No. I asked some of the chairmen myself if they had any actual revision, and they said not. They produced the book, and asked if there was any objection by any person whose name was in it; but they had no means of getting the information, which I think is one of the defects of the Act.

2160. As to the qualification, what is your opinion; in the first place, do you approve of a rating qualification?—Yes, I do; I first thought the qualification was very much too low, but on looking into the matter carefully and examining the books I came to the conclusion that a 30 *l.* rating would give a very good class of jurors in counties.

2161. That would be in the rural districts and towns?—Yes.

2162. Would you say that there should be any other qualification for occupiers of houses in towns?—Yes; I think in towns from 12 *l.* to 15 *l.* a year house rating would give a very intelligent class of jurors.

2163. If the qualification is in respect of a holding within a town, it probably is a house, is it not?—Yes; there may be lands, or a field, or so, with it; I would rather separate it, and confine it to the house qualification; I think you are certain to have a better class of jurors.

2164. You would say that the occupier rated at from 12 *l.* to 15 *l.* for a house in towns, would be as competent a juror as a 30 *l.* occupier in the country?—I should say so.

2165. Perhaps more so?—Perhaps more so; you have a very intelligent class among the shopkeepers in country towns, generally speaking.

2166. Would you add any persons to the list who were not rated?—Yes, I would be disposed to do so; for instance, every one holding the commission of the peace in a county, whether he was rated or not, I would put on the jurors' list; I would put the sons of peers, and the sons of country gentlemen on, if there were any means of coming at them; I would place all those on the list, because you would thereby to some extent ensure an intelligent class of jurors.

2167. They are already on the special jurors' list?—I do not think they are, unless they are rated; but whether rated or not, I should be disposed to put them on; for instance, every man holding the commission of the peace for a county I would put on the jurors' list, to discharge some of the duties of the county in that respect.

2168. Mr. *Bourke.*] Would you add his son?—Yes, if his son was of age.

2169. Colonel *Vandeleur.*] Whether he resided or not?—Yes; if he was a magistrate for the county, I would have him on the list, so that if he did at any time come into the county he should be there to discharge the duties; I think the present Act provides that all these shall be first placed on the special list, but to justify that they must be rated, as I take it, under the Act; they must be first rated, and put on the general jurors' book; those parties are all now authorised and qualified to act as grand jurors; you frequently have them on grand juries, and why not put them on the other juries.

2170. Mr. *Bruen.*] Do you mean you would put them both on the special jurors' list and on the general jurors' list?—They must be first on the general jurors' list and then on the special list.

2171. *Chairman.*] Is that class now placed upon the common jurors' list, or only on the special

Mr. *W. H. M'Grath.*

12 May 1873.

special jurors' list?—If rated, they are first placed on the jurors' book, and then from that on the special jurors' list, but they cannot be placed at all, as I take it, unless they are rated.

2172. It has been already suggested to the Committee that in certain cases (and I believe by one witness it was suggested that in all criminal cases) the Crown should have the right to require a special jury?—I think that would be a desirable provision; but I would also give the same permission to the prisoner, so that he should have the power of applying to the Queen's Bench for a special jury to try him.

2173. Would the prisoner be at all likely to claim such a right?—I do not know that he would in the general class of cases.

2174. Mr. *Bourke.*] In some political cases he might?—Yes, certainly; I think that would get rid of a course that has always appeared to me very objectionable; that of telling a juror, when he comes up, to stand aside, which in practice, although quite necessary, is, I think, objectionable.

2175. *Chairman.*] Do you think it would not be a very invidious power, if exercised by the Crown, the right of asking for a special jury?—I do not think it would, because the object would be to get an intelligent class of jurors, and there ought to be no objection to that, I think.

2176. But in the majority of criminal cases, would not the practical effect be to try a man by a jury composed of persons very much his superiors in station?—It would have that effect.

2177. You do not think it would be so invidious a power as that of ordering jurors to stand aside?—I do not think it would.

2178. Have you had to make use of that right frequently?—Yes, I have had very often, and particularly at the last assizes I had to exercise it.

2179. Dr. *Ball.*] Did you prosecute?—Yes, in one case particularly; but the prisoner has to be tried again, and therefore I should not like to say anything about that case.

2180. *Chairman.*] Have you found it necessary to make use of that power under the old Act?—I have, frequently.

2181. Do you consider that you would have to use it much more frequently under the present Act than under the old one?—Yes; I was at the last assizes obliged to tell a great number to stand aside, who appeared to me quite incompetent to act as jurymen.

2182. Whatever system might be adopted you do not think it is a power which could be dispensed with?—I think not. I think that power ought always to remain with the Crown.

2183. I believe that in civil cases either party may ask for a special jury?—Yes, in a civil case, no matter what the amount involved is, either party can apply to have it tried by a special jury. I do not see why that same principle ought not to apply to a criminal case.

2184. It would be said, would it not, that it was no longer trying a man by his peers?—To some extent, no doubt.

2185. Would it not have the effect of throwing almost the whole of the work upon the special jurors' panel?—I do not know; that would depend upon the exercise of it. I do not think the Crown would in all cases apply for a special jury, only in special cases. I know there was a case in the County Fermanagh, in which it would have been very desirable to have had an intelligent jury. There was a case there which there ought to have been no difficulty about, but the jury thought proper to disagree.

2186. Would not the exercise of this power be still more invidious, if it were the ordinary practice to have a common jury, if in cases of murder, or attempt to murder, or agrarianism, or any political case, resort were had to a special jury, would not then the exercise of the power be rather an invidious one?—I do not know; I cannot see that. You would have a class of jurors in the box who you cannot suppose would find verdicts against the evidence laid before them.

2187. You said, I think, that verdicts obtained under the old system did not always command the confidence of the public; you do not think that that would at all be the case if the alteration were adopted which you are now recommending?—I think not.

2188. You think it would tend, perhaps, to increase the confidence of the public?—I should say so.

2189. As to the revision of the list, would you extend the disqualifications or exemptions?—I would disqualify all publicans; in fact, now it is one of our duties to put them aside. I would disqualify them by the Act, because it is very invidious, when they are called up, to be always told to stand aside. I would also disqualify all illiterate persons. Another class I would exclude would be attorneys' clerks; I think they ought to be excluded from juries.

2190. We will go through the list; you would disqualify all illiterate persons; what means would you take to ascertain the illiteracy of a person?—I would be disposed very much to put upon the clerk of the peace the duty of getting information through the ratepayers, or the police, or through any other channel, as to every man upon the jury; the collectors know almost every man in their district, and they would know at once whether he was illiterate or not.

2191. The barony collectors have now nothing to do with the preparation of the list?—The poor-rate collector, the barony cess collector, have not, I think.

2192. Would you throw on the clerk of the peace the duty of making himself acquainted with the circumstances and character of every man on the lists?—Certainly; and collecting evidence where necessary, and bringing that before the chairman at the quarter sessions so as to have an actual revision of the list.

2193. Is it not the case that in most counties the duties of clerk of the peace are performed by deputy?—Yes, it is so.

2194. The clerk of the peace would hardly be able in many instances to discharge this duty, would he; should it be discharged in those cases also by deputy?—I think so. In a great many cases the deputies are very competent men; I have met several of them that are very competent.

2195. You think either the clerk of the peace or his deputy would be able to collect the necessary information?—Yes; in some counties the clerk of the peace acts himself, in the county Clare for instance.

2196. Then you mentioned publicans?—I would exclude them as a rule; they are, in point of fact, excluded at present, but they are on the list, and you are obliged to tell them to stand aside.

2197. For what reason would you make that a ground of exclusion?—Every Attorney General that I have had to do with has made it a point with the Crown Solicitors that they will put off the jury

Mr. W. H. M'Grath.

12 May 1873.

jury all those people; publicans as a rule are not allowed to serve, therefore what we are obliged to do now I would do by the Act.

2198. Is it your opinion that there is any good ground for the exclusion?—I think there is; in criminal cases I think there is a very good ground, because all sorts of people meet in public-houses, and the publican on a jury would necessarily have his mind distracted between his duty to act on evidence, and the private feeling of injury thereby to his trade, and other matters which he might by accident be aware of, as connected with his trade.

2199. Would you make it a ground of exemption or of absolute exclusion; there is a difficulty, is not there?—Yes.

2200. Do you consider, that without casting any slur upon their character as a body of tradesmen, it places them in rather an invidious position?—I think it does; I do not mean to cast the slightest imputation on them, because I have known some very respectable and proper men having houses of the sort, but I would exclude them in the same way that I exclude doctors and attorneys, and people of that class.

2201. *Mr. Bourke.*] They would be a different class altogether than those represented by the Licensed Victuallers Association?—Yes.

2202. People of a lower class altogether?—Yes.

2203. (*Chairman.*) Did you say you would exclude doctors?—I think they are excluded already.

2204. What is your opinion about the present exemptions; do you think that they are in any respect too extensive?—I do not think they are.

2205. The present exemptions exclude a great number of very competent jurors, do they not?—Yes, certainly.

2206. You think that in the public interest it is better that they should remain excluded?—I should say so.

2207. Why would you propose to add attorneys' clerks to the list?—Because, in criminal cases in the county, in the case of attorneys' practising at quarter sessions, and at assizes, and acting for prisoners, their clerks know a great deal about the affairs generally, and I would exclude them on that ground. Besides, it would be excessively inconvenient to their employers to have them taken away.

2208. Would you give any more general power to the chairman to strike the names of persons off the list?—I would be disposed to give the Judge of Assize, or the chairman of quarter sessions, power to excuse a juror upon sufficient cause; that is, cause that would appear to the judge or to the chairman sufficient.

2209. But at the annual revision would you give the chairman power to strike the name of any juror off who, for some reason which might not have been specified in the Act, did not appear to him properly qualified?—Yes, certainly I would; I should be quite disposed to give that power to the chairman.

2210. For any cause which appeared to him sufficient?—Yes; I am sure it would be properly exercised.

2211. The evidence, I suppose, to be on oath?—Yes, if the chairman require it; in ordinary cases he would not require that; if a man came up before him, and he saw from his appearance that he was incompetent, in that case it would not be necessary to go into evidence.

2212. I think a witness was asked whether the fact of a man being a Fenian would be a special ground of exclusion; what would be your opinion?—I do not know how you are to discover that.

2213. You would not be satisfied with the mere assertion of the constabulary that he was a reputed Fenian?—If the constabulary had satisfactory proof of the matter, and evidence of it, I would be disposed to act upon that, or to give the chairman the power of acting upon that.

2214. You would rather trust to a high qualification and the retention of the power of setting aside, to keep any persons of that sort off the jury?—I would; I think with a 30 *l.* rating you would get a very good class of jurors.

2215. In the counties with which you are acquainted?—Yes.

2216. Colonel *Wilson Patten.*] Do you think that would be the case all over Ireland?—Generally speaking, I think it would be.

2217. There are no counties where you think 30 *l.* would be too low a rate?—I am not aware of that; I should not like to say.

2218. *Chairman.*] I understand you would not recommend, under any circumstances, reverting to the old plan of selection by the sheriff?—Certainly not.

2219. Do you think, even supposing it were a mistake to have abandoned that power, it would be more difficult now to revert to it?—I think it would be much more, and I think it would be very objectionable to go back to the old system; I think that uncontrolled selection by the sheriff, or by any person in the position of a sheriff, of a jury panel is open to great objection.

2220. And most stringent and thorough revision of the list by the chairman, and the exclusion of all disqualified persons, is a very different thing from reverting to selection from that list by any person whatever, is it not?—A very different thing.

2221. Do you know anything of the working of this Act in the matter of expense?—No; not at all.

2222. There are no new duties thrown upon you?—No, none at all.

2223. Of course, for the purpose of using the power of ordering jurors to stand by, it is necessary that you should have a tolerably complete knowledge of the persons on the panel?—Yes.

2224. Under the old system, I suppose, you generally had that knowledge?—Yes; when I go down to assizes I generally get information about the list, and the men on it.

2225. Could you obtain that knowledge at the last assizes?—I did, as far as I could.

2226. It was more difficult, of course, in consequence of so many new jurors being on the panel?—Yes; there were a number of men called on the list that nobody knew anything about, that were never on the list before. Some men that were called were dead for a length of time; very old men came up, and it was only necessary to look at them to see that they were incompetent, and that was all in consequence of revision not taking place.

2227. You attribute great importance to a more careful revision?—I do; I think if there had been a proper revision even under the present Bill, it would not have been so bad as it was.

2228. Do you think that you would have much difficulty in finding out as much as might be necessary for the purpose as to the character of the

Mr. *W. H. M'Grath.*

19 May 1873.

the panel, so as to exercise your right of ordering jurors to stand aside?—I can get the information through the constabulary, and in other respects which would enable me to discharge that duty.

2229. Colonel *Wilson Patten.*] You say the defect you have last alluded to was in consequence of the absence of the power of revision; what power of revision would you give; you say you could see by the looks of the parties standing around that they were incompetent to be on the jury?—Yes, some of them that were considerably over age; for instance, the Act of Parliament excludes every person over 60, and there were men there upwards of 70.

2230. You would not give the power to the revising authority to strike a man off because of his looks?—Not without information, certainly; not of his mere whim, I would not.

2231. But for some positive defect of intelligence or qualification?—Yes; some information that would justify him sitting there as judge in excluding the man.

2232. Dr. *Ball.*] You say that you have often seen magistrates on the common juries in Clare?—Yes.

2233. And also in Limerick, I think; you did not say Limerick, but I ask you that?—I have seen them in Limerick.

2234. Were not there most excellent juries under the old system, both at Clare and Limerick?—Yes.

2235. From what you know of the Irish peasantry, do not you think they have much more respect for justice administered by persons of education and intelligence than they ever can have if the persons administering it are uneducated, and of their own class?—I think they have.

2236. Your object as to qualification would be to have it as high as would admit of a sufficient number of jurors?—Yes.

2237. That is all you aim at?—That is all; I think it is most desirable to have an intelligent jury.

2238. In taking a 30 *l.* qualification the number it would give would be very considerable; is it one of your motives that you think the same person should not be called on to serve too often?—No; I do not think it is any grievance at all to a juror to be called upon to serve once or twice in the year; I think he ought.

2239. Excepting in Cork, Belfast, and, perhaps, Derry, or Galway; is it not the fact that in most of the assize towns in Ireland the assizes last only a day or two?—Yes, except in the places you have mentioned.

2240. How long in Tyrone, and Fermanagh, except you get a case like Montgomery's?—In Fermanagh the assizes of late are generally over in half a day, or a day; I mean as regards criminal business.

2241. The civil business is not long?—I have known the judges remain in Omagh over a week in civil cases.

2242. You would agree with the view I take, that it is no hardship on a gentleman of property that he should be made to discharge a certain duty to the public twice a year?—I think not; there is a great objection on the part of gentlemen to attend.

2243. Can you give any reason for that?—They state they have great objection to go upon juries in some cases, and in other cases to mix with the class of jurors.

2244. Looking at the juries which you saw, do you think it is not an unfair objection?—In some cases it is not.

2245. As to that proposition of yours about the Crown having a special jury, I would ask you whether you would have any objection to add to it that a special jury should only be obtained on the direct application of the Attorney General by a counsel in the Queen's Bench?—I would only grant it to the Crown in that instance, certainly.

2246. You would confine the right to great cases in which the Attorney General personally thought it proper to have it?—Certainly, and I would give the same right to the prisoner.

2247. There is a class of cases which was occurring to me in which power might be very useful, cases connected with the revenue; have you ever had any of those cases?—No.

2248. If there was a process for illicit distillation, are the lower classes likely to be very attentive to the interests of the Crown?—I think you would find it very difficult in some cases to satisfy them.

2249. There would be no harm in having that power to get a special jury?—No.

2250. In political and agrarian and all that class of cases?—Yes.

2251. You know Clare very well?—Yes.

2252. Did you look at all at the panel?—No.

2253. You only examined the two counties with which you were officially connected?—I only examined one, because I was first under the impression that 30 *l.* would be too low, and I thought a much higher qualification would be necessary, but when I looked into the Tyrone list, in which there are over 3,000 on the jurors' book, and I found that the difference between 20 *l.* and 30 *l.* rating would strike off about 1,500, I altered my views. I could scarcely credit such a result.

2254. Could you believe that it would have that effect in the other counties, that such a small difference as between 30 *l.* and 40 *l.* would strike off that proportion?—I should not like to say it would; I am not aware.

2255. Mr. *Bruen.*] The system of calling jurors by alphabetical rotation throws exactly the same burden upon the man who lives a great distance from the assize town as upon the man who lives near?—Yes.

2256. Is it not a very much greater burden upon the distant man to attend?—Of course it is.

2257. Is not that throwing an unfair proportion of public duty upon him?—I think it is one of the duties that a man resident in a county ought to be prepared to discharge at personal inconvenience to himself.

2258. If you are to discharge a public duty in that way you cannot consider your personal convenience?—I should so.

2259. So long as the personal convenience were equalised probably that would be a very just view; but do not you think it ought to be equalised as far as possible?—I think it ought to be equalised, and in that way I think you have it. You take a name from each letter. You spread it over the whole county.

2260. The distant man has to serve as often as the man who lives near?—Of course when his name comes, but it is very often desirable to get a distant man to try a case in preference to a man who is on the spot.

2261. Taking the question of convenience, I suppose you admit that the distant man being summoned as often as the near man throws a greater burden, inconvenience, and expense upon him?—It puts the additional travelling on him, and, of course, some additional expense. I do not see how that can be avoided.

Mr. W. H. M'Grath.

16 May 1873.

2262. You think it cannot be avoided by the alphabetical system of rotation?—I think not.

2263. Are you not aware that persons employed in business, whose time is very necessary for the superintendence of that business, would lose more by being called upon to attend a case which would last three weeks, than a person who is not engaged in business?—Of course it is a necessary consequence.

2264. Is not that an unequal burden thrown upon one which is not thrown upon another?—It is, certainly; but I cannot see how that is to be avoided.

2265. You said that the uncontrolled selection of the jury panel by the sub-sheriff was open to great objections, but I think you also said you had never known instances of a sub-sheriff exercising that power unfairly?—I am not aware of any case.

2266. Then that objection which you have advanced is rather a theoretical than a practical objection?—I have often heard the matter discussed, and statements made about it, but I am not myself personally aware of any case.

2267. So that, in fact, in your experience the objection is a theoretical objection and not a practical one?—As far as I myself am concerned it is so.

2268. You are obliged to call upon the jurors to stand by in Crown cases?—Yes.

2269. I suppose you exercise that power from knowledge of the jurors?—Yes.

2270. Under the old Act had you a pretty good knowledge of the jurors that appeared?—Yes, it was part of my duty to make myself acquainted with the men returned on the panel.

2271. Under the new Act a very great addition is made to the numbers?—Yes.

2272. Do you mean to say that you can exercise your right of calling on jurors to stand by from personal knowledge?—Not from a personal knowledge certainly, but from the information which I acquire from the constabulary, and others who are able to give it to me.

2273. Do you exercise that right upon the information given by the constabulary?—And others; any other information I can get from other parties; it is the duty of the sessional Crown Solicitor, for instance, to give me information if he is aware of any circumstance.

2274. Do you call upon the constabulary when they give you information for the grounds of their objections?—Yes, I generally ask the reason.

2275. You take the information they give you as a fact?—Generally I do; I generally get the information through the county inspector or the sub-inspector of constabulary; I do not get it from the men.

2276. Do you think that the county inspector and the sub-inspector have themselves the personal knowledge of this great number of new jurymen which would enable them to give you that information of their own knowledge?—They get the information from the men in the neighbourhood.

2277. *Chairman.*] If a man were a bad character they probably would have personal knowledge themselves?—No doubt.

2278. Mr. *Bruen.*] In the counties for which you are Crown Solicitor, I imagine there is not much Fenianism, is there?—I am not aware of any.

2279. And that objection has never been made to you by the constabulary; have the constabulary ever objected to a man being sworn upon a jury, and called upon you to make him stand aside on the ground of his being a Fenian?—Never.

2280. Supposing that Fenianism existed in the district, and that the constabulary objected to a man, owing to his being a Fenian, would you consider that a sufficient ground for the exercise of your power to make him stand aside?—Certainly; without the slightest hesitation.

2281. You know the county Clare?—Yes.

2282. In that county is not there a considerable amount of the Fenian conspiracy?—I understand there is, but I am very happy to say I have not seen any of it yet myself.

2283. Do you think that the jury franchise, if I may use that expression, the 30 *l.* qualification, would absolutely exclude all Fenians?—I do not mean to say so at all; I do not know anything about Fenians; what their qualification or valuation is.

2284. You think that there ought to be a right of claiming a special jury given in all cases, and if demanded it should be given both to the Crown and the prisoner?—In all cases of magnitude.

2285. Do you think a prisoner would ever ask for a special jury?—I do not know; I cannot imagine what a prisoner would do in a particular case.

2286. You do not wish to give an opinion?—I do not think they would apply as frequently as the Crown would.

2287. Do you think they ever would apply?—I do not know.

2288. Did I understand you to say that the qualification which you considered would be a good one to add to the Act, would be a 12 *l.* to 15 *l.* qualification for houses or buildings?—Yes, in towns.

2289. You would limit it to towns?—Yes.

2290. Do you think a man living in the country, who lived in a house valued from 12 *l.* to 15 *l.*, would not be fit to perform the duties of a juryman?—I did not say so; in the country the house is generally valued with the land.

2291. Putting the land aside and taking a house qualification merely?—I think a man that lives in a house in the country valued at 12 *l.* to 15 *l* would be, generally speaking, an intelligent man.

2292. Perhaps it would simplify the matter if a man who possesses a house rated at 12 *l.* to 15 *l.* a year, no matter where he lived, should be a fit man to serve as a juryman?—Yes, I should think he would.

2293. You need not put in any denomination of towns or villages in that respect?—I think it quite unnecessary in that view of it.

2294. Is not there a difficulty in putting in that denomination of towns and villages, in knowing what a village is?—It would not be necessary if it were a mere house even in the country.

2295. That is the suggestion I put to you: according to your proposition, that in towns and villages a 12 *l.* or 15 *l.* house qualification should be the qualification for a juryman, it would be necessary that the towns and the villages should be properly defined?—I think, generally speaking, they are. I think the difference between towns and villages at present is pretty well defined.

2296. *Chairman.*] They are defined in the rate book, are they not?—"A net annual value of 20 *l.* or upwards in respect of lands, tenements,

Mr. *W. H. M'Grath.*

12 May 1873.

ments, or hereditaments, within any of the said counties; or a net annual value of 12 *l.* or upwards, in respect of lands, tenements, or hereditaments, appearing on the rate book of any union, to be situate in any city, town, or village, within any of the said counties."

2297. Mr. *Bruen.*] That is an arbitrary definition, which depends entirely on the man who makes the valuation, as to what is a village. You would actually leave it to the valuation officer to decide whether a man was to be a juryman or not?—If you give 12 *l.* as the rating of a house, I do not think it signifies whether it is in a village or a town; it is "in any city, town, or village."

2298. Villages included?—Yes; in any of those places, if he is rated at 12 *l.*, he would be on the list.

2299. Who is to judge of what a village is?—It is not necessary to judge of that; it is the rating which would give the qualification: it is not its being in a village or a town.

2300. If the qualification is conveyed by a 20 *l.* rating in the country, or a 30 *l.* rating in the country, and a 15 *l.* rating in a village, of course it does depend on whether it is a village or not?—Yes; it says "the respective tenements or hereditaments;" that is, houses.

2301. Mr. *Bourke.*] Is there not a definition, something like "houses and offices"?—Yes, in the rate books.

2302. That is the kind of qualification you propose?—Yes.

2303. Therefore it would be no matter, as long as you fixed on the sum, whether you exclude the words "town or village" or not?—No.

2304. Because if it were to be a good qualification in the town, *à fortiori* it would be a good qualification in the country?—Yes; whether the houses and offices were in the country or in the town, it does not matter if they were rated.

2305. Mr. *Bruen.*] Do you think that a rating of 12 *l.* or 15 *l.* in some country towns in Ireland invariably shows that it proceeds from a house?—No.

2306. Are there not town parks included in many towns in Ireland which are land and rated up to 12 *l.* or 15 *l.*?—I think not; it would be put down as "houses and lands"; but "houses and offices" does not include land.

2307. *Chairman.*] Will you look at the 4th Schedule of the Act?—It says, "A net annual value of 20 *l.* or upwards in respect of lands, tenements, or hereditaments within any of the said counties, or a net annual value of 12 *l.* or upwards in respect of lands, tenements, or hereditaments appearing on the rate book of any union to be situate in any city, town, or village within any of the said counties." That takes lands, tenements, or hereditaments of the value of 12 *l.* in a town or village.

2308. Mr. *Bruen.*] The case I wish to put to you is this, whether it is within your knowledge that in any town a qualification may perhaps be 30 *s.* or 2 *l.* rating for the house and the balance made up of land; town parks?—It may be, no doubt, but then it would be put down as land; "houses and land."

2309. Do not you think that a qualification for buildings only would be a better qualification than for lands?—I think so. The 12 *l.* qualification ought to be upon a house only, and not to include any land. The occupier of that house, generally speaking, is an intelligent person.

2310. With regard to the exemptions, you said you thought that the exemptions which appeared in this Act were in the interests of the public; do you think that the exemption of public notaries and actuaries is one which, if it were taken out of the Act, and those gentlemen were not excepted, would cause the public to suffer very much?—I do not think so.

2311. Their exemption is rather in the interests of the gentlemen exempted than in the interest of the public?—I should say so, the exemptions generally speaking were in the interest of the public.

2312. It is the second schedule to the Act. There are a great number of those exemptions which we agree are necessary, but that was one which I thought you might consider not altogether in the interests of the public. Then there is another exemption as to persons holding any public office under Her Majesty's Government, or any public department, or any local authority?—There exclusion is a matter of public convenience.

2313. It includes gentlemen who hold any public office under any local authority?—The public in general would suffer if a man were taken away from his office.

2314. Mr. *Herbert.*] You said you thought 30 *l.* was the rating which ought to be in counties?—Yes.

2315. When you gave that opinion did you take into consideration the rise there would be in the value of holdings after the new valuation which the Government have brought in?—No, I did not.

2316. Do not you think if you took that into consideration you ought to put a higher qualification?—I think if you put a higher qualification you get a better class of jurors, no doubt, the higher you go, but then it is matter for consideration whether you get a sufficient number.

2317. In the south of Ireland, I believe, the valuation would be very much raised, therefore a number of men of 25 *l.* and 20 *l.* now, would become men of 30 *l.*; the rating I consider too low, and, therefore, you would be getting the same class in again?—In that case I would raise the qualification, certainly.

2318. That 30 *l.* is only under the present valuation; Griffiths' valuation?—Yes.

2319. Colonel *Vandeleur.*] The notices and summonses are served at present by the special bailiffs of the sheriff?—Yes.

2320. Would you approve of serving them by the police?—I would certainly; I think it desirable to have a certainty of the summons or notice getting into the hands of the man for whom it is intended, and I think you have a better security for that through the constabulary.

2321. At the same time the constabulary would attend at the sessions, or assizes, and would be able to give you information respecting the party summoned?—Yes.

2322. It is their duty to attend?—It is; for instance, the constabulary serve all the Crown summonses in criminal cases.

2323. Are you aware that in the valuation book the house and office were always rated separate from land?—Yes.

2324. There is no difficulty in the clerk of the union separating them?—I think not.

2325. It is for convenience sake that they amalgamate the land and the house?—Yes, they are always rated separately.

2326. Would you suggest that the juror should receive a notice that he has been put upon the list, and at the same time to be called upon to object to himself if he thought fit?—I think he ought

Mr. *W. H. M'Grath.*

12 May 1873.

ought to have notice of the revision by the chairman, or whoever is to revise the list; I think he ought to have notice, so that he may attend, if he thinks proper, either to object to himself or to have himself put on if he is not on.

2327. *Chairman.*] It has been suggested that summonses should be served by post, by registered letter?—I think service through the post with gentlemen, and that class of jurors, would answer; but I think with countrymen they rarely go to the post, and some of them live very far away from the post, they never think of going to get a letter. I think in that case it would be more satisfactory to have the summons served.

2328. Did I understand you to recommend that the summons should be served by the constabulary?—Yes, either through the constabulary or through the process servers at quarter sessions, who are appointed by the chairman.

2329. I do not think I asked you whether you found the operation of the present Act decidedly contrary to the interests of justice at the late assizes?—I should say so, with the class of jurors that we have under it.

2330. Do I understand you to be of opinion, that with the class of jurors whom you saw, you would be apprehensive as to the verdicts that would be given?—Yes.

2331. Rather than that you had found reason to complain of any verdict which had been given?—Yes; I have had no reason to complain of verdicts, unless in one or two cases. In Fermanagh I had no occasion to try the effect of the Jury Bills, because most of the prisoners pleaded guilty.

2332. Colonel *Vandeleur.*] Were you in Clare at the time of the last assizes?—No.

2333. You are not aware whether the verdicts there gave satisfaction or not?—I rather suspect they did not.

2334. Was anybody found guilty there?—I think not; I think if an alteration were made in the quarter sessions it would be desirable to dispense with the grand jurors at quarter sessions, which I think is a very idle sort of system, having grand jurors there at every quarter sessions finding bills for the pettiest offences before you put the accused on trial. If you get rid of that system you would save a great deal of the jurors; you would not require so extensive a list.

2335. Dr. *Ball.*] That would prevent the exhaustion of the special jury panel?—Yes; there is another alteration, I do not know whether I ought to mention it, which I think would be very desirable, and that is, if all persons were tried in the county town, where the gaol is, at quarter sessions, because at present they are sent about the country from the county gaol; they are sent all over the county to be tried. I think it would be desirable, if there were any alteration in the system, to try them where the gaol was.

2336. *Chairman.*] What is the reason of their being sent from one town to another?—They are tried wherever the informations were taken; they are generally sent back to that district to be tried at the quarter sessions.

2337. What would be the effect of their being tried at the county town?—It would save sending prisoners through the county to the quarter sessions towns, and then sending them back again.

2338. It would have nothing to do with the operation of this Act?—Except saving the special jurors; it would not exhaust the panel so rapidly.

2339. Colonel *Vandeleur.*] It would give the common jury in that particular division too much to do; they would complain of it?—You try them all at once in the town.

2340. *Chairman.*] Do I understand you would have no criminal cases tried at the quarter sessions in the county, except at the county town?—Yes, where the gaol is, and where all the prisoners are confined.

2341. Would that lead to no inconvenience?—I do not think it would, I think it would rather lead to convenience.

2342. Colonel *Vandeleur.*] You do not include prisoners on bail?—It might put them to some inconvenience.

2343. They might be tried at the usual quarter sessions? Yes.

2344. Would not what you propose give a great deal of additional trouble to witnesses?—They must go into the town, and it would be just as short for them to go into the county town; there is some inconvenience.

2345. *Chairman.*] Perhaps you are aware that the Bill which the Attorney General for England has introduced, proposes that a certain number of special jurors, say three, should serve upon every jury; do you think that would be an improvement?—I think it would; I think the more intelligent you make a jury the better.

2346. Would you see any objection to it?—I do not see any objection to that.

2347. Were you present at the revision of the lists?—No.

2348. It is not your duty?—No, I have nothing at all to say to it; I think it would be very objectionable that the Crown solicitor should have anything to say to the selection of the jury; I think Captain Buchanan meant the Sessional Crown solicitor. I think it would be objectionable as to him also, because he has the prosecution of criminals at quarter sessions; I think it would be better to have the officer of the chairman, which I consider the clerk of the peace, an independent officer to discharge that duty.

2349. Mr. *Bruen.*] You would put on the clerk of the peace the duty of ascertaining the case of each juror as to illiteracy or otherwise?—I would put upon him the getting the information so as to bring it before the chairman.

2350. Would you give him any extra remuneration for that; it would be a very troublesome business, would it not?—Yes, I think he ought to be paid something additional for that.

2351. You say you would give the chairman power to strike off names for sufficient reason; would you give him that power to be exercised in open court, or in *camera*?—It must be in open court, I should say.

2352. Mr. *Herbert.*] In the counties with which you have had anything to do; do you think there was any organised system on the part of the respectable jurors to defeat the working of this Act?—I would rather not answer that; I think there was a very great prejudice against the Act, and I think that, perhaps, led to matters that were not desirable, but I should be far from saying that the respectable class of jurors formed any resolution against it.

2353. Dr. *Ball.*] That case of Montgomery lasted 10 or 12 days?—Twelve days.

2354. Do not you think that a great many men would stay away from that?—Of course they would; there was a magistrate called upon that jury, and he did not answer, he preferred, if to be levied, paying the fine; you cannot blame him for that.

Thursday, 15*th May* 1873.

MEMBERS PRESENT:

Mr. Attorney General.
Dr. Ball.
Sir Rowland Blennerhassett.
Mr. Bourke.
Mr. Bruen.
Viscount Crichton.
Colonel Forde.
Marquis of Hartington.
Henry Arthur Herbert.
Mr. Heron.
Mr. Charles Lewis.
The O'Conor Don.
The O'Donoghue.
Colonel Wilson Patten.
Colonel Vandeleur.

THE MARQUIS OF HARTINGTON, IN THE CHAIR.

Mr. JAMES MURLAND, called in; and Examined.

Mr. J. Murland.

15 May 1873.

2355. *Chairman.*] YOU are Crown Solicitor for the county of Down, are you not?—Yes.

2356. For what period?—I was appointed in 1868.

2357. And you have had experience of the working of the present and the former Acts?—Yes. I have had experience during the last assizes, since this Act came into operation, and at the quarter sessions as well.

2358. What opinion have you formed of the principle and working of the present Act?—The principle of the Act I conceive to be a most excellent one, that is, taking away from the sub-sheriff the power of selection of the jury; and as far as the working of the Act is concerned, I think, with some amendments, it would also prove to be very advantageous.

2359. Did you observe at the last assizes any defects in the working of the Act, which required to be corrected?—I did. In my opinion the qualification of the jurors ought to be raised, because, certainly the class of jurors that were summoned at the last assizes were not so intelligent at all, as those that were summoned by the sheriff under the old Act.

2360. They were very inexperienced, were they not, in their duties as jurors?—There were very few of them that had served as jurors before, and I think those that had served as jurors did not attend upon their summonses; at all events, those who did attend seemed to me not to have served as jurors before. As I said before, they were certainly an inferior class.

2361. Are you of opinion that the class admitted was decidedly too low, or that there was material for good jurors if they had sufficient experience?—I think that the class was too low.

2362. Do you think, that by raising the qualification the principle of the Act which you have referred to might be maintained?—I think so, and with some amendment it would work admirably.

2363. How much would you suggest that the qualification should be raised?—I would suggest in the county of Down, the county which I know myself, that there ought to be a household qualification. I would say a household qualification of 12 *l.* in the country and towns under a certain population, and a household qualification of 20 *l.* where the population exceeded a certain number.

2364. Would you have no merely rated qualification?—I would have a general rating qualification of 30 *l.* at least; that is, including both houses and land.

2365. Have you any suggestion to make as to the selection in alphabetical order?—The selection by alphabetical order in the county of Down would work in this way. In the letter "M" on the juror's list, in the county of Down, there are, I am informed, by the sub-sheriff, 870 more names than in any other letter. The result of that would be, that in a short time (it would take some time, perhaps a couple of years) the list would be reduced to the letter M, and there would be left of the letter M, after exhausting all the others, some 500 or 600 names. For instance, there are 47 Moores on the panel, 35 Marroughs, 35 Murrays, and 20 Murphys, and so on. So that you might have a jury composed, perhaps of relatives, or of all of the same name. I would suggest that could be remedied in this way: that instead of having the list in alphabetical order when the clerk of the union sends in his returns to the clerk of the peace, each list as it is revised by the chairman should be numbered consecutively and so on, until the whole of the numbers of the list were found. Say that there are 5,000, or whatever numbers there may be on the list, the whole of those numbers written upon cards should be put into a box to be drawn in the presence of the chairman, and upon the reverse side of the card, as the number is drawn, I would put Number 1, and Number 2, and so on, and in that way they might be put upon the list of jurors. That card should be preserved, and it would show at once how the list had been framed, and then in those lists of the clerks of the union I would have those numbers entered after each name as a matter of reference. Having so got the revised list of jurors, instead of requiring as is proposed by this Act of Parliament, the clerks of the union to send in all the names of rated occupiers qualified to serve as jurors under whatever Act may be passed; the jurors' list so revised in the last year should be sent

Mr. J. Murland.

15 May 1873.

sent to the clerks of the unions, who should make their observations as to whether the parties on it had parted with their qualification or become otherwise disqualified, and the chairman could strike out of the list of jurors for the previous year the names of those who had become disqualified, or who had died or gone away. In addition, I would require the clerks of the unions to make, as in the case of the Parliamentary voters' list, a supplemental list of any parties that have been put upon the rate-book since the last return made by them, and I would let that list be revised, in the same way as the previous list was, and balloted for, in the way I have suggested, and added at the end of the list of the previous year. By that means the sheriff would not have to go in the way that he now has, from from letter to letter, but simply to take the names in the rotation in which he finds them upon the list; every man is brought forward in his turn. I take the list for the county of Down, for example, this year; it would take three or four years to exhaust, but when the sheriff gets another list, entirely new and framed from a new return, made irrespective of the old list altogether; there may be men of the same name put on, that never served before, and it is very hard for him to know exactly how to act: but the plan that I propose prevents all difficulty of that kind; every man will have to serve in his turn.

2366. The first panel would be selected according to your method, entirely by chance?—Yes; by ballot. I mean the jurors list.

2367. And the second panel would also be selected by chance, excluding the names of those that had served before?—The second list would exclude all the names upon the former list; there would be what is called a supplemental list in precisely the same way as the Parliamentary list is now framed; it will save a great deal of trouble, and also save a great deal of expense.

2368. Have you any suggestion to make as to balloting for the jury in criminal cases?—I would also think that the jury ought in a criminal case to be balloted for in the same way as in a civil case. I do not see any reason why it should not be so; but I think that there is very good reason why it should. Just take a case: if the panel is published, as I think it is, eight days before the assizes, any one can have a copy of the panel, and the prisoner sees the first names upon the panel, and his friends see the first names upon the panel. We will suppose that it is a case involving some party feeling, and as in the case of a misdemeanor, there is no challenge, that would lead perhaps to the canvassing of the jurors, and it would be well to avoid that by balloting for them in the way that I suggest. It would be impossible that people would then know who would be upon the jury, and therefore, I think it would be a safeguard; and it would cause no additional trouble in the world, because the sheriff has only to give cards with the name and address of each juror upon it, who is upon his panel; and those being taken from the box, the clerk of the court could as easily call them from the cards as from the panel itself, and he could put the cards, with the names of those who answer, down on one side of him and call them out again.

2369. Would that involve the giving up of the power of the Crown Solicitor to order jurors to stand aside?—It would not have the slightest effect upon that at all, because they are not sworn on the jury as they are called in the first instance, but are then merely called to see the number who answer, and on second calling, if it is a case of felony that is to be tried, where the party has a right to challenge peremptorily, let the prisoner, before the juror is sworn, challenge him if he likes, and so on, until a jury of twelve is formed.

2370. Do I understand that the panel has to be called over first, and that challenges or directions to stand aside are to be made when the panel is first called over?—No; that is done afterwards. At present they call the panel at first, and all the parties that answer are marked by the Clerk of the Court; the first calling is simply to see the number of jurors that may be in attendance, and then they are called a second time for the purpose of forming the jury. Then the prisoner is called upon to look upon the juror, and if he has no objection to him or the Crown, do not direct him to stand aside, they place him upon the jury, and so on until 12 are selected. It is just the same as at present, excepting that, instead of calling them, in the order in which they are upon the panel, it is calling them by ballot in the first instance.

2371. Are you aware whether the names of many illiterate persons were placed upon the jury book?—I am afraid that a great deal of confusion arose at the last assizes; indeed I am sure it did, owing to the chairman, who revised the list, not having proper information supplied to him for the purpose of having the list revised, according to the Act of Parliament. Many persons that were suffering from bodily infirmity, many persons above 60 years of age, and persons disqualified, got upon it. Also another matter in the revising of the list caused a great deal of trouble. They did not attend to the instructions with regard to giving the proper descriptions of the parties on the list. In one case there was a gentleman, a magistrate, and a man of very high position in the county, who happened to be rated in two places in the county, and whose name appeared twice on the list; he was called a farmer, and he was summoned to the Downpatrick Quarter Sessions, and also to the Newtownards Quarter Sessions, as a petty juror, just merely because they had not put "J. P." after his name in the list of jurors.

2372. Why should not the person you have alluded to have been summoned?—Because he was not liable to serve at the quarter sessions. Of course, at the assizes he should, and would have been summoned.

2373. How do you suggest that the necessary information should be laid before the chairman?—I think that the Sessional Crown Prosecutor ought to be supplied with those lists from the clerks of the union, and that he ought to attend himself, say at the unions and examine the poor-rate collectors, and get the necessary proofs or necessary information to enable him to assist the court of revision in revising and making the list as accurate as possible.

2374. Do not you think that there is any objection to the Crown Solicitor who is engaged in the prosecutions being mixed up with the preparation of the jury lists?—For my own part I would rather not be mixed up with it. I think that the Sessional Crown Prosecutor should attend to this matter. I do not see that there would be any objection to him, because no person can know what case will be tried at the time

Mr. *J. Murland.*

15 May 1873.

time of the revision. I think there could be no objection whatever.

2375. Could not the clerks of unions give the information?—No doubt they could, but we have found from experience that it is not done unless there is some responsible person to look after these things. I have always found that really at this revision no person takes the slightest trouble about it.

2376. That revision, I presume, has merely taken place once?—There was always a revision of the jurors' list, but there never was a particle of pains taken in seeing that it was properly framed.

2377. But it was not so essential under the old Act as it is under the new Act, that it should be carefully revised?—It was not at all so essential, because now the power of selection is taken away, whereas before, the sheriff had the power of selection.

2378. If it were made known to the clerks of unions, that it is their duty, and that they are bound by law to afford all necessary information to the chairman, do not you think that you may rely upon them to give that information?—My experience is that, unless there is some person charged with the duty, it is not done.

2379. Why not charge them with the duty?—They have not done it.

2380. Mr. *Bourke.*] Are they interested in the administration of justice at all in any other way?—Not in the slightest degree, any further than any other member of the community.

2381. *Chairman.*] Would you add to the disqualifications or exemptions which are mentioned in the present Act?—I certainly would; I would not return a man as a juror who could neither read nor write.

2382. Are there any others that you would omit?—I am not aware of any other. I think that the exemptions that are mentioned in the Act would be quite sufficient.

2383. Would you give the chairman any power of granting exemption for what he considered a sufficient cause?—I would not. I think that the chairman should have the grounds of disqualification given in the Act of Parliament, whatever Parliament may decide upon, and that he ought to follow those. It ought to be no general discretion.

2384. You would not give him a discretion?—I would not.

2385. What qualification would you suggest for a special juror?—In the county of Down, I would say, from my knowledge of the county, that for a special juror, a household qualification of 40 *l.* or a general rating of 100 *l.* would be sufficient.

2386. Have you considered what number of jurors the qualifications that you propose would admit in the county of Down?—Strange to say there is no return from the county of Down, and it would take a long time to find that out, but of course, if that qualification would not give a sufficient number it would alter my opinion; but I think that it would give a sufficient number by a 40 *l.* household qualification.

2387. What do you consider a sufficient number for the common jury book and the special jury list?—In order not to make them serve too often, I think if we had between 2,000 and 3,000 upon the common jury list, and from 500 to 600 upon the special jury list, it would not entail too much trouble upon them.

2388. How many quarter sessions division are there in the county of Down?—There are two divisions; there is the Downpatrick division, and the Newry division, and in each division there are two quarter sessions towns. I see that there is a provision in the Act of Parliament that jurors are not to be summoned to quarter sessions out of their own division. If the criminal business is still to be transacted in both towns, I would suggest that it ought still more to be limited, that is to say, the jurors for the quarter sessions should only be summoned from the baronies adjoining the sessions town in which they reside. The reason I mention that, is this, that I saw at the last Downpatrick session the jury were composed of men who resided 25 and 27 miles from Downpatrick, and who resided just convenient to the other quarter sessions town at which the sessions were held the following week for the same division, and therefore a great inconvenience arose. People from Downpatrick were summoned to Newtownards, and people from Newtownards were summoned to Downpatrick; whereas, if the suggestion that I have made were adopted, and it was confined to the baronies surrounding the quarter sessions town, there would be no practical inconvenience; they would not have far to go, and it would be only extending the provision to the baronies instead of to the division.

2389. Would there be any difference in practice in what you suggest from a re-division of the county into four quarter sessions districts instead of two?—There would not be any, if you made that arrangement for criminal business; but under the present system there is a great convenience in civil business, because parties can go to either quarter session town in the division, and sometimes it is convenient for them to do it; but I think, in order to obviate the inconvenience as to jurors that I have mentioned, it would be better that there should be only one town in each division for criminal business, and thus save the attendance of 25 or 30 grand jurors, and 40 or 50 petty jurors, four times in each year; at present, grand and petty jurors are sometimes brought to a town where there is no case to try. The criminal business, having so much decreased at quarter sessions, it might be worth considering whether it would not be better to have the entire criminal business of each quarter disposed of in the county town where the gaol is, and where the officials all are. It would save expense, and be very little practical inconvenience to any one.

2390. The quarter session grand jury is entirely composed of those in the special list, is it not?—That is so; and that is another reason too why I would suggest it, because it is a great matter not to exhaust the special list and take them off the general list of jurors.

2391. Under the existing system the special list becomes very speedily exhausted, does it not?—It would become very speedily exhausted; and I also think it is very desirable to have sitting together and trying a case at the assizes farmers and magistrates and shopkeepers together. I am quite sure that in the county of Down there would not be the slightest objection to it.

2392. You would reduce as much as practicable the number of jurors required to serve on the grand juries?—I would at quarter sessions, for the reasons I have mentioned.

2393. Have you any suggestion to make as to the

Mr. *J. Marland.*

15 May 1873.

the peremptory challenges that are allowed at present in criminal cases?—I think that if such pains as are prescribed by this Act were taken for the purpose of having the jury panel arranged, 20 peremptory challenges are too many, and I certainly would reduce the number of challenges allowed to a prisoner.

2394. You would not propose to alter the power of the Crown to order jurors to stand aside?—No, I would not like to alter that.

2395. Is there any other suggestion which you wish to make?—With regard to the serving of summonses upon the jurors, I think that if they were served by post in a registered letter, and if the receipt of the postmaster to the sheriff, the same as in the case of Parliamentary Notices for Private Bills are now allowed to be served, it would be a great boon to the sheriffs, and also they would be sure that the summons would reach the juror. There is a difficulty where there is no delivery of letters, and that I was just thinking might be obviated in this way. There is always a post office now-a-days very near to where any juror would be; and where there is no delivery, perhaps there might be some arrangement made that the postmaster should send those registered letters, which he could do for a very small sum, to any people who did not call for them the day after they came there, and that he should charge for it. In that way it would insure the people getting the notices; and a list so signed by the postmaster, given into the hands of the sheriff, should be *primâ facie* evidence that all the jurors named in that list had received their summonses. I do not think that the expense would be very great in delivering those where there is no regular delivery. As I said before, there are very few jurors who reside very distant from a post town, and the postmaster could get the letters delivered to them, and let him be paid for it. Of course, if that were done, it would require the post town to be put down on the List of Jurors opposite to each juror's name.

2396. Colonel *Wilson Patten*.] Have you stated the number of jurors that would be required to transact the business at the assizes and quarter sessions in your county?—Yes; I have had it given me by the sub-sheriff; I think it is 6,100; and he says that that will do for him for upwards of three years.

2397. Supposing that in your county you were to adopt the 30 *l.* franchise, would that leave a sufficient number of jurors on the list for the transaction of the county business?—I am quite sure it would.

2398. Supposing that you were to raise it to a 50 *l.* franchise, would that be the case?—That would depend upon the return. I believe there is no return from Down. It would be simply a question of supply. I would like to raise the qualification, but not too high; I would only like to raise it so as to get intelligent men upon the jury, and also to make it so that we should have a sufficient number, and not to require men to serve too often.

2399. What should you say would be the qualification which would secure the proper discharge of the duty?—My impression would be, that 30 *l.* general rating and 12 *l.* for the household franchise in the country districts and small towns, and 20 *l.* where the population exceeded a certain number, say 5,000, would be a proper qualification.

2400. At the last assizes and quarter sessions in your county, did you find any detriment to the administration of justice owing to the want of intelligence on the part of the jurors?—All I can say as regards that, is, that I did not hear the judge find fault with any verdict that was delivered, nor did the Crown counsel, nor had I any reason to find fault with any verdict. I am speaking now of the assizes, because I do not attend the quarter sessions. I believe there was scarcely a trial at all at the quarter sessions.

2401. Mr. *Bruen*.] Do you think that the Sessional Crown Prosecutor ought to attend the court of revision and give information to the chairman?—Not to give information merely, but to conduct the case before the chairman, and to produce what would be necessary to enable him to strike off the names of unqualified persons.

2402. But not to collect the information?—Yes, to collect it; and of course to give the necessary proofs to the chairman.

2403. That duty you would give to the Sessional Crown Prosecutor, and not to the gentlemen who perform those duties at the assizes?—I would have the Sessional Crown Prosecutor do it.

2404. That duty of collecting information would involve a great amount of trouble and time, would it not?—I think not. I think that perhaps he could do the whole of it within a week or 10 days, by appointing a day to meet the rate collectors at the board-room in each of the workhouses in the county, and going over the list with them, and hearing what they had to say, and telling them really what their duties were, and afterwards his duties would become very light.

2405. Do you think that he ought to go to the constabulary for that information?—I think that he ought; and that when he does go to get information, he ought to ask a member of the constabulary from each of the stations in the union to be present to give him any information that he could.

2406. When he has collected this information and given it to the court, do you think that he ought to give notice to any of the persons to whom he objects, that he is going to object to them?—I do not see that any notice would be required for anything of that kind. The Clerk of the union might put "objected" after the name, but I do not see that for any of the causes that are mentioned in the Act, any notice would be necessary to be given to the party. There is a provision in the Act, that if any party feels aggrieved by either being improperly put on, or being improperly kept off the list, he can immediately after apply to have himself either omitted or inserted in the list.

2407. But you think that the causes which would be operative for displacing a man from the list, are only those which are stated in the Act at present?—Yes; and also illiterates.

2408. In the case of a district where there were people disaffected towards the law, would you imagine that that cause would be sufficient for excluding a man from the jury list?—I do not see how that could be proved, because it would be trying a man for an offence against the law, before you put him on the list on a vague rumour of that kind, and I do not see how that could be done. If a man is disaffected in that way, or has done anything that brings him within the law, I would prosecute him.

2409. But

Mr. *J. Murland.*

15 May 1873.

2409. But you do not think that the fact of a man being disaffected to the law, if he has not been guilty of an overt act, is a sufficient reason for keeping him off the jury lists?—If a man is disaffected to the law he certainly ought to be kept off the jury list, but I do not see how it could be proved. Certainly, if I, as Crown Solicitor, had any good reason to believe that a man was disaffected to the law, I would desire him to stand aside.

2410. But you do not think that that exclusion ought to be exercised so as to prevent him being put upon the jury list?—I would be very glad if it could be, but I cannot see any way in which it could.

2411. In certain districts in Ireland would there not be a danger of having a considerable number of men on the jury lists, who actually were known to be disaffected to the law, and although no overt act had been proved against them, those men would be liable to be upon the jury panels?—I am not in a position to speak of those districts; I am happy to say that in the county in which I live, there would be no danger of that.

2412. In any of those cases in which the chairman was to exercise his power of striking off the jury lists, would you have that power exercised in open court, or would you give power to the chairman to conduct the proceedings in secret?—I would have it in open court clearly.

2413. Some witnesses have made suggestions to the Committee, that there should be a right to either side to call for a special jury in criminal cases, do you think that that would be a good right to give? I am afraid that that would not be very popular. It is very seldom that the accused would take advantage of it, and perhaps it would look harsh on the part of the Crown to try people by others than their peers.

2414. Then you object to that power being given?—I would not like to say that I object to that power, but certainly I would rather not recommend it.

2415. Have you frequently had occasion to exercise your right of calling upon jurors to stand aside when they were called?—Very seldom have I had to do that, except at the last assizes, and I should tell you, perhaps, the reason I did it at the last assizes.

2416. As it happened, I suppose, since the Act came into operation, perhaps you will be so good as to tell the Committee why it was?—There were two parties put upon their trial for murder. It was a case entirely of circumstantial evidence, that required intelligent men to try it. As I said before, the jury were not of as intelligent a class as formerly. Generally, the course adopted, and it was adopted in this case, was, that the solicitor for the prisoners peremptorily challenged any man of the slightest intelligence. Then when I saw a man called whom I did not believe fit to try a case of that kind, not intelligent enough, I desired him to stand aside, in order to get some men of intelligence upon the jury, and when there are 40 taken off the panel by peremptory challenges, with only, perhaps, 96 answering, it leaves it very difficult for the Crown to get an intelligent jury. The sole reason I had for telling jurors to stand aside, was not against their honesty, or anything of that kind, but to get men of intelligence.

2417. Were you at all restricted in your right of calling upon those jurors to stand aside by the fact that you found that the panel was nearly exhausted?—I cannot say that I was. If it had been exhausted, they would have had to go over it again. My object was simply to get men of fair intelligence upon the jury.

2418. May I gather from your answer then, that if the panel had been larger, you would have exercised your right of calling upon those jurors to stand aside, more extensively than you really did?—I will not say that, because I think that the men would be of the same class as the former ones; yet I think I got 12 honest men on the jury, though certainly a good number of them were not so intelligent as I should wish to see to try the case, but a more anxious set of men I never saw try a case. They were nervously anxious to come, as I believe, to the right conclusion.

2419. How often do you think that the turn of a juror ought to come round to serve?—That would greatly depend upon the supply of jurors in the county. I think if, as I hear, there are some counties where you cannot get very many jurors, that are intelligent and fit to be upon juries, they ought not to complain at serving oftener, and I do not think they would complain of serving oftener, if they saw that there was fair play done them, that is to say, if they were not brought out of their turn to serve. That is what the great complaint was before, that men were selected and summoned for convenience sake, over and over again to the court. I really do not think that men would object to serve upon the jury if they thought that it was necessary that they should serve, and that they were fairly summoned in rotation.

2420. I want to ascertain not so much what the practice is, but your abstract opinion upon how often a man ought to be summoned to serve upon a jury?—That would entirely depend upon the number of jurors in the county who were qualified to serve.

2421. But could you give the Committee your own opinion in the matter, in an abstract point of view?—I am of opinion that a juror would like to serve as seldom as he could; but it is impossible for me to say what my opinion is, as to how often they should be summoned. I can only say this, that they would like to serve as seldom as they could. But I do not think that jurors would object to serve when it was absolutely necessary for them to serve, when the county required their services on such occasions, provided they were not brought oftener than was necessary for the ends of justice.

2422. Mr. *Heron.*] In the county of Down for many years, under the old system, party cases had to be tried very often, had they not?—No doubt.

2423. From what you know of the county in party cases, was there public dissatisfaction at the formation of the panel under the old system?—I never heard it; certainly not justly. I have known the county for 40 years, and I think I have been perfectly acquainted with it. I have been on both sides in party cases, and I never yet heard the sheriff accused of partiality in the county of Down; I really believe that there was no reason to accuse him.

2424. You know the north of Ireland very well; have you heard dissatisfaction expressed in other counties?—I do not know the north of Ireland very well; I know my own county very well; but I really do not know the other counties, and I would not speak as to the other counties.

2425. In the formation of the panel under the old

Mr. *J. Morland.*

15 May 1873.

old system, the sheriff always selected, did he not, his panel at a time when he knew the cases that would be tried?—Sometimes after he had selected his panel, cases would come in; but there is no doubt that the sheriff would know before he selected his panel, what probable amount of business was to be done. It was necessary for him to know that, in order to know the number that he ought properly to summon.

2426. At the time that he returned his panel he would know the business that would be likely to be transacted at the coming assizes?—He would know the quantity of business to be transacted.

2427. Under the old system the sheriff had the absolute selection of the panel, had he not?—No doubt about that.

2428. You do not consider it desirable to return to that system?—Certainly not. Just as much on account of the sheriff as any one else, for I am quite sure that it is a great boon to the sheriff to be released from the responsibility of selection.

2429. From what you know of the sheriffs in the north of Ireland, would you say that they do not wish the old system to be returned to?—I have never spoken to any but one sub-sheriff. I have spoken to several high sheriffs upon it, but I am perfectly sure, from what I know of them, that they would not like it; at least, I should suppose so. The high sheriffs would be very glad to be relieved from the responsibility, and I think the sub-sheriffs would be very much gratified to be relieved from the responsibility of selection.

2430. With regard to balloting the jury in criminal cases, are you aware that in calling from the panel in regular order, commencing at the top of the panel, has been resorted to for convenience as regards the challenging, and that that is a very general practice?—I was not aware that it was. It is only latterly that the balloting system has come in force.

2431. Have you often both challenged for the prisoner, and also as Crown Solicitor directed jurors to stand by?—Yes.

2432. It is a matter of convenience to you to know the order in which they are coming on both sides. There would be a tremendous delay in calling over the panel when for the first time a name is called from the card?—I do not think that there would be a particle of delay, because the name and place of abode of each man upon the panel can be written distinctly upon a card and put into the box, and the officer of the court can draw it out and read it just as quickly as he could from the panel itself, and if the man answers, he just puts it down in that way, and then afterwards calls the names of the jurors as they answered.

2433. But either side is ready for the names so as to know whom to challenge or to order to stand by?—That is not the time that they would require them to challenge. At present the officer of the court reads out the names from the panel before there can be any challenges, and then those that answer are called again, and then commences the challenging.

2434. When they have answered, in balloting the names, would you have them called in their balloting order?—Yes.

2435. Called as they have answered?—Yes, certainly.

2436. First of all called from the balloting box, and then called over again for the purpose of being sworn?—Precisely; called in the order in which they came out of the balloting box, and then challenged if the parties desired it.

2437. Colonel *Forde.*] Does the solicitor of each party have a copy of the panel?—I think that it must be lodged with the clerk of the peace immediately after it is finished; but either party can have a copy of the panel several days before the assizes.

2438. Therefore, either the solicitor for the prisoner, or the solicitor for the Crown, knows every one on that panel, and is, or ought to be, perfectly prepared either to challenge him or to set aside, as the case may be?—That is quite right. The time for them to know the parties that they ought to challenge, is before they are called at all.

2439. They ought to be prepared at once to do it?—Yes, quite so.

2440. I think you said that you could only speak as far as the county Down is concerned, and in reply to the honourable Member for Carlow, you stated that you did not exhaust the panel when you challenged in those murder cases that you referred to?—No; there were several parties that answered, and that were not called upon to serve.

2441. Should you say that in other parts of Ireland if the Crown were to challenge they would exhaust the panel?—They might; but I have not spoken as regards other parts of Ireland at all; I am confining myself to my own county.

2442. You recommended, I think, that the Sessional Crown Solicitor should be the party to give instructions to the assistant barrister in selecting the panel?—To conduct the revision of the list before him, and to produce the evidence.

2443. In some counties does that officer reside in, and does he know, the circumstances of the county?—I believe that in some counties the Sessional Crown Solicitor does not reside in the county. At all events, he is a professional man, and he ought to go and get information so as really to be able to afford it to the chairman.

2444. And the Crown Solicitor just in the same way?—The Crown Solicitor, I believe, does not so often reside in the county as the Sessional Crown Solicitor does.

2445. Colonel *Vandeleur.*] You mentioned that the clerks of the unions would be dependent upon the rate collectors for their information?—Clearly, because they do not themselves know the people personally; it is the rate collectors that they are dependent upon for their information.

2446. The rate collectors now put objections on the voters list, do they not?—Yes.

2447. Could not they at the same time that they object to a man on the voters list object equally to a rated occupier being a juror?—Precisely the same.

2448. That could be done at one and the same time, could it not?—Precisely the same.

2449. And the two lists could be equally revised by the barrister at the same time?—No; because the Parliamentary list is quite a different list and depending upon a great number of other circumstances.

2450. The clerk of the union could afterwards make out two separate lists, could he not, and place them before the barrister at one and the same time?—Yes, he could, certainly; he might place them at the same time before him, but then the barrister must revise them separately, because there are a great number of objections to the

Parliamentary

Mr. *J. Murland.*

15 May 1873.

Parliamentary list that would not arise in the jurors' list.

2451. In going over the lists, it would save a great deal of time, trouble, and expense, would it not, if he revised them at the same time that he had both lists before him, so that when he heard one case of objection he could hear the other case of objection?—I do not see that; I do not see how it would be convenient at all, because he must revise the lists separately. There is a different set of professional men before him for the Parliamentary list, and different objections altogether to it from what there are to the jurors' list. I do not see that any time would be saved by going to a name on the Parliamentary list, and then to a name on the jurors' list; I think it would create confusion.

2452. Would not it save the barrister from going over the same names, and save him from doing the same work over again?—I think they generally appoint the time for the revision of the Parliamentary voters' lists, and the time for the revision of the jurors' lists at the same time. I think I scarcely understand the honourable Member's question.

2453. You think that all criminal cases arising in the county, and returnable at the quarter sessions, should be tried at the county town?—I think it would be a great convenience.

2454. Would you include cases out on bail?—Yes; I would include cases out on bail; but there are very few now.

2455. We think that one quarter sessions grand jury would be sufficient for the whole country?—Quite sufficient, and it would save a vast deal of trouble.

2456. It has been suggested that the grand jury might be done away with altogether at quarter sessions, do you approve of that?—I certainly would not recommend that.

2457. You recommend the service of notices upon jurors by registered letters through the post?—I think so, in the same way as Parliamentary Notices are served; but to secure attendance where the letters are not delivered, instructions should be given to the postmaster, if this could be carried out, to have them delivered.

2458. Would you consider whether they could not be served by the police in each district, in the same way that the service of voting papers for the guardians of unions are served?—I would rather not impose that duty upon the police. I do not think the jurors would like it so well.

2459. Surely they are accustomed to see the police serve the notices which I have referred to?—Yes; but I think that the police have quite enough to do without serving notices to jurors.

2460. Mr. *Attorney General.*] You say, I think, you would diminish the number of the prisoners' challenges?—I would.

2461. But reserving the right of the Crown to set aside?—That is a matter for consideration, but still I would not like to take away the right of the Crown.

2462. Would not the effect of that be that you would place the prosecution of the prisoner at a still greater disadvantage apparently, than they now stand at?—Apparently, that might be so.

2463. Is it not very important that justice should not only be done, but appear to be done?—I think it would be. I merely throw that out as a suggestion for the Committee.

2464. The object, I presume, of having a special jury in any case, is to secure a jury of higher intelligence?—Yes.

2465. And it is thought worth while in cases which require the application of high intelligence to go to the expense in civil cases of having a special jury?—Yes.

2466. However small the stake may be, yet if either party has sufficient interest in the stake, he can by going through a certain process, and taking a certain expense upon himself, obtain a special jury?—Quite so.

2467. May not the issues in criminal cases often be quite as great, and the difficulty of determining it quite as extreme as in civil cases?—No doubt.

2468. Do you think it defensible in theory or in logic, that you should not be able under any circumstances to secure juries of high intelligence on the trial of criminal cases?—In theory, I do not think it is; but still for the reason which you have suggested, people themselves might think that it was not fair that they should not be tried by ordinary jurors, and that the Crown should do away in that case with men in humbler circumstances, and try them by a special jury. I think that people would not like it so well. In theory, I cannot see any reason against it, because they would have a fair trial.

2469. Would not that mitigate your objection to the expense, if the special jury in a criminal case was always paid by the State, and if the prisoner had an equal right to a special jury with the prosecutor upon cause shown to the judge at chambers? I think not; I do not think that the prisoner would ever avail himself of a special jury. I think that a special jury for a prisoner would rather aggravate matters, so far as popular opinion would go. I thoroughly agree that there could be no objection whatever to the fairness of a trial by special jury; but still, people of the lower orders might think that justice was not fairly administered to them.

2470. Are you aware that in a certain class of cases, which although not called by the technical name of felony, may yet raise the most important issues, by the use of the *certiorari*, special juries may now be had by either party?—I am aware of that.

2471. Do you think that there is any intelligible or defensible distinction?—When there is a special jury, there is always a special case made out for it, and the party tried, hears what the reason is for it.

2472. Are you aware that the Crown can in any case try a misdemeanor at Nisi Prius?—Yes.

2473. And that the Crown gives the right to the prisoner to be tried by a special jury if he thinks fit?—Quite so.

2474. Do you think that an intelligible or defensible distinction to maintain?—I can only say that, as far as I am concerned, I think it would be very well to give to either party the right to it, but I would not like to make the innovation just for the reason I have given you. If you alter the law as regards special jury, and if you say this in the Act of Parliament that the prisoner at his option may have a special jury, I could understand it; but if you go to put it further, and say in every case, either the Crown or the prisoner may have it, if that be necessary in the Act of Parliament, I would rather not put it in for the reason that I have given.

2475. But it would be protecting both sides if it were enacted it should not be done in any case without the leave of the Court or the Judge?—

If

Mr. J. Murland.

15 May 1873.

If that qualification was put in that it must be upon application and with express leave of the Judge, I can see not the slightest objection either in theory or in practice.

2476. You mentioned that as far as you were aware there had been never any objections made to the selections by the sheriff?—Never in the county of Down.

2477. In Ireland?—I must say in a case in which I was in myself that appeared to be so.

2478. As an Irish gentleman, of course you have some means of knowing the public opinion of Ireland as any other gentleman; what I want to know is this; am I to take it from you that there was no opinion in Ireland generally as to the subject of occasional partial selections?—I could not well answer that question. I have heard of two or three cases; but if I was going to be asked what the general opinion was amongst those well affected people in the country, I think that the opinion was that the sheriff did his duty and fairly selected the panel.

2479. When you say the well affected people, they would probably be persons like those who were selected by the sheriff for jurors?—I should say this further; I think that this was said by parties that wished to create grievances where there really were none; as a rule I do think that the sheriffs fairly selected the juries.

2480. I did not ask, as a fact, whether it was so or not, but what I asked you was, whether there was any opinion upon the subject, because I think that you admitted to me fairly enough just now, that a man should not only be tried fairly, but should think that he was tried fairly; what I ask you is whether upon the whole you would say, that in Ireland there was no general feeling that there were occasionally partial selections made?—I could not say that there was not a general feeling that there were occasionally partial selections made, but those were very few.

2481. The selection is made in practice, I presume, by the person whom you call the sub-sheriff, and whom we call here the under-sheriff?—Yes.

2482. With us generally speaking, the sub-sheriff is not permanent, but in Ireland, as far as you are aware, is the sub-sheriff practically a permanent person?—Latterly, he has been generally permanent.

2483. How many counties are there in Ireland?—Thirty-two counties.

2484. Are they in all the 32 counties permanent?—Yes, generally.

2485. And every one of those 32 men, has, at least, the means of being partial?—Clearly.

2486. Are you so singularly blessed in Ireland, that you have always had 32 men in that responsible position who are uniformly impartial?—I can only say, that as a general rule, I believe that they have been impartial, that is all I can say.

2487. Do they always resist the strongest temptation?—I do not know what temptation there could be, for they are all men of very high respectability. I think that there is no temptation to do it, but it is all the other way.

2488. In framing the panel might not some of the very best men, and men of the highest principle, feel it from strong opinions to be their duty to prevent persons of different opinions from their own, being upon juries; when opinions run up into very important differences, and when people entertain those differences as matters of principle?—I can scarcely imagine a gentleman holding that responsible office would ever think in framing the jury of putting men off because they hold different opinions from him. I think the only selection would be to secure a fair trial to the prisoner.

2489. Not where the question was the trial of persons, because they entertained opinions and sentiments different from their own?—I can hardly imagine that they would do it; there is a great temptation.

2490. Take the case of a trial of a prisoner, for I will not use any particular form of offence, but for some offence, the trial of which was disaffection to the law; do you mean to say that you think that a high principled man in Ireland might not think it his duty, to take care that a man who he thought was disaffected to the law, should form no part of the jury to try that prisoner?—I think very likely he would.

2491. Do you think that if that was done, the prisoner who was disaffected to the law would be well satisfied with the jury?—I quite agree with you upon that. I think myself, that to take away the power of selection is perfectly right, and that the principle of this Act is excellent, as it removes all grounds for suspicion.

2492. I could not quite follow you because, as I understood you, you said that you had never heard this objected to at all, and yet you would not go back to the principle; if it had never been objected to, I cannot quite see why you should wish it altered?—I misunderstood you. I objected myself to the framing of the panel by the sub-sheriff in the case I before alluded to, and why I objected to it was this, it was a party case, and I was for a private prosecutor, and when I went to the assizes I was informed that there were about 30 men at the top of a panel of 200, favourable to, and likely to acquit the traverser; and it being a case of misdemeanour where I had no power of challenge, I did not go on with the case for that reason. I did not say that I never heard of such a thing as packing a jury; I said that I had heard of two or three instances where there was just cause for the imputation.

2493. Mr. *Bruen*.] On this point which you have just mentioned to the Attorney General, do you believe that the sheriff put those 30 men on the top of the jury for the purpose of acquitting the prisoner?—It is possible it may have occurred without design, but I can scarcely believe it. I was told when I went there that there was no use in my going; so I removed the indictment by *certiorari*. Of course I am only giving you my impression from what I was told.

2494. Were you for the prisoner, or were you prosecuting?—I was prosecuting for a gentleman in that case, a gentleman of position

2495. Colonel *Forde*.] Have you any information to give to the Committee as to the expense of the jury lists in the county of Down?—The expense presented to the grand jury for carrying out the Act at the last assizes was 268 *l*. 11 *s*. 8 *d*.

2496. That was what the grand jury paid?—Yes.

2497. But the clerks of the unions were paid extra for their duty done by the unions themselves, were they not?—Of course.

2498. So that that would add so much more to the expense?—Of course it would.

2499. *The O'Conner Don*.] Were the jury lists in the County of Down printed?—I think not. The jury book is not printed, but there was a good deal of printing to do in the way of forms and notices, and all that; but I do not think that the names were printed.

2500. *Chairman*.]

Mr. WILLIAM ROCHE, called in; and Examined.

Mr. *W. Roche.*

15 May 1873.

2500. *Chairman.*] You are a Crown Solicitor, are you not?—I am.

2501. For what county?—For the county and city of Limerick.

2502. For what period?—For 12 years.

2503. Will you state to the Committee what your experience of the working of the present Act has been?—It has only been in operation at the last assizes, and then it was not satisfactory.

2504. In what respect?—I think that the jurors were not of sufficient intelligence to be upon a jury, and I think that they were influenced probably by the position that they occupied, in arriving at decisions on the issues that were sent to them.

2505. Then really there was a want of intelligence?—Yes, there was a want of intelligence; and there was I believe an apprehension on behalf of the men themselves, as to the exercise of their discretion, and that they often were of an inferior class.

2506. You think that they were not of an independent class?—I think not.

2507. What is your opinion of the old system?—I think that this is a great improvement upon the old system, and that by modifying and altering in some degree the present Act of Parliament, I think it is an immense improvement.

2508. What you have seen does not induce you to wish to revert to the old system?—Certainly not.

2509. What would you suggest for the improvement of the present jury list?—I would raise the qualification in the county. Speaking of my own county, I would not touch it in the city, for I find it work exceedingly well in the city, and I have nothing to complain of; the jurors discharged their duties on the last occasion just as well, and appeared to me to be quite as intelligent as at any previous time, the qualification in the city being 12 *l.*

2510. You found that the city qualification of 12 *l.* gave you a good panel?—Certainly; in my opinion, it did.

2511. But the county panel was composed, I suppose, chiefly of farmers?—Yes.

2512. And of farmers of a very low class?—Yes; there were upon that panel men of a different class too, but they did not attend or they did not answer to their call, and the Judge imposed fines upon them. I had not them upon the jury in the cases which I was trying.

2513. Were the fines levied?—No, they were not, they were remitted; there was an excuse tendered, and it was accepted.

2514. Have you considered how high you would raise the qualification in your county?—I have given it some consideration, and I would raise it to 50 *l.*

2515. Would that give you a sufficient number of jurors?—I understand that it would; I have not had an opportunity of analysing the return, but I have been told that it would afford a sufficient number.

2516. Would you have a 50 *l.* rating irrespective of town or country?—No; I would leave the town qualification as it is.

2517. The county of Limerick, I suppose, contains other towns besides the city of Limerick?—Yes; in the towns and villages I would not increase it beyond a few pounds, if at all.

2518. Have you any suggestion to make as to the revision of the lists by the chairman?—Yes; I would have the chairman act as the judge, and I would give him very large powers indeed.

2519. Would you extend the powers that he has now?—I would; I would afford him ample opportunity of exercising his judgment in every case that he thought fit, and I do not think that there would be any dissatisfaction follow.

2520. Would you extend the statutory grounds of exemption?—I hardly think that would be necessary. I do not recollect the exact exemptions.

2521. Would you make inability to read or write a ground of exemption?—Yes, I would certainly do that.

2522. You would also give the chairman a discretionary power to strike off any juror whom for any cause he did not consider qualified?—I would.

2523. How would you suggest that the chairman should obtain the necessary knowledge?—I would have his court attended by the collectors of the poor rate, and the barony collectors, and the constabulary, and, I think that he would get a great deal of the information that he would require from them, if not all.

2524. Would you suggest that the clerk of the union in preparing the list, should make any mark opposite the name of a juror whom he considered to be unfit?—Yes; that might be so; but I think the clerk of the union or the poor law collectors, being on the spot, it would be their duty to call the attention of the chairman as the name was called, whether there was a mark opposite it or not.

2525. Have you ever been present at the revision of a list?—I never have.

2526. But you would make it a real revision, and make it incumbent upon the chairman to go through the list almost name by name?—Yes: although I have not been there, it is a matter of public notoriety, that the revision was a mere nominal revision heretofore.

2527. Would you make political opinions of any description a ground of exemption?—Not all; I would not, I think, when the Crown Solicitor comes to examine the panel, it is his duty to make a careful examination of the panel that is presented to him by the sheriff, and to go over every name, and then if he finds a person that he supposed was a Ribbonman, or Fenian, he should exercise his discretion and tell him to stand by.

2528. But you would not suggest that any information that the chairman might receive as to the supposed political opinions of jurors, should form a ground of exemption?—No; I would be careful how I would do that.

2529. Have you always had to exercise the power of ordering jurors to stand by?—I always possess the power, but I always used it very sparingly. I thought it my duty to be very careful how I told men to stand by, because I was answerable to the Attorney General as to my conduct, and I took very good care, as far as my ability went, to carefully examine the panel, and investigate it, and to be in a position, if I told a man to stand by, to explain why I took that course.

2530. Were you able to use that power at the last assizes, or did you find a difficulty of obtaining

Mr. W. Roche. — 15 May 1873.

ing information as to the jurors on the panel?—I had more difficulty last assizes, though I consulted the best persons I could obtain information from, as I always do.

2531. Were you able to obtain sufficient information respecting the jurors on the new panel?—Not at all to the extent that I was on former occasions; they were unknown men as it were. I knew a great many men myself in the county, and with the aid of the other sources of information that I applied, I was able at all times to examine carefully the panel before I went into court.

2532. Did you find it necessary to exercise that power more freely than usual at the last occasion?—Yes; on the last occasion I did.

2533. I understand that even after exercising that power you did not obtain a satisfactory jury?—I did not.

2534. It was partly, I presume, the consequence of the absence of the better class of jurors?—To a small extent; not to a very large extent, but to a certain extent it was, because men of intelligence and acquaintance with the duty of a juror were not there. Many of those men never had been in the jury box before. If they had got an intelligent man with them he would have assisted them no doubt.

2535. There were persons on the panel, who, if they had attended, would have formed a competent jury?—I could not have formed it of them, because I had not a sufficient number of that particular class.

2536. Men of that particular class did not attend?—They did not.

2537. Mr. *Bruen.*] Were they on the panel?—There were a good many of them on it, but not to a sufficient extent. I said there were not a sufficient number on the panel of that class of intelligent men that I was in the habit of having upon panels.

2538. Mr. *Attorney General.*] It could only have been those who were on the panel that did not attend?—Yes; but who did not serve, I meant.

2539. *Chairman.*] I understood you to say, that of the better class of jurors who were on the panel, many did not attend?—Certainly.

2540. And if they had attended you would have had a better jury?—Of course I should.

2541. Would you suggest any way of compelling the poor-rate collectors and the clerks of unions to give information to the chairman?—I would give the chairman the power of obliging them to attend and furnish such information as was within their reach. We know very well that they must possess a very great deal of information, because they know everybody.

2542. Mr. Murland has just suggested that he would prefer balloting for the jury, in criminal cases to calling them from the panel as now. Are you of the same opinion?—Certainly. I think that that would be a very great improvement. Under the 41st section, they call them from the panel now as they did at all times heretofore; but I think that it would be far better to ballot for the juries, as in civil cases in fact.

2543. For what reason?—First, it would get rid of the system of the friends of the accused going amongst the earlier numbers on the panel to secure their attendance. I think that it would give great public confidence, seeing that they were called without any reference to their position on the panel.

2544. Would not you reduce the number of the peremptory challenges of the prisoner?—No; I would not. I do not see any objection to the present number.

2545. Mr. *Attorney General.*] They are not called upon the panel under the Act now, are they?—I thought, when I read it, that they were not; but it was decided in Ireland, and they were called, upon the last occasion, from the panel in the way that they had been for very many years before.

2546. The 41st Section is: "The name of each man who shall be summoned and empanneled, either as a common or special juror, in any court of assize or Nisi Prius, with the place of his abode and addition, shall be written on a distinct piece of parchment or card, being all as nearly as may be of an equal size, which shall be delivered unto the clerk or registrar of the judge who is to try the cause, by the sheriff or other officer returning the process, and shall, by direction and care of such clerk or registrar, be put together in a box to be provided for that purpose; and when any issue shall be brought on to be tried, such clerk or registrar shall, in open court, draw out twelve of the said parchments or cards, one after another, after having shaken them together"?—I read that section so; but the judges held otherwise, that it only applied to civil cases. That was the construction put upon it by the judges. My opinion was of very little worth as compared with theirs.

2547. It says a court of assize as well as Nisi Prius? -Yes.

2548. *Chairman.*] Is there not less necessity under the present Act than under the old Act for allowing a prisoner a great number of challenges?—It may be held so; but I would not make any alteration.

2549. The panel cannot be packed against a prisoner now, can it?—No, I do not think it can, if it is properly worked out. As I said before, I think it is a vast improvement.

2550 Would you suggest that publicans should be excluded, or that they should be allowed to serve on juries?—Practically, they are excluded now, because I am bound to tell them to stand by; and I was rather surprised at reading in a paper the other day that some letter had been written to you complaining of this, because I think it is rather a benefit than anything else to them. They were brought to the assize town at some expense, and as a matter of course, it is not a pleasant thing, because they are always desired to stand by when they are called from the panel. The inconvenience and disagreeableness to themselves of that would be saved, I think, by excluding them.

2551. You would make that a ground of exemption?—Yes, certainly; though there are very respectable men in that class, I may say.

2552. Would you call it an exemption or a disqualification?—I would call it a disqualification. I would disqualify them entirely; it is the more correct word.

2553. Colonel *Wilson Patten.*] Did you say that you would not extend the statutory exclusion, or that you would not recommend any such exclusion on the part of the chairman?—I would give him very extensive power; in fact, I would not limit his power at all.

2554. You have not given the Committee any idea of the limitation; will you kindly state the limit that you would impose upon the chairman?—A man

Mr. *W. Roche.*

15 May 1873.

—A man being over age or a man being illiterate, a person convicted of a previous criminal offence, an habitual drunkard, should be excluded.

2555. *Chairman.*] Most of those are disqualifications now?—Yes, they are. I do not recollect exactly the statutory disqualifications, and consequently I am not very well able to state any additional ones.

2556. Colonel *Wilson Patten.*] There would be no objection to those circumstances being stated, and to its being made the custom or the law that the chairmen should have the power of excluding jurymen on those grounds?—No.

2557. You stated that under the present system there is a system of canvassing of the jurors; is that custom very extensive in Ireland?—I think it has been always known to exist. I have known it of my own knowledge, and I hear people speak of it. It did not occur to myself, but I have always heard that men have been anxious to know who were upon the jury, and who, as they express it, they could "speak to."

2558. Mr. *Bruen.*] In speaking of canvassing jurors, when was that canvass performed; was it after the juries were sworn?—No; not after they were sworn, but when the panel was seen. They saw twenty names upon the panel, and the prisoner saw whether he had any friends there, and he spoke to his friends, as they expressed it, or to the friend of a friend.

2559. Under the former system the panels were not known until the sheriff had summoned them, and published the names?—The panel has been supplied to us for the last four or five years, a fortnight before, by the direction, I think, of the Attorney General, as I recollect.

2560. But before it was furnished to you, it was not known to the prisoner?—It was not.

2561. Under the present system, does not the alphabetical selection give to the parties the power of knowing who will be upon the panels a long time before?—They can conjecture, but that is the very reason why I suggest the ballot, because if there were 140 or 150 on the panel, it would be rather a difficult thing to canvass the whole 150, for the 149th man might be the first man drawn; whereas, if you called them from the panel, they would commence at Abram, and so on, and they would make a calculation as to how far the Crown would be able to form a jury.

2562. But the panel is known beforehand?—Yes; it is known beforehand.

2563. Therefore there is a long opportunity for the prisoners' friends to get at those who will serve on the panel, is there not?—The same opportunity, if they wish to have recourse to it, no doubt.

2564. Not the same opportunity, because there was no opportunity before?—I beg your pardon, there was. Four years ago, I think it was; that the Attorney General directed that the panel should be distinctly furnished. I think it was fourteen days before, and then any man who wished, could go and pay a shilling and get the panel.

2565. But it was limited to the time of a fortnight?—I do not think that I got the panel this last time, even so early as a fortnight.

2566. Is it not a fact that by the alphabetical system of selection, the list of those who are to be on the panel, are to be known long before the assizes; perhaps a year before?—No; because they change each time.

2567. They do, but the change is laid out beforehand by this alphabetical selection?—But the same men will not be upon the panel at the next assizes.

2568. But it would be known who would be the next men, would it not?—No; it would not.

2569. Is not the exact series and method by which the sheriff is to return his panel laid down in the Act of Parliament?—It is.

2570. And therefore, the former panel being known, it is also known of whom the next panel will be composed?—That is hardly so, because they must go to the jurors' book to ascertain that fact.

2571. Why not; is there any difficulty in it?—There is no difficulty in it; but a man may be dead, or left the county, or twenty other contingencies may have taken place.

2572. But failing those contingencies, the panel is perfectly known?—I do not see that it could be possible.

2573. It has been suggested by some witnesses that there ought to be given to the prisoner and to the Crown an equal right of trying criminal cases by a special jury; is it your opinion that that power ought to be given?—I see no real objection to it. Of course, by leave of the court, we have the power now in misdemeanour cases in the Queen's Bench.

2574. Have you ever known the sub sheriff's power of selecting the panels abused?—In my own county, I never knew it, but I have heard of it in other places. Whether it is true or false, I cannot say; that is all.

2575. Only as a matter of rumour?—That is all.

2576. Taking it as a practical question; it is a theoretical objection, and not a practical one in your own view?—I cannot say one word beyond what I have heard. The report is current enough, but I would not venture to state whether it was correct or not. I have no means of knowing it.

2577. Colonel *Forde.*] Did you order many jurors to stand aside at the last assizes?—I did; more than I ever did before.

2578. How many convictions did you get, do you remember?—I only got one conviction; I did not try all the cases.

2579. If respectable jurors had answered to their names, do not you think it would have been very likely that they would have been challenged by the prisoner?—It may be; I dare say they would.

2580. In agrarian or other cases, where there are perhaps two or three tried at the same time, have all the prisoners a right to challenge?—Yes; but we do not try them at the same time, because they would exhaust the panel. We are obliged to take one at a time. If you put three on trial, there would be three times twenty peremptory challenges. We cannot try them all; we must only put one or two on.

2581. Have not the Crown had to challenge more now, than they formerly had under the old system?—On the last occasion, I had.

2582. The challenging by the Crown is not a very popular thing, is it?—Of course it is not a popular thing; but I never heard a complaint made of it in my county in my life.

2583. Mr. *H. A. Herbert.*] How many jurors are there on the panel at Limerick?—One hundred and forty, I think.

Mr. *W. Roche.*

15 May 1873.

2584. How many respectable men remained away that were on that panel?—I have not computed that.

2585. You never thought of counting them?—I never did.

2586. How many of those jurors were absent?—Some of them were actually in court, or about the court, and they were fined on account of it.

2587. Do you think that many stopped away, or did not answer to their names, in order to throw discredit upon this Act?—I should be very sorry to say anything of the kind. I would not venture to make any such assertion.

2588. Colonel *Vandeleur.*] Did you conceive that there was a failure of justice in Limerick at the last assizes?—I did.

2589. Have you ever known anything equal to that in the county of Limerick?—I never have.

2590. I think you stated that you had adjourned or put off several cases?—I did.

2591. Was that in consequence of the great failure of justice?—No, certainly not; I had to put off cases. With the best panel that could have been framed I would have put them off. It was irrespective entirely of the panel.

2592. Mr. *Attorney General.*] You stated that you did not think that the jurors were independent; what do you mean by independent?—I do think that they were apprehensive of exercising their own judgments.

2593. Did they find verdicts as the judge told them, or how?—No; they did not find verdicts as the judge told them. They were independent as far as that went; but they said that they would not find verdicts as the judge told them.

2594. How did they show their want of independence?—Probably I expressed myself wrong, but I will explain it. A man living in a small thatched house is on the trial of a man of, probably his own party or faction; if he find him guilty he might make a discovery afterwards not very comfortable to him.

2595. You mean that they acquitted men of their own party?—I mean they would be likely to do so.

Monday, 19*th May* 1873.

MEMBERS PRESENT:

Mr. Attorney General.	Mr. Herbert.
Sir Rowland Blennerhassett.	Mr. Heron.
Mr. Bruen.	The O'Conor Don.
Viscount Crichton.	The O'Donoghue.
Mr. Downing.	Colonel Wilson Patten.
Colonel Forde.	Colonel Vandeleur.
The Marquis of Hartington.	

THE MARQUIS OF HARTINGTON, IN THE CHAIR.

The Right Honourable JAMES HENRY MONAHAN, called in; and Examined.

Right Hon. *J. H. Monahan.* 19 May 1873.

2596. *Chairman.*] I BELIEVE you are the Chief Justice of the Court of Common Pleas in Ireland?—Yes.

2597. Do you recollect for what time?—For more than 20 years. I believe 21 or 22 years.

2598. You have had a very large experience of the working of the former Jury Act?—I necessarily had some experience. I did all the business of my own court, and I always went circuit. I never missed a circuit.

2599. You went circuit at the last assizes?—I did.

2600. Will you be good enough to state to the Committee whether you formed an impression that the former Jury Act required amendment?—My impression is that it did require very serious amendment, and that the present Act has amended it to some extent.

2601. Will you state in what particulars you thought that the old Jury Act was especially in need of amendment?—There was a general impression that the sheriff might do as he pleased; and in cases of excitement, if a jury were returned unfavourable to any particular party, it was always attributed to the sheriff. I think it very bad that there should be a possibility of such a thing existing, and I think it is of the greatest possible advantage that the thing should be regulated in some way, so that no person would have that power. I do not mean to say that the sheriff exercised the power in every instance, but I think it is just as bad that he should be suspected of doing it, which I think it is necessary to avoid.

2602. Have you reason to think that there ever was partiality in the selection of the panel?—To be sure there was partiality. I cannot give many instances, but there is no doubt there was partiality, and I recollect, going back to ancient history, when I was at the bar; I recollect a circumstance occurring to my own knowledge, and I was very sorry to know it and hear of it, but I was obliged to hear of it.

2603. Should you have any objection to state that case?—I should have an objection to state particular names, but I believe most of the parties are dead. I could generally state what I mean. It was this. There was a particular trial going on. The parties were most anxious that there should not be jurors from a particular part of the country. We happened to say so, and the result was that, to our astonishment, when we came into court the court was crowded with jurors from the other part of the country, and not a single man from the place we did not wish to get them from.

2604. At all events, whether that partiality was common or not, there was an impression on the minds of the public that the sub-sheriffs were not impartial in the selection of the panel?—There was an impression to that effect, and I think that in a great many instances it was unfounded, but there was room for the impression, and it did a great deal of mischief.

2605. Do you think the mere fact that such an impression existed was injurious to the due administration of the law in public opinion?—I am perfectly sure it was. I think it is of as great consequence that the people should have confidence in the administration, as that it should in fact be pure.

2606. Do you recollect many instances in which there was a challenge to the array?—No; it so happened that since I was on the bench there has never been any such thing at all in my particular court, or before me.

2607. As to the working of the old jury system in Dublin?—The effect of it in Dublin was this, that we always had the same jury before us. We had some very bad; and I recollect a few years ago getting rid of half a dozen of them, by telling the sheriff that if ever he sent them to me again I would send him somewhere, and accordingly the result was that I never saw one of them afterwards.

2608. Practically, in Dublin a very small number of jurors were on the jury in every case?—Very few. It was uniformly in the Court of Common Pleas, the sittings after term. There were five or six men constantly there; and I think that the sheriff was induced to summon them, not through any corrupt motive at all, but for convenience sake; that he found they were anxious to attend, and got their guineas in special causes.

Right Hon. *J. H. Monahan.*

19 May 1873.

causes. They were what we call "guinea-pigs;" they were anxious to get the guinea, and they were sure to attend; there was no difficulty in procuring their attendances, and therefore they attended.

2609. Was that, in your opinion, a very bad state of things?—I leave that to you to form your own opinion upon. I do not express an opinion on such a subject.

2610. In such a state of things a suitor might form a very good guess as to the jurymen who would try his case?—He could know it very well.

2611. There was the inducement, at all events, to try to secure the favour of a juryman?—Of course, the men might wish to try to get a favourable jury; but I must say that I did not find much of that in fact, for I found that the juries did tolerably well, in fact very well. There was no complaint of them.

2612. What circuit did you go last assizes?—The Home Circuit.

2613. What opinion did you form of the juries under the present Act?—I formed the opinion that they got on extremely well; I had no scene before me; there was a scene in the next court that caused a great deal of laughter, about a particular juror being unable to read or write, or to sign his name, which I heard of, but no such thing occurred in my court; and I have been many years in the habit, under the old system, and I adopted it in the present, if a juror was called, and 12 men about being sworn, and if I saw that the first man on the list was likely not to be as intelligent as the second, third, or fourth man, I would say, "Mr. So-and-so, you have no objection to let Mr. So-and-so act as foreman." There is no law to prevent it, and I always get one of the most intelligent men to be foreman.

2614. Colonel *Wilson Patten.*] There was no objection of the juror to that?—None whatever: I never found the least objection.

2615. *Chairman.*] Did the jurors appear to consist of a lower class than formerly?—I believe they did, to some extent, though I did not perceive it much, because things went on smoothly with me, and there was nothing to direct my attention to it; I daresay they were somewhat of a lower class; they were certainly all strangers to me. I may mention that the term before, on the last day of my sittings at Nisi Prius, I was quite surprised when the foreman of the jury came up to take leave of me; I really did not know what he was about. He prefaced it by saying, "We have come to take our leave of you, and to return you thanks for your kindness." I asked what was it all about Well, they said their vocation was gone; and it turned out, on inquiry from one of the officers of the court, the crier, or somebody who knows a great deal more about it than I do, what was the reason of this, that of the whole jury there was only one man on the new panel, and therefore that they had taken leave.

2616. From what you have heard, more than perhaps from what you have actually seen on circuit, have you formed any opinion as to too low a class having been admitted by the present Act?—Nothing having occurred in my own court, and things having gone on satisfactorily, I did not observe anything, I did not hear anything particular; but I daresay they were something of a lower class, but I do not know that of my own knowledge.

2617. What are the counties included in the Home Circuit?—We commenced with Meath, then Westmeath, King's County, Queen's County, Carlow, and Kildare.

2618. Of course, you have a very great knowledge of the whole of the country. Should you say that in Connaught or in some other parts of Ireland a 20*l.* qualification would include men of less intelligence than those who were returned by a 20*l.* qualification in those counties?—That is very possible. There is a general notion that men whose business is altogether amongst cattle are not as intelligent as others, but I did not see anything particular of it.

2619. Were any cases tried before you of either a party or an agrarian character?—No; I had no party cases or agrarian cases, but I may observe I had some heavy civil cases. There was one case, a case of very considerable importance, and the jury acted perfectly right. I may mention that from the whole of the circuit, and from the sittings after term, there was not a single new trial motion. The parties were satisfied with the result.

2620 Mr. *Downing.*] From the whole circuit?—The entire of my circuit; there was not a single new trial motion last term, neither was there from my sittings after term; that is, my sittings in court, which involved the sittings after term.

2621. *Chairman.*] Would you have any apprehension that in cases of either a party or a political, or an agrarian character, the new class of jurors could, perhaps, not possess the independence which was necessary?—I really did not consider that much.

2622. Supposing that, in the opinion of the Committee, it should become necessary to make some alterations in the present law, in what direction would you suggest that they should be made; would you suggest that they should be made in the direction of raising the qualification, or of a more careful revision of the lists, or of returning to the old principle of selection by the sheriff.

2623. As to going back to the old principle, you may put that out of the question. I think, once having adopted the new principle, going back to the old would be so monstrous that it could not be thought of for a moment. My impression is that there might be an alteration; for instance, I have heard it stated that in some cases men could not read or write. I think that would be very easy to make that a disqualification. The Act strikes off persons incompetent or incapable of giving evidence, and I think it would be very simple to add that. The words of the Act are, "Shall, upon sworn testimony, or any other evidence satisfactory to such chairman or barrister, amend the said lists by expunging therefrom the name of every man whose name shall appear thereon respectively, who shall be exempted, or who shall not be qualified, under this Act, or who, from lunacy, imbecility of mind, deafness, blindness, or other permanent infirmity shall be unfit to serve as a juror." I think it would be very easy and simple and proper to include, amongst the persons not proper to serve as jurors, those being unable to read or write. I think that would be very proper.

2624. Not but what there may be persons of considerable intelligence who are not able to read or write?—I confess I think their intelligence might keep them at home. I think a man at the present day, who is not able to read or write, cannot

Right Hon. *J. H. Monahan.*

19 May 1873.

cannot complain if he is not to try on a jury complicated questions.

2625. As a matter of fact, they would not complain?—They would be delighted to get rid of it. There is no such thing as a complaint of a juror; they are always infesting the court, and saying, "I am not fit to serve as a juror. I cannot read or write; sure I cannot serve as a juror."

2626. I understand you see no objection to any alteration of the Act, which, by raising the qualification, would secure a higher and more intelligent class?—None whatever.

2627. Or by increased stringency of revision would secure that unqualified persons were struck off the list?—Certainly.

2628. Do you think that the chairman's court is a good one for the revision of the jurors' list?—I think if he takes the trouble he is an excellent one; but whether he will take the trouble or not I do not know. If he will take the trouble to inquire and to strike off he is perfectly competent to do it, and I hope will discharge his duty properly, but whether he will or not I do not know.

2629. Have you considered at all whether the duty of revision of the lists could be entrusted better to any other person?—I really have not considered that.

2630. It was nominally the duty of the magistrates formerly?—Under the old system, I believe, it was everyone's duty, and no one's duty; there was no such thing as a revision before at all. A parcel of people attended, whose duty it was. It was asked, "does anybody object;" nobody objects, and it is all right, and there is no more said about it. There should be on some person the duty imposed, and I suppose the chairman would discharge it properly when it is really made his duty.

2631. The chairman might be furnished with a good deal of information by the clerks of the unions?—He might.

2632. By the poor rate collectors?—Yes.

2633. By the constabulary, do you think?—Yes, the constabulary could give information, if they chose to do it.

2634. Would you be in favour of the chairman having a discretionary power?—No; he should exercise the power he has by fixed rules prescribed.

2635. The disqualifications or exemptions should all be statutory?—I should say so.

2636. Under no circumstances, even as a temporary measurement pending the revision of the whole subject, would you be disposed to revert to the principle of selection?—As to the principle of selection, it is abominable; it cannot be tolerated at all, or thought of.

2637. Have you considered at all the question of requiring unanimity upon juries?—That is not really a question for a judge; it is more a question for the Legislature to do what they like.

2638. If the principle were adopted that is proposed by the Attorney General for England, would you see any objection to extending it to Ireland? I should like to see how it worked in England first.

2639. Colonel *Wilson Patten.*] You stated that there were no motions for new trials from the last circuit?—Certainly.

2640 Were there many civil causes tried during the last circuit?—I do not recollect the exact number, but there were the average number for the home circuit, and there was the average number of cases in the Court of Common Pleas.

2641. Does that amount to any great number?—"Great number" is a comparative term; it would be very little in England, I dare say, but it is tolerable there.

2642. Were there any very serious cases?—There were some very heavy causes. There was one very heavy cause which the parties thought a great deal of, a case of Lord Greville against some company.

2643. You stated that you would make all the objections statutory; would you allow no discretion at all beyond what was allowed by statute?—Upon my word, I do not know, and it is very hard to say. My impression would be to confine it to the statutory objections, and to make them a little more extensive than at present.

2644. Nothing that came to the knowledge of the judge or the chairman you would allow, to enable him to tell a man to stand by?—You might say, supposing you found a man drunk, or a thing of that sort, it would be very right to let a man of that kind stand by.

2645. Supposing a judge or a chairman had reason to believe that a man was privately or personally interested in the case?—The lists are formed without knowing of cases at all. The list is formed generally. You cannot know that a man will be interested in a particular case.

2646. Supposing that it came to the knowledge of the judge that there was some objection of that kind, would not you allow the judge to exercise his own discretion?—I will tell you how I would act if the case came before myself. When the party objects to a juror for any fanciful ground, I always say, "You would much rather not serve;" and I get them off that way quietly. I could not do that, perhaps, if the parties objected; but they have an objection to object.

2647. On the whole, you think the exemption from serving on juries would be considered an advantage?—Quite; there is not a man in Ireland, unless the "guinea pigs," that would not be obliged to you for excluding them.

2648. Therefore this Committee need entertain no scruples in placing a higher limit?—Certainly not, there is not a man in Ireland wishes to be on a jury.

2649. Mr. *Bruen.*] Would you give a statutory power of excusing a juror, for any cause, to the judge; entirely at the judges discretion?—The judge would find it very hard to exercise that discretion, unless he saw what you were aiming at.

2650. You do not think it would be right to give that absolute discretion to the judge to excuse a juror without assigned cause?—I really do not quite see how that could come into operation.

2651. We will say, supposing a juror came forward and said to the judge it was very inconvenient for him to serve?—I should be very much disposed to let him go if I could. It frequently happens a man says, "It is very inconvenient to me to attend." Well, I suspect that he may be romancing, and ask him what is the inconvenience, and if he satisfies me that he really has very important business to attend to, I always say to the parties present in court, "There is no objection; we can get a juror without this gentleman, and we will let him go." I never find the parties object to that.

2652. That

Right Hon. J. H. Monahan.

19 May 1873.

2652. That is not actually a statutory power that is now in your hands?—It is not, but it does as well as any statute; it is every day practice in Ireland.

2653. Have you ever known the system of selection of jury panels by the sheriff to act prejudicially to the prisoner?—I know nothing at all about that, but I suspect a great deal.

2654. Have you had any suspicion, or have you had any good cause for believing that that system was exercised prejudicially to the prisoner?—I have heard so, and I have been told it; I have no means of investigating, and I did not investigate it, and I cannot know anything about it.

2655. I think you mentioned that there had been no case of appeal from any sentence or verdict which had been given on the Home Circuit?—No motion for new trial.

2656. If there had been a motion for a new trial I suppose that that case would have been tried again in the same way, would not it?—The first question is, whether it would be tried at all again? and I should hope it would not, for I try to be right the first time; I do not think it would be tried any more.

2657. Supposing there was a good ground for a new trial, that trial would take place under the same circumstances?—Certainly.

2658. Before a jury chosen in the same way?—No; if it were a case tried under the present Jury Act, and there was a new trial directed, it would be tried under the same Act.

2659. Supposing the parties had not confidence in the verdict which the jury had given, and they called for a new trial, it would be, in fact, exposing themselves to a verdict given, perhaps equally unintelligently, by a jury chosen in the same way?—Not at all; because the objection to a verdict of a jury is, that on the evidence the jury came to a wrong conclusion. Well, it does not follow at all, that because 12 men came to that wrong conclusion, another 12 men will come to the same conclusion.

2660. At the same time, if distrust were felt of the system under which these jurors were brought together, a person who felt that distrust would naturally not appeal to a jury chosen again in the same way?—He would not be influenced by that at all; he would appeal because he thought some one or other invisible to him on the jury came to a wrong conclusion; it would be a matter of chance whether there would be one on the next jury of the same way of thinking. There was no such thing at all.

2661. As a matter of objection to the intelligence of the jury?—He could not appeal on the ground of the unintelligence of the jury; that is not a ground of appeal.

2662. You were satisfied with the verdicts that were given?—Perfectly.

2663. Do you think the jury were at all swayed in their verdict by the direction of the judge more than in former years?—I do not think they were really, because there were always on the jury some intelligent men, who I know acted on their own opinion; but I think perhaps, as a rule, if there was a parcel of people who were incapable of forming an opinion, they would be influenced by the opinion of the judge.

2664. Do you think that, at the last assizes on your circuit, as a matter of fact, the jury seemed to be more under the influence of the judge's directions than they were before?—I did not observe that they were. I did not observe one way or the other.

2665. Do you consider the alphabetical selection of jury panels a perfect system?—I think it is as good a system as can be suggested.

2666. Do you think there is any chance of injustice and inequality of burden on the juror by reason of that system?—In any case in the world, if you have 12 men on the jury, there is a chance that some one of the 12 may be unfavourable to the plaintiff or to the defendant.

2667. That is not the point I wish to put. I wish to ask you whether you thought there was a chance of injustice and inequality of burden on the jurors who were summoned?—Of course, in common sense it is so. Except that they liked it, there was a great injustice on those men who attended in the Court of Common Pleas; the same always constantly attended, except three or four of them, of whom I got rid, that I was ashamed of. Of course, it was an injustice to them, if their time was of more value than the remuneration they got, but they considered it a great act of justice. I am told that their emoluments as jurors were a very serious consideration to them.

2668. That was with reference to the old system?—Yes.

2669. Do you think there is not a chance of injustice and inequality of burden under the new system upon some jurors more than upon others?—No; I do not see how it can exist.

2670. For instance, a juror who has a valuable business depending upon his own superintendence would, no doubt, lose more than a man who has not very much to do?—Yes, certainly; but I do not see how that will influence the verdict.

2671. It was not all with reference to that point, but as to the burden on the juror himself?—Yes, it might be a burden on the juror, of course.

2672. And a greater burden on some than on others?—Certainly; but then it is to happen but occasionally, it seems.

2673. With reference to what I suppose you may call the failure of the old jury system in Dublin, were not all those defects you mention caused rather by the officers entrusted with the law not carrying it out according to the statute?—But they did carry it out according to the statute; because the statute merely directed that they should take the jury from the jurors' book. Well, then, they did take it from the jurors' book.

2673*. Did they not summon merchants and persons of good position on the panel?—Scarcely.

2674. Can you give the Committee any idea of the number of men accustomed to act in this way, and who are called "guinea pigs"?—I cannot give any number at all.

2675. There surely would be more on the sheriff's panel than would be comprised in that description?—Certainly; but though they would be on the sheriff's panel, they would not attend under the old system.

2676. They ought to have attended under the statute?—They ought. If people did as they ought we should have no laws at all.

2677. There was a power reserved in the statute for compelling their attendance?—Yes; but who in the world would set about compelling

Right Hon. *J. H. Monahan.*

19 May 1873.

ling their attendance when he could do without them?

2678. I thought the objection your Lordship made was that you did not wish these men to attend?—When I had them there I found them very good, and I worked away with them.

2679. At the same time it is hardly fair to make an objection to a system when you could have compelled the attendance of better men under it?—I could compel their attendance, but you are not aware, perhaps, of the bother and confusion, which people do not like to get into. You call over the list of the panel. Scarcely more than the 12 used to answer. They used to have it arranged so that 12 or 13 men would answer. When I got 12 or 13 men ready to try the case, and who would try it tolerably well, it was not my business to be fining the others, or meddling with them at all.

2680. If there was an objection to these 12 or 13 men?—If there was an objection to them, but I was not to find that out.

2681. Then, in fact, there was not an objection to them?—You may say so.

2682. Your Lordship mentioned in the first part of your evidence a case in which partiality was without doubt exercised by the sheriff?—I do not like to go into that case any more.

2683. How long ago was it?—It was when I was at the Bar, over 20 years ago.

2684. Colonel *Forde*.] Supposing the jurors had been summoned from the part of the country which you said they were not summoned from, would there, in your opinion, have been a fair trial?—I think it would have been too fair.

2685. Mr. *Bruen*.] The objection you made to that case was, not that there was a failure of justice, it did not produce a failure of justice?—You say so, and you may fancy so, and I was bound to think so at the time.

2686. There has been a doubt thrown upon the power the sheriff has under the new system of choosing his panels after the first panel has been chosen. It is held, I understand, by some, that after the first panel has been chosen, the sheriff may take the other panels from the different letters in the alphabet rather at his discretion; that is to say, instead of taking the next man under letter A., he may take a man from letter A., standing three or four names down the list if he chooses. Is it your opinion that that is still in the power of the sheriff?—When the question arises, I will tell you; but if it be possible that that is the construction of the Act, I think it ought to be altered.

2687. Mr. *Downing*.] I think this is about the purport of your evidence, that under the old system you were not satisfied with it, nor were the other judges generally?—I do not know what the others thought.

2688. Was that your own case?—Yes.

2689. And under the present Act, so far as you have had any cognisance of its working, you have found it work very well?—I found it work sufficiently well. There was an outcry made against it, and if a man cannot read or write, we all cry out against it.

2690. I suppose you do not think it possible that any human tribunal can make a perfect system?—Not without a great many trials; they must go about from time to time.

2691. I think you were Attorney General a good many years ago, and you had some State trials yourself?—I had enough of them; I convicted Smith O'Brien.

2692. On the occasions of those trials, were there any complaints that men were excluded from the jury who ought not to have been excluded?—There were no complaints at all; there was no good in complaining.

2693. Serjeant Armstrong is a man of very large experience at the Bar?—Very great.

2694. Both civil and criminal?—I believe so; he is a man of great experience.

2695. He gave this reply to a question put to him. He says: "That is the great merit of the Act as it stands, that it strikes a decided blow at such a system. I have not the slightest hesitation in saying that, under the old system, cases occurred in which you could have a jury to order, and if you prescribed your jury, you might get it." Do you believe that?—I believe anything the Serjeant says of his own knowledge. He has means of knowledge that I have not.

2696. With regard to the qualification. Do you think you would get a better class of jurors by raising the qualification to 30 *l.* than by leaving it as it is at 20 *l.*?—I should suppose so, but I do not know. That is more a matter for statistics. Before you can raise the qualification from 20 *l.* to 30 *l.*, you must ascertain how many you will have of the increased qualification, and if you find it will not give you a sufficient number you cannot have it.

2697. With regard to the unanimity of a jury in criminal cases. Have you known from your knowledge that one man out of 12 has refused to convict where the party afterwards was acquitted?—I know a strong instance of that, which relieved me from a very serious responsibility as judge. I recollect a case in which two men were tried for murder. It was a special commission. In the first jury that tried the case there was one man who held out for an acquittal. We heard this afterwards. The jury disagreed; Mr. Justice Blackburn was my companion in the commission. He tried the first case. They were put on trial again the following day, and the result was another jury disagreed. I think the evidence was not quite so strong and convincing on the second occasion as it was on the first, but the jury disagreed. Afterwards the prisoners were put on trial again, and the jury disagreed. It afterwards appeared on very clear, distinct evidence, and men were convicted upon it, that these were not the men who had committed the offence.

2698. That was a case of murder?—It was.

2699. If those men had been convicted on the first trial, it would have been the duty of the judge to have sentenced them to execution?—They would have been sentenced as sure as two and two make four.

2700. And, according to all law, it is better that 99 guilty men should escape than that one innocent man should suffer?—Yes; perhaps that man may not have been innocent altogether, he may have had a knowledge of it.

2701. You have heard, I am quite sure, of the celebrated Dunrail conspiracy?—Yes.

2702. In which, on the first trial, four men were convicted, and sentenced to be hanged?—I believe so.

2703. Are you aware that on the second trial one man held out against 11, on the second batch being tried?—I suppose I have heard of it, but I do not recollect it.

Right Hon. *J. H. Monahan.*

19 May 1873.

2704. And that subsequently, the very next day, before a fresh jury, they were acquitted?—I heard so, but I do not know anything about it.

2705. So that under these circumstances, perhaps you would say you were not in favour of having a verdict in criminal cases by a majority?—If I am to give an opinion upon it; but I would rather not give an opinion; I really do not approve of the system at all.

2706. Mr. *Heron.*] We understood you to say, that under the old system in civil cases, there was opportunity both for partiality and corruption?—There was opportunity, but whether it was exercised or not I do not know.

2707. Do you remember a very remarkable case you tried very recently; the case of Meldon *v.* Lawless?—I do.

2708. Do you remember Mr. James Dillon Meldon, proving in the witness box, that a man came to him before the trial, and said a juror would be on the jury, and that he wanted the price of a new pair of boots?—I recollect hearing something of that sort.

2709. That man actually was forced on the jury although we tried to keep him off?—That was not before me.

2710. Yes, it was?—I do not think there was any question before me about forcing him on the jury.

2711. No, we had no legal objection to him; we tried to say there was an objection to that man before the trial, and failed?—I do not recollect that.

2712. Was there any application made last term in your court for a new trial on the ground of misconduct of the jury?—No, not that I am aware of.

2713. Of course if a jury misconducted themselves in any way, the setting aside the verdict would be a matter of course?—Yes.

2714. A suggestion has been made in the course of the evidence before this Committee, that in criminal cases the Crown or the prisoner should have the opportunity of striking a special jury; do you wish to give any opinion on that suggestion?—No, indeed I do not. I see the present Act makes a difference as to jurors in the case of a special commission. As I understand the section of the Act, it says that in case of a special commission, the panel is to be taken both from the special jury and the common jury list. Well, I would improve that certainly in the case of a special commission; I would let the jury be taken altogether from the special jurors. It is the 19th section which contains the provision I refer to: "Provided further that the sheriff or other officer shall, according to the mode of selection hereinbefore in this section prescribed, select the persons to be returned to serve as *petit* or common jurors at any special commission of oyer and terminer, or at the assizes, from the general jurors' book without omitting from such selection persons whose names are marked on the general jurors' book as special jurors." That provision of course would have the effect, that where there is a special commission, they are to be taken from the general body and not from any particular body. I think if there is a special commission, it might be proper that the jury should be taken from the special jury portion of the panel.

2715. *The O'Donoghue.*] I gather from your evidence, that you think the opinion generally entertained in Ireland of the old jury system was that it was an unfair system?—Yes.

2716. And that that arises from the knowledge of the people that the sheriff had the power of selecting who were to be on the jury?—Yes.

2717. Without asking your Lordship to say whether anything could be stated in extenuation of such a practice, I will ask you, do not you think that it must be assumed, that under such a system, a trial by jury could not be described as being fair or just?—That is a very general way. My impression is that the misconduct of the sheriff, if you may so call it, did not exist so generally as was supposed, and I think in several cases, they have returned the panel fairly and properly, without any selection whatever; but I say, the possibility of selecting makes the people suspicious, and we are a suspicious set in Ireland. We do not hesitate to form opinions as to what people do, although we may not have legal grounds for it.

2718. Colonel *Forde.*] You would not give any one a power of selection?—Certainly not.

2719. Not even the chairman?—Not even the judge himself. At present we are a little hampered in this way: a man applies to be excused on some ground on which really it would be better to get rid of him, and I always let him go. I am not right perhaps in doing it, but I let the man go about his business.

2720. The Committee presented a report to the House of Commons, in which they suggested that power should be given to the judge to exercise a discretion to make a juror stand by. Do you or do you not agree to that?—I would not like to have that power myself of making a man necessarily stand by.

2721. Mr. *Bourke.*] The opinion you have given to the Committee is the opinion you have formed from your own judicial experience?—Clearly.

2722. And nothing else?—And nothing else.

2723. Therefore, the opinion you have formed of the new Act, is the opinion you have formed from the experience you have had of the working of the Act in your own court?—Certainly.

2724. You have not ascertained the opinion of the body of persons who form the great body of jurors in the country on the working of the Act?—No, I have nothing to do with them. I do not know anything about them.

2725. In a political point of view, do you think it would be desirable for the due administration of justice, that as far as possible, the system that is pursued in England, with regard to the selection of juries, should be the system in Ireland?—I do not know what it is.

2726. Simply, as a matter of fact, do you think that it would be desirable that the people of Ireland could say, that they were tried exactly in the same way, and by the same kind of jury, selected in the same manner as people in England?—I should like to know what is the rule in England, and I would then tell you whether I thought it right or not.

2727. I will give you a little sketch of the system. Supposing the parish officers, in the first instance, make out a list of everybody who is entitled to serve on a jury in the parish; supposing, then, that that list is published upon the usual places, chapels and churches, and so on, and that after a certain time the justices meet in petty sessions,

Right Hon. *J. H. Monahan.*

19 May 1873.

sessions, as a special sessions, and settle those lists which have been published by the overseers, the parochial officers, and also that they are to append to that list a notice to all persons qualified to serve as jurors in the parish, that unless they make objections and claim exemptions before the justices, they will be struck off, or not put on, the jurors' list. Supposing, then, that the justices of the peace sent that list so corrected by them, and corrected by the parties that they may call before them, to the clerk of the peace, and the clerk of the peace then sends it to the sheriff, and the sheriff then takes that as the jurors' book for one year, and then that that same process should be gone through from year to year, and so the jurors' book and the panel afterwards be made out from that. Do you think that a good system?—Indeed, I do not.

2728. Will you tell us what you object to in it?—In the first place, it would never act in Ireland, because I do not think, if you published your notices, they would ever take the least notice of them; nobody would read them in Ireland.

2729. Suppose you gave notice, the first time a man was put on the jurors' list, by post?—He would put it in his pocket, or on the dresser; he would never hear of it again. We are not such particular people at all.

2730. You attach no importance whatever to a juror being put upon the list without notice?—Not at all; he thinks it is time to complain when the grievance comes.

2731. Would you give to the justices of the peace any power of striking people off?—Not a bit.

2732. How would you take the list?—I would have a responsible officer. I would have the chairman, or the assistant barrister, as we call him, and I would give him the power to select, and I would make it more stringent than it is.

2733. You would give exactly the same power to the chairman of the county that is proposed to be given in England to the justice of the peace?—I do not exactly know what that is; it is too complicated, you will find.

2734. You would simplify it as much as possible?—Yes, I would come to the point.

2735. As I understand you, you would confer all the powers of getting a good jurors' book upon the chairman of the counties?—I would to a great extent. He cannot have knowledge of himself; but give him the means, and I would impose it upon him.

2736. You would give him power to call before him the different officers of the county, the constabulary?—And every one he likes.

2737. It has been suggested by the honourable Member for Tipperary that clerks of the petty sessions should supply the convictions?—Yes.

2738. *The O'Donoghue.*] Would you suggest that it should be done in open court?—Certainly.

2739. Mr. *Bourke.*] You think it would be advisable to send the convictions?—Yes.

2740. You would give him all the information you could?—Yes.

2741. Mr. *Attorney General.*] I suppose most men of common sense would agree that the object is to get a reasonably good list?—Yes.

2742. Whatever machinery may be simplest and best for that purpose, probably, you would say should be employed?—Most certainly. I do not care what it is, provided it has that effect.

2743. The conditions of the two countries may be very different in those respects?—So they are, I believe, but I do not know.

2744. At any rate, whether they are or are not, they might be?—They might be.

2745. As I understand the Irish law now, as to juries, I do not want to get a judicial opinion from you for nothing; the old habit of selecting special jurors and not allowing them to serve on the juries is at an end?—I believe so.

2746. Every one who ought to serve, whether special or common, now serves indifferently?—No, I believe not.

2747. Is not that so?—I rather think the ordinary common juries have a particular qualification.

2748. I really ask for information, because I do not pretend to know; is it not this, that with regard to civil trials everybody is liable to serve, whether special or not?—No.

2749. But if there is to be a special jury, then the special jurors only have to serve on that trial and have to be paid more, because they have to serve only on that trial?—I do not know really how it is.

2750. Would it, in your judgment, be a good thing that on every trial, whether civil or criminal, there should be some higher intelligence?—I think it is impossible to have difference between them. I should like to have men of intelligence, but they must come in by chance.

2751. What I mean is this, supposing the individuals to be equally selected by chance, what should you say to the notion of having a definite proportion of one class, and of another class upon each jury?—My impression is that that would not be a good plan in Ireland. I think in the jury box they would say, "I am a better juror than you."

2752. It would introduce class feeling?—Yes, and matters of that sort.

2753. On the whole, I understand you to say that you are strongly against having an uncontrolled principle of selection anywhere or to anybody?—I would not leave it to any one whatever. No one whatever should have an uncontrolled selection.

2754. If I may presume to translate your evidence, that is rather because it is important, not only that persons should be tried, but that they should think that they are tried fairly, than from any feeling that they have not been in fact tried fairly?—Precisely so. I think it is of the greatest importance that they should have confidence in their trial, and in the persons who are to try them. They will have that perfect confidence if there is no selection, but if there is a selection you destroy the confidence.

2755. You would be of the same opinion, however few the actually ascertained instances of unfair selection were?—Precisely. I believe, as a matter of fact, there are very few instances; but I think the power existing creates the suspicion.

2756. *Chairman.*] Do you think it is necessary to retain the power of the Crown to order jurors to stand by in criminal cases?—To be sure it is.

2757. Whatever system you adopt?—Yes; the Crown should have the power of ordering any man they please to stand by.

2758. Mr. *Downing.*] Unlimited?—Not unlimited, but within certain bounds.

Right Hon. *J. H. Monahan.*

19 May 1873.

2759. You would trust to that power to exclude from the jury persons, if there be any, who are supposed, in the opinion of the Crown advisers, to be disaffected to the law?—Certainly; the officer of the Crown would not discharge his duty if he had any hesitation in making to stand by all men of that class.

2760. You would rather trust to that power than to the power of striking the names of such men off the jurors' book?—Certainly.

2761. For instance, you could not, in your opinion, make the allegation that a man was a Ribbonman or a Fenian a ground for striking his name off the list?—I could not make it, but I would get rid of him.

2762. Through the process of ordering him to stand by?—Exactly.

2763. *The O'Conor Don.*] On your circuit at the last assizes did any question come before you as to the legality of the grand juries paying the sub-sheriffs for any additional trouble thrown on them by this new Act?—I do not think any question of that sort arose before me.

2764. You did not consider that?—Not at all.

The Right Honourable JAMES ANTHONY LAWSON, called in; and Examined.

Right Hon. *J. A. Lawson.*

2765. *Chairman.*] You are a Judge of the Court of Common Pleas of Ireland?—Yes.

2766. For what time?—Four or five years.

2767. More than that, is it not?—Perhaps, but I am not quite certain about dates.

2768. I believe you went on circuit the last assizes?—Yes; I went the North East Circuit.

2769. That includes what counties?—Drogheda, Louth, Monaghan, Armagh, Down, and Antrim.

2770. What opinion did you form of the operation of the new Juries Act?—I formed a very bad opinion of it. I thought it introduced a very bad class of jurors, which I had never seen before. I think I had gone that circuit three or four times before, and I saw upon this last occasion a class of jurors who were quite illiterate, and, in my judgment, totally incompetent to act as jurors. I may mention that that circuit is the heaviest circuit in Ireland. I rather think I tried more cases in one town than would be tried on the whole of the Home Circuit.

2771. Was that Belfast?—Yes.

2772. The business was very heavy at Belfast?—Very heavy indeed.

2773. You stated, I think, that the jurors were unintelligent and illiterate?—Yes, very much so; and in very poor circumstances, many of them. Many of them came to me during the assizes, and implored me to allow them to go home. They said they were not able to pay their expenses in the town, and asked me to order them some money. They really appeared a very poor class of men, whom it was a hardship to bring away from their little farms, perhaps some 60 or 70 miles away.

2774. Did you observe that the class was uniform throughout the circuit, or did you observe a difference in different counties?—They were better in some counties than in others. There generally was on each jury, perhaps, one or two men of a better class; but as a general rule, they were very ignorant men.

2775. Did any abstention of the better class of jurors become known to you?—There were very few of the better class on the panel. In the county of Antrim I know the names of the jurors and the gentry pretty well; and I think there were only about 10 persons on the panel of at all a better class. All the rest were very small farmers.

2776. Did they attend?—They did not attend.

2777. Did you on any occasion find it necessary to fine jurors for non-attendance?—No, I did not fine jurors for non-attendance. The attendance was always large. When the Belfast Assizes had lasted a week, I felt the hardship so great on these poor men from the remote ends of the county, that I took upon myself to allow them to go home, and finished the assizes with the jurors from the neighbourhood of Belfast.

2778. Do not you think some means ought to be adopted to compel the attendance of the better class of jurors as well as of the inferior class who may be summoned?—I think they ought all to be compelled to attend; but if the better class attended on this occasion, they were such a small proportion that it could not make any difference.

2779. Of course you will not answer any questions which you have any objections to, or any difficulty in answering; but should you have any objection to state whether you had any fault to find with the verdicts which were given?—I had no particular fault to find with the verdicts. I think the men appeared to be disposed to find fair verdicts, generally speaking. I had no fault to find with them.

2780. Did they generally follow your directions?—A judge does not generally give directions. He leaves the question to the jury, and generally speaking they found verdicts which I approved of.

2781. You formed the opinion that they were generally not men capable of forming an intelligent opinion upon a difficult case?—They manifestly, most of them, were quite incapable of understanding any case of difficulty. I tried a civil case in Dundalk, which was an action on a charter-party, rather a nice question, and I think there was scarcely a man on the jury who was capable of comprehending what was going on.

2782. Did they appear to you to be an independent class?—They appeared to me to be a very decent class for men of their position, and to be very well disposed. I found no fault with them, except that they were not intelligent; not educated. It was with some difficulty that we used to be able to select a man from among them who would act as foreman and sign the verdict; we had to look out for such a man generally.

2783. Sir *R. Blennerhassett.*] Were they generally persons who could not read or write?—Apparently so.

2784. *Chairman.*] You had a large number of party cases to try?—Yes.

2785. Were the verdicts in those cases generally satisfactory?—The verdicts were generally satisfactory.

2786. Do you think that the qualification ought decidedly to be raised?—I think the qualification ought to be raised, and I think a diversity of qualifications ought to be introduced. I think it is a mistake to have only one qualification, viz., a rating

Right Hon. *J. A. Lawson.*

19 May 1873.

a rating qualification. I think there ought to be a diversity of qualifications in order to get a good class of jurors.

2787. Could you suggest what new qualifications you would introduce? — In the Bill now passing through the House, introduced by Sir John Coleridge, there are a number of excellent qualifications given which might be adapted to Ireland.

2788. Mr. *Bourke.*] Do you mean those in the first clause?—Yes, in the earlier clauses.

2789. Mr. *Attorney General.*] In the first four clauses?—Yes, I have read all those; you could form a very nice variety of qualifications from those. It is a mistake to have only one qualification.

2790. *Chairman.*] You would retain the rating qualification as one?—I would raise it to such a point as would give you the adequate number of jurors, and join with that these other qualifications, some of which are contained in Sir John Coleridge's Bill. In some counties of Ireland those other qualifications would give you but very few additional jurors.

2791. Would they not?—I have not examined the statistics, and therefore I speak with reserve upon this matter of raising the qualifications.

2792. Are you acquainted with the county of Leitrim?—No; it would be very difficult to get a jury there at all, I believe.

2793. What opinion have you formed of the alphabetical arrangement system?—I think the alphabetical arrangement is a very bad system. It led to two rather disagreeable matters upon that circuit. In the county of Down, upon the trial of the Hollywood murder, the whole of the jury was challenged, because the sub-sheriff departed in a small particular from the alphabetical arrangement. That challenge was allowed by the Crown, which led to a postponement of the assizes. I was not Crown Judge there. I was Crown Judge in Belfast. The array of the jury was challenged again before me in Belfast upon this ground; a very curious ground; it appeared that in making out the list they took the liberty of adding a letter to the alphabet; that is, they made Mc a letter as well as M, which is a thing you constantly see in directories. It is a very convenient arrangement. The sheriff found it there, and accordingly he chose to consider Mc as a separate letter. On that ground the array was challenged before me. Well, I overruled that challenge; but I can only say that in all the cases that were tried there, counsel handed in a challenge on parchment to the array of the jury, in consequence of this point. I thought it was not a good ground of challenge, and I overruled it. I do not perceive that any writ of error has been brought upon it since. The alphabetical arrangement necessarily leads to mistakes. You cannot convert a man into a machine, and when you work by men you must allow some little discretion and some latitude. I may mention another curious effect of that alphabetical arrangement, which was this: I was told that in the county of Down, after some time, when the book had been gone through to a certain extent, all the remaining jurors that would be returned would be persons of the name of Murphy, because the letters M were so numerous that if you took an equal number from each letter, when you exhausted all the other letters, you left a residue of Murphys; therefore any gentleman of the name of Murphy that happened to be tried under those circumstances would have the advantage of being tried by his peers.

2794. Then, if the principle of the selection of the panel from the jury book be maintained, you would recommend some other system than the alphabetical system?—I would substitute another system which I am prepared to state. I will mention another inconvenience from that alphabetical system: there might be three members of a firm, all of whom have the same name. They would all be in order, one after another, upon the book. They might all be summoned upon the same panel. There is now, I believe, at this moment, a trial proceeding in Dublin in which there is an eminent wine merchant on the jury, and I observe that his two partners were called on the jury. They did not attend, and they have been fined; so that the effect, according to that, is to take all the men of business away from the establishment. Those are, of course, little inconveniences which could not be foreseen, but which, in practice, have led to very unpleasant consequences.

2795. I think you stated you would be prepared to recommend an alternative scheme?—Yes; before I go to that I should like to mention this: I have been speaking hitherto of the common jury; the special jury system has been greatly injured by the late Act. I never heard of any one under the former law complain of the special jury system; they were all excellent men, and in Belfast particularly there was a first class special jury. That is all altered now, and every man who is rated at 50*l.* a year is on a special jury panel. I have reason to know that the consequence of that has been that many mercantile cases were actually withdrawn or compromised at the last Belfast Assizes, the parties not choosing to submit them to such a special jury as is now there in place of the old one. I saw a very curious thing, which I may mention, occur in my own presence, which illustrates that. There were a number of men put on their trial before me for a riot; I think 14 or 15. They were all called, and they all answered except one man, and his name was called very often in court. At last one man in the dock said, "Oh, he is on a jury in the next court." I sent into the next court to know whether that was the case, and I found that he was not actually serving upon the jury, but was waiting to be called, and was actually on the special jury panel in the next court; I thought that certainly showed that the special jury had very much altered for the worse.

2796. What would you suggest, that the qualification should be raised?—I would suggest that the qualification should be raised, and that there should be a discretion in some one not to summon any one on the special jury, except a person known to be a person of intelligence of a very high order.

2797. What is your opinion of the abolition of the power of selection by the sheriff?—I am clearly of opinion that there must be somewhere a power of selection; there must be somewhere a power of striking off illiterate, incompetent, and improper persons, and I think it does not much matter whether it is in the sheriff or in some other authority.

2798. Is it the same thing to give to the chairman, or some other person, the power of striking off the names of incompetent persons, and giving it to any person, the power of selecting the panel from

Right Hon. *J. A. Lawson.* 19 May 1873.

from the list?—No, it is not. I think the striking off of incompetent persons, if that is done by a proper authority, gives you a jurors' book upon which you may rely, and all you need do then is as is done in this Bill of Sir John Coleridge's, to provide that the sheriff should summon them from that book by fair rotation.

2799. Then, I understand that you would advocate returning to the old system under which the sheriff or the sub-sheriff should actually select the panel from the list?—I have heard so much said about that, that I hesitate to give an opinion, but I confess I never could see any reason for departing from what has been the constitutional system in England and Ireland as long as we have had laws. I never could see the reason for it. I do not see the reason for exceptional legislation in Ireland upon this point. If that system is not to be returned to, I think there must be an authority vested in some one to strike off incompetent persons.

2800. Mr. *Attorney General.*] It has not been the case in England since the 5th George 4, the power of selection?—The sheriff has the power of summoning anyone he pleases.

2801. By ballot?—No; I looked at the new Bill carefully.

2802. You say, as I understood you, that it has always been the constitutional practice for the sheriff to select whom he pleased; I do not think that has been so since 5 Geo. 4; it is by ballot?—He forms his panel by ballot.

2803. Yes?—That is not the provision in the new Bill.

2804. *Chairman.*] Selection by rotation is not selection at all; it is another form of chance?—It is no selection at all if you must take the names in alphabetical order.

2805. With reference to special juries, you said you never heard any fault found with the special juries under the old system?—No.

2806. Does that statement extend to Dublin also?—I am not speaking of Dublin at all; I do not sit at Nisi Prius in Dublin; I am only speaking of the circuits.

2807. You have no knowledge except hearsay of what has been stated to us, that the special juries in Dublin were almost always composed of the same persons, or of limited numbers?—I do not know anything of the Dublin juries; but on the circuits the special juries always appeared to me to give great satisfaction, and to work very well.

2808. Have you not heard great fault found with the previous system of selection by the sheriff, on the ground of partiality?—I have heard that stated very often; but I am bound to say, that in my experience I never knew an instance of the kind. I remember, on a special commission in Cork, there was a challenge taken to the array on the ground of the partiality of the sheriff having improperly arrayed it, and it was most properly found in favour of the sheriff. I have heard a great many things stated, as you will hear in Ireland, but I never knew an instance of a sheriff being partial in arraying a panel. I only speak from my own experience.

2809. It was a very large power, was it not, to put into the hands of any man?—It is a large power.

2810. And practically it was not exercised by the sheriff, but by the sub-sheriff?—Yes.

2811. Do not you think that whether it were a good or a bad system, there would be great difficulty in reverting to it, now that it has been abandoned?—I should think so.

2812. Supposing it be decided to abandon altogether the power of selection, you would then revert to a very stringent revision of the list?—Yes, I think if you abandon the power of selection in the sheriff, and make him summon by rotation, you must have a careful revision of the list.

2813. Have you any suggestion to make as to how that should be done, and by whom?—Yes; I have very carefully read this Bill of Sir John Coleridge's, and I think its provisions would work very well indeed with us. I should propose that the justices in each petty sessions district should revise the lists, that they should be sent in to the clerks of the union, and so on; and that they should be revised in each petty sessions district, by striking off all persons who were disqualified, or who were entitled to exemption, or who, by reason of want of education or other cause should, in the opinion of the justices, be unfit men to serve as jurors.

2814. Would you give the magistrates a power of striking off the name for any cause that might, in their opinion, be sufficient?—I would.

2815. You would not exhaustively define them?—No, I think it is impossible to do that. It may be perfectly well known that a man is a disorderly character, and a drunken character; but you cannot put that in a Bill, and if we cannot trust our magistrates to revise the list, I am sure I do not know whom we can trust.

2816. Mr. *Attorney General.*] I think that in one of the clauses of the Bill there is some very generally expressed power?—Yes.

2817. "For any cause that may seem to them fit," or something like that?—Yes; upon that point it is quite true, that under the former jury system in Ireland, that revision had degenerated into a form, because there was no discretion given to the justices at all, but it was merely a question whether the man was statutorily disqualified or not; therefore, in addition to that, I would propose that just as is proposed in Sir John Coleridge's Bill, there should be proper notice given of the holding of the sessions, and the lists of the persons returned as jurors should be printed, and posted in the district, with a notice that persons claiming to be struck off the list, or to be inserted on the list, should attend at that sessions. If that were the case, I think you would have an effectual revision. I was greatly struck in Belfast with this circumstance, that several persons came before me as jurors, and complained of the great hardship of being summoned there. One of them was a schoolmaster; another was a professor in one of the colleges; another was a clerk in a merchant's office, men whose time was not their own. I said, "Why did you not go and claim exemption?" The answer was, "I never knew I was on the list of jurors at all, until I received the summons to attend." Well, I thought it very hard to believe that, but on looking into this Act which the Committee are now considering, I found that there is no provision at all that a man should receive notice that his name is about to be put on the list. That is the provision in Sir John Coleridge's Bill, and it is only fair to give a man an opportunity of claiming exemption by giving him notice in some way or other that he is to be called as a juror.

2818. *Chairman.*] Would you give him notice by

Right Hon. *J. A. Lawson.*

19 May 1873.

by post?—If he were on the list for the first time he ought to get notice by post; on a future occasion it would be enough to print the list, and post it up in the usual places in the district.

2819. In the revision by the magistrates, would you give the magistrates power to strike off, or exempt a juror, without stating a reason?—Yes.

2820. If a juror himself, or any person claimed to know on what grounds So-and-so had been struck off, would you not make it necessary for the magistrates to assign a cause?—I would have a second revision of the lists by the chairman of quarter sessions, who would receive at quarter sessions all the various lists returned from the districts, revise them all, hear any complaints, put any person on who he thought ought to be on, and strike any person off who ought to be struck off, and correct anything in which the magistrates had erred. I think if such a list were framed, such a book as that, first revised by the magistrates in petty sessions, and then again by the chairman of quarter sessions, it might be allowed to be in force for two years.

2821. *The O'Donoghue.*] You would leave it open for a person to come and complain?—Yes.

2822. How would they know that they had been struck off if the first revision had been done privately?—I do not propose to have anything done privately, but in open court.

2823. Then notice must be served on all the jurors?—Yes, that is one of the provisions, that notice should be served; that a special session would be held on such a day to revise the list of jurors; that is the provision in this Bill.

2824. *Chairman.*] Would not it be almost essential at the first revision by the magistrates that some cause should be assigned by the magistrate for every name struck off, otherwise how is the chairman to know, on his second revision, what reason has induced the magistrate to take off the name of any juror?—Of course, unless some one comes and complains that he was improperly struck off, the chairman will endorse what the magistrates have done. If he thinks he was improperly struck off, he can come and complain; but I never found any anxiety on the part of people to be jurors; on the contrary, they are very anxious to escape it.

2825. What process would you recommend for forming the panels?—When the jurors' book was made, I would propose to divide it into fifties. If there were 1,000 names on the book, there would be 20 fifties. I would compel the sheriff, in selecting his panel, to take an equal number of names out of each fifty, and so to go in rotation through the whole panel. That would obviate these anomalies that arise from the alphabetical arrangement, and it would make it certain that the panel would be gone through in order.

2826. You would let him select any name he pleased out of each fifty?—I would.

2827. He would have to exhaust the fifty before he called a juror the second time?—He could not call any juror a second time until he had called all the book. You must allow some little discretion. A sheriff may know that a man is dead, or that he has left the country, therefore you cannot safely direct that he must summon them in a particular order, such as the alphabetical order; you must leave him some little latitude. I would leave him as little as possible, and I would say that in selecting his panel he should take, as nearly as might be, an equal number of names from each fifty on the list. Then there would be no going out of his way to select any particular persons.

2828. Would not that still leave to the sheriff the power, if he happened to know that a particular class of cases were coming on for trial at the next assizes, to select his panel accordingly?—I scarcely think it would. I do not think it would. I can only say that I do not know of such things having occurred.

2829. That is a plan which you propose in substitution for the selection in alphabetical order?—Yes.

2830. Have you any suggestion to make as to returning jurors for quarter sessions?—I have heard sub-sheriffs complain very much of the hardship upon jurors, that for the quarter sessions, where there is very little business, they are obliged to summon men from the remotest ends of the county, because they happen to be the next in alphabetical order. They ought to have a discretion in the case of summoning jurors for quarter sessions.

2831. *Mr. Downing.*] That is provided for in the Act we are now discussing. He cannot go out of the district?—I know the sub-sheriff of the county of Down told me that he was obliged to summon persons a long way off. Perhaps if he had the discretion of summoning a man within two or three miles of the town, that would be quite enough.

2832. That is an exceptional case?—Yes.

2833. *Chairman.*] In general would not the necessity of the case be met by the provision in the present Act, that jurors for quarter sessions should be only summoned from that quarter sessions district?—Yes, I think so.

2834. Do you consider that there is any very pressing necessity for a temporary measure, pending a reconsideration of the whole question?—I think any measure that is to be framed ought to be a very well-considered measure, and to be a permanent measure, and I think there ought to to be a temporary measure until that can be done.

2835. What would you suggest as to that?—I cannot suggest anything as a temporary measure, except authorising the sheriff not to summon any persons who are illiterate, and so on; that is the only suggestion I can make as to a temporary measure.

2836. Would you doubt whether a mere raising of the qualification would be sufficient?—As I said before, if you raise the qualification to such an extent as to make it quite certain that you would get no bad jurors, then you would raise it to such an extent that you would not have enough of jurors. I think there would be a great deal of difficulty about that.

2837. Did you have an opportunity of observing whether the juries were better when there were a considerable number of jurors from towns?—Yes, decidedly; the jurors from towns are always better; they are more intelligent men, though they are rated lower; shopkeepers, and people of that kind, who are accustomed to business, are much more intelligent jurors than a man who has been all his life long sowing potatoes and that sort of thing.

2838. In Clause 1 of the 4th Schedule, the rating qualification is 20 *l.* annual value in the country and 12 *l.* in towns?—Yes.

2839. Would you be disposed to retain that 12 *l.* town qualification?—I cannot speak as to figures,

Right Hon. *J. A. Lawson.*

19 May 1873.

figures, for I have not the statistics. I only know that you may go safely lower for men in towns as compared with what you can in the country.

2840. From your general knowledge of the country, you would be of opinion that a man rated at 12 *l.* in a town, would probably be superior in intelligence to a 20 *l.* farmer?—Decidedly. You can form very little conception of what a 20 *l.* farmer in the county of Antrim is, unless you saw him.

2841. I believe you have given some attention to the question of unanimity of jurors?—I really have not given very much attention to it. I have been rather in favour of taking the majority, but I do not think public opinion seems to be ripe for that yet. I can only say whatever the law in England is, I hope we shall have the same in Ireland upon that subject.

2842. It has been suggested here that the Crown or the prisoner should have the power of requiring a special jury in criminal cases; what is your view of that?—I do not see much objection to it. The Crown now, if they think fit by removing a case on certiorari, can get a special jury; at least in some cases.

2843. Mr. *Attorney General.*] That is only in misdemeanours?—Yes; I do not see why they should not have the power of getting a special jury in any case.

2844. You have given us very strong evidence indeed on the subject of the class of persons who, taking your circuit through, appeared before you. I will take it for the purpose of this question, that no doubt the qualification is low; but, as I read that 5th section, every man, whether highly or lowly qualified, between 21 and 60 years of age, who is rated at a certain sum, is liable to serve?—Yes.

2845. Can you account for the fact that the persons who formerly used to serve, and who were intelligent, and who, I presume, in point of rating, were qualified under the new Act, did not present themselves?—The fact is, the jurors' book of Antrim contains 7,836 names; the sheriff on his panel, a large panel, returned 339 names, and then, of course, it so happened that the great majority of those were small farmers.

2846. *Chairman.*] You stated that the jurors' book contained 7,836 names?—Yes.

2847. It appears from a return the Committee have before them that on the average of the last three years the book contained 5,285 names; the new Act undoubtedly admitted a great number of new jurors?—Yes.

2848. But, probably, the increase would have been much greater if the Act had not operated also in striking off names of a number of jurors who were on the book?—Yes.

2849. That must have been the operation of the Act in the county Antrim?—Yes.

2850. Mr. *Attorney General.*] One would treat anything you say with the greatest respect. I wanted to gather from you, upon what ground, and I have no doubt you have a good one, you put it. I assume competent and incompetent existing, and both being alike qualified under the Act; how do you account for it, if you can account for it, that the incompetent alone appear to have attended?—I can only account for it by there being a great number of small holders in that county, and they being the vast proportion, the others did not turn up.

2851. Mr. *Bourke.*] Under the new Act there is no power of selection. You think that the intelligence of the jurors, generally, so far as you could observe, was not so great under the new system as under the old. Would you attribute that absence of intelligence so much to the absence of the power of selection, or would you attribute it to the non-appearance of those persons who were bound to appear under the old system, but who did not make their appearance under the new?—I attribute it to the absence of the power of selection. If the sheriff had the power of selection he would not have returned a man rated at 20 *l.* per year.

2852. If under the new system you would have had exactly the same system as under the old, if you had not the power of selection, you would have just as bad jurors under the old as under the new?—You would not have quite as bad, because, I suppose, the qualification is lower now.

2853. Mr. *Attorney General.*] The old jurors' book being 5,285, and the new jurors' book being 7,836, what I understand the honourable Member to mean is, that if all the 5,285 had been summoned as all the 7,836 are now summoned, you might have had pretty nearly as bad a jury?—Yes.

2854. Of course, under the former system, it is of course quite true the sheriff knew who the good and experienced jurors were, and he used to summon them?—Yes.

2855. How do you account for this, that nevertheless, though you say they were unintelligent, yet you have no reason to be dissatisfied with the results?—I think there were always one or two men of intelligence on each jury; and where there is no prejudice or bias swaying them, they generally go by the feeling of the most intelligent.

2856. I do not know whether it has ever happened to you, possibly not; did it ever happen to you to be present at an assize, either in Wales or in some of the more purely agricultural counties of England?—No.

2857. You cannot compare the amount of intelligence which we put up with in Wales and in the agricultural counties of England with what you have to put up with on the North Eastern Circuit?—No, I cannot.

2858. Colonel *Wilson Patten.*] Did your remark on the want of intelligence on the part of jurors apply to all the places on your circuit?—Yes, very much.

2859. You thought at all those places it was a want of intelligence on the part of jurors that rendered it necessary to alter the present law?—Yes.

2860. Do you think that any power should be given to the judge or the chairman of quarter sessions to tell a juryman to stand by for any other than statutory reasons?—I do not think there should be any new power conferred on the judge or chairman in that respect.

2861. With regard to the objection you have just stated, that in an alphabetical system it often happens that two or three men of a firm may serve on the same jury; would not you allow the judge, or chairman of quarter sessions, to interpose in such a case?—The judge always has a power of saying he will not fine a man under such circumstances for not attending.

2862. Is it not possible that if there was any corrupt motive, it might be necessary to oblige him

Right Hon. *J. A. Lawson.*

19 May 1873.

him to stand by?—In a Crown case the Crown Solicitor has power to tell a man to stand by; he does exercise it, and that is sufficient, I think.

2863. You would object to anything that prevented a judge from telling a man to stand by if he knew that there were two or three members of the same family on the jury, or three members of the same firm?—I do not think it is a matter for the judge to deal with at all.

2864. Would you leave that to the discretion of the judge?—I would.

2865. Mr. *Bruen.*] Do you think that in the circuits you went, you remarked a great amount of want of independence in the jury?—I did not see a want of independence, but a want of education and intelligence; the northern people are generally very independent.

2866. So that the experience you derived was derived from a part of the country in which you might expect a favourable result?—Yes, certainly; I would expect a much more favourable result there than in any other part of the country.

2867. Do you testify to the general joy and rejoicing in Ireland which some witnesses here have spoken of, in consequence of the abolition of the sheriff's power of selection?—I never heard of anything of the kind.

2868. That satisfaction was attributed to the idea that juries were packed, by the sub-sheriff, I suppose; do you think there was any suspicion in the public mind that that packing of juries, if I may so call it, was produced rather by the power of the Crown applied through the Crown Solicitor?—The complaints I have been in the habit of hearing were of the Crown Solicitor telling the people to stand by, whom he ought not to tell to stand by; that is the way it has been said that juries were packed. I think that complaints about the sheriff, in my experience, have been very rare.

2869. Under the new system of alphabetical selection, is it not much more necessary for the Crown Solicitor to exercise that power of calling upon jurors to stand aside, than under the old system?—Yes, he must exercise it, and does exercise it now, to a greater extent than I ever saw before; because, on the very view of a juror, many of them, the Crown Solicitor would not feel himself justified in letting him try a serious case. I have seen more jurors made to stand aside in the last circuit than I used to see before; in truth, summoning men of that kind is summoning them there almost for the purpose of telling them to stand aside.

2870. In the exercise of the power of revising the books, which you recommend to be placed in the hands of the justices, and also in the hands of the chairman, you would give to both of those courts power to strike the names of men off the jurors' list who, in the opinion of the court, were unfit to serve, without actually stating the reason?—Certainly I would.

2871. The justices acting in a petty sessions district, I suppose, would be more likely to have a personal knowledge of the jurors on the jurors' list, than the chairman of quarter sessions?—Certainly, the revision before the chairman of quarter sessions under his act must be a very defective one, because he cannot know as the justices at petty sessions would know the men in his own district.

2872. The previous revision by the justices would lighten the duties of a chairman very much?—It would.

2873. And consequently it would be likely to save expense to the county?—Yes.

2874. There has been a suggestion made by one of the witnesses here, that the number of challenges which the prisoner has now a right to exercise should be reduced; are you of opinion that the prisoner's right of challenge should be reduced?—No, I am not. I should not alter the law in that respect.

2875. Upon the whole, you are of opinion that it is absolutely necessary to leave in some officer a discretionary power of selection, to some degree in forming the jury panels?—I think so.

2876. Sir *A. Hervey-Bruce* [?] Sir *A. Hhennerhassett.*] You said you would propose a diversity of qualifications; I do not quite understand that?—If you refer to the Bill of Sir John Coleridge, you will find in the earlier sections a great variety of qualifications; in the first three clauses.

2877. Do you remember the juries in Kerry under the old system?—No, I never went circuit in Kerry.

2878. Was there any great difference of degrees of incompetency in the juries in the counties you went into?—No, they were all pretty much the same, I think.

2879. The general result was that you had a class of jurors who could not read or write?—Many of them.

2880. So that you had a difficulty in getting a foreman?—Yes.

2881. Mr. *Downing.*] I believe you had not very much practice in criminal business at the bar?—Yes, I had a great deal.

2882. Before you were Attorney General?—Yes; I was Crown Prosecutor of my own circuit for a great number of years.

2883. When were you Attorney General?—I cannot remember those dates.

2884. It is a thing which people do generally remember?—I do not remember it.

2885. You were satisfied with the verdicts returned on the last circuit?—I have stated so.

2886. And there were party trials at Belfast of a very angry character?—Yes, I have stated I thought the verdicts on the whole were satisfactory, and such as I approved of.

2887. You consider that that they were a bad class of jurors, because they were illiterate?—Yes, they were ignorant, illiterate, and uneducated men.

2888. If a provision were made to get rid of illiterate jurors, that objection would fade away?—It would be a very great improvement.

2889. Would you draw any distinction between a man who cannot read and a man who cannot write?—I declare, I think a man is not fit to be on a jury, who cannot both read and write.

2890. Have you looked at the returns for county Antrim, with regard to the number of jurors?—No, I have not had the advantage of seeing any of those returns. I have heard of such things, but I have not seen them.

2891. You will find that in the year 1870, there were 6,090 jurors returned for the county of Antrim; the number, as you stated correctly for 1873, was 7,836; the increase there was not very much?—No.

2892. You had 339 on the panel?—That is so, I am informed.

2893. Did I understand you to say, that on all the

Right Hon. *J. A. Lawson.*

19 May 1873.

the juries you found one or two intelligent men?—Yes, always; I know the look of an intelligent man on a jury very well; there were always a couple of men to whom I could direct my observations with the certainty that they would understand what I was saying.

2894. From your experience as a judge and at the bar, did not you find that one or two intelligent men, generally speaking, led the others?—Indeed they do, unless there is some bias or prejudice.

2895. If there were not an intelligent man or two on the jury, the jury would take the judge's direction, generally speaking?—They would not understand a judge's direction if they were that kind of men.

2896. If they were all illiterate?—Yes.

2897. Did you ever bring in a Bill yourself to amend the jury laws?—I do not think I ever did. I do not remember it.

2898. Were you not Attorney General when that Act was brought in (*handing same to his Lordship*); in 1866, I think you were Attorney General; I think you went out in July 1866?—I forget.

2899. We may take it for granted you were Attorney General?—Of course, those are all public facts which anyone can inform themselves of, but you cannot expect me to recollect the date at which I became Attorney General.

2900. Were you always of opinion that the alphabetical order was a bad one?—I do not know whether I was or not.

2901. I find in this Bill, brought in by you in 1866, that the alphabetical system is one of the clauses in your Bill; Clause 13?—I have no recollection of anything of the kind.

2902. If you brought in the Bill in 1866, you must then have been of opinion that the alphabetical order——?—I decline to answer those sort of questions.

2903. *Chairman.*] The Committee do not wish to press you on any subject you do not like to answer, but I think there would be some little misapprehension probably if the examination were to stop exactly where it is. If you will allow me, I will just ask you for a few words of explanation. I have had an opportunity of looking at the Bill which you brought in when you were Attorney General, as to the mode of formation of the panel for the jury-book. The system which you appear to have adopted was this: those were the words of your clause, "Such sheriff or other officer shall select, as far as may be practicable, the names of such persons only as shall not have been summoned, or shall not have attended as jurors for the longest period before the time of such selection." You do not appear to have adopted the alphabetical mode of selection which is adopted in the present Act. I want to ask you whether that principle which you adopt would not practically have taken away from the sheriff all power of selecting at his discretion?—It is very hard for me to answer without seeing the Bill. The thing has passed altogether from my memory.

2904. Would not this have been the effect; supposing the sheriff, in selecting his first panel, had passed over the name of So-and-so, as in his opinion an unfit person. Suppose, in selecting his second panel, he had again passed him over, would not the effect of that clause in your Bill have been to have left the last panel entirely composed, or almost exclusively composed, of persons who had been passed over for some cause upon previous panels?—Will you allow me to look at the clause? (*The Act was handed to his Lordship.*) You are to return the names of such persons only "as shall not have been summoned, or shall not have been appointed, as jurors for the longest period before the time of such selection;" that was for the purpose of not summoning the same man over again, I suppose.

2905. If you actually compel him to summon every juror who has not been summoned before, it does in practice, does it not, take away all discretion in the matter?—I think it would leave him such a discretion as was given in Sir John Coleridge's Bill; that is, that he might summon persons, but he must summon them in rotation.

2906. He must exhaust the book?—Yes, of course he must. Is there anything about alphabetical arrangement in this Bill.

2907. Mr. *Downing.*] So far as regards the list being returned and settled by the clerk of the peace?—I was quite misled by the question. I understood that this Bill contained a statement that the jurors were to be summoned by the sheriff in alphabetical order; that appears now not to be the case.

2908. I did not say one word as to the sheriff; you would give a power to the justices at the petty sessions to revise the list?—Yes.

2909. You are aware that they have that power up to the recent Act?—Yes.

2910. Do you think that people have that confidence in the justices of petty sessions that they would be satisfied with their selection?—I answer matters from my own knowledge; I do not answer questions of that kind, whether people have confidence or not; I know nothing about it.

2911. Do you not think it is desirable and necessary that people should have confidence in the administration of the law?—I think it is.

2912. If you go to a tribunal ——?—I really must say to the Chairman, I have not come here to argue with you, or any other Member; I have come to give any information in my power, but I decline any argument; put any question, and I will answer it.

2913. Do not you believe that the people of Ireland have much more confidence in the chairman of quarter sessions than in the magistrates?—I do not.

2914. You said you did not think that the chairman would have the means of revising the lists properly; supposing that the clerk of the poor law union, the rate collector, and the other barony officers were in attendance on the chairman, and that he was obliged to read each name upon the list, and to ask if there was any objection, do not you think that then he would have sufficient information to revise the list properly?—No; I do not think he would have the same information as the magistrates in the district would have.

2915. You would give him a power, even in their revision, to revise further?—Certainly.

2916. You said you thought there ought to be proper notice of the lists published, so as to enable parties to come and object; have you read the precept which is in the very Act we are now dealing with; the precept in that Act is compulsory on the clerk of the peace: "the said clerk of the peace to cause a sufficient number

Right Hon. *J. A. Lawson.*

19 May 1873.

ber of copies of the said list to be printed, published, and posted within the barony for which the said list shall have been prepared;" so that you see this Act provides for that very difficulty which struck you?—So much the better.

2917. You also gave an instance of how this alphabetical order interfered with the administration of justice, by saying that parties were summoned under the letter "M," and that the sheriff made another for himself "Mc"; that, of course, can be easily rectified, and will be for the future; there was a challenge to that?—Yes.

2918. You disallowed the challenge?—Yes.

2919. There was no failure of justice there?—No.

2920. Now that it is known that the names must be alphabetically on the panel, that will not arise again?—I cannot tell whether it will arise or not.

2921. You have been, I think, very often judge in the county of Monaghan; you have gone circuit?—I have gone the north-east circuit several times.

2922. I think you were on circuit when the panel there was quashed?—I was not in the Crown Court at all I never sat in the Crown Court at Monaghan.

2923. Have you ever known a challenge to the array succeed but that one in Monaghan?—I do not remember any other.

2924. It is a very difficult thing, in fact, to establish corruption or want of impartiality in the sheriffs on an inquiry of that kind?—I suppose it is, especially if it does not exist.

2925. Mr. *Heron.*] In reference to the last north-eastern circuit, do you know how many cases there are in which applications have been made for new trials, on the ground either of misconduct of the jury, or the verdict being against evidence?—I do not know; I was principally in the Crown Court on the last circuit. I did not try the records.

2926. The last assizes, as we know, were the heaviest?—Yes; but I was exclusively engaged in the criminal business.

2927. On the whole the trial of those party cases in Belfast was satisfactory as regards the convictions?—I have said so; I have said that I find no fault with anything the juries have done

2928. In reference to your plan of selection by fifties, did you intend that ultimately the whole of the jurors' book should be gone through in that way, so that every one should serve?—I do distinctly.

2929. Therefore, in that way the sheriff, although to a limited extent he may be said to have the power of selection, yet ultimately he must call the entire jurors' book?—Yes, and in my opinion if the jurors' book is properly revised beforehand by striking off improper persons, that is quite sufficient.

2930. Supposing there to be a proper jurors' book; I will read you this passage from Bentham, and ask you do you agree with it. It is section 7 on Jury Trial, "By whom should the members of a jury be appointed. A. By no man, but by fortune. Man has sinister interests; fortune has no sinister interests. Under man's appointment justice would have no even chance; under fortune's appointment she would have an even chance, and that is the best chance that can be given to her"?—What is your question on that?

2931. Do you consider the entire jurors' book should be ultimately exhausted; do you think that they should be taken from it by chance, or alphabetical selection, or by the selection of the sheriff?—I have given you my answer about that already; I do not know that I can give you any other. I cannot give an opinion in a moment upon a passage in Bentham which I have not seen for a long time.

2932. *The O'Donoghue.*] I think I understood you to say that you had more cases at Belfast than were tried on the whole of the home circuit?—I should think very likely.

2933. Was that owing to any exceptional circumstances?—Yes, very exceptional circumstances.

2934. It would not be the general rule, I suppose?—As a general rule, I think there is more business in Belfast, both civil and criminal, than on some circuits.

2935. I understood you to approve of taking away from the sheriff the power he had under the old law of selecting the jury?—If you give it to another person I approve of it.

2936. You suggested that no one should be struck off without hearing why he was considered incompetent, and without having any opportunity of objecting to his removal from the list?—Yes; I said that any one who objected to his removal from the list should have the right to do so; he should come before the chairman and ask to be reinstated.

2937. That is a very different think, is it not, from the old system, when the sheriff decided in his private room, at his pleasure, or on what might be mere gossip, as to who would be the jurors?—It is different.

2938. Would not this proposed revision throw upon all who wish to serve as jurors the necessity of attending this revision, as frivolous or groundless charges of incompetence might be brought against them?—I do not think so.

2939. Do you not think it possible that frivolous charges might be brought?—Indeed I do not.

2940. You think that is impossible?—I do.

2941. That men cannot be mistaken?—I do not think anyone has an interest in bringing frivolous charges, and therefore I do not think they would be likely to bring them.

2942. You would not suggest that it should be the duty of some public officer to see that no one was struck off on charges of such a nature?—I think the thing ought to be done in the presence of the magistrates, and of the proper authorities.

2943. Would it not be very inconvenient for people to attend these revisions twice in the year?—I did not say twice in the year; according to my system, it would be only once in the year. I would make the jurors' book last for two years.

2944. I thought you said the assisting barrister was to have the power?—Of course no one need to attend the court unless they have been aggrieved by what has been done below, and then they can come and complain.

2945. Would you say, from your experience as a judge, that there is a great prevalence of ordinary crime in Ireland, or the contrary?—I think Ireland is reasonably free from what you call ordinary crime. I think, having regard to its population and all that, it is very favourable.

2946. Those who say there is sympathy in Ireland

Right Hon. *J. A. Lawson.*

19 May 1873.

Ireland with crime, so far as you know, have no grounds for such a statement, and sympathy with crime cannot be urged as a disqualification against the new class of jurors created by this Act?—I am not prepared to answer that question at all.

2947. You admit there is little ordinary crime in Ireland, and no grounds, therefore, for those who say there is sympathy with crime?—I do not think there is any sympathy with ordinary crime, but there is often sympathy with extraordinary crime.

2948. You have been on the bench four years?—I think so.

2949. Have you tried any persons for agrarian crimes?—I generally am sent the Northern Circuit. I do not think there is much agrarian crime there; I do not remember any.

2950. These cases are the great exceptions, are they not?—Yes.

2951. You would not frame a law that it might deal, according to the opinion of some people, better with exceptional cases?—I would frame a law for the general benefit of the community.

2952. Mr. *Herbert.*] Do you think it is true, or would it be true, if it were stated here that the failure of this Act arose from the respectable part of the jury on the panel remaining away from the court?—I think not at all; as I have said already, they formed such an insignificant proportion, those who were on the panel before me, that their attendance could make no sensible difference.

2953. How many jurors did you say there were in the County Antrim?—I think there were 7,600 on the jurors' book, and that there was a panel of 339.

2954. How many jurors do you think would be sufficient for a county of that size?—For the jurors' book?

2955. Yes; for the jurors' book for the whole county?—I should think that a thousand jurors on a jurors' book would yield a sufficient number of jurors.

2956. How would you name those thousand jurors?—I have not proposed that at all.

2957. Can you suggest anything to the Committee for that; you would have a rating qualification as well as an educational one, I suppose.—I have suggested a rating qualification and other qualifications, but I have not suggested any machinery for reducing the jurors' book to a smaller number. I think, if it could be done, it might be a good thing to do.

2958 Do you think the higher the qualification goes the better class of jurors you get?—Generally speaking, I suppose so.

2959. Are you in favour of a ballot in Crown cases, subject afterwards to the power to stand by, by a challenge?—No, I am in favour of leaving the law as it is.

2960. Mr. *Bourke.*] With regard to the answer you gave as to the jurors generally under this Act, as far as you had experience of it, being of an inferior kind, and at the same time that the verdicts given before you were not altogether unsatisfactory, do you attribute that to the providential circumstance that there were two or three respectable jurors, generally speaking, on the jury?—Yes, I think so; I have stated that I think a couple of intelligent men generally led the other men; at the same time I do not think that any of those men, though they were uneducated, had the desire to go wrong.

2961. It was more from incapacity than unwillingness?—I think they were incapable of understanding nice distinctions and nice questions that arose.

2962. Assuming that the alphabetical system should be the basis of the jurors' book, you are of opinion that in some way or another you must have resort to a system of intelligent expurgation?—I think so.

2963. That is the great principle?—That is the principle I go upon; that I think there must be an expurgation of the list somewhere by someone having authority to remove persons who, from want of education, or otherwise, are manifestly unfit.

2964. Colonel *Vandeleur.*] Did you ever find any difficulty about the nomination of foremen with the juries?—I had a very good officer with me at Belfast; he always knew the man that ought to be foreman, and he always invited him down to the front, and said, "Mr. So-and-so, will you act as foreman?"

2965. Then it is not the custom that the first man named on the jury should stand as foreman?—It is the ordinary custom that the first man should serve as foreman, and so he would, in an ordinary way, but my officer, the clerk of the Crown, will pick out a man he knew was intelligent, and he will say, "You will be good enough to act as foreman."

2966. Would it be desirable to make that imperative that the clerk of the Crown should pick him out, or that the jurors should arrange it among themselves?—It is not necessary to legislate on that subject, it is always done; every man is quite willing to be relieved of the duty of acting as foreman.

2967. We have had evidence that in some cases in the southern circuits that the foreman could neither read nor write?—Yes. I should ask the officer did he think that man could read or write, and he would say no, and then he would ask another man to act.

2968. Did any question come before you on your circuit as to the legality of the grand jury presenting for the expenses of the sub sheriff under this Act?—I think there was some question about it.

2969. Was it your opinion that the grand jury had the right of presentment?—I think I told the grand jury so. I am not quite sure; but I have some recollection of that.

2970. Mr. *Bruen.*] The suggestion was made that, by the system of summoning the panels which you recommended the sheriff by summoning the best men first, would leave a residuum which he would be obliged to summon on the last panels before he began again; that is not at all necessary under your system, is it; the sheriff is not obliged to summon all the best men at once?—You mean under what I have now suggested.

2971. Yes?—No; I take it for granted the sheriff would, in the ordinary way, summon them as they were; he would take the first names out of each 50.

2972. He would probably take care to summon his panels in such a way that there should not be a residuum of incompetent jurors left for his last panel?—I assume that there would be no incompetent jurors, if there was a good system of revision.

2973. Even supposing that there were, it would not be necessary for the sheriff to leave them all to the last?—No.

2974. He

Right Hon. *J. A. Lawson.*

19 May 1873.

2974. He would very easily take care to summon some of those who had not experience?—The sub-sheriffs are not fond of incurring any responsibility, and I think under that system they would summon the men as they found them; they would not go out of their way to do anything else.

2975. *Chairman.*] If it is made incumbent on the sheriff to summon every man on the jurors' book who has not served before, there is no use, is there, in passing over a man for any cause affecting his character or intelligence?—No.

2976. Because he must go sooner or later?—Yes, he must go through the whole book.

2977. So that the power of selection, as now understood, is practically given up?—Practically, and ought to be given up, I think, if there is a proper expurgation of the list originally; that is my idea.

The Right Honourable MICHAEL MORRIS, called in; and Examined.

Right Hon. *M. Morris.*

2978. *Chairman.*] YOU are a Judge of the Court of Common Pleas, in Ireland?—Yes.

2979. From what time?—Easter Term 1867; that is six years past.

2980. What circuit did you go last assizes?—I went the Connaught Circuit. I have gone every circuit in Ireland.

2981. Your experience of the present Act is derived from the Connaught Circuit?—My experience of the present Act is as large as any judge's, because I went the Connaught Circuit, and I also sat at the last Commission court for the county and city of Dublin, under the new Act.

2982. What counties are included in the Connaught Circuit?—The whole province of Connaught, which, probably, English gentlemen may not exactly remember. It includes Leitrim, Sligo, Roscommon, Mayo and Galway.

2983. Will you state what opinion you have formed of the operation of the Act?—A very bad opinion.

2984. In what respect?—From the paralysis, in my opinion, of the administration of law, either in the civil court or the criminal court.

2985. From the inferior character of the juries?—From the inferior character of the juries, and from the extraordinary change that had taken place under the system of the new Act from what had been. I was on the Connaught Circuit for 32 circuits as a practising barrister, and of late years, I may take the liberty of saying, did the largest business upon it. The contrast was the more remarkable to me, being so intimately acquainted with the circuit. I am myself a native of the county of Galway, and knew most of the jurors personally. In that way I consider I had peculiar opportunity of perceiving the contrast.

2986. In what respect did you consider the late juries deficient?—In intelligence and position.

2987. Did the jurors appear to be of a very low class?—In some places most extraordinarily so. In the county of Roscommon, the honourable Member for which county is one of this Committee, the sub-sheriff informed me that he had been 29½ years sub-sheriff, which I myself knew to be the fact, and that a particular jury which was trying a case there, he was ready to declare he had never seen before in his life, to his knowledge. He had never seen one of them. He is a very large farmer, and, I thought, a man who knew almost everybody in the county. I think they must have been from a very peculiar class. I tried a case there, an action of ejectment brought by the present Member for the county of Roscommon, to which there was not a shadow of defence that I could perceive, except substantially that no landlord ought to bring ejectment now-a-days. It was against a lady of position, so that the element of poor person did not enter into it at all. She was a lady of position equal to his own. The jury found a verdict for the defendant; or rather, they gave in the strange verdict, "We will find no verdict for the plaintiff." I asked them why would they find no verdict for the plaintiff; they said they were not satisfied of the service of the notice to quit. I asked them, "Are you satisfied that it was served on Thomas McDermott?" the name of one of the defendants. They said, "No." "Why," said I, "he was examined here himself, and admitted that it was." They had a conference then, rather puzzled at that; and then they said they would find the service on him, but apparently on no other person. I had to take the verdict. There was an application made to the Court of Queen's Bench to set it aside, and they set it aside without hearing counsel for The O'Conor Don. It will have to go to a new trial. I may say that I was informed by the registrar of Baron Deasy, my colleague, I think it was from him or some officer, that the jury had stated that they would not find any verdict for the plaintiff, because it was suggested that I should, what is called in law, direct a verdict; and, as I understood, they said that, knowing me for some time, they would have felt rather unpleasant if I had ordered them to find a verdict for the plaintiff, and they certainly would not have done it. I was civil judge in Roscommon. In the county of Sligo there was a very heavy criminal calendar. Except in one or two trifling cases, there was either an acquittal or a disagreement.

2988. During the whole assizes?—Yes; I think there were nearly 20 cases, and there were only two or three convictions. I believe some person was foolish enough to plead guilty, not seeing what a chance he would have had.

2989. This is in County Sligo?—Yes; in County Leitrim Baron Deasy was in the Criminal Court. In the first case tried before him the jury convicted the prisoner. It was in some way connected with an assault on the police. The judge did that which sometimes is done where it may be thought right. He said he entirely approved of the verdict, and in the presence of the jury he sentenced the man to, I think, 12 months imprisonment. The next morning he and I were at breakfast at the judge's lodgings, when five of the jury appeared to state that they had not agreed at all, and that they were prepared to make a declaration of that fact. They did make a declaration of the fact, and the man was released by the executive. In Mayo many of the jury were only Irish-speaking people, and there

Right Hon. *M. Morris.*

19 May 1873.

there were continual observations from the gallery in Irish, which I have the rather unusual advantage of understanding a little. There the matter was not very bad, because I excused a great number, I believe, without any strict right; but as the Attorney General for England said, as is quite common with the judge, excusing a man from the necessity of the case. We had one jury trying a rather important case; the jury retired; they came back in 5 or 10 minutes, and asked me, would it make any difference if one of them had not been sworn at all? I asked the Clerk of the Crown how such a miscarriage could have taken place; he said no miscarriage had taken place. "We called over the names of the 12 persons whom he had sworn," and it appeared that one of them had gone into a far-off gallery; he thought he had a better view there I suppose, and that some other man had gone into the jury box and taken his seat there. He may have offered an excellent opinion on the whole thing in the jury-room for aught I know, but that caused a mis-trial in that case. In my own county, Galway, there was a most marvellous change, particularly in the special jury. We were rather proud of the special jury of the county Galway, and in all the courts their character stood A 1, I may say. It was composed principally of magistrates, and persons at all events in that position. I have the special jury panel in my pocket, and having an intimate acquaintance with the people, I can say there is only about a fourth of the special jury panel of the class that used to be there. Some miscarriages took place, I believe, in the Crown Court, but I was not the Crown judge. A leading article in the "Times," upon one of these miscarriages, alluded to me as being the judge; I was not in the court at all; however, that is not very unusual in an English paper. The comments were very strong about it. I am giving the Committee my own practical experience of a few instances only, but I think they are a pretty good sample.

2990. You mentioned that in county Sligo the verdicts were almost all acquittals?—Disagreements principally. Some cases were so plain, that of course there was an agreement to disagree.

2991. I understand you to have been dissatisfied with a great number of those verdicts?—Principally with non-verdicts, most distinctly. The thing was so plain, that the mere recital of it was sufficient.

2992. They were clear cases?—Some of them; I do not give any names, because it would not be right.

2993. You consider that in the county Sligo, there was a miscarriage of justice?—Most distinctly; in an experience of 32 circuits as a barrister, and 12 as a judge, the most extraordinary I ever saw or could have imagined; in fact, there was no administration of the law at all, and in addition to that, there was a great deal of what I think is very dangerous; the whole thing being turned into a burlesque; so many grotesque incidents occurred that really there was no possibility of even pretending to keep decorum; the thing had reached such a stage, and so many absurd incidents arose.

2994. There always were good stories about juries even under the old system?—Yes, there were occasionally good stories, but now it is all one good story; a consecutive good story.

2995. As to the Galway special jury panel, I think you said about a fourth of the special jury who were on the panel, were on it now?—Of the class. I had no special jury case to try, but I got the panel from the sheriff, which I have in my pocket, as I considered it a curiosity, from the extraordinary incongruity of the persons upon it. I was informed, that a gentleman and his coachman who drove him to Sligo, were both upon the panel; which would create a difficulty about someone looking after the horses.

2996. The qualification is 50 *l.*?—No, 20 *l.*

2997. For the special jury panel?—I am speaking of a Sligo common jury panel. In Roscommon, I think it was, a gentleman and his butler were on the panel. I am aware that the tipstaff of my brother Lawson is upon the special jury panel in Dublin for the Probate Court, where men of superior intelligence are required for will cases, &c. At the Commission Court in Dublin, the variety of persons who appeared to remonstrate against being put on the panel, and the roars of laughter at the exhibitions really in my mind were very indecorous. The hall porter of the Hibernian Hotel made a strong case, I thought. A soldier appeared in uniform; different clerks in some of the law offices appeared; one came from the Bankruptcy Court, and intimated to me that all the bankrupts would make away if he did not get off, and that sort of thing took place. I had some very important cases to try there; several of the jury were challenged by the prisoner, or by those advising him, with great discretion. Any man who appeared to have a good coat was challenged. So few, comparatively, had them, that the thing became, as a gentleman facetiously remarked, rather a challenge of the array. All these incidents led my mind, not as a matter of opinion, but as a matter of clear induction from recognised facts, to the opinion that there must be, at all events, a great reformation in the Act if there is to be any administration of law at all, either for property or person.

2998. Must not a good many of the cases to which you refer have arisen from an insufficient revision of the list?—I suppose so, but I do not think you will ever have any efficient revision; you never, in my mind, will have a revision in which there is not some person personally interested. There is what is called a revision of voters now, in which you would think persons would take much more interest than in being on a jury, because they dislike being on a jury, and they like having a vote. The revision of voters is a mere form unless there are political parties watching it, and each striking off persons who have no right to be on it on the opposite side. In the case of jurors it is nobody's business, and accordingly nobody will do it; I mean it is nobody's peculiar business.

2999. You do not think it could be made the business of the clerks of the unions?—I think it might be made their business to a certain extent; but I do not think it will be carried out, because they may incur some sort of odium in meddling, and they cannot incur any by letting the thing alone. It appears to me that was one of the grounds upon which a great many of these juries disagreed. Judge Lawson mentioned the juries on the north eastern circuit. I can make the same observation on the Connaught circuit. I think it was from want of intelligence and position adequate to make them not so amenable to the

Right Hon. *M. Morris.*

19 May 1873.

the friends of the persons they were trying that prevented them from doing their duty. Those persons are anxious never to do anything; by disagreeing and finding no verdict they disoblige nobody.

3000. You say the jurors do not wish to be on the list?—Distinctly they do not.

3001. Will they not come forward themselves to get their names struck off the list?—I think they might if there were sufficient notice given of it. I think that would be the best way by which it could be arrived at, that the persons would come forward themselves. There is a great objection in Ireland, a very natural one, to be on a jury, for you may incur a great deal of odium, a great deal of unpleasantness, and you never incur anything advantageous to yourself.

3002. That would be one way of improving the revision?—It would.

3003. To give sufficient notice to the juror that he was to be put on the list?—Yes, certainly.

3004. I do not know whether you wish to add anything as to what you saw of the operation of the Act?—Nothing occurs to me at the present moment. I have merely given this as a sample. I have delayed you so long in giving a sample of it, but probably other questions might bring to my recollection other anecdotes.

3005. Have you considered in what way the Act should be amended?—I do not adopt the principle of the Act; I mean one of the principles of it. I think there ought to be some power in somebody, if not of selecting, of excluding, at all events; and I think the alphabetical mode is open to every objection; I think it is even a bad mode of going by rotation; for, as has been already explained, it is well known that in some letters of the alphabet there will be very few names. In the south of Ireland the M and the O will predominate to a most extraordinary degree, and the end of it will be, that you will have a jury substantially consisting of persons of the same name. To such an extent has that gone, that in a somewhat remarkable case, that I dare say most people have heard of, "O'Keeffe *v.* Cullen," which is now on trial in the Court of Queen's Bench in Dublin, of the jury of 48 persons (that is the panel for the Queen's Bench), I observe in the newspapers that there were three gentlemen of rather the unusual name of Turbot upon it. I suppose they were brothers; one of them answered to his name, and the other two have been fined 100*l.* each. There were, I think, three persons of the name of Fitzsimons out of the 48; and considering the size of the county of Dublin, and the thousands of jurors who must be on it, that shows you exactly the absurd result which this alphabetical rota brings up, that three members of a wine merchant's firm should be selected out of 48, and that 48 selected out of thousands. The reason will be, that there will not be a great many persons whose names begin with the letter T, and accordingly being obliged to go A, B, C, D, and so on, the only person he meets with is Turbot; he begins again, until he comes to another Turbot, then he begins again and meets another Turbot, and it is a very fishy transaction at the end of it. The same applies to the Fitzsimons. All the gentlemen whose names begin with X, if there were any beginning with that letter, would be sure to be on the first panel; father, son, and grandson, and uncle, and nephew, and cousin, if there were five or six persons whose names begin with that letter; some Greek name, I suppose, would be the only patronymic.

3006. Even supposing these smaller inconveniences were got rid of, you object to the principle of selecting the panel from the book by chance?—I do.

3007. Do you approve of the old principle of selection?—I think it might be modified fairly, but I should like no change to have been made until there had been an Act passed in England. I object very strongly, as a general rule, to passing Acts of Parliament peculiarly for Ireland; if there is a jury system here, I should wish to see the same in Ireland. I stand up for the Attorney General's Bill. If it is a good Bill, apply it to Ireland, *mutatis mutandis*.

3008. The practice of selection did not prevail in England?—I thought it did, but I heard the Attorney General say it did not. He, of course, knows, and I do not pretend to know, never having studied the English system, though I think I am very well acquainted with the Irish mode. I thought it did; but if it did not, then have the English plan.

3009. Do not you think there were any objections to the practice of selection by the sub-sheriff?—In theory, it is obvious that there is; and accordingly, a theoretical writer has been cited by my friend here. I may say, all Bentham's views have not been carried out in practice; but, practically, I have no recollection of anything that called for or demanded a change. As I said, I went 32 circuits as a barrister; I think I may say I was in as large a *nisi prius* business in Dublin as any gentleman, and I had therefore, I think, as much acquaintance for the 25 years I was at the bar as anybody, and I never heard of any substantial objection to the panels.

3010. You do not think there was partiality?—I do not think so, distinctly; as a matter of opinion, of course.

3011. Do you think there was a suspicion, or a generally received suspicion?—I think there is a suspicion of everything nearly. I saw that an honourable Member in his place in Parliament suspected the formation of this very Committee. If you are to legislate for all the suspicions, I do not envy the legislator. Indeed, I do not envy him in many other respects, but certainly not in that.

3012. Do not you think it did any harm to the administration of justice, that it could be alleged that the selection of a jury panel was in the hands of the sub-sheriff, who might be a person of very decided political or party opinion?—I think it would be better if you could reach a state of optimism; but I am a disbeliever that you can ever reach such a stage in any matter in this world.

3013. Your opinion is that, practically, it did not do much harm?—As far as I can form an opinion upon anything, I am satisfied it did not, and I do not think you ought to sacrifice the ninety-nine cases in which it is doing a great deal of good to get rid of the suspicion in the hundredth case.

3014. Do you think it is more difficult to revert to that principle now, having once abandoned it?—I do; accordingly I would take the liberty of suggesting a compromise of views, that there should be an expurgation, or an exclusion by the sheriff of persons whom he did not think fit to go on the jury; which, in my opinion, would throw very

Right Hon. *M. Morris.*

19 May 1873.

very much greater responsibility upon him, make him very much more open to public opinion, and make it much more dangerous than the late power he had of mere selection. No man could complain of not being selected, but he could complain of being put out.

3015. Would you have an expurgation of the list by the sheriff?—I would.

3016. And make the remainder serve in rotation?—And make the remainder serve in rotation. I would have the sheriff have power of not calling or putting on his panel persons that he thinks right to exclude for good and wise reasons; subject to public opinion; subject to a challenge; subject to the animadversion of the judge, who, if a case were brought before him, and he thought justified to remark upon it, I think that would be quite sufficient, with the respectable body of gentlemen who now serve the office of sub-sheriff in Ireland. I have been through the 32 counties of Ireland as judge; I know most of the sub-sheriffs, and I can say, as to some of them, that in my opinion they are quite incorruptible, and the equals in social position, and in every way, not alone to the chairmen but of the judges, except in so far as you get official rank.

3017. That would be, practically, giving the revision of the list to the sub-sheriff, instead of to the chairman?—As to the revision by the chairman, I look upon it as a mere matter of form. The chairman signs his name to a lot of lists. What can he know about it? The chairman is very often a stranger.

3018. If it is only a form it had better be given up altogether?—I think so; I am a great opponent of mere forms which are supposed to be a guard, and which are really not.

3019. Have you heard Mr. Justice Lawson's suggestion of a preliminary revision by the magistrate?—Certainly; I think if there were to be any revision at all it should be by some one who knows something about it. I think it is generally a good thing to have it done by the person who understands it. The chairman knows very few people; the chairman would be only the machinery to carry out the views of persons who would be about; some officials. Then, possibly, or probably, it would be good to have an appeal to the chairman, as I heard suggested by Judge Lawson. It did not occur to me, but I heard him suggest it, and I agree it would be a good thing; that would be an appeal upon some particular case. I think, if you want to have any revision at all, you must have it done by the magistrates who know the people.

3020. The magistrates or the sub-sheriff?—I think by the magistrates. I do not think it would be a duty for the sub-sheriff at all. I think there is some confusion between the juror's book, which would be done at the revision and the panel which the sheriff takes from the jurors' book. They are two distinct things. I think the sheriff should take the panel from the jurors' book, but the jurors' book should be revised at the petty sessions.

3021. I understand you to be of opinion that, after the book had been as thoroughly expurgated as possible, it should be the duty of the sheriff to summon jurors from it in rotation?—In rotation, he having the power even still, from the jurors' book, of not summoning persons who he did not think ought to be summoned, and who may have remained on either from inadequate revision or from other causes, from having died or emigrated. In fact, I think the precept of the sheriff should follow this form, which I find in a Bill introduced in the year 1856, I presume by Mr. Justice Fitzgerald and Mr. Justice Keogh. If it was not by Mr. Justice Keogh, it was by Mr. Justice Fitzgerald, for it is by the Attorney General and the Solicitor General. This form of precept struck me as an admirable one, "That the sheriff shall be directed to return a sufficient number of the most competent persons named in the jurors' book, selecting, so far as practicable, but having regard to competence, such jurors as shall not have been summoned at preceding assizes;" that is, that he should go through the whole book, but selecting as far as practicable only competent persons. That Bill, in my opinion, hits the happy mean. As to the alphabetical plan, I would take the liberty of saying I do not see how it can stand at all. It appears to me to lead in such practical absurdities.

3022. Would you suggest the raising the qualification?—If there were the power of expurgation at the sessions, and also that the sheriff was not obliged to summon persons he knew to be incompetent, I would not care about raising the qualification, because, you observe, he would then be to a certain extent master of the position, and he need not summon the illiterate and ignorant people whom he would know, therefore there would be no necessity in that case of raising the qualification. Of course, if you do not do that, but you keep up either this alphabetical plan or some plan substantially the same, then, I say, raise the qualification.

3023. Sir *R. Blennerhassett.*] Would you keep the rating qualification only?—No; that is a matter which I intended by and bye to mention in detail. The other qualifications of the Act 3rd William the 4th, and the qualifications stated in Sir John Coleridge's Bill, should be left in, in addition to a mere rating qualification. You lose a very good class of jurors very often who cannot be rated at that. It appears to me, that there should be an opportunity given of having them. The question of qualification only arises if you get rid of the power of expurgation. In fact, the principle of the Bill, which I take exception to is, that it is a matter of indiscriminate machinery, that is my description of it. I put intelligence against indiscriminate machinery; I take my stand on intelligence, and any other body may take it upon indiscriminate machinery, in which you take in the halt, and the blind, and the lame, the imbecile, and the criminal, the incompetent, and all, as if it were some natural right of a man to be a juror.

3024. *Chairman.*] If you introduce any new qualifications the lists must be prepared by some other person than the clerk of the union, must it not?—The clerk of the peace would be the better person, I should say, to include the names of the other qualifications, such as the eldest sons of magistrates, the sons of baronets, and large merchants, and various other qualifications, which are in the 3 & 4 Will. 4, c. 91.

3025. I think you said you were not satisfied with the operation of the Act in Dublin?—No, decidedly not.

3026. Were you satisfied with the working of the old law in Dublin?—No, it was always more or less unsatisfactory in Dublin, and I think the interests of the rest of Ireland have been to some extent sacrificed towards repairing some obvious defects in Dublin. I never heard of

any

Right Hon. *M. Morris.*

19 May 1873.

any allegation against juries in the province of Connaught during the 32 circuits I went as barrister, in which I was engaged in almost every civil case; and as I said before, the pre-eminence, and intelligence, and position of a county Galway jury was a matter of history. Cases which had no connection with the county Galway were sent by the courts in Dublin, and by other courts, to be tried by a Galway jury; as having a great prestige the juries were upon their metal; it was known there was that prestige. I have seen cases in which a mixed jury has found a verdict that I believe could scarcely be attained in any other county in Ireland, under the same circumstances. I have the special jury panel, and I see a great number of farmers on it, a great number of men in Galway, who are rated at 300 *l.* or 400 *l.* a year, cannot speak English. I let off special jurors in Galway that could not speak English; one of them, I understand, pays 500 *l.* or 600 *l.* a year rent. I know one to pay 400 *l.* He appeared in court and addressed me, as the people all know me very well, and I know everybody, I believe I may say.

3027. Are there many persons in Galway or elsewhere, under 60 years of age, who cannot speak English?—There are a number of persons. I do not know whether they are jurors, but there are thousands of persons, under 60 years of age, who cannot speak English; I do not say jurors, but people. I remember in my younger days, in the place where my property lies, very few of my father's tenants at all spoke English. I believe about half of them do not speak it well at this moment. That is one reason why it appears to me to be plain that an indiscriminate machinery must end in a smash, as it has.

3028. Colonel *Wilson Patten.*] I do not quite understand that last answer. What do you mean by an indiscriminate machinery ending in a smash?—The plan of taking the jurors alphabetically, which is a mere piece of machinery; anybody might as well do it as the sheriff. It has ended in a smash. I applied that word to the machinery, because I considered at the last assizes I went, the greater portion of it was a legal smash.

3029. Did you consider that the failure of justice in the instances you have stated to the Committee arose entirely from want of intelligence on the part of jurors, or was there any perversity of disposition?—I think it arose principally from want of intelligence; not from any perversity of disposition, but from the class from which a great many of the jurors came. They did not want to make an enemy of anybody; they would be going to the next fair, and by not finding a verdict they did not make themselves unpopular with anybody. If they found a verdict they thought the friends of the prisoner might be at the next fair, and that they would not make it very pleasant for them, I suppose.

3030. Do you think that that feeling would be at all done away with or diminished if the qualification of the jurors was raised, so as to get another class?—Distinctly, there was a want of intelligence and a want of position, because a poor humble man who has to go back to a thatched house is much more afraid than a man who has to go back to a country town. We judges, who drive into the town and drive out, expect too much Spartan virtue from these jurors sometimes; a foolish thing to expect, I think.

3031. I think you stated that you had private property in county Galway?—Yes, all the property I have in the world is there.

3032. Has that led you to have knowledge of the circumstances of the people there?—Yes; I served the office of high sheriff myself, and sat on a grand jury before I practised at the bar.

3033. Can you state to the Committee on what qualification you think the county of Galway would furnish an intelligent jury?—I think scarcely any qualification that would not make it so meagre as that it would be really practically useless. There are men paying four, five, and six, and I believe eight hundred a year, who cannot speak English.

3034. Those are exceptions, I presume?—That man of 800 *l.* may be an exception, but there are a great many men of 100 *l.* a year, and if they are able to speak English they are illiterate.

3035. *The O'Donoghue.*] They are old men?—A good many old men. I believe it has occurred in a family, the old people can scarcely speak English, and the young people can scarcely speak Irish. I have tenants who fill that capacity. The old people scarcely understand their children, and the children scarcely understand them; such is the progress of education; I attribute the speaking of English to the National Schools.

3036. In the county of Galway the number would be sufficient to enable you to get a sufficient number of jurymen of rather a high qualification, would it not?—Yes, there are very large farmers there; it is a great grazing county. In that respect it would be different from the northern counties, because the northern counties are principally small farmers. We are, principally, very large farmers; men holding a thousand and two thousand acres, and you drop very soon from that to very small farmers.

3037. I think Leitrim is in your circuit?—Yes.

3038. Leitrim is a very small county?—It is not so small in area; it is a poor county.

3039. That would not stand a very high qualification?—No, it would not stand as high a qualification as Galway or Roscommon.

3040. Have you any knowledge of what a 30 *l.* qualification would give in County Leitrim?—No; you could get a return from the valuation office, and then it becomes a matter of fact. It is always better to have fact, and not mind the opinion.

3041. Do you believe that the intelligence of persons rated at 30 *l.* in Leitrim would be equal to the intelligence of the persons rated at 30 *l.* in Galway?—I do distinctly. I think their intelligence would be quite equal; with a great number their want of intelligence would be quite equal, probably.

3042. It has been stated before this Committee that if you raised the qualification very much there would be considerable danger of not having a sufficient number of jurymen to transact the business at the assizes and the quarter sessions?—I dare say; and that is one of the reasons why I say that your qualification mode of amending this Act of Parliament, in my opinion, never will meet the evil; if you raise it so high you will make the number so small that you cannot work, whereas there might be a great number of men rated at a small rate who would be intelligent people, and if some official had the power of calling them, I think it would be better.

Right Hon. *M. Morris.*

19 May 1873.

3043. That would only be the case in a small number of counties, I presume?—Yes; the *Act* of Parliament is a bed of *Procrustes*. Every county and everything is put under these schedules.

3044. Sir *R. Blennerhassett.*] A compound qualification would make some difference?—A slight difference.

3045. Colonel *Wilson Patten.*] Is it your opinion that under the peculiar circumstances you have stated, a temporary Act is necessary, so as to insure proper justice being administered at the next assizes?—Most decidedly.

3046. You think that it is necessary?—I think there ought to be a temporary Act; but I think it would be just as easy to pass a good Act at once, as pass a temporary Act. I see no difficulty in passing a general Act. A temporary Act is better than nothing.

3047. You ought to be acquainted with the forms it goes through in the House of Commons?—Yes, I believe I saw brought in a Bill when I was in the House, which, I think, passed all in one night.

3048. I believe that is an exceptional case?—Yes.

3049. *The O'Conor Don.*] A Jury Bill?—No.

Thursday, 22nd May 1873.

MEMBERS PRESENT:

Mr. Attorney General.	Mr. Arthur Henry Herbert.
Sir Rowland Blennerhassett.	Mr. Heron.
Mr. Bourke.	Mr. Charles Lewis.
Mr. Bruen.	The O'Conor Don.
Viscount Crichton.	The O'Donoghue.
Mr. Downing.	Colonel Wilson Patten.
Colonel Forde.	Colonel Vandeleur.
Marquis of Hartington.	

THE RIGHT HONOURABLE THE MARQUIS OF HARTINGTON, IN THE CHAIR.

The Right Honourable MICHAEL MORRIS, re-called; and further Examined.

Right Hon. *M. Morris.*

22 May 1873.

3050. Mr. *Bruen.*] THERE has been an opinion given to the Committee upon the mode of selecting the jury panels by the sub-sheriff after the first panel has been selected, that opinion seeming to imply that the sub-sheriff had still the selection, so long as he kept within the different letters of the alphabet; has any case come before you upon that point?—No case has come before me; but I know that it has been mooted as to whether, under this present Act, the sheriff is bound to take any A.'s, or whether he is bound to take the dictionary A.'s, which of course you are aware are quite different things; in other words, whether he can select anybody that he likes out of the letter A., or anybody he likes out of the letter B.; or whether he must select the first out of the letter A. and the first out of the letter B., and then again the second out of the letter A. and the second out of the letter B. I have heard it talked about, but no case has come before me about it. I believe that the intention obviously was that he should go through the dictionary A.'s, because the history of the Act would show that; for otherwise, what was sought for would not be carried out, namely, that he should be merely a piece of machinery in the doing of it; but if he had the selection in each letter it would give him a very wide discretion in some letters.

3051. In your opinion, without going very closely into the matter, you believe that it would be in accordance with the spirit of the Act that there should be no sort of discretion whatever left to the sheriff in the selection of his panels?—I believe that was the intention of the Juries Act upon which you have been questioning me. I have said that the question has arisen, whether that intention was exactly carried out, and whether he had not a discretion, provided he called a person from each letter in the alphabet; in other words, whether he was obliged to go to the A.'s, or whether he was obliged to go alphabetically, like a dictionary. I understand that Mr. Justice Fitzgerald in Cork, but I only know this by public report, rather threw out something about it. I do not know whether it came before him judicially or not. It did not come before me judicially; and where a thing does not come before me judicially, I always decline to offer any opinion about it.

3052. It is that rigid, mechanical form which is imposed upon the sub-sheriff to which you object?—Yes; I think he ought to have a discretion.

3053 I think you said you thought that the provision of the Bill, which was introduced in 1856 by Mr. Justice Fitzgerald when he was Attorney General, with regard to the precept to the sheriff, was one that you thought would meet the case?—Yes; I thought that that was the happy mean; it deprives him of the unlimited selection that he had up to the passing of this Juries Act, and it obliges him, substantially, to go through the whole of the jurors' book in rotation, selecting, as far as practicable, having regard to competency. I believe those are the words, and I think the words, "having regard to competency," ought always to be added on to every mode of selection; I also think that taking away from the sheriff the power of exclusion (which is all I ask to be left to him) of incompetent persons, largely increases the necessity for the Crown Solicitor, who is the mere official of the executive Government of the day, to order persons to stand aside, and I consider that that is a far more dangerous power, particularly from the popular point of view, than that of the sheriff, who is an officer not so immediately under the control of the executive Government, or rather, who ought not to be under their control at all. If you take away the power from the sheriff of expurgating incompetent persons, it necessarily increases the necessity of the Crown Solicitor ordering incompetent persons to stand aside; that, as I have said before, I think, is one objection. In the next place it seems rather a stupid way, I take the liberty of saying, of doing the thing, that you invite a number of persons to attend, and then you turn away a given number of them at once; persons who have been probably summoned from immense distances in some of those large counties, such as Cork, or my own county, which is next in point of size, and of course, I suppose, next in point of importance. Persons summoned from vast distances of 60 or 70 miles are summoned for the purpose of being sent off, by being ordered by the Crown Solicitor

Right Hon. *M. Morris.*

22 May 1873.

licitor to stand aside. If they are ignorant persons they ought never to have been there. It appears to me that I am not using too strong an expression when I say that it is a very stupid way of arriving at such a conclusion.

3054. It has been said that the confidence of the public has not been reposed in the system in which that power of selection existed; do you know any instance in which the confidence of the public has evidently been withheld under the present system?—I think that the confidence of a great portion of the public is being withheld from the system under the present Act. I think it behoves anybody who has any property, or thinks that he is an unpopular person for any reason, to look sharp now-a-days.

3055. A case has been mentioned to me by a gentleman in a letter, in which he says, "I think the following fact bears strongly on the case, and you may possibly consider it worth bringing before the Committee who will be appointed to consider this question. I am plaintiff in two actions at law, one of them involving a sum of 500 *l.*, and the other smaller. In both these cases I have written to my country and Dublin solicitors, saying that I think it would not be advisable to proceed to trial, on account of the incapacity of juries under the present system. Both said solicitors have written to me saying that they quite approved of my not going on with the actions at present." Do you think that that is a fair exposition of the want of confidence which appears to exist with regard to the present system?—The question is, should I be surprised to hear it. I have lived long enough to be surprised to hear nothing; but I think, in large commercial cases, I have heard eminent merchants, particularly from Belfast and places where there are important trials, complain very much as to the mode in which they would now be obliged to resort to a *special* jury under this new Act, in which, necessarily, a considerable number of the jurors would be persons wanting in adequate capacity to deal with heavy and important commercial questions. I do not like to pin myself to approving of any gentleman's dictum, and I suppose you have got that from some gentleman who sends it to you. I, however, confine myself to the expression of my own opinion. If I concur with it, I approve of it to that extent, and to the extent that my opinion does not concur with his, I do not.

3056. Before the introduction of the Bill of 1871, were you aware that there was any public outcry against the exercise of the sheriff's power?—I never heard of it, and that is one of the reasons why I think that the Bill of 1871 passed in such a quiet sort of way, which has amazed me. It passed the House of Lords without anybody making any remark at all about it, and I believe it passed the House of Commons at the end of the Session in a similar way. I believe nobody made any remark at all about it; it passed like a sort of Turnpike Bill, or, at least, I believe so, for I read no debates on it, and I believe there was no amendment moved in the House on it. If I am wrong, of course I can be corrected. If there were amendments, I suspect the amendments would have been in an opposite direction to that in which it was passed, probably. I believe that the papers do not report, now, certain subjects after certain hours, and I suppose that that is peculiarly applicable to Irish subjects. I can only say that I did not see in the papers any opposition to the Bill, and it was passed *sub silentio*, like a Turnpike Bill.

3057. You mentioned in your evidence on Monday the case of three gentlemen who had all been summoned together on the panel in Dublin to serve on juries?—Yes, I did, on last Monday; and this moment, when I came into the room, the clerk to the Committee handed me a letter, which is written by one of those gentlemen, in which he says he is much obliged for my mentioning to the Juries' Committee that three members of one firm were summoned to the present trial; such is the great hardship of the alteration. He then refers to several matters, and says, "My name is well known as being a member of a firm established over 80 years." It is the firm of Turbett Brothers, one of the oldest established and most respectable wine merchant's firms in Dublin. By this alphabetical process of rotation, the three brothers that compose that firm are turned up on a panel of 48 names; so that instead of this being a panel that is to take in a large number, it turns out that there are three brothers upon it in such a large place as Dublin; and as I call attention to already, from the necessity of the case, anybody who can understand the alphabet, must see the necessary results that must follow.

3058. I do not know whether the alphabetical system is particularly onerous in the case of wine merchants, but I have here a letter from another firm of wine merchants, who it appears have been also treated in a very uncomfortable manner, though perhaps not exactly in the same way; and they say, "During the after sittings following Hilary Term, I was summoned to attend as a juror simultaneously both to the Court of Probate and the Consolidated Nisi Prius Court; and my partner received at the same time a summons to the same court; and as if inconvenience of both partners of one firm being absent from business together was not enough, our accountant was at the same time summoned to attend on the same day at the Court of Common Pleas." This is a letter signed by Frederick R. Rambaut, a member of a respectable firm of wine merchants in Dublin?—I am not personally acquainted with them, but I believe the firm to be a highly respectable one.

3059. It appears that those gentlemen were summoned to different courts at the same time, so that it would have been almost impossible for the judge to have excused them, because he would not have known of the fact of the other partners having been sworn on the jury, and there would not have been ground for asking the judge to excuse them, unless the other members of the firm had been sworn on the jury panel?—I see continually the same idea in letters in the Dublin papers from firms, complaining that two members were summoned in consequence of the letter which heads their surname, being a letter, I suppose, that contained very few names, and necessarily they must turn up. I was looking since I was here on the last occasion at the special jury panel for the county of Galway, containing 48 names out of that second largest county in Ireland, and I found a father and son on it, because, I suppose, there were very few of that letter in the county. I think it would look very odd to the public to find three brothers on a jury, and if it had happened in the old times, it would have been said that there had been rare packing.

3060. That is the inevitable result, is it not, of the alphabetical rotation?—In certain letters it

seems,

Right Hon. *M. Morris.*

21 May 1873.

seems to me to be the necessary result, so long as the letters of the English alphabet remain the same as they are.

3061. Do you think that it is impossible by any special division of the jury lists, so to make the jurors who are on that list of so excellent a class as to render it unnecessary to have some method of selection?—No; I think that there must be a method of expurgation. I prefer using that word to "selection," because "selection" has got blown upon, and I think "expurgation" is a better word; and I think it means a different thing. It is one thing for the sheriff to have the power of selecting without giving any reason at all, and it is quite a different thing only to leave him the power of putting off persons, which involves, I think, much greater responsibility. A man may complain of being put off; he cannot complain of not being invited; at least not so fairly.

3062. Viscount *Crichton.*] Your practice I understand at the bar was very considerable, before you were on the bench; what opinion did you form of the jurors, under the old system, before this Act came into operation?—On the Connaught Circuit, upon which I went regularly, and I never missed a circuit from the time I went to the bar until I became a law officer, my experience was that they were very good. In Dublin, as I mentioned the last day, and I repeat it, as long as I can remember there were always objections to the juries, that is to say, they were too much of what you would call stock jurors, that is to say, men who made a sort of trade of being jurors. That arose from a variety of reasons. In the first place, they attended more readily, and it was easier for the sheriff to have them. In the next place, mercantile people complained in Dublin of having cases from the country tried very much in Dublin, instead of being tried in the locality; a matter which I have, as far as I could, since I went on the bench, always endeavoured to oppose, and to insist that cases should be tried as a general rule, where they ought to be tried, in my opinion, namely, where the cause of action occurred, as far as the nature of things would admit of it. Therefore, the mercantile people complained that they were kept there for weeks trying some wretched assault case, between people from a remote part of Ireland. Then, those stock jurors, as I call them, that had nothing to do to occupy their time but to serve on the jury, got some little payment for attending on the jury and combining their want of occupation with getting a little advantage by it; they were always there. Therefore there was always a feeling about the jurors in Dublin, and I think that an amendment was required in the case of the jurors in Dublin.

3063. But your experience of the country jurors was favourable, was it not?—My experience of the country jurors was favourable. I have gone every circuit in Ireland, as judge, and I have had scarcely any reason, or I have no recollection of any case of having had much reason to differ with the decision of the juries. Of course sometimes they may have taken a different view from what I would have done, if I had been on the jury; but it may be that they were right, and that I was wrong.

3064. In point of fact, you think that the demand for this Act was confined to the Dublin jurors?—I thought so; I think that this theoretical change, even if it was nothing else, might have been a good one, if there had been no practical grievance, namely, if it was to be done in England, it might be as well to do it in Ireland, and not to leave so wide a selection to the sheriff. As I have already said, I object most emphatically, as far as my views are concerned, to having peculiar legislation for Ireland. If it is a good thing here, let us have it in Ireland. At all events, let it be modified, so as to render it as nearly as possible the same.

3065. I think you stated that you had been every circuit in Ireland; may I ask you what is your experience of the sub-sheriffs; do you think that they are men who are likely to use wrongfully the power that was entrusted to them under the late Act?—I do not. Taking them as a class, I think that they are as little likely as any other class. I know most of the sub-sheriffs, as I have already stated, and I do not think, as a class, they have done so. I know several sheriffs who, in my opinion, are just as respectable, socially and in every way, as any chairman who would be revising the list, or any judge on the bench either, except as far as official position and rank give precedence to the two latter.

3066. Do you know many cases of challenge to the array of panels?—I have no recollection of any challenge to the array since I have been on the bench, except a rather remarkable one that took place before myself in the county of Monaghan, in the spring assizes of 1869, and I remember that case quite well.

3067. Would you have any objection to tell the Committee whether you approved of the verdict that the triers gave?—I did not; most emphatically not; for I charged the opposite way, and they took a different view of it; as I have said already, that is the good of a jury, I suppose.

3068. Do you remember the grounds that were alleged by Mr. Mitchell, the sub-sheriff, on that occasion, in defence of the constitution of the panel?—I do not remember the detailed grounds, because they were numerous; but they culminated in alleging that he had framed the panel, as well as I remember, partially in consequence of some trials that were to have come off; but I have not seen the challenge lately, and therefore, of course, I need not say that I have only a general recollection; but I think that that is substantially the case, or that is what it turned upon, at all events. There were several grounds assigned, as they are bound to do upon the challenge. One was, I remember, that the Orange Society had subscribed funds for the prosecution of a man named McKenna, who was to be tried for an alleged murder, and I think that the sub-sheriff himself had either subscribed, or was a member of the society that subscribed. It turned out that there was no foundation at all for the allegation that that society had subscribed; at least, when I say that there was no foundation, it was sworn, and there was nobody to contradict it.

3069. Was not the sheriff dismissed in consequence of the finding of the triers?—No; the high-sheriff was dismissed, because he would not dismiss the sub-sheriff.

3070. Were you consulted about it?—Distinctly not.

3071. It is usual to consult the judge is it not, when any step of that kind is taken?—On the matter of challenge to the array, it occurs so seldom that I do not know. I never remember seeing

Right Hon. *M. Morris.*

22 May 1873.

seeing another challenge to the array; but in ordinary cases, when there is an application made to the executive connected with any criminal case, there is a printed form sent by the executive, by his Excellency the Lord Lieutenant, or rather in his name, by his Under Secretary, for the judge's report of the case; first a report of the facts, and then observations such as he may think fit to add. Sometimes the judge sends in a bare naked report, and offers no observations, but he sometimes sends in a report and adds observations.

3072. *Mr. Attorney General.*] That is only in cases, is it not, in Ireland, where the sentence upon a prisoner is in question?—So I have said, in criminal cases. The question was put by Lord Crichton to me, and I thought that I guarded myself by saying that I was not aware of any practice.

3073. I rather thought that the noble lord was asking you whether it was not the practice to consult the judge about such matters as the partiality of the sheriff, it being supposed that that was a question of the partiality of the sheriff in the production of the jury list; that would not be a matter in England upon which the judge would be consulted at all; although, no doubt, he would be consulted as to the sentence upon a prisoner?—I have already stated that I am not aware of what the practice would be about the challenge to the array, for I never remember one. I confine my observations to the ordinary criminal cases to which the Attorney General has already alluded.

3074. Viscount *Crichton.*] You have been a good many circuits in the north of Ireland, have you not, since you have been on the bench?—I have gone five circuits in the north, and I went three of them consecutively on the north-east.

3075. Was it your experience that the jurors in that part of Ireland returned fair verdicts?—They just appeared to me as fair as in any other part of Ireland, and I have been on all the circuits.

3076. You were also the presiding judge at a trial which caused a great deal of notoriety some years ago, the trial of the present Member for Belfast, for taking part in a party procession which was then illegal, but which is now legal; do you recollect the composition of the jury upon that trial?—Yes; I tried Mr. Johnston, the present Member for Belfast, for a violation of the Party Processions Act. It was a statutable misdemeanour. It would have been no crime at common law, or socially and morally, apparently; but, of course, it was a statutable misdemeanour, and as such, in that sense, a moral crime, and a social crime, that everybody is guilty of who violates the law. But, however, it was a case in which a jury, above all others, if they wished to go against the strict rule, would be more naturally biassed to do so, and influenced by the speeches of counsel. Accordingly, the jury in Downpatrick were addressed by a very eloquent counsel, who in a very decided manner suggested that they ought to acquit Mr. Johnston; but they did not do so. I am not aware of their composition as a matter of fact myself, but I understood, and I believe, that they were all Protestants, of the same denomination and religious faith as he was, and that some of them were members of the Orange Society; at least I was so informed. But they returned a verdict of guilty against him in, I should say, about five minutes. That case excited a good deal of interest, and I think rightly so; for it used to be said that a jury of that class would not convict a man like him, who was a sort of leader amongst a certain section. However, they did convict him, and he was imprisoned. It is supposed that it had an important result, the opposite of what may have been expected.

3077. As to the charges of jury packing, were they not generally addressed against the law officers and other Crown officials more than against the sheriff?—According to my experience, distinctly so. In all the cases that I recollect of jury packing what was complained of, was the Attorney General or the Crown Solicitor of the day, excluding persons off the juries; and it appears to me a strange thing now talking about jury packing as regards the sheriff, when the necessity for exclusion, I am told, will arise much more; the very circumstance which, according to my observation, was what always excited special complaint. For instance, in the famous trial of Mr. O'Connell, although it took place long before my day, I believe there was no accusation at all against the sheriff, the accusation was against the making up of the jurors' book by the officials, and against the Attorney General, or the executive of the day, for striking the Roman Catholics off it; and I believe that was what my Lord Denman describes as a mockery, a delusion, and a snare, words which have become a sort of household words in speeches upon these subjects in Ireland. I am not aware that the sheriff's conduct was at all impugned. I must say, of course I cannot recollect it, for I was very young at the time, but I have read the thing, and I do not remember that there was anything about the sheriff. In all the State Trials in 1848, and subsequently, what I used to see of the complaints in the newspapers, the persons against whom the complaint was directed were the executive officials, and, as I understand it, there is to be a greater necessity now thrown upon the executive officials of putting people aside, which appears to me to be a strange result.

3078. It has been said that the Act has not been fairly tried; do you think that any further trial would produce any better result?—If there was to be no change in the Act as regards the qualification or otherwise, to say that it is not "fairly tried," seems to me to be just a confusion of ideas. Surely, if it is an alphabetical thing, it must just always turn up the same as if you tried a bag of oats, and the next time you tried it, it must be the same, unless it really was packed. The first trial of this thing must be the same as the second and third, and so on. I do not understand that phrase "a fair trial."

3079. *Sir R. Blennerhassett.*] You have heard of the old juries in Kerry, have you not?—I never went as a judge into Kerry but once, and that was under the old jury system, and very excellent juries they were. It was after a very hotly contested election in which your namesake was one of the candidates.

3080. Do you happen to know that there were people upon those juries who would have been kept off, if there had been a higher rating qualification?—I think that that would occur in all the counties nearly in Ireland, particularly in the western counties. I have already said that I think that various qualifications in the Act of the 3rd and 4th of William the Fourth ought not to have

Right Hon. *M. Morris.*

22 May 1873.

have been got rid of, and that it should not have been made a solely rating qualification. The Act of the 3rd and 4th William the Fourth provides for the sons of baronets and persons who have served the office of sheriff and magistrates, and I think the sons of magistrates being on the jury, I forget exactly what it was; but there was a variety of qualifications, at all events, which I think was useful. It might so happen that there might be some excellent jurors that were not rated, and it might happen that there were some very bad jurors that were rated.

3081. *Mr. Downing.*] Can you tell me when you were appointed Attorney General?—I was appointed Solicitor General in the month of July 1866, and I was appointed Attorney General in October of the same year.

3082. That was very rapid?—Yes, very rapid indeed.

3083. And when were you appointed judge?—I was appointed judge in Easter Term 1867.

3084. That was rather rapid, was it not?—I did not object to that. I served the office, I believe, nine months during the most troublesome time that ever any man had, who was Attorney General in Ireland; at least for the last 50 years; so that if it was a short term of office, on the other hand you see there was more done.

3085. You have described in the earlier part of your evidence the state of things at Sligo during the last assizes, which was very bad, was it not?—I described the results of the trials, which, in my opinion, were very bad, naturally when there were a number of disagreements.

3086. Could you tell the Committee how many cases were tried at the assizes?—I cannot. I should say vaguely about 15; but it is only a general statement; it might be more.

3087. Or it might be less?—I think scarcely less.

3088. How many disagreements were there?—I do not remember; but I remember that there were disagreements in two very remarkable cases; but as the parties will be tried again, I do not think it would be right to go into a detailed discussion of them.

3089. Do you think that there were a greater number of disagreements at the last assizes for Sligo than there were at any other period within your recollection?—I do not pretend to offer any opinion at all upon that point. I think that there were a greater number of disagreements with me presiding as judge than there would have been at any previous assizes.

3090. Are you aware that there has been a Return made to the House upon this very question?—I saw something about it, but I have not studied it.

3091. I will just read the numbers from a Return made to the House, which has not been printed, if you will allow me?—I do not see any use in reading it to me.

3092. Because you were the judge that tried the cases, and I see that the number of cases tried by jury were 11?—I do not know what that Return is, but I say that, so far as I have it in my recollection, there were about 15.

3093. We might take the Return to be correct, might we not, because it is signed by the Clerk of the Crown for the county?—I never take anything to be correct unless I read the document myself.

3094. I will give you the document signed by the Clerk of the Crown (*handing the same to the Witness*); you know the gentleman, do you not?—I do not know him, because I believe that the Clerk of the Crown there is a gentleman who does not attend very often.

3095. Do you know the deputy?—I do not know the deputy there at all.

3096. Will you tell the Committee, from that Return, how many cases you tried at the last assizes?—It says that the number of cases tried before a jury at the spring assizes of 1873 were 11; number of persons tried, 18; number of persons found guilty, 3; number of persons acquitted, 9; and number of persons as to whom the jury disagreed, 6.

3097. Will you go to the assizes before that, and see how many disagreements there were?—Four.

3098. And at the assizes before?—Four; at the assizes before that, none; and at the assizes before that, four.

3099. Those disagreements were before the new Act, were they not?—Certainly; but, as I said before, not before the same judge; and you cannot always collate things with reference to individuals.

3100. Of course there may have been disagreements or convictions or acquittals, according to the judge who presides?—I do not know that; but I am not able to give you any information upon that subject, nor had I the means of judging, except the last time; I never went the Connaught Circuit before as judge.

3101. In answer to a question from the noble Lord, you said that previous to that Act of Parliament you were quite satisfied with the jurors on the Connaught Circuit, including Sligo?—I do not know whether I did say that or not. There is no use in reciting what I said through me. If that be so, you are repeating correctly what I did say; if it is not, you are not.

3102. That was under what is called Perrin's Act?—I never knew that it was Perrin's Act; I know that it was the 3 & 4 of Will. 4. You know I did not live in those days, and I do not remember who the parties were that brought in Acts. I know that it was the 3 & 4 Will. 4, c. 91, but I did not know whether it was Perrin's Act, or whose it was; and until I heard somebody in this Committee call it Perrin's Act, I never knew whose Act it was. There are various Acts of George 3 and George 4, but I have not the wildest dream who the Attorney Generals were who brought them in.

3103. After the passing of that Act, which we will call Perrin's Act, are you aware that that Act was very much condemned?—How can I be aware of what occurred when I was only six or seven years old.

3104. Did you hear that there was a Committee of the House of Lords upon it?—Never heard anything at all about it. The only things that I heard of the incidents of that period are matters of history, such as the Reform Bill; matters that happened in 1832 and 1833 are matters of history to me.

3105. Will you allow me to give you some information about the state of Sligo?—I prefer reading it myself; I deprecate very much, with the permission of the Committee, being instructed.

3106. I wish to read from a Report of a Committee of the House of Lords?—What is the use of reading to me a thing which I know nothing about. You might as well read to me, to compare

Right Hon. *M. Morris.*

22 May 1873.

pare small things with great, Clarendon's "History of the Great Rebellion," and ask my opinion of Lord Falkland. It only makes me the conduit pipe for Mr. Downing's observations when I do not know anything about the words he reads.

3107. Who was the Attorney General before you?—Mr. Walsh, afterwards the Master of the Rolls.

3108. Are you aware that a Bill was brought in by the present Chief Justice Whiteside, in the year 1858?—I am not.

3109. Have you not read the Bill brought in by him?—No; I looked over the Bill brought in by him in 1854.

3110. Are you not aware that he brought in another in the year 1858?—I do not know it.

3111. Are you aware that the Act which we are now discussing was founded upon the Bill brought in by Chief Justice Whiteside, when he was Attorney General?—I believe that that portion of it about the alphabet takes its origin from a Bill brought in by the Lord Chief Justice in the year 1854.

3112. Are you aware that in 1854 he brought in a Bill in which the alphabetical order was provided for?—Yes; having heard such a thing, I went the other day to the library at the Castle, and I asked the librarian if he would be good enough to let me look at it.

3113. I understood you, in your examination, to say that you approved of the mode suggested in the Bill brought in by Mr. Justice Fitzgerald, in the year 1856?—Yes; you told me it was Mr. Justice Fitzgerald's Bill. I think that is Mr. Justice Keogh's Bill. The back of the Bill has on it the Attorney General and the Solicitor General, and unless you cast back very clearly, you forget sometimes. I think it was about the time that Mr. Justice Keogh was the Attorney General, that is my own impression.

3114. Will you allow me to ask you, are you opposed to the system of calling the jurors by alphabetical order?—I am opposed to the panel being called out of the jurors' book by the letters of the alphabet. I am opposed to an indiscriminate machinery, as I called it on Monday; I do not see what is the use of the sheriff settling the panel at all. Anyone could take No. 1, letter A, as well as the sheriff, and No. 1, letter B.

3115. Have you read the whole of that Bill?—No; I just looked at that particular clause of it.

3116. Will you allow me to ask you, do you approve of Section 27 of that Bill, which says, "The name of each man who shall be empanelled to try any issues, civil or criminal, in any of the courts, with the place of his abode and addition, shall be written on a distinct piece of parchment or card, all as nearly as may be of an equal size, and shall be delivered unto the clerk or registrar of the judge who is to try the cause by the sheriff or under sheriff or other officer returning the process, and shall by direction and care of such clerk or registrar be put together in a box to be provided for that purpose; and when any issues, civil or criminal, shall be brought on to be tried, such clerk or registrar shall in open court draw out 12 of the said parchments or cards one after another, after having shaken them together, or in civil cases where any view shall have been directed," and so on, and a jury of 12 shall be formed?—That is the Ballot; in fact, I did not consider it, but as at present advised, I would not object to that, if you kept the rest of it, namely, that the sheriff would have the power of placing upon the panel only competent persons; then I do not think I would object to the Ballot, reserving always of course the privilege of the Crown to set aside, and of the prisoner to challenge; as at present advised, I would not object to it.

3117. Would not it get rid of your objection, which is so strong to having the panel arranged alphabetically and called out alphabetically, if all the names were put into a box and shaken, and 12 names drawn?—I did not object to the panel being arranged alphabetically; but what I objected to was the panel being called out of the jurors' book, not by any exercise of intelligence, but by the letters of the alphabet as the machinery for doing it. The mode of selecting the jury out of the panel is the point that we are upon. The selection of the panel out of the jurors' book was entirely a distinct thing. Give me a decently good panel, and I do not think it makes much difference how you call the panel, whether by ballot or alphabetically; of course, giving the prisoner his power of challenge, and the Crown its right to set aside; but the point is getting a good panel.

3118. You would not object, would you, to balloting in criminal cases?—As at present advised, under such circumstances, I would not. I object to the ballot distinctly, excepting under the circumstances which I have mentioned; but with these reservations I do not, and I especially do not object to it, as the Attorney General for England mentioned here on the last day that that was the mode in England; and I looked at the 6 Geo. 4, c. 50, s. 26, at the club of which I am a member, and I found that the jury are balloted for in England, although I was not aware of it before.

3119. Would you approve also of the suggestion in the same section, that the Crown should be limited as well as the prisoner to 20 peremptory challenges in cases of treason?—I have not considered those wide questions like the unanimity of juries and otherwise, and I would not like to offer an opinion upon those constitutional subjects.

3120. I think you said that you would approve of the magistrates at petty sessions having the power to revise the lists rather than the sheriff?—No; the sheriff has nothing to say to the revising of the lists at all; the sheriff never comes into action until the jurors' book had been revised, and then he takes his panel from it. There often seems to me to be some confusion between the two lists.

3121. I meant the chairman?—That is true; because I do not think that the chairman has any knowledge of the thing at all. I have seen chairmen revising the voters' lists where there are no parties, I mean no political parties, and it is a mere turning over the sheets and signing his name to them; and it appears to me to be a waste of pen and ink.

3122. You are aware that the chairmen have only that power since this Act passed?—I believe so.

3123. I suppose that it was made a more solemn act upon his part that he was attended by the clerk of the union, and attended by the poor rate collector, and attended by the county cess collector, all of whom had a thorough knowledge of the people, and who were bound to answer him upon oath as regards the disqualifications in the

Right Hon. *M. Morris.*

22 May 1873.

the Act; but you do not think that he would be the most impartial and best person to revise the list?—It provides a machinery which I do not know that this present Act does; about the solemnity of it, I do not much mind that at all, because that is more according to the appearance of the gentleman, or that one may do the thing more solemnly than another; but, as regards the details of the matter, as to whether the poor rate collector should attend, and all that, I quite agree with you that, if it is to be so, it would be most useful for the poor rate collectors to attend, because they know most of the persons. But then there is always an objection, which you know as well as I do, that people in Ireland do not want to be meddling at all. There is a great desire in Ireland just to keep out of meddling with things, unless they are obliged to be in them, and I think that there would be a great unwillingness on the part of the poor rate collector to object to persons being on the list.

3124. He cannot object if he is obliged by the Act of Parliament to attend and to answer all questions upon oath?—How is a chairman to know what questions to put to him at all, unless he gets a hint?

3125. Any person may object in court?—You know that that will never be done; that nobody will bother their heads to go to the revision of the jurors' book. I think you know your county as well as most people, and I take it that it is the same in other counties, that most people will not go into these sort of things, and be meddling in public business unless they have a direct interest in it, particularly in that class of life. The poor rate collector is putting in his potatoes, or his oats, and do you think that he would go into the next quarter sessions town and spend days in arguing whether Pat Brown or John Smith is to be put upon the jury panel? Not at all; he will go home and attend to his business, if he is a sensible man.

3126. You were asked a question by the noble Lord with regard to quashing a panel before you in 1869, and it was said that you were not satisfied with the panel?—I said that I was not satisfied with the finding.

3127. Is that the only occasion on which you ever knew a panel to be quashed?—I think it is. I have no recollection of any other, and I have a pretty good memory.

3128. Do you remember that one of the grounds for quashing that panel was that the sub-sheriff was an Orangeman?—No, I do not remember that; I do not know whether that was in the challenge. I think it was, but rather indirectly, because I do not think that a man being an Orangeman would be a ground of challenge. Being of a different religious faith myself, I may not take the best view of an Orangeman, but I am not aware that it is a legal ground of challenge. I believe that it would not be any ground of challenge, and I believe that the way in which it was introduced was this: they said that an Orange society was prosecuting this man, and that therefore the sub-sheriff, being an Orangeman, was mixed up in it. I doubt whether I should have taken the challenge if it was merely that the man was an Orangeman.

3129. I have the report here in the "Northern Whig;" will you allow me to read it to you?—I do not know what may be in that paper. I remember that it was proved that the sub-sheriff was an Orangeman, and the challenge, I think, stated that the high sheriff was an Orangeman, but the high sheriff stated that he was not an Orangeman. I have a very good recollection of the case now, without any newspapers, and I am sure a far more accurate one.

3130. There were two jurors, I think, who tried it?—Yes, there were two triers, and the strange part of it was this: the complaint was that there were not enough Roman Catholics on the panel, and the two common jurors that tried whether it was a partial or an impartial panel were both Roman Catholics. I never saw a greater *argumentum ad absurdum* in my life.

3131. Were not the triers the two first that answered?—Yes; the complaint was that they were influenced in their decision; but surely their verdict was open to the gravest rebuke if the challenge was to be on the question of the proportion of religion.

3132. Has not that been a dispute which has arisen from the earliest time when a petty jury has been called?—I believe not; and it was not, I believe, allowed at any time. I know that Mr. Butt, who was for the prisoner, wished it to be tried by two of the grand jury, and the Crown counsel, who is now the Solicitor General, opposed it most vehemently, and said that it should be tried by the first two that answered. I have a very strong impression that if Mr. Butt, who was for the prisoner, had succeeded in convincing me that it ought to be two of the grand jury, there would have been a verdict against him; but the Crown counsel succeeded in convincing me that it ought to be the two first that answered; I did not know them at all; there was a verdict for Mr. Butt, so that it was in that respect also most extraordinary.

3133. Can you remember how the jury was constituted in that case of the Bairds?—No; McKinna was the name of the man in this case.

3134. The Bairds were tried a few days before this at the same assizes, were they not?—The Bairds were persons connected with what was called the Orange party, and they were tried for the alleged firing out of a house when the mob attacked the house. The defence of the Bairds was two-fold. In the case of the man who was tried, it was a question of identification; and then there was a question as to whether he had not fired in self-defence, if that was the case. Both questions, in my opinion, raised a fair question for the jury, who acquitted the prisoner.

3135. As a matter of fact, is it so, that there were 12 Protestants upon that jury?—I have not the wildest notion. I would not know a Protestant face from a Catholic face in the court. They appear to me to have all very much the same sort of face; there is no difference even in their hair; and I have not the wildest notion. I never heard anything of the religious portion of the matter until the challenge was handed in. When the challenge was handed in the Crown counsel retired, as they usually do, to consider. I did not know whether they were going to demur to the challenge or take issue upon it; but they took issue upon it, and insisted that it should be the first two that answered who were to try it, and as the first two that answered were Roman Catholics, it appeared to me that they practically came to the conclusion that there were not enough Roman Catholics on the panel.

3136. That was one of the causes of the challenge?—No. If I understand the challenge, you cannot put as a ground of challenge that there

Right Hon. *M. Morris.*

22 May 1873.

there are not enough of any particular religion, and I certainly would have refused to take such a challenge myself; I think that it is no ground of challenge to say that there are not enough of men of a particular religion on the panel. You might as well say that there were not enough black-haired men on it; it was quite absurd; but the challenge is, that it is partially arrayed, and when that is given in evidence, of course that would be a fact which might lead to such a conclusion; as if the proportion was so extravagantly absurd, it might go to show that it could not have occurred either by accident or by a reasonable supervision of the panel. As that case has been mentioned, it is right to say that it did not appear to me to be an extraordinary proportion. I have heard that question canvassed before, and stated that there were 80,000 Roman Catholics in the county and 30,000 Protestants. The sheriff had to take the panel from the jurors' book, and in the jurors' book there were 1,200, of whom 800 were Protestants and 400 were Catholics, and the proportion on the panel in that case, as I remember, was 49 out of 200.

3137. That is three-and-a-half to one?—You may get your pen, and as I told the jury, it is a nice sum in the rule of three.

3138. You complained very much of the three brothers who were summoned in Dublin?—I did not complain at all. If I had to be tried I would be delighted to have had them, because those three gentlemen of the Turbett family are three most respectable men in Dublin, and I think that there will be lack enough of such men upon the jury under the new system. Do not you think people would come and say, I have heard of packing, but I never knew of such an instance before in which three brothers, in the city of Dublin, were together upon the one panel of 48 names.

3139. Would it not easily remedy that by giving the judge power to dispense with them?—Why should the judge be embarrassed with these things. Why put him in that position; because, of all countries in the world, in Ireland a judge ought not to be dragged into these fights at all.

3140. Suppose that these three brothers were summoned, and that one of them came and served upon the jury; if the next was called he would say that he had been summoned, and that his brother was on the jury; and then might not the judge have power to excuse him?—What is the use of creating a difficulty in order to give the judge an opportunity of getting rid of it. I want to get rid of the difficulty altogether, and you want to try to cure the difficulty when it arises.

3141. You took the case of three names in a particular house?—I took that case because it was a case that everybody had been speaking about, and it was a remarkable sort of case.

3142. *The O'Conor Don.*] At the last assizes at Sligo the grand jury consulted you, did they not, as to the legality of paying the sub-sheriff for his expenses?—I do not know whether it was in Sligo, but I have it in my mind that some grand jury did. I think nearly all the grand juries sent in very strong resolutions against this new Jury Act. I distinctly remember that, and I remember being asked by, I think, more than one grand jury, as to the enormous expense that they were obliged to present for applying that which they thought, and in which I confess I joined then, a great change for the worse.

3143. You do not remember the particular application that was made to you in Sligo, with respect to the payment of the sub-sheriff's expenses?—I remember such an application, but not whether it was in Sligo or not.

3144. I believe your decision upon that was, that the grand jury had power to present sums to the sub-sheriff?—I thought that the words "reasonable expenses attendant on the Act," it might be held to come under that. I think you will find that it provides for the payment of poor-rate collectors and others, and then it says, "of all reasonable expenses attendant upon the Act." I thought that that would be, at all event, a fair way of looking at it when the sheriff was put to such expenses.

3145. If any doubt exists with regard to that clause, I suppose you think it desirable that it should be set at rest?—I do most distinctly, because it was argued before me. I think it is by no means clear, because, when all the other officers are named, and when the sheriff is not named, a sort of impression arises whether or not we are right. The maxim that the expression of one thing is rather supposed to be exclusion of another might be applied to it. However, I took rather an equitable view of "all reasonable expenses." I thought it was reasonably applied to such expenses as sending a car with a person all round the country looking for jurors, and trying to dig them up from the earth.

3146. You think that the section is a doubtful one?—I do. I think there is another objection to this Act; I think that the mode of service could be very easily altered into a service by letter. I see no reason why there should not be service by registered letter. Every humble man in Ireland now, owing to the communication with America, if it was nothing else, has letters by the post office, and particularly a person who is the subject of a substantial qualification. I think that a registered letter would be far better than a summons. In a county like Cork or Galway, sending summonses by men in cars into the most extreme angles and peninsulars of a county that may be 120 miles from one end of it to the other, is an enormous expense, which the ratepayers complain of very justly. I think that service by registered letter, as it is in Dublin, would be quite sufficient; and I have the authority of several sub-sheriffs for saying that, in addition to my own belief, they think that that is an arrangement by which everybody would get notice.

3147. Have they that service in Dublin now? They have, I believe, under this Act; if it is not it ought to be, but I think it is under this Act. I do not see any reason why it should not be in other counties as well as Dublin. Another matter which I would beg to remark upon is, that if this Act is to remain as it is, I think that persons who are merely summoned should not be excused for two or three years, and that it should be persons who either served, or attended to serve, at all events. Now it is said that several who are called good jurors, in contradistinction to bad ones, that is, persons in a higher position, do not attend at all; and you are giving them all the advantage of that now by excusing them for three years. In Section 19, which forms the alphabetical rota, in my opinion it should be at least amended so as only to exonerate for two years persons who have either served or attended to serve, and not merely persons who have been summoned.

3148. How

Right Hon. *M. Morris.*

21 May 1873.

3148. How would you carry that out in forming the panels?—The sheriff now leaves out those who were summoned before.

3149. In making out the panel of the next year, does he leave out all those who were summoned or on the panel of the last year?—Yes; I think that ought to be changed, and that he should only leave out those who had either served or attended to serve, a list of whom could be very easily taken. Otherwise, the jurors that did not choose to attend get all the advantage of not attending by being excused for two years. In Mr. Justice Fitzgerald's Bill, as well as I remember, in 1856, it was those who had either served or attended to serve; I think it was not those who were summoned. In the Attorney General for England's Bill, I take the liberty of suggesting, under Clause 19 of the Bill, which I think is one for a rota, it excuses jurors who either served or attended to serve, because if a man attends to serve, I think it is the same thing as serving.

3150. By attendance to serve, you mean answering to their name?—Yes, and that men are entitled to be excused if they were either set aside, or if they were not called, but they were there.

3151. With respect to the qualification for jurors, do I understand you to object to the indiscriminate rating qualification which it is in this Act?—If you gave the power of the exclusion of incompetent persons, to my mind the qualification then would be a secondary consideration. Of course it ought always to be a substantial one. If you do not give the power of exclusion the question of qualification becomes of more importance.

3152. Have you at all considered the relative qualifications of the jurors in small towns and in the counties?—Yes; of course a juror in a small town that would be rated at 15 *l.* as a general rule, would be more intelligent probably than a bucolic juror with double that rating upon land. From time immemorial it has always been the notion that those who drive fat oxen should themselves be fat.

3153. From your experience at the bar, and as a judge, are you aware that many householders in towns rated even as low as 8 *l.* or 10 *l.* are very often qualified to act as jurors? — Yes, but I would draw the line higher than that. Of course you may get occasionally a competent person at that rating, but I think that 12 *l.* or 15 *l.* would be the lowest that I would go to, and that in towns also. I see in this Act the word villages, which is a very vague phrase; I would confine it to persons living in cities or towns. Nearly every town in Ireland of 3,000 inhabitants has town commissioners.

3154. Would you find persons living in those villages who would have a household qualification of 12 *l.*?—Probably not.

3155. Would not the household qualification itself, no matter where it was situated, of 12 *l.*, be more likely to give you a qualified juror than 30 *l.* or even 40 *l.* land valuation qualification?—Yes, I would like the household qualification pure and simple, because any man who was really well off as a general rule has a decent house.

3156. Do not you think that a household qualification would have a tendency to give you a better class of jurors than a mere land valuation qualification? — Yes, but I think I would have both. I could understand a land qualification of a considerable amount and also a household qualification which would take in a different class of persons, and I would have both, but as I said before, I do not go upon the qualification so much.

3157. Colonel *Forde*.] As far as that goes, may I understand you that a town qualification should only be a house valuation?—Distinctly.

3158. It should not take land in with the house? — No, a man must live in a house somewhere, of course.

3159. A man may have a house in a town, and it may only be valued, we will say, at 6 *l.*, and he may have a town park in the neighbourhood, which may be valued, say, at 6 *l.* more, that would make a 12 *l.* valuation; but it would not be a 12 *l.* valuation of the class that you approve of, which is a house qualification pure and simple?—No doubt it would not.

3160. You would not recommend a double qualification in a town, but that it should be merely a single qualification of 12 *l.*?—Precisely; I would recommend a rating qualification of 30 *l.* or 40 *l.*, whatever it consisted of, and a simple household qualification of, say 12 *l.*, if a man lives in a house at 12 *l.*, whether he had land or not. Many a respectable shopkeeper in those country towns in Ireland has no land at all; he buys his milk, or he has the grass of a cow, or something, but no land.

3161. Mr. *Attorney General*.] Under the old system, the jurors' list was generally smaller, was it not, than it is under the new, in point of number?—I do not know how that is, because I never saw a jurors' list. The jurors' lists, you see, never come before the judge; all that comes before the judge is the panel.

3162. I mean that I should have thought that, as a country gentleman, and as a person acquainted with the state of Ireland, you would know whether the number of persons liable to serve under the old system was more or less than the persons liable to serve under the new?—The persons liable to serve, or who were competent to serve, if that was examined into strictly under the old system, had become very few, in consequence of the 3 & 4 Will. 4, being principally grounded on a freehold or leasehold qualification. Now, the giving of leases has ceased very much in Ireland from a variety of causes, to mention which would be to getting into political questions.

3163. Do you set much store upon bringing as many people as possible within the area of jury service; do you think it a good thing, nationally and generally, that as many people as possible, always assuming that they are competent, should be passed into the jury box?—I think it would be a good thing if as many persons as were competent were called upon always, and in everything to participate in all public business; I think that it gives greater solidity to the State.

3164. You think, therefore, the competency being assumed, the larger the number that you can bring within the area of the juries the better?—No doubt.

3165. I also rather gather that no practical rating qualification alone will secure intelligence?—No.

3166. I mean that no personal qualification would in all cases secure intelligence?—No.

3167. And you would be rather in favour of a mixed system of qualification?—I would.

3168. And,

Right Hon. *M. Morris.*

22 May 1873.

3168. And, as I understand, there should be some power of exclusion?—Precisely; that the sheriff, in taking the names, should leave out the men whom, when he came to form his panel, he would have to inquire into, and who he knew were persons who from a variety of motives were not fit.

3169. In reason, the number of qualified jurors having become somewhat small, and the new system being for good or bad reasons initiated, you would expect, would you not, that in the first instance there would be difficulties, and that people who were not used to it would be raw, and unequal to the work at first?—No doubt that would be a consideration with regard to anything new, that it would not work very smoothly at first. Nothing physical or moral works as smoothly at the beginning as it does afterwards.

3170. I understood you to say that the old system of leaving the selection in the hands of the sheriff has been blown upon?—I think so.

3171. I would not for a moment question whether rightly or wrongly blown upon; but as a fact, being blown upon, do you think it possible to go back to it?—That is the reason why I suggested some intermediate course. I am always a person anxious to defer to the opinions of others even when I have a strong view upon the subject. I would venture almost to wish it to be gone back to, but I doubt whether it would be attainable.

3172. Would not you agree, as I put it before, and I think with acceptance from other learned judges, that it is very important that men should not only be tried fairly, but should think they were tried fairly?—I say so distinctly; but I think that my recollection of Ireland (which does not go back to those olden times, but goes back for a quarter of a century) is that, in all cases in which I have heard as a general rule allegations of unfairness, it was in setting aside jurors, the very process which I am told is to be the corrective to this Bill.

3173. I do not presume to question whether it is rightly or wrongly, but as a matter of fact it is so, is it not, that leaving in the hands of 32 men the power of making up the panel, does leave in the hands of 32 men the power of being unfair?—Yes; but I declare, if I was a popular leader in Ireland I think I would as soon be in the hands of the present body of sub-sheriffs that I know, as in the hands of the Government. I am speaking of all Governments.

3174. But, at any rate, it does leave, as a matter of fact, the power of being unfair in those hands?—Any man that has power can be unfair. The discretion of a judge has been said to be the law of a tyrant.

3175. Further than that, it gives the power of being unfair in private, and without discussion, does it not?—No, I think there would be just as much discussion if there was some partial panel put forward. That was the very allegation that arose in Monaghan.

3176. You say that all people may be unfair, judges included?—"They might be," I said.

3177. If a judge is unfair he must be unfair in public, and upon argument?—Yes.

3178. Whereas, if a sub-sheriff is unfair he may be unfair in private, and without argument?—No, because there would be great argument before the judge about his unfairness when they came in with the challenge to the array.

3179. Surely you do not mean to say that a man may be unfair, without being so unfair as to give rise to legal argument?—I am sure that a judge, sitting in public, may be unfair, and not be so unfair as that the public will see it.

3180. That is true, unfortunately; but do you really make no distinction between the corrective applied by public discussion and public argument, and that which a man may do without any discussion and without argument?—Certainly I do, inasmuch as I believe that our law would never have lived through all its various phases, except it was administered in public, and with a listening bar and public to control the judges. Public opinion, I believe, is a most admirable corrective, and I believe that, owing to our human nature, we should degenerate largely if we were not controlled by a listening, learned bar, and by the public. That is an abstract thing, but in this question about the sheriff I do not see that it would apply.

3181. You say that you think that the power of setting aside may be exercised invidiously, but I did not understand you to say that you think that in any country it could be safely foregone?—I do not; and I do not say that it may be exercised invidiously; but I say that the public outcry or complaints in Ireland have been, according to my experience, more addressed to that than to the sheriff.

3182. Still that is a power which no Government in any country could forego?—No; I am the last man even to suggest that it should be foregone.

3183. But whether it may have been exercised fairly or not, or whether it may have been observed upon or not, it is nevertheless a power which every Government must maintain?—Certainly.

3184. Therefore it is not a matter for argument?—No; but I wish to explain. I was asked as to the suspicions attaching, properly or not, to the selection by the sheriff; and of legislating to get rid of suspicion, whether it was correct or not; I say that you are not legislating to get rid of suspicion; but you are in reality, in my opinion, going the other way, increasing suspicion; for you are creating a greater necessity for setting aside, which, according to my recollection, has been always the greatest ground of popular complaint in Ireland.

3185. You must always admit this proposition, "if it is reasonably possible"?—That was my point, that it was not reasonably possible; but I was asked whether the thing was not to be like Cæsar's wife.

3186. I observe you speak very strongly about the want of speaking English; were there a very large number, or anything like a large number, of jurors brought in upon this circuit that you went who could not speak English?—Not what I would call a very large number; but there was a substantial number. It is a portion of Ireland in which there is the most Irish spoken, and it would be in that respect analogous to Wales.

3187. I asked Mr. Justice Lawson whether he had had the good or bad fortune to attend the Welsh Assizes; have you ever done so?—No; but I have read some Welsh verdicts, and I think I might reasonably say that I do not want to assume a monopoly for ourselves of stupidity at all.

3188. That is the more unfair; because if they do not understand, they may be forgiven for not coming to a very good verdict?—Distinctly.

3189. Would

Right Hon. *M. Morris.*

22 May 1873.

3189. Would you make it a positive disqualification for serving in a court of justice in Ireland, that a man could not speak English?—I would distinctly now-a-days, particularly because, from the spread of national schools now, all the younger population that would be at all within the jury qualification can speak English, I think.

3190. Then it is a thing which will wear itself out?—Yes, it will wear itself out, and that is the inutility, I believe, of bringing in a temporary Act, of which I see that is an element, the removal of which appears to me to be worth about as much as *lana caprina*.

3191. Would you say the same thing about reading and writing?—No, I would not; I think that no man ought to be allowed to be upon a jury who could not read or write; no man, particularly in the age that we live in. Of course you may meet with single exceptions in everything, but you must always pass an Act of Parliament, in my opinion, for what will suit the average bulk of cases, and not for the *rare ones*.

3192. Is there not in Ireland a considerable body of people who do not read and write, and yet who are shrewd and intelligent people, and capable of forming a very good judgment upon facts?—Unquestionably there are a certain number, but they are diminishing every day. I do not mean that the number of shrewd people are diminishing, but the number of persons who cannot read nor write is diminishing.

3193. You would make the non speaking of English, and the inability to read and write, a positive disqualification?—I would; but I do not consider that after a few years it would have any material effect at all upon the thing.

3194. You were mentioning this matter about the alphabetical selection, and I think you said that there was a case in which persons of the same name, or belonging to the same firm, have been summoned in three different courts, and that therefore, even if the judge had been disposed, they could not very well, any of them, have been excused?—No, I did not; I said that there were three gentlemen of the name of Turbett summoned in the same case.

3195. In answer to one of the honourable Members of the Committee, you said to-day, I think, that there were three gentlemen who were members of the same firm who had been summoned, and as they were not in the same court, each judge could not say that any of them should be excused?—I did not say that; Mr. Bruen said it. He addressed that observation to me, and I gave him the same answer as I did to several questions of Mr. Downing, that if that was so, it was so, and if it was not, it was not.

3196. I was going to ask you whether inconveniences of that kind will not happen from time to time under any system of working?—Inconveniences will occur, but I do not think that it would have ever occurred to any proper system of rotation that the three members of any firm in a town should have turned up on the same jury of 48 names in the same court, out of 1,000 names. No such doctrine of chances has ever been heard of, and any man that could learn that would make his fortune at Homburg.

3197. How would it be to summon alphabetically, with this qualification, that the persons should not be taken from the same parish, but that the A's, for example, of all the parishes within the district, should be first exhausted?—I think that that would be better than the present system of alphabetical order, because at present, men are summoned 60 or 70 miles off, because you are obliged to go through the letter A, and you see those letters have no regard for geography at all. The next letter A may live 60 miles away from the other man next before him on the list.

3198. If there were to be a rotation that A, B, C, D, E, and F should come from the first parish, and that another set of A, B, C, D, E, and F, should come from the next parish, and so on, how would that do?—I think that there would be great objections raised in the country to that, because very often parishes and localities differ in their population very much, particularly in some of those border northern counties such as Monaghan. Some parishes, nay, some baronies, are exclusively Protestant, and there is one barony, the barony of Farney, which is almost exclusively Catholic, and I think that the Protestants would find fault if the names were all outside their barony, and the Farney men would find fault *vice versâ*.

3199. I do not mean contiguous parishes, but parishes that happened to stand next on the book; how would it be to take the first name in letter A, we will say, in parish A, and then in the letters B, C, D, E, and so on; and then the first name in parish B, which might not be by any means the next parish in point of locality, but might be a great way off; would you not get a reasonable shuffling of the cards in that way?—I think that that would be better than the present system.

3200. Then, as I understand, nobody could say that anyone was packing or choosing the jury?—As to that, they would say it to the end of time. I am only guarding you against supposing that you have reached the state of optimism even by this plan.

3201. They could not say it with justice, nor indeed with any pretence of justice?—No; but I hear a great many things said that have no pretence of justice in them.

3202. Mr. *Bruen*.] As a matter of fact, I think that there are no such districts as parishes recognised by the law since the disestablishment of the Episcopal Church?—I do not know that at all; you must go to the representative synod for that.

3203. *Chairman*.] I think you stated that in your opinion there was not any strong popular demand for this change?—I never heard of any. I heard no one talking about it at all, and I did not see anything in the papers about it, until it was brought in at the end of the Session, and then there was a chorus of approbation of it, it is but right to say, from all the papers; I wish to say that to the advantage of the Bill; that there seemed to be a general chorus of approbation of it, but there was a general chorus of disapprobation very soon after.

3204. Are you aware that the Select Committee of the House reported in 1852 in favour of an alteration in the Jury Act?—I am sure that everyone must have reported in favour of an alteration of the Jury Act from this fact, that the qualification had almost practically disappeared. The great qualification in the old Jury Act was a freehold and a leasehold one. Freeholds and leaseholds have almost disappeared in Ireland, and there was scarcely a jury panel in Ireland that was a legal one, or that could not

Right Hon. *M. Morris.*

22 May 1873.

not have been properly challenged for that reason.

3205. This was not a Committee on juries; it was a Committee appointed to inquire into the state of certain parts of Ireland?—I am aware that it was the Outrages Committee.

3206. That Committee recommended unanimously that measures should be adopted to secure strict impartiality in the selection of the jury panel in Ireland, and it was a very important Committee, was it not?—I do not know who was on it, but I would have added my humble name to the same recommendation, but they by no means recommended the alphabetical order, for I have turned it up since I came to London, and I read Hansard for the year 1855, and I see the present Lord Chief Justice, then Mr. Whiteside, relied upon that recommendation for the alphabetical arrangement, and that he was met by Mr. Justice Fitzgerald who showed that this alphabetical arrangement was not at all endorsed by that Committee. I take the liberty of saying that I entirely agree with Mr. Justice Fitzgerald's view upon that point.

3207. It was probably in consequence of the recommendation of that Committee that the Attorney General of almost every Government since that time has introduced a measure?—Distinctly; I think that even during my own short reign I had to consider the subject, but all until this one were founded on not taking away from the sheriff some control over the panel. Mr. Justice Fitzgerald and Mr. Justice Keogh both agree in that reservation. I saw five or six of them in the library at the Castle in Dublin, and they all left some selection, or some power of expurgation or exclusion to the sheriff until this one.

3208. But none of those left to the sheriff the power of selecting as he could under the late Act; that is to say, of selecting the same name over and over again?—No, I think not; that is one of the matters which ought to be carefully guarded against, and which I disapprove of. In the first place, the qualification was absolutely gone, and it was a monstrous thing that for many years persons were serving on juries who had not the qualification in the Act, because that qualification had disappeared, and in addition to that, there was some reform as regards the selection; but what I object to is, that it has run to such an extreme in the other direction, that I would like to bring it back again.

3209. You were asked a question about Mr. Johnston's trial, and you said that you heard that the jury was entirely composed of Protestants?—I did.

3210. Although the verdict in that case may have been very satisfactory, supposing Mr. Johnston had been acquitted, and perhaps very properly acquitted, would not it have been an unfortunate circumstance for him, and for the interests of justice generally, that he should have been acquitted by an exclusively Protestant jury?—I think that it would have been an unfortunate thing for him, because I believe that his conviction had a very material result in his being returned for Belfast immediately after.

3211. In what county was he tried?—He was tried at Downpatrick, within 26 miles of Belfast; the county of Down is the largest county in Ireland as regards the Protestant population; I think that the Protestants are two to one in the county of Down.

3212. Still, do not you think that it would be an objectionable thing that even in such a Protestant county as Down, a party case should be tried by an exclusively Protestant jury?—I think so; supposing I were asked my impression, my answer would be, that if such a jury as that were trying a gentleman who had taken a popular part in their view, they would have all the elements that would lead to a disagreement, if it was nothing else, as often occurs in other places; but after hearing my charge, in which I told them that the Act had been violated, of course they might find that it had not been, if they chose.

3213. Colonel *Forde*.] I think, if I remember rightly, there were not more than three Roman Catholics on that jury?—I understood that it was the reverse; at all events, they did not disagree, which is enough for me. I think there were men of extreme party views upon it, and it was a peculiar case, in which a jury might have been led to disagree, because there was no commission of any common law crime, or of any social crime, as I said, excepting so far as the violation of an Act of Parliament necessarily is so.

The Right Hon. JOHN DAVID FITZGERALD, called in; and Examined.

Right Hon. *J. D. Fitzgerald.*

3214. *Chairman.*] I BELIEVE you are a Judge of the Court of Queen's Bench?—Yes.

3215. And have been so for some considerable time?—For 13½ years.

3216. On what circuit did you go at the last assizes?—The Munster Circuit, which is the most extensive, territorially and in population.

3217. Have you had any experience of the working of the present Jury Act, except upon that circuit?—There, and at the previous commission in Dublin; my only experience of the country parts has been that one circuit.

3218. Will you state to the Committee, generally, what impression you have formed of the working of the new Act?—I should state, before coming exactly to the operation of the Act itself, that in one respect I differ from the evidence that has just been given by Mr. Justice Morris, in this, that my impression is that for many years there has been a public demand for an alteration of the Jury Act, 3rd and 4th of William the Fourth. I state that from my experience in Parliament, and from what I know as a public man, and I have had occasion more than once, myself, from the bench, publicly to call attention to its defects, and to recommend that there should be some alteration in the Jury Act. When I came into office myself, in the year 1856, I found that my predecessor had introduced a Jury Bill which was prepared, I think, under the direction of Mr. Brewster, who had been Attorney General, and that either Sir Joseph Napier or the present Chief Justice had also introduced a Jury Bill; and so it went on from year to year, every successive law officer introduced a Jury Bill, having as its basis an extensive alteration of the Act of the 3rd and 4th of William the Fourth. My Bill has been alluded to, but I am scarcely responsible for it, for I merely took the Bill that had been handed over

Right Hon. *J. D. Fitzgerald.*

22 May 1873.

over to me by my predecessor in office, and amended it.

3219. Who was that?—The present Mr. Justice Keogh and Mr. Brewster, and, furthermore, if the pages of Hansard are referred to, I also, in introducing the Bill, proposed to refer it, and what I might call a rival Bill, a Bill introduced upon the other side of the House (for there were always two Bills, one on each side), to a Select Committee. I was anxious to take the whole question out of the region of party, and have it settled by a Committee of Irish Members in the manner which would be the best for the country; it continued in that state up to the time that I left Parliament. Since I have been upon the Bench I have seen that the Act required alteration. There was no real revision of the jury list. It was entrusted to the magistrates at quarter sessions, but there was no real revision. My experience is, that there were men on the jury list who ought not to have been there, who were disqualified, and who had no qualification. There were men, of course, who were qualified.

3220. Would you say that they were legally disqualified?—I mean that there was an absence of qualification, they had no qualification.

3221. Do you think that there were jurors who were not qualified in point of intelligence, or that they were merely disqualified for want of a legal qualification?—They had no statutory qualification. Furthermore, there were a number left off who were qualified, and there was at least a suspicion in many instances that some of them had been left off by design. I mean that they were to be moving parties in it themselves to avoid the trouble of being jurors. I have known both on the jurors' book and on jury panels, the names of a number of persons who were dead, and of men who had left the country. In one remarkable instance, in a case that excited some public attention, I had occasion myself to enforce the attendance of jurors; it was known that they would avoid the unpleasant duty which the case involved, and in consequence of that I had to impose fines. Then, afterwards, upon examination into those fines, I found that I had imposed fines on a number of people who were dead. Such are the grounds upon which I thought, and still think, that an amendment of that law was necessary. The Act with which we are now dealing, when it was in the shape of a Bill before the House of Parliament, seemed, so far as I could judge, to excite universal public approval. It was considered absolutely necessary, and it was not until it became law, and until its operation was seen in the large extent to which it added to the jurors' book, that there was any expression of public apprehension and dissatisfaction. There is no doubt whatever that the present Act has gone far beyond what was anticipated, and very likely what was intended, and it has brought upon the jurors' books, as they at present exist, a great number of persons who, from defects of intelligence, and education, and independence, are not at present, at least, fit to be there, having regard to the public safety. You have asked me my experience of the working of the Act on the Munster Circuit. In Dublin it appears to have done pretty fairly well. In the first county of the Munster Circuit, which is Clare, certainly its operation was not satisfactory. A particular case came before me there for trial; it was a case of that character that the result created a good deal of public uneasiness. I may allude to the case, because the man was acquitted, and therefore he cannot be tried again in any shape. If it were a case of mere disagreement I would not mention it; a man was tried for what is called an agrarian offence; that is to say, he was charged with attempting to shoot his landlord, in consequence of some dispute about land. I do not know what it was, but it was something connected with land, and that man was acquitted. The evidence was all one way, and it was perfectly clear that he ought to have been convicted; it was a disastrous failure of justice, and caused very considerable uneasiness in the district, and I attribute that very much either to the whole of the jury consisting of such persons, or to there being at least persons upon that jury who, either from defect of intelligence or from sympathising with that class of crime, or from their being influenced by apprehension or pressure, pronounced a verdict which nothing in the case warranted. In other respects my experience in Clare was satisfactory. In all the civil cases there, and I tried the whole of the civil business, there was no verdict that I disapproved of; but, at the same time, I should add, or I shall be misleading the Committee, that I felt it necessary, from the change which had taken place in the law, not alone to obviate any defects that existed, but to give the jury a great deal more assistance than I have thought it necessary to do under ordinary circumstances; that is to say, I formed my own opinion upon the facts of the case as to the result that ought to be arrived at, and in putting the case to the jury I endeavoured, as powerfully as I could, to bring them to that conclusion, and in most of the instances they took the view of the case that I adopted. In the county of Limerick my experience was more satisfactory than in Clare. Though there were some disagreements in Limerick, I cannot say that there was any case in which there was a failure of justice, or anything that I would attribute to any defect in this Act of Parliament. There was one case in Limerick which has been already alluded to, and which, I saw in the public papers, has been brought before the Committee, where a man was tried and there was a disagreement, and I was obliged to use very strong language. The evidence was all one way. It was a case of no importance, and involved no party or political consideration; though it was a homicide, there was nothing of malignity in it, or anything important in the case, but the jury disagreed. The whole thing depended upon a statement made by the prisoner himself; immediately after the homicide he admitted that he was guilty of it. The jury told me that they believed the witness who made that statement, that there could be no reason for doubting him at all, and yet they disagreed, and would not convict; but I do not attribute that case in the least to this Act of Parliament. The prisoner in that case was one whose relations in the county were very extensive indeed. He was one of a very numerous family, who stood in a particular position in the locality, and commanded more influence than his humble rank would leave one to suppose; and it altogether arose from this, that some friends of his got upon the jury, and would not convict. It had nothing to do with the working of this Act.

3222. That case might have happened, might it

Right Hon. *J. D. Fitzgerald.*

27 May 1873.

it not, under the old Act?—I have known the same thing repeatedly occur under the old Act in other parts of Ireland, especially in the north of Ireland. I mean that, notwithstanding the evidence being all one way, you could not secure unanimity upon the jury. Kerry I may altogether exclude from consideration for this reason, that the sheriff there took the view of the Act of Parliament, that his discretion was not taken away, and accordingly he returned such a jury as he thought fit. I did not censure him for it, because he did it from the very best motives; smallpox was very prevalent in the county town, and he took the jury from the surrounding district, so that they should not be obliged to remain in the town at night; and the consequence was, that we had a class of either town jurors or jurors from the immediate vicinity of the county town. It was no doubt a violation of the Act of Parliament, but it was done with a good motive, and we had very good juries, and they tried all the cases very satisfactorily.

3223. Objection might have been taken, might it not, to that panel?—Objection was taken, but they did not put it upon the right ground, and I helped the sheriff out of his difficulty. I would not have done so in a criminal case, but in a civil case. In fact, objections were taken in two civil cases, but there were practical difficulties in the way, and that panel was not quashed. In the county of Cork I had very considerable experience, both civil and criminal, and I should say that in the county of Cork, at the last assizes, both on the Crown side and on the civil side (for my observation applies equally to both) the verdicts generally were satisfactory. I took the trouble of again going through my note-books, with a view to see the character of each case, and I am prepared to answer the Committee as to each case, its character, and its result. Upon the whole, in the county of Cork, in my view, the conduct of the jurors was satisfactory. But again, I would possibly be misleading the Committee if I did not accompany that with the observation that the panel in the county of Cork was very considerable; and I observed myself that there were a great many jurors in attendance, some of great poverty; some infirm, and wholly unfit to be there from infirmity; and some plainly in that position in life that ought not to have been upon the jurors' book at all; and I took a liberty with the Act of Parliament, and quietly allowed them to go home. Probably, in that respect, I overstepped the limit of the law, but by the assistance of the sub-sheriff, when complaints were made by the jurors, an intimation was given that they would not be called on fines. For instance, one juror applied to me there, and he told me he had come from Cape Clear and, with the exception of the sea passage to the main land, he represented that he had walked nearly the whole way to Cork, a distance, I think, of some fifty or sixty miles, and that he had not the means of subsistence. I thought it not unwise to let that man go home; that is to say, to intimate that he would not be called upon and fined. A similar course was taken in some other instances, and we got juries which were very satisfactory. But in addition, at the opening of the assizes, when addressing the grand jury, I appealed to the gentlemen of the county. I had found in the earlier towns that the better class of jurors, gentlemen in the position of magistrates and others, had not attended, and that was a very great defect, and they had failed to perform their duty. Therefore I appealed to the gentlemen of the county of Cork. In addressing the grand jury, I took the opportunity of appealing to the gentlemen who would be upon that jury panel, and in consequence of that appeal, they did attend, and did perform their duty; and I have no doubt that they assisted the less educated jurors in enabling them to carry out the administration of justice in the satisfactory manner that I have described. I have before me here two panels for the county of Limerick, in order to show practically the working of the Act of Parliament. The one is the jury panel for the summer assizes of 1872, and the other is the panel for the spring assizes of 1873, being the last assizes. They happen to be nearly similar in number; the one in 1872 has a total of 141 upon it, and the one of 1873 has a total of 140. Upon the one of 1872 there were, according to classification, 37 jurors with the addition of "esquire," which would probably represent magistrates or gentlemen of position. There were 34 described as gentlemen or shopkeepers. Many of them I know by name, though not being magistrates, to be quite their equal in rank; and there were 70 men described as farmers, making the whole 141. The panel of 1873 has a total of 140, and upon the whole of that panel there were but five justices of the peace, seven gentlemen, and 128 farmers. That at once shows compendiously the practical operation of the Act. In the same way, in the county of Cork, I have brought the panels for two assizes there. At the summer assizes of 1872 there was a total, I think, of 189 on the panel, of whom there are returned as farmers about 22, leaving 167 under the various classifications of justices of the peace, esquires, gentlemen, and shopkeepers. In the spring of 1873 the total number on the panel is 240, and those returned as farmers upon it are 174, as against 22 on the previous panel. However, for the information of the Committee, in calling attention to this, I would wish not to be misunderstood, or let it be inferred in any degree that I entertain myself an opinion adverse to the main principle of this Act, which I look upon as the rating principle, and that is the extending of the ambit, if I may use the expression, from which you are to take the persons qualified, and extending it so as to include the humbler and less wealthy classes. On the contrary, I think that we ought to go as far as we can in that direction, consistently with the public safety. I am speaking now only for myself; but I look upon it as of the utmost constitutional importance to bring that class of people (I speak of the humbler and less wealthy classes) as far as you safely can, in connection with the administration of justice, and, above all, in connection with it by serving as jurors. It has a tendency very much to elevate them in their own estimation, if you put them in a position of dignity and responsibility in making them aid in the administration of the law, and that has a direct effect in creating confidence in the law itself, and it tends to teach them what they have yet to learn, that the laws of the country have been made, and are administered for them, and not against them. There was in the olden times, at least some 40 years ago, a strong feeling which has not yet died out, that the laws were made against the people, and administered in a hostile spirit, whereas, if they are brought in connection with its administration, they cannot fail to see, not

alone,

Right Hon. *J. D. Fitzgerald.*

22 May 1873.

alone, that they live under an excellent system of laws, which will bear comparison with any in the world, but that they are administered in the mildest and best spirit for their benefit. I would look upon those as very great advantages in a constitutional point of view; and I am entirely for going as far as you possibly can in that direction, consistently with public safety. I therefore approve entirely of the principle of resting the main qualification upon rating, but the Act has gone undoubtedly too far, and has brought in a class of men who, as yet are not suitable to serve on juries. I understand from the public papers that the Committee are proposing, in a Bill before Parliament, to increase the amount of the qualification.

3224. That is a temporary measure?—I have no doubt of its usefulness: it will probably exclude a number of the less educated, the less independent, and the less qualified, and you will principally find them, of course, in the lowest stratum. There is a thing also which we must all recollect, and that is, that the national system of education which is bringing up an entirely new class of people, has only been potentially in extensive operation for about 30 years, and it never has affected, or brought within its limits those who at that period were beyond the age of school boys; so that it has not affected the old people, and has left untouched a great many who would be on those jury panels. That will gradually wear away, and probably hereafter it may be found that the limit in the present Act is not too low, but at present it seems to me to be advisable to raise it again.

3225. Would you look rather for the improvement of the class of jurors to raising the qualification than to a more careful revision?—I should always take the two together. I think that the qualification ought at least temporarily to be raised; and furthermore, it is one of the things that I entirely approve of in this Act, that it has substituted for the previous wholly inefficient revision what, as at least would appear by the Act to be intended to be, a proper revision by a competent judge acting under judicial responsibility. I think there ought to be, in addition to raising the qualification, a most rigid revision with a view to exclude those who are not entitled to be there. And for that purpose I would leave it to the chairman, as the judge who is to exercise that power of revision. The chairmen of counties are a body as to whom we have perfect confidence in their judicial ability, impartiality, and every quality that you would expect to find in a person holding a judicial office, but it will be necessary to arm them with strong powers by Act of Parliament; and I think it will be necessary to have some person or persons who will have the responsibility of bringing the case before the chairman. It will not do to hand in the jurors' list to the chairman and say, "Revise this as best you can." He must not alone be attended by public officers, but I think there ought to be some officer whose duty it should be to do what a counsel or agent does in court, and to bring up cases before the chairman, and submit to him whether they ought to be on the jurors' book or not. I am entirly in favour of a rigid revision in addition to increasing the qualification.

3226. Have you considered who would be the proper person to furnish the chairman with the necessary information?—Already I have seen that it is recommended that he should be attended by certain public officers, such as the poor rate collectors, who are locally the officers of the county; but that is not exactly what I have been pointing at; it is some one to have the carriage of the proceedings before him. I do not know of any officers better to entrust it to than the clerk of the peace and the clerk of the Crown. The one represents, to some extent, the administration of criminal justice, and the other acts on the civil side. Also they are officers who attend the chairman at his sittings; one of them, at least, does; and possibly you could not select better persons to conduct the revision before him.

3227. You would not re-introduce the sheriff?—No; the officers I have named are both general county officers assisting in the administration of justice. I once entertained the view that the offices ought to be amalgamated. However, we have them now, one on the civil side, and one on the Crown side; I tried to carry it out when I was Attorney General; by, in two or three instances, appointing the same officers to both places; but you have them now separate, and I conceive that they would be the best persons to whom to intrust the conduct of this revision.

3228. Under the Act it is the duty, I believe, of the clerk of the peace to make the final jury list?—Yes, from the materials which he gets.

3229. And you would throw upon him the duty of taking such measures as might be necessary to strike out the names of imperfectly qualified jurors?—Yes; from information that he would derive either from the officers of the constabulary, or other public officials by whom the chairman's court would be attended.

3230. I think that Mr. Justice Morris suggested that the sheriff should still have the power of expurgating the list, by striking off the names of unqualified jurors?—That is in framing his panel, that he should have restored to him the old power. I call it selection; I think it is a better word, because, call it exclusion, expurgation, or what you will, it was the exercise of selection by the sub-sheriff. It was not the high sheriff that did it, for the high sheriff had no control at all. It was done by the under sheriff; and the under sheriff did it, as has been properly described, in private; that is to say, he took the jury panel from any portion of the jurors' book he thought fit. He was not tied down by any rule; he took it from any place that he thought fit, and I certainly would not be for restoring that power to the under sheriff. If it had been a new matter, if I had been framing this Act of Parliament myself, I do not think that I should have ventured to have gone so far as to have removed that authority of the under sheriff entirely. I am averse myself to very violent changes; and what probably I should have recommended would have been, not to have removed that power of selection altogether, not to have taken away his responsibility, but to have edged it round with safeguards, which would have lessened the danger of its abuse. For instance, a great deal would be done in that way when you say that a juror shall only be summoned once in a year, or once in two years; that takes away a great deal from his power. Again I should have made the framing of the panels to be the act not of the under sheriff, but of

Right Hon. *J. D. Fitzgerald.*

16 May 1873.

of the high sheriff. The high sheriff has now no responsibility for it, either moral or legal. To be sure, if the under sheriff commits anything that would be actionably wrong, the action is brought against the high sheriff; but the high sheriff deputes to the under sheriff the power of framing the jury panel; it is part of his deputation, and the high sheriff has no responsibility. His name is signed to the panel, but he has no responsibility for it; and one of the checks that I would have provided would have been that the high sheriff himself should frame the panel. He would, of course, in that have the assistance of the under sheriff, and of his experience; but I would have made him responsible. There are other safeguards which might be suggested, so as to reduce the power of abuse. It was too great a power to vest in a single hand, and from my experience there was, at least, a prevalent strong public opinion, not that the power was generally abused, but that it had been in individual instances. For instance, if a particular class of cases was known to be coming on, any that excited special attention, as political cases, or involving a question of party or religion, there did prevail an opinion that sometimes the panel was framed to meet them, and the suspicion of such an evil, is almost as bad as the existence of the evil itself; I mean as a general public mischief. Therefore I would have provided, as far as I could, to prevent the possibility of that taking place. It would be very difficult to do so, and any alteration of the law must have been in the direction of depriving the under-sheriff of that power. That has been done by this Act of Parliament, and in my judgment it would not be wise now to reverse it.

3231. Not in any limited degree?—No, not in any limited degree. I would leave it as it is now; but provide otherwise for securing a good jury.

3232. You do not think that it would be possible even now to revert to what was proposed in some of the earlier bills, that the sheriff should select the panel of names in rotation, omitting any that he considered disqualified?—If the question put is as to the possibility, of course it would be practicable to do it, but I scarcely think it would be wise. My opinion now is, that as the alteration has taken place, it is better to adhere to it, and see in what other way you can provide for securing a good jury. It is a matter that we are all vitally interested in, and I would propose therefore to adhere to the rating, but I would supplement it. There are classes who are left out, and who might well be added. According to the present Act of Parliament, there must be an occupation of property and a rating by name; that is to say, the name of the party must appear upon the rate book, both as the occupier and the party rated, before he comes on the jury list at all. I daresay that that will really bring in a great body of persons who ought to serve as jurors, but no doubt some will be omitted, and there are classes who ought, irrespective of the qualification entirely, beyond all question to be on the jury list; for instance, all magistrates. There are some 300 or 400 justices of the peace in the county of Cork; if the jury list is examined, many of those will be found not to be upon it at all, and some of them may not be rated in respect of any property. I propose to add all those. I would put on the general panel and on the special panel all magistrates. You cannot make the special panel too high in its standard. I should bring in a number of other qualifications, such as merchants and bankers, if you can get them, and if they are not already on the ratebook.

3233. There are some special qualifications, are there not, for the special jury list?—Still, you have one common foundation of rating by name, and the point that I am calling attention to is, that many persons, qualified in every respect to be jurors, and above all, qualified to be special jurors, may not be rated by name, and if you could get at them, I think it would be a very great advantage.

3234. Colonel *W. Patten.*] How are they rated?—They may have to pay their proportion of rates, and yet not be rated by name. Again, you may frequently meet, for instance, with merchants and men of undoubted wealth, and yet they may not be rated by name in respect of property that will qualify them. There has been a suggestion that the sons of Peers ought to be on the jury list. I should say yes, they should be on the jury list, and the special jury list, whether rated or not, but the proposition is only to put them on if they are rated. I would put them on whether rated or not. So I would put the eldest son of a baronet along with justices of the peace. There are a number of persons who may be chairmen or directors of public companies, and a great number of those may already be on the rate-book, but you will find that there are many who are not. With regard to special jurors, provided you can secure a sufficient number of special jurors, you cannot make the qualification too high. The object should be to put on the special jury list the most intelligent and independent class, provided you could get them in sufficient number. And furthermore, I have an impression that it would be wise to adopt the principle of the Scotch plan, of having at least one-third of the ordinary panel selected from the special jurors' book. The Scotch practice is subject to this objection. As I understand it, what is done is this: there are two panels summoned for trials, one from the common jurors' book and the other from the special jurors' book, and then at the trial a certain proportion is taken of special jurors and a certain proportion of common jurors. That is open to the objection that it may seem to array class against class. I see another error that has crept into the evidence before the Committee; the idea that there are two panels of jurors; one for civil and the other for criminal cases. That is not so; there is but one panel for the two classes of cases, and I would suggest that whoever frames the general panel for the assizes should take at least one-third of the general from the special jurors' book; that he should then put them all into one general panel, and when they come to be balloted for, you will find a proportion of special jurors for every jury that has to try civil or criminal cases.

3235. You would ballot for the jury from the panel instead of calling them?—I am entirely in favour of the ballot, both in civil and criminal cases.

3236. The practice is now, I believe, to call the names from the top of the list?—There is a ballot

Right Hon. J. D. Fitzgerald.

22 May 1873.

ballot now in every civil case, but in criminal cases there is no ballot, and they are called as they appear alphabetically on the list, and the jury is formed from those who answer first. I think that that is open to very serious objection, and I should entirely approve of the adoption of the ballot both in civil and criminal cases.

3237. You would not, I think you say, dispense with the power of the Crown to set aside jurors?—I do not think you can do that with safety. I may instance it thus: there may be a man whom you could not exclude from the jurors' book, because, probably, there may be nothing but suspicion against him. You might suspect a man to be a leading member of some secret organisation, or to belong to some illegal society, but you could not, on mere suspicion, with propriety exclude him from the jury list or from the jurors' book, but it would be very wise that the officer of the Crown, who had the grave responsibility of conducting public prosecutions, should be at liberty to direct such a person to stand aside. He may be a very good juror in civil cases, but in a particular class of criminal cases he may be entirely unfit for that duty.

3238. Do you think that the exercise of that power is a very invidious one?—I think not, generally speaking. It has been very sparingly exercised. I have known it occasionally to go beyond that limit, but only where there was a necessity. I think one of the good things done by this Act is taking that power away from a private prosecutor.

3239. *Chairman.*] Have you any other general suggestion to make to the Committee?—With reference to the substitution of the alphabetical rotation in the Act, I look upon the two great principles of the Act to be the rating qualification and the taking away from the under-sheriff the power of selection. Those are the two objects of the Act, but there is also that of alphabetical rotation; that is a matter which was very often before the House of Commons; I am not able to say that it was ever gravely considered there, but it is not new to us. I remember as far back as the year 1854 it was proposed, but if you take away the sheriff's power of selection, and if you do not transfer that power to some other public officer, I do not see how you are to dispense with the alphabetical or some other rotation, and upon the whole I think that the alphabetical system of rotation is possibly the best.

3240. It is only a particular form of machinery for getting a chance selection of a panel from the jury list. I see no reason to think that, if fairly carried out, it would operate unfairly. I think that the instance which has been referred to to-day, of three brothers of the same name being on one special panel, may be accounted for very readily without its being any blot upon the Act of Parliament. You will recollect that there are, in the after sittings in Dublin, six courts sitting for trials, and possibly, for four of those, at least, special panels, probably exhausting particular letters. It may so happen that in following out this alphabetical rotation that you will have persons of the same name, or members of the same firm. I have known that occur before under the old Act; I have had repeated applications to excuse a particular member of a firm from serving, because another member of the same firm was already acting before me, and I yielded to the application: it is not peculiar to this Act; and in the exercise of judicial discretion, when I found two members of a firm upon the panel, I took the opportunity of letting one go.

3241. Would not drawing the number out of a box equally secure the object?—Certainly; that is to say, putting the whole of the names on the jurors' book into the ballot-box.

3242. The whole of the unexhausted jurors?—I see no objection whatever to that.

3243. Have you heard the objection that was taken to the alphabetical arrangement in the case of some counties where the same names greatly predominate, for instance, names beginning with some letter which greatly outnumbers all the others, for instance, M's and O's?—M is a very large letter with us, because it involves the name of Murphy, and those commencing with Mac.

3244. It would be rather ludicrous, would it not, if the last panel should be found to be composed almost exclusively of Murphys?—That could scarcely ever arise; it might be a little ludicrous, nothing more than that, because it would not follow that because they were of the name of Murphy or MacDonald that they had the slightest connection the one with the other. But you see you commence each year with a new jurors' book. As I read this Act of Parliament, and in dealing with the new jurors' book, a great many new names may come in at the head of each letter. The sheriff deals with the jurors' book, and he has to go along the letters in alphabetical selection, and the effect of that will be that he cannot summon those who had served before, otherwise I do not think that such an occurrence as that pointed out is likely to arise; and if it did, I see no great evil in it; it is more in the arrangement than anything else.

3245. Have you anything further to suggest to the Committee?—I would be further inclined to deal with the exemptions; that is to say, I would reduce them in one direction and increase them in another. I should not exempt a man simply because he was over 60; I should carry it up to 70. Some of the best men that I have seen serving on juries, and many who have applied to me to claim exemption because they were over 60, were the very men that I desired to have, and I see no reason because a man is over 60 that he is not to serve upon a jury. I should also give considerable power to the judge who presides at any trial, civil or criminal, to excuse jurors. I mentioned in the early part of my evidence, that I had taken upon myself a power of that kind, especially in Cork, which the law did not give me, but it was only a *bonâ fide* effort to give full effect to this Act of Parliament. I should be inclined to give the judge very large power for sufficient cause, such as would appear to him to be a sufficient reason at the trial, to excuse a juror, and to allow him to withdraw, and even to set him aside. There is another class that I would very much wish to be exempt, which has often come before me, and that is the class of persons who are only depending upon their daily labour for their subsistence. Cruel cases have come up before me in which I have been unable to let the jurors withdraw, although the evidence was quite satisfactory that they were in that position in life that they depended upon their daily labour for their subsistence.

3246. Has that been entirely under the new Act?—No, I have known it under both, but less frequently under the old Act. I had frequent applications

Right Hon. *J. D. Fitzgerald.*

22 May 1873.

applications from jurors under the old Act under such circumstances that it was cruel to them to detain them. I should be very much inclined to give to the revising officer and to the judge the power to excuse such persons who from being dependent upon their daily labour, or from some other feature in their circumstances, were unable to attend the office of juror, without great injury to themselves. Then, possibly, the disqualification in consequence of crime might be judiciously enlarged; at least there might be a power given to the revising judge to exclude from the juror's book persons who have been convicted of crime. At present, I think, in the Act of Parliament, it is only where the parties have been found guilty of felony or of some infamous crime. It is very difficult to define what infamous crime is. I suppose perjury and forgery, and matters of that kind, would be considered so, but I should be inclined very much to adopt the French system, which is, that any person who has been convicted of any crime in respect of which he has been subject to a sentence of over twelvemonths' imprisonment may be excluded. I would not say positively that he should, but that he may be excluded from it; and I would even go lower than that. I should be inclined to give the revising judge power to deal with parties convicted of crime, but which would not come within the category of infamous crime, such as indecent assaults and offences of an aggravated character, that did not come within the class of felonies or infamous crimes. I should be very much inclined to exclude such parties, and make it a disgrace to exclude him from the jury list, a disgrace attaching upon the crime.

3247. You would make that a disqualification and not a ground of exemption?—No, it should be a disqualification. The period of exemption from serving, having once served, is two years; but I am inclined to think that that is too long a period, as I think that in the working out of this Act, if it is allowed, it will create embarrassment hereafter. I entirely agree with what Mr. Justice Morris has said, that a man should not be exempted from serving by reason of his having been summoned, but by reason of having served, that he has either served by attendance, or by actually acting upon the jury.

3248. Colonel *Wilson Patten.*] You would not allow him to be exempted if he has been summoned, but has not served?—No, unless he has attended; a very large proportion of those who are summoned do not attend at all; they take the risk, and their having taken the risk they get the benefit of exemption, because they have been summoned.

3249. But you would not recommend that the exemption should be for two years?—I would confine it to those who have attended or served; I should rather be inclined to adopt the limit of a year.

3250. *Chairman.*] Under the existing Act they may serve oftener, may they not, than two years, if the book is exhausted?—Yes, if the book is exhausted; but probably in many counties it would not be, having regard to the great number that are upon the jurors' book. The right to peremptory challenge has excited a good deal of attention. At present the right of peremptory challenge is a matter which stands upon an unsound basis, and in my judgment it ought to be altered. The peremptory challenge was given originally in favour of life; it was given in cases of felonies, but it was established at the time when all felonies were capital, and it existed in all cases of felony without benefit of clergy; that is, where the punishment was death. A great many felonies, I am happy to say, 19-20ths of them, are now not punishable capitally; but the right to challenge 20 peremptorily is retained. In my judgment, either the right to challenge peremptorily should be confined to cases which are now capital, or you should modify the right and extend it to all criminal cases. I have repeatedly had this before me. The Crown have preferred an indictment against a prisoner for an offence, which might be either treated as a felony, or as a misdemeanor, and have had Bills found for felony and misdemeanor; but to avoid the challenge, they would put him on trial only for the misdemeanor. That seems highly objectionable; and, again, some wretched case of larceny in which, for a first offence, you would very likely impose two months' imprisonment; the prisoner had the right of 20 peremptory challenges, because larceny was felony, but in the next case that you would have to try, which would be a misdemeanour only, for which probably you would inflict seven years' penal servitude, the prisoner would have no right of challenge. Therefore, whilst I would not at all interfere with the power of peremptory challenge, in capital cases I would leave it as it is. I would give the prisoner, in such cases, his 20 peremptory challenges simply upon the look of a juror, and say, I do not like you, and I will not have you, but I would certainly either abolish the right in other cases, or modify and extend it to all criminal cases. In my opinion it would be desirable to reduce the number of peremptory challenges, but also to extend it to all criminal cases; that is to say, I would give a right of peremptory challenge in every criminal case to a limited extent; I would not interfere with the right in capital cases where the punishment is death. If I may add, before parting with this subject, my own impression that a limited right of peremptory challenge should also be given in civil cases; I have known this repeatedly happen, that a juror in a civil case was known to be the intimate friend of the plaintiff or defendant, and there was no power of setting him aside; the judge could not do it except by consent, and yet you would know that there was going upon the jury a person who would never consent to a verdict in favour of one party, no matter how much he might be entitled to it by law. One of the great evils in the administration of the civil law is in the frequent occurrence of disagreements, by reason of some friend of either party very frequently having got upon the jury, and my own opinion is, that that right of peremptory challenge to a limited extent should also be given in civil cases.

3251. *Chairman.*] There are an unlimited number of challenges for cause, are there not?—Yes.

3252. Would you limit the right of the Crown's peremptory challenges?—The Crown has no peremptory challenges; it has the power to set aside; that power may be hereafter limited, but at present I do not think you could, with due regard to the safety of the public, interfere with the right of the public prosecutor to set aside. He only directs to stand aside, and if the panel should be exhausted, then the persons whom he has directed to stand aside will be called up, and sworn, unless he can show legal cause of challenge.

Then,

Right Hon. *J. D. Fitzgerald.*

22 May 1873.

Then, following out the observation that I made, the public evil, the great expense and loss to both parties (I am speaking now of Ireland alone), which has arisen by reason of disagreement in civil cases, is a very great grievance. I should be very much inclined in civil cases to take the verdict of a majority. I am not prepared to adopt it in criminal cases for Ireland, and certainly not in any case that is capital. I have known so many instances where even a single juror, by holding against the opinion of his brethren, has saved life, and prevented the perpetration of a judicial murder.

3253. Sir *Rowland Blennerhassett*.] Would you have a bare majority in civil cases?—That is a matter of detail which I have not considered.

3254. *Chairman*.] To take the verdict of a majority would also frequently in Ireland, would it not, act in a different way, and would secure an acquittal in some cases to a prisoner, where now there has only been a disagreement?—Yes; it might in criminal cases.

3255. Probably there have been cases where, after a disagreement, conviction has followed?—Certainly, although in criminal cases, I think, it is rare after a disagreement to get a conviction, but I have known it in some cases; but generally speaking, disagreement is followed by disagreement, and the final discharge of the prisoner in criminal cases; but in capital cases, as I mentioned, I have known the disagreement of juries in many instances operate most beneficially.

3256. Have you known cases where the minority were subsequently proved to be right?—Yes, and in one remarkable case, the minority was one. It was a case which occurred when I was a junior barrister myself, and I recollect sitting by at the trial in Limerick when a young man was charged with murder. The evidence was apparently conclusive against him, and the jury retired after a long trial. They were locked up for the night, having announced in the early part of the evening that they were not likely to agree, or, as the expression was, one man was standing out. They were locked up for the night, and finally they were discharged the next day, being unable to agree, and there was a great outcry against that one juror. I was present at the second trial of the prisoner, and it was clearly proved that the principal witness against him was the murderer, and the prisoner was perfectly innocent, and he was acquitted by a first-class jury in Limerick without turning round. On one or two occasions I have met with cases of that kind, and that is the reason why I would not accept the verdict of a majority in a capital case. I should mention that the dissentient juror in that case was afterwards a Member of the House of Commons, Mr. Stephen De Vere, Member for Limerick.

3257. Colonel *W. Patten*.] When you recommend that the peremptory challenge should be taken away in certain criminal cases, do you not think that in the present state of Ireland that would meet with considerable opposition?—I proposed that it should be reduced, and extended to all criminal cases; in cases not capital it is not much exercised, but it is an anomaly that it should exist in one class of criminal cases and not in another. What I propose is that it should be reduced, but extended to all criminal cases.

3258. You do not think that at trials where crime and politics are mixed up together, it would be looked upon as diminishing the rights of the people at all?—Of course any alteration that would take place in that way would, for a time, be regarded with jealousy, but the right to challenge for cause remains.

3259. You have mentioned a certain number of cases in which you would give discretion to the judges; in what mode would you give them that discretion, would you do it all by statute, or would you do it by regulation, or would you have it to be done by practice?—The discretion that I alluded to was a discretion to discharge a juror when he appeared before the judge, and that should be given to him by statute.

3260. At the same time, would it be possible to put into the statute all the exemptions?—No; what I propose to do would be independent of the Revision Court entirely, but to give the judge at the trial the power to discharge a juror for sufficient cause; of course he would investigate the case.

3261. You think that that would be sufficient for the safety of the subjects without assailing any privilege?—Yes; he would investigate the case in open court.

3262. You stated that you would give the power to the Clerk of the Peace and the Clerk of the Crown to exercise their judgment on the list of jurors; are those officers in Ireland in a position to know much about the qualifications of jurors?—The Clerk of the Crown is not very much; indeed, there is this objection, that both of these officers do the duty by deputy; but the deputy who does the duty ought to have, if he has been long enough in the county, a very extensive knowledge of the county; what I wished to call the attention of the Committee to was, that if you constitute the chairman's court as a court of revision, there certainly should be some one to bring the case before him, as you have in the matter of prosecutions; there must be some one charged with that duty; if it is left at large, what is everybody's duty will be nobody's duty.

3263. But the question is, with whom should it be left; it is very desirable that there should be such a power somewhere or other, for the reasons which you have stated; but the question is, who is the officer who has the greatest knowledge of the jurymen in the county?—Probably the parties who would have the most extensive knowledge would be the officers of the constabulary; but I would not think of entrusting the carriage of this proceeding to them; I would make them the means of communicating information, and make it their duty to give to whoever is to be the public officer having charge of this particular duty the fullest information, and I would compel them to attend to give evidence before the court. You have to select some one, say the Clerk of the Crown, or the sessional Crown Prosecutor; the sessional Crown Prosecutor would be a very good officer, and a man of intelligence; but it is open to this objection, that, as he has the conduct of the quarter sessions Crown prosecutions, it might be alleged that he objected to people and got them off the jurors' list who would be favourable or unfavourable in particular cases; he might be regarded with suspicion, in other words.

3264. You have stated to the Committee that in consequence of the increase of education in Ireland the number of illiterate persons is daily diminishing?—Yes, daily, I should say.

Right Hon. *J. D. Fitzgerald.*

22 May 1873.

3265. In the course of the circuit to which you have alluded, where the juries were not in a satisfactory state, did you find that that want of education was confined to the elder branches, or generally was it common to the younger branches as well?—I am unable to answer the question; the place that I objected to principally was Clare, and as I have stated to the Committee I was the civil judge in Clare, and as far as the civil cases were concerned the conduct of the juries was exemplary, and they found proper verdicts in cases, some of them of very considerable difficulty, assisted of course by the judge. It is one great advantage of having persons of that class assisting in justice that they are brought into communication with people of a higher rank, both with the barristers and with the judge, who assists and instructs them, and in the civil cases their conduct was very good. I was not the criminal judge, but as it happened, from the pressure of business in the Crown Court, my colleague, Mr. Justice O'Brien, was obliged to send one very important case to me for trial, and I will just describe the process that took place. When the jurors came into court many of them appeared of the humblest farming class, and the prisoner had the right of challenge; he challenged 20 peremptorily, and it was a joke at the time that I heard it, but it was not without foundation, that on the part of the prisoner every one was challenged who had a necktie on. The result of exercising the challenge in that way was that you had a jury apparently of a very indifferent class. I cannot say whether those were illiterate or not, but certainly they either were illiterate and incapable of understanding the case, or they were terrified into finding a false verdict, or some of them sympathised with the crime, for undoubtedly the decision which they came to was wholly inexcusable.

3266. The discretion which you say should be given to the judge to exempt a juryman for cause shown, you would allow, would you not, to the chairman of quarter sessions as well as to the judge of assize?—Yes, in any case coming before them.

3267. Mr. *Bruen.*] I suppose you would not limit the judge to any number of cases in which he could excuse for those reasons?—No.

3268. Colonel *Wilson Patten.*] The discretion, I presume, that you recommend is not to strike off a juryman, but to exempt him?—To exempt him *pro hac vice.*

3269. Would you give no discretion to the judge to strike off a juryman from the panel or jurors' book, and not merely to exempt him?—What I applied my statement to was simply to the panel. A person may be subject to infirmity, or 50 causes may arise so that the judge might often wish himself to have the authority of excusing a particular juror and leaving him off the panel when the parties would not consent, and at present he could not do it without consent.

3270. Have you seen instances where you would have been glad to have struck a juror off the panel, but you had not the power to do it?—Yes, and I see no objection whatever to having that power. The Court of Queen's Bench has the power at present, or any judge of that court, upon an application to examine into the case of any juror and striking him off the books. I see no objection to extending that power to all the judges, whether sitting in the superior courts at Dublin or at assizes.

3271. Mr. *Bruen.*] Would you have the reason assigned in open court?—Yes, certainly, I would have the thing done openly and above board.

3272. It would be brought before you by some public officer?—If there is an application to strike a juror off the jurors' book, he ought to have notice of it, and the case brought before the judge by somebody or other.

3273. You would not give the judge, upon such application, power to excuse a juror?—The power to excuse a juror is different, and that is merely from serving upon that occasion. It arises generally in this way, the juror himself comes forward and either objects himself or makes some excuse to be allowed to go away on proof that he is unfit. It is in those cases which the juror himself brings forward, that I propose to entrust that discretion in the judge.

3274. But not without an application from the juror?—No, not without an application from the juror; it usually comes from the juror.

3275. You did exercise that power, you told us, in Cork?—Yes, with the assistance of the under sheriff, in whom I had great confidence.

3276. Could you give us any idea about how many you excused in that way?—No, I could not tell. There may have been some 20 or 30, the panel was very large; the panel was about 240 or 250; I could not tell the number.

3277. Still it was a very considerable number?—Yes, it was a substantial number.

3278. But those, I suppose, were probably men whom the sheriff himself would have excluded from his panel if he had been framing it according to his own discretion?—Probably; some of those men were subject to infirmity; poverty and inability to remain; I examined into the cases myself.

3279. I think you said that in theory, looking at the present position of affairs, you have personally no great objection to allowing to the high sheriff a modified power of selection?—I said that if I were introducing this as a Bill, that is the course that I would have adopted myself; I would not have taken the large step of taking away that discretion altogether, but would have modified it, and hedged it round with safeguards to prevent abuse, and one of the things that I suggested would be making the high sheriff, who is generally a gentleman of considerable position in the county, personally responsible for it.

3280. So that in theory, at all events, you think that it would not be an unconstitutional power to give to the sheriff so guarded?—I could not call it unconstitutional; but I think that the tendency must be eventually to take away his authority altogether, and as you have done it I would prefer adhering to it.

3281. You think that it would be impossible to revert; would you mind my asking you why you think it impossible to revert to a limited power of selection given to the sheriff?—It is a returning upon a system which I have no hesitation in saying has been the subject of abuse, and may, no matter what safeguards you put round it, still be abused, and I am unwilling to recreate what the Legislature has abolished.

3282. Having expressed that in theory, you have no objection to this limited power of selection hedged round with those safeguards which you have named, do you think that there are no possible circumstances in which it would be wise to revert to that selection, so guarded?—I am afraid

Right Hon. *J. D. Fitzgerald.*

21 May 1873.

afraid that I have expressed myself incorrectly, if I am taken as saying that there was no objection in theory; I think there is great objection in theory to leaving this authority anywhere above the control of the law. What I intended to convey was this, that if I had been framing this Bill I should not have taken so large a leap myself, because I am averse to violent changes, and above all averse to tampering or dealing unnecessarily with the great institution of trial by jury.

3283. There is very considerable objection, is there not, to the knowledge, a long time beforehand, of who will be upon the panel?—It gives an opportunity of tampering with particular jurors.

3284. The present system of alphabetical selection is open to that objection in some degree, is it not?—Certainly; but I should add, that under the old system it was only a question of time, for the panel must have been published, and in the hands of everyone that wanted to get it, many days before any trial could take place; I forget the number of days.

3285. The revision of the jurors' lists you would give to the chairman of the county, because you think that he is acting under judicial responsibility. If the magistrates were empowered at petty sessions to revise the lists in their petty sessions districts, would you not consider that they were acting under judicial responsibility?—I did not at all mean to suggest that; I have no doubt that they would feel that they were. But what I desire to point out is that the magistrates have been tried, and failed; the revision, under the old law, was in the hands of the magistrates potentially, but it was nominal only in most counties.

3286. The qualification under the old law being rather obsolete, it would have been very different for the magistrates, I suppose, to have run through the lists without reducing them so much as almost to leave insufficient lists?—I mentioned that, certainly; but I mentioned the cases of dead men, for years dead. Under the old system, once on the jurors' book they remained there, although the men went to America, or were all dead, or whatever became of them.

3287. Do not you think that the carelessness in the revising the lists might have been due, perhaps, to the fact of the magistrates sitting for the whole county in one court, and that if they sat for their own petty sessions districts it would be more likely to be carefully performed?—I think it would be; do not suppose that I imply the least distrust in the magistrates. There would be an advantage in a primary revision at the petty sessions, that you would have it done by a class of gentlemen who very likely would know all the circumstances of their district; still I would bring it in the end to the chairman's court, whether there was a primary revision at the petty sessions, or not.

3288. Have you any objection to my asking you a question with regard to a charge which you are reported to have given to a jury in the county of Cork, at the assizes, respecting the framing of the panels?—No; I should be very glad to answer it.

3289. It is reported that you spoke in these words: "You are aware, under the old law, that the high sheriff, or his deputy, in selecting the jury panel, had an unlimited discretion. He took whom he pleased from the jurors' book; and it has been supposed that the new Jury Act reversed completely that system, and deprived the sheriff of all discretion, and relieved him from all responsibility: but that is not so. That I find to have been the view taken by the sheriffs, in two of the counties of this circuit. In my judgment, but not having the question discussed before me, I offer my opinion, with some hesitation, that is a mistake. The sheriff still has a discretion, and has a responsibility; and that discretion of his may be usefully applied. For instance, as I saw the panel framed, and as I examined it in other counties, the sheriff proceeded in this way: he commenced, say, with a panel of 100, and very likely, such as in the letter Y, he had no name in it. He would take from each letter, and would commence by taking the first letter in A, the first in B, and so on; and when he went to the end of the alphabet, he began with the second number. That is not the mode of selection; the Statute, at least, does not impose that mode of selection. He has a discretion still, and when, after framing the panel, he selects, for instance, from the letter A, he may select any four he pleases within the limit of that letter who have not served before. So I wish to point out that the sheriff has still, in framing the jury panel, a power of selection, and also a responsibility cast upon him to select persons who are fit and proper to serve as jurors"; will you allow me to ask whether that is a correct exposition of your view?—It is a correct statement of some observations which I addressed to the grand jury. It states my individual opinion, which opinion I still entertain. I have not the slightest doubt that the framers of this Act of Parliament intended to exclude the discretion of the sheriff altogether; but then I can only take their intention from the language of the Act, and not from what I may know historically was their intention. And it seems to me (I do not know whether I stand alone amongst the judges in this respect or not) that the language of the Act is capable of another construction. I call your attention to section 19 of the Act. "The sheriff in selecting the jurors." I pause first upon the term "selecting," which is inapplicable; if he is merely to take them as they are in the book. Then, again, it says, that he is to select them "in a regular alphabetical series." How is he to do that? "By returning one name from each letter in succession," not returning the first name in each letter, but "one name from each letter;" that is to say, one from A. and one from B. Then it goes on further to say, that he is to go on "through the letters of the alphabet from first to last, as often as may be necessary, and so far as the number of names in each letter will admit," and further, having gone through them, he has then to "commence with the letter next following that from which the last name in the preceding panel was taken;" but in no place does it say till you come to a later sentence (which no doubt creates ambiguity) that he is to do anything else than take a name from each letter. The view that I took was this, that in taking a name from a letter, he performed his duty if he took any name from letter A., and it was not necessary that he took the first name; and so when he passed the letter B. he could take any name from it. As as we get lower down in section 19, there is a sentence which creates ambiguity; but still, upon the whole, I thought the fair construction

Right Hon. *J. D. Fitzgerald.*

22 May 1873.

construction of the Act was this, that the sheriff had a modified discretion, that he was obliged to pursue the alphabetical order, but that in taking the names from letter A. he was at liberty to take any names from any persons who had not served before, and so when he came to letter B. he had discretion again within that letter, and took any names from it of jurors who had not served before. Lower down you will find this passage, "So that the name of every juror shall be returned on the panels of jurors in its proper turn and order." That is the only passage in the clause that creates any ambiguity, but I do not think that the ambiguity is sufficient to overturn the clear construction of the previous matter, that in selecting the jurors in a certain series, he is to do it "by returning one name from each letter in succession;" that is, any name from each letter. I do not mean to say that that is the opinion of any other judge than myself. I formed the best opinion I could; it was never discussed before me; I acted upon it on the spot, and told the grand jury of Cork that such was my view.

3290. May I ask whether in your opinion it is a safe limit of discretion to allow to the sheriff?—I thought, under the circumstances in Cork, it was a wholesome limit if he did exercise it, but he did not.

3291. You have no wish to see that limited discretion entirely reduced by his taking the names in strict dictionary order?—No; that is one of the things that I would have not done myself. If I had been framing this Act, I would have limited the discretion, but not abolished it. I intimated, too, that I thought that the obligation ought to be imposed upon the high sheriff. Then there was this further, that in adopting the alphabetical series, the discretion that would be left with the sheriff would be simply a discretion to select the names within the letter.

3292. You have made a suggestion, I think, if I understood you aright, that it might be advisable to select the panel by ballot from the list; was I mistaken in supposing that you made that suggestion?—I said I can see no objection at all if the whole of the names of the jurors who have not served were put in a ballot box, and the selection of the jury panel was by ballot.

3293. Should you prefer that mode of choosing the jury panel to the strict dictionary order of selection from the list?—I should be rather inclined to adopt the ballot.

3294. Mr. *Downing.*] That would get rid of all this difficulty about alphabetical order?—It never was suggested to my mind before so as to consider it, but apparently, taking it at the moment, it would get rid of it.

3295. With regard to the opinion which you have given upon the 19th section, do not you think that you ought to read the 13th section in connection with the 19th, where it says that it shall be arranged as in the dictionary?—I have read every section carefully.

3296. Would not that alter your opinion?—Not in the least.

3297. You said that there was rather a serious case relegated to you by Mr. Justice O'Brien; was that a case in which a man's finger was taken off by an explosion?—Yes, in trying to shoot his landlord he shot his own hand off; the gun burst in his hand.

3298. Was not it an indictment for firing what was calculated to deprive the man of his life?—Yes.

3299. Was there any evidence that it was loaded?—The clearest evidence that you could possibly have in a case of the kind. The gentleman fired at deposed (and I had no reason whatever to disbelieve him, for he gave his evidence in a very fair way) that he heard the rush of missiles pass his head.

3300. Was not it really a question for the jury whether they believed that the gun was loaded?—Certainly it was, and I put it to them, and called their attention to the evidence, but I do not conceive that there was any ground upon which a reasonable man could go but that. What did the man go there to fire the blunderbuss for; did he go to fire at a man with only powder in it? People must look at those cases with common sense.

3301. What was the indictment?—The indictment was the firing of a gun loaded with some deadly missile; no matter whether it was a bullet or a button, or piece of iron, or anything else.

3302. You stated that where for any crime the imposition of 12 months' imprisonment could be inflicted, you would consider that that was one of those cases where the chairman or judge should have the power of exclusion?—I would not propose that it should be an absolute disqualification.

3303. Taking the present category in the Act of Parliament, would you make felony one of the crimes which should disqualify a man?—Yes, undoubtedly; but I would go beyond that, and render a man liable as a matter of disgrace to be excluded from the jurors' book if he had been found guilty of a crime which subjected him to a certain degree of punishment. I would not make it an absolute disqualification, for we know that sentences are occasionally passed with reference to crime; for instance, the Party Processions Act; and I would not exclude a man because he had been convicted of a crime which involves no moral turpitude; therefore I would give the revising officer discretion to inquire what the charge was.

3304. You would not disqualify a man because he was convicted of assault, for which he might get two years?—Sometimes I would for assault; it is often a very bad crime.

3305. That would depend on circumstances, I presume?—Sometimes in the case of an assault, where five or six men attack one man going to a fair, and nearly beat the life out of him, I would keep all of them off the jurors' list, and I would make that a part of their punishment.

3306. I see in the Bill which you introduced, you would deprive the Crown of the right to stand by, and limit the number to the same as the prisoner has a right of peremptory challenge?—I take it for granted that you are right as to that. Whatever I did was very carefully considered.

3307. It is Section 27, and it says: "In all cases of indictment for any treason or felony, the clerk or registrar shall draw out of the box 52 of such parchments or cards, or if any of the men whose names shall be so drawn shall not appear, or shall be challenged for a cause, then such further number until 52 be drawn who shall appear, and who after all just causes of challenge allowed, shall remain as fair and indifferent, and thereupon the names of such jurors shall be called over a second time in the order in which they were drawn from such box; and the person so indicted

indicted for such treason or felony shall be admitted to challenge peremptorily 20 of such jurors and no more, and those who prosecute for the Crown shall be admitted to challenge peremptorily 20 of such jurors and no more"?—No doubt that section is there as you read it to me. I have no recollection of it; but I have a strong impression on my mind that that section is not mine, and that I am not responsible for it, and that it did not express any opinion that I entertained, because, as I stated, I got the Bill from my predecessors, and I made some alteration where I thought alteration was necessary; but, after all, that was only a step towards what I wanted to have done, and you will find in "Hansard" that more than once I asked the House to refer both Bills to a Select Committee, and let them make a good one out of them.

3308. Do you happen to know that, by the law of Scotland, the Crown have only the same right to stand by an equal number with the right of the prisoner to challenge?—I am not at all prepared to say. Again, I should mention that the circumstances of the country have very much altered since that time. There has been a great deal of insurrectionary crime, which did not exist at all then. Indeed all the time that I was in office was a period of unexampled peace and quiet, and it was a very proper time to consider amendments and alterations of the law when you were at peace and quiet; but what I might have recommended then I would not recommend now that we have the experience of 1856 and 1857. There may be on the jury panel parties whom you cannot reach, but who we all know are not fit in particular cases to serve as jurors. I hope the day will come when the right may be dispensed with; but I am not inclined at present to interfere with the right of the Crown to direct jurors to stand aside.

3309. You seem to agree with a great majority of the witnesses, that the principal thing to arrive at is the strict revision of the jurors' list? —Yes.

3310. I think that you have stated that you think that the chairman of quarter sessions is really the very best person to perform that function?—Yes, in my judgment he is; I have great confidence in him.

3311. An opinion was expressed by the Chief Justice of the Common Pleas, and by Mr. Serjeant Armstrong, that if, after the list came from the clerk of the union, and after the clerk of the union prepared it, with the assistance of the rate collectors, it was brought before the chairman at the quarter sessions, say on the first day of the quarter sessions, or on the first day of the Crown business, the clerk of the union and the clerk of the peace being always in attendance, the local Crown Prosecutor being always in attendance, the sub-sheriff being always in attendance, or his deputy being always in attendance, and each name was called out by the clerk of the peace in public court, and with the attendance of those different officers, do not you think that you would have, as far as it is possible, a correct and properly-revised list?—I entertain a strong view that you must impose the duty on some one individual of bringing forward the objections to particular names, and I have stated that I contemplate that the chairman should be attended by all those officers, who should give him every information; but that will not do unless you impose on some public officer the obligation of bringing the cases forward, and making him responsible for doing that. I do not care who that public officer is, but there must be some one for the purpose.

Right Hon. *J. D. Fitzgerald.*

22 May 1873.

3312. Do you conceive of any public officer now that would have such knowledge of the jury panel as to be enabled to publicly put forward objections to certain jurors?—I do not think that that is required. What I want is to have some active agent to bring the cases forward, whose duty it would be to get information, and who would have the officers of the constabulary and other public officers about him, who would inform him, either then or beforehand, that such a man ought to be objected to, and the grounds of objection. But if you leave it indiscriminately to all to do it, nobody will do it.

3313. Do not you think that persons are very anxious to get off the jury list?—Generally speaking, they are anxious to avoid that duty; but I confess that I would wish to alter that feeling. I would wish to bring them to that condition that they would consider it a discredit to be left off; for instance, I should leave off, as I think I ought, all men who cannot read or write, and that a man should feel at once that it is discreditable to him to be off the jurors' list. There is at present the wish to avoid that duty; but I wish to change that feeling, and to make it an honour, as I believe it to be.

3314. Colonel *Forde*.] I think I understood you to say that you would give the judge the power of allowing a juror, on his application, or proving an objection, to be excused; but I think that you further said that you would give a power to the judge to set aside a juror if he thought it was necessary?—That is to say, to strike him off the jurors' book.

3315. No, on the trial?—Yes, to set him aside, if in his judgment he is an improper juror.

3316. That power you have not at present?—No, unless upon a challenge.

3317. You would like to get that power?—Yes, and to be able to exercise it without a challenge.

3318. The high sheriffs do not always live in the county, I think, and they may not be always there?—In the contemplation of the law, the high sheriff ought to be always in his county, and never out of it.

3319. Perhaps he might not like the duty to be imposed upon him?—He would have the assistance of the under-sheriff; but it should be done on his responsibility.

3320. The present Act, the 3rd and 4th of William the Fourth, makes the sheriff responsible?—No, I am afraid not. I think that it is one of the duties that goes to the under-sheriff by his deputation, and in which the high sheriff cannot interfere, or if he does he violates the law. I would reverse it, and make him responsible.

3321. Colonel *Vandeleur*.] You stated that you were satisfied with the jurors in your court, except in the case of Mr. Creagh, in the county of Clare; you were sitting there in the civil court, were you not?—Yes.

3322. Were the rest of the cases civil or criminal?—I tried, as I said, only one criminal case, all the others were civil; but the one in which I was quite satisfied with the verdict was of a criminal character. It involved a question that was afterwards tried in the Crown Court, and the man's name was Foundation.

Right Hon. *J. D. Fitzgerald.*

12 May 1873.

3323. Was Mr. Justice O'Brien satisfied with the verdict in the Crown Court?—I heard Mr. Justice O'Brien speak with strong disapproval of one case of acquittal in his court at Clare. It was a case in which the parties were charged with assaulting a police officer in the discharge of his duty, of which there was no doubt at all upon the evidence, and yet they acquitted the man.

3324. Being partly connected with Clare, and going that circuit very often, can you state whether the jurors in Clare hitherto have been generally very respectable and very satisfactory?—Certainly, very; the only objection that I would have taken to the Clare jurors before this was, that I pretty generally always saw the same faces; they appeared to be the same body of men certainly, assizes after assizes, and I thought that was very unfair. It was putting on a small section of the community a duty that ought to have been spread over a large portion of it.

3325. Colonel *Forde.*] Did you see many old faces amongst the jury panel at Clare?—No; I think the few that were on the panel absented themselves.

3326. How was the difficulty got over in Kerry with regard to the jury panel?—In most cases an objection was taken in the Crown court, but the judge there proposed to send the cases to be tried to the quarter sessions, and forthwith the objection to the jury was withdrawn. In the civil court, with me, they were not anxious to raise the objection.

3327. Colonel *Vandeleur.*] You spoke about the difficulty that would be experienced in bringing objections to jurors before the court; you are aware that in the case of the voters' list the rate collectors, who assist the clerks of the unions, insert before every man's name the word "objected;" might not in the same way on the jury's list the word "objected" be posted up by the rate collector or by the head constable of the district?—I see not the least objection to that. It would be a very invidious duty, but it would only tell the chairman that a man was objected to.

3328. It would tell the parties, if they did not choose to appear, that they need not; and if the parties chose to be struck off without remonstrance, they need not attend the court?—I see no objection whatever to that. I believe that that has been objected to by some witnesses; but I see none at all to it.

Monday, 26th May 1873.

MEMBERS PRESENT:

Mr. Attorney General.
Sir Rowland Blennerhassett.
Mr. Bruen.
Viscount Crichton.
Mr. Downing.
Colonel Forde.
Mr. Henry Arthur Herbert.
The Marquis of Hartington.
Mr. Heron.
The O'Donoghue.
Colonel Wilson Patten.

THE RIGHT HONOURABLE THE MARQUIS OF HARTINGTON, IN THE CHAIR.

Mr. HENRY HAIGH BOTTOMLEY, called in; and Examined.

Mr. H. H. Bottomley.
26 May 1873.

3329. *Chairman.*] I BELIEVE you are Sub-Sheriff of the county of Antrim?—I am.

3330. For what time have you held that office?—I am entering my fifteenth year of office.

3331. Have you held it continuously?—Yes, consecutively, without interruption.

3332. Are you aware of any meeting that has taken place of the sub-sheriffs in Ireland with reference to the Juries Act?—There was a meeting held in Dublin, about a month ago, in which the subject was discussed amongst the sub-sheriffs.

3333. Were you present at that meeting?—I was not; I was not able to be present.

3334. But have you the means of knowing what the views of the sub-sheriffs are with reference to this Act, or with reference to any evidence which has been given before this Committee?—So far as I can learn, the sub-sheriffs are not opposed to the principle of the Act, provided that some modifications could be made, and some improvements, especially with regard to the service of the summonses, which touches them more particularly.

3335. Can you state what modifications they desire to see?—In order to produce a better class of jurors, the sub-sheriffs are of opinion that the qualification should be raised. With regard to the county of Antrim, I could give my impression as to the deterioration of the jurors at the last assizes, compared with what they were formerly in point of intelligence. With regard to the jurors generally of the county of Antrim, it has been already stated by some of the witnesses here since I came, that they were always particularly distinguished for their general intelligence; and the judges who have come on the circuit have frequently expressed the same opinion with regard to the jurors of the county of Antrim under the old system. At the last assizes, as regards the special jurors, the class was entirely changed. There were very few of those who formerly served as special jurors on the panel, and the remainder were taken up from a class who had previously not been on a special jury panel at all. There were farmers, publicans, and cattle dealers on the special jury list, which had previously been for the most part composed of the merchants in Belfast, and also of the large ratepayers throughout the county generally. As regards the common jurors, I was particularly struck with the immense number of aged persons, that is, people above 60 years of age; and also with the number of illiterate persons, which was quite a novelty as regards the common jury in Antrim.

3336. Were those special jurors, whom you used to summon, not on the special jury list at the last assizes?—There were very few of them on the new special jury list prepared under the Act of 1871.

3337. Do you mean that the class who used to serve as special jurors were not included on the new special jury list, or that so many others were included that they did not happen to be summoned upon the panel?—I should fancy that they were all included in the general list, but there was such a large addition made to the number by the new qualification that there were very few appeared on the panel.

3338. In the discharge of your duty as sub-sheriff how used you to select the jurors that you placed on the panel, both common and special jurors?—With regard to the special jurors, under the old system the sheriff had under the Act of William the Fourth a power of making out what was called a special jurors' list for the county at the beginning of his year of office. That list comprised perhaps some 300 or 400 names. There were certain qualifications given in the Act of the 3rd & 4th Will. 4, to which the sheriff was required to attend in making out those special jury lists so far as he had knowledge on the subject.

3339. Do I understand you to say that it was the duty of the sheriff, not only to select the panel from the list, but also to make a list of special jurors?—It was under the former Act.

3340. And practically that was done by you?—Practically it was done by all the under sheriffs at the beginning of the year; it was the duty of the sheriffs to do so.

3341. How did you form first of all the list that

Mr. H. H. Bottomley.

26 May 1873.

that you selected the panel from; what steps used you to take to do it?—I took from the general jurors' book, which was furnished to me, the names of the persons who were included in the qualification clause for special jurors in the former Act, the Act of William the Fourth.

3342. What was the qualification?—There were a variety of qualifications in the Act.

3343. Having framed your list, how did you then proceed to select the panel?—With regard to special jurors I was obliged to furnish a panel of 48 names, and I generally took them in a sort of alphabetical selection as regards the special jurors, and also from different parts of the county. It was not incumbent upon me to select them alphabetically; and I took them from different parts of the county. Of course the majority of the special jurors were from Belfast, being a place of large population.

3344. Did you endeavour to go through the list, so as to give each a turn?—I did, and I succeeded in doing so to a very great extent. In point of fact, the special jurors were seldom called on to serve again, at least, until the third year.

3345. You stated that the general jurors' book was handed to you, by whom was that done?—By the clerk of the peace.

3346. And you had nothing to do with the preparation of that book?—Nothing whatever.

3347. But it was your duty to select the common jurors' panel from that book?—Yes; it was my duty to select the common jurors' panel after selecting the special jurors.

3348. Can you state how you did that?—I was in the habit of selecting them from particular districts throughout the county. I do not mean one particular district, but several districts, including a large number from Belfast. I took two or three districts in the county for the Spring assizes, and two or three for the Summer assizes, perhaps, in another part of the county. I did not go in any regular routine; but I merely made a general selection from the book.

3349. In that selection did you have regard to the fact of jurors having served previously?—I always did so. I took the names at the beginning of each year myself, with the assistance of my clerk, and discovered the names of those who had served on the previous year from the entries in the book. I put a mark opposite to them, and I did not call them again.

3350. Did you endeavour to go through the whole list, or were there a certain number upon the list who, from your knowledge of them, were more intelligent than others, and the rest you never summoned at all?—I endeavoured to go through the entire list to exhaust the general jurors' book, and between the panels summoned at the assizes and those at the sessions, I have to a very great extent succeeded at the end of the year in having a very large proportion of the jurors summoned out of the book; but sometimes I entrusted to two of my principal officers, who were men whom I could rely upon, the right (subject to my revision on reports from them) of rejecting those who were above age, as far as possible, or who might be held to be unable to attend from sickness or permanent infirmity, and those who were labouring under any physical defect, and also as far as possible to exclude illiterate men. In consequence of these steps the jurors were of a very superior class in the county.

3351. Has your panel ever been challenged?—My panel was challenged twice.

3352. Can you give the instance?—It was challenged in the year 1865, at the instance of Mr. John Rea, on the ground of there being no jurors' book, and on the ground of fraudulent omission by the high constables of names on the jurors' book in preparing the same, and on the ground of non-service of summons to jurors by the sheriff in time.

3353. What was the result?—The result was that the challenge was overruled, and the judge stated that there was no ground of complaint against the sheriff in the formation of the panel.

3354. What was the next occasion?—The next was the spring assizes of 1873, the present year.

3355. On what ground?—On the ground of the panel not being arranged in strictly alphabetical order.

3356. What was the result of that?—The ground of challenge was that I had placed the letter M and the letter Mc on the panel, that being the arrangement which was made in the jurors' book which was supplied to me.

3357. Viscount *Crichton*.] Whom were they challenged by?—By the prisoner.

3358. Who was his counsel?—The first challenge taken was by Mr. Walter Boyd. It was a riot case; it was not connected with the Belfast riots, but a riot in Lisburn, as far as I recollect; subsequently the same challenge was lodged in a number of cases connected with the Belfast riots.

3359. *Chairman*.] What was the result?—The judge overruled the challenge, and the trials proceeded.

3360. Did he express any opinion as to whether you had been right in making two letters of M and Mc?—His general observations were to the effect that the Act had converted the sheriff into a machine, and that machinery sometimes went out of order without any fault. He said there was no fault; he thought that I had properly followed the arrangement in the jurors' book, as if I had not done so all the names under Mc would have been practically excluded from the panels for several years to come, in fact, until the book was exhausted, the Mc's would not appear at all.

3361. And when they did begin to appear very few others would appear, I suppose?—They would be all Mc's or they would be left out entirely until the other letters were all exhausted, and I thought that that was not in accordance with the spirit of the Act of Parliament.

3362. Then you would suggest some alteration in the mode prescribed by the Act of forming the panel by this alphabetical process?—So far as I can learn, the sub-sheriffs have no desire to have a return to the old system giving them an absolute power of selection. I believe for my own part and on the part of those whom I know, that it was carried out very fairly indeed under the old system. Under the present they think that there cannot be a perfect, or anything approaching to a perfect panel of jurors, unless there is some power of rejection or exclusion vested in some officer before the panel is finally returned.

3363. I was asking you, whether in your opinion

Mr. H. H. Bottomley.

26 May 1873.

opinion some other mode of impartial selection should be substituted for this process of taking the names alphabetically?—If the view taken by Judge Fitzgerald, as reported, that the sheriff might take one name from each letter without going strictly, and taking the first name from A, and the first name from B, and the first name from C, were held to be correct, there would be no objection on the part of the sub-sheriffs to the alphabetical selection. There is a difficulty created by requiring the sheriff to take the first name from A, the first name from B, and the first name from C, because when he sends out his summonses he is not made aware until close upon the assizes whether A can be served or B can be served, or whether they may not have been dead or left the country, and that creates a difficulty and a very great difficulty too. In consequence of that, I was obliged to send out a second and a third time to serve jurors throughout the county for the last assizes, at an enormous expense; at least, enormous compared with what it had been formerly.

3364. You are in favour of retaining in the hands of the sheriff a limited power of rejection? —I cannot see that by any process of revision, no matter how carefully it is attended to, there will not remain some jurors who ought fairly to be excluded from the panel as being illiterate, or above age, or from other reasons; and I think the sheriff has the means of obtaining information with regard to the jurors throughout his county as large as any other person.

3365. How used you practically to obtain the information; was it from your own personal knowledge of the jurors, or through any third person?—My own personal knowledge of jurors in the county of Antrim, considering that there were on the average 4,000 names on the jurors' book, was very small; but I took the means of ascertaining all the particulars that I could from the barony constables. The lists were returned by the barony constables formerly, and I ascertained some particulars from them, and I also relied in a great measure on my own principal officers.

3366. Who were they?—I have two of them, one resides in Belfast, and another in the centre of the county, whom I have had a considerable number of years under me; a superior class of men, to whom I have paid a salary.

3367. What is their official position?—They are sheriffs' officers, or sheriffs' bailiffs; they were head bailiffs.

3368. You think that no revision of the jurors' list can thoroughly exclude disqualified persons; but do you think that the revision could be carried further than it was on the last occasion?—Undoubtedly it could be carried much further, provided that there was some official, as suggested here by some of the witnesses, whose duty it was exclusively to look after the revision, and to raise objections to jurors.

3369. Are not the clerks of unions and the poor-law collectors directed by the Act to attend the revision?—They are directed by the Act to attend the revision, which, I presume, they do attend; but I was not at the last revision. I had been at previous revisions of jurors, not officially, but to see how it was done.

3370. Would it not be possible for the chairmen to exclude from the list such persons as you say remained on the list on the last occasion over age and illiterate, and so on?—Yes, provided that they had information.

3371. Had they not the information from the clerks of unions and the poor rate collectors?—The clerks of unions may, to some extent, have the means of giving information, if they are asked, upon the subject; but unless an objection is made by someone, I cannot see how they would be called upon to give information in each particular case. The man himself who is illiterate is not at all likely to come forward and declare his incompetency in the presence of his neighbours and friends.

3372. Was not the foundation of the jurors' list a list prepared by the poor rate collectors?—That is the foundation of the present jurors' list.

3373. Were they not directed by the Act to leave out of that list persons over age?—They were so directed; but it could not have been done on the last occasion, because there was an extremely large proportion of the entire panel in Antrim composed of aged persons; I should say one-fourth.

3374. That was not done; but it might have been done, had they the means of knowing who were over age?—If they had the means of knowing that, it could have been done.

3375. Would anybody have better means of knowing such facts than the poor rate collectors? —I really cannot answer the question; if they had all the sources of information available, I should fancy that they would be able to get a great deal of information.

3376. Is there anyone who is more likely to know the age of the ratepayers than the poor rate collectors; is there anyone better acquainted with that class?—If they applied to the agents of the different landed proprietors, the agents generally know the ages of their tenants; and if they had the means of getting information in that way, I think they could obtain it.

3377. But from what you saw at the last assizes, I gather that you are of opinion that the poor rate collectors cannot have taken any pains to exclude from the list those who were disqualified under the Act?—I certainly do not think they could have taken much pains.

3378. If the power of rejection were restored to the sheriff, would you make him responsible for the omission of any names on account of reasons which, in his opinion, disqualified them? —Undoubtedly, he ought to be made responsible.

3379. In what way?—At present the high sheriffs are responsible for all the official acts of their deputies, and they would be made, on a challenge to the array, as far as public opinion would go, by having the question raised against them.

3380. Under the late Act the sheriff was not in any way bound, was he, to summon all the qualified jurors in turn?—He was not bound to summon the jurors in turn.

3381. You now, as I understand, would make it incumbent upon him to summon all properly qualified jurors in turn?—Yes, I should think that that would be right.

3382. Can you suggest any means by which he should be called upon to account for his omission of any person?—The only suggestion that I have to make with regard to the omission of jurors would be, that he might be required to state in a schedule or list, the reasons of his rejection,

Mr. *H. H. Bottomley.*

26 May 1873.

jection, which might be verified on oath, and might be handed to the clerk of the Crown to be kept there, in case there was a question raised upon his selection.

3383. In the county of Antrim, what qualification would you suggest for common jurors?—I think the rating qualification of common jurors should be raised to 30 *l.* and upwards.

3384. Would you have any house rating qualification?—The house rating, I think, I would fix at 20 *l.*

3385. You do not mean that you would require, as a necessary part of the qualification, that a juror should be rated in respect of house or buildings, 20 *l.* in towns?—Yes; that would give a sufficiently large list in the county of Antrim. Of course different counties are under very different circumstances.

3386. What qualification would you suggest for special jurors?—The qualification for special jurors, I think, in the county of Antrim, should be raised to 100 *l.* and upwards.

3387. Would you have any different qualification for jurors resident in towns?—There is no different qualification in the Act.

3388. Would you suggest any difference?—I have no suggestion to make as regards special jurors.

3389. You would not admit upon the special jurors' list anyone non-resident in a town rated at less than 100 *l.*?—Not in the county of Antrim.

3390. Have you any means of knowing what diminution of the list would be caused by those alterations in the law?—As regards common jurors, if the first three ratings were excluded, that is, 12 *l.* and under 15 *l.*, 15 *l.* and under 20 *l.*, 20 *l.* and under 30 *l.*, to bring them above 30 *l.*, that would cause a diminution of 4,012 names, which, deducted from 7,836 names, the number on the jurors' book, would leave a residue of 3,824. I have taken that from the Return before the Committee.

3391. Do you think that that would be sufficient for the county of Antrim?—Yes; the average number of jurors formerly were 4,000 on the jurors' book, and that was found more than sufficient.

3392. Do you know what diminution in the special jurors' list would be caused?—The total number of the jurors on the special jurors' book is 1,982; striking off the number rated at 50 *l.* and under 80 *l.*, 935; and the number rated at 80 *l.* and under 100 *l.* 282, there would be 765 special jurors left, and I think that that number would be quite sufficient.

3393. Do you think that raising the qualification alone would be a sufficient amendment of the law?—I have already stated to the Committee that the mere raising of the qualification I do not think would be sufficient without a more perfect revision, and also a limited power of exclusion.

3394. Do you suggest that it would be desirable to exempt grand jurors at the assizes from liability to serve as common jurors?—I certainly should.

3395. On what ground?—On the ground that there might be an impression, on the part of the prisoners, that a grand juror, who had assisted in finding the bills against them, should not be placed upon the jury to try them.

3396. The assizes at Belfast last generally a long time, do they not?—They invariably last upwards of a week, and sometimes so long as three or four weeks.

3397. At the last assizes did many jurors appear who could not bear the expense of so long an absence from home?—It was a matter of daily occurrence at the conclusion of the business in the Crown Court, for a number of jurors to come up towards the bench, in a body consisting of about a dozen, and apply for liberty to go, on various grounds, many of them on the ground that they could not bear the expense of remaining from their farms, and the majority of those who applied were over 60 years of age.

3398. Had the judge the power of excusing them?—I am not aware whether he had the power, but he did excuse them; he allowed them to go home in great numbers. I may mention that there was a very large panel summoned in consequence of the number of cases that were coming on of a party nature at the assizes.

3399. You would think it desirable that the judge should have the power of excusing any juror who might come before him and show sufficient ground?—Yes, I should certainly think so. They generally apply to the sheriff first, and the sheriff refers them to the judge.

3400. Have you any suggestion to make as to the area from which jurors are taken for the assizes and quarter sessions?—Any suggestion that I would venture to make would be more with regard to jurors who are summoned to quarter sessions. At the last quarter sessions there were many instances of very great hardship inflicted on jurors in requiring them to come a very considerable distance, both grand and common jurors, to the quarter session town where there was no criminal business.

3401. They are summoned, are they not, under the Act from the quarter sessions district only?—They are; but the divisions in the county of Antrim are very large.

3402. What would you suggest?—As regards the quarter sessions' jurors, I was never aware that there was any complaint made with regard to the jurors who were summoned under the former system. They were summoned from a very limited area, and there was no inconvenience caused; and the class of jurors certainly were much better than we have now. The grand jurors were summoned principally from the towns where the quarter sessions were being held, and the common jurors from a small area round the towns.

3403. Then for quarter sessions juries, do I understand that you would propose to revert absolutely to the old system of summoning?—I do not know whether a distinction could be made between jurors at quarter sessions and jurors at assizes; I certainly think that the area should be diminished by some means as regards quarter sessions' jurors, merely for the purpose of lessening the inconveniences to which they are subjected.

3404. Colonel *Forde.*] In Antrim the divisions are the same as in the county of Down, large; but the quarter sessions are held in two towns in the same division?—The divisions are very large, and the quarter sessions are held in two towns in a division; but under the system in the Act of 1871, the jurors had to be summoned from the extreme ends of the division, very frequently to the first quarter sessions town.

3405. Could not you suggest that the jurors of certain baronies, we will say, around the town of the

Mr. *H. H. Bottomley.*

26 May 1873.

the quarter session, should be summoned for that time, and *vice versa*?—I should certainly say, that if there is a distinction made between quarter sessions jurors and those summoned at assizes, they should be summoned from particular baronies.

3406. *Chairman.*] But a distinction is made now, is there not, under the Act, the jurors are summoned for the assizes from the whole county, are they not?—Yes.

3407. And for the quarter sessions from the quarter sessions divisions?—Yes, from the quarter sessions divisions.

3408. Therefore, there is a distinction?—That being so, I would suggest that the district should be still more limited than the division.

3409. Would not the grievance of which you complain be met by reducing the size of the quarter sessions divisions?—To a great extent, I think it would.

3410. In many instances at the quarter sessions, I understood you to say that grand and common jurors were summoned from great distances, and they had nothing to do when they came?—That was the case. In two of the quarter sessions towns there is a great absence of criminal business generally.

3411. I understand that you and other sub-sheriffs have a great grievance as regards the summoning of jurors?—We certainly felt it very much as to summoning the jurors to the last assizes.

3412. You were put to very heavy expense, were you not?—Not only that, but we were put into a state of uncertainty as to whether we should get our summonses served or not in time.

3413. Were they served by your officers?—In the first instance I endeavoured to serve them through my own officers, but I found that it was impossible to do so. I then had to revert in some cases to the Civil Bill officers, as a matter of favour, to ask them to serve the summonses, and found great difficulty in getting it accomplished. The employment of a large number of persons to serve the summonses entails an additional expense upon the sheriff, as he is obliged, by the rules of the judges, to bring those persons to the assize town, and keep them there during the assizes.

3414. In order to prove the summons?—Yes, in order to prove the summons; the judges require it to be done by their rules.

3415. On whom did the additional expense fall: on the sheriff or on the county?—In my own county the grand jury allowed me a portion of the expenses of service, but at the same time, I believe that they passed a resolution, protesting against the extra expense of carrying out the Act being thrown on the county.

3416. Can you state what sum the grand jury of Antrim allowed you?—They allowed me 40 *l.*

3417. Did that cover all your expenses?—No, it did not.

3418. That was a new expense altogether, was it not?—It was a new expense, but not altogether new.

3419. I mean the expense on the county; was not that new?—Yes, it was new to the county.

3420. It has been suggested here that the summons should be served by a registered letter; do you approve of that?—I certainly do approve of it. I think that in the majority of counties it would be a very effective mode of service.

3421. In the county of Antrim would it be a very effective mode of service?—It certainly would be there, and I should fancy that there would be very few instances in which any difficulty would be felt that could not be overcome, provided the summonses were sent out by the post in proper time. I mean that if they were returned, and could not be served, the sheriff would have an opportunity of sending out additional summonses, so as to complete his panel.

3422. If they were not returned, you would make the fact of the summonses having been sent in a registered letter sufficient proof that the jurors had been summoned?—Yes, provided the letters were not returned, I would make it a proof that the jurors had been summoned. The receipt of the postmaster should be a proof.

3423. Do you know what has been the cost of service in any county besides your own?—From information which I have received, the cost has been much heavier in some counties than in my own county; for instance, in Tipperary, where there are two Ridings.

3424. Do you know what it was in the county of Tipperary?—It has been stated to me as 80 *l.*

3425. It has been suggested that the summonses might be served by the constabulary; do you approve of that suggestion?—I do not approve of it at all.

3426. For what reason?—I think that it would have a tendency to render the constabulary unpopular with the people. I also think that the fact of their acting under the sheriff would have a bad effect. I may add, that in case the postal system is not adopted, which I decidedly think would be the best and cheapest, I think the best machinery for serving jurors' summonses would be the Civil Bill officers, the process servers, provided they were compelled to serve them at a certain estimated rate for service; but there would be occasional difficulties about it, because sometimes, in some parts of Ireland and in the county of Antrim, I know the doors are shut when a process server appears.

3427. You have already referred to the interpretation of the 19th section of the Act by Mr. Justice Fitzgerald; I understand that he is of opinion that the sheriff still has a discretion?—Yes; the words of the section are, "In a regular alphabetical series, by returning one name from each letter in succession." His view seemed to be, that the sheriff might range about in a particular letter; that he was to take one name, but that he was not bound to select the first name; however, I thought that that was not in accordance with the Act, as I understood it, and I selected the first name from each letter, and had very great difficulty in getting my panel arranged in time. In the 18th section the sheriff is required to place on the panel the name of the place of abode, and the additions of the persons summoned. I considered that he should be prepared to prove that every man placed on the panel had been so summoned.

3428. Although he might know that the juror whose name was on the panel was dead, or had changed his place of abode?—I certainly would not place him upon the panel if he were dead, or had changed his place of abode, and I did not do so.

3429. Do you think that the Act, literally interpreted, requires you to do so?—The 18th section does so, I think. It appears to me to require a draft panel to be made out in strict alphabetical

Mr. *H. H. Bottomley.*

26 May 1873.

tical order, and that the sheriff should send out his summonses, and when he came to frame his final panel under the 18th section, he should only place on it the names of persons who had actually been summoned, as the word summoned is used there.

3430. Do you find any difficulty as to the exhaustion of the names on the jurors' book, and as to the direction not to summon persons who had served in the three preceding years?—As to the exhaustion of the names on the jurors' book, there is a much larger number of names under particular letters than others, and in the county of Antrim that will lead to the names on the panels in some years being all under one particular letter of the alphabet; and in other counties the same result will appear.

3431. Do you find any difficulty as to the direction not to summon persons who have served in the three preceding years?—I think that there will be a difficulty, for under the new Act there is a new jurors' book to be furnished, as I understand, each year, and it will be exceedingly difficult for the sheriff to determine whether a person's name in the new jurors' book is the same person who has been summoned in the previous year.

3432. Owing to the great number of the same name?—Yes, owing to the great number of the same name, and also to the different residences; and sometimes a man is returned from one particular townland one year, and he is returned from another townland the next year. There are also very frequent changes of abode, especially in a large town like Belfast, and there would be great difficulty in determining whether a man who has a certain description this year is the same man who has an entirely different description last year, and who has served.

3433. Do you find any difficulty as to the time named for summoning your jurors, preparing your panel, and giving it to the returning officer?—There is a difficulty. There is a section of the Act as regards special jurors, which states that the sheriff need not serve any special juror unless he gets an eight-day notice. His panel must be in Dublin seven days before the assizes, and if he were to rely on that section with regard to the notice, he would only have one day, or a fraction of a day, in which to serve his 48 jurors, and have his panel in Dublin the next morning printed, which would be an impossibility.

3434. You have already stated that, so far as you are aware, the power hitherto confided to the sub-sheriff has been impartially exercised?—Such is my belief.

3435. And you know of no case in which that power has been systematically abused?—I do not.

3436. Or corruptly used?—I do not.

3437. Have you any document that you wish to hand in to the Committee on the subject?—I have a return of the number of the challenges to jury panels throughout Ireland previous to the passing of the Act, returned from 29 counties from the present holders of office, some of whom have been in office for 27 and 28 years, and others for shorter periods. The challenges and the results are given. (*The same was handed in, vide Appendix.*)

3438. Have you any other document which you wish to hand in to the Committee?—I have a statement, signed by a number of the sub-sheriffs, protesting against some evidence which was given previous to the passing of this Act. (*The same was handed in, vide Appendix.*)

3439. Do you know by how many sub-sheriffs this is signed?—Twenty-seven.

3440. Do you know whether those 27 signatures were attached in the year 1871, or have they been lately attached?—The majority of them were attached in the year 1871.

3441. But others have been added lately?—Yes.

3442. Since the inquiry of this Committee was commenced?—Yes, since the inquiry was commenced; at an earlier part of this inquiry.

3443. Was any use made of this paper in 1871?—None.

3444. Was it not forwarded to anyone?—Not that I am aware of.

3445. In whose charge has it been since 1871?—That duplicate of it has been in my custody.

3446. Where is the other?—I do not really know where the other is.

3447. One copy was given to you, and you do not know what became of the other?—I do not know.

3448. Have you no knowledge of the purpose for which this was signed; was not it intended to be sent to anyone?—My recollection is, that it was intended to be forwarded.

3449. To whom?—I really forget now to whom it was to be forwarded.

3450. When papers of this sort are signed, it is generally intended to make some use of them?—I presume so, but I forget at the moment.

3451. Mr. *Bruen.*] Was there any opportunity of making use of it?—There was no opportunity of making use of it.

3452. *Chairman.*] Is there anything that you wish to add before other honourable Members of the Committee ask you any questions?—I would merely wish to express the hope that some change may be made or some greater facilities given as regards the mode of service of jurors' summonses. My own impression is that there will be a difficulty found at the next assizes in having the jurors served in time.

3453. Mr. *Bruen.*] You said, did you not, that the sub-sheriffs you thought were rather favourable, to some extent, to the principle of the Act, which relieves them from the responsibility of framing the jury panels?—I stated so.

3454. Does that satisfaction which they express arise from any consciousness that they had not done their duty in framing the panels, or from any fear that they could not exercise their duty for the future, if that duty was thrown upon them?—Not the slightest.

3455. You are here to state that, as far as your own personal conduct in framing the panels is concerned, and from what you know of many of the sub-sheriffs, they have not been guilty of any partiality in exercising that duty?—I have a personal knowledge of the majority of the sub-sheriffs who have acted for long periods in Ireland, and I believe that they would be quite incapable of acting with partiality or corruption in the discharge of their duty, as regards the summoning of jurors or the selection of them.

3456. You have been in this room, I think, for a good many days, and you have heard the expression "jury packing"; has it ever come to your knowledge, or have you been at all aware that that expression has been directed towards the

the sub-sheriffs in forming their jury panels?—No. Any statement as to the packing of jurors seemed to refer to the rejection of jurors by the Crown solicitors, if there was any complaint made, so far as I know or have heard.

3457. I think I may gather from you that the satisfaction which the sub-sheriffs feel, is more at being relieved from a very onerous and difficult duty?—It is; they would sooner be relieved of it.

3458. Naturally they would much rather not have to perform a very onerous and difficult duty?—Yes, if it is one that exposes them to any suspicion, they would so much the more wish to get rid of it, although they believe that it is not founded on fact.

3459. But it is not from any fear that any one of them would be at all guilty of unfairness in the exercise of their duty?—No, I believe it is not in any case that I know.

3460. As regards the charges against the sub-sheriffs, you have given in a paper of the number of challenges to panels which have been made through many counties in Ireland previous to the passing of this Act; how many years does it go back to?—It goes back in many counties to a period of 28 years.

3461. I see that in some the period of 28 years is mentioned; but does it go back to 28 years in all the counties mentioned?—No, it does not.

3462. Take the county of Mayo; there was one challenge there three years ago; does that period to which this paper refers include the previous 28 years; that in the 28 years there has only been one challenge to the jury panel in the county of Mayo?—That is seven years.

3463. That was the time when the challenge was actually made?—That was the period in which the sub-sheriff was in office.

3464. I want to know how long a period this paper includes?—In some counties it includes a period of 28 years, which is the longest. There are periods of 27 years and 17 years. It is only the present holders of office who have given me that information; but the lowest period is three years. There is only one three years; all the rest are much longer.

3465. In the whole, how many challenges have there been during the periods of office of the present sub-sheriffs?—Seven.

3466. How many of them were allowed?—One was partially allowed by the judge at the last assizes in Kerry.

3467. I think you will find that there were two allowed in Mayo and in Down?—Yes, in Down, that was so.

3468. In Mayo, I see by the note that, although the challenge was allowed, the judge stated that he was satisfied that the panel was fair and impartial?—Yes, that is the statement given to me.

3469. So that from that it would appear that whatever the ground of challenge was, it did not succeed on account of any malfeasance on the part of the sub-sheriff?—So it would appear.

3470. In the Down case, are you conversant with it; what was the reason that that succeeded?—The challenge was taken on the ground that the jurors were not alphabetically selected, the sub-sheriff having put on the panel the Ms and the Macs.

3471. That had no reference, had it, to the want of impartiality of the sub-sheriff?—No.

3472. Before the present Act was passed, the sheriff, when preparing his panel, was to some extent responsible to the judge that proper persons were on the panel, because if improper persons were found to be on the panel, he might be liable to be fined by the judge, might he not?—He might be liable to be censured by the bench.

3473. Supposing that improper persons were put on a panel, I suppose the judge could fine the sheriff, could he not?—There is the power of fining given by the present Act.

3474. There is no person now actually responsible for the preparation of the panel, because the sheriff being guided by those strict rules, if he carried them out, is not responsible at all if there are improper persons upon the panel?—No.

3475. Supposing, if by any means, a person was summoned a second year running on the panel by the sheriff, owing to his name being the same as another man's name, what would happen, would the whole panel be liable to be quashed, on account of the sheriff having framed it improperly?—I should think not. The juror would be very much dissatisfied, and he possibly might have a remedy against some person.

3476. As regards the county of Antrim, is there a large proportion of the jurors on the present jurors' list unintelligent?—At the last assizes there was a very large proportion of unintelligent jurors, much larger than ever I saw before.

3477. Can you give any explanation why that should have been so?—The number of jurors on the general jurors' book was so vastly increased that necessarily a large number of persons were summoned who had a low qualification, that was one reason. There was always a great disinclination on the part of those who were rated highly to attend the assizes.

3478. Do you think that the revision of the jurors' lists under the chairman of the county will be sufficient to purge those lists from the persons who are incompetent, or who from other reasons are incapable of serving?—I have stated previously that I do not consider that there would be a complete purging of the lists of those persons, unless there is in addition some limited power of rejection reposed in some officer.

3479. The reason why you think that it would not be a sufficient revision is, that you think that people would be unwilling to come forward to confess that they are incapable or illiterate?—I think that that would be one difficulty in the way.

3480. Do you think that that would be got rid of by imposing upon the poor rate collectors and other officers the duty of coming before the chairmen and giving them information?—It may be got rid of to some extent. I do not think that it would be got rid of entirely. They may discover a number of illiterate persons.

3481. Have the Chamber of Commerce at Belfast given any opinion as to their confidence in the juries under this new Act?—I am not aware that they have given any official opinion; I have heard the subject referred to; it was referred to in the retiring address of the president of last year of the Chamber of Commerce, and since I came to London the present holder of the office of president of the Chamber of Commerce made me a communication with regard to the present jury system, which he said I was at liberty to use.

Mr. *H. H. Bottomley.*

26 May 1873.

3482. Will you state what that opinion was?—He said that his own opinion, and the opinion of the members of the council of the Chamber of Commerce, so far as he could learn it, was that they had no confidence in submitting mercantile cases to the present class of jurors, either special or common. He also stated that he knew of a number of cases that had been withdrawn in consequence of the state of the jury list.

3483. As to the question which I think was mentioned by Mr. Justice Fitzgerald at the last meeting of the Committee, when he proposed that the high sheriff should be entrusted with the duties of forming the panels, has the deputation which the high sheriff gives to his deputy included in it any authority as to the jury panels?—The deputation given by the high sheriff to his deputy authorises him to do all official acts as the high sheriff can do himself. There is no limitation that I am aware of.

3484. So that the sub-sheriff always acts under complete authority in this case from the high sheriff?—He does, under complete authority.

3485. You have, I believe, to choose panels for four quarter sessions and for two assizes in the year; that is, 16 panels in the year, and to return them?—I have to return more than that; I have to return the special jurors' panel and the common jurors' panel for each assizes; that is, four jury panels. In addition to that, there are four quarter sessions towns, and they hold sessions four times a year. I have to return panels for each of them.

3486. The quarter sessions panels are only chosen from their own districts?—From the quarter sessions divisions.

3487. So that, taking the whole county, you have to return two panels for the assizes from the whole county, and you have then to return four panels from each division for the quarter sessions?—Two panels from each division for each quarter sessions. There is only one panel returned for the quarter sessions. The grand and the common jurors are on the same piece of parchment; the grand jurors come first and then the common jurors follow. There are two quarter sessions' towns in each division, and there are two panels consequently returned from each division.

3488. What I want to ascertain from you is, whether you could give the Committee any near estimate of the number of common jurors that you require to choose from the jurors' list in the year, taking the whole county, for the assizes and the sessions together?—At each assizes, on the average, I return a panel of 300 names, and sometimes a larger number, when there are a great number of cases. For instance, at the last assizes, in the cases connected with the Belfast riots, when there were a great number of prisoners to be tried, and where the number of challenges might be very great, I returned a larger panel.

3489. Would 300 be the average?—Yes, it would; 250 or 300 I returned to each assizes in Antrim. The number of grand jurors summoned at each quarter sessions town would be about 30, in order that from 30 a panel of 23 might be obtained. The number of common jurors summoned at each quarter sessions, I believe, would be about 45 or 50.

3490. Are there four of those?—There are four of those quarter sessions four times a year; that is, 16 quarter sessions panels.

3491. How soon do you calculate that the whole jurors' list would be exhausted?—I have not made that calculation.

3492. Sir *R. Blennerhassett.*] What did you mean by saying that the challenge to the array in Kerry was partially allowed?—I merely stated that from the return furnished me from the sub-sheriff of Kerry. I have no knowledge on the subject at all; but that is what he said, that it was partly allowed.

3493. Mr. *Downing.*] You have been 14½ years sub-sheriff, I think you say? Yes; this is my fifteenth year.

3494. Notwithstanding that you have been 14½ years sub-sheriff, your personal knowledge was rather limited with regard to personally knowing the jurors in the county?—Considering the large population of the county, and the varying population of Belfast, my personal knowledge of the jurors is very limited.

3495. The poor rate collector and the collector of the jury cess must have a more intimate knowledge of the people than you possibly could have?—Yes, within his own district.

3496. Are there a poor rate collector and a collector of jury cess in every district and every barony?—Yes; but they have not such a large general knowledge as I have.

3497. But the collectors of the county rates and of the poor rates have an intimate knowledge of every man, because they receive the money and give receipts?—I presume they have.

3498. Did I understand you to say that on the jurors' books for this year there were one-fourth of the number who ought not to be returned who were over the age?—I said one-fourth in the panel, not on the jurors' book.

3499. Would that apply generally to the jurors' book?—I am not aware of that; I only judged of those that were there and the number that came up every day.

3500. If they were eliminated from the panel and from the jurors' book, that would considerably reduce the number for the county of Antrim, would it not?—The general number of jurors undoubtedly would be reduced.

3501. There is now only one general book in which the special jurors are marked?—There is one general jurors' book, and there is one book called the special jurors' book of the county. Formerly they were all in one book.

3502. I think you said that raising the qualification would, in Antrim, according to your account, reduce the number from 7,836 to 3,824?—Yes, I think that that is the statement that I made.

3503. Then there are 765 special jurors that must be also deducted?—Yes.

3504. That would leave you 3,059?—Yes.

3505. There being a large number of persons returned over age and illiterate, if they were excluded, it would reduce the number to a still lower figure?—It certainly would. I was assuming that those would be all taken away.

3506. You returned, I think you said, a panel of 300 names for the last assizes?—Yes; 338 was the exact number.

3507. If the number in the county of Antrim is reduced largely, and if you would return 300 on the panel, the jurors must serve more frequently than they would desire; that is to say, more frequently than two years?—I suppose they would.

3508. With regard to the quarter sessions, I think there is some little mistake about that; which

Mr. *H. H. Ballantry.*

26 May 1873.

which town do you refer to in which parties have been summoned from a long distance?—The town of Ballymoney is one.

3509. Is that the name of the division?—Ballymena is the division.

3510. Are there two quarter sessions towns in that division?—Yes.

3511. The Lord Lieutenant and the Privy Council have power to divide a division into districts, and there is a special town for each district?—I summoned them out of the division at the last sessions.

3512. What is the other town?—Antrim.

3513. Antrim is one sessions town, and Ballymoney the other?—Yes.

3514. Do you mean to say that you summoned for the Antrim quarter sessions men residing in the district of Ballymoney?—No, certainly not; I summoned them from Belfast divisions.

3515. There is one part of the division of Ballymoney, and another part of the division where the special sessions are held, and you only summon persons in that district, and not from the division at large?—I summon them from the division wherever they were found alphabetically.

3516. It would be very easy to remedy that, by limiting the return from each sessions town district?—If you mean to restrict the area, that is what I suggest.

3517. That suggestion would meet your difficulty upon that point, would it not?—It would remove the hardship complained of by the jurors; I was not aware of any division into districts made under any order of the Lord Lieutenant as regards Antrim.

3518. It struck you personally before this Act at all, that it was an admirable arrangement to summon parties in alphabetical order, because you selected 48 names for the special jury by alphabetical order?—I did to a certain extent, not confining myself altogether to that.

3519. But it struck you yourself as a very good system?—It was a fair enough system.

3520. Do you think it would get rid of the difficulty of this alphabetical order, if the whole of the names were put into a box, and they were drawn as is done in civil cases?—Not as far as the sheriff is concerned, it would not.

3521. Supposing, as you say, that by the alphabetical order you are obliged to pursue a certain course, and to summon certain parties, and supposing when you came to the assizes you returned your 300 names, and supposing that they were put into a ballot-box and balloted for in criminal as well as in civil cases, that would meet the difficulty, would it not?—I think it would be a very fair course towards the prisoner, and the Crown too.

3522. I think you said that you have very little criminal business in your quarter sessions in your county?—There is a great deal at one; but I said in some towns. In Belfast the chairman of quarter sessions has a great deal to do, both criminal and civil.

3523. *The O'Donoghue.*] Am I not right in assuming that, whether rightly or wrongly, the power vested in the sheriff by the old Act exposed him to a great deal of suspicion?—I am not aware of any being exposed to suspicion.

3524. Are you not aware that they were suspected of acting unfairly at any time?—No, I am not, and I can scarcely understand by whom they were suspected.

3525. You surely understand what I mean, when I ask if they were suspected?—I never heard of any suspicion.

3526. You stated in answer to the right honourable Chairman, that the sheriffs had an absolute power of selection under the old Act?—They had.

3527. Is there any doubt that this power of selection was exercised?—They must have exercised that power of selection in order to frame their jury panels.

3528. If that power of selections was not exercised, it would have been a matter of indifference, would it not, to the sheriffs, whether the new system was retained or whether the old system was reverted to?—The new system exposes the sheriff to increased difficulties in every way.

3529. Does it increase his power of selection?—It takes away his power of selection.

3530. And it is in that respect different from the old Act, is it not?—Yes.

3531. When you stated that the sheriffs did not wish to return to the old system, you meant, of course, that they were glad to be relieved from doing that which custom had imposed upon them as a duty?—I think they were glad to be relieved.

3532. Is it not the fact that under the old system the sheriffs had not only to see that there was a sufficient number of jurors in attendance, but they had also occasionally to select the jurors with a view to particular trials which might come off at the assizes?—I never heard of a selection of a jury being made in contemplation of any trials coming off at the assizes.

3533. If it was a political trial, for example, or an agrarian trial, or a trial for a mob of Catholics and Orangemen, you do not think that the process of selection differed then from what it did upon ordinary occasions?—I only know that I have had, in my own county, all those several descriptions of cases, except agrarian cases. I have had plenty of cases of every complexion, where people were charged with Ribbonism and Fenianism, and different classes of party processions, and I never made the slightest difference, or was influenced in any way by the class of cases coming for trial, nor did I know anything about them until they were tried.

3534. Are you not aware that there was a very general impression that the trials very much affected the nature of the duty thrown on the sheriff with regard to his selection?—I was not aware that there was any such general impression. I should think the sheriff who lent himself to any such practice would be very unworthy of holding the post.

3535. You do not think the general impression is that the sheriff was influenced by those considerations?—No, I never heard of it.

3536. At all events, is it not the case that, under the new Act, suspicion, even of partiality, is taken away; that there cannot be any partiality or any unfair selecting?—I do not know whether the suspicion would be taken away, because, though it was unfounded, there might still be a suspicion. A prisoner might not know much about what the system of selection was, but it certainly does take away any grounds, if any such grounds did exist.

3537. Mr. *Attorney General.*] The power of selection was absolute formerly, was it not?—Yes.

3538. I presume

Mr. H. H. Bottomley.

26 May 1873.

3538. I presume the object of selection was to get a jury fit for the cases that were to be tried?—Fit as to general intelligence.

3539. I suppose they might vary, might they not, according to the cases that were to be tried; and the class of persons whom you would select to try one sort of case would not be precisely the same class of persons that you would select to try another, would they?—Precisely the same.

3540. Do not cases vary in Ireland?—They vary most materially, but the panel is the same.

3541. What I want to know is, whether you really mean to say that you think that the same class of persons are fit to try all classes of cases?—I stated that the class of persons summoned on the common jury panel in my own county were highly qualified to serve as jurors.

3542. I am not asking you as to the practice in any particular case, but upon the general state of things, in which as I understand you, there was an absolute power of selection, and the object of the selection was to get a fit jury to try the cases?—To get an intelligent jury, and to exclude those who were unintelligent for their want of intelligence.

3543. Do you really mean to say, that when there was a class of cases which the sheriff upon the best grounds had reason to think that a set of men were unfit from any reason to try them, he would not exclude such men from trying them?—Do you mean on religious or political grounds.

3544. Supposing there was a trial of a man or men for an offence against the Government of the country, whatever that Government might be, and the sheriff knew that two particular men were strongly disaffected to the Government of the day, whatever that Government might be, do you really mean to say, that that gentleman, having the power of absolute selection in his hands, would not exercise that power of selection in such a case as that against such persons?—I mean to say that I never did so, nor had I the means of doing it.

3545. Had you ever occasion?—I might have had occasion.

3546. Had you?—I have had cases in which I knew that persons were going to be tried who were charged with disaffection to the Government.

3547. Do you mean to say that you selected the panel without the slightest reference to notorious disaffection on the part of the jury who were going to try them?—If I had known of my own knowledge that any person was disaffected, I would have passed him over in making the panel.

3548. Then I rather gather from you that the reason that such persons were not passed over, if they were not, was not want of intention, but want of knowledge?—Want of knowledge. I said that in such a large population my knowledge is necessarily limited.

3549. May I take it that if there had been the knowledge, there would have been the action?—Certainly; I would have thought it right in that extreme case to have done so.

3550 That being so, do you really mean to say that it was not felt in Ireland that that power was occasionally exercised unduly. I do not say rightly or wrongly; it may have been upon very imperfect and insufficient grounds, but as an abstract question, do you really mean to say that that being the case, there was no feeling from time to time, in Ireland, whether well or ill founded, that that selection was made, which you admit would have been made, if the knowledge had existed on the part of the person that made it?—I am not aware of any such feeling existing in the several counties in the north of Ireland.

3551. Do you confine your answer to the north?—I am not so much acquainted with the south and west of Ireland.

3552. Do not you know, as an Irish gentleman, what the feeling in Ireland has been?—I have only the same means of seeing the newspapers that others have.

3553. However, you really mean to leave the Committee under the impression that, whether well or ill founded, there were no feelings that those selections which you admit would not have been made if knowledge had existed to make them, were from time to time made?—Not as against the sheriffs, I think.

3554. Against anybody?—I have stated to the Committee before, that I thought if there was any feeling it was rather with regard to the rejection made by the Crown Solicitor at the trial.

3555. There was none upon the selection of persons to begin with?—I am not aware of any such feeling as against the sheriffs.

3556. You say that they may be suspected now; but at any rate, if the law is followed, they could not be suspected now with any show of reason, could they?—There would be no grounds in the mind of any sensible person.

3557. If a person was guilty of selection now for an improper object, he must break the law to do it?—Certainly.

3558. He must exercise a power which the law does not give him?—Certainly he would go beyond the power that the law gives him.

3559. And that would not have been the case before?—No, he would have been within the law then.

Mr. Joseph B. Johnson, called in; and Examined.

Mr. J. B. Johnson.

3560. Mr. *Heron.*] You are Sub-Sheriff of the county of Cork?—I am.

3561. How long have you been Sub-Sheriff?—I have held that office 15 years.

3562. During that time you have had great experience in the arranging of jury panels at assizes and sessions?—I have had very considerable experience.

3563. Will you state to the Committee what mode you adopted in selecting the jurors for the assizes under the old system?—I made it a rule to avoid summoning the same individual more than once every third assizes, and then to the best of my judgment as regards a man's qualification, I selected him for assize purposes, either on the long panel or the special jury panel.

3564. At that time you knew that you had the most absolute power of selection of the men upon the jurors' book?—I was perfectly aware that I had.

Mr. *J. B. Johnson*.

26 May 1873.

3565. Had you ever occasion for any class of trials to make a selection excluding a certain class of jurors?—The only exceptional case that I ever had was the Special Commission of 1867. I was not in office in the year 1865.

3566. Was that the trial of the Fenians?—Yes, that was a special commission for the purpose of trying the Fenians.

3567. What did you do at that Special Commission in the way of selection?—I selected, irrespective of their previous service, those whom I considered most intelligent, and totally irrespective of religion. I confess that I did go to some little trouble to select as many as I could of the Roman Catholic persuasion, in order to divide the numbers as fairly as possible. That was the only manner in which I did deviate, if in any way, I did so, in forming the panel; of course I used my utmost exertions to select the most intelligent. Had I known that any juror was of Fenian tendency, I feel bound to say, that I certainly should not have selected him.

3568. Have you formed any opinion as to the desirability of going back to the old system of selection?—I have a very strong opinion, and I am very strongly opposed to going back to the old system, that is unless you repeal the present Act in toto.

3569. Is that opinion of yours shared by other sheriffs and sub-sheriffs?—I cannot say that. I have had no communication from them; I did write to one or two other sheriffs, but I have not as yet received their replies giving me any information as regards their experience, and therefore as my experience merely refers to the county of Cork, I do not wish to go at all beyond that county.

3570. Will you state why you think it undesirable that the old system of selection by the sheriff should be reverted to?—If I were to exercise my own judgment to the utmost of my skill and with the greatest integrity, the result would be that at the end of two years I would still have to come back to those individual jurors on the jury book who had been previously passed over as being ignorant and unqualified, and from that class and that class only I should then have to select the panels; that would be my first objection. I have a further objection, that I think it would place the sheriff in a very invidious position. The public are under the impression that the power of selection being taken away from the sheriff, he is bound to take them in their alphabetical order, and if he therefore takes upon himself to disqualify a person, he may possibly light on the name of the person that he intended, but not exactly on the individual person himself; he may therefore pass over that individual with the best intention, believing that he was unqualified; and afterwards, upon discovering that he had committed a mistake, he would be liable to censure from that person whom he had taken upon himself the responsibility of disqualifying. Further, I think that, by that selection, he would arrive at the name of another gentleman whose name would otherwise not have appeared on the panel if he had not passed over the names of the previous juror.

3571. You mentioned the word "invidious"; in your experience, did the power of selection, as it was exercised before, ever place the sheriff in an invidious position?—I confess that I think it did, and I am satisfied that I made far more enemies than ever I made friends by having exercised the power of selection, and I have no wish whatever to return to it.

3572. As regards the south of Ireland, which you know so well, do you think that other sheriffs were placed in a similarly invidious position?—I am quite sure that they must have been, at times.

3573. Irrespective of the invidious position of the sheriff, do you consider that the power of selection, exercised as it was, cast a suspicion upon the administration of justice?—Yes; I would go that far.

3574. Will you explain to the Committee why you think so?—Because I think that, if the sheriff wishes to act improperly, it is quite within his power to do so; and if you again conferred upon him the partial power of selection, it would be, in point of fact, quite within his power to pack a jury, if he wished to do so; therefore I think it is but fair that that power should be removed from the sheriff, so as to place him above suspicion.

3575. Did you ever know of any instance in your county where your bailiffs did not serve jurors in particular districts of the county, with a view to save costs?—Yes; I confess that there have been instances, and too many, perhaps, where bailiffs have omitted to serve jurors whose names were returned to them on the list by me. I had occasion to dismiss one of my bailiffs for such.

3576. Very often that would not appear?—It would very often not appear; but I made it a rule to return the names of all the jurors, even before I knew whether they had been served or not, for the purpose, if possible, of preventing that practice by the bailiffs; and the bailiffs being aware of that being my rule, find it absolutely necessary to serve them, because, in case a juror was afterwards fined, he came before the judge, or he appealed at the next quarter sessions, and the juror then explained that he has not been served, therefore the conduct of the bailiff would come before the court.

3577. But the judge could not fine a juror unless the bailiff proved service?—I do not know that. I think the practice in our county has been to fine for non-attendance in the first instance.

3578. Have you ever known any instance in your county of fines actually levied?—I think three fines only were levied through me. I believe that others may have been received by the clerk of the peace, and clerk of the Crown, but through me not more than three have been levied during the whole of my term of office.

3579. Do you remember the amount of them? One of them, I think, was 5 *l.* I forget what the others were, but 2 *l.* is the general fine.

3580. The county of Cork, as we all know, is the largest in Ireland?—Yes.

3581. Has your attention been directed to the inconvenience which arises as to the quarter sessions juries and the assizes juries, owing to the distances that they have to travel?—That is particulars to which my attention has been directed.

3582. Will you state to the Committee what plan you have originated to obviate the great inconvenience which now exists in that county? —What I state applies entirely to the county of Cork. I am very strongly impressed with the idea that we should have two jurors' books, a general jurors' book for sessions purposes, and a general

Mr. J. D. Johnson.

26 May 1873.

general jurors' book for assize purposes, and I do not think that a juror serving at sessions should have credit for that service as against his liability to serve at the assizes. The principal object in that is this: we have in the county of Cork, 816 special jurors, and from those we are obliged to select the grand jurors for session purposes, as well as the assize special jurors. At the expiration of the first year of the working of this Act, we would have exhausted the entire special jurors' book in forming the sessions grand juries, excepting the names of such magistrates as may remain on it, and would not be qualified to serve at sessions. We would then have to form our assize panel exclusively from the general jurors' book, without the assistance of any of the special jurors. That would be obviated by having two general jurors' books, one I would have for sessions purposes, and for that I would have a lower qualification than I would for the general jurors' book for assize purposes; and I would have upon the general jurors' book for sessions purposes the names both of the grand and the petty jurors. I would wish that the sessions jurors' book should, if possible, be framed in sessions districts, each district to be in its own alphabetical order. Not only would I suggest that for simplicity, but to prevent the possibility of the sheriff travelling outside the quarter sessions district in which the sessions were to be held. The service of jurors at quarter sessions would not appear in the general jurors' book for assize purposes at any time, and I would suggest a higher qualification for the jurors for assize purposes.

3583. Have you calculated how many jurors are required for the county of Cork?—Yes; I have made some calculations. There are 8,425 at present, and there are 816 special jurors who are included in the 8,425.

3584. How many would be enough for the service of the county?—I should think we may safely go down to 3,000; that would be quite sufficient for assize purposes. That would not require a juror to attend at assizes more than once in six years, which would be a very limited attendance indeed. That, of course, is assuming that we have separate jurors' books, the one for sessions and the other for assize purposes.

3585. Then you think that the service on the grand jury at quarter sessions should not exempt a special juror from serving at the assizes?—Certainly not. In the case of the grand jurors who are summoned to the quarter sessions, their attendance will very frequently not be more than three or four hours; and as that service is marked on the jurors' book now, it exempts them from further service at the assizes; whereas if such juror was summoned to the assizes, he would probably have to remain there a fortnight, or possibly three weeks. I therefore do not think it fair that a juror, serving for a very short period of a few hours at the sessions, should be entitled to be exempted from service at the assizes; because I think it is unfair to the other jurors upon whom the burden of the assize work is cast. I also say that, because it takes from the sheriff the better class of jurors on the special jurors' book, and exhausts it within a year.

3586. As regards the letters of the alphabet in the jurors' book of the county of Cork, in which letter is there the largest number of jurors?—I think in the letter "C," in which we have no less than 1,251 names, and in the letter "M," in which we have 1,123.

3587. Do you happen to remember the name in the letter "C" in which there is the great preponderance?—I do not remember exactly; but I should say that the Callaghans would be the largest number in our county.

3588. Do you see any objection to the alphabetical order being pursued until nothing but Ms come into the panel?—That is an objection; and eventually you would exhaust all the other names, and would have to form the panel exclusively from those names; therefore I would suggest that any letter which contained double the amount of the average number contained in the other letters should be divided; take, for instance, the letter "C," which has 1,251 names, I would say that there should be 625 of those written into the jurors' book by the clerk of the peace in the ordinary manner, and the remaining 626 should be written in in red ink, and should form a separate letter in itself, and that the sheriff be entitled to regard them as two distinct and separate letters, and that when forming his panel he should place the second half, which were in red ink, in italics in the panel, in contradistinction from the others; and the same remark would, of course, apply to the other letters referred to.

3589. In that way you would add three letters in your county?—Yes.

3590. Are you of opinion that that is far more convenient than throwing all the names into one balloting box, and drawing them from it?—I think there would be great objection to throwing them all into one ballot box, unless you adopted the system of having separate jurors' books. I would see grave objection to the balloting system, if you balloted on the present system of one general jurors' book, you of course then would be liable to summon jurors for sessions purposes from districts in which they did not reside at all. But if you adopted a separate jurors' book for assize and sessions purposes there would be no such difficulty; because, when you ballot for assizes purposes, you would draw out of that box only those intended for assize purposes, and it would not make any difference what portion of the county they came from.

3591. Do you consider that, if the names on a panel of 400 or 500 were to be written upon separate cards, and thrown into a large bag or box, there would be great danger of confusion?—I think there would; the thing would be possible. I never heard of it until I read the evidence of Mr. Justice Fitzgerald to-day; but I think it would be quite possible. The balloting box may be left in the custody of the clerk of the Crown, and may be locked and kept there and used at each assizes; the names of all the jurors on the general jurors' book for assize purposes having been previously placed in it; but I think the other system would be decidedly better. I also think that it should be the "Dictionary" order, and not the alphabetical order, and that there should be no mistake upon that point. The sheriff should summon his jury and form his panel in the "Dictionary" order, and not in the alphabetical order.

3592. Under the new system, at the last assizes did you find great trouble to get the jurors served?—Very great indeed; and the expense of summoning jurors has very considerably increased. For quarter sessions purposes I was enabled formerly to summon jurors for a very moderate sum, from 1 *l.* to 30 *s.*, whereas I had

to

Mr. *J. B. Johnson.*

26 May 1873.

to pay for the service of each quarter sessions jury, on the last occasion, 5 *l.*, and in some instances, even more.

3593. What was your entire expense for service of jurors up to the present year?—I have not calculated what it was up to the present year, but what it would be if some amendment was not made in the Act, and it were to continue for a year. I consider that the service of jurors alone for the year, in the county of Cork, would cost me 106 *l.* under the present Act.

3594. With regard to the system of service by registered letter, which has been suggested, do you see any objection to that?—I see no objection whatever to it; but I would not wish to press upon the Committee the fact that the service by registered letter would be absolutely available any further than in the cases of special jurors and grand jurors for sessions purposes. I would not wish to say that there would be security that a registered letter directed to a petty juror for quarter sessions purposes would with certainty be received by the juror.

3595. Is there not in the county of Cork, as regards the towns, a letter-carrier service?—Yes, clearly in the towns there is.

3596. And there would be no objection to the registered-letter system where the letters are delivered?—Certainly not in any town, because the registered letter would be returned more quickly through the Dead-Letter Office if it was not received by the juror. I would suggest three modes of service. First service by the constabulary; and, as far as I am individually concerned, I see no objection whatever to it. The sheriff might prepare a list and the summonses, which he should deliver to the officers of each district for quarter sessions purposes, the same for assizes purposes; that list to be returned to the sheriff again within a specified time, and from that list he should frame his panel. The great difficulty of service of jurors at present, necessitated my employing four bailiffs to summon the jury for sessional purposes, whereas one bailiff performed the duty under the old Act. The next mode that I would suggest, if that was not thought advisable, would be, that the process servers at quarter sessions should be employed; that is to say, that two or more of them should be appointed in each quarter sessions district by the chairman of quarter sessions, for the special purpose of summoning the jurors, and that they be paid a specific salary for the performance of that duty; the sheriff to deliver to them lists of the jurors to be summoned, with summonses, from which lists when duly returned by them, the panels should subsequently be formed by the sheriff from such lists. The third mode is that which has been first referred to, namely, by registered letter.

3597. That is only available, in your opinion, in the towns?—I should not wish to press the matter beyond that; but I am afraid that there would not be a certainty with regard to petty jurors in the rural districts; undoubtedly there would be with the grand jurors for the sessions, and with the special jurors for the assizes. I have no hesitation in saying that it would reach those; but I would not wish to lead the Committee to believe that in the county of Cork there would be a certainty that every summons would be delivered by registered letter. It would unquestionably be a very considerable convenience to the sheriff; I know it would in my case.

3598. I understood you to say that, as regards the jurors at quarter sessions, you do not think that the qualification requires to be raised?—Very slightly; I would suggest that the qualification should be raised to 20 *l.* and upwards; but in doing that, I would only wish that the names of all farmers rated under 20 *l.* should be erased, because, if you erase all under 20 *l.*, you exclude a very large proportion of most intelligent men, the shopkeepers in towns. I have found on going through the statistics, and working out accurately the number that would be affected in that way under a rating of 20 *l.*, that several gentlemen would be excluded, and therefore, if it was thought favourable that the Act should apply to farmers, I would suggest that for quarter sessions purposes, the names of all farmers rated under 20 *l.*, should be struck out of the present jurors' book; that is the only change which I would make in the present jurors' book for quarter sessions purposes?—A great number of the farmers, it must be remembered, reside in the villages.

3599. Mr. *Attorney General.*] "Villages" would be, as in England, a very vague word; there is a village sometimes with 2,000 or 3,000 people, and some villages with only 20?—In Ireland I am afraid that the same remark would not apply; we do not regard a place with such an amount of population a village.

3600. Is there any definite idea attached to the word village in Ireland?—No, not that I am aware of, except that it describes a very small number of houses in one locality.

3601. Mr. *Heron.*] As regards the jurors for the assizes, do you think that the qualification ought to be raised?—I think that it may very safely be raised, striking out the names, as I suggested before, in the common jurors' list of all farmers rated under 40 *l.*

3602. Your evidence relates to the county of Cork?—Yes, to the county of Cork only; I do not presume to know the state of things in other counties.

3603. As regards special jurors, what would you suggest?—As regards special jurors, I would suggest several different qualifications. As regards rating, I would suggest a house rating for special jurors; and I would suggest, in the country that all farmers, or the occupants of all houses rated at 35 *l.* a year and upwards, should be entitled to be placed upon the special jurors' book, and in towns I would put it at 40 *l.* or 45 *l.* Irrespective of the rating qualification, I would also place in the special jurors' book the names of all the magistrates of the county, and the names of all retired professional gentlemen not otherwise exempt, and the names of all half-pay officers in the Army and Navy, and of all officers of the Militia not actually on service. I would suggest that there be added, irrespective of qualification, to the special jurors' book the names of the eldest sons of all noblemen and baronets, and I think I might also suggest that the eldest sons of all magistrates might be placed in the special jurors' book, if within the prescribed age, and not otherwise excluded.

3604. Have you considered what persons should be disqualified or exempted from serving, even though they have the rating qualification; for instance, would you exclude a person unable to read or write?—Yes, certainly; then, instead of imposing upon the sheriff the obligation of selection, I would suggest that that obligation should

Mr. *J. B. Johnson.*

26 May 1873.

be placed on those who have the revising of the jurors' lists; and I would further suggest, that the revision should first take place at the petty sessions, before a stipendiary magistrate, and two or more other magistrates.

3605. Mr. *Attorney General.*] You mean exclusion, not selection?—Quite so. I adopt the fact of the book being already proved, and of course my observation now alludes to exclusion.

3606. Mr. *Heron.*] Do you think that people in the neighbourhood of the petty sessions would attend at the revision?—I think they would. I think they would be better known to the local magistrates, who would be personally acquainted with a great number of them by having this revision first take place at petty sessions, and a further revision to take place at the quarter sessions before the chairman, which would be in the shape of an appeal; but I would, in the first instance, suggest that the revision of the jurors' list should take place at petty sessions for convenience; it could there be gone through by means of the attendance of the clerk of the unions and the poor-rate collectors of the district, who should be bound to attend at those petty sessions.

3607. Who, then would return the list from the petty sessions to the quarter sessions?—The clerk of the union. I would suggest that it should not reach the hands of the clerk of the peace until after the first revision had taken place at the petty sessions.

3608. Would that revision at petty sessions be attended with any expense?—I do not think that it would be attended with any expense whatever. The clerk of the union and the poor rate collector would attend at very little inconvenience, as it would be merely in their district There might be some trifling travelling expenses for them, but there would be nothing else.

3609. On what fund would you throw that expense?—On the county; it would be a very trifling one.

3610. Mr. *H. A. Herbert.*] Do not you think that those officers would immediately apply for a rise of salary in consequence of the extra work?—I think that that would be met by other officers offering to perform the duty at the previous salary. I do not think that the extra work cast upon them would entitle them to a large amount of remuneration, or that they would ask for it.

3611. Mr. *Heron.*] Would there be another revision at the quarter sessions?—Yes; I would have the final revision of the jurors' list at the quarter sessions before the chairman. It would be more in the shape of an appeal, for I fear that if the revision were to take place solely before the chairman at quarter sessions, the notice of the revision would never reach the eyes of those for whom it was intended; they would be the ignorant class, incapable of reading and writing, and they would never see the notice of it in the paper, and would know nothing of the court being held, or the purpose for which it was held, and the consequence would be, that they would absent themselves; whereas if they were aware that it took place in their own petty session district, they could, without any personal inconvenience, attend there and satisfy the magistrates that they were incapable of reading or writing, or that they could not speak the English language. I would make that another subject of disqualification.

3612. Would you give the magistrates at sessions, or the chairman, the power of striking off the list persons who have been convicted of assaults or drunkenness?—I certainly would. I would extend to them that power also. I do not mean to say for a solitary case of drunkenness, but for serious assaults and habitual drunkenness it would be a question whether, if a man was convicted once at petty sessions, he should be excluded altogether from the jurors' list.

3613 Have you any further suggestion to make to the Committee?—I have taken the number of Jurors on my jurors' book, within a certain rating, who are farmers, and also those who are not farmers, and I find that the numbers rated who are farmers only, between 12 *l.* and 15 *l.*, are 88, and between 15 *l* and 20 *l.*, I find there are 138. Those are all the farmers at those ratings in the entire county. Then I find the number between 12 *l.* and 15 *l.*, who are other than farmers, such as shopkeepers, are 195, and between 15 *l.* and 20 *l.* I find the numbers to be 199. By striking off only the names of the farmers so rated, you reduce the jurors' book for sessions purposes by only 226 names. Then for assize purposes, if you were to raise the qualification to 40 *l.* and upwards, you would reduce the present jurors' book from 8,425 to 3,510, and thereby exclude the names of 852 most intelligent men; whereas if you strike out the names of all farmers rated under 40 *l.* you will only reduce the jurors' book for assize purposes by 4,063 names, leaving 4,362 available; the 852, which by this mode would not be excluded, I would regard as most intelligent and valuable jurors, and I think it would be very injudicious that their names should be erased from the jurors' book. I really do not see any means of keeping these on, and excluding the others, except that which I have already suggested, namely, raising the qualification for farmers. I look on the farmers rated under a certain valuation as the most ignorant on the present jurors' book, and I regard the shopkeepers as an intelligent class.

3614. Do you consider that it is the general opinion in the county of Cork that the power of selection under the old system should not be restored to the sheriff in the formation of the panel?—I do not like to undertake to say what the opinion of the county of Cork is. Probably there may be an opinion in favour of the old system, with people who may not thoroughly understand it; but I think I may say that those who thoroughly understand the question would say that the power of selection should not be restored. There may be those who have not carefully considered the case, and who know that under the old system we had in the county of Cork an intelligent class of jurors, and who may think for that reason that it would be better that the power was restored to the sheriff of selecting the jurors, but I think that with a careful revision of the jurors' list, and with the subsequent revision which would of course take place at each assizes and sessions, the farmers who would not attend at the sessions for the purpose of having their names taken off would be summoned, and would appear at the assizes, and would then be relieved from attendance by the judge of assize, a note of which should be taken by the sheriff, and the names of all such persons considered by the judge of assize or the chairman of quarter sessions as disqualified, should be taken down by the sheriff, and after each assizes a copy of such names should be transmitted by him to the clerk of

Mr. *J. B. Johnson.*

26 May 1873.

of the peace, for the purpose of having those names erased from the jurors' book. I further think that at the end of a year, or two years at the farthest, the jurors' book for our county would become so perfect that the necessity which some people think may now exist for restoring to the sheriff the power of selection would not then exist.

3615. Did you notice at the last assizes that some of the gentry of the county who were summoned on the panels did not attend?—Yes, I am aware that they did not attend; and they gave as their reason that they would not sit in the box with the class of jurors whom they saw there.

3616. I presume that that feeling will wear away in time?—I am quite sure that the feeling will wear away at the expiration of a year or two at the farthest, for the reason which I have mentioned.

3617. From your great experience of trial by jury, do not you think it an advantage that persons of a comparatively inferior class should be brought into association with the administration of justice?—I do; but that is one of the strongest reasons why I say there should be two separate jurors' books; for I say that by having a general jurors' book for the sessions, they will see how the work is performed, and they will there be schooled up and educated, as it were, for the duties which they will afterwards have to fulfil at the assizes; but I do not think that it would be judicious that those of the humbler class should be at once brought up for assize purposes. I would exclude all farmers rated under 40 *l.* for assize purposes, and all under 20 *l.* for sessions purposes.

3618. Mr. *Bruen.*] I think you have just told the Committee that it was only those who were ignorant of the question who wished to have the power of selection restored to the sheriff?—In our county I said that that was my impression. I did not mean ignorance of the question, I meant ignorance of the working of the system.

3619. You say that suspicion has been cast upon the administration of justice, by reason of the power of selection exercised by the sheriff?—May be cast, I think I said; if I have said that it had been cast, I should wish to correct that. I am not aware that that ever was the case in our county.

3620. Do you wish to extend that further than your county; do you think that it has been cast upon the administration of justice in other parts of Ireland?—I should prefer not to extend my evidence beyond my own county. I have no practical experience of the working of the system in any other county than Cork.

3621. When you say that suspicion may be cast, do you think it may be cast justly?—No, I do not; I do not think, as far as my knowledge goes, that I have ever been aware, with one exception, that a sheriff has acted improperly. I have heard of one instance; I do not wish to mention names, but it was not in our county.

3622. Mr. *Attorney General.*] In a state of the law under which selection may be exercised irresponsibly, of course it is possible that that power of selection may be abused, and it is also possible, that that power of selection may not be abused; whether it has been or not, is a question of fact, but that it may be abused as a matter of possibility is obvious, from the state of the law?—That has been already my evidence.

3623. Mr. *Bruen.*] Do you consider that the possibility of an abuse of power is a reason why all power should be taken away from individuals?—I think it would be a reason.

3624. I rather gathered from you, that this power of selection had to you personally become rather invidious, and that you had felt that you had made enemies through the use of it?—I stated that I am satisfied that I have made far more enemies than friends by exercising the power. Men have frequently applied to me to excuse them from service, and I have refused to do so, and they have always looked upon me afterwards as having done a very unkind act.

3625. It is quite natural to suppose that the power of selection should not have made you any friends, and therefore you are quite safe in saying, that you had made more enemies than friends; but do you suppose that you have made any enemies in consequence of it?—I am aware that I have made enemies, and not in one individual case only.

3626. Do you mean persons who wish to be on the jury panel, and who thought that they ought to have been on it?—No, persons who wished not to be on the panel, and who were placed on the panel: that is the way in which I put it.

3627. You mean, that by putting persons on the panel, you have made yourself invidious to them?—That is what I mean to convey.

3628. Persons who wanted to avoid a public duty?—Quite so.

3629. That was the hostility to which you referred, if it was hostility at all?—Yes.

3630. *The O'Donoghue.*] They knew that if you pleased you might have exempted them?—Yes; I was going to add that observation.

3631. Mr. *Bruen.*] Therefore it was not from the exercise of the power of exclusion that you incurred any hostility?—No.

3632. If that power of exclusion was still to be in your hands, do you think that it would occasion hostility to you?—I do; for the reason that I explained a short time since. The public are under the impression that that power is taken from the sheriff by his direction to follow the alphabetical system, and if he passes over the name of one man, believing him to be ignorant, and he afterwards finds out that he has committed a mistake, and that the man was not ignorant, I think that he is liable to very great censure from the party whom he has so stigmatised as an ignorant man; and in doing that, I think he does a further injury for which he is made responsible, because he takes the name of another man instead, whose name would not have appeared upon the panel if the proper rotation had been observed, and for that he makes himself liable to the penalty mentioned in the latter part of the section.

3633. If the power of selection were restored, and the sheriff were entirely freed from the necessity of alphabetical selection, do you think that he would still be subject to hostility?—I would object to having any power restored, if it was not restored *in toto* as before.

3634. Supposing that it was restored *in toto*, do you think that there would be any danger at all to the community, or to the administration of justice, by that restoration?—Not in my county, for it has never yet suffered in that way.

3635. I have not inferred from your evidence that you object to the power of selection, theoretically, as at all dangerous to the administration of

Mr. J. B. Johnson.

26 May 1873.

of justice?—No, I did not put it in that light. I say that if the power is to be restored to the sheriff, the present Act must be repealed.

3636. Why should the present Act be repealed?—The alphabetical system, I think, is the essence of the present Act.

3637. You consider that the principle and essence of the present Act to be the taking away from the sheriff of the power of selection?—I think that that is the principle and essence of the present Act.

3638. Do not you think that placing the qualification upon the basis of rating is also a very important change from the old rule?—It is an important change; but if the suggestions that I have made with reference to special jurors were adopted, I think that would be remedied; otherwise, I think it would be absolutely necessary, irrespective of any rating qualification, that there should be names added to the special jurors' panel, and if that was done, I think the injury done by the present rating qualification would be obviated in the special jurors' list.

3639. I do not quite understand the qualifications that you wish to give for the petty jury lists for the county of Cork. I see by the fourth schedule to the Act, that at present a person, to be upon the petty jury panel, must be rated at the annual value of 20 *l.* or upwards; you do not wish to change that, do you?—No.

3640. But if he resides in a city, town, or village, then the rating of 12 *l.* is sufficient to place him upon the jury lists?—Provided he be not a farmer.

3641. But there is nothing about a farmer here, and you wish to put that in?—Yes: I say that 226 of those rated between 12 *l.* and 20 *l.* are farmers, and are so described in the jurors' book. I find that of those rated between 15 *l.* and 20 *l.*, 226 are farmers, although they may reside in villages.

3642. Do you think that to be a farmer is a disqualification, primarily?—I think that the ignorant class in our county are the farmers, under the circumstances that I have already mentioned. Then, as to the 40 *l.* for assizes purposes, I think that the shopkeeper class are much more intelligent, and therefore I would allow the rating to stand for them. I beg to add to what I before said, that I would exclude on same scale with farmers working tradesmen or mechanics. I found at the last assizes we had a few that were under that qualification, and I do not think they were able to bear the expense of attending the assizes.

3643. But you think that a man who possesses property to the value of 12 *l.*, residing in a city, town, or village, and whose property is situated in a city, town, or village, must of necessity be a farmer?—No; I have them described in the jurors' book under two heads, some as farmers and others as shopkeepers. I consider that a man rated between 12 *l.* and 20 *l.*, and described as a shopkeeper, an intelligent man.

3644. But there is no such description given in the valuation books from which the returns are compiled?—I think it must have been, or they would never have been able to furnish it to me if it were not; my jurors' book contains it.

3645. You are not acquainted with the valuation book from which the jurors' book is compiled?—No, I am not; but I fancy that it must have appeared upon it, or else the clerk of the peace would never have arrived at that knowledge.

3646. If a man was a shopkeeper possessing a property valued at 12 *l.*, you would place him on the jurors' list, but if he was a farmer possessing that qualification you would not?—Precisely so.

3647. Mr. *H. A. Herbert.*] You said, I think, that you would exclude the class of working tradesmen?—Yes; I would exclude them with farmers, on account of the expense which they would have to incur.

3648. For no other reason?—For no other reason whatever. They came up on the last occasion and presented themselves at the assizes, but I do not think that they could bear the expense of attending the assizes.

3649. So far as intelligence is concerned, you see no reason to exclude them?—I think they were quite as intelligent, but I think it would be great hardship to impose upon them the necessity of attending at the assizes.

3650. Mr. *Brown.*] There is one portion of your evidence to which I wish to call your attention. You say that it does not matter from what portion of the county jurors come for assizes purposes?—I meant that as contra-distinguished from the jurors for sessions purposes.

3651. Does not it much matter to the jurors themselves being summoned from the far end of the county?—Of course it does; but I think that the sheriff has no right to take any cognizance of that whatever. I never did even under the old Act.

3652. Under the old Act, did you give any preference to men who resided near the town where the assizes would be held?—The only instance in which I ever exercised that power was with regard to the barony of Bear, which is so distant that I never brought a man from that barony to our Spring assizes. I think it is too great a distance at that season of the year. From our court-house, it would be at least 70 miles.

3653. You thought that it was an unfair thing, taking a man in winter 70 miles to the assize town?—Yes, I did.

3654. Do you think that it still remains an unfair thing?—Of course it is not altered by the present Act.

3655. The present Act has not diminished the hardship?—No, it has not in any way.

3656. Therefore the present Act does impose a hardship upon those persons which was not imposed under the old Act?—It does, undoubtedly. But if there were two separate jurors' books for our county, their attendance at the assizes would be so very limited, even though the number were reduced to 3,000, that I do not believe we should require their attendance at an assizes more than once in seven years; that would be so very long an interval that I do not think it would ever create a hardship, even though they were summoned to the Spring Assizes.

3657. You referred to a case in which you actually discharged some of your bailiffs who had omitted to serve jurors with summonses from improper motives?—Yes.

3658. That was independent of the former law, and whatever injustice happened from that cause was not at all to be attributed to the former law?—I think my evidence was that it took place under the former Act; no doubt it was an infringement of it.

3659. Therefore any injustice that arose from that ought not to be attributed to the former Act?—I do not think it ought: of course, the sheriff is responsible for the acts of his bailiff.

3660. But

Mr. *J. B. Johnson.*

26 May 1873.

3660. But it in no way arose from the imperfection of the law?—No, I do not think it did. It is possible still that a bailiff, wishing to act corruptly, may do the same; but if it came under the observation of the court, the sheriff would be made responsible.

3661. Mr. *Downing*.] You are aware that the magistrates had the power of revision before this Act was passed?—Yes.

3662. I believe you are aware that it was very imperfectly done?—It was very imperfectly done, but the revision took place under the former Act at certain districts, not at petty sessions, as I would now suggest, and I think that that was where the mistake occurred. There was very little trouble taken at the revision of the jurors' lists under the old Act, for the simple reason, as I said before, that in the case of the ignorant class it did not come within their knowledge; they never saw the advertisements placed in the paper by the clerk of the peace convening a sessions for the purpose.

3663. Are you aware that the revision did take place in the petty sessions court?—Yes, in some instances.

3664. From your knowledge of the country, do not you think that there is rather a prejudice against giving the magistrates any interference whatsoever in the selection of jurors?—I would not go that length at all.

3665. Do you think that it would be satisfactory to the people?—I do not see why it should not be. I would insist upon the stipendiary magistrate attending at the sessions, with any other number of magistrates in the district.

3666. The stipendiary magistrate has a very limited knowledge of the people, has he not?—Quite so, and that is why I would ask that he should be assisted by the knowledge of the other local magistrates.

3667. Are you a member of a board of guardians?—No, I am not.

3668. Are you aware that there is an elected guardian representing a particular division?—Yes, I am.

3669. He must have a very intimate knowledge of all the people residing in that division?—No doubt he has.

3670. Would you not approve of the clerk of the union, after he has made out his list upon a given day, bringing the list before the board of guardians, and each guardian bringing his local knowledge to bear, to say, "I know that A. B. is a man in great poverty, and that he is a man who is unfit to serve as a juror;" would you not have that remark placed before his name, and afterwards brought before the chairman?—No; I do not think that would do. I would suggest that the guardian of the district may be added to the court in which the revision should take place, as a member of the court.

3671. You do not expect that a guardian who gives his attendance once a week at the board room would afterwards attend at the petty sessions to constitute a court to revise the jurors' list?—I do not think that he would, as a rule, always do so; there are some individual guardians who would; but as a general rule I think they would not.

3672. Do not you think that every duty is best performed by a man who is paid for it?—Unquestionably.

3673. Do not you think that the magistrates who are not paid for it would consider it a very thankless office that they should sit at petty sessions to revise the jurors' lists?—I would fix the date of the petty sessions days, so as to make it obligatory on them attending on the day in which the revision would take place.

3674. You could not compel the magistrates who are not paid to attend?—They would be compelled to attend on the petty sessions day in their different courts. The only difficulty that I can see about it is that you could hardly bring them all within one month, which should be the case, in order that the revision should subsequently take place before the chairman of quarter sessions.

3675. Your experience is very large with regard to the county of Cork; that county is divided, is it not, into two Ridings?—Yes; the East and the West Riding.

3676. There is one clerk for the West Riding and another for the East Riding?—Quite so.

3677. Are you not aware that they have a very intimate knowledge of the people in both Ridings?—I think they have a very intimate knowledge of them.

3678. Let us suppose that at the quarter sessions it was the duty of the chairman, say, upon the first day of the sessions, or the first day of the Crown business, to have the lists placed before him by the clerk of the peace, the poor-rate collector, the collector of the county cess, and the clerk of the union being present; do not you think that that would be such a revision as must of necessity be satisfactory to all parties?—Clearly, if you can secure the attendance of the individual jurors whose names should be excluded; but that is where I am afraid the difficulty would be found. If you merely had it at the quarter sessions, the knowledge of the sessions would never reach those for whom it was intended, that is the ignorant class; and that is the difficulty that I see in having it at the quarter sessions.

3679. Do you think that the jurors would attend at all, either at the petty sessions or at the quarter sessions?—My impression is, that they would attend at the petty sessions, and be disposed to attend there, if there were notice given, and there would be much more district and local knowledge obtained at the petty sessions.

3680. Do not you think that the judge having the power at the assizes to discharge a person from attendance from any cause that may appear to him to be fit, proper, and just, would be a very right measure?—I think so. I have said that already. I think that a note should be taken of that by the sheriff of all people so excluded by the judge of assize, or the chairman of quarter sessions, and then the sheriff after each assizes should send a list of the names so excluded, to the clerk of the peace, for the purpose of having their names erased from the books.

3681. Are you aware that you will reduce the number in the county of Cork by excluding those who are rated under 40 *l.* from 8,425 to 3,510?—Quite so, and that would do for assize purposes by excluding all farmers rated under 20 *l.*

3682. Are you not aware that a great number of persons were summoned at the last assizes who were over age?—Yes; in answer to your former question, by striking off the jurors' book the names of all those irrespective of whether they were farmers or shopkeepers, that would reduce the number to 3,510, but if you struck off only the names of the farmers there would remain still

Mr. *J. B. Johnson.*

26 May 1873.

still on the general jurors' book for assizes purposes 4,362, excluding from the panel farmers rated under 40 *l.*

3683. You do not mean to say, that because a man is convicted of a common assault that is a reason why he should be excluded from the jurors' book?—I do not mean a common assault; but if a man is convicted of an assault or any very serious offence, that should be a cause of disqualification, and equally so for habitual drunkenness.

3684. Mr. *Attorney General.*] The expression in the Bill now before Parliament, is "infamous crime;" would that do? I quite concur in that. With regard to the formation of the general quarter sessions jurors' book at present, there certainly is very great difficulty; for as I read the present Act, I am impressed with the idea that I am bound to summon all the jurors in their strict alphabetical rotation; and I am afraid that I am bound to summon them out of the division and not out of the district. I have so acted up to the present time. I think it would be most desirable that the district should be adopted, and not the division; that is to say, the quarter sessions town and the baronies immediately surrounding the town in which the quarter sessions are held. In the county of Cork, for instance, there is the division of Mallow, which comprises the quarter sessions town of Kanturk, and the quarter sessions town of Mallow, in which each alternate sessions are held. I therefore think it hard that a man living in the quarter sessions town of Kanturk should be brought up to serve at the quarter sessions in the town of Mallow. I would wish, if possible, that there should be a distinction made, and that each quarter sessions district should be, as it were, a division in itself for the purposes of the jurors. And the way I would suggest is this; that if there be a general jurors' book for sessions purposes, each quarter sessions district should be placed in its own alphabetical order in that jurors' book. There would be no difficulty about that, I am satisfied. It may appear rather difficult and complicated at first, but I am satisfied that any smart clerk would accomplish what I suggest within two days. I would suggest that in that sessions general jurors' book each division should be in its own alphabetical order, and that the sheriff should take them according as he finds them, in alphabetical order; for one of the great objections to the present system would be the complication that would be caused at the end of the year. The constant attendance of the same jurors being marked at the quarter sessions and at the assizes, it would be found at the end of the two years most difficult to ascertain whether the panel had been formed in accordance with the Act, and whether the sheriff had not summoned any juror out of his turn. We have in our county but 816 special jurors, and from those were are obliged to form the quarter sessions grand jurors. We have 24 quarter sessions grand jurors in the county of Cork annually, and for them we would require for grand jury purposes at quarter sessions 864 jurors, and as they must be taken from the special jurors' book, the same parties must attend more constantly, and their service becomes more complicated when marked upon the jurors' books. That is my further reason for wishing that there should be separate jurors' books for the sessions as distinct from the assizes.

3685. *The O'Donoghue.*] With regard to the revision of the jurors' lists by the magistrates at petty sessions, I suppose there would be some means of letting all persons know on what day the revision might take place?—There would be no difficulty about that; the clerk of the peace could cause an advertisement to appear in the local papers.

3686. Do you think that such a system of revision would be regarded with confidence in the north of Ireland, where the magistrates, as a body, hold one set of religious and political opinions, and a vast number of people another?—I do not know. I do not wish to say anything with regard to the north. My experience has never extended to the north. What I meant to convey was entirely with regard to the county of Cork, which is a very large county. There is one special Act for the county of Cork, and I find very great convenience through this Act, which empowers the judge to direct the sheriff at the assizes to form the jury into two panels. It was an Act brought in by the present Lord Chief Baron, and it enables the sheriff, or directs him, to summon the first set for a limited time. The judge then has power to discharge that set at the expiration of a given number of days, which is mentioned in his precept, and the second set are summoned to attend at a future day. Where our assizes have sometimes lasted three weeks that has been found a very great advantage.

3687. I gather from your evidence that you think that the absolute power of selection exercised by the sheriff exposes him, whether rightly or wrongly, sometimes to the suspicion of acting unfairly?—I think it does, and I think it is objectionable that it should do so.

3688. Where there were trials of an unusual character, such as political or agrarian trials, is it not within your knowledge that the prisoner, whether rightly or wrongly, thought that he was certain to be tried by men of a certain bias, and whose verdict would reflect that bias?—The only instance of that kind, and to which I referred in the earlier part of my evidence, was, as I stated at the Special Commission of 1867. That was the only instance that we ever had during my experience. There was a Special Commissioner for the county of Cork in the year 1865, but I was not in office when it happened. I believe that panel was challenged.

3689. With regard to the Fenian trials which you referred to, may I ask whether your selection of jurors was influenced by your previous political leanings?—If I found that a man was a reputed Fenian, I undoubtedly would have excluded him from the list. I cannot remember any individual case, but I know that my exertions were, as far as religion was concerned, to have both persuasions fairly represented

3690. Is it not the case that in political trials, the result has always been treated as a foregone conclusion; and that trial by jury is looked upon as a more form, inasmuch as it is divested of that impartial character which is held to be its chief recommendation?—I cannot go that length with you; I do not think that that observation applies to the county of Cork; I do not know what may have been the result in other counties; but I do not think that such a feeling existed in the county of Cork.

3691. But you will admit that there was room for suspicion?—Yes, I will admit that.

3692. Would you admit that all that ground of suspicion is removed as far as possibly could be

Mr. *J. R. Johnson.*

26 May 1873.

be by the present Act?—Yes, I concur in that. Decidedly, the present Act, if it is worked according to the alphabetical system leaves no ground of suspicion attaching to the sheriff.

3693. In fact, impartiality is provided for under the new Act as far as it is possible to conceive that it could be?—I think so.

3694. Mr. *H. A. Herbert.*] Mr. Downing asked you whether you would disqualify a man for certain assaults; and I think the Attorney General asked you whether you would adopt the expression "infamous crime"?—Yes, I would adopt the words mentioned by the Attorney General, "infamous crime."

3695. Is there not a class of serious assaults in Ireland which ought to disqualify a man from serving on a jury?—I think that there were in former times in our country. There used to be a great many faction fights, in which very serious assaults took place, but that is dying out to a great extent.

3696. Are there no assaults of a serious nature of that kind in the county of Cork?—I will not say that there are none, of course there are very serious ones, but not of that very serious nature which could come under the category described by the Attorney General.

3697. You would not allow those men who committed those serious assaults to be qualified as jurors?—No. I will adopt the words used by the Attorney General; I think that some of them would come within the meaning of that expression.

3698. Mr. *Attorney General.*] Any assault with an intent would be an infamous crime?—Yes, certainly.

Mr. Alexander Morphy, called in; and Examined.

Mr. *A. Morphy.*

3699. Mr. *H. A. Herbert.*] How long have you been Crown Solicitor?—Twelve years Circuit Crown Solicitor for Clare and Kerry. I had been previously Sessional Crown Solicitor for Kerry for some years.

3700. You were at the assizes at Clare and Kerry on the last occasion?—Yes, I was.

3701. Will you state to the Committee what took place during the assizes in the county of Clare?—In Clare, the juries in some of the cases gave verdicts contrary to the evidence. Unquestionably, in two cases, I should say that the verdicts were opposed to the evidence. In the other cases all the trials in Clare resulted in acquittals at the last assizes in those five or six cases that were tried; but there were only two of them in which I could say that the verdicts were opposed to the evidence diametrically.

3702. One of those cases was a case of murder, was it not?—It was a case of shooting with intent to murder; it was the case referred to the other day by Judge Fitzgerald, who tried it.

3703. Do you think that that was owing to the class of jurors who were on the panel?—Certainly; in fact I am quite satisfied that if that case had been tried by jurors of the same class who previously were jurors in Clare, there would have been a conviction without a moment's hesitation.

3704. How many jurors were on that panel?—There were, I think, 230 or 236 on the panel in Clare at the last assizes.

3705. Out of that number, how many were jurors who had served before?—There were under 20; I think only 14.

3706. Did those jurors object to serve?—The case did not arise; they were not called; they had no opportunity of declining. The numbers were so small in proportion to those who had never been jurors before, that the question did not arise.

3707. Therefore, as a test of the present Act, those cases were not on account of that class of jurors not being willing to serve?—There was no unwillingness expressed, that I am aware of, by any person to serve as a juror at the Clare assizes, the question did not arise. I say that out of the 230 or 240 jurors on the panel, I believe there were only 14 who had ever been on a jury panel previously.

3708. What took place in Kerry at the assizes?—In Kerry the panel was a very small one, I think about 90, and the jurors were brought in from one particular district in the immediate neighbourhood of the county town, and they were very good jurors; but that was no test of the working of the Jurors Act.

3709. They were challenged, I believe?—Yes, they were challenged, and the challenges were allowed, and only those were tried who consented to be tried.

3710. How was that got over?—Certain accused persons consented to be tried, and they were tried; and the trials of those who did not consent to be tried were postponed to the coming assizes.

3711. In fact the working of the Act in Kerry during those assizes, had nothing to do with the Act?—I do not think it was any test or criterion of the working of the Act at all; they were excellent jurors, but they were all from the Barony of Trughanacmy, in the immediate neighbourhood of the county town.

3712. What change, if any, would you suggest in the qualification of jurors?—The present qualification for common jurors under the Statute in Clare and Kerry, is 20 *l.* I would be disposed to suggest that in the rural districts it should be raised to 50 *l.*, and in towns reduced to 14 *l.*, possibly to 12 *l.* I think that we lose a most valuable class of jurors by the high qualification in towns, because the valuation on buildings is very low. I may instance Ennis, which is a very thriving town of about 6,000 inhabitants, all highly intelligent and orderly-thriving people; all the buildings in the union, which extends beyond the borough, rated at 20 *l.*, are only 63, and I should say would not give 30 jurors; I think that is a great loss to the public.

3713. What was the case in Tralee; how many jurors were there there?—In Tralee the number of inhabitants is about 10,000. In the whole union of Tralee, which extends beyond the borough, there are only 150 houses or buildings of any sort rated at 20 *l.* and perhaps they would not give more than 50 jurors.

3714. When you state the qualification at 50 *l.*, do you take into consideration the number that is likely to be added to the panel under the new Valuation Bill?—Yes, I suggest 50 *l.* anticipating that there will be a revision of the valuation, and as I believe in Clare and Kerry it will be

Mr. *A. Murphy.*

26 May 1873.

be raised. I think that a valuation of, perhaps 40 *l.*, would give a good class of jurors in the rural districts.

3715. Do you know how many jurors Tralee gives at present?—I think Tralee gives at present about 50 jurors. If the qualification were reduced to 14 *l.* it would give 150 jurors, and they would be first-rate jurors for intelligence.

3716. What qualification would you give to special jurors?—I would include all those who are now mentioned in the 11th section of the Jurors Act, whether they were rated or not. That is to say, magistrates and their eldest sons, and those other persons enumerated in that section of the Act of Parliament, which I think is the 11th. I would have those jurors whether they were rated or not. I know that that would give an ample number in the two counties that I am acquainted with for special jurors purposes.

3717. What exemptions would you make from those jurors?—I think those already exempted are fair enough: except that I heard Mr. Johnson here speak of militia officers and half-pay officers, and I think that they would be an admirable addition to the special jury list.

3718. And the sons of magistrates?—Yes, and all those who are now mentioned in the 11th section. Magistrates and their eldest sons, baronets and their sons, and the sons of peers and others, but I think that at present they would be only on the special jury list, provided they were rated. I would suggest that they should be on the special jury list, whether they are rated or not. I would not make it a rating qualification for special jurors in that particular. I would have it of classes.

3719. Do you consider it advisable that the jurors should be balloted for in criminal cases?—Unquestionably. I think that in the administration of our criminal trials it would be an excellent thing if selection were abolished, and they were balloted for, because then there could be no canvassing of the jurors, as would now be the case. Anyone now can get the panel for the accused person previous to the trial, and some persons would go about amongst their friends and acquaintances, and the jurors might be canvassed, I am sure that they would be canvassed; but that could not occur, and it would not be attempted if there was a ballot.

3720. Have you heard any of the suggestions that have been made with reference to summoning jurors by post?—Yes, I have heard one or two of the gentlemen who have given evidence here suggest it. I believe that in the counties of Clare and Kerry it would not work at all; and instead of that, I should suggest service by hand, effected through the constabulary, who would be, I am sure, very glad to undertake it, for perhaps a less remuneration than the expense of summoning by registered letter would involve.

3721. I suppose you refer to the remote districts chiefly?—Yes, to the remote districts of both Clare and Kerry. In the western part of Kerry the letters might be a long time for the jurors in the post-office without being called for. Regarding it from the point of view which a Crown Solicitor might take, I think it would be very desirable indeed that some persons should inquire before the assizes, who could tell something about the jurors, whether they were related to the prisoners on trial, and other very important circumstances that ought to be known.

3722. What is your opinion as to how the jurors' books should be revised?—I think that they should be revised by the magistrates at petty sessions. Every person on them would be known by some of the magistrates, and if any juror felt himself aggrieved at being struck off or being kept on, he might go to the chairman at quarter sessions afterwards alone; that is to say, I would not allow the magistrates at quarter sessions to interfere at all with the chairman; but I would get the jurors' list in the first list revised at petty sessions by the magistrates.

3723. Do not you think that that would cast an invidious duty upon the magistrates?—Not in the slightest degree; no more than sending a trespasser to prison, and not so much; or any other magisterial duty.

3724. Would you have them give their reasons in public for excluding a man?—I would. I do not see why they should not do it.

3725. Do you think generally that that could be done?—I do. There are magistrates in the counties of Clare and Kerry that take a vital interest in the working of this Juries Act, so far as I am aware, and I have heard it expressed widely, at all events.

3726. Did you observe any reluctance on the part of gentlemen summoned as jurors at the last assizes to be associated with jurors of a low class?—No, I did not; that did not arise in Clare; they did not happen to be called. I heard gentlemen who had been formerly jurors state, not from any pride or superciliousness but from other reasons, that they did not think they would like to sit on the same juries.

3727. Therefore the failure of the working of this Act is not attributable to those jurors not wishing to serve with them?—No, they were not summoned. In Kerry, we had excellent jurors, but they afforded no test of the working of the Act for they were culled. In Clare the jurors were very bad, and there were only, as I say, about 14 gentlemen who ever had been on a jury panel before summoned out of 240.

3728. Mr. *Bruen*.] Had you experience of the working of the former Jury Act?—Yes, for 19 years.

3729. Did it work well in Clare and Kerry?—Admirably; I have never heard of any person dissatisfied with a verdict on the criminal side of the court.

3730. Was the working of the Act, as regards the civil business, as satisfactory also under the old system?—Yes, it worked admirably; there could not be better jurors than the jurors in Clare and Kerry under the old system.

3731. Did you hear great public dissatisfaction expressed at the power of the sub-sheriff in framing the jury panels formerly?—I never did in either of the counties that I am connected with, but I am quite well aware and I think that every person who knows anything of public opinion in Ireland must be aware, whether rightly or wrongly that such an opinion prevails in some parts of Ireland.

3732. There was an opinion prevailing that the sub-sheriffs packed the juries?—That they did not summon a fair proportion of Roman Catholics; I think that is the plain way of expressing it.

3733. But that did not come within your own observation in the district with which you are officially connected?—There never was the slightest question about the fairness of the constitution

Mr. *A. Murphy.*

26 May 1873.

stitution of the juries of Clare and Kerry in my time.

3734. It is not an uncommon thing in Ireland for reports of a discreditable and party kind to be spread, and when you come to inquire into them you find that the persons who spread those reports have had no personal experience of them?—I think always.

3735. Would you be inclined, on account of reports of that kind that are not substantiated, to change an old system that works well?—No, I should not; but I would be inclined to change this particular system.

3736. You do not think that the new system works well?—I think it can be made to work very well. I should be very sorry to suggest reverting to the old system, although in the counties that I am acquainted with, the old system worked admirably.

3737. During the time that you have been in office have you had to exercise the power of calling upon jurors to stand aside?—Yes.

3738. Did you have occasion to exercise that power frequently under the old Act?—No, I had not. During the Fenian prosecutions I did exercise that power, but not in many instances, and I know that in Kerry there were verdicts which gave great satisfaction, and convictions by juries entirely composed of persons who would be supposed to hold popular opinions, and those convictions were of very great value in the vindication of the law.

3739. At the last assizes had you to exercise your power of calling upon jurors to stand aside more extensively than usual?—I tried, in Clare, to ascertain something about the jurors, and really I failed to get anything like reliable information. The grand jurors did not know them, and they appeared not to be known by anyone as a class. In one case I put aside persons who, I heard, were either connections of the accused, or residing in his immediate vicinity. I think if the mode of serving summonses on jurors, which I have taken the liberty of suggesting, was adopted, it would afford an opportunity for persons interested for the accused or for the prosecution, knowing what jurors, from local circumstances, should not sit upon particular trials.

3740. You think that there are local circumstances that would unfit jurors from serving on particular trials?—Unquestionably; and particularly now under the recent change of the law, it would be most desirable to have that power.

3741. The only way by which those persons could be prevented from sitting on juries would be by the exercise of that power of calling upon them to stand aside?—Either by challenge on the part of the accused, or the putting them aside on the part of the Crown.

3742. Then, I suppose, you anticipate to be obliged to exercise that power more frequently under the new Act than under the old?—To do it more now than under the old system, but still not very much if the qualification is raised.

3743. Supposing that cases of political excitement were to arise, such as the Fenian troubles, which we had in 1867, do you anticipate that you would be obliged to exercise your power of calling upon jurors to stand aside more extensively?—I believe I should.

3744. Of course, if it came to your knowledge that a man was at all implicated in the Fenian conspiracy, and there were a Fenian to be tried, you would think it your duty to call such a juror to stand aside?—Of course I should.

3745. Under the old system, I suppose it would be not unlikely that men of that class would not have been placed upon the jury panel at all?—Perhaps a good many that had Fenian tendencies may have been placed upon it.

3746. At all events, in the case of the jurors under the old system, there was a double sifting process; there was first of all an officer who was bound to place upon his jury panels those whom he knew to be well affected to the law; and then again, when the juries were empanelled, it was your duty to call upon those to stand aside whom you knew to be disaffected?—It was clearly my duty to put aside any juror that I thought would not act honestly upon the evidence.

3747. So that, as regards the old system, as compared with the new, there was a greater facility, and the administration of justice would be better exercised, and the juries would be more freed from partisans than under the new?—I think that the old jurors were subject to the pressure of public opinion, which a great many of the new jurors would not be. They were perfectly independent of public opinion, and independent of influence, because those who were taken from the old jurors' books were generally taken from the upper middle classes of society; and if they attempted openly to violate the obligation of their oath as jurors, they would be shunned. At present, with the juries constituted under this Act, I think that many a juror would consider that he upheld his position by sticking to his neighbours or friends, and not sending them to gaol.

3748. Under this system, supposing a juror had manifestly violated the obligations of his oath, when it came round to his turn to serve again, would there be any power of excluding him from the panel?—But there would be a power to exclude him from the jury by the Crown Solicitor.

3749. Except that power there would be none; he must be summoned upon the jury panel?—Yes, certainly he must be summoned. After a little while of the working of this Act, if the qualification is raised at all, so as to limit the number of jurors somewhat, the Crown Solicitor will become familiar with almost every one of the jurors, and know all about them, and will act accordingly. At present, with the very large number in Kerry, for instance, the jurors who were on the last assizes, I do not think will come there again for about 15 years, and the Crown Solicitor, or any other official, could not know anything about them.

3750. Do you think that in the counties of Clare and Kerry there are a great number of jurors on the jury list who are not qualified, as to independence of feeling, for the exercise of their duties?—I know that there are a great many who are wholly unfit to be jurors as far as independence of feeling goes.

3751. Do you think that if the qualification was raised to the extent that you propose, even then there would be a considerable number of men on the jury lists not qualified to serve?—I think not; I think that if the qualification was raised to the extent which I have ventured to suggest, we should then have the class of jurors that we were in the habit of meeting with frequently, either in the Poor Law Board rooms, and at fairs and markets, or as associated ratepayers, and in other ways,

Mr. *A. Murphy.* 26 May 1873.

ways, who are amenable to quite a different public opinion from the small farmers.

3752-3. Mr. *Downing.*] You would rather not have farmers on juries at all, I fancy?—No, I think that the small farmers that were tested in Clare showed themselves unequal to the obligations which were imposed upon them, and I think they gave verdicts diametrically opposed, in two cases, to the evidence.

3754. We have had that from the judge; but you were satisfied with the jury panel in Kerry?—I was.

3755. Did you analyse that panel?—I did.

3756. Is that it (*handing a Paper to the Witness*)?—Yes.

3757. On that panel of 91, are there not 61 farmers that are described as small farmers?—No, there are not; not small farmers.

3758. Are there 61 farmers?—There may be 61 persons with the name of farmer added to them, but for the most part they are in the immediate vicinity of Tralee. I believe there are only five, on the whole, outside the barony of Trughanacmy.

3759. Your sheriff altogether forgot his duty by not summoning from the entire county?—Yes, he did, and the array was challenged successfully in consequence.

3760. You would like to have all the magistrates and their sons on the panel?—Yes, on the special jurors' panel.

3761. Are you aware that in Kerry, by your qualification of 40 *l.*, you would reduce the number from 2,440 to 493?—I did not think it could be so many.

3762. Your qualification would be 40 *l.*?—Yes, in the rural districts, and 14 *l.* or 12 *l.* in the towns.

3763. If you take from the list all up to 40 *l.*, you will find that the panel for the whole county will be reduced to 449?—I do not think that that will be so.

3764. Would not that be too small a number to have on the jurors' book for the county of Kerry?—I think not. I think that 500 would be amply sufficient for the assize work of the whole county.

Monday, 9th June 1873.

MEMBERS PRESENT:

Sir Rowland Blennerhassett.	Mr. Charles Lewis.
Mr. Bruen.	The O'Conor Don.
Viscount Crichton.	Major O'Reilly.
Mr. Downing.	Colonel Wilson Patten.
The Marquis of Hartington.	

THE RIGHT HONOURABLE THE MARQUIS OF HARTINGTON, IN THE CHAIR.

Mr. JAMES ROBINSON, called in; and Examined.

Mr. *J. Robinson.*

9 June 1873.

3765. Mr. *Bruen.*] I THINK you are a Queen's Counsel, and Chairman of Quarter Sessions of the county of Cavan?—Yes.

3766. You go the Connaught circuit, and are the leader of it?—Yes.

3767. Do you practice also at the bar in Dublin?—Yes.

3768. You had been chairman of other counties, had you not, before you were chairman of the county of Cavan?—Yes; I was four years chairman in Roscommon, six years in the county of Tyrone, and I have been four years chairman of the county of Cavan.

3769. You were very conversant, were you not, with the operation of the jury law before the change which was made by the late Act?—Yes, I naturally saw a great deal of it, as well in Dublin as on circuit.

3770. Are you of opinion that in some degree a change was required?—It was, because the leasehold and freehold qualifications had to a large extent ceased to exist, that is to say, the 10*l.* freeholders and the 15*l.* leaseholders had ceased to exist; and, besides that, it was difficult to make out in any shape a correct list of jurors; and therefore a change in that respect was absolutely necessary. Besides that, in Dublin, there were some irregularities; for instance, merchants and traders complained that they were frequently summoned, and that their time was wasted in that way, the same person being summoned over and over again. Several men in Dublin also attended constantly, men whose faces you always saw; but, as a rule, their verdicts were satisfactory. I heard no objection made to their verdicts; but there was an objection, and a strong one, made by the merchants and traders, as to being compelled to attend time after time. I think, as far as I can judge, that was what caused considerable outcry against the old system.

3771. The judges were satisfied, were they not?—They took the men that presented themselves; I do not know whether they were satisfied or not.

3772. As regards the Connaught circuit, you think that the jurors were good under the old Act?—Yes, they certainly were, and in the county of Galway they were pre-eminently so; in fact, in almost all cases where there was a controversy as to where the venue should be changed to in order to have a good jury, beyond exception Galway was always selected; still one saw there what I have always seen time after time, a great number of the same faces in the box, but there was no objection to them, because every one knew, whether it was a party case, or anything connected with religion or politics, whether the men were Catholics or Protestants, they gave honest verdicts, beyond exception.

3773. Then the sheriffs' selection gave satisfaction to the public?—Most clearly on the Connaught circuit.

3774. There was no complaint about the formation of the panel?—I never heard of any.

3775. Under the existing Act have you remarked that there has been any change in that respect?—I have seen it in Dublin, and I have seen it also on the last Connaught circuit; at the quarter sessions, there was very little business to be done in that way, because it followed immediately on the assizes; in fact, only three small cases came before me; one at Cavan, a small assault case, and two cases at Cootehill, and in those cases at Cootehill, from the class of men who appeared in the box, I should say the whole of them, it was clear to anyone who saw them, that there had been no revision whatever; there were a vast number of old men, and a number of men wretchedly poor. One of the cases at Cootehill was a case in which a man was accused by the Crown of having committed larceny; he was also charged with receiving. The jury were locked up for a long time; I sent the sub-sheriff to know what kept them, and he came down to say that they could not agree; so I called them down, and found that 11 of them said they would agree, but the twelfth said that he would not. It was clearly proved that the man had stolen coal and hid it in a field, but this juror's idea was that he had only asked for it, and he thought that there was no offence committed; finally, I said that I was very sorry for it, but I should lock them up until the morning, when the man said at once, "I will agree," and they returned a verdict.

3776. Do you think that there is the same confidence in the execution of the law under the present jury system that there was under the old system?

Mr. J. Robinson.

9 June 1873.

system?—I do not think there is the same class of intelligent men on the juries; as to the matter of confidence I cannot say that I have asked many questions about it, but I know that there is not the same class of intelligent men; that is a matter that all of us can see. It is a large question as to whether the juries have the public confidence or not.

3777. In the other counties in that circuit, for instance, in Roscommon, was there any particular case to which you would refer?—What I have just now spoken of was with regard to the quarter sessions in Cavan, but on the Connaught circuit I saw several matters which showed prejudice and want of intelligence. For instance, in Roscommon I was leading counsel for The O'Conor Don in a case in which nothing particular turned up, but where the service of notices to quit was properly proved, and in that case, although the evidence was clear that the notices had been served, the verdict returned, after a few minutes, and after a strong charge from the judge in favour of The O'Conor Don, was in these words, "No verdict for the plaintiff." Then the judge took them categorically through the services, and said, "Do you believe the man who swore that he himself was served," and after a little hesitation they said, "Yes." Then he said, "Do you believe that the man who was proved to have come into Mr. Stapleton's office to be served was served," and they said that they did not. The judge stayed execution to enable me to move the Court of Queen's Bench, in Dublin, to have the verdict set aside, and by the leave of the court, without hearing the counsel for The O'Conor Don, the verdict was set aside as being utterly opposed to anything like what it ought to have been. There was another case in which the judge's report showed that there was a want of intelligence in the jury; that was the case of Judge *against* Lowe. It was a case with regard to the obstruction of some lights, and the plea that was put in was that by the leave of the plaintiff the defendant had erected a building which obstructed the lights. This being so, the matter was very simple indeed, and the judge charged strongly for the plaintiff; the latter part of the report just gives an idea of what the jury was. He said that the jury came out several times, and said that they could not agree, and at last they came out to ask him to tell them what his opinion was, and finally they found for the defendant; and that case, the moment it came to Dublin, was set aside as a matter of course. That is what I saw there, and I should say that the juries on the circuit were not so good as they were before the change in the law; many of the jurors were wretchedly poor, but it was most noticeable in the three counties of Mayo, Roscommon, and Leitrim.

3778. Do you consider that the deterioration of the jurors as to intelligence, and the other qualities which are necessary for the proper discharge of their duties, was most marked?—I think so; those two instances prove that as far as they go; but a most absurd thing occurred in Leitrim in the Crown Court, where a man was convicted. Baron Deasy told me (for I do not practice in the Crown Court) that a man was charged with assaulting a constable, was found guilty, and sentenced to 12 months' imprisonment with hard labour; but the next morning five of the jurymen called upon the judge, and said that they had not agreed to the verdict at all; and having made a declaration to that effect, the result was that the man was set at large.

3779. Sir *R. Blennerhassett.*] When was this?—At the last assizes in the county of Leitrim; and Baron Deasy told me of it himself.

3780. Mr. *Bruen.*] Have you heard lately of anything that has occurred in the other counties, for instance, a statement by a Queen's counsel in relation to a jury returned for the city of Cork?—Last Friday Mr. Gerald Fitzgibbon, who was opposed to me in a motion to change the venue to Sligo, said, in arguing before the court, that what the sheriff of the city of Cork had done was this, to select from the letter A. any name that he thought fit, and so on dealing with the other letters of the alphabet, and not taking them in dictionary order. He said that the juries were remarkably good and intelligent, and stated before the Court of Common Pleas, Chief Justice Monahan and the other judges presiding, that such was the true construction of the Act; and Mr. Justice Keogh said, do you mean to say that any judge except Mr. Justice Fitzgerald takes that view; and Mr. Justice Keogh announced that the other 11 judges were unanimous in holding that according to the existing Act the sheriff must take the names in dictionary order. There was another matter that occurred in the county of Mayo when I was on circuit, which was rather absurd; a jury had been empanelled before Mr. Justice Morris in the Crown Court. The court adjourned, and when it resumed the trial proceeded, 12 men being in the box, but after a considerable time, it was discovered that one of the 12 jurors was sitting in the gallery opposite, whereupon there was a mistrial, and the trial had to commence again.

3781. Major *O'Reilly.*] Who were the 12 that were sitting in the box?—One person who was by saw a vacant seat, and sat down in it.

3782. Mr. *Bruen.*] Will not the application of the alphabetical and dictionary order in some parts of the country produce a very injurious effect?—Yes; in the part that I know it must, that is to say, in the west of Ireland, where it is quite possible that a jury might be entirely composed of M's or O's, owing to the great preponderance of those letters. Take the letter A, any man familiar with the thing will see at once that the names in that letter must, as a matter of course, be exhausted in a short time, and it must come eventually to persons, all of whose names commence with the letter M or the letter O.

3783. Besides that there is a very great inconvenience in the system, in that it summons persons from a distance, whereas otherwise people might be summoned to serve near at hand?—Yes; in the county of Cavan, at quarter sessions, by the Act, as it stands, the dictionary order is merely pursued in the division of the county. This I have known to occur, for the sheriff has told me so. Ballyconnell is the name of one of our quarter sessions towns, at the extreme northwest of Cavan, and the county town is Cavan. At those two places quarter sessions are held, and at the April quarter sessions, men who perhaps lived miles away up the county near Ballyconnell, were brought down to serve at Cavan, whereas men at Cavan could have been got quite as conveniently, and men from the Cavan side were brought to serve at Ballyconnell.

3784. Major *O'Reilly.*] Is it not possible to have the county divided into districts by the authority

Mr. J. Robinson.

9 June 1873.

authority of the Lord Lieutenant for quarter sessions purposes?—Yes, that is the way that it is divided.

3785. This would not have occurred, would it, if it had been so divided?—Yes, it would; it must occur; if you had a fresh division, of course, it might not; that is to say, if you divided the Cavan quarter sessions district into two, of course, according to the Act of Parliament as it stands you would not have that unpleasantness.

3786. But there is power to do that, is there not?—Yes, clearly.

3787. The Lord Lieutenant may divide a county for quarter sessions purposes, but the dictionary order is followed in the division, is it not?—Yes, but that would lead to absurd results in another way; if it was divided following out your Act of Parliament you would only select men from the divided district, but still this absurdity would follow that you would be cutting a district, which is not too large as it is, into two, merely for the purpose of sustaining that provision in the Act of Parliament, because there would not be the work to be done; recollect the waste of power, if I may use the term, which you would have in this small division if it were cut into two; you would summon a number of men to serve on the grand jury, and you would summon a number of men to do the work of common jurors; you would have double the waste of power going on, and you would have that waste in both districts; your proposition would divide the district into two, and then double the work.

3788. But it could be so arranged, could it not, as to have the jurors at Ballyconnell summoned from the Ballyconnell district only?—If you stood by your existing Act of Parliament it would be to arrange it so that men should be taken from convenient baronies, but I do not see how you could carry out that proposition, because it would lead to this result, that it would cut up a small district into two.

3789. My proposition is this, that the juries for the quarter sessions towns should be summoned in the order prescribed in the present Act from the convenient baronies for their quarter sessions towns?—That would be much better, no doubt.

3790. Mr. *Bruen.*] Have you any suggestion to make with regard to additional qualifications for jurors?—Yes, I do not refer to the late Act, because it mentions some additional qualifications, namely, the sons of peers and baronets, and so on; but there are qualifications omitted altogether from the present Act of Parliament, which in my humble judgment should be added, as I think that they would give an increase of power, and be a better class, perhaps; for instance, I believe that the persons mentioned in the Bill, which was brought in by Sir John Young, now Lord Lisgar, in the year 1854, would be very desirable, but the qualifications which, I think, would be proper to add would be those which you will find on the register in every county, and do not require occupation, namely, 50 *l.* freeholders, 50 *l.* rent-chargers, 20 *l.* freeholders, 20 *l.* rent-chargers, and 20 *l.* leaseholders; by the Act of the 3 & 4 Vict. c. 69, which is the Act under which the registration is carried on, the franchises which I have just told you of were preserved; they are not mentioned in the Jury Act which is in force; but they are still in existence.

3791. What is the difference between a 50 *l.* freehold and a 20 *l.* freehold?—The former Acts of Parliament created two different franchises; there was the 50 *l.* freehold, arising from land or rent; that is one thing created by the Act of Parliament, and therefore it is an existing thing; and there was the 50 *l.* freehold arising from rent-charge; that was created by Act of Parliament, and is an existing thing; there was the 20 *l.* freehold arising from land or rent, created by Act of Parliament, and that is an existing thing.

3792. *Chairman.*] Does not the franchise of 20 *l.* freehold and upwards include the 50 *l.* freehold?—No, certainly not, because the 20 *l.* freehold goes up as high as 50 *l.*, and stops there; the 50 *l.* freehold may be only 50 *l.* and may run up to 200 *l.*; they are distinct things created by Act of Parliament. On the register, as it stands now, those things are to be found: the 50 *l.* and 20 *l.* freehold arising from land and rent, the 50 *l.* and 20 *l.* rent-charge, and the 20 *l.* leasehold, and to none of those franchises is occupation essential.

3793. Viscount *Crichton.*] Do all those qualifications confer the Parliamentary franchise?—Yes, they confer the franchise on every one who happens to possess them; I believe you will find in every county of Ireland that there are more or less of them, and in some more than others.

3794. Mr. *Bruen.*] Are all of those on the register?—Yes, they are every one on the register; therefore you could, if you thought fit, call for a return from the clerk of the peace of the persons who would be eligible to serve as jurors, namely, those persons so qualified residing within the county.

3795. With regard to the amount of qualification, have you any suggestion to make as to raising of it?—As far as I have heard, and as far as Cavan is concerned, I should fancy that the 20 *l.* rating in the towns and the 30 *l.* rating in the country would produce a very fair jury, and for special jurors 50 *l* rating in towns and 80 *l.* in the country; as far as I can understand, that would give a good class of jurors in Cavan.

3796. You think it is desirable that the qualification should be raised so long as a sufficient number of jurors were supplied for the service of the county?—Yes, for this reason, that, as a rule, you are more likely to secure intelligence, and most certainly independence, the higher you go.

3797. And not only so, but the poorer class of jurors find it hard, do they not, to support themselves when in attendance upon their duties as jurors?—Yes; I should say that the humbler classes are most anxious to be free from this burden altogether. I know, as a matter of fact, in Cavan particularly, when humble men attend some of them are in a wretched condition as far as poverty is concerned. It is a serious hardship upon them to be obliged, with their narrow means, to spend a couple of days sometimes, in one of those quarter sessions towns.

3798. With regard to exemptions, who do you think ought to be exempted?—I would exempt publicans, because, I may mention this. I was Crown prosecutor on the entire Connaught circuit, from June 1852 to the spring of 1855, when I gave it up, and during that time it was an inflexible rule that publicans were desired to stand aside by the Crown. I always understood that was the rule Sir Michael O'Loghlen, when Attorney General, laid down, and that it was followed

Mr. *J. Robinson.*

9 June 1873.

followed and enforced by every succeeding Attorney General.

3799. Would you exempt law clerks?—Yes; law clerks and sheriffs' officers I think it would be very proper to exempt.

3800. Can you suggest any other exemptions?—Except publicans and sheriffs' officers and law clerks, it does not occur to me to suggest any other, except that I would exempt domestic servants. In Dublin some of the judges' servants are on the jurors' book. I know, as a fact, that one of Judge Keogh's servants is a special juror, and I think that that is a great absurdity.

3801. What have you to say with regard to disqualifications?—I should not be disposed to add anything to the disqualifications that are in the Act, except those that I find in Sir John Young's Bill, in the 6th Section of that Bill, the words are these, "No man who shall have been convicted within seven years of any offence against the Act passed in the session of Parliament holden in the first and second years of the reign of his late Majesty King William the Fourth, chapter 44, or of any crimes resulting from illegal combination, and who has undergone punishment, is or shall be qualified to serve on juries or inquests in any court or on any occasion whatsoever." That is only a disqualification for seven years, because a man may be quite a different man at the end of seven years from what he was before. It would be absurd if you were not to exclude men of that class, and I will tell you why. The 1st and 2nd of William 4, chap. 44, is an Act of Parliament that disqualifies persons who have committed misdemeanours; for instance, any person or persons rising or assembling as described in the 15th and 16th of George the 3rd, chapter 21, or in any other manner, and unlawfully compelling, or by force, threats, or menaces, attempting to compel anyone to quit his dwelling-house, habitation, farm possession, place of abode, service, or lawful employment; or maliciously assaulting or injuring the dwelling-house, place of abode or habitation of any person, or breaking into his house, habitation, barn or outhouse, or causing any door to be opened by threats or menaces; or maliciously injuring the goods, chattels, lands, or property of any person; or taking away any horse, gelding, mare, or mule, or any gun, sword, or other weapon, or any money, goods, or chattels, without the consent of the owner; or causing the same to be delivered by threats or menaces; or maliciously digging, turning up, cutting down, or injuring the lands or crops growing or secured, or the walls or other fences, or the cattle, goods, or chattels of any person. That is a misdemeanour; it is not a felony; it is a misdemeanour of a formidable class. You may observe that this very misdemeanour would meet the case of the Belfast rioters, a number of whom compelled people by threats to leave their dwelling-houses. It seems to be certainly fitting that a man committing a very atrocious offence in the midst of a quiet district should be deprived of the privilege of sitting as a juror to try matters involving questions of property and agrarian offences, and therefore, that offences of that class should create, at all events, a seven years' disqualification.

3802. With regard to the revision of the jury lists, what do you propose as to the proceedings preliminary to the revision of the lists of Parliamentary voters and jurymen combined; I think you have said that there might be a combination of the two lists?—My proposition would be that all matters preliminary to the revision of Parliamentary voters, and the jury should be combined; that there should be added to the Parliamentary register and the supplemental list, two columns headed, "Common Jurors," and "Special Jurors;" and that in the two columns which deal with the objections by the clerk of the peace, and the union clerk, there should be some words added which would restrict the objections to the Parliamentary voters; then, instead of two precepts issuing, as is the case now, from the clerk of the peace to the different clerks of the unions, one precept would go, and there would be one return, those two columns of jurors and special jurors being filled up; and when they were returned to the clerks of the peace he would make the list out in alphabetical order, and print it; I will take the county of Cavan as an instance, just to show how the thing would work, and what an enormous saving there would be in the expense to each county, and I think perfection in the way of revision; there are 18 petty sessions districts in that county, and in respect of each under the late Act of Parliament there exists a perfect register applicable to that district. On that register there is the name of every 12 *l.* rated occupier and every freeholder and leaseholder entitled to vote. Therefore, when it would come returned to the clerk of the peace with the two columns filled up, which I would propose to add to the register and the supplemental list, there would appear on the face of it a perfect list, as far as the voters and the jurors are concerned. Then what I would propose would be, that when the whole of that is printed, and sent back, a copy of it should be sent to every clerk of every poor-law union, and there are four in that county, and to every sub-inspector in the county, of whom there are seven, and I should propose that copies of those should be published in each district, and that, at the foot of this list, there should be a copy printed of the exemptions and disqualifications, and a notice appended informing everyone in that district that on a day specified, at the petty sessions court, the list would be revised by the magistrates, and that anyone who claimed to be inserted in that list or struck off that list should attend. A copy should be also given to the sessional Crown solicitor, and his business would be to inform himself in relation to that jury list, and for that purpose he could easily appoint a day with the four clerks of the unions in each union to meet the individual clerk and the rate collectors referable to that union, and he could easily, by correspondence, be informed by the sub-inspectors to whom a copy of the list had been sent, of all the information that the constabulary and the sub-inspectors could give. Then, armed with this information, he could on that day for which the court was appointed attend and inform the magistrates.

3803. You would have a summary means by which the knowledge of all these circumstances could be brought to the Bench at the public revision?—Yes; I would make it imperative on the resident magistrates to attend, and the local magistrates would attend, because they would not have to go more than four or five miles; the people themselves would attend, because, for the first time, notice would be brought to their mind that there was such a thing as a revision; heretofore they have had no notice whatever. They would

Mr. *J. Robinson.*

9 June 1873.

would have notice then for the first time, and would attend, and would see if they could bring themselves within the exemptions; and would get free from the onerous duty of attending as jurors. I believe that that revision would be perfect. And again, there is this very important thing, as far as county purposes are concerned, that the expense most clearly would be diminished one-half; because now you send two precepts to the clerks of the unions, and the clerks of the unions make out double lists, and double printings are done through the agency of the clerk of the peace.

3804. The duty of the sessional Crown Solicitor would be especially to inform himself, would it not, of all those matters with regard to the jurors?—Yes, clearly. I would impose it on him as a duty; but his duty would be small in reality, except attending at those different petty sessions courts. There are some 18 in Cavan, and it would impose some extra trouble upon him, no doubt.

3805. Would you reserve any right of appeal from this revision court to the original revision court?—I would in this way. I would give the right of appeal to any one whose name was struck off, and to any one who claimed to be inserted on the list, and I would give the right of appeal to the sessional Crown Solicitor, but in each of those cases only on their serving a notice on the clerk of the peace, and for this obvious reason, that giving an appeal without a provision compelling them to serve a notice, the sessional Crown Solicitor would not know what to do when he came to the chairman's court, what cases he was to fight, or what he was to do, and he could give no information. When notice is served he sees what it will be necessary for him to do, and what witnesses he should come prepared with when the matter was brought before the chairman. I have no doubt that in that way the revision would be perfect.

3806. With regard to the first revision, I should ask you whether you would strictly define by law the magistrate's power to strike off jurors?—I would certainly, because whoever is struck off, I think it is of the last importance that it should be done in open court, and for reasons assigned.

3807. In the second court of revision, by way of appeal, would you have it an independent court of the chairman of quarter sessions?—Yes; he could take up the whole list and revise the whole at the same time, and when revised the jurors and voters names could be separated. The jurors' book would show the jurors' names and the register the voters' names; there would be no practical difficulty whatever about it.

3808. With regard to the service of the summons on jurors, do you think that service by registered letter would be a good form of service?—Yes; I think wherever there is a postal service, that would be the mode to adopt most clearly, because there could be no mistake about it, and you would get rid, in that way, of the bailiff, who has been a very corrupt agent when employed for the purpose of serving those notices.

3809. There does not exist in all places a facility for service by post, does there?—No; in a very large portion of the rural parts of Ireland there is no postal service.

3810. What would you do in such a case as that?—Then I think that the constabulary would be the proper persons to serve the notices; they would be incorruptible, and the notices would be certainly served; I think there could not be a possibility of extending the registered letter system to all the rural districts, because every one who knows any part of Ireland knows, in fact common sense would tell him, that the farmers, as a class, have no correspondence; they do not send to the post, and they have no letters, and it would be an absurdity to impose a fine upon a man who no one could say had really received the letter, and therefore inasmuch as the summons server has been found in many cases to have been a very corrupt agent, I think you must resort to something else, and I do not see anything but the constabulary; as to the idea that people would be terrified by seeing them going about, I do not think there is anything at all in that.

3811. Colonel *Wilson Patten*.] In what way do you believe that the process server has been a corrupt agent?—He has been told that he would get half-a-crown for not serving, and having got that he would not serve the summons at all; sometimes a man would say to another, "I expect to come round to your place on such a day," "Very well, here is half-a-crown for you, do not come," and he would hear no more about it; that has been constantly done, and any one who has attended at assizes and quarter sessions has seen, supposing the judge or the chairman were determined to fine jurors, how difficult a thing it was to fine them, because it was a matter of rare occurrence that the sheriff was in a condition to be able to prove that he had served the juror, simply because he had a set of agents who did not do their duty.

3812. Mr. *Bruen*.] The constabulary are already employed, are they not, in different services collecting information, and their going about the country for that purpose does not excite any alarm?—No, the Irish are a very acute people, and they are not frightened easily. The constabulary go among them to collect statistical information, and when there is to be a poor law election they go about and serve notices, and supposing one of these men was seen going round, the whole of the people in the county would know what he was going about perfectly well.

3813. With regard to the summons of the jurors by the sheriff and the formation of the panel, do you think that there is any document or any Bill existing which would form a machinery of a fair description for doing what ought to be done in that way?—It occurred to me that the great thing would be, if you could do it, to secure men who would do their duty, and who would be competent to serve in the real sense of the word. I have seen a Bill that was brought in by Sir John Young and Mr. Solicitor General for Ireland, now Mr. Justice Keogh, on the 14th December 1854, and that Bill by one of the sections, namely the 13th, contains a direction that the judges of assize shall issue a precept to the respective sheriffs of such counties, cities, and so on, "requiring them to summon for the trial of all issues, whether civil or criminal, which may come on for trial at the assizes, or general sessions of the peace, or other sittings, a sufficient number of the most competent persons named in the jurors' book, so to be delivered by the clerk of the peace, selecting, so far as may be practicable, having regard to their competency, the names of such jurors as shall not have been summoned and attended as such at the

Mr. *J. Robinson.*

9 June 1873.

the last preceding assizes or sessions." The scope of that section, as I understand it, was this: that inasmuch as it must be admitted that no matter how you revise the jurors list (keeping out of view inquiring into a man's opinions, I do not think that you ever could do that at any revision court), it is utterly impossible that you can test capacity at any revision. I understand this Bill to provide in this way, that substantially the book shall be gone through, and that the important thing is that a sufficient number of the most competent persons should be named upon the panel, selecting, as far as may be practicable, having regard to their competency, the names of such jurors as shall not have been summoned and attended as such at the last preceding assizes or sessions. There is a provision also in this Act of Parliament very much to the same effect.

3814. Mr. *Downing.*] What is the qualification in that Bill?—£. 20; and, as regards the part of the Bill of which I spoke some few minutes ago, namely, the second section, it speaks thus: that the rating is to be 20 *l.* or upwards of yearly value; then there is also this provision: "As a freeholder, or lessee, or assignee of any lease of any lands, tenements, or hereditaments, of the yearly value of 20 *l.* or upwards, shall be qualified as to property." Therefore, that Section 2 shows this: that Sir John Young and the Solicitor General of that day thought that, besides the rating qualification, there should be a freehold and leasehold qualification also; therefore, it sustains so far the view that I mentioned a few moments ago, as to the addition to the qualification in the Act of Parliament at the present time. But there is another provision in Section 8, which was copied from Perrin's Act, and which would, if it could be adopted in the way which it occurs to me, lead to almost using, or perhaps entirely using every name to be found upon the jurors' book, and it is this: namely, that the clerk of the peace is, from the lists which he gets, "required to cause one general printed list, arranged according to rank and property, to be made out from the lists so made by and furnished to him as aforesaid." No alphabetical arrangement was pursued there at all; it was not pursued in Perrin's Act, and it is not pursued in this Bill of Sir John Young's, but a "general printed list arranged according to rank and property, to be made out from the lists so made by and furnished to him." I presume that the idea that passed through Mr. Perrin's mind and the minds of the framers of this Bill was this, that the sheriff, knowing how the jurors' book was made up, would see at a glance that the men of larger property qualification, and, to be assumed, of larger intelligence, were at the head of the jurors' book. But, assuming that that was done by legislation, what might occur would be that, to a great extent, all the jurors' book, if framed with that clause governing it, might be utilised in this way: The men at the lower part of the book would, one might fairly say, being lower in rating, be more liable to intimidation or solicitation from persons who are prisoners; in other words, less independent. All that class could be utilised at the quarter sessions, because at quarter sessions no agrarian offences, party cases, treasons, murder, or serious felonies are tried. Those are the cases which involve exasperated and strong feeling in Ireland; and it is, to some extent, a cruel thing, as well as I think an absurd thing, if you look at it, to expose any man of humble circumstances to the hazard of sitting on juries in misdemeanour cases, where he has no power to resist the intimidation which might be brought to bear against him, or, perhaps, to resist the solicitation of the friends of the prisoner. Therefore, in this clause, which Sir John Young introduced into his Bill, and which was copied from Mr. Perrin's Act, I presume that was the idea that passed through the minds of the framers of both; and, as I said before, if that clause were adopted, it would appear to me that the whole of this book, as made up and arranged according to actual rank and property, might be utilised in the way that I suggest.

3815. Major *O'Reilly.*] What is the way in which you propose that the book should be used?—It would simplify it in this sort of way. In Cavan, as I understand it, you have by your new Bill proposed that the rural franchise for common juries should be 30 *l.*, and that the building franchise, if I may call it so, shall be 20 *l.* Then, as I understand, the Bill provides that the special jurors' franchise shall be 75 *l.*, I believe that is it; then ranging up from 20 *l.* and from 30 *l.* to 75 *l.* would be the common jurors' book, but if you arrange them according to rank and property, the man of 75 *l.* rating would head the list; and you descend on the book from 75 *l.* rating, going gradually down through the ratings till you finally reach the 20 *l.* man. My idea is simply this, that if you adopted this clause, copied from Perrin's Act, and introduced into Sir John Young's Bill of arranging the jurors' book according to rank and property, taking all the common jurors below 75 *l.*, you would have a heading in your common jurors' book, and you would descend through the different ratings of men on the common jurors' book from 75 *l.* to 20 *l.*

3816. I understand entirely how you propose the names to be arranged in the jurors' book; what I want to know is, how you propose that the panel should be taken out of that jurors' book for the assizes and for quarter sessions?—That would occupy a very short time. Supposing you divide the common jurors' panel, beginning just below 75 *l.*, until you reached 20 *l.*, and you divided it so in the middle line between 75 *l.* and 20 *l.*, and 30 *l.* for the assizes, you would naturally have men more independent in circumstances, and less liable to intimidation and solicitation; that is my idea.

3817. *Chairman.*] And below that line you would have the jurors for quarter sessions?—Yes.

3818. Major *O'Reilly.*] Then do I understand you to propose that the panels for the assizes should be taken from the upper half of the jurors' book, and that the panels for the quarter sessions should be taken from the lower half?—I do not propose that, nor do I think that it would operate in that way. What I propose would be simply this, to carry out that which Sir John Young proposed in the 13th section, that the Judges should issue their precept requiring the sheriff to summon a sufficient number of the most competent persons, and so on; and then I say, not that you should enact anything beyond that, because my idea would be to take this pure and simple; but in the working out of that, the sheriff, I should fancy, might and could utilize the entire book; not that you should enact anything about it, but that he could utilize it. Supposing that

he

Mr. *J. Robinson.*

9 June 1873.

he was in the discharge of his duty, and he wished to do it, there naturally would be a great number of the humbler classes at the quarter sessions, where no party or agrarian case can arise as a matter of practice (they might arise if it was not for the universal practice to send such cases to the assizes), and where the law says no treason or murder case can be tried. That is my idea.

3819. Then do I understand that you would propose that having arranged the jurors' book in the way that you have described, so far as the law is concerned; you would leave it with that general direction in Sir John Young's Bill to the sheriff to take the names from any part of the panel that he chose; but you would say that the sheriff would take them in the way that you describe for special jurors?—That would be my idea, with this also which is passing in my mind, that up to this time the high sheriff has never taken any part in the preparation of the panel at all, and I think that it would be perhaps a desirable thing, if at the foot of every panel that was made up, the high sheriff was to certify under his hand that he had examined the jurors' book, and examined the panel and had read the section of the Act of Parliament, and that he believed that the panel was made up in accordance with the Act of Parliament?—I have met the magistrates at quarter sessions, in Roscommon, in Tyrone, and in my present county of Cavan; The O'Conor Don amongst others, in his own county often sitting beside me; and from what I know of them, they are men who if the duty were cast upon them would endeavour to discharge it; and beyond exception the sheriff is the only officer who is entirely independent of the Crown.

3820. Mr. *Bruen.*] Before leaving the question of the formation of the panel, you wish to adhere still to that part of the clause in the Bill which you have read which runs thus: that the sheriff should select "a sufficient number of the most competent persons named in the jurors' book, selecting so far as may be practicable, having regard to their competency, the names of such jurors as shall not have been summoned at the last preceding assizes or sessions?—That is my idea, and I would wish him still to go through the book.

3821. And you would approve of a different mode of service of the jurors?—Yes, similar to the mode which exists in Dublin; supposing you employ the constabulary to serve the notices in the rural districts, where there is no postal service; having adopted the system of service by registered letter, you take away from the sub-sheriff every motive almost, except any corrupt one, which he had heretofore not to serve a juror, because the thing is done by their local agency; it puts the sub-sheriff to no inconvenience, and, therefore, he naturally would be inclined to do his duty, even if there was not an additional check imposed upon him by the suggestion with regard to the high sheriff being brought into operation in these matters; he would have no motive to do otherwise, because there would be no trouble imposed upon him.

3822. You mentioned that that would take away from the sub-sheriff every corrupt motive; I do not suppose that you meant by that to imply that the sub-sheriffs have acted upon corrupt motives heretofore?—On my circuit I never knew an instance of it, and I never heard it talked of; with respect to one case that I have heard of, in which it was said that the sheriff was corrupt, I know as a matter of fact that the sheriff was not corrupt, and that was O'Connell's case; every lawyer knows what that case was, and it was this: the Recorder of Dublin was obliged judicially to decide what names should be on the jurors' list; he had simply ministerially to send out those lists to the Clerk of the Peace to be made up in the jurors' book; either in the transit to the Clerk of the Peace's office, or in the Clerk of the Peace's office, a list containing 59 names comprised in the letter M were omitted from the making up of the jurors' book, and the jurors' book was handed over to the sheriff, but there was no pretence for saying that he had anything to do with it in anywise, nor had he any power; there was a challenge to the array in that case, and on these facts which I have told the Committee, three judges in Ireland overruled that challenge, and when the judges were summoned to the Bar of the House of Lords, they unanimously held the challenge to be bad on this ground, that no corruption or impropriety was imputed to the sheriff. Therefore, that case conclusively shows, when it is examined, that the allegation which is popularly made based on that case against the sheriffs has no foundation in fact at all; in fact, one might push the argument higher, and say that inasmuch as there was no imputation against him *ex concessis* he was pure in that transaction.

3823. You also stated that the high sheriff never took any part in the formation of the jury panels, but, I suppose, you only state that as being rather a matter of rumour than anything that has come within your personal knowledge; I think that cases have been brought before the Committee in which the high sheriff has been mentioned as having taken a part in the formation of the panel?—That may be so, but I have never heard of it, and I can only speak from my own knowledge; I never heard of it in my own circuit, and I never heard of it in Dublin.

3824. You consider that the high sheriff would be very much assisted by the sub-sheriff; he could not do without his assistance?—No; the sub-sheriff would naturally be the man to assist him, but if the high sheriff was brought in privity with the book in that way, from what I know of the gentlemen that I speak of, I think that they would be desirous to do their duty, and they would see that the book was substantially gone through. They would see that there should be some very substantial reason why any name was omitted. As I said before, I think that the whole panel could be utilised by sending the men of inferior status to the quarter sessions, where no disturbing element would exist.

3825. Would anything be gained in this way; do you think that they would be thoroughly subject to public opinion, and that that would be a great safeguard to the proper carrying out of the provisions which you propose?—I am quite satisfied that it would, and I think that those men would do their duty.

3826. With regard to the safety of a prisoner, he would have all the safeguards that he has now, would he not?—I should say that he would have far more protection than if any of the theories which I have heard advocated were adopted. One theory advanced is this, that the chairman of sessions should retire into a room, and with the constabulary, who are under the control of and paid by the Crown, should revise the lists. That is one gentleman's proposition, and adopted by a certain

Mr. *J. Robinson.*

9 June 1873.

certain school of thought, if I may use the word, but it would appear to me that if that clause were introduced into the Bill, there would be a shout of execration in Ireland. Again, another proposition is just as monstrous, in my opinion, and that is, that, *ex parte*, the Crown of its mere motion, in Dublin, at the commission court or at the assizes, should at any moment obtain a special jury. I believe if that was put forward there would be a cry of execration throughout the country. I believe this, that every man knows that the sheriff is entirely independent of the Crown, and if he, as a gentleman living in his own county, was brought in privity with this book and looked to see that the Act of Parliament was honestly carried out, I believe that the parties in civil cases, as well as prisoners, would be safer than if there was unlimited power given to the Crown, as it would be by the propositions which have been put forward.

3827. The propositions which have been put forward, though they do not give larger power to the Crown, at all events throw upon the Crown officers a larger duty of operating upon the jury panels than they have hitherto exercised?—No doubt.

3828. Do you think that there should be any ballot for jurors in criminal cases?—I think that it would disserve both the Crown and the prisoner; I have heard no argument advanced for that change, but just see how it would operate; as a rule the long panel, as we call it, is called, and a certain number of men answer, and as they answer, persons employed for the prisoner put a mark opposite a name that he considers is a friend or a partisan, or for some other reason, he thinks him an enemy, and he may challenge him when he comes to the book; the Crown does the like. The Crown Solicitor puts a mark opposite the name of some man who has answered, and who he believes will not be an impartial juror, and whom he wishes to get rid of, and therefore I think that it would be inconvenient, and I have heard no reason advanced for the change.

3829. With regard to special juries, you have stated that there ought not to be that right which was suggested by some of the witnesses, that *ex parte*, a special jury should be called for by either side?—I certainly think that they should not; there should be a special jury of course, when a special commission issued, but they are never issued except under grave circumstances.

3830. With regard to a proportion of special jurors serving with common jurors, what is your opinion?—I am perfectly satisfied that that would be a very bad arrangement indeed; I am quite satisfied that they would be placed in a position in which they would be in antagonism when it came to any matter in which there could be any disturbing element introduced, and it would be a class antagonism, and I am quite convinced that it would not work at all.

3831. With regard to the unanimity of juries in their verdict, do you think that that principle should be continued?—I am quite satisfied that it should; I think that it would be a disastrous thing to introduce into Ireland, in Crown cases, any principle which would get rid of the unanimity of juries, and for this reason, that I think that the majority in a case like that would be exposed to imminent danger. Besides, independently of that, I think there is a sort of feeling amongst people that, although they may think a case sometimes, when decided, a hard case, still they say 12 men disposed of it, and after awhile they forget it. But I think, supposing seven or eight men decided against four, supposing 12 should be the tribunal, I would not like to be one of the eight men, especially in a disturbed time; I think that it would be fraught with imminent peril.

3832. Some opinions have been stated before this Committee with regard to the judge discharging a juror or exempting him from service; what have you to say upon that point?—Vesting in the judge the power of dispensing with the services of jurors would be very fatal to the administration of justice; I think it is beyond everything necessary that the judge should have nothing to do with the jury panel; I should define strictly in the Act of Parliament what his duties were, and I would give him permission to let a man stand aside if he was ill, or if any member of his family was seriously ill, or he might desire him to stand aside if he was drunk, but beyond that I cannot call to mind any other point; there is this also, that if any man was called on a jury in a civil case, who was a relative of either of the litigant parties, or of the attorney of either party litigant, I think that it would be a very proper case, but I would strictly limit and define the rights of the judge in such a matter.

3833. Would not that be a ground of challenge even in a civil case?—Yes, but recollect a challenge is a cumbrous matter, whereas I would propose to give him so much power without any challenge at all.

3834. You do not think that it would be right to interfere with the present power enjoyed by the Crown of calling upon jurors to stand aside?—Certainly not; notwithstanding any amount of revision in summoning competent jurors, supposing this proposition was adopted, still it might happen that some man connected with some secret society might be on the jury, and the Crown might desire to get rid of him; I think that you cannot make the system perfect, and you must leave that power with the Crown.

3835. Your suggestions would probably diminish the necessity for the exercise of that power?—The more you secure competent men by that machinery, the less necessity is there for the Crown exercising that power which they have always had.

3836. With regard to fines for non-attendance, do you propose any change in that respect in the present law?—I am disposed to say, in order to carry out this Act of Parliament to secure the regular attendance of men to serve as jurors, I think it would be desirable to make it a matter of necessity that a fine to some amount should be imposed upon every man who did not answer to his name, and that the judge should direct it to be so recorded by the officers of the court; the judge, of course, to have his present power of remitting the fine, or of increasing the fine.

3837. Is there any danger of embarrassment in Section 19 of the present Juries Act, that is, for excusing those already summoned during the current and next two preceding years, in the rotation of service?—I am satisfied, no matter what you do, whether you retain the existing law or change it, that that would be a useless section, for this reason: virtually, it says that a juror is not to serve for three years. That depends upon the number of men that you have. How can you predicate till you see what number of men you would have, that you can exempt a man after

having

having served once, for three years; and, besides that, supposing that the rotation system is carried through, you do not want that section.

3838. There appears to be a pretty general concurrence of opinion amongst the witnesses who have appeared before the Committee, that there should be some additional power of exercising, or exempting, or relieving from service certain jurors; that is to say, an extension of the power of selection which is now given in the Act; do you concur that the Act could not be made to work well without some power of selection being committed to somebody?—That seems to be a universal theory. I fail to see it, and as far as I understand from the cursory view of the evidence that I have seen, the only question is, who is to have the power of selection? One set of men propose that there should be a selection by the chairman, with the help of the constabulary, in his private chamber; I think that a disastrous course. Another set of men say that there ought to be special jurors in all cases at the mere motion of the Crown, either at assizes or at sessions. I think, standing on the old system, I do not see, as far as my judgment goes, a better scheme than this of Sir John Young when he introduced this Bill; besides, if I am rightly informed, in the Bill which the Attorney General for England is passing through a Committee, as I see by the newspapers, there is no clause which takes away from the sheriff the power of selection. I understand that that is so; and if it be so, it seems to me to afford an additional reason for thinking that this 13th section would be a wise section to adopt in any Bill for the purpose of being passed into an Act of Parliament; because we see that the law officers, people eminent for their knowledge of the law, are prepared to leave this power with the old constituted authority of the county.

3839. Mr. *Downing*.] I think you stated that one of Judge Keogh's servants was one of the jurors?—I heard that he was on the special jurors' list in Dublin.

3840. It would be very easy, would it not, to obviate a recurrence of that by introducing into any Act of Parliament that may be passed hereafter an exemption with regard to persons in such employment?—That is what I said.

3841. We have had evidence from Mr. Serjeant Armstrong, that in one of the most important cases tried perhaps in Ireland, in which the succession to the Mount Garratt title and property was involved, there was a farmer upon the jury with his collar open, and his breast red from the sun, so that under the former Act there were similar cases to those which occur under the present?—I do not think that that exactly proves your proposition; it only shows that one out of 12 was a man of that class. As I understand the proposition of persons who dissent from the working of the present Act, it is this, that there might be nine or 10 of that class out of the 12, which is a widely different state of things.

3842. You would not object to a man who was not quite educated if he could read and write, because he was a mere farmer?—I do not object to any man's rank in life, far from it. There may be honesty and intelligence in the lowest rank as well as in the highest, but you may more reasonably expect to reach that intelligence by going higher in the scale of a man's qualification in the way of property. That would be the more reasonable expectation. I do not object to any man because he is not a man of wealth.

Mr. *J. Robinson.*

9 June 1873.

3843. Did I understand you to say that in revising the lists you would have the two lists made into one, containing the Parliamentary voters as well as those who would be returned for the jurors' book?—Yes, I would.

3844. Did I understand you that you would have objections made to persons who were entitled to the franchise upon that list, or was it merely to jurors?—I said that in the two columns on the register and the supplemental list, giving power to the clerk of the peace and the clerk of the Crown to object to a voter. I would insert words restricting objections to the voter alone; but I think it would be very improper that the clerk of the peace or the clerk of the Crown should have the power to object to a juror, because there are disqualifications to the juror, and many people might say many things hard of a man if they saw "objected" opposite to his name.

3845. You did not intend to apply to those several persons whom you named as being compelled by Act of Parliament to attend upon the magistrates, that they should have the power to object in any way whatsoever to a voter, as they have the power under the present Act of Parliament?—My proposition was quite wide of the revision of voters. You have the present register and the supplemental list, and what I propose is (and it is the simplest thing in the world) two additional columns, one headed "Common Jurors," and the other headed "Special Jurors," to be added to these two matters. I propose to insert certain words in the two lists which deal with the objections by the clerk of the peace, and the clerk of the Crown, so as to restrict the objection simply to the voter; according to my idea I think that it would be a very improper thing, which would give rise to bad feeling, if you allowed objections to be placed opposite a juror's name, for there are so many matters of disqualification that the world is bad enough to impute all sorts of things without the least foundation. Therefore, I distinctly guarded against that in my proposition.

3846. As I understand you, you would have one general list, and when you came to the jurors who were valued at 20 *l.* and under, you would have those returned for quarter sessions, and you would have those between the higher qualification and 20 *l.* returned for assize purposes?—I do not say that I would make it part of the Act of Parliament, but I think that it would be reasonable that the sheriff in working out the Act should have power to do so.

3847. Did not I understand you to say that you would put upon the jurors' book the names according to their rank and position, which you afterwards explained by saying that you would take a man of 75 *l.* and put him at the head of the list, and you would take those others according to their valuations?—What I said was this, that taking 75 *l.* as the under limit of the special jurors, we will say in the county of Cavan, all men of 70 *l.* we will suppose would be the first common jurors, and that you would run down the list till you reached the 20 *l.* and 30 *l.* men; then I merely say, not for the purpose of framing the Act in this way, but theoretically, if I was a sheriff, supposing this 13th Section was adopted as part of the Act of Parliament, and obligatory upon the sheriff, I should in the discharge of my duty summon men of the lower qualification to the quarter sessions, where no disturbing element could

Mr. J. Robinson.

9 June 1873.

could arise, and in that way I think practically the whole book could be gone through.

3848. That is merely giving the sheriff a discretion which you, if you were sheriff, would exercise?—Yes, that is the way in which I would carry it out.

3849. Supposing you did exercise it, did I understand you to say that men valued at 18*l.* or 20*l.* a year were more open to intimidation and solicitation than men in a better position of life, say at a valuation of 30*l.* or 40*l.*?—As a rule I would say that they are more independent, and from their circumstances they are perhaps to some extent a more highly educated class. We see that in the world, and besides that every one knows that a man according to the affluence of his means is less likely to be intimidated or to yield to solicitation.

3850. Do you think there is much difference between two men, one valued at 20*l.* and another at 25*l.* or 30*l.*?—No; but you cannot work out anything by looking at a pound or two. You can only take the large idea that I put forward. You cannot test the principle by saying that; take a man of 20*l.*, there is not much difference between him and a man of 30*l.*; there is no principle in that.

3851. In the county of Cavan I find that there are on the jury list at present 1835, and if you pick out the number whose qualification is under 30*l.*, namely, 1086, that would reduce the panel to 749?—You have done that by your late Act.

3852. You would disapprove of that, would you?—No, I would not disapprove of it.

3853. I understood you to say that you adopt this Bill of Sir John Young with the valuation of 30*l.*?—I said that I adopted the 13th section of the Bill of Sir John Young.

3854. Deducting 1036 in the county of Cavan of those who are valued under 30*l.*, that would reduce the panel to 749; supposing that you, as sub-sheriff, selected the panel according to your own discretion, as you have just now mentioned, you would take the men of 70*l.*, 60*l.*, 50*l.*, and so on, until you came down to the lowest number?—I am afraid that I have not conveyed my proposition very clearly, because you and I are not *ad idem*. What I meant to say was this, that I would adopt this Bill as far as arranging the names in the general list according to rank and property. That is what Sir John Young thought, copying Perrin's Act; and then as to the practical working of it, I thought it would be easy to get through the entire jurors' book, because I said that if I was the sheriff, wishing to do my duty, I would take the men of the under classes as far as they went. You cannot draw a hard and fast line in the middle of any class or classes. I would take them as far as I could utilize them. My opinion was that a quarter sessions, where no disturbing element could arise, as far as I could, I would summon the lower qualified jurors, and sending the men of more independent means to the assizes, where a disturbing element would arise.

3855. You do not mean to take them alphabetically?—I am assuming that the alphabet is rejected, because if Sir John Young's Bill was adopted the alphabetical question does not arise.

3856. Then the sheriff would have full discretion to select the jury from the jurors' book?—Yes, because there is no other injunction upon him, but to select competent names with this proviso, that he is never to fall back upon the men who have previously served if he can get competent men still to serve.

3857. Do you think that the gentleman who usually occupies the position of high sheriff would take the trouble of going over the lists, and that he would not depend upon his sub-sheriff and say, you are acquainted with the county, you have been so many years sub-sheriff, and I rely upon you to make out a proper panel?—I am perfectly satisfied, from what I know of those gentlemen in those three counties, that that would not be so. I have sat for four years in Roscommon, six years in Tyrone, and four in Cavan, and I am perfectly satisfied that if that duty was imposed upon them they would see that the duty was discharged.

3858. But the high sheriff has no acquaintance with the people of the county?—But he has intelligence, as a rule, and he would require the sub-sheriff to inform him why certain names were passed by.

3859. Mr. *Bruen.*] Do you think that the high sheriff, as a rule, has not any acquaintance with the people?—Most of the high sheriffs that I have seen in the west of Ireland were denizens of the county, and, therefore, I should say that they were dull men indeed if they did not know the people to some extent.

3860. Mr. *Downing.*] Do you not know that sheriffs have been appointed from other counties?—I cannot answer that from my own knowledge, but I believe that it is so.

3861. You stated, did you not, that you thought it would be a bad thing to give the judge the power to put people off the panel without sufficient cause?—I think that it would be very injurious to the administration of justice.

3862. You would say that whatever was done by the judge in that way ought to be done publicly?—Yes, that is of the last importance, most assuredly.

3863. Major *O'Reilly.*] You stated that juries in Galway, from your experience hitherto, have always given satisfactory verdicts?—I have always found it so.

3864. You would not say that that applies universally to every case; there have been cases in which the verdicts of the juries have been at least strongly criticised; for instance, the Barrett's case?—I was not at the assizes, and I cannot speak of that case, but I remember Barrett's case, and that there was great excitement about it and bad feeling; they were not the class of men that I spoke of; I spoke of the class of jurors whom I saw at the assizes, and who were first class men.

3865. In that case perhaps you would allow that the result was not what you would call satisfactory?—I think they were what you would call a low class of men; but I do not like to say that, for I know nothing of them from my own knowledge. I have seen 12 Catholics in the box, and if any Protestant in the county wished to be tried in any question affecting his property, or his life, or his honour, he might have selected them, for they were men of the highest class.

3866. In Cavan, you said that under the new Act there evidently had been no revision of the jurors' book at all, and that old men over the legal age apparently, and others who ought to be there even under the present Act, were there?—Yes; because there was, in fact, before us chairmen no revision. What occurred was just this: when we sat at the revision, the clerks of the

unions

Mr. *J. Robinson.* 9 June 1873.

unions and the rate collectors appeared. I asked, could any one give me information as to whether there were persons over the age to be struck off, and they all said they could not. Again I asked, could any one inform me whether any of them were disqualified, and they said "No." And, therefore, our tribunal of revision failed, just as the tribunal of revision of magistrates under the older Act failed. We had no materials to carry out the revision.

3867. May I not fairly conclude from your evidence that under the existing Act, if the revision was improved, we might expect a better class of jurors, without saying that they would be entirely satisfactory?—I think not; you would get rid of the old men, but you would retain the men between 21 and 60 years, but I do not see what more you could do.

3868. Would you not get rid of the dead and the blind?—Yes, certainly under the last Act.

3869. Under the existing Act?—Yes, possibly, and the illiterate under the fresh Bill, which is before the House.

3870. You suggested that it would be desirable that the sheriffs, in the exercise of their discretion, should take the panel for the assizes substantially from the upper part of the jurors' book when arranged according to the qualification, and the panels for the quarter sessions from the lower part of the same book?—Yes.

3871. You also said in answer to another question that you thought that if special jurors served on the same jury with common jurors there would be at once a class antagonism set up?—I think so.

3872. Does not that suggest that if the assize juries are all taken from the *quasi* special class there would be this class antagonism, not in the jury box, but outside it?—I do not think so, I do not exactly understand what you mean by outside.

3873. I mean that there would be prejudice in the popular mind against juries taken substantially from a special class?—I do not propose that; what I said was this, if I was sheriff and this 13th Section in the Bill of Sir John Young were made the law of the land I should work it out in that way; that is all I said; I do not propose that you should legislate in that way.

3874. I asked you whether if it was worked out by the sheriff, as you suggest, it would not be liable to that danger and difficulty that there would be prejudice against the jury panel as being selected from people who in Ireland would undoubtedly, in certain instances, be a separate class?—I do not see what you are to do, because you must adopt something.

3875. You are chairman of the county of Cavan, but I do not know whether you are well acquainted with what I may call the local politics of the county of Cavan; I mean with regard to the construction of the jurors' book or the panel, or whether you are only acquainted with the county as chairman?—That is all; I only know it as chairman.

3876. You do not know whether any discussions have taken place in the county as to the formation of the jurors' book or the panels?—I never heard any discussion about it.

3877. You are aware, as every other man is perfectly well aware, that Cavan is one of the counties where parties are to some extent marked by religion, or are very strongly opposed to each other?—I have heard of that.

3878. And, consequently, it is one of the counties in which great feeling might probably exist on the subject of the formation of the jurors' book and the panel?—I do not see how that could be, because I should say that the vast majority would be Catholics.

3879. Is it really your impression that the vast majority of jurors in the county of Cavan would be Catholics?—That is my idea, and I only give that as an idea; I do not know it positively.

3880. From your knowledge of the county of Cavan would you think it not unnatural that there should be prejudice in the county of Cavan as to the formation of the juries, if it turned out that the vast majority of the jurors were of an opposite view?—I have no knowledge of their local opinions.

3881. *Chairman.*] I understand that you would leave the sheriff the power in his selection of the jury panel of excluding any person who in his opinion did not possess the necessary qualification for being a juror?—In one sense, yes; I would require that he should always have a panel of the most competent persons; the disqualification is one thing which is specified in the Act of Parliament.

3882. I understand that you would give him the power of leaving out of his panels any persons who he did not think would make a good juror?—I think that you must leave some power of selection somewhere, and therefore I think that leaving it with the sub-sheriff, controlled by the high sheriff's attention being brought to it in the way I have expressed, is a safer thing than to deal with it by directing the chairman to retire into a private room with the constabulary, or to give the power *ex parte* to the Crown in every case of having a special jury.

3883. That would leave room, would it not, for the sheriff when so disposed, to exercise partiality in the selection of the panel?—Yes, just as in England he may do the same. The law is so in England, and I understand that it is not to be changed.

3884. Would you provide any legal mode of challenging the discretion so exercised by the sheriff?—The challenge to the array for partiality or for malpractice is the law of the land, and it always lies; and the challenge to the polls, that is, to individual jurors, always lies. You can challenge the array for unindifferency of the sheriff; that is the law of the land, and it is every man's right.

3885. You would trust to that right of challenge to restrain the sheriff from anything in the nature of partiality?—I would trust to that law of challenge, and to the additional matter that I have spoken of, namely, bringing the high sheriff in privity with the book, and his certifying, as I have suggested at the foot of each panel, that the panel was in accordance with the Act of Parliament, which, supposing my proposition to be adopted, would compel the going through of the book substantially.

3886. Supposing that the provision in the Bill of Sir John Young were law, and under that provision the sheriff had in many successive panels omitted the name of one or more very properly qualified jurors, would that be a ground for challenge?—If it was done corruptly, of course it would; you could challenge the array.

3887. Would it not be very difficult to prove that it had been done corruptly?—That is a question which it is very difficult to answer. It depends

Mr. *J. Robinson.*

9 June 1873.

depends upon what the corruption is. In the O'Connell case, the corruption somehow was plainly proved, although it clearly was not the sheriff, because the demurrer having been taken to the challenge in that case, of course, as we lawyers say, they admitted the truth of everything contained in it, and therefore there was corruption in some one, though not in the sheriff.

3888. You would trust, would you, to the action of public opinion upon the sheriff?—I would trust to public opinion, and I would trust to the fact, which is a very important one, of the high sheriff himself of every county being brought into privity with the panel in the way that I have described.

3889. You think that, under that section, the sheriff would not, in practice, omit the names of any jurors on the list who were qualified in point of intelligence?—I am perfectly satisfied that he would not, as far as my idea goes.

3890. That would be a considerable alteration in the law and practice as it stood before the passing of the late Act, would it not?—It would be in this way, that the old duty of the sheriff at all times was this, to return a competent panel; but he might return, under the old law, the same panel time after time.

3891. There was no necessity thrown upon him of going through the jurors' book?—Never. According to the old law of England, he might return the same panel continually. It was enough if he returned a competent panel, which he was bound by the law of England to do; that was compulsory on him. This Bill, if it had been passed into law, would have advanced him a stage; it would have said this in other words, pursue your duty as the old law said that you should; return a competent panel, but in doing so do it in this wise, go through the book as far as you can, still seeking for the administration of justice a competent panel. Perrin's Act simply cast upon the clerk of the peace, upon the rate collectors, and upon the recorder, and other functionaries, the duty of revising the lists. Then those revised lists were put into a book, and then the book was given to the sheriff, and his duty was simply to select the names of competent jurors from that book.

3892. With regard to giving the judge any power of excusing jurors, has not the Court of Queen's Bench now some power which is not possessed by the other courts?—No; all the courts are equal in that way; the only difference between the Court of Queen's Bench and the other courts is this, that it has a Crown jurisdiction, and they have only civil jurisdictions; it has control over all the magistrates of the country, that is to say, a criminal jurisdiction, whereas the other courts have not, they have nothing but a civil jurisdiction; but as far as *nisi prius* trials are concerned all the judges are equal.

3893. Looking at the 6th clause of the Bill now before the House, which is in these terms, "Whereas doubts have been entertained as to the power of judges to excuse jurors from serving, and it is expedient to remove such doubts; it is hereby declared and enacted, that it shall be lawful for the judge, if he shall so think fit, of any court before which any person may be summoned as a juror to discharge such person from further attendance on such court, or to excuse such person from attendance for any period during the sittings of such court;" what difference do you understand that that will make in the power of the judge?—I think that this enables the judge for any reason to excuse a juror, or for no reason; I think it gives him absolute power to do what he likes.

3894. That power does not exist, does it, in the Court of Queen's Bench now?—It exists in no court in this country or in Ireland; that clause gives unlimited power to any judge without any reason at all, no matter what his motive is, to allow a man to go away; prior to this he could not do so.

3895. You object to that power being given?—I think, for the sake of the judges, and for the sake of the administration of justice, it is a very disastrous power.

3896. Major *O'Reilly.*] Does not it rather aim at this, that where there is no question about the desirability of a juror being allowed to go away, the judge may exempt him and allow him to go home in case of illness, or something else; or allow, as is frequently done in civil cases, by consent, a juror to be passed over?—No; I can only consider an Act of Parliament by its language, and the language of the 6th section is so large, that any judge sitting has power to dispense with the attendance of any man for any cause, or for no cause; it gives him absolute power, and my proposition for the sake of the judge himself would be this, to mention in terms in any section that you introduce in relation to that power, the instances in which any judge should exercise that power.

3897. *Chairman.*] What inconvenience do you think that would impose upon the judge?—In this way; because supposing a man was called on a jury, and he had a wish to go home and to attend to his own business, one of the litigants might wish to have him kept; he might think that he would be a useful juror for him; but you first give the judge absolute power to let the man go home, and then you put him in this unfortunate position as far as the administration of justice is concerned, that the judge is a suspected man by the party who has an interest in retaining the juror in the box.

3898. Would anyone expect the judge to use that power, except in the case where it was absolutely for the convenience of the juror himself and of all parties, and not to the detriment of any party, that the juror should be excused?—Human nature is such, and the atmosphere in Ireland is so full of suspicion, that if you confer upon a judge unlimited power, and if he exempts a man who appears in the box, because he says, "I have important business, and wish to get home, will you excuse me?" as he would have power to do under that clause, I think that the litigant in the case, if he knew the man and thought that he was friendly to him, would suspect the administration of justice.

3899. Why should not a litigant object to that juror being excused?—But you give the judge unlimited power, and he might say, "I don't care if you do object; I will let him go home"; there is nothing to check him; whereas I would, as I said before, suggest that you ought to define, for the sake of the judge expressly in any enactment, in what cases he should have the right to allow a man of his own motion to retire.

3900. Mr. Justice Fitzgerald told the Committee the other day that he did allow a number of jurors who had been summoned, and who appeared to be very poor, and who would not probably be required to act as jurors, to go home?—I suppose that he had jurors enough without them.

3901. What

Mr. *J. Robinson.*

9 June 1873.

3901. What objection do you see to that exercise of power on the part of Judge Fitzgerald?—I do not wish to criticise anything that a judge does; but what I do say is, that I think giving the judge absolute power in relation to allowing jurors to retire, would be an unfortunate enactment, because I think one should strive to do all he could do to place a judge in a position where he would not be suspected; and, in my opinion, the moment that in any case of excitement a judge approaches the panel to touch it in the slightest way, you destroy his usefulness in that cause.

3902. You would define the reasons?—Yes.

3903. For what reason would you give the judge the power of excusing?—For instance, if a man said that he was ill I should allow him to retire, or if he said that any member of his family was labouring under a dangerous illness I should allow him to retire; or if it was stated that one of the jurors was a relative of one of the parties litigant, or of the attorney of one of the parties litigant, I should allow him to retire; at present, I cannot see precisely that I should extend that power beyond that.

3904. That would be a good ground of disqualification for him in that particular case, but why should he on that account be excused from further attendance on the panel?—I would excuse him in that particular case.

3905. The power that is sought to be given is to excuse him altogether from attendance at the assizes?—If I have not forgotten the section I think it goes further than that; it says, "It shall be lawful for the judge if he shall so think fit, of any court before which any person may be summoned as a juror to discharge such person from further attendance on such court, or to excuse such person from attendance for any period during the sittings of such court"; the power that you have given him is an absolute power to retire from further attendance on the court.

3906. Why do you desire to limit so strictly the power of the judge to discharge a juror from further attendance at the assizes, if he is related to one of the parties in a particular suit?—My idea would be, not to discharge him from attendance at the assizes or sessions, but to discharge him from serving on that particular cause.

3907. You think you would not give the judge power to excuse any juror from further attendance, except in a case of urgent necessity?—I should say so; it would be better for the judge himself, and for the administration of justice I am quite satisfied; I do not think that the judges would wish to have that power; I have spoken to several of them, and they do not desire it.

3908. Colonel *Wilson Patten.*] Would it be possible to define all the circumstances under which you would give the power of excusing a man from serving on a jury?—I think they could be defined; I doubt if they should be put beyond the instances that I have given the Committee, because I think that the interference of the judge with the panel would be looked on with great jealousy.

3909. We have had brought before us on this Committee instances in which two men out of a firm of three have been put upon the same jury, and three men of the same family and a number of other cases have been stated to the Committee which would clearly render a jury objectionable; what have you to say to those cases?—But supposing the propositions which I have put forward were adopted the case could not arise. The case that you allude to is the case of O'Keeffe and Cullen, where three Turbetts and three Fitzsimons were on a panel of 48 (and there are several cases in the north of Ireland), but that was because the alphabetical system is adopted; get rid of the alphabetical rotation and the thing could not arise, because no sheriff would summon three of a firm.

3910. It is possible that under any circumstances three men of the same firm in Dublin might be summoned to attend at different courts in Dublin, only one of them being in one court, an instance of which was brought before the Committee the other day; if a man under such circumstances were to state in the court that his two partners were summoned to serve on a jury in the other two courts, would you not in such a case give the judge a discretion?—Yes, I would get rid of that certainly; I was not aware that under the old law it was possible; it is quite clear that it is possible under the new law, because we have several cases in which the thing has arisen, and it must arise from the necessity of the case; the M's and the O's are so largely preponderating that it would arise, but if you get rid of the dictionary order I do not see how it can arise, because no sheriff would summon three members of a firm.

3911. *Chairman.*] If a number of jurors had been summoned who actually would not be required for the business of the assizes, you would not give the judge any power to allow them to go home?—Every judge does that if he has enough and he requires no more; that is an inherent power in the judge.

3912. That is all, as I understand, that this section is intended to allow him to do?—I think it goes much beyond that.

3913. You say that it is an inherent power in the judge; Mr. Justice Fitzgerald appeared to think that it was very doubtful whether he did possess the power, but he exercised it?—He took the men that answered in the box that he found intelligent, and let all the needy men go home, but he compelled those men whom he retained to serve time after time. It was a large exercise of power in that case; but I am assuming a widely different thing, that he had enough men to serve in rotation, and that there was no extreme pressure put upon him.

3914. You think that he has that power now?—I do not think that he has the power now, but under this Bill, if it passes, he would have the power.

3915. What is the inherent power which you think he has now?—I ought to correct myself a little about that, because if you come to that I do not think that he has any power to discharge a man until the business is done.

3916. As I understand you, you would not give him that power?—After all, if a set of jurors are summoned, I would compel them to take their share of duty. It is very hard on some men that they should do the whole of the work, and that a certain number should be allowed to go home; it is very hard on those that remain. Independently of that, the section in the Bill goes vastly beyond that, because it enables the judge without any cause assigned, to permit any individual juror in the box to retire if he thinks fit.

3917. *Mr. Downing.*] Does not that section give him power at his own lodgings if the sheriff goes to him in the morning and says, here are

Mr. J. Robinson.

9 June 1873.

four jurors that wish to go home to their family, to allow them to do so?—I will not express an opinion about that. He can do it in court at all events.

3918. *Chairman.*] I should like to know what power you think might be safely or advantageously given to the judge?—Whatever powers you give him I would define them.

3919. But you would not give him power to excuse a juror simply because he thought he would not be wanted?—I think not.

3920. If there were 100 jurors present at the assizes, and it was not probable that more than 20 or 30 would be wanted, would you have all those 100 kept until the assizes were over?—You never can assume at an assize how many will be wanted. The jurors are locked up sometimes for a considerable time, and the prisoner has his challenges; he has 20 peremptory challenges, and as many more as he can show cause for, and you do not know what number will be wanted. You will see this very often, that when the civil business is light, two courts will be sitting for the discharge of criminal business, and the system of challenging and setting aside will be going on simultaneously. I do not think that you can legislate in that way. I have spoken to several judges as to this large power that is proposed to be given in the Bill, and I have not observed that any of them wish to have it.

3921. Mr. *Downing.*] Mr. Justice Fitzgerald in his evidence at Question 3273 was asked, "You would not give the judge upon such application power to excuse a juror," and his answer was, "The power to excuse a juror is different, and that is merely from serving upon that occasion; it arises generally in this way, the juror himself comes forward and either objects himself or makes some excuse to be allowed to go away on proof that he is unfit; it is in those cases which the juror himself brings forward that I propose to entrust that discretion to the judge." And in a question put by the honourable Member for Carlow, Question 3271, he was asked, "Would you have the reason assigned in open court," and his answer was, "Yes, certainly; I would have the thing done openly and above board;" you do not see any objection, do you, to what Mr. Justice Fitzgerald said there?—I think that whatever is done ought to be done above board and in open court. I think it is always satisfactory that everything should be as much as possible done before the public.

3922. *Chairman.*] Did I understand you to say that you did not see any objection to that?—I do not think that that goes much beyond what I have said.

3923. Colonel *Wilson Patten.*] Would you be satisfied if the words "for cause assigned" were added?—I think that it would be reasonable to say so; I do not think, as far as I have seen of the judges, that they desire to have that power. I think that as a rule, so far as I have seen of them, they do not; they wish, excepting in extreme cases, to keep away from touching the panel.

3924. Mr. *Bruen.*] You object on theory to giving to the judges this power, and you say that it would not be necessary for them to have it, if you take away the alphabetical selection; but supposing that the alphabetical selection was retained, do not you think it necessary to lodge in some person the power to get rid of an objectionable juror?—If the dictionary order system remains, you must give an absolute power to the judge to provide against many cases which may arise.

Mr. Thomas Wilkinson, called in; and Examined.

Mr. T. Wilkinson.

3925. *Chairman.*] You are the Sub-sheriff of the County of Wexford, are you not?—Yes.

3926. When were you first appointed?—In 1854.

3927. Have you held the office continuously?—Yes, continuously, except that there were two years, 1855 and 1856, when I was not in office; I came in again in 1857, and have continued so ever since, and am so still.

3928. I believe, however, that in every case, the appointment has been by the high sheriff?—Yes, and renewed every year just as if it were a perfect stranger brought in; I am re-appointed and re-sworn each time.

3929. Have you ever had any case of challenge to your jury panel?—Never.

3930. On what principle have you selected your panels?—On the principle of having every class, creed, and party, represented on the panel, so that they were invariably well mixed, and I believe that they gave very general satisfaction.

3931. Did you go upon the principle of going through the book as completely as you could?—No.

3932. Did you summon the same jurors over and over again?—Not always, I varied them as much as the number of eligible jurors on the book permitted me; but the juror books were so very badly compiled, that we always had a very large number of jurors on it that we did not think, when there was discretion allowed us, ought to be summoned as jurors at all.

3933. Did you select the panels on the principle of going through those whom you considered eligible as jurors as fairly as you could?—Yes, as fairly as I possibly could from the beginning to the end, that was the very first duty of the sub-sheriff when he got the juror book, he had to go through it, and select from it certain persons, and put them in a separate list that was called the special jurors' list; they were defined in the old Act of Parliament, as the sons of peers, magistrates, grand jurors, knights, baronets, merchants, and traders, supposed to be worth 5,000 *l.*, and if they were not sufficient, there was a discretionary power given to the sheriff, having regard to their position, to put on a sufficient number, that review of the book brought them all under my eye, and I marked off those that I thought in every case, were eligible for service for that year.

3934. You stated that the jurors' books were very carelessly compiled and revised; in what particular do you mean?—There was a large number of such persons of the small farming class as are now being got rid of by the Bill that has been passing through the House, raising the qualification; those persons were not generally summoned, if at all, at the assizes, but we summoned as many as possible at the quarter sessions for convenience sake, because they were in the duties

Mr. T. Wilkinson.

9 June 1873.

district immediately surrounding the sessions town.

3935. You said that the book which you had heretofore used was generally very carelessly compiled; in what respect was that the case?—That the barony constable who made out the book did not make it out of those that had leaseholds and freeholds, as far as I could see. I have been at revision courts, and I have seen that they simply handed in a list that had been made out principally from the freeholders' list of the county, and such persons, and it was signed as a matter of course. I never saw anyone struck off or put on at the revision court by the magistrates. I did not attend there officially, but I have been present at several of them.

3936. The effect of this careless compilation was, that there were many disqualified persons on the book, were there not?—Yes; the jurors' book only contained about 1,600 names, and fully 30 per cent. of those were never summoned, on the ground that we considered that they were of a class below what in point of position and intelligence a juror ought to be; and it would be expected from the sheriff that he would do so.

3937. Did you prepare a statement for the information of the Grand Jury, previous to the last assizes on working of the new Act?—Yes; there were several grand juries at the assizes that were held, and they were passing resolutions, and I thought that I would just prepare a short summary, more statistical than otherwise, for them, but they did not pass any resolution at Wexford, and therefore it was never made use of. The Paper before your Lordship is what I prepared.

3938. You state in that Paper that the number, both of special jurors and of common jurors, was in excess of the number required?—Yes; I think I stated so.

3939. Do you recollect what those numbers were?—The gross number on the general juror book is 3,295, and of those, 985 are special and 2,310 common jurors.

3940. What is the number that is required?—The number of special jurors required for the assizes and sessions every year is about 340, that is taking twice the 48 names, that we use at the assizes and the grand juries at the quarter sessions. There are eight quarter sessions held in the county of Wexford, and the number of petty jurors, I think, would be about 780.

3941. How long would it, under those circumstances, have taken to exhaust the list?—About three years.

3942. So that the jurors would only have been required to serve once in three years?—That is all, according to that calculation.

3943. You think that that is more seldom than they might be required to serve?—Yes; I think that the jurors might serve more frequently than that.

3944. Was the effect of the Act to alter the character of the two panels at the last assizes?—It did alter them, considerably. I will just give a comparison. In the special panel, for instance, there were of magistrates and grand jurors in 1872 (at the spring assizes, comparing one spring spring assizes with the other), 38, in 1873 there were but three, of merchants, there were nine in 1872, and in 1873 there were but six. There were of shopkeepers one in both cases. There were farmers 38 in 1873; and no farmers in 1872 in the special jurors' panel, as they were not then eligible.

3945. Was there a great difference made in the common panel?—Yes, there were gentlemen and esquires, 30 in 1872, and there were five in 1873. Of merchants there were 11 in 1872, and at the last assizes one. Of shopkeepers there were 21 in 1872, and 10 in 1873. Of farmers there were 38 in 1872, and 87 in 1873. You will observe in that that the classification of trades and businesses was as liberally made up as possible.

3946. Have you anything to say as to the inconvenience that is imposed upon jurors attending at quarter sessions?—Yes; many of them have to come from a very great distance, from 20, and 30, and even 35 miles, to attend at the quarter sessions.

3947. They cannot under the Act be summoned out of their own division, can they?—No; but the divisions are sometimes very inconvenient. In some cases it might be that the sessions town is on the extreme edge of the division, and therefore they must come from the opposite extreme of the county division.

3948. Colonel *Wilson Patten*.] What was the greatest distance that any of your jurors might have to come?—About 35 miles; and there were some very poor men who attended at the last sessions. I have been thinking of a remedy for that, and you will see in the Paper in your hand that I recommend the old polling districts for election purposes, which covered the whole county, and which would leave out no one. No juror would be omitted by adopting that plan, and the jurors resident within the old polling districts would be brought to the sessions town in which the polling place formerly was. It is the simplest mode of remedying the difficulty, without omitting any part of the county, so that no persons would be exempted from service; but it would make it as convenient to them as possible.

3949. What suggestions did you prepare for the grand jury for the amendment of the Act?—Without altering the principle of the Act at all as to the alphabetical arrangement, I would suggest that the special jurors' book and the general jurors' book should be separate, and that the special jurors should be kept for special purposes. That was with the view of economising the jurors, because in the course of the change that is taking place now in the law, as I understand, the qualification of a special juror would be 100 *l.* valuation, and there would be no more than about 300 perhaps in the county of Wexford, and they would be exhausted within a year.

3950. Do not you think that it is an advantage that the best class of jurors who are included in the special list should also serve on common juries?—I think it would be very desirable to have serving on juries jurors of the best and most intelligent class. I think that that gives the jury a more honourable character.

3951. But you propose to make that impossible?—That is by raising the qualification so far that they would not be in sufficient number, or by taking them as general jurors first, because you must select the special jurors as is provided by the 19th section of the Act, where we must take the general jurors from the book first, and after that is done, begin and take the special ones. It would not last in that way, I fear, for a year.

3952. How many special jurors would there be in Wexford above 100 *l.* qualification?—Speaking from memory, I would say about 300.

Mr. T. Wilkinson.

9 June 1873.

In the return that I made, it shows that I was proposing that the qualification for a special juror should be 90 *l.*

3953. *Chairman.*] You stated at the beginning of your evidence that the number of special jurors required at the assizes and sessions every year is about 340; is that the case?—Yes, about that; that is exclusive of the jurors that would be taken in the general jurors' book before I could select those 340. The 19th section of the Act says, "provided, further, that the sheriff or other officer shall, according to the mode of selection hereinbefore in this section prescribed, select the persons to be returned to serve as petit or common jurors at any special commission of oyer and terminer, or at the assizes, from the general jurors' book, without omitting from such selection persons whose names are marked on the general jurors' book as special jurors." That being done it would exhaust the jurors that I select out of the 340; I should not have them.

3954. What do you mean by your selection out of the 340?—For the two assizes there would be 48 names, that is, say 100 in round numbers, and 240 would be required to make up the eight grand juries and quarter sessions afterwards.

3955. But you do not select those?—If I select them and they serve, I cannot turn back upon any of those to serve again.

3956. You do not select anybody now, do you?—The mode of selecting in this section is by alphabetical arrangement.

3957. You mean if they are called upon to serve?—Yes, if they are called upon to serve.

3958. You propose, as I understand, first of all, that the special jurors should not be summoned to attend on common juries?—Yes; that is if the qualification be raised to 90 *l.*, as I propose; because I think that that would qualify about 400.

3959. The qualification that you propose is 90 *l.* in country holdings and 40 *l.* in towns and villages?—Yes; and that would give about 400.

3960. What qualification do you propose for common jurors?—I was proposing 40 *l.*, because we have a very large number of qualified persons in that class in the county. A qualification of 40 *l.* in the country, and 20 *l.* in towns and villages, I calculated would create about 1,300 jurors.

3961. Would that be sufficient?—Yes, I think it would be sufficient; it would last for nearly two years.

3962. You have spoken about the question of the division of the county for quarter sessions purposes, have you any suggestion to make as to the summoning of jurors?—I think that the postal arrangement, the same as it is for the county of Dublin, might be very fairly applied to Wexford.

3963. Is there postal service to every district?—Yes, a very complete service indeed; I do not think that there is a man, perhaps, in the country that is not within three miles at the very most of a post office; but if that be not enacted I would be in favour of letting the jury summonses be served by the constabulary.

3964. Do you think that the constabulary might be employed, as has been suggested by some of the witnesses before this Committee?—I think they might very well be so employed. Their arrangements are so very good, and their organisation so complete, that I think they would give to the summons the appearance of law, and give it a character that it does not take when it is served by a bailiff.

3965. Would there not be great objections to mixing up the establishment of the constabulary with the composition of the jury?—I think that it would not affect the composition of the jury.

3966. Do not the constabulary in many cases almost occupy the position of prosecutors?—They do; they serve the summonses of the Crown, and they serve the summonses for coroners' juries, and they get up the juries for inquests.

3967. I am asking you whether, in cases tried at the assizes, the constabulary are not almost in the position of prosecutors?—They are, generally.

3968. They are generally the most important witnesses, are they not?—They are.

3969. Do you see no objection to the constabulary being supposed to be engaged, however indirectly, in the preparation of the jury panel?—I do not think that they would be engaged in the preparation of the jury panel; the panel would be formed by the Act of Parliament and taken out, and they would get nothing but the mere summonses to serve; they should enter them in a book, and give evidence that they served them.

3970. Do not you think that an imputation would perhaps be made upon them that they did not serve a summons upon a juror who they thought would be unfavourable to the prosecution?—That never occurred to me, and I scarcely think it would.

3971. You see no objection to mixing them up in this matter?—Not with the service of the summons merely.

3972. Are you in favour of returning to the old practice of selection by the sheriff?—No; I think where the sheriff is relieved of that responsibility, as far as I am personally concerned, I would rather that it would remain so; but I would have it arranged in other respects so that the jurors would be fairly called in proportion; I will not say merely in the order in which they are placed on the jurors' book, but that they should be called in some regular order by which all parties and all classes would be fairly called upon in their turn.

3973. Are you in favour of restoring to the sheriff any power of rejection?—I would give him some power, in fact, to reconcile his duties with his oath, and with the precept that he gets to execute. He swears on taking office that he will make the panels of men able and sufficient to serve, and that are not suspected or procured, and then when the precept comes, that is the command to him.

3974. Does he still take that oath?—Yes, I took that oath on taking office this year. There is the precept, which you will find recited in the 30th section of the Act, which commands "the sheriff or other officer to whom the same shall be issued, to summon and return, on a day to be named therein, for the trial of all issues, whether civil or criminal, which may come on for trial before the said Court, a sufficient number of good and lawful men;" this implies some discretion in the officer in summoning, otherwise he might be going against his oath, and going against the exigencies of the writ.

3975. Mr. *Downing.*] Does the high sheriff take that oath?—Yes, he does. We both take it together; and both oaths are filed in the Court of Exchequer.

3976. *Chairman.*]

Mr. T. Wilkinson.

9 June 1873.

3976. *Chairman.*] Have you got the oath of office with you?—Yes, I have.

3977. Will you read that part of it?—It is a very ancient document. "I swear that I will truly act and return reasonable and due issues of them that be in bailiwick, according to their estate and circumstances, and make due panels of persons able and sufficient, and not suspected or procured, as is appointed by the statutes of this realm." Then the words of the precept are in the 30th section, where the sheriff is commanded to return "a sufficient number of good and lawful men of the body of the county qualified according to law." I do not think that very much discretion need be given to the sheriff, but sufficient to reconcile this precept and this oath with his acts. He has some discretion in this way indirectly now under this Act, because he is left still the sole judge of what is a sufficient number; and supposing that a sheriff found that there were on the panel taken out, as he is coerced to take them from the book exactly in alphabetical order, persons incapable of attending from physical or mental causes, he might add the same number to the panel to make up for those without omitting them; he has that discretion. Supposing that there were 100 men on the panel, and he saw that four or five of them would not be able, from mental or physical causes, to attend, he might make his panel 105 or 110 or 120, because he is commanded to summon a sufficient number.

3978. Mr. *Downing.*] Then he is liable, is he not, to be fined by the judge for not returning the proper number?—Yes; for returning too few he would be liable to be fined.

3979. *Chairman.*] The sheriff may now make his panel consist of as many as he pleases, may he not?—Yes, as many as he could justify, in fact, because he might be accountable for summoning too many.

3980. What limited power of rejection do you propose to restore to the sheriff?—The power of rejection that I would think advisable would be this, that if he met with the names of dead men, or the names of men out of the county, to his own knowledge, or of a man that was mentally or physically incapacitated, he might omit those names, and enter on the jurors' book the cause of his so omitting them. I think he would be accountable in law for that entry, because it would be a return to the writ.

3981. You would not give him any further discretion than that?—If the principle of the Act is to be carried out, I think that that would be perhaps sufficient.

3982. You stated that you did not wish to return to the old system; are you in favour of the principle of the Act?—I think that with those safeguards it would work very well in Wexford. I will show you that the alphabetical arrangement will work most injuriously just now, but also that that can be remedied.

3983. What do you propose as a substitute for the alphabetical arrangement?—I will show the Committee exactly how the alphabetical arrangement will act in the County of Wexford.—(*The Witness produced a Diagram, and explained the same to the Committee.*)—The 19th section was introduced with a view to get rid of the sheriff's selecting, because it was thought in many places that he selected too many of one party, and put them on according to his own fancy, or from some other object that he had in view. In the county of Wexford, in a religious sense the Catholics are 80 per cent. and the Protestants 20 per cent. upon the jurors' book as near as possible; but up to the present time, where the juries have been taken for six sessions and the assizes, they have been admirably mixed, and fully 35 per cent. of Protestants have been mixed up with the jurors on the panel; and how to account for that was what struck me at first, and induced me to make this diagram for the purpose of ascertaining how it was, and I found that nearly all the Protestant names were in the small letters and the Catholic names in the large ones. Of course the very reverse would be the case in the north of Ireland, and therefore you may look forward to a certain period coming round every second year, when there will be a total exclusion of one party or the other upon the juries by the alphabetical arrangement. That seems to be, I think, almost a mechanical law that cannot be got over. I do not undertake to say how the names are arranged in any county but my own, but from communicating with one or two sub-sheriffs I find that they are very much the same. For instance, in Londonderry the letter M has double the number of any other letter in the jurors' book; in fact, it contains nearly 300 names above any other letter.

3984. Have you any suggestion to make as to substituting some other mode of selection?—Yes; the remedy that I was about to suggest was, not to disturb the alphabetical arrangement of the book, but to make use of the numbers prefixed to the jurors' names as we would do in striking a special jury under the old system, and I have had a Table made out with figures, just to show the Committee how the plan would work (*producing a Table and explaining it to the Committee*).

3985. In fact, as I understand you, you make one column of the number of the letter which has the most names, and you make up the remaining columns of several letters?—Yes; there could be no unfairness, and juries could be struck in Dublin Castle, if that would be any recommendation, and sent down to the sheriff.

3986. Do you wish to make any observation on the imputations which have been cast upon the sub-sheriffs as to partiality?—No further observation than this, that I believe that the evidence that will be taken, and that has been taken, will fully exonerate them from any charges that were made against them. I look at the result as being very much in their favour; I should have said in the beginning, that I have served under sheriffs in their turn; no matter what their religion or what their political principles have been, there has been no difference. I have served under all, and I believe I have given them all satisfaction; but the dictionary form will certainly introduce both creed and party spirit into the jury box, to the exclusion of the others.

3987. Do you think that, as a body, the sheriffs were exposed to any imputation of partiality under the old system?—I think they were; it was very often said, I think, that any officer that has absolute control in responsible duties will be suspected as to the manner in which he will discharge them.

3988. It was a system which admitted of the exercise of partiality?—There are a great many checks against it; the sub-sheriff, on taking office, has to take an oath, and I had to give a bond for 5,000 *l.* that everything should be done fairly and impartially to the best of my skill and judgment,

Mr. *T. Wilkinson.*

9 June 1873.

ment, and all the interest, and all the motives, that can actuate a man in the way of self interest go in the direction of making the sub-sheriff act fairly, honestly, and properly. Of course if I did such a thing as pack a jury, in the sense in which it has been attributed to them, I do not think that I should ever get office again if that was done in Wexford.

3989. You wish to say that whatever imputations may have been made, you do not suppose that there was any foundation for them?—Not within my own knowledge, certainly; I do not go any further than that.

3990. Do you wish to add anything else on this point?—No, except that if I have made those Tables sufficiently plain that the Committee can understand them, I think that they might contain some valuable suggestions.

3991. Colonel *Wilson Patten.*] Have you ever known an instance of a sheriff returning a list of jurors insufficient for the purposes of the assizes?—No, I never did.

3992. In case a sheriff should return too small a number of jurymen, is he subject to any penalty?—Any penalty that the judge would wish to place upon him. The judge has absolute power in that respect. It is in the Act, I think amongst the consolidated clauses.

3993. Has a sheriff in Ireland the same power as an English sheriff has, of nominating his own sub-sheriff?—Yes.

3994. Uncontrolled by anybody?—Yes, it is absolutely in his own hands; he may appoint whoever he chooses.

3995. With that power, you have held the office of sub-sheriff how many years?—Nineteen years, with two exceptions. I have been seventeen years in succession.

3996. Could you state what the proportion has been with Roman Catholic and with Protestant sheriffs?—The proportion is very small of Roman Catholics in Wexford amongst the landed gentry. I think I have served under three Catholics.

3997. Have you served as sub-sheriff under sheriffs of all political opinions and all religious opinions?—Yes, under all.

3998. Mr. *Bruen.*] Do you think that, under the Act of 1871, the sheriff may be coerced to violate his oath in the discharge of the exigencies of the precept?—I have to consider that. Seeing that he has discretion still left him to add to the panel any number that he thinks would be sufficient, it goes to some extent to the same point; but I do think that it ought to be made more direct, and not to be left to be inferred.

3999. I see that in your oath of office you say that you will not, in making out your panels, summon any man who is suspected; is there any possibility by which you can avoid summoning a man whom you know to be open to suspicion?—A very extraordinary case occurred at the last assizes in Wexford, of a man who, within two years before that assizes, had been committed for trial on a charge of murder, and who was not tried or acquitted; but who, I believe, stands out, either on his own recognizances or on entrance by the Crown of a *nolle prosequi*, they not having sufficient evidence. That man was actually summoned on a jury, and, for anything I know, served at the last assizes. I was coerced to put that man on the jury, as I had no power to reject him.

4000. I think that the language of the Act itself says that you are to summon "lawful" men?—Yes; the precept, which is a command from the Crown to the sheriff, says that he is to do that.

4001. Have you any power of avoiding summoning those whom you know to be disaffected to the law?—No.

4002. That is the effect, is it not, of the alphabetical system?—That is the effect of it. I do not think that even that which was suggested here to-day, namely, the sheriff taking the names out of their order in the book, could be at all resorted to; for it would have this effect: if he did it at these assizes, at the next he could only take the jury from the refuse, because every man on the book has to be returned in his proper turn and order. The sheriff has no power of leaving off, or omitting, or rejecting anyone, as I read the section when reading it with the view of discharging my duties.

4003. There was some Fenianism in Wexford some few years ago, was there not?—Very little, there were some suspected cases.

4004. Were there any persons arrested under the Act?—Yes, there were.

4005. Were they brought to trial?—I think there were one or two brought to trial.

4006. Were any of them, after being arrested, let out again?—Yes; I think so.

4007. Those persons are now liable, are they not, to be summoned on the jury panel, if they possess the necessary qualification?—Yes; I would not like to reject or prevent any man being summoned on account of political opinions or religious opinions; I think he ought to be there; and even a man that might be suspected of Fenianism or membership of any other political society might be a very good juror in cases where political questions would not arise.

4008. But in cases where political issues of that class did arise, in the exercise of your duty under the former Acts, I suppose that you would not put upon the panel, when cases of that sort were coming to be tried at the assizes, a man that you had known to be arrested and set at large again without having the issue tried?—I think if he had had the proper qualification on the book that would not prevent my returning him and letting him be challenged. I do not think that the sheriff would take upon him to do that.

4009. The exercise of your discretion under the former Act was one in which you gave the largest possible interpretation to the right of a person to hold his own political opinions as long as he was not adjudged a criminal?—So long as he was not tried.

4010. You say that the sheriff has now the power to add to his panel *ad libitum*?—I think so; that is to say, he has power to put what he believes and what he can justify as a sufficient number.

4011. Do you think that he would be accountable for returning too many?—I think he would be; that is to say, if there was any improper motive attributable; but if his desire was merely to give the court a sufficient number of jurors, he would not.

4012. But that is the only way by which it appears to you that you can evade the difficulty which your oath of office and the form of the precept impose upon you?—That is the only way that occurs to me.

4013. Do you think that it is a desirable way of avoiding that difficulty?—No. I think that the limited power of rejection that I have suggested would be better. I think that the sheriff would

Mr. *T. Wilkinson*

9 June 1873.

would be very slow to exercise any power of rejection if they had it; but I believe that if they were put in a position to reject and to enter the cause of rejection upon the jurors' book, it would be a record against them of which use might be made, and perhaps might make them liable to an action.

4014. Your authority, of course, in summoning those jury panels is derived from the precept which comes from the judge?—Yes.

4015. Do you think that this would be a good form of precept, and of which you would approve, that the judge of assize shall issue a precept to the respective sheriffs, requiring them to return at the assizes or general sessions of the peace a sufficient number of the most competent persons named in the jurors' book, selecting, so far as may be practicable, having regard to their competency, the names of such jurors as shall not have been summoned and attended as such at the last preceding assizes, sessions, or other sittings?—That would be a very good form to adopt if the sheriff had the power to obey it. As a suggestion to him as to what he should do, it would be very good.

4016. Would that form of precept meet with your approval?—Yes; that form of precept would be very explicit.

4017. You said that you approved of the discretion having been taken away from the sheriff, that is to say, the discretion which he enjoyed under the former Act; does that approval arise from your satisfaction at being relieved from an onerous and responsible duty?—It does, more than from any evil consequences that I ever knew to ensue for the exercise of the discretion.

4018. It does not arise from your disapproval of the discretionary power being lodged in the hands of some responsible officer?—No.

4019. May I go further, and say that you do approve of a limited power of discretion in the choice of jury panels being lodged in the hands of some responsible officer?—I would be in favour of whatever plan would produce the best jury, and I think that that would give a better class of jurors, but it would reject a large class, because the sheriff would omit a great number. A great deal depends upon the revision. If there was such a revision, it would be more what I think the law contemplates, that every man in the jurors' book would be really like a soldier, that he would be disciplined and ready to take the field at any call, if they were all of that class of jurors that would be approved of in point of intelligence and position, and everything else that makes up the qualification of a juror. I think then it does not much matter whether there is discretion in anyone or not.

4020. You do not require discretion if the materials are all equally perfect?—No; it is actually to get that good material that the discretion has been given.

4021. But the fact being that the materials are not all equal and perfect, is it not necessary that there should be some system of selection before you can get satisfactory jury panels?—I think it is; you know it undergoes another process after the sheriff has done with it, because it is liable to be challenged, and individuals to stand aside; the jurors, before they are sworn in, 12 in the box, undergo many processes, beginning with the revision, then coming to the empanelling, and then being brought into court.

4022. The expense of the service of the summons by the sheriff under the new Act is very considerable, is it not?—It is very considerable, because we have to send so many men to people who live in remote corners of the county, more than we did before, and we have to employ such a number of persons for that purpose; heretofore they were taken from a circle around the sessions town; now we take in the whole of two or three baronies that make up a division, and we have to send to every process officer within that area, a certain number of jury summonses, and they make their own terms, and get very large fees indeed from the sheriff for serving them, because we must have them served; we cannot leave the court without the jurors.

4023. I see that in your statement which you have handed in, you instance the districts of Enniscorthy and New Ross, and you say that 206 jurors would be summoned, and that of those 64 would be taken from the old districts, and the remaining 142 will be brought from distances varying from 10 to 35 miles; that shows, does it not, that the districts are not fairly constituted now, and that they require some alteration in the constitution of the districts?—Yes; that is why I suggest that there should be some provision with regard to the old polling districts into which the county was divided; four of them; the sessions towns stand in a very central situation in each of them, in a very large district, and the whole county would be so arranged that the jurors would not be summoned to a greater distance than some 10 or 12 miles at the most.

4024. Can you give the Committee any idea of the increase of expense that has been thrown upon you in the service of summonses since the passing of the Act?—Not with sufficient accuracy until after the next assizes, because I shall not have paid them, but the expense will be more than double; some of them I pay by a regular stated salary in the case of bailiffs who attend at the assizes; and others are brought in as auxiliaries.

4025. *The O'Conor Don.*] Do you receive any additional payment from the grand jury in consequence of the expense thrown upon you under this Act?—No; we made no application for it; I do not think that the 16th section of the Act was sufficient to entitle us to do so; in fact, it omitted the sheriff, and I thought that was very hard dealing with us; if he had been included like the clerk of the peace, and other officers that assist in the discharge of the duties, it would have been to us a very great boon.

4026. Mr. *Bruen.*] You do not intend to make any application on behalf of the sheriff's expenses?—I think that there would be a difficulty with the grand jury, and on that account I do not think there is any use in doing it; the sub-sheriffs are very badly treated in that way I think; and not only in this but in other legislative measures; and the only remedy we have is to make the high sheriff, on entering on his office, to pay us a little more, which I believe is not fair; but it is strange that in the late Act, the 22nd section, for serving juries by post in the city of Dublin, and extending to the county of Dublin, gives to the sheriff there the power of going and getting all that it costs him from the grand jury, the same as the clerk of the peace does, yet the country sheriffs have not that privilege of postage; they are made to do it at 10 times the expense, and they have no power to get it back again.

4027. You heard the suggestion made by Mr. Robinson before the Committee to-day, as to the combination

Mr. T. Wilkinson.

9 June 1873.

combination of the first list of jurors with the list of Parliamentary voters; I am aware that it is not quite within your province, but are you inclined to give any opinion upon that proposition?—Originally the jurors were taken from the freeholders' list simply before the jury books were prepared under the Act of Parliament, and I do not see anything to prevent that being done, but it would tend to economy if there was a column for jurors and a column for voters.

4028. How would that economise the expense?—If there was only one printing it would save the county a very large sum; it is simply a question of economy; it would save some counties 500*l.* a year.

4029. Mr. *Downing*.] For the 17 years that you have been the sub-sheriff, have you yourself prepared the panel?—Yes, in all cases the grand jury of the county I submitted to the high sheriff, and the other panels that were prepared by me I submitted too, but it was very seldom that he looked at it.

4030. The high sheriff, during your 17 years of office, never interfered with you in preparing the common panel?—No; at least he always had that confidence that it was right; it is always given to him, and returned in his name.

4031. Mr. *Bruen*.] Can you tell me whether the high sheriff, although he may not have corrected the list, has ever gone over it generally with you?—I do not remember that at any time.

4032. Mr. *Downing*.] Have you never been a sheriff in the North of Ireland?—No; never in any county but Wexford.

4033. I think you stated to the Committee that the proportion of Roman Catholics and Protestants which exists in Wexford would exist in an adverse ratio in the North of Ireland?—I should infer that.

4034. Supposing that the sub-sheriff, instead of acting as you did, in selecting fairly from the different creeds, wished to put upon the panel 200 names, 100 of whom he knew to be Orangemen, upon a panel when there was an Orangeman to be tried on a party on a religious quarrel, would that be fair?—I do not think it would be fair. I do not say that the proportion would be unfair for this reason, that I do not think that the proportion of jurors put upon the panel should ever be the proportion that they bear one to another in the county, because it is not with each other that they have to do; it is the prisoner in the dock and the suitor at the bar that has to look to the jury, and that expects to find them mixed and composed of representatives of all creeds and parties there.

4035. But the sheriff under the old system could have done that which I have suggested in my question?—He could have done it if he were fool enough.

4036. With regard to the distance, which you say the jurors have been obliged to attend at quarter sessions, what is the quarter sessions town to which you refer?—New Ross and Enniscorthy.

4037. Are those both in one division?—New Ross is in one division and Enniscorthy in the other.

4038. Is not each division divided into districts?—No.

4039. Have you not two quarter sessions towns in each division?—Yes; but they are not in the same division; there are two divisions of the county, and the sessions are held alternately in the two places.

4040. Could not it be so arranged that the jurors should not be summoned from a greater distance than within a certain number of miles of the sessions town?—Yes; if there were an Act of Parliament for it, but not otherwise; that would completely cure my objection; and I think that something of the kind ought to be done for the sake of the poorer jurors.

4041. With regard to the service of summonses upon jurors through the police, perhaps you would alter your opinion when I put a case to you?—Recollect the police with me is an alternative; the post is, I believe, much better.

4042. Do not you see a most insurmountable objection to having policemen serving summonses upon jurors for the assizes where those police may be the prosecuting parties themselves?—That did not occur to me before, but if that was an objection I would not approve of it.

4043. Do not you think it a very strong objection?—I do not think it would have much effect.

4044. Would you give policemen an opportunity of talking to jurors, perhaps, that attended at the assizes, and on a trial that causes very great excitement?—He has the power now to go and speak to any one beforehand if he knew that he was a juror.

4045. You do not mean to suggest that any policeman should be allowed to look at the jury panel, and be allowed to go and talk to the jurors beforehand?—No.

4046. If you sent him with a summons to serve upon a juror to attend at the assizes, and being him into contact with a juror, he might have an opportunity of talking about the particular trial?—That might be so.

4047. Do not you think that that would be the case?—I do not think that the police would speak to a juror upon the subject; I think if they got a summons to serve, they would do so simply as a matter of duty, without attempting to do such a thing as that.

4048. What you would recommend would be the service by a registered letter through the post office?—Yes, I believe that what is extended to the county of Dublin might fairly be extended to the county of Wexford, and I suppose to other counties.

4049. I suppose you do not know any part of the county of Wexford with which you are acquainted, in which there is not a post office sufficiently near to bring home to every party living there, easy access to the post office?—Just so. By raising the qualification now, you bring a class of men that get their newspaper, and get their letters like other people. I find in my official duties in writing to them on other subjects, that I never have any miscarriages through the post office.

4050. Supposing that all the arrangements which you have suggested in this plan were carried out, that, in your opinion, would get rid of many of the objections that have been made to the Act now in operation?—It would.

4051. I understand that in this Paper which you have handed in it would amount to this; that you would take one from the letter A., and you would take from the next column D. and D.?—No, no letter can occur twice.

4052. By that arrangement you would get rid of the possibility of having men of the same family

family called upon the jury panel?—There is a difficulty that I see might occur in the end with the dictionary form, that it will throw in, perhaps, two of the same name on the panel, but they will be some distance from each other; there is another thing to be remembered, that the smaller letters would be so mixed up with the others as to keep the relative proportions nearly all through the same.

4053. This Paper contains 900 names, and you have in each column 100?—Yes, because there are 100 exactly in the letter C.

4054. Supposing that you were in a county where there are not 400, how would you arrange the column?—In the same way, by the largest letter, and dividing the gross number by it, you would have the number of columns; for instance, to show you the difference of the letters, the letter L. contains 40 names, there are 28 Protestants and 12 Roman Catholics; the letter M., I think, contains over 500 names; there are not more than 25 Protestants among them; a person's name is often an indication of his party, and it will be so I am sure all over Ireland, and by that means you mix the small letters with the great, and in mixing certain letters you mix the parties; there is no one accountable, no one is responsible, and no one has done it, and I think that is saying a great deal; it is carrying out the principle of the Act fairly, although it is not an alphabetical arrangement; but inasmuch as the letters would never be equal you would take them by the numbers, and you would not know what names you were taking out until it was done.

4055. Do you see any objection to selecting the jury in criminal cases by ballot?—What I propose is a sort of ballot in itself.

4056. Supposing that was not carried out, would you object to the ballot?—I do not think there is any objection either way; I see the ballot just turn up as bad juries as any other way; but if that is done it is a complete ballot; and it might be done in Dublin, or it might be done here.

4057. *Mr. Bruen.*] Would that system which you recommend avoid the difficulty which has occurred, of three gentlemen, members of the same firm, appearing upon the same panel?—It might not entirely, but I think it would to a great degree.

Thursday, 12*th June* 1873.

MEMBERS PRESENT:

Dr. Ball.	Mr. Arthur Henry Herbert.
Sir Rowland Blennerhassett.	Mr. Heron.
Mr. Bruen.	Major O'Reilly.
Viscount Crichton.	Colonel Wilson Patten.
Mr. Downing.	Colonel Vandeleur.
Marquis of Hartington.	

THE RIGHT HONOURABLE THE MARQUIS OF HARTINGTON, IN THE CHAIR.

Mr. MICHAEL FLYNN, called in; and Examined.

Mr. *M. Flynn.* 12 June 1873.

4058. *Chairman.*] You are Clerk of the Poor Law Union of Strokestown, in the county of Roscommon?—Yes.

4059. You have had a good deal to do, have you not, with the working of the late Jury Act?—Yes, I have had the preparation of a set of returns for my own union for the clerk of the peace, and had them revised.

4060. Have you any knowledge of the expense incurred in the working of the Act?—I have; at least I can form a very fair estimate.

4061. What opinion have you formed upon that subject?—My opinion is that the amount paid in expenses has been considerably more than was necessary; more than was an equivalent remuneration for the work done.

4062. How do you arrive at that conclusion?—I will take the case of the clerks of unions. There are few clerks of unions in Ireland paid as high as 200*l.* a year, I should imagine; and at the rate at which I know some clerks of unions were remunerated, it would be more than 20*l.* a week.

4063. Major *O'Reilly.*] Were they remunerated for the job, or by task?—By the job. But it is scarcely fair to debit the amount so paid to the account of the Juries Act. Generally speaking, Boards of Guardians who know that the salaries they pay their clerks are insufficient remuneration for the class of men they have to employ, take advantage of opportunities such as this Act affords, in an indirect shape to increase the remuneration.

4064. *Chairman.*] What are the duties of the clerks of the unions under the Act?—To prepare, with the assistance of the poor rate collectors, and arrange, in alphabetical order, the list of persons qualified to be jurors, and make inquiries as to their residence, whether they reside within the distance prescribed by the Act, whether they are over 60 years of age, and whether they are otherwise qualified or disqualified. They arrange this list alphabetically, and send a copy of it to the clerk of the peace, and get copies of it printed and circulated in the baronies to which the lists relate. Then they attend the revising sessions, but at those sessions the clerks of unions are also bound to attend for the revision of the Parliamentary Voters' List, for they go hand in hand together.

4065. What do you estimate the pay that the clerks of the unions receive?—I estimate that the clerks of the unions all over Ireland have received at least 20*l.* on the average.

4066. From what do you form that conclusion?—I know that in most of the unions with which I am acquainted the amount allowed has been more than that. I have seen by the papers that in some cases as high as 50*l.* has been allowed.

4067. Do you know what the average number of jurors that each clerk of a union has had to return has been?—I could only estimate that; I should say that my estimate of the average number is not over 300; in my own union the number is 209.

4068. How much labour should you conceive there has been thrown upon the clerks by this duty?—I am perfectly sure that in my own case I would have no difficulty at all in revising the list for the union in two days, that is, a day for every 100 names, and if there were 300 names I would do it in three days.

4069. Do you think that it is not likely to have taken any clerk more than a week?—I should say not; not unless his number was very much over the average, or unless he was somewhat deficient in the local knowledge of his union.

4070. You conceive that 20*l.* is good pay for that amount of work, considering the rate at which the clerks of unions are generally paid in Ireland?—Yes, I do.

4071. Have you any objection to state what you received yourself?—I received 15*l.*, and out of that I paid 5*l.* for printing the lists and publishing them. In reality, I might have made a separate claim for the cost of printing, because the Act so provides; but I was perfectly ashamed to ask even 15*l.* for that amount of work. I would not have taken it from the guardians without explaining to them fully, that so far as the remuneration for that particular duty went, it was in excess of what I should have got.

4072. Then you have formed the opinion that the remuneration which has been granted to the clerks of the unions for their duties under the Juries Act, has been an indirect way of making up their salaries?—Yes, I have.

4073. And that is a practice which you would not approve of?—Certainly not, because I know that boards of guardians, as a rule, must take their

Mr. M. Flynn.

12 June 1873.

their information on all matters affecting the union principally from their clerks, and in my opinion it is highly undesirable that the clerk of the union should be placed in a position where his self-interest would seem to conflict with the manifest duty.

4074. Were the poor-rate collectors separately remunerated for their labour?—Yes, the Act provides that the grand juries should present to them something which the grand juries were satisfied was sufficient, and I believe that there has been an allegation that the allowance did not seem to be based on a very great general knowledge of the duty performed.

4075. Do you know what the rate collectors in your union received?—I know that one collector got 4 *l.* 10 *s.*, and I know the entire extent of his duty was scarcely work for that amount. He lives about a mile from my office, and about the same distance from the court-house, and the entire duty performed by him was attendance at my office for about three hours each on two days, and about half-an-hour at the court-house on the day of the revision of the list. I am sure that the grand jury did not exactly understand the nature of the work. I believe that, in Roscommon, the arrangements with the grand jury was that they gave 10 *s.* each electoral division, and this man had nine electoral divisions in his district, and I heard that there was some arrangement of that kind that they based their calculation upon.

4076. That was granted by the grand jury, I think, you say?—Yes.

4077. But your remuneration was granted by the board of guardians?—Yes, by the board of guardians; and it does appear that the board of guardians would be better able to remunerate the collectors, at least they would be better able to understand the duties performed than the grand jury.

4078. And to decide upon the amount of remuneration to which they were entitled?—Yes.

4079. Could you suggest any way in which the expenses of working the Act could be reduced?—I think that if there were a tariff rate of remuneration fixed it would be somewhat more equitably in the distribution of the expenses, and I am sure it could be fixed at such a rate as would seem sufficient, and yet be very much less than the allowance made last year.

4080. Do you mean that you would propose to fix a certain rate of pay per day for each person employed?—No, by the number of names on the lists; that is what I should think would be the most equitable way.

4081. And I understand that you would suggest that the remuneration should be fixed by the guardians rather than by the grand jury?—Yes, for the poor-rate collectors. Besides there does not appear to be any reasonable ground that I can see why the poor rates, one-half of which is paid by the landlord, should pay a share, and that the county cess, the whole of which is paid by the occupying tenant, should pay the other expenses. That is the principal difference between allowing the grand jury or the board of guardians to fix the amount.

4082. Mr. *A. H. Herbert.*] Is that the case always?—Yes, that is so in every case, except those of new lettings, since the late Land Act, but those are very few and they scarcely constitute an exception.

4083. Have you any knowledge of the duties required by the Act of the clerks of the peace?—Yes, I have.

4084. Can you state what they are?—If I had my memorandum before me I could pretty well state them, because it refers to particular sections of the Act. The clerk of the peace issues his precepts to the clerks of the unions. Those precepts are a very simple matter; they are printed forms and the blanks are to be filled in. The clerk of the peace receives from the clerks of the unions the several alphabetical lists, and he prepares from those and from other sources of information the special jurors' list. When I speak of other sources of information I mean he has to ascertain from other sources the names of the eldest sons of magistrates and the sons of peers, and so on, who are special jurors in right of their position. These need not necessarily be on the clerks of the unions' lists; and he has to arrange a separate list for them, and the lists of the clerks of the unions, and this list he has to submit for revision at the ordinary revising sessions where they are revised. He then prepares his general jurors' book, arranging in alphabetical order the names in the general list from the several alphabetical lists supplied by the clerk of the unions.

4085. Then the clerk of the peace has to be present at the court of revision, has he not?—Yes, he is obliged to be there otherwise, because he has to attend the revision of the voters' lists as well.

4086. Do you know what the number of names on both the lists in the county of Roscommon were?—My idea is, I have not been able to get the number accurately, but taking into account that my union, which is fully one-sixth the county, supplies only 209 for the general list, I take it that if I put 1,400 names for the general list of the entire county, that would about make it up; I should think that I am pretty safe in saying that it does not exceed 1,400, and the special jurors would not number 400; and under the provisional Bill which has been passed now, I believe the number would be very considerably reduced. I noted the result of my revision before I came off here, and I had to take off 81 names from the general list of 209.

4087. Do you know what remuneration the clerk of the peace of the county of Roscommon receives for his expenses, under the Act?—£. 50 from the grand jury.

4088. Do you consider that he also was well paid?—I do; the clerks of the unions and the clerks of the peace, would be much obliged to Her Majesty's Government if they would pass a few more Juries Acts, or something of the sort.

4089. Had the clerks of the peace any duties at all, in connection with the Juries Act, previous to the passing of this Act?—They had very nearly as much as they now have; then they had to get their lists from the barony constables, and arrange them, and have them revised, but the numbers were not so great.

4090. But they had no special payment for that?—They had not.

4091. It was included in their salary, was it?—Yes. And with regard to the salaries and fees of the clerks of the peace, I should imagine, judging from what I know of the county of Roscommon, that perhaps the average for Ireland could not be much, if anything, short of 600 *l.* a year.

4092. You stated, did you not, that you would recommend

Mr. *M. Flynn.*

12 June 1873.

recommend tariff rates for the remuneration of all parties concerned?—Yes, I think that that would be a very equitable way.

4093. Are you prepared to recommend any particular sum?—I have thought over the matter, and I believe that 6 *d.* per name to the clerks of unions would fully compensate them for all the inquiries that they have to make, and for the trouble of preparing the lists, and revising them and getting them printed; of course, the cost of printing is a separate charge; I think that 6 *d.* per line should remunerate the clerks of the peace for the duty of preparing their special jurors' lists, which involves the trouble of making inquiries; and that 3 *d.* per line would be ample for preparing the general jurors' list, which is merely a mechanical duty; arranging in alphabetical order one general list from the several alphabetical lists received from the union clerks; and that 3 *d.* a line would pay the rate collectors, who act under the direction of the clerks of unions.

4094. Have you made any estimate of what the expense of preparing the list for the county of Roscommon upon your principle would have been?—Yes, I have. It can be but an estimate, because the union boundaries are not coterminous with the boundaries of the counties; as, for instance, in the case of the clerk of the union of Castlerea, a portion of the duty for which he is remunerated relates to Galway, Mayo, and Roscommon. I estimate that in the county of Roscommon clerks of unions have received 100 *l.*, and I know that the clerks of the peace received 50 *l.*, and the rate collectors 65 *l.*

4095. *Mr. Bruen.*] That is the pay that they have received?—That is what was presented for them; they have not received it yet, but they will receive it.

4096. *Chairman.*] That makes a total of 215 *l.*?—Yes.

4097. What do you think it would be under your system?—The clerks of the unions 35 *l.*, and the clerk of the peace 27 *l.* 10 *s.* I think that would be my calculation for both.

4098. Would those be the figures under your plan: to the clerks of the unions 35 *l.*; to the clerk of the peace, for special jurors, 10 *l.*; to the same, for the general list, 17 *l.* 10 *s.*; and to the rate collectors 17 *l.* 10 *s.*; making a total of 80 *l.*?—Yes.

4099. Have you framed that estimate on the assumption that there would not be more than 1,400 names on the general jurors' book?—Yes; and 400 on the special jurors' book.

4100. From the returns it appears that your estimate for the general jurors' book was in excess of the number, because the return shows that there were only 1,054 names on the general list; that would take off something from your estimate, would it not?—Yes; about 10 *l.*, I should think.

4101. You think that your estimate of 80 *l.* would have paid the various officials sufficiently in the place of the 215 *l.* which you believe was paid?—I do.

4102. Do you know anything about the printers' accounts, and other expenses?—Yes, I do. The system provided by the Act is rather expensive, of requiring the entire lists to be printed every year before the revision. The Act provides that there must be a perfectly new list supplied by the clerk of the union to the clerk of the peace every year, and that a perfectly new list must be printed and published. I conceive that the work would be very much lessened, both of the clerks of unions and the clerks of the peace, if the procedure adopted under the Parliamentary Voters' Act were followed; that is to say, that the general list, when revised, would be printed, and would be supplied to the clerks of the unions for revision, just as the Parliamentary voters' lists are sent to them for revision, and then that they should strike out all those who were dead, or had lost their qualification, and return on a supplementary list all new names. The old lists, with the objections in writing, could be posted up, and that would comply with the condition as to publication required by the Act, and the printing of the new supplementary list in a small county of the size of Roscommon, where there never would be 100 names, I am sure, on the supplementary list, would be a mere trifle; and, if done by contract, it would not be very much over 1 *l.* By having the jurors' list printed, I think another advantage would accrue, that is, that it would be in the power of the clerk of the peace to supply solicitors and all others concerned with the full jurors' list at a mere nominal fee of 1 *s.* or 1 *s.* 6 *d.*, such as he charges for copies of the voters' list. The work could be very much lessened, because the copying and arranging of a new list every year would be avoided, and the work of revision by the clerk of the peace would be lessened too.

4103. Can you state to the Committee any fact from your own union to show the necessity for fixing a tariff rate for payment for services in connection with the Act?—I can; I have already mentioned the amount that I received myself, that is 15 *l.*, which 15 *l.* covered 5 *l.* which I paid out of pocket for printing and publication. In a neighbouring union, 30 miles off (I do not care to mention the name), I happened to be in the place some time ago, and I ascertained that the clerk of the union there, for his list, which was not three times the size of my list, got 40 *l.* for himself, and that his printer's bill amounted to 34 *l.* There must be something paid for posting up the notices, and if that was paid with the same proportionate liberality, I should say that it must have brought the whole thing up to 80 *l.* I should say that there could be no better evidence of the necessity for fixing some scale by which the remuneration could be gauged than the contrast between these sums.

4104. Did anything come under your notice in connection with the payments for printing?—Yes. In my own particular union I was rather badly circumstanced. One of my collectors had left the country, and was dismissed, and another was ill, so ill that he was unable to attend, and I was obliged to do the entire work of the preparation of the list for 11 out of the 20 divisions of which the union was formed, but I have a great deal of local knowledge of the union, for I was born in it, and I know nearly everybody in it. It took me so much longer time to get my lists prepared that I had not time to bargain with the printer (we had no printer in the town of Strokestown), and I was obliged to send to the county printer and pay him what he chose to ask, 4 *l.*; but if I had had the time to make a contract for the printing I would not have given more than 2 *l.*

4105. Do you wish to make any suggestion to the Committee on any other part of the Act?—Yes; there is just one other point which I should like to mention. I saw by the papers that the Committee seemed to have some difficulty about the manner of summoning the jurors. By taking them as the Act provides, that is, a name from each

Mr. *M. Flynn.*

2 June 1873.

each letter, in consequence of the disproportion of the names under the various letters, after a few rotations, some letters would be run out, and at the wind-up of the list the jurors would be called altogether from one or two or three letters, which might involve the possibility of a jury being composed entirely of one family. I have seen it has been suggested that these letters having most names under them should have the names divided, and be treated as if two or more letters, but I think I could suggest a simpler plan. By the Act the lists are not only arranged alphabetically, but they are consecutively numbered, and it strikes me that if every tenth or twentieth name were summoned, throwing overboard altogether the initial letter, you would avoid anything like what you fear. There would be no chance of their being confined to one village, or to one name or family, and I think it would be just as little liable to objection on the score of the possibility of being abused as the present system.

4106. Of course, if your plan were adopted, any raising of the qualification and consequent reduction in the number of the jurors would diminish the expenses of the Act?—Yes, very considerably.

4107. Can you state to the Committee what was the social position of the jurors who were placed upon the list for the first time under this Act in your union?—The social position has been something under that of the previous jurors, because necessarily it must be so, as the number was so very much increased; but I think that the outcry against the jurors has been rather greater than, as far as my experience went, the merits of the case warranted.

4108. Did the Act place upon the list in the county of Roscommon a considerable number of very small farmers?—I would not call a small farmer a man with 20 *l.* valuation, but it placed a number, if not a very considerable number, of people that are perhaps not yet up to the mark of being very good jurors, but I believe that perhaps their faults have had more attention paid to them than need have been. From my experience of the Poor Law, I should say that you could safely come to the conclusion that even without any amendment, if time were given to it, the old Act as it stood would work itself free of the hitches and faults which have been so much dwelt upon. I know that in 1846 when the real amount of heavy work came to be imposed upon boards of guardians, there were very few boards of guardians in Ireland that were equal to the emergency, and I am quite aware, as my experience extends as far back as the formation of the new unions in 1850, the guardians in the new unions when they were elected, as a rule, would be perfectly incapable of administering the Poor Law efficiently if it had not been for the assistance of the large staff of Poor Law inspectors, and the qualification of a Poor Law guardian is being rated on a 20 *l.* valuation.

4109. That was at the beginning of the working of the Act?—Yes, I have known several men who are now most excellent public men as Poor Law guardians, who on their first term of office seemed to be a class very much below what the position required; but I think I can safely say now, and I speak from a very wide experience extending outside of my own union, that I do not believe that there are any other public bodies in Ireland endowed with public fiscal functions with whom the board of guardians cannot favourably contrast at present, and taking into account that the qualification of a common juror in the county of Roscommon, which is 20 *l.* valuation, is the same qualification as that of a Poor Law guardian, I do not see why, under similar circumstances, similar results might not ultimately be expected to be realised. No doubt, from the very great number of new men who, for the first time in their lives, had the duties of jurors imposed on them; who had grown up with the impression that they were not regarded by the State as fit to be entrusted with the functions of jurors, and who had no previous training or technical knowledge, and in some cases formed the entire jury, things did not in every case go on satisfactorily, or as smoothly as they would after the jurors had acquired a little experience.

4110. From the returns which the Committee have received from the county of Roscommon, have you calculated that by raising the qualification from 20 *l.* to 50 *l.*, it would strike off a very large number in that county?—I think it would strike off 40 per cent.

4111. Could you, from your knowledge of the county, say what qualification in the towns would give the same class of men as a 30 *l.* rating in the country?—I think that a 12 *l.* house qualification in the towns would give a very good class of jurors.

4112. Do you think that it would give as intelligent jurors as 30 *l.* in the country?—I do; they are much smarter men; they are so much more in contact with the world, and their wits are so much more sharpened, that I think they would be better calculated to reason even than a 30 *l.* farmer.

4113. Could you make any suggestion as to improving the revision by the chairman; as it is now, I believe, it is very ill-performed?—Really, I do not think there is anything necessary beyond what it is at present; at present, although the lists are very generally published, no one seems to read them or to pay any attention to them; and people who might have got their names struck off had they attended were left on, and those people having been summoned at the sessions 10 or 12 or 14 miles away, have had their wits sharpened, so that they are not likely to fail to attend the next revision, if their names should be on the list.

4114. You think that the jurors who are not qualified under the Act will take measures themselves to get their names struck off the list?—I do; I think that the fact that they have been put to the trouble and expense of attending the sessions, and, in some cases, fined for non-attendance, will bring about that result.

4115. Mr. *Bruen.*] As to the qualification, do you think that the 12 *l.* qualification in a town would produce an intelligent juror?—I do.

4116. I think you limited that by saying that it ought to be a house qualification?—Yes.

4117. And you do not think that a qualification of 12 *l.* valuation made up partly of house property, and partly of land, would be sufficient; you would not wish to place upon the juror's list men in that position?—No, because we might find in the suburbs of a town men who live chiefly by land, and a man of that sort with a 12 *l.* valuation would not be a bit better qualified than a country juror of the same valuation.

4118. Referring to your opinion that the jurors who have lately been placed upon the jurors' lists will,

Mr. *M. Flynn.*

19 June 1873.

will, in time, become fully qualified to perform their duties, because they are men of the same standing as the Poor Law guardians, is it not the fact that although the qualification for a Poor Law guardian may be the same, that is 20 *l.*, yet that a guardian is a man who is selected by his fellows as being the best of the whole class in his electoral division?—Yes, he is selected because of some particular reason that may be analogous to that.

4119. He is selected, is he not, as being the most intelligent, and probably the best educated, and a man most fitted to represent his fellows?—He may be selected because being the most popular man.

4120. Would there not also be the consideration that he is thoroughly qualified by education, and also by intelligence, to occupy the position?—That does not follow; there is no educational qualification provided by the Poor Law Act.

4121. I ask you from your experience whether it is not the fact that guardians are generally elected with those qualifications?—Yes, it is the general fact; but I have mentioned in my statement before, that I have known from time to time men who are now very excellent public men as Poor Law guardians, who, on their first term of office, did not appear men of the stamp that one would have thought would have produced satisfactory results.

4122. But they were the select men; they had been chosen as being the best of their class, had they not?—I wish to correct that; it does not follow that they are chosen as the best of their class, because it is the majority of the votes that elect them; although a man may have a great majority of votes in his favour, he need not necessarily be the best of his class.

4123. Do you mean to say that they are not the best of their class?—As a rule I think they are the best of their class.

4124. Are you aware that there are any elected guardians in your union whose qualification is so low as to be limited by 20 *l.*?—No; I do not think at present there are, but there have been.

4125. In your experience, is it not a fact that the elected guardians that are selected by their fellows have a much higher qualification than that?—Yes; but I have known a case where a man had barely possessed that qualification, and had been elected. I have known a case where a man has been elected in the last few years possessing merely the qualification of a 25 *l.* valuation.

4126. I ask you whether the fact which you mentioned, that the elected guardians of unions, although they were selected men from their class, were hardly able to perform the duties imposed upon them, is not a strong reason for supposing that those men who are not selected in that way might not be incapable of performing the duties of jurors, owing to their want of intelligence?—If I understand your question aright, I think I answered it before; I said that at the formation of the new unions the boards of guardians, generally speaking, elected in the new unions, were quite unequal to the task of the administration of the law, as it was required to be then administered, and they would not have been able to succeed if it had not been for the help received from the poor law inspectors. I adduced the fact that they are now so thoroughly satisfactory in the performance of their work, as a reason why I arrived at the conclusion, that given the same opportunities to jurors of acquiring knowledge of their business, and of the importance of the trust reposed in them, you may expect results very much akin to those.

4127. But the fact is that those guardians were all of them selected men, and you admit that they are selected generally on account of their superior intelligence?—I said generally speaking they are men of a good class, but from my own experience of my own union it does not necessarily follow that it should be so every year, because there is nothing in the Act that causes it to be so. The only qualification for a poor law guardian is that he shall not have been convicted of felony, or some other indictable offences, and that he should possess the qualification of a certain rating.

4128. Certainly that is in the Act, but I have already called your attention to the fact, that all those men are selected, and elected by their fellows for a certain position, and you admit that they are generally selected because they are the fittest men?—I do generally.

4129. Therefore there is no parallel to be drawn as to their capacity for performing that duty between a man who is selected out of a certain number as being the fittest man, and a man who is not so selected?—If his selection was because of his being the fittest, but his selection is not because of his being the fittest, his selection is a mere accident, and it may have no relation to fitness at all.

4130. You say that you have a knowledge of the duty performed by clerks of the peace; have you ever acted as a clerk of the peace?—No.

4131. Are you authorised here to represent the clerks of the peace?—I am not, but I have a thorough general knowledge of the entire fiscal working of the county of Roscommon, because in addition to being clerk of the union, I have other positions. I represent the treasurer of the county of Roscommon who is non-resident, and I do all his local business, and I have some land agencies, so that altogether I am brought more into connection with the public affairs of the county than I would be if I were merely clerk of the union.

4132. Have you any knowledge of the rate of payment which has been given to the clerks of the peace throughout Ireland?—I know what is given in Sligo and Roscommon, it has been 50 *l.* in each case.

4133. You do not mean to represent, I suppose, that you are authorised to say that the clerks of the peace were well paid; it is only your own private opinion?—Certainly. I only take my own authority. I take the facts of the case. I think that I can price scrivener's work pretty fairly from my long acquaintance with it. I have read the Act very attentively, and I have seen what the duties are, and I understand what the terms mean.

4134. You would prefer that the remuneration which is paid for the duties performed under the Juries Act should be fixed partly by a schedule of prices?—I would.

4135. And that that remuneration should be placed upon the poor-rates and not upon the county cess?—I did not offer an opinion upon that. I merely said that I did not see any reason why a part of the expenses should be paid out of the poor-rates, and part out of the county cess. I did not presume to offer an opinion upon that point at all.

4136. Have you formed an opinion as to whether it would be possible to combine the lists of voters

Mr. *M. Flynn.*

12 June 1873.

voters and the lists of jurors so as to save printing?—I do not think that it could be done. Really the cost of printing would be very little as soon as the thing came to be thoroughly understood. I should say that under the new Bill, by increasing the qualification, taking the county of Roscommon, there would be 800 names in the general jurors' book, and I am perfectly aware that the cost of printing need not be more than 1 *l.* for every 100 names, and 8 *l.* is not a matter that there need be very much economy about; there is not much room for economy in an expense of 8 *l.* over an entire county.

4137. That is to say the printing of the lists that you prepare?—No, the lists that the clerk of the peace prepares.

4138. Can you mention the rate of payment which is now made in preparing the Parliamentary Voters' List?—In passing through Dublin I called on a printer, and I asked him to give me a rough estimate of what the cost of printing would be. I did not want it to be very accurate, or anything like a tender, and he said that in round figures it would be about 1 *l.* for every 100 names.

4139. That is the estimate which he formed, supposing it to be printed in Dublin?—Yes.

4140. That would be only on the supposition that all the printing was done in Dublin?—As far as that is concerned it would be always done at the cheapest market, and there is no reason why it should not be done as cheaply in the country.

4141. You propose a plan by which the difficulty which occurs in the alphabetical selection might be avoided, that is to say, the difficulty when you come to the end of the list, having the panels formed out of one name or two names, and you are of opinion that that alphabetical process of selection is not a satisfactory one?—I think it is open to the objections which I mentioned, because the letter E goes out very soon, and the letter I goes out very soon, and there are a few other letters that will disappear ultimately. In Connaught, for instance, it would be left to the B's and C's and M's. You would have the whole of the names in those letters, and at the wind-up the M's would beat all the other letters.

4142. When you make out a list of jurors, you do not put them in the dictionary order; I presume that you put them only in alphabetical order?—I put them in dictionary order myself. The clerks of union, by the Act, are absolutely bound to put them in alphabetical order, but not in dictionary order; but in the lists that I prepared I arranged them in dictionary order.

4143. But you only prepared the lists for your own union?—Yes, but I know that it did not involve any great additional trouble.

4144. *Mr. Downing.*] Is it not a fact that every union in Ireland receives from the Valuation Office a list annually of all the valuations in that particular union?—Yes, that is last year's list as altered, and as soon as they exhaust all the various colours in which the corrections are made new lists are prepared.

4145. Is it not from that list that you make out your poor rate books and your warrants for the collection of rates?—Yes.

4146. And that is paid for distinct from any other charge upon the rates?—Yes, it is.

4147. And it amounts to rather a heavy item, I believe, in several counties?—It comes to between 400 *l.* and 500 *l.* a year in Roscommon.

4148. In fact, that is the origin of the valuation system?—Yes.

4149. When the list is sent to the clerk of the peace under the precept directed to you, is it printed?—That is the list sent by the clerks of the unions; the clerks of the unions have to get them printed themselves, and the Act throws upon the clerk of the union the duty of printing them.

4150. Had not the clerk of the peace to discharge that same duty before?—Yes, but the numbers were very much smaller.

4151. Although the numbers were smaller, was not his duty rather more difficult, because he had to deal with the baronial constables?—So far as the number of names were concerned it was more difficult as the lists were not so perfectly presented to him as they are at present; but as the numbers are very much greater at present the duty is now heavier.

4152. In your opinion has the clerk of the peace now to discharge any duty that he had not to discharge before?—Very little more.

4153. Does not the clerk of the peace always get from the grand jury a presentment for his printing expenses?—Yes.

4154. Then there would be no very great additional duty, if any, thrown upon him, and you do not see why the clerk of the peace is entitled to very much remuneration under the Act?—Precisely so.

4155. Did I understand you to say that you would pay the clerk of the peace 6 *d.* per name for every name upon the list?—Upon the special jurors' list only, because the special jurors are not merely made up of names returned in the general list by the clerks of the unions, but of the eldest sons of magistrates and the sons of peers and baronets, and so on, and the clerk of the peace has to seek out from other sources the information that enables him to make that list perfect.

4156. Then do I understand you to say that you would not give him any remuneration for the general list?—Three-pence a line. The clerk of the peace has to prepare his list in dictionary order; he has a good deal of copying work and comparing, and altogether it is more troublesome to him at present than it was before.

4157. Do you know what it would amount to in a large county, in the county of Antrim, for instance, where there are nearly 8,000 on the list?—I think if the number was very large I would reduce the rate.

4158. You would not pay more in proportion, that is to say, if you paid him 6 *d.* for each line in a small county you would not pay him the same in a large county?—Not altogether, but very nearly I would.

4159. *Mr. Bruen.*] A line and a name are synonymous terms, are they not, because there is only one name in each line?—Yes, only one name in each line.

4160. *Mr. Downing.*] There is annually a revision, is there not, of that book which is sent down from the General Valuation Office in Dublin, by the officer sent down from that department?—Yes.

4161. And that is returned to the clerk of the union?—Yes, and a copy also to the county treasurer.

4162. A notice is given before he comes down, for a considerable period, that he is coming down, and that he will revise the valuation of any person

Mr. M. Flynn.

12 June 1873.

son who gives notice of a desire to do so?—No, that is not so, that notice is not given generally.

4163. Is it not given in the board room of the board of guardians?—He writes a special letter to the board of guardians informing them that he will come on a particular day, but it is not usual to publish it in the shape of an advertisement.

4164. But do you, as clerk of the union, when you get the notice of it, inform the several guardians who are present, both the elected and the *ex officio* guardians?—I do.

4165. With a view to their communicating that fact in their different electoral divisions?—Yes.

4166. When the list so revised is returned to you, there is nothing more to be done but merely to copy it?—Yes, that is so.

4167. I take it for granted that in your union as in unions that I am acquainted with, the clerk of the union generally gets hold of a boy or two amongst the paupers who can read very well, and write, and he employs them as clerks to copy the list?—No, that is not the case anywhere now, although it may be in Dublin, because the services of boys of that class are much too highly prized now; they do not remain as paupers.

6168. Do you think that a qualification of 12 *l.* for houses in towns is not too high a qualification for the purpose of obtaining the best jurors?—I do not mean to say that it is not too high, but I mean to say that the 12 *l.* qualification would give, from my experience, very intelligent jurors.

4169. What town do you reside in?—Strokestown, but I know nearly every town in the county.

4170. Have you made a calculation of the number of houses in Strokestown valued at 12 *l.*?—I have not; I have not the memorandum with me, but I have it for the whole county.

4171. I have here the number in the citizen towns in the whole of Connaught at 12 *l.* and upwards, as 1,575?—I am not aware of the number; but the O'Conor Don asked me to let him know what additional number of jurors would be added, by giving a 6 *l.*, 8 *l.*, 10 *l.* and 12 *l.* household qualification, and I went over the list supplied to me as the representative of the county treasurer, where there is a separate valuation of the houses given.

4172. Did you take it from the valuation of towns and villages only?—Yes, in towns and villages only, in 6 *l.* and not 20 *l.* there were 451 in the county of Roscommon; 8 *l.* and not 20 *l.*, 354; 10 *l.* and not 20 *l.*, 246; and 12 *l.* and not 20 *l.*, 173.

4173. That would give the number of qualified jurors in the whole county as 1,224?—That would not be the number, because the number would be less than that, for a man occupying a 12 *l.* house may be on the jurors' lists in right of some other qualification, and some of the occupiers may be exempted from serving on juries.

4174. You seemed to be under the impression that there was a general uniform qualification for the election of guardians throughout Ireland?—That was the general impression that I had.

4175. I will just call your attention to the table of unions in Ireland, under the orders of the Poor Law Commissioners in 1858; for instance, in Bandon, the qualification for an elect guardian is 20 *l.*, and in the very next, Castletown, it is 12 *l.*; and then I go on and I find that it is as low as 10 *l.* in the county of Waterford; so that you see that the qualification is not uniform, and that the qualification is so low as 10 *l.*, and I may state that in one instance it is as low as 6 *l.*; do not you think that the most intelligent and the best jurors to be found are those who reside in towns and in large villages?—I do.

4176. They are a much superior class in point of general knowledge of the world, and better educated, are they not?—They are, and they can reason more accurately.

4177. I think I understood you to say that you thought there was a greater outcry against this Act than there need be, considering that it was the first assizes, and the first quarter sessions at which it was brought into operation?—Yes, I think so.

4178. I think I also understood you to say that you did not think there was anything essentially necessary with regard to making the revision more perfect than the operation of this Act as it stands?—So I say.

4179. I will take yourself as a clerk of a union; you must have a most intimate knowledge of all the people in your union?—Yes, and I think I can best explain that by saying that in going over the list there was scarcely any information even as to reading and writing that the collectors were capable of giving me that I did not previously possess.

4180. The rate collector, who comes constantly in contact with the people, and receives the money, and goes to their residences, must also have a very thorough knowledge of them?—He must have a better knowledge even than I can have, and yet my own knowledge was sufficient to enable me in the Strokestown Union to know every man who could not read or write, at least to the extent of raising such a doubt as induced me to make inquiry.

4181. You convey to the Committee that there should be no difficulty whatever in your, and the collector of your union, from communicating to the chairman at the revision the objections that are stated in the Act of Parliament, objections that would apply to every person upon the list?—Not the slightest difficulty.

4182. It has been stated here by some witnesses that they thought the clerks of the unions and rate collectors would rather not be asked those questions; do you think that there would be any possible object in reason why they should object?—No object would occur to me, at least; I would neither object to answer the question nor to volunteer the information.

4183. Do you not think that those persons who would be objected to would rather be objected to than otherwise?—Yes; I believe they would rather be objected to.

4184. Do not you know that, generally speaking, men desire to be left off of the jury?—Certainly they do.

4185. Have you not heard that they actually bribed the bailiffs to induce them not to serve the summons?—I know that very well. The other day the sheriff's bailiff was drunk, and he said, the sheriff who at one time was the king of the county is now no more than any other ordinary man, and the bailiff cannot make a single sixpence. I believe that under the old system bailiffs used to prepare unauthorised summonses for the purpose of exacting black-mail for not serving them.

4186. Have you considered with regard to the service of summonses upon jurors, what would be the best mode of doing it?—I think the best way would be by registered letter; the post offices are distributed everywhere, and people are so much

Mr. *M. Flynn.*

12 June 1873.

much in the habit of looking for their letters now, that if a few additional days' notice were granted, it would be certain that the summonses would reach everyone.

4187. In fact, do you know any part of your county where there is not a post office within a very reasonable distance wherever a man is living?—I do not know any part of the county where there is not a post office within three miles.

4188. You know, do you not, that letters are coming from America to every quarter of Ireland, and that they are delivered within a very short time after their arrival?—Yes; I do not believe that letters ever remain four days in the post office.

4189. If a letter remains in the post office, is it not usual on a Sunday for the postmaster, or some one else, to communicate to some one from the neighbourhood that a letter is lying in the post office?—Yes, it is a very common thing; I have been at the post office, and I have sympathised deeply with the postmaster in consequence. I have seen 20 people in a large village come to the post office in succession, and they will first ask for their own letters, and then they will go the round and say, are there any letters for this person, and that person, and the same question is put by 20 different individuals in the same day.

4190. With regard to the mode of paying expenses under this Act, you said that you did not express an opinion upon it; I want to ask you whether you do not think it very hard, and perhaps very unjust that any portion of the expense of this Act of Parliament, which is for the benefit of the community at large, should be placed solely and entirely upon the occupiers?—I do.

4191. Which is the case, is it not, when it is put upon the county cess?—Yes; I consider, in fact, that all new charges that were not contemplated at the time of the letting of land, ought not to be placed exclusively on either the occupier or the proprietor, and certainly not on the occupier.

4192. Do not you think that where it is an Act which affects the general interests, not only of Ireland, but of the United Kingdom, an expense of that kind ought to be put upon the Consolidated Fund?—I do think so, because I think that jurors are a part of the machinery of the criminal law, and that they do as much service for merchants and manufacturers as they do for the farmers.

4193. Mr. *H. A. Herbert.*] Have you a very large attendance of guardians on your board?—There is a very fair attendance.

4194. What would you say is the average attendance?—I should say that the average attendance would be very close up to 12.

4195. How many of those are *ex officio*, and how many are elected guardians?—Between two and three are *ex officio*, and the remainder are elected guardians; that is, taking the average attendance.

4196. Could you mention to the Committee the average rating of the greater number of those men who attend the board; I presume that in every union in Ireland there are a certain number of gentlemen who devote themselves to the work of the board?—Yes.

4197. Could you tell the valuation of those 10 men who generally attend on the average?—The elected guardians are not the highest rated.

4198. But could you mention about the average rating?—I should suppose that the average would be about 60 *l.*; in fact, some of the lowest rated guardians are perhaps the most punctual in their attendance. In the Stokestown Union, some of the guardians are rated on a very large valuation, and their valuation would bring up the average very considerably. Some men are rated as high as 1,000 *l.*

4199. Occasionally, I suppose, you have a very much larger attendance of guardians?—Yes, occasionally. I suppose the largest attendance that I ever saw was 27.

4200. That large attendance, I suppose, would be when there was an election, or an increase of salary, or something of that kind?—Yes.

4201. You stated that raising the qualification of jurors from 20 *l.* to 30 *l.* would knock off about 40 per cent.?—Yes, it would knock off about 40 per cent. in my own union.

4202. On what did you base that calculation?—I have taken 80 names off the 200, and I think that would be about 40 per cent.

4203. When you make that calculation do you take into account the increase that would take place, supposing the new Valuation Bill were passed?—No.

4204. I presume that you know that there is a new Valuation Bill before the House?—Yes.

4205. What number would that Valuation Bill, do you think, add to this number which you have just stated?—Keeping the qualification as provided in the amended Bill, I do not think that the increase of valuation would do no more than bring up the numbers to what they originally were.

4206. That is to say, 1,400 in your county?—Yes.

4207. You just now stated that summonses going through the post in a registered letter would be sure to reach the different parties for whom they were posted; is it not the fact that numbers of letters from America are sent to land agents and to landlords, and to different people, rather than to the post-office, for delivery?—No, not in my experience.

4208. Colonel *Vandeleur.*] You prepare the voters' list, do you not?—Yes.

4209. In the list of voters, I believe, the post-office direction of each voter is not given?—No, it is not.

4210. And in the same way, in the list of jurors, you merely put the townlands in which the jurors reside?—Yes.

4211. How is the sheriff, or anybody, to know what the post-office nearest to each person is?—There could be no difficulty in adding a column in the list when it is prepared; of course it would be essential to do that, or else the sheriff could not comply with the law, I apprehend, if you alter the law in one respect you must do so in other respects as well.

4212. To carry out your view, you must add the post office of each party who is to be summoned as a juror?—Yes.

4213. Would you say that the services of the police might be made use of in summoning jurors?—I do not see any objection to the police, but at the same time I believe that perhaps the less the police are called in to interfere, generally speaking, the better it would be, and the better people would be pleased. There is a certain amount of terror caused by the appearance of a couple of policemen coming across a man's farm, because

Mr. *M. Flynn.*

12 June 1873.

because he does not know whether they are going to search for whisky or something of that sort.

4214. Do not the police perform any duties now under the Poor Law Act?—Yes, they do; they have the distribution of the voting papers and the collection of them, but that duty is so very well known at the time, that the people know what they are coming for.

4215. That might be equally well known, might it not, in the case of summoning jurors?—No, I do not think that there would be the same interest in making that known, because in the case of poor law elections the candidates are out, and apprising their friends that a visit may be expected. I know that there is, in remote places particularly, rather a fear of the presence of the police.

4216. Major *O'Reilly*.] A suggestion was made by another witness with regard to printing the lists, which I would like to ask your opinion upon, and it was, that a list should be made out of both voters and jurors by adding two other columns, or as many other columns that were necessary upon the sheet for the jurors?—I really believe that there would be no economy in that case, because the sheets would be so much larger, and in a large county where, as Mr. Downing said, there would be 8,000 jurors, there would be a proportionately large number of voters, and it would add to the voluminous shape of the lists, and the cost of printing would in the end be found to be about the same.

4217. You would propose to economise the printing, as I understand you, by not reprinting the new list until it is revised?—Yes, that is my idea; if the list, after it is revised, is printed, a sufficient number of copies could be kept to be sold to anybody who wanted the panel, and also copies to be sent to the clerks of the unions for the publication required by the Act, and nothing would require to be newly printed previous to the revision, except the supplemental list, which could be printed by the clerk of the peace, which, in a county of the size of Roscommon, need not cost more than 1 *l.* for its printing.

4218. It has been stated that frequently persons who ought not to have been on the jurors' list, not in respect of rating qualification, but for other disqualification, such as being of an age over 60, blind, deaf, and other infirmities, did get on the jurors' list, and did come up as jurors on the panel; do I gather from you that you think that if the poor rate collectors and clerks of unions did their duty in supplying the information that was necessary for revising the lists, such names should have been struck off?—Certainly.

4219. And you think that there would not be any practical difficulty in doing that?—Just so; I can safely say that no such difficulty occurred in the union of which I prepared the list.

The Lord Chief Justice the Right Honourable JAMES WHITESIDE, called in; and Examined.

Right Hon. *J. Whiteside.*

4220. *Chairman.*] YOU are the Chief Justice of the Court of Queen's Bench?—Yes.

4221. Do you recollect what time you have held that office?—I think I was appointed about six or seven years ago.

4222. Will you be so good as to give the Committee the result of your experience of the working of the present Jury Act?—The result of my experience, is to lead me to a very unfavourable opinion of the existing system.

4223. Will you state first what experience you have had of it?—My experience is almost daily. I believe I have tried more jury cases than most judges, and I, unfortunately, have had an experience which the judges in other courts have not, because all Government cases are brought into the Court of Queen's Bench, and the first class of cases of that kind that I had to deal with, and with juries under the present system, were the prosecutions directed under the Act, with regard to undue influence, and cases of prosecution arising upon Mr. Justice Keogh's report; and I should add, not by a jury of the city of Dublin, but by a jury of the county; there is a cardinal distinction to be made between the city jurors and the county jurors. As far as I have seen of the present Act, the city juries are very good; I forget at this moment what the rating is, but I should say it is 50 *l.* or 60 *l.* upon a house; and I need hardly say that that would insure intelligence. Generally, they are highly intelligent men; and I have no complaint to make of them as jurors, nor have I any complaint to make of the city special jurors who were there before this Act; but as to the county special jurors that were summoned in those important cases, it was rather a painful matter to me to witness what occurred; they were quite strangers to the situation in which they were placed; there was a constant titter going on in the court while we were endeavouring to get the panel of the jurymen arranged; the first man who was called to act as foreman declined, and I conceived that it was because he could not read or write; I desired the official to put that gentleman aside as foreman; he was called as foreman, and he objected, and he pushed aside a paper that was near him, and I at once concluded that the man could not read or write, and his appearance confirmed my conjecture; then he was sworn, and that was the person who afterwards, when we adjourned for luncheon, did not appear; we waited half an hour, and we sent to search for him; and one juryman said that he thought he could find him in Pill-lane; I was very awkwardly placed: there was constant laughter going on in the court whilst this affair was proceeding, until at last the man was discovered and brought into court. He really did not appear to know the ways of the place, or what he ought to do, or what he ought not to do; I asked him, of course, what he had to say for himself, and I felt it my duty to fine him; he told me very plainly, that he had been eating a roll of bread and drinking a glass of beer in Pill-lane; that was the answer he made me. I did fine him 20 *l.*; but when I came out of the court the high sheriff spoke to me, and said, "I have met an old friend here in that juryman;" "An old friend!" said I. "How is he your friend?" He said, "He has carried me on his back many a time; he was a carter," or some such thing, I think he said, "of an uncle of mine, and he is a very decent, good fellow;" he spoke to me, and interceded with me about the fine, and perceiving that the juryman erred merely from ignorance, and that the man was put into a situation for which he was entirely unfitted, I remitted the fine. I believe there were several persons on those juries who

sum

Right Hon. J. Whiteside.

12 June 1873.

were totally unfitted to be on a special jury to try any case; I have inquired into the lists, and I have asked the sheriff once or twice to send me the names of the persons, and who they were; I found that they were nearly all new men, and I had never seen them on a special jury before, except, perhaps, one or two upon each jury, or some three at the most, who were men of some mark. On inquiry, I found that in one case one of them was a dairyman. I was also told by the sheriff that a person appeared on a jury, who was a very industrious clever man in his way; he had been a cab driver and made money, and bought more cabs, and got up in the world, and was rated to the amount required, and, therefore, was summoned as a special juror; I have no doubt that that was quite accurate. My objection is not at all that many of them were not innocent men; I do not impute to them any corruption, but I say that they had not intelligence adequate to perform the duty imposed upon them.

4224. The special jurors, before the passing of this Act, I believe, were a very limited class in Dublin, were they not?—Limited in this way, that a certain set of gentlemen were willing to attend; for instance, a retired merchant, or sometimes a retired officer, or a country gentleman who had nothing better to do, and had a house in town, very often attended, and then the very busy men absented themselves; but I have to mention that those jurors gave very moderate and judicious verdicts. They were trained men, and trained jurymen are a great comfort to a judge, because they do not waste time in asking foolish questions. I have seen one of these jurymen offend a very eloquent counsel while he was speaking, by taking out his watch and looking at the advocate, who immediately observed, "Oh, I perceive that you are not influenced by the speech." He was not so much influenced by the speech as by the facts, but at present eloquent and ingenious counsel address speeches to jurymen that, in my opinion, they would never address to an educated and qualified class of special jurymen.

4225. I understand your Lordship's objection to the present special jurors to be partly that they are inexperienced?—That is true.

4226. That is the natural result, is it not, of the extremely limited number of those who formerly discharged those duties?—But I should say that there must be a mistake about the limited number, because, on one occasion, in speaking to the sheriff in the Queen's Bench about the want of attendance of jurymen, he said to me, "Perhaps you are not aware that I have had to supply eight juries to day." I said, "How is that?" He said, "The Probate Court has a jury, the Master of the Rolls has a jury" (as under the new law they may have), "and our three courts, with the two courts assisting the chief justice, have juries;" and if the commission at Green-street was sitting, sometimes he would have to supply a jury of a somewhat different class perhaps, but all from the same book; but that which you have mentioned unquestionably existed, to a certain extent, that some gentlemen attended regularly when called, and those who might attend avoided attending when they knew, or supposed, that their places would be supplied by others.

4227. You have hitherto, I think, only spoken of special juries?—Only special juries.

4228. Have you had some experience of common juries under the Act?—Latterly in Dublin, I very rarely am able to try a common jury case, and I therefore cannot speak of common juries, except what I have seen at the Commission in Green-street, and on two or three circuits.

4229. Did your Lordship at the last assizes go on the Home circuit?—No the Leinster circuit, and for the first time.

4230. Will you give the Committee the result of your experience on that circuit?—I was Crown Judge at Clonmel, and I found the criminal business rather heavy there, and I was seven days in court, from 10 to 7 o'clock each day. I can give you an account of the state of affairs in that county. The first fact that I observed was, that a number of very ill-dressed and poor looking persons were in the court; these, I found out, were jurymen. Then we got into work, and we got a panel. We generally begin with small cases, and at the end, I believe, of the first or second day, a man glided up to the side of the Bench, and asked me to let him remain at home to-morrow. I asked him, Why? and he said, that he had two pigs to sell. Another man came up, and told me that he would be greatly obliged if I would let him stay at home, because car hire was very expensive to him. I spoke to the sub-sheriff as I was a stranger there myself, and he told me, "All those statements made to your Lordship are quite true." I have only the authority of this official for the statement that I am now about to make, but he assured me, that he believed that several of those poor men had been obliged to pawn their clothes to support themselves in the town of Clonmel, and added that it was a very cruel thing to bring them in that situation a great distance to the assize town. It is right that the Committee should understand what the exact state of procedure in a Crown case of any little importance is. You will then clearly see into the whole system. We may have 80 or 90 jurymen; I think that is quite a sufficient panel, and ordinarily we do not want more. On that occasion at Clonmel, there were certainly 20 out of the 80, who, as far as I could judge, were substantial men, and quite competent to be jurymen. Then the prisoner's attorney, a local agent, is thoroughly conversant with everything and every juryman in the court, and if it is a felony he has the right to challenge, and he challenges every man, according to my observations, in a rough way according to the coat he wore; if he wore a good coat he was challenged, and so the 20 good men are sure, if called, to be challenged. Then those who are conducting the case for the Crown are left to the residuum of the panel. I observed that the solicitor for the Crown, Mr. Bolton, was a clever man; I had never seen him before, but he did set aside jurors, and he exercised his right, I should say, as far as it was right to exercise it, and he set aside several. I can show you now how it operates in a very remarkable instance that occurred before me. There were three persons, I think, tried for a felonious assault on a farmer who was accompanied by his wife. Being a felony the attorney for the prisoner did what I have described; he challenged all those people, and there was a very inferior jury sworn to try the felony, and the defendants were all acquitted against my opinion of the evidence. I was about to order their discharge when the Crown counsel informed me that there was an indictment pending for an assault upon the wife who had accompanied her husband, and who

was

Right Hon. J. Whiteside.

19 June 1873.

was also beaten, but not so severely. The next day (it was late in the evening, and we could not proceed on the same day with the trial), the trial proceeded for a misdemeanour, an assault upon the wife; 15 of those respectable men that I have before described were called, and the prisoner's attorney had no power of challenging, and 12 were sworn. The very same witnesses were examined, and the same facts, and the same occurrences exactly proved to have taken place, and on that occasion the same three men were convicted, so that they were both convicted and acquitted upon the same evidence, and the conviction naturally arose from the superior intelligence and honesty of purpose of the jurors last sworn; there is no doubt of that, and the same thing might occur I have no doubt in other instances of a like nature. There was a capital case in Tipperary of a respectable farmer who was tried for the murder of his wife. The case involved questions of the treatment which was resorted to and of the skill of the medical man in operating upon the injured person, which questions are becoming not unusual in Ireland. This man was of course defended by able counsel, and we got a jury, but the challenges prevailed. In that case the trial went on until 7 in the evening, and I was obliged then to lock up the jurymen in the usual manner. The next morning, at 10 o'clock, I resumed the case, and it fell to Mr. Hemphill, one of the Queen's counsel who was concerned for the Crown, to address the jury in reply, and whilst he was speaking, one of the jurymen stood up and blurted out something that I could not understand; I looked at him, and he sat down. Mr. Hemphill resumed his speech, but the man got up again, and spoke incoherently to the counsel. I looked at him again, and then I suspected that he must be intoxicated; it was so early (it was only 12 o'clock), and as the man had been locked up all night under the charge of the sheriff, I was a little surprised at it; therefore I directed the jury to withdraw, and I called the county infirmary surgeon, Dr. Hemphill, a highly educated gentleman, and I had him sworn, and then I sent him into the jury-room to examine that juryman, as if he had got a fit, or was suddenly taken ill. He returned and informed me that the juryman was suffering under the effects of intoxication arising from whisky, and that he had found a whisky bottle in the jury-room. I was very much annoyed at this affair; things occuring in court, such are very detrimental to the administration of justice. I asked, "What is your evidence?" He gave me his evidence that in his opinion the juryman would require three or four hours' repose before we could resume the trial, it being a capital case. I then ordered the sheriff to take charge of the whole 12, as they could not be separated, the 11 who were sober, and this unfortunate juryman, and I gave them three or four hours' rest. Then I sent Dr. Hemphill to examine the man again, and he returned and was examined in court, and declared to me that he had examined the juror again, and that the man was comatose; that was Dr. Hemphill's expression; and furthermore, he swore that in his opinion the juryman had not understood one word of the evidence that had been given that day in court; it was impossible then to begin and try the case over again. My Brother Fitzgerald was occupied in trying a heavy fishery case, and had some other business to dispose of, and I was obliged to go on to Waterford to open the commission. We had allowed seven days for Clonmel, and that was the eighth day, and therefore I made this order in the Crown book (*produces same*) which discloses the whole of the facts, and which I drew up myself. I state "on Friday, the 7th day of March 1873, pending the trial, and before the charge a juror, named Maurice Wall, misconducted himself in presence of the court, and when rebuked exhibited symptoms of intoxication; whereupon the Lord Chief Justice had Dr. William Hemphill, surgeon to the gaol, sworn to examine and report on the state of Maurice Wall, the said juror, and to ascertain and depose whether, from the use of intoxicating drinks or any other cause, he was in a fit state to understand the evidence and perform his duty as a juror. And the said Dr. Hemphill, having examined the said juror, then deposed to the Court that he had seen and examined the juror, Maurice Wall; that the said juror was then labouring under the effects of drink, of whisky; that he would require the entire of the day to rest before his brain would be clear. Whereupon the jury were ordered to retire for some hours, and the said juror had repose; after which the said Dr. Hemphill further deposed, that he had just seen and again examined the juror, Maurice Wall (who had been, with the other jurors, confined to the jurors' apartments during the night); that he was apparently in a comatose state, that he was not capable of understanding anything, and that he had been incapable all the morning; that he had taken a great deal of spirituous liquor during last night and this morning, and that it would take a considerable time until his brain became clear. Whereupon all the foregoing matters so appearing to the Court, the jury were then called into court and discharged." It is a painful thing to discharge a jury on such grounds stated in open court. The jury were discharged then, and I was obliged to leave the case over for the next assizes. Whether it was right or wrong, I gave an order to the sheriff never to summon that drunken man again upon a jury; I am not sure that I had authority to do it; but, however, I did it.

4231. That was in Tipperary?—Yes, it was at Clonmel. I should mention that it was stated to me by some of the bar that there was a returned convict upon one of the juries, that it had not been discovered in time to have him set aside. He was a returned convict, and he would be on the jurors' book if he was sufficiently rated.

4232. At other assize towns did the juries appear to be of the same character?—No; Clonmell is the heavy town in that circuit. The business at Kilkenny was very light; Waterford also surprised me; when I went in to open the commission for my Brother Fitzgerald, I found that there were only two or three cases, and those of a very trifling character, for trial in the county. I had no experience of anything useful on this inquiry there. I have spoken of criminal cases, but before we quit that subject it is right to say that I have seen before this last Jury Act great miscarriages of justice in criminal cases from the formation of the common jury panel, and in very serious cases. There was a great deal to be rectified in the system before this Act dealt with the subject. I tried a case in Cavan about two years ago for a threatening notice; it was clearly proved, and it was a very bad case. We had a jury under the old system. It was not so bad

Right Hon. J. Whiteside.

12 June 1873.

had a jury as you might get now, perhaps; but, however, after the thing was finished, and the jury were locked up, I went into another case. Two or three hours after I asked if the jury agreed, and they came out, and said, "Eleven of us are agreed, but there is a juryman that will not speak, except to say that he will not agree; he will not reason with us, or state any argument for his opinion." I said that I must beg them to retire, and I left them shut up till between 11 and 12 at night, then I returned and called them out, and they repeated the statement that they had before made, and as I could not put the health of the 11 jurymen in jeopardy, of course I discharged them; but in coming home I asked the sheriff in the carriage who was the dissentient man, and if he knew him. "Yes," he said, "I know him very well; he is a pawnbroker, and he dare not give a verdict of guilty; he depends upon the people, and therefore he behaved as he did behave." Then it occurred to me that that very proper clause which, I believe, was in the Act of Parliament of Sir Michael O'Loghlen, excluding publicans, might be extended, inasmuch as a publican is excluded because he depends upon the people in a great degree. Here was a man who was a pawnbroker, who defeated justice, and perhaps did it more thoroughly than it would be done by a publican, for what I know. I have tried other cases where 11 men have agreed, and one has dissented against the justice of the case.

4233. Would you propose to disqualify, absolutely, all publicans?—Yes, certainly, beyond all doubt. I am not quite sure whether I have made a mistake, whether that was in a statute or whether it was by the authority of Sir Michael O'Loghlen.

4234. *Mr. Heron.*] It was what he recommended when he was Attorney General?—The noble Chairman has asked me a very proper question. It would be very useful to disqualify, absolutely, such persons, and prevent them being on the panel, for this reason, that if they are on the panel it necessitates the Crown Solicitor desiring them to stand by, and that lessens the strength of the panel, because you must exercise the right of directing those publicans to stand by, and the oftener you do that the more unpleasant it is for the prosecution. I should also mention to the Committee a matter which has struck me very forcibly. In later times the difficulty has been increased of getting a verdict upon what we call circumstantial evidence. When I speak of circumstantial evidence I mean a case of this kind; a man is walking home at night at 10 or 11 o'clock, and a person comes behind him and shoots him in the back of the head and he perhaps fires from a revolver a second bullet into his head and then runs down the street. There is immediately a cry raised, and he is caught at the end of the street by a constable. This may happen (and I have tried a case very like it), that there is a struggle, and the constable twists the pistol out of the prisoner's hand and holds him fast; the pistol is examined, and it is a six-chamber revolver, we will say; two barrels appear to have been recently discharged, and the other four are undischarged; the injured man is lying at the top of the street with the two bullets in the back of his head; but nobody saw the murderer actually fire the shot. The two shots have been heard, and the persons that followed him have appeared and say, "We saw a man run down the street with a pistol in his hand;" and the constable at the end of the street appears and says, "I had a struggle with this man, and took the pistol out of his hand, and here it is." The argument that I have heard used by counsel in a case of that kind is this, "To be sure this is a case of suspicion, but nobody saw this man fire the pistol and *non constat*, but another man fired it and gave the pistol to him, and then he ran down the street with the pistol and was caught in the way described;" and an argument of that nature will be, when required, strenuously insisted upon. Of course no judge could interfere to prevent a barrister doing the best he can for his client, but I do not think that an argument of that kind would be addressed to 12 gentlemen such as I see before me in this Committee, and I think again that the evil is apparently the want of intelligence; but in such cases as I have referred to I must add other circumstances as well. I think that there is, in such cases, a sympathy for the crime and the criminal.

4235. *Chairman.*] The case which you refer to was tried by a jury under the old Act, was it not?—It does not matter much, as far as sympathy is concerned, whether it was or not.

4236. I mean that the verdict given in that case was not a result of the present Act?—Perhaps not; I have already said distinctly that there were evils of this nature to be cured before this Act was passed. In the cases that are brought before us in the Court of Queen's Bench we see them. In motions to change the place of trial, in criminal cases and in bail motions, we have questions coming before us constantly that prove to us the difficulty of obtaining convictions, particularly in cases of the description to which I refer, which would include a Ribbon case in the county, or a case arising out of a confederacy in a city, or a plan to put out of the way a bailiff, or an agent, or a thing of that kind; and you will find that if the case depends upon circumstantial evidence, although it may be of a very strong character, the difficulty of getting a verdict is almost insuperable.

4237. I think you also stated that the City special jurors were more satisfactory than the county ones?—Yes, I have no complaint to make about them at all; I think they are very good. I should mention to the Committee about the city and county of Dublin, that the right to nominate or to recommend the sheriff for the city and county, belongs to the individual who fills my office; he has that privilege, if it be one, of recommending the sheriffs for appointment by the Crown. I have had, I think, very respectable men as high sheriffs; I tried to have men that every one would respect. My last high sheriff was Mr. Darcy, who I believe is a Member of Parliament. He and his sub-sheriff, under the old system, gave me very good juries; I mean juries that did their business well. What you look to is to get the business of the county done, and done satisfactorily, and the sheriffs gave me very good juries. The gentleman who succeeded Mr. Darcy is, I believe, of opposite opinions; but if he had an opportunity, I am satisfied that he would give me just as good juries as the sheriff who preceded him. A former high sheriff of the city informed me (and I told him that he was only doing his duty) that he examined the book himself, and that he looked carefully at the names and the fitness of the jurors who were returned, and I have a confident opinion that if the high sheriff of every county would really do his duty, and not leave it to

Right Hon. *J. Whiteside.*

12 June 1873.

to be performed by the sub-sheriff, but would examine the book with the knowledge that he has of the country in which he lives, and see that fit and competent jurors were returned, that duty would be faithfully performed, because if you mean to trust anybody (it may be difficult to know who you would trust in Ireland with any discretion in this matter), but if you do trust anybody, I cannot conceive that there is any one so fit to be trusted as the high sheriff, who is a gentleman independent of the Crown, or ought to be so, and of the people; and if there were high treason trials to-morrow in Devonshire, I know of no one so fit to be trusted with the selection of the jury as the noble Lord whom I see in the chair; but I think if that power is given, and there was a great dispute about it long ago whether it ought or ought not, I think the high sheriff should be bound to sign on the panel a declaration that he has read the panel, and compared it with the jurors' book, and to certify that it is impartially chosen, in accordance with the Act of Parliament, as he verily believes.

4238. Just to return for a moment to the Dublin juries; has the special jury panel, prepared under the provisions of this Act, given you satisfactory juries?—Perfectly so. The jury differed from me in a case of the running down of a ship, but I thought afterwards that they were right. The ship that took out Lord Dufferin ran down a brig in Loch Foyle. I thought, perhaps, that the steamer ought to suffer, but a number of gentlemen were on the jury whom I had not seen before, some of whom happened to be acquainted with yachting, and with the sailing rules. They put questions, and conducted themselves like men of ability, and found a verdict for the steam packet company (which is not very usual) charged with running down a brig in daylight in Loch Foyle. I noticed that many of their questions were practical, and that their manner and behaviour were good. At present it is right that you should understand, if you are alluding to civil cases, that when we are on circuit trying a civil case under the present system, if we get two or three good jurymen we are fortunate. You look to that one or two sensible men, and you point his or their attention to the facts, and to the law of the case. In the instances I refer to, the one or two appeared to lead the other 10 or 11, who were quite puzzled-looking innocent farmers, who did not seem to know much about the affair. They asked no questions, whereas the intelligent jurors did; and I think that the best chance we have in commercial cases in the country is the chance of getting one or two town jurors or merchants, and so on, who will lead the others, and I think they are willing to be led.

4239. Did you happen to hear how the jury in the late case of O'Keeffe and Cullen was composed, as to the proportion of Roman Catholics and Protestants?—I am not sure that I know correctly, and therefore I cannot answer that question positively.

4240. I have been told that it was composed of five Protestants and seven Roman Catholics?—I should have thought that there were fewer Protestants, but I did not ask the question. When the jurors had given their verdict, I was addressed by some of them, and they asked me whether I could give them any relief under the circumstances in which they were placed. I think it was Mr. Turbit who applied to me (there were two or three Turbits under this alphabetical system upon the jury), and he is a very intelligent gentleman; he is a merchant, and a respectable man. He said to me, "Is this fair, that two or three of the firm are summoned at once; here I have been eight days, and as there is a Committee sitting to inquire into this jury system, would you not mention our grievances, and would you not also say that we think it very unfair, as we understand the rule in England is that the special jurors are paid something for every day that they attend; here, at the end of 10 or 12 days, a special juryman gets one guinea only." Another juryman addressed me, and said, "There are other evils, my Lord, to be rectified; a juryman," he said, "ought to have sense," and I think he said, "intelligence for the office." A third juryman said that they were deceived by the operation of the late Act. I think he said that they were called more frequently than it was expected they would be under the new Act. So I turned round to the sub sheriff, and said, "After the long and fatiguing service of these gentlemen, I do not think that you ought to call them again." He immediately protested to me that that could not be; "I beg to inform your Lordship," replied the sheriff, "that I have gone through the book already, and notwithstanding the theory of the two years, I shall have to summon all these gentlemen soon again." How that is I am not able to say, and I therefore could not get the wearied jurors even a little indulgence; but I promised to represent their grievances to the Committee, and I do so accordingly, the grievance being, I think, practically one for mercantile men, that it is a hard case to summon at one time all the partners or members of a firm. And I must say that the practice in England as to the remuneration of a jury ought to be the practice in Ireland; and that whatever is the general law in England as to the formation of juries should be the general law in Ireland.

4241. That case might have come on in the previous term, might it not, but was it not postponed for a good reason?—Yes, a principal witness, it was stated, of the cardinal was ill, and on his application I postponed it twice.

4242. It has been stated that if the case had come on in the previous term, it would have have been tried by a jury selected from a panel consisting of 47 Protestants, and only one Roman Catholic; are you aware whether that would have been the case?—I have not the least notion how that would be.

4243. Supposing that were the fact, would you not consider it very greatly to be regretted?—Not at all; I would try the case; I think that Catholic jurors give excellent verdicts, and I think that Protestant juries give very good verdicts. When they differed, as they did in some of these prosecutions, with regard to undue influence, I have a strong conviction that they differed sincerely.

4244. If under the old Act the sheriff or the sub-sheriff selected a panel which would have to try such a case as that of O'Keeffe and Cullen, consisting, in the town of Dublin, of 47 Protestants, and only one Roman Catholic, would not you consider that to be regretted?—If he did it designedly you are quite right, but if the names were on the book, whether they were Quakers or Episcopalians, or Presbyterians, there is no principle in the law that justifies anybody in inquiring into the religion of a juror, but I quite

I quite agree with you that if with the knowledge of the case, and the peculiarities of the case, the sheriff did it for the purpose of defeating justice, and if he thought that it would accomplish that object, then I think the law ought to quash the panel decidedly.

4245. That has not been proved before the Committee; but supposing that were the case, was it not conduct that could hardly have been by accident?—I do not know. There is a special jurors' book for the City of Dublin, and you must take the jurors out of the book; but what are the component parts of the sheriff's book I am unable to explain to you.

4246. It could hardly have been in the proproportion of 47 to 1?—I do not know how the names are upon the special jurors' book for the city. I have never asked the question, and have never been informed. Perhaps some gentleman in the Committee knows whether the Roman Catholic jurors are in a majority or a minority, but I wish to state distinctly that I would trust equally Mr. Darcy, Mr. Kinahan, the next sheriff, Mr. Martin, the eminent merchant, whom I named myself. I believe that they have their different opinions, but I would trust any one of them to return a panel, and I do believe that he would return it honestly if he had the power of selecting; that is my observation of their conduct, at least of such of them as I have seen.

4247. I understand your Lordship to be of opinion, that the present Act requires considerable amendment?—Yes, I do. May I make an observation with reference to what you have just asked me about the sheriff and his authority, if he was to have any. I think the way in which Sir John Young proposed to deal with that was a very judicious way, in leaving to the sheriff, not the selection, but the formation of the panel, he, Sir John, included in the clause of his Bill that the sheriff should return fit and competent persons, and I believe that he required also that the sheriff should do what I understand the Committee have judiciously approved of, that is, that he should go substantially through the jurors' book, and that is my view, that the sheriff should be required to go substantially through the jurors' book, and that he should certify that his panel was impartially constructed from names in the book, and that he should be at liberty not to call unfit persons who may appear upon the ratebook, and whom you never can get excluded from the jurors' panel, except by some such authority.

4248. That would be a considerable alteration of the old practice; it was not in any way incumbent upon him to go substantially or otherwise through the book?—No; it would, however, be a great improvement, because, as has been rightly observed, either in evidence or by a Member of the Committee, that the labour is severe enough, and that it should be cast over as large a number of jurymen as would be competent to perform the duty. If every juror named in the book were like every gentleman on this Committee, educated and intelligent, then the principle of the present Act would be quite right; but, as it is not so, and as you have not the material, you must in some way deal with the facts as they are; and I do not know anybody so safe to be trusted, in a modified way, as the sheriff.

4249. But you would direct the sheriff to go through the book as well as he could?—I would require him to do so. If Sir John Young's Bill of 1854 is here you will find that that is his proposal.

4250. Mr. *Bruen.*] That Bill contains a direction that the Judges of Assize shall issue a precept to the respective sheriffs of such counties, cities, and so on, "requiring them to summon for the trial of all issues, whether civil or criminal, which may come on for trial at the assizes or general sessions of the peace, or other sittings, a sufficient number of the most competent persons named in the jurors' book so to be delivered by the clerk of the peace, selecting, so far as may be practicable, having regard to their competency, the names of such jurors as shall not have been summoned, and attended as such at the last preceding assizes or sessions"?—That seems very sensible and practical.

4251. *Chairman.*] Your Lordship advocates that partly, as I understand, on the ground of the severity of the labour which is cast upon the juries?—Yes, partly.

4252. And partly also on account of the importance of securing the impartiality of juries?—Yes; I should add to that that my opinion from observation is that no system of revision that you can contrive will prevent persons being on the jurors' book who ought not to be jurors, because even a returned convict, if he recovers himself, and is rated sufficiently, will appear; publicans will appear there, and pawnbrokers will appear there. My principal tipstaff is a special juror of the city at this moment I have no doubt. I agree that it is disagreeable to legislate nominally against persons of that class, but if your Lordship was high sheriff, and you had to do that duty in the manner that Sir John Young points out, you would, with the aid of your sub-sheriff, say, Do not summon such and such persons; and, furthermore, I think it not improbable that you would say, Such a person, I believe, though he is on that panel, has been suspected of Fenianism, or he has been connected with a confederacy of an unlawful character in the country, and he ought not to be summoned; and therefore you would omit him. But no system of revision that you can contrive will avert that evil, which is an evil existing in the present system, and which existed in the former system just as much, and which has been met, or limited to a certain extent, by the authority of the Crown Solicitor, or that which he exercises, of bidding jurymen to stand by. Perhaps the Committee will allow me to mention a thing which occurred when I was Attorney General. If I remember rightly there was a case of a threatening letter, threatening the late Duke of Leinster, or some man of that character, in Kildare. The Crown Solicitor waited on me (and I believe he is still the Crown Solicitor, Mr. Seed), with a book under his arm, and the late Mr. Berwick with him, who was Crown prosecutor on the circuit. They came to me (I was very much engaged at the time) to ask for authority to do a certain thing; I requested them to tell me what it was, and to do it as briefly as possible, but the Crown Solicitor opened the book containing a long list of regulations made by different Attorney Generals, and I said I had not time to go through that book, but that if he would tell me what he wanted, I would answer his question. He said, "We have been so fortunate as to get the manuscript of the threatening notice (the threatening notice was printed at a shabby

Right Hon. J. Whiteside.

12 June 1873.

shabby printer's office in Dublin); we have clear proof of the handwriting of this person, and he is a respectable person, apparently, in Kildare. If we have not authority to desire certain jurors as they may come up, to stand aside, this man, who is clearly guilty, will, in all probability, be acquitted, and what we want from you is this authority." I believe that these gentlemen were apprehensive that some question would be asked in the House of Commons upon the subject, and they wanted me to give them authority to set aside such persons if they should appear as jurymen. I said, "I can only tell you shortly, that anybody who appears as a juryman, that you conscientiously believe will not do his duty between the Crown and the prisoner, you have my authority to set him aside, and I will defend the act for you in the House of Commons, if it should, as you anticipate, be brought before the House." Mr. Seed accordingly, I believe not unfairly, exercised his right of putting aside some jurors; the prisoner was tried before my Brother Monahan, and was convicted, and sentenced to seven years' penal servitude; we did not hear anything more of threatening notices in Kildare for a long time afterwards, and unless that course were pursued in such cases it is, in my opinion, quite idle to expect a verdict; you get a difference of opinion the first time, and a difference of opinion the second time, and then, in many very serious cases, there will ensue a discharge of the prisoner.

4253. I believe that when you were Attorney General you introduced one or two Bills into the House of Commons upon this subject?—Yes; I daresay if you have looked at the book in the Irish Office for the year 1852, you will have seen that there was a Crime and Outrages Committee appointed; that there were very many dreadful crimes committed in different parts of the country, I believe chiefly in Louth and Armagh. There was a Resolution passed by the Committee, and then, as the Government of the day did not do anything, I attempted, with the present Sir Joseph Napier, to carry a Jury Bill. When we were preparing the Bill I looked about for some mode of revision, but I did not know of any mode of revision that I could fasten upon, except the revision by the chairman of the list of the electors for each country town, for at that time the electoral list was fought out very keenly before the chairman by the two great parties in the State. I took that list that he had revised, and endeavoured to construct a jury system upon it, but I was afterwards told in debate, either by Mr. Justice Keogh or by Mr. Justice Fitzgerald, if I mistake not, that the effect of that revision was to weed out the rate book by nearly five-sixths. I think they said that it reduced it to one-sixth of the names appearing upon the rate book. In that Bill I proposed the plan of taking the names as they stood in that revised list.

4254. You adopted the principle of alphabetical selection of the panel from the jury book?—Yes, and that was vehemently opposed, so that I dropped it. I think Mr. Justice Fitzgerald opposed it, and certainly Mr. Justice Keogh, and I believe Sir John Young, who was Chief Secretary at the time, said, "I will deal with the subject." He brought in, I think, while he was Chief Secretary, his Bill of 1854, and he said and argued that the right of forming the panel, you may call it selection, ought to be certainly reposed in the high sheriff, and then I believe we dropped the Bills altogether, and nothing was done. But I now, from my experience, think that the alphabetical arrangement is altogether erroneous.

4255. And you are of opinion that however as list may be revised it will be necessary to give to some one a limited power, not of selection but of rejection?—A modified power of framing the panel; I would confer upon the person that you may trust ultimately with the formation of the panel, having first revised your jury book with the utmost care that you can apply to it, a modified authority which must be lodged in somebody, in returning the panel, at the same time requiring him to go substantially through the jurors' book. I was asked whether I had any remedies to suggest; I may observe since I came into the room I heard a witness speaking of serving jurymen by letter. Yesterday I was deciding whether or not I should fine a juror for non-attendance. I believe the fine was 50 *l.* in the county of Dublin. He made out his case to this effect: "I never got the letter; and, in order to satisfy you upon that point, I say it was sent back from the Dead Letter Office as a returned letter;" a declaration in lieu of an affidavit accompanied it in which this person declared that he lived at such a place; that the post office was three or four miles beyond his residence; that he was not in the habit of going for letters; and that he never got it; he positively affirmed that. I sent for the sub-sheriff, and I put this paper into his hand and asked him for his report upon it. He said that he took the address from the Directory, but the fact was clear that the man never got the letter, and it was equally clear to me that men in that class are not likely, having no commercial affairs or business, to send for the letters to the post office. And having looked into the case, and considering it an honest case, I remitted the fine. I am afraid if you summon men in the country at a distance from the local post office they will all escape, for they would not send for letters if they suspected there was a letter summoning them on the jury; they would rather leave it there. So far as that matter is concerned it requires a little attention. With regard to the remedies that I have noted down, the first I do not know whether it would be called a remedy or a principle, but I am strongly of opinion that the general law, whatever it may be decided by Parliament to be with regard to the jury system of England, should be the same as in Ireland. I am next of opinion that there should be a considerable increase in the rating qualification of jurors. I also think that you should include the five classes of voters who are specified in the 3 & 4 Vict. c. 69. I would include 50 *l.* and 20 *l.* freeholders, and 50 *l.* and 20 *l.* rent-charges, and 20 *l.* leaseholders. If there be a power of selection preserved, and if that is the way in which the discretion is expressed and reserved to the high sheriff in England, I think it would be mischievous to have a different principle applied to Ireland. I heard your Lordship ask a question of a former witness, about deaf people. I have the pleasure of having deaf people constantly appearing before me. At Clonmel I had one or two men who said that they were deaf; I tried speaking to them in a moderate tone of voice and one heard me very well, so that I secured him; but deaf people are put on the panel, and blind people, and sick people, and dying people, and dead people. I heard a witness here to-day speak of the revision before the

the assistant barrister, I am sure that he spoke sincerely; but, as the matter now stands, as far as I can discover, unless the chairman regularly inquires into the subject, it would be perfectly futile; for instance, take the assistant barrister in Cork, sitting in that town with ever so many thousand names before him; the list is read out, and it is all over in a couple of hours; the chairman is told that the names are right and he signs the book. Those deaf people, those incompetent persons, and those blind persons and publicans are all on the panel, and when the judge is about to get a jury he is constantly delayed by all sorts of excuses and it may be pretences, which might have been inquired into if there was any real revision, which there is not.

4256. I think a witness stated to-day that when the operation of the Act was more generally known a large number of jurors who were not qualified under the Act, would themselves ask to be excused from the inconvenience of attending as jurors; does your Lordship agree in that opinion?—I have been asked in this way very recently at Clonmel; a juryman was called, and he said, "I am unable to read or write;" and I looked at him, and then said that it was a creditable thing for him to say so. I was satisfied from his appearance that it was true, and I excused him; but I do not think that those persons should be put on the list at all. I think that the list should be carefully revised in some way or other, with the assistance of officials and witnesses who would take the trouble to get or give the evidence, which the overseers never do.

4257. What was suggested by the witness, I think, was that serving as a juror was not a privilege which was much coveted; but that when the effect of the Act is better understood the jurors would come forward to the Revision Court and ask to be excused?—That is quite possible; but I should receive their evidence with some little suspicion. I would rather have more impartial evidence; because we have found all sorts of excuses often made. You cannot imagine the number of certificates of doctors that I get when a case such as O'Keeffe and Cullen is coming on, or other cases of the like character. Latterly we refuse to accept them unless verified by affidavit. From the observations that have been made here, the judges will be more strict, and if you will be good enough to put into the Act, if you think fit to do that, a moderate fine is to be imposed upon every juror who does not attend without reference to the judges at all (giving them the power, if you choose, to modify the fine), I think it would do good. But it struck me that if it appeared wise in the judgment of the Committee, you might do something of this kind; you might train those jurymen who are the lowest on the rate book by obliging them to attend in the division of their county at the Quarter Sessions. Serious crimes are not investigated there, and there are lesser matters even of a civil kind in which they might be summoned as jurymen, and in that way they might become fitted to become jurymen at the assizes. But you cannot imagine the erroneous notions entertained upon the difference between civil and criminal cases. Criminal cases sometimes become the most involved, and the most difficult, and most critical, of all inquiries, and you have got by a perversion of reason the most ill-educated men to try such cases. Their superiors in position and in education, think it in Ireland a great indignity to be forced to sit upon criminal cases; whereas I would force them to sit there if I could.

4258. Is there any other suggestion that you would wish to make?—I have mentioned the regular illiterate persons, and returned convicts, and domestics, and clerks, all of whom ought, I think, to be excluded, and I have explained to the Committee what I mean by a modified discretion in the sheriff, and I rest my opinion upon the ground that the sheriffs are recommended by the judges, that they are independent gentlemen of the country, whom I think it is well to associate with the administration of justice, and that in my opinion they perform their duties faithfully; but I believe they have been in the habit of reposing too much upon their sub-sheriffs. That, I think, should be checked. I think that the revision of the list at the Petty Sessions, with an appeal to the chairman, would be a thing perfectly feasible, because it is a small area, and the magistrates attending the district would be likely to know the persons residing within the area, and you could thoroughly revise the list in that way. I think that there must be a certain amount of discretion left to your officials, to your Crown solicitors, especially in cases that are tried of a particular kind, such a case as we had yesterday in the Crown Court. The question was whether the conviction was good or bad; but the case was of this nature; it was what we call a Ribbon case. A man waited upon the agent of Lord Leitrim, and said, "I wish to speak with you in a friendly manner. I have no particular enmity to you; but," taking out a revolver, and laying it beside him on the bed, he said, "I have been employed to shoot you." Then he took out a purse, and jerked it in his hand. "This is not silver, it is gold," said the visitor, "and I now tell you that I do not want to shoot you. I do not wish it myself; but if you serve any more ejectment processes for Lord Leitrim you will certainly be shot, and only that your wife was with you as you were coming on last Sunday night, you would have been shot; so be advised by me, and do not meddle with these things any more, for if you do, you will be a dead man." Then he walked out and fired two shots in the daylight. The question before the Court was, whether he was rightly convicted upon a question reserved by Baron Deasy under the Whiteboy Act. Those are the cases that I allude to when I say that there are a certain class of cases in which you must allow your officials a reasonable discretion to set aside jurymen. For instance, in that very case, the man said that he was employed by a body of tenants to do the thing, and it would be a most absurd arrangement to put on the panel jurymen living near the scene of a transaction of that kind. I say that in that and all other Ribbon or agrarian outrages, there ought to be, and must be, a discretion left with your officials, in order that your panel may be composed of men who have no fear, and who are in a better position of life; if they be so, it does not much matter what district of the country they come from. That is what I mean by saying that you must leave a certain discretion in a certain class of cases, from the unfortunate fact, that there is a sympathy in such cases with the accused.

4259. Colonel *Wilson Patten*.] You stated just now that a case had failed from one juryman holding out against the rest, and that was a pawnbroker?—So they told me.

Right Hon. J. Whiteside.

12 June 1873.

4260. Is there anything in the business of a pawnbroker in Ireland which would disqualify a man from serving on a jury?—Not to disqualify him in point of law; but that he is supported mainly by the people, and dependent upon them, just as a publican is.

4261. You are in favour of publicans being excluded?—Yes.

4262. But you would not recommend the exclusion of pawnbrokers?—No; but I would leave a discretion with the official of the Crown in such a case to say, "Stand by; I am quite sure that such a man ought not to be on such a jury." It is an awkward thing, legislating against classes of individuals; but in a case where a man who depends entirely on the people is summoned on a trial of that sort, it would be much better to tell him to stand by.

4263. Are the class of pawnbrokers a respectable class in Ireland?—Yes; I would not wish to suggest that they should be disqualified.

4264. What is the discretion which you think that the judge or the chairman should have with regard to exempting jurymen from serving?—I should never dream of exercising, and I would respectfully ask the Committee never to give, any such authority to a judge as to exclude any one for his political opinions, and if I had such authority, I do not think that I would ever exercise it. The judges have no authority except in the case of sickness or infirmity at present. A man says he is deaf or blind, and if he really is so, and a surgeon comes up and gives a satisfactory affidavit or affirmation that if that gentleman sat on a jury for a day or two he might lose his life, we would excuse such a person.

4265. Several instances have been brought before this Committee in which great hardship has been done to parties from being placed in the jurors' list in different courts in Dublin and in other places; would you give no discretion to the judge when he hears of a case of great hardship, to enable him to exempt a man from serving on the jury?—We often hear of those things. A juryman says, I was yesterday in the Probate Court, and I was the day before in another court; but we cannot therefore excuse him, for without him we may not be able to get a jury. That is our difficulty very often, but when we have got a good, a working jury, composed of the very men who have served in the way which you have described, you would be surprised to see how promptly they come to the desired conclusion. The very fact of their serving so frequently, although it is very troublesome to them, and although it is very unfair to give them so much work to do, makes them so familiar with their duty that they do it very well.

4266. In a case of this kind which has been mentioned before this Committee, where three individuals of a firm have been summoned on the jury list at the same time, and the business of the firm has been materially interfered with in consequence, would it not be advisable that some one should have the discretion of exempting those parties?—I think it might not be unfair to put it into the Act of Parliament that the sheriff should not summon in such a case all the members of the jurors; the old sheriff would not do it; I do not think he would summon three gentlemen of the name of Turbit: I am quite certain he would not. He would say this is a very great hardship on the members of this firm, and I will not do it, I will summon only one; I think that somehow or other that ought to be prevented.

4267. You would give some remedy in the case of three brothers being upon the same jury?—Yes, I think so; I have heard the complaint often made, and it is a very just complaint.

4268. Dr. *Ball*.] As I understand, your Lordship advocates uniformity in the provisions of the law, not of course as to qualification, but in other respects for England and Ireland in respect of the jury system?—Unquestionably.

4269. Generally you would advocate that?—Certainly, and for this reason, that if it is a bad law it is much more likely to be corrected if it applied to England, than if it only extended to Ireland.

4270. You would extend it, I take it, also to a litigated or doubtful question in which there is a great difference of opinion, that the majority of the jury or a proportion of the jury should be capable of giving a verdict?—Certainly.

4271. Whatever is done for England you would agree to for Ireland?—Yes, but I do not advocate any unnecessary departure from the present system in that respect; that is all.

4272. You mentioned that Mr. Turbit complained of more than one of the firm being taken from the business of the firm on a particular day for that trial, and kept there for 10 days?—He did.

4273. Does not it occur to your Lordship that there is another objection to a matter of that kind being possible as regards mercantile cases, that three persons of the same firm, all intimately connected and having the same class of interest, should be on the same jury to decide an important mercantile case?—That is a very just observation, and I think it is an evil which should be avoided or remedied.

4274. A judge occasionally at a Nisi Prius trial, if counsel objects to a person, may say, why you may as well not press this, but is it not the fact that in a criminal trial you cannot do that?—I cannot do that.

4275. The Crown solicitor must put him aside or the attorney for the prisoner must put him aside?—Yes; I do decide very strictly the question of challenge; the right of challenging must be exercised according to strict law in a criminal trial; you have no right to depart from that one iota.

4276. You mentioned a case of circumstantial evidence which struck me as one of very nearly direct evidence; but suppose a case requiring a very much more critical appreciation of facts being requisite, a case of circumstantial evidence say, in which the aggregate occurrences out of which you were to infer guilt, occupied four, five, or six days in evidence, is it not your opinion that without any perverseness an uneducated juror would fail in capacity to deal with such a case?—It is decidedly my opinion; I have heard from a brother judge that in an important trial in Ireland, which was entirely dependent upon circumstantial evidence, after he had charged for a day and a half, and he had been eight days engaged in listening to circumstantial evidence, the jury came out and put the question formally to him: "Could a man be convicted by the law of the country upon circumstantial evidence"; so that they had not caught up the very object of their inquiry, and yet I believe they were innocent men.

4277. Mr. *Bruen*.] Under the old law your Lordship

Right Hon. *J. Whiteside.*

14 June 1873.

Lordship had a great many opportunities of observation of the way in which the sheriffs performed their duty in summoning jurors on the panels; had you any occasion to find fault with the sheriffs, or had you observed that they failed in their duty, or acted partially in the formation of those panels?—No; I have gone the circuit in the county which you represent, several times, but I did not observe any misconduct or inattention to their duties, or any injustice; they were very attentive and respectable men.

4278. Have any cases of challenges to the array on account of the unindifference of the sheriff come before you?—Never. I have had challenges of course. We generally begin the trial with challenges, but not to the array of the sheriffs.

4279. There has been a suggestion made before this Committee, that there should be a right given to the Crown or to the prisoner to claim a special jury to try the case; what is your opinion upon that proposition?—I am not quite so sure about that; the idea of a prisoner wishing to be tried by a special jury is such a thing as never could by possibility occur. I am apprehensive that if the Crown had the power of applying for special juries to try prisoners, the prisoners, or their friends, might say that they had not had fair play shown them. Although it is remarkable that when a special commission is issued, the high sheriff thinks himself at liberty to begin with the first men in the county, and he puts them all at the head of the panel. It is not his clerk, but I understand the sheriff himself does so; he puts all the most respectable gentlemen at the head of the panel, but they will then be challenged as far as twenty of them are concerned at first. But then the panel is so constructed, and there are so many men of position and fortune upon it, that the challenges of the prisoner do not avail to prevent a very high class panel being constituted. That only occurs in the formation of a special commission. I went down on a special commission to try a man of the name of Barrett, at Galway; it was not a panel of that kind, and I thought I had but a very indifferent jury.

4280. There has also been a proposition made that there should be a certain proportion of special jurymen placed upon every jury; what is your opinion upon that proposition?—I cannot say that I am in favour of that, because the result would be that those special jurymen would lead the others by the nose, I should say, in the main; and then whether the other jurymen would be quite pleased or satisfied at having some three or four gentlemen of superior position with them, I do not know. I should mention, lest I be misunderstood about Galway, that as to the special juries in civil cases at Galway, there could not be better in any part of the world. I tried a case or two for a brother judge there by special juries, and they were gentlemen of the county, who tried the cases admirably.

4281. Under the old system of the jury laws, as a general rule, you had never, I think, to complain of a want of impartiality in the juries that came before you?—In civil cases I cannot say that I ever had; but I could not say the same in a certain class of criminal cases. I do not include in that the cases of difference of opinion, as in your county, where a respectable man was tried for sending a threatening notice, and the jury differed, and when I returned the next time to try him, though I doubled the bail, he had vanished. There were once three threatening notices only in Carlow, whereas there would be 50 in Westmeath, perhaps. I have had as many as 25 in King's County; but in Carlow two of the offenders were convicted, and the third disappeared; and there has not been, I believe, any there since, showing how much better the application of the ordinary law of the land is where you can rely upon it than any other contrivance.

4282. Mr. *Downing.*] You were asked with regard to the power that might be given to the judge, to excuse jurors from serving, and I understood you rather to disapprove of it?—Yes, for anything, except in the case of deafness, we will say, or blindness, or ill-health, or inability to attend, or a matter of that description, certainly.

4283. You would have the grounds upon which the judge should have the right to exempt jurors defined in the Act?—Yes; but leaving it as it is would be quite sufficient, because we never dream of inquiring into anybody's opinions, because it could not be done.

4284. And you would make that order in court?—Certainly.

4285. Are you aware that in the Bill which has now passed the third reading in the House of Commons, very large power is given to the judge?—I am sorry to hear it.

4286. It says, "Whereas doubts have been entertained as to the power of judges to excuse jurors from serving, and it is expedient to remove such doubts: It is hereby declared and enacted that it shall be lawful for the judge, if he shall so think fit, of any court before which any person may be summoned as a juror, to discharge such person from further attendance on such court, or to excuse such person from attendance for any period during the sittings of such court." Your Lordship sees that that is a general power given to the judge to excuse anyone he pleases, or when and where he pleases?—I was not aware of that. Perhaps it only means to legalise that which we do at present. I am not aware that it does go further than that.

4287. I will read to your Lordship an answer of Mr. Robinson, whom your Lordship knows, the Chairman of Cavan, upon that point, at Question No. 3893, where he says, "I think that this enables the Judge for any reason to excuse a juror, or for no reason; I think it gives him absolute power to do what he likes;" do you agree with that?—Upon that, I would just make an observation. When discretion is given to a judge, I would understand it to be judicial discretion, quite contradistinguished from a vague arbitrary exercise of power. But I quite agree that if this is meant to apply to political opinions, it is a power that I for one would never exercise. "If he shall so think fit, to discharge such person from further attendance on such court." That might mean this: that, supposing a man were summoned who had been convicted, we will say as a Fenian, or something of that sort, although he had got upon the panel, yet the judge in that case, if it was brought under his notice, might discharge him. I would also say, that if it means that, supposing one of our own attendants was summoned as a juryman (which might happen in this unfortunate state of things, as these men are very respectable, and have houses), if it applies to such a case as that for a temporary purpose, then I could understand

Right Hon. J. Whiteside.

12 June 1873.

understand it, and we might delicately say to him, "You are not wanted." But if it means to exclude anybody on the score of his political opinions, and that that is to be done by the judges sitting alone, I should say that it was in principle inadmissible. The officials of the Crown in criminal cases have information, and they can exercise that right which ought to be given them of challenging or setting aside jurors. They are the officers to whom this clause might be applied; but I do not think that that power should be bestowed upon the judge. I understand that clause to point to this state of things that many men, as a fact, are on the book at this moment who ought not to be there, and until that abuse is corrected, looking about, I presume, for some impartial person to whom the power might be entrusted of desiring such persons to stand by, it was through respect for the bench confided to the judges on the part of the framers of the Bill.

4288. Dr. *Ball.*] Would you not go the length of saying that, supposing the case of a man becoming disqualified for discharging his duty by drinking, the judge should have power of saying to the sheriff, "Do not return that man again"?—I think I should have such power as I exercised in that instance to which I have referred, in a criminal case, and as I might do if I had seen a juryman fall down in an epileptic fit. I have a right to deal with that case, and empanel a new jury, and I should have power to put such juror off the panel. To the extent to which you put it, it would be a very reasonable thing, but if it means vaguely the discretion of a judge to inquire into the opinions of jurors, then it would be, I think, a power that the judges would not wish to assume or exercise.

4289. Mr. *Downing.*] With regard to those parties who you were under the impression were at this moment upon the special jury panel, such as a man who you were informed was a carter to the sheriff's uncle, or cabman who by his industry got into position, if those were really intelligent men, you would not object to them because they happened to succeed in the world?—A man may have capacities to judge of the qualities of a cow or a horse, and yet if you put him into a jury box to try a difficult and complicated commercial case, or to try one of those important cases that I have referred to, his intelligence fails; his ideas are limited, his experience is narrow and confined to his own sphere, and he would not have the qualities that would constitute him a proper juryman to decide upon property, or upon a commercial case. What could be more absurd than to place before such a man ancient documents, muniments, and patents, as evidence to establish the right to a fishery, or anything of that kind; he has never seen such things before, and he is puzzled, and when counsel begin to reason upon them, he is entirely astray as to the effect and meaning of the documents, and he fails to understand the arguments, not having that intelligence which I think be ought to have.

4290. Do you think that you can ever have a jury on ordinary occasions in which you will not have one or two men who lack that intelligence which you would wish to see them all have?—That is true; but I think that in these cases rather the majority were in that position. In Wicklow I thought they were very amiable, innocent looking men; but one or two clever men did the whole business.

4291. You were counsel in the great Mount Garrett case, were you not?—Yes.

4292. We have had it stated here on evidence that upon that jury, which I believe settled the title of the estates, there was a man upon the jury who came into court with his breast open, and red from the sun; have you any recollection of that case?—I cannot remember the colour of his complexion exactly at this distance of time; but there were two trials, and I believe, at the first trial, we succeeded for the brother. The second time the case was tried the jury reversed that decision, and that decision was upheld by the House of Lords.

4293. With regard to the man who you said got drunk at Clonmel, did I understand you to say that that was on the second day of the trial?—It was; but he had provided himself with a bottle of whisky, which he brought into the jury box with him. I guarded the jury particularly, because I, as you perhaps know, swear the bailiffs before I leave the bench, and they are put on guard over the jury, to take care that they shall not get any intoxicating drink, and they are watched very closely. I never saw such a thing occur before. The man did not get the whisky from the sheriff, as I mentioned to the Committee. Dr. Hemphill swore that he found the bottle concealed by the juror, and put it to his nose, and discovered that it was not medicine, but whisky.

4294. You also said that, in your experience, you had known many cases of miscarriage of justice before the passing of this Act?—Yes, certainly; I mean in a certain class of cases.

4295. When at the bar, I believe you had one of the largest practices, and that you were most successful in criminal cases yourself?—Cases of a certain kind.

4296. Very important cases, were they not?—For instance, in high treason I did defend a great many; but I remember Mr. Smith O'Brien's case, and I remember that the jury were all the first gentlemen of the county, whom the high sheriff, Mr. Pennefather, returned under the system of the grand panel, they were gentlemen who felt for him, which might be seen in that recommendation which they gave for mercy; I have no doubt that they found the verdict that they thought right; but you must observe in some of those high treason cases, the juries somehow or other are not of that low class, because the sheriff, as I have observed before, thinks himself entitled to return what we call the grand panel of the county, and then 20 challenges is a small matter.

4297. I think if I am not mistaken, you attended special in the north of Ireland?—Very frequently.

4298. I think I remember that you defended a man of the name of Sam Gray?—I did, several times.

4299. He was tried, was he not, for murder?—Yes, he was; and nothing could furnish a more striking illustration of the jury law than that case, and your question reminds me of this circumstance; he was acquitted of the murder, but he was afterwards arrested and tried for firing at a person whom be was accused of having fired at and missed on the same occasion. The same facts, therefore, were investigated again, and the jury differed; on a third trial a juryman fell down in a fit; a fourth trial took place, for the Government were properly anxious, although

it

Right Hon. *J. Whiteside.*

12 June 1873.

it was a very unusual attempt, to bring him, if possible, to justice. But what did they do then, showing the difference between the juries of one class and another? They brought the case by *certiorari* into the Queen's Bench, and they sent it down to be tried at Monaghan by the jury that try civil cases, namely, by the gentry of the county. The result that I feared happened. There was a conviction. The jury of gentry who were not influenced by Mr. Gray's party predelictions, found him guilty on that fifth occasion; and the only chance that we had in defending him, was this: that the Attorney General was so far misled as to refuse the right to challenge, and we put in a challenge to the array (he was not tried for his life then); that was overruled in Ireland, but it came to the House of Lords, and the House of Lords affirmed our objection and reversed the verdict. Mr. Gray, I believe, died in his bed, having been five times tried.

4300. I was alluding to another case in which you defended him, in which he was tried for the murder of a man named Murphy, in 1836?—But the jury of gentlemen, you observe, convicted him, and the common jury either differed or acquitted him. That is just the way that that matter stands.

4301. He was acquitted in this case of Murphy's, was he not?—He was.

4302. Do you remember that there were four witnesses examined in that case who identified him as the man who fired the shot?—It must have occurred 30 years ago. It is quite certain that a man whose name I do not remember, and who was not shot, did identify him as being the man who fired it. Murphy, I think, was the name of the schoolmaster. It arose out of a will that disinherited his family.

4303. You have already given your opinion, I think, with regard to the alphabetical order?—I am against it entirely. I think that it is an inconvenient and embarrassing thing.

4304. There was another Bill which you brought in in 1858, which had the alphabetical order, I think?—But none of those Bills ever passed. The Government said that they would bring in a Bill, and mine was adopted.

4305. The qualification in that Bill which you brought in was 30 *l.*, and the Committee reduced it to 20 *l.*, did they not?—That was against my opinion. We had a 30 *l.* rating for common jurymen, and I think 60 *l.* for special jurymen; "a proportionate number alphabetically" is what it is in the Bill you produce, and you see that that makes a great difference, because there are some letters in which there are not many names, and if you exhausted those names you would then have men of all one class perhaps of opinions. This is "a proportionate number."

4306. The language of the Bill of 1858 is "as far as possible in regular alphabetical order"?—May I ask what became of it ultimately?

4307. It passed through Committee and was amended in Committee, but I could not trace it afterwards?—If you look at the debates, I remember being met by the opinions of several gentlemen, and I must honestly say that in listening to them I thought that they had a good deal to justify their opinions. I thought ultimately that there should be some discretion left somewhere in the formation of the jury panel, and that is certainly my opinion. I do not know that Sir John Young carried his Bill. I believe he did not.

4308. As far as I understand you, you would like to see the same law applied to Ireland as may be applied in England?—Certainly.

4309. Are you aware that the Attorney General has at this moment a notice of amendment on the paper to introduce the alphabetical rotation in the English Bill?—I am sorry to hear it.

4310. If it should be carried, would you wish to see it applied to Ireland?—Upon the principle which I have before mentioned, that I think when a Bill that is mischievous is extended to England as well as to Ireland, if once it is found to be inconvenient in England, it will be speedily rectified; we would then get it corrected in Ireland; but if you pass a Bill that is mischievous for Ireland, I am not so sure that it will be promptly remedied, and therefore, although I quite differ from the Attorney General in his alphabetical arrangement, yet, if it is adopted, I should almost, for the sake of the principle that I advocate, take it in Ireland; but I should very much regret it.

4311. Might I ask you whether, supposing that the ballot was applied in criminal cases as well as civil cases, that would not get rid altogether of the whole question of the alphabetical order?—I do not know that I would like the ballot in criminal cases, for the present system is a fair one; take a man on trial for his life. The officer reads slowly the whole panel, and the attorney for the prisoner, and the parties have an opportunity of considering the names, and they see the persons answering to those names, and then they have an opportunity of considering how they will exercise the right of challenge. You might do injustice to a prisoner if you called the jurors out by ballot, and bound him by the ballot as the names came out, if he is to be tried for his life by a juror so balloted for, suddenly, even if he has then a right to challenge, which right is the old law of the land, and very fair to the prisoner, and I do not see any reason to change it.

4312. I do not suppose for a moment that you are to alter the present system; I am supposing that the name is drawn from the ballot box, and as the juror is called, and the prisoner, or his counsel, or his solicitor, is asked in the same way to look upon him, and he would look upon him, and see if he had any objection to him?—I think that the old system is better; it is a direct and consistent course of proceeding, and if you have a fair jury, I would give the prisoner every benefit that the law confers upon him, and I would give him time to exercise his privilege of challenging.

4313. I will read to you a question and an answer, to show Mr. Justice Fitzgerald's opinion. At Question 3235 he was asked, "You would ballot for the jury from the panel, instead of calling them?" and his answer was, "I am entirely in favour of the ballot, both in civil and criminal cases"?—That is a very respectable opinion, but I incline to the old practice of calling over the names. It is of use both to the Crown and to the prisoner, for you find out then what the ballot will not tell you, namely, who you have got in court. If you put a number of cards into the ballot box, and you draw out a name, as you do in civil cases, it becomes of little importance who is drawn, but in criminal cases, particularly in serious cases, it is but right both for the Crown

Right Hon. J. *Whiteside.*

19 June 1873.

and the prisoner to know who you have in court as jurymen, and then having once called over the names and noted down the answers, they being present, you have an opportunity of observing and of exercising the challenge fairly.

4314. With regard to publicans, would you not draw a distinction between a man who had a respectable house, supposing he was a grocer who also had a spirit license, but did not sell spirits in the ordinary way, and an ordinary publican?—I do not think that he would be considered to be an ordinary publican.

4315. You would not exclude him?—No; I think there are a good many grocers who do sometimes sell spirits by retail, who are at the same time not like those country publicans in whose houses conspirators may assemble, and in which latter case it is as much for the benefit of the man himself that his exclusion takes place, as it is for the justice of the country.

4316. Although in answer to the honourable Member for Carlow, you stated that you had no reason either at the bar or from the bench to say that you were aware of any corruption on the part of any sheriff, yet I understand you to say that you thought the high sheriff generally left too much to the sub-sheriffs in the discharge of their duty?—So I have understood in the formation of the panel. I think that a great security for the country, both for the subject and for the crown, would be that the high sheriff in each county, particularly where he is resident, should examine the panel, and in the city these merchants, that I referred to, know all the people perfectly, and I would like to force them when sheriffs to do the work themselves of revising the panel, and to make them personally responsible for what they do, so that their fellow citizens should know that they had certified that the panel was fairly and impartially constructed. I do not see in the city of Dublin that we have any apprehension that these gentlemen whom I have named would not make a perfectly fair panel.

4317. We have had the sub-sheriff of Wexford, and he told us that for 17 years he was sub-sheriff, and the high sheriff never interfered one way or the other, and that he had the complete control of the panel?—Wexford is a very well circumstanced county, but at the same time I may make the observation that I think that the juries there might be improved. I tried a compensation case (respecting the new works that are going on) between the railway company and a proprietor through whose ground the railway went, taking it from him, and leading to the new harbour that they are constructing in that part of the county. In that case the engineers and people of that sort were examined, and it occurred to me that the jury might be improved. It was a Crown jury, I believe, as it is Crown juries that try all those compensation cases. I do not think that in this case they were quite up to the mark of understanding all the scientific evidence that was given.

4318. Have you known in your long experience that a dissentient juror has been very often right?—I cannot say that I have met with cases of that description; I have heard that there have been such cases. For instance, there is a gentleman, a minister of a state now abroad, Mr. Duffy, who was saved by a dissentient juryman. Of course one is very glad to find that it should have produced such a good result to the individual, but whether the eleven were right or wrong, or whether the dissentient juryman was right or not, I am not prepared to say. One has heard of such cases as you put, but I do not recollect having met with any one myself.

4319. I will just read to you Question 3236, which was put to Mr. Justice Fitzgerald: "Have you known cases where the minority were subsequently proved to be right?" And his answer is, "Yes;" and in one remarkable case with which all who are connected with law are perfectly familiar, the minority was one. It was a case which occurred when I was a junior barrister myself, and I recollect sitting by at the trial in Limerick when a young man was charged with murder. The evidence was apparently conclusive against him, and the jury retired after a long trial: they were locked up for the night, having announced in the early part of the evening that they were not likely to agree, or as the expression was, one man was standing out; they were locked up for the night, and finally they were discharged the next day, being unable to agree, and there was a great outcry against that one juror; I was present at the second trial of the prisoner, and it was as clearly proved as that we have sunlight now that the principal witness against him was the murderer, and the prisoner was perfectly innocent, and he was acquitted by a first-class jury in Limerick without turning round. On one or two occasions I have met with cases of that kind, and that is the reason why I would not, with my present views, accept the verdict of a majority in a capital case; I should mention that the dissentient juror in that case was afterwards a Member of the House of Commons, being no less than Mr. Stephen De Vere, who was the Member for Limerick?—All I can say is, that the prisoner was fortunate to have a man of superior intelligence on the jury; I did not say that I was not in favour of unanimity; I guarded myself against having any novelties in Ireland, as far as the general law is concerned, that are not adopted in England.

Mr. Frederick Hamilton, called in; and Examined.

Mr. F. Hamilton.

4320. (Mr. *Heron.*) You are a practising solicitor in Dublin, are you not?—I am.

4321. Have you brought over the panel of special jurors for the Court of Queen's Bench in the county of Dublin, Michaelmas Term 1872?—I have.

[*The same was delivered in, and is as follows:*]

County of Dublin, to wit.

Queen's Bench.—Special Jurors. Michaelmas Term, 1872.

Names of Special Jurors to try Issue, wherein Walter Trevor Stannus, Plaintiff, Francis Dalzell Finlay, Defendant.

1. Nicholas Wade Monserratt, 10, St. James-terrace, Clonskea, wine merchant.

2. George

2. George McMaster Brookville, Simmons Court-road, druggist.
3. Timothy O'Brien, Aylesbury House, Merrion, baker.
4. Andrew William Reid, 66, Pembroke-road, gentleman.
5. Henry Shaw, 1, Waterloo-road, flour merchant.
6. Robert William Smyth, 50, Morehampton-road, merchant.
7. Charles Uniacke Townsend, 10, Burlington-road, gentleman.
8. William Turner, Hammersmith Works, Pembroke-road, engineer and ironfounder.
9. Thomas Thouton, 12, St. James's-terrace, Clonskea, insurance agent.
10. Charles H. Wogan, 87, Pembroke-road, stationer.
11. Samuel Warren, Jun., 1, Abercorn-terrace, Sidney-parade, merchant.
12. Richard Wright, Ossory Lodge, Strand-road, merchant.
13. Samuel McComas, Dalkey, gentleman, J. P.
14. Andrew McCullagh, Brookville, wine merchant.
15. Andrew Todd, Jones'-road, merchant.
16. Evory Carmichael, Longford-terrace, gentleman.
17. Richard Seymour Guinness, Donnybrook, gentleman.
18. John Hayes Woodtown, Rathfarnham, gentleman.
19. Isaac Molone, 3, Palmerston-villas, merchant.
20. William Frederick Bewley, 36, Muckross-terrace, Bushfield-avenue, merchant.
21. George W. McQuestion, Ashbrooke, Sallymount-avenue, Esquire.
22. Thomas Sibthorpe, 46, Upper Leeson-street, Esquire.
23. David Drummond, Drumfeller, Orwell-road, gardener.
24. John Hawker Frane, 73, Leinster-road, Esquire.
25. William Deals Brewer, 15, Raglan-road, gentleman.
26. Henry Hayes, Stradford Orwell-road, tanner.
27. William Hayes, 24, Garville avenue, merchant.
28. Joseph Maguire, 67, Kenilworth-square, architect.
29. George Mitchell Hopetown, Roundtown-road, tobacconist.
30. Adam Millar, Monkstown, merchant.
31. George Sykes, 13 Garville avenue, woollen draper.
32. Charles Allen, Trafalgar-terrace, merchant.
33. Henry Carleton, Seapoint, Monkstown, gentleman.
34. Joseph H. Ferguson, 10, Waltham-terrace, gentleman.
35. William Foot, 1, Belgrave-square, gentleman.
36. William E. Garner, Monkstown, gentleman.
37. Lewis Hemcky, East View, Monkstown, merchant.
38. Harry Hodges, Alma-road, merchant.
39. John Inglis, Belgrave-square, gentleman.
40. Alphonso Busby, 4, Burlington-road, distiller.
41. Henry Morrison, Monkstown, hat manufacturer.
42. Valentine O'Brien O'Connor, Newtown Park, merchant.
43. Eldred Oldham, Sea-point, merchant.
44. Benjamin Ormsby, Waltham-terrace, merchant.
45. Alexander Orr, Merrion-avenue, gentleman.
46. Stewart K. Overend, Sidney-avenue, gentleman.
47. William Williamson, Merrion-avenue, gentleman.
48. John McEvoy, Lower George street, chandler.

So answers John Hely Hutchinson, sheriff.

County Dublin, Sheriff's Office.

True copy of Panel,
Hugh Lane.

0.78.

Mr. F. Hamilton.

12 June 1873.

4322. Have you a thorough acquaintance with the persons on that panel, who they are, and what they are?—I have.

4323. Have you been for many years conducting the revision of the Parliamentary Voters' Lists for the county of Dublin?—I have for 17 years.

4324. You know who all those persons are on that panel?—Nearly all the persons.

4325. There are 48 on that panel, are there not?—There are.

4326. How many of those are Protestants?—Forty-five.

4327. What are the other denominations?—There are two of the Society of Friends, or Quakers, and there is one Roman Catholic.

4328. And the other 45 are members of what we now term the Church of Ireland; Episcopal Protestants?—Yes.

4329. Mr. Ormsby was sub-sheriff then, was he not?—No; John Mallet Williamson was sub-sheriff, and John Heley Hutchinson high sheriff.

4330. Have you brought over an order postponing the trial of O'Keeffe and Cullen for that term?—I have.

4331. Is it an attested copy?—It is an official copy of the order from the Queen's Bench, signed by the proper officer, dated the 23rd of November 1872.

[*The same was delivered in, and is as follows:*]

Rev. Robert O'Keefe
v.
His Eminence Paul Cardinal Cullen.

Queen's Bench, Saturday, 23rd November 1872.

On motion of Serjeant Armstrong of Counsel for Defendant, who moved that the trial of this cause be postponed, so that same shall not come on in the next after sittings upon the ground of the impossibility of having the evidence of a witness material and necessary for the defence, and on hearing notice of motion and affidavits of Defendant, of Doctor Cruise, and of Plaintiff read, and on hearing Mr. Butt, Q.C., and Mr. Purcell, Q.C., of Counsel for Plaintiff, Mr. Carton of Counsel for Defendants, it is ordered, that the trial of this cause be postponed, so that same shall not come on in the sittings after the present Term, and that Plaintiff's costs of this motion be costs in the cause.

By the Court—
Thomas F. Yeo.

Arthur O'Hagan, } Attorneys.
Wm. R. Meredith, }

W. R. M.

4332. Have you any other papers to hand in?—None that I think are necessary; merely the formal preliminary papers, such as the notice of trial, showing that the trial was at issue, and ripe for trial.

4333. Do you produce the notice dated the 11th of November 1872, for the trial to take place on the 26th of November, in the case of O'Keeffe against Cullen?—Yes.

[The

Mr. F. Hamilton.

10 June 1873.

[*The same was delivered in, and is as follows:*]

Notice of Trial at Dublin—Special.

Reverend Robert O'Keeffe, P.P., Plaintiff; His Eminence Paul Cardinal Cullen, Defendant.

Sir,

Take notice, that this cause being at issue in Her Majesty's Court of Queen's Bench in Ireland, the same will receive a trial by Nisi Prius, before the Right Honourable James Whiteside, Lord Chief Justice of said Court, or in his absence, before one of his brethren Justices of the said Court, on Tuesday, the twenty-sixth day of November, at the place called the Court of Queen's Bench, in the Four Courts, Dublin, between the hours of ten and eleven o'clock in the forenoon of the said day; and also take notice that this cause will be tried by a special jury.

Dated this 11th day of November 1872.

William Rice Meredith,
Attorney for the Plaintiff,
No. 19, Upper Ormond Quay, Dublin.

To Arthur O'Hagan, Esq.,
Attorney for Defendant,
No. 9, Harcourt-street, Dublin.

4334. Do you also produce a notice of the 15th of November 1872, from Mr. Meredith, the plaintiff's attorney, in O'Keeffe against Cullen, declining to withdraw notice of trial?—Yes.

[*The same was handed in, and is as follows:*]

Reverend Robert O'Keefe, Plaintiff; His Eminence, Paul, Cardinal Cullen, Defendant.

Sir, Queen's Bench.

In reply to your notice of the 12th instant, I hereby inform you that the Plaintiff will not withdraw the notice of trial in this case, nor consent to any postponement thereof.

Wm. Rice Meredith,
Plaintiff's Attorney,
19, Upper Ormond Quay.

Dated this 15th day of November 1872.

To Arthur O'Hagan, Esq.,
Defendant's Attorney, 9, Harcourt-street.

4335. Mr. *Bruen*.] Was that order postponing the trial made by one of the superior judges?—Certainly such order must be made by one of the judges, but the copy of his order is never signed by him, but it is signed by the proper officer of the court, Mr. Thomas F. Yeo.

4336. [*Chairman*.] Have you any knowledge of the special jurors' book from which this panel was selected?—I have, but I do not know the exact number that were upon it; I have got a general knowledge of the gentlemen in the county of Dublin who are competent, and who generally serve upon special juries.

4337. What sort of number would there be on the book?—I should not like to hazard the exact number.

4338. Would there be several hundreds?—Yes, certainly; about 450.

4339. Have you any idea as to the proportions of Protestants and Roman Catholics that would be on that list?—I have; I think there would be three Protestants to one Roman Catholic.

4340. But you are quite sure that there could be nothing on the whole of the special jurors' list like that proportion of 47 to 1?—I cannot tell how that occurred; certainly no such proportion.

4341. But there could not possibly be upon the whole special jury list, the same preponderance of Protestants over Roman Catholics?—Certainly not.

4342. I did not understand you to say that this panel was struck with any particular reference to the case of O'Keeffe against Cullen?—Certainly not; it was an ordinary panel struck to try all the special jury cases that would come on that term.

4343. But it is a fact that if the trial had not been postponed, that case would have been tried by a jury selected from this panel?—Certainly, by 12 gentlemen selected out of that panel.

4344. Mr. *Heron*.] By the 12 who first answered to their names as being called?—Yes, that is the practice.

4345. Mr. *Bruen*.] You do not impute to the sub-sheriff partiality, do you, in forming the panel?—Certainly not; I have no grounds for doing so.

4346. And it is quite possible that the sub-sheriff might not have known the religion of the gentlemen whom he placed upon the panel?—If the sub-sheriff either read the names out from any book, or wrote them, I am quite satisfied that he did know their religion just as well or better than I know it myself, if possible better, because I know Mr. Williamson to be a man of great experience; he is living in the centre of the city or county, and he has conducted political business for a great many years; I know him to be a man of intelligence and a gentleman of high education, and I am satisfied that he knows every single man in the county competent to sit upon special juries, that is to say, if they were resident for any period of time.

4347. Do you mean to say that it is your belief that, knowing their religious opinions, he deliberately put on this panel 47 men who were Protestants?—No, I never imputed any such thing; but I am perfectly satisfied that he knew the politics and the religion of every gentleman put on the list.

4348 But knowing their religion, and putting them, you say that it was done deliberately?—I cannot say the motive; I did not impute that.

4349. Your assertion is that he knowingly put on this panel 47 Protestants and one Roman Catholic?—I should say so. I say that he must have known their religion, for he knows, in my opinion, the religion of every man upon that panel, in which there are 45 Protestant Episcopalians, two Friends, and one Catholic. I know every one of those persons, most of them personally.

4350. Have you examined previous special jury panels?—I have frequently had occasion to do so in the way of my professional practice.

4351. Can you give the Committee any information as the composition of the previous special jury panels as regards religion?—Not in my recollection.

4352. It is only to this particular panel that your attention has been directed?—Yes, very recently.

4353. Colonel *Vandeleur*.] Have you ever found

found fault with the panel previously for the same reason?—Not personally, but I have frequently heard the panels complained of.

4354. Did that come under your knowledge before?—It never came under my knowledge in the case of any particular panel, but I have often been fully aware that the panels, and the special panels particularly, have been more largely composed of Protestants than they should have been.

4355. That is to say, in the county of Dublin?—Yes, particularly in the county of Dublin, and the reason I say so is that I have a great knowledge of the gentlemen in the county.

4356. I think you stated that the Protestants are in as great a disproportion as three to one?—Yes, my opinion is that there are three Protestants to one Catholic in the county of the class of gentlemen that you are referring to who would be competent to serve on special juries. If you are referring to the other class it would be quite the other way.

4357. Mr. *Bruen*.] Is it your belief that the case which you have mentioned of O'Keeffe against Cullen, would not have been fairly tried by a jury chosen out of that panel?—I should say certainly that it would have been fairly tried; those gentleman are all very respectable, and would have tried the case on their oath.

4358. Viscount *Crichton*.] Your attention was directed to this particular panel?—It was.

4359. With a view to giving evidence upon it here?—It was.

4360. Mr. *Heron*.] Are you quite sure that Mr. Ormsby was sub-sheriff last year?—No, Mr. Williamson was the sub-sheriff, a prominent Conservative agent.

4361. I think there was a change last year?—I am not aware of that, but believe Mr. Ormsby was re-appointed.

Mr. *F. Hamilton.*

12 June 1873.

Monday, 16th June 1873.

MEMBERS PRESENT:

Mr. Attorney General.	Mr. Henry Herbert.
Dr. Ball.	The O'Conor Don.
Mr. Bruen.	Colonel Wilson Patten.
Mr. Downing.	Colonel Vandeleur.
Marquis of Hartington.	

THE MARQUIS OF HARTINGTON, IN THE CHAIR.

Mr. JOHN REILLY, called in; and Examined.

Mr. *J. Reilly.*

16 June 1873.

4362. Mr. *Downing.*] I BELIEVE you are a professional gentleman of some 25 years' standing? —Yes.

4363. Were you born in the county of Monaghan?—I was.

4364. Have you since the year 1850, filled any position in the county with regard to its politics? —I have been since 1850, agent for the late Colonel Leslie, for the registry of voters; now for his brother.

4365. You are what is known as the Conservative agent?—Yes.

4366. Can you tell the Committee what is the population of the county of Monaghan?—About 112,000.

4367. Can you give the relative proportions of Roman Catholics and other religionists in the county?—Almost three to one, I think; almost three Roman Catholics to one of every other denomination.

4368. Your return here is two-thirds and one-third?—That is what I mean.

4369. Did you fill the office of sub-sheriff in the year 1846 and 1847?—I did.

4370. For the county of Monaghan?—Yes.

4371. How did you prepare your panel for that year?—According to the numbers of the different religious denominations on the jurors' book returned to me. They were two of every other denomination to one of Roman Catholics.

4372. Did you so arrange them on your panel? —I so arranged them as near as possible on my panel.

4373. Did you give them in their position on the panel itself; did you place them accordingly? —I took first two Protestants, then one Catholic, then two Protestants, then one Catholic, and so on.

4374. You are aware that generally, a jury is selected from the first 70 names?—Yes.

4375. That is allowing the prisoner the right to 20 peremptory challenges, and the Crown to put a number aside. The jury is almost invariably taken from the first 70 names on the panel?—Yes, they have the best chance of being on the jury.

4376. Then by your arrangement, out of the first 70 names you give 23 Catholics out of 70? —Yes.

4377. Do you know Mr. Mitchell?—I do; I did, rather.

4378. He was sub-sheriff about the year 1861, and before it, I believe?—Some time shortly before 1861 he commenced.

4379. Did he continue as the sub-sheriff up to the year 1864?—I think he did.

4380. Were you in the habit of taking criminal business and defending prisoners?—Yes.

4381. Had you reason to believe, and was there a strong opinion in the county that panels were not fairly formed when there were any political trials?—By him?

4382. Yes?—Yes, very great complaints on the subject.

4383. Who was the sheriff in 1864?—Dacre Hamilton.

4384. Who was his sub-sheriff?—Mr. Harry Rogers.

4385. Who was the returning officer for that year?—I was.

4386. Did the sub-sheriff, with your assistance, and upon your suggestion, prepare the panel in 1864 as you prepared it in 1846?—I advised him to do so, and he took my advice.

4387. He did so?—He did so.

4388. Did Mr. Mitchell come in in the year afterwards; in the year 1865?—He did.

4389. Do you know how many Roman Catholics were on the panel for the year 1865, prepared by Mr. Mitchell; of the first 67 names how many Catholics?—In the spring assize of 1869 there were seven Catholics in the first 70 names.

4390. In 1865?—In 1868 and 1869.

4391. You put three here?—That was previous.

4392. That was in 1865?—The three in the 67 names refer to the panel I talk of; that was on a previous panel; I am now adverting to the panels which were the subject of contention.

4393. 1865 and 1866?—My answer to that is, that before 1865 there was a panel. One of the panels complained of which contained only three Catholic names on the first 67 names; before 1865.

4394. Mr. *Bruen.*] What year was that?—I cannot tell you exactly. It was between 1861 and 1865.

4395. Mr. *Downing.*] It was before you were returning officer in 1864?—Yes.

4396. *Chairman.*] Returning officer for what? —For the sheriff. The sheriff appoints the returning

turning officer, to whom he sends all his writs in Dublin to return to the courts. I was that man.

4397. Mr. *Downing.*] And to whom all communications are made with reference to the writs?—Yes.

4398. Was there a very remarkable trial in that year, 1866, of Mr. Gray, for the murder of a man of the name of Shevlin?—There was, Edward Warren Gray.

4399. Shevlin was a Roman Catholic?—Yes.

4400. And he lost his life in one of these party riots?—He lost his life coming from an election at Castle Blayney.

4401. How was that jury composed?—Twelve Protestants.

4402. Was he acquitted?—He was.

4403. Was there a general feeling of dissatisfaction upon that trial?—There was at the result of the trial.

4404. A very strong feeling?—A very strong feeling.

4405. Did Mr. Mitchell continue sub-sheriff till 1869?—Yes.

4406. Was there in 1869, in Monaghan, a very heavy calendar arising out of party rights?—Yes; a great number of people to be tried arising out of a riot in an Orange walk.

4407. There were a number of Orangemen and a number of Roman Catholics returned for trial for party riots and assaults?—Yes.

4408. Were there persons of the name of Baird, to be tried for the murder of a man of the name of Hughes?—Yes; father and son.

4409. Hughes being a Roman Catholic?—Yes.

4410. And there was a man of the name of McKenna to be tried for the murder of a man of the name of Clarke, who was a Protestant?—Yes.

4411. Were seven of those Roman Catholics, four women and three men, tried at those Assizes for one of those riots?—Yes; at the Spring Assizes.

4412. At the Spring Assizes for 1869?—Yes.

4413. Taken from that panel?—Taken from a panel.

4414. The panel of 1869?—The panel of 1869.

4415. Is that the issue containing the names of the jury which tried that case (*handing same to the Witness*)?—This is a copy of issues sent to a jury on the 5th of March 1869. This is, the greater part of it, in the handwriting of Mr. Bourne, the Clerk of the Crown.

4416. And signed by him?—I do not see his signature; it is in his own handwriting. I know it.

4417. Was that an exclusively Protestant jury?—There is one name here I am doubtful of, No. 3; all the rest are Protestants.

4418. Were the Bairds tried at those same Spring Assizes for the murder of Hughes?—They were.

4419. Were they tried by an exclusively Protestant jury?—They were.

4420. Were they acquitted?—They were.

4421. McKenna was then, afterwards, put to the bar charged with the murder of Clarke?—Yes.

4422. And there was a challenge to the array?—Yes.

4423. Were you examined upon that challenge?—I was.

4424. And the panel was quashed?—It was.

4425. What was the consequence of the quashing of that panel; were all the prisoners in custody for trial enlarged?—The assizes were adjourned; the next morning all that were on bail were allowed to stand out on bail till the next assizes.

4426. And the seven who were tried by a jury from that panel were sentenced, I believe, to very heavy punishments?—They were tried by Judge Lawson, and they got heavy punishments, as mostly every man that he sentences does get.

4427. Of course, there were no further criminal trials at the Spring Assizes?—No; McKenna's ended the whole affair.

4428. Have you got the original panel of that assizes?—I have.

4429. Will you produce it?—I have not got the original panel; that is the sheriff's, but I have a printed copy.

4430. Will you tell the Committee, of the first 70 names, how many Roman Catholics there are upon that panel?—No. 7 is a Roman Catholic.

4431. Tell us the number?—Seven out of the 70.

4432. Were two of those men who had spirit licenses?—One.

4433. He, as a matter of course, was put by by the Crown?—I do not recollect the fact whether he was or not.

4434. Do not you know publicans are always objected to by the Crown?—I know that it is the rule.

4435. Were you employed professionally to defend McKenna?—I was.

4436. Did you, previously to the assizes, communicate with the high sheriff; did you write him a letter on the subject of returning a fair and impartial panel?—I wrote to both the high sheriff and the sub-sheriff.

4437. Did you get a reply from the high sheriff?—I got a reply in writing from the high sheriff.

4438. What was the purport of it?—That he knew nothing of it; that he left the matter in the hands of the sub-sheriff.

4439. Did you then communicate with the Lord Lieutenant?—I did.

4440. What reply did you get from the Castle?—That the Lord Lieutenant could not interfere.

4441. This was previously to the Spring Assizes of 1869?—My letters to the sheriffs and Lord Lieutenant were previously to the Spring Assizes; but I cannot answer whether my reply from the Lord Lieutenant was previous.

4442. What was the result of your having written those several letters; was there any addition made to the panel in consequence?—I do not know whether in consequence; but the panel that Dr. Ball has was the panel for the assizes.

4443. What was the usual number of jurors returned for the assizes upon the panel?—Two hundred.

4444. And this consists of how many?—Two hundred and fifty.

4445. How many baronies are there in the county Monaghan?—Five.

4446. I believe there is one barony that is particularly called a Catholic barony, the Barony of Farney?—Yes.

4447. Can you tell me how many were returned from that barony upon that panel?—I think, 20.

4448. What position have they on the panel?—With

Mr. *J. Reilly.*

16 June 1873.

—With the exception of one, all at the end of the panel.

4449. Can you tell me what is the rating valuation of the large number of those upon that panel?—I can; I have a copy of the panel.

4450. Is the rating so low as 15 *l.*, and less?—I prefer referring to it. No. 10 is 13 *l.*

4451. The rating is so low as 13 *l.*?—Nos. 27 and 29 are 13 *l.* 10 *s.* No. 36 is 13 *l.* 5 *s.*

4452. Are you aware that in consequence of the quashing of the panel, and in consequence of a discussion in the House of Commons, the high sheriff was removed from his office, because he would not remove Mr. Mitchell, his sub-sheriff?—I am aware that the high sheriff was removed from his office; but I cannot give you the reasons of the Government for doing so; that was Mr. Thomas Coote.

4453. He having been removed, who was appointed sheriff in his place?—I should state he was not removed till after the Summer Assizes. When he was removed Mr. Langdale was appointed in his place.

4454. Who was appointed as sub-sheriff?—Mr. Edward Fay Donelly.

4455. And who was his returning officer?—I was.

4456. The panel for the Summer Assizes, you say, was made out before Mr. Langdale was appointed?—Mr. Langdale was not appointed till after the assizes.

4457. Have you got the panel for the Summer Assizes?—I have.

4458. Will you produce it?—I will.

4459. Dr. *Ball.*] What year was that panel for?—For the Spring Assizes of 1869. This is the panel for the Summer Assizes of 1869.

4460. Mr. *Downing.*] Having got that panel for the Summer Assizes of 1869, I believe you find 200 names upon it?—Yes.

4461. Is there any difference between the panel of 1869, which was quashed, and the panel for the Summer Assizes of the same year, which you now hold in your hand?—There is.

4462. What is the difference?—The 50 special jurors are excluded from this panel.

4463. Which were upon the other?—Which were upon the other. The two triers who tried that panel are excluded also, and there are five new jurors added, four of whom are Catholics.

4464. And except that the persons on that panel are identical with the parties on that?—Identical, but put in different order.

4465. That is the panel that was quashed?—That is the panel that was quashed.

4466. Colonel *Wilson Patten.*] Merely in different order?—If I knew number five on that, I would tell you what number he is on this.

4467. Mr. *Attorney General.*] Upon what grounds was it quashed?—The want of impartiality.

4468. Partiality in the sheriff?—Yes.

4469. Dr. *Ball.*] I think the verdict was against the charge of Judge Morris?—It was, distinctly.

4470. Mr. *Downing.*] You were examined?—I was examined.

4471. Did you hear Mr. Mitchell examined?—I did.

4472. Did you hear him admit that he was an Orangeman?—I did.

4473. Did you hear him admit that he subscribed to the funds for the defence of Orange prisoners?—I do not recollect.

4474. At all events, the panel was quashed?—It was.

4475. When you found this panel was the same as the panel which was quashed at the March assizes, did you make an application to the Queen's Bench in Dublin to change the venue for the trial of McKenna?—The application was pending when I got this panel; I compared this panel with that panel, and I put them both in the hands of Mr. Butt, who was our leading counsel.

4476. Do you see the endorsement?—Yes.

4477. That was used as an exhibit before the judges in the Queen's Bench?—It was.

4478. In consequence of the affidavit and the facts that came out, was the venue in that case changed?—It was.

4479. To what county?—To Louth.

4480. Was McKenna tried there?—He was.

4481. Was he acquitted?—He was.

4482. After Mr. Langdale was sworn in sheriff, did you, as it was your duty, and the right of the sheriff, demand the jurors' book for the year at Mr. Mitchell's office?—By directions of Mr. Donelly, the sheriff, I did demand from the outgoing sheriff the jurors' book, and all writs unreturned.

4483. Did you get the jurors' book?—I got the jurors' book, and all writs unreturned.

4484. Have you got that jurors' book here?—It is here.

4485. Just produce it. Is that book in the same state in which you received it from Mr. Mitchell's office?—It is.

4486. Now, will you open it. (*The Witness did so.*) Do you see as you throw your eye along the columns a cross opposite to a number of names?—Yes.

4487. Do you happen to know to what religion those persons belong who are marked that way with the cross?—Exclusively Catholics.

4488. Is every Roman Catholic on the panel marked with a cross?—Every Roman Catholic in this book is marked with a cross, and seven of those were on the panel in the first 70 names.

4489. How many Roman Catholics are in that book?—I cannot tell you.

4490. Mr. *Attorney General.*] But about?—I cannot give you the relative numbers.

4491-2. Can you tell upon the jurors' book at all approximately, not binding you to 10 or 20, but approximately, can you tell the numbers of the proportions of the two religions?—I cannot without counting; I have never done so.

4493. But you could let us know?—I can let you know in half an hour's time, by counting.

4494. The way the argument stands is this: you have the book which belonged to a sheriff who was dismissed for want of impartiality, and it is produced before the Committee; that book shows that the members of a particular religion are throughout marked with a cross; then the two facts we want to get, are the proportions of the two religions, roughly speaking. Having ascertained what the proportions of the two religions are upon the book, then see what the proportions of the two religions are upon the panel, then you have the case complete, and you have a reasonable ground for what the crosses mean?—I can give you the names and the number of Roman Catholics in this book in five minutes.

4495. Colonel

Mr. *J. Reilly.*

16 June 1873.

4495. Colonel *Vandeleur.*] You said there were three to two?—Yes.

4496. Mr. *Attorney General.*] If you have the rough proportion on the book, you can have the accurate proportion on the panel, and then different minds will put different conclusions as to what the crosses meant?—I can do it in an instant.

4497. Mr. *Downing.*] Will you put that in afterwards?—I should mention that in addition to their names being crossed on every counter leaf, the numbers are given in pencil. The number of Catholics on this page is here in pencil, and was so when the book was returned to me.

[Number of Names on Jurors' Book, County Monaghan, for Year 1869 -	1,269
Number marked with × - - -	493
Of those marked with ×,	
There are - Roman Catholics -	492
Protestant - -	1
	493]

4498. Just show it to the Chairman. (*The Witness showed the book to the Chairman*)?—You can do it without me. There are 10 Catholics on that page.

4499. Who is the sub-sheriff for Monaghan this year?—Mr. Mitchell.

4500. From your knowledge as returning officer, I ask you, if you were so inclined, could you so arrange the panel for an assizes that you could have any jury you pleased; that is, I mean of politics and feeling?—On the old system.

4501. Yes?—I could make a jury to order.

4502. That being the case, would you go back to that system?—Decidedly not.

4503. Do you think that if the Chairman of the Quarter Sessions paid proper attention to the revision of the lists, and that he was attended there by the clerks of the unions, and the poor rate collectors, and other officials that may be convenient, that they would not have sufficient information to enable them to suggest and prove all those persons who ought not to be put on the jury, either from ill-health or poverty, or crime, or other causes that might be specified?—I think, through the clerks of the unions and the poor rate collectors, every man against whom there was a fair objection could be known at the revision sessions.

4504. And after one careful revision there would be very little to be done afterwards?—The work is merely the deaths, and parties who get into the position of criminals afterwards.

4505. Had you any experience of the working of the present Act?—No; there was very little to do at the last Monaghan assizes.

4506. Do you approve of the alphabetical system?—Decidedly.

4507. An objection has been made that some of the letters contain but very few names, and that after an assizes or two, you then have to take the names for juries from a few letters, and that therefore, that would be objectionable, that there might be relatives and friends on the jury?—I can only speak for the one county. I do not profess any knowledge of other counties; it would not go to that extent, but there are letters which contain a great many names. I would divide those letters and deal with each separate number, whatever number were settled upon, as a separate letter.

4508. Did you read the evidence of Mr. Wilkinson who was examined here?—No.

4509. The sheriff of Wexford?—No, I never heard of the man.

4510. Have you made a calculation of the number of jurors you would require as sub-sheriff to discharge the duties of that county both at assizes and quarter sessions for a year?—I have.

4511. Perhaps you will give it to the Committee; state what number you would require on the panel to discharge the duties for one year?—This is my writing. There are two divisions for criminal business in the county; there would be required four petty panels for the Castle Blayney division; and I would put on each panel four juries; 48 names multiplied by four would be 192.

4512. That would be for Quarter Sessions purposes?—For that division. The same number for Monaghan division, 192.

4513. That would be 384?—There would be four grand juries required for the Castle Blayney division; I put the numbers for the grand jury at 30; there should be 23 men on the grand jury. Well, four times 30 would be 120, and the same number for the Monaghan division. That is what would be required for Quarter Sessions. Then for the assizes there would be two petty panels required for the county for each year, and I put down the number of each petty panel as 200. Twice 200 would be 400. There would be two special panels required for the assizes; I put down the number in each panel at 50; that is 100. That makes the gross number that I would consider necessary for the discharge of the duty of the juries in the county, in one year, 1,124.

4514. Have you taken from the Returns made to this Committee the number for Monaghan at present?—Some of the numbers. If you will allow me to see that Paper, I will tell you what I have taken. (*The Paper was handed to the Witness*).

4515. How many are returned now for Monaghan, the rating being 20 *l.* and upwards?—The rating being under 30 *l.*

4516. The first is at 20 *l.* and upwards?—One thousand eight hundred and eighty-five.

4517. How many are valued under 30 *l.*?—One thousand and ninety-two.

4518. How many will that leave qualified at a rating of 30 *l.* and over?—Seven hundred and ninety-three.

4519. So that you would not have sufficient number on the panel for one year?—No; it would be more than 300 short.

4520. Mr. *Herbert.*] According to your calculation?—These numbers state from a printed return.

4521. Your calculation was that 1,124 would be necessary?—Yes.

4522. Mr. *Attorney General.*] What average number of causes do you try at the assizes?—A few; you mean the civil business.

4523. Yes?—I would say averaging not more than five.

4524. Colonel *Wilson Patten.*] Is that five at each assizes?—Yes.

4525. Mr. *Attorney General.*] What is the number

Mr. *J. Reilly.*

16 June 1873.

number of prisoners at the assizes?—It varies very much.

4526. But what is the average when there is no particular thing, no bad winter, to increase crime?—I would say a dozen cases.

4527. And at Quarter Sessions?—Sometimes very few, and sometimes a great many more than 12.

4528. Can you average it at all?—I cannot on the instant; I would average it at a higher average.

4529. Would 20 at each, that is 80 persons in the year, at Quarter Sessions, be enough?—I think that is a large average.

4530. That is 120 prisoners, and 10 causes; do you really require 1,124 jurors to do that?—You require a great number to be summoned.

4531. I am quite aware of that; you must have a margin for challenges, and so on; but surely that is an extravagant margin, is it not?—Recollect there are two divisions in the county for sessions. You asked me for an average; I merely talk of one division, but I must add to that the same average for Castle Blaney division.

4532. There are only four Quarter Sessions of course in the year. You do not hold an intermediate Session in Ireland as we do here?—Four Quarter Sessions.

4533. They are at different places?—Yes.

4534. Still the number of persons tried is what you represent?—Four Quarter Sessions, and at each Quarter Sessions there is criminal business in two of the towns; that is you may say, there are eight Quarter Sessions for criminal business.

4535. The number of prisoners is not greater than you state?—I think on the average, 12 for Quarter Sessions.

4536. Twenty I gave you?—Taking the average of the two towns, I think 20 would be fair.

4537. Then that comes to what I say; that comes to 120 prisoners and 10 causes; that is 130 issues, 130 verdicts in the year; surely you do not want 1,124 jurors for that?—Multiply 130 by 12, because it takes 12 men to each issue.

4538. Surely you do not want a fresh jury for each issue?—No.

4539. Unless you are very different there to what we are here, I suppose a jury sits for the day?—Yes.

4540. If the cases are light, they would dispose of a dozen prisoners in a day easily?—Sometimes you will, and sometimes you will not; often I have seen one case take the whole day.

4541. I have been circuit for 15 or 16 years, so that I know what it would be; the average would be seven or eight a day, taking one day with another?—Seven or eight prisoners?

4542. Yes; that is rather a low average, I should say?—Yes.

4523. You do not want anything like 12 jurors for each issue?—You test the number by the number of persons to be tried, and the number of issues to be tried. I merely test it by the number that should be on each panel.

4544. Surely you do not mean to represent that in Ireland you want 12 jurors for every issue. You want to have 12 jurors, I know, but you do not want 12 different jurors for the 130 issues you try?—No; because in fact the same 12 jurors very often try all the prisoners.

4545. Colonel *Vandeleur.*] You stated that you would require 192 for each division?—I gave you the numbers.

4546. Mr. *Downing.*] With regard to the jurors from towns and villages, do you consider that they are, generally speaking, more intelligent than jurors taken from the rural districts?—I think men in towns and villages, men in business, are more intelligent.

4547. What rating do you think would be a reasonable rating, so as to secure a fair number of those on the jurors' books?—£. 8.

4548. A rating of 12 *l.* will not give you many such jurors from the small towns?—It would exclude a great many that I think are fit men to be on the jury.

4549. The *O'Conor Don.*] Do you not think that there are many men rated at 8 *l.* in the towns and villages who are more competent to act as jurors than men in the country who are rated at 30 *l.*?—I do; I think, as a class, the mercantile class, which is the chief class in towns and villages, are more competent than those in the country.

4550. Mr. *Downing.*] Do you think that the rating is at all a guide to the intelligence of the juror?—Not as regards country jurors.

4551. Do not you think it depends much more upon age?—Yes, because when you come to jurors of a certain age, a great many of them are illiterate, but a great number of men under a certain age have learned to read and write.

4552. In consequence of the introduction of the national schools, the proportion of persons who can read and write is very much in excess of what it was formerly?—Yes.

4553. With regard to the service of summonses, would you employ the police?—No.

4554. Do you think that would be objectionable?—I do.

4655. Have you considered the question of summoning jurors by a registered letter?—Yes.

4556. What is your opinion of that?—That the great majority of the summonses would never reach them.

4557. Have you any suggestion to make to the Committee on the question of the service of jurors?—Yes.

4558. What is it?—I think that the summons servers of the different petty sessions districts would be very good people to summon.

4559. Every magistrate's district in Ireland has a summons server?—Yes.

4560. You would have the summonses in that district sent to the summons server for service?—Yes.

4561. I suppose you would have a column in which you would make an entry of the mode of service?—There would be a tabulated form; in one column the name and residence of the jurors, and for the summons server, a column to state when he served them, and how he served them.

4562. Would you have that service verified by an affidavit, and that affidavit forwarded to the sheriff?—Verified by an oath and forwarded to the sheriff.

4563. That would not require the attendance of the summons server at the assizes?—No.

4564. Would you make any distinction between the jurors that serve at the quarter sessions and at the assizes?—No.

4565. You would have only one jurors' book?—Only one.

4566. You would make no difference as regards the qualification for the assizes and the sessions?—No, decidedly not, there are very many heavy cases tried at the sessions.

4567. And

Mr. *J. Reilly.*

16 June 1873.

4567. And some very serious cases?—Very serious.

4568. *Dr. Ball.*] In Monaghan, I suppose, the same as in most of the northern counties, the labouring class is all Catholic?—The greater portion.

4569. According as you ascend in the social scale, do not the Protestants preponderate?—They do.

4570. Therefore the higher the rating the more Protestants?—The more Protestants, and the less Roman Catholics.

4571. I think you mentioned that this barony of Farney is all Catholic?—Nearly all.

4572. It is a peculiar place, separate from the rest of the county somewhat?—It is the southern end of the county.

4573. And has been at times a very disturbed place, has it not?—Yes.

4574. Have you seen Mr. Trench's book?—That is a long time ago. I read the book; but I think there is a great deal of story in the book as well as fact.

4575. With reference to the trial to which you referred, I must tell you, Judge Morris was asked about the fairness of the jury; he was asked would he tell what was his opinion as to the verdict of the triers. He said he did not approve of it, "Most emphatically not, for I directed the opposite way, and they took a different view"?—Yes.

4576. Is Mr. Mitchell, the sub-sheriff, still acting?—Yes.

4577. We can have him to examine?—To be sure you can.

4578. In this book I see several marks, can you explain the other marks?—I cannot. I have been thinking about the other marks, and I cannot explain them.

4579. I think the other mark is more frequently repeated than the one you alluded to; which do you think is the mark which marks those of the Catholic religion?—(*The Witness pointed out the mark to which he referred.*)

4580. What do you say to those marks (*pointing to some other marks in the book*)?—I do not know. There are four Catholics on that page.

4581. If you were selecting a jury, merely on the principle of respectability, would not that give a preponderance of Protestants?—I do not know what you mean by "respectability."

4582. I mean higher in the social scale and richer?—The higher the rating the more Protestants.

4583. Suppose you thought in selecting your panel, that you ought as much as possible, to get the jury from persons of a higher position even though they were of the farming class; if you acted upon that principle it would lead to the result of having a preponderance of Protestants?—It would; the more you eliminate the lower rating, the more you take out the Catholics.

4584. That is the same, I believe, all over the north?—I do not know. I will only speak for the one county.

4585. *Mr. Bruen.*] I did not quite understand what you said was the proportion between the Roman Catholics and Protestants in the population of the County Monaghan?—The Catholics are almost three to one; almost three Catholics to one Protestant in the whole of the county.—(*See* "Thom," p. 774.)

4586. Have you any idea of the proportion of the Catholics on the jury list?—Yes, I have, or I had an idea of what it was in 1869.

4587. What was it then?—There were three Protestants to two Catholics on the jury list; it is just reversed.

4588. *Dr. Ball.*] In the barony of Farney are the holdings small?—Not now.

4589. But they were?—They were weeded out; I know one part where there is a large district, and not a man in it.

4590. *Mr. Downing.*] That is many years ago?—Yes.

4591. *Mr. Bruen.*] How many years was Mr. Mitchell sub-sheriff?—I cannot tell you. I see that he commenced to be sub-sheriff before 1861, and I think, with the exception of the year that Mr. Hamilton was sheriff, he was sheriff until he was removed in 1869; that is my recollection.

4592. Then he must have served under a great number of high sheriffs?—He did.

4593. Were there any high sheriffs during that time that were of the Roman Catholic religion?—Not that he was sub-sheriff to; I think the last high sheriff that was a Catholic was Mr. Kenny. It was Mr. Kenny's brother that was his sub-sheriff till after 1869.

4594. Were there any sheriffs of different political opinions to Mr. Mitchell?—I think Mr. Coote, the sheriff who was dismissed, was of different political opinions from Mr. Mitchell. I am very sorry he was dismissed on account of the matter.

4595. Were there any others besides Mr. Coote under whom Mr. Mitchell served, who were of different political opinions from him?—Not that I recollect.

4596. You say there was a suspicion in the county that jurors were not impartially empanelled by Mr. Mitchell?—I do not think I used the word "suspicion" at all; I said there were complaints made.

4597. Do you think those complaints were well founded?—I always thought so.

4598. Then you had a suspicion?—I complained. If I had not a suspicion and a well-grounded suspicion, I would not complain.

4599. You had a suspicion that the jurors were not impartially empanelled by Mr. Mitchell?—My answer is, I complained and if I had not a well-grounded suspicion, I would not complain. I object to that word; I never used the word; it was founded on more than suspicion. I object to the word "suspicion" being used.

4600. It was a certainty?—In my mind.

4601. *Dr. Ball.*] Your complaint was as to the relative proportions of the two religions on the panel, and the improper position of the Catholics?——

4602. *Mr. Bruen.*] Your complaint was founded entirely upon the alleged disproportion on the panel of the two religions?—That was one ground.

4603. Will you mention another?—I have mentioned it; the improper position of the Catholics on the panel.

4604. As regards the proportionate numbers of the two religions, you said that the course you followed was to put upon the panel exactly the same proportion of Roman Catholics which appeared on the jurors book?—Yes.

4605. Do you think that in every county in Ireland that is a fair rule to follow?—I do not know anything about any county but my own.

4606. You think that is a fair rule?—I think that is a fair rule, and *the* fair rule.

4607. And therefore it follows that a sub-sheriff

Mr. *J. Reilly.*

16 June 1873.

sheriff ought, under the former law, to have made himself acquainted with the religion of those on the jurors' book?—I do not think he ought to be sub-sheriff if he did not know it.

4608. You know it?—Well.

4609. You inquired, and made yourself acquainted with it?—Tell me any man's name, and where he lives, and I will tell you what he is.

4610. In going over this jurors' book which you have handed in, as to which you say that every Catholic name is marked in a peculiar way——?—Yes, with a cross.

4611. Did you gain that knowledge, and come to that conclusion, entirely from your own knowledge, or did you get the assistance of others?—I gained that knowledge from my own knowledge; I saw, to my astonishment, when I got the book, that every Catholic name was marked. I know the Catholics, and I know the people of the county, having been working at the registry for upwards of 20 years.

4612. You know the religion of every man in that book?—I can tell you the religion of every man. I know one mistake that was made in the book, and I will show it to you if you wish.

4613. I shall be obliged to you if you will?—That man (*pointing to a name in the book*) is marked as a Catholic, and I do not think he is one.

4614. Dr. *Ball.*] If you find a mark put to a Protestant, how do you know it is exclusively put to the Catholics?—Every other mark is put to a Catholic; I know the name as well as I know who you are.

4615. Mr. *Bruen.*] I see the name you have pointed out to me as being wrongly marked, is Alexander Boyd; I see another name, William Boyd, who is not so marked?—Because he ought not to be marked as a Catholic.

4616. You do not go by the name, but simply by your knowledge of the individuals?—I do go by the names.

4617. Is Mulligan a Roman Catholic name?—Both Catholic and Protestant.

4618. And Neill?—Both Catholic and Protestant; I know both Orangemen and Papists of that name.

4619. And Smith?—We have every sort of Smith, Catholic, Presbyterian, and everything but a Quaker.

4620 You are sure you cannot be mistaken when you say that, with the exception of this one name, all the others that are marked with a cross in the book are the names of Roman Catholics?—Decidedly so.

4621. You having been sub-sheriff, of course have had the custody of juries' books?—I have had the custody of one.

4622. They are kept in your office, I suppose?—Under lock and key, mine was.

4623. Are you sure that Mr. Mitchell put these marks himself?—No, I do not know who put those marks.

4624. Are you sure it was done in his office?—I got it in his office in that state from his clerk, who he directed to hand it over to me.

4625. Dr. *Ball.*] When did you get it?—In the month of August 1869, when Mr. Langdale was appointed in the place of Mr. Coote.

4626. Mr. *Bruen.*] Can you tell me when the book was prepared?—That book was prepared in the month of December 1868, and was the jurors' book from February 1869 till February 1870.

4627. And you got it in August 1869?—In August 1869, and from that book I assisted Mr. Donnelly to make out the panels for the sessions of October 1869 and January 1870.

4628. You consider that it is a fair principle that on a panel the same proportion of religions should be observed as exists upon the jurors' book?—I do.

4629. Would it be possible to preserve and carry out that order under the alphabetical process?—No, you must adhere to the alphabetical system, and you must take them then in the regular alphabetical order.

4630. It might be possible then that, under the alphabetical system, there might be a preponderance of Protestants upon a jury?—Faith, I think it is very likely. I think it is not only possible, but very likely.

4631. In your view that would not be a fair mode of selection?—I would have the alphabetical system, no matter what the consequence, because nobody could say that there was any unfairness used; I would as soon myself be tried by 12 Protestants as by 12 Catholics; but the lower orders who are those that are mostly tried, would not like that.

4632. It is simply the case of suspicion, and not of a well-grounded suspicion in the minds of the lower orders?—No, I do not agree with you at all.

4633. You say you would just as soon be tried by 12 Protestants as by 12 Roman Catholics?—I would, because I feel that I am very well liked by both sides.

4634. Mr. *Attorney General.*] Perhaps you would add to that, that you would do so if they were taken by chance?—Decidedly, I am altogether for taking men by chance.

4635. Dr. *Ball.*] Except in the Orange cases, do you think it signifies the least about the religion?—I think it is in Orange cases, and in party cases that the mischief is done.

4636. As to the rest, it would not signify whether all were Protestants or all Catholics?—Where there is no party feeling arising it is very different.

4637. *Chairman.*] Does not party feeling arise in the north even upon ordinary cases?—Very often; it is brought into nearly everything, unfortunately.

4638. Mr. *Bruen.*] I believe you defended Mr. McKenna, the prisoner who was accused of the murder of Clark?—I did.

4639. By the change of the venue that trial took place in Louth?—It did.

4640. Did you make it your business to inquire into the panel at Louth?—Very accurately.

4641. What did you discover?—I got a jury

4642. Did you inquire into the religion of the jurors who tried that case?—Yes.

4643. And can you give the Committee information as to what the composition of it was, as regards religion?—I can.

4644. What was it?—Twelve Roman Catholics.

4645. You spoke of the rating of some of the jurors?—I spoke of the rating of some of the jurors that were on the panel of the Spring Assizes of 1869.

4646. You spoke of No. 10 a 13 *l.* rating?—£. 13 rating; Edward Blackburn, of Monaghan.

4647. Can you tell the Committee what his social position was?—He is a very respectable man;

man; he is a mercantile man living in the town of Monaghan.

4648. Is he a shopkeeper?—A shopkeeper.

4649. There was another one you spoke of, 13 *l.* 10 *s.* rating?—Yes, then there is No. 27.

4650. What is he?—A farmer, Alexander Armer Cappog.

4651. Was he a man of education?—No; do not take from me that he could not read and write. I do not mean to say that.

4652. Had he any other qualifications except his farm which was rated at 13 *l.* 10 *s.*?—None on this panel, and none that I know of.

4653. You mentioned another, 13 *l.* 5 *s.*?—Yes, I may have mentioned 13 *l.* 5 *s.*, but the next that occurs to me is No. 29, 13 *l.* 10 *s.*

4654. Who was he?—Eben Miller, Bannaghroe, farmer.

4655. Was that 13 *l.* 5 *s.* the only qualification he had?—The only one that I know of or knew of.

4656. Was he a man of education?—Not saying whether he could read or write, I say he was not, and is not.

4657. Those that you speak of as having those low rating qualifications, are they, generally speaking, simple farmers?—Yes; the next man I come to is No. 36, 13 *l.* 5 *s.*; he is a farmer. I have one 12 *l.* 5 *s.*, a farmer.

4658. With no other qualification that you are aware of?—No. Next, 12 *l.* 6 *s.*, farmer.

4659. *The O'Conor Don.*] Were these all Protestants?—No; the man I am going to mention now I think is a Roman Catholic. No. 68, 13 *l.* 15 *s.*; he is called here Jordan. I have marked that his surname should be Jardine. I think he is a Catholic. All the rest were Protestants.

4660. I think you said those names were on the panel; but they were on the jurors' book first?—Decidedly; I do not mean to insinuate that there was any name on the panel that was not on the jurors' book first.

4661. These men being on the jurors' book, the sheriff had a right to take them out, had he not, and to put them on the panel?—A perfect right to take them out.

4662. Were there a great number on the panel lower rated in this way?—No, the greater number were higher rated.

4663. Are the first few names on the panel more highly rated than the others?—The first name on the panel is one of the special jury that was added to this panel.

4664. He was one of the special jurors' panel?—To this panel there are added 50 special jurors' names; the first name on it is one of those, and he is a magistrate.

4665. What is the second name?—The second name is a common juror; a very respectable man.

4666. Could you say what qualification he possesses?—He is a farmer. I have not marked opposite to his name. I know he is a farmer.

4667. Running down the first dozen names, are they all pretty highly qualified as jurors?—They are all above 13 *l.* The first, I think, is 16 *l.*; the next 25 *l.*; the next, a special juror, 149 *l.*; the next 24 *l.*; the next, the Catholic that was the trier, William McPhillips; the next 23 *l.* 15 *s.*; the next 43 *l.*; the next 13 *l.*; the next 20 *l.*; the next 28 *l.*; the next 16 *l.* 15 *s.*; the next 14 *l.* 10 *s.*; the next is a special juror; the next is 40 *l.* 13 *s.*; the next is a special juror.

4668. I will not trouble you to go any further; it was only to gain some general knowledge of the position. Do those gentlemen live at a great distance, or near the assize town?—The first man lives in the town of Castle Blayney, 12 miles away; the next man lives six miles from the town; the next man lives in the town; the next man five miles from the town; the next 10 miles from the town; the next lives within a mile of the town; the next lives six miles from the town; the next lives within a mile of the town; the next lives eight miles from the town; the next man lives in the town; I do not know where the next man lives; I cannot tell the distance from the town; the next man lives about eight miles from the town.

4669. Was this the panel for the summer assizes?—No, for the spring assizes.

4670. When you formed your panel, did you pay any attention to the convenience of the jurors attending, to take them during the spring assizes from anywhere near, and for the summer assizes to choose those that were more distant?—No; I took each barony, and I selected the proportions from each barony to make the number on the panel meet the correct number of jurors from each barony, and the proportions according to their religious belief.

4671. You attempted to form your panel as much as possible in strict proportion to the names on the jurors' book, according to religion, and according to barony?—Yes, I considered I should do so, and I did do so.

4672. You thought it was your duty to have regard to religion in forming the panel?—I thought so; to give a fair panel.

4673. Colonel *Vandeleur.*] You said just now you approved of the alphabetical system?—Yes.

4674. You have heard some objections made to the alphabetical system, that there may be three names only in A., and that there may be 50 in M.?—Yes.

4675. Would you approve of taking it by numbers, say one of the first 10, or one of the first 15; to go down the list by numbers, and not by letters. All the names are numbered consecutively?—I prefer the alphabetical system.

4676. Some contain only five names in each, and others may contain 30 or 40 names?—I know that is so.

4677. Taking it in numbers, would you prevent these family réunions which may take place by taking it in the alphabetical order?—I do not think I should.

4678. It has happened that there have been three brothers summoned?—Yes, I heard about three brothers being on a special jury.

4679. If there are only a few of that name, say Abbott for instance, you go down to the end of the panel, and then you go up again and take the first, second, and third, and there might be no other A. on the panel?—There might be.

4680. If you take it by numbers, you avoid that?—Yes, but I fall into as great a mess in another way. Taking it by numbers, I take the first 24 numbers, go back and then take the second 24, and then the third 24, till I make up my panel, take 200 names. Then I have taken the first 200 names. In the second 200 names I may perhaps meet 50 of one name. We will suppose the arbitrary number 50. Out of my panel of 200 I would have a great proportion of that name. I think the fairest way, and the way to which there can be the least objection, and the least manufacturing of panels, is by taking it alphabetically,

Mr. *J. Reilly.*

16 June 1873.

alphabetically, and let everybody take their chance. That is my opinion.

4681. You do not think taking it by numbers would be an improvement?—I do not think it would be a bit of an improvement.

4682. In your county, after you have taken the grand jury out of the panel, do all magistrates, and all persons upon the panel, serve indiscriminately?—Not latterly; the jury law was amended some years ago; I do not recollect the exact year. Before that, I have seen magistrates upon the petty jury. I have not seen magistrates latterly on the petty jury.

4683. You are aware it is the case in many counties?—I do not know; I do not profess to know anything except about my own county.

4684. You have spoken about the summons; you object to the service of the summons by the police?—I do not think the police should be brought into it; they have a particular duty to do; they get up, I do not say improperly, it is their duty to do so, the cases for the Crown against the prisoner.

4685. Who sends out the summonses?—The sheriff.

4686. Has not the sheriff officers of his own; that is to say, a process server?—No; bailiffs.

4687. Bailiffs in each district who would serve his own summonses?—That is the way it is done. But I being an old sheriff, know that a great many are not summoned, from whom they get half-a-crown.

4688. Might not that be the same with the process servers?—No; not according to what I suggested. There is a list made out, and I should have the summonses filled and given to them for service, and a penalty put upon them for non-service, unless they showed good cause. I think also they should be paid a fair sum for the service. It is not fair to impose a duty upon men without paying them.

4689. Who pays for this at present?—Nobody.

4690. Mr. *Downing*.] The sheriff does himself?—Not expressly; there is no payment for the service, but it is part of the duty of the bailiff.

4691. Colonel *Vandeleur*.] The county pays nothing?—The county pays the sheriff 92 *l.* 6 *s.* 8 *d.* each half year.

4692. There is no extra charge?—No.

4693. Under this new Bill there is an extra charge for everything?—Well, I like people to be paid, I must say.

4694. Mr. *Attorney General*.] I understand you to object to the principle of selection altogether?—That is on the old system?

4695. Yes?—I do decidedly.

4696. When you say that you would be perfectly indifferent as to the religion of persons who tried you or anyone else, I understand you to assume in that, that the persons are chosen indifferently, and not for the special purpose of trying a particular person?—No, not at all; indifferently.

4697. I have looked at these panels; you say you cannot tell me anything beyond Monaghan, but it is the universal practice, as far as you know in Monaghan, to have the panels in this way, and not alphabetically?—On the old system.

4698. This is 1869?—The panel is not to be alphabetical· I never knew the panel made alphabetically

4699. It s entirely contrary to the English practice as far as I know it?—I do not know the English practice.

4700. The panel is always alphabetical whatever the jury book is; but that is not so in Ireland?—I never knew it to be the practice.

4701. You pointed very truly at what, I suppose, in all places has been a great practical evil; that is to say, the summonses not being delivered for improper reasons, the summoning officer getting something not to deliver them, or to forget that he delivers them, or something of that sort; I ask honestly for information. Do you really think the post would break down in Ireland?—I will tell you why it would break down with the class of people you have to deal with as common jurors. You have to deal with a great many farmers, living not in towns or villages, but where they are far from a country post-office. They are people who, some of them at least, receive perhaps not more than half-a-dozen letters in their lives. They never go to a post-office to look for their letters. There is no individual whose duty it would be to go round as a postman would go round to houses in towns, and deliver registered letters.

4702. Have you any country postmen in Ireland?—No, not for the delivery of letters; in towns there are postmen.

4703. In the ordinary run of agricultural parishes in Monaghan, for instance, there are no postmen?—No postmen for the delivery of letters.

4704. I mean persons to go round the country and deliver them?—No; there is a postman to carry a letter bag from an office to a sub-office; but that is a different thing.

4705. I do not mean that; there is no person to go round the country districts to deliver to the various cottagers?—There is not in Monaghan; and I do not believe there is in any county in Ireland.

4706. Colonel *Wilson Patten*.] Are there not in the county of Monaghan several districts of small posts in the town?—Yes.

4707. In villages?—And out of villages.

4708. Are those pretty well spread out over the country?—I think you may say they are pretty well spread over the country. I do not think there is any square distance of six miles without one.

4709. There is nobody attached to these local post offices who could be deputed to carry a registered letter?—There is nobody.

4710. You stated to the Attorney General just now, the number of cases, civil and criminal, tried at different assizes and sessions?—I stated to the Attorney General an average on the instant. I may be wrong either way in that average; I do not like to average either the number to be tried or the number of jurors. I told you what I think is the average number of jurors summoned on the panel, 200 on each panel for the assizes, and as well as my recollection serves me, I had always a panel of 150 names for the sessions.

4711. Can you tell the Committee about what proportion of the jurors summoned have been called upon to serve within your knowledge?—I would average it at one-half.

4712. Have you ever known instances where there has been an absence of jurymen?—Yes, I recollect a case of mine.

4713. Where there were not sufficient jurymen present?—Where a man was to be tried for an

Mr. *J. Reilly.*

16 June 1873.

an offence where he had a right of challenge, and got a very energetic attorney who challenged the whole panel out.

4714. Colonel *Vandeleur.*] That could not be provided for?—It was for the purpose of going to the assizes; they thought they would get better off, and they got worse off.

4715. Colonel *Wilson Patten.*] Having answered the question put to you as to the number of jurymen required for the county Monaghan, are you still of opinion that 1,124 is the number that would be absolutely necessary?—Yes; I do not think the assizes should depend upon the chance of having the same jury to try several cases; I think you should have a proper number to try all; I think it is not the sheriff's business to look to that; the sheriff might render himself liable to a heavy fine from the judge if there were jurors wanting.

4716. *The O'Conor Don.*] Do you undertake to say that, on an average, there are as many as 80 criminal cases at the assizes in Monaghan in a year? -There are eight criminal sessions. No, I think 80 is too much; I would say 60 is an average.

4717. Supposing the alphabetical order were departed from in the selection of the jury from the panel, would you approve of ballotting in criminal cases?—I think it would be the next best thing.

4718. Colonel *Vandeleur.*] Did you mean to say that you had 400 for each assizes; 200 for each court?—One common panel does for both courts.

4719. You said 400 for the assizes?—That is for two assizes.

4720. Two hundred for each assizes?—Yes.

Tuesday, 24th June 1873.

MEMBERS PRESENT:

Dr. Ball.	Marquis of Hartington.
Mr. Bruen.	The O'Conor Don.
Viscount Crichton.	Colonel Wilson Patten.
Mr. Downing.	Colonel Vandeleur.

THE RIGHT HONOURABLE THE MARQUIS OF HARTINGTON, IN THE CHAIR.

Mr. WILLIAM ORMSBY, called in; and Examined.

Mr. *W. Ormsby.* — 24 June 1873.

4721. Mr. *Bruen.*] You have filled the office of Sub-Sheriff both in the county and city of Dublin, I think, on many occasions?—Yes, I have.

4722. Are you now sub-sheriff of the city of Dublin?—I am.

4723. Were you sub-sheriff of the county of Dublin in the year 1872?—I was not.

4724. Can you tell the Committee who was sub-sheriff then?—Mr. John Malet Williamson.

4725. Has your attention been drawn to some evidence which was given before this Committee by Mr. Frederick Hamilton?—It has.

4726. What do you wish to say with regard to his evidence as respects the preparation of the panel to which he referred?—I had nothing to do with the formation of that panel.

4727. But you have on many occasions, of course, had to summon panels?—Yes, a great many. I have been sub-sheriff for 12 years for the county, and a good many years for the city.

4728. Are you aware of any complaint having been made against you, on account of the proportion of the different religions of the jurors summoned upon these panels?—Never. I can say that on some occasions during the Fenian trials, I have had six Catholics and six Protestants on a jury, and they always agreed; there never was any complaint, and there were several Fenian cases tried.

4729. Have you ever made it your business to inquire into the religion of the jurors, before you put them on the panels?—Never.

4730. Do you think it is a proper thing for the sheriff or the sub-sheriff to inquire into the religion of jurors before summoning them to serve?—I do not.

4731. Since Mr. Hamilton's evidence has been brought to your notice, have you made any inquiries as to the formation as regards religion of that panel which you are supposed to have summoned?—I did not ask any one, but I looked over it myself since reading that evidence, and I have got a copy of the panel.

4732. Dr. *Ball.*] What was the panel for?—It was for the Queen's Bench in the county of Dublin, for Michaelmas Term, 1872, to try all cases.

4733. Mr. *Bruen.*] Looking at that panel, without having obtained any extra information from others upon it, do you believe that the assertion is true that it was composed of 47 Protestants and one Roman Catholic?—No; I know that there were more than one myself. I know of my own knowledge that there were two Roman Catholics: there was Valentine O'Connor, a man very well known in Dublin, and the last man on the panel, is chairman to the Kingstown Commissioners. I know them both personally, but I could not speak as to the religion of the persons on the panel in general, although I believe that most of them are Protestants.

4734. Since that evidence has been given, have you ascertained in any way, or attempted to ascertain what the proportion of Protestants and Roman Catholics is upon the Jury Lists of the county of Dublin, for instance; how was it in the year 1872?—Not in 1872; I could not say that; but I have brought them with me here, several panels, which I have made out myself, for 1871 and 1870. I could not tell with regard to anything about the panels for the county in 1872.

4735. My question was as regards the jury book?—I have not the jury book either in 1872.

4736. But previously in the composition of the jury book, I suppose the Protestants are largely in excess of the Roman Catholics?—They are.

4737. Do you think that the evidence given by Mr. Hamilton, that the proportion of three Protestants to one Roman Catholic is correct?—I should say that there are more Protestants.

4738. I do not wish to press you to give an answer as to the relative proportions of the two religions, because you have already stated that you did not inquire into it, but have you any idea of the relative proportions of the two religions upon the Jury Lists during the years that you were sub-sheriff?—I could not say, but I am quite sure that the proportions are fully what Mr. Hamilton said they were in his evidence, that is to say, in the Special Jury.

4739. But as regards the panels which you say you have brought with you, can you give the Committee any information as to the composition of those panels?—I can; I went to a gentleman who knows the county very well, Mr. Smart; he is deputy clerk of the peace under Mr. Gale, and has been for years; and I thought that he knew the religion of the jurors as well as any person that I could go to; and I got him to go over them and mark them with me. Before that I did not know their religion generally; I knew

Mr. W. Ormsby.

24 June 1873.

knew the religion of a few that I knew intimately, like Mr. O'Connor, but I did not know the others. I have brought a copy of the Michaelmas panel of the county of Dublin for 1870, in which year Mr. Hone was the high sheriff, and I was his sub-sheriff.

4740. What is the proportion on that panel?—Sixteen Roman Catholics out of the 48.

4741. Dr. *Ball.*] That is the special jury panel, is it not?—Yes; I have also brought a copy of the panel for 1871, and the proportion in that was 10 Roman Catholics out of the same number.

4742. Mr. *Downing.*] Was that also the special jury panel?—Yes.

4743. Mr. *Bruen.*] Have you other panels?—I have brought the panels for the city; it was just by the merest chance that I got them, for I do not keep them. There are very few county cases; they are mostly city cases. At some of the after sittings there are no county cases tried at all.

4744. Will you give the information to the Committee with regard to those other panels?—I have brought six special jury panels for the city. Mr. Stirling was high sheriff in 1870, and on this one which I have in my hand, there were 17 Roman Catholics.

4745. Those special jury panels, of which you are now giving evidence, are formed by the sub-sheriff, by selection from the jury lists, are they not?—Yes, from the jurors' book.

4746. Will you have the goodness just to go over the different panels, and name the year and name the proportions of the Roman Catholics on them?—I have three for the year 1870, for different terms for the Queen's Bench, and there are 15 Roman Catholics on one, 17 on another, and 17 on another. In 1871 I have three, and there are 25 Roman Catholics on one, 21 on another, and 17 on another.

4747. Those panels are not picked ones, I presume?—Certainly not.

4748. They are just those that you happened to have been able to obtain, in order to give information before this Committee?—They are; I told my clerk to get them, and what is more I think it is but fair to say that I myself have not a Protestant in my employment in my office, and they are all Roman Catholics; I have in my office three clerks, all Roman Catholics.

4749. As far as you are aware the composition of the other jury panels, of which you have had the formation, was similar to these?—Yes, it was; I never made any distinction.

4750. As regards the system of alphabetical selection, have you any objection to that system?—It will never do in Dublin; it is impossible for it to do in the county.

4751. Can you give the Committee any reasons why you think it will not succeed?—The principal people that are on the grand jury now are both illiterate and men that are not fit to be on a petty jury; I can give an instance, I was sent up by a judge the other day, in the last week, to tell the grand jury to send down a bill; the court were waiting many hours for them to send down a bill; they had not examined one witness, and they did not know how to examine him, and one of the jurors said, "It may be, your honour will examine them yourself, and find the bills for us, and we will do what you bid us."

4752. Dr. *Ball.*] That was in the county, was it not?—Yes, that was in the county; they were composed of dairymen, and market gardeners, and poor farmers that held from 15 to 30 acres of ground, and pay from 4 *l.* to 5 *l.* an acre rent.

4753. Mr. *Bruen.*] The valuation there is very high, is it not?—Yes, the valuation is very high.

4754. Do you think it would be an improvement for the county of Dublin, if there was added an exclusively household qualification?—I think it would be a very great improvement, a great many of the villa holders that pay some 70 *l.*, or 80 *l.*, or 90 *l.* a year, have houses valued at 40 *l.* or 50 *l.*, and they are all men of respectability, and gentlemen who would make a good class of jurors, especially in Rathmines, and Rathgar, and Kingstown.

4755. You probably might go much lower in the scale of valuation if you had a strictly household qualification, and not a compound qualification of house and land?—I think so.

4756. Dr. *Ball.*] Is it not the case that many of the tenants of those villa-residences at Rathmines and Rathgar have no land?—They have no land generally, and the same may be said of Blackrock and Longford-terrace, and all down there; they are very fine houses but with no land.

4757. Mr. *Bruen.*] As an officer of considerable experience in the working of the jury laws, what is your opinion as to the advisability of lodging in the hands of some officer the duty of selecting the jury panels and jury lists?—I think it would be very desirable; I do not think that the jury system will ever work well without it; for instance, summoning four people, which I have done, out of the same firm, and three out of another, is a very great inconvenience indeed. The Barringtons and the Williamsons, and several others, complain that it is very hard, and it really is so in the case of men of business to summon every one in a firm.

4758. Is it a fact, that at the late sittings of the court, the sheriff was obliged to summon himself?—Yes, the high sheriff, George Kinahan was; and I had to summon several people whom I knew were dead; for instance, Major Knox; I had to send summonses according to the Act, to people that I knew were quite incapable.

4759. Are there any other facts that you wish to bring before the Committee with regard to the duties of your office as sub-sheriff?—I would be very glad if the Committee would fix a scale of fees for the sheriff, if they are going to change the Act, or bring in a new Bill; I may mention that personally, I have had to bring the matter before the Court of Queen's Bench, and it is to be on again to-morrow with regard to the fees which Mr. Joint has refused to pay me, in the case of the late trial of the clergymen from Galway, who were tried under the old system.

4760. *Chairman.*] Fees for what?—For the sheriff for striking the juries under the old system, amounting to three guineas for each case; I may mention, that I have had the opinion of as eminent a man as any at the bar, I believe, Mr. Butt, who says, that I am entitled to them.

4761. Dr. *Ball.*] The fees that you claim, are in the case of a criminal trial at one side of the court, brought up by certiorari?—Yes.

4762. Your contention is, that the Crown, in a case of that character, is in the same position as a private suitor?—Yes, and the Custom-house always pay me in revenue cases; and if they withdraw a case after serving me with notice, they always pay me my fees. I have to attend, and

Mr. W. Ormsby.

24 June 1873.

and the name of every man on the jury must be counted over to me first, and their names must be put into the box, and the first 24 names of the 48 are called out and written down, and then each party takes off 12.

4763. The same in criminal as in civil cases?—Yes, exactly.

4764. You might have to put 800 names into the box, must you not?—Yes, and more; as many as 3,900 names.

4765. *The O'Conor Don.*] You consider that you should receive special fees for that?—I consider that I am entitled to them, and I have been paid them for the last 23 years until now.

4766. Dr. *Ball.*] You are always paid in a civil case, are you not?—Yes.

4767. Mr. *Bruen.*] In the city of Dublin, how soon do you think that the jury book would be exhausted?—It is very nearly exhausted at present; there are about six or seven letters only that are not exhausted now.

4768. *Chairman.*] Do you mean the Common Jury List?—Yes; the General Jurors' Book.

4769. Mr. *Bruen.*] How long do you anticipate that it will take to exhaust those names which are left?—The next after sittings will exhaust them.

4770. And then you will have to begin again, and take those that have served before?—Yes.

4771. How often in a year, or in two years will it impose service upon each juror?—I should say in two years about three times; the year is not out yet; I should remark that it is quite impossible for the sheriff to carry out the present Act as far as initialling and marking the jurors who have served, for there is no space left in the book that I have got to do it, and it is quite impossible for me to do it; there is no margin left by the clerk of the peace in the jurors' book.

4772. Mr. *Downing.*] I suppose that that would be very easily remedied by having a margin?—Yes, in a new book; I had to get it bound myself.

4773. I take it for granted that that is not the most serious objection to the present system?—Certainly not.

4774. I understand you to say, that you yourself, and I think very properly, never make any inquiry as to the religion or the party of those on the jury book?—Never; I never put them on with any reference to their religion.

4775. I presume that you are not very well acquainted with the religion of the parties on the jurors' book?—No, I am not; there are a great many that I am not.

4776. Mr. Hamilton stated that he was for 17 years attending to the registry, and that he had a most intimate knowledge of every one that was upon the panel to which he referred, and that there was but one Roman Catholic in the 48?—I have named two that I know personally.

4777. Can you name more than two?—No; I know those personally; one of them is a commissioner of the Kingstown township, and the other is Mr. Valentine O'Connor.

4778. If you were so disposed under the old system, and the panel had been left to you, you might as sub-sheriff have returned such a jury as a party might desire to have upon a party trial or a religious question?—I would perjure myself if I did so, I consider.

4779. But you might do it?—Yes, of course.

4780. Have you never heard that imputations of that kind were made upon sub-sheriffs?—Never made to me or of me.

4781. Have you never heard that such imputations were made of the sheriffs in Ireland?—I have not, until I heard that the imputation was made here; never, I may say.

4782. Are the inhabitants of the county of Dublin a particular ignorant class?—No, quite the reverse.

4783. Did I understand you to say that the grand jury for the county Dublin, to which you referred, was at the sessions?—No, at the commission the other day at Green-street.

4784. Did I understand you to say that that grand jury, composed of 23, were all so ignorant that they did not know how to examine a witness?—No, I did not say that; I said that I was asked by a grand juror to examine the witnesses, and to tell them what to find, and they would have the cases tried very quickly, and send them down.

4785. Must they not have been a particularly ignorant body to ask you, the sub-sheriff, to tell them what bills to find?—I think that they were very ignorant, a great number of them; I think there were even some that could not read or write, and some that did not know how to administer an oath.

4787. Were they all dairymen?—Certainly not.

4786. Were they all market gardeners?—No.

4788. Have you got a list of the grand jury?—Not here, but I can very easily get it.

4789. Were there no men of respectability and intelligence upon that grand jury?—Yes, there were.

4790. Who was the poor man?—I could not from recollection tell you, but I do not think that he knew much about the case; he was a stranger; they were mostly all strangers; they were not the class of grand jurors that I would have summoned.

4791. *Chairman.*] Were the grand jurors at the commission summoned alphabetically?—Yes.

4792. Mr. *Downing.*] You would have no difficulty in procuring a list of that grand jury and sending it to the Committee?—Certainly not; I have a copy of it at home, and I will furnish it to the Committee.

4793. With regard to summoning four out of the same house, it would be very easy to get rid of that matter by creating a new Act of Parliament, and saying that no two persons out of the same house should be summoned at the same assizes, or the same quarter sessions?—Yes, of course that might be done.

4794. I presume that the sheriff did not suffer very much by having himself returned upon the panel?—He did not suffer, but virtually instead of 48 there were only 47 names, because he was serving as sheriff in another place; he was served for the commission; it was at the Queen's Bench that he was summoned.

4795. Do you think that it is likely to take place again for a great many years, that the sheriff himself will be summoned on a special jury?—I would not be surprised at the same thing taking place after a year or two.

4796. Do you think that it would not be difficult to remedy that in an Act of Parliament?—No, I do not; I only thought it right to mention the circumstance.

4797. Have you any other grievance under this Act of Parliament, except the matters which you have stated?—I am only just mentioning these

these as instances; I am not complaining, for it makes no difference to me.

4798. Do not you approve of the new system of taking from the sheriff the power to select?—I do not.

4799. You would like to retain that power, would you?—I would not, but I think there is no man more competent to form those panels than he is; he is the responsible person. With regard to attorneys' clerks being on juries, I know a person now who is an attorney's clerk who is on the grand jury, and I know there are judges' tipstaffs who are on grand juries.

4800. Notwithstanding all that, I understand you to say that you would not wish to see the sheriff still have the power of selection?—I do not care about it; I have no wish one way or the other.

4801. My question went beyond that; I asked you whether you would wish to retain the power of selection still?—I have not the slightest wish on the subject.

4802. Mr. *Bruen*.] You are speaking personally, are you not?—I am.

4803. Mr. *Downing*.] You have heard, no doubt, what we have heard, here, that there were jurors in Dublin called guinea pigs?—Yes.

4804. You understand perfectly well what that means?—Yes, perfectly well.

4805. Were not they a class of jurors that somehow or other contrived to get constantly upon the juries, and who were paid a guinea for each trial?—I do not think that the sheriff would have put them on if he had a good attendance, but he knew that they were the more skilful, and they were the best men that could be put on the juries I believe, for they were so well up to the cases, and there was no trouble as there is now.

4806. Do you think that the suitors had confidence in them?—Certainly I do.

4807. And the bar?—And the bar; I never heard them complain about them.

4808. Have you read Mr. Serjeant Armstrong's evidence?—I have not.

4809. Would you be surprised if he stated here that when he saw a juror about to be sworn, and who was sworn, he actually withdrew the record, knowing perfectly well that he could not get a verdict?—I never knew of such an instance.

4810. Did the high sheriff ever interfere with you in the forming of your panels?—One high sheriff did.

4811. Who was he?—Mr. Darcy.

4812. He was high sheriff last year, was he not?—Yes.

4813. He is a Roman Catholic, I believe?—Yes, he is.

4814. And he was the only high sheriff during your whole experience that ever interfered with you with regard to your selection of the panels?—I think he was; I have been sub-sheriff to several Roman Catholics; I was sub-sheriff to the Honourable Jenico Preston, to Mr. Malach Hussey, and to Mr. Darcy, and Sir Charles Domvile was the first person whom I served under at all in Dublin. I was sheriff for Sligo 10 years before I came to Dublin.

4815. In returning your special jury panels, did the recorders ever interfere with you?—Never.

4816. Are you aware that under the law previously to Perrin's Act, you could not summon a juror in the city of Dublin until the third term after he had once served on a jury?—No; I was not aware of that.

4817. And that you were obliged to give him a certificate of his attendance, which protected him from being summoned again?—I never was aware of that.

4818. Time after time were those guinea pigs on your panel?—Some of what you call guinea pigs, and some of the men that I have put on have been most respectable men and good jurors; but I never make any distinction about their religion; I put on both Catholics and Protestants. I never make any distinction.

4819. If that course was pursued strictly by every sub-sheriff in Ireland, probably we should have heard no complaint?—I do not know as to that.

4820. *The O'Conor Don*.] You stated in answer to the honourable Member for Carlow, that the jurors' book in Dublin would be exhausted at the next after sittings?—Yes.

4821. Do you mean to say that all the jurors on that book have actually served?—No.

4822. What proportion of them have actually served?—Not one-fourth of them, I should say.

4823. Then it does not follow, from what you have stated with respect to the jurors' book being exhausted, that the same gentlemen would be obliged to serve three times in two years?—I do think so, and I will tell you why; I summon 48 on the special jury and 48 on the petty jury, but in all probability one half of them sometimes do not attend.

4824. *Chairman*.] Do you only summon 48 on the petty jury panel?—Yes; that is all.

4825. Mr. *Downing*.] Do you mean for the Green-street Commission?—No, that is the long panel, but I mean for the juries for civil cases, I summoned 170 on the long panel this time for Green-street; I made my clerk take a memorandum of the number. The prisoner has the power of challenging 20, and the Crown so many, and I summoned 48 special and 48 petty. There are four courts independently of the other courts that sometimes now require juries, that did not before; I had one the other day in the Rolls' Court.

4826. *The O'Conor Don*.] Do you think it desirable that jurors who have actually served, should not be called upon again until the other jurors who have not served, have put in an appearance?—If it could be managed, I think it would; but I think it would be very difficult to manage it, for there are a great many other jurors that never put in an appearance, and who are disqualified for different reasons, who are over age or deaf, and so on.

4827. Do you think it possible by any system to discover these disqualified jurors, and to have their names struck off the list?—I think that that should be done.

4828. If that were done, if disqualified jurors were taken off the list, of course that objection would not continue?—Of course that would make a great difference.

4829. In that case would you think it desirable that jurors who have served before should be exempted from serving again, until others have also served?—I think so; I think it is but fair to make each take a portion of the work, and I think that they should be paid also; a special juror is sometimes engaged for a fortnight or three weeks, and now he only gets a guinea for the whole time; and I think that is a very great hardship

Mr. *W. Ormsby.*

24 June 1873.

hardship for men of business, who lose a great deal of time, and some of them are poor men.

4830. Colonel *Vandeleur.*] You stated, did you not, that the grand jury in Green-street was very bad?—Very bad.

4831. And I think you said, that neither the foreman nor any of the grand jury appeared to be able to conduct the business?—They conconducted the business, but they required to be told what to do. I believe that they did not know anything about it until they were told, and some of them, I do not think, can even read or write.

4832. They were also called, were they not, in alphabetical order?—Yes.

4833. Not by selection?—No.

4834. Is that the case with other grand juries, for instance, the grand juries at the sessions?—No; they are not selected by the sheriff.

4835. That is to try county cases?—Yes; if there are any cases in the county they come before them. The present time is the only time that they have had cases of any importance.

4836. What description of cases were there to try at Green-street?—Manslaughter cases and criminal cases.

4837. You mentioned also, that you would prefer a household qualification as producing a very good description of jurors?—Yes.

4838. What rating would you put upon that for the county of Dublin for special jurors or common jurors to try the questions that come before the courts?—The common jury are the best jury now in the county of Dublin.

4839. Do you mean those selected under the new Act?—Yes; I know very respectable gentlemen who are summoned there on the grand jury, all men in business; Mr. Alley, for instance, men who always served before as common jurors.

4840. You said that in the neighbourhood of Rathmines and the different suburbs of Dublin, there are a large number of jurors with a rating which would produce in your opinion a good description of jurors?—Yes; I should say a 40 *l.* household rating for special jurors.

4841. And those special jurors could also serve upon common juries if required?—Yes; on the long panel.

4842. They would answer for both in fact?—Yes.

4843. With regard to the fees, what expenses have been created which are now chargeable to the county under the new Act in the county of Dublin?—There is no fee to the county, excepting summoning the juries, and the stamp that goes on the summons.

4844. The sheriff receives nothing from the county rates for any of the duties that he performs?—No; nothing under the new Act at all, excepting 3 *d.* for the stamp, which he puts upon each summons by post. I serve them by post now in the county and the city generally, but that is different from other counties.

4845. Have you found that in practice to answer?—Very well.

4846. Are the letters ever refused?—Some are; for instance, if a man is in a large way of business. I have been told when a letter is sent to him by post that he is out of the country, and I have known it to occur that letters have been sent to men who are dead.

4847. There have been cases in which registered letters have been sent, and the parties suspecting what they were, have not received them or have refused them?—Yes; but I find it to answer very well in Dublin to serve the summonses by registered letter. It is very hard to get men, no matter how you may pay them, to serve some persons, for a great many people if you send a man, will say to him, "Here is 5 *s.*," or, "Here is 10 *s.*, do not serve me," and the man may come back to me and say, "That man has left the place, he is away." I have no means of discovering it and I have not time to find it out.

4848. The service of the summonses was paid for by the sheriff up to this time, was it not?—Yes.

4849. Are you aware of the expenses the clerks of the peace were paid for forming the new lists?—No, I am not.

4850. Dr. *Ball.*] In the county of Dublin the principal part of the farming class live on the north side, do they not, or at least they used to do so?—Yes, they do.

4851. It never struck me that they were at all an intelligent class; what is your experience?—I am quite sure that they are not.

4852. Do not you think that the county of Dublin is altogether exceptional on account of the number of villas belonging to merchants and gentlemen who occupy them?—Yes, and private gentlemen also.

4853. Legislation therefore as to that county should be confined to itself, and exceptional?—I should say so.

4854. In consequence of the number of the inhabitants of the city who live in the country, it should have some approximation, should it not, to the mode in which you deal with the city?—Yes.

4855. And of the crime that is in the county, is not that principally crime that comes from the city?—Very often.

4856. In fact all round Dublin, Rathmines, Clontarf, and all those suburban districts, are nothing in reality but an extension of the city?—No doubt.

4857. And they have much more analogy to that than they have to the general condition of the rural counties?—Yes. I may mention that sometimes I have summoned the same person twice, because he may be rated in two different places, but his name is put down and I have had to summons him twice over.

4858. What do you think should be the household qualification for special jurors?—I should say from 40 *l.* upwards.

4859. And for a common jury what would you say?—From 20 *l.* and upwards.

4860. Do you think that you would get an excellent panel in this way?—Yes, I think that a person rated at 20 *l.* is likely to be a very good juror.

4861. With respect to your own panels, there are a great many exemptions, are there not, from liability to serve, which shut out professional men in Dublin, so that no attorneys and no barristers can serve?—Certainly, but under the new law there are lots of attorneys' clerks and lots of people in that class who are liable to serve.

4862. In your own panels you were excluded from the professional class?—Yes.

4863. Was not the effect, therefore, that you had to come to the mercantile class?—Yes.

4864. If you took a very high standard of the trading

Mr. W. Ormsby.

24 June 1873.

trading and mercantile class, the preponderance would be Protestants, would it not?—Yes, certainly.

4865. And that without any design on your part?—Certainly.

4866. *Chairman.*] I think you said that you had nothing to do with the selection of the panel in Michaelmas Term, 1872, to which attention has been called?—I had nothing to say to it at all.

4867. By whom was that panel prepared?—The sub-sheriff was Mr. John Malet Williamson, who was sub-sheriff to Mr. Hutchinson.

4868. You are sub-sheriff now, are you not?—I am.

4869. And you have been sub-sheriff for many years?—For 12 years. I was only out one year. In 1860 I came to Dublin first, and I have been ever since sub-sheriff for the county, except last year.

4870. You have produced, I think, two or three special jury panels which you have struck?—Yes, I have produced two from the county and six from the city.

4871. Were those two from the county, as far as you remember, average specimens of the jury panels which you struck?—They were.

4872. And both of them contained, I think, a considerable number of Roman Catholics?—Yes.

4873. Can you account at all for the circumstance that in this panel to which attention has been called, there should be only two Roman Catholics?—I am sure that there were two. I cannot account for the number. Mr. Williamson and I were not very thick, and I did not give him any assistance or advice upon the matter. He asked me if I would, and I refused to give him any advice or assistance. He never was sub-sheriff before, and I think he never will be again; he was never sub-sheriff for either the county or the city before.

4874. By whom was that special jury list from which that panel was taken prepared?—I got it from the clerk of the peace.

4875. Was it prepared by him?—I do not know who prepared it for him, or how it was prepared.

4876. It is now a very different book from the old book, is it not?—It is.

4877. At all events it would be quite impossible, would it not, under the present law, that the special jury panel should contain only two Catholics out of 48 names?—I do not think it could possibly occur.

4878. Have you any other statement which you wish to make to the Committee?—No, I am not aware of anything further.

Mr. William Mitchell, called in; and Examined.

Mr. W. Mitchell.

4879. *Chairman.*] Are you at present sub-sheriff of the county of Monaghan?—I am.

4880. Have you previously been sub-sheriff?—I have.

4881. In what years?—In the years 1861, 1862, 1863, 1865, 1866, 1867, 1868, part of 1869, and in 1871 and 1872.

4882. Has your attention been called to the evidence given by Mr. Reilly before this Committee?—It has.

4883. With reference to the composition of the jury panel in the year 1869?—With reference to that and other portions of his evidence.

4884. Do you wish to make any statement upon it?—I wish to make a statement relative to those marks or crosses opposite the Roman Catholics' names; the high sheriff was dismissed in 1869, and after the quashing of the panel at the spring assizes in that year I went over the jury book for the purpose of ascertaining the proportions of Protestants and Roman Catholics on that book, and I placed opposite the name of every Roman Catholic a cross; the other marks to which Mr. Reilly alludes, and which he says he could not explain, were marks to distinguish sessional grand jurors at the quarter sessions, special jurors at the assizes, and petty jurors at the assizes and quarter sessions.

4885. You formed the panel which was quashed?—I did.

4886. Do you wish to state anything to the Committee upon the subject of that panel?—I do; that panel that was quashed was a counterpart of the panel which I made for the summer assizes of 1868, with some exceptions; I have a copy of the calendar of that assizes, by which it appears that there were only three trifling cases to be tried, two of assault, and one of the larceny of a shilling, three custody cases, and no bail cases; I got the calendar and information from the governor of the gaol; riots occurred of a party nature in Monaghan immediately after those assizes; they were riots at the contested election in November 1868, and I followed the panel of that assizes as closely as I could, putting on as nearly as I could persons in the place of those who had emigrated or had died, or who were not in fact on the new jury book.

4887. Do you mean that you summoned the same jury panel for the spring assizes of 1869 as you had summoned for the summer assizes of 1868?—As closely as I could.

4888. Was it your practice always to summon the same jurors?—In that case I did so summon them, as there had been some remark made that there would not be a fair panel at the spring assizes of 1869. The panel of 200 I considered too small; it was 200, and I increased it by 50 of the special jury panel, and placed them at regular intervals on the panel.

4889. Dr. *Ball.*] That is to say you put 50 from the special jury panel in the other panel?—The panel of special jurors was about 50 at each assizes.

4890. When you increased the panel did you take 50 names that were special jurors and put them up and down the common jury panel?—Yes, I did so at regular intervals on the common jury panel.

4891. *Chairman.*] What else did you do?—I did nothing else.

4892. Do you remember what the composition of that jury panel was as to religion?—I can refer to that from memorandums that I have. There were 49 Roman Catholics out of 250.

4893. Do you know how many Roman Catholics there were upon the jury that was struck to try the case of McKenna?—There was no jury empanelled to try McKenna; the jury was called over, but not empanelled.

4894. Do you know what jury is referred to in Question 4417 of Mr. Reilly's evidence, where he was asked, "Was that an exclusively Protestant

Mr. W. *Mitchell.*

24 June 1873.

testant jury"?—I remember that trial and that jury, but I cannot tell how it was composed.

4895. Is it probable that although there were 49 Roman Catholics upon the panel, the jury might be composed on that panel exclusively of Protestants?—It is possible.

4896. The names of the Protestants would have come first, would they?—No, I do not say that.

4897. They would be a large proportion, would they not?—I cannot say; I never formed a panel according to religion.

4898. Upon what principle were they arranged upon the panel?—I raised them from the different baronies. I took them in the baronies, and I called so many jurors from each barony, one or two persons who I believed were intelligent first of all, and then I took them, some from one barony and some from another; and, as well as I recollect, I mixed them from the different baronies.

4899. Were they arranged in their ordinary qualification from the top to the bottom?—No.

4900. You did not put all the highest rated jurors at the top?—No; I knew nothing about the rating when I formed the panel.

4901. Will you explain exactly how you arranged the panel?—I arranged the panel by putting one or two men of respectability at the top of the panel that I knew were respectable men, and the others, I took a man here, and a man there, from the different baronies.

4902. Did you take them perfectly promiscuously?—From the baronies, perfectly promiscuously, one here and another there; and if I saw a respectable man, I would put him on the panel, and mark the jury book at his name; generally, I summon so many from each barony.

4903. So that, as far as you are aware, the 49 Roman Catholics upon that panel, were scattered about here and there through the panel?—Yes, as far as I am aware, but I cannot say now what position they were in, unless I saw the panel. I may mention that on that panel of 1869, the first two men that answered, when the panel was called over, were Roman Catholics.

4904. Is it a fact, as stated by Mr. Reilly, that of the first 70 names, there were only seven Roman Catholics?—I cannot say.

4905. You have the panel, have you not?—No, I have not; I left immediately after getting the summons, and I had not time to get it after receiving the summons.

4906. Mr. *Downing.*] Is this the panel (*handing a paper to the Witness*)?—Yes; this is the panel.

4907. Having the panel in your hand, I ask you whether it is a fact, as your attention has been called to the evidence, that of the first 70 names, there were only seven Roman Catholics?—I see that it is a fact, as far as I can judge from this panel.

4908. Would it be probable that the jury would be struck out of the first 70 names?—No.

4909. What is the process of forming the jury?—Calling the panel over, left about 60 or 70 names; that panel, as well as I recollect, was called, and 70 answered when it was called over first.

4910. How would the juries be struck?—By striking the first 70 names that would answer; the panel was generally exhausted before there was enough got, and from those that answered the jury was struck; a great many jurors would not answer.

4911. Would the first man who answered be put on the jury if he was not ordered to stand by or challenged?—If he answered he would.

4912. And so on with regard to the others?—Yes, and so on with the others.

4913. Then those jurors at the top would have a better chance of serving on the jury than those at the bottom, would they not?—They have a better chance. In my experience I have almost invariably seen the panel exhausted before a sufficient number would answer.

4914. You do not know whether that jury to which I have called your attention referred to in Question 4417, was or was not an exclusively Protestant jury?—I do not. I cannot say from recollection.

4915. You have not come here to contradict that?—No, I have not.

4916. Is there any other part of Mr. Reilly's evidence upon which you wish to make any observation, especially with regard to the jurors from the barony of Farney, which he said was a particularly Catholic barony, and the number of jurors returned upon the panel were 20?—That is correct. I never saw in any assizes more than 20 from Farney, it is a long way from Monaghan, and they almost invariably attend badly.

4917. You think that 20 was the average number summoned from that barony?—As an average not so many as 20. I generally summoned 60 from the barony of Monaghan, 50 from the barony of Cremorne, 40 from Dartree, 30 from Trough, and 20 from Farney; I think that makes up the 200.

4918. Was the reason of summoning so few from Farney, its distance from the county town?—Yes; and as a rule they did not attend.

4919. Is it a fact that it is particularly called a Catholic barony?—There is no doubt that it is so. I never heard it called that name, but there are a great many Roman Catholics in it, more so than in any other barony in the county.

4920. In answer to the next question, No. 4448, "What position have they on the panel?" he stated, "With the exception of one, all at the end of the panel." Can you explain why, with the exception of one, they were all at the end of the panel?—Except in that assizes I put them there, knowing that they would not attend; it was the panel of summer assizes of 1868 that I followed, which was a panel composed previously to those outrages.

4921. You placed them at the end of the panel because you knew that they would not attend?—That is the only reason that I can give. I do not remember.

4922. Being placed there, would they be likely to be empaneled on the jury?—They would not be likely to be empaneled at the summer assizes of 1868, which panel I followed.

4923. We are talking of the spring assizes of 1869?—Yes, but it is the same panel. There are other jurors near the end, respectable men from the barony of Dartree.

4924. Are you here to make any statement to the Committee about the operation of the new Act?—So far as I have seen of the operation of the new Act in Monaghan at the sessions and assizes, it has appeared with some few exceptions to work very fairly. I think that the 20 *l.* qualification will get respectable enough petty jurors, and

Mr. W. Mitchell.

24 June 1873.

and the 50 *l.* qualification will get very fair special jurors.

4925. Would it make a very large addition to the number on the common jurors' book?—The common jurors' book in 1869, had generally about from 1,200 to 1,300 names on it; after 1869, from some reason, I suppose looking more particularly to the qualification of the jurors, the juror's book was reduced to something between 700 and 900 names, which was the number of the petty jurors for 1871 and 1872. There were only, I think, between 700 and 800 names on the jurors' book, of men qualified under the old law. Now the new Act has increased it, I think, to a little over 1,800, and I should say, that in revising under the late temporary Act, they have been reduced to about 750. Those would be all on the jurors' book. There is a difficulty now in summoning the jurors. The expense has increased, and there are some jurors on the book that should not be on it at all.

4926. Of what class?—In some cases a juror is qualified in two baronies, and he is on the jurors' book for both, and sometimes summoned at the same assizes or the same sessions for both; but I have no power to put him off; and dead men also are summoned. In making out the list of the last summonses, the bailiff told me that in the case of one man, they would be obliged to have him carried out of his house, because he was permanently crippled. A change in the way of summoning the jurors, I think, would be very desirable.

4927. Dr. *Ball.*] In the county of Monaghan the higher you ascend in the social scale do they not become more Protestant?—They do.

4928. Therefore, when you took 50 names from the special jury panel, and inserted them into the common jury panel of 200 that were there before, you increased the preponderance of Protestants?—I did.

4929. Mr. *Bruen.*] But that was not done with a view of increasing the preponderance of Protestants on the jury?—It was not; it was to increase the panel by the addition of respectable jurors.

4930. Knowing that there were eight cases to be tried?—Yes, knowing that there were some heavy cases to be tried.

4931. You say that at the assizes of the summer of 1869, the cases were of a very trivial nature?—The cases at the summer assizes of 1868 were of a very trivial nature.

4932. In answer to the right honourable Chairman, with regard to the Farney men having a bad chance at that assizes of being put upon the jury, you say that they would have a bad chance?—They would.

4933. Was that owing to the fact that the whole panel was not gone through?—The whole panel was not gone through then, and I knew that there were no cases in which there was likely to be a challenge.

4934. Were there Farney men summoned upon the panel of 1869?—Yes, they were the same men that were summoned in 1868.

4935. *Chairman.*] As I understand, they were at the bottom of the panel?—Some of them were. I remember that the second man that answered to his name, when the panel was called over, was a Farney man.

4936. Mr. *Bruen.*] The assertion of Mr. Reilly is that, with the exception of one, all the Farney men are at the end of the panel; is that true?—It is not; there were only three out of the last 20 names who were from the barony of Farney.

4937. Then, take the next 20 names upwards, and see how many there are?—I only make out two.

4938. We have got five Farney men out of the last 40; take the next 20?—I think in the next 10 there are only two; I know a great many of the men, and the names of the places I know.

4939. There was no process of ascertaining how many Farney men there were in the third 20, counting from the bottom of the list?—I may have made a mistake in one or two; in the third 20 names there are two that I know.

4940. The evidence that you have given as to these numbers is not intended to be absolutely and entirely accurate; it is to the best of your belief, and you think that within one or two, the numbers that you have stated to us are correct?—Yes, I do. I may mention that there are some most respectable men at the end of the panel from Farney, and other places.

4941. *Chairman.*] I asked you a question which at first I understood you to answer in the affirmative, whether it was a fact that, with the exception of one, they are all at the end of the panel?—It is not correct.

4942. *The O'Conor Don.*] Could you tick off 20 names belonging to Farney on that panel?—I could very nearly give you them, I might make a mistake in two or three, but I think it would be very nearly accurate.

4943. Mr. *Bruen.*] At all events in the panel in the spring of 1869, you said the whole of that panel was gone through?—The long panel was called over and only 70 jurors answered, and then the panel was exhausted.

4944. If the men from the barony of Farney had attended, and wished to answer to their names, they could have done so?—They could.

4945. I want to draw your attention to Question 4386 of Mr. Reilly's evidence; that has reference, has it not, to Mr. Rogers?—Yes.

4946. The question is, "Did the sub-sheriff," that is Mr. Rogers, "with your assistance, and upon your suggestion, prepare the panel in 1864, as you prepared it in 1868?" Did Mr. Reilly prepare the panel in 1866?—He did not.

4947. You were sub-sheriff at that time, were you not?—I was sub-sheriff in 1866.

4948. Turning to Question 4369, you will see there that Mr. Reilly said that he filled the office of sub-sheriff in 1846?—He did.

4949. It is quite possible that 1866 may have been a misprint for 1846?—Yes it is.

4950. Had you had any communications with Mr. Rogers upon the subject?—I had.

4951. I believe Mr. Reilly did apply to you in February 1869?—He did.

4952. Is this his letter: "Dear Mitchell,—I called at your office, but finding you are not expected in, I now write that no time may be lost; I claim from you a fair panel of jurors for the next assizes; I know myself you can put the Protestants and Roman Catholics on alternately from your book, as I did so myself when returning officer for Harry Rogers; I expect you will do this, you cannot be blind to the state of excitement existing in this and neighbouring districts since the riots of July; I trust you will so frame your panel that my many clients may get a fair and impartial trial, and that no complaint be made to your conduct." That is a letter dated the

Mr. W. Mitchell.

24 June 1873.

the 5th February 1869, and in that the assertion is made that the Protestants and Roman Catholics were put on alternately by Mr. Reilly advising Mr. Rogers?—Yes.

4953. And in August 1869, when this panel was quashed, did you write a letter to Mr. Rogers in these terms: "10th August, 1869. My dear Sir,—Will you be good enough to let me know if in the year 1864, when you were sub-sheriff of this county, the jury panel was arranged by Mr. Reilly, by placing Protestants and Roman Catholics alternately on it"?—That is a copy of the letter I wrote.

4954. Is this the reply which you received: "12th of August 1869.—Dear Sir, In reply to your note of the 10th instant, asking me if in the year 1864 the jury panel was arranged by Mr. Reilly by placing Protestants and Roman Catholics alternately on it, I beg to say that when making out the panel for spring assizes 1864, I was assisted by Mr. Reilly, and, as far as I can recollect, the question of the religion of the jurors was never thought of by us. I enclose a copy of the panel, which will show you that they were not arranged Protestant and Roman Catholic alternately. In fact, it could not be so, as out of the 200 names on it, 140 at least are those of Protestants. The panel for the summer assizes was made out entirely by myself." Did you see that panel of 1864?—I did.

4955. Then that is a statement which Mr. Rogers absolutely contradicts?—It is.

4956. That letter says that there was no such consideration employed in the formation of the panel?—It does.

4957. Did you on that accusation against you inquire into the formation of the panel of 1864 and its composition?—I did.

4958. Did you find that it appears to be composed almost in the identical manner, as regards religion, as the previous panels?—I did.

4959. And those previous panels were selected by you, were they not?—They were.

4960. You were sub-sheriff first in 1861?—Yes, in 1861.

4961. What was the number of Roman Catholics on the panel in that year?—There were 66 out of the whole 200; as near as I can recollect, that was the number at that assizes.

4962. In 1862 you were sub-sheriff?—Yes, I was.

4963. What was the number of Roman Catholics upon the panel in that year?—Forty.

4964. In 1863 you were sub-sheriff?—I was.

4965. What was the number of Roman Catholics upon the panel in that year?—Fifty.

4966. In 1864 Mr. Rogers was sub-sheriff?—Yes.

4967. That was the year in which Mr. Reilly says that the panel was composed in strict proportion to the numbers of Protestants and Roman Catholics upon the jury list?—Yes.

4968. What was the number of Roman Catholics upon that panel?—Fifty.

4969. The same number as was on the panel the year before?—Yes, the same number as the year before.

4970. In 1865 you were sub-sheriff?—I was.

4971. What was the number on the panel that year?—Fifty-three.

4972. In 1866 you were sub-sheriff?—I was.

4973. The number of Roman Catholics that year was what?—Sixty-six.

4974. In 1867 you were sub-sheriff, how many Roman Catholics were there then?—Fifty-four.

4975. In 1868, how many?—Forty-eight.

4976. In 1869, how many?—Forty-nine.

4977. I suppose you were obliged, under the old law, to have regard to the rating qualification of the jurors?—No.

4978. When I say that you were obliged, you were not absolutely obliged by the law, but you did have some regard to that?—I had regard to their position and intelligence.

4979. It was with regard to their position and intelligence, coupled with a fair distribution of service throughout the county, as regards the baronies, that you formed your panels?—Yes, it was. I generally took a better class of jurors for the assizes, if anything, than for the quarter sessions.

4980. But as regards religion, do you tell the Committee, most emphatically, that that element did not enter into your calculations when you formed the panels?—Never; nor do I believe that it should enter into the calculations of any sheriff.

4981. As to the change made by the new law, are you personally glad to be relieved from the responsibility of forming the panels?—I am.

4982. Is it entirely a personal consideration?—Entirely a personal consideration.

4983. But is it your opinion that the duty of selecting jurors, or summoning them upon the panel, should be entrusted to some official?—It should be vested in some one.

4984. Colonel *Vandeleur*.] Will you state how the county jurors' book was formed at that time?—There were revising sessions, at which the magistrates of the county presided, and the different barony constables brought their lists of jurors.

4985. How many names in each? I could not tell how many each barony constable brought; but there were something like between 1,200 and 1,300 jurors' names on the book. I am speaking now under the old Act; but of those 1,200 or 1,300 there were not more than one-half of them who were duly qualified by law. In Monaghan there were very few leases.

4986. Of late years the high constables returned according to their qualifications, generally the highest rated?—Yes; and those that they considered more eligible to serve on jurors, and men of intelligence.

4987. Had you anything to say to putting those men on the jury list?—Nothing.

4988. I mean as to who were Roman Catholics and who were Protestants?—No; the book was handed to me from the clerk of the peace office.

4989. Those lists were returned, were they not, not in dictionary order, but in alphabetical order?—They were returned in the different baronies.

4990. Each barony was returned to you in alphabetical order?—Yes, as well as I recollect, by the high constables of that barony; I should say not to me, but returned to the clerk of the peace; and I got the book from the clerk of the peace, arranged in baronies.

4991. You made out your panels from that book?—Yes, from that book.

4992. Taking so many from each barony, I presume?—Yes, so many from each barony; in fact, I might take all from one barony. There was an indiscriminate power left in the hands of the sheriff in that respect.

4993. In that book there was no reference made, was there, to the religion of any of the parties?—None.

4495. Will

Mr. *W. Mitchell.*

24 June 1873.

4994. Will you now state your opinion as to the formation of the new book, as to the dictionary arrangement?—I think, as far as Monaghan has gone, it works very well; we only experienced it at one quarter sessions, and part of another quarter sessions, and at the assizes, and it seemed, as far as I could judge, to work well enough. There should be a little discretion left with some person, for I may mention that at the last quarter sessions in Monaghan last week, in the case of one very respectable farmer, who had been accustomed to be foreman to the grand jury at the quarter sessions, his qualifications did not entitle him to be a grand juror any longer, and he was summoned as a petty juror, although, from intelligence and position, he had for years acted as foreman of the grand jury at the sessions.

4995. You think that the power of selection ought to be given as to placing men as foremen upon juries?—I do not mean as foremen alone; I mean that the power of selection should be vested in some one.

4996. You mentioned also, that you would suggest some change in summoning; will you now state what you referred to?—I referred to the way of summoning jurors to attend at the sessions and assizes, which is a most unsatisfactory way at present; I would recommend that it should be done by the constabulary; they have plenty of opportunity in the fairs and markets to serve the jurors, and the returns could be given in through the sub inspectors.

4997. Mr. *Downing.*] I understand that you have had the evidence of Mr. Reilly sent to you for the purpose of becoming acquainted with the evidence which he gave here?—It was.

4998. Is there any portion of it that you would wish to explain, save and except that portion with regard to the panel for 1864?—The principal thing that I wish to explain about is, the crosses opposite the Roman Catholic names. There is another statement which he makes; he says that the county pays the sheriff 92 *l.* 6 *s.* 8 *d.* each half year; that is wrong, it is only 37 *l.* each half year; but that is not very material.

4999. If I understood your explanation, it was this, that after the high sheriff had been dismissed in August 1869, your attention was called to the jurors' book, and that you then marked off the Roman Catholics that were upon that panel?—No; it was previous to his dismissal; it was after the quashing of the panel that I did it, at the spring assizes of 1869.

5000. You wish to qualify what you did say?—I do not think there is any qualification; it was after the quashing of the panel in 1869.

5001. You said that there were some other marks upon the jurors' book?—Yes.

5002. Could you inform the Committee what they were?—I believe the book is not here. In some of the jurors' books I have marked opposite the jurors that I considered qualified to act as special jurors at the assizes an "S," and a "G" opposite those whom I considered qualified to serve as grand jurors. On one of the jurors' books, and I believe on this one, I made a red mark on one class of jurors, and a blue mark on another class of jurors, on some jurors' books, and on that book which is in question I believe there are blue and red marks; I heard so, but I have not seen the jurors' book since 1869.

5003. You have admitted in answer to the noble Chairman, that there were only seven Roman Catholics in the first 70 names of the panel of the spring assizes of 1869?—Yes.

5004. I believe that amongst those seven, there are two publicans, or licensed to sell spirits?—I did not look over them; I dare say there are two or more licensed publicans in the first 70 names.

5005. As a matter of course, publicans are not called, but are put off?—I cannot say that; I know nothing at all about it.

5006. The Crown has the power, has it not, to set aside jurors?—Yes.

5007. And the prisoner has the right to challenge 20?—Yes, I believe so.

5008. What did you mean in answer to the noble Chairman, by saying that it was not likely that a jury to try a prisoner would be struck out of the first 70 names, the prisoner could only challenge 20?—I do not quite understand the honourable Member's question.

5009. You were asked whether it was not probable that a jury to try a criminal would be obtained out of the first 70 names, and you said that you did not think so; what was your reason for that opinion?—Because a great many jurors do not answer, and before the first 70 have answered, the panel is generally called over.

5010. Does not that apply to the jurors from number one to the last on the panel?—It does.

5011. If the numbers are called upon the panel, and if number one answers, and you go on to number six and he answers, and number 12 answers, and number 18 answers, would not the proportion of Roman Catholics and Protestants be likely to be the same amongst those who answer?—I do not understand what you mean.

5012. (*Chairman.*] Is it more likely that a jury would be taken out of the first 70 names, than out of the last 70?—I should think it is more likely out of the first 70; there would be more jurors to answer to their names than out of the last 70.

5013. Would not they be able out of the first 70?—I should think not; I never heard a panel called over, that I recollect, that all answered.

5014. Those would have to answer in order to get a jury out of the first 70?—I think it will take at least 70 jurors to answer to the challenges; the panel was exhausted in that assizes; 250 names were called over before 70 answered.

5015. Colonel *Vandeleur.*] That is a special case, is it not?—In many other cases I have seen the panel exhausted before 70 answered.

5016. Mr. *Downing.*] Surely the prisoner has only 20 peremptory challenges?—Yes, that is so.

5017. Then 50 must remain?—Yes.

5018. Could not the Crown set aside any out of that 50?—It was the custom in Monaghan that the prisoner could challenge any that he could show just cause against also.

5019. You have handed in the panel of 1864, and I see marks upon that panel, will you inform me what they mean; there is a star after a certain number of names, do those stars intimate that the names after which they are placed are Roman Catholics?—I think they do.

5020. Have you any doubt about that?—No; it is the panel that Mr. Rogers sent to me.

5021. If you count them, I think you will find that there are 19 Roman Catholics in the first 70 names?—Yes, there are 19 in the first 70.

5022. That is the panel Mr. Reilly called your attention to?—It is, but I never saw the panel till I got it from Mr. Rogers.

Mr. W. Mitchell.

24 June 1873.

5023. When Mr. Reilly called upon you to put a fair proportion of Roman Catholics upon the panel and referred to that panel, if you had referred to it would you have acted upon it?—I would not; I did not think it my duty, and I never did, look to the religion of the jurors.

5024. After the panel of the spring of 1869 was quashed, did you make out a perfectly distinct panel?—No.

5025. The panel of the spring of 1869 was almost identical, was it not, with that of the summer of 1868?—Yes, with the exception of the special jurors.

5026. Is it usual to summon the same men at three assizes, one following the other?—It is not.

5027. Did not you prepare the panel for the summer of 1869, with the exception of five or six names, identically the same as the panel that was quashed in the spring of 1869?—I did not, for 50 special jurors were taken off.

5028. Excepting that, was it not the same?—Yes, except that.

5029. And, although it was unusual to have the same jurors summoned for three assizes alternately, you did it in this case, leaving off 50 special jurors?—Yes, leaving off 50 special jurors it was almost a copy of the panel that was made in 1868.

5030. Although it was not usual to do that?—I generally followed the panel from one assize to another, because jurors were so scarce in Monaghan.

5031. You appear to know perfectly well the number of Roman Catholics in your panels which you have referred to here; in answer to the honourable Member for Carlow, you appeared to understand perfectly well the number of Roman Catholics and Protestants upon the jury?—I did; I took them from a statement which I made out at the time.

5032. In the 50 names that you added to the panel of the spring of 1869, upon the letter of Mr. Reilly, did you put more than one Roman Catholic amongst 50?—I think that there was only one Roman Catholic upon the special jury panel. To the best of my recollection there was only one Roman Catholic upon it.

5033. In the special jury list for the county of Monaghan how many were there?—There was only one on the panel.

5034. How many on the jurors' book were there?—There was no separate list of special and common jurors in the book.

5035. Where did you take them from?—I marked the men of position whom I considered suitable to act as special jurors.

5036. You had marked the men whom you knew to be men of position?—Yes.

5037. You marked off as men of position whom you would place upon the special list, 50 for trying important trials, and but one was a Roman Catholic?—I see only one.

5038. Who was he?—Mr. Downes, he is a shopkeeper in Carrickmacross.

5039. Mr. Downes of Carrickmacross was the only one Roman Catholic in the county of Monaghan who was a man of sufficient note and position to be put upon the common jury panel amongst the 50 specials?—I do not say that.

5040. Why did you not put more?—As I said before, the barony of Farney is the furthest from Monaghan, and very few jurors attend from it, and most of the Roman Catholics of position and independence, and qualified to be special jurors are in that barony.

5041. I thought you told the honourable and learned Member for the University of Dublin that the small farmers were in Farney, Roman Catholics?—I did not. There are many Roman Catholics in the barony of Farney, very respectable men.

5042. Are there no Roman Catholics in the barony of Monaghan itself that are fit to be put on the special jurors' list?—Yes, there are indeed.

5043. Why did you not put them on?—Those were men taken from the old panel. I never looked at their religion at all.

5044. We have this fact that in the 50 additional names that you put on, there was only one Roman Catholic?—Only one.

5045. We have also this fact, that upon that panel of 250 there were 49 Roman Catholics?—Yes.

5046. And they would be in the proportion of four to one?—Yes, about that.

5047. Upon all the previous panels that you have given us from 1861 to 1868, was not the proportion only three to one, if you take 50 from 200?—I think that in 1866 there were 66 on, and as well as I recollect there were 300 on that panel.

5048. Then the proportion at least was larger upon the previous panel?—You can calculate it. I have given the figures.

5049. I believe that you were examined before the trials when the panels were quashed?—Yes.

5050. There was a very strong feeling at that time, as stated by Mr. Reilly in his letter to Mr. Mitchell?—There is generally a strong feeling after contested elections.

5051. And more particularly strong on this occasion, because there were three Roman Catholics and one Protestant, each to be tried for murder?—Yes, a very strong feeling.

5052. That was the occasion upon which the sheriff would be particularly cautious and anxious to have a fair panel?—Yes.

5053. I believe that you admitted upon that trial that you were a member of an Orange Lodge?—I did.

5054. Do you hold rank in that?—Yes.

5055. You are deputy grand master, I believe?—Yes.

5056. Is that for the county?—Yes, for the county.

5057. Which is divided, I believe, into districts?—Yes.

5058. The grand master is Captain Madden, is he not?—Yes.

5059. You did admit that you were an Orangeman?—I did.

5060. You are aware that there was a subscription made for the purpose of defending the Bairds, who were to be tried at that spring assizes, and a subscription to prosecute McKenna?—I heard of a subscription to defend the Bairds. I never heard of a subscription to prosecute McKenna.

5061. You know that there was a subscription to defend the Bairds?—I do.

5062. Do you know whether there were any Orangemen upon the panel?—I am sure there were some on it.

5063. Do you remember being asked whether there were not over 600 Orangemen upon that panel before the trial?—I do not remember.

5064. But

Mr. *W. Mitchell.*

21 June 1873.

5064. But there were a number on it?—I have no doubt there were a number on it.

5065. Some of them probably subscribed to defend the Bairds?—I cannot say whether they did that or not; it is possible.

5066. Do you approve of the system which existed, of giving the sub-sheriff power to select from the jurors' book as he pleased?—I believe that the power is in the hands of the high sheriff.

5067. Does the high sheriff exercise it generally?—No.

5068. Then he left it entirely in your hands?—Almost always, except on one occasion.

5069. Do you think that it was likely to give confidence to the Roman Catholics of Monaghan, that you should be the sub-sheriff, and have power to select the jury to try those very party cases?—I can give no opinion upon that subject.

5070. Would you wish to go back to that system?—I much prefer this system, as far as I am personally concerned.

5071. Are you satisfied with the system as far you have had experience of it?—Excepting for trifling details which could be easily amended.

5072. And which you would always find under any system?—Yes, under any system, and which would work out in time as far as the county of Monaghan is concerned.

5073. You cannot have a perfect system?—No.

5074. Mr. *Bruen.*] With regard to the trial of those prisoners at the assizes of 1869 for murder, and for party riots, there is no right of challenging jurors except by the Crown, is there; there is of course the right of the prisoners to challenge, but on the other side, the Crown has the exclusive hold of the right of challenging jurors?—The Crown has.

5075. The whole panel, you have told us, was gone over before 70 names could be got to answer?—Yes, before 70 names could be got to answer.

5076. Consequently the whole 49 Roman Catholics who were on the panel were called, and could have served if they had answered?—They could.

5077. There was no reason, except that of non-attendance and not answering, why the whole jury could not have been composed of Roman Catholics?—There was not.

5078. Unless it was that the Crown might have challenged some of them as being unfit persons to be on the jury?—Yes; perhaps I may mention that in the county of Monaghan I do not believe there is a juror of any religious denomination that would wish to get on a jury to convict a man of murder.

5079. Mr. *Downing.*] With regard to the question of the honourable member for Carlow, the prisoner has the right of peremptorily challenging 20?—Yes.

5080. And the Crown is unlimited in the power of ordering to stand by?—It is.

Mr. Joseph D. Cope, called in; and Examined.

Mr. *J. D. Cope.*

5081. *Chairman.*] You are Clerk to the Rathdown Union, are you not?—I am.

5082. You can state to the Committee, can you not, the general opinion of the clerks of the unions with regard to the evidence given by Mr. Flynn before this Committee?—I can. Upon reading the evidence of Mr. Flynn, as it appeared in the Irish newspapers, I at once communicated with the clerks of the several unions in Ireland, and also with your Lordship and I forwarded to the clerk of each union a copy of the circular which I hold in my hand, with a request to each clerk to inform me whether he acquiesced in the statements made by Mr. Flynn or not, and, without exception, they are of opinion that his evidence was most fallacious in every respect. From 163 unions in Ireland I received 147 replies, not one of which coincided with the views put forward by Mr. Flynn.

5083. Will you read the circular?—It is in these terms: "Dear Sir, Having read a report of the evidence of Mr. Flynn, the clerk of the Strokestown Union before the Select Committee of the House of Commons in the Juries (Ireland) Act, in the Dublin morning papers of yesterday, to the effect that the preparation of the jurors' lists would not take any clerk of a union more than a week to perform, and he thought that 6 *d.* per name on the general list of jurors furnished to the clerk of the peace, would fully compensate us for the additional labour, responsibility, and expenses incurred thereby. As it is the intention of some of our body to proceed to London to negative that evidence, I will thank you to let me know by return of post, whether you acquiesce in his statement or not, and oblige yours truly, *J. D. Cope.*" To that circular I received 147 replies.

5084. Have you only a general statement of their disagreement to give to the Committee, or can you go into any particulars upon the subject?—They do not agree with Mr. Flynn's evidence as is stated in that circular, namely, that the preparation of the list could be done by the clerks of the unions within a week. I may mention to the Committee, that having received a communication from the Irish office, I addressed another circular to the clerks of unions, embodying a number of queries, and the queries were as follows: (1.) "How many ratings are there in your rate books?" (2.) "How many names of jurors did you give in your return to the clerk of the peace?" (3.) "How many revision courts did you attend?" (4.) "How many miles did you travel attending these courts?" (5.) "What time did it take you to complete the lists?" (6.) "If an assistant was employed, how long was he engaged?" (7.) "What amount of remuneration did you receive from your board of guardians for this work?" (8.) "State whether you would wish to be paid by a fixed scale of fees for each name returned to the clerk of the peace, or to be remunerated as at present?" (9.) "Should you prefer a fixed scale of fees, state the amount you consider would pay you for each name returned to the clerk of the peace; this sum to include all expenses, excepting printing?" I received 108 replies to that circular, and I have summarised the information sent to me in the answers.

5085. Will you give that information to the Committee?—In reply to the first of the queries I ascertained that in 108 unions there are 806,122 ratings, and that the average number of ratings in each union is 7,463. In answer to the second query, I ascertained that there were 63,675 jurors returned, and that the average number for each union was 589. The number of

Mr. J. D. Cope.

24 June 1873.

of revision courts attended by them was 315, making an average of three to each. That the number of miles travelled by these 108 to attend revision courts was 7,100, and that the average number of miles travelled was 71. That the total number of weeks employed by the clerks of unions, and by their assistants, to prepare the lists, was 539, making an average time of five weeks to each clerk of the union. That the amount of remuneration awarded to those 108 clerks amounted to 2,631 *l.*, and that the average amount was 30 *l.* Then the answer to the query, whether they would wish to be paid by a fixed scale of fees or as at present, leaving it to the discretion of the board of guardians, I have ascertained that 17 were for a fixed scale of fees, whilst there were 67 who wished to be left as at present; the amount of fees which the clerks of the unions state vary so much, viz., from 6 *d.* to 3 *s.* per name; and that the average would be 1 *s.* 6 *d.* per name.

5086. Colonel *Vandeleur.*] How many at 6 *d.*, and how many at 3 *s.*?—I have nothing to show that; there were only two that mentioned 6 *d.*, as far as I recollect.

5087. *Chairman.*] What is your opinion as to being paid by a fixed scale, or leaving it to the discretion of the boards of guardians?—Personally, I prefer to have a fixed scale.

5088. What amount should you put it at?—Nothing less, in my opinion, for the amount of labour, responsibility, and expenses attending the preparation of this list, than 1 *s.* 3 *d.* per name would compensate the clerks of the unions; and I may mention, that I do not think in some unions that that sum would at all be adequate, for this reason; that I know in one union the number of jurors sent to me was only 40, and if that man was only allowed 1 *s.* 3 *d.* for each name, the amount would not possibly defray his travelling expenses.

5089. Will you state to the Committee what are the duties of the clerks of the unions in connection with this Act?—The first step that the clerk of a union was obliged to take was, to ascertain under the Act, who were qualified to serve, and who were disqualified, of the names of those appearing upon the rate books as rated occupiers; I had first to prepare a list of every male person appearing upon my rate books; that list I handed to the collector to report to me who were qualified and who were disqualified under the Act; having ascertained that fact, I then arranged the names in alphabetical order of surnames; and having again, with the assistance of the collectors, revised the list in that form, fearing that some names might appear upon the list twice and others that were not qualified, I then had a copy prepared for the clerk of the peace, and another copy for the printer.

5090. In the lists which you furnished to the collector you only had to include the names of the occupiers who were rated at a sufficient amount?—Quite so; that is all I did do.

5091. *The O'Conor Don.*] You had everything of that kind on the voters' list before, had you not?—No, not at all, in my opinion not one out of every 50.

5092 How was that?—I cannot say.

5093 Is not the qualification under the Act for a juror higher than that for a voter?—It is higher than for a Parliamentary voter, but it is not every person whose name appears upon the rate book that appears upon the Parliamentary voters' list.

5094. Does not every man who is rated at 20 *l.* appear upon the voters' list?—No.

5095. Ought not the clerk of the union to return the name of every person rated 20 *l.* to the revising barrister for insertion on the voters' register?—The clerk of the union returns the name of every male rated occupier valued at 12 *l.* and upwards on the supplemental list, whose name does not appear upon the register of Parliamentary voters. That supplemental list contains the name of every male person not appearing upon the register, and the chairman of the county then strikes off a number of those, in consequence of objections raised, and parties not coming forward to support their *prima facie* case.

5096. Does the revising barrister strike off any one except he is objected to by the clerk of the union?—He does.

5097. Upon what grounds?—On the ground that any person appearing upon the register of voters, and entitled to his franchise can object to a person's name appearing upon the Parliamentary Voters' Register.

5098 Any ratepayer who is entitled to be a juror would be entitled to be a Parliamentary voter, would he not?—Yes, in point of rating.

5099. Therefore the barrister cannot strike off that Parliamentary voters' list any one whom you would, under this Act, be obliged to put upon the jurors' list?—Yes, the barrister has the power of striking off the Parliamentary voters' list any person's name that is objected to upon the supplemental list.

5100. Objected to and the objection sustained?—Yes, and the objection sustained; the rule of the Chairman of the county of Dublin is this, the clerk of the union furnishes the clerk of the peace with the name of every male person appearing upon the rate books, and not appearing upon the register; the agents on the Conservative and on the Liberal side of the franchise *pro forma*, object to almost every person appearing upon my supplemental list; the chairman would not admit any person upon the register who is objected to, that does not attend to support his claim, or produces some evidence to satisfy the chairman that he is entitled to his franchise.

5101. Are you aware whether that is a peculiar practice in Dublin, or is it general in the country?—I can only speak for my own county, and I might speak for the county of Wicklow; it is not the practice in the county of Wicklow, for this reason, that the agents in the county of Wicklow do not object to them in the Revising Court, as much as they do in the county of Dublin.

5102. Do you mean to say that in the county of Dublin the chairman in revising the voters' list strikes off every one against whom objection is raised, unless that person comes forward and substantiates his claim?—Or some person to represent him, to satisfy the chairman that the party is entitled to the franchise.

5103. I understood you to state in the first part of your evidence that a very large proportion of those whom you under this Act would be obliged to put upon a jurors' list are not upon the voters' list?—Yes.

5104 And you attribute that to the fact that the barrister has struck them off the voters' list, in consequence of their being objected to, and not appearing?—Yes.

5105. *Chairman.*] How many names had you to extract from the list of occupiers for the lists which

which you furnished to the collectors?—As far as I recollect, I think something about 7,000; that is the first list prepared by me.

5106 What was the next work which you had to do?—Having furnished the collectors with that list, I then received from them their report as to who was qualified and who was disqualified under the Act, or exempted under the provisions of the Act, and having received their reports, I then arranged the lists in strict alphabetical order of surname, as required by the Act. That list having again been revised by me was finally copied, one copy for the clerk of the peace, and another copy for the printer.

5107. Had the rate collectors no lists in their own possession which would answer the purpose?—They had their warrants containing the name of every ratepayer, but not the calling of each. They were obliged to go round with the lists to ascertain who was who.

5108. I do not understand why you were obliged to begin by furnishing the rate-collectors with new lists when they had lists of the occupiers already in their possession?—It was only those who were qualified according to the rating that I furnished them a list of. I believed that that was the shortest and most accurate way of preparing the lists.

5109. Under the Act you might call upon your collectors to furnish you with lists of qualified persons in that district, might you not?—No, I think that the assistance which the collectors would be obliged to give the clerks of the union would be the calling of each person and whether he was over age or not. That is the class of information that I required from my collectors.

5110. For what purpose did you require the calling?—Because the Act of Parliament, or the form which I am obliged to furnish the clerk of the peace with, requires the calling or vocation of each person to be given.

5111 The rate book does not give that?—No, it does not.

5112. Have you stated all the work that fell upon you?—I have stated all the work that fell upon me.

5113. What remuneration did you receive from the union?—I received 100 *l.* as my remuneration. The guardians in awarding me that sum had a special committee of the board summoned to ascertain the amount of work performed by me, and having counted the number of entries made by me, 2 *d.* for each entry in the preparation of the lists would have awarded me a sum of over 98 *l.*

5114. Mr. *Bruen.*] When you speak of an entry, do you mean each name?—Yes; 2 *d.* for each name.

5115. *Chairman.*] Can you state to the Committee how long you were occupied in those various operations?—At intervals, I was engaged from the 3rd day of February up to August; putting it altogether, I calculate that I was engaged better than three months myself and my assistants.

5116. Not three months the whole time?—Yes, three months the whole time, working eight hours each day; it is a very tedious process to arrange those names in alphabetical order of surnames. Having taken out the names in alphabetical order according to the first letter, you are obliged to go through the list for instance, and put Cooper before Cope and so on, in dictionary order, which we are now obliged to do under the Act; it is a very tedious operation.

5117. Had you to employ special assistance?—I had an assistant, not a special assistant, for this particular work; I had other assistance

5118 You had not to employ any extra assistance?—No; but I utilised a great deal of pauper labour in the house. I have had always a man in the house, a pauper, who could write a good hand; and I got him to assist me.

5119 Had you any printing to do out of the 100 *l.* which you received?—No.

5120. The 100 *l.* which you received was remuneration to yourself and to your assistant?—For myself, my assistants, and for my travelling expenses.

5121. Did you say that 2 *d.* an entry would have given you 98 *l.*?—Yes, about 98 *l.*

5122. Colonel *Vandeleur.*] How many names did you return to the clerk of the peace?—The number of names returned to the clerk of the peace in my union, I think, was about 1,700.

5123. *Chairman.*] Did I understand you to say that you thought that 1 *s.* 3 *d.* would be a proper remuneration?—Yes; upon the lists furnished to the clerk of the peace in my union it would be, but in other unions I believe it would not be at all adequate.

5124. What would 1 *s.* 3 *d.* have given in your own union?—One shilling and threepence in my own union, upon the number of returns to the clerk of the peace would be, I think, something about 100 *l.*

5125. What is the 2 *d.*; upon what?—The 2 *d.* was upon all the entries that I made, amounting to nearly 7,000, as near as I can recollect in the first instance, and subsequently reduced to the number sent to the clerk of the peace and printer.

5126. The 2 *d.*, as I understand you, would have given you above 98 *l.*?—The number of entries that I made at 2 *d.* would have amounted to that.

5127. One shilling and threepence would have given you 100 *l.*?—One shilling and threepence upon the number returned to the clerk of the peace.

5128. How did the number of entries become so reduced?—They were reduced in this way. The first list that was supplied to the collectors contained the name of every person who was qualified and not qualified.

5129. Do you mean qualified in point of rating?—Yes, in point of valuation.

5130. Were the persons qualified in point of rating subsequently reduced one-sixth?—They were reduced to about one-third, and no more, I should think.

5131. By what causes?—By different causes; double entries, non-residence, and illness—deafness, for instance, was one.

5132. What sort of people were disqualified?—The first would be for being over 60 years of age; the next class were professional gentlemen, doctors, barristers, solicitors, ministers of religion, teachers, public officers, and others.

5133. Was the list reduced to one-sixth of those qualified by rating, merely by those exemptions?—I do not think, perhaps, I have explained what caused the great number of entries in the first instance; I may tell the Committee the process to be gone through to ascertain who were properly qualified and who were not.

5134. Mr. *Downing.*] When you speak of the number of 7,000 odd, you speak of the whole list

Mr. *J. D. Cope.*

24 June 1873.

Mr. *J. D. Cope.*

24 June 1873.

list of persons rated at the smallest sums?—No; I speak only of male persons appearing upon the rate books, as holding a rating qualification under the Act, namely, 20 *l.* and upwards.

5135. *The O'Conor Don.*] You make out this large number of names because you had to enter the same names over and over again?—Yes; I had to enter them four times, which caused a large number of entries.

5136. *Chairman.*] Do you mean in respect of different occupations?—No, in respect of the lists; I was obliged to prepare four lists; first of all a list of the persons who appeared upon the rate books as holding the rating qualification; that list was furnished to the collectors to report to me who were qualified and who were not, and having ascertained their report, it was revised, and the names of those excepted were struck out; it was then arranged in alphabetical order in the book for me to produce in court in case of any question arising; another copy of the book was furnished to the printer, and another copy was furnished to the clerk of the peace.

5137. By entry, do you mean one name that appears several times as an entry?—One name appears several times; for instance, there were a number of persons who were rated for several ratings; they were returned in the list to the collectors to report as to whether they were the same person or not.

5138. In fact, before the juror was returned to the clerk of the peace, his name had been entered by you three or four times?—Yes, four times.

5139. Colonel *Vandeleur.*] And you charged separately for each entry?—The rate of 2 *d.* for each entry was allowed me by the guardians.

5140. *Chairman.*] Did the guardians pay you upon any calculation such as you have made?—The guardians paid me upon the calculation which I have just mentioned. The finance committee, in determining the amount which should be awarded to me as remuneration under this Act, had before them all my lists, and having satisfied themselves as to the number of entries, and having made a calculation, the amount that I was awarded would have amounted to about 2 *d.* for each entry made, not for each entry sent to the clerk of the peace, but for each entry that was separately made independent and including those sent to the clerk of the peace

5141. Colonel *Vandeleur.*] Instead of being 2 *d.* for each entry, you ought to have charged 8 *d.*, what was the real sum that you received?—It amounted to 8 *d.* for an entry on the number sent to the clerk of the peace, but in this calculation the names rejected are not included.

5142. I understood you to say, that 1 *s.* 3 *d.* per name furnished to the clerk of the peace would have paid you the same amount?—Yes, about that; what I mean by returned to the clerk of the peace is, only those that were qualified.

5143. Would the labour be anything like the same on future occasions?—I do not anticipate that the labour will be so great next year; in some unions it will not be, and in other unions it will be almost as great; for instance, in my union the duty will be very little lessened. I am aware that in other unions the duties will not vary very much, and I will give you my reasons for saying so. My union is situated in the county of Dublin, in the suburbs of the city, and as the principal towns in it are watering places, there is a large number of changes in the names of the occupiers of rated premises, which takes place annually, and which does not take place in an agricultural or a rural district. To give the Committee an illustration of that, I may take, for instance, the changes which have been officially sent by me to the Valuation Office as compared with the Strokestown Union. The annual number of changes which take place in my union amount to 1,800, whereas in the Strokestown Union, according to the return furnished to me from the Local Government Board, it was 350.

5144. Have you with you the books showing the work which was done in connection with the preparation of the list?—I have.

5145. Will you just show them to the Committee. (*The Witness produced the books, and explained the preparation of them to the Committee.*)

5146. Dr. *Ball.*] In the union that you are concerned with, do you know what proportion the rating of a house bears to the rental generally?—I think about two-thirds.

5147. Then a 40 *l.* rating would be equivalent to a 60 *l.* rental?—Yes.

5148. *Chairman.*] Have you any suggestion to make as to the qualification or otherwise?—I think I would like to see property represented in the jury box. I think there are a class of persons who could be placed upon the jurors' lists that do not appear as rated occupiers, many of them appearing on the Parliamentary Voters' Register as rent-chargers, freeholders, and householders, who are not occupiers but owners of property in those capacities.

5149. Their names could not be got at from the rate book?—No, they could not be got at from the rate book, but they could be got at by the machinery at the disposal of the clerks of unions. They are obliged to revise the Parliamentary Voters' Register each year, and they have a copy of the register, and likewise it contains the names of those persons who appear registered as freeholders and leaseholders, and rent-chargers.

5150. Would you suggest that the Parliamentary Register should be made the foundation of the jurors' book?—According to the ruling in the county of Dublin, every one appearing upon the register would not include all the rated occupiers in the union; for instance, I suppose that out of every 100 names returned annually in the supplementary list as rated occupiers, there are not more than perhaps 20 per cent. of those admitted upon the register.

5151. You mean that a person may be qualified to be a juror who is not qualified to be a voter?—Not if you take the Parliamentary Voters' Register as your basis of qualification.

5152. *The O'Conor Don.*] Then you have him upon the supplemental list of voters?—Yes, on the supplemental list, that is, the list supplied by the clerk of the union.

5153. You have him either on the register of voters, or upon the supplemental list, the one or the other?—Yes, he would appear upon either the one or the other, but it must be recollected that the supplemental list is sent to the clerk of the peace a month before the jurors' list is finished and the supplemental list is not again seen, until the revision court in October following.

5154. *Chairman.*] Have you formed any opinion as to the qualification which would provide a respectable class of jurors?—As far as I can judge from my experience of the county of Dublin,

Mr. *J. D. Cope.*

24 June 1873.

lin, and I will say also of the county of Wicklow, a part of that county being in my union, and having some knowledge also of the county of Carlow, being almost a native of it, I think that the qualification as set out in the Act of the present Session, ought to secure a respectable and intelligent, and I would say, an impartial, class of jurors. You have in the county of Wicklow raised the qualification from 20 *l.*, in the Act of 1871, to 20 *l.* and 30 *l.*; that is, 20 *l.* in a village, and 30 *l.* in the country, and you have raised the special jurors from 50 *l.* to 100 *l.* in the county of Wicklow; in the county of Dublin you have left the qualification of common jurors in the villages or cities or towns the same; but you have raised those residing in the country from 20 *l.* to 30 *l.*, and that I think is a movement in the right direction; you have also increased the qualification of a special juror in the county of Dublin from 50 *l.* to 150 *l.*, that is, 50 *l.* in a village or city, and 150 *l.* in the country.

5155. Dr. *Ball.*] Do not you see that the qualification in the county of Dublin excludes many householders in the city, and is it not quite well known that the county of Dublin furnishes a highly intelligent class of persons?—It does not exclude them from the common jurors' list.

5156. But it does from the special; the 50 *l.* household qualification shuts them out, and lets in the market gardeners?—A 50 *l.* qualification in the county of Dublin is a class of house occupied by merchants in my union, and I think the majority of them would be rated between 40 *l.* and 50 *l.*

5157. As Mr. Ormsby suggested 40 *l.*, would you agree with that?—Yes, between 40 *l.* and 50 *l.*, in my union; but there must necessarily be very few persons whom you would call market gardeners, qualified as special jurors, rated at 50 *l.*

5158. That may be so on the south side of Dublin, but do you know of any on the north side of Dublin?—I know that it is a more agricultural union than Rathdown.

5159. Mr. *Bruen.*] The Rathdown Union, I think, according to the census of 1861, had about 50,000, or 52,000 inhabitants in it?—Yes, that was about the population, but it has considerably increased since the census of 1861.

5160. Have you any idea what the population is now?—The population of the county of Dublin has increased by some thousands; I do not exactly know the number; I do not believe that the census returns for the county of Wicklow are yet complete; at least, I have not got them in my office.

5161. I see that Rathdown, in 1861, is put at 53,000 inhabitants, and I see that the North Dublin Union is put down at 134,000 inhabitants?—Yes, but that includes the city.

5162. Your union you may almost call a suburban rather than a county union?—Yes, it is a suburban union; it is, in point of fact, a continuation of the city of Dublin, with the exception of very few districts.

5163. In showing the books that you have just shown to the Committee, you mentioned that the collector only fills in one column?—That is all the information that was required from him.

5164. *Chairman.*] Do you know what the collectors received in your union?—No, I do not; but I heard them complain very much of the amount of the remuneration that was given them by the grand jury.

5165. Mr. *Bruen.*] Can you tell the Committee whether there is a considerable amount of research and inquiry required in filling in that column?—Of course there must be a great deal of inquiry to be made on the part of the collector; each name requires to be separately inquired into, and very often the collectors get wrong information. For instance, there is a great objection on the part of some ratepayers to be placed upon the jurors' list, and they will give wrong information, with a view to get off; some will say that they are over 60 years of age, others will say, I am a teacher, and others, I am a public officer, when they are really not so, and others will give wrong christian names.

5166. You rely entirely upon the collectors for all this information, I suppose?—Not entirely, because I have considerable local knowlege myself of the persons; as to the callings of the persons, I rely entirely upon the collectors.

5167. The collectors of course had all this duty imposed upon them, under the Juries Act of 1871, which they had not to do before?—They never had to do it before.

5168. You could not say how much they received?—No, I could not in my union; but I have heard them complaining one to another.

5169. I did not quite understand as to the 1 *s.* 3 *d.* per name, which you thought was a fair remuneration; were those the names that appeared on the general jurors' book when it was formed?—Yes, quite so, what I sent in to the clerk of the peace; the names sent to the clerk of the peace consisted of the general jurors' book.

5170. *Chairman.*] Subject to revision, are they not, by the chairman?—Yes, subject to revision by the chairman. There were very few struck out. The information was so complete that there were very few names struck out on the revision.

5171. Mr. *Bruen.*] As to the 1 *s.* 3 *d.* per name, how much would it have given to you if it had been followed out?—Something about the sum that the guardians awarded me for the duties; something about 100 *l.*

5172. You do not complain of insufficient remuneration?—No, I do not complain. Perhaps I may be permitted to observe that while that sum, namely, 1 *s.* 3 *d.* per name, would have amply compensated me for my duties, I believe that in other unions it would not.

5173. The larger the number of course the smaller the rate of remuneration would be per name?—The larger the remuneration would be.

5174. How do you arrive at that; is not the research, the inquiry, and the trouble in strict proportion to the number of names entered?—I know that in one union there were only 40 names returned by the clerk of the union, and if that official received but 1 *s.* 3 *d.* for his trouble it would not pay his travelling expenses; probably he may have to attend three or four revision courts.

5175. Is not that a very extreme case?—No; there are many instances of it.

5176. *Chairman.*] He could have very little trouble except attending the revision courts?—Very little trouble indeed.

5177. Do you mean to say that a man who had 40 names to give would actually ever have to attend more than one revision court?—Yes; it is according to baronies; for instance, a man may have five or six names in one barony. I know a case in my own union in the Barony of Dublin where I had only 10 names, and to attend the

Mr. J. D. Cope. 24 June 1873.

the revision court there I had to go to Kilmainham from Rathdown, and there are very many other instances of this class.

5178. But it is principally with respect to the travelling expenses that you think that a small number of names would render a higher rate of remuneration necessary?—I think that 1 s. 3 d. would compensate the clerks of the unions independently of their travelling expenses; that is to say, over and above their travelling charges.

5179. In large unions that would be included, would it not?—In large unions it might not, for this reason, that the clerk of the union is obliged to employ some assistant. The duties are so severe and heavy that he would be obliged to employ an assistant for getting the work done, and the one would balance the other.

5180. I suppose you are hardly disposed to give any evidence with regard to the grievances of the poor-rate collectors themselves?—As to my own experience, and I have had twenty-two years' experience of the Poor Laws, I believe that the rate collectors of Ireland are a respectable and trustworthy class of officials, and I believe that they are a very ill-used class also. With regard to what they should receive under the Juries Act, I cannot speak.

5181. Colonel *Vandeleur*.] Are you aware what the collectors asked for their service?—I am aware that they asked for more than they received; but as to the exact amount that they asked, I cannot say.

5182. Or what amount they received?—No.

5183. *The O'Conor Don*.] What is your salary as clerk of the union?—£. 200 per annum.

5184. You say that it took you five weeks to do the work under the Juries Act?—It took me longer than that; it took me three months: it took me on and off from February up to August. Altogether, I calculate that I was employed about three months.

5185. For that three months you got 100 *l.*?—Yes.

5186. Your salary for the whole year's service being only 200 *l.*?—Yes; but that includes all my expenses for my assistants, and a portion of my travelling expenses.

5187. What additional expense had you outside the travelling expenses?—I had my assistant, and I paid my assistant 50 *s.*

5188. Had you to get that assistant specially?—No. I may mention that the guardians allow me 50 *l.* a year for an assistant, and I supplemented that by, I suppose, something between 30 *l.* and 40 *l.* a year additional for the other labour.

5189. Did you pay him anything special for this work under the Juries Act?—I gave him a premium for it.

5190. Will you state how much it was?—I gave him 5 *l.*

5191. Then you received 95 *l.* for yourself, excluding your travelling expenses?—No. I gave him that for the work he had done, but there was other assistance that I had to pay for. While I was employed doing this work, he was employed doing the general business of my office, and it was only for a portion of the work that he got this.

5192. What additional remuneration did you give him this last year beyond what you gave him in any previous year in consequence of the additional work thrown either upon you or upon him under this Juries Act?—To him I gave 5 *l.*, and to others, I suppose, on and off, as far as I can recollect the amount, something about 15 *l.* a year more.

5193. Altogether you paid, for clerks' work, 20 *l.* out of this 100 *l.*?—I think, as far as I can recollect, it would be about that.

5194. Could you give the Committee any idea what your travelling expenses amounted to?—I daresay my travelling expenses amounted to about 10 *l.*, perhaps not so much; I should say, about 7 *l.*

5195. For this additional work which you say you estimate took you three months, you received 70 *l.*, your salary for the whole year being 200 *l.*?—Yes; I daresay the guardians awarded me 70 *l.* for my labour.

5196. Do you think that the 70 *l.* for the three months was a fair remuneration, considering that you got only 200 *l.* for your salary?—I do not think it at all excessive.

5197. I understood you to say, when you were referring to those books, that a clerk would copy about 50 of those names in an hour?—Yes, in alphabetical order, but not in dictionary order; he could not do it. In some hours a clerk may be able to do more than 50, but he is not constantly employed at it; it is a most monotonous class of work, and a man cannot stick at it constantly without making errors; he is obliged to take a rest and go on, and do other work. Since I gave this answer I have timed the matter, and found that the mere copying, much less to arrange the names in alphabetical order, that no man can copy more than 25 names an hour, and he will work but a very few hours each day at this work.

5198. Calculating it at 2 *d.* an entry, it would be 8 *s.* 4 *d.* an hour for this work, which would be 3 *l.* 6 *s.* 8 *d.* a day?—Yes; but you must recollect that that is not for mere copying, it is for seeking information, making returns, and all the responsibilities attaching to the preparation of the lists.

5199. Calculating it in the way that I put it, if it were for mere copying work it would be at the rate of 3 *l.* 6 *s.* 8 *d.* a day?—For mere copying work it would be at about the rate of 8 *s.* 4 *d.* an hour.

5200. And calculating it at the rate of eight hours a day, it would be 3 *l.* 6 *s.* 8 *d.*?—But I would not allow for the mere scrivenery work 2 *d.* an entry; the 2 *d.* would cover the responsibilities attached to the work.

5201. What would you allow for the mere copying work?—I suppose for the mere copying work I would allow about half of that.

5202. So that for the copying you would allow at the rate of 1 *l.* 13 *s.* 4 *d.* a day?—But no man could possibly work eight hours constantly at copying those lists.

5203. But you see, whether he does it constantly or not, he should be paid, according to your evidence, to this rate, for doing this work?—If he was able to copy constantly, he would be able to earn that amount.

5204. In your calculation, how many hours a day would he be able to work at this copying work?—To work at it constantly, I should say that he would be employed about two hours and a half or three hours. I do not believe that any man could do it for more than two or three hours constantly.

5205. With respect to the travelling expenses, have you not been obliged to attend the sessions to revise the voters' list?—Yes.

5206. Is it not at the same time that those jurors' list will be revised?—It is after the

Parliamentary

Mr. *J. D. Cope.*

14 June 1873.

Parliamentary Register is revised that the jurors' lists are revised, and at a separate time altogether.

5207. Is it not at the same sessions?—It is at the same sessions, but then you are obliged to attend different days for it.

5208. Then one travelling to the particular place where the sessions are held would do, would it not?—No; in some cases, where the distance is very far, people would stop out all night, and the one travelling would do.

5209. Do not you think that it could be easily arranged that the revision of the two lists, the Parliamentary Voters' List and the jurors' list, should be taken one after the other, so as not to necessitate the two journeys on the part of the clerks of the unions and the other officials?—No, because the time is occupied by the court.

5210. Do you think that is general throughout the country?—I cannot say. I only speak for the county of Dublin.

5211. In the country, where the revision of the voters' list occupied sometimes only an hour or two, do not you think the jurors' list could be done immediately after the voters' list, and thereby save the travelling expenses?—In some unions it could be done, I believe.

5212. Do you receive any special remuneration for travelling, with regard to the voters' list?—Yes, an income of 50 *l.* a year is allowed me for my duties under the Parliamentary Voters' Act.

5213. Are not your duties under the Parliamentary Voters' Act more onerous than those under the Juries Act?—No, they are not.

5214. Have you not to make out a much larger number of names?—No.

5215. How do you explain that?—Because we are not obliged to return the names to the clerk of the peace in our supplementary list of Parliamentary voters; it is not names that appear upon the register; it is only such names as appear upon the books, and do not appear upon the register, that you are obliged to return to the clerk of the peace for the Parliamentary voters; but by the Juries Act, no matter whether the name appears before, you are obliged to repeat the name year after year, and send it in in writing.

5216. But all the difficulties which you indicated as attending the making out of the jurors' book in the first instance would not recur year after year?—In some unions that observation would apply.

5217. Would not it apply in every union where, in the same manner, people remain on the registry for years?—Yes, in some unions, I say that it would; for instance, in the agricultural districts, where a man seldom changes his residence, but remains there say for 12 years, it may be.

5218. In the unions where many changes take place in the occupation of dwellings, the work is equally great with regard to the revision of the Parliamentary Voters' List, is it not?—Not so great with regard to the Parliamentary voters.

5219. If a Parliamentary voter changes his rating, he is struck off the list?—Yes.

5220. If a new one comes he has to be put on the list?—Yes.

5221. Therefore, as far as those unions where the changes are very great are concerned, the additional work with regard to the Parliamentary Voters' List is equally great, is it not?—No, not at all so great, for the reason that I have given you, that a ratepayer's name appearing on the Parliamentary Voters' Register is not obliged to be copied, and sent to the clerk of the peace annually, whilst the new jurors' list is.

5222. I am not speaking of copying, I am speaking of making inquiries, and all the other difficulties you have alluded to; when a juror is put upon the jurors' book, all inquiries have been made regarding him, have they not?—Yes, they have.

5223. With regard to that juror next year, there would be nothing required except to copy the name again?—Except to know whether he is in occupation or not; we know his calling from the previous return.

5224. But have you not to obtain the same information for the Parliamentary Register?—No, the Parliamentary Register, in any case, would be no index to it at all, for the reason that there is not perhaps more than half the number of rated occupiers qualified to serve upon the register.

5225. But the Parliamentary Register and the supplemental list will tell you?—No, for this reason, that there are many instances where the collector has not information of the party having left his residence, his name is put upon the supplemental list, because he appears rated, and the collector has no information, and it is only after the Revision Court is over, that the collector has ascertained whether the party is in occupation or not, when it is too late to take notice of it; in preparing the jurors' list, the jurors' list is sent in in August, and the revision takes place in October.

5226. You are prepared to state, I suppose, that your union is very exceptional with respect to the alteration of occupancy?—There are, I believe many other unions in Ireland similarly circumstanced; I know that the South Dublin Union is so, and I know that a portion of the North Dublin Union is so, and I know that Rathdrum is so, and I have heard that in the Belfast, Cork, and Limerick Unions the same thing occurs.

5227. Those unions are very dissimilar from the ordinary agricultural unions?—Yes; very much so.

5228. And the expenses in the latter need not be so high as in those partly city unions?—Not in the rural districts certainly, because the same trouble is not necessary to be taken by the officials.

5229. Colonel *Vandeleur.*] What would the printing expenses be?—With regard to the printing expenses of my union, the list was so large that a contract was entered into, and it amounted to, I think, 45 *l.*

5230. Did you print the 7,000 names?—No; only the names returned to the clerk of the peace; that would be about 1,700, as far as I can recollect.

5231. In answer to a question by the honourable Member for Roscommon, you stated that you were put to 15 *l.* extra expenses, besides the 5 *l.* that you allowed to your regular assistants; and you also mentioned that you employed pauper boys to do the rest of the work which was not done by your assistants; did that 15 *l.* go to the pauper boys?—It is contrary to the rule to give them anything, but I could not depend upon them to do the work without giving them something. They did not get it, but others did. I gave them half-a-crown now and then

M. *J. D. Cope.* 24 June 1875.

5232. It is not the general custom of the union for the clerk to pay pauper boys?—It is I believe.

5233. In fact, it is against the rule, is it not?—It is against the rule, I know, but I did it for the purpose of having the work accurately done; and these people will not do that unless you give them something.

5234. You could have got the work done by a person outside, could you not?—I could.

5235. You could have brought in a scrivener or a schoolmaster, for instance; and could you not have got the work done for less?—No, that would be considerably higher in expense.

5236. Speaking of the Parliamentary revision which you make every year, that is with regard to the changes of occupancy, is it not?—As far as the Parliamentary revision is concerned, it is the changes of occupancy, and the payment of rates.

5237. And sub-division of polling districts also?—Yes.

5238. That is all returned to you, is it not, by the collectors, as a matter of duty, and as a part of their business?—Yes.

5239. And you also enter that in your own book, in the regular course of business; you would enter all those changes of occupancy in revising your own books?—Not in revising my books, but in revising the Parliamentary voters' register.

5240. And in revising your rate books?—No, those lists are sent up to the Valuation Office.

5241. In the regular course of your business, as clerk of the union, all those alterations would be made in your rate books, would they not?—They are made in the rate books through the Valuation Office.

5242. Free of any charge?—Yes, free of any charge.

5243. Therefore there is no reason why you should charge the guardians over again for making the very alterations which you are bound to do as clerk of the union?—No, and I have made no charge for it.

5244. You put that forward, did you not, as one of the grounds for that very heavy additional charge upon the rates?—No; I can explain the reason why that was done to the rate books in my union; the rate is struck in June; if I were to revise the list, or commence the revision of the list from the rate struck in June this year, it would be quite impossible for me to go through the lists with the rate struck at this late period of the year, and therefore I was obliged to take up the previous year's rate book, and from the information of the collectors as to the parties who were rated, and who were new, and who they knew were gone, I had then to take up the new rate books to see when the change took place, and whether additional names were placed upon them.

5245. You would have to do that in any case, would you not?—Not with the jurors' lists; I make out the rate books, and I certainly should be obliged to do that.

5246. It is from the rates book, is it not, that you make out the jury book?—Yes; it is from the rate book.

5247. *The O'Conor Don.*] Have you any idea what is the average salary of the clerks of unions in Ireland?—I could not speak with certainty, but I dare say that on an average it would be between 120 *l.* and 150 *l.* altogether; it may not be so much.

LIST OF APPENDIX.

Appendix, No. 1.

Appendix, No. 2.

Appendix, No. 3.

Appendix, No. 4.

Appendix, No. 5.

Appendix, No. 6.

Appendix, No. 7.

Appendix, No. 8.

APPENDIX.

Appendix, No. 1.

PAPERS handed in by the *Chairman.*

Appendix, No. 1.

RETURN, by the Clerks of the Peace, of the Number of JURORS on the "JURORS BOOK" for the last Three Years, and for the Present Year.

No.	COUNTY.	1870	1871.	1872.	Average of Three Years.	1873.
1	Antrim	6,090	4,861	4,895	5,285	7,846
2	Armagh	864	880	850	858	2,000
3	Belfast	*	–	–	–	1,063
4	Carlow	1,155	1,110	1,248	1,171	1,219
5	Carrickfergus	301	301	320	307	928
6	Cavan	847	773	733	784	1,835
7	Clare	1,070	1,038	1,025	1,051	2,036
8	Cork	4,081	4,392	4,211	4,228	8,425
9	Cork City	1,122	1,383	1,206	1,240	808
10	Donegal	977	830	869	895	1,608
11	Down	1,471	1,449	1,172	1,164	5,651
12	Drogheda	240	243	199	227	94
13	Dublin	4,842	3,413	3,015	3,757	3,000
14	Dublin City	4,018	4,308	3,901	4,076	3,421
15	Fermanagh	1,414	1,439	1,514	1,455	1,096
16	Galway	887	938	920	911	1,855
17	Galway Town	189	191	194	191	214
18	Kerry	916	899	1,011	942	2,440
19	Kildare	1,161	1,130	1,113	1,136	1,397
20	Kilkenny	1,680	1,770	1,771	1,742	3,273
21	Kilkenny City	180	176	186	183	146
22	King's County	361	370	364	365	1,527
23	Leitrim	804	717	716	745	1,103
24	Limerick	2,105	2,036	1,999	2,046	3,864
25	Limerick City	510	450	480	478	331
26	Londonderry	2,120	2,149	2,105	2,124	2,530
27	Londonderry City	293	288	277	286	194
28	Longford	385	390	374	383	934
29	Louth	358	379	380	373	902
30	Mayo	1,144	1,146	1,166	1,152	985
31	Meath	1,490	1,497	1,495	1,494	2,010
32	Monaghan	1,097	517	491	678	1,838
33	Queen's County	1,110	1,137	1,165	1,137	1,484
34	Roscommon	711	697	761	723	1,054
35	Sligo	342	428	413	394	1,010
36	Tipperary	1,207	1,252	1,260	1,239	6,429
37	Tyrone	1,160	1,133	1,167	1,133	3,073
38	Waterford	1,042	903	1,000	981	2,380
39	Waterford City	461	469	452	461	360
40	Westmeath	960	975	940	958	1,705
41	Wexford	1,663	1,580	1,537	1,600	2,998
					Average of two years.	
42	Wicklow	690	697	†	693	1,200

* There was no "Jurors' Book" for Belfast till the passing of the late Act.

† No Jurors' Book for Wicklow for 1872.

I.—RETURN by Sheriffs of the Number of JURORS in the "GENERAL JURORS' BOOK," classified as hereunder.

No.	COUNTY.	Number Rated at £.12 and under £.15.	Number Rated at £.15 and under £.20.	Number Rated at £.20 and under £.30.	Number Rated at £.30 and under £.40.	Number Rated at £.40 and under £.50.	Number Rated at £.50 and under £.80.	Number Rated at £.80 and under £.100.	Number Rated at £.100 and under £.150.	Number Rated at £.150 and under £.200.	Number Rated at £.200 and upwards.	Total Number of Jurors in General Jurors' Book.
1	Antrim - - -	794	650	2,308	1,108	674	955	282	314	141	330	7,636
2	Armagh - - -	–	–	1,357	608	897	438	88	95	34	40	2,964
3	Carlow - - -	–	–	360	286	147	234	65	68	46	38	1,315
4	Carrickfergus - -	–	56	64	31	15	10	1	18	2	5	214
5	Cavan - - -	–	–	1,080	318	129	100	41	51	16	94	1,835
6	Clare - - - -	–	–	916	374	196	300	68	90	46	98	2,088
7	Cork - - - -	285	307	2,777	1,518	934	1,348	390	430	165	101	8,436
8	Cork City - - -	–	–	350	115	56	169	45	34	16	85	808
9	Donegal - - -	–	–	730	380	186	244	56	65	28	17	1,063
10	Down - - -	–	–	–	–	–	–	–	–	–	–	–
11	Drogheda - - -	–	38	31	15	5	5	2	–	2	–	94
12	Dublin - - -	–	–	–	–	–	–	–	–	–	–	–
13	Dublin City - -	–	–	–	–	–	–	–	–	–	–	–
14	Fermanagh - -	–	–	31	263	125	168	48	96	13	21	783
15	Galway - - -	–	–	734	312	159	291	80	117	78	149	1,553
16	Galway Town - -	–	61	41	38	43	7	22	5	10	17	253
17	Kerry - - -	–	–	1,163	383	250	388	74	61	15	15	2,440
18	Kildare - - -	47	37	306	220	153	258	109	100	80	106	1,536
19	Kilkenny - - -	–	30	1,057	741	410	373	146	168	71	74	3,260
20	Kilkenny City - -	–	36	55	25	9	18	4	3	–	–	148
21	King's County - -	6	4	573	267	186	231	63	90	53	72	1,296
22	Leitrim - - -	–	494	375	135	57	82	13	15	5	14	1,198
23	Limerick - - -	17	20	1,343	715	383	694	182	237	110	107	3,546
24	Limerick City - -	–	–	122	68	44	84	11	15	3	6	371
25	Londonderry - -	–	–	1,168	402	249	340	103	93	33	45	2,336
26	Longford - - -	–	–	438	166	91	231	56	43	19	25	950
27	Louth - - -	–	–	315	166	91	136	44	67	30	69	902
28	Mayo - - -	–	–	414	120	103	144	32	56	43	50	965
29	Meath - - -	34	19	404	265	153	326	127	205	105	262	2,007
30	Monaghan - - -	–	–	1,069	356	153	172	45	30	11	18	1,855
31	Queen's County - -	–	2	527	251	161	234	72	108	50	30	1,484
32	Roscommon - -	–	–	539	165	85	107	33	61	26	41	1,076
33	Sligo - - - -	–	–	406	188	94	143	42	29	20	39	1,019
34	Tipperary - - -	128	137	1,850	1,025	600	775	233	278	121	210	5,363
35	Tyrone - - -	–	–	1,639	706	347	312	84	69	21	25	3,003
36	Waterford - - -	–	–	539	490	297	350	181	206	55	87	2,153
37	Waterford City - -	–	–	95	44	38	22	10	14	8	7	230
38	Westmeath - - -	48	34	536	302	174	248	85	124	53	96	1,700
39	Wexford - - -	80	80	1,098	689	303	549	140	170	53	65	3,295
40	Wicklow - - -	–	–	393	257	184	211	61	97	72	56	1,203

II.—RETURN by Sheriffs of the Number of JURORS in the "SPECIAL JURORS' BOOK," classified as hereunder.

No.	COUNTY.	Number Rated under £. 30.	Number Rated at £. 30 and under £. 40.	Number Rated at £. 40 and under £. 50.	Number Rated at £. 50 and under £. 80.	Number Rated at £. 80 and under £. 100.	Number Rated at £. 100 and under £. 150.	Number Rated at £. 150 and under £. 200.	Number Rated at £. 200 and upwards.	Total Number of Jurors in Special Jurors' Book.	Number of Jurors in the "Special Jurors' Book" who are Sons of Peers, Baronets, Knights, Magistrates, Eldest Sons of Baronets, Knights or Magistrates, classified as under: Number Rated at a Net Annual Value under that fixed as to Special Jurors' Qualification, in 5th Schedule of Act of 1871, stating Qualifications	Total Number of such Persons, however Rated.
1	Antrim - - -	–	–	–	935	282	314	141	310	1,982	Jurors' book does not show.	
2	Armagh - - -	–	–	–	452	88	97	34	47	718	No information given by sheriff.	
3	Carlow - - -	1	2	1	214	65	66	40	52	443	4	28
4	Carrickfergus - -	–	39	15	19	9	12	3	5	85	—	—
5	Cavan - - -	–	–	–	108	41	51	16	24	200	Jurors' book does not show.	
6	Clare - - -	–	–	–	309	62	90	46	68	572	No information given by sheriff.	
7	Cork - - -	–	–	–	–	–	420	185	101	815	- - ditto - - ditto.	
8	Cork City - -	–	–	–	183	45	84	15	35	288	1	25
9	Donegal - - -	1	4	2	243	57	65	37	10	418	- - -	27
10	Down - - -	–	–	–	–	–	–	–	–	–	—	—
11	Drogheda - - -	–	13	5	5	2	1	3	1	28	3 £. 30	- none.
12	Dublin - - -	–	–	–	–	–	–	–	–	–	—	—
13	Dublin City - -	–	–	–	–	–	–	–	–	–	—	- -
14	Fermanagh - -	–	–	–	46	48	46	12	20	175	—	.
15	Galway - - -	–	–	–	234	74	116	85	150	655	- none - -	38
16	Galway Town - -	–	37	13	27	8	15	5	14	119	2 rated under 30 l.	19
17	Kerry - - -	–	–	–	329	69	60	18	20	503	- - -	8
18	Kildare - - -	–	–	–	–	–	104	75	158	337	Jurors' book does not show.	
19	Kilkenny - - -	–	–	–	572	146	182	72	74	1,046	- - none - -	- none.
20	Kilkenny City - -	–	23	9	18	4	3	–	–	57	1 rated under 30 l.	4
21	King's County - -	–	–	–	221	62	60	55	78	476	- - none - -	24
22	Leitrim - - -	5	122	37	82	13	18	8	14	304	3	20
23	Limerick - - -	1	–	–	4	3	297	116	109	458	6	40
24	Limerick City - -	–	2	44	59	12	17	5	7	148	1	1
25	Londonderry - -	–	1	1	345	95	90	33	45	610	2	34
26	Longford - - -	–	–	–	184	36	80	21	24	354	- - none - -	- none.
27	Louth - - -	–	–	2	142	39	64	31	61	309	No information given by sheriff.	
28	Mayo - - -	–	1	1	141	28	53	43	50	309	2	60
29	Meath - - -	–	–	–	–	–	208	100	285	593	- - -	57
30	Monaghan - - -	–	–	2	167	45	90	11	19	260	2	20
31	Queen's County - -	–	–	–	254	72	114	47	63	550	- - -	33
32	Roscommon - -	–	–	–	119	81	55	25	64	294	- Not stated -	41
33	Sligo - - -	–	2	–	141	40	29	22	42	276	3	3
34	Tipperary - - -	–	–	–	–	–	286	156	217	676	—	—
35	Tyrone - - -	–	–	–	310	94	61	24	35	518	No information given.	
36	Waterford - - -	1	3	5	550	151	200	83	57	1,004	- - -	- 7
37	Waterford City - -	–	39	21	92	7	14	4	8	183	- - none - -	- none.
38	Westmeath - - -	–	–	–	–	–	194	53	26	275	- - -	45
39	Wexford - - -	–	–	–	542	146	170	53	65	985	None; qualification, 20 l. and upwards.	78
40	Wicklow - - -	–	–	–	211	61	87	73	55	489	Jurors' book does not show.	

RETURN of the Number of all HOUSES (Residences) according to the following Classification.

COUNTIES (BY PROVINCES).	Rural Districts. Number Valued at £ 6 and upwards.	Cities and Towns. Number Valued at £ 12 and upwards.	TOTAL.
LEINSTER:			
Carlow	304	232	536
Dublin	—	—	—
Dublin City	—	—	—
Drogheda Town	- -	372	372
Kildare	651	319	970
Kilkenny	656	64	720
Kilkenny City	- -	264	264
King's County	445	279	724
Longford	238	127	365
Louth	435	316	751
Meath	970	197	1,167
Queen's County	464	219	683
Westmeath	622	227	849
Wexford	853	526	1,379
Wicklow	652	463	1,115
TOTAL for LEINSTER (excluding Dublin County and City)	6,290	3,605	9,895
MUNSTER:			
Clare	516	200	716
Cork, East Riding	2,115	1,435	3,550
Cork, West Riding	653	350	1,003
Cork City	- -	1,848	1,848
Kerry	343	403	746
Limerick	655	138	793
Limerick City	- -	940	940
Tipperary, North Riding	427	322	749
Tipperary, South Riding	458	614	1,072
Waterford	768	286	1,054
Waterford City	- -	502	502
TOTAL for MUNSTER	5,965	7,038	13,003
ULSTER:			
Antrim	1,641	1,072	2,713
Armagh	1,051	917	1,968
Belfast Town	- -	4,233	4,233
Carrickfergus Town	- -	147	147
Cavan	349	271	620
Donegal	629	331	960
Down	2,742	1,859	4,601
Fermanagh	364	304	668
Londonderry	742	501	1,243
Londonderry City	- -	903	903
Monaghan	324	386	710
Tyrone	757	770	1,527
TOTAL for ULSTER	8,659	11,794	20,453
CONNAUGHT:			
Galway	621	293	914
Galway Town	- -	370	370
Leitrim	151	126	277
Mayo	363	280	643
Roscommon	366	232	598
Sligo	268	274	542
TOTAL for CONNAUGHT	1,769	1,575	3,344

SUMMARY.

COUNTIES (BY PROVINCES).	Rural Districts. Number Valued at £ 6 and upwards.	Cities and Towns. Number Valued at £ 12 and upwards.	TOTAL.
PROVINCE OF LEINSTER	6,290	3,605	9,895
PROVINCE OF MUNSTER	5,965	7,038	13,003
PROVINCE OF ULSTER	8,659	11,794	20,453
PROVINCE OF CONNAUGHT	1,769	1,575	3,344
TOTAL for IRELAND (excluding Dublin County and City)	22,683	24,012	46,695

RETURN of the Number of all Houses (Residences) according to the following Classification.

COUNTIES (BY PROVINCES).	NUMBER OF HOUSES, OR HOUSES AND OFFICES (RESIDENCES) VALUED AT: £. 6 and under £. 8.		£. 8 and under £. 10.		£. 10 and under £. 12.		£. 12 and under £. 15.		£. 15 and under £. 20.		£. 20 and under £. 30.		£. 30 and under £. 40.		£. 40 and under £. 50.		£. 50 and upwards.		TOTAL.		GRAND TOTAL.
	Rural.	Cities, &c.	Rural.	Cities, &c.	Rural.	Cities, &c.	Rural.	Cities, &c.	Rural.	Cities, &c.	Rural.	Cities, &c.	Rural.	Cities, &c.	Rural.	Cities, &c.	Rural.	Cities, &c.	Rural.	Cities, &c.	
LEINSTER:																					
Carlow - - -	80	113	56	75	27	54	43	66	36	78	31	60	13	16	9	7	9	1	304	474	778
Dublin - - -	–	–	–	–	–	–	–	–	–	–	–	–	–	–	–	–	–	–	–	–	–
Dublin City - -	–	–	–	–	–	–	–	–	–	–	–	–	–	–	–	–	–	–	–	–	–
Drogheda Town - -	–	117	–	103	–	53	–	90	–	121	–	103	–	26	–	11	–	12	–	644	644
Kildare - - -	155	176	87	122	94	62	82	120	61	106	84	73	23	11	10	5	35	2	651	679	1,330
Kilkenny - - -	226	111	85	60	78	37	63	34	59	22	75	7	25	2	10	2	27	–	656	272	928
Kilkenny City - -	–	74	–	71	–	40	–	60	–	54	–	67	–	42	–	9	–	12	–	449	449
King's County - -	117	140	49	124	47	80	65	82	68	73	50	82	29	31	11	7	9	4	445	623	1,068
Longford - - -	59	81	30	60	31	28	24	37	32	42	35	29	12	17	7	2	8	–	238	296	534
Louth - - -	102	129	66	144	52	65	51	61	53	84	47	93	15	42	20	16	26	18	435	654	1,089
Meath - - -	217	117	141	77	120	51	108	56	124	68	116	57	62	16	35	1	42	3	970	442	1,412
Queen's County - -	118	170	73	96	41	85	65	70	68	79	63	45	22	15	16	5	13	5	464	570	1,034
Westmeath - - -	188	136	120	69	76	62	72	77	76	54	64	70	29	18	17	6	30	2	622	494	1,116
Wexford - - -	209	257	156	177	124	116	93	176	107	170	98	143	37	30	9	4	20	3	853	1,056	1,909
Wicklow - - -	148	153	107	111	78	92	63	101	74	90	97	105	44	61	13	23	28	61	652	809	1,461
TOTAL for LEINSTER, excluding Dublin County and City -	1,368	1,754	970	1,288	768	815	719	1,029	773	1,048	750	962	319	329	166	119	257	123	6,290	7,469	13,759
MUNSTER:																					
Clare - - -	91	174	61	126	30	81	70	84	79	56	73	57	35	4	15	2	13	–	516	581	1,097
Cork, East Riding -	449	474	255	441	258	282	206	368	227	401	328	396	177	144	87	78	120	54	2,115	2,633	4,748
Cork, West Riding -	190	274	101	193	50	166	79	120	75	107	93	93	85	21	14	6	16	1	653	983	1,636
Cork City - -	–	577	–	456	–	346	–	398	–	421	–	615	–	234	–	111	–	171	–	3,327	3,327
Kerry - - -	88	211	56	165	40	100	38	124	42	96	42	112	11	44	6	10	12	7	343	897	1,240
Limerick - - -	161	147	95	96	78	52	74	62	68	43	114	25	49	6	19	1	27	1	685	437	1,119
Limerick, City - -	–	215	–	190	–	134	–	156	–	204	–	251	–	115	–	69	–	118	–	1,479	1,479
Tipperary, North Riding	36	162	40	56	64	65	48	113	79	86	61	86	34	21	8	10	18	6	427	644	1,071
Tipperary, South Riding	118	220	80	132	44	92	43	190	58	168	54	173	32	44	11	22	23	17	488	1,060	1,548
Waterford - - -	240	131	119	89	96	76	67	78	66	97	60	84	47	17	10	7	24	8	705	582	1,350
Waterford City - -	–	192	–	166	–	112	–	115	–	126	–	150	–	64	–	28	–	19	–	977	977
TOTAL for MUNSTER -	1,422	2,777	830	2,164	607	1,311	625	1,618	718	1,807	820	1,931	492	744	170	348	260	392	6,965	13,190	19,135

Return of the Number of all Houses (Residences) according to the following Classification—*continued.*

COUNTIES (BY PROVINCES)	Number of Houses, or Houses and Offices (Residences), valued at: £. 6 and under £. 8		£. 8 and under £. 10		£. 10 and under £. 12		£. 12 and under £. 15		£. 15 and under £. 20		£. 20 and under £. 30		£. 30 and under £. 40		£. 40 and under £. 50		£. 50 and upwards		TOTAL		GRAND TOTAL
	Rural	Cities, &c.	Rural	Cities, &c.	Rural	Cities, &c.	Rural	Cities, &c.	Rural	Cities, &c.	Rural	Cities, &c.	Rural	Cities, &c.	Rural	Cities, &c.	Rural	Cities, &c.	Rural	Cities, &c.	
ULSTER:																					
Antrim	465	347	224	393	179	297	159	295	136	313	164	306	93	109	48	42	181	47	1,641	2,239	3,880
Armagh	302	483	164	873	113	207	117	241	127	232	107	226	40	90	34	51	67	81	1,081	1,982	3,063
Belfast, Town	–	2,545	–	1,818	–	638	–	1,063	–	1,196	–	1,083	–	513	–	980	–	268	–	9,744	9,751
Carrickfergus Town	–	67	–	44	–	20	–	28	–	56	–	35	–	29	–	8	–	11	–	284	284
Cavan	28	149	56	174	43	48	39	163	32	87	45	60	21	17	7	9	18	5	349	602	951
Donegal	172	247	84	168	65	128	75	123	79	111	95	63	29	26	16	4	21	2	639	874	1,503
Down	783	697	415	502	259	375	272	498	230	460	265	495	157	185	106	96	245	105	2,742	3,453	6,195
Fermanagh	109	198	60	121	96	70	39	74	43	59	82	62	12	47	10	20	53	12	364	629	993
Londonderry	176	180	107	171	78	106	89	155	100	128	68	137	47	52	22	19	42	12	742	958	1,700
Londonderry City	–	353	–	209	–	160	–	215	–	179	–	227	–	108	–	70	–	104	–	1,712	1,712
Monaghan	97	159	42	101	41	50	36	117	20	111	45	95	19	32	6	14	16	17	324	720	1,044
Tyrone	297	343	118	278	81	183	106	212	77	231	96	190	54	63	31	36	86	36	787	1,577	2,364
Total for Ulster	2,394	6,035	1,290	4,415	885	2,490	973	2,127	844	2,117	981	3,098	475	1,272	276	649	657	700	8,689	24,754	33,443
CONNAUGHT:																					
Galway	165	192	76	123	70	70	92	109	88	95	77	67	59	19	36	1	31	2	621	678	1,299
Galway, Town	–	81	–	96	–	79	–	90	–	26	–	99	–	48	–	18	–	19	–	626	626
Leitrim	43	56	29	33	18	25	15	46	21	59	13	29	6	5	5	2	3	3	151	240	391
Mayo	78	200	52	136	54	77	56	85	43	92	59	77	19	16	8	5	14	5	363	693	1,056
Roscommon	74	105	68	98	39	65	14	52	56	59	46	70	18	16	8	4	13	1	366	499	865
Sligo	60	97	44	106	28	41	47	70	34	79	25	91	13	16	6	11	11	7	258	520	778
Total for Connaught	380	732	269	592	216	357	244	484	242	420	300	433	109	120	57	41	79	37	1,769	3,256	5,025

SUMMARY.

RETURN of the Number of all HOUSES (Residences) according to the following Classification.

COUNTIES AND PROVINCES.	NUMBER OF HOUSES, OR HOUSES AND OFFICES (RESIDENCES), VALUED AT									TOTAL.
	£. 5 and under £. 8.	£. 8 and under £. 10.	£. 10 and under £. 12.	£. 12 and under £. 15.	£. 15 and under £. 20.	£. 20 and under £. 30.	£. 30 and under £. 40.	£. 40 and under £. 50.	£. 50 and upwards.	
LEINSTER:										
Carlow	103	181	81	111	114	61	31	16	10	778
Drogheda, Town	117	108	55	60	121	108	30	11	12	644
Dublin	770	604	560	800	1,251	1,646	1,307	750	983	8,678
Dublin, City	—	—	—	—	—	—	—	—		—
Kildare	331	300	156	303	180	157	34	15	57	1,330
Kilkenny	280	145	115	94	81	88	27	81	27	898
Kilkenny, City	74	71	40	60	54	87	42	9	12	449
King's County	257	175	197	147	141	158	60	18	13	1,064
Longford	140	90	50	61	74	64	20	9	8	654
Louth	231	210	117	112	137	140	60	36	44	1,083
Meath	334	218	171	164	193	173	79	89	45	1,412
Queen's County	286	169	186	125	142	108	37	21	14	1,034
Westmeath	274	180	158	149	130	134	47	23	33	1,110
Wexford	440	330	240	200	277	241	67	13	23	1,900
Wicklow	301	218	100	104	164	195	105	55	90	1,401
TOTAL for LEINSTER (excluding Dublin City)	4,009	2,678	2,149	2,548	2,937	3,260	1,855	1,015	1,263	22,274
MUNSTER:										
Clare	225	173	114	184	110	127	38	17	13	941
Cork, East Riding	898	690	504	520	630	718	310	164	100	4,089
Cork, West Riding	484	294	210	193	188	160	56	29	17	1,816
Cork City	377	456	360	398	427	415	234	111	171	2,987
Kerry	305	237	147	108	136	158	54	18	19	1,181
Limerick	308	165	130	120	111	139	55	20	28	1,112
Limerick City	315	190	184	158	204	251	145	60	115	1,472
Tipperary, North Riding	226	197	125	106	155	134	59	19	29	1,025
Tipperary, South Riding	308	217	151	245	233	228	79	60	33	1,544
Waterford	375	208	174	145	198	144	64	17	37	1,352
Waterford City	198	108	115	115	195	150	61	28	19	977
TOTAL for MUNSTER	4,116	2,947	2,150	2,300	2,490	2,728	1,165	518	641	19,145
ULSTER.										
Antrim	1,012	617	409	446	449	430	202	68	228	3,880
Armagh	775	539	390	358	335	333	130	85	146	3,093
Belfast Town	2,745	1,656	636	1,063	1,190	1,063	519	280	208	9,154
Carrickfergus Town	67	44	26	28	30	55	20	8	11	284
Cavan	242	170	111	142	110	95	38	16	18	931
Donegal	419	252	193	201	190	157	48	29	21	1,503
Down	1,480	927	634	770	710	790	352	202	350	6,106
Fermanagh	237	181	128	113	132	94	50	30	45	998
Londonderry	350	278	184	237	226	235	90	41	54	1,690
Londonderry City	358	200	102	215	179	247	106	70	104	1,712
Monaghan	250	145	121	158	131	140	51	28	53	1,044
Tyrone	563	336	204	312	308	280	119	67	75	2,304
TOTAL for ULSTER	8,449	5,705	3,265	4,040	3,901	3,830	1,748	910	1,357	33,443
CONNAUGHT.										
Galway	207	190	149	101	163	144	72	31	33	1,090
Galway Town	81	90	79	60	97	100	46	18	10	520
Leitrim	90	69	41	63	60	42	11	7	6	389
Mayo	247	166	122	196	104	98	30	10	16	1,098
Roscommon	180	164	104	185	115	116	34	13	14	925
Sligo	157	152	69	117	113	116	29	17	18	788
TOTAL for CONNAUGHT	1,061	841	564	713	673	615	227	96	106	4,897

SUMMARY.

	£. 5 and under £. 8.	£. 8 and under £. 10.	£. 10 and under £. 12.	£. 12 and under £. 15.	£. 15 and under £. 20.	£. 20 and under £. 30.	£. 30 and under £. 40.	£. 40 and under £. 50.	£. 50 and upwards.	TOTAL.
LEINSTER (excluding Dublin City)	4,098	3,603	2,149	2,548	2,937	3,260	1,860	1,015	1,260	22,274
MUNSTER	4,110	2,947	2,150	2,306	2,496	2,722	1,165	518	641	19,145
ULSTER	8,480	5,705	3,265	4,040	3,901	3,780	1,743	910	1,357	33,443
CONNAUGHT	1,061	841	564	713	673	615	227	96	106	4,897
TOTAL for IRELAND (excluding Dublin City)	17,758	12,355	8,227	9,607	10,000	10,750	4,995	2,340	3,407	73,633

Appendix, No. 2.

LETTER from Mr. *T. H. Burke* to Mr. *B. Banks*.

Sir, Dublin Castle, 19 April 1873.

I AM directed by the Lord Lieutenant to request that the Local Government Board will be good enough to state their opinion, for his Excellency's information, whether, when the clerks of the several poor law unions in Ireland are preparing, pursuant to the 9th section of the Juries (Ireland) Act, 1871, the lists in the Form B. set forth in the Third Schedule to that Act, there would be any practical difficulty in the way of their ascertaining (with the assistance of the collectors of poor rate and the relieving officers) and stating whether each rated person entered on the lists is or is not over 60 years of age, whether he can read and write, whether he can speak English, and whether he is unfit to serve as a juror, either from lunacy, imbecility of mind, deafness, blindness, or other permanent infirmity, or for any other reason; and if, in the opinion of the Board, such information could be obtained and afforded by the clerks of the unions, whether it could not be conveniently supplied by the amendment of Form B. in the manner given in the enclosed form.

I am, &c.
(signed) *T. H. Burke.*

B. Banks, Esq., Local Government Board,
Custom House.

FORM B.

County of (*) and Poor Law Union of

"GENERAL LIST OF JURORS" for the (†) in the said County, prepared this day of , 18 , by the Clerk of the said Union.

Consecutive Numbers.	Surnames in Alphabetical Order.	Christian Names.	Place of Abode.	Barony, Half-barony or Ward in which Place of Abode is situate.	Title, Quality, Calling, or Business.	Annual Value of Rated Property.	Place of Property.	Disqualification or Unfitness (if any). (‡)

(*) [County of the City of , or County of the Town of , or Borough of , as the case may be.]
(†) [Barony, Division of a Barony, or other district, and in counties of cities or counties of towns, or boroughs, "Ward".]
(‡) If any such person is disqualified or unfit to serve as a juror by reason of his being over 60 years of age, being unable to read and write, not understanding English, lunacy, imbecility of mind, deafness, blindness, or other permanent infirmity, or for any other reason, such disqualification or unfitness should be here stated.

Appendix, No. 2.

LETTER from Mr. *B. Banks* to Mr. *T. H. Burke.*

Local Government Board, Dublin,
23 April 1873.

Sir,

THE Local Government Board for Ireland acknowledge the receipt of your letter of the 19th instant, in which you request, for the information of His Excellency the Lord Lieutenant, the opinion of the Board as to whether, when clerks of unions are preparing the lists of jurors in the Form B., under the provisions of the Jurors (Ireland) Act, 1871, there would be any practical difficulty in the way of their ascertaining (with the assistance of the poor rate collectors and the relieving officers) and stating whether each rated person entered on the lists is or is not over 60 years of age, whether he can read and write, whether he can speak English, and whether he is unfit to serve as a juror either from lunacy, imbecility of mind, deafness, blindness, or other permanent infirmity, or for any other reason; and if, in the opinion of the Board, the information could be so obtained, whether it could not be conveniently supplied by the amendment of Form B. in the manner given in the Form which is enclosed with your letter.

In reply, the Local Government Board have the honour to state, for His Excellency's information, that they do not apprehend any practical difficulty on the part of the clerks of unions, with the aid of the collectors, doing what is proposed; and the amended Form which accompanied your letter seems to be perfectly adapted to the purpose.

By order of the Board,
(signed) *B. Banks.*

To T. H. Burke, Esq., &c. &c.
Dublin Castle.

Appendix, No. 3.

Appendix, No. 3.

RETURN showing the Estimated Number of COMMON and SPECIAL JURORS in each County at large in *Ireland*, qualified [according to the Scale of Property Qualification stated below, estimated from Tables laid before Committee, and where no Return has been made in such Tables, from Tenure Return, 1870, c. 32.

I.—COMMON JURORS.

Estimated Number of Jurors in the following Counties.		Scale of Property Qualification.
Number.	Counties.	
	CLASS I:	
4,928	Antrim - - - -	A net annual value of 20 *l.* or upwards in respect of lands, tenements, or hereditaments, within any of the said counties, or a net annual value of 12 *l.* or upwards in respect of lands, tenements, or hereditaments appearing on the rate book of any union to be situate in any city, town, or village within any of the said counties.
2,084	Armagh - - -	
930	Carlow - - - -	
880	Cavan - - - -	
1,258	Clare - - - -	
5,038	Cork - - - -	
1,119	Donegal - - - -	
4,262	Down* - - - -	
4,867	Dublin* - - -	
830	Fermanagh* - - -	
1,573	Galway* - - -	
1,580	Kerry - - - -	
1,207	Kildare - - - -	
1,230	Kilkenny - - -	
1,092	King's County - -	
2,518	Limerick* - - -	
1,906	Londonderry - - -	
578	Longford - - -	
730	Louth - - - -	
932	Mayo* - - - -	
1,577	Meath - - - -	
987	Monaghan - - -	
1,080	Queen's County - -	
970	Roscommon* - - -	
687	Sligo - - - -	
3,385	Tipperary - - -	
1,940	Tyrone - - - -	
1,945	Waterford - - -	
1,306	Westmeath - - -	
2,263	Wexford - - -	
1,046	Wicklow - - -	
	CLASS II:	
731	Leitrim - - - -	A net annual value of 20 *l.* or upwards in respect of lands, tenements, or hereditaments within any of the said counties, or a net annual value of 12 *l.* or upwards in respect of lands, tenements, or hereditaments appearing on the rate book of any union to be situate in any city, town, or village within the said county.

* In the case of these counties the Tables (Appendix, No. 1) laid before the Committee contain no returns as to the number of jurors of different classes.

II.—Special Jurors.

Appendix, No. 3.

Estimated Number of Jurors in the following Counties. Number.	Counties.	Scale of Property Qualification.
	Class I.:	
040	Antrim - - - -	A net annual value of 150 *l.* or upwards in respect of lands, tenements, or hereditaments within any of the said counties, or a net annual value of 50 *l.* or upwards in respect of lands, tenements, or hereditaments appearing on the rate book of any union to be situate in any city, town, or village within any of the said counties.
600	Dublin* - - -	
	Class II.:	
560	Cork - - - -	A net annual value of 150 *l.* or upwards in respect of lands, tenements, or hereditaments within any of the said counties, or a net annual value of 30 *l.* or upwards in respect of lands, tenements, or hereditaments appearing on the rate book of any union to be situate in any city, town, or village within any of the said counties.
431	Down* - - - -	
244	Kildare - - - -	
303	Limerick - - -	
235	Londonderry - - -	
395	Meath - - - -	
414	Tipperary - - -	
225	Wicklow - - -	
	Class III.:	
311	Armagh - - -	A net annual value of 100 *l.* or upwards in respect of lands, tenements, or hereditaments within any of the said counties, or a net annual value of 20 *l.* or upwards in respect of lands, tenements, or hereditaments appearing on the rate book of any union to be situate in any city, town, or village within any of the said counties.
190	Carlow - - - -	
214	Clare - - - -	
313	Galway* - - -	
339	Kilkenny - - -	
240	King's County - -	
203	Louth - - - -	
239	Queen's County - -	
253	Roscommon* - - -	
193	Tyrone - - - -	
352	Waterford - - -	
385	Westmeath - - -	
389	Wexford - - -	
	Class IV.:	
151	Cavan - - - -	A net annual value of 80 *l.* or upwards in respect of lands, tenements, or hereditaments within any of the said counties, or a net annual value of 20 *l.* and upwards in respect of lands, tenements, or hereditaments appearing on the rate book of any union to be situate in any city, town, or village within any of the said counties.
187	Donegal - - -	
130	Fermanagh* - - -	
211	Kerry - - - -	
130	Longford - - -	
230	Mayo* - - - -	
159	Monaghan - - -	
155	Sligo - - - -	
	Class V.:	
146	Leitrim - - - -	A net annual value of 50 *l.* and upwards in respect of lands, tenements, or hereditaments within any of the said counties, or a net annual value of 20 *l.* or upwards in respect of lands, tenements, or hereditaments appearing on the rate book of any union to be situate in any city, town, or village within the said county.

* In the case of these counties, the Tables laid before the Committee contain no returns as to the number of jurors of the different classes.

London, 6 May 1873.

W. Neilson Hancock.
Constantine Molloy.

Appendix, No. 4.

MEMORANDUM by Mr. *Constantine Molloy.*

THE RIGHT OF THE CROWN TO CHALLENGE JURORS.

THE right of challenge to jurors appears to be coeval with the institution of trial by jury. It was probably borrowed from the Roman law, for it was in use amongst the Romans. The Lex Servilia, B.C. 104, enacted that the accuser and accused should severally propose 100 judices, and that each might reject fifty from the list of the other, so that 100 would remain to try the alleged crime.

By the common law the Crown had an unrestricted right of peremptory challenge, but the Statute 33 Edward 1 deprived the Crown of the right of peremptory challenge, and confined the right of the Crown to challenge for cause. The 33 Edward 1, statute 4, enacted as follows:—"Of inquests to be taken before any of the justices, and wherein our Lord the King is party, however it be: It is agreed and ordained by the King and all his counsel, that from henceforth, notwithstanding it be alleged by them that sue for the King that the jurors of those inquests, or some of them, be not indifferent for the King, yet such inquests shall not remain untaken for that cause; but if they that sue for the King will challenge any of those jurors, they shall assign of their challenge a cause certain, and the truth of the same challenge shall be inquired of according to the custom of the court."

The plain and fair construction of this statute would appear to be, that when a challenge to any juror was taken on behalf of the Crown, the cause of such challenge should be stated and then tried in the ordinary way. But in the course of time the Statute received a different construction, and judges held that the Crown was not bound to state the cause of challenge to a juror until the whole panel was called over, and that in the meantime the Crown might, on a juror being called, direct the juror to stand aside for the present, until the whole panel was gone through. In this way the Crown, if a jury could be obtained without again calling on the person so set aside, obtained and exercised a peremptory power of putting particular individuals off juries.

The earliest authority I have been able to find for the construction which has been put on the Statute of Edward 1 is Staundforde, who wrote in the reign of Philip and Mary. In his Pleas of the Crown, fol. 162, he says:—"By the Statute of Edward 1 the King cannot challenge without cause; but this cause he need not show immediately upon his challenge (as a common person must if he was party against the King), but he must show it when he has perused all the panel." Staundforde, it must be observed, does not cite any authority or give any reason for the proposition he thus lays down. Sir Edward Coke wrote some time after Staundforde, yet he does not, in his Institutes, although he treats very fully of the subject of challenges, make any mention of the doctrine propounded by Staundforde.

This question came before the Court of Queen's Bench in the 33rd of Elizabeth, on the trial of an indictment for murder, as appears from the case of "Savage *v.* Brooks, Moor," 595; the report states:—"In the Queen's Bench three justices held that the Queen can challenge peremptorily, without cause shown, the jurors empannelled to try a felony, but they sent Fenner to the Common Bench, to have the opinion of the justices there, and they were of a contrary opinion, that is, that she could not challenge without cause shown."

The next case in which this question was considered was in "Rex. *v.* Morgan, 1 Bulstrode, 84, in the 8th year of James 1. The court said that the counsel for the King ought not to show cause of challenge till the other jurors on the panel are sworn.

In "Anon, 1 Ventris," which was an information for forgery, the counsel for the King challenged, and were pressed to allege the cause for. 33 Edward 1 does take away the general challenge, *quia non sunt boni pro Rege,* "but all the court (save Wylde, who seemed to be of another opinion), ordered the panel to be gone through, and if they were enough the King is not to show any cause."

In "Ford, Lord Grey's Case, Sir Thomas Raymond's Reports, 473":—"In a trial at bar of an information against Lord Grey, of Warke, and others, for taking away Lady Henrietta Berkley, 20th August, 34 Charles 2, the counsel for the King challenged some of the jurors, and Lord Grey's counsel insisted that the cause of challenge ought to be *presently* shown according to the 33rd Edward 1, and to enforce them to do so the counsel for Lord Grey challenged *tous par avail,* but it was resolved by the whole court that the King ought by that Statute to show his cause of the challenge, but not before all the jurors of the panel

are

are called over, for if there be enough besides those which are challenged no cause shall be shown of that challenge."

These four cases in "Moor, Bulstrode, Ventris," and "Sir Thomas Raymond's Reports" are the authorities, with Staundforde, for the construction which has been given to the Statute 33 Edward 1. If the construction thus put on that Statute had not since been adopted by eminent and upright judges, these cases, having regard to the times when they occurred, and some at least of the judges who decided them, might well be regarded as of little or no authority. In the case in "Moor," the Common Bench was of a different opinion. In the case in "Ventris," Wylde dissented from the decision, and Sir Thomas Jones, who formed one of the majority of the court, was included in the impeachment against Scroggs, "for having traitorously and wickedly endeavoured to subvert the fundamental laws of England." He also presided at the trial of Cornish, and Sir Francis Pemberton, who was Chief Justice of the King's Bench when the case in "Sir Thomas Raymond's Reports" was decided, presided at the trial of Lord Russell, and the Legislature afterwards solemnly stigmatised both these trials of Cornish and Lord Russell as having been obtained "by partial and unjust constructions of law."

It is right, however, to mention that Lord Hale in his "Pleas of the Crown," vol. ii., p. 271, adopts this construction of the Statute of 33 Edward 1, and quotes Staundforde as the authority for it. Throughout the State trials, and down to the most recent times, this construction of the Statute has been always questioned, and invariably upheld. Lord Holt, when at the bar, impugned it, but he afterwards, when presiding at Sir Richard Graham's trial in 1691 (12 "State Trials," p. 675), declared that "there is not any more clear case in all our law than that cause is not to be shown by the King's counsel till all the panel is gone through, and then, if there be not 12 left to try, they are bound to show cause;" and he was so clear and decisive on the point, that he told Sir Richard Graham he would not have the time of the court spent by assigning counsel to argue it. In Frost's case, Sir Frederick Pollock and Mr. Fitzroy Kelly impugned this construction of the Statute of Edward 1, but the court maintained it. It was again impugned, and with the like result, in 1857, in the case of "Mansell v. The Queen in error;" "Dearsley and Bell," 375; "8 Ell. and Bl.," 155.

The 33 Edward 1 was re-enacted by the 29th section of the English Jury Act, 6 Geo. 4, c. 50, which enacts "That in all inquests to be taken before any of the courts hereinbefore mentioned, wherein the King is a party, howsoever it be, notwithstanding it be alleged by them that sue for the King, that the jurors of these inquests, or some of them, be not indifferent for the King, yet such inquests shall not remain untaken for that cause, but if they that sue for the King will challenge any of those jurors, they shall assign of their challenge a cause certain, and the truth of the same challenge shall be inquired of according to the custom of the court, and it shall be proceeded to the taking of the same inquisitions as it shall be found if the challenges be true or not after the discretion of the court."

After the long series of decisions, in which the construction originally put on the Statute of 33 Edw. 1 has been invariably upheld, and after the Legislature, by the 29th section of the 6 Geo. 4, c. 50, has in almost similar words re-enacted the provisions of the Statute of Edw. 1, without condemning or declaring such construction to have been erroneous, I think it must now be taken beyond any question that the Crown cannot be obliged to state the grounds of challenge until the whole panel has been gone through.

In Ireland this right of the Crown to postpone the time for stating the ground of challenge does not rest merely, as it does in England, upon judicial decision, but is conferred by the express words of the 9th section of the 0 Geo. 4, c. 54; that section re-enacts in the same words as the 29th section of the English Jury Act (6 Geo. 4, c. 50), the provisions of the 33 Edw. 1, and adds the following proviso, which is not contained in the 6 Geo. 4, c. 54: "Provided always, that nothing herein contained shall affect or be construed to affect the power of any court in Ireland to order any juror to stand by until the panel shall be gone through at the prayer of them that prosecute for the King, as has been heretofore accustomed."

In the United States of America the public prosecutor has not the right of peremptory challenge, but he may challenge for cause, and is not obliged to state the ground of challenge until the challenge has been gone through. "Wharton's Criminal Law," section 2936; 4th edition, 1857.

The effect of the right of the Crown to order jurors to stand by until the panel has been gone through depends on the number of jurors returned by the sheriff. Where the panel is a large one the Crown virtually obtains the right of peremptory challenge, as it is very unlikely that the prisoner by his challenges would be able to exhaust the panel before 12 jurors would be obtained to whom the Crown would not object. Of course, where the panel is a limited one, it may be exhausted before the 12 jurors are sworn, and then the Crown will have to state its ground of challenge.

As the effect of this right on the part of the Crown depends so much upon the number of jurors returned upon the panel, I have endeavoured to ascertain what number of jurors was usually returned by the sheriff in those early times when the construction of the Statute of Edw. 1 was fixed by the judges, but I have been unable to do so; indeed, I think it would be impossible at this day to ascertain it; however, I think I am justified in saying that the practice of sheriffs at the present day is to return a far greater number of jurors than in former times, in proof of which I may refer to the following authorities:—"The general precept that issues before a sessions of gaol delivery, oyer and terminer, and of the peace is to return 24, and commonly the sheriff returns upon that precept 48." Hale,

Appendix, No. 4.

"Pleas of the Crown," vol. ii., p. 263. "The *venire facias* to the sheriff at common law was to return only 12 to serve on the petit jury, but as there would have been great inconvenience from merely summoning the number to be actually employed, and the full jury would be very seldom assembled, it seems to have been always the practice for the sheriff to return 24 on the panel. He might, however, at any time have returned more than that number, for the Statute of Westminster the second, which limits the panel in civil cases to 24, does not extend to criminal cases." Chitty's "Criminal Law," fol. 1, p. 505, ed. 1816.

Upon the trial of Sir Harry Vane, the number of jurors to be returned by the sheriff was considered, as appears from the following memorandum in Sir John Kelyng's "Reports," p. 16:—"Memorandum that in this case of Sir Henry Vane, he being to be tried at the King's Bench bar. Before he came to his trial it was considered by myself and others, then of the King's counsel, that it was possible that he might challenge peremptorily, and so defeat his trial at that day at which it was appointed, if there should be only 24 jurors returned. And thereupon search was made in the Crown Office, and it did appear that in trials on the Crown side for criminals the sheriff might be commanded to return any number the court pleased; and, accordingly, at his trial the sheriff returned 60 of the jury." Upon the trial of Layer, 16 Howell's State Trials, p. 93, 100 jurors were returned; upon Charnock's trial, 12 State Trials, p. 1377, 160 were returned; and upon Townley's trial, 18 State Trials, p. 332, 108 were returned. At the present day the same precept issues for the return of jurors for both civil and criminal cases, by which the sheriff is directed to return a competent number of jurors for the trial of all issues; and in practice on circuit the sheriff rarely, if ever, returns less than 100; the usual number is from 150 to 200; and where important cases are to be tried, the number generally exceeds 200; and in the case of State prosecutions it is still larger.

It is manifest that from the increase in the number of jurors returned by the sheriff, this right of the Crown has been materially altered, so that the Crown has again, for all practical purposes, virtually the right of peremptory challenge.

This right of the Crown to order jurors to stand by until the whole panel has been gone through is claimed and exercised by the private prosecutor in this country.

In the year 1857 Mr. M'Gowan, Mayor of Sligo, was prosecuted by a private prosecutor for conspiracy in tampering with poll-books at an election. The right to order jurors to stand by was extensively exercised by the private prosecutor; and Mr. Justice Christian, who tried the case, reserved the question, whether a private prosecutor has such a right, for the Court of Criminal Appeal. That court decided (Mr. Justice Perrin, *dubitante*) that it was the privilege of the prosecutor, whether public or private, not to assign cause for his challenge until the panel had been gone through and exhausted. That court also decided (but from this part of the judgment Mr. Justice Perrin dissented) that the judge was bound, at the instance of the prosecutor, to order the juror to stand by; such an order not being optional with him, he having no discretion in the matter.—Reg. v. M'Gowan, 3 Ir. Jur., N. S. 403.

In 1862, on the trial of an indictment for libel at the Armagh Assizes, preferred by a private prosecutor against a Roman Catholic priest, for a letter which he had written commenting on the conduct of the prosecutor towards his tenants, the private prosecutor largely exercised this right. Mr., now Chief Justice, Whiteside, the prisoner's counsel, strongly protested against its exercise; and it was not approved of by Mr. Justice Fitzgerald, who tried the case.

As there is hardly, if ever, a case in this country which is properly the subject of a criminal prosecution that is not taken up by the Crown, and as private prosecutions in the majority of cases are instituted either for the purpose of establishing a civil right by means of a criminal prosecution, or of obtaining for the private prosecutor some advantage which he would not have if he adopted a civil proceeding to obtain redress for the injury of which he complains, I think that a privilege of such great magnitude as the right to order jurors to stand by, and one which is liable to be abused, ought not to be entrusted to an irresponsible private prosecutor, and should, by express legislation, be confined to the cases where the prosecution is conducted by the Attorney General in person, or by his direction.

As regards the right of the Crown to order jurors to stand by until the whole panel has been gone through and exhausted, I believe that it is a privilege which is necessary to be entrusted to the public prosecutor, in order to secure the due administration of justice. That this privilege has been sometimes grossly abused there can be no question, and thereby convictions obtained in cases where this right has been abused have lost all that moral weight which is so essentially necessary to give due effect to the administration of the law. This abuse had reached such a height in 1835, when Mr. Justice Perrin was Attorney-General, that he deemed it necessary to issue a circular to the Crown Solicitors for their guidance; and Sir Maziere Brady, when Attorney General, in 1839, issued a similar circular. And if the instructions contained in those circulars are faithfully observed, there is little danger of this privilege being abused.

2 March 1871. *Constantine Molloy.*

Appendix, No. 5.

PAPERS handed in by the *Chairman*.

REPORTS received from the INSPECTORS of POOR LAW UNIONS in *Ireland* in Reply to Circular Letter from the LOCAL GOVERNMENT BOARD, *Ireland*, relative to the working of the JURIES (IRELAND) ACT, 1871. Appendix, No. 5.

Mr. Richard Bourke.	Mr. William P. O'Brien.
Mr. William James Hamilton.	Mr. Terence Brodie.
Mr. Samuel Horsley.	Mr. Charles Croker King.
Mr. Richard T. Hamilton.	Mr. George F. Roughan.
Mr. Henry Robinson.	Mr. Thomas Hamilton Burke.

REPORT of Mr. *Richard Bourke*.

(No. 11,648–73.—Miscellaneous.)

Gentlemen, Kilkee, 28 April 1873.

WITH reference to your letter of the 10th instant, transmitting the copy of a communication from the Under Secretary to the Lord Lieutenant, upon the subject of the working of the recent Jurors Act, in which it is stated that his Excellency desires to obtain information which may be of practical value in fixing a proper qualification for jurors and special jurors, I have the honour to state that, having, in accordance with the suggestion contained in this letter, consulted the most intelligent of the clerks in my district, and brought their local knowledge to bear in scrutinising the lists in localities with which they or I were personally acquainted, the following are the conclusions which have been arrived at:—

1. That no increase in the rating qualification (unless the number of jurors for each county were reduced below 1,000), would secure the return of men more fit and proper than those now on the list. The clerks of the unions are unanimous in thinking that no rating qualification will, of itself, procure an uniformly efficient jurors' list. They recognise in the large majority of persons rated between 20 *l.* and 30 *l.*, men in every way qualified to serve as jurors, while among those of higher valuations they are able to point out several who would be utterly incompetent. As one instance may be taken, the case of Denis Kean, which created no little excitement at the Ennis Spring Assizes, where he was placed as foreman of a petit jury, and found unable to speak English, and otherwise quite illiterate, that man is rated in the electoral division of St. Martin's and Union of Kilrush at 50 *l.* 15 *s.* Again, in the same union, a man named Patrick Shanasy (recently dead) was equally ignorant and unsuited for a juror, though rated at 93 *l.* Instances such as these could easily be multiplied, whilst, on the other hand, hundreds of names could be given of men rated at about 20 *l.*, qualified by education, intelligence, and probity, to discharge all a juryman's duties with credit and efficiency.

2. That, in the present state of the valuation books, no household qualification in rural districts, whether by itself or in conjunction with the rated value of land, could be employed in fixing the qualification of jurors, because the changes and improvements in houses since the last valuation, where they were separately entered, have been so considerable, that those valuations, at no time very discriminative, bear less relation now than they ever did to the real value of the tenements. It is no uncommon occurrence to find highly rated occupiers whose houses are valued at 20 *s.* or 30 *s.* only, and a 6 *l.* household qualification, would exclude nine-tenths of the present common jurors.

3. That, as regards special jurors, the limit in the County Clare might perhaps be better fixed at 80 *l.* than at 50 *l.*, but left in Limerick and Tipperary at 100 *l.* as at present.

4. With reference to the 12 *l.* town and village qualification some difference of opinion prevails between the clerks of Limerick and Tipperary, to which counties it applies.

Appendix, No. 5.

applies. In Limerick the general opinion seems to be that the qualification might with advantage be lowered to 8 *l.* or 10 *l.*, which would bring in an intelligent class of shopkeepers. But in Roscrea, the clerk, a very well-informed man, is in favour of raising it above 12 *l.* My own opinion coincides with that of the clerks who favour a reduction, and I think such a household qualification should be extended to the County Clare, and I presume to the other counties in Ireland which do not now possess it, if (as I see suggested by Mr. Hemphill in his examination before the Committee) publicans are excluded.

As regards the amount of qualification generally, I entirely agree with the clerks whose opinion I have reported, and I am quite unable to see why any higher qualification should be required for common jurors than for elected guardians of the poor, in whose case a valuation ranging from 10 *l.* to 30 *l.* provides men in all respects suited for the duty. But as the expenses attending service on juries are beyond the means of very poor men, and they may be assumed to be in easier circumstances as their valuation increases, it might be proper, as a relief to the very poor, if the qualification were raised to 30 *l.* which in the counties of Limerick and Clare (where I am acquainted with the particulars) would leave the numbers above the point fixed in the communication forwarded to me. And as even in this class some might still be found incompetent to the discharge of these duties, whether from want of education or from such physical disability as deafness or infirmity of body, it might be possible to require clerks of unions to mark such cases on their lists, giving the parties a right of appeal to the chairman at the revising sessions. I am informed by the clerks of unions that with the assistance of the collectors they would find no difficulty in discharging this duty.

Having now stated all the points regarding qualification which have resulted from the inquiries I have been directed to make, I may be allowed to add a few observations on the general question of the operation of the recent Act.

It seemed to me from the commencement that the numerous unfavourable judgments pronounced about it after the last assizes were premature and somewhat rash. It is not to be wondered at if some of the men, brought for the first time in their lives to the discharge of duties of a complicated and technical nature, should have shown some inaptitude for the task. It was so at first with regard to elected guardians of the poor, but a short experience corrected the evil, and it is remarkable that even at the present Quarter Sessions a great improvement has been observed in the conduct of jurymen, who have in several counties been complimented by the chairman for the intelligence they displayed. Neither should it be forgotten that, under the previous system of arbitrary selection by barony constables and sub-sheriffs, complaints were common of the difficulty of obtaining convictions in criminal cases, and it cannot fairly be attributed to defects in the present law if similar obstructions to the course of justice have occasionally been observed under the measure recently introduced.

I have, &c.

To the Local Government Board. (signed) *R. Bourke.*

REPORT of Mr. *William James Hamilton.*

(No. 11,423–73.—Miscellaneous.)

Gentlemen, Fiddown, Piltown, 24 April 1873.

I BEG to state that I have consulted the clerks of the unions in my district on the subject of the qualifications which should be fixed for securing a class of fit and proper jurors, bearing in mind the necessity of providing a sufficient number; and as to what would be the effect of a household qualification of 6 *l.* in rural districts and 12 *l.* in cities, towns, and villages.

I have likewise procured from each union in my district, excepting Clogheen, a copy of the general list of jurors. There are in all 10,354 jurors in the unions in my district comprising 63 portions of baronies in portions of the

Queen's County.
County Wexford.
County Carlow.
County Kilkenny.
County Limerick.
County Tipperary, North and South Riding.
County Waterford.

I had intended to classify the jurors according to the annual value of rated property, so as to show the number of jurors and special jurors at each amount as under:—

£.		£.	£.		£.
20	to	25	70	to	80
25	to	30	80	to	90
30	to	40	90	to	100
40	to	50	100	to	200
50	to	60	200 and upwards,		
60	to	70			

but

but I doubt whether any benefit would result from my doing so, for I have now reason to believe that somewhat similar particulars have been already furnished from each county; boundaries of the unions are so different from the boundaries of the counties, and baronies are so interlaced that, with the county as the unit of area, any returns which were not of a general nature would not be worth the time they would occupy in the preparation, and would possibly not give any further information than may be obtained with sufficient accuracy from such a cursory examination of the lists as I have already made. I can send the lists to you if you desire.

I think I may say there is a general concurrence of testimony amongst those I have consulted on the subject as to the principle of the Act being right; of course the point of view from which I, and those whose opinions I propose to quote, is almost entirely limited to our experience of the classes we are brought in contact with; few of us know anything of the alleged effects of the Act beyond what we have read in the newspapers. No doubt reliable information on this point has been obtained from those who are able to give it and who are able to make the allowances which ought to be made for inexperience, but there still remains the difficulty of guarding against ignorance, incompetence, partisanship and other disqualifications for a jury box, and I apprehend that no rating qualification will effectually prevent the occurrence of cases which may bring undeserved discredit in any of these respects upon what I nevertheless believe to be a fair, just, and impartial Act.

The clerk of Clogheen Union says, "I do not think that, consistently with the necessity of providing a sufficient number of jurors, any qualification that may be fixed will exclude unfit and improper jurors."

The clerk of Castlecomer Union says, "I am of opinion that raising the rating qualification will not give a better class of jurors."

The clerk of Carrick-on-Suir Union says, "The rating qualification is no criterion whatever as to who are the illiterate. I know of occupiers of holdings valued at over 100 *l.* who are quite illiterate."

The clerk of New Ross Union says, "The valuation in very many cases is not any test of the occupiers' intelligence of fitness to act as jurors."

The clerk of Thomastown Union says, "No manipulation or arrangement of the valuation will remove the objections which have been urged to the working of the Act, but of course the objections would be more limited by raising the standard of qualification; but then, though there might be a sufficient number of jurors provided, the burden of work would be unduly and unnecessarily placed upon the reduced number."

The clerk of Kilkenny Union says, "There are many men wholly illiterate, or nearly so, who are rated so high as to fit them to be special jurors, and who not unfrequently possess more common sense and sound judgment than those apparently much smarter and better educated, so that it is difficult to make a rule to meet all cases."

The clerk of Tipperary Union says, "It is generally assumed that by raising the rating qualification, a better class of jurors could be had; this, no doubt, would solve the problem at once, did intelligence and a high qualification go hand in hand? But unfortunately this generally is not the case, as I know of my own knowledge that in a great many instances they bear an inverse ratio to each other."

The clerk of Waterford Union says, "The property qualification in this union is as good as any that could be adopted."

The clerk of Kilmacthomas Union says, "I do not think that a rating qualification is a correct test."

The clerk of Clonmel Union "Is in favour of raising the qualification of a country juror to 50 *l.*, to be reduced after six years' training so as to admit such further admixture of lower valuations as would not appreciably deteriorate the intelligence and the business qualities of the body, but would gradually recruit and considerably increase the number without lessening their efficiency, and so in time relieve the body of jurors of excessive duty." In his opinion, "No scale of rating could be solely relied on for the selection of persons so qualified."

The clerk of Cashel Union, too, advises a "Somewhat higher qualification for general jurors and somewhat lower for special jurors," and the clerk of Donaghmore Union "Recommends 35 *l.* for common jurors, and 100 *l.* for special jurors."

Though I think it would have been better if provision had been made for gradual admission and gradual training, I am not now prepared to advise any retrograde step as regards the amount of qualification, not only because I do not think it will meet the exigencies of the case, but because I think the remedy must be sought in another direction.

For the present, I think there must be such a weeding of the lists in an open manner, and by competent authority, as will set aside notoriously incompetent persons. The Act has brought forcibly to light the necessity for fitting a greater number of persons to fulfil their duties to the State in return for the protection which they are entitled to. "An instructed and intelligent people are always more decent and orderly than an ignorant and stupid one; they feel themselves each individually more respectable, and more likely to obtain the respect of their lawful superiors, and they are therefore more disposed to respect those superiors; they are more disposed to examine, and more capable of seeing through the interested complaints of faction and sedition; and they are upon that account less apt to be misled into any wanton or unnecessary opposition to the measures of Government."

Appendix, No. 5.

I desire very much to see my countrymen of all classes trained to fill their respective stations, and I welcome the Juries Act as one that must tend to have that effect.

The clerk of Thomastown Union says, "To say that men who have not been in the habit of serving on juries, previous to the commencement of the operation of the new Act, do not discharge the duties satisfactorily, is no argument against allowing the present scale of qualification to stand, for if the duty be new to them, that is no reason why they might not after a little experience, and being improved by serving with their fellow jurors who had served before, become expert and intelligent. Men whose valuation is from 20 *l.* to 30 *l.* are quite as intelligent in matters of justice as men whose valuation is three times as great, and I hold that they ought to be obliged to take a share in such work as that in question; it is calculated to gradually make them better citizens, and have greater respect for the laws. Persons of the class I refer to, I have known to be as useful and as intelligent at a Board of Guardians."

The clerk of New Ross Union says, "The fact of making these men attend occasionally as jurors, will tend greatly to make them try to improve themselves, as they feel rather proud of the privileges, and I doubt now very much the wisdom of the policy, if such be the intention, of striking their names off the lists."

The clerk of Kilkenny Union says, "The present qualification will, in my opinion, right itself after a little time, as soon as jurors acquire experience and talk among themselves of the nature of their duties. Besides, old men will gradually fall off and be succeeded by their sons, who are generally somewhat more enlightened, thanks to the national system of education, and by such an admixture they are certain to become nearly all (if not all) ere long, good jurors."

The clerk of Kilmacthomas Union thinks "That primarily the mode of preparing the lists of jurors is excellent."

The clerk of Urlingford Union says, "The present generation have not been educated as jurors; the rising generation may be fully competent; but this will take some years."

The clerk of Castlecomer Union says, "No doubt there may be some amongst the list of special jurors not possessing as high a degree of intelligence as would be desirable, but year by year those will be diminishing, and their places become occupied by younger and better educated men."

Concurring as I do in these views, I am not prepared to recommend any alteration as regards the qualifications of the general jurors so far as the amount of rating.

I do not know whether I may be permitted to offer suggestions respecting any other point, but it has occurred to me that if the petty sessions districts were made the unit of intermediate registry of jurors, it would be easier to deal with the disqualifications than can now be possible.

The disqualifications, in addition to those specified in the Act, are, chiefly,—

Illiteracy; physical disability; being unable to speak or understand the English language.

I think if a register with suitable headings were kept by the clerk of each petty sessions, and that each juror was required to sign and verify its contents within a limited and convenient time, and that such registers were produced annually at the quarter sessions of the district, and were then thoroughly revised and corrected in open court, much, if not all, of what is now complained of, might be remedied without any interference with the really important provisions of the Act. A set of simple general rules which everybody could understand could effectually guard against any unnecessary hardship or injustice.

The details of the Act might be more nearly assimilated to the Parliamentary Voters Act as regards the working out, publishing, and revision; much of the expense of the existing provisions in these respects would be saved, and would suffice to pay a moderate fee to each petty sessions clerk for the trouble imposed on him.

The sheriff could summon the number of jurors from each petty sessions district in proportion to the number on each register, and care should be taken to put the jurors to the least inconvenience, so far as distance from their homes, in reference to facilities of locomotion, that ordinary circumstances would admit of.

In the event of any extraordinary amount of crime, the general body would of course be available, so as to avoid intimidation or other disturbing influences.

Each register should be capable of being used for several years. At present, so far as I understand the matter, there will have to be a new register of some thousands of names each year, and even then the names will be alphabetically arranged in baronies, rather than in counties, or ridings of counties.

Holding these views, I see no objection to the admission of a household qualification at 12 *l.* in cities, towns, and villages. Neither the rate books nor valuation books give the house valuation separately; hence, the effect of the addition of a household qualification of 6 *l.* in rural districts cannot be ascertained from them. I do not attach much importance to such an addition. I do not believe it would operate injuriously, provided that some such check as I have referred to were introduced, and that full powers be given to the chairman of counties and judges in the superior courts, to deal with each case of disability and unfitness on its own merits, and for the public good.

As to special jurors, there are certain classes of cases requiring technical knowledge and intelligence; and while I should regret to see the rating qualification of general jurors increased beyond its present amount, I see no such objections to raising the qualifications for special jurors to any amount that will give a sufficient number; but I think that

that no jurors should be classed as a special juror until he shall have served as a general juror. Anything which tends to associate classes rather than to separate them, works for good.

I have, &c.
To the Local Government Board. (signed) *W. J. Hamilton.*

Report of Mr. *Samuel Horsley.*

(11,835-73—Miscellaneous.)

My Lord and Gentlemen, 30 April 1873.

Adverting to your communication (with Enclosure) of the 10th instant, I have the honour to report, that in my district, comprising the entire county of Kerry, and a large portion of the county of Cork, I have reason to believe, from information afforded to me by clerks of unions, and other persons capable of forming a sound opinion on the subject, strongly confirmed as that information is by my own observation and knowledge of the people, the amount of qualification, namely, a 20 *l.* rating, fixed for those counties in Schedule 4 of 34 & 35 Vict. c. 65, is far too low to admit of jurymen of sufficient intelligence and education being secured to try satisfactorily the common run of cases, either in the civil or criminal tribunals of the country.

The number of "Illiterates," persons who cannot read or write, but who are rated on a 20 *l.* valuation, is very large; and it might, therefore, be expedient to eliminate that class from the Juries Lists, and to raise the qualification for a general juror from a 20 *l.* rating to one of 30 *l.*, at least; and in the case of the county of Kerry, the qualification for a special juror from a 50 *l.* rating to one of 80 *l.*

As the total number, however, on the general list of jurors for the county of Kerry is, at present, only 2,440, I am not prepared to say that the increase of the qualification, as above suggested, might not reduce that list to less than 1,000.

It might also be expedient that persons, whatever the amount of their rating qualification, who do not speak or understand the English language, should be exempted from serving on juries.

There is a considerable class of persons, namely, retail shopkeepers in towns and villages, who, from want of a sufficient rating qualification, are excluded from the juries' lists, but who would, I think, generally speaking, make intelligent and conscientious jurors, were some course or plan devised for placing them on the general panel.

I have, &c.
(signed) *Samuel Horsley,*
Local Government Inspector.

Report of Mr. *Richard T. Hamilton.*

(No. 11,556-73—Miscellaneous).

My Lord and Gentlemen, Strabane, 25 April 1873.

In reference to your letter of the 10th instant, No. 9903, forwarding a copy of a letter from the Under Secretary, relating to the working of the Juries (Ireland) Act, 1871, and communicating his Excellency's desire to obtain information which may be of practical value in fixing a proper qualification for jurors and special jurors, I have the honour to inform you that, immediately after I received your letter, I wrote to the clerk of each union in my district, requesting him to furnish me with his views on the subject.

I have now received reports from the following unions, and herewith forward them for your information; viz.:—

Milford - -	Donegal.	Londonderry - -	County Derry.
Stranorlar - -		Coleraine - -	
Letterkenny - -		Newtownlimavady -	
Ballyshannon -			
Inishowen - -		Lisnaskea - -	County Fermanagh.
Glenties - -		Irvinestown - -	
Donegal - -		Enniskillen - -	
Gortin - - -	County Tyrone.	Ballycastle - -	County Antrim.
Castlederg - -		Ballymoney - -	
Omagh - - -			
Strabane - -			

The writers of these reports have had the opportunity of acquiring practical knowledge on the subject, and their opinions are entitled to some weight.

The clerk of the Dunfanaghy Union has not replied to my letter, and the clerk of Clogher Union has had no experience in the matter.

I am of opinion that if the rating qualification in the counties of Donegal, Tyrone, Derry, and Antrim be raised from 20 *l.* to 30 *l.*, a more intelligent class of jurors would be secured; but I fear the county Fermanagh is too small to admit of a corresponding rise.

I would strongly recommend for each county, in addition to the rating qualification, a household qualification of 12 *l.* in cities, towns, and villages.

This latter qualification will add, I think, a very intelligent class of business men to the panel.

There seems to be a general feeling that illiterate persons who can neither read nor write, should be disqualified from acting on juries.

I think the union officers who prepare the lists could, without much difficulty, find out such parties, and a note to that effect might be placed opposite the name, in order to draw the attention of the Chairman of Quarter Sessions, or whoever may be authorised to revise the lists, to the case.

If the qualification of jurors be raised, I think there should be a corresponding rise in the qualification of special jurors.

A household qualification in rural districts could not be adopted in this part of the country.

I have, &c.
The Local Government Board, Dublin. (signed) *R. Hamilton.*

County of Donegal.

(11,556–73.)

Reports from Clerks of Milford, Stranorlar, Letterkenny, Ballyshannon, Inishowen, Glenties, and Donegal Unions.

Sir, Milford Union, Milford, 18 April 1873.

I beg to acknowledge receipt of your letter of the 16th instant, requesting to obtain information regarding the jurors' lists, with a view to an amendment of the Juries Act, 1871.

1st. With reference to the amount of rating value, I am of opinion that the rating qualification, 20 *l.* for the above union, excludes a good number of persons who are better fitted to be jurors than some of those rated at 20 *l.*, or even some over 20 *l.* (and who reside in the villages within the union).

For such, a rating or rental of 6 *l.* would be sufficient for all purposes in this union, and would be found quite high enough; and for farmers, I think 15 *l.* would have been better. In my opinion, you will find as many intelligent men rated at 12 *l.* as some of those over 20 *l.*; many persons rated at 20 *l.* are to be found who cannot write.

I think the selection or rejection of any of those persons should rest with the clerks of unions, assisted by the poor rate collectors, who are also generally county cess collectors.

Power should be given to the clerks of unions to exempt persons rated at 20 *l.*, or upwards, who are illiterate, viz., who can neither read nor write. This information could be easily obtained from the collectors, and they should be bound to make due inquiry on their rounds when applying for payment to the persons rated to the proper qualification that may hereafter be fixed, should the present qualification be amended.

The clerk of union should have power to omit from the list of jurors the names of persons suffering from constitutional infirmity of body, deafness, blindness, decrepit, &c.

By the 12th section of 34 & 35 Vict. c. 71, Juries Act, 1871, the chairman of the county has the power to expunge from the general list of jurors, made out by the clerk of the peace, so furnished to and made out by him, all such persons, but it does not state who is to bring those cases under the notice of the court, if the persons themselves do not attend (which they will not do).

If the clerk of union is bound to place all on who are of the rated value (except persons over 60 years of age, &c.), then he should be called on to place a distinguishing mark, thus *, on the margin of the list furnished, opposite to the person's name, or to write on the margin the word "objected," opposite the name of such person; this would call the attention of the court to make inquiry what were the objections, and the court could amend the list accordingly, as it would see proper.

At the revision sessions at which I attended, no questions were put by anyone, except to a person making personal application for exemption on account of age.

A greater publicity should be given to the publishing and posting of the lists of jurors; the posting of the lists should be done by the constabulary in their respective unions, and should also be posted or suspended at the outer door or gate of each constabulary station, for one month at least prior to the holding the revision sessions, a notice of which should be published in one or more newspapers circulating in the union, stating that the objections of persons returned on said list of jurors will be received by the clerk of union up to a stated day.

A class of persons who live at lodgings should also be included; this would apply to cities and large towns more than this union.

I have, &c.
R. Hamilton, Esq., (signed) *Wm. Reid,*
Poor Law Inspector, &c. &c. Clerk of Union.

Appendix, No. 5.

Sir, Stranorlar Union Workhouse, 18 April 1873.

I HAVE the honour to acknowledge the receipt of your letter of the 16th instant, with its enclosure, as to the proper qualifications which should be fixed for securing a class of fit and proper jurors.

I have deemed it best in place of speculating as to the working of different descriptions of qualifications, to select that which to me appears best, and show its working in the union of which I am clerk; my object being to select the highest possible qualification which will produce the required number of jurors.

I would first remark that the valuation of this union is about 30,000 *l.*, and that of the county 300,000 *l.*; this union, if a fair sample of those embraced in the county, should supply one-tenth of the number of jurors; and as it is stated in the letter from the Under Secretary that the total number for each county should not be under 1,000, it will require the qualification to be arranged to produce the requisite proportion, say 100, at least.

I find that the suggested household qualification of 6 *l.* for the rural districts, and 12 *l.* for cities, towns, and villages, would in this union produce under the first about 30, and under the latter about 28 jurors, total 58, a number much below the requisite proportion. Of the above numbers only about 10 live exclusively by farming, the others are gentlemen, shopkeepers, &c.

The required addition to the above numbers should in my opinion be selected from the substantial yeomanry of the country, whose interest in its welfare is likely to be of a permanent character. What I would suggest then is, that a 30 *l.* rating under the Tenement Valuation Acts in addition to the household qualification be adopted; this will produce about 94 additional jurors, or 152 in all. Allowing 20 per cent. for females and persons over 60 years of age, there will remain about 122 available jurors.

I am, &c.

R. Hamilton, Esq., (signed) *Andrew Millar*,
Poor Law Inspector, Galway. Union Clerk.

Letterkenny Union, Board Room,
18 April 1873.

Sir,

I BEG to acknowledge receipt of your letter of the 16th instant, and copy of communication from the Under Secretary, relative to the working of the "Juries (Ireland) Act, 1871." I respectfully submit the following as my views on the subject.

I have had considerable opportunities of observing the working of the jury system, both under the former and the recent Acts; and I am not ignorant of the difficulties that surround the problem.

Any rating, or even household qualification, must include a number of illiterates, inebriates, and other mental incapables; and I doubt not, were the panels compared, that the Act of 1871, as regards such, would show a marked improvement. Formerly the sheriff and his assistants selected from the entire panel a sufficient number of jurors, whom, from personal knowledge, they believed best qualified; hence the same persons were successively summoned, and thereby came to possess a considerable acquaintance with the forms and language of the court, and some knowledge of their duties. This exercise of discretional power on the part of the sheriff, however necessary, became rather invidious when the cry of a "packed jury" arose. A change in the law was deemed needful, and the recent Act was passed. Here the sheriff has no option but to summon alphabetically; hence large numbers were for the first time called on to serve, and even some juries had few or none among them who had any experience in that capacity; and the sheriff, as formerly, had no power to eliminate those who were mentally or physically incapacitated. How best to remedy this state of matters, and to secure the dignity and efficiency of the jury system, is the problem to be solved.

I am convinced, if a sufficient number of jurors could be obtained, that the rating qualification should, for this county, be raised to at least 30 *l.*, and there should be, as a collateral qualification, the educational test that the party should be able to "read and write." This would have the additional effect of stimulating education more generally.

I think that the qualification of a "dwelling house," rated at 12 *l.* in towns and villages, and at 6 *l.* in the rural districts, an excellent suggestion; and I am persuaded that a more intelligent class of jurors could be obtained on this basis; as a man's civilisation and moral elevation is in some degree commensurate with the class of house he occupies, and where such qualifications would not supply a sufficient number of jurors for the county, I would supplement some from ratings of 30 *l.* and upwards. Power to exclude those who are mentally or physically disqualified should be vested in the sheriff, the chairman of the county, or some other competent authority.

I have, &c.

R. K. Hamilton, Esq., (signed) *John Storey*, Clerk.
Inspector under the Local Government Board.

Appendix, No. 5.

Sir, Workhouse, Ballyshannon, 18 April 1873.

I HAVE received your letter enclosing a copy of a communication addressed by the Under Secretary for Ireland to the Local Government Board, relative to the qualification of jurors under the Juries (Ireland) Act, and, in reply thereto, I beg leave to say that I am not quite clear as to the meaning of "household qualification, limited to 6 *l.* in rural districts, and 12 *l.* in towns." Some change is certainly greatly wanted, as, under the present rating qualifications, fixed for the portions of Leitrim, Fermanagh, and Donegal, contained in this union, there have been men returned as jurors who are not fit and proper persons to act on any jury, from want of intelligence and education; some of them can barely write their names, and some cannot write at all. The clerk of the union, although aware of their incapacity, is bound to return the names of such persons if their valuation be sufficient, and if they are within the limits of age; and the sheriff must summon them in rotation, having no liberty to omit any, no matter how unfit. The only remedy I can think of for this is to give the sheriffs power to strike the names of unfit persons off the jurors' lists. The rating qualification also excludes a good many business men in small towns, who are intelligent men, and who would make far better jurors than farmers of far higher valuations.

There is a point in the Act on which there appears to be a difference of opinion, and which should be put beyond doubt, namely, whether magistrates ought to be returned by union clerks on the jurors' lists. Section 29 of the Act implies that a justice may be summoned to serve as a juror, except in the district of which he is justice; the second schedule contradicts this, as it exempts persons holding "any paid, judicial, or other office belonging to any court of justice in Ireland." Some of the precepts received by me had not a comma after the word "paid," in the Schedule; but the copy of the Act printed by the Queen's printers has, thus making "paid" and "judicial" two separate classes of exempted persons.

I am also of opinion that clerks of unions ought to be allowed to remove the names of persons claiming exemption on the ground of age, &c., from lists, when making them out yearly, on being satisfied as to the validity of the grounds on which the parties claim to be exempted, as it would be more convenient than to oblige persons to go 16 or 20 miles to attend the Revision Sessions for the purpose of having their names struck off. With regard to the payment of poor rate collectors for their services under the Act, there should be a better provision made than leaving it to the grand juries to present such sum as they "deem reasonable." No collector in this union has, as yet, been paid one penny for his services; and, as the collecting fees of some of them are very small, it is hard to put extra duty on them, without even paying their car hire to the Revision Sessions.

I remain, &c.
(signed) *J. R. Chism,*
Clerk of Union.

R. Hamilton,
Local Government Board Inspector.

Inishowen Union,
Sir, Workhouse, Carndonagh, 22 April 1873.

I HAVE the honour to acknowledge receipt of your letter of the 16th instant, asking my views and any information I can afford as to the qualification of jurors, and special jurors, prescribed by the Juries Act of 1871.

I beg to say, that, having regard to the circumstances of this union, and the necessity for returning a sufficient number of jurors, I am of opinion that the rating qualification (viz., 20 *l.*) is about right; but I am strongly of opinion that there should also be an educational qualification, and that none should be returned as a juror who could not read and write. I think the age might properly be made 70, instead of 60 years, leaving the chairman of the county the discretion of striking out any name in which he considered the party had a disqualifying infirmity of body or mind.

I may state that I am supported in these opinions by several parties here, who have given the subject some consideration.

I remain, &c.
(signed) *Robt. Moore,*
Clerk of Union.

Sir, Glenties Union, Glenties, 19 April 1873.

I BEG to acknowledge the receipt of your letter, dated the 16th instant, together with a copy of a letter addressed to the Local Government by the Under Secretary to his Excellency the Lord Lieutenant, relative to the working of the Juries (Ireland) Act, 1871.

In reply, I beg to inform you that the qualification of jurors for this union was fixed at 20 *l.*, and for special jurors 50 *l.* Poor law valuation, which in my opinion, excluded a great number of intelligent men having a less poor law valuation, I would suggest that if the

the qualification of jurors for this union were fixed at 10 *l.*, and for special jurors at 30 *l.* and upward, it would increase their number and also secure a better class of men. And that a juror, who cannot read and write, should be disqualified from serving on juries.

Of course these observations are entirely confined to this union.

I have, &c.
(signed) *Alexander Hill*,
Clerk of the Union.

R. Hamilton, Esq.,
Local Government Board Inspector.

Sir, Donegal Union, 19 April 1873.

I BEG to acknowledge receipt of your letter of the 16th instant, enclosing copy of a letter from the Under Secretary.

In reply, I beg to state that from my knowledge of this country, I believe that no limit at which a rating qualification could be fixed would insure a sufficient number of intelligent jurors without having as many ignorant (or what is worse, unprincipled) men, as will totally frustrate, or at least, very much clog the ends of justice. My own opinion (and I know that it is shared by a very great number of the jurors and grand jurors of this county) is that nothing but deciding by majority, so long as the qualification is solely a rating one, will obtain convictions. No matter almost how clearly a case is proved, I have known men to go into the jury box, in this town, with the openly avowed determination not to convict any person.

To make the best of a bad case, however, I think that a 15 *l.* qualification would be the best for this county; this would of course shut out a great many intelligent men and admit a great many who are totally unfit for the position; but I think it would supply a sufficient number. And if the judges of the different courts had power to strike a name off the list when a case of decided unfitness comes before him, it would tend to purify the panel.

To fix the qualification at any stated sum will give a very unequal supply of jurors in different counties, if nearly the same number are required for each county. I would think that the best plan would be to apportion that number over the different unions, according to population or valuation, and let each union supply that number of its highest ratepayers, commencing with the highest and going down the scale as far as is necessary.

I remain, &c.
(signed) *D. C. Pearson*,
Clerk of Union.

To R. Hamilton, Esq.

COUNTY OF TYRONE.

REPORTS from Clerks of Gortin, Castlederg, Omagh, and Strabane Unions.

Sir, Gortin Union Workhouse, 18 April 1873.

IN reply to your letter of the 16th instant, relating to the Juries (Ireland) Act, 1871, I beg respectfully to say that I really do not see what improvement can possibly be made (especially in small unions) in the qualification of jurors, except that it would be advantageous to reduce the qualification from 20 *l.* to 10 *l.* valuation in the case of villages and towns; this would have the effect of increasing the number, and allow of the putting on the lists a good many business people, but any increase in the rating, while diminishing the number, would not, in my opinion, ensure a higher standard of intelligence. Out of 52 persons returned on the list for the barony of Upper Strabane in this union, not more than four are wholly illiterate.

I think all persons who can neither read nor write, or could only read, should be exempt.

If the qualification was raised to 30 *l.*, it would reduce the part of the barony abovenamed from 52 to 16.

I have, &c.
(signed) *Dan M'Farland*, Jun.,
Clerk of Union.

Richard Hamilton, Esq.

Board Room, Castlederg Union,
21 April 1873.

Sir,

I AM in receipt of your letter of the 16th instant, respecting a communication from the Local Government Board with reference to information that may be obtained from clerks of unions relative to the present Juries (Ireland) Act, 1871, and requesting any suggestion from me with a view to amend the same.

With reference thereto, I beg to state, for your information, that after careful examination of the present jurors' list of this union, and I am satisfied that by taking in the 12 *l.* householders in towns and villages, and increasing the amount in other cases to 30 *l.*

Appendix, No. 5.

or upwards, would ensure a far superior class of jurors than at present. The 12 *l.* householders are generally men of intelligence and business habits. There is no class of 6 *l.* householders in the rural part of this union that I am aware of. The two former would, in my opinion, I think, meet all the requirements, and give general satisfaction.

I am, &c.
(signed) *William Hamilton*,
Union Clerk.

To R. Hamilton, Esq.

Poor Law Union Office, Omagh,
21 April 1873.

Sir,

I BEG leave to acknowledge the receipt of your letter of the 16th instant, enclosing copy of one from the Under Secretary of the Lord Lieutenant to the Local Government Board, on the subject of the working of the Juries (Ireland) Act, 1871.

In reply, I beg leave to state that while a high rating qualification will not in all cases secure intelligent and efficient jurors, still I believe that, if the standard of qualification were raised from 20 *l.* to 30 *l.*, there would be, on the whole, a better class than at present.

In the general list of jurors, prepared by me for this union on the 1st of August last, there are 817 names, of this number, 459 appear at a valuation of 30 *l.* and upwards, so that there would be no difficulty in obtaining, in the county of Tyrone at least, a sufficient number of jurors at the proposed increased qualification.

I would take the liberty of suggesting that there should be in each county an officer, say the sub-sheriff, responsible directly to the Government for the exercise of a discretionary power of excluding from juries persons who may appear on the jurors' list, but who, from want of education, or otherwise, are found to be incompetent for the office, the officer referred to, seeing at the same time that all competent jurors are summoned and required to serve by regular rotation as provided for by this Act.

I have, &c.
(signed) *John Knight*,
Clerk of the Union.

To R. Hamilton, Esq.,
Local Government Inspector, Galloway House,
Strabane.

Sir, Strabane Union Board Room, 17 April 1873.

I BEG to acknowledge receipt of your letter of the 16th instant, enclosing copy of a letter from the Under Secretary to the Local Government Board communicating his Excellency's desire to obtain information which may be of practical value in fixing a proper qualification for jurors and special jurors.

In reply, I have to state that in my opinion a rating qualification, as a general rule can never be a criterion to ensure a competent class of jurors, further than that it affords a guarantee that the persons possessed of that qualification may fairly be considered capable of a standing without serious injury to his circumstances. But in order to secure competent jurors, I would suggest that the lists be made out, as at present provided by the clerks of unions, with the assistance of the rate collectors, and before publication be submitted to a meeting of the board of guardians called for the purpose at which all the collectors should be called upon to attend, and the entire lists be then carefully examined; and any person found not competent or incapable, from any known disability, could be struck out.

This plan would secure a class of men competent to discharge the duty and at the same time not lessen the number of competent persons; but should a household qualification be adopted, there would be very few persons from the country districts, and the lists would be chiefly composed of low traders in the towns, whose connexion in the rural districts might materially hinder them in the proper discharge of their duty.

I have, &c.
(signed) *David M'Menamin*,
Clerk of Union.

To R. T. Hamilton, Esq.,
Poor Law Inspector.

COUNTY OF LONDONDERRY.

REPORTS from Clerks of Londonderry, Coleraine, and Newtownlimivady Unions.

Sir, Poor Law Office, Londonderry, 21 April 1873.

I HAVE consulted with the sheriff and clerk of the peace in reference to the working of the Juries Act, 1871, and the latter, who has just returned from the quarter sessions, informs me it has worked very satisfactorily throughout the entire county, the juries in every case doing their work well, notwithstanding many of them never having served before.

With

Appendix, No. 5.

With respect to the jurors summoned for the assizes, Mr. Chambers found them, on the whole, to work fairly; and it is only reasonable to assume that they will be found to improve with experience, the work being new to many of them.

I am of opinion that if the qualification of all jurors general and special in rural districts was raised, say, by 10 *l.*, the Act would give satisfaction so far as this county is concerned both as regards the quality and number of the jurors required. With such a reduction as above, there would still remain nearly 2,000 jurors on the lists.

The household qualification mentioned in the Under Secretary's letter would, as I understand it, have little effect in this part of the country, as such a thing seldom occurs here.

I consider the present mode of revising the lists, namely, by the chairman of the county, works very fairly, and if a discretionary power of excluding some names from the lists could be exercised, it might prove of advantage; but I am not prepared to say in whom such power should be vested, whether in the Chairman, on proof being produced to him, or otherwise.

I have, &c.
(signed) *J. T. Russell.*

R. T. Hamilton, Esq.,
Poor Law Inspector.

Board Room, Coleraine Union,
18 April 1873.

Sir,

In reply to your communication of the 16th instant, requesting my views, for the information of the Local Government Board, in reference to fixing a proper qualification for jurors, I beg leave to state that by raising the qualification in rural districts to a 30 *l.* annual rating, and in towns and villages fixing a minimum household rating of 12 *l.* per annum, a sufficient number of duly qualified jurors would, in my opinion, be obtained in this part of the country at any rate.

By raising the qualification in rural districts to 30 *l.*, about one-half of the present number would be struck off the lists here; but, on the other hand, a uniform household rating of 12 *l.* in towns, &c., would very considerably increase the number in these districts, and add a highly intelligent body of jurors to the lists. I say a household rating of 12 *l.* in towns, &c., as I do not mean to include rated occupiers of houses valued below 12 *l.*, but whose total valuation amounts to, or exceeds, 12 *l.*, from holding land in the neighbourhood.

With respect to special jurors, I am not so qualified to express an opinion; but I consider that a qualification of 60 *l.* rating in rural districts, and 25 *l.* in towns, &c., would be sufficient.

From my own observation I cannot altogether agree with the general condemnation of the new system; no doubt the jurors in most cases are as yet unacquainted with their duties, having never heretofore served as jurors.

I may observe that jurors complain much of being taken from one extremity of the county to the other to serve as jurors at quarter sessions. This could be easily remedied.

I am, &c.
(signed) *John V. Fleming,*
Clerk of Coleraine Union.

Richard Hamilton, Esq.,
Poor Law Inspector.

Newtownlimavady Union,
19 April 1873.

Sir,

I beg to acknowledge the receipt of your letter of the 15th instant, with copy of letter from the Under Secretary for Ireland, with reference to the qualification for jurors.

The fourth schedule of the Juries Act fixes the qualification for such in this union at the net annual valuation of 20 *l.* and upwards, and the number of names returned on the general jurors' list in July last was 789, a large number for so small a union. Had a valuation of 30 *l.* been adopted, the number returned would have been 315. Those valued at the latter sum are, generally speaking, men of a somewhat higher social status, and perhaps of greater intelligence.

As regards the suggestion of a household qualification for jurors fixing the limit at 6 *l.* in rural districts and 12 *l.* in towns and villages, the latter might give a very fair class of jurors for the town of Newtownlimavady; but the former would, in my opinion, without some other qualification is added, be utterly unsuited to the circumstances of this union, and would exclude many otherwise well qualified both as regards social position and intelligence to act as jurors.

I am unable to give reliable statistics on those points, as the valuation in force in this union does not give the valuation of the house separate from that of the land attached, merely giving the total valuation of the property described as "house, offices, and land." This would in any case present a serious, if not fatal, obstacle to the adoption of the scheme of a household qualification, that is, if it be proposed to work it by the same machinery as that is used for giving effect to the present Act. The printed primary valuation does indeed give the value of the entire buildings on each holding, but in very many

Appendix, No. 5.

many instances changes in the way of improvement that would considerably alter the value of these have taken place since it was issued.

Taking into account all the circumstances of this district, I cannot suggest any remedy for the present state of things other than the raising of the standard of qualification, and that although it would undoubtedly give a better selection of jurors, in a social point of view, would not, I am afraid, very materially alter the present panel as regards intelligence.

I am, &c.
(signed) *W. P. Hunter*,
Clerk of Union.

R. T. Hamilton, Esq.,
Strabane.

COUNTY OF FERMANAGH.

REPORTS from Clerks of Lisnaskea, Irvinestown, and Enniskillen Unions.

Poor Law Office, Lisnaskea Union,
19 April 1873.

Sir,

I HAVE the honour to acknowledge receipt of your communication of 16th instant, with enclosed copy of letter from the Under Secretary to the Lord Lieutenant, relative to the "Juries (Ireland) Act, 1871," and requesting information on the subject. After having given the matter due consideration, and had the opinion of persons of experience, as to the class of persons of which juries are composed, I desire to say that I consider the qualification might, with advantage be raised from 20 *l.* to 30 *l.* for common jurors, and from 50 *l.* to 80 *l.* for special jurors, in the county Fermanagh.

This qualification would leave the number of common jurors in this union about 200, and of special jurors about 30. The number of common jurors in the county qualified as above would not, I believe, exceed 1,000; and of special jurors would not be much over 100; and I presume this is as low a number as could safely be estimated for.

With regard to the propriety of establishing a household qualification, whatever might be its advantage in towns, I do not consider it either necessary or desirable in rural districts; and I am of opinion that the qualification indicated in the letter of the Under Secretary, would not provide anything like a sufficient number of jurors.

I have, &c.
To R. Hamilton, Esq., &c. (signed) *Jo. R. Hogg*, Clerk of Union.

Irvinestown Poor Law Union,
19 April 1873.

Sir,

I BEG to acknowledge receipt of your letter of 16th instant, with copy of a letter from the Under Secretary to the Local Government Board, requiring information on the subject of the qualification for jurors and special jurors, and in reply have to state, that so far as this union is concerned, I consider the Juries (Ireland) Act, with very few exceptions, would work well; I would say there should be some means of excepting illiterate jurors from serving, and consider a household qualification of 12 *l.* (supplemental to the rating qualification) would furnish a number of a proper class of jurors.

I am, &c.
R. Hamilton, Esq., &c. &c. (signed) *C. Graham*, Clerk of Union.

Sir, Workhouse, Enniskillen, 17 April 1873.

IN reply to your communication of the 15th instant, on the subject of qualification for jurors, I beg most respectfully to say, that (if rating can be considered to be in any sense a qualification for the office of juror) the qualification fixed in this county, viz., 20 *l.* for a petty juror (the qualification for the office of poor law guardian), and 50 *l.* for a special juror, can hardly be amended, as a higher qualification would reduce the number of jurors very much; and a household qualification of 6 *l.* would produce a still less number, because the average value of houses in the rural districts of this union is between 1 *l.* and 4 *l.*

I am bold to say that the conception of the Juries (Ireland) Act, 1871, was the inauguration of a better system than that which previously obtained, and which was so deservedly expunged from the Statute Book; but it embodies a principle which presupposes that the generality of country farmers have sufficient intelligence to enable them to discharge functions which the low state of their educational attainments entirely unfits them for, the mass of the people of Ireland being to this day lamentably deficient in the educational qualifications necessary for the proper discharge of the duties devolving upon jurors, a small minority only being in the possession of intellectual acquirements fitting them for the due exercise of such an office.

It

Appendix, No. 5.

It is to be greatly regretted that such haste was made to condemn a measure founded upon a wise policy, but brought to trial probably half a century before its time; and it would be a deplorable mistake to set it precipitately aside without further experience of its effects upon the jury system of this country. Allowance, however, might, with great propriety, be made for the present transition state of the education of the people; and to the Act, as it now stands, an addition might be made, giving the high sheriff, or some other properly qualified official, the power, for some years to come, of making a selection, within carefully considered well guarded limitations, from the names upon the general list of jurors, of those known to be by their education and intelligence peculiarly qualified to serve, and I am certain that the result will prove satisfactory.

I have, &c.
To Richard S. Hamilton, Esq., (signed) *William Henry Morrison,*
Inspector, Gallony House, Strabane. Clerk of the Union.

COUNTY OF ANTRIM.

REPORTS from Clerks of Ballycastle and Ballymoney Unions.

Sir, Ballycastle, 19 April 1873.

I RECEIVED your letter of the 16th instant, with enclosures, and in reply I beg to inform you that the present qualification for jurors in this county is 12*l.* in towns and villages, and 20*l.* in rural districts. The qualification for special jurors is 50*l.*

I find the general impression is (and it is my opinion) that the present qualification of 12*l.* in towns and villages is a proper one, and should not be changed.

It is, however, considered, that in the country districts the present qualification is much too low, and that it would require to be increased to a rating qualification of, say, 40*l.*

The qualification for special jurors is also considered low, and in my opinion should be increased to 80*l.*

I believe that the qualifications mentioned would afford a sufficient number of jurors in this county, and also that it would give a class of jurors generally more intelligent than those returned under the present qualifications.

I have, &c.
(signed) *Charles McVaughan,*
R. Hamilton, Esq. Union Clerk.

Sir, Board Room, Ballymoney, 22 April 1873.

I BEG to acknowledge receipt of your favour of 15th instant, enclosing copy of letter from the Under Secretary to the Local Government Board, with reference to the working of the "Juries (Ireland) Act, 1871."

I think that if the qualification for ordinary jurors in the counties of Antrim and Derry were settled at 16*l.* in towns, and 30*l.* in rural districts, a sufficient number of jurors would be provided; a class of men would be on the lists who could better afford the time for such duties, and more likely to prove intelligent than jurors drawn from a lower scale of society.

Something more would be necessary than raising the qualification; there should be some discretionary power left in the hands either of the chairman of the county or the clerks of the Poor Law Unions to strike out of the lists of those qualified to be jurors, by the amount of their valuation, the names of any persons known to be illiterate, or those who, while mentally capable of managing their own business, would, in the opinion of any man of common sense, be incapable of forming a correct opinion on most subjects, or persons known to be habitually drunkards; if it could be so arranged that the sifting process could be carried out privately it would be more thorough, as local men with the requisite knowledge might object to state publicly their reasons why they considered certain names should not be on the lists, though those reasons might be none the less valid and known to everybody.

There is one grievance complained of by jurors, viz., being summoned for Quarter Sessions business out of their own district; it appears to me that the law should be so amended that no juror should be summoned for such business out of the Quarter Sessions district in which his dwelling place is situated.

I have heard many complaints from jurors because they were detained for many days at assizes, though never called to serve on a jury; would it not be possible to summon a certain number of jurors for the first four days, a second lot for the second four days, and so on for the period during which it is thought the assizes will last.

I am not sure that a household qualification of 6*l.* in rural districts would be an improvement; the valuation of the houses is not shown in the Government valuation books separate from the valuation of the land, so that new books would require to be prepared before any change could be made in this direction. I also consider that a qualification

Appendix, No. 5. fication by house valuation of 6 *l.* would be too high; the number of jurors qualified in this union would, if this scale were adopted, be insufficient.

I have, &c.
(signed) *T. Berris Hume*, M.D.,
Clerk of Union.

R. Hamilton, Esq.

REPORT of Mr. *Henry Robinson.*

(No. 11,032/73—Miscellaneous.)

7, St. George's-square, Belgravia, London,
21 April 1873.

My Lord and Gentlemen,

I HAVE the honour to acknowledge the receipt of a copy of the letter addressed to you by the Under Secretary of the Lord Lieutenant on the 7th instant with reference to the working of the Juries (Ireland) Act, 1871, communicating his Excellency's desire to obtain information which may be of practical value in fixing a proper qualification for jurors and special jurors, and stating that it has occurred to his Excellency that the Inspectors under the Local Government Board, who might consult the clerks of unions on the subject, may be able to afford useful information as to the proper qualifications which should be fixed for securing a class of fit and proper jurors.

With reference to this communication, I beg to inform you that, in consequence of my absence from Ireland, I have been unable to make personal inquiries as to the working of the Juries Act, but that I wrote to the clerks of some of the unions in my district, with a view to obtain some information for his Excellency with as little delay as possible; I selected one clerk in each county comprised in my district, as well as the clerks of the two Dublin Unions, and I now forward to you the letters which I have received from them on the subject.

I have, &c.
(signed) *Henry Robinson.*

To the Local Government Board,
Dublin.

From Mr. *Jameson*, Clerk of Carlow Union, County Carlow.

Sir,
Hermitage, Carlow, 16 April 1873.

I AM in receipt of your letter of the 12th instant, in which you ask my opinion "as to the proper qualifications which should be fixed for securing a class of fit and proper jurors."

In reply, I beg to state that in my opinion a qualification of 30 *l.* would in this county secure a good class of jurors.

Last week I furnished a return to the Chief Secretary of the number of jurors on the jurors' book whose respective valuations exceeded 20 *l.* and under 30 *l.*, and from 30 *l.* to 40 *l.*, &c. Of the former there are 399, and the total number on the jurors' book is 1,215. This would leave upwards of 800 jurors, which ought to be sufficient for the business of this small county. This number might be increased if the qualification in the towns of Carlow, Tullow, and Bagenalstown was reduced to one-half, say 15 *l.* On the clerk of the union's list for the Barony of Carlow, Carlow Town, with a population of upwards of 6,000, has returned only 80 jurors. Now, I think, that house property in towns is valued at a low rate, and that the class who inhabit houses valued at 15 *l.* would be fully as respectable and intelligent as rural jurors, the valuation of whose holdings is 30 *l.*

I also think that the qualification for special jurors ought to be raised in this county, and would suggest that it should be increased to 70 *l.* or 75 *l.*

The present qualification is 50 *l.*, which is certainly too low.

I am, &c.
(signed) *Edward L. Jameson*,
Sub-Sheriff, County Carlow.

To Henry Robinson, Esq.
London.

From Mr. *Cope*, Clerk of Rathdown Union, County of Dublin.

Sir,
Clerk's Office, Loughlinstown, 18 April 1873.

I DELAYED answering your letter of 12th instant until now, in order to enable me to consider fully the subject you referred for an expression of my opinion, viz., the qualifications which should be fixed for securing fit and proper persons to serve as jurors in this country.

In reply, I beg to say that from my own observations, and from inquiries I have made, I am of opinion that in the county of Dublin a 20 *l.* rating would secure a proper jury for the trial of larceny or common assault cases, but for the trial of capital, political, or offences of a semi-political, religious, or riotous character, a jury should be formed from the list of special

special jurors, whose rating qualification should not be less than 50 *l.*; but in *all* cases I would suggest that an educational qualification be applied, which could very easily be done at the time of swearing the jury.

I have, &c.
(signed) *Joseph D. Cope.*

To Henry Robinson, Esq.
Junior United Service Club, London.

From Mr. *Molloy*, Clerk of Naas Union, County Kildare.

Sir, Abbeyfield, Naas, 18 April 1873.

THE question of the working of "The Juries (Ireland) Act, 1871," is, I believe, the most difficult of the day, and the solution of it the hardest to arrive at.

There are 751 jurors in Naas Union, rated, 171 ranging from 100 *l.* to 1,156 *l.*, 169 between 50 *l.* and 100 *l.*, 260 between 25 *l.* and 50 *l.*, 151 between 12 *l.* 10 *s.* and 25 *l.*

In my opinion there is as fair a per-centage of good jurors to be found amongst those rated between 12 *l.* 10 *s.* and 50 *l.* (that is, if you exempt the magistrates and a few others, who are generally classed amongst the largest rated), and any of the other classes. That is mainly attributable to the fact that business people in towns, whom I look upon as about the most intelligent jurors, are generally rated between 12 *l.* 10 *s.* and 50 *l.*

I have no hesitation in stating that there are as many illiterate persons to be found amongst those largest rated as there are amongst any of the other classes.

My opinion is, that so far as the Union of Naas is concerned, rating is no test of intelligence, therefore I think the sheriff should be allowed to exercise his discretion in the selection of jurors.

From inquiries I have made I have ascertained that no fault was to be found with the jurors who attended at the assizes and sessions recently held at Naas, but so good a class did not attend the sessions at Kildare.

I am, &c.
(signed) *E. Molloy.*

To Henry Robinson, Esq.

From Mr. *Lacy*, Clerk of Navan Union, County Meath.

Sir, Navan Union, 18 April 1873.

IN reply to yours of the 12th instant on the subject of the "Juries Act," I beg to say that in my opinion the qualification for jurors in this county, namely, 20 *l.*, and 12 *l.* in a town or village, should not be altered until the Act is fairly tested.

There are close on 400 names returned on the "General List of Jurors" for this union, and the most of those persons whose names are so returned are personally known to me; and on a careful examination of the subject, I have come to the conclusion that, with the exception of some 30 persons who should be excluded on account of being illiterate, they are quite capable of forming a sound opinion upon any subject which they might be called on to decide as jurors. As my experience of the working of the Act is so limited, I do not feel warranted in giving an opinion regarding any other county than this, but I am strongly of opinion that if the Act be fairly tried, that it will be found to work well here.

Yours, &c.
(signed) *George Lacy,*
Clerk of Union.

To Henry Robinson, Esq.,
Local Government Inspector.

From Mr. *Prendergast*, Clerk of Wexford Union, County Wexford.

Sir, Wexford Union, 17 April 1873.

I HAVE the honour to acknowledge the receipt of your letter of the 12th instant, and in reply to state that, although I am aware the Juries (Ireland) Act of 1871 has not worked efficiently, I am unable to offer any suggestion as to how it could be amended. A higher rating qualification will not, in my opinion, insure competent jurors; and until the farmers' sons, who have been and are being educated (at least to some extent), take the place of their fathers, very little improvement can, in my mind, be made in the jurors of Ireland.

I am, &c.
(signed) *Thomas Prendergast,*
Clerk of Union.

To Henry Robinson, Esq.,
&c. &c.

From Mr. *Cooke*, Clerk of the Baltinglass Union, County Wicklow.

Sir, Baltinglass Workhouse, 15 April 1873.

I BEG leave to acknowledge the receipt of your letter of the 12th instant, and to inform you, in reply, that I have given a great deal of consideration to the working of the Juries (Ireland) Act, 1871. I have also consulted with men of experience on the subject, and these persons perfectly agree with me that it would be injudicious to raise the qualifications for jurors over the present amount, 20 *l.* and upwards, for the counties of Carlow, Kildare,

Appendix, No. 5.

Kildare, and Wicklow. I have a perfect knowledge of the counties above mentioned, and I do believe that if the qualification was raised, say, from 20 *l.* to 40 *l.* or 50 *l.*, it would not remedy the Act, inasmuch as I know several persons valued from 20 *l.*, 30 *l.*, and 40 *l.*, just as intelligent as those valued over 50 *l.* and 100 *l.*

The Act is only in its infancy, and I have no doubt, after some short time, it will work well. The only alteration I would suggest is, that no juror should be placed on a jury that could not read and write, and the latter could be ascertained by the judge or sheriff at the swearing of a jury.

I am, &c.
(signed) *Michael Cooke*,
Clerk of the Union.

To Henry Robinson, Esq.

From Mr. *Atkinson*, Clerk of North Dublin Union.

Suggestions, in case Juries (Ireland) Act of 1871 is Amended.	Observations.
1. One general panel, including petit, special, and grand jurors.	
2. In order to please the grand jurors, I would suggest two panels; one to be called the grand panel, and the other the general panel; those not sworn as grand jurors to be compelled to serve as petit or special jurors on a specified penalty, say, 50 *l.* or 100 *l.*	By inflicting a penalty of 50 *l.* or 100 *l.*, grand jurors will serve on petit or special juries, but with a less penalty some would prefer paying it rather than serve with persons of inferior rank.
3. The qualification of jurors to be raised according to the classification of counties. Counties must be classified for that purpose.	For the purpose of classifying the counties, returns should be made from every union of all male persons (only) rated at 20 *l.* to 50 *l.*, and at 50 *l.* to 100 *l.*, and upwards.
4. Dublin city and county should be in a class for itself, as more jurors are required in Dublin than any other place, consequently the rating should not be so high as the other counties and cities, say, 25 *l.* rating, as the minimum for the county and city.	My reason for not stating a higher rating than 25 *l.* as the minimum is, that some of the most intelligent jurors to be found anywhere occupy houses in the city and suburbs, viz.: Rathmines, Rathgar, Clontarf, Blackrock, Kingstown, &c., at that valuation. This valuation, I calculate, would leave 2,500 or 3,000 jurors for the county of Dublin.
5. The amended Act, to make it imperative on rate collectors, under penalty to supply, in addition to what is now required from them, a return or list of the persons who are not educated, which list the clerk of the union should be required to transmit a copy of to the clerk of the peace, for the information of the chairman or revising barristers, for which the collectors should be adequately remunerated by the respective grand juries and town council.	It should be made the collector's interest to take an active part in the faithful discharge of the duties imposed on him under this Act, by compensating him fairly for his trouble; and they should be facilitated in that duty by the clerk of the union, having columns inserted in their warrant books for age, calling, profession, and business; whether party can read, and write, and speak, the English language.
6. Additional powers to be given to the chairman or revising barrister to expunge the names of any jurors returned not qualified by education, &c.	The return or list named in No. 5 Suggestion, would enable the chairman or revising barrister to do this in the court of revision, on the collector being present.
7. Some provision should be made in the amended Act not to drag a juror from one end of a county to the other end to attend a quarter sessions court, and to meet this it should be left optional with the sheriff to summon a sufficient number in the neighbourhood of the quarter sessions town on those occasions: this rule should only apply to quarter sessions, and not to assizes, special commissions, commissions in Green-street, law terms in Four Courts, &c.	As the law now stands, a man may be summoned from Tallaght down to Balbriggan. However, a great deal may be said for and against this, but the convenience of jurors should be regarded.

Appendix, No. 5.

From Mr. *Hepburn*, Clerk of South Dublin Union, County Dublin.

South Dublin Union,
Clerk's Office, Board Room, James-street,
10 April 1873.

Sir,

I am favoured with your letter of 12th instant, requesting my opinion as to the proper qualification which should be fixed for securing a class of fit and proper persons to serve as jurors for the county of Dublin.

I have carefully examined the lists prepared by me in July last for the portion of the county in this union, and I find that a qualification of 40 *l.* and upwards valuation would give about 600 jurors, and a qualification of 30 *l.* and upwards would give about 900.

Assuming that this union is equal to the North Dublin and Balrothery Union together, with that portion of Rathdown Union situated in county Dublin, there would, on a qualification of 40 *l.* and upwards, be about 1,200, and on a 30 *l.* qualification, 1,800 jurors. The latter would, I think, effectually exclude nearly all objectionable persons, but I believe it would be injudicious to go lower.

I have, &c.
(signed) *Geo. Hepburn*,
Clerk of the Union.

To Henry Robinson, Esq.,
7, St. George's-square, Belgravia,
London.

Report of Mr. *William P. O'Brien.*

My Lord and Gentlemen, Malahide, 23 April 1873.

I have the the honour to acknowledge the receipt of your letter of the 10th instant, enclosing a copy of a communication from the Under Secretary, conveying the desire of his Excellency the Lord Lieutenant to receive any information in the power of your inspectors to afford, with reference to the subject of fixing a proper qualification for jurors and special jurors.

As a certain number of jurors, at least amounting in every case to 1,000, is stated to be indispensable, it would not be possible, in my opinion, to name with any approach to accuracy a definite qualification for this purpose without first obtaining full statistical returns complete for each county, classifying the numbers at present rated under certain specified heads. The clerks of unions being conversant only with particular portions of their respective counties, can afford little or no assistance in this matter, nor do the valuation books now supplied to the various unions exhibit at all the separate valuations of houses rated jointly with land.

Any general opinion I here venture to offer must, therefore, be taken as being given subject to its being hereafter ascertained, in the manner just indicated, that a number of persons sufficient for the purposes of the Act, and having the qualification which appears to me to be desirable, can be obtained in each county.

So far as I am competent to form an opinion on the matter, I am disposed to think the suggestion that a household qualification would be advantageous is entitled to the utmost weight; and I would say further, that I think the limits suggested towards this end are judicious and well considered, viz., 6 *l.* in rural districts, and 12 *l.* in cities, towns, and villages.

The latter class will be found, I am satisfied, to supply by far the best description of jurors to be found in each county; those resident in towns being usually far better educated and more conversant with business matters, both public and private, than the rural population; but I am at the same time of opinion that a general rating qualification should be combined with this, not only for the object of providing a sufficiently ample panel, but also to avoid in many cases the total exclusion of a class of persons fully entitled to the position of jurors. I think a 12 *l.* household qualification will give a very fair class of town jurors; and I also incline to think that 6 *l.*, though it at first sight looks a somewhat low limit to take, will be likely to give a similar result in the rural districts; the valuation of farmhouses being invariably, I believe, regulated by a very much lower standard than that applied to houses rated apart from land; but as it is certain that in various parts of Ireland substantial farmers are still content to live in very miserable houses, which would not be valued as high as 6 *l.*, the effect of confining the qualification to a household one would be to deprive this class altogether of their proper status, which I should consider in every point of view as an undesirable arrangement.

What the general rating qualification should be is, for the reason I have already mentioned, a matter on which no positive opinion can be at present pronounced; but should the returns I have referred to, as being a necessary element in the case, sustain my view, I should consider that the amount set forth in the Schedule to the Act, 34 & 35 Vict. c. 65, might be doubled advantageously in every case in regard to the ordinary jury panel; and in regard to special juries, I should consider that a total rating of 100 *l.*, or a household qualification of 50 *l.* in towns and 30 *l.* in the county, would not, if practicable, be at all higher than a due regard for the functions to be discharged would seem to call for.

I have, &c.
(signed) *W. P. O'Brien*,
Local Government Inspector.

To the
Local Government Board.

Appendix, No. 5.

Report of Mr. *Terence Brodie*.

(No. 10,911/73.—Miscellaneous.)

Gentlemen, Galway, 19 April 1873.

I have the honour to acknowledge the receipt of your letter, dated 10th instant, with a copy of letter from the Under Secretary to his Excellency the Lord Lieutenant, with reference to the working of the Juries (Ireland) Act, 1871.

The subject-matter under consideration is one of much importance, and as such requires long and careful investigation into the advantages and disadvantages that have arisen since its introduction, and the result that may be arrived at by the Committee of the House of Commons, about to commence their inquiries, will, I trust, be favourable to the principle of the Bill, which, notwithstanding any drawbacks, has effected a complete reformation, and put an end to abuses and alleged corruptions on the part of sheriffs' bailiffs, which pressed heavily and unfairly on some people.

My experience of the operation of the Poor Law Acts leads me to the conclusion that the Juries Act might be expected, without any great amendment, to work itself free of those hitches and faults of which so much remark has been made. When the famine of 1846 threw an amount of practical duty on boards of guardians to which they were previously strangers, how few were the boards which stood the test? On the formation of new unions in 1850, the boards of guardians which were then formed in the majority of cases, could not, but for the assistance of the large staff of Poor Law Inspectors, have been made to administer the law in a satisfactory manner. Their mistakes, if exposed with the same assiduity now applied to the publication of the faults of the Juries Act, would have been found to be more numerous as well as serious. Yet I think I can say that at the present time those boards can contrast favourably with any existing organisation entrusted with public fiscal functions. The teachings of experience have wrought this change.

A new machinery has been set in motion for the first time, and it is conceded, as might be naturally expected, that it has not worked with perfect smoothness. A new class of jurors has been introduced, awkward from their inexperience, and including some undoubtedly not qualified for the office. The desirability of removing defects is admitted on all hands, but at the same time it is conceded that the essential principles of the Bill should not be destroyed.

As regards the rating qualification for jurors, I confess I cannot see what great good could be effected by raising the qualification. A juryman valued at 20 *l.* is, in the great majority of cases, as intelligent and competent for the office as his neighbour valued at 30 *l.*, so that a higher standard of rating would not insure a better class of jurors, and at the same time provide a sufficient number. The object of any amendments of the law should, therefore, be to provide for removing from the lists, framed under the existing law, persons not qualified to act as jurors.

Men who cannot read and write may have a large amount of shrewdness and common sense in transacting their ordinary business, but these qualities must be distinguished from the intelligence necessary in a juryman.

The poor rate collectors and clerks of unions perform their duties under the sense of obligations and penalties, and they might be entrusted with the power to omit from the list of jurors those whom they know cannot read and write. Power should also be given to the chairman of quarter sessions and to the judges of assize to direct the removal of incompetent persons from the lists, and to make it the duty of the clerks of peace and Crown to notify such orders to the clerks of unions, so that the names should not be again returned.

Persons not able to speak the English language should be dealt with in like manner.

In this way the lists would be gradually and very soon purged of the most incompetent class now returned, and in the meantime the other new jurors would be gaining the knowledge and experience necessary for the due performance of their duties.

A household qualification I consider to be quite unsuitable to rural districts. For the most part the dwellings of landholders rated at from 20 *l.* to 30 *l.* are valued at a very low figure, probably not exceeding 4 *l.* on the average. A 6 *l.* household qualification would exclude so many, that a sufficient number of jurors could not be returned.

I think, however, the principle could be advantageously applied in towns. A 10 *l.* house-rating in the larger towns having, say, a population of over 3,000, and an 8 *l.* rating in smaller towns, would bring in an intelligent class of jurors, excluded by the present rating qualification.

With regard to special jurors for counties, I am in favour of raising the qualification from 50 *l.* to 100 *l.*, while in towns I am in favour of reducing the qualification, as at present many of the principal merchants and traders are debarred from acting as special jurors, in consequence of their premises not being sufficiently rated. Those men must act as petty jurors, though of course competent to deal with the most important cases.

In conclusion, I may be permitted to remark that the present quarter sessions districts could

could be re-arranged with much convenience to jurors, and the prevention of long, expensive, and unnecessary journeys. Appendix, No. 5.

Under existing circumstances, a juror can be brought under a penalty from Clifden to Galway, a distance of 50 statute miles.

I have, &c.

To the Local Government Board. (signed) *T. Brodie.*

(No. 11,836-73.—Miscellaneous.)

REPORT of Mr. *Charles Croker-King.*

My Lord and Gentlemen, Cork, 30 April 1873.

IN reply to your letter (No. 9903-73—Miscellaneous) of the 10th instant, respecting the proper qualification for jurors, I have the honour to submit the following observations for consideration:—

Previous to the passing of "The Juries (Ireland) Act, 1871," jurors were selected by the baronial constables as fit and proper persons to serve irrespective of any rating qualification; the number of jurors returned under this system, in 1872, was 4,226 for the county of Cork, to which all my observations apply.

Under the Juries Act referred to above, a property qualification of 20 *l.* in rural districts, and 12 *l.* in towns, &c., is required for ordinary jurors, and 100 *l.* for special jurors; the number of jurors returned under the Act is 8,425, or nearly double the number under the former system.

Of the 8,425 jurors returned, 5,028 are valued at 30 *l.* and upwards, consequently the property qualification might be raised to that amount in this county, and a sufficient number of jurors would appear on the list, but a mere property qualification is not sufficient, as many farmers rated at 30 *l.* and upwards are totally illiterate.

In addition to the disqualifications set forth in Section 7 of Juries Act, I would suggest that inability to read and write, or to speak the English language, or having been frequently convicted of drunkenness, or being notoriously of intemperate habits, should be disqualifying circumstances.

The revision of the general list of jurors, as at present conducted before the assistant barrister (who does not possess any local knowledge), is a mere form.

I would suggest that the revision of the jurors' list should be conducted at petty sessions specially convened for the purpose, at which the local magistrates should be invited, and the stipendiary magistrate of the district required, to attend, and at which the barony cess and poor-rate collectors should be obliged to attend, the list so revised being subject to correction (for cause shown) by the assistant barrister; and I would further give a judge of assize, or an assistant barrister at quarter sessions, a discretionary power of removing any juror's name from the list if he should appear to be ineligible or incapable.

The number of persons qualified to act as special jurors in the county of Cork is 816, which number is insufficient; and, furthermore, I am informed that many persons on this list are totally unfit to act as special jurors.

I would recommend that the following classes of persons be qualified to act as special and as ordinary jurors, irrespective of any property qualification whatever: barristers, solicitors, medical men not practising their professions, retired officers of the Army, Navy, or Constabulary, and persons holding degrees from any University authorised to confer them.

At present the grand jurors at quarter sessions are taken from the special jurors' list, and any person who has served as a juror at quarter sessions is exempt from serving at assizes. This rule acts obstructively, the list is so exhausted by service at sessions, that a sufficient number of jurors cannot be obtained to act as special jurors at assizes, at which cases of great moment have frequently to be tried; but the remedy is simple: let jurors be not exempt from serving as special jurors at assizes on the ground that they have served on juries at quarter sessions. The adoption of this rule would not be oppressive in this county, as a juror would not in all probability be required to attend at assizes more frequently than once in four years.

I may remark that the clerk of the peace is required to make a general list of jurors of every barony in the county, in alphabetical order, same as would be arranged in a dictionary (see Section 13, Juries Act), but the sheriff or other officer in selecting jurors, although required to take the names from the general jurors' list in alphabetical order, is not obliged to place them in the order as arranged in a dictionary.

With respect to the question of adopting a household qualification in rural districts, difficulty would arise in ascertaining the value of a house distinct from the adjoining land, and, furthermore, if the suggestions I have made be approved of, a household qualification would be unnecessary.

I have, &c.

To the Local Government Board. (signed) *Charles Croker-King.*

Appendix, No. 5.

REPORT of Mr. *George F. Roughan.*

(11,550-73—Miscellaneous.)

Sir, Sligo, 26 April 1873.

I HAVE the honour to acknowledge the receipt of your leter of the 10th instant, No. 9903, forwarding a copy of a letter which had been received by the Local Government Board from the Under Secretary of his Excellency the Lord Lieutenant with reference to the working of "The Juries (Ireland) Act, 1871," and communicating his Excellency's desire to obtain information which may be of practical value in fixing a proper qualification for jurors and special jurors; and stating that it has occurred to his Excellency that the inspectors under the Local Government Board might be able to afford such information.

I feel much diffidence in venturing to write or offer any suggestion on this very important subject, which is at present under the consideration of a Committee of the House of Commons, where judges of assize, chairmen of counties, and county officers will afford ample information on the working of the Juries Act of 1871, and the portions of it that require amendment; nevertheless, I doubt not the information rendered by the inspectors, derived from personal knowledge of the class likely to constitute good and intelligent jurors, will be of a practical nature, and not altogether without value.

The working of the Juries Act, 1871, has up to this failed to sustain the intentions of the Legislature, and the expectations of the public, chiefly owing to want of education and consequent want of intelligence of some of the persons whose names were permitted to remain on the revised list, because the Revising Barrister had not power to remove them.

Property qualification alone should not constitute the sole basis for the formation of the jurors' list; there are many persons rated much higher than the amount fixed by the statute, whose want of education totally unfits them for discharging the duties of jurors or special jurors.

Property qualification should, in my opinion, in every instance be combined with house rating, and if properly done would go far to exclude the illiterate class who are now on the jurors' list, and would supply a class of jurors whom it would be impossible to equal by any other mode of selection.

In fixing the household qualification in conjunction with land, it must be borne in mind that farmhouses valued as low as 2 *l.* are of a superior class, and generally occupied by intelligent and well-informed people. If the household valuation in rural districts were fixed at a limit of 8 *l.*, it would be very much too high, and would exclude some of the most intelligent of the middle class. The owner of a house valued from 2 *l.* to 4 *l.* in the country is a man of better position and superior intelligence to the occupier of a 20 *l.* town house, so that the qualification of common jurors in rural districts might, I think, with advantage, be fixed at a limit of 2 *l.* for house rating, in conjunction with 20 *l.* for land rating; and in towns and villages, occupiers of houses rated at 12 *l.*, and occupiers of houses rated from 7 *l.*, who may possess additional rating up to 20 *l.* This basis would, I think, supply the number, or very nearly the number, of jurors for each of the counties with which I am officially connected, viz., Mayo, Sligo, and Leitrim, mentioned in the Under Secretary's letter.

The qualification of special jurors should, I think, be based on house rating, and on house rating combined with land. Occupiers of 8 *l.* houses in rural districts, and 12 *l.* in towns, and occupiers of 4 *l.* houses in rural districts, with a land rating of 50 *l.*, would, I think, provide a superior class of special jurors.

For the purpose of revision, and the ultimate issue of a complete list of competent jurors, the clerk of the peace would, as is provided for in the 8th section of the Juries (Ireland) Act, issue his precept to the clerk of the union, who would prepare a list in the manner provided by the 9th section of the same Act, of persons having the required qualification between the ages of 21 and 60 years, and excluding those disqualified by the 7th section of the present Act, and exempting all owners of public-houses from serving as jurors. I am fully satisfied they themselves would desire it, as, from their position, they cannot, without injury to their business, return an adverse verdict in criminal cases. To aid in a perfect revision, I would suggest, that on an early date, after the clerk of the union has completed his list, and had it printed, a special meeting of the board of guardians should be convened, at which the rate collectors should be required to attend, and that the list be submitted to that meeting for observations to be entered in a column left for that purpose, so that full information as to the want of intelligence or character of any person whose name might be on the list would be placed before the Revising Barrister, whose duty it would be, after proper inquiry, to remove the name of any person whom he considered disqualified by want of intelligence, or other sufficient cause.

I have, &c.
(signed) *George F. Roughan.*

B. Banks, Esq., &c. &c.,
Local Government Board, Dublin.

Appendix, No. 5.

REPORT of Mr. *Thomas Hamilton Burke*.

(No. 11,773–73—Miscellaneous.)

Sir, Belmont, Mullingar, 29 April 1873.

I HAVE had the honour to receive in due course your letter of the 10th instant, No. 9903/73, forwarding, by directions of the Local Government Board, the copy of a letter received from the Under Secretary of his Excellency the Lord Lieutenant relating to the working of the Juries (Ireland) Act, 1871, communicating his Excellency's desire to obtain information which may be of practical value, in fixing a proper qualification for jurors and special jurors through the Board's inspectors, who might consult the clerks of unions on the subject, with reference to which I beg to state that after communicating, by letter (and in many instances personally as well), with the several clerks of unions in my districts; from information thus and otherwise obtained, it would appear to me that the present qualification of jurors, as set forth in the Schedule (common and special), is fair and sufficiently high for the object intended.

The principal complaints as to the practical working of "the Act" appear to have arisen in consequence of parties being placed on the jurors' lists, who, though they possessed the necessary rating qualification, were found to be quite unsuited for the proper discharge of the responsible duties devolving upon them as jurors, by reason of mental or physical incapacity in some instances, and the total want of the common educational requirements in others; to obviate which I would beg to leave to suggest as a remedy, that in the framing of any amended Act there might be inserted a clause (to the effect) requiring all poor-rate collectors, after a careful scrutiny of the lists of ratepayers in their several districts, to enter "Objected" after, or opposite, to the names of any (to their knowledge) ineligible, by reason of either mental or physical incapacity, their being unable to read and write, or other just cause (to be defined); such lists (when completed) to be forwarded to the clerk of the union, by whom, after due publication, they would be forwarded to the clerk of the peace, and laid before the county chairman at a special revision sessions, where the parties so objected to would have an opportunity of showing cause why their names should not be struck off; thus affording a safeguard against the successful attempt of any party who might be influenced by corrupt or improper motives in the framing of the list of jurors.

With those exceptions, the measure (so far as I can ascertain) appears to have given general satisfaction.

I remain, &c.
(signed) *T. H. Burke*,
Local Government Board
Inspector.

R. Banks, Esq.,
Local Government Board,
Dublin.

Appendix, No. 6.

Appendix, No. 6.

PAPERS handed in by Mr. *Bottomley.*

THE JURIES (IRELAND) BILL.

EXTRACT from the SPEECH of the Right Honourable the Lord Chancellor of *Ireland*, delivered in the House of Lords, on Friday, the 19th May 1871, and reported in the "Freeman's Journal" of 22nd May 1871.

"And the oldest Crown Solicitor in Ireland, who has discharged the duties of that office for nearly 30 years, says:—

"The formation of the petty jury panel is now entirely at the discretion of the sub-sheriff, who is often the friend of and influenced by the attorney for the prisoners.

"And, again, in answer to questions put by the Committee—

"Did I understand you to say that the sub-sheriff was frequently influenced by the solicitor employed for the accused?—Most frequently. I know cases of it myself. . . . . . I have seen by the acts of the sub-sheriff that he was influenced by the prisoner's attorney. I cannot prove that he receives money, or that he is bribed by him, but for a person who attends the criminal courts so constantly as I do, it is very easy to observe the influence the attorney has with the sub-sheriff."

We, the undersigned sub-sheriffs of the counties in Ireland, opposite to which our names are placed, with the periods during which we have respectively held office, do hereby declare that the foregoing statement of the Crown Solicitor in question, as quoted and relied on by the Lord Chancellor, is absolutely untrue, and that we have invariably formed our jury panels fairly and impartially, as bound so to do by our oath of office, uninfluenced by any individual, or by any corrupt or unworthy motives, and we respectfully ask that the above measure may be referred to a Committee of Parliament, before which we may have an opportunity of refuting the foregoing statements, which we regard as a cruel slander, and calculated to injure us in our official positions.

COUNTIES.	Period of Office.	Signature of Sub-Sheriffs.
Antrim - - - - -	12 years - -	H. H. Bottomley.
Armagh - - - - -	20 " - -	Wm. Hardy.
Monaghan - - - - -	9 " - -	William Mitchell.
Tyrone - - - - -	6 " - -	Jas. Mackay.
Londonderry - - - -	26 " - -	Thos. Chambers.
Donegal - - - - -	5 " - -	John S. M'Coy.
Fermanagh - - - -	8 " - -	M. H. Murphy.
Cavan - - - - -	14 " - -	Ralph Harman.
Meath - - - - -	6 " - -	Harcourt Lighburne.
Westmeath - - - -	7 " - -	Thos. Murray.
Longford - - - -	4 " - -	P. M. Carnan.
Leitrim - - - - -	9 " - -	A. Harrison.
Sligo - - - - -	16 " - -	Bernard Owen Cogan.
Roscommon - - - -	25 " - -	John S. Hackett.
Clare - - - - -	3 " - -	John Cullinan, Jun.
Kerry - - - - -	10 " - -	W. Harnett.
Limerick City - - - -	1 " - -	James Nash.
Limerick County - - -	5 " - -	John Ryan.
Cork County - - - -	14 " - -	J. B. Johnson.
Cork City - - - -	4 " - -	Wm. B. Galwey.
Waterford County - - -	7 " - -	Richard Hudson.
Waterford City - - -	2 " - -	Joseph K. Barrow.
Wexford - - - - -	15 " - -	Thos. Wilkinson.
Wicklow - - - - -	10 " - -	J. K. Toomey.
Mayo - - - - -	9 " - -	Jas. C. Macdonnell.
Galway - - - - -	25 " - -	John M. O'Hara.
Tipperary, North and South Riding - - - -	17 " - -	Gerald Fitzgerald.

THE JURIES (IRELAND) ACT, 1871.

STATEMENT as to Challenges to Jury Panels throughout *Ireland* previous to the passing of this Act.

County.	Name of Sub-Sheriff.	How long in Office.	Number of Challenges made during that Period.	Cause of Challenge.	Result.
Mayo - -	James C. Macdonnell	7 years -	Once - -	On ground that sub-sheriff was prosecutor in a criminal case.	Allowed; though judge stated he was satisfied panel was fair and impartial.
Queen's County	John Malcolmson -	5 years -	Never.		
Wicklow -	John K. Toomey -	11 years -	Twice - -	1. In traverse of award under Lands Clauses Act, on ground that traverser's attorney was father of sub-sheriff. 2. In an ejectment, on ground that sub-sheriff personally interested.	Traverse found against the challenge. Abandoned.
Kerry - -	William Hanson -	21 years -	Once - - Last Assizes	Not alphabetically arranged - -	Partly allowed
Roscommon -	John L. Hackett -	27 years -	Never.		
Galway - -	John M. O'Hara -	20 years -	Never.		
Limerick -	John Ryan - -	4 years -	Once - - Special Commission in year 1865.	Under proportion of Protestants -	Disallowed.
Limerick City -	Ambrose Hall - -	4 years -	Never.		
Cork - -	J. B. Johnston -	15 years -	Never.		
Longford -	P. M. Cutchison -	6 years -	Never.		
Monaghan -	William Mitchell -	9½ years -	Once - - Spring 1869.	Partially formed - - - -	Traverse found in favour of challenge, and panel quashed.
Leitrim - -	Arthur Harrison -	11 years -	Never.		
Wexford - -	Thos. Wilkinson -	17 years -	Never.		
Kilkenny -	P. M'Dermott -	4 years -	Never.		
Londonderry -	Thomas Chambers -	25 years -	Once - -	Civil case on ground of sheriff being interested	Trial postponed
Westmeath -	Thomas Murray -	9 years -	Never.		
Carlow - -	Edward L. Jameson	27 years -	Never.		
Cavan - -	Ralph Harman -	16 years -	Never.		
Clare - -	John Cullinan - -	4 years -	Never.		
Tipperary -	Gerald Fitzgerald -	17 years -	Never		
Louth - -	B. Brabazon - -	30 years -	Never.		
King's County	Robert Whelan -	13 years -	Never.		
Sligo - -	William Alexander -	3 years -	Never.		
Armagh - -	William Hardy -	20 years -	Never.		
Down - -	Hutchinson Boyd -	8 years -	Once - - Spring 1872.	On ground that jurors not alphabetically selected	Panel quashed.
Waterford -	Richard G. Wilson -	8 years -	Never.		
Donegal - -	John S. M'Coy -	7 years -	Never.		
Antrim - -	H. H. Bottomley -	15 years -	Twice - - Once in 1865.	On ground of there being no jurors' book, and fraudulent omission by high constables of names, and non-service of jurors.	Challenge overruled.
			And at Spring Assizes 1872.	On ground of panel not being alphabetically arranged.	Like result.

Appendix, No. 7.

Appendix, No. 7.

PAPERS handed in by Mr. *Thomas Wilkinson*, 9 June 1873.

SPECIAL JURORS' BOOK.

Gross Number of Jurors in Book - - - - - - -	985
Number Letter C., being the largest letter - - - - -	100
Number of Figures in each Column save last - - - - -	100

Table showing the action of the Machinery created by Act 10 for selecting Jurors by taking one name in each letter in regular Alphabetical Series so that the name of every Juror shall be returned in its proper turn and order

Letter	U	V	Q	A	O	E	I	T	N	G	L	P	H	F	W	S	R	K	D	B	M	C		Number of Names
Number	1	2	7	23	25	31	40	57	68	95	110	129	187	205	210	236	247	257	300	345	355	360		
																							10	200
																							20	180
																							30	169
																							40	160
																							50	150
																							60	147
																							70	138
																							80	130
																							90	129
																							100	128
																							110	120
																							120	110
																							130	109
																							140	100
																							150	101
																							160	100
																							170	100
																							180	100
																							190	100
																							200	100
																							210	90
																							220	80
																							230	70
																							240	67
																							250	57
																							260	45
																							270	40
																							280	40
																							290	40
																							300	40
																							310	33
																							320	30
																							330	30
																							340	30
																							350	20
																							360	15
																							4	4
	1	2	3	4	5	6	7	8	9	10	11	12	13	14	15	16	17	18	19	20	21	22		3295

Margin notes: 1374 (beside 30), 2304 (beside 80), 2304 (beside 190)

10 Large letters contain 2686
12 Small letters . 609

3295

Summary

4	Letters exceed	300
6	— . —	200
2	.	100
3	.	50
7	. under	50

Wm. Wilkinson
Sub Sheriff Wexford

THE JURIES ACT (IRELAND), 1871.—COUNTY OF WEXFORD.

1		101		201		301		401		501		601		701		801		901
2		102		202		302		402		502		602		702		802		902
3		103		203		303		403		503		603		703		803		903
4		104		204		304		404		504		604		704		804	T	904
5		105		205		305		405		505		605		705	R	805		905
6		106		206		306		406		506		606		706		806		906
7		107		207		307		407		507		607		707		807		907
8		108		208		308		408		508		608		708		808	U	908
9		109		209		309		409		509		609		709		809	V	909
10		110		210		310		410		510		610		710		810		910
11		111		211		311		411		511		611		711		811		911
12		112		212		312		412		512		612	P	712		812		912
13		113		213		313		413		513		613		713		813		913
14		114		214		314		414		514		614		714		814		914
15		115		215		315		415		515		615		715		815		915
16		116		216		316		416	K	516		616		716		816		916
17		117		217		317		417		517		617		717		817		917
18		118		218		318		418		518		618		718		818		918
19		119		219		319		419		519		619		719		819		919
20		120		220		320		420		520		620		720		820		920
21		121		221		321		421		521		621		721		821		921
22		122		222		322		422		522		622		722		822		922
23		123		223		323		423		523		623		723		823		923
24		124		224	F	324		424		524		624	Q	724		824		924
25		125		225		325		425		525		625		725		825		925
26		126		226		326		426		526	M	626		726		826		926
27		127		227		327	H	427		527		627		727		827		927
28		128		228		328		428		528		628		728		828		928
29		129		229		329		429		529		629		729		829		929
30		130		230		330		430		530		630		730		830		930
31		131		231		331		431		531		631		731		831		931
32		132		232		332		432		532		632		732		832		932
33		133		233		333		433		533		633		733		833		933
34		134		234		334		434		534		634		734		834		934
35		135		235		335		435		535		635		735		835		935
36		136		236		336		436		536		636		736		836		936
37		137	D	237		337		437		537		637		737		837		937
38		138		238		338		438		538		638		738		838		938
39		139		239		339		439		539		639		739		839		939
40		140		240		340		440		540		640		740		840		940
41		141		241		341		441		541		641		741		841		941
42		142		242		342		442		542		642		742		842		942
43		143		243		343		443		543		643		743		843		943
44		144		244		344		444		544		644		744		844		944
45		145		245		345		445		545		645		745		845		945
46		146		246		346		446		546		646		746		846		946
47	C	147		247		347		447		547		647		747		847	W	947
48		148		248		348		448		548		648		748		848		948
49		149		249		349		449		549		649		749		849		949
50		150		250		350		450		550		650		750	S	850		950
51		151		251		351		451	L	551		651		751		851		951
52		152		252		352		452		552		652		752		852		952
53		153		253		353		453		553		653		753		853		953
54		154		254		354		454		554		654		754		854		954
55		155		255		355		455		555		655		755		855		955
56		156		256		356		456		556		656		756		856		956
57		157		257		357		457		557		657		757		857		957
58		158		258		358		458		558		658		758		858		958
59		159		259		359		459		559		659		759		859		959
60		160		260		360		460		560	N	660		760		860		960
61		161		261		361		461		561		661		761		861		961
62		162		262		362		462		562		662		762		862		962
63		163		263		363	J	463		563		663	R	763		863		963
64		164		264		364		464		564		664		764		864		964
65		165		265		365		465		565		665		765		865		965
66		166		266		366		466		566		666		766		866		966
67		167		267	G	367		467		567		667		767		867		967
68		168		268		368		468		568		668		768		868		968
69		169		269		369		469		569		669		769		869		969
70		170		270		370		470		570		670		770		870		970
71		171		271		371		471		571		671		771		871		971
72		172		272		372		472		572		672		772		872		972
73		173		273		373		473		573		673		773		873		973
74		174		274		374		474		574	O	674		774		874		974
75		175		275		375		475		575		675		775		875		975
76		176		276		376		476		576		676		776		876		976
77		177		277		377		477		577		677		777		877		977
78		178		278		378		478		578		678		778		878		978
79		179	E	279		379		479		579		679		779		879		979
80		180		280		380		480		580		680		780		880		980
81		181		281		381		481		581		681		781		881		981
82		182		282		382		482		582		682		782		882		982
83		183		283		383		483		583		683		783		883		983
84		184		284		384		484		584		684		784		884		984
85		185		285		385		485	M	585		685		785		885		985
86		186		286		386	K	486		586		686		786		886		
87		187		287		387		487		587		687		787		887		
88		188		288		388		488		588		688		788		888		
89		189		289		389		489		589		689		789		889		
90		190		290		390		490		590	P	690		790		890		
91		191		291		391		491		591		691		791		891		
92		192	F	292		392		492		592		692		792		892		
93		193		293		393		493		593		693		793		893		
94		194		294	H	394		494		594		694		794		894		
95		195		295		395		495		595		695		795	T	895		
96		196		296		396		496		596		696		796		896		
97		197		297		397		497		597		697		797		897		
98	D	198		298		398		498		598		698		798		898		
99		199		299		399		499		599		699		799		899		
100		200		300		400		500		600		700		800		900		

Appendix, No. 8.

Appendix, No. 8.

PAPER handed in by Mr. *William Ormsby*, 24 June 1873, in answer to Question 4792.

County Dublin.—Grand Jury.

Commission Court, Green-street, June Commission, 1873.

1	Laurence B. Rorke - - - -	Knockmitten, Clondalkin - -	Gentleman.
2	Beverley Smyth - - -	Tymon North, Tallaght - -	Farmer.
3	Patrick Ross - - - -	1, Clyde-road, Dublin - - -	Merchant.
4	Michael Smyth - - -	Beaverstown, Donabate - -	Farmer.
5	Peter Wilson - - - -	Drinan, Malahide - - -	Farmer.
6	Benjamin Coghlan - - -	Lospipple, Swords - - -	Farmer.
7	Joseph Hoey - - - -	Cloghran, Swords - - -	Publican.
8	Peter Knowles - - - -	10, Arran Quay and Palmerstown -	Victualler.
9	William M'Cullagh - - -	Gerrardstown, Oldtown - -	Farmer.
10	Thomas Smith - - - -	Corballis, Donabate - - -	Publican and farmer.
11	Richard Wilson - - -	Diswellstown, Castleknock - -	Farmer.
12	Charles Coghlan - - -	Kilbarrack, Upper - - -	Farmer.
13	Thomas Knox - - - -	Walshestown, Balbriggan - -	Farmer.
14	Thomas W. Rossiter - - -	Churchtown, Dundrum - -	Gentleman.
15	William Sneyd - - - -	Forrest, Little, Swords - - -	Farmer.
16	Michael Coghlan - - -	Kilbarrack, Upper - - -	Farmer.
17	John Doyle - - - -	Tibradden, Whitechurch - -	Farmer.
18	Patrick Hoey - - - -	Buzzardstown, Cloghranhuddart -	Farmer.
19	Edward M'Donald - - -	Ronanstown, Clondalkin - -	Gentleman.
20	John Hogan - - - -	Baldwinstown - - - -	Farmer.
21	Simon J. Brazill - - -	82, St. George's-street, Kingstown	Hotel keeper.
22	Thomas Rourke - - -	Lusk - - - - - -	Farmer.
23	Edward Hogan - - -	Sutton, North, Sutton - - -	Farmer and oyster-bed proprietor.

Robert Warren, Sheriff.

INDEX

TO THE

REPORTS

FROM THE

SELECT COMMITTEE

ON

JURIES (IRELAND).

Ordered, by The House of Commons, to be Printed,
7 July 1873.

INDEX.

ANALYSIS OF INDEX.

LIST of the PRINCIPAL HEADINGS in the following INDEX, with the Pages at which they may be found.

INDEX.

[*N.B.*—In this Index the Figures following the Names of the Witnesses refer to the Questions in the Evidence; those following *App.* to the Pages in the Appendix; and the Numerals following *First Rep.*, *Second Rep.*, and *Special Rep.*, respectively, to the Pages in the several Reports.]

A.

ACT 34 & 35 *VICT. c.* 65 (1871). Grounds for the opinion that the Act of 1871 has worked well as regards the selection of jurors; intelligence displayed by juries in Kerry under the new system, *Hemphill* 4–7. 106. 138–142. 171——Considerable amount of prejudice against the Act, *De Moleyns* 338. 342. 555. 556——Strong approval of the Act both in its principle and its conception, *ib.* 454–456——Evidence to the effect that the Act has not received fair play, *Coffey* 627–635——Witness considers the Act a most valuable step in the right direction, *ib.* 638.

Strong approval of the principle of the Act; urgent want, however, of improvement in its administration as regards the qualifications of jurors, *Armstrong* 765. 768. 822, 823. 865, 866. 1007.

Decided deterioration of the juries under the new Act; the operation of the Act has, in fact, created a burlesque of justice, *J. Hamilton* 1024. 1028–1035. 1096–1098. 1101. 1111, 1112. 1134——Self-acting character of the Act, whilst it cannot be properly administered, *ib.* 1195–1198.

Unfavourable experience of witness as to the working of the new Jury Act; opinion that life and property are not safe in the hands of the new class of jurors, *Battersby* 1439–1441.

Witness drafted the Juries Act in conjunction with Mr. White and Dr. Hancock, *Molloy* 1698, 1699. 1755–1758——Considerable objections to the old system; absolute necessity for a change in the law, *ib.* 1700–1703——Explanations in connection with the defective operation of the new system; great carelessness in making out the jury lists, *ib.* 1708 *et seq.*——Objections to the suggestion that the old law should be reverted to until the necessary amendments can be carried out, *ib.* 1860–1871.

Approval of the change of system instituted by the new Act, *Buchanan* 1894, 1895——Unsatisfactory working of the present Act; approval, however, of its principle, *M'Grath* 2154. 2155——Approval of the principle of the present Act; expediency of taking away from the sheriff the power of the selection of the jury, *Murland* 2358. 2428. 2491, 2492——Opinion that the new Act is a great improvement upon the old system, *Roche* 2507, 2508.

Concurrence in the view that the Act of 1871 has not operated satisfactorily, and requires amendment; grounds for this conclusion, *Right Hon. J. A. Lawson* 2770 *et seq.*; *Right Hon. J. D. Fitzgerald* 3221 *et seq.*; *Right Hon. M. Morris* 2983 *et seq.*; *Right Hon. J. Whiteside* 4222 *et seq.*

See also the Headings generally throughout the Index.

Age of Exemption. Jurors struck off the list as a matter of course, if they can prove that they are above sixty years of age, *Hemphill* 128, 129——Suggestion as to the expediency of a lower age than sixty as the limit, *De Moleyns* 477–479——Strong opinion that the limit of age to entitle to exemption should be raised from sixty to seventy years, *Right Hon. J. D. Fitzgerald* 3243.

Agrarian Outrages. Belief that there would be no fear of special jurors in agrarian or political cases becoming marked men, *Hemphill* 319, 320.

ALPHABETICAL SELECTION (JURY PANEL):

Under the old Act, the sheriff might select any juror on the list; selection under the new law abolished, and the juror summoned alphabetically, *Hemphill* 63–70——Improbability

Alphabetical Selection (Jury Panel)—continued.

bability of selecting interested jurors under the dictionary order; abundant power of the court to change the venue on the slightest suggestion of partiality, *Hemphill* 101-104. 278-280——Great advantage in the jurors being selected alphabetically from the list, *De Moleyns* 455——Alphabetical selection very generally approved of throughout Ireland; advantage thereof as compared with the system of balloting, *Armstrong* 766. 769. 922-925. 930, 931.

Grounds for disapproval of the alphabetical process of selection, *J. Hamilton* 1045. 1110. 1172-1175. 1188-1197——The burden of service upon jurors is not equally distributed by the system of alphabetical rotation, *ib.* 1172-1175——Inconvenience inasmuch as the jurors' book might in some cases consist of but one letter, *ib.* 1355-1359.

Suggestions for obviating the evil attendant upon summoning by alphabetical rotation, as regards business men, *Battersby* 1498-1503——Facility in forming the panel by alphabetical selection, *Molloy* 1881-1888——Contention that no difficulty would arise from occasional preponderance of names commencing with the same letter, *ib.* 1883-1888——Examination as to the effect of alphabetical selection on the attendance of jurors; occasional advantage in having jurors from a distance, *M'Grath* 2255-2264.

Inexpediency of selecting jurors by alphabetical rotation; approval of a system of balloting as the more impartial process, *Murland* 2365-2368. 2430. 2434-2438——Opinion that the jurors on the panel are not known long before the assizes on account of the alphabetical selection, *Roche* 2562-2572.

Examination as to the extra burden and inconvenience put upon individual jurors by the adoption of alphabetical selection, *Right Hon. J. Monahan* 2665-2672——Grounds for disapproving of alphabetical selection; case in point, *Right Hon. J. A. Lawson* 2787-2791——Disapproval of the alphabetical mode of selecting jurors; predominance in some counties of names commencing with a certain letter, *Right Hon. M. Morris* 3005. 3021. 3057-3060. 3114-3117. 3138-3141. 3194-3198. 3206——Possible advantage of adopting a system of alphabetical selection from parishes; difficulties in the cases of baronies and parishes that are either exclusively Protestant or Catholic, *ib.* 3197-3199——Doubt as to any mischief arising from a predominance of the same name, *Right Hon. J. D. Fitzgerald* 3243, 3244.

Suggestions as to overcoming the difficulty of the presence on the list of a preponderance of names commencing with the letters "C" and "M," *Johnson* 3586-3591——Expediency of selecting the panel in dictionary and not in strict alphabetical order, *ib.* 3591——If worked according to the alphabetical system, the Act will leave no ground of suspicion against the sheriff, *ib.* 3692, 3693——Injurious effect of the alphabetical and dictionary order of selection; necessity under such system of bringing persons from a distance, whereas otherwise they would be summoned from the neighbourhood, *Robinson* 3782-3789.

Examination as to the arrangements proposed by witness as an alternative to the selection of the panel in alphabetical order, *Wilkinson* 3983-3985. 4050-4054——The proposed system would avoid in a great degree the difficulty of three persons of the same firm appearing on the same panel, *ib.* 4057——Proposal for obviating the difficulty of summoning jurors by the alphabetical system, *Flynn* 4105. 4141-4143.

Disapproval of the alphabetical selection of the panel from the jury book; the system is inconvenient and embarrassing, *Right Hon. J. Whiteside* 4254. 4303-4307. 4309, 4310.

Decided approval of the alphabetical system; probability, however, of there being, under such a system, a preponderance of Protestants, *J. Reilly* 4506, 4507. 4629. 4631. 4673-4680——Desirability of taking jurors by chance; approval of the ballot system in the event of the alphabetical system not being adopted, *ib.* 4634. 4717——The dictionary arrangement has worked fairly, *Mitchell* 4904.

Table and diagram submitted by Mr. Wilkinson showing the action of the machinery for selecting jurors, by taking one name from each letter in regular alphabetical series, *App.* 324, 325.

See also Antrim. Carson Brothers. Turbett, Messrs.

Antrim. Examination as to the number of jurors it would be practicable to obtain in the county Antrim, *J. Hamilton* 1340-1346——The great majority of the jurors in the county are small farmers; the smallness of the holdings accounts for the absence of a superior class at the assizes, *Right Hon. J. A. Lawson* 2844-2850.

Deterioration of the jurors in the county of Antrim, both common and special, since the new Act, *Bottomley* 3334-3337. 3476, 3477——Statement as to the principle which actuated witness (as sub-sheriff) in the selection of the panel from the common jurors' list, *ib.* 3338-3341. 3526-3528——Method adopted in selecting the panel from the special jurors' list; special jurors seldom called on to serve oftener than once in three years, *ib.* 3343-3346. 3518, 3519——Absence of routine in selecting the panel from the common

Antrim—continued.

common jurors' list; the fact of jurors having served previously is always taken into consideration, *Bottomley* 3347–3350.

Statement that the panel selected by witness has been twice challenged; grounds upon which the challenges were made, and their results, *Bottomley* 3351–3361——Opinion that in the county of Antrim the rating qualification should be 30 *l.* and upwards, and the house qualification 10 *l.* for common jurors, *ib.* 3386–3389——Sufficient number of jurors left on the Antrim list, notwithstanding the raising of the qualification, *ib.* 3390–3392——Considerable number of jurors discharged from attending by the Judge at the last assizes on the plea of poverty, *ib.* 3397, 3398——Disadvantage of the alphabetical system on account of the large numbers of names under certain letters in the county, *ib.* 3430–3432.

See also ***Belfast Assizes.***

Appeal. Power of appeal should be given in the case of any objection against a juror, *De Moleyns* 375. 474. 554——Concurrence in the view that the right of appeal should be given to any person whose name has been struck off the lists, *De Moleyns* 499–501; *Robinson* 3805.

Area (*Jury Lists*). Instances in which the juror can only be selected from certain divisions and not from the county generally, *Hemphill* 68–70——Propriety of distributing the business of jurymen over the whole county, *Armstrong* 766. 768. 794, 795——Political view of the question of extending the area for the selection of jurors, *ib.* 769.

Armstrong, Mr. Serjeant. (Analysis of his Evidence.)—Is a Queen's Counsel and first Serjeant of Law in Ireland, 764——Considerable experience of witness as to the working of the Juries Act, 765. 767——Strong approval of the principle of the Act; great improvement upon the former system, if the Act be properly administered, and the qualifications improved, 766 *et seq.*; 822, 823. 865. 1007——Propriety of distributing the business of jurymen over the whole country, 766. 768. 964, 965——Decided opinion that the qualification for a juror should not be altogether dependent upon property, but that there should be an educational qualification, 766. 776. 779. 872. 877.

Alphabetical selection very generally approved of throughout Ireland, 766. 769——Contention in favour of a qualification for a common jury of not less than 50 *l.*, 769. 824, 825. 994, 995——Political view of the question of extending the area for the selection of jurors, 769——Small shopkeepers are proud to act upon juries as identifying them with the institutions of the country, 769——Unsatisfactory character of the special juries in Dublin; absence of pressure put upon the better classes with a view to compel them to serve, 771, 772. 776. 837–839. 1009.

Necessity for altering the machinery of summoning; easy evasion of the service by intercepting the summonses by means of servants, 772–774. 1008——Expediency of adopting the postal services all over the country; the fact of posting a summons should be considered *primâ facie* evidence of service, 772. 792–795. 904–907. 944–946——Argument that any person who is so obscure as to be beyond the reach of the post is not fit to serve upon a jury at all, 772. 792.

Decided opinion that a man who is unable to read or write should be *ipso facto* disqualified, 779. 873–876. 956–959——Authority to revise the jurors' list should be vested in the chairman upon information to be afforded by various country officials; large amount of confidence reposed in the chairman of counties by every class in Ireland, 779–782. 857–864. 870, 871. 970. 1001——Inexpediency of giving any member of the board of guardians the power of selection or rejection, 779.

Opinion that the word "objected" should not be placed against the name of any person for fear of giving offence, 780, 781. 970——Doubtful expediency of making it absolute that no juror shall serve oftener than once in three years; convenience in having one or two jurors who are familiar with the routine business, 783. 816. 867–869——Strong disapproval of introducing a certain number of special jurors upon every jury; difficulty thereby obviated by raising the qualification, 784–786. 791.

Belief that a system of special juries for criminal trials would be regarded in Ireland as the worst kind of packing possible, 788. 856——The Crown should resort to special commissions in cases of great public interest, instead of requiring special juries, 788–791. 1012, 1013——Under no circumstances should the old system of selection by the sheriff be reverted to; absence of confidence in such system on the part of the lower orders, 796. 799. 844–847. 940–943.

Considerable extent to which challenges to array have been resorted to by Crown counsel; explanation of the meaning of such challenges, 797–799. 841–846. 908–910. 939. 1008——Instances under the old system by which a jury could have been obtained to order; withdrawal by witness of a case from trial in consequence of the state of the panel, 799. 837——The selection of juries was practically in the hands of the sub-sheriffs; observations with reference to the alleged partiality on the part of a sub-sheriff, as noticed by Mr. Seed, 800–805. 831–835. 912.

Armstrong, Mr. Serjeant. (Analysis of his Evidence)—*continued.*

Blemish in the Act with regard to view-juries consisting only of six persons; opinion that the whole twelve should form the jury, 805——Desirability of giving the power to either side of having a special jury without application to the court, 806——The qualification for a special juror should in no case be under a rating of 100 *l.* a year in counties, 807. 808. 890-893——Excellent juries obtained in the county of the city of Dublin under the present system, 809. 865, 868.

Favourable opinion of a compound rating qualification; household qualification a surer test of intelligence than that of land or other property, 810-814. 961-963——Minimum household qualification should be 10 *l.* or 12 *l.*; belief that with such a qualification there would be an ample number of jurors, 811-815. 817. 966——Difficulties with regard to praying a *tales* owing to the peculiar wording of Perrin's Act; expediency of giving both plaintiff and defendant in civil cases the power to pray a *tales*, 817, 818.

Doubtful wisdom in accepting the verdict of a majority; such alteration in the law might be introduced into Ireland if it were found to answer well in England, 819, 820. 827-829——The occasional result of the power of challenging under the old system was that the most respectable jurors were struck out, 828. 830——Evil effect of the present system upon the public mind caused more by the conduct and character of the jurors than by the verdicts they return, 836.

Frequent challenging the natural result of a low qualification, 836——Statement that the dereliction of attendance on the part of the higher class of jurors in Dublin was chiefly caused by the non-imposition of fines by the judges, 839. 1009——Opinion that the duty of setting aside jurors by the Crown counsel is not regarded at all in an odious light, 851-855. 926-929——Great improvement in Dublin under the new law, 865, 866——Computation showing the difficulty in laying down a rule by which no juror would be called more than once in two years, as regards the county of Tyrone, 879-889.

Evidence showing that in the several jury Bills brought into the House of Commons, no qualification of a higher value than 30 *l.* a year was contemplated, 896-901——Questionable policy in employing the constabulary in serving summonses on jurors; service by registered letter for which a receipt would be given, would be preferable, 903-907. 944-946. 982-985——Inexpediency of compelling the Crown to assign a cause for challenging jurors and having a contest thereon in open court, 915. 920——The right of challenging exercised by the Crown solicitor upon his own responsibility without consultation with any Crown counsel, 921.

Doubtful expediency in having the jurors balloted for; opinion in favour of selecting them in true alphabetical order, 922-925. 930, 931——Antagonistic feeling towards the sub-sheriffs on account of the active part they take at elections, 932-938——Strong opinion in favour of the evidence as to objections to jurors being taken upon oath and in open court; high reputation for impartiality in such cases enjoyed by the chairman, 947-955. 972-974. 1000——Power should be given to the judge to set aside a juror upon an objection being made, 960. 975.

Expediency of adding to the panel certain persons who, though not qualified by property, would still be eminently fit to serve on juries, 968, 969——Opinion that the office of sub-sheriff should not be made permanent; remuneration of the sub-sheriff should be a matter of arrangement between himself and the high sheriff, 986-993.

Suitability of the county surveyor to give assistance to the chairman when revising the lists, 998, 999——The labour of revision by the chairman would be very materially lessened after the first time, as the revision would be confined to the new names, 1001.

Further opinion that the lowness of the qualification leads to an exhibition of burlesque on the part of the juries, expediency of endeavouring to get a higher qualification for the next assizes, 1003. 1008. 1010, 1011——Right of the Crown to bring cases to the Queen's Bench for trial by special jury; power to remove the trial of a case from one county to another vested in the court, 1014, 1015.

Assizes. Suggestion that all prisoners should be sent for trial to the county town as a means of saving expense, *M'Grath* 2335-2341——Expediency of having two jurors' books, one for sessions and the other for assize purposes; higher qualification necessary for assize jurors, *Johnson* 3582-3584. 3617. 3656. 3684——Opinion that a higher class of jurors should be selected for the assizes and the lower class utilised at the quarter sessions, *Robinson* 3813-3819. 3824. 3849-3854. 3870.

Expediency of making the qualification the same both for the assizes and for the sessions, *J. Reilly* 4564-4567.

See also Qualifications. Revision of Jury Lists.

Atkinson, Mr. Report from Mr. Atkinson, clerk of the North Dublin Union, relative to the qualifications to be required in jurors, and the amendments desirable in the Act of 1871, *App.* 316.

Reports, 1873—*continued.*

Attendance of Jurors. Opinion that in Clare and other counties the new Act has not received fair play; strong disapprobation expressed by Mr. Justice Fitzgerald of the conduct of the country gentlemen in absenting themselves as jurors, *Coffey* 627–633—— Belief that the attention of the country gentlemen has been aroused by the remarks of the Judges, and that the attendance will be better at the next assizes, *ib.* 631. 692.

Importance of relieving jurors from constant attendance; complaints made by them as to the great distance they have to travel, *J. Hamilton* 1088, 1204——Power of a judge to excuse a juror from attendance; power also to fine him for non-attendance when summoned, *ib.* 1179–1188.

Belief that the cause of the absence of the better class of jurors at the last assizes was a desire on their part to bring discredit upon the new Act, *Molloy* 1807. 1830–1835—— Examination as to the possibility of the better class of jurors absenting themselves on account of disinclination to associate with the very low class that were summoned, *ib.* 1832–1836.

Non-attendance of the better class of jurors, *Roche* 2535–2540——Desirability of giving the judge at the assizes power to discharge any juror from attendance, *Johnson* 3680.

See also Cork. Dublin, 3. Fines. Lower Classes. MKenna's Trial. Public, The. Resident Jurors. Service of Jurors. Summonses, &c.

Attorneys' Clerks. Decided opinion that attorneys' clerks should be exempted from serving on juries, *Hemphill* 190–193.——*See also Exemptions.*

B.

Bailiffs. Blackmail exacted under the old system by bailiffs by means of unauthorised summonses to persons, *Flynn* 4185.

Bairds' Trial. Examination as to the preponderance of the religious element in the jury that tried the Bairds, *Right Hon. M. Morris* 3133–3137.

BALLOT (JURY PANEL):

Selection of jurors by ballot for the trial of civil causes, *Hemphill* 89——Desirability of introducing a system of balloting in criminal cases; impression that before the present Act jurors were taken by ballot both in civil and criminal cases, *De Moleyns* 388–390. 450–453.

Contention in favour of balloting for the panel in criminal as well as in civil cases; such a course would take away the frequent necessity which exists for challenging; *Coffey* 654. 655. 717–726—— Balloting would not take away the right of the Crown or that of the prisoner to challenge, *ib.* 655, 656.

Doubtful expediency in having the jurors balloted for; opinion in favour of selecting them in true alphabetical order, *Armstrong* 922–925. 930, 931——Examination as to the probability of obtaining impartial juries by a system of ballot or other chance selection; conclusion as to the expediency of balloting for special jurors, *Battersby* 1457, 1458. 1681–1690. 1696—— Advantage of balloting in criminal cases; canvassing jurors by the friends of prisoners would be thereby avoided, *Roche* 2542, 2543. 2545–2547; *Murphy* 3719.

Desirability of a system of ballot, reserving both to the Crown and to the prisoner the right of challenge; objection to the ballot except with such reservation, *Right Hon. M. Morris* 3116–3119——Entire approval of the selection of jurors both in criminal and civil cases by means of the ballot, *Right Hon. J. D. Fitzgerald* 3235, 3236. 3241, 3242. 3292–3294. 3307.

Opinion that a system of ballot would be fair both towards the Crown and the prisoner, *Bottomley* 3520, 3521 —— Approval of balloting if there were a separate jurors' book for sessions and assizes purposes, *Johnson* 3590, 3591.

Inexpediency of a system of ballot in criminal cases; opinion that the privilege of the prisoner to challenge, and the power of the Crown to set aside, answers every purpose, *Robinson* 3828——Evidence in favour of a selection of the panel in criminal cases by means of the ballot, *Wilkinson* 4055. 4056——Disapproving of adopting the ballot in criminal cases; opinion that the present system is the fairest to the prisoner, *Right Hon. J. Whiteside* 4311–4313.

Battersby, George, LL.D. (Analysis of his Evidence.)—Is a Queen's Counsel and Senior of the Home Bar, 1436——Is also a judge in the Consistorial Court, and is Crown Counsel for three counties, 1437, 1438——Unfavourable experience of the working of the new Jury Law Act; opinion that life and property are not safe in the hands of the new class of jurors, 1439–1441.

Battersby, George, LL.D. (Analysis of his Evidence)—*continued.*

Ludicrous conduct of the jurors at the last assizes for the Home Circuit; the foreman of a special jury at Trim, unable to write, 1442–1445——Under the old law, the foreman of that jury would have been a gentleman of education and property, 1445–1447——The rating qualification is not a sufficient test of the fitness of a juror; necessity for the adoption of other tests as far as possible, 1448, 1449.

Extreme poverty of the jurors at the last assizes; their desire to be exonerated from serving, and to be permitted to return home, 1450–1452——Unjust verdicts found by the lowest class of jurors; opinion that a higher class are to be depended upon in spite of their prejudices, 1453, 1454.

Suggestion of remedies to be applied, so as to bring the present law into better shape; expediency of raising the rating qualification for common jurors to 100 *l.*, and for special jurors to 200 *l.*, 1455–1468. 1555——Imposition of fines necessary to ensure the attendance of jurors, 1455. 1475–1477——Considerable advantage in using the post office as a means for summoning jurors, *ib.* 1456. 1512–1515.

Recommendation that either party both in civil and criminal cases should be entitled to have a special jury struck; belief that such an arrangement would not be unpopular in the country, 1455, 1456. 1485–1489. 1593–1598. 1678–1682——Expediency of balloting for special jurors as is the case in the Court of Chancery, 1457, 1458——Suggestions as to placing certain persons of good position on the jurors' book who have no property qualification at all, 1458. 1467–1471. 1506, 1507. 1592. 1627.

Statement as to persons who should be disqualified from serving; information thereto should be given by the poor rate collectors and by the constables in charge of districts, 1458. 1565. 1568, 1569. 1629–1638——Assumption that the chairman is to continue to be the revising officer under the new Act, 1459. 1628.

Expediency of giving the sheriff power to omit names and form the panel generally on his own responsibility; the county surveyor would be entirely incompetent for such duty, 1459–1466. 1556, 1557. 1643–1646. 1649–1652——Instance of partiality of a juror at Mullingar upon the occasion of the first conviction of a Fenian, 1462. 1661——A lower qualification might be adopted, if the sheriff be given power to select the panel, 1472–1474——Great objection to the present system of serving summonses upon jurors; expediency of employing the constabulary for the purpose, 1484. 1524–1535.

Evidence to the effect that there was no ground for the imputations of Mr. Seed as regards the sub-sheriff of Westmeath, 1489–1494——Opinion as to the impartiality of the sub-sheriffs in forming the panel, 1493–1497. 1599, 1600. 1649–1653——Suggestions for obviating the evil attendant upon summoning by alphabetical rotation as regards business men, 1498–1503——Inexpediency of adopting the so-called compound qualification, 1504, 1505——Approval of the exemption of law clerks, publicans, and domestic servants, 1508——Examination as to the effect of an increased qualification on the numbers of jurors in certain counties, 1516–1523. 1540–1547. 1553, 1554. 1559–1561. 1617–1621.

Facility with which the jurors' lists could be revised by the assistant barrister when engaged upon the revision of the voters' lists, 1536–1539——Contention that the valuation of 100 *l.* for common jurors, and 200 *l.* for special jurors, would be a sufficiently low qualification, 1549–1552——Expediency of lowering the rate where a sufficient number of jurors cannot be obtained, 1558——Evidence as to the suitability of leasehold qualification, 1562–1591.

Inexpediency of doing away altogether with the exemptions under the Act; grounds for this conclusion, 1603–1609. 1674, 1675——Additional evidence as to the omission, not selection, of names by the sheriff, 1611. 1676, 1677——Approval of an arrangement by which the high sheriff would sign the panel with his own hand, 1612. 1647, 1648.

Decided opinion that the sooner the present law is altered the better; suitability of the present time for carrying out the necessary changes, 1626——Statement as to the method of making the lists of Parliamentary voters, 1639, 1640——Disinclination of the Irish people to serve on juries, 1641——Objection to leaving the formation of the panel to the discretion of any person; it is, however, impossible to avoid this, 1654–1657.

Impossibility of satisfactorily purging the jury book by any process, 1658, 1659. 1695——Invidious character of the power exercised by the Crown solicitor in challenging jurors; difficulties in the way of his obtaining information as to particular persons on the panel, 1662–1673——Panel struck seven days before the assizes, 1668.

Statement that some of the exemptions in the second schedule, are on account of the interference with other public duties, 1674, 1675——Examination as to the probability of obtaining impartial juries by a system of ballot or other chance selection, 1681–1690. 1696——Desirability of obtaining a considerable degree of intelligence as well as impartiality; opinion that a revision by the chairman will not secure sufficient intelligence, 1691–1693.

Belfast

Reports, 1873—*continued.*

Belfast Assizes. Heavy character of the business at the last Belfast assizes, *Right Hon. J. A. Lawson* 2770–2772. 2784. 2932. 2934——Large attendance of jurors, in consequence of which there was no imposition of fines upon those absent; opinion that the better class should be compelled to attend, *ib.* 2777, 2778——Disposition of the jurors who attended to find fair verdicts; advantage in having had one or two intelligent men on nearly every jury, *ib.* 2779, 2780. 2785. 2855. 2885, 2886. 2893–2896. 2927. 2960, 2961.——*See* also *Antrim.*

Belfast Chamber of Commerce. Communication from the President of the Chamber of Commerce at Belfast, as to the confidence extended to the juries under the new Act, *Bottomley* 3481, 3482.

Boards of Guardians. Inexpediency of giving any member of the board of guardians the power of selection or rejection of jurors, *Armstrong* 779.

See also *Revision of Jury Lists.*

Bottomley, Henry Haigh. (Analysis of his Evidence.)—Has held the office of sub-sheriff for the county of Antrim for fifteen years without interruption, 3329–3331——Operation of the new Act discussed at a meeting of the sub-sheriffs held in Dublin; absence of opposition on their part to the principle of the Act, 3332–3334——Expediency of some modification in the method of serving summonses; considerable difficulty in serving the summonses in time, 3334. 3411–3414. 3452.

Deterioration of the jurors in the county of Antrim, both common and special, since the new Act, 3335–3337. 3476, 3477——Statement as to the principle which actuated witness in the selection of the common and special panels from the jurors' list; special jurors' list also made out by witness, 3338–3341. 3526–3528——Method adopted in selecting the panel from the special jurors' list; special jurors seldom called on to serve oftener than once in three years, 3343–3346. 3518, 3519.

Absence of routine in selecting the panel from the common jurors' list; the fact of jurors having served previously is always taken into consideration, 3347–3350——Statement that the panel selected by witness has been twice challenged; grounds upon which the challenges were made, and their results, 3351–3361.

Impossibility of there being a perfect panel unless there is a power of selection by some public officer; approval of the alphabetical selection as laid down by Mr. Justice Fitzgerald, 3362, 3363. 3497–3499——Expediency of the sheriff retaining a limited power of rejection on account of his possessing the largest means of obtaining information, 3364–3367. 3393——Belief that no revision can thoroughly exclude disqualified persons, 3368. 3478–3480.

Examination as to the information which can be given to the chairman by the poor law collector, 3369–3377. 3494–3497——Importance of making the sheriff responsible for the correctness of the lists in the event of the power of rejection being restored to him, 3378–3382——Opinion that in the county of Antrim the rating qualification should be 30 *l.* and upwards, and the house qualification 20 *l.* for common jurors, 3383–3385——The qualification for special jurors should be raised to 100 *l.* and upwards, 3386–3389.

Sufficient number of jurors left on the list, notwithstanding the raising of the qualification, 3390–3392——Approval of exempting grand jurors from serving on common juries, 3391. 3395——Considerable number of jurors discharged from attending by the judge at the last assizes on the plea of poverty, 3397, 3398——Suggestion as to the course to be adopted with a view to relieving jurors who have to come a long distance, 3400–3410. 3508–3517.

Difficulties as to the payment of expenses in carrying out the new Act, 3415–3419. 3423, 3424——Approval of the service of summonses by means of registered letters; disapproval of summoning by the constabulary, 3420–3422. 3425, 3426——Disadvantages of the alphabetical system on account of the large number of names under certain letters in the county of Antrim, 3430–3432.

Impossibility of adhering to the Act as regards the time for summoning special jurors, 3433——Belief that the sub-sheriffs would be incapable of exercising partiality in the exercise of their duty as regards the selection of jurors, 3434–3437. 3454–3456. 3460–3471——Statement that any suspicion that existed as to the packing of jurors was directed more to the setting aside of jurors by the Crown solicitors than to unfair conduct upon the part of the sheriffs, 3450. 3523–3525. 3532–3535. 3553–3565.

Satisfaction felt by the sub-sheriffs at being relieved from an onerous and difficult duty in selecting the panel, 3457–3459. 3531–3536——Absence of responsibility in any official as to returning improper persons on the panel under the present Act, 3472–3475——Communication from the President of the Chamber of Commerce at Belfast as to the confidence extended to the juries under the new Act, 3481, 3482.

Full powers entrusted to the sub-sheriff in the deputation given by the high sheriff, 3483, 3484——Examination as to the method adopted in selecting panels for the quarter sessions and the assizes respectively, 3485–3491——Further evidence as to the necessity for

Bottomley, Henry Haigh. (Analysis of his Evidence)—*continued.*

for revising the jurors' lists; admission that such revision would so reduce the number of jurors that they would be obliged to serve more frequently, 3498–3507.

Opinion that a system of ballot would be fair both towards the Crown and the prisoner, 3520, 3521——Examination as to the expediency of the sheriff selecting jurors for particular trials; statement that absence of knowledge was the only thing to prevent such selection, 3537–3552.

Bourke, Richard. Report by Mr. Richard Bourke, poor law inspector, submitting the views arrived at by him, after consulting various clerks of unions, relative to the qualification desirable for jurors, *App.* 301, 302.

Brodie, Terence. Report by Mr. Brodie relative to the working of the Juries Act of 1871, and the qualifications desirable for common jurors and special jurors respectively, *App.* 318, 319.

Buchanan, Lewis M. (Analysis of his Evidence.)—Is deputy clerk of the peace and of the Crown for the county of Tyrone, 1889. 1975–1977——Initiatory preparation of the jurors' lists undertaken by witness, 1890——The qualifications under the old list had become so obsolete that sufficient jurors could not be obtained, 1891, 1892——Under the present Act, with a qualification of 20 *l.*, the number of jurors is 3092; 1893.

Approval of the change instituted by the new Act, 1894. 1895——Opinion that the qualification is too low, and should be raised; qualification for house property in towns should be 15 *l.*, 1895–1899. 1902. 2026——Qualification for the county should not be under 30 *l.*; expediency of keeping house and land ratings distinct both in towns and counties, 1903–1906.

Statement that a list of 1,000 names for the county of Tyrone would be amply sufficient if jurors were required to serve once a year, 1910——Universal approval of the principle of the new Act in the county; objection, however, that the qualification is too low, thereby bringing upon the lists persons who are unfit every way to act as jurors, 1911–1916. 1940–1942. 2042–2046.

Essential necessity for a rule by which the foreman of a jury should be selected by an officer of the court and not by the jury themselves, 1916–1920. 2038. 2068–2070——Suggestions as to the examination of lists, previously to coming before the court; expediency of informing jurors that their names have been placed on the lists, 1921.

Objection upon the part of many people to be excluded from juries, 1922——Desirability of limiting the right of challenge to twelve, thereby obviating the necessity of a large list; this right should be given to every prisoner in every description of trial, 1923. 1996–2007. 2113——Argument in favour of having a less number on the jury list, that the jurors will be of a much higher class, 1924, 1925. 1927. 2011, 2012, 2032, 2033.

Over anxiety of inexperienced jurors to be guided more by the opinion of the Bench than by their own judgment, 1926, 1927. 2034–2037——Expediency of a modification in the system of requiring unanimous verdicts from juries, 1930–1932——Decided opinion that no official should be given the power of selection as regards the jury lists; the sheriff should have power to omit the names of unfit persons, but not to select, 1933–1935.

Elimination of improper persons should be by means of raising the qualification and by stringently revising the lists, 1937, 1938. 1991–1994——Instances of cases at the last assizes in which the jurors were of a class quite unfit for further duties, 1941–1945. 1966——Examination as to the class of jurors to be obtained by a rating of 30 *l.* in the county Tyrone, 1946–1965.

Belief that the county Tyrone is quite equal to the average of the rest of Ireland in point of education, 1967–1970——Large numbers of jurors set aside, both by the Crown and the prisoner, at the trial of Montgomery, 1972–1974——Expediency of combining the lists of electors and voters for the purposes of revision by the chairman; grounds for arriving at this opinion, 1978–1987. 2108–2113——Statement of the method of revising the electors' list, 1980–1985.

Difficulties in the case of several prisoners being tried together, and each exercising the right to challenge, in order to exhaust the panel, 2008–2110——Further suggestions as to the manner to be adopted for economising the summoning of jurors; necessity for diminishing the number of places where quarter sessions are held, 2013–2023——Diminution of the quarter sessions divisions would not add to the duty of the jurors of one division over another, 2024, 2025.

Approval of the compound qualification if it were feasible; opinion that the rating of a man's homestead and farm buildings are a criterion of his respectability and fitness to serve, 2027–2029——Expediency of a certain number of special jurors being required to serve on every jury, 2039–2041——Further evidence upon the subject of increasing the qualification for special jurors, both in towns and in the county, 2047–2053.

Rating qualification for the county based upon Griffith's valuation; opinion that if the existing valuation is changed it ought to be considerably augmented, 2054–2057——

Desirability

Buchanan, Lewis M. (Analysis of his Evidence)—*continued.*

Desirability of including villages in the new Act as a basis for qualification; contention that a man rated at 20 *l.* in a village is as fit to be a juror as a man rated at the same amount in a town, 2058–2063.

Absence of any difficulty for the chairman to revise the jurors' book against the next assizes, 2064–2066——Statement as to the exhaustion of the jury panel in Tyrone for this year, 2071–2075. 2083——Duties of the grand jury at the quarter sessions, 2076–2082——Opinion that the expenses under the new will not be so great as they were under the old Act; detailed statement of the cost of preparing the jury list, 2084–2092. 2114–2121. 2128–2130——Character of the work performed by the clerks of unions in connection with the lists, 2093–2096. 2122–2128——The work of witness will be materially reduced by raising the qualification, as this will have the effect of reducing the number of jurors, 2097–2105——Enormous predonderance of names in the county Tyrone, beginning with the letter "M," 2131–2134.

Burke, Thomas Hamilton. Report by Mr. Burke, poor law inspector, relative to the qualification desirable in jurors, and the amendments required in the Act of 1871, *App.* 381.

C.

Carson, Brothers. Letter from the firm of Carson, Brothers, of Dublin, complaining that both members of the firm had been summoned to serve on juries on the same day, *J. Hamilton* 1176.

Cavan. Excellent juries formerly supplied in Cavan on the civil side, *J. Hamilton* 1030——With regard to certain comments by the judges on the course pursued by the sub-sheriff in selecting juries at Cavan, witness submits that under the old system the juries did their duty very well, *ib.* 1318, 1319——Existence of party feeling in the county as regards the formation of the jury list, *Robinson* 3878–3880.

Chairman of Quarter Sessions. See *Revision of Jury Lists.*

CHALLENGE OF *JURORS*:

1. *Challenges by the Crown.*
2. *Challenges by Prisoners.*
3. *Statistics of Challenges previously to* 1871.
4. *Challenges to the Array.*

1. *Challenges by the Crown.*

Crown counsel can order jurors to stand aside, without alleging any cause, in trials for felony, *Hemphill* 91. 130——Selection of jurors by the sheriff does not in any way dispense with the necessity of exercising the right of challenge by the Crown solicitor, *ib.* 181–184——Unpleasant and invidious duty of Crown counsel under the old system as to challenge of jurors; the efficient administration of justice endangered thereby, *ib.* 643–646. 654.

The occasional result of the power of challenging under the old system was that the most respectable jurors were struck out, *Armstrong* 826. 830——Extensive challenging the natural result of a low qualification, *ib.* 836——Opinion that the duty of setting aside jurors by the Crown counsel is not regarded at all in an odious light, *ib.* 851–155. 926–929——Inexpediency of compelling the Crown to assign a cause for challenging, and having a contest thereon in open court, *ib.* 915–920——The right of challenging is exercised by the Crown solicitor upon his own responsibility, without consultation with any Crown counsel, *ib.* 921.

Security for an impartial jury by means of the system of challenging; inexpediency of exercising such power too largely, *J. Hamilton* 1053——The offices of Crown solicitor and Crown prosecutor are invariably the rewards of political services, but no suspicion ever attached itself to them on that account, *ib.* 1168, 1169——Examination as to the probable extent to which the Crown would have to exercise the power of setting jurors aside under the present Act, *ib.* 1405–1411.

Invidious character of the power exercised by the Crown solicitor in challenging jurors; difficulties in the way of his obtaining information as to particular persons on the panel, *Battersby* 1662–1673.

Belief that, under all circumstances, unfit jurors will occasionally be returned to the panel; in such cases the Crown should have the right to order them to stand by, *Malley* 1742. 1796–1799——Decided opinion that the exercise of the power is not invidious; paper handed in showing the way in which the power was acquired by the Crown, *ib.* 1743–1745. 1754——Facility with which the Crown solicitors can inform themselves of the

CHALLENGE OF JURORS—continued.

1. *Challenges by the Crown*—continued.

character of the panel previous to the assizes, *Molloy* 1746. 1800–1804——Rules for the guidance of the Crown solicitors as to the duty of directing jurors to stand by, *ib.* 1746, 1747.

Frequent exercise by witness of the power to order jurors to stand by; means of acquiring the knowledge necessary for the purpose, *MGrath*, 2177–2182. 2265–2280——Examination as regards the power and practice of ordering jurors to stand by; witness exercises the power very sparingly, *Roche* 2529–2533. 2577–2582.

Inexpediency of limiting the power of the Crown to order jurors to stand by, *Right Hon. J. H. Monahan* 2756–2762; *Right Hon. J. D. Fitzgerald* 3252. 3308; *Robinson* 3834, 3835——Increased necessity for the Crown to order jurors to stand by consequent upon the new system of alphabetical selection, *Right Hon. J. A. Lawson* 2869.

Argument that taking away the power of selection from the sheriff will throw upon the Crown solicitor the duty of more frequently ordering jurors to stand by, which is a far more dangerous power from a popular point of view, *Right Hon. M. Morris* 3053. 3066–3073. 3077. 3126–3132. 3181–3185——The power of the Crown to set aside jurors cannot safely be dispensed with; beneficial clause in the present Act which removes the power from a private prosecutor, *Right Hon. J. D. Fitzgerald* 3237, 3238.

Opinion that the power of the Crown to order jurors to stand by will be more frequently exercised under the new Act, *Murphy* 3737–3746——Necessity of giving the Crown officials considerable discretion as to setting jurors aside, *Right Hon. J. Whiteside* 4258. 4262——The right of challenging in a criminal trial must be exercised according to strict law, *ib.* 4275——Unlimited power of the Crown to challenge jurors, *Mitchell* 5074. 5080.

Paper prepared by Mr. Constantine Molloy, dated 2nd March 1871, on the subject of the right of the Crown to challenge jurors, *App.* 298–300.

2. *Challenges by Prisoners:*

Desirability of limiting the prisoner's right of challenge to twelve, thereby obviating the necessity of a large list; this right should be given to every prisoner in every description of trial, *Buchanan* 1923. 1996–2007. 2113——Difficulties in the case of several prisoners being tried, and each exercising the right to challenge, in order to exhaust the panel, *ib.* 2008–2110.

Way in which the system of challenging is carried out; the number of challenges allowed to the prisoner should be diminished, *Morland* 2369, 2370. 2393, 2394. 2415–2418. 2431–2441. 2460–2463——Peremptory challenges by the prisoners should not be reduced in number, *Roche* 2544. 2548.

Inexpediency of diminishing the right of a prisoner to challenge, *Right Hon. J. A. Lawson* 2874——Necessity for an alteration in the right of peremptory challenge by the prisoner; opinion that such right should not be interfered with in capital cases, *Right Hon. J. D. Fitzgerald* 3250, 3251. 3257, 3258——Right of the prisoner to challenge twenty jurors peremptorily, *Mitchell* 5079.

3. *Statistics of Challenges previously to 1871:*

Statement as to challenges to jury panels throughout Ireland previously to the Act of 1871 showing in each case the name of the sub-sheriff, the cause of challenge, and the result, *App.* 323.

4. *Challenges to the Array:*

Considerable extent to which challenges to array have been resorted to by Crown counsel; explanation of the meaning of such challenges, *Armstrong* 797–799. 841–846. 905–910. 939–1008——Expediency of giving the judge power to name the tiers in the case of a challenge to the array, *J. Hamilton* 1062, 1063.

Statement that the challenges to the array have been of very rare occurrence; ridiculous system of the appointment of tiers, *Hamilton* 1072–1078. 1200, 1201. 1371. 1377–1380——Instance in which a remarkable challenge to the array was drawn by witness, *ib.* 1072–1076. 1081. 1327–1334.

Challenge to the array has never occurred in the experience of witness, *Right Hon. James H. Monahan*, 2606.

Efficacy of challenge to the array as a safeguard against the exercise of partiality by the sheriff; circumstances under which a challenge to the array can be exercised, *Robinson* 3884–3887.

See also Antrim. Kerry. Leinster Circuit. Monaghan.

Chism, J. R. Report from Mr. Chism, Clerk of the Ballyshannon Union, relative to the qualifications to be required in jurors, and the amendments desirable in the Act of 1871, *App.* 308.

Circumstantial Evidence. Difficulties in Ireland of getting verdicts upon circumstantial evidence; difficulty of uneducated jurors dealing with such evidence, *Right Hon. J. Whiteside* 4234-4236. 4276.

Clare. Illiterate and ragged jury which were in the box at the last Clare assizes, *Coffey* 627. 647. 748, 749——Very good jurors formerly; attendance of the country gentlemen as a rule, *ib.* 629-631——Opinion that no legally disqualified persons had been placed on the jurors' list, *ib.* 636, 637. 670.

Superior class of jurors in the counties of Clare and Limerick to those placed on the panel in Fermanagh and Tyrone, *M'Grath* 2148-2150. 2232-2234.

Remarkable instance of a failure of justice in the county of Clare, *Right Hon. J. D. Fitzgerald* 3221. 3297-3301——Satisfactory character of the jurors at the last Clare assizes; large proportion of civil cases at these assizes, *ib.* 3321, 3322——Strong disapproval expressed by Mr. Justice O'Brien relative to a case of acquittal, *ib.* 3323——The only objection to be made against the Clare jurors was that they re-appeared too constantly, *ib.* 3324, 3325.

Unsatisfactory verdicts at the last Clare assizes, *Murphy* 3700-3707. 3727.

Clerks of the Peace. The duty of giving the chairman information for the revision of the lists should devolve upon the clerk of the peace, *Morland* 2347-2351——Statement of the duties imposed upon the clerks of the peace by the new Act; special payments made to these officers by the grand jury, *Flynn* 4083-4091. 4130-4133. 4149-4154.

Clerks of Unions. Character of the work performed by the clerks of unions in connection with the jury lists; extent of labour entailed, *Buchanan* 2093-2096. 2122-2128; *Flynn* 4084——Opinion that the remuneration paid to clerks of unions for duties under the Act has been an indirect way of making up their salaries; disapproval of this practice, *Flynn* 4063. 4071-4073——Intimate knowledge of all the people in the unions possessed both by the clerks of the unions and by the rate collectors; facility of imparting this knowledge to the chairman when revising the lists, *ib.* 4179-4182. 4218, 4219.

Evidence in contradiction of that given by Mr. Flynn as to the labour entailed upon clerks of unions by the preparation of the jurors' lists, *Cope* 5082-5088——Detailed statement as to certain queries put to the clerks in connection with this service, *ib.* 5084-5086——Description of the duties of the clerks of unions in connection with the Jury Act, *ib.* 5089, 5090. 5095. 5100, 5101. 5105-5112. 5219-5225. 5236-5246——The average salary of clerks of unions in Ireland is between 120 *l.* and 130 *l.*, *ib.* 5247.

Correspondence in April 1873 between the Irish Government and the Local Government Board on the subject of the clerks of unions obtaining certain information as to the qualifications of persons on the rated lists to serve as jurors, *App.* 294, 295.

Reports from the Inspectors of Poor Law Unions, and from several clerks of unions, relative to the working of the Juries Act of 1871, and the qualifications desirable for common jurors and special jurors respectively, *App.* 301-321.

Clonmel Assizes. Impoverished condition of the jurors at the last assizes at Clonmel; statement that several of them were obliged to pawn their clothes for their support while in the town, *Right Hon. J. Whiteside* 4230.

Coffey, James Charles, Q.C. (Analysis of his Evidence.) Is chairman of the County and City of Londonderry and Crown prosecutor for the county of Clare, 620-623——Large experience of witness as regards the working of the Jury Act, and of the old Act in the City of Dublin, 624-626——Opinion that the new Act has not received fair play; strong disapprobation expressed by Mr. Justice Fitzgerald of the conduct of the country gentlemen in absenting themselves, 627-633——Admixture of classes upon the jury panels under the old system; frequent appearance of magistrates upon juries, 629, 630. 633. 744. 750——Belief that the attention of the country gentlemen has been aroused by the remarks of the judges, 631. 692.

Statement that the special jury is formed from a special class taken from the long panel, 633——Illustration of the disfavour with which the new Act has been regarded in Clare, 634, 635——Opinion that no legally disqualified persons had been placed on the jurors' list for the county, 636, 637. 670——Great advantage of the new Act in taking the selection of the panel from the sub-sheriff; the official who selected the jurors under the old system was always liable to a suspicion of partiality, especially in political or party cases, 638-641. 645, 646. 755-758.

Non-interference in the selection of the panel by the high sheriff; impossibility for an official in his position to perform the duty satisfactorily, 642. 705-708——Unpleasant and invidious duty of counsel under the old system as to challenge of jurors; the efficient

Coffey, James Charles, Q.C. (Analysis of his Evidence)—*continued.*
administration of justice endangered by that system, 643–646. 654——Opinion that the rating qualification under the new Act is too low; expediency of a household franchise by which a valuable class of jurors is obtained, 647, 652.

Considerable advantage in having a town element upon a jury, 649–651——Contention in favour of balloting for the panel in criminal as well as in civil cases; such a course would take away the frequent necessity which exists for challenging, 654, 655. 717–726——Balloting would not take away the right of the Crown, or that of the prisoner, to challenge, 655, 656.

Approval of Mr. Hemphill's suggestion that a certain number of special jurors should serve on every jury, 657. 660——Anomalous state of the law whereby in a civil case a special jury may be obtained, but in a case affecting a man's life or liberty, there is no such power, 657——Conclusion that in all serious and heavy cases there should be power given both to the Crown and to the prisoner to have a special jury, 657–659. 700–702. 717. 736–743——Persons of social position chosen to act on grand juries irrespectively of rating qualification, 660, 661.

Opinion that the rating qualification for common jurors should be raised to 30 *l.*, and that the household qualification should be 12 *l.*, 662–666. 729, 730. 761–763——Approval of entrusting the revision of the list to the chairman upon information afforded by the poor law collectors and the sub-sheriffs; the power of the chairman to exempt jurors should be largely extended, 667–669. 672–675. 685. 709, 710——The poor law collector should state the objection, and not write only the word "objected" against the juror's name, 676–684——Hardship in bringing jurors from a great distance to the towns where they are to serve, 686.

Unsuitability of the post office as a means of serving notices upon the jurors, 687, 688——Expediency of exempting publicans and attorneys' clerks, 689–691——Suggestions amending the present system before the next assizes, 692–696. 703, 704——Objection to a principle of accepting the verdict of a majority, 697–699——Expediency of adopting the qualification for special jurors as laid down in the Act, 711–713.

Belief that a man who can read but cannot write would be a proper juror, 727, 728——Argument in favour of dividing the sessions into districts for the convenience of jurors, by taking them from the immediate neighbourhood, 731–735——Illiterate and ragged jury which were in the box at the last Clare assizes, 748, 749.

Common Juries. See the *Headings generally throughout the Index.*

Compound Qualification. Expediency of introducing a compound qualification, composed of a rating of 40 *s.*, and a land qualification of 30 *l.*, *J. Hamilton* 1036–1038–1041. 1084–1086——Opinion as to the inexpediency of the so-called compound qualification, *Battersby* 1504, 1505——Approval of the compound qualification if it were feasible; opinion that the rating of a man's homestead and farm buildings are a criterion of his respectability and fitness to serve, *Buchanan* 2027–2029.

The qualification for common jurors should be 12 *l.* in the country and 20 *l.* in towns, in addition to 30 *l.* general rating; belief that such a qualification would procure a sufficient number of jurors, *Murland* 2383, 2384. 2396–2399.

Favourable opinion of a mixed system of qualification, *Right Hon. M. Morris* 3167——Opinion of the inexpediency of a qualification of 12 *l.* made up partly of house property and partly of land, *Flynn* 4116, 4117.

Connaught Circuit. Low class of intelligence evinced by the juries on the Connaught Circuit, *Right Hon. M. Morris* 2985–2987.——Instances of the unsatisfactory nature of the verdicts returned, *ib.* 2987–2989.

Favourable opinion of the selection of jurors by the sheriff on the Connaught Circuit under the old Act, *Robinson* 3773, 3774.

Cooke, Michael. Report from Mr. Cooke, Clerk of the Baltinglass Union, relative to the qualifications to be required in jurors, and the amendments desirable in the Act of 1871, *App.* 315, 316.

Cope, Joseph D. (Analysis of his Evidence.)—Is clerk to the Rathdown Union, 5081——Evidence in contradiction of that given by Mr. Flynn as to the labour entailed upon clerks of unions by the preparation of the jurors' lists, 5082–5086——Detailed statement as to certain queries put to the clerks in connection with this service, 5084–5086.

Desirability of a fixed scale of remuneration for the duties of making up the jurors' book; opinion that 1 *s.* 3 *d.* per name should be the minimum rate, 5087, 5088. 5123–5127. 5169–5179——Statement that in very small unions the allowance of 1 *s.* 3 *d.* a name would be altogether inadequate, 5088. 5174–5178.

Cope, Joseph D. (Analysis of his Evidence)—*continued.*

Description of the duties of the clerks of unions in connection with the Jury Act, 5080, 5090. 5095. 5100, 5101. 5105–5112——Statement that a large proportion of jurors are not upon the Parliamentary Voters' Lists, notwithstanding that the qualification is higher for jurors than for voters, 5091–5099. 5103, 5104.

Payment of 100*l.* to witness, by the Board of Guardians, for making out the new book; 1*d.* an entry would have amounted to about 98*l.*, 5113, 5114. 5119–5122. 5125, 5126. 5139–5141——Calculation that it took three months to arrange the names, 5115, 5116. 5184——Utilisation of the paupers in the preparation of the list; system of remunerating them, 5118. 5231–5235.

Reduction of the original lists by about one-third, on account of the elimination of unqualified persons, 5128–5138——Belief that the labour of making out the lists in the future will not be materially reduced as regards the suburbs of Dublin on account of the number of changes of residence, 5143. 5226–5228——Expediency of having property represented in the jury box; opinion that owners as well as occupiers should serve as jurors, 5148–5153.

Approval of the qualification as laid down in the list for common and special jurors, 5154–5158——Increase of population in the county of Dublin since the census of 1861; 5159–5162——Onerous duties imposed upon the collectors; complaints by those officers of the small amount of remuneration paid to them by the grand jury, 5164–5168. 5180–5182.

Comparison drawn between the amount paid to witness for the jury list business and his salary as clerk of the union, 5183–5196——Examination as to the amount of remuneration to be paid for the copying work, 5197–5204——Opinion that the revision of the jurors' and the voters' lists could not be undertaken upon the same occasion, so as to save the expense of two journeys, 5205–5211——Statement of the duties developing upon the clerk of the unions in regard to the revision of the Parliamentary Lists, 5212–5225. 5236–5246——The printing expenses under the Act in the Rathdown Union amounted to 45*l.*, under contract, 5229, 5230——The average salary of clerks of unions in Ireland is between 120*l.* and 130*l.*, 5247.

Cope, J. D.—Report from Mr. Cope relative to the qualifications to be required in jurors, and the amendments desirable in the Act of 1871, *App.* 314, 315.

Cork. Wretched state of the jurors who attended at the last assizes in the county of Cork, *Right Hon. J. D. Fitzgerald* 3223. 3265.

Instances of improper conduct on the part of the bailiffs in the county in neglecting to serve summonses with a view to saving costs, *Johnson* 3575, 3576. 3657–3660——Few cases of fines being levied for non-attendance of jurors, *ib.* 3578–3580.

Considerable inconvenience arising from jurors having great distances to travel in the county of Cork; suggestions for obviating this inconvenience, *Johnson* 3582–3584. 3650–3656. 3684——Statement as to the rating qualification and the numbers of jurors available for assize purposes, *ib.* 3613. 3639–3641. 3681, 3682——Cause of the non-attendance of the gentry at the last assizes, *ib.* 3615, 3616.

Country Districts. Difference as regards intelligence between the jurors in Dublin and those in the country under the new Act; belief that the jurors who answered to their names in the country were not a fair specimen of those on the panel, *Molloy* 1705–1707.
See also Qualifications. Town Jurors.

Crime. Satisfactory state of Ireland as regards freedom from ordinary crime, *Right Hon. J. A. Lawson* 2945.

Criminal Cases. Strong opinion that in criminal cases the panel should contain more special jurors than in civil cases, *De Moleyns* 407–410——Belief that a system of special juries for criminal trials would be regarded in Ireland as the worst possible system of packing, *Armstrong* 788–856——Strong disapproval of the Crown having power to try a criminal case by a special jury, *J. Hamilton* 1089–1093——Evidence in opposition to the proposal to give the right to either side to call for special jurors in criminal cases, *Murland* 2413, 2414. 2464–2475.

Opinion that in the case of a special commission only it would be expedient to have a special jury in a criminal trial, *Right Hon. J. H. Monahan* 2714——Special juries may be granted to the prisoners in criminal cases when demanded, *Right Hon. J. A. Lawson* 2842, 2843——Occasional instances of partiality in juries in criminal cases, *Right Hon. J. Whiteside* 4281.

See also Agrarian Outrages. Ballot. Special Jurors, 2. Verdicts.

Croker-King, Charles. Report, of Mr. Croker-King relative to the working of the Jurors Act of 1871, and the qualifications desirable for common jurors and special jurors respectively, *App.* 319.

Crown, The. *See Challenge of Jurors.*

D.

De Moleyns, Thomas. (Analysis of his Evidence.)—Is a Queen's Counsel, and is chairman of the county of Kilkenny, and prosecutor for the city and county of Limerick, 329–331 ——Correct statement made by Mr. Hemphill in relation to the changes which have been effected in the law as to juries in Ireland, 332–334——Unsatisfactory results of cases tried at the last Limerick assizes; opinion, that the Act did not receive a fair trial upon the occasion, 335–342. 346, 347. 449. 457–460. 555, 556.

Considerable amount of prejudice against the Act, 338. 342. 555, 556——Absence of the better class of jurors at the Limerick assizes; strong observations made by Mr. Justice Fitzgerald thereon, 338–341. 347. 481–484——Special jurors of the county before the passing of the Act belonged to the highest class of country gentlemen and were remarkable for their intelligence and experience, 338. 340. 347. 557–561——Power of setting jurors aside by the Crown extensively used in a particular case at the Limerick assizes, 343–345.

Approval of the principle and conception of the new Act; opinion that jurors should be persons who are above the usual class of offenders, 348——Absence of any great objection on the score of want of qualification of the jurors under the old system, with the exception of the city of Dublin, 349, 350——Expediency of depriving the sheriff of the power of selecting jurors; possibility of an exercise of partiality under such system, 351–354. 509–513.

Propriety of considering the personal fitness of jurors as well as their rated qualification; deficiency in the Act in this respect, 355, 358. 429——Desirability of the chairman having power to go beyond the strict disqualifications in expunging the names of unsuitable jurors; revision by the chairman under the present system is purely nominal, 356–365. 430–436. 444–446. 456. 461. 587. 601——Advantage to the chairman of the assistance of the poor law collectors and the local crown solicitors when revising the jurors' lists, 358–360. 365. 495–498.

Inexpediency of giving the poor rate collector the power to put the word "objected" against the juror's name; information should be given by him to the chairman as to any objection, 359, 360. 377–380. 462–466. 587–589——Opinion that conviction for certain offences should disqualify a man from serving on a jury; information as to such convictions might be given to the chairman by the petty session clerks or by the constabulary, 361. 535–539. 619.

Statement that it is part of the duty of the chairman to revise the jury lists, 366–371——Inability to read and write should be considered a ground of disqualification; circumstances under which it is essentially necessary that a juror should be able to read and write, 372. 374. 447, 448. 505–507——Belief that educated intelligence is becoming very generally diffused throughout Ireland, 374, 375——Power of appeal should be given in the case of any objection against a juror, 375. 474. 554.

Contention that a publican should be positively excluded from serving on a jury, 376. 521. 523. 567——The duty of serving on a jury is more generally avoided than sought for, 381, 382. 471. 600. 609, 610——Uncertainty of jurors themselves coming forward to claim exemption, 382, 383——Expediency of adopting a qualification for a general juror of a net annual value of 12 *l.* for house and offices in a town, and 30 *l.* in the county, 384–388. 425. 489–491. 554–550——The limit of serving on juries should be once in a year and a half or two years, 386. 551, 552. 592–597.

Opinion that the grievance of frequent attendances should be subservient to raising the qualification, by which a more intelligent class of jurors would be obtained, 386. 597——Desirability of introducing a system of balloting in criminal cases; impression that before the present Act jurors were taken by ballot both in civil and criminal cases, 388–390. 450–453——Power of the judge to empanel juries in all cases but ejectment and land cases, 396–403——Strong opinion that in criminal cases the panel should contain more special jurors than in criminal cases, 407–410.

Question considered as to the expediency of compelling certain special jurors to serve on all cases; the advantage of the system lies in the fact of indiscriminate selection, 417. 604–606——Superior class of jurymen selected for the sessions as compared with the assizes, 418–422——Definition of a village in the meaning of the Act, 426–428——Necessity of the officials, whose duty it is to make objections to jurors being furnished with instructions; the chairman should have the power to give these instructions, 436–438. 586——Doubtful expediency of employing the constabulary in making objections to the qualifications of jurors; invidious character of such duty, 439–443.

Strong approval of the Act both in its principle and its conception, 454–456——Great advantage in the jurors being selected alphabetically from the list, 455——Unsuitability of an elected guardian of the union being appointed to make objections; opinion that such

Reports, 1873—*continued.*

De Molyns, Thomas. (Analysis of his Evidence)—*continued.*

such duty should be imposed on the poor law collector, 467–470. 582, 583——Expediency of giving the judge power to strike any one off the jurors' list upon proper representations of unfitness; extreme poverty should be one of the reasons for disqualification, 473. 474. 533.

Further evidence in favour of a higher rating qualification as being likely to result in a more intelligent class of jurymen, 475–477. 617——Suggestion as to the expediency of a lower age than sixty as the limit, 477–479——Numerous instances of houses being valued as low as 30 s. a year, which are upon lands valued to the extent of 60 *l.* and 70 *l.* a year, 492–494——Persons whose names have been struck off the lists should have power of appeal against the objection, 499–501.

Likelihood of persons being tampered with who are employed by the sheriff to summon jurors, 502——Difficulties in summoning jurors by means of registered letters; incompetency of the post offices to perform such a duty, 503. 526, 527. 607——Considerable expense thrown upon the sheriff in summoning jurors; opinion that the serving of summonses might be fairly performed by the constabulary, 503, 504. 526. 530, 531.

Evil of unqualified persons being upon the jurors' list obviated by the present system, 508——Chairman should have the power to exempt persons from serving who are either very poor or who have to come long distances to the sessions, 514–518. 533, 534——Convenience of a system of summoning jurors only who are resident in the neighbourhood of the court, 515–520.

Approval of the exemption of attorneys and bankers' clerks, and of veterinary surgeons, from serving on juries, 524. 540–543——Expediency of permitting exemptions by the chairman upon declarations made by the jurors themselves, and transmitted through the post, 537. 553——Remarkable instance of a notorious failure of justice at the Limerick assizes in a case of manslaughter under the new Jury Act, 562–565. 572–579. 598, 599.

Further evidence as to the method adopted in revising the jurors' lists by the chairman, 566–571——Opinion that no extra remuneration can be claimed by the poor law collector for the duty of stating objections to the chairman when revising the lists, 584–586. 590, 591——Further reference to the question of special jurors serving with common jurors in all ordinary cases, 604–608——Lists of persons entitled to serve on juries should be posted up in public places, 608.

Difficulty in carrying out any amendment in the law which would come into effect immediately; no alteration in the jurors' list could be made for two years unless an Act is passed in the present Session, 617–618——No difficulty in directing the sheriff to omit any name from the list, 616.

Disqualification. Difficulty in defining the crimes that entail disqualification from serving on juries, *Hemphill* 96, 97. 274–276——Opinion that conviction for certain offences should disqualify a man from serving on a jury; information as to such convictions might be given to the chairman by the petty sessions clerks or by the constabulary, *De Molyns* 361. 535–539. 619——Expediency of giving the judge power to strike any one off the jurors' list upon proper representation of unfitness; extreme poverty should be one of the reasons for disqualification, *ib.* 473, 474. 533——Evil of unqualified persons being upon the jurors' list obviated by the present system, *ib.* 508.

Statement as to the persons who should be disqualified from serving; information thereto should be given by the poor rate collectors and by the constables in charge of districts, *Battersby* 1458. 1565. 1568, 1569. 1629–1638——Absence of complaints by jurors when disqualified, *Right Hon. J. H. Monahan* 2625. 2647, 2648——Importance of the disqualifications and exemptions being in every case statutory, *ib.* 2635. 2643–2646.

Persons who have been subject to imprisonment for certain offences should be disqualified, *Right Hon. J. D. Fitzgerald* 3146. 3302–3305——Expediency of rendering exclusion from the jury a disgrace when connected with punishment for a crime; opinion that conviction for crime involving no moral turpitude should not entail disqualification, *ib.* 3302–3305——Suggestion for a seven years' disqualification of persons who have been convicted of certain offences, *Robinson* 3801.

See also Educational Qualification. Exemption. Pawnbrokers. Publicans.

Distant Jurors. Suggestions as to the course to be adopted with a view to relieving jurors who have to come a long distance, *Bottomley* 3400–3410. 3508–3517——Serious inconvenience imposed upon the jurors in being summoned to attend the quarter sessions from great distances, *Wilkinson* 3946–3948——Considerable expense in summoning jurors under the new Act, on account of distances to be travelled, *ib.* 4022–4024.

See also Summonses.

Donegal. Very inferior juries in Donegal under the Act of 1871; needy character of the jurors at the last assizes, *J. Hamilton* 1030. 1129. 1346, 1347.

Reports, 1873—*continued.*

Downshire. Unsatisfactory manner in which the revision of the lists for the County Down was carried out at the last assizes; absence of proper information to the chairman of the county as to the character of the panel, *Murland* 2371, 2372——Belief as regards the qualification necessary for a special juror, that in the County Down a 40 *l.* household qualification would give a sufficient number, *ib.* 2385, 2386——The lists should contain between 2,000 and 3,000 common and between 500 and 600 special jurors, *ib.* 2387.

Suggested alterations in the quarter sessions divisions; expediency of having the entire criminal business of each division transacted in the county town, *Murland* 2388, 2389. 2453. 2454——Expense of forming the jury lists in the county, *ib.* 2494–2499.

***Dublin* (*County and City*):**

1. *Special Juries.*
2. *Formation of the Panel.*
3. *Attendance.*
4. *Character of the Common Juries for the County and City respectively.*
5. *Qualification.*
6. *Preparation of Jury Lists.*
7. *Grand Jury.*
8. *Suggestions by Clerks of Unions for an Amendment of the Law.*

1. *Special Juries*:

Existence of a necessitous class of persons who serve in the city of Dublin on special juries for the sake of the guinea fee, *Hemphill* 25. 115. 143–147——Unsatisfactory character of the special juries in Dublin; absence of pressure upon the better classes with a view to compel them to serve, *Armstrong* 771, 772. 837–839. 1009; *J. Hamilton* 1135–1138. 1211–1213——Constant recurrence of the same juries in the Dublin courts; attendance on special juries chiefly on account of the guinea fee, *Right Hon. J. H. Monahan* 2607–2611——Certain amount of usefulness of the guinea-a-day jurors (or "guinea pigs"), *ib.* 2673–2681.

Remarkable ignorance and want of intelligence of the county special jurors; instances of men who had been in very humble positions, now on the special panels for the county, *Right Hon. J. Whiteside* 4223–4227——Limited class of special jurors before the present Act; moderate and judicious verdict given by them, *ib.* 4224–4227.

Instance in which the high sheriff was obliged to summon himself as a special juror; facility of remedying this difficulty in the Act of Parliament, *Ormsby* 4758. 4793–4796 —Useful character of the jurors who from serving constantly on the special juries have obtained the sobriquet of "guinea pigs," *ib.* 4803–4809. 4818.

2. *Formation of the Panel*:

Production of the special jury panel of the Court of Queen's Bench for the county of Dublin for Michaelmas Term, 1872; thorough acquaintance of witness with the persons composing the panel, *F. Hamilton* 4321–4325. 4336–4338——Statement of the religious denominations to which the persons composing the panel belong, *ib.* 4326–4328. 4349–4352——Favourable opinion as to the impartiality of the sub-sheriff in the selection of jurors to serve on the panel; opinion, notwithstanding, that the special jury panels have been more largely composed of Protestants than they should have been, *ib.* 4345. 4355. 4357. 4359.

Explanation that Mr. J. M. Williamson was the sub-sheriff who prepared the panel in the year 1872, which has been referred to by Mr. Hamilton, *Ormsby* 4723–4726. 4866, 4867. 4873. 4877——Absence of any complaint as regards the formation of the panels prepared by witness from a religious point of view, *ib.* 4727, 4728. 4780, 4781——Preponderance of Protestants on the jurors' book of the county of Dublin, *ib.* 4731–4738.

Impartial manner in which Roman Catholics have been summoned upon the special panels for the city of Dublin, *Ormsby* 4739–4749——Inexpediency of adopting the alphabetical system of selection in Dublin; grounds for this opinion, *ib.* 4750–4753——Statement that Mr. Darcy was the only high sheriff who interfered with witness in the formation of the panel, *ib.* 4810–4814.

3. *Attendance*:

Statement that the dereliction of attendance on the part of the higher class of jurors in Dublin has been chiefly caused by the non-imposition of fines by the judges, *Armstrong* 839. 1009——Disgraceful state of the jury panel in the city of Dublin; absolute necessity for the imposition of fines as a means for compelling a respectable class of jurors to attend, *J. Hamilton* 1135–1138. 1211–1213.

Examination as to the time in which the jury book would be exhausted, and as to the frequency of imposing service on the jurors, *Ormsby* 4765–4773. 4820–4829.

Instances

DUBLIN (COUNTY AND CITY)—continued.

4. *Character of the Common Juries for the County and City respectively:*

Instances formerly in Dublin of jurors asking for loans from counsel, *Hemphill* 149——Marked improvement in the common juries in the county and city of Dublin under the new Act, *ib.* 200–203——Excellent juries obtained in the county of the city of Dublin under the present system, *Armstrong* 809. 865, 866——Under the old system there have been waiters and domestic servants upon juries in the Four Courts, *Molloy* 1877, 1878.

Superiority of country jurors over those in Dublin under the old system; belief that the demand for the present Act is confined to Dublin alone, *Right Hon. M. Morris* 3062–3064——Unsatisfactory character of the Dublin jurors, *Robinson* 3769, 3770——Suggestions as to persons who should be exempted from serving; statement hereon, that one of Judge Keogh's servants is upon the special jurors' list in Dublin, *ib.* 3798–3800. 3839, 3840.

Cardinal distinction to be drawn between the jurors of the city and those of the county of Dublin; the former have been in every way satisfactory, *Right Hon. J. Whiteside* 4223, 4224. 4237, 4238——High class of intelligent jurors who reside in the county of Dublin, *Ormsby* 4850–4857.

5. *Qualification:*

Desirability of an exclusive household qualification for the county of Dublin; expediency of going much lower in the valuation if a strictly household qualification is adopted, *Ormsby* 4754–4756. 4837–4842——A high qualification in Dublin would result in a preponderance of Protestant jurors, *ib.* 4863–4865.

6. *Preparation of Jury Lists:*

Reduction of the original lists by about one-third on account of the elimination of unqualified persons, *Cope* 5128–5138——Belief that the labour of making out the lists in the future will not be materially reduced as regards the suburbs of Dublin, on account of the number of changes of residences, *ib.* 5142. 5226–5228——Increase of population in the county of Dublin since the census of 1861, *ib.* 5159–5162.

7. *Grand Jury:*

Nominal list of the grand jury of the county of Dublin, *App.* 326.

8. *Suggestions by Clerks of Unions for an Amendment of the Law:*

Reports from the clerks of the North Dublin and South Dublin unions, relative to the amendments required in the Act of 1871, *App.* 316, 317.

Duffy, Sir Gavan. Statement that Mr. (now Sir Gavan) Duffy, who is a Minister of State abroad, was saved by one dissentient juror from conviction, *Right Hon. J. Whiteside* 4318.

E.

EDUCATIONAL QUALIFICATION:

Concurrence of opinion in favour of disqualification in the case of a man unable to read or write, or to speak English, *Hemphill* 9–17. 85–88. 167–170. 256, 257. 307–314; *Armstrong* 779. 873–876. 956–959; *J. Hamilton* 1426; *Right Hon. J. H. Monahan* 2642–2644; *Right Hon. M. Morris* 3186.

Opinion that the word "objected" should be placed by the Poor Law collector before the name of any juror who is unable to read and write and speak English, and that the objection should then be inquired into by the chairman, *Hemphill* 41–49. 81–83. 152–157. 220–236. 281——Instance in which a whole jury might consist of persons incapable of reading and writing, *ib.* 90——Expediency of there being in the schedule to the Act an educational and a property disqualification, *ib.* 93, 94.

Inability to read and write should be considered a ground of disqualification; circumstances under which it is essentially necessary that a juror should be able to read and write, *De Moleyns* 372. 374. 447, 448. 505–507——Belief that a man who can read but cannot write would be a proper juror, *Caffey* 727, 728.

Decided opinion that the qualification for a juror should not be altogether dependent upon property, but that there should be also an educational qualification, *Armstrong* 766. 778. 779. 872. 877——The exclusion of unintelligent persons from the panel would not constitute a sufficient revision; ignorant jurors, however, do good by following the directions of the judge, *J. Hamilton* 1049——The effect of the system of ignorant juries has been to alarm the orderly and to encourage the disorderly part of the population, *ib.* 1142–1147.

Educational Qualification—continued.

Desirability of obtaining a considerable degree of intelligence as well as impartiality; opinion that a revision by the chairman will not secure sufficient intelligence, *Battersby* 1691–1693——Method to be adopted for ascertaining the illiteracy of jurors, with a view to their disqualification, *M'Grath* 2190–2195. 2223–2228. 2310–2313——Expediency of excluding from the jury list persons who are unable to read or write; with this addition the exemptions in the present Act are sufficient, *Murland* 2381–2383. 2407——Approval of disqualifying persons who are unable to read and write, and who have been convicted of certain crimes, *Johnson* 3604. 3611, 3612. 3683, 3684. 3694–3698.

Views of various poor law inspectors and clerks of unions in favour of the disqualification of persons who can neither read nor write, *App.* 301–321.

Conclusion of the Committee that persons unable to read or write the English language should be exempted from serving on juries, and that a judge should have the power of excusing a juror from serving in his court, *First Rep.* iii.

See also Meath. Qualifications.

Ejectment Cases. Power of the judge to empanel juries in all cases but ejectment and land cases, *De Moleyns* 396–403——Statement as to the failure of the Act in ejectment cases; inexpediency of changing the venue in such cases under the present Act, *Hamilton* 1412, 1413.

England (Assimilation of the Law). Opinion that the system of choosing jurors should be assimilated to the law of England in every particular, *Right Hon. M. Morris* 3006–3008——Emphatic objection to peculiar legislation for Ireland; further opinion that the law should be the same in both countries, *ib.* 3064——Decided opinion that the law of England as regards juries should be the same as in Ireland, *Right Hon. J. Whiteside* 4255. 4268–4271. 4308–4310. 4319.

Exemptions. Absence of difficulty in exempting jurors who can show any remote pecuniary or other interest in a cause to be tried, *Hemphill* 114——Inexpediency of destroying all exemptions; admission that a large number of intelligent jurors are eliminated by the present system of exemptions, *ib.* 162–165.

Uncertainty of jurors themselves coming forward to claim exemption, *De Moleyns* 382, 383——The chairman of the county should have power to exempt persons from serving who are either very poor, or who have to come long distances to the sessions, *ib.* 514–518. 533, 534——Approval of the exemption of attorneys' clerks, bankers' clerks, and of veterinary surgeons, from serving on juries, *ib.* 524. 540–543——Expediency of permitting exemptions by the chairman upon declarations made by the jurors themselves, and transmitted through the post, *ib.* 532. 553.

Expediency of exempting publicans and attorneys' clerks, *Coffey* 689–691——Opinion that law clerks and publicans should be exempted from serving; bank clerks, on the other hand, should not be exempted, *J. Hamilton* 1205–1207.

Approval of the exemption of law clerks, publicans, and domestic servants, *Battersby* 1508——Inexpediency of doing away altogether with the exemptions under the Act; grounds for this conclusion, *ib.* 1603–1609. 1674, 1675——Statement that some of the exemptions in the second schedule are on account of the interference with other public duties, *ib.* 1674, 1675.

Expediency of excluding publicans, illiterate persons, and attorneys' clerks from the panel; grounds for this conclusion, *M'Grath* 2189, 2190. 2196–2202. 2207. 2223–2228. 2310–2313——Opinion that the existing exemptions are not in any way too numerous, *ib.* 2203–2206——The chairman should have no further power of exemption than that allowed by the Act, *Murland* 2383, 2384.

Desirability of the judge having power by Statute to exempt or set aside a juror for sufficient cause; examination generally as to the class of persons who should be exempted from serving on juries, *Right Hon. J. D. Fitzgerald* 3245–3249. 3259–3261. 3268–3278. 3314–3317.

Advantage in disqualifying small farmers, as being the most unintelligent members of the community; also working tradesmen, who, though intelligent, cannot afford the expense of attending the assizes, *Johnson* 3613. 3640–3647——Approval of excluding small farmers from the jury list, on account of their want of intelligence, *Morphy* 3752–3758.

See also Age of Exemption. Disqualification.

Expenses (Jury List). Expenses of the jurors' list fall on the sheriff; those of the voters' list upon the county, *Hemphill* 133–137——Opinion that the expenses will not be so great under the new Act as they were under the old; detailed statement of the cost of preparing the jury list, *Buchanan* 2084–2090. 2114–2121. 2128–2130.

Absence

Expenses (Jury List)—continued.

Absence of any question at the last assizes as to the legality of grand juries paying the sub-sheriffs for additional trouble, *Right Hon. J. H. Monahan* 2763, 2764——Previous revision by the justices would lighten the duties of the chairman, and would save expense to the county, *Right Hon. J. A. Lawson* 2872, 2873——Expediency of the grand jury having power to pay the sub-sheriff for the expenses incurred by him attendant upon the Act, *Right Hon. M. Morris* 3142–3146.

Difficulties as to the payment of expenses in carrying out the new Act, *Bottomley* 3415–3419. 3423. 3424——Difficulties of the sub-sheriffs in obtaining any additional remuneration from the grand juries in consequence of the extra expenses thrown upon them, *Wilkinson* 4025, 4026——Statement that the expenses incurred in the working of the Act have been considerably more than was necessary; grounds for this conclusion, *Flynn* 4050–4063. 4065–4075. 4094–4096——Contention that the board of guardians is a more suitable body than the grand jury to arrange the payments to the rate collectors, *ib.* 4076–4078. 4081——Suggestions for the reduction of expenses under the Act; expediency of adopting a tariff rate of remuneration, *ib.* 4079–4082. 4092–4094. 4097–4101. 4103. 4104. 4155–4159——Hardship of imposing solely on the occupiers the expenses under the Act, *ib.* 4190–4192.

Proposition that the present Committee should fix a scale of fees for the sheriff, *Ormsby* 4759–4766. 4843. 4844. 4848, 4849.

Desirability of a fixed scale of remuneration for the duties of making up the jurors' book; opinion that 1 *s.* 3 *d.* per name should be the maximum rate, *Cope* 5087, 5088. 5123–5127. 5169. 5179——In very small unions the allowance of 1 *s.* 3 *d.* per name would be altogether inadequate, *ib.* 5088. 5174–5178——The remuneration paid to witness as clerk of Rathdown union by the board of guardians, for making out the new book, is 100 *l.*; 2 *d.* an entry would have amounted to about 98 *l.*, *ib.* 5113, 5114. 5116–5122, 5125, 5126. 5139–5141——Calculation that it took three months to arrange the names, *ib.* 5115, 5116. 5184——Utilisation of the paupers in the preparation of the lists; system of remunerating them, *ib.* 5118. 5231–5235.

Onerous duties imposed upon the collectors; complaints by these officers of the small amount of remuneration paid to them by the grand jury, *Cope* 5164–5168. 5180–5182——Comparison drawn between the amount paid to witness for the jury list business and his salary as clerk of the union, *ib.* 5183–5196——Examination as to the amount of remuneration to be paid for the copying work, *ib.* 5197–5204.

F.

Fay, John. See *Summonses (Attendance of Witnesses).*

Fenian Trials. Instance of partiality of a juror at the Mullingar assizes upon the occasion of the first conviction of a Fenian, *Battersby* 1462. 1661——Necessity, during the Fenian trials in Cork, of exercising the power of selection, by excluding improper persons from the jury panel, *Johnson* 3535–3567. 3689.

Fines (Non-attendance of Jurors). Considerable disinclination to serve on juries; imposition of fines in case of non-attendance is the only means to overcome such disinclination, *Hemphill* 116–118. 122. 127. 158, 159——Fines upon jurors go to the Queen through a process called "Green Wax," *ib.* 121——Fines are not levied upon jurors systematically; if so levied jurors would be more punctual in their attendance, *ib.* 122.

Imposition of fines necessary to ensure the attendance of jurors, *Battersby* 1455. 1475–1477——Desirability of imposing fines upon jurors who do not answer to their names; expediency of the judge having power to remit or increase the fine, *Robinson* 3836——Expediency of giving the judges power to impose moderate fines, *Right Hon. J. Whiteside* 4267——Fines are imposed upon recalcitrant jurors, but may be remitted by the judges upon satisfactory excuses being tendered, *Roche* 2513.

See also Attendance of Jurors.

Fitzgerald, Right Hon. John David (Analysis of his Evidence.)—Has been Judge of the Court of Queen's Bench for thirteen years, 3214, 3215——His experience as to the operation of the new Jury Act is confined to the Munster circuit, 3216, 3217——Opinion that for many years past there existed a strong necessity for an alteration in the law relating to juries; grounds for this conclusion, 3217–3223——The principal defect in the old Act was that there was no real revision, 3219–3221.

Statement that the present Act has, in admitting improper jurors, gone beyond what was anticipated when it was in the shape of a Bill before Parliament, 3221——Remarkable instance of a failure of justice in the county of Clare, 3221. 3297–3301——Instance of disagreement of a jury in the county of Limerick which called forth strong remarks from witness, 3221–3223——Wretched state of the jurors who attended at the last assizes in the county of Cork, 3223. 3265

Reports, 1873—*continued.*

Fitzgerald, Right Hon. John David. (Analysis of his Evidence)—*continued.*

Importance of bringing the humbler classes as much as possible into connection with the administration of justice; expediency, on this account, of resting the main qualification upon rating, 3223. 3239——Advisability of raising the qualification, and at the same time establishing a system of careful revision, 3224, 3295. 3309——Power of revision of the lists should be exercised by the chairman; inexpediency of entrusting this duty to the magistrates, 3225. 3285–3287. 3310, 3311.

Necessary information for the revision should be furnished to the chairman by the clerk of the peace and the clerk of the Crown; inexpediency of reverting to the system of selection by the sub-sheriff, 3226–3230. 3239. 3262, 3263. 3318——Decided opinion that the high sheriff should be charged with the framing of the panel, 3230. 3279. 3291. 3318–3320——Doubtful wisdom of adopting a system of selection by rotation, 3232.

Special qualifications other than rating necessary for putting a superior class of persons on the jury list, 3232–3234 — Expediency of the introduction of a proportion of special jurors into every jury for civil and criminal cases, 3234——Entire approval of the selection of jurors both in criminal and civil cases by means of the ballot, 3235, 3236. 3241, 3242. 3292–3294. 3307——Power of the Crown to set aside jurors cannot safely be dispensed with; beneficial clause in the present Act which removes that power from a private prosecutor, 3237, 3238.

Doubt as to any mischief from a system of alphabetical rotation through a preponderance of the same names, 3240. 3243, 3244——Strong opinion that the limit of age to entitle jurors to exemption should be raised from sixty to seventy years, 3243——Desirability of the judge having power by statute to exempt or set aside a juror for sufficient cause; examination generally as to the class of persons who should be exempted from serving on juries, 3245–3249. 3259–3261. 3266–3278. 3314–3317.

Statement that persons who have been subjected to imprisonment for certain offences should be disqualified, 3248. 3302–3305——Necessity for an alteration of the right of peremptory challenge by the prisoner; such right should not be interfered with in capital cases, 3250, 3251. 3257, 3258——Inexpediency of limiting the power of the Crown to order jurors to stand by, 3252. 3308.

Approval of accepting the verdict of the majority in civil cases only; remarkable instance in which an innocent man escaped a capital conviction by a majority of one, 3252–3256——Grounds for disapproving of a return to the system of selection by the sheriff, 3280–3282——Objection to the previous publication of the names of those jurors who will be upon the panel, 3283, 3284.

Examination as to certain observations by witness respecting the propriety of limiting the discretion of the sheriffs, 3288–3291——Expediency of rendering exclusion from the jury lists a disgrace when connected with punishment for a crime; opinion that conviction for crime involving no moral turpitude should not entail disqualification, 3302–3305.

Strong opinion as to the absolute necessity of imposing on some public officer the obligation of bringing before the chairman objections to particular persons, 3311, 3312——Belief that at the present time there is a general desire to avoid serving on juries; expediency of such feeling being altered by making it discreditable to be excluded from the list, 3313.

Evil of the present state of the law, whereby the responsibility which should be vested in the high sheriff is deputed to the sub-sheriff, 3319, 3320——Further statement as to the satisfactory character of the jurors at the last Clare assizes; large proportion of civil cases at these assizes, 3321, 3322——Strong disapproval expressed by Mr. Justice O'Brien relative to a case of acquittal in the county of Clare, 3323.

The only objection to be made against the Clare jurors was that they reappeared too constantly, 3324. 3325——A difficulty in the county of Kerry as to the panel was surmounted by the judge proposing to remit the case to the quarter sessions, 3326——Statement that though it would be an invidious duty to place the word "objected" against a juror's name, there is no real reason why it should not be done, 3327, 3328.

Fleming, John F. Report from Mr. Fleming, clerk of the Coleraine Union, relative to the qualifications to be required in jurors, and the amendments desirable in the Act of 1871, *App.* 311.

Flynn, Michael. (Analysis of his Evidence.)—Is clerk of the Poor Law Union at Strokestown, in the county of Roscommon, 4058——Preparation, by witness, of returns having reference to the working of the new Jury Act, 4059——Statement that the expenses incurred in the working of the Act have been considerably more than was necessary; grounds for this conclusion, 4060–4063. 4065–4075. 4094–4096.

Opinion that the remuneration paid to clerks of unions for duties under the Act has been an indirect way of making up their salaries; disapproval of this practice, 4063. 4071–4073——Description of the duties imposed upon clerks of the unions under the Act, 4064——Contention that the Board of Guardians is a more suitable body than the Grand Jury to arrange the payments to the rate collectors, 4076–4078. 4081.

Suggestions

Flynn, Michael. (Analysis of his Evidence)—*continued.*

Suggestions for the reduction of expenses under the Act; expediency of adopting a tariff rate of remuneration, 4079–4082. 4088–4094. 4097–4101. 4103. 4134. 4155–4159——Statement of the duties imposed upon the clerks of the peace by the new Act; special payments made to these officers by the Grand Jury, 4083–4091. 4132–4133. 4149–4154——Estimate of the expense necessary for preparing the list for the county of Roscommon, 4094–4101.

Information as to the expenditure necessary for printing the jury lists, 4102–4104——Proposal for obviating the difficulty of summoning jurors by the alphabetical system, 4105. 4141–4143——Disapproval of the outcry against the jurors who have attended under the new Act; argument that they will in time become fully qualified, being of the same standing as the Poor Law guardians, 4107–4109. 4118–4129.

Calculation that raising the qualification from 20 *l.* to 50 *l.* in the county of Roscommon would strike forty per cent. off the list, 4110. 4201–4203——Belief that a 12 *l.* house qualification in towns would give a high class juror; superiority of the town juror over the juror from the country, though the latter is rated much higher, 4111, 4112. 4115–4117. 4168. 4175, 4176.

Absence of necessity for any further revision of the lists; opinion that jurors who are not qualified will themselves take measures to be struck off the lists, 4113, 4114. 4178——Inexpediency of adopting a qualification of 12 *l.* made up partly of house property and partly of land, 4116, 4117——Examination as to the qualifications necessary for a Poor Law guardian; evidence in favour of their general intelligence and capacity, 4118–4130.

Impracticability of combining the jurors' and the voters' lists so as to save the cost of printing, 4136, 4137. 4216, 4217——Statement that the charge for printing the list of Parliamentary voters is about 1 *l.* per 100 names, 4138–4140——Annual transmission by the Valuation Office of lists of valuations in all the unions; poor rate books and warrants made out from this list, 4144–4148. 4160–4167.

Evidence as to the numbers of jurors which would be placed on the list by a household qualification of 6 *l.*, 8 *l.*, 10 *l.*, and 12 *l.* respectively in the county of Roscommon, 4170–4173——Variable nature of the qualifications for Poor Law guardians in different parts of Ireland, 4174. 4176. 4193–4200——Intimate knowledge of all the people in the unions possessed both by the clerks of the unions and by the rate collectors; facility of imparting this knowledge to the chairman when revising the lists, 4179–4182. 4218, 4219.

Objections upon the part of the people to serve on juries, 4183–4185——Black mail exacted under the old system by bailiffs by means of unauthorised summonses, 4185——Expediency of using the post office as a means for serving the jurors, 4186–4189. 4207–4212——Hardship of imposing solely on the occupiers the expenses under the Act, 4190–4192——Doubtful expediency of employing the police in summoning jurors, 4213–4215.

Foreman of Jury. Essential necessity for a rule by which the foreman of a jury should be selected by an officer of the court, and not by the jury themselves, *Buchanan* 1916–1920. 2038. 2068–2070——It is unnecessary to make it imperative upon the clerk of the crown to nominate the foreman of a jury, *Right Hon. J. A. Lawson* 2964–2967.

G.

Galway. Existence in Galway of special jurors rated as high as 300 *l.* a year, who were unable to speak English, *Right Hon. M. Morris,* 3027. 3033–3035——High character of the Galway jurors; impartial verdicts given by jurors in that county, whether Catholics or Protestants, *Robinson* 3772. 3862, 3863.

Graham, C. Report from Mr. Graham, clerk of the Irvinestown Union, relative to the qualifications to be required in jurors, and the amendments desirable in the Act of 1871, *App.* 312.

Grand Jury. Selection of the grand jurors from the special jurors' lists by the sheriffs *Hemphill* 6, 7——The grand jury at the assizes is drawn from all parts of the county; while that for the quarter sessions is taken from the immediate district, *ib.* 107, 108——Persons of social position chosen to act on grand juries, irrespectively of rating qualification, *Coffey* 660, 661.

Statement as to the duties of the grand jury at the quarter sessions, *Buchanan* 2076–2082——Inexpediency of doing away with the grand jury at quarter sessions, *Morland,* 2455, 2456——Approval of exempting grand jurors from serving on common juries, *Bottomley* 3394. 3395.

Decided opinion that a quarter sessions grand juror should not be exempted from serving at the assizes as a special juror, *Johnson* 3585——Extraordinary instance of ignorance upon the part of the grand jury for the county of Dublin, *Ormsby* 4751–4755. 4783–4791. 4830–4836.

Reports, 1873—*continued.*

Griffith's Valuation. The rating qualification for the county is now based upon Griffith's valuation; opinion that if the valuation be changed at all, it ought to be considerably augmented, *Buchanan* 2054–2057.

H.

Hamilton, Frederick. (Analysis of his Evidence.)—Is a practising solicitor in Dublin; has for seventeen years conducted the revision of the Parliamentary Voters' Lists for the county of Dublin, 4320. 4323—Production of the special jury panel of the Court of Queen's Bench for the county, for Michaelmas term 1872; thorough acquaintance of witness with the persons composing that panel, 4321–4325. 4336–4338.

Statement of the religious denominations to which the persons composing the Dublin panel belong, 4326–4328. 4349–4352——Production by witness of the order postponing the trial of O'Keeffe *versus* Cullen, the notice for trial, and the notice declining to withdraw the notice for trial, 4330–4335——Preponderance of Protestants over Roman Catholics on the special jurors' book; absence of any reference to the case of O'Keeffe *versus* Cullen, in the formation of that particular panel, 4339–4344. 4356.

Favourable opinion of the impartiality of the sub-sheriff in the selection of jurors to serve on this panel; opinion, notwithstanding, that the special jury panels have been more largely composed of Protestants than they should have been, 4345–4355. 4357–4359.

Hamilton, James. (Analysis of his Evidence.)—Is a Queen's Counsel, and has been Chairman of the county of Sligo for five years, 1016, 1017. 1114——Considerable experience of witness as to the operation of the new Jury Act, 1019——Opinion that the present Act is an excellent one, in so far as the preparation of the jury lists is concerned, 1020——Approval of the substitution of rating for the old qualification, 1021——Statement that the revision in the chairman's court is a mere mechanical operation, 1022.

Strong disapproval of the change of system by depriving the sub-sheriff of the power of selecting the panel, 1023. 1048. 1066. 1095. 1100. 1119, 1120——The operation of the present Act has created a burlesque of justice; general inferiority of the new to the old Act, 1024. 1096–1098. 1101. 1111, 1112——Deterioration of the juries under the new Act; contemptuous tone adopted by counsel when addressing them, 1028–1033——Verdicts given by juries in obedience to the judge, or else in accordance with their own prejudices or fears, 1034, 1035.

Almost entire agreement with the principles laid down by Mr. Serjeant Armstrong for the improvement of juries, 1036——Expediency of raising the qualification under the new Act; desirability of introducing a compound qualification composed of a rating of 40 *s.*, and a land qualification of 30 *l.*, 1036. 1038–1041. 1084–1086——The exclusion of improper persons from the jury-box should be in the preparation of the panel by the sub-sheriff, 1037–1040. 1043. 1102, 1103. 1107–1109.

Disapproval of the alphabetical process of selection, 1045. 1110——Impossibility of purging the jurors' book by any practicable means so as to leave no improper person on the panel, 1046–1048——Elimination of improper persons from the panel must be carried out in private by a responsible official, 1048——The exclusion of unintelligent persons from the panel would not constitute a sufficient revision; statement that ignorant jurors often do good by following the directions of the judge, 1049.

Necessity of adopting some means whereby Ribbonmen, Fenians, and Orangemen should be excluded, 1050, 1051——Explanation that the special and general panels are prepared without reference to any particular case, 1052——Security for impartial jury by means of a system of challenging by the Crown solicitor; inexpediency of exercising such power too largely, 1053——Instance of an acquittal for murder on account of relations and friends of the prisoner being upon the jury, 1058.

Further evidence as to the probity and impartiality of the sub-sheriffs; challenges to the array a strong safeguard against the malconstruction of a jury, 1060–1062. 1065. 1070, 1071. 1081——Expediency of giving the judge power to name the triers in the case of a challenge to the array, 1062, 1063.

Statement that Perrin's Act became inapplicable on account of the diminution of freeholders and leaseholders, 1066——Opinion that the duty of serving on juries should not be confined to persons living contiguous to the assize towns, but that all men should serve in their turn, 1067, 1068——Instance in which a remarkable challenge to the array was drawn by witness, 1072–1078. 1082.

Impossibility of bringing the Irish peasantry to a belief in the impartiality of the law by any change in the present system, 1079, 1080——Importance of relieving jurors from constant attendance, 1088——Strong disapproval of the Crown having power to try a criminal case by a special jury, 1089–1093——Difficulties in the way of revising the lists by the chairman, and of obtaining information from the county officers for the purposes of such revision, 1115–1118.

Opinion that the grievance to the jurors is more from the fact of their being put upon the

Hamilton, James. (Analysis of his Evidence)—*continued.*

the list than from being expunged from it, 1121——Needy character of the jurors at the last Donegal assizes, 1122.

[Second Examination.]—Additional safeguards suggested against the mal-construction of the jury panel; high approval of Perrin's Act as a means for amending and forming the panel, 1125–1133. 1162. 1209, 1210. 1214, 1215——Further disapproval of the change in the jury law by the Act of 1871; 1134——Disgraceful state formerly of the jury panel in the city of Dublin, absolute necessity for the imposition of fines as a means for compelling a respectable class of jurors to attend, 1135–1138. 1211–1213.

Further observations as to the ignorance displayed by the jurors in the country; fortunately for the interests of justice the verdicts were those of the judges, 1139–1141. 1170. 1247——The effect of the system of ignorant juries has been to alarm the orderly and to encourage the disorderly part of the population, 1142–1147——Liability of the present class of jurors to intimidation on the part of secret societies, 1143–1148.

A larger attendance on the part of the higher class of jurors would not prevent disagreement as regards the verdict; inexpediency of having a jury of gentlemen to try a peasant, 1149–1152——The right of the Crown to try certain cases by a special jury would be inconsistent with the principle of trial by jury, by which a man is tried by his peers, 1153–1155.

Considerable difficulties in exercising the power of selection; impossibility of the chairman having sufficient knowledge to revise the lists, 1156–1160——Impropriety of a system by which the chairman should revise the lists in secret; opinion that such an arrangement would be degrading, and would throw odium upon the administration of justice, 1160. 1348, 1349. 1424, 1425.

Strong evidence as to the impartiality and moderation of the sub-sheriffs; belief that there is no unfavourable prejudice against the preparation of the panel by them, 1161–1167. 1169. 1227–1232. 1298–1301. 1350–1354. 1372–1378. 1393–1404. 1422, 1423. 1434, 1435——Statement that the offices of Crown Solicitor and Crown Prosecutor are invariably the rewards of political services, but no suspicion ever attaches itself to them on that account, 1168, 1169——Extraordinary instance of an unjust verdict found by a jury in the county of Roscommon, 1171. 1304–1306.

Statement that the burden of service upon juries is not equally distributed by the system of alphabetical rotation, 1172–1175——Letter from the firm of Carson Brothers, complaining that both members of the firm had been summoned to serve on juries on the same day, 1176——Notwithstanding the obvious inconvenience of the alphabetical system, it is highly expedient that mercantile men should be compelled to serve on juries, 1177.

Expediency of a power to clear the panel of bad men, and to avoid inconveniences to individuals; belief that no sheriff would summon two members of the same firm, 1178——Power of a judge to excuse a juror from attendance; power also to fine him for non-attendance when summoned, 1179–1188——Desirability of summoning every man on the panel who has not served, before any juror is summoned for the second time, as is proposed by the English Bill, 1189, 1190.

Curious effect of Perrin's Act that in the county of Dublin it was as prejudicial as it was beneficial in the city, 1191–1193——The abuse of the administration of that Act had the effect of encouraging speculative actions, and so degrading the legal profession; opinion that there is no security in the present Act against the recurrence of similar abuses, 1193, 1194.

Contention that the present Act is self-acting, and that it is incapable of being administered, 1195–1198——Further statement that the challenges to the array have been of very rare occurrence; ridiculous system of the appointment of tiers, 1200, 1201. 1371. 1377–1389——Belief that the service of the summons might be undertaken by the Post Office with advantage; inexpediency of employing the constabulary upon such duty, 1202, 1203.

Further evidence as to the complaints made by jurors as to the great distances that they were obliged to travel; recommendation that no juror should be summoned to attend at quarter sessions out of his own division, 1204——Opinion that law clerks and publicans should be exempted from serving; bank clerks, on the other hand, should not be exempted, 1205–1207.

Condemnatory evidence given by Mr. Fausset before the House of Lords as to the jurors summoned under Judge Perrin's Act in the county of Sligo, 1217–1221——One of the means to secure strict impartiality would be to keep off the panel men who would not honestly do their duty, 1225, 1226. 1249——Evidence in approval of the jurors of of the county Sligo, 1234——Statement as to the intellectual capacity of the jurors in the various towns that witness has been professionally engaged in, 1235–1243. 1317, 1318.

Hamilton, James. (Analysis of his Evidence)—*continued.*

Removal from office of the high sheriff of the county Monaghan for the reason that he would not dismiss the sub-sheriff because a challenge to the array had succeeded at Monaghan, 1250–1257——Circumstances under which this challenge to the array was made, 1258–1269. 1308–1315. 1432, 1433——Examination as to the expediency of having twelve Protestants or Orangemen upon a jury, 1273–1282.

Absence of practical difficulty in arriving at the fact as to whether a man is a Ribbonman or an Orangeman, 1284——Further statement as to the desirability of raising the qualification as proposed by Mr. Serjeant Armstrong; strong opposition, however, to his suggestion as to the revision of the lists by the chairman, 1285, 1286.

Opinion that the sheriff should form the panel without reference to alphabetical order; expediency of retaining the old system on account of the difficulty of getting a fair jury under the proposed qualification, 1288–1297——The adoption of the principle by which the Crown may try all serious cases by special juries will do away altogether with the necessity for selection, 1302, 1303.

With regard to certain comments by the judges on the course pursued by the sub-sheriff in selecting juries at Cavan, witness submits that the juries under the old system were very fair, 1318, 1319——Novel expedient adopted at Omagh to obtain conviction in the case of a trial for riot between Protestants and Catholics, 1322–1326——Further statement as to the remarkable challenge to the array drawn by witness, 1327–1334——Under the old system the sub-sheriff had theoretically but not practically the power of packing the panel, 1335, 1336.

Examination as to the numbers of jurors it would be practicable to obtain in the county Antrim; inferior character of jurors in the county Donegal, not one half of those on the list being fit to serve, 1340–1347——Inconvenience in the alphabetical system by which the jurors' book might in some cases consist of but one letter, 1355–1359.

Practice of the judge in civil cases to cause a juror who is shown to be interested to stand aside, 1368–1371——Possibility of there being good grounds for an objection to a panel which would, however, be incapable of proof; in the majority of instances the objection would be capable of proof, 1390–1392.

Examination as to the extent to which the Crown would have to exercise the power of setting jurors aside under the present Act, 1405–1411——Further statement as to the failure of the Act in ejectment cases; inexpediency of changing the venue in such cases under the present Act, 1413, 1413.

Process by which the sub-sheriff frames the jury panel; qualification for the duty by reason of his thorough knowledge of the residents in the county, 1414–1421——Unanimity in juries should be invariably required in criminal cases; possible expediency of accepting in civil cases a majority if concurred in by the judge, 1426.

Opinion that a system of having a certain number of special jurors upon every jury would have a tendency to prevent unanimity, 1427——Expediency of disqualifying any man who could not read or write, 1428.

Further statement that one of the greatest causes of the failure of justice is the sympathy or terrorism evinced by the jury, 1429, 1430——Advantage of interesting as many people as possible in the administration of the law, 1431.

Hamilton, Richard T. Report by Mr. R. T. Hamilton, poor law inspector, relative to the qualification desirable in jurors, and the amendments required in the Act of 1871, *App.* 305, 306.

Hamilton William. Report from Mr. Hamilton, clerk of the Castlederg Union, relative to the qualifications to be required in jurors, and the amendments desirable in the Act of 1871, *App.* 309, 310.

Hamilton, William James. Report by Mr. W. J. Hamilton, poor law inspector, relative to the working of the Jurors' Act of 1871, and the qualifications desirable for common jurors and special jurors respectively, *App.* 302–305.

Hemphill, Charles Hare. (Analysis of his Evidence.)—Is a Queen's Counsel, and chairman of the county of Kerry, 1, 2——Considerable experience of witness as to the practical working of the Jurors' Act, Ireland, 3——Opinion that the Act has worked well as regards the selection of jurors; intelligence displayed by the jurors, both grand and petty, under the new system, 4–7. 106. 138–142. 171——Selection of the grand jurors from the special jurors' lists by the sheriff, 6, 7——Petty jurors at Quarter Sessions under the new system belong more to the agricultural and farming class than was the case formerly, 8.

Strong opinion in favour of disqualification in the case of a man unable to read or write or speak English, 9–17. 85–88. 167–170. 307–314——Suggestion that there should be a higher household qualification for special and common jurors, 18. 28–32. 250——Expediency of a higher test for special juries; facility of adopting these suggestions without alteration in the present Act, *ib.* 18. 28——Descriptions of the qualifications under

Hemphill, Charles Hare. (Analysis of his Evidence)—*continued*.

under the old Act; honorary qualifications under the old nearly the same as under the new Act, 19–22. 112.

Opinion that an ex-grand juror, or an ex-sheriff should be qualified as a special juror, 22——The principle of the present Bill is that the poor law valuation is made the basis of the qualification; approval of such basis, 23. 26——Machinery by which the old qualifications were ascertained; unsatisfactory nature of such machinery, by which persons were put upon the jurors' book who were totally devoid of property qualification, 24. 113. 143.

Impossibility of objecting to a juror on the ground of want of qualification after his name has been placed on the list, 25——Existence of a mercenary class of persons who serve in the city of Dublin on special juries for the sake of the guinea fee, 25. 115. 143–147——The household qualification should be quite distinct from rating; the qualification for a common juror might be from 12 *l.* to 15 *l.*, and for a special juror from 25 *l.* to 30 *l.* a year rent, 29–31. 208. 252.

Opinion that a house does not improve in proportion to the increase of valuation of a farm, 30. 199. 218, 219——Household qualification would have the effect of adding in county towns intelligent persons to the panel, 32. 210–217——Fitness of jurors not to be tested so much by raising the valuation or the qualification, as by giving the chairman of quarter sessions more power in forming the list, 33. 34. 40–41. 92, 93——Revision of the jury lists under the old system by the magistrates, under the new by the chairman of quarter sessions; considerable advantages resulting from the latter arrangement, 35–39.

Opinion that the word "objected" should be placed by the poor law collector before the name of any juror who is unable to read and write and speak English, and the objection then inquired into by the chairman, 41–49. 81–83. 152–157. 220–236. 261——The chairman of quarter sessions should be empowered to strike off the name of any juror upon full proof of his unfitness, 50–52. 150, 151. 177, 178——Decided approval of the clause depriving the sheriff of discretion in summoning jurors; general idea in Ireland that in a political trial the sheriff would select a jury for a special purpose, 53–61. 104–111. 204–206. 277, 278, 281–289.

Statement as to the position held by the sub-sheriffs in Ireland, 57–59——Additional labour and expense thrown upon the sheriff by the present Act; great distances to which he is obliged to send to serve summonses personally, 62. 131–137. 237–243——Under the old Act the sheriff might select any juror on the list; selection under the new law abolished, and the jurors summoned alphabetically, 63–70——Instances in which the jurors can only be selected from certain divisions, and not from the county generally, 68–70.

Expediency of serving summonses by means of registered letters to jurors at a distance, as is the practice in the county and the city of Dublin, 71–80. 119, 120. 166. 179, 180. 194, 195——Opinion that the judges should have power to strike off the name of a juror whom they considered unfit to serve, 84–88——Three operations to be gone through before a jury is got into the box; jurors selected by ballot for the trial of a civil cause, 89.

Instance in which, a whole jury might consist of persons incapable of reading and writing, 90——Crown counsel can order jurors to stand aside without alleging any cause in trials for felony, 91. 130——Formation of the general jurors' book should be entirely in the hands of the chairman of quarter sessions; expediency of there being in the Schedule to the Act an educational and a property disqualification, 93, 94.

Difficulty in defining the crimes that entail disqualification from serving on juries, 96, 97. 274–276——Decided opinion that publicans should be exempted from serving, inasmuch as they are intimately connected with the witnesses and friends of the prisoners, 98, 99. 160, 161. 185–189——Veterinary surgeons are entitled to be exempted, 100.

Improbability of selecting interested jurors by adopting the dictionary order; abundant power of the court to change the venue on the slightest suggestion of partiality, 101–104. 278–280——The grand jury at the assizes is drawn from all parts of the county; while that for the quarter sessions is taken from the immediate district, 107, 108——Advantage of the present system, by which a juror will not be summoned more than once in three years in a large county, 110, 111. 244–247.

Absence of difficulty in exempting jurors who can show any remote pecuniary or other interest in a cause to be tried, 114——Considerable disinclination to serve on juries; imposition of fines in the case of non-attendance is the only means to overcome such disinclination, 116–118. 127. 158, 159——Proof of sending a registered letter should be *primâ facie* evidence against a juror that he had received it, 120.

Fines upon jurors go to the Queen through a process called "Green Wax," 121——Facility by which jurors can obtain information as to whether their names are upon the lists or not; lists of jurors posted on all the chapels through the district, 123–126——

Reports, 1873—*continued.*

Hemphill, Charles Hare. (Analysis of his Evidence)—*continued.*

Jurors struck off the list as a matter of course if they can prove that they are above sixty years of age, 128, 129.

Great advantage in having an admixture of classes in ordinary juries; power over the verdict exercised by one or two leading minds, 130——Impossibility of making a common list for the qualifications of a voter and a juror, 131, 132——Expenses of the jurors' list fall upon the sheriff; those of the voters list fall upon the county, 133–137——Very objectionable class now found on the special jury list, 143–149——A rating of 50 *l.* a year to the poor rate is, however, some check to necessitous persons getting on the special list, 148, 149.

Inexpediency of destroying all exemptions; admission that a large number of intelligent jurors are eliminated by the present system of exemptions, 162–165——Larger amount of publicity given to the revision by the chairman of quarter sessions than could possibly be given by the magistrates, 173–176——Selection of jurors by the sheriff does not in any way dispense with the necessity of exercising the right of challenge by the Crown Solicitor, 181–184.

Strong opinion that attorneys' clerks should be exempted from serving on juries, 190–193——Marked improvement in the common juries in the county and city of Dublin under the new Act, 200–203——Impossibility in some rural districts of getting a household test on account of the valuation being so very low, 248, 249——Further evidence in favour of giving a general discretion to the chairman of quarter sessions to strike off the name of unsuitable jurors from the list, 253–255.

Further statement as to the expediency of giving the judge power to set a juror aside who is unable to read or write or speak English, 256, 257——Inexpediency of imposing a penalty upon the poor rate collector for lists improperly made out; suggestions with regard to insuring the lists being correctly made, 258–273——Reference to certain evidence of Mr. Seed to the effect that the former selection by the sub-sheriff was very unsatisfactory, 285–289——Special jurors withdrawn from the list as regards civil causes, but remain on it for criminal purposes, 290–298.

Opinion in favour of unanimity of juries; inexpediency of the verdict of the majority being accepted, 299–306. 318——Contention that in Ireland there would be no fear of special jurors in agrarian or political cases becoming marked men, 319, 320——Suggestions with regard to the insertion of special jurors in the general jurors' book, 321–328.

Hepburn, George. Report from Mr. Hepburn, clerk of the South Dublin Union, relative to the qualifications to be required in jurors, and the amendments desirable in the Act of 1871, *App.* 317.

High Sheriff. Non-interference in the selection of the panel by the high sheriff; impossibility for an official in his position to perform the duty satisfactorily, *Coffey* 642. 705–708——Approval of an arrangement by which the high sheriff would sign the panel with his own hand, *Battersby* 1612. 1647, 1648——Non-interference by the high-sheriff with the jury panel, on account of his not possessing sufficient local knowledge, *M'Grath*, 2151–2153.

Importance of imposing on the high sheriff the duty of examining and certifying as to the correctness of the panel; statement hereon that the sheriff is the only officer who is entirely independent of the Crown, *Robinson* 3819. 3821. 3824–3826. 3857–3860. 3882–3885. 3888——Non-interference at present of the high sheriff in the formation of the panel, *Robinson* 3819. 3823; *Wilkinson* 4029–4031.

Decided opinion that the high sheriff should be charged with or responsible for the framing of the panel, *Right Hon. J. D. Fitzgerald* 3232. 3279. 3291. 3318–3320——Concurrence in the opinion that the high sheriff should examine and certify as to the impartial selection of the panel, *Right Hon. J. Whiteside* 4237.

See also Monaghan. Sheriffs, or Sub-Sheriffs.

Hill, Alexander. Report from Mr. Hill, clerk of the Glenties Union, relative to the qualifications to be required in jurors, and the amendments desirable in the Act of 1871, *App.* 308, 309.

Hoey, J. R. Suggestions by Mr. Hoey, clerk of the Lisnaskea Union, relative to the qualifications of jurors, and the amendments desirable in the Act of 1871, *App.* 312.

Home Circuit. Satisfactory character of the jurors at the last assizes on the home circuit; from those assizes there was not a single new trial motion, *Right Hon. J. H. Monahan* 2612–2621. 2635–2642. 2655–2664.

Horsley, Samuel. Report by Mr. Horsley, Poor Law Inspector, relative to the qualification desirable in jurors, and the amendments required in the Act of 1871, *App.* 305.

Household Qualification. Suggestion that there be a higher household qualification for special and common jurors, *Hemphill* 18. 28–32. 250——Facility of adopting this suggestion

Household Qualification—continued.

tion without causing alteration in the present Act, *Hemphill* 18–28——The household qualification should be quite distinct from rating; the qualification for a common juror might be from 12 *l.* to 15 *l.*, and for a special juror from 25 *l.* to 30 *l.* a year rent, *ib.* 29–31. 208. 252.

Opinion that a house does not improve in proportion to the increase of valuation of a farm, *Hemphill* 30. 199. 218, 219——Household qualification would have the effect of adding in county towns intelligent persons to the panel, *ib.* 32. 210–217——Impossibility in some rural districts of getting a householder test on account of the valuation being so very low, *ib.* 248, 249.

Numerous instances of houses being valued so low as 30 *s.* a year, which are upon lands valued to the extent of 60 *l.* and 70 *l.* a year, *De Moleyns* 492 494——Opinion that the rating qualification under the new Act is too low; expediency of a household franchise, by which a valuable class of jurors is obtained, *Coffey* 647–652.

Favourable opinion of a compound rating qualification; a household qualification is a surer test of intelligence than that of land or other property, *Armstrong* 810–814. 961–963——The minimum household qualification should be 10 *l.* or 12 *l.*; belief that with such a qualification there would be an ample number of jurors, *ib.* 811–815. 817. 966——Approval of house qualification for special jurors, *Molloy* 1767–1776.

Advantages of a simple household qualification in towns, *Right Hon. M. Morris* 3153–3160——Preference for the household qualification pure and simple, on the ground that a man with a decent house will probably make a good juror, *ib.* 3155–3160.

Return of the number of all houses or residences valued at 6 *l.* and upwards in rural districts, and at 12 *l.* and upwards in cities and towns, *App.* 290——Returns containing details relative to the number of houses in rural districts, and in cities and towns respectively, and in counties and provinces, classified according to different rates of value, *ib.* 291–293.

See also Compound Qualification. Qualifications.

Hume, T. Borris, M.D. Report from Dr. Hume, clerk of the Ballymoney Union, relative to the qualifications to be required in jurors, and the amendments desirable in the Act of 1871, *App.* 313. 314.

Hunter, W. P. Suggestions by Mr. Hunter, clerk of the Newtownlimavady Union, relative to the qualifications of jurors, and the amendments desirable in the Act of 1871, *App.* 311, 312.

I.

Interested Jurors. Instances under the old system by which a jury could have been obtained to order; withdrawal by witness of a case from trial in consequence of the state of the panel, *Armstrong* 799–837——Instance of an acquittal for murder on account of relations and friends of the prisoner being upon the jury, *J. Hamilton* 1058——Practice of the judge in civil cases to cause a juror who is shown to be interested to stand aside, *ib.* 1368–1371.

Intimidation. Liability of the present class of jurors to intimidation on the part of secret societies, *J. Hamilton* 1143–1148——One of the greatest causes of the failure of justice is the sympathy or terrorism evinced by the jury, *ib.* 1429, 1430.

J.

Jameson, Edward. Report from Mr. Jameson, clerk of the Carlow Union, relative to the qualifications to be required in jurors, and the amendments desirable in the Act of 1871, *App.* 314.

Johnson, Joseph B. (Analysis of his Evidence.)—Has been sub-sheriff of the county of Cork for fifteen years, 3560, 3561——Considerable experience of witness in the formation of jury panels both at the assizes and the sessions, 3562——Method adopted in selecting the jurors under the old system; statement that the sub-sheriff possessed an almost absolute power of selection, 3563, 3564——Necessity during the Fenian trials of exercising the power of selection by excluding improper persons from the jury panel, 3565–3567. 3689.

Strong disapproval of reverting to the old system; grounds for this conclusion, 3568–3572. 3614. 3618——Invidious position in which the sheriff was placed by possessing the power of selection; hostile feeling on the part of the people engendered by the exercise of this power, 3571–3573. 3624–3633——Reference to the possibility of suspicion being

Reports, 1873—*continued.*

Johnson, Joseph B. (Analysis of his Evidence)—*continued.*

being cast upon the irresponsible selection of the panel by the sheriff as a reason for a change in the system, 3573, 3574. 3619–3623. 3687–3693.

Instances of improper conduct on the part of the bailiffs in neglecting to serve summonses with a view to saving costs, 3575, 3576. 3657–3660——Few cases of fines being levied in witness' county for non-attendance of jurors, 3578–3580——Considerable inconvenience arising from jurors having great distances to travel in the county of Cork; suggestions for obviating this inconvenience, 3581–3584. 3650–3656. 3684.

Expediency of having two jurors' books, one for sessions and the other for assize purposes; higher qualification necessary for assize jurors, 3582–3584. 3617. 3656. 3684——Decided opinion that a quarter sessions' grand juror should not be exempted from serving at the assizes as a special juror, 3585——Suggestions as to overcoming the difficulty of the presence on the list of a preponderance of names commencing with the letters "C" and "M," 3586–3591.

Expediency of selecting the panel in "dictionary" and not in alphabetical order, 3591——Augmentation of trouble and expense in summoning the jurors under the new system, 3592, 3593——Absence of objection to serving by registered letters; suggestions as to other modes, 3594–3597——Slight alteration required in the amount of the present rating qualification, 3598–3602.

Variety of qualifications essential for special jurors, 3603. 3638——Approval of disqualifying persons who are unable to read and write, and who have been convicted of certain crimes, 3604. 3611, 3612. 3683, 3684. 3694–3698——Opinion that the revision of the lists should be entrusted first to the magistrates and then finally to the chairman, 3604–3611. 3662–3666. 3685, 3686——Revision at petty sessions would be attended by no appreciable expense, 3608–3610.

Further evidence as to the rating qualification and the numbers of jurors available in Cork for assize purposes, 3613. 3639–3641. 3681, 3682——Expediency of disqualifying small farmers, as being the most unintelligent members of the community, and working tradesmen, who, though intelligent, cannot afford the expense of attending the assizes, 3613. 3640–3649——Cause of the non-attendance of the gentry at the last Cork assizes, 3615, 3616.

Statement that if the power of selection be restored to the sheriff, the present Act must be repealed, 3634–3637——Suggestion as regards revision being aided by Poor Law guardians; opinion that a revision by the chairman of the county at quarter sessions would not be attended by the jurors, 3667–3679——Desirability of giving the judge at the assizes power to discharge any juror from attendance, 3680——If worked according to the alphabetical system, the Act will leave no ground of suspicion against the sheriff, 3692, 3693.

Johnson, W., M.P. Examination as to the trial of Mr. Johnson, the member for Belfast, for taking part in an illegal procession, *Right Hon. M. Morris* 3076. 3209–3213——Belief that the conviction of Mr. Johnson had a material result in his being returned for Belfast immediately afterwards, *ib.* 3210.

Judges. Concurrence in the opinion that the judges should have power to strike off the name of any juror whom they may consider unfit to serve, *Hemphill* 84. 88; *Armstrong* 96c. 975; *Molloy* 1702; *Right Hon. J. H. Monahan* 2770——Power to strike the name of a juror off the list for sufficient cause should be given to the judge or to the chairman of the county, *M'Grath* 2208–2213——Practice of the judge to excuse a juror when necessary, *Right Hon. J. Monahan* 2649–2652.

Objection to any additional power being given to the judge or the chairman as to ordering a juror to stand by, *Right Hon. J. A. Lawson* 2860–2864.

Disapproval of giving the judge power to discharge a juror from service except for very sufficient cause; argument that a judge should have nothing to do with the jury panel, *Robinson* 3832, 3833. 3861, 3862——Further examination as regards the power of the judge to excuse jurors from attendance; necessity for defining in the Act the cases in which he should exercise that power, *ib.* 3892–3924——Disapproval of giving the judge this power, as well for his own sake as for the sake of the proper administration of justice, *ib.* 3895–3901. 3907.

Statement of the cases in which a judge should have power to excuse a juror from serving, *Robinson* 3903–3908——Inherent power in the judge to excuse jurors above a sufficient number for the purposes of the assizes, *ib.* 3911–3915——Decided opinion that whatever decision a judge arrives at as regards excusing a juror should be stated in open court, *ib.* 3921. 3922——Expediency of giving the judge absolute power in many cases in the event of the dictionary order system of selection being established, *ib.* 3924.

Strong disapproval of the judge having power to exclude any juror on account of his political opinions, or for any other cause than physical infirmity, *Right Hon. J. Whiteside* 4264, 4265. 4282–4288.

Reports, 1873—*continued.*

Juries Act (Ireland), 1871. See *Act* 34 & 35 *Vict. c.* 15.

Juries (Ireland) Act, 1873. Recommendation that a temporary Bill be immediately passed for amending the Act of 1871, in certain particulars, in order that the jurors' books may be corrected so as to be available at the approaching quarter sessions and assizes, *First Rep.* iii.

Passing of the proposed Bill in accordance with the previous recommendation of the Committee, *Second Rep.* iv.

Anticipated necessity of the examination of witnesses as to the practical operation of the Act; recommended re-appointment of the Committee next Session for this purpose, *Second Rep.* iv.

See also Legislation.

Jury Lists (generally). Facility by which jurors can obtain information as to whether their names are upon the lists or not; the lists are posted on all the chapels throughout the district, *Hemphill* 123–126——Inexpediency of imposing a penalty upon the poor-rate collector for lists improperly made out; suggestions with regard to insuring the lists being correctly made, *ib.* 258–273.

Lists of persons entitled to serve on juries should be posted up in public-houses, *De Moleyns* 608— Opinion that the present Act is an excellent one, in so far as the preparation of the jury lists is concerned, *J. Hamilton* 1020——The grievance with jurors arises more from the fact of their being put upon the list than from being expunged from it, *ib.* 1121.

Defects of the new system under the Act of 1871; great carelessness exhibited in making out the lists, *Molloy* 1708–1714. 1829–1845. 1859——Suggestions as to the examination of the lists previously to their coming before the court; expediency of informing jurors that their names have been placed on the lists, *Buchanan* 1921——Opinion that the jury list, when carefully revised, might be allowed to remain in force for two years, *Rt. Hon. J. A. Lawson* 2820. 2943——Expediency of the special and general jurors' books being separate, as a means of economising the numbers of the special jurors, *Wilkinson* 3949.

See also Area (Jury Lists). Clerks of the Peace. Clerks of Unions. Expenses. Legislation. Notice to Jurors. Number of Jurors. Objections to Jurors. Printing Expenses. Responsibility. Revision of Jury Lists. Special Jurors. Voters' Lists.

K.

Kerry. Satisfactory working of the Act of 1871 in the county of Kerry, *Hemphill* 4–8——A difficulty in the county as to the panel was surmounted by the judge proposing to remit the case to the quarter sessions, *Right Hon. J. D. Fitzgerald* 3326.

Challenge to the array at the Kerry Assizes on account of the jurors having been summoned from one barony and not from the whole county; they were, however, excellent jurors, *Murphy* 3708–3711. 3727. 3758, 3759.

Knight, John. Report from Mr. Knight, clerk of the Omagh Union, relative to the qualification to be required in jurors, and the amendments desirable in the Act of 1871, *App.* 310.

L.

Lacy, George. Suggestions by Mr. Lacy, clerk of the Navan Union, relative to the qualifications of jurors, and the amendments desirable in the Act of 1871, *App.* 315.

Lawson, Right Hon. James Anthony. (Analysis of his Evidence.)—Has been judge of the Court of Common Pleas for four or five years; went the North East Circuit at the last assizes, 2765–2769——Unfavourable opinion of the new Juries Act; illiterate and unintelligent character of the jurors at the last assizes, 2770–2775. 2781–2783. 2851–2854. 2865, 2866. 2877–2880. 2887. 2952——Heavy character of the business at the last Belfast assizes, 2770–2772. 2784. 2932–2934.

Large attendance of jurors at Belfast, in consequence of which there was no imposition of fines upon those absent; opinion that the better class should be compelled to attend, 2777, 2778——Disposition of the jurors who attended to find fair verdicts; advantage in having had one or two intelligent men on nearly every jury, 2779, 2780. 2785. 2865. 2885, 2886. 2893–2896. 2927. 2960, 2961——Opinion in favour of raising the qualification; expediency of introducing a diversity of qualifications, 2786–2791. 2796. 2836. 2876.

Reports, 1873—*continued.*

Lawson, Right Hon. James Anthony. (Analysis of his Evidence)—*continued.*

Excellent qualifications in Sir John Coleridge's Bill which might be adapted to Ireland, 2787–2791——Disapproval of a selection by alphabetical arrangement; instance in which such selection of names interfered with the administration of justice, 2793. 2794. 2900–2907. 2931——Considerable injury to the special jury system by the Act; every man who is rated at 50 *l.* is now on the special jury panel, 2795. 2805–2807.

Strong opinion that there must be, somewhere, a power of selection, and a power of striking off illiterate, incompetent, and improper persons, 2796–2804. 2888, 2889. 2962, 2963——Evidence as to the partiality of the sheriff in selecting the panel, 2808–2811. 2828. 2867, 2868. 2924——Stringent revision necessary upon the abandonment of the system of selection by the sheriff, 2812.

Officials who should be charged with this revision; power should be given to the magistrates to strike off a juror without stating a reason, 2813–2817. 2819, 2860. 2870–2872. 2914——Expediency of sending a juror notice through the post on the occasion of his being first placed on the list, 2817, 2818. 2823. 2916. 2936–2938——Opinion that the jury list, when carefully revised, might be allowed to remain in force for two years, 2820. 2943.

The revision of the lists should not be undertaken privately, but in open court, 2822. 2942——Suggestions as to the process of forming the panel; proposed division of the jurors' book into fifties, from which numbers the panel should be selected by the sheriff, 2825–2833. 2928–2931——Desirability of framing a temporary measure pending a reconsideration of the whole question, 2834. 2835——Higher class of intelligence in jurors from towns than in those in the country, 2837–2840.

Favourable opinion as to taking the verdict of the majority; importance of assimilating the law of Ireland to that of England on the subject, 2841——Special juries may be granted to the prisoners in criminal cases when demanded, 2842, 2843——The great majority of the jurors in the county of Antrim are small farmers; the smallness of the holdings accounts for the absence of a superior class at the assizes, 2844–2850.

Disapproval of any additional power being given to the judge or the chairman as to ordering a juror to stand by, 2860–2864——Increased necessity for the Crown to order jurors to stand by consequent upon the new system of alphabetical selection, 2869——Previous revision by the justices would lighten the duties of the chairman, and save expense to the county, 2872, 2873.

Inexpediency of diminishing the right of a prisoner to challenge, 2874——Disinclination of witness to argue any question as to the confidence of the people in the administration of the law, 2910–2914——Opinion that the chairman would not have information for the purpose of revising the lists equal to that possessed by the magistrates, 2911——Satisfactory state of Ireland as regards freedom from ordinary crime, 2945.

It is unnecessary to make it imperative upon the clerk of the Crown to nominate the foreman of a jury, 2964–2967——Further statement as to the advantage of the sheriff selecting the jury panel in fifties, 2970–2974——Opinion that the sub-sheriffs are not inclined to incur responsibility, and that they would simply summon the jurors as they found them, 2974——Decided opinion that if there be a proper expurgation of the list originally the power of selection by the sheriff will be practically given up, 2975–2977.

Leasehold Qualification. Evidence as to the suitability of leasehold qualification, *Battersby* 1589–1591.

Legislation. Difficulty in carrying out any amendment in the law which would come into effect immediately; no alteration in the jurors' lists would be made for two years unless an Act is passed in the present session, *Dr Molyneux* 612–618——Suggestions for amending the present system before the next assizes, *Coffey* 692–696. 703, 704; *Armstrong* 1003–1006. 1010, 1011——Decided opinion that the sooner the law is altered the better; suitability of the present time for carrying out the necessary changes, *Battersby* 1626.

Any general amendment of the law would not be possible for a considerable time; feasibility of passing a temporary measure to come into operation before the next assizes, *Molloy* 1718, 1719. 1735. 1805. 1822–1829. 1846, 1847. 1858, 1859.

Desirability of framing a temporary measure pending a reconsideration of the whole question, *Right Hon. J. A. Lawson* 2834, 2835——Decided opinion that a temporary Act is necessary to ensure that the law will be properly administered at the next assizes; belief that there would be no difficulty in passing a general Act with the same object, *Right Hon. M. Morris* 3045–3049——Examination as to certain jury bills brought in by various Attorneys-general, *ib.* 3107–3113.

Opinion that for many years past there has existed a strong necessity for alterations in the law relating to juries; grounds for this conclusion, *Right Hon. J. D. Fitzgerald* 3217–3223——Explanation as to the principles of the Bills introduced by witness when Attorney-general, *Right Hon. J. Whiteside* 4253, 4254. 4304–4307.

See also Juries (Ireland) Act, 1872.

Reports, 1873—*continued*.

Leinster Circuit. Fair and reasonable verdicts found by the juries on the Leinster circuit under the new system, *Hemphill* 7——Systematic challenge of the respectable jurors by the prisoners on the Leinster circuit; expedient adopted by the Crown solicitor to counteract this practice, *Right Hon. J. Whiteside* 4230.

Leitrim. Peculiar position of Leitrim county as regards the number of small holdings; opinion that if the 100 *l.* qualification were adopted in the county, there would be no possibility of obtaining a special jury, *Molloy* 1787–1792. 1795. 1855–1857——Town qualification in county of Leitrim should not be different from the rest of Ireland, *ib.* 1854——Impossibility of adopting a high qualification for the county, *Right Hon. M. Morris* 3037. 3041.

Limerick. Unsatisfactory results of cases tried at the last Limerick assizes; opinion notwithstanding that the Act did not receive a fair trial upon the occasion, *De Moleyns* 335–342. 346, 347. 449. 457–469. 555, 556——Absence of the better class of jurors at the assizes; strong observations made by Mr. Justice Fitzgerald thereon, *ib.* 338–341. 347. 481. 484——Special jurors of the county, before the passing of the Act, belonged to the higher class of country gentlemen, and were remarkable for their intelligence and experience, *ib.* 338. 340. 347. 557–561.

Power of setting jurors aside by the Crown extensively used in a particular case at the Limerick assizes, *De Moleyns* 343–345——Remarkable instance of a notorious failure of justice at the assizes in a case of manslaughter, under the new Jury Act, *ib.* 562–565. 572–579. 598, 599.

Unsatisfactory operation of the present Act at the last assizes; low and unintelligent class of jurors which attended, *Roche* 2503–2508. 2533, 2534. 2586–2595——Expediency of raising the qualification in the county by 50 *l.*; the existing qualification of 12 *l.* for the city should not be disturbed, *ib.* 2509–2517——Statement as to the number of jurors on the panel in Limerick, *ib.* 2583–2588.

Instance of a disagreement of a jury in the county which called forth strong comments by witness, *Right Hon. J. D. Fitzgerald* 3221–3223.

Londonderry County. Fairly good juries in this county, though they have deteriorated under the Act of 1871, *J. Hamilton* 1030, 1031.

Lower Classes. Belief that the humbler classes are most anxious to be relieved from the duty of serving on juries; serious hardship imposed on them by being detained at quarter sessions towns, *Robinson* 3797.——*See also Public, The.*

M.

M'Farland, D. Report from Mr. M'Farland, clerk to the Gortin Union, relative to the qualifications to be required in jurors, and the amendment desirable in the Act of 1871, *App.* 309.

M'Grath, William Henry. (Analysis of his Evidence.)—Is Crown Solicitor for the counties of Fermanagh and Tyrone, 2135–2137——Opinion that the selection of the jury panel by the sheriff was open to great objection; grounds for this conclusion, 2138–2143. 2218–2220. 2265–2267——Statement that the same jurors were to be found from year to year at the assizes in Tyrone; complaints by the jurors of the hardship of having to serve so often, 2144–2147.

Superior class of jurors in the counties of Clare and Limerick to those placed on the panel in Fermanagh and Tyrone, 2148–2150. 2232–2234——Non-interference by the high sheriff with the jury panel, on account of his not possessing sufficient local knowledge, 2151–2153——Unsatisfactory working of the present jury Act; approval, however, of its principle, 2154, 2155.

Absence of proper revision of the jury lists; jurors of advanced age excused upon their own application, 2155–2160——Opinion that a 30 *l.* rating in the counties, and from 12 *l.* to 15 *l.* in towns generally throughout Ireland, would give an intelligent class of jurors, 2162–2165. 2214–2217. 2236–2238. 2253. 2254. 2288. 2292. 2305–2309. 2314–2318.

Expediency of adding to the panel certain persons of good position who do not possess a property qualification, 2166–2171——Desirability of giving the Crown and the prisoner equal rights to demand a special jury; opinion that the prisoner would not apply for the privilege so often as the Crown, 2172–2176. 2183–2188. 2245–2250. 2284–2286.

Frequent exercise by witness of the power to order jurors to stand by; means of acquiring the knowledge necessary for such action, 2177–2182. 2268–2280——Expediency of excluding publicans, illiterate persons, and attornies' clerks from the panel; grounds for this conclusion, 2189, 2190. 2196–2202. 2207. 2223–2228. 2310–2313——Method to be adopted for ascertaining the illiteracy of jurors, 2190–2195——Exclusion of doctors

Reports, 1873—*continued.*

M'Grath, William Henry. (Analysis of his Evidence)—*continued.*

under the present law; opinion that the existing exemptions are not in any way too numerous, 2203–2206.

Power to strike the name of a juror off the list for sufficient cause should be given to the judge or to the chairman, 2208–2213——Statement as to the power of revision necessary for the proper formation of the jury list, 2229–2231——Disinclination felt by persons of high standing to serve on juries; opinion that there is no hardship in requiring the attendance of such persons twice a year, 2239–2244.

Examination as to the effect of alphabetical selection on the attendance of jurors; occasional advantage in having jurors from a distance, 2255–2264——Absence of any necessity to make a distinction between "towns" and "villages" as regards qualifications, 2291–2307——Approval of a system of serving summonses by means of the constabulary, and not through the post office, 2319–2322. 2327, 2328.

Opinion that the juror should have notice that his name has been placed on the list, 2326——Apprehensions as to the verdicts given by jurors of the class required by the present law, 2329–2334——Suggestion that all prisoners should be sent for trial to the county town as a means of saving expense, 2335–2344.

Approval of having a certain number of special jurors upon all juries, 2345, 2346——Duty of giving the chairman information for the revision of the lists should devolve upon the clerk of the peace, 2347–2351.

M'Kennan's Trial (*Monaghan*). Successful challenge to the array in the case of M'Kennan, charged with the murder of Clarke; the result of this challenge was that the high sheriff was removed, because he would not dismiss Mr. Mitchell, the sub-sheriff, *Reilly* 4421–4427. 4452——Examination as to the character of the panel from which the M'Kennan jury was selected, *ib.* 4428–4431.

Statement as to the venue for the trial of M'Kennan having been changed, *Reilly* 4453–4466. 4475–4481——Want of impartiality the ground upon which the panel was quashed; admission by the sub-sheriff that he was an Orangeman, *ib.* 4467–4474——Statement that upon the change of venue in the case of M'Kennan he was tried in Louth by twelve Roman Catholics, *ib.* 4638–4644.

M'Menamin, David. Report from Mr. M'Menamin, clerk of the Strabane Union, relative to the qualifications to be required in jurors, and the amendments desirable in the Act of 1871, *App.* 310.

M'Vaughan, Charles. Suggestions by Mr. M'Vaughan, clerk of the Ballycastle Union, relative to the qualifications of jurors, and the amendments desirable in the Act of 1871, *App.* 313.

Magistrates. Non-attendance of the magistrates upon the juries in the county Monaghan, *J. Reilly* 4682, 4683.——*See also* *Revising Jury Lists*, 3.

Meath. Ludicrous conduct of the juries at the last assizes for the Home Circuit; the foreman of a special jury at Trim was unable to write, *Battersby* 1442–1445——Under the old law the foremen of this jury would have been a gentleman of education and property, *ib.* 1445–1447.

Meldon v. *Lawless.* Remarkable instance of corruption, in the case of Meldon v. Lawless, *Right Honourable J. H. Monahan* 2706–2711.

Mercantile Classes. Notwithstanding the obvious inconvenience of the alphabetical system, it is highly expedient that mercantile men should be compelled to serve on juries, *Hamilton* 1177.

Millar, Andrew. Report from Mr. Millar, clerk of the Stranorlar Union, relative to the qualifications to be required in jurors, and the amendments desirable in the Act of 1871, *App.* 307.

Mitchell, William. (Analysis of his Evidence.)—Holds the office of sub-sheriff of the county of Monaghan, 4879–4881——Explanatory statement in regard to the marks placed opposite the names of Roman Catholics in the jurors' book referred to by Mr. Reilly, 4882–4884. 4997–5002. 5019——The jury panel that was quashed was a counterpart of that for the preceding assizes, with the addition of fifty special jurors, 4885–4891. 5025.

Examination as to the composition of the 1869 panel with regard to religion; statement that there were forty-nine Roman Catholics out of 250; 4892–4897. 4903–4907. 4914. 4927–4930. 5003. 5019–5023. 5031, 5032. 5037–5048. 5076, 5077——Promiscuous arrangement of the Roman Catholics on the 1869 panel, 4898–4903——Principle which actuated witness in his selection of jurors, 4909–4913. 4977–4980.

Non-attendance of jurors from the barony of Farney; denial of Mr. Reilly's statement that all the Farney jurors were at the end of the panel, 4916–4923. 4932–4944——Opinion

Reports, 1873—*continued.*

Mitchell, William. **(Analysis of his Evidence)—*continued.***

Opinion that with a few exceptions the new Act has worked very fairly; approval of a 20 *l.* qualification for common, and a 50 *l.* qualification for special jurors, 4944, 4925. 5071, 5072.

Difficulty which exists as to summoning jurors; desirability of employing the constabulary upon that duty, 4925, 4926. 4996——Correspondence of witness with Mr. Rogers contradicting statements by Mr. Reilly as to the formation of the Monaghan panel in the year 1864; 4945-4959——Examination as to the number of Roman Catholics on the panels from the year 1861 to 1869; 4960-4976.

Decided opinion that religion should never be considered in selecting jurors for the panel, 4980. 5023——Satisfaction of witness at being relieved from the responsibility of forming the panels, 4981, 4982——Expediency of entrusting the selection of suitable persons to serve on juries to some official, 4983. 4994, 4995——Description of the formation of the county jurors' book under the old Act; indiscriminate power of selection in the hands of the sheriff, 4984-4993.

Statement that the dictionary arrangement in making out the new book has worked fairly, 4994——Opinion that it is more probable that a jury will be selected from the first seventy names than from the last seventy names on the panel, 5008-5018——The panel for the summer assizes of 1869 was almost identical with that for the year 1868; 5024-5030——Admission that upon the special jury panel at the spring assizes of 1869, there was but one Roman Catholic, 5031-5039. 5044.

Existence of strong party feeling in Monaghan after contested elections, 5050, 5051——Orange proclivities of witness; statement that some Orangemen were upon the 1869 panel, 5053-5065——Non-interference by the high sheriff with the arrangements of witness for selecting jurors from the book, 5066-5069——Unlimited power of the Crown to challenge jurors; right of the prisoner to challenge twenty peremptorily, 5074-5080.

Mixture of Classes. Great advantage in having an admixture of classes in ordinary juries; power over the verdict exercised by one or two leading minds, *Hemphill* 130——Admixture of classes upon the jury panels under the old system; frequent appearance of magistrates upon juries, *Coffey* 629, 630. 633. 744. 759.

Molloy, Constantine. **(Analysis of his Evidence.)**—Is a practising barrister and a member of the Home Circuit, 1697——Witness drafted the Juries Act in conjunction with Mr. White and Dr. Hancock, 1698, 1699. 1754-1758——Considerable objections to the old system; absolute necessity for change in the law, 1700-1703——Well-founded complaints as to the manner in which the panel was formed by the sheriff, 1704.

Difference as regards intelligence between the jurors in Dublin and those in the country under the new Act; belief that the jurors who answered to their names in the country were not a fair specimen of those on the panel, 1705-1707——Causes of the defects of the new system; great carelessness exhibited in making out the lists, 1708-1714. 1829. 1845. 1869.

Revision of the lists the duty of the chairman under the Act; necessary information regarding the jurors to be given by the clerks of the unions and the poor law collectors, 1711-1714——Desirability of raising the qualification for common jurors in counties to 30 *l.* and in towns to 12 *l.*; the town qualification to include house and garden, 1715, 1716. 1736. 1741. 1806. 1850-1853. 1869.

Any general amendment of the law would not be possible for a considerable time; feasibility of passing a temporary measure to come into operation before the next assizes, 1718, 1719. 1735. 1805. 1819-1829. 1846, 1847. 1858, 1859——Correction of the jury lists for the next assizes would be the only possible amendment; means by which this revision could be carried out, 1720-1733. 1816, 1817. 1839-1844. 1859. 1875. 1879, 1880.

Opinion that the proposed correction of the lists could be accomplished in less than a week, 1726——The temporary correction of the lists would not involve the insertion of any new names, 1734, 1735—— Expediency of giving the judge at the next assizes power to set aside a juror on account of unfitness, 1738——Division of qualification for special jurors into six classes, this division necessarily having regard to the number of jurors to be obtained, 1739, 1740. 1777. 1837, 1838.

Belief that under all circumstances unfit jurors will occasionally be returned on the panel; in such cases the Crown should have the right to order them to stand by, 1742-1745. 1796-1799——History of the manner in which such right was acquired by the Crown; paper handed in on the subject, 1743-1745. 1754.

Facility with which the Crown solicitors can inform themselves of the character of the panel previous to the assizes, 1746. 1800-1804——Rules for the guidance of Crown solicitors as to the duty of directing jurors to stand by, 1746, 1747——Statistical information afforded by Dr. Hancock as to the numbers of jurors under the raised qualifications, 1748, 1749.

Molloy, Constantine. (Analysis of his Evidence)—*continued.*

Clause in the new Act by which Mr. Serjeant Armstrong's objection as to a view-jury is obviated, 1750–1752——Statement that the system of praying a *tales* is the same under the new as it was under the old Act, 1753——Changes made by the House of Commons in the qualifications as laid down by the House of Lords, 1760–1766——Approval of house qualification for special jurors, 1767–1776.

Contention that the qualification for common jurors in the Act is too low; grounds for this conclusion, 1778–1786. 1813–1815——Peculiar position of Leitrim county as regards the number of small holdings; opinion that if the 100 *l.* qualification were adopted in the county there would be no possibility of obtaining a special jury, 1787–1792. 1795. 1855–1857——Inexpediency of adopting the same uniform rule as to qualifications for all counties, 1793–1795.

Belief that the cause of the absence of the better class of jurors at the last assizes was a desire on their part to bring discredit upon the new Act, 1807. 1830–1835——Opinion that the rating qualification is the best means to be adopted for the selection of jurors, 1808–1812——Examination as to the possibility of the better class of jurors absenting themselves on account of disinclination to associate with the very low class that were summoned, 1832–1836.

Admirable manner in which the lists of Parliamentary voters are made out by the clerks of unions; argument therefrom that those persons should be charged with the duty of preparing the jurors' lists, 1845–1849——Statement that town qualifications in the county of Leitrim should not be different from the rest of Ireland, 1854——Evidence in opposition to the suggestion that the old law should be reverted to until the necessary amendments in the new Act can be carried out, 1860–1871——Under the old system there have been waiters and domestic servants upon juries in the Four Courts, 1877, 1878.

Facility in forming the panel by alphabetical selection, 1881. 1886——Contention that no difficulty would arise from the occasional preponderance of names commencing with the same letter, 1883–1888.

Molloy, Mr. Memorandum by Mr. Constantine Molloy, dated 2nd March 1871, on the subject of the right of the Crown to challenge jurors, *App.* 298–300.

Molloy, E. Report from Mr. E. Molloy, clerk of the Naas Union, relative to the qualifications to be required in jurors and the amendments desirable in the Act of 1871, *App.* 315.

MONAGHAN:

Removal from office of the high sheriff of the county of Monaghan for the reason that he would not dismiss the sub-sheriff because a challenge to the array had succeeded, *J. Hamilton* 1250–1257——Circumstances under which this challenge to the array was made, *ib.* 1258–1269. 1308–1315. 1452, 1453.

Statement that the proportion of Roman Catholics in the county of Monaghan is about three to one as regards other denominations; the population of the county is about 112,000, *Reilly* 4366, 4367. 4585–4587——Formation of the panel by witness when sub-sheriff, according to the religious denominations of the persons on the jury lists, *ib.* 4371–4376. 4604–4609. 4628. 4670–4672——Complaints as to partiality in the formation of the panel by Mr. Mitchell, who was sub-sheriff of the county for several years up to 1869, *ib.* 4377–4382. 4405. 4499. 4591–4603.

Statement in detail of the grounds for dissatisfaction with Mr. Mitchell, *J. Reilly* 4388 *et seq.*——Correspondence with the high sheriff and the sub-sheriff on the subject of returning an impartial panel for the year 1869 assizes; subsequent communication with the Lord Lieutenant, *ib.* 4435–4441——Position of the Farney jurors, who are chiefly Roman Catholics, at the end of the panel, *ib.* 4440–4448. 4571–4574——Information as to the rating valuation of the jurors upon the panel, *ib.* 4449–4451. 4645–4668——Significant fact that in the jurors' book for the year 1869 there is a cross placed against the name of every Roman Catholic, *ib.* 4489–4498. 4578–4580. 4610–4627.

Examination as to the number of jurors required for the purposes of the assizes and the quarter sessions for one year; statement of the numbers available under certain ratings, *Reilly* 4510–4521. 4715, 4716. 4718–4720——Average number of cases tried at the assizes and quarter sessions; opinion that 1,124 jurors is not too large a number for these trials, *ib.* 4522–4545. 4710——The higher the rating so much the more does the Protestant element preponderate, *ib.* 4568–4570. 4581–4584——The average of the jurors called upon to serve has been about one-half of those summoned, *ib.* 4711——Instance in which the challenges by a prisoner exhausted the panel, there not being a sufficient number of jurymen present, *ib.* 4712–4714.

Explanatory statement in regard to the marks placed opposite the names of Roman Catholics in the jurors' book referred to by Mr. Reilly, *Mitchell* 4882–4884. 4997–5002. 5019——The jury panel that was quashed was a counterpart of that for the preceding assizes, with the addition of fifty special jurors, *ib.* 4885–4891. 5025——Examination as to the composition of the 1869 panel with regard to religion; there were forty-nine Roman

Monaghan—continued.

Roman Catholics out of 250, *Mitchell* 4892–4897. 4903–4907. 4914. 4927–4930. 5003. 5019–5023. 5031, 5032. 5037–5048. 5076, 5077——Promiscuous arrangement of the Roman Catholics on the 1869 jury panel, *ib.* 4898–4903.

Process of forming a jury from the panel; principles which actuated witness in his selection of jurors, *Mitchell* 4909–4913. 4977–4980——Non-attendance of jurors from the barony of Farney; denial of Mr. Reilly's statement that all the Farney jurors were at the end of the panel, *ib.* 4916–4923. 4932–4944——Correspondence of witness and Mr. Rogers contradicting statements by Mr. Reilly as to the formation of the panel in the year 1864, *ib.* 4945–4959.

Examination as to the number of Roman Catholics on the panels from 1861 to 1869, *Mitchell* 4960–4976——Opinion that it is more probable that a jury will be selected from the first seventy names than from the last seventy names on the panel, *ib.* 5008–5018——The panel for the summer assizes of 1869 was almost identical with that for the year 1868, *ib.* 5024–5030.

Admission that upon the special jury panel at the spring assizes of 1869 there was but one Roman Catholic, *Mitchell* 5032–5039. 5044——Orange proclivities of witness; statement that some Orangemen were upon the 1869 panel, *ib.* 5053–5065——Non-interference by the high sheriff with the arrangements of witness for selecting jurors from the book, *ib.* 5066–5069.

See also M'Kennan's Trial.

Monahan, Right Hon. James Henry. (Analysis of his Evidence.)—Has been chief justice of the Court of Common Pleas in Ireland for twenty-two years, 2596. 2597——Large experience of witness in the operation of the former Jury Act, 2598, 2599——Considerable amendment required in the old Act; great evil in the fact that the sheriff had uncontrolled discretion in the election of the panel, 2600, 2601. 2696. 2706–2711. 2715–2719. 2753–2755.

Undoubted partiality in the selection of the panel under the old system; great importance that the people should have confidence in the administration of the law, 2602–2605. 2682–2685. 2754. 2755——Challenge to the array has never occurred in the experience of witness, 2606——Constant recurrence of the same juries in the Dublin courts; attendance on special juries chiefly on account of the guinea fee, 2607–2611.

Satisfactory character of the jurors at the last assizes on the home circuit; statement that from those assizes there was not a single new trial motion, 2612–2621. 2639–2642. 2655–2664——Expediency of disqualifying persons who are unable to read and write, 2622–2624——Absence of complaint by jurors when disqualified, 2625. 2647, 2648——Desirability of raising the qualification, so as to secure higher intelligence, and of providing a more stringent revision by which unsuitable persons would be struck off the lists, 2626, 2627.

Approval of the Chairman's Court as a court of revision; opinion that the chairman should decide by fixed rules, and should not act upon his own discretion, 2628–2634. 2737–2742——Importance of the disqualifications and exemptions being in every case statutory, 2635. 2643–2646——Disapproval of accepting the verdict of a majority, 2637, 2638. 2697–2705.

Practice of the judge to excuse a juror when necessary, 2649–2652——Examination as to the extra burden and inconvenience put upon individual jurors by the adoption of alphabetical selection, 2665–2672——Usefulness of the system of paying a guinea a day to special jurors in Dublin, 2673–2681.

Remarkable instance of corruption in the case of Meldon *v.* Lawless, 2706–2711——Opinion that in the case of a special commission only it would be expedient to have a special jury in a criminal trial, 2714——Disapproval of the judge having the power to order a juror to stand by, 2720——The opinion of witness upon the working of the new Act has been formed from judicial experience, and not from any knowledge of the feelings of the jurors themselves, 2721–2724.

Inapplicability of the English rule of summoning jurors to Ireland, 2726–2730. 2743, 2744——Revision of the lists by the Chairman should be carried out in open court, 2738——Inexpediency of introducing the "special" element into every jury, on account of class feeling, 2745–2752.

Power of ordering any juror to stand by should be retained by the Crown; persons who are supposed to be disaffected to the law should be excluded from juries by these means, 2756–2762——Absence of any question at the last assizes as to the legality of grand juries paying the sub-sheriffs for additional trouble, 2763, 2764.

Montgomery's Trial. Large numbers of jurors set aside both by the Crown and the prisoner at the recent trial of Montgomery for murder, *Buchanan* 1972–1974.

Reports, 1873—*continued.*

Moore, Robert. Report from Mr. Moore, clerk of the Inishowen Union, relative to the qualifications to be required in jurors, and the amendments desirable in the Act of 1871, *App.* 308.

Morphy, Alexander. (Analysis of his Evidence.)—Has held the office of Crown Solicitor for the counties of Clare and Kerry for many years, 3699——Unsatisfactory nature of the verdicts at the last Clare assizes, 3700–3707. 3727——Statement that the jurors at the Kerry assizes were challenged because they were all from one barony, but that, notwithstanding, they were excellent jurors, 3708–3711. 3727.

Expediency of raising the qualification for jurors in the rural districts to 40 *l.* and lowering it in towns to 12 *l.* or 14 *l.*; belief that this qualification will secure an adequate number of jurors, 3712–3715. 3750. 3751. 3761–3764——Approval of a qualification of classes, not of rating, for special jurors, 3716–3718. 3760——Desirability of balloting in criminal cases; canvassing jurors by the friends of prisoners would be thereby avoided, 3719.

Belief that summoning jurors by post would be wholly impracticable; suggestion that the constabulary should be employed upon this duty, 3720, 3721——Revision of the lists should be undertaken by the magistrates at petty sessions, who should give their reasons publicly in the case of the exclusion of any person, 3722–3725.

Examination as to suspicion of partiality on the part of the sheriff in framing the jury panels, 3728–3734——Disapproval of reverting to the old system, 3735. 3736——Opinion that the power of the Crown to order jurors to stand by will be more frequently exercised under the new Act, 3737–3746——Advantage of the old juries in being more subject to public opinion than those summoned under the present Act, 3747–3749.

Expediency of excluding small farmers from the jury list, on account of their want of intelligence, 3752–3758——Challenge to the array at the Kerry assizes on account of the jurors having been summoned from one barony, and not from the whole county, 3758, 3759.

Morris, Right Honourable Michael. (Analysis of his Evidence.)—Has been judge of the Court of Common Pleas in Ireland since 1867; has had large experience of the working of the Jury Act, 2978–2982——Unfavourable opinion of the operation of the Act; grounds for this conclusion, 2983–2998——Low class of intelligence evinced by the juries on the Connaught circuit, 2985–2987——Instances of the unsatisfactory nature of the verdicts returned by these juries, 2987–2989.

Deterioration of the special jury panel; case in which a gentleman and his coachman were upon the same panel, 2989. 2995–2997——Miscarriage of justice in Sligo, the result of the present state of the law, 2993–2997——Opinion that there never will be an efficient revision of the list as long as it is nobody's peculiar business, 2998.

Great objection in Ireland to serve on juries, on account of the desire to avoid becoming unpopular, 2999–3001. 3029, 3030——Expediency of giving the juror notice that he is to be on the list, 3001–3003——Disapproval of the alphabetical mode of selecting jurors; predominance in some counties of names commencing with a certain letter, 3005–3021.

Opinion that the system of choosing jurors should be assimilated to the law of England in every particular, 3006–3008——Theoretical rather than practical objection to the system of selection by the sub-sheriff; necessity for an expurgation of the list by the sheriff, 3009–3016. 3021——Revision by the chairman is a mere matter of form; approval of a preliminary revision by the magistrates, with an appeal to the chairman, 3017–3020.

Probability that in raising the qualification a sufficient number of jurors will not be obtained, 3023. 3042——Expediency of introducing a system of qualification other than mere rating, 3023. 3024——Existence in Galway of special jurors rated as high as 300 *l.* or a year, who are unable to speak English, 3026, 3027. 3033–3035——Impossibility of adopting a high qualification for the county of Leitrim, 3037–3041——Decided opinion that a temporary Act is necessary to ensure that the law will be properly administered at the next assizes; belief that there would be no difficulty in passing a general Act with the same object, 3045–3049.

[Second Examination.]—Further evidence relative to the selection of the jury panels by the sub-sheriff; opinion that a certain discretion should be vested in that official, 3050–3058——Argument that taking away the power of selection from the sheriff will throw upon the Crown Solicitor the duty of ordering jurors to stand by, which is a far more dangerous power from a popular point of view, 3053.

Absence of public confidence in the present system, 3054–3056——Further evidence in disapproval of the alphabetical system of selection; hard case of Messrs. Turbett, where three brothers, members of the same firm, were summoned upon the same panel, 3057–3060. 3114–3117. 3138–3141. 3194–3198. 3206——Absolute necessity of a process of expurgation by the sheriff; "Expurgation" and "Selection" being different things, 3061. 3168. 3170——Superiority of country jurors over those in Dublin under the old system; belief that the demand for the present Act is confined to Dublin alone, 3063, 3064.

Emphatic

Morris, Right Honourable Michael. (Analysis of his Evidence)—*continued.*

Emphatic objection to peculiar legislation for Ireland; further opinion that the law should be the same in both countries, 3064——Evidence as to the impartiality of the sub-sheriffs; public opinion is an admirable safeguard against any unfairness on their part, 3065. 3173–3180. 3200, 3201——Statement as to a remarkable instance of a challenge to the array at the Monaghan assizes; conclusion as to the necessity of a more frequent exercise by the Crown of the power to order jurors to stand aside in the event of the power of selection being taken from the sheriff, 3066–3073. 3077. 3126–3132. 3181–3185.

Fairness of verdicts returned by Irish juries, 3074, 3075——Examination as to the trial of Mr. Johnston, the Member for Belfast, for taking part in an illegal procession, 3076. 3209–3213——Complaints as to jury-packing made more frequently against the Crown officers than against the sheriff; complaint of this kind in the famous trial of O'Connell, 3077. 3181. 3184.

Additional evidence in favour of a variety of qualifications besides rating which would place the sons of baronets, sheriffs, and magistrates, upon the panel, 3079–3081——Further evidence on the unsatisfactory state of things during the last assizes at Sligo, 3085–3106——Examination as to certain jury bills brought in by various attorneys general, 3107–3113.

Desirability of a system of ballot, reserving both to the Crown and to the prisoner the right of challenge; objection to the ballot except with such reservation, 3116–3119——Opinion that the present revision by the chairman is quite valueless on account of his want of local knowledge, 3120–3125——Examination as to the preponderance of the religious element in the jury that tried the Bairds, 3133–3137.

Statement that there is no ground for challenge in the fact that there is not enough of any particular religion on a jury; the only ground for challenge is that the panel is partially arrayed, 3138——Expediency of the grand jury having power to pay the sub-sheriff for the expenses incurred by him attendant upon the Act, 3142–3146.

Suitability and economy of the Post Office as a means of summoning jurors by registered letters, 3146, 3147——Opinion that jurors who have been only summoned and have not served should not be exonerated from serving for two years, 3147–3150——Secondary importance of the qualification if the power be given to exclude incompetent persons, 3151. 3165. 3166.

Relative qualifications of town and county jurors; advantage of the former over the latter as regards intelligence, 3152——Inexpediency of going below 12 *l.* or 15 *l.* for the rating qualification for either towns or counties, 3153——Vagueness of the phrase "Village" in the Act; qualification should be confined to towns and cities, *ib.*——Preference for the household qualification pure and simple, 3155–3160.

Considerable advantage in calling competent persons to participate in all public business as much as possible, 3163, 3164——Favourable opinion of a mixed system of qualification, 3167——Approval of the absolute disqualification of every person who is unable to speak English; inability to read or write should also be considered a ground for disqualification, 3186–3193.

Possible advantage of adopting a system of alphabetical selection from parishes; difficulties in the cases of baronies and parishes that are either exclusively Protestant or Catholic, 3197–3199. 3201——Further statement as to the public disapprobation of the present Bill, 3203.

Selection by the sheriff was contemplated in every Bill brought in since the year 1852 until the present, 3207, 3208——Belief that the conviction of Mr. Johnston had a material result in his being returned for Belfast immediately afterwards, 3210——Opinion that it is not desirable that a party case should be tried by a jury composed entirely of Protestants, 3212.

Morrison, William Henry. Suggestions by Mr. Morris, clerk of the Enniskillen Union, relative to the qualifications of jurors, and the amendments desirable in the Act of 1871, *App.* 312, 313.

Murland, James. (Analysis of his Evidence.)—Has been Crown Solicitor for the county Down since 1868; 2355, 2356——Has had considerable experience in the working of the present and former Acts both at assizes and quarter sessions, 2357——Approval of the principle of the present Act; expediency of taking away from the sheriff the power of the selection of the jury, 2358. 2428. 2491, 2492.

Statement that the jurors under the new Act are not equal in intelligence to those who were formerly summoned by the sheriff; opinion that the present qualification is decidedly too low, 2359–2362. 2398——Qualification for jurors should be 12 *l.* in the county and 20 *l.* in towns, in addition to 30 *l.* general rating; belief that such a qualification would procure a sufficient number of jurors, 2363, 2364. 2396–2399.

Inexpediency of selecting jurors by alphabetical rotation; approval of a system of

 balloting

Murland, James. (Analysis of his Evidence)—*continued*.

balloting as the most impartial process, 2365-2368. 2430. 2434-2436——Method in which the system of challenging is carried out; the number of challenges allowed to the prisoner should be diminished, 2369, 2370. 2393, 2394. 2415-2418. 2431-2441. 2460-2463.

Unsatisfactory manner in which the revision of the lists was carried out at the last assizes for Down; absence of proper information to the chairman as to the character of the panel, 2371, 2372——Suggestions as to the manner of affording the necessary information to the chairman; opinion that the sessional Crown Prosecutor should be charged with this duty, 2373-2380. 2401-2405. 2442-2444.

Desirability of excluding from the jury list persons who are unable to read and write; with this addition the exemptions in the present Act are sufficient, 2381-2383. 2407——The chairman should have no further power of exemption than that allowed by the Act, 2383, 2384——Qualifications necessary for a special juror; belief that in the county Down a 40 *l.* household qualification would give a sufficient number, 2385, 2386.

Statement that the lists for Downshire should contain between 2,000 and 3,000 common, and between 500 and 600 special jurors, 2387——Suggested alterations in the quarter sessions divisions in the county Down; expediency of having the entire criminal business of each division transacted in the county town, 2388, 2389. 2453, 2454——Importance of not exhausting the special jury list, as it will have the effect of taking jurors off the general list of jurors, 2390-2392.

Great advantage in summoning the jurors by means of registered letters through the Post Office; inexpediency of employing the constabulary upon this duty, 2395. 2457-2459——Disapproval of notice being given to any juror as to objections made against him, 2406——The proceedings of the chairman as to striking names off the list should be carried out in open court, 2412.

Evidence in opposition to the proposal to give the right to either side to call for special juries in criminal cases, 2413, 2414. 2464-2475——Disinclination generally of persons to serve on juries, 2419-2421——Decided opinion as to the impartiality of the sub-sheriff in forming the jury panel under the old system; notwithstanding this belief, the removal of selection by that official is highly expedient, 2422-2429. 2476-2491——Impossibility of the voters' and the jurors' lists being revised by one operation before the barrister at the same time, 2448-2452——Inexpediency of doing away with the grand jury at quarter sessions, 2455-2456——Statement as to the expense of forming the jury lists in the county Down, 2494-2499.

N.

Non-Property Qualification. Expediency of adding to the panel certain persons who, though not qualified by property, would be still eminently fit to serve on juries, *Armstrong* 968, 969; *Battersby* 1458. 1492. 1506, 1507. 1627; *M'Grath* 2166-2171——Statement that the non-property qualifications would be a considerable set off against the diminution of the general panel by reason of the raising of the rating qualifications, *Battersby* 1467-1471.

North-East Circuit. Unfavourable opinion of witness as to the working of the new Act; illiterate and unintelligent character of the jurors at the last assizes on the north-east circuit, *Right Hon. J. A. Lawson* 2770-2775. 2781-2783. 2851-2854. 2865, 2866. 2877-2880. 2887-2952.

Notice to Jurors. Expediency of sending a juror notice through the post on the occasion of his being first placed on the list, *M'Grath* 2326; *Right Hon. J. A. Lawson*, 2817, 2818. 2823. 2916. 2936-2938; *Right Hon. M. Morris* 3001-3003——Disapproval of notice being given to any juror as to objections made against him, *Murland* 2406.

Number of Jurors. Examination as to the effect of an increased qualification on the number of jurors in certain counties, *Battersby* 1516-1523. 1540-1547. 1553, 1554. 1559-1561. 1617-1621——Expediency of lowering the rate where a sufficient number of jurors cannot be obtained, *ib.* 1358——Statistical information offered by Mr. Hancock as to the numbers of jurors under the raised qualification, *Molloy* 1748, 1749——Argument in favour of having a less number on the jury list, that the jurors will be of a much higher class, *Buchanan* 1924, 1925. 1987. 2011, 2012. 2032, 2033——The work of witness (as clerk of the peace) will be materially reduced by raising the qualification, as this will have the effect of reducing the number of jurors, *ib.* 2105.

Probability that in raising the qualification a sufficient number of jurors will not be obtained, *Right Hon. M. Morris* 3023. 3042——Admission that revision would so reduce the number of jurors that they would be obliged to serve more frequently, *Bottomley* 3498-3507.

Reports, 1873—*continued.*

Number of Jurors—continued.

Return, by the clerks of the peace, of the number of jurors on the jurors' book for the several years 1870–73; large increase in many counties in 1873, *App.* 287.

Return showing the estimated number of common jurors in each county at large, qualified according to a certain scale of property qualification, *App.* 296——Similar return as regards special jurors, *ib.* 297.

See also Qualifications. Roscommon. Service of Jurors. Special Jurors, 4.

Numerical Selection. Objections to a system of selection of the jury panel by numbers, *J. Reilly* 4675–4681.

O.

O'Brien, Smith. High class of persons on the jury that tried Mr. Smith O'Brien for high treason, *Right Hon. J. Whiteside* 4296.

O'Brien, William P. Report by Mr. O'Brien relative to the working of the Juries Act of 1871, and the qualifications desirable for common jurors and special jurors respectively, *App.* 317.

O'Connell Trial. Complaint made of jury packing in the trial of Mr. O'Connell, *Right Hon. M. Morris* 3077. 3181. 3184——Statement as to the impartiality of the selection by the sheriff in the case of the jury in the O'Connell trial, *Robinson* 3822.

O'Keeffe v. *Cullen.* Explanations in connection with the proportion of Roman Catholics and Protestants on the jury in this case, *Right Hon. J. Whiteside* 4239–4246.

Production by witness of the order for stopping the trial of O'Keeffe *v.* Cullen, the notice for trial, and the notice declining to withdraw the notice for trial, *J. Hamilton* 4330–4335——Preponderance of Protestants over Roman Catholics on the special jurors' book; absence of any reference to the case of O'Keeffe *v.* Cullen in the formation of that particular panel, *ib.* 4339–4344. 4356.

Objections to Jurors. Impossibility of objecting to a juror on the ground of want of qualification after his name has been placed on the list, *Hemphill* 25——Inexpediency of giving the poor-rate collector the power to put the word "objected" against a juror's name; information should be given by him to the chairman of the county as to any objection, *De Moleyns* 359, 360. 377–380. 462–466. 587–539——Necessity of the officials, whose duty it is to make objections to jurors, being furnished with instructions; the chairman should have the power to give these instructions, *ib.* 436–438. 586——Unsuitability of an elected guardian of the union being appointed to make objections; the duty should be imposed on the Poor Law collector, *ib.* 467–470. 582, 583——Opinion that no extra remuneration can be claimed by the Poor Law collector for the duty of stating objections to the chairman when revising the lists, *ib.* 584–586. 590, 591.

The Poor Law collector should state the objection, and not merely write the word "objected" against the juror's name, *Coffey* 676–684——Opinion that the word "objected" should not be placed against the name of any person for fear of giving offence, *Armstrong* 780, 781. 970——Possibility of there being good grounds for an objection to a panel which would, however, be incapable of proof, *J. Hamilton* 1390–1392.

Statement that though it would be an invidious duty to place the word "objected" against a juror's name, there is no real reason why it should not be done, *Right Hon. J. D. Fitzgerald* 3327, 3328.

See also Appeal. Revision of Jury Lists.

Omagh Assizes. Novel expedient adopted at Omagh to obtain convictions in the case of a trial for riot between Protestants and Catholics, *Hamilton* 1322–1326.

Ormsby, William. (Analysis of his Evidence.)—Has been sub-sheriff of the city of Dublin for twelve years, 4721, 4722. 4868, 4869——Statement that Mr. J. M. Williamson was the sub-sheriff who prepared the panel in the year 1872 which has been referred to by Mr. Frederick Hamilton, 4723–4726. 4866, 4867. 4873–4877——Absence of any complaint as regards the formation of the panels prepared by witness from a religious point of view, 4727. 4728. 4780, 4781.

Disapproval of the sheriff inquiring into the religion of jurors before summoning them, 4729, 4730. 4774–4779. 4818, 4819——Preponderance of Protestants on the jurors book of the county of Dublin, 4731–4738——Impartial manner in which Roman Catholics have been summoned on the special panels for the city of Dublin, 4739–4749.

Inexpediency of adopting the alphabetical system of selection in Dublin; grounds for this opinion, 4750–4753——Extraordinary instance of ignorance upon the part of the grand jury for the county of Dublin, 4751–4758. 4783–4791. 4830–4836——Desirability of an exclusive household qualification for the county of Dublin; expediency of going much

Ormsby, William. (Analysis of his Evidence)—*continued.*

much lower in the valuation if a strictly household qualification is adopted, 4754–4756. 4837–4842.

Inexpediency of taking from the sheriff the power of selecting the panels, 4757, 4758. 4798–4802——Instance in which the high sheriff was obliged to summon himself as a special juror; facility of remedying this difficulty in the Act of Parliament, 4758. 4793–4796——Proposition that the Committee should fix a scale of fees for the sheriff, 4759–4766. 4843, 4844. 4848, 4849.

Examination as to the time in which the Dublin jury book would be exhausted, and as to the frequency of imposing service on the jurors, 4765–4773. 4820–4829——Useful character of the jurors who, from serving constantly at the special juries, have obtained the *soubriquet* of "guinea pigs," 4803–4809. 4818——Statement that Mr. Darcy was the only high sheriff who ever interfered with witness in the formation of the panel, 4810–4814——Efficacy of the post as a means for serving summonses; difficulty in the case of personal service on account of persons paying money to avoid being summoned, 4844–4848——High class of intelligent jurors who reside in the county of Dublin, 4850–4857——Statement that a high qualification in Dublin would result in a preponderance of Protestant jurors, 4863–4865.

Owners. Expediency of having property represented in the jury box; opinion that owners as well as occupiers should serve as jurors, *Cope* 5148. 5158.

P.

Packing of Juries. Complaints as to jury-packing made more frequently against the Crown officers than against the sheriff; complaint of this kind in the famous trial of Mr. O'Connell, *Right Hon. M. Morris* 3077. 3181. 3184——Any suspicion as to the packing of jurors has been directed more to the setting aside of jurors by the Crown solicitor than to unfair conduct upon the part of the sheriffs, *Bottomley* 3456. 3523–3525. 3532–3535. 3553–3558. *See also* ***Sheriffs, or Sub-Sheriffs.***

Panel (generally). Opinion that the elimination of improper persons from the panel should be carried out in private by a responsible official, *J. Hamilton* 1048——Additional safeguards suggested against the malconstruction of the jury panel; approval of Perrin's Act as a means for amending and forming the panel, *ib.* 1125–1133. 1162. 1209, 1210. 1214, 1215——One of the means to secure impartiality would be to keep off the panel men who would not honestly do their duty, *ib.* 1225, 1226. 1249——Disinclination of witness to leave the formation of the panel to to the discretion of any person; it is, however, impossible to avoid this, *Battersby* 1654–1657——The jury panel is struck seven days before the Assizes, *ib.* 1664.

Suggestions as to the process of forming the panel; proposed division of the jurors' book into fifties, from which numbers the panel should be selected by the sheriff, *Right Hon. J. A. Lawson* 2825–2833. 2928–2931. 2970–2974——Objection to the principle of selecting the panel by chance, *Right Hon. M. Morris* 3006–3008——Approval of the panel being formed on an improved alphabetical arrangement, *Right Hon. J. D. Fitzgerald* 3243. 3244——Objection to the previous publication of the names of those jurors who will be upon the panel, *ib.* 3283, 3284.

Impossibility of there being a perfect panel unless there is a power of selection by some public officer; approval of the alphabetical selection as contemplated by Mr. Justice Fitzgerald, *Bottomley* 3362, 3363. 3427–3429——Suggestions as to the method to be adopted in selecting panels for the quarter sessions and the assizes respectively, *ib.* 3485–3491.

Liability of the sheriff to be fined by the judge for returning an insufficient number on the panel, *Wilkinson* 3978, 3979. 3991, 3992——Disadvantages inherent to the system of alphabetical selection; suggestions for an alternative scheme, *ib.* 3983–3985. 4050–4054——Statement that the sheriff would be accountable for returning too large a number of jurors, if it were shown that there had been any improper motive in so doing, *ib.* 4010–4013.

See also ***Alphabetical Selection. Ballot. Dublin. Judges. Legislation. Monaghan. Numerical Selection. Packing of Juries. Responsibility. Revision of Jury Lists. Sheriffs, or Sub-Sheriffs.***

Pawnbrokers. Unsuitability of a pawnbroker to perform the duties of a juror on account of his dependence on the public; doubtful expediency, notwithstanding, of absolutely disqualifying him, *Right Hon. J. Whiteside* 4252. 4260. 4262, 4263.

Pearson, D. C. Report from Mr. Pearson, clerk of the Donegal Union, relative to the qualifications to be required in jurors, and the amendments desirable in the Act of 1871, *App.* 309.

Peasantry. Impossibility of bringing the Irish peasantry to a belief in the impartiality of the law by any change in the present system, *Hamilton* 1079, 1080.

Perrin's

Reports, 1873—*continued.*

Perrin's Act. Description of the former qualifications, under the old Act; honorary qualifications under the old nearly the same as under the new Act, *Hemphill* 19–22. 112——Machinery by which the old qualifications were ascertained; unsatisfactory nature of such machinery by which persons were put on the jurors' book who were totally devoid of property qualification, *ib.* 24. 113. 143.

Insufficient materials for forming the panel under Perrin's Act, on account of the diminution of freeholders and leaseholders, *J. Hamilton* 1020. 1066. 1191——Curious effect of Perrin's Act that in the county Dublin it was as prejudicial as it was beneficial in the city, *ib.* 1191–1193——The abuse of the administration of the Act had the effect of encouraging speculative actions, and so degrading the legal profession; opinion that there is no security in the present Act against the recurrence of similar abuses, *ib.* 1193. 1194.

Objections to a return to the old law pending the amendment of the Act of 1871; *Molloy* 1860–1871; *Murphy* 3735, 3736——Statement that a change from the old law was absolutely necessary, *Robinson* 3769, 3770.

Police. Doubtful expediency of employing the constabulary in making objections to the qualifications of jurors; invidious character of such duty, *De Moleyns* 439–443.

See also Summonses.

Political or Party Feeling. Necessity of adopting some means whereby Ribbonmen Fenians, and Orangemen should be excluded, *J. Hamilton* 1050, 1051——Examination as to the inexpediency of having twelve Protestants or Orangemen upon a jury, *ib.* 1273–1282——Absence of practical difficulty in arriving at the fact as to whether a man is a Ribbonman or an Orangeman, *ib.* 1284——Questionable expediency of removing a juror's name on account of his political opinions, *Roche* 2527, 2528.

Persons who are supposed to be disaffected to the law should be excluded from juries by the right of challenge, *Right Hon. J. H. Monahan* 2756–2762——Opinion that it is not desirable that a party case should be tried by a jury composed entirely of Protestants, *Right Hon. M. Morris* 3212.

Examination as to the power of the sheriff in rejecting any juror who may be suspected of being disaffected to the law, *Wilkinson* 4000–4010——Existence of strong party feeling after contested elections, *Mitchell* 5050, 5051.

See also Fenian Trials. Johnston, W., M.P.

Poor Law Officials. Examination as to the qualifications necessary for a poor law guardian; evidence in favour of their general intelligence and capacity, *Flynn* 4118–4130——Annual transmission by the Valuation Office of lists of valuations in all the unions; poor-rate books and warrants made out from this list, *ib.* 4144–4148. 4160–4167——Variable nature of the qualifications for poor law guardians in different parts of Ireland, *ib.* 4174. 4176. 4193–4200.

Reports from the inspectors of poor law unions, and from several clerks of unions, relative to the working of the Juries Act of 1871, and the qualifications desirable for common jurors and special jurors respectively, *App.* 301–321.

See also Objections to Jurors. Revision of Jury Lists.

Poverty of Jurors. Extreme poverty of the jurors at the last assizes for Kildare, &c.; their desire to be exonerated from serving, and to be permitted to return home, *Battersby* 1450–1452.——*See also Clonmel Assizes. Qualifications.*

Prendergast, Thomas. Report from Mr. Prendergast, clerk of the Wexford Union, relative to the qualifications to be required in jurors, and the amendments desirable in the Act of 1871, *App.* 315.

Printing Expenses. Information as to the expenditure necessary for printing the jury lists for the county of Roscommon, *Flynn* 4102–4104——Impracticability of combining the jurors' and the voters' lists so as to save the cost of printing, *ib.* 4136, 4137. 4216, 4217——Statement that the charge for printing the list of Parliamentary voters is about 1 *l.* per 100 names, *ib.* 4138–4140.

The printing expenses under the Act in the Rathdown Union amounted to 45 *l.*, under contract, *Cope* 5229, 5230.

Public, The. The duty of serving on a jury is more generally avoided than sought for by the public at large, *De Moleyns* 381, 382. 471. 600, 609, 610——Advantage in interesting as many people as possible in the administration of the law, *J. Hamilton* 1431——Disinclination of the Irish people to serve on juries, *Battersby* 1641——Belief that there is a considerable objection upon the part of many people to be excluded from juries, *Buchanan* 1922.

Disinclination generally to serve on juries, *Marland* 2419–2421; *Flynn* 4183–4185——Great objection in Ireland to serve on juries on account of the desire to avoid becoming unpopular,

Public, The—continued.

unpopular, *Right Hon. M. Morris* 2999–3001. 3029, 3030——Absence of public confidence in the present system, *ib.* 3054–3056. 3200.

Belief that at the present time there is a general desire to avoid serving on juries; expediency of such feeling being altered by making it discreditable to be excluded from the list, *Right Hon. J. D. Fitzgerald* 3313——Advantage of the old juries in being more subject to public opinion than those summoned under the present Act, *Morphy* 3747–3749.

See also Attendance of Jurors. Fines. Upper Classes.

Publicans. Decided opinion that publicans should be exempted from serving, inasmuch as they are intimately connected with the witnesses and friends of the prisoners, *Hemphill* 98, 99. 160, 161. 185–189——A publican should be positively excluded from serving, *De Moleyns* 376. 521–523. 567——Expediency of absolutely disqualifying publicans; distinction drawn between publicans and grocers who sell spirits by retail, *Right Hon. J. Whiteside* 4230–4234. 4261. 4314, 4315.——*See* also *Exemptions.*

Q.

QUALIFICATIONS (COMMON JURORS):

1. *As to the Operation of the present System.*
2. *As to the Amendments suggested.*

1. *As to the Operation of the present System:*

The principle of the present Bill is that the poor law valuation is made the basis of the qualification; approval of such basis, *Hemphill* 2326——Contention that the qualification for common jurors in the Act is too low; grounds for this conclusion, *Coffey* 647–652; *Molloy* 1778–1786. 1813–1815; *Buchanan* 1895–1899——Opinion that the lowness of the qualification leads to an exhibition of burlesque on the part of the juries, amendment being urgently required, *Armstrong* 1003–1006. 1010, 1011.

Changes made by the House of Commons in the qualifications as laid down by the House of Lords under the Bill of 1871, *Molloy* 1760–1766——Instances of cases at the last assizes in which the jurors were of a class quite unfit for their duties, *Battersby* 1450–1452; *Buchanan* 1941–1945——Statement that the jurors under the new Act are not equal in intelligence to those who were formerly summoned by the sheriff; opinion that the present qualification is decidedly too low, *Murland* 2359–2362. 2398——The higher the qualification the more reasonable is it to expect a higher class of intelligence, *Robinson* 3841, 3842. 3849, 3850.

Disapproval of the outcry against the jurors who have attended under the new Act; argument that they will in time become fully qualified, being of the same standing as the poor law guardians, *Flynn* 4107–4109. 4118–4129.

Description of a case in which the jury was discharged on account of the intoxication of one of their number; instance also of a case in which a returned convict was sworn on the jury, *Right Hon. J. Whiteside* 4230, 4231. 4293——Opinion that with a few exceptions the new Act has worked very fairly; approval of a 20 *l.* qualification for common and a 50 *l.* qualification for special jurors, *Mitchell* 4924, 4925. 5071, 5072——Approval of the qualification as laid down in the Act for common and special jurors, *Coke* 5154–5158.

Return of sheriffs of the number of jurors on the general jurors' book classified according to various amounts of rating qualification, *App.* 288.

Reports from the inspectors of poor law unions, and from several clerks of unions, relative to the working of the Juries Act of 1871, *App* 301–321.

Conclusion of the Committee that the rating qualification has placed on the jurors' books the names of persons who are not qualified in point of intelligence to serve as jurors, *First Report* iii.

2. *As to the Amendments suggested:*

Evidence in favour of a higher rating qualification as being likely to result in a more intelligent class of jurymen, *De Moleyns* 348 *et seq.*; 475–477. 617——Opinion that jurors should be persons who are above the usual class of offenders, *ib.* 348——Propriety of considering the personal fitness of jurors as well as their rated qualification; deficiency in the Act in this respect, *ib.* 355, 366. 429——Expediency of adopting a qualification for a general juror, of a net annual value of 12 *l.* for house and offices in a town and 30 *l.* in the county, *ib.* 384–388. 425. 489–491. 554–560——The grievance of frequent attendances should be subservient to raising the qualification, by which a more intelligent class of jurors would be obtained, *ib.* 386. 597.

Opinion

QUALIFICATIONS (COMMON JURORS)—continued.

2. *As to the Amendments suggested*—continued.

Opinion that the rating qualification for common juries should be raised to 30 *l.*, and that the household qualification should be 12 *l.*, *Coffey* 662–666. 729, 730. 751–763——Contention in favour of a qualification for a common juror of not less than 50 *l.*, *Armstrong* 769. 824, 825. 991. 995——Evidence showing that in the several jury bills brought into the House of Commons no qualification of a higher value than 30 *l.* a year was contemplated, witness submitting suggestions for an improved qualification, *Armstrong* 896 *et seq.*

Expediency of substitutions of rating for the old qualification, *J. Hamilton* 1021——Concurrence in the opinion as to the desirability of raising the qualification, *ib.* 1038; *et seq.*; 1285, 1286.

Suggested remedies to be applied so as to bring the present law into better shape; expediency of raising the rating qualification for common jurors to 100 *l.*, and for special jurors to 200 *l.*, *Battersby* 1448, 1449. 1455–1468. 1555——The rating qualified is not a sufficient test of the fitness of a juror; necessity for the adoption of other tests as far as possible, *ib.* 1448, 1449——Admission that a lower qualification might be adopted if the sheriff be given power to select the panel, *ib.* 1467–1471——Contention that the valuation of 100 *l.* for common jurors, and 200 *l.* for special jurors, would be a sufficiently low qualification, *ib* 1549–1552.

Desirability of raising the qualification for common jurors in counties to 30 *l.*, and in towns to 12 *l.*; the town qualification to include house and garden, *Molloy* 1715, 1716. 1736. 1741. 1808. 1850–1853. 1859——Opinion that the qualification is too low, and should be raised; the qualification for house property in towns should be 15 *l.*, *Buchanan* 1895–1899. 1902. 1906——The qualification for the county should not be under 30 *l.*; expediency of keeping house and land ratings distinct, both in towns and counties, *ib.* 1903–1906——Elimination of improper persons should be by means of raising the qualification, and by stringently revising the lists, *ib.* 1937, 1938.

Opinion that a 30 *l.* rating in the counties, and from 12 *l.* to 15 *l.* in towns generally throughout Ireland, would give an intelligent class of jurors, *M'Grath* 2162–2165. 2214–2217. 2236–2238. 2253, 2254. 2288–2292. 2305–2309. 2314–2318.

Desirability of a higher qualification, so as to secure higher intelligence, and of a more stringent revision, by which unsuitable persons would be struck off the lists, *Rt. Hon. J. Monahan* 2626, 2627——Opinion in favour of raising the qualification; expediency of introducing a diversity of qualifications, *Rt. Hon. J. A. Lawson* 2786–2791. 2796. 2836. 2878——Excellent qualifications necessary in Sir John Coleridge's Bill, which should be extended to Ireland, *ib.* 2787–2791.

Expediency of introducing a system of qualification other than rating, *Rt. Hon. M. Morris* 3023, 3024——Evidence in favour of a variety of qualifications besides rating, which would place the sons of baronets, sheriffs, and magistrates upon the panel, *ib.* 3079–3081——Inexpediency of going below 12 *l.* or 15 *l.* as the rating qualification for either towns or counties, *ib.* 3153——Considerable advantage in calling competent persons to participate in all public business as much as possible, *ib.* 3163, 3164.

Constitutional importance of bringing the humbler classes as much as possible into connection with the administration of justice; expediency, on this account, of resting the main qualification upon rating, *Rt. Hon. J. D. Fitzgerald* 3223. 3239——Advisability of raising the qualification, and at the same time establishing a system of careful revision, *ib.* 3224, 3225. 3209——Special qualifications other than rating necessary for putting a superior class of persons on the jury list, *ib.* 3232–3234.

Expediency of raising the qualification for jurors in the rural districts to 40 *l.*, and lowering it in towns to 12 *l.* or 14 *l.*; belief that this qualification will secure an adequate number of jurors, *Murphy* 3712. 3715. 3750, 3751. 3761–3764——Slight alteration required in the amount of the present rating qualification, *Johnson* 3598–3602——Expediency of adopting additional qualifications, similar to those which confer the Parliamentary franchise; approval of raising the rating qualification, *Robinson* 3790–3796. 3814——Calculation that a qualification of 40 *l.* in the country and 20 *l.* in the towns, would supply an inadequate number of common jurors, *Wilkinson* 3960, 3961.

Desirability of a considerable increase in the rating qualifications of jurors, *Rt. Hon. J. Whiteside* 4755——Opinion that as regards a country juror, the rating qualification is no test of intelligence, *J. Reilly* 4550–4552.

Reports from the inspectors of poor law unions, and from several clerks of union, relative to the qualification desirable for common jurors, *App.* 301–321.

Recommendation by the Committee that the amount of property qualification for common jurors in counties at large, in respect of premises which do not appear on the

QUALIFICATIONS (COMMON JURORS)—continued.

2. *As to the Amendments suggested*—continued.

the rate-book to be situate in any city, town, or village, should be raised, *First Rep.* iii.

See also Alphabetical Selection. **Antrim.** **Ballot.** *Belfast Assizes.* *Clare.* *Compound Qualification* **Disqualification.** *Dublin.* *Exemption.* *Galway.* *Household Qualification.* **Interested Jurors.** *Intimidation.* *Leasehold Qualification.* *Legislation.* **Limerick.** **Meath.** *Monaghan.* *Non-Property Qualification.* **Number of Jurors.** *Owners.* *Perrin's Act.* *Political or Party Feeling.* **Poverty of Jurors.** *Public, The.* *Religious Element.* *Revision of* **Jury Lists.** **Sheriffs,** *or Sub-Sheriffs.* *Sligo.* *Special Jurors.* *Town* **Jurors.** **Tyrone.** *Uniformity of Qualification.* **Verdicts.** *Villages.* **Wexford.**

Qualifications (*Special Jurors*). See *Special Jurors.*

Quarter Sessions. Petty jurors at quarter sessions under the new system belong more to the agricultural and farming class than was the case formerly, *Hemphill* 8——Superior class of jurymen selected for the sessions, as compared with the assizes, *De Moleyns* 418-422——Contemplated diminution in the number of places where quarter sessions are held; that is, with a view to economy in the system of summoning, *Buchanan* 2013-2023——Diminution of the quarter sessions to divisions would not add to the duty of the jurors of one division over another, *ib.* 2024, 2025——*See also Revision of Jury Lists.*

R.

Rating Qualification. See *Qualifications.* *Special Jurors.*

Re-appointment of Committee. Recommended re-appointment of the Committee in the next Session of Parliament, in order to consider the practical operation of the Juries (Ireland) Act, 1873, *Second Rep.* iv.

Reid, William. Report from Mr. Reid, clerk of the Milford Union, relative to the qualifications to be required in jurors, and the amendments desirable in the Act of 1871, *App.* 306.

Reilly, John. (Analysis of his Evidence.)—Has been Conservative agent for the late Colonel Leslie and his brother since the year 1850, held the office of sub-sheriff for the county of Monaghan in the years 1846 and 1847; 4362-4365. 4369, 4370——Statement that the proportion of Roman Catholics in the county of Monaghan is about three to one as regards other denominations; the population of the county is about 112,000; 4366, 4367. 4585-4587——Formation of the panel by witness when sub-sheriff, with due reference to the religious denominations of the persons on the jury lists, 4371-4376. 4604-4609. 4628. 4670-4672.

Complaints as to partiality in the formation of the jury panel by Mr. Mitchell, who was sub-sheriff of the county Monaghan for several years up to 1869; 4377-4382. 4405. 4499. 4591-4603——Statement of the grounds for this dissatisfaction with Mr. Mitchell, 4388 *et seq.*——Successful challenge to the array in the case of McKenna, charged with the murder of Clarke; the result of this challenge was that the high sheriff was removed because he would not dismiss Mr. Mitchell, 4412-4427. 4452.

Examination as to the character of the panel from which the McKenna jury was selected, 4428-4434——Correspondence with the high sheriff and the sub-sheriff on the subject of returning an impartial panel for the 1869 assizes; subsequent communication with the Lord Lieutenant, 4435-4442——Position of the Farney jurors, who are chiefly Roman Catholics, at the end of the panel, 4446-4448. 4571-4574——Information as to the rating valuation of the jurors upon the panel, 4449-4451. 4645-4668.

Evidence as to the similarity of the succeeding panel to that which was quashed; venue for the trial of McKenna changed on that account, 4453-4466. 4475-4481——Want of impartiality the ground upon which the panel was quashed; admission by the sub-sheriff that he was an Orangeman, 4467-4474——Significant fact that in the jurors' book for the year 1869, there is a cross placed against the name of every Roman Catholic, 4482 4498. 4578-4580. 4610-4627——Statement that under the old system it was quite feasible for the sub-sheriff to return a jury to order, if so inclined; disapproval of reverting to that system, 4500-4502. 4694, 4695——Absence of difficulty in a complete revision of the lists; opinion that after one careful revision there would be very little trouble afterwards, 4503, 4504——Decided approval of the alphabetical system; probability of there being, under such system, a preponderance of Protestants upon the panel, 4506, 4507. 4629. 4631. 4673-4680.

Examination as to the number of jurors required for the purposes of the Monaghan assizes and the quarter sessions for one year; statement of the numbers available under certain

Reilly, John. (Analysis of his Evidence)—*continued.*

certain ratings, 4510–4521. 4715. 4716. 4718–4720——Average number of cases tried at the assizes and quarter sessions; opinion that 1,124 jurors is not too large a number for these trials, 4532–4546. 4710——Superior class of jurors obtained from towns, as compared with those from the rural districts, 4546–4549.

Opinion that as regards a country juror, the rating qualification is no test of intelligence, 4550–4552——Inexpediency of employing the police upon the duty of summoning jurors, 4553. 4554. 4684——Impracticability of serving jurors by means of registered letters through the post, 4555. 4556. 4701–4709——Suggestions as to the best means for serving the summonses; opinion that the service should be verified by oath, 4557–4563. 4685–4693.

Expediency of making the qualification the same both for the assizes and for the sessions, 4564–4567——Statement that the higher the rating, so much the more does the Protestant element preponderate, 4568–4570. 4581–4584——Impartiality of Protestant or Catholic juries, except in cases of a party character, 4631–4637. 4696——Desirability of taking jurors by chance; approval of the ballot system in the event of the alphabetical system not being adopted, 4634. 4717.

Statement that upon the change of venue in the case of McKenna, he was tried in Louth by twelve Roman Catholics, 4638–4644——Objections to a system of selection by numbers, 4675–4681——Non-attendance of magistrates upon the petty juries in the county Monaghan, 4682. 4683——The average of the jurors called upon to serve has been about one-half of those summoned, 4711——Instance in which the challenges by a prisoner exhausted the panel, 4712–4714.

Religious Element. Statement that there is no ground for challenge in the fact that there is not enough of any particular religious element on a jury; the only ground for challenge is that the panel is partially arrayed, *Right Hon. M. Morris* 3136——Proportion of Roman Catholics and Protestants on the jury in the case of O'Keeffe *v.* Cullen; belief in the impartiality of jurors professing either of those religions, *Right Hon. J. Whiteside* 4239–4246——Impartiality of Protestant or Catholic juries, except in cases of a party character, *J. Reilly* 4631–4637. 4696——Disapproval of the sheriff inquiring into the religion of jurors before summoning them, *Ormsby* 4729. 4730. 4774–4779. 4818. 4819——Decided opinion that religion should never be considered in selecting jurors for the panel, *Mitchell* 4980. 5023.——*See also Monaghan.*

Removal of Trials. Right of the Crown to bring cases to the Queen's Bench for trial by special jury; power to remove the trial of a case from one county to another vested in the court, *Armstrong* 1014, 1015.

Resident Jurors. Convenience of a system of summoning jurors only who are resident in the neighbourhood of the court, *De Moleyns* 515–520——Hardship in bringing jurors from a great distance to the towns where they are to serve, *Coffey* 687, 688——Argument in favour of dividing the sessions into districts, for the convenience of jurors, by taking them from the immediate neighbourhood, *ib.* 731–735.

Opinion that the duty of serving on juries should not be confined to persons living contiguous to the assize towns, but that all men should serve in their turn, *J. Hamilton* 1067. 1068——Complaints made by jurors as to the great distances that they are obliged to travel; recommendation that no jurors should be summoned to attend at quarter sessions out of his own division, *ib.* 1088. 1204.

Responsibility. Opinion that there never will be an efficient revision of the list as long as it is not the special business of some official, *Right Hon. M. Morris* 2998——Absence of responsibility in any official as to returning improper persons on the panel under the present Act, *Bottomley* 3472–3475——Reference to the possibility of suspicion being cast upon the irresponsible selection of the panel by the sheriff as a reason for a change in the system, *Johnson* 3573. 3574. 3619–3623. 3657. 3693——Statement that it will be impossible for the present Act to work well if the power of selection is not committed to some responsible person, *Robinson* 3838——Expediency of entrusting to some official the selection of suitable persons to serve on juries, *Mitchell* 4983. 4994. 4995.

See also Revision of Jury Lists. Sheriffs, or Sub-Sheriffs.

Revision of Jury Lists:

1. *System of Revision hitherto.*
2. *Suggestions for an amended System; Question more especially of enlarged Powers to the Chairman of Quarter Sessions, aided by different Officials.*
3. *Question of Revision by the Magistrates.*
4. *Suggested Revision before the next Assizes.*

1. *System of Revision hitherto:*

Revision of the jury lists under the old system by the magistrates, under the new by the chairman of quarter sessions; considerable advantage resulting from the latter arrangement, *Hemphill* 35–39. 173–175——Larger amount of publicity given to the revision

Reports, 1873—*continued.*

REVISION OF JURY LISTS—continued.

1. *System of Revision hitherto*—continued.

revision by the chairman of quarter sessions than could possibly be given by the magistrates, *Hemphill* 173-176——Explanation of the present duty of the chairman as to revision of the jury lists, *De Moleyns* 366-371. 566-571.

Statement that the revision in the chairman's court is a mere mechanical operation, *J. Hamilton* 1022——Difficulties in the way of revising the lists by the chairman, and of obtaining information from the county officers for the purposes of such revision, *ib.* 1115-1118. 1158-1166——Revision of the lists the duty of the chairman under the Act; necessary information regarding the jurors to be given by the clerks of the unions and the poor law collectors, *Molloy* 1711-1714——Absence, at present, of a proper revision of the jury lists, *M'Grath* 2155-2160.

Opinion that the present revision by the chairman is a mere matter of form, and is quite valueless on account of his want of local knowledge, *Right Hon. M. Morris* 3017, 3018. 3120-3125——The principal defect in the old Act was that there was no real revision; persons were placed on the jury list who were wholly unqualified, *Right Hon. J. D. Fitzgerald* 3219-3221.

Very imperfect revision of the jury list under the new Act; want of intelligence on the part of the new jurors, *Robinson* 3775-3781. 3866-3869——Absence of necessity for any further revision of the lists; opinion that jurors who are not qualified will themselves take measures to get themselves struck off the lists, *Flynn* 4113, 4114. 4178——Obstacles to a real revision before the assistant barrister, *Right Hon. J. Whiteside* 4255.

2. *Suggestions for an amended System; Question more especially of enlarged Powers in the Chairmen of Quarter Sessions, aided by different Officials:*

Conclusion that the fitness of jurors is not to be tested so much by raising the valuation or rating qualification as by giving the chairman of quarter sessions more power in revising the list, *Hemphill* 33, 34. 40, 41. 92, 93——The chairman should be empowered to strike off the name of any juror upon full proof of his unfitness, *ib.* 50-52. 150, 151. 177, 178——The formation of the general jurors' book should be entirely in the hands of the chairman, *ib.* 93——Further evidence in favour of giving a general discretion to the chairman of quarter sessions to strike off the name of unsuitable jurors, *ib.* 253-255.

Desirability of the chairman having power to go beyond the strict qualifications in expunging the names of unsuitable jurors; the revision by the chairman under the present system is purely nominal, *De Moleyns* 356-365. 430-436. 444-446. 458. 461. 587. 602——Advantage to the chairman of the assistance of the poor law collectors and the local Crown solicitors when revising the jurors' list, *ib.* 358-360. 365. 495-498.

Approval of entrusting the revision of the list to the chairman upon information afforded by the poor law collectors and the sub-sheriffs; the power of the chairman to exempt jurors should be largely extended, *Coffey* 667-669. 672-675. 685. 709, 710.

Authority to revise the jurors' list should be vested in the chairman upon information to be afforded by various county officials; large amount of confidence reposed in the chairmen of counties by every class in Ireland, *Armstrong* 779-782. 857-864. 870, 871. 970-1001——Objections to jurors being taken upon oath, and in open court; high reputation for impartiality in such cases enjoyed by the chairman, *ib.* 947-955. 972-974. 1000——Suitability of the county surveyor to give assistance to the chairman when revising the lists, *ib.* 998, 999——The labour of revision would be very materially lessened after the first time, as the revision would be confined to the new names, *ib.* 1001.

Impossibility of purging the jurors' book by any practicable means, so as to leave no improper person on the panel, *J. Hamilton* 1046-1048——Impropriety of a system by which the chairman should revise the lists in secret; opinion that such an arrangement would be degrading, and would throw odium upon the administration of justice, *ib.* 1160. 1348, 1349. 1424, 1425.

Assumption that the chairman is to be continued as the revising officer, *Battersby* 1459. 1628——Impossibility of satisfactorily purging the jury book by any process, *ib.* 1658, 1659. 1695——Statement as to the power of revision necessary for the proper formation of the jury list, *M'Grath* 2229-2231.

Suggestions as to the manner of affording the necessary information to the chairman; opinion that the sessional Crown prosecutor should be charged with this duty, *Murland* 2373-2380. 2401-2405. 2412-2444——Revision of the lists by the chairman should be carried out in open court, *Murland* 2412; *Right Hon. J. H. Monahan* 2738——Desirability of giving unlimited power to the chairman in the revision of the lists, *Roche* 2518, 2519. 2522. 2526. 2553-2556——Statement as to the means to be adopted for giving the chairman the requisite information in revising the lists, *ib.* 2523, 2524. 2541.

Approval

REVISION ON JURY LISTS—continued.

2. *Suggestions for an amended System; &c.*—continued.

Approval of the chairman's court as a court of revision; opinion that the chairman should decide by fixed rules, and not upon his own discretion, *Right Hon. J. Monahan*, 2628–2634. 2732–2742——Strong opinion that there must be, somewhere, a power of selection and a power of striking off illiterate, incompetent, and improper persons, *Right Hon. J. A. Lawson* 2796–2804. 2888, 2889. 2962, 2963——Stringent revision necessary upon the abandonment of the system of selection by the sheriff, *ib.* 2812——The revision of the lists should not be undertaken privately, but in open court, *ib.* 2822. 2942.

Necessary information for the revision should be furnished to the chairman by the clerk of the peace and the clerk of the Crown; inexpediency of reverting to the system of selection by the sub-sheriff, *Right Hon. J. D. Fitzgerald* 3226–3230. 3262, 3263. 3312——Strong opinion as to the absolute necessity of imposing on some public officer the obligation of bringing before the chairman objections to particular persons, *ib.* 3311, 3312.

Belief that no revision can thoroughly exclude disqualified persons, *Bottomley* 3368. 3478–3480——Examination as to the information which can be given to the chairman by the poor law collector, *ib.* 3369–3377. 3494–3497——Suggestions as to the guardians aiding in the revision, *Johnson* 3667–3674——Opinion that a revision by the chairman of the county, at quarter sessions, would not be attended by the jurors, *ib.* 3675–3679.

Emphatic disapproval of a revision of the lists by the chairman, privately, assisted by the constabulary, *Robinson* 3826. 3838. 3882——Absence of difficulty in a complete revision of the lists; opinion that after one careful revision there could be very little trouble afterwards, *J. Reilly* 4503, 4504.

3. *Question of Revision by the Magistrates:*

Disadvantages of revision by the magistrates as compared with revision by the chairman, *Hemphill* 35–39. 173–176——Power should be given to the magistrates to strike off a juror without stating a reason; officials who should aid the magistrates in the matter, *Right Hon. J. A. Lawson* 2813–2817. 2819, 2820. 2870–2872. 2914——Opinion that the Chairman has not such information for revising the lists as is possessed by the magistrates, *ib.* 2914.

Approval of preliminary revision by the magistrates, with an appeal to the chairman, *Right Hon. M. Morris* 3017–3020——Inexpediency of entrusting the duty to the magistrates instead of to the chairman, *Right Hon. J. D. Fitzgerald* 3225. 3285–3287. 3310, 3311——Opinion that the revision of the lists should be entrusted first to the magistrates and then, finally, to the chairman, *Johnson* 3604–3611. 3662–3666. 3685, 3686.

Suggestions as to the magistrates assisting in the revision, *Johnson* 3661–3674——The revision at petty sessions would be attended by no appreciable expense, *ib.* 3608–3610——Revision of the lists should be undertaken by the magistrates at petty sessions, who should give their reasons publicly in the case of the exclusion of any person, *Murphy* 3722–3725.

4. *Suggested Revision before the next Assizes:*

Correction of the jury lists for the next assizes would be the only practicable and speedy amendment; means by which this revision could be carried out, *Molloy* 1720–1735. 1816, 1817. 1839–1844. 1859. 1875. 1879, 1880——Opinion that the proposed correction of the lists could be accomplished in less than a week, *ib.* 1726——The temporary correction of the lists would not involve the insertion of any new names, *ib.* 1734, 1735——Absence of any difficulty for the chairman to revise the jurors' book against the next assizes, *Buchanan* 2064–2066.

See also Clerks of the Peace. Clerks of Unions. Legislation. Notice to Jurors. Objections to Jurors. Public, The. Responsibility. Voters' Lists.

Robinson, Henry. Letter from Mr. Robinson, Poor Law Inspector, submitting reports from clerks of unions relative to the amendments desirable in the Juries Act, *App.* 314.

Robinson, James. (Analysis of his Evidence.)—Is a Queen's Counsel and Chairman of Quarter Sessions for the County of Cavan, 3765–3768——Statement that a change in the old law was absolutely necessary; unsatisfactory character of the Dublin jurors, 3769, 3770——High character of the Galway jurors; impartial verdicts given by jurors in that county, whether Catholics or Protestants, 3772. 3883–3885——Favourable opinion of the selection by the sheriff on the Connaught circuit under the old Act, 3773, 3774.

Absence of revision of the jury list, the result of the new Act; want of intelligence on the part of the new jurors, 3775–3781. 3866–3869——Injurious effect of the alphabetical and dictionary order of selection, 3782–3789.

Robinson, James. (Analysis of his Evidence)—*continued*.

Expediency of adopting additional qualifications similar to those which confer the Parliamentary franchise; approval of raising the rating qualification, 3790–3796. 3814——Belief that the humbler classes are most anxious to be relieved from the duty of serving on juries; serious hardship imposed on them by being detained at quarter sessions towns, 3797.

Suggestions as to persons who should be exempted from serving; statement hereon that one of Judge Keogh's servants is upon the special jurors' list in Dublin, 3798–3800. 3839. 3840——Desirability of a seven years' disqualification of persons who have been convicted of certain offences, 3801——Proposition that the revision of the jurors and the Parliamentary lists should be combined; method by which this revision should be carried out, 3802–3807. 3843–3850.

Statement that the right of appeal should be given to any person whose name has been struck off the list, 3805——Desirability of summoning the jurors by means of registered letters; where there is no facility for postal service the constabulary should be employed, 3808–3813. 3821.

Approval of framing the jurors' list upon the principle laid down in Sir John Young's Bill; opinion that a higher class of jurors should be selected for the assizes, and the lower class utilised at the quarter sessions, 3813–3819. 3824. 3849–3854. 3870——Importance of imposing on the high sheriff the duty of examining and certifying as to the correctness of the panel; the sheriff is, in fact, the only officer who is entirely independent of the Crown, 3819. 3821. 3823–3826. 3857–3860. 3882. 3885. 3888.

Decided opinion that the sheriff should still make a selection of the most competent jurors from the jurors' book, 3820. 3881, 3882——Impartiality of the sub-sheriffs in the selection of the panel; remarkable instance of a challenge to the array in the case of O'Connell which was overruled by the judges and the House of Lords, 3821, 3822. 3837.

Emphatic disapproval of a revision of the lists by the chairman, privately, assisted by the constabulary, 3826. 3838. 3882——Impropriety of the proposal that either side should be given the right to have a special jury, 3827. 3829. 3838——Inexpediency of a system of ballot in criminal cases, 3828.

Disapproval of the proposal that a proportion of special jurors should serve with common jurors, 3830. 3871. 3874——Decided opinion in favour of unanimity of juries; conviction that any change in the present system would be most disastrous, 3831——Disapproval of giving the judge power to discharge a juror from service except for very sufficient cause; argument that a judge should have nothing to do with the jury panel, 3832, 3833. 3861, 3862.

Importance of not interfering with the right of the Crown to order jurors to stand by, 3834, 3835——Desirability of imposing fines upon jurors who do not answer to their names; expediency of the judge having power to remit or increase the fine, 3835——Further statement that it will be impossible for the present Act to work well if the power of selection is not committed to some responsible person, 3838.

The higher the qualification the more reasonable is it to expect a higher class of intelligence, 3841, 3842. 3849, 3850——Examination as to the existence of party feeling in the county Cavan as regards the formation of the jury list, 3878–3880——Efficacy of challenges to the array and to polls as a safeguard against the exercise of partiality by the sheriff, 3884–3887.

Evidence in further support of a system of selection by the sheriff; corruption on the part of that officer prevented by the action of public opinion, 3886–3890——Statement, that under the old law the sheriff might return the same panel time after time, 3890, 3891.

Further examination as regards the power of the judge to excuse jurors from attendance; necessity for defining in the Act the cases in which he should exercise that power, 3892–3924——Decided opinion that, whatever decision a judge arrives at as regards excusing a juror, should be stated in open court, 3921, 3922——Expediency of giving the judge absolute power in many cases in the event of the discretionary system of selection being established, 3924.

Roche, William. (Analysis of his Evidence.)—Has been Crown Solicitor for the county and city of Limerick for twelve years, 2500–2502——Unsatisfactory operation of the present Act at the last Limerick assizes; low and unintelligent class of jurors which attended, 2503–2506. 2533. 2534. 2588–2595——Opinion however that the new Act is a great improvement upon the old system, 2507, 2508.

Expediency of raising the qualification in the county to 50 *l.*; the existing qualification of 12 *l.* for the city should not be disturbed, 2509–2517——Fines imposed upon recalcitrant jurors, but remitted by the judges upon excuses being tendered, 2513——Desirability of giving unlimited power to the chairman in the revision of the lists, 2518, 2519. 2522. 2525, 2526. 2553–2556.

Statement

Reports, 1873—*continued.*

Roche, William. (Analysis of his Evidence)—*continued.*

Statement as to the means to be adopted for giving the chairman the requisite information in revising the list, 2523, 2524. 2541——Questionable expediency of removing a juror's name on account of his political opinions, 2527, 2528——Examination as regards the power and practice of ordering jurors to stand by, 2529–2533. 2577–2582.

Non-attendance of the better class of jurors, 2535–2540——Approval of a system of balloting for the jury in criminal cases; this would get rid of the canvassing of jurors on the part of the prisoners, 2542, 2543. 2545–2547——Peremptory challenges of the prisoner should not be reduced in number, 2544. 2548——Expediency of disqualifying publicans from serving, 2550–2552.

Opinion that the jurors on the panel are not known long before the assizes on account of the alphabetical selection, 2562–2572——Absence of objection to giving the Crown and the prisoner equal right to call for a special jury, 2573——Statement as to the number of jurors on the panel in Limerick, 2583–2585.

Roscommon. Estimate of the expense necessary for preparing the jurors' list for the county of Roscommon, *Flynn* 4094–4101——Calculation that raising the qualification from 20 *l.* to 50 *l.* in the county of Roscommon, would strike forty per cent. off the list, *ib.* 4110. 4201–4203——Number of jurors which would be placed on the list by a household qualification of 6 *l.*, 8 *l.*, 10 *l.*, and 12 *l.* respectively, *ib.* 4170–4173.

Rotation (Selection of Panel). Doubtful wisdom of adopting a system of selection by rotation, *Right Hon. J. D. Fitzgerald* 3932.——*See also Alphabetical Selection.*

Roughan, George F. Report by Mr. Roughan relative to the working of the Juries Act of 1871, and the qualifications desirable for common jurors and special jurors respectively, *App.* 320.

Russell, J. T. Suggestions by Mr. Russell, clerk of the Londonderry Union, relative to the qualifications of jurors, and the amendments desirable in the Act of 1871, *App.* 310, 311.

S.

Seed, Mr. See *Sheriffs, or Sub-Sheriffs.*

Selection of Panel. See *Alphabetical Selection.* *Ballot (Jury Panel).* *Dublin High Sheriff.* *Judges.* *Legislation.* *Monaghan.* *Numerical Selection.* *Packing of Juries.* *Responsibility.* *Rotation.* *Sheriffs, or Sub-Sheriffs.*

Service of Jurors. Advantage of the present system by which a juror will not be summoned more than once in three years in a large county, *Hemphill* 110, 111. 244–247——Desirability of summoning every man on the panel who has not served, before any juror is summoned for the second time, as is proposed by the English Bill, *J. Hamilton* 1189, 1193——The limit of serving on juries should be once in a year and a half, or two years, *De Moleyns* 386. 551, 552. 592–597.

Doubtful expediency of making it absolute that no juror shall serve oftener than once in three years; convenience in having one or two jurors who are familiar with the routine business, *Armstrong* 783. 816. 867–869——Opinion that jurors who have been only summoned and have not served should not be exonerated from serving for two years, *Right Hon. M. Morris* 3147–3150——Jurors should serve oftener than once in three years, *Wilkinson* 3941–3943.

See also *Attendance of Jurors.* *Summonses.*

SHERIFFS, OR SUB-SHERIFFS (SELECTION OF PANEL):

1. *Evidence in Approval generally of the Removal from the Sheriffs of the Power of Selection; partiality in the Exercise of such Power.*
2. *Evidence to a contrary purport; denial of the Charge of Partiality.*
3. *Suggestions for a modified form of Selection or Expurgation by the Sheriff.*
4. *Satisfaction of the Sheriffs in being relieved from Selection of the Panel.*
5. *Remuneration and Duties of the Sheriffs.*

1. *Evidence in Approval generally of the Removal from the Sheriffs of the Power of Selection; partiality in the Exercise of such Power.*

Decided approval of the clause depriving the sheriff of discretion in summoning jurors; general idea in Ireland that in a political trial the sheriff would select a jury for a special purpose, *Hemphill* 53–61. 104–111. 204–206. 277, 278. 281–289——Expediency of depriving the sheriff of the power of selecting jurors; possibility of the exercise of partiality under such system, *De Moleyns* 351–354. 509–513——Great advantage of the new Act in taking the selection of the panel from the sub-sheriff; the official who selected

Reports, 1873—*continued.*

SHERIFFS OR SUB-SHERIFFS (SELECTION OF PANEL)—continued.

1. *Evidence in approval generally of the Removal from the Sheriffs, &c.*—cont.

the juries under the old system was always liable to a suspicion of partiality, especially in political or party cases, *Coffey* 638–641. 645, 646. 755–758.

Under no circumstances should the old system of selection by the sheriff be resorted to; absence of confidence in such system on the part of the lower orders, *Armstrong* 798. 799. 844–847. 940–943——The selection of juries was practically in the hands of the sub-sheriffs; observations with reference to the alleged partiality on the part of sub-sheriffs, as noticed by Mr. Seed, *ib.* 800–805. 831–835. 912——Antagonistic feeling of the people towards the sub-sheriffs on account of the active part they take at elections, *ib.* 932–938.

Well-founded complaints as to the manner in which the panel was formed by the sheriff, *Molloy* 1704——Opinion that the selection of the jury panel by the sheriff was open to great objection; grounds for the conclusion, *M'Grath* 2138–2143. 2218–2220. 2265–2267.

Considerable amendment required in the old Act; great evil in the fact that the sheriff had uncontrolled discretion in the selection of the panel, *Right Hon. J. H. Monahan* 2600, 2601. 2636. 2706–2711. 2715–2719. 2753–2755——Undoubted partiality in the selection of the panel under the old system; great importance that the people should have confidence in the administration of the law, *ib.* 2602–2605. 2652–2685. 2754, 2755.

Evidence as to the partiality of the sheriff in selecting the panel, *Right Hon. J. A. Lawson* 2808–2811. 2828. 2867, 2868. 2924——Opinion that the sub-sheriffs are not inclined to incur responsibility, and that they would simply summon the jurors as they found them, *ib.* 2974——If there be a proper expurgation of the list originally the power of selection by the sheriff may well be given up, *ib.* 2975–2977.

Grounds for disapproving of a return to the system of selection by the sheriff, *Right Hon. J. D. Fitzgerald* 3280–3282——Examination as to certain observations by witness respecting the propriety of limiting the discretion of the sheriffs, *ib.* 3288–3291——Impartiality of the sub-sheriff in forming the jury panel under the old system; notwithstanding this, the power of selection by that official was highly expedient, *Morland* 2422–2429. 2476–2494.

Method adopted in selecting the jurors under the old system; the sub-sheriff possessed an almost absolute power of selection, *Johnson* 3563. 3564——Strong disapproval of reverting to the old system; grounds for this conclusion, *ib.* 3568–3592. 3614–3618——Invidious position in which the sheriff was placed by possessing the power of selection; hostile feeling on the part of the people engendered by the exercise of this power, *ib.* 3571–3573. 3624–3633——If the power of selection be restored to the sheriff the present Act must be repealed, *ib.* 3634–3637.

Examination as to suspicion of partiality on the part of the sheriff in framing the jury panels, *Murphy* 3728–3734——Inexpediency of returning to the old practice of selection by the sheriff, *Wilkinson* 3972. 3982. 4017——Statement that under the old system it was quite feasible for the sub-sheriff to return a jury to order if so inclined; disapproval of reverting to such system, *J. Reilly* 4500–4502. 4694, 4695.

2. *Evidence to a contrary purport; denial of the Charge of Partiality:*

Strong disapproval of the removal from the sub-sheriff of the power of selecting the panels, *J. Hamilton* 1023. 1048. 1056. 1095. 1100. 1119, 1120——The exclusion of improper persons from the jury-box should be in the preparation of the panel by the sub-sheriff, *ib.* 1037–1040. 1043. 1102, 1103. 1107–1109——Strong evidence as to the impartiality and moderation of the sub-sheriffs; belief that there is no unfavourable prejudice against the preparation of the panel by them, *ib.* 1060–1062. 1070. 1081. 1161–1167. 1169. 1227–1232. 1298–1301. 1350–1354. 1372–1376. 1393–1404. 1422, 1423. 1434, 1435——Expediency of a power to clear the panel of bad men and to avoid inconveniences to individuals; belief that no sheriff would summon two members of the same firm, *ib.* 1170–1188.

Opinion that the sheriff should form the panel without reference to alphabetical order; expediency of retaining the old system on account of the difficulty of getting a fair jury under the amended qualification proposed, *J. Hamilton* 1288–1297——Under the old system the sub-sheriff had theoretically, but not practically, the power of packing the panel, *ib.* 1335, 1336——Process by which the sub-sheriff frames the jury panel; qualification for the duty by reason of his thorough knowledge of the residents in the county, *ib.* 1414–1421.

Inaccuracy of the imputations of Mr. Seed as regards the sub-sheriff in Westmeath, *Battersby* 1489–1494——Impartiality of the sub-sheriffs in forming the panel; witness never knew a jury packed, *ib.* 1493–1497. 1599, 1600. 1649–1653——Belief that the sub-sheriffs would be incapable of exercising partiality in the exercise of their duty as regards the selection of jurors, *Bottomley* 3434–3437. 3454–3456. 3460–3471——

Examination

SHERIFFS OR SUB-SHERIFFS (SELECTION OF PANEL)—continued.

2. *Evidence to a contrary purport; denial of the Charge of Partiality*—continued.

Examination as to the expediency of the sheriff selecting jurors for particular trials; statement that absence of knowledge was the only thing to prevent such selection, *Bottomley* 3537–3552.

Decided opinion that the sheriff should still make a selection of the most competent jurors from the juror's book, *Robinson* 3820, 3831, 3832——Favourable opinion as to the impartiality of the sub-sheriffs in the selection of the panel, *ib.* 3821, 3822. 3837——Further support of a system of selection by the sheriff; corruption on the part of that officer prevented by the action of public opinion, *ib.* 3886–3890——Under the old law the sheriff might return the same panel time after time, *ib.* 3890, 3891.

Evidence as to the impartiality of sub-sheriffs in the formation of the panel, *Wilkinson* 3988–3989. 4034, 4035——Inexpediency of taking from the sheriff the power of selecting the panels, *Ormsby* 4757, 4758. 4798–4802——Description of the formation of the county jurors' book under the old Act; indiscriminate power of selection in the hands of the sheriff, *Mitchell* 4984–4993.

Protest by numerous sub-sheriffs in positive denial of a charge by a Crown solicitor that the sub-sheriffs were unduly influenced in forming the jury panels, *App.* 322, 323.

3. *Suggestions for a modified form of Selection or Expurgation by the Sheriff:*

Conclusion that there would be no difficulty in directing the sheriff to omit any name from the list, *De Moleyns* 616——Expediency of giving the sheriff power to omit names and form the panel generally on his own responsibility; distinction drawn between "omission" and "selection," *Battersby* 1459–1466. 1556, 1557. 1611. 1643–1648. 1649–1652. 1676, 1677——Decided opinion that no official should be given the power of selection as regards the jury lists; the sheriff should have power to omit the names of unfit persons, but not to select, *Buchanan* 1933–1935.

Expediency of the sheriff retaining a limited power of rejection on account of his possessing the largest means of obtaining information, *Bottomley* 3364–3367. 3397——Importance of making the sheriff responsible for the correctness of the lists in the event of the power of rejection being restored to him, *ib.* 3378–3382.

Theoretical, rather than practical objection to the system of selection by the sub-sheriff; necessity for an expurgation of the list by the sheriff, *Right Hon. M. Morris* 3009. 3016. 3021——Further evidence relative to the selection of the jury panels by the sub-sheriff; opinion that a certain discretion should be vested in that official, *ib.* 3050. 3056——Evidence as to the impartiality of the sub-sheriffs; public opinion is an admirable safeguard against any unfairness on their part, *ib.* 3065. 3173–3180. 3200, 3201——Secondary importance of the qualification if the power be given to exclude incompetent persons, *ib.* 3151. 3158. 3165. 3166——Absolute necessity of a process of expurgation by the sheriff; "expurgation" and "selection" being different things, *ib.* 3161. 3168. 3170——Selection by the sheriff was in every Bill brought in since 1852, until the present year, *ib.* 3207, 3208.

Argument that the oath of office imposes a certain discretion upon the officer in selecting the panel, and that he should have consequently a certain power of selection and rejection, *Wilkinson* 3973–3977. 3980, 3981. 4014–4016. 4019–4021.

Impossibility of so revising the jurors' book as that no improper person will be retained on the list; contention therefrom that the sheriff should exercise a certain discretion in the selection of competent persons, *Right Hon. J. Whiteside* 4250–4252. 4256. 4307——Question considered as to the partiality of the sheriffs in the formation of the panel, *ib.* 4277, 4278. 4316.

4. *Satisfaction of the Sheriffs in being relieved from Selection of the Panel:*

Operation of the new Act discussed at a meeting of the sub-sheriffs held in Dublin; absence of opposition on their part to the principle of the Act, *Bottomley* 3332–3334——Satisfaction felt by the sub-sheriffs at being relieved from an onerous and difficult duty in selecting the panel, *Bottomley* 3457–3459. 3531–3536; *Mitchell* 4981, 4982.

5. *Remuneration and Duties of the Sheriffs:*

Information as to the position held by sub-sheriffs in Ireland, and as to the duties entrusted to them, *Hemphill* 57–59. 62. 131–137——Additional labour and expense thrown upon the sheriff by the Jurors Act; great distances to which he is obliged to send to serve summonses personally, *ib.* 62. 131–137. 237–243.

Opinion that the office of sub-sheriff should not be permanent; the remuneration of the sub-sheriff should be a matter of arrangement between himself and the high sheriff, *Armstrong* 986–993——Full powers entrusted to the sub-sheriff in the deputation given by the high sheriff, *Bottomley* 3483, 3484——The appointment of sub-sheriff by the high sheriff is an annual one, *Wilkinson* 3928.

See also Alphabetical Selection. Antrim. Ballot. Dublin. High Sheriff. Monaghan. Packing of Juries. Panel (Generally).

Shopkeepers. Small shopkeepers are proud to act upon juries, as identifying them with the institutions of the country, *Armstrong* 769.

Sligo. Information relative to a remarkable challenge to the array drawn by witness as chairman of the county of Sligo, *J. Hamilton* 1072–1078. 1327–1334——Condemnatory evidence given by Mr. Fausset before the House of Lords as to the jurors summoned in the county under Judge Perrin's Act, *ib.* 1217–1221——Evidence in approval of the jurors of the county under the present Act, *ib.* 1234——Statement as to the intellectual capacity of the juries in the various towns that witness has been professionally engaged in, *ib.* 1235–1243. 1317, 1318.

Unsatisfactory state of things during the last Sligo assizes; miscarriage of justice in consequence, *Right Hon. M. Morris* 2993–2997. 3085–3108.

Special Commissions. The Crown should resort to special commissions in cases of great public interest, instead of requiring special juries, *Armstrong* 788–791. 1012, 1013.

SPECIAL JURORS:

1. *Present Qualifications; Amendments proposed.*
2. *Question of Special Jurors serving on Common Juries.*
3. *Question of Special Juries in other than Civil Cases, and of increased facilities for obtaining Special Juries.*
4. *Statistics of the Number and Rating Qualifications of Special Jurors.*

1. *Present Qualifications; Amendments proposed.*

Opinion that an ex-grand juror or an ex-sheriff should be qualified as a special juror, *Hemphill* 22——Objectionable and necessitous class of persons sometimes found on the special jury list, *ib.* 143–149——A rating of 50 *l.* a year to the poor rate is, however, some check to necessitous persons getting on the list, *ib.* 148, 149——Special jurors withdrawn from the list as regards civil causes, but remain on it for criminal purposes, *ib.* 258–273.

Statement that the special jury is formed from a special class taken from the long panel, *Coffey* 633——Expediency of the qualification for special jurors as laid down in the Act, *ib.* 711–713——The qualification for a special juror should in no case be under a rating of 100 *l.* a year in counties, *Armstrong* 807, 808. 890 893——Explanation that the special and general panels are prepared without reference to any particular case, *J. Hamilton* 1052.

Division of qualification for special jurors into six classes; this division necessary having regard to the number of jurors to be obtained, *Molloy* 1739, 1740. 1777. 1837, 1838——Evidence upon the subject of increasing the qualification for special jurors both in town and in the country, *Buchanan* 2047–2053.

Considerable injury to the special jury system by the Act; every man who is rated at 50 *l.* is now on the special jury panel, *Right Hon. J. A. Lawson* 2795. 2805–2807——Deterioration of the special jury panel; case in which a gentleman and his coachman were upon the same panel, *Right Hon. M. Morris* 2989. 2995–2997.

The qualification for special jurors should be raised to 100 *l.* and upwards, *Bottomley* 3386–3389——Variety of qualifications essential for special jurors, *Johnson* 3603. 3618——Approval of a qualification of classes, not of rating, for special jurors, *Morphy* 3716–3718. 3760.

Report from the inspectors of poor law unions and from several clerks of unions, relative to the working of the Juries Act of 1871, and the qualifications desirable for common jurors and special jurors respectively, *App.* 301–391.

Recommendation by the Committee that the amount of property qualification for special jurors in counties at large in respect of premises not situate in towns should be raised, *First Rep.* iii.

2. *Question of Special Jurors serving on Common Juries:*

Suggestions with regard to the insertion of special jurors in the general jurors' book, *Hemphill* 321–328——Question considered as to the inexpediency of compelling certain special jurors to serve on all cases; the advantage of the system lies in the fact of indiscriminate selection, *De Moleyns* 417——Further reference to the question of special jurors serving with common jurors in all ordinary cases, *ib.* 604–606——Approval of Mr. Hemphill's suggestion that a certain number of special jurors should serve on every jury, *Coffey* 657. 660.

Strong disapproval of introducing a certain number of special jurors upon every jury; difficulty thereby obviated by raising the qualification, *Armstrong* 784–786. 791——Expediency of a certain number of special jurors being required to serve on every jury. *Buchanan* 2039–2041——Approval of having a certain number of special jurors upon all juries, *M'Grath* 2345, 2346——Importance in not exhausting the special jury list as it would have the effect of taking jurors off the general list of jurors, *Murland* 2390–2392.

Conclusion

SPECIAL JURORS—continued.

2. *Question of Special Jurors serving on Common Juries*—continued.

Conclusion as to the inexpediency of introducing the "special" element into every jury, *Right Hon. J. H. Monahan* 2745–2752; *Right Hon. J. Whiteside* 4279, 4280——Opinion as to the expediency of the introduction of a proportion of special jurors into every jury for civil and criminal cases, *Right Hon. J. D. Fitzgerald* 3234.

Injudicious character of the proposal that a proportion of special jurors should serve with common jurors; belief that such arrangement would create a class antagonism, *Robinson* 3830. 3871–3874——Desirability of the best class of Jurors who are included on the special list being called upon to serve on common juries, *Wilkinson* 3950, 3951.

3. *Question of Special Juries in other than Civil Cases, and of increased Facilities for obtaining Special Juries:*

Anomalous state of the law whereby in a civil case a special jury may be obtained, whilst in a case affecting a man's life or liberty there is no such power, *Coffey* 657——Conclusion that in all serious and heavy cases there should be power given both to the Crown and to the prisoner to have a special jury, *ib.* 657–659. 700–702. 717. 738–743——Desirability of giving power to either side of having a special jury without application to the court, *Armstrong* 806.

The right of the Crown to try certain cases by a special jury would be inconsistent with the principle of trial by jury, by which a man is tried by his peers, *J. Hamilton* 1153–1155——The adoption of the principle by which the Crown may try all serious cases by special juries would do away altogether with the necessity for selection, *ib.* 1302, 1303.

Recommendation that either party, both in civil and criminal cases, should be entitled to have a special jury struck; belief that such an arrangement would not be unpopular in the country, *Battersby* 1455. 1456. 1485–1489. 1593–1598. 1678–1682.

Desirability of giving the Crown and the prisoner equal rights to demand a special jury; opinion that the prisoner would not apply for the privilege as often as the Crown, *M'Grath* 2172–2176. 2183–2188. 2245–2250. 2284–2286——Absence of objection to giving the Crown and the prisoner equal right to call for a special jury, *Roche* 2573.

Disapproval of the proposal that either side should be given the right to have a special jury, *Robinson* 3827. 3829. 3838——Questionable expediency of the Crown or the prisoner having the right to claim a special jury, *Right Hon. J. Whiteside* 4279, 4280.

4. *Statistics of the Number and Rating Qualifications of Special Jurors:*

Return by sheriffs of the number of jurors on the special jurors' book, classified according to various amounts of rating qualification, *App.* 289——Total number of jurors in the special jurors' book in each county, *ib.*——Number of jurors in the special jurors' book who are sons of peers, baronets, magistrates, &c., *ib.*

See also Agrarian Outrages. Antrim. Criminal Cases. Dublin, 1. *Galway. Legislation. Responsibility. Wexford.*

Storey, John. Report from Mr. Storey, clerk of the Letterkenny Union, relative to the qualifications required in jurors, and the amendments desirable in the Act of 1871, *App.* 307.

Sub-Sheriffs. See *Sheriffs, or Sub-Sheriffs.*

Summonses (*Attendance of Witnesses before Committee*). Special Report relative to two fictitious documents, purporting to be summonses issued by the direction of the Chairman of the Committee for the attendance of Mr. John Fay, high sheriff of Cavan, and Mr. Theophilus Thompson, magistrate, of Cavan, *Special Rep.* v.

Copies of the documents in question, and of communications thereupon from Mr. Fay and Mr. Thompson, *Special Rep.* vi, vii.

SUMMONSES (ATTENDANCE OF JURORS):

Expediency of serving summonses by means of registered letters to jurors at a distance, as is the practice in the county and the city of Dublin, *Hemphill* 71–80. 119, 120. 168. 179, 180. 194, 195——Proof of sending a registered letter should be *primâ facie* evidence against a juror that he had received it, *ib.* 120.

Likelihood of persons being tampered with who are employed by the sheriff to summon jurors, *De Moleyns* 502——Difficulties in summoning jurors by means of registered letters, incompetency of the Post Office to perform such a duty, *ib.* 503. 526. 527. 607——Considerable expense thrown upon the sheriff in summoning jurors; opinion that the serving of summonses might be fairly performed by the constabulary, *ib.* 503, 504. 525. 530, 531. *ib.*

SUMMONSES (ATTENDANCE OF JURORS)—continued.

Necessity for altering the machinery of summoning; easy evasion of the service by intercepting the summonses by means of servants, *Armstrong* 772–774. 1008——Expediency of adopting the postal services all over the country; the fact of posting a summons should be considered *primâ facie* evidence of service, *ib.* 772. 792–795. 904–907. 944–946—— Argument that any person who is so obscure as to be beyond the reach of the post is not fit to serve upon a jury at all, *ib.* 772–792.

Questionable policy in employing the constabulary in serving summonses on jurors; service by registered letter, for which a receipt would be given, would be preferable, *Armstrong* 902–907. 914–966. 982–985; *J. Hamilton* 1202, 1203; *Bottomley* 3420–3422. 3425. 3426——Considerable advantage in using the post office as a means for summoning jurors, *Battersby* 1455. 1512–1515; *Wilkinson* 3962, 3963. 4048, 4049; *Flynn* 4186–4189. 4207–4212——Great objection to the present system of serving summonses upon jurors; expediency of employing the constabulary for the purpose, *Battersby* 1484. 1524–1535——Suggestions as to the means to be adopted for economising the summoning of jurors; advantage of diminishing the number of places where quarter sessions are held, *Buchanan* 2013–2023.

Approval of a system of serving summonses by means of the constabulary, and not through the post office, *M'Grath* 2319–2322. 2327, 2328——Great advantage in summoning the jurors by means of registered letters through the post office; inexpediency of employing the constabulary upon this duty, *Murland* 2395. 2457–2459.

Inapplicability of the English rule of summoning jurors to Ireland, *Right Hon. J. H. Monahan* 2725–2730. 2743, 2744——Suitability of the post office as a means of summoning jurors by registered letters; belief that such an arrangement would not only be sure, but would save a large amount of expense, *Right Hon. M. Morris* 3146, 3147.

Expediency of some modification in the method of serving summonses; considerable difficulty in serving the summonses in time, *Bottomley* 3334. 3411–3414. 3452——Impossibility of adhering to the Act as regards the time for summoning special jurors, *ib.* 3433——Augmentation of trouble and expense in serving the jurors under the new system, *Johnson* 3592, 3593——Absence of objection in serving by registered letters; suggestion as to other modes, *ib.* 3594–3597.

Belief that summoning jurors by post would be wholly impracticable; suggestion that the constabulary should be employed upon this duty, *Murphy* 3720, 3721——Desirability of summoning the jurors by means of registered letters; where there is no facility for postal service, the constabulary should be employed, *Robinson* 3808–3813. 3821——Advisability of employing the constabulary in summoning jurors in the event of the postal service not being carried out, *Wilkinson* 3963–3971. 4041–4049——Inexpediency of employing the police in summoning jurors, *Flynn* 4213–4215; *Reilly* 4553, 4554. 4684.

Doubtful expediency of adopting the postal system for summoning jurors, *Right Hon. J. Whiteside* 4255——Impracticability of serving jurors by means of registered letters through the post, *J. Reilly* 4555, 4556. 4701–4709——Efficacy of the post as a means of serving summonses; difficulty of persons paying money to avoid being summoned, *Ormsby* 4844–4848——Difficulty which exists as to summoning jurors; desirability of employing the constabulary upon that duty, *Mitchell* 4925, 4926. 4996.

See also Bailiffs. Resident Jurors. Service of Jurors.

T

Tales (Perrin's Act). Difficulties with regard to praying a *tales* owing to the peculiar wording of Perrin's Act; expediency of giving both plaintiff and defendant in civil cases the power to pray a *tales*, *Armstrong* 817, 818——Statement that the system of praying a *tales* is the same under the new Act as it was under the old Act, *Molloy* 1753.

Temporary Legislation. See *Juries (Ireland) Act*, 1873. *Legislation.*

Thompson, Theophilus. See *Summonses (Attendance of Witnesses).*

Town Jurors. Considerable advantage in having a town element upon a jury, *Caffry* 649–651——Higher class of intelligence in jurors from towns than in those from country districts, *Right Hon. J. A. Lawson* 2837–2840; *Reilly* 4546–4549——Relative qualifications of town and country jurors; advantage of the former over the latter, as regards intelligence, *Right Hon. M. Morris* 3152——Belief that a 12 *l.* house qualification would give a high class juror; superiority of the town juror over the juror from the country, though the latter is rated much higher, *Flynn* 4111, 4112. 4115–4117. 4168. 4175, 4176.

See also Household Qualification. Qualifications. Special Jurors.

Turbett, Messrs. Hard case of Messrs. Turbett, where three brothers, members of the same firm, were summoned upon the same panel, *Right Hon. M. Morris* 3057–3060. 3114–

Turbett, Messrs.—continued.

3114–3117. 3138–3141. 3194–3198——Strong complaints made by Messrs. Turbett and other jurors in Dublin as to the unfair burden thrown upon them under the alphabetical system of selection, *Rt. Hon. J. Whiteside* 4240. 4266, 4267. 4272, 4273.

Tyrone. Computation showing the difficulty of laying down a rule by which no juror would be called more than once in two years as regards the county of Tyrone, *Armstrong* 879–889.

Initiatory preparation of the jurors' lists in Tyrone undertaken by witness, as clerk of the peace for the county, *Buchanan* 1890——The qualifications under the old Act had become so obsolete that sufficient jurors could not be obtained, *ib.* 1891, 1892——Under the present Act, with a qualification of 20 *l.*, the number of jurors is 3092; *ib.* 1893——A list of 1,000 names for the county would be amply sufficient if jurors were required to serve once a year, *ib.* 1910.

Universal approval of the principle of the new Act in the county; objection, however, that the qualification is too low, thereby bringing upon the lists persons who are unfit in every way to act as jurors, *Buchanan* 1911–1916. 1940–1942. 2042–2046——Examination as to the class of jurors to be obtained by a rating of 30 *l.*, *ib.* 1946–1965——Belief that the county of Tyrone is quite equal to the average of Ireland in point of education, *ib.* 1967–1969——Statement as to the exhaustion of the jury panel in Tyrone for this year, *ib.* 2071–2075. 2083——Enormous preponderance of names in the county beginning with the letter "M," *ib.* 2131–2134.

Statement that the same jurors were to be found from year to year at the Assizes in Tyrone; complaints by the jurors of the hardship to serve so often, *M'Grath* 2144–2147.

U.

Unanimity of Juries. See *Verdicts.*

Uniformity of Qualification. Inexpediency of adopting the same uniform rule as to qualifications for all counties, *Molloy* 1793–1795.

Upper Classes. Disinclination felt by persons of high standing to serve on juries; opinion that there is no hardship in requiring the attendance of such persons twice a year, *M'Grath* 2239–2244.

V.

Verdicts. Concurrence of opinion in favour of unanimity of juries; inexpediency of the verdict of the majority being accepted, *Hemphill* 299–306. 318; *Coffey* 697–699; *Right Hon. J. H. Monahan* 2637, 2638. 2697–2705——Doubtful wisdom in accepting the verdict of a majority, such alteration in the law might be introduced into Ireland if it were found to answer well in England, *Armstrong* 819, 820. 827–829——Evil effect of the present jury system upon the public mind, caused more by the conduct and character of the jurors than by the verdicts they return, *ib.* 836.

Verdicts given by juries in obedience to the judge, or else in accordance with their own prejudices or fears, *J. Hamilton* 1034, 1035——Further observations as to the ignorance displayed by the jurors in the country; fortunately for the interests of justice the verdicts were those of the judges, *ib.* 1139–1141. 1170. 1247——Extraordinary instance of an unjust verdict found by a jury in the county of Roscommon, *ib.* 1171. 1304–1306——Unanimity in juries should be invariably required in criminal cases; possible expediency of accepting in civil cases a majority, if concurred in by the judge, *ib.* 1426——Opinion that a system of having a certain number of special jurors upon every jury would have a tendency to prevent unanimity, *ib.* 1427.

Unjust verdicts found by the lowest class of jurors; opinion that a higher class are to be depended upon in spite of their prejudices, *Battersby* 1453, 1454——Over anxiety of inexperienced jurors to be guided more by the opinion of the Bench than by their own judgment, *Buchanan* 1926, 1927. 2034–2037——Expediency of a modification in the system of requiring unanimous verdicts from juries, *ib.* 1930–1932——Apprehensions as to the verdicts given by jurors of the class required by the present law, *M'Grath* 2329–2334.

Favourable opinion as to taking the verdict of the majority; importance of assimilating the law of Ireland to that of England in the matter, *Right Hon. J. A. Lawson* 2841——Fairness of verdicts returned by Irish juries, *Right Hon. M. Morris* 3074, 3075——Approval of accepting the verdict of the majority in civil cases only; remarkable instance in which an innocent man escaped a capital conviction by a majority of one, *Right Hon. J. D. Fitzgerald* 3252–3256——Decided opinion in favour of unanimity of juries; conviction that any change in the present system would be most dangerous, *Robinson* 3831.

Verdicts—continued.

Occasional miscarriage of justice under the old system; notable failure occasioned by a pawnbroker holding out against eleven other jurymen, *Right Hon. J. Whiteside* 4232. 4236. 4294——Approval of receiving the verdict of the majority in a doubtful or litigated case, *ib.* 4270——Case of a man having been tried five times, and but once convicted, when the House of Lords reversed the verdict on the challenge to the array, *ib.* 4298–4302.

Veterinary Surgeons. Veterinary surgeons are entitled to be exempted from serving on juries, *Hemphill* 100.

View Juries. Blemish in the Act with regard to view juries consisting only of six persons; opinion that the whole twelve should form the jury, *Armstrong* 805.

Clause in the Act by which Mr. Serjeant Armstrong's objection as to a view jury is obviated, *Molloy* 1750–1752.

Villages. Definition of a village in the meaning of the Act, *De Moleyns* 426–428——Desirability of including villages in the new Act as a basis for qualification; contention that a man rated at 20 *l.* in a village is as fit to be a juror as a man rated at the same amount in a town, *Buchanan* 2058–2063——Absence of any necessity to make a distinction between towns and villages as regards qualifications, *M'Grath* 2274–2307——Vagueness of the phrase "village" in the Act; qualifications should be confined to towns and cities, *Right Hon. M. Morris* 3153.

Voters' Lists. Impossibility of making a common list for the qualifications of a voter and a juror, *Hemphill* 131, 132——Facility with which the jurors' lists could be revised by the assistant barrister when engaged upon the revision of the voters' lists, *Battersby* 1536–1539——Statement of the method of making and revising the electors' lists, *Battersby* 1639, 1640; *Buchanan* 1980–1986.

Admirable manner in which the lists of Parliamentary voters are made out by the clerks of unions; argument therefrom that those persons should be charged with the duty of preparing the jurors' lists, *Molloy* 1845–1849——Expediency of combining the lists of electors and voters for the purposes of revision by the chairman; grounds for this opinion, *Buchanan* 1978–1987. 2108–2113——Impracticability of the voters' and the jurors' lists being revised by one operation before the barrister at the same time, *Murland* 2448–2452.

Proposition that the revision of the jurors' and the Parliamentary lists should be combined: method by which this revision should be carried out, *Robinson* 3802–3807. 3843–3859——Combination of the first list of jurors with the list of Parliamentary voters would be expedient and tend to economy, *Wilkinson* 4027, 4028.

Statement that a large proportion of jurors are not upon the Parliamentary voters' lists, notwithstanding that the qualification is higher for jurors than for voters, *Cope* 5091–5099. 5103, 5104——Opinion that the revision of the jurors and the voters lists could not be undertaken upon the same occasion so as to save the expenses of two journeys, *ib.* 5205–5211.

W.

Wexford. General satisfaction as to the impartiality of witness (as sub-sheriff) in the selection of the panel for Wexford; principles which actuated the selection, *Wilkinson* 3929–3983. 3986——Examination as to a statement prepared by witness for the information of the grand jury on the working of the new Act; opinion that the special and common jurors in the county are in excess of the numbers required, *ib.* 3937–3940——Careless compilation of the jurors' book; large number of disqualified persons on the list, *ib.* 3932. 3934–3936.

Statement of the number of special jurors required for the two assizes; opinion that a qualification of 90 *l.* for country and 40 *l.* in towns would give about 400, *Wilkinson* 3952–3959——Considerable alteration caused by the new Act in the character of the panels at the late assizes, *ib.* 3944, 3945.

Considerable room for improvement in the juries in the county of Wexford, *Right Hon. J. Whiteside* 4317.

Total of 985 jurors on the special jurors' book, *App.* 324.

Whiteside, Rt. Hon. James. (Analysis of his Evidence.)—Has held the office of Chief Justice of the Court of Queen's Bench for seven years, 4220, 4221——Unfavourable opinion of the working of the present Jury Act, 4222——Cardinal distinction to be drawn between the jurors of the city and those of the county of Dublin; those of the city of Dublin have been in every way satisfactory, 4223, 4224. 4237, 4238.

Remarkable ignorance and want of intelligence of the county special jurors; instances of men who had been in very humble positions, now on the special panel for the county, 4223.

Whiteside, Rt. Hon. James. (Analysis of his Evidence)—*continued.*

4223. 4225. 4289, 4290——Limited class of special jurors before the present Act-moderate and judicious verdicts given them, 4224-4227.

Impoverished condition of the jurors at the last assizes at Clonmel; statement that several of them were obliged to pawn their clothes for their support while in the town, 4230——Systematic challenge of the respectable jurors by the prisoners on the Leinster circuit, 4230.

Description of a case in which the jury were discharged on account of the intoxication of one of their number; instance of a case in which a returned convict was sworn on a jury, 4230, 4231. 4293——Occasional miscarriages of justice under the old system; notable failure occasioned by a pawnbroker holding out against eleven other jurymen, 4232. 4236. 4294.

Unsuitability of a pawnbroker to perform the duties of a juryman on account of his dependence on the public; doubtful expediency, notwithstanding, of absolutely disqualifying him, 4232. 4260. 4262, 4263——Decided opinion as to the expediency of absolutely disqualifying publicans; distinction drawn between publicans and grocers who sell spirits by retail, 4232. 4234. 4261. 4314, 4315.

Difficulties in Ireland of getting verdicts upon circumstantial evidence, 4234-4236. 4276——Opinion that the High Sheriff for the city of Dublin should examine and certify as to the impartial selection of the jury panel, 4237. 4247-4272. 4316.

Statement as to the proportion of Roman Catholics and Protestants on the jury in the case of O'Keeffe *versus* Cullen; belief in the impartiality of jurors professing either of those religions, 4239-4246——Strong complaints made by the Messrs. Turbett and other jurors as to the unfair burden thrown upon them under the alphabetical system of selection, 4240. 4266, 4267. 4272, 4273.

Considerable amendment required in the present Act, 4247——Impossibility of so revising the jurors' book as that no improper person will be retained on the list; contention therefrom that the Sheriff should exercise a certain discretion in the selection of competent persons, 4250-4252. 4255. 4307.

Explanation as to the principles of the Bills introduced by witness when Attorney General, 4253, 4254. 4304-4307——Disapproval of the alphabetical selection of the panel from the jury book, 4254. 4302-4307. 4309. 4310.

Desirability of a considerable increase in the rating qualifications of jurors, 4255——Impossibility of carrying out a real revision before the assistant barrister, *ib.*——Expediency of giving the judges power to impose moderate fines upon non-attending jurors, 4257——Necessity of giving the Crown officials considerable discretion as to setting jurors aside, 4258. 4262.

Strong disapproval of the judge having power to exclude any juror on account of his political opinions, or for any other cause than physical infirmity, 4264, 4265. 4282-4288——Approval of receiving the verdict of the majority in a doubtful or litigated case, 4270——Statement that the right of challenging in a criminal trial must be exercised according to strict law, 4275.

Question considered as to the partiality of the sheriffs in the formation of the panel, 4277, 4278. 4316——Questionable expediency of the Crown or the prisoner having the right to claim a special jury; disapproval, also, of having a proportion of special jurors on every jury, 4279, 4280——Occasional instances of partiality in juries in criminal cases, 4281——High class of persons on the jury that tried Mr. Smith O'Brien for high treason, 4296.

Remarkable case of a man having been tried five times, and but once convicted, when the House of Lords reversed the verdict on a challenge to the array, 4298-4302——Disapproval of adopting the ballot in criminal cases; opinion that the present system is the fairest to the prisoner, 4311-4313——Considerable room for improvement in the juries in the county of Wexford, 4317——Statement that Mr. Duffy, who is now a Minister of State abroad, was saved by one dissentient juror, 4318.

Wilkinson, Thomas. (Analysis of his Evidence.)—Has held the office of sub-sheriff of the county of Wexford since the year 1854; 3925-3927. 3995-3997——The appointment of sub-sheriff by the high sheriff is an annual one, 3928——General satisfaction as to the impartiality of witness in the selection of the panel; principles which have actuated him in making the selection, 3929-3933. 3986——Careless compilation of the jurors' book; large number of disqualified persons on the list, 3932. 3934-3936.

Examination as to a statement prepared by witness for the information of the grand jury on the working of the new Act, 3937-3940——Contention that jurors should serve oftener than once in three years, 3941-3943——Considerable alteration in the character of the panels at the late assizes caused by the new Act, 3944, 3945——Serious inconvenience imposed upon the jurors in being summoned to attend the quarter sessions from great distances, 3946-3948——Expediency of the special and general jurors' books being separate, as a means of economising the numbers of the special jurors, 3949.

 Desirability

Wilkinson, Thomas. (Analysis of his Evidence)—*continued*.

Desirability of the best class of jurors who are included in the special list being called upon to serve on common juries, 3950, 3951——Statement of the number of special jurors required for the two assizes in Wexford; opinion that a qualification of 90 *l.* for country, and 40 *l.* in towns, would give about 400; 3952–3959.

Calculation that a qualification of 40 *l.* in the country and 20 *l.* in towns would supply an adequate number of common jurors, 3960, 3961——Approval of adopting the postal system of summoning jurors, 3962, 3963. 4048, 4049——Advisability of employing the constabulary in summoning jurors in the event of the postal service not being carried out, 3963–3971. 4041–4049.

Inexpediency of returning to the old practice of selection by the sheriff, 3972. 3982. 4017——Argument that the oath of office imposes a certain discretion upon the officer in selecting the panel, and that he should have consequently a certain power of selection and rejection, 3973–3977. 3980, 3981. 4014–4016. 4019–4021——Liability of the sheriff to be fined by the judge for returning an insufficient number on the panel, 3978, 3979. 3991, 3992.

Disadvantages inherent to the system of alphabetical selection; suggestions as to an alternative scheme, 3983–3985——Evidence as to the impartiality of sub-sheriffs in the formation of the panel, 3986–3989. 4034, 4035——Examination as to the power of the sheriff as to rejecting any juror who may be suspected of being disaffected to the law, 4000–4010——Statement that the sheriff would be accountable for returning too large a number of jurors, if it were shown that there had been any improper motive in so doing, 4010–4013.

Considerable expense in summoning jurors under the new Act on account of the distances to be travelled, 4022–4024——Difficulties of the sub-sheriffs in obtaining any additional remuneration from the grand juries in consequence of the extra expenses thrown upon them, 4025–4026——Combination of the first list of jurors with the list of Parliamentary voters would be expedient and tend to economy, 4027, 4028——Non-interference of the high sheriff in the formation of the panel, 4029, 4031.

Examination as to the arrangements proposed by witness as an alternative to the selection of the panel in alphabetical order, 4050–4054——Evidence in favour of a selection of the panel in criminal cases by means of the ballot, 4055, 4056——The system recommended by witness would avoid in a great degree the difficulty of three persons of the same firm appearing on the same panel, 4057.

INDEX

TO THE

REPORTS

FROM THE

SELECT COMMITTEE

ON

JURIES (IRELAND).

Ordered, by The House of Commons, to be Printed,
7 July 1873.

[*Price* 8 *d.*]

283.

Under 6 *oz.*

www.ingramcontent.com/pod-product-compliance
Lightning Source LLC
Chambersburg PA
CBHW051742300426
44115CB00007B/665